Contents

Introduction	4
International Civil Aircraft Markings	6
Aircraft Type Designations & Abbreviations	8
British Civil Aircraft Registration	9
Isle of Man Civil Registrations	309
Channel Islands Civil Registrations	315
Military to Civil Cross-Reference	325
Republic of Ireland Civil Registrations	331
Overseas Airliner Registrations	351
Radio Frequencies	438
Airline Flight Codes	439
BAPC Register	441
Future Allocations Log	446
Future Allocation Groups	447
Overseas Airliners Registration Log	448

This 65th edition first published 2014

ISBN 978 0 7110 3797 7

© Ian Allan Publishing Ltd 2014

Published by Ian Allan Publishing
an imprint of Ian Allan Publishing Ltd,
Hersham, Surrey KT12 4RG.
Printed in England by TJ Interational.

Visit the Ian Allan Publishing website at
www.ianallanpublishing.com

Front cover: iStockphotos © carterdayne

Advertising: Dave Smith, Tel/Fax 01775 767184
6 Sunningdale Avenue, Spalding, Lincs, PE9 2PP, UK.

Introduction

The familiar 'G' prefixed four-letter registration system was adopted in 1919 after a short-lived spell with serial numbers commencing at K-100. Until July 1928 the UK allocations were issued in the G-Exxx range but, as a result of further international agreements, this series ended at G-EBZZ, the replacement being G-Axxx. From this point registrations were issued in a reasonably orderly manner through to G-AZZZ, the position reached in July 1972. There were, however, two exceptions. In order to prevent possible confusion with signal codes, the G-AQxx sequence was omitted, while G-AUxx was reserved for Australian use originally. In recent years however, individual requests for a mark in the latter range have been granted by the Authorities.

Although the next logical sequence was started at G-Bxxx, it was not long before the strictly applied rules relating to aircraft registration began to be relaxed. Permission was readily given for personalised marks to be issued, incorporating virtually any four-letter combination, while re-registration also became a common feature – a practice almost unheard of in the past. In this book, where this has taken place at some time, all previous UK identities carried appear in parenthesis after the operator's/owner's name. For example, during its career Twin Squirrel G-NTWK has also carried the identities G-BMUS, G-OJOR and G-FTWO.

Some aircraft have also been allowed to wear military markings without displaying their civil identity. In this case the serial number actually carried is shown in parenthesis after the type's name. For example Auster 6A G-ARRX flies in military colours as VF512, its genuine previous identity. As an aid to the identification of such machines, a conversion list is provided.

Other factors caused a sudden acceleration in the number of registrations allocated by the Civil Aviation Authority in the early 1980s. The first surge followed the discovery that it was possible to register plastic bags, and other items even less likely to fly, on payment of the standard fee. This erosion of the main register was checked in early 1982 by the issue of a special sequence for such devices commencing with G-FYAA. Powered hang-gliders provided the second glut of allocations as a result of the decision that these types should be officially registered. Although a few of the early examples penetrated the current in-sequence register, in due course all new applicants were given marks in special ranges, this time G-MBxx, G-MGxx, G-MJxx, G-MMxx, G-MNxx, G-MTxx, G-MVxx, G-MWxx, G-MYxx and G-MZxx. It took some time before all microlights displayed an official mark but gradually the registration was carried, the size and position depending on the dimensions of the component to which it was applied.

There was news of a further change in mid-1998 when the CAA announced that with immediate effect microlights would be issued with registrations in the normal sequence alongside aircraft in other classes. In addition, it meant that owners could also apply for a personalised identity upon payment of the then current fee of £170 from April 1999, a low price for those wishing to display their status symbol. These various changes played their part in exhausting the current G-Bxxx range after some 26 years, with G-BZxx coming into use before the end of 1999. As this batch approached completion the next series to be used began at G-CBxx instead of the anticipated G-CAxx. The reason for this step was to avoid the re-use of marks issued in Canada during the 1920s, although a few have appeared more recently as personalised UK registrations.

Another large increase in the number of aircraft registered has resulted from the EU-inspired changes in glider registration. After many years of self-regulation by the British Gliding Association, new gliders must now comply with EASA regulations and hence receive registrations in the main G-Cxxx sequence. The phasing-in of EASA registration for the existing glider fleet was a fairly lengthy process but has now come to an end and by the beginning of 2012 there were over 2,250 examples on the Register.

September 2007 saw the issue of the 50,000th UK aircraft registration with G-MITC being allocated to a Robinson R44 Raven. The total number of aircraft on the Register has risen over the past 25 years from just under 10,000 at the beginning of 1985 to in excess of 21,300 by January 2009. Numbers have fallen back slightly since that time with the figure as at 1st January 2014 standing at 19,851. Of these, 4,029 were microlights, 1,232 were helicopters, 2,247 were gliders and 1,625 were balloons.

The Isle of Man launched its own aircraft register in May 2007 aimed mainly at private and corporate business jets and helicopters and the first to be allocated was Cessna 525B Citation M-ELON. By the end of 2013 over 650 aircraft had been registered. This has now been followed by the Channel Islands Aircraft Registry which was launched by the States of Guernsey on 9 December 2013 and is likely to be followed in 2014 by a Jersey register. The M- (Isle of Man) and 2- (Guernsey) registers can be found at the end of the British Civil Aircraft Registrations section of this book.

Non-airworthy and preserved aircraft are shown with a star (★) after the type.

The three-letter codes used by airlines to prefix flight numbers are included for those carriers most likely to appear in the UK. Radio frequencies for the larger airfields/airports are also listed.

ASW

ACKNOWLEDGEMENTS: Once again thanks are extended to the Registration Department of the Civil Aviation Authority for its assistance and allowing access to its files and thanks are also given to all those who have contributed items for possible use in this edition.

International Civil Aircraft Markings

A2-	Botswana		M-	Isle of Man
A3-	Tonga		N-	United States of America
A4O-	Oman		OB-	Peru
A5-	Bhutan		OD-	Lebanon
A6-	United Arab Emirates		OE-	Austria
A7-	Qatar		OH-	Finland
A8-	Liberia		OK-	Czech Republic
A9C-	Bahrain		OM-	Slovakia
AP-	Pakistan		OO-	Belgium
B-	China/Taiwan/Hong Kong/Macao		OY-	Denmark
C-	Canada		P-	North Korea
C2-	Nauru		P2-	Papua New Guinea
C3-	Andorra		P4-	Aruba
C5-	Gambia		PH-	Netherlands
C6-	Bahamas		PJ-	Netherlands Antilles
C9-	Mozambique		PK-	Indonesia
CC-	Chile		PP-	Brazil
CN-	Morocco		PR-	Brazil
CP-	Bolivia		PT-	Brazil
CS-	Portugal		PU-	Brazil
CU-	Cuba		PZ-	Surinam
CX-	Uruguay		RA-	Russia
D-	Germany		RDPL-	Laos
D2-	Angola		RP-	Philippines
D4-	Cape Verde Islands		S2-	Bangladesh
D6-	Comores Islands		S5-	Slovenia
DQ-	Fiji		S7-	Seychelles
E3-	Eritrea		S9-	São Tomé
E5-	Cook Islands		SE-	Sweden
EC-	Spain		SP-	Poland
EI-	Republic of Ireland		ST-	Sudan
EK-	Armenia		SU-	Egypt
EP-	Iran		SX-	Greece
ER-	Moldova		T2-	Tuvalu
ES-	Estonia		T3-	Kiribati
ET-	Ethiopia		T7-	San Marino
EW-	Belarus		T8A-	Palau
EX-	Kyrgyzstan		T9-	Bosnia and Herzegovina
EY-	Tajikistan		TC-	Turkey
EZ-	Turkmenistan		TF-	Iceland
F-	France, inc Colonies and Protectorates		TG-	Guatemala
G-	United Kingdom		TI-	Costa Rica
H4-	Solomon Islands		TJ-	Cameroon
HA-	Hungary		TL-	Central African Republic
HB-	Switzerland and Liechtenstein		TN-	Republic of Congo
HC-	Ecuador		TR-	Gabon
HH-	Haiti		TS-	Tunisia
HI-	Dominican Republic		TT-	Tchad
HK-	Colombia		TU-	Ivory Coast
HL-	South Korea		TY-	Benin
HP-	Panama		TZ-	Mali
HR-	Honduras		UK-	Uzbekistan
HS-	Thailand		UN-	Kazakhstan
HZ-	Saudi Arabia		UR-	Ukraine
I-	Italy		V2-	Antigua
J2-	Djibouti		V3-	Belize
J3-	Grenada		V4-	St. Kitts & Nevis
J5-	Guinea Bissau		V5-	Namibia
J6-	St. Lucia		V6-	Micronesia
J7-	Dominica		V7-	Marshall Islands
J8-	St. Vincent		V8-	Brunei
JA-	Japan		VH-	Australia
JU-	Mongolia		VN-	Vietnam
JY-	Jordan		VP-A	Anguilla
LN-	Norway		VP-B	Bermuda
LV-	Argentina		VP-C	Cayman Islands
LX-	Luxembourg		VP-F	Falkland Islands
LY-	Lithuania		VP-G	Gibraltar
LZ-	Bulgaria		VP-L	British Virgin Islands

VP-M	Montserrat	4R-	Sri Lanka
VQ-B	Bermuda	4X-	Israel
VQ-H	Saint Helena/Ascension	5A-	Libya
VQ-T	Turks & Caicos Islands	5B-	Cyprus
VT-	India	5H-	Tanzania
XA-	Mexico	5N-	Nigeria
XB-	Mexico	5R-	Malagasy Republic (Madagascar)
XC-	Mexico	5T-	Mauritania
XT-	Burkina Faso	5U-	Niger
XU-	Cambodia	5V-	Togo
XW-	Laos	5W-	Western Samoa (Polynesia)
XY-	Myanmar	5X-	Uganda
YA-	Afghanistan	5Y-	Kenya
YI-	Iraq	6O-	Somalia
YJ-	Vanuatu	6V-	Senegal
YK-	Syria	6Y-	Jamaica
YL-	Latvia	7O-	Yemen
YN-	Nicaragua	7P-	Lesotho
YR-	Romania	7Q-	Malawi
YS-	El Salvador	7T-	Algeria
YU-	Serbia	8P-	Barbados
YV-	Venezuela	8Q-	Maldives
Z-	Zimbabwe	8R-	Guyana
Z3-	Macedonia	9A-	Croatia
ZA-	Albania	9G-	Ghana
ZK-	New Zealand	9H-	Malta
ZP-	Paraguay	9J-	Zambia
ZS-	South Africa	9K-	Kuwait
3A-	Monaco	9L-	Sierra Leone
3B-	Mauritius	9M-	Malaysia
3C-	Equatorial Guinea	9N-	Nepal
3D-	Swaziland	9Q-	Congo Kinshasa
3X-	Guinea	9U-	Burundi
4K-	Azerbaijan	9V-	Singapore
4L-	Georgia	9XR-	Rwanda
4O-	Montenegro	9Y	Trinidad and Tobago

Aircraft Type Designations & Abbreviations

(for example PA-28 Piper Type 28)

A.	Beagle, Auster, Airbus
AAC	Army Air Corps
AA-	American Aviation, Grumman American
AB	Agusta-Bell
AESL	Aero Engine Services Ltd
AG	American General
An	Antonov
ANEC	Air Navigation & Engineering Co
ANG	Air National Guard
AS	Aérospatiale
A.S.	Airspeed
A.W.	Armstrong Whitworth
B.	Blackburn, Bristol, Boeing, Beagle
BA	British Airways
BAC	British Aircraft Company
BAC	British Aircraft Corporation
BAe	British Aerospace
BAPC	British Aviation Preservation Council
BAT	British Aerial Transport
B.K.	British Klemm
BN	Britten-Norman
Bo	Bölkow
Bü	Bücker
CAARP	Co-operatives des Ateliers Aéronautiques de la Région Parisienne
CAC	Commonwealth Aircraft Corporation
CAF	Canadian Air Force
CASA	Construcciones Aeronautics SA
CCF	Canadian Car & Foundry Co
CEA	Centre-Est Aviation
CH.	Chrislea
CHABA	Cambridge Hot-Air Ballooning Association
CLA.	Comper
CP.	Piel
CUAS	Cambridge University Air Squadron
Cycl	Cyclone
D.	Druine
DC-	Douglas Commercial
DH.	de Havilland
DHA.	de Havilland Australia
DHC.	de Havilland Canada
DR.	Jodel (Robin-built)
EE	English Electric
EAA	Experimental Aircraft Association
EMB	Embraer Empresa Brasileira de Aeronautica SA
EoN	Elliotts of Newbury
EP	Edgar Percival
ETPS	Empire Test Pilots School
F.	Fairchild, Fokker
F.A.A.	Fleet Air Arm
FFA	Flug und Fahrzeugwerke AG
FH	Fairchild-Hiller
FrAF	French Air Force
FRED	Flying Runabout Experimental Design
Fw	Focke-Wulf
G.	Grumman
GA	Gulfstream American
GAL.	General Aircraft
GC	Globe Aircraft
GECAS	General Electric Capital Aviation Services
GY	Gardan
H	Helio
HM.	Henri Mignet
HP.	Handley Page
HPR.	Handley Page Reading
HR.	Robin
HS.	Hawker Siddeley

ICA	Intreprinderea de Constructii Aeronau
IHM	International Helicopter Museum
I.I.I.	Iniziative Industriali Italiane
IL	Ilyushin
ILFC	International Lease Finance Corporation
IMCO	Intermountain Manufacturing Co
IWM	Imperial War Museum
KR	Rand-Robinson
L.	Lockheed
L.A.	Luton, Lake
LET	Letecky Narodny Podnik
LLP	Limited Liability Partnership
L.V.G.	Luft-Verkehrs Gesellschaft
M.	Miles, Mooney
MBA	Micro Biplane Aviation
MBB	Messerschmitt-Bölkow-Blohm
McD	McDonnell
MDH	McDonnell Douglas Helicopters
MH.	Max Holste
MHCA	Manhole Cover
MJ	Jurca
MS.	Morane-Saulnier
NA	North American
NC	Nord
NE	North East
P.	Hunting (formerly Percival), Piaggio
PA-	Piper
PC.	Pilatus
PZL	Panstwowe Zaklady Lotnicze
QAC	Quickie Aircraft Co
R.	Rockwell
RAF	Rotary Air Force
RAAF	Royal Australian Air Force
RAFGSA	Royal Air Force Gliding & Soaring Association
RCAF	Royal Canadian Air Force
RF	Fournier
R.N.	Royal Navy
S.	Short, Sikorsky
SA,SE,SO	Sud-Aviation, Aérospatiale, Scottish Aviation
SAAB	Svenska Aeroplan Aktieboleg
SC	Short
SCD	Side Cargo Door
SNCAN	Société Nationale de Constructions Aéronautiques du Nord
SOCATA	Société de Construction d'Avions de Tourisme et d'Affaires
SpA	Societa per Azioni
SPP	Strojirny Prvni Petiletky
S.R.	Saunders-Roe, Stinson
SS	Special Shape
ST	SOCATA
SW	Solar Wings
T.	Tipsy
TB	SOCATA
Tu	Tupolev
UH.	United Helicopters (Hiller)
UK	United Kingdom
USAF	United States Air Force
USAAC	United States Army Air Corps
USN	United States Navy
V.	Vickers-Armstrongs
VLM	Vlaamse Luchttransportmaatschappij
VS.	Vickers-Supermarine
WA	Wassmer
WAR	War Aircraft Replicas
WHE	W.H.Ekin
WS	Westland
Z	Zlin

British Civil Registrations

Reg.	Type	Owner or Operator	Notes
G-AAAH†	DH.60G Moth (replica) (BAPC 168) ★	Yorkshire Air Museum/Elvington	
G-AAAH	DH.60G Moth ★	Science Museum *Jason*/South Kensington	
G-AACA†	Avro 504K (BAPC 177) ★	Brooklands Museum of Aviation/Weybridge	
G-AACN	HP.39 Gugnunc ★	Science Museum/Wroughton	
G-AADR	DH.60GM Moth	E. V. Moffatt	
G-AAEG	DH.60G Gipsy Moth	I. B. Grace	
G-AAHI	DH.60G Moth	Nigel John Western Reid Discretionary Settlement 2008	
G-AAHY	DH.60M Moth	D. J. Elliott	
G-AAIN	Parnall Elf II	The Shuttleworth Collection/Old Warden	
G-AAJT	DH.60G Moth	M. R. Paul	
G-AALY	DH.60G Moth	K. M. Fresson	
G-AAMX	DH.60GM Moth ★	RAF Museum/Hendon	
G-AAMY	DH.60GMW Moth	Totalsure Ltd	
G-AANG	Blériot XI	The Shuttleworth Collection/Old Warden	
G-AANH	Deperdussin Monoplane	The Shuttleworth Collection/Old Warden	
G-AANI	Blackburn Monoplane	The Shuttleworth Collection/Old Warden	
G-AANJ	L.V.G. C VI (7198/18)	Aerospace Museum/Cosford	
G-AANL	DH.60M Moth	R. A. Palmer	
G-AANO	DH.60GMW Moth	A. W. & M. E. Jenkins	
G-AANV	DH.60G Moth	R. A. Seeley	
G-AAOK	Curtiss Wright Travel Air 12Q	Shipping & Airlines Ltd	
G-AAOR	DH.60G Moth	B. R. Cox	
G-AAPZ	Desoutter I (mod.)	The Shuttleworth Collection	
G-AATC	DH.80A Puss Moth	R. A. Palmer	
G-AAUP	Klemm L.25-1A	J. I. Cooper	
G-AAWO	DH.60G Moth	Iain Charles Reid Discretionary Settlement 2009	
G-AAXG	DH 60M Moth	S. H. Kidston	
G-AAXK	Klemm L.25-1A ★	C. C. Russell-Vick (stored)	
G-AAYT	DH.60G Moth	P. Groves	
G-AAYX	Southern Martlet	The Shuttleworth Collection	
G-AAZG	DH.60G Moth	E. G. & N. S. C. English	
G-AAZP	DH.80A Puss Moth	R. P. Williams	
G-ABAA	Avro 504K ★	Manchester Museum of Science & Industry	
G-ABAG	DH.60G Moth	A. & P. A. Wood	
G-ABBB	B.105A Bulldog IIA (K2227) ★	RAF Museum/Hendon	
G-ABDA	DH.60G Moth	R. A. Palmer	
G-ABDW	DH.80A Puss Moth (VH-UQB) ★	Museum of Flight/East Fortune	
G-ABDX	DH.60G Moth	M. D. Souch	
G-ABEV	DH.60G Moth	S. L. G. Darch	
G-ABHE	Aeronca C.2	N. S. Chittenden	
G-ABLM	Cierva C.24 ★	De Havilland Heritage Museum/London Colney	
G-ABLS	DH.80A Puss Moth	R. A. Seeley	
G-ABMR	Hart 2 (J9941) ★	RAF Museum/Hendon	
G-ABNT	Civilian C.A.C.1 Coupe	Shipping & Airlines Ltd	
G-ABNX	Redwing 2	Redwing Syndicate	
G-ABOI	Wheeler Slymph ★	Midland Air Museum/Coventry	
G-ABOX	Sopwith Pup (N5195)	C. M. D. & A. P. St. Cyrien	
G-ABSD	DHA.60G Moth	M. E. Vaisey	
G-ABUL†	DH.82A Tiger Moth ★	F.A.A. Museum/Yeovilton (G-AOXG)	
G-ABUS	Comper CLA.7 Swift	R. C. F. Bailey	
G-ABVE	Arrow Active 2	Real Aircraft Co	
G-ABWD	DH.83 Fox Moth	R. I. Souch	
G-ABWP	Spartan Arrow	R. T. Blain	
G-ABXL	Granger Archaeopteryx ★	J. R. Granger	
G-ABYA	DH.60G Gipsy Moth	M. J. Saggers	
G-ABZB	DH.60G-III Moth Major	G. M. Turner	
G-ACBH	Blackburn B.2 ★	South Yorkshire Aircraft Museum/Doncaster	
G-ACCB	DH.83 Fox Moth	E. A. Gautrey	
G-ACDA	DH.82A Tiger Moth	J. Turnball	
G-ACDC	DH.82A Tiger Moth	Tiger Club Ltd	
G-ACDI	DH.82A Tiger Moth	Doublecube Aviation LLP	
G-ACDJ	DH.82A Tiger Moth	R. H. & J. A. Cooper	
G-ACEJ	DH.83 Fox Moth	I. G. Barnett & G. R. Williams	
G-ACET	DH.84 Dragon	G. Cormack	

Notes	Reg.	Type	Owner or Operator
	G-ACGT	Avro 594 Avian IIIA ★	Yorkshire Light Aircraft Ltd/Leeds
	G-ACGZ	DH.60G-III Moth Major	N. H. Lemon
	G-ACIT	DH.84 Dragon ★	Science Museum/Wroughton
	G-ACLL	DH.85 Leopard Moth	V. M & D. C. M. Stiles
	G-ACMA	DH.85 Leopard Moth	P. A. Vacher
	G-ACMD	DH.82A Tiger Moth	M. J. Bonnick
	G-ACMN	DH.85 Leopard Moth	M. R. & K. E. Slack
	G-ACNS	DH.60G-III Moth Major	C. T. Parry
	G-ACOJ	DH.85 Leopard Moth	Norman Aeroplane Trust
	G-ACSP	DH.88 Comet ★	T. M., M. L., D. A. & P. M. Jones
	G-ACSS	DH.88 Comet ★	The Shuttleworth Collection *Grosvenor House*/Old Warden
	G-ACSS†	DH.88 Comet (replica) ★	G. Gayward (BAPC216)
	G-ACSS†	DH.88 Comet (replica)	The Galleria Hatfield (BAPC257)
	G-ACTF	Comper CLA.7 Swift ★	The Shuttleworth Collection/Old Warden
	G-ACUS	DH.85 Leopard Moth	R. A. & V. A. Gammons
	G-ACUU	Cierva C.30A (HM580) ★	G. S. Baker/Duxford
	G-ACUX	S.16 Scion (VH-UUP) ★	Ulster Folk & Transport Museum
	G-ACVA	Kay Gyroplane ★	Museum of Flight/East Fortune
	G-ACWM	Cierva C.30A (AP506) ★	IHM/Weston-super-Mare
	G-ACWP	Cierva C.30A (AP507) ★	Science Museum/South Kensington
	G-ACXB	DH.60G-III Moth Major	D. F. Hodgkinson
	G-ACXE	B.K. L-25C Swallow	J. G. Wakeford
	G-ACYK	Spartan Cruiser III ★	Museum of Flight (front fuselage)/East Fortune
	G-ADAH	DH.89A Dragon Rapide ★	Manchester Museum of Science & Industry *Pioneer*
	G-ADEV	Avro 504K (E3273)	The Shuttleworth Collection/Old Warden (G-ACNB)
	G-ADGP	M.2L Hawk Speed Six	R. A. Mills
	G-ADGT	DH.82A Tiger Moth (BB697)	The Tiger Club 1990 Ltd
	G-ADGV	DH.82A Tiger Moth	M. van Dijk & M. R. Van der Straaten (G-BACW)
	G-ADHD	DH.60G-III Moth Major	M. E. Vaisey
	G-ADIA	DH.82A Tiger Moth	S. J. Beaty
	G-ADJJ	DH.82A Tiger Moth	J. M. Preston
	G-ADKC	DH.87B Hornet Moth	C. G. Winch & J. W. Davy
	G-ADKK	DH.87B Hornet Moth	S. J. Sykes
	G-ADKL	DH.87B Hornet Moth	J. S. & P. R. Johnson
	G-ADKM	DH.87B Hornet Moth	S. G. Collyer
	G-ADLY	DH.87B Hornet Moth	Totalsure Ltd
	G-ADMT	DH.87B Hornet Moth	D. C. Reid
	G-ADMW	M.2H Hawk Major (DG590) ★	RAF Museum Storage & Restoration Centre/RAF Stafford
	G-ADND	DH.87B Hornet Moth (W9385)	D. M. & S. M. Weston
	G-ADNE	DH.87B Hornet Moth	G-ADNE Group
	G-ADNZ	DH.82A Tiger Moth (DE673)	D. C. Wall
	G-ADOT	DH.87B Hornet Moth ★	De Havilland Heritage Museum/London Colney
	G-ADPC	DH.82A Tiger Moth	Baxterley Flying Group
	G-ADPJ	B.A.C. Drone ★	M. J. Aubrey
	G-ADPS	B.A. Swallow 2	J. F. Hopkins
	G-ADRA	Pietenpol Air Camper	A. J. Mason
	G-ADRG†	Mignet HM.14 (replica) ★	Lower Stondon Transport Museum (BAPC77)
	G-ADRR	Aeronca C.3	C. J. & M. A. Essex
	G-ADRX†	Mignet HM.14 (replica) ★	S. Copeland Aviation Group (BAPC231)
	G-ADRY†	Mignet HM.14 (replica) (BAPC29)★	Brooklands Museum of Aviation/Weybridge
	G-ADVU†	Mignet HM.14 (replica) ★	North East Aircraft Museum/Usworth (BAPC211)
	G-ADWJ	DH.82A Tiger Moth	K. F. Crumplin
	G-ADWO	DH.82A Tiger Moth (BB807) ★	Solent Sky, Southampton
	G-ADWT	M.2W Hawk Trainer	R. Earl & B. Morris
	G-ADXS	Mignet HM.14 ★	Thameside Aviation Museum/Shoreham
	G-ADXT	DH.82A Tiger Moth	DH Heritage Flights Ltd
	G-ADYS	Aeronca C.3	E. P. & P. A. Gliddon
	G-ADYV†	Mignet HM.14 (replica) ★	P. Ward (BAPC243)
	G-ADZW†	Mignet HM.14 (replica) ★	Solent Sky/Southampton (BAPC253)
	G-AEBB	Mignet HM.14 ★	The Shuttleworth Collection/Old Warden
	G-AEBJ	Blackburn B-2	BAe Systems (Operations) Ltd
	G-AEDB	B.A.C. Drone 2	M. J. & S. Honeychurch
	G-AEDU	DH.90 Dragonfly	Norman Aeroplane Trust
	G-AEEG	M.3A Falcon Skysport	P. R. Holloway
	G-AEEH	Mignet HM.14 ★	Aerospace Museum/Cosford
	G-AEFG	Mignet HM.14 (BAPC75) ★	N. H. Ponsford/Breighton

Reg.	Type	Owner or Operator	Notes
G-AEFT	Aeronca C.3	N. S. Chittenden	
G-AEGV	Mignet HM.14 ★	Midland Air Museum/Coventry	
G-AEHM	Mignet HM.14 ★	Science Museum/Wroughton	
G-AEJZ	Mignet HM.14 (BAPC120) ★	Aero Venture	
G-AEKR	Mignet HM.14 (BAPC121) ★	Doncaster Museum & Art Gallery	
G-AEKV	Kronfeld Drone ★	Brooklands Museum of Aviation/Weybridge	
G-AEKW	M.12 Mohawk ★	RAF Museum	
G-AELO	DH.87B Hornet Moth	M. J. Miller	
G-AEML	DH.89 Dragon Rapide ★	Fundacion Infante de Orleans/Spain	
G-AENP	Hawker Hind (K5414) (BAPC78)	The Shuttleworth Collection	
G-AEOA	DH.80A Puss Moth	P. & A. Wood/Old Warden	
G-AEOF†	Mignet HM.14 (BAPC22) ★	Aviodrome/Lelystad, Netherlands	
G-AEOF	Rearwin 8500	Shipping & Airlines Ltd	
G-AEPH	Bristol F.2B (D8096)	The Shuttleworth Collection	
G-AERV	M.11A Whitney Straight	R. A. Seeley	
G-AESB	Aeronca C.3	R. J. M. Turnbull	
G-AESE	DH.87B Hornet Moth	B. R. Cox	
G-AESZ	Chilton D.W.1	R. E. Nerou	
G-AETA	Caudron G.3 (3066) ★	RAF Museum/Hendon	
G-AETG	Aeronca 100	J. Teagle and Partners	
G-AEUJ	M.11A Whitney Straight	R. E. Mitchell	
G-AEVS	Aeronca 100	R. A. Fleming	
G-AEXD	Aeronca 100	M. A. & N. Mills	
G-AEXF	P.6 Mew Gull	Richard Shuttleworth Trustees	
G-AEXT	Dart Kitten II	R. A. Fleming	
G-AEXZ	Piper J-2 Cub	M. & J. R. Dowson	
G-AEZF	S.16 Scion 2 ★	Acebell Aviation/Redhill	
G-AEZJ	P.10 Vega Gull	D. P. H. Hulme	
G-AFAP†	CASA C.352L ★	Aerospace Museum/Cosford	
G-AFBS	M.14A Hawk Trainer 3 ★	G. D. Durbridge-Freeman/Duxford (G-AKKU)	
G-AFCL	B. A. Swallow 2	D. & J. Cresswell	
G-AFDO	Piper J-3F-60 Cub	R. Wald	
G-AFDX	Hanriot HD.1 (HD-75) ★	RAF Museum/Hendon	
G-AFEL	Monocoupe 90A	M. Rieser	
G-AFFD	Percival Type Q Six	G-AFFD Restoration Group	
G-AFFH	Piper J-2 Cub	M. J. Honeychurch	
G-AFFI†	Mignet HM.14 (replica) (BAPC76) ★	Yorkshire Air Museum/Elvington	
G-AFGD	B. A. Swallow 2	South Wales Swallow Group	
G-AFGE	B. A. Swallow 2	A. A. M. & C. W. N. Huke	
G-AFGH	Chilton D.W.1.	M. L. & G. L. Joseph	
G-AFGI	Chilton D.W.1.	K. A. A. McDonald	
G-AFGM	Piper J-4A Cub Coupé	P. H. Wilkinson	
G-AFGZ	DH.82A Tiger Moth	M. R. Paul (G-AMHI)	
G-AFHA	Mosscraft MA.1. ★	C. V. Butler	
G-AFIN	Chrislea LC.1 Airguard (BAPC203) ★	T. W. J. Carnall	
G-AFIR	Luton LA-4 Minor	J. Cresswell	
G-AFIU	Parker CA-4 Parasol ★	The Aeroplane Collection/Hooton Park	
G-AFJA	Watkinson Dingbat ★	A. T. Christian	
G-AFJB	Foster-Wikner G.M.1. Wicko	J. Dible	
G-AFJR	Tipsy Trainer 1	M. E. Vaisey (stored)	
G-AFJU	M.17 Monarch	Museum of Flight/East Fortune	
G-AFJV	Mosscraft MA.2 ★	C. V. Butler	
G-AFNI	DH.94 Moth Minor	J. Jennings	
G-AFOB	DH.94 Moth Minor	K. Cantwell	
G-AFOJ	DH.94 Moth Minor	A. H. Soper	
G-AFPN	DH.94 Moth Minor	A. A. A. Maitland & R. S. Jones	
G-AFRZ	M.17 Monarch	R. E. Mitchell/Sleap (G-AIDE)	
G-AFSC	Tipsy Trainer 1	D. M. Forshaw	
G-AFSV	Chilton D.W.1A	R. E. Nerou	
G-AFTA	Hawker Tomtit (K1786)	The Shuttleworth Collection	
G-AFTN	Taylorcraft Plus C2 ★	Leicestershire County Council Museums/ Snibston	
G-AFUP	Luscombe 8A Silvaire	R. Dispain	
G-AFVE	DH.82A Tiger Moth (T7230)	J. Mainka	
G-AFWH	Piper J-4A Cub Coupé	C. W. Stearn & R. D. W. Norton	
G-AFWI	DH.82A Tiger Moth	P. R. Harvey	
G-AFWT	Tipsy Trainer 1	N. Parkhouse	
G-AFYD	Luscombe 8F Silvaire	J. D. Iliffe	
G-AFYO	Stinson H.W.75	M. Lodge	
G-AFZA	Piper J-4A Cub Coupe	R. A. Benson	

Notes	Reg.	Type	Owner or Operator
	G-AFZK	Luscombe 8A Silvaire	M. G. Byrnes
	G-AFZL	Porterfield CP.50	P. G. Lucas & S. H. Sharpe
	G-AFZN	Luscombe 8A Silvaire	A. & B. Garcia
	G-AGAT	Piper J-3F-50 Cub	A. S. Bathgate
	G-AGBN	GAL.42 Cygnet 2 ★	Museum of Flight/East Fortune
	G-AGEG	DH.82A Tiger Moth	Norman Aeroplane Trust
	G-AGHY	DH.82A Tiger Moth	P. Groves
	G-AGIV	Piper J-3C-65 Cub	J-3 Cub Group
	G-AGJG	DH.89A Dragon Rapide	M. J. & D. J. T. Miller
	G-AGLK	Auster 5D	M. A. Farrelly & D. K. Chambers
	G-AGMI	Luscombe 8A Silvaire	Oscar Flying Group
	G-AGNJ	DH.82A Tiger Moth	B. P. Borsberry & ptnrs
	G-AGNV	Avro 685 York 1 (TS798) ★	Aerospace Museum/Cosford
	G-AGOS	R.S.4 Desford Trainer (VZ728) ★	Leicestershire County Council Museums
	G-AGPG	Avro 19 Srs 2 ★	The Aeroplane Collection/Hooton Park
	G-AGPK	DH.82A Tiger Moth	T. K. Butcher
	G-AGRU	V.498 Viking 1A ★	Brooklands Museum of Aviation/Weybridge
	G-AGSH	DH.89A Dragon Rapide 6	Bournemouth Aviation Museum
	G-AGTM	DH.89A Dragon Rapide 6	Air Atlantique Ltd
	G-AGTO	Auster 5 J/1 Autocrat	M. J. Barnett & D. J. T. Miller
	G-AGTT	Auster J/1 Autocrat	C. Norfolk
	G-AGVG	Auster 5 J/1 Autocrat (modified)	P. J. & S. J. Benest
	G-AGXN	Auster J/1N Alpha	Gentleman's Aerial Touring Carriage Group
	G-AGXU	Auster J/1N Alpha	L. J. Kingscott
	G-AGXV	Auster J/1 Autocrat	B. S. Dowsett & I. M. Oliver
	G-AGYD	Auster J/1N Alpha	P. D. Hodson
	G-AGYH	Auster J/1N Alpha	I. M. Staves
	G-AGYT	Auster J/1N Alpha	P. J. Barrett
	G-AGYU	DH.82A Tiger Moth (DE208)	S. A. Firth
	G-AGYY	Ryan ST3KR (27)	H. de Vries/Holland
	G-AGZZ	DH.82A Tiger Moth	M. C. Jordan
	G-AHAG	DH.89A Rapide	D. E. Findon
	G-AHAL	Auster J/1N Alpha	Wickenby Aviation
	G-AHAM	Auster J/1 Autocrat	Interna Engineering BVBA/Belgium
	G-AHAN	DH.82A Tiger Moth	Tiger Associates Ltd
	G-AHAP	Auster J/1 Autocrat	W. D. Hill
	G-AHAT	Auster J/1N Alpha ★	Dumfries & Galloway Aviation Museum
	G-AHAU	Auster 5 J/1 Autocrat	Andreas Auster Group
	G-AHBL	DH.87B Hornet Moth	Shipping and Airlines Ltd
	G-AHBM	DH.87B Hornet Moth	P. A. & E. P. Gliddon
	G-AHCL	Auster J/1N Alpha (modified)	N. Musgrave
	G-AHCN	Auster J/1N Alpha	C. L. Towell & A. G. Boon
	G-AHCR	Gould-Taylorcraft Plus D Special	D. E. H. Balmford & D. R. Shepherd
	G-AHEC	Luscombe 8A Silvaire	C. G. Dodds
	G-AHED	DH.89A Dragon Rapide (RL962) ★	RAF Museum Storage & Restoration Centre/ RAF Stafford
	G-AHGW	Taylorcraft Plus D (LB375)	C. V. Butler
	G-AHGZ	Taylorcraft Plus D (LB367)	M. Pocock
	G-AHHH	Auster J/1 Autocrat	K. Moore & G. J. Molloy
	G-AHHT	Auster J/1N Alpha	A. C. Barber & N. J. Hudson
	G-AHIP	Piper J-3C-65 Cub	A. D. Pearce
	G-AHIZ	DH.82A Tiger Moth	C.F.G. Flying Ltd
	G-AHKX	Avro 19 Srs 2	The Shuttleworth Collection
	G-AHKY	Miles M.18 Series 2 ★	Museum of Flight/East Fortune
	G-AHLK	Auster 3 (NJ889)	J. H. Powell-Tuck
	G-AHLT	DH.82A Tiger Moth	M. P. Waring
	G-AHNR	Taylorcraft BC-12D	T. M. Buick
	G-AHOO	DH.82A Tiger Moth	J. T. Milsom
	G-AHPZ	DH.82A Tiger Moth	N. J. Wareing
	G-AHRI	DH.104 Dove 1 ★	Newark Air Museum
	G-AHSA	Avro 621 Tutor (K3241)	The Shuttleworth Collection
	G-AHSD	Taylorcraft Plus D (LB323)	A. L. Hall-Carpenter
	G-AHSP	Auster J/1 Autocrat	R. M. Weeks
	G-AHSS	Auster J/1N Alpha	A. M. Roche
	G-AHST	Auster J/1N Alpha	A. C. Frost
	G-AHTE	P.44 Proctor V	D. K. Tregilgas
	G-AHTW	A.S.40 Oxford (V3388) ★	Skyfame Collection/Duxford
	G-AHUF	DH.Tiger Moth	Dream Ventures Ltd
	G-AHUG	Taylorcraft Plus D	D. Nieman

Reg.	Type	Owner or Operator	Notes
G-AHUI	M.38 Messenger 2A ★	The Aeroplane Collection/Hooton Park	
G-AHUJ	M.14A Hawk Trainer 3 (R1914) ★	Strathallan Aircraft Collection	
G-AHUN	Globe GC-1B Swift	R. J. Hamlett	
G-AHUV	DH.82A Tiger Moth	A. D. Gordon	
G-AHVU	DH.82A Tiger Moth	J. B. Steel	
G-AHVV	DH.82A Tiger Moth	M. Arter	
G-AHXE	Taylorcraft Plus D (LB312)	J. M. C. Pothecary	
G-AIBE	Fulmar II (N1854) ★	F.A.A. Museum/Yeovilton	
G-AIBH	Auster J/1N Alpha	M. J. Bonnick	
G-AIBM	Auster J/1 Autocrat	R. Greatrex	
G-AIBR	Auster J/1 Autocrat	P. R. Hodson	
G-AIBW	Auster J/1N Alpha	C. R. Sunter	
G-AIBX	Auster J/1 Autocrat	Wasp Flying Group	
G-AIBY	Auster J/1 Autocrat	D. Morris	
G-AICX	Luscombe 8A Silvaire	C. C. & J. M. Lovell	
G-AIDL	DH.89A Dragon Rapide 6 (TX310)	Air Atlantique Ltd	
G-AIDN	VS.502 Spitfire Tr.VII (MT818)	P. M. Andrews	
G-AIDS	DH.82A Tiger Moth	K. D. Pogmore & T. Dann	
G-AIEK	M.38 Messenger 2A (RG333)	P. E. Beaver	
G-AIFZ	Auster J/1N Alpha	M. D. Ansley	
G-AIGD	Auster V J/1 Autocrat	R. B. Webber	
G-AIGF	Auster J/1N Alpha	D. W. Mathie	
G-AIGT	Auster J/1N Alpha	R. R. Harris	
G-AIIH	Piper J-3C-65 Cub	The G-AIIH Group	
G-AIJI	Auster J/1N Alpha ★	C. J. Baker	
G-AIJM	Auster J/4	N. Huxtable	
G-AIJT	Auster J/4 Srs 100	Aberdeen Auster Flying Group	
G-AIKE	Auster 5	R. H. Cooper & T. K. Rumble	
G-AIPR	Auster J/4	M. A. & N. Mills	
G-AIPV	Auster J/1 Autocrat	W. P. Miller	
G-AIRC	Auster J/1 Autocrat	N. O'Brien	
G-AIRK	DH.82A Tiger Moth	J. S. & P. R. Johnson	
G-AISA	Tipsy B Srs 1	S. Slater	
G-AISC	Tipsy B Srs 1	Wagtail Flying Group	
G-AISS	Piper J-3C-65 Cub	K. W. Wood & F. Watson	
G-AIST	VS.300 Spitfire 1A (AR213/PR-D)	Spitfire The One Ltd	
G-AISX	Piper J-3C-65 Cub	Cubfly	
G-AITB	A.S.10 Oxford (MP425) ★	RAF Museum/Hendon	
G-AIUA	M.14A Hawk Trainer 3 (T9768) ★	D. S. Hunt	
G-AIUL	DH.89A Dragon Rapide 6	I. Jones	
G-AIXA	Taylorcraft Plus D (LB264)★	RAF Museum/Hendon	
G-AIXJ	DH.82A Tiger Moth	D. Green	
G-AIXN	Benes-Mraz M.1C Sokol	A. J. Wood	
G-AIYG	SNCAN Stampe SV.4B	J. E. Henny/Belgium	
G-AIYR	DH.89A Dragon Rapide (HG691)	Spectrum Leisure Ltd	
G-AIYS	DH.85 Leopard Moth	R. A. & V. A. Gammons	
G-AIZE	Fairchild F.24W Argus 2 (FS628) ★	Aerospace Museum/Cosford	
G-AIZG	VS.236 Walrus 1 (L2301) ★	F.A.A. Museum/Yeovilton	
G-AIZU	Auster J/1 Autocrat★	C. J. & J. G. B. Morley	
G-AJAD	Piper J-3C-65 Cub	C. R. Shipley	
G-AJAE	Auster J/1N Alpha	J. W. Wolfe	
G-AJAJ	Auster J/1N Alpha	G-AJAJ Group	
G-AJAM	Auster J/2 Arrow	D. A. Porter	
G-AJAP	Luscombe 8A Silvaire	M. Flint	
G-AJAS	Auster J/1N Alpha	P. Ferguson & L. & R. Ferguson-Dalling	
G-AJCP	D.31 Turbulent	B. R. Pearson	
G-AJDW	Auster J/1 Autocrat	D. R. Hunt	
G-AJDY	Auster J/1N Alpha	W. Bayman	
G-AJEB	Auster J/1N Alpha ★	The Aeroplane Collection/Hooton Park	
G-AJEE	Auster J/1 Autocrat	A. C. Whitehead	
G-AJEH	Auster J/1N Alpha	J. T. Powell-Tuck	
G-AJEI	Auster J/1N Alpha	J. Siddall	
G-AJEM	Auster J/1 Autocrat	A. L. Aish	
G-AJES	Piper J-3C-65 Cub (330485:C-44)	D. E. Jarvis	
G-AJGJ	Auster 5 (RT486)	British Classic Aircraft Restoration Flying Group	
G-AJHS	DH.82A Tiger Moth	Flying Wires/Netherlands	
G-AJIH	Auster J/1 Autocrat	A. J. Collins	
G-AJIS	Auster J/1N Alpha	Husthwaite Auster Group	

Notes	Reg.	Type	Owner or Operator
	G-AJIT	Auster J/1 Kingsland Autocrat	G-AJIT Group
	G-AJIU	Auster J/1 Autocrat	M. D. Greenhalgh
	G-AJIW	Auster J/1N Alpha	W. C. Walters & R. J. Guess
	G-AJJP	Fairey Jet Gyrodyne (XJ389) ★	Museum of Berkshire Aviation/Woodley
	G-AJJS	Cessna 120	Juliet Sierra Group
	G-AJJT	Cessna 120	Juliet Tango Group
	G-AJJU	Luscombe 8E Silvaire	Enstone Luscombe Group
	G-AJKB	Luscombe 8E Silvaire	T. Carter
	G-AJOC	M.38 Messenger 2A ★	Ulster Folk & Transport Museum
	G-AJOE	M.38 Messenger 2A	P. W. Bishop
	G-AJON	Aeronca 7AC Champion	J. M. Gale
	G-AJOV†	Westland WS-51 Dragonfly ★	Aerospace Museum/Cosford
	G-AJOZ	Fairchild F.24W Argus 2 ★	Yorkshire Air Museum/Elvington
	G-AJPI	Fairchild F.24R-41a Argus 3 (314887)	R. Sijben/Netherlands
	G-AJRB	Auster J/1 Autocrat	R. W. Vince
	G-AJRH	Auster J/1N Alpha ★	Charnwood Museum/Loughborough
	G-AJRS	M.14A Hawk Trainer 3 (P6382:C)	The Shuttleworth Collection
	G-AJTW	DH.82A Tiger Moth (N6965:FL-J)	J. A. Barker
	G-AJUE	Auster J/1 Autocrat	P. H. B. Cole
	G-AJUL	Auster J/1N Alpha	M. J. Crees
	G-AJVE	DH.82A Tiger Moth	R. A. Gammons
	G-AJWB	M.38 Messenger 2A	P. W. Bishop
	G-AJXC	Auster 5	R. D. Helliar-Symonds, K. A. & S. E. W. Williams
	G-AJXV	Auster 4 (NJ695)	B. A. Farries
	G-AJXY	Auster 4	X-Ray Yankee Group
	G-AJYB	Auster J/1N Alpha	P. J. Shotbolt
	G-AKAT	M.14A Hawk Trainer 3 (T9738)	R. A. Fleming
	G-AKAZ	Piper J-3C-65 Cub (57-G)	Frazerblades Ltd
	G-AKBO	M.38 Messenger 2A	D. O. Blackburn & P. A. Fenton
	G-AKDF	M.38 Messenger 2A	C. W. P. Turner
	G-AKDK	M.65 Gemini 1A	C. W. P. Turner
	G-AKDN	DHC.1A-1 Chipmunk	P. S. Derry/Canada
	G-AKDW	DH.89A Dragon Rapide ★	De Havilland Heritage Museum/London Colney
	G-AKEL	M.65 Gemini 1A ★	Ulster Folk & Transport Museum
	G-AKEN	M.65 Gemini 1A	C. W. P. Turner
	G-AKEX	Percival Proctor III	M. Biddulph (G-AKIU)
	G-AKGE	M.65 Gemini 3C ★	Ulster Folk & Transport Museum
	G-AKHP	M.65 Gemini 1A	M. A. McCallum
	G-AKHU	M.65 Gemini 1A	C. W. P. Turner
	G-AKHZ	M.65 Gemini 7 ★	The Aeroplane Collection/Hooton Park
	G-AKIB	Piper J-3C-90 Cub (480015:M-44)	R. Horner
	G-AKIF	DH.89A Dragon Rapide	Airborne Taxi Services Ltd
	G-AKIN	M.38 Messenger 2A	Sywell Messenger Group
	G-AKIU	P.44 Proctor V	Air Atlantique Ltd
	G-AKKB	M.65 Gemini 1A	D. R. Gray
	G-AKKH	M.65 Gemini 1A	J. S. Allison
	G-AKKR	M.14A Magister (T9707) ★	Museum of Army Flying/Middle Wallop
	G-AKKY	M.14A Hawk Trainer 3 (L6906) ★ (BAPC44)	Museum of Berkshire Aviation/Woodley
	G-AKLW	Short SA.6 Sealand 1 ★	Ulster Folk & Transport Museum
	G-AKOW	Auster 5 (TJ569) ★	Museum of Army Flying/Middle Wallop
	G-AKPF	M.14A Hawk Trainer 3 (N3788)	P. R. Holloway
	G-AKPI	Auster 5	R. H. & J. A. Cooper
	G-AKRA	Piper J-3C-65 Cub	W. R. Savin
	G-AKRP	DH.89A Dragon Rapide 4	Eaglescott Dominie Group
	G-AKSY	Auster 5 (TJ534)	A. Brier
	G-AKSZ	Auster 5D (modified)	P. W. Yates & R. G. Darbyshire
	G-AKTH	Piper J-3C-65 Cub	OFL4 Group
	G-AKTI	Luscombe 8A Silvaire	C. Chambers
	G-AKTO	Aeronca 7BCM Champion	R. M. Davies
	G-AKTP	PA-17 Vagabond	Golf Tango Papa Group
	G-AKTR	Aeronca 7AC Champion	T. White
	G-AKTS	Cessna 120	M. Isterling
	G-AKTT	Luscombe 8A Silvaire	S. J. Charters
	G-AKUE	DH.82A Tiger Moth	D. F. Hodgkinson
	G-AKUF	Luscombe 8E Silvaire	M. O. Loxton
	G-AKUH	Luscombe 8E Silvaire	A. G. Palmer (G-GIST)
	G-AKUJ	Luscombe 8E Silvaire	P. R. Bentley
	G-AKUK	Luscombe 8A Silvaire	O. R. Watts
	G-AKUL	Luscombe 8A Silvaire	E. A. Taylor

Reg.	Type	Owner or Operator	Notes
G-AKUM	Luscombe 8F Silvaire	D. A. Young	
G-AKUN	Piper J-3F-65 Cub	W. R. Savin	
G-AKUO	Aeronca 11AC Chief	L. W. Richardson	
G-AKUP	Luscombe 8E Silvaire	D. A. Young	
G-AKUR	Cessna 140	J. Greenaway & C. A. Davies	
G-AKUW	Chrislea CH.3 Super Ace 2	J. & S. Rickett	
G-AKVF	Chrislea CH.3 Super Ace 2	Aviation Heritage Ltd	
G-AKVM	Cessna 120	N. Wise & S. Walker	
G-AKVN	Aeronca 11AC Chief	P. A. Jackson	
G-AKVO	Taylorcraft BC-12D	T. P. Hancock	
G-AKVP	Luscombe 8A Silvaire	J. M. Edis	
G-AKVR	Chrislea CH.3 Skyjeep 4	R. B. Webber	
G-AKVZ	M.38 Messenger 4B	Shipping & Airlines Ltd	
G-AKWS	Auster 5A-160 (RT610)	M. C. Hayes	
G-AKWT	Auster 5 ★	C. Baker	
G-AKXP	Auster 5 (NJ633)	M. J. Nicholson	
G-AKXS	DH.82A Tiger Moth	J. & G. J. Eagles	
G-AKZN	P.34A Proctor 3 (Z7197) ★	RAF Museum/Hendon	
G-ALAR	Miles M.38 Messenger 4A	C. W. P. Turner	
G-ALAX	DH.89A Dragon Rapide ★	Durney Aeronautical Collection/Andover	
G-ALBJ	Auster 5 (TW501)	B. M. Vigor	
G-ALBK	Auster 5	J. S. Allison	
G-ALBN	Bristol 173 (XF785) ★	RAF Museum Storage & Restoration Centre/ Cardington	
G-ALCK	P.34A Proctor 3 (LZ766) ★	Skyfame Collection/Duxford	
G-ALCU	DH.104 Dove 2 ★	Midland Air Museum/Coventry	
G-ALDG	HP.81 Hermes 4 ★	Duxford Aviation Society (fuselage only)	
G-ALEH	PA-17 Vagabond	A. D. Pearce	
G-ALFA	Auster 5	A. E. Jones	
G-ALFU	DH.104 Dove 6 ★	Duxford Aviation Society	
G-ALGA	PA-15 Vagabond	S. T. Gilbert	
G-ALGT	VS.379 Spitfire F.XIVH (RM689)	Rolls-Royce PLC	
G-ALIJ	PA-17 Vagabond	G-ALIJ Flying Group	
G-ALIW	DH.82A Tiger Moth	F. R. Curry	
G-ALJF	P.34A Proctor 3	J. F. Moore	
G-ALJL	DH.82A Tiger Moth	R. I. & D. Souch	
G-ALJR	Abbott-Baynes Scud III	The Gliding Heritage Centre	
G-ALLF	Slingsby T.30A Prefect (ARK)	J. F. Hopkins & K. M. Fresson	
G-ALMA	Piper J3C-65 Cub	M. J. Butler (G-BBXS)	
G-ALNA	DH.82A Tiger Moth	R. J. Doughton	
G-ALND	DH.82A Tiger Moth (N9191)	J. T. Powell-Tuck	
G-ALOD	Cessna 140	H. Merkado	
G-ALSP	Bristol 171 Sycamore (WV783) ★	RAF Museum/Hendon	
G-ALSS	Bristol 171 Sycamore (WA576) ★	Dumfries & Galloway Aviation Museum	
G-ALST	Bristol 171 Sycamore (WA577) ★	North East Aircraft Museum/Usworth	
G-ALSW	Bristol 171 Sycamore (WT933) ★	Newark Air Museum	
G-ALSX	Bristol 171 Sycamore (G-48-1) ★	IHM/Weston-super-Mare	
G-ALTO	Cessna 140	T. M. Jones & ptnrs	
G-ALUC	DH.82A Tiger Moth	Tiger Moth Experience Ltd	
G-ALWB	DHC.1 Chipmunk 22A	D. M. Neville	
G-ALWF	V.701 Viscount ★	Duxford Aviation Society *RMA Sir John Franklin*	
G-ALWS	DH.82A Tiger Moth	K. F. Crumplin	
G-ALWW	DH.82A Tiger Moth	D. E. Findon	
G-ALXT	DH.89A Dragon Rapide ★	Science Museum/Wroughton	
G-ALXZ	Auster 5-150	P. J. Tyler	
G-ALYB	Auster 5 (RT520) ★	South Yorkshire Aviation Museum/Doncaster	
G-ALYG	Auster 5D	A. L. Young	
G-ALYW	DH.106 Comet 1 ★	RAF Exhibition Flight (fuselage converted to 'Nimrod')	
G-ALZE	BN-1F ★	M. R. Short/Solent Sky, Southampton	
G-ALZO	A.S.57 Ambassador ★	Duxford Aviation Society	
G-AMAW	Luton LA-4 Minor	The Real Aeroplane Co.Ltd	
G-AMBB	DH.82A Tiger Moth	J. Eagles	
G-AMCK	DH.82A Tiger Moth	Stamp Aviation Ltd	
G-AMCM	DH.82A Tiger Moth	A. K. & J. I. Cooper	
G-AMDA	Avro 652A Anson 1 (N4877:MK-V) ★	Skyfame Collection/Duxford	
G-AMEN	PA-18 Super Cub 95	The G-AMEN Flying Group	
G-AMHF	DH.82A Tiger Moth	A. J. West	

Notes	Reg.	Type	Owner or Operator
	G-AMHJ	Douglas C-47A Dakota 6 (KG651) ★	Assault Glider Association/Shawbury
	G-AMKU	Auster J/1B Aiglet	P. G. Lipman
	G-AMLZ	P.50 Prince 6E ★	The Jetstream Club
	G-AMMS	Auster J/5K Aiglet Trainer	M. C. Jordan
	G-AMNN	DH.82A Tiger Moth	I. J. Perry
	G-AMOG	V.701 Viscount ★	Museum of Flight/East Fortune
	G-AMPG	PA-12 Super Cruiser	A. G. & S. M. Measey
	G-AMPI	SNCAN Stampe SV.4C	T. W. Harris
	G-AMPO	Douglas C-47B (FZ626/YS-DH) ★	(gate guardian)/RAF Lyneham
	G-AMPY	Douglas C-47B (KK116)	Air Atlantique Ltd
	G-AMRA	Douglas C-47B	Air Atlantique Ltd
	G-AMRF	Auster J/5F Aiglet Trainer	D. A. Hill
	G-AMRK	G.37 Gladiator I (K7985)	The Shuttleworth Collection
	G-AMSG	SIPA 903	S. W. Markham
	G-AMSN	Douglas C-47B ★	Aceball Aviation/Redhill
	G-AMTA	Auster J/5F Aiglet Trainer	J. D. Manson
	G-AMTF	DH.82A Tiger Moth (T7842)	H. A. D. Monro
	G-AMTK	DH.82A Tiger Moth	S. W. McKay & M. E. Vaisey
	G-AMTM	Auster J/1 Autocrat	R. J. Stobo (G-AJUJ)
	G-AMTV	DH.82A Tiger Moth	G-AMTV Flying Group
	G-AMUF	DHC.1 Chipmunk 21	Redhill Tailwheel Flying Club Ltd
	G-AMUI	Auster J/5F Aiglet Trainer	R. B. Webber
	G-AMVD	Auster 5 (TJ652)	M.Hammond
	G-AMVP	Tipsy Junior	A. R. Wershat
	G-AMVS	DH.82A Tiger Moth	J. T. Powell-Tuck
	G-AMXA	DH.106 Comet 2 (nose only) ★	(stored)
	G-AMYD	Auster J/5L Aiglet Trainer	R. D. Thomasson
	G-AMYJ	Douglas C-47B (KN353) ★	Yorkshire Air Museum/Elvington
	G-AMZI	Auster J/5F Aiglet Trainer	J. F. Moore
	G-AMZT	Auster J/5F Aiglet Trainer	D. Hyde, J. W. Saull & J. C. Hutchinson
	G-ANAF	Douglas C-47B	Air Atlantique Ltd
	G-ANAP	DH.104 Dove 6 ★	Brunel Technical College/Lulsgate
	G-ANCF	B.175 Britannia 308 ★	Bristol Aero Collection (stored)/Kemble
	G-ANCS	DH.82A Tiger Moth	C. E. Edwards & E. A. Higgins
	G-ANCX	DH.82A Tiger Moth	E. N. K. Lison
	G-ANDE	DH.82A Tiger Moth	D. A. Nisbet
	G-ANDM	DH.82A Tiger Moth	N. J. Stagg
	G-ANEH	DH.82A Tiger Moth (N6797)	G. J. Wells
	G-ANEL	DH.82A Tiger Moth	Totalsure Ltd
	G-ANEM	DH.82A Tiger Moth	P. J. Benest
	G-ANEN	DH.82A Tiger Moth	G-ANEN Group
	G-ANEW	DH.82A Tiger Moth (NM138)	K. F. Crumplin
	G-ANEZ	DH.82A Tiger Moth	C. D. J. Bland
	G-ANFH	Westland WS-55 Whirlwind ★	IHM/Weston-super-Mare
	G-ANFI	DH.82A Tiger Moth (DE623)	G. P. Graham
	G-ANFL	DH.82A Tiger Moth	Felthorpe Tiger Group Ltd
	G-ANFM	DH.82A Tiger Moth	Reading Flying Group
	G-ANFP	DH.82A Tiger Moth	K. F. Crumplin
	G-ANFU	Auster 5 (NJ719) ★	North East Aircraft Museum/Usworth
	G-ANHK	DH.82A Tiger Moth	J. D. Iliffe
	G-ANHR	Auster 5	H. L. Swallow
	G-ANHS	Auster 4 (MT197)	Mike Tango Group
	G-ANHU	Auster 4	J. Mainka
	G-ANHX	Auster 5D	D. J. Baker
	G-ANIE	Auster 5 (TW467)	R. T. Ingram
	G-ANIJ	Auster 5D (TJ672)	G. M. Rundle
	G-ANIS	Auster 5	J. Clarke-Cockburn
	G-ANJA	DH.82A Tiger Moth	A. D. Hodgkinson
	G-ANJD	DH.82A Tiger Moth	D. O. Lewis
	G-ANKK	DH.82A Tiger Moth (T5854)	Halfpenny Green Tiger Group
	G-ANKT	DH.82A Tiger Moth (K2585)	The Shuttleworth Collection
	G-ANKV	DH.82A Tiger Moth (T7793)	J. A. Cooper
	G-ANKZ	DH.82A Tiger Moth (N6466)	T. D. Le Mesurier
	G-ANLD	DH.82A Tiger Moth	K. Peters
	G-ANLS	DH.82A Tiger Moth	P. A. Gliddon
	G-ANLW	Westland WS-51/2 Widgeon ★	Norfolk & Suffolk Museum/Flixton
	G-ANMO	DH.82A Tiger Moth (K4259:71)	R. J. Moore & B. S. Floodgate
	G-ANMY	DH.82A Tiger Moth (DE470)	Dog Easy Ltd
	G-ANNB	DH.82A Tiger Moth	J. P. Brown

Reg.	Type	Owner or Operator	Notes
G-ANNG	DH.82A Tiger Moth	P. F. Walter	
G-ANNI	DH.82A Tiger Moth (T6953)	C. E. Ponsford & ptnrs	
G-ANNK	DH.82A Tiger Moth (T7290)	J. Y. Kaye	
G-ANOA	Hiller UH-12A ★	Redhill Technical College	
G-ANOD	DH.82A Tiger Moth	P. G. Watson	
G-ANOH	DH.82A Tiger Moth	N. Parkhouse	
G-ANOK	SAAB S.91C Safir ★	A. F. Galt & Co (stored)	
G-ANOM	DH.82A Tiger Moth	W. J. Pitts	
G-ANON	DH.82A Tiger Moth (T7909)	M. Kelly	
G-ANOO	DH.82A Tiger Moth	R. K. Packman	
G-ANOV	DH.104 Dove 6 ★	Museum of Flight/East Fortune	
G-ANPE	DH.82A Tiger Moth	T. K. Butcher (G-IESH)	
G-ANPK	DH.82A Tiger Moth	A. D. Hodgkinson	
G-ANPP	P.34A Proctor 3	C. P. A. & J. Jeffrey	
G-ANRF	DH.82A Tiger Moth	C. D. Cyster	
G-ANRM	DH.82A Tiger Moth (DF112)	Spectrum Leisure Ltd	
G-ANRN	DH.82A Tiger Moth	J. J. V. Elwes	
G-ANRP	Auster 5 (TW439)	S. D. & S. P. Allen	
G-ANRX	DH.82A Tiger Moth ★	De Havilland Heritage Museum/London Colney	
G-ANSM	DH.82A Tiger Moth	Douglas Aviation	
G-ANTE	DH.82A Tiger Moth (T6562)	G-ANTE Flyers Ltd	
G-ANTK	Avro 685 York ★	Duxford Aviation Society	
G-ANUO	DH.114 Heron 2D (G-AOXL) ★	Westmead Business Group/Croydon Airport	
G-ANUW	DH.104 Dove 6 ★	Jet Aviation Preservation Group	
G-ANVY	P.31 Proctor 4	J. W. Tregilgas	
G-ANWB	DHC.1 Chipmunk 21	G. Briggs	
G-ANXB	DH.114 Heron 1B ★	Newark Air Museum	
G-ANXC	Auster J/5R Alpine	Alpine Group	
G-ANXR	P.31C Proctor 4 (RM221)	N. H. T. Cottrell	
G-ANZT	Thruxton Jackaroo (T7798)	D. J. Neville & P. A. Dear	
G-ANZU	DH.82A Tiger Moth	M. I. Lodge	
G-ANZZ	DH.82A Tiger Moth	T. K. Butcher	
G-AOAA	DH.82A Tiger Moth	R. C. P. Brookhouse	
G-AOBG	Somers-Kendall SK.1	P. W. Bishop	
G-AOBH	DH.82A Tiger Moth (NL750)	P. Nutley	
G-AOBJ	DH.82A Tiger Moth	A. D. Hodgkinson	
G-AOBU	P.84 Jet Provost T.1 (XD693)	T. J. Manna	
G-AOBX	DH.82A Tiger Moth	David Ross Flying Group	
G-AOCP	Auster 5 ★	C. J. Baker (stored)	
G-AOCR	Auster 5D (NJ673)	D. A. Hill	
G-AOCU	Auster 5	S. J. Ball	
G-AODA	Westland S-55 Srs 3 ★	IHM/Weston-super-Mare	
G-AODR	DH.82A Tiger Moth	G-AODR Group (G-ISIS)	
G-AODT	DH.82A Tiger Moth (R5250)	R. A. Harrowven	
G-AOEH	Aeronca 7AC Champion	A. Gregori	
G-AOEI	DH.82A Tiger Moth	C.F.G. Flying Ltd	
G-AOEL	DH.82A Tiger Moth ★	Museum of Flight/East Fortune	
G-AOES	DH.82A Tiger Moth	K. A. & A. J. Broomfield	
G-AOET	DH.82A Tiger Moth	Venom Jet Promotions Ltd	
G-AOEX	Thruxton Jackaroo	A. T. Christian	
G-AOFE	DHC.1 Chipmunk 22A (WB702)	W. J. Quinn	
G-AOFS	Auster J/5L Aiglet Trainer	P. N. A. Whitehead	
G-AOGA	M.75 Aries ★	Irish Aviation Museum (stored)	
G-AOGI	DH.82A Tiger Moth	W. J. Taylor	
G-AOGR	DH.82A Tiger Moth (XL714)	R. J. S. G. Clark	
G-AOGV	Auster J/5R Alpine	R. E. Heading	
G-AOHY	DH.82A Tiger Moth (N6537)	S. W. Turley	
G-AOHZ	Auster J/5P Autocar	A. D. Hodgkinson	
G-AOIM	DH.82A Tiger Moth	R. C. P. Brookhouse	
G-AOIR	Thruxton Jackaroo	K. A. & A. J. Broomfield	
G-AOIS	DH.82A Tiger Moth (R5172)	J. K. Ellwood	
G-AOJH	DH.83C Fox Moth	Connect Properties Ltd	
G-AOJJ	DH.82A Tiger Moth (DF128)	JJ Flying Group	
G-AOJK	DH.82A Tiger Moth	R. J. Willies	
G-AOJR	DHC.1 Chipmunk 22	G. J-H. Caubergs & N. Marien/Belgium	
G-AOJT	DH.106 Comet 1 (F-BGNX) ★	De Havilland Heritage Museum (fuselage only)	
G-AOKH	P.40 Prentice 1	J. F. Moore	
G-AOKL	P.40 Prentice 1 (VS610)	N. J. Butler	
G-AOKO	P.40 Prentice 1 ★	Aero Venture	

BRITISH CIVIL REGISTRATIONS

Notes	Reg.	Type	Owner or Operator
	G-AOKZ	P.40 Prentice 1 (VS623) ★	Midland Air Museum/Coventry
	G-AOLK	P.40 Prentice 1 ★	RAF Museum
	G-AOLU	P.40 Prentice 1 (VS356)	N. J. Butler
	G-AORG	DH.114 Heron 2	Duchess of Brittany (Jersey) Ltd
	G-AORW	DHC.1 Chipmunk 22A	Skylark Aviation Ltd
	G-AOSK	DHC.1 Chipmunk 22 (WB726)	P. McMillan
	G-AOSY	DHC.1 Chipmunk 22 (WB585:M)	Chippy Sierra Yankee Group
	G-AOTD	DHC.1 Chipmunk 22 (WB588)	S. Piech
	G-AOTF	DHC.1 Chipmunk 23 (Lycoming)	A. C. Darby
	G-AOTI	DH.114 Heron 2D ★	De Havilland Heritage Museum/London Colney
	G-AOTK	D.53 Turbi	J. S. & P. R. Johnson
	G-AOTR	DHC.1 Chipmunk 22	Ace Leasing Ltd
	G-AOTY	DHC.1 Chipmunk 22A (WG472)	A. A. Hodgson
	G-AOUJ	Fairey Ultra-Light ★	IHM/Weston-super-Mare
	G-AOUO	DHC.1 Chipmunk 22 (Lycoming)	M. F. Cuming
	G-AOUP	DHC.1 Chipmunk 22	A. R. Harding
	G-AOUR	DH.82A Tiger Moth ★	Ulster Folk & Transport Museum
	G-AOVF	B.175 Britannia 312F ★	Aerospace Museum/Cosford
	G-AOVS	B.175 Britannia 312F ★	Airport Fire Section/Luton
	G-AOVT	B.175 Britannia 312F ★	Duxford Aviation Society
	G-AOVW	Auster 5	B. Marriott
	G-AOXN	DH.82A Tiger Moth	S. L. G. Darch
	G-AOZH	DH.82A Tiger Moth (K2572)	M. H. Blois-Brooke
	G-AOZL	Auster J/5Q Alpine	R. M. Weeks
	G-AOZP	DHC.1 Chipmunk 22	S. J. Davies
	G-APAF	Auster 5 (TW511)	J. J. J. Mostyn (G-CMAL)
	G-APAH	Auster 5	T. J. Goodwin
	G-APAJ	Thruxton Jackaroo	J. T. H. Page
	G-APAL	DH.82A Tiger Moth (N6847)	P. J. Shotbolt
	G-APAM	DH.82A Tiger Moth	R. P. Williams
	G-APAO	DH.82A Tiger Moth (R4922)	H. J. Maguire
	G-APAP	DH.82A Tiger Moth (R5136)	Tiger Leasing Co Ltd
	G-APAS	DH.106 Comet 1XB ★	Aerospace Museum/Cosford
	G-APBE	Auster 5	E. G. & G. R. Woods
	G-APBI	DH.82A Tiger Moth	C. J. Zeal
	G-APBO	D.53 Turbi	R. C. Hibberd
	G-APBW	Auster 5	N. Huxtable
	G-APCB	Auster J/5Q Alpine	A. A. Beswick
	G-APCC	DH.82A Tiger Moth	L. J. Rice/Henstridge
	G-APDB	DH.106 Comet 4 ★	Duxford Aviation Society
	G-APEP	V.953C Merchantman ★	Brooklands Museum of Aviation/Weybridge
	G-APFA	D.54 Turbi	F. J. Keitch
	G-APFJ	Boeing 707-436 ★	Museum of Flight/East Fortune
	G-APFU	DH.82A Tiger Moth	Leisure Assets Ltd
	G-APFV	PA-23-160 Apache	J. L. Thorogood (G-MOLY)
	G-APHV	Avro 19 Srs 2 (VM360) ★	Museum of Flight/East Fortune
	G-APIE	Tipsy Belfair B	D. Beale
	G-APIH	DH.82A Tiger Moth	K. Stewering
	G-APIK	Auster J/1N Alpha	J. H. Powell-Tuck
	G-APIM	V.806 Viscount ★	Brooklands Museum of Aviation/Weybridge
	G-APIT	P.40 Prentice 1 (VR192) ★	WWII Aircraft Preservation Society/Lasham
	G-APIY	P.40 Prentice 1 (VR249) ★	Newark Air Museum
	G-APIZ	D.31 Turbulent	R. G. Meredith
	G-APJB	P.40 Prentice 1 (VR259)	Air Atlantique Ltd
	G-APJJ	Fairey Ultra-light ★	Midland Aircraft Preservation Society
	G-APJZ	Auster J/1N Alpha	P. G. Lipman
	G-APKM	Auster J/1N Alpha	C. M. Tyers
	G-APLG	Auster J/5L Aiglet Trainer ★	Solway Aviation Society
	G-APLO	DHC.1 Chipmunk 22A (WD379)	Lindholme Aircraft Ltd
	G-APLU	DH.82A Tiger Moth	M. E. Vaisey
	G-APMB	DH.106 Comet 4B ★	Gatwick Handling Ltd (ground trainer)
	G-APMH	Auster J/1U Workmaster	M. R. P. Thorogood
	G-APMX	DH.82A Tiger Moth	R. A. L. Hubbard
	G-APMY	PA-23 Apache 160 ★	Aero Venture
	G-APNJ	Cessna 310 ★	Newark Air Museum
	G-APNT	Currie Wot	B. J. Dunford
	G-APNZ	D.31 Turbulent	Turbulent G-APNZ Preservation Society
	G-APPA	DHC.1 Chipmunk 22	J. Miller
	G-APPL	P.40 Prentice 1	S. J. Saggers

Reg.	Type	Owner or Operator	Notes
G-APPM	DHC.1 Chipmunk 22 (WB711)	S. D. Wilch	
G-APRL	AW.650 Argosy 101 ★	Midland Air Museum/Coventry	
G-APRO	Auster 6A	A. F. & H. Wankowski	
G-APRS	SA Twin Pioneer Srs 3	Aviation Heritage Ltd (G-BCWF)	
G-APRT	Taylor JT.1 Monoplane ★	Newark Air Museum	
G-APSA	Douglas DC-6A	G-APSA Ltd	
G-APSR	Auster J/1U Workmaster	D. & K. Aero Services Ltd	
G-APTR	Auster J/1N Alpha	C. R. Shipley	
G-APTU	Auster 5	G-APTU Flying Group	
G-APTW	Westland WS-51/2 Widgeon ★	North East Aircraft Museum/Usworth	
G-APTY	Beech G.35 Bonanza	G. E. Brennand	
G-APTZ	D.31 Turbulent	The Tiger Club (1990) Ltd	
G-APUD	Bensen B.7M (modified) ★	Manchester Museum of Science & Industry	
G-APUE	L.40 Meta Sokol	S. E. & M. J. Aherne	
G-APUP	Sopwith Pup (replica) (N5182) ★	RAF Museum/Hendon	
G-APUR	PA-22 Tri-Pacer 160	S. T. A. Hutchinson	
G-APUW	Auster J/5V-160 Autocar	E. S. E. & P. B. Hibbard	
G-APUY	D.31 Turbulent	C. Jones	
G-APVF	Putzer Elster B (97+04)	A. Wiseman	
G-APVG	Auster J/5L Aiglet Trainer	R. E. Tyers	
G-APVN	D.31 Turbulent	R. Sherwin	
G-APVS	Cessna 170B	N. Simpson Stormin' Norman	
G-APVT	DH.82A Tiger Moth	M. C. Boddington	
G-APVU	L.40 Meta Sokol	S. E. & M. J. Aherne	
G-APVZ	D.31 Turbulent	The Tiger Club (1990) Ltd	
G-APWA	HPR.7 Herald 101 ★	Museum of Berkshire Aviation/Woodley	
G-APWJ	HPR.7 Herald 201 ★	Duxford Aviation Society	
G-APWN	Westland WS-55 Whirlwind 3 ★	Midland Air Museum/Coventry	
G-APWY	Piaggio P.166 ★	Science Museum/Wroughton	
G-APXJ	PA-24 Comanche 250	T. Wildsmith	
G-APXR	PA-22 Tri-Pacer 160	A. Troughton	
G-APXT	PA-22 Tri-Pacer 150 (modified)	A. E. Cuttler	
G-APXU	PA-22 Tri-Pacer 125 (modified)	C. J. Cauwood	
G-APXW	EP.9 Prospector (XM819) ★	Museum of Army Flying/Middle Wallop	
G-APXX	DHA.3 Drover 2 (VH-FDT) ★	WWII Aircraft Preservation Society/Lasham	
G-APYB	Tipsy T.66 Nipper 3	B. O. Smith	
G-APYD	DH.106 Comet 4B ★	Science Museum/Wroughton	
G-APYG	DHC.1 Chipmunk 22	P. A. & J. M. Doyle	
G-APYI	PA-22 Tri-Pacer 135	D. R. Gibby	
G-APYT	Champion 7FC Tri-Traveller	B. J. Anning	
G-APZJ	PA-18 Super Cub 150	S. G. Jones	
G-APZL	PA-22 Tri-Pacer 160	B. Robins	
G-APZX	PA-22 Tri-Pacer 150	V. A. Holliday	
G-ARAD	Luton LA-5 Major ★	North East Aircraft Museum	
G-ARAM	PA-18 Super Cub 150	Skymax (Aviation) Ltd	
G-ARAN	PA-18 Super Cub 150	G-ARAN Group	
G-ARAS	Champion 7FC Tri-Traveller	Alpha Sierra Flying Group	
G-ARAW	Cessna 182C Skylane	Ximango UK	
G-ARAZ	DH.82A Tiger Moth (R4959:59)	D. A. Porter	
G-ARBE	DH.104 Dove 8	M. Whale & M. M. W. A. Lunn	
G-ARBG	Tipsy T.66 Nipper 2	D. Shrimpton	
G-ARBM	Auster V J1B Aiglet	A. D. Hodgkinson	
G-ARBS	PA-22 Tri-Pacer 160 (tailwheel)	S. D. Rowell	
G-ARBV	PA-22 Tri-Pacer 160	L. M. Williams	
G-ARBZ	D.31 Turbulent	G. Richards	
G-ARCF	PA-22 Tri-Pacer 150	M. J. Speakman	
G-ARCS	Auster D6/180	R. J. Fray	
G-ARCT	PA-18 Super Cub 95	A. H. Diver	
G-ARCV	Cessna 175A	R. Francis & C. Campbell	
G-ARCW	PA-23 Apache 160	F. W. Ellis	
G-ARCX	A.W. Meteor 14 ★	Museum of Flight/East Fortune	
G-ARDB	PA-24 Comanche 250	P. Crook	
G-ARDD	CP.301C1 Emeraude	K. N. P. Higgs	
G-ARDE	DH.104 Dove 6 ★	T. E. Evans	
G-ARDJ	Auster D.6/180	P. N. A. Whitehead	
G-ARDO	Jodel D.112	W. R. Prescott	
G-ARDS	PA-22 Caribbean 150	S. A. Rennison	
G-ARDV	PA-22 Tri-Pacer 160	M. D. N. Fisher	
G-ARDY	Tipsy T.66 Nipper 2	J. K. Davies	
G-ARDZ	Jodel D.140A	M. J. Wright	

BRITISH CIVIL REGISTRATIONS

Notes	Reg.	Type	Owner or Operator
	G-AREA	DH.104 Dove 8 ★	De Havilland Heritage Museum/London Colney
	G-AREH	DH.82A Tiger Moth	A. J. Hastings & A. Mustard
	G-AREI	Auster 3 (MT438)	R. B. Webber
	G-AREL	PA-22 Caribbean 150	The Caribbean Flying Club
	G-AREO	PA-18 Super Cub 150	E. P. Parkin
	G-ARET	PA-22 Tri-Pacer 160	L. A. Runnalls
	G-AREV	PA-22 Tri-Pacer 160	D. J. Ash
	G-AREX	Aeronca 15AC Sedan	R. J. M. Turnbull
	G-AREZ	D.31 Turbulent	R. E. Garforth
	G-ARFB	PA-22 Caribbean 150	The Tri Pacer Group
	G-ARFD	PA-22 Tri-Pacer 160	N. I. M. Mackintosh
	G-ARFG	Cessna 175°	G. C. Rogers
	G-ARFI	Cessna 150A	J. D. Woodward
	G-ARFO	Cessna 150A	A. P. Amor
	G-ARFT	Jodel DR.1050	R. Shaw
	G-ARFV	Tipsy T.66 Nipper 2	J. J. Austin
	G-ARGG	DHC.1 Chipmunk 22 (WD305)	D. Curtis
	G-ARGO	PA-22 Colt 108	Kauri Group
	G-ARGV	PA-18 Super Cub 180	Wolds Gliding Club Ltd
	G-ARGY	PA-22 Tri-Pacer 160	G-ARGY Flying Group (G-JEST)
	G-ARGZ	D.31 Turbulent	The Tiger Club (1990) Ltd
	G-ARHB	Forney F-1A Aircoupe	K. J. Peacock & S. F. Turner
	G-ARHC	Forney F-1A Aircoupe	E. G. Girardey
	G-ARHL	PA-23 Aztec 250	C. J. Freeman
	G-ARHM	Auster 6A	R. C. P. Brookhouse
	G-ARHR	PA-22 Caribbean 150	A. R. Wyatt
	G-ARHW	DH.104 Dove 8	Aviation Heritage Ltd
	G-ARHX	DH.104 Dove 8 ★	North East Aircraft Museum
	G-ARHZ	D.62 Condor	E. Shouler
	G-ARID	Cessna 172B	L. M. Edwards
	G-ARIF	Ord-Hume O-H.7 Minor Coupé ★	M. J. Aubrey
	G-ARIH	Auster 6A (TW591)	M. C. Jordan
	G-ARIK	PA-22 Caribbean 150	A. Taylor
	G-ARIL	PA-22 Caribbean 150	S. Eustathiou
	G-ARIM	D.31 Turbulent	S. R. P. Harper & J. C. Holland
	G-ARJB	DH.104 Dove 8	M. Whale & M. W. A. Lunn
	G-ARJE	PA-22 Colt 108	C. I. Fray
	G-ARJH	PA-22 Colt 108	F. Vogels/France
	G-ARJR	PA-23 Apache 160G ★	Instructional airframe/Kidlington
	G-ARJS	PA-23 Apache 160G	Bencray Ltd
	G-ARJT	PA-23 Apache 160G	J. H. Ashcroft
	G-ARJU	PA-23 Apache 160G	F. W. & I. F. Ellis
	G-ARKD	CAC CA-18 Mk.22 Mustang P-51D	Classic Flying Machine Collection Ltd
	G-ARKG	Auster J/5G Autocar (A11-301/931)	A. G. Boon & C. L. Towell
	G-ARKJ	Beech N35 Bonanza	G. D. E. Macdonald
	G-ARKK	PA-22 Colt 108	R. D. Welfare
	G-ARKM	PA-22 Colt 108	Kilo Mike Group
	G-ARKN	PA-22 Colt 108	D. A. Flood
	G-ARKP	PA-22 Colt 108	D. S. White & I. J. Mitchell
	G-ARKS	PA-22 Colt 108	A. J. Silvester
	G-ARLB	PA-24 Comanche 250	D. Heater (G-BUTL)
	G-ARLG	Auster D.4/108	Auster D4 Group
	G-ARLK	PA-24 Comanche 250	R. P. Jackson
	G-ARLP	Beagle A.61 Terrier 1	Gemini Flying Group
	G-ARLR	Beagle A.61 Terrier 2	M. Palfreman
	G-ARLU	Cessna 172B Skyhawk ★	Instructional airframe/Irish Air Corps
	G-ARLZ	D.31A Turbulent	A. D. Wilson
	G-ARMC	DHC.1 Chipmunk 22A (WB703)	John Henderson Children's Trust
	G-ARMD	DHC.1 Chipmunk 22A	A. L. Grisay
	G-ARMF	DHC.1 Chipmunk 22A (WZ868:H)	J. Miller
	G-ARMG	DHC.1 Chipmunk 22A	G-ARMG Group
	G-ARML	Cessna 175B Skylark	M. P. Wiseman & A. Parker
	G-ARMN	Cessna 175B Skylark	G-ARMN Group
	G-ARMO	Cessna 172B Skyhawk	R. D. Leigh
	G-ARMR	Cessna 172B Skyhawk	Mike Romeo Group
	G-ARMZ	D.31 Turbulent	The Tiger Club (1990) Ltd
	G-ARNB	Auster J/5G Autocar	R. F. Tolhurst
	G-ARND	PA-22 Colt 108	G-ARND Group
	G-ARNE	PA-22 Colt 108	The Shiny Colt Group
	G-ARNG	PA-22 Colt 108	F. B. Rothera

Reg.	Type	Owner or Operator	Notes
G-ARNJ	PA-22 Colt 108	R. A. Keech	
G-ARNK	PA-22 Colt 108 (tailwheel)	S. J. Smith	
G-ARNL	PA-22 Colt 108	J. A. Dodsworth	
G-ARNO	Beagle A.61 Terrier 1 (VX113)	M. C. R. Wills	
G-ARNP	Beagle A.109 Airedale	S. W. & M. Isbister	
G-ARNY	Jodel D.117	G-ARNY Flying Group	
G-ARNZ	D.31 Turbulent	The Tiger Club (1990) Ltd	
G-AROA	Cessna 172B Skyhawk	F. J. L. Kendall	
G-AROC	Cessna 175B	A. J. Symes (G-OTOW)	
G-AROJ	Beagle A.109 Airedale ★	D. J. Shaw (stored)	
G-ARON	PA-22 Colt 108	M. Hayter	
G-AROO	Forney F-1A Aircoupe	K. J. Harron & W. J. McMeekan	
G-AROW	Jodel D.140B	A. R. Crome	
G-AROY	Boeing Stearman A75N.1	I. T. Whitaker-Bethel & J. Mann	
G-ARPH	HS.121 Trident 1C ★	Museum of Flight/East Fortune	
G-ARPK	HS.121 Trident 1C ★	Manchester Airport Authority	
G-ARPO	HS.121 Trident 1C ★	CAA Fire School/Teesside	
G-ARRD	Jodel DR.1050	P. R. Watkins	
G-ARRE	Jodel DR.1050	West of Leicester Flyers	
G-ARRI	Cessna 175B	G-ARRI Partnership	
G-ARRL	Auster J/1N Alpha	A. C. Ladd	
G-ARRM	Beagle B.206-X ★	Bristol Aero Collection (stored)	
G-ARRO	Beagle A.109 Airedale	M. & S. W. Isbister	
G-ARRS	CP.301A Emeraude	J. F. Sully	
G-ARRT	Wallis WA-116-1	K. H. Wallis	
G-ARRU	D.31 Turbulent	D. G. Huck	
G-ARRX	Auster 6A (VF512)	J. E. D. Mackie	
G-ARRY	Jodel D.140B	C. Thomas	
G-ARRZ	D.31 Turbulent	T. A. Stambach	
G-ARSG	Roe Triplane Type IV (replica)	The Shuttleworth Collection/Old Warden	
G-ARSL	Beagle A.61 Terrier 1 (VF581)	D. J. Colclough	
G-ARSU	PA-22 Colt 108	Sierra Uniform Flying Group	
G-ARTH	PA-12 Super Cruiser	R. I. Souch	
G-ARTJ	Bensen B.8M ★	Museum of Flight/East Fortune	
G-ARTL	DH.82A Tiger Moth (T7281)	F. G. Clacherty	
G-ARTT	MS.880B Rallye Club	R. N. Scott	
G-ARTZ	McCandless M.4 gyroplane	W. R. Partridge	
G-ARUG	Auster J/5G Autocar	D. P. H. Hulme	
G-ARUH	Jodel DR.1050	A. F. Vizoso	
G-ARUI	Beagle A.61 Terrier	T. W. J. Dann	
G-ARUL	LeVier Cosmic Wind	P. G. Kynsey	
G-ARUV	CP.301A Emeraude	D. A. Healey	
G-ARUY	Auster J/1N Alpha	D. Burnham	
G-ARVM	V.1101 VC10 ★	Brooklands Museum of Aviation/Weybridge	
G-ARVO	PA-18 Super Cub 95	M. Ali	
G-ARVT	PA-28 Cherokee 160	Red Rose Aviation Ltd	
G-ARVU	PA-28 Cherokee 160	T. W. Mitchell	
G-ARVV	PA-28 Cherokee 160	G. E. Hopkins	
G-ARVZ	D.62B Condor	A. A. M. Huke	
G-ARWB	DHC.1 Chipmunk 22 (WK611)	Thruxton Chipmunk Flying Club	
G-ARWR	Cessna 172C	Devanha Flying Group	
G-ARWS	Cessna 175C	M. D. Fage	
G-ARXB	Beagle A.109 Airedale	S. W. & M. Isbister	
G-ARXD	Beagle A.109 Airedale	D. Howden	
G-ARXG	PA-24 Comanche 250	R. F. Corstin	
G-ARXH	Bell 47G	A. B. Searle	
G-ARXP	Luton LA-4 Minor	R. M. Weeks	
G-ARXT	Jodel DR.1050	CJM Flying Group	
G-ARXU	Auster 6A (VF526)	A. B. Taylor-Roberts and E. M. Le Gresley	
G-ARXW	MS.885 Super Rallye	M. J. Kirk	
G-ARYB	HS.125 Srs 1 ★	Midland Air Museum/Coventry	
G-ARYC	HS.125 Srs 1 ★	De Havilland Heritage Museum/London Colney	
G-ARYD	Auster AOP.6 (WJ358) ★	Museum of Army Flying/Middle Wallop	
G-ARYH	PA-22 Tri-Pacer 160	C. Watt	
G-ARYK	Cessna 172C	M. James	
G-ARYR	PA-28 Cherokee 180	G-ARYR Flying Group	
G-ARYS	Cessna 172C	B. & S. Aviation Ltd	
G-ARYV	PA-24 Comanche 250	D. C. Hanss	
G-ARYZ	Beagle A.109 Airedale	C. W. Tomkins	
G-ARZB	Wallis WA-116 Srs 1	K. H. Wallis	
G-ARZS	Beagle A.109 Airedale	M. & S. W. Isbister	

Notes	Reg.	Type	Owner or Operator
	G-ARZW	Currie Wot	B. R. Pearson
	G-ASAA	Luton LA-4 Minor	M. J. Aubrey (stored)
	G-ASAI	Beagle A.109 Airedale	K. R. Howden
	G-ASAJ	Beagle A.61 Terrier 2 (WE569)	T. Bailey
	G-ASAL	SA Bulldog Srs 120/124	Pioneer Flying Co Ltd
	G-ASAU	MS.880B Rallye Club	Juliet Tango Group
	G-ASAX	Beagle A.61 Terrier 2	A. D. Hodgkinson
	G-ASAZ	Hiller UH-12E4 (XS165)	Hields Aviation
	G-ASBA	Phoenix Currie Wot	J. C. Lister
	G-ASBH	Beagle A.109 Airedale	D. T. Smollett
	G-ASCC	Beagle E3 Mk 11 (XP254)	R. Warner
	G-ASCD	Beagle A.61 Terrier 2 (TJ704) ★	Yorkshire Air Museum/Elvington
	G-ASCH	Beagle A.61 Terrier 2	G-ASCH Group
	G-ASCM	Isaacs Fury II (K2050)	R. F. Redknap
	G-ASCZ	CP.301A Emeraude	I. Denham-Brown
	G-ASDF	Edwards Gyrocopter ★	B. King
	G-ASDK	Beagle A.61 Terrier 2	J. Swallow (G-ARLM)
	G-ASDY	Wallis WA-116/F	K. H. Wallis
	G-ASEA	Luton LA-4A Minor	D. Underwood
	G-ASEB	Luton LA-4A Minor	S. R. P. Harper
	G-ASEO	PA-24 Comanche 250	M. Scott
	G-ASEP	PA-23 Apache 235	Arrowstate Ltd
	G-ASEU	D.62A Condor	W. M. Grant
	G-ASFA	Cessna 172D	D. Austin
	G-ASFD	L-200A Morava	M. Emery
	G-ASFL	PA-28 Cherokee 180	G-ASFL Group
	G-ASFR	Bölkow Bö.208A1 Junior	S. T. Dauncey
	G-ASFX	D.31 Turbulent	E. F. Clapham & W. B. S. Dobie
	G-ASGC	V.1151 Super VC10 ★	Duxford Aviation Society
	G-ASHD	Brantly B.2A ★	IHM/Weston-super-Mare
	G-ASHS	SNCAN Stampe SV.4C	J. W. Beaty
	G-ASHT	D.31 Turbulent	C. W. N. Huke
	G-ASHU	PA-15 Vagabond (modified)	The Calybe Flying Group
	G-ASHX	PA-28 Cherokee 180	Powertheme Ltd
	G-ASII	PA-28 Cherokee 180	T. N. & T. R. Hart & R. W. S. Matthews
	G-ASIJ	PA-28 Cherokee 180	MK Aero Support Ltd
	G-ASIL	PA-28 Cherokee 180	G. R. Plant & A. D. Harwin
	G-ASIS	Jodel D.112	W. R. Prescott
	G-ASIT	Cessna 180	R. A. Seeley
	G-ASIY	PA-25 Pawnee 235	The Royal Air Force Gliding and Soaring Association
	G-ASJL	Beech H.35 Bonanza	R. L. Dargue
	G-ASJV	VS.361 Spitfire IX (MH434/PK-K)	Merlin Aviation Ltd
	G-ASJZ	Jodel D.117A	M. A. Watts
	G-ASKC	DH.98 Mosquito 35 (TA719) ★	Skyfame Collection/Duxford
	G-ASKK	HPR.7 Herald 211 ★	Norwich Aviation Museum
	G-ASKL	Jodel D.150	J. M. Graty
	G-ASKP	DH.82A Tiger Moth	Tiger Club (1990) Ltd
	G-ASKT	PA-28 Cherokee 180	T. J. Herbert
	G-ASLV	PA-28 Cherokee 235	S. W. Goodswen
	G-ASLX	CP.301A Emeraude	J. J. Reilly
	G-ASMA	PA-30 Twin Comanche 160 C/R	K. Cooper
	G-ASMF	Beech D.95A Travel Air	M. J. A. Hornblower
	G-ASMJ	Cessna F.172E	Aeroscene Ltd
	G-ASML	Luton LA-4A Minor	G. D. Gunby
	G-ASMM	D.31 Tubulent	W. J. Browning
	G-ASMS	Cessna 150A	M. & W. Long
	G-ASMT	Fairtravel Linnet 2	P. Harrison
	G-ASMV	CP.1310-C3 Super Emeraude	D. G. Hammersley
	G-ASMW	Cessna 150D	Dukeries Aviation
	G-ASMY	PA-23 Apache 160 ★	R. D. Forster
	G-ASMZ	Beagle A.61 Terrier 2 (VF516)	B. Andrews
	G-ASNC	Beagle D.5/180 Husky	Peterborough & Spalding Gliding Club Ltd
	G-ASNI	CP.1310-C3 Super Emeraude	D. Chapman
	G-ASNK	Cessna 205	Justgold Ltd
	G-ASNW	Cessna F.172E	G-ASNW Group
	G-ASNY	Campbell-Bensen B.8M gyroplane ★	Newark Air Museum
	G-ASOH	Beech 95-B55A Baron	G. Davis & C. Middlemiss
	G-ASOI	Beagle A.61 Terrier 2	G.D.B. Delmege
	G-ASOK	Cessna F.172E	D. W. Disney

Reg.	Type	Owner or Operator	Notes
G-ASOL	Bell 47D ★	North East Aircraft Museum	
G-ASOM	Beagle A.61 Terrier 2	GASOM.org (G-JETS)	
G-ASOX	Cessna 205A	S. M. C. Harvey	
G-ASPF	Jodel D.120	G. W. Street	
G-ASPP	Bristol Boxkite (replica)	The Shuttleworth Collection/Old Warden	
G-ASPS	Piper J-3C-90 Cub	A. J. Chalkley/Blackbushe	
G-ASPV	DH.82A Tiger Moth (T7794)	P. Zanardo	
G-ASRB	D.62B Condor	B. J. Douglas/Ireland	
G-ASRC	D.62C Condor	C. R. Isbell	
G-ASRK	Beagle A.109 Airedale	Bio Pathica Ltd	
G-ASRO	PA-30 Twin Comanche 160	D. W. Blake	
G-ASRT	Jodel 150	P. Turton	
G-ASRW	PA-28 Cherokee 180	G. N. Smith	
G-ASSM	HS.125 Srs 1/522 ★	Science Museum/South Kensington	
G-ASSP	PA-30 Twin Comanche 160	P. H. Tavener	
G-ASSS	Cessna 172E	P. R. March & P. Turner	
G-ASST	Cessna 150D	F. R. H. Parker	
G-ASSV	Kensinger KF	C. I. Jefferson	
G-ASSW	PA-28 Cherokee 140	E. R. Curry	
G-ASSY	D.31 Turbulent	C. M. Bracewell	
G-ASTG	Nord 1002 Pingouin II	R. J. Fray	
G-ASTI	Auster 6A	S. J. Partridge	
G-ASTL	Fairey Firefly I (Z2033) ★	F. A. A. Museum/Yeovilton	
G-ASTP	Hiller UH-12C ★	IHM/Weston-super-Mare	
G-ASUB	Mooney M.20E Super 21	S. C. Coulbeck	
G-ASUD	PA-28 Cherokee 180	G-ASUD Group	
G-ASUE	Cessna 150D	D. Huckle	
G-ASUG	Beech E18S ★	Museum of Flight/East Fortune	
G-ASUI	Beagle A.61 Terrier 2	A. L. Aish	
G-ASUP	Cessna F.172E	GASUP Air	
G-ASUS	Jurca MJ.2B Tempete	M. P. Grimshaw	
G-ASVG	CP.301B Emeraude	K. R. H. Wingate	
G-ASVM	Cessna F.172E	R. H. Bennett	
G-ASVO	HPR.7 Herald 214 ★	Archive Visitor Centre/Shoreham (cockpit section)	
G-ASVZ	PA-28 Cherokee 140	T. D. Jackman	
G-ASWJ	Beagle 206 Srs 1 (8449M) ★	Brunel Technical College/Bristol	
G-ASWN	Bensen B.8M	D. R. Shepherd	
G-ASWX	PA-28 Cherokee 180	Gasworks Flying Group Ltd	
G-ASXC	SIPA 903	A. L. Hall-Carpenter (G-DWEL)	
G-ASXD	Brantly B.2B	Lousada PLC	
G-ASXI	Tipsy T.66 Nipper 3	E. Martin	
G-ASXS	Jodel DR.1050	R. A. Hunter	
G-ASXU	Jodel D.120A	G-ASXU Group	
G-ASXX	Avro 683 Lancaster 7 (NX611) ★	Panton Family Trust/East Kirkby	
G-ASXZ	Cessna 182G Skylane	Last Refuge Ltd	
G-ASYD	BAC One-Eleven 475 ★	Brooklands Museum of Aviation/Weybridge	
G-ASYG	Beagle A.61 Terrier 2 (VX927)	Terrane Auster Group	
G-ASYJ	Beech D.95A Travel Air	Crosby Aviation (Jersey) Ltd	
G-ASYP	Cessna 150E	Henlow Flying Group	
G-ASZB	Cessna 150E	R. J. Scott	
G-ASZD	Bölkow Bö.208A2 Junior	M. J. Ayers	
G-ASZE	Beagle A.61 Terrier 2	D. R. Ockleton	
G-ASZR	Fairtravel Linnet 2	R. Hodgson	
G-ASZS	Gardan GY-80 Horizon 160	ZS Group	
G-ASZU	Cessna 150E	L. J. Baker, R. Hall & C. Davies	
G-ASZV	Tipsy T.66 Nipper 2	J. K. Davies	
G-ASZX	Beagle A.61 Terrier 1 (WJ368)	R. B. Webber	
G-ATAG	Jodel DR.1050	T. M. Dawes-Gamble	
G-ATAS	PA-28 Cherokee 180	ATAS Group	
G-ATAU	D.62B Condor	M. C. Burlock	
G-ATAV	D.62C Condor	V. A. Holliday	
G-ATBG	Nord 1002 (NJ+C11)	Ardmore Aviation Service	
G-ATBH	Aero 145	P. D. Aberbach	
G-ATBJ	Sikorsky S-61N	British International	
G-ATBL	DH.60G Moth	E. G. & N. S. C. English	
G-ATBP	Fournier RF-3	D. McNicholl	
G-ATBS	D.31 Turbulent	J. A. Lear	
G-ATBU	Beagle A.61 Terrier 2	T. Jarvis	

Notes	Reg.	Type	Owner or Operator
	G-ATBW	Tipsy T.66 Nipper 2	Stapleford Nipper Group
	G-ATBX	PA-20 Pacer 135	G. D. & P. M. Thomson
	G-ATBZ	Westland WS-58 Wessex 60 ★	IHM/Weston-super-Mare
	G-ATCC	Beagle A.109 Airedale	North East Flight Training Ltd
	G-ATCD	Beagle D.5/180 Husky	T. C. O'Gorman
	G-ATCE	Cessna U.206	A. J. Hickling
	G-ATCJ	Luton LA-4A Minor	Flanders Flyers
	G-ATCL	Victa Airtourer 100	A. D. Goodall
	G-ATCN	Luton LA-4A Minor	The Real Aeroplane Co.Ltd
	G-ATCX	Cessna 182H	S. M. C. Harvey
	G-ATDA	PA-28 Cherokee 160	Portway Aviation Ltd
	G-ATDN	Beagle A.61 Terrier 2 (TW641)	S. J. Saggers
	G-ATDO	Bölkow Bö.208C1 Junior	P. Thompson
	G-ATEF	Cessna 150E	Swans Aviation
	G-ATEM	PA-28 Cherokee 180	G. D. Wyles
	G-ATEP	EAA Biplane ★	E. L. Martin (red)/Guernsey
	G-ATEV	Jodel DR.1050	J. C. Carter & J. L. Altrip
	G-ATEW	PA-30 Twin Comanche 160	Air Northumbria (Woolsington) Ltd
	G-ATEZ	PA-28 Cherokee 140	EFI Aviation Ltd
	G-ATFD	Jodel DR.1050	G-ATFD Group
	G-ATFF	PA-23 Aztec 250C	T. J. Wassell
	G-ATFG	Brantly B.2B ★	Museum of Flight/East Fortune
	G-ATFM	Sikorsky S-61N	British International Helicopter Services Ltd
	G-ATFR	PA-25 Pawnee 150	Borders (Milfield) Gliding Club Ltd
	G-ATFV	Agusta-Bell 47J-2A ★	Caernarfon Air World
	G-ATFY	Cessna F.172G	J. M. Vinall
	G-ATGN	Thorn Coal Gas Balloon	British Balloon Museum/Newbury
	G-ATGP	Jodel DR.1050	Madley Flying Group
	G-ATGY	Gardan GY-80 Horizon	D. H. Mackay
	G-ATHA	PA-23 Apache 235 ★	Brunel Technical College/Bristol
	G-ATHD	DHC.1 Chipmunk 22 (WP971)	Spartan Flying Group Ltd
	G-ATHK	Aeronca 7AC Champion	T. C. Barron
	G-ATHM	Wallis WA-116 Srs 1	Wallis Autogyros Ltd
	G-ATHN	Nord 1101 Noralpha ★	E. L. Martin (stored)/Guernsey
	G-ATHR	PA-28 Cherokee 180	Azure Flying Club Ltd
	G-ATHT	Victa Airtourer 115	Cotswold Flying Group
	G-ATHU	Beagle A.61 Terrier 1	J. A. L. Irwin
	G-ATHV	Cessna 150F	Cessna Hotel Victor Group
	G-ATHZ	Cessna 150F	R. D. Forster
	G-ATIC	Jodel DR.1050	T. A. Major
	G-ATIG	HPR.7 Herald 214 ★	Norwich Airport towing trainer
	G-ATIN	Jodel D.117	A. Ayre
	G-ATIR	AIA Stampe SV.4C	A. Trueman
	G-ATIS	PA-28 Cherokee 160	D. E. Skertchly
	G-ATIZ	Jodel D.117	R. A. Smith
	G-ATJA	Jodel DR.1050	Bicester Flying Group
	G-ATJC	Victa Airtourer 100 (modfied)	Aviation West Ltd
	G-ATJG	PA-28 Cherokee 140	C. A. McGee
	G-ATJL	PA-24 Comanche 260	S. J. Ollier
	G-ATJN	Jodel D.119	J. Upex
	G-ATJV	PA-32 Cherokee Six 260	Wingglider Ltd
	G-ATKF	Cessna 150F	Holdcroft Aviation Services Ltd (G-HPFT)
	G-ATKH	Luton LA-4A Minor	H. E. Jenner
	G-ATKI	Piper J-3C-65 Cub	J. C. Holland
	G-ATKT	Cessna F.172G	R. J. D. Blois
	G-ATKX	Jodel D.140C	Kilo Xray Syndicate
	G-ATLA	Cessna 182J Skylane	J. W. & J. T. Whicher
	G-ATLB	Jodel DR.1050/M1	Le Syndicate du Petit Oiseau
	G-ATLM	Cessna F.172G	N. A. Baxter
	G-ATLP	Bensen B.8M	R. F. G. Moyle
	G-ATLT	Cessna U.206A	Skydive Jersey Ltd
	G-ATLV	Jodel D.120	G. Constantine & A. Y. Leung
	G-ATMC	Cessna F.150F	G. H. Farrah & D. Cunnane
	G-ATMH	Beagle D.5/180 Husky	Dorset Gliding Club Ltd
	G-ATMM	Cessna F.150F	Cranfield Aviation Training School Ltd
	G-ATMT	PA-30 Twin Comanche 160	Montagu-Smith & Co Ltd
	G-ATNB	PA-28 Cherokee 180	Ken Macdonald
	G-ATNE	Cessna F.150F	G-ATNE Flying Group
	G-ATNL	Cessna F.150F	PVI Power Services Ltd
	G-ATNV	PA-24 Comanche 260	K. Powell
	G-ATOH	D.62B Condor	Three Spires Flying Group

Reg.	Type	Owner or Operator	Notes
G-ATOI	PA-28 Cherokee 140	R. Ronaldson	
G-ATOJ	PA-28 Cherokee 140	British NorthWest Airways Ltd	
G-ATOK	PA-28 Cherokee 140	ILC Flying Group	
G-ATOM	PA-28 Cherokee 140	A. Flight Aviation Ltd	
G-ATON	PA-28 Cherokee 140	Stirling Flying Syndicate	
G-ATOO	PA-28 Cherokee 140	Caralair Aviation	
G-ATOP	PA-28 Cherokee 140	P. R. Coombs	
G-ATOR	PA-28 Cherokee 140	Aligator Group	
G-ATOT	PA-28 Cherokee 180	Sirius Aviation Ltd	
G-ATOU	Mooney M.20E Super 21	DbProf Doo	
G-ATOY	PA-24 Comanche 260 ★	Museum of Flight/East Fortune	
G-ATOZ	Bensen B.8M	C. R. Gordon	
G-ATPN	PA-28 Cherokee 140	M. F. Hatt & ptnrs	
G-ATPT	Cessna 182J Skylane	C. Beer t/a Papa Tango Group	
G-ATPV	JB.01 Minicab	D. H. G. Cotter	
G-ATRG	PA-18 Super Cub 150	Lasham Gliding Society Ltd	
G-ATRK	Cessna F.150F	Falcon Aviation Ltd	
G-ATRL	Cessna F.150F	A. A. W. Stevens	
G-ATRM	Cessna F.150F	J. Redfearn	
G-ATRW	PA-32 Cherokee Six 260	Pringle Brandon Architects	
G-ATRX	PA-32 Cherokee Six 260	S. P. Vincent	
G-ATSI	Bölkow Bö.208C1 Junior	GATSI Bolkow Ltd	
G-ATSL	Cessna F.172G	Aircraft Engineers Ltd	
G-ATSR	Beech M.35 Bonanza	C. B. Linton	
G-ATSX	Bölkow Bö.208C1 Junior	Little Bear Ltd	
G-ATSY	Wassmer Wa.41 Super Baladou IV	McLean Aviation	
G-ATSZ	PA-30 Twin Comanche 160B	Sierra Zulu Aviation Ltd	
G-ATTB	Wallis WA-116-1 (XR944)	D. A. Wallis	
G-ATTI	PA-28 Cherokee 140	G-ATTI Flying Group	
G-ATTK	PA-28 Cherokee 140	G-ATTK Flying Group	
G-ATTM	Jodel DR.250-160	C. P. Tomkinson	
G-ATTN	Piccard HA Balloon ★	Science Museum/South Kensington	
G-ATTR	Bölkow Bö.208C1 Junior	S. Luck	
G-ATTV	PA-28 Cherokee 140	G-ATTV Group	
G-ATTX	PA-28 Cherokee 180	G-ATTX Flying Group	
G-ATUB	PA-28 Cherokee 140	P. Sharpe	
G-ATUF	Cessna F.150F	D. P. Williams	
G-ATUG	D.62B Condor	C. Gill	
G-ATUH	Tipsy T.66 Nipper 1	C. & M. D. Barnard	
G-ATUI	Bölkow Bö.208C1 Junior	M. J. Grundy	
G-ATUL	PA-28 Cherokee 180	Barry Fielding Aviation Ltd	
G-ATVF	DHC.1 Chipmunk 22 (WD327)	The Royal Air Force Gliding and Soaring Association	
G-ATVK	PA-28 Cherokee 140	P. Ratcliffe	
G-ATVO	PA-28 Cherokee 140	Pilot Flying Group	
G-ATVP	Vickers FB.5 Gunbus replica (2345) ★	RAF Museum/Hendon	
G-ATVS	PA-28 Cherokee 180	D. S. Olson	
G-ATVW	D.62B Condor	C. Gartland	
G-ATVX	Bölkow Bö.208C1 Junior	A. M. Witt	
G-ATWA	Jodel DR.1050	One Twenty Group	
G-ATWB	Jodel D.117	Andrewsfield Whisky Bravo Group	
G-ATWJ	Cessna F.172F	J. P. A. Freeman	
G-ATXA	PA-22 Tri-Pacer 150	S. Hildrop	
G-ATXD	PA-30 Twin Comanche 160B	M. Bagshaw	
G-ATXJ	HP.137 Jetstream 300 ★	Fire Service training airframe/Cardiff	
G-ATXN	Mitchell-Proctor Kittiwake 1	R. G. Day	
G-ATXO	SIPA 903	C. H. Morris	
G-ATXZ	McCandless M.4 gyroplane ★	Ulster Folk & Transport Museum	
G-ATXZ	Bölkow Bö.208C1 Junior	B. F. Hill	
G-ATYM	Cessna F.150G	P. W. Fisher	
G-ATYN	Cessna F.150G	J. S. Grant	
G-ATYS	PA-28 Cherokee 180	A. J. Hardy	
G-ATZM	Piper J-3C-90 Cub	N. D. Marshall	
G-ATZS	Wassmer Wa.41 Super Baladou IV	I. R. Siddell	
G-AVAW	D.62B Condor	Condor Aircraft Group	
G-AVBG	PA-28 Cherokee 180	M. C. Plomer-Roberts	
G-AVBH	PA-28 Cherokee 180	Tenterfield (Holdings) Ltd	
G-AVBS	PA-28 Cherokee 180	Bravo Sierra Flying Group	
G-AVBT	PA-28 Cherokee 180	J. F. Mitchell	
G-AVCM	PA-24 Comanche 260	R. F. Smith	
G-AVCN	BN-26A-8 Islander	Britten-Norman Aircraft Preservation Society	

BRITISH CIVIL REGISTRATIONS

Notes	Reg.	Type	Owner or Operator
	G-AVCV	Cessna 182J Skylane	University of Manchester, School of Earth, Atmospheric and Environmental Sciences
	G-AVDA	Cessna 182K Skylane	F. W. Ellis
	G-AVDG	Wallis WA-116 Srs 1	K. H. Wallis
	G-AVDS	Beech 65-B80 Queen Air ★	Airport Fire Service/Filton
	G-AVDT	Aeronca 7AC Champion	D. & N. Cheney
	G-AVDV	PA-22-150 Tri-Pacer	L. Beardmore & R. W. Taberner
	G-AVDY	Luton LA-4A Minor	J. Goodband
	G-AVEC	Cessna F.172 ★	S. M. Furner
	G-AVEF	Jodel 150	C. E. Bellhouse
	G-AVEH	SIAI-Marchetti S.205	EH Aviation
	G-AVEM	Cessna F.150G	N. M. Robinson
	G-AVEN	Cessna F.150G	J. M. Hough
	G-AVEO	Cessna F.150G	G-AVEO Flying Group (G-DENA)
	G-AVER	Cessna F.150G	LAC Flying School
	G-AVEU	Wassmer Wa.41 Baladou IV	The Baladou Flying Group
	G-AVEX	D.62B Condor	C. A. Macleod
	G-AVEY	Currie Super Wot	M. C. Jordan
	G-AVEZ	HPR.7 Herald 210 ★	Rescue trainer/Norwich
	G-AVFB	HS.121 Trident 2E ★	Duxford Aviation Society
	G-AVFE	HS.121 Trident 2E ★	Belfast Airport Authority
	G-AVFH	HS.121 Trident 2E ★	De Havilland Heritage Museum (fuselage only)/ London Colney
	G-AVFM	HS.121 Trident 2E ★	Brunel Technical College/Bristol
	G-AVFR	PA-28 Cherokee 140	G. Cockerton
	G-AVFU	PA-32 Cherokee Six 300	Barry Fielding Aviation Ltd
	G-AVFX	PA-28 Cherokee 140	A. E. Fielding
	G-AVFZ	PA-28 Cherokee 140	G-AVFZ Flying Group
	G-AVGA	PA-24 Comanche 260	G. McD. Moir
	G-AVGC	PA-28 Cherokee 140	D. Matthews
	G-AVGE	PA-28 Cherokee 140	Spirit of Flight Ltd
	G-AVGU	Cessna F.150G	R. D. Luper
	G-AVGZ	Jodel DR.1050	A. F. & S. Williams
	G-AVHH	Cessna F.172	B. C. Costin
	G-AVHL	Jodel DR.105A	Seething Jodel Group
	G-AVHM	Cessna F.150G	D. A. & W. D. Hill
	G-AVHT	Auster AOP.9 (WZ711)	C. W. Romkins LtdSeething Jodel Group
	G-AVHY	Fournier RF.4D	I. G. K. Mitchell
	G-AVIA	Cessna F.150G	American Airplane Breakers
	G-AVIB	Cessna F.150G	Far North Aviation
	G-AVIC	Cessna F.172 ★	Leeside Flying Ltd
	G-AVIL	Alon A.2 Aircoupe (VX147)	G. D. J. Wilson
	G-AVIN	MS.880B Rallye Club	R. A. C. Stephens
	G-AVIP	Brantly B.2B	Eaglescott Brantly Group
	G-AVIS	Cessna F.172 ★	J. P. A. Freeman
	G-AVIT	Cessna F.150G	P. Cottrell
	G-AVJF	Cessna F.172H	J. A. & D. T. A. Rees
	G-AVJJ	PA-30 Twin Comanche 160B	A. H. Manser
	G-AVJK	Jodel DR.1050/M1	Juliet Kilo Syndicate
	G-AVJO	Fokker E.III (replica) (422/15)	Flying Aces Movie Aircraft Collection
	G-AVJV	Wallis WA-117 Srs 1	K. H. Wallis (G-ATCV)
	G-AVJW	Wallis WA-118 Srs 2	K. H. Wallis (G-ATPW)
	G-AVKD	Fournier RF-4D	Lasham RF4 Group
	G-AVKE	Gadfly HDW.1 ★	IHM/Weston-super-Mare
	G-AVKG	Cessna F.172H	P. R. Brown-John
	G-AVKI	Slingsby T.66 Nipper 3	Team Nipper
	G-AVKK	Slingsby T.66 Nipper 3	C. Watson
	G-AVKP	Beagle A.109 Airedale	D. R. Williams
	G-AVKR	Bölkow Bö.208C1 Junior	L. Hawkins
	G-AVLB	PA-28 Cherokee 140	M. Wilson
	G-AVLC	PA-28 Cherokee 140	D. P. McCullagh
	G-AVLE	PA-28 Cherokee 140	G. E. Wright
	G-AVLF	PA-28 Cherokee 140	Woodbine Group
	G-AVLG	PA-28 Cherokee 140	R. J. Everett
	G-AVLI	PA-28 Cherokee 140	Lima India Aviation Group
	G-AVLJ	PA-28 Cherokee 140	Cherokee Aviation Holdings Jersey Ltd
	G-AVLM	Beagle B.121 Pup 3	T. M. & D. A. Jones
	G-AVLN	Beagle B.121 Pup 2	Dogs Flying Group
	G-AVLO	Bölkow Bö.208C1 Junior	G. D. Price & P. R. Teager
	G-AVLT	PA-28-140 Cherokee	Turweston Flying School Ltd (G-KELC)
	G-AVLW	Fournier RF-4D	J. C. A. C. da Silva

Reg.	Type	Owner or Operator	Notes
G-AVLY	Jodel D.120A	S. M. S. Smith	
G-AVMA	Gardan GY-80 Horizon 180	Z. R. Hildick	
G-AVMB	D.62B Condor	L. J. Dray	
G-AVMD	Cessna 150G	E. M. Wood	
G-AVMF	Cessna F. 150G	J. F. Marsh	
G-AVMJ	BAC One-Eleven 510ED ★	European Aviation Ltd (cabin trainer)	
G-AVMK	BAC One-Eleven 510ED ★	Gravesend College (fuselage only)	
G-AVMO	BAC One-Eleven 510ED ★	Museum of Flight/East Fortune	
G-AVMU	BAC One-Eleven 510ED ★	Duxford Aviation Society	
G-AVNC	Cessna F.150G	J. Turner	
G-AVNE	Westland WS-58 Wessex Mk 60 Srs 1 ★	IHM/Weston-super-Mare	
G-AVNN	PA-28 Cherokee 180	G-AVNN Flying Group	
G-AVNO	PA-28 Cherokee 180	November Oscar Flying Group	
G-AVNS	PA-28 Cherokee 180	P. T. Osborne	
G-AVNU	PA-28 Cherokee 180	D. Durrant	
G-AVNW	PA-28 Cherokee 180	Len Smith's (Aviation) Ltd	
G-AVNY	Fournier RF-4D	J. B. Giddins (G-IVEL)	
G-AVNZ	Fournier RF-4D	C. D. Pidler	
G-AVOA	Jodel DR.1050	D. A. Willies	
G-AVOH	D.62B Condor	Condor Group	
G-AVOM	CEA Jodel DR.221	Avon Flying Group	
G-AVOO	PA-18 Super Cub 150	Dublin Gliding Club Ltd	
G-AVOZ	PA-28 Cherokee 180	Oscar Zulu Flying Group	
G-AVPD	Jodel D.9 Bébé ★	S. W. McKay (stored)	
G-AVPI	Cessna F.172H	Air-Tech	
G-AVPJ	DH.82A Tiger Moth	C. C. Silk	
G-AVPM	Jodel D.117	L. B. Clark & J. C. Haynes	
G-AVPN	HPR.7 Herald 213 ★	Yorkshire Air Museum/Elvington	
G-AVPO	Hindustan HAL-26 Pushpak	B. Johns	
G-AVPV	PA-18 Cherokee 180	K. A. Passmore	
G-AVPY	PA-25 Pawnee 235C	Southdown Gliding Club Ltd	
G-AVRK	PA-28 Cherokee 180	Air Romeo Kilo Ltd	
G-AVRS	Gardan GY-80 Horizon 180	N. M. Robbins	
G-AVRU	PA-28-Cherokee 180	Lanpro	
G-AVRW	Gardan GY-20 Minicab	Kestrel Flying Group	
G-AVRZ	PA-28 Cherokee 180	Mantavia Group Ltd	
G-AVSA	PA-28 Cherokee 180	M. C. Bellamy	
G-AVSB	PA-28 Cherokee 180	D. L. Macdonald	
G-AVSC	PA-28 Cherokee 180	G-AVSC Syndicate	
G-AVSD	PA-28 Cherokee 180	C. B. D. Owen	
G-AVSE	PA-28 Cherokee 180	F. Glendon/Ireland	
G-AVSF	PA-28 Cherokee 180	Monday Club	
G-AVSI	PA-28 Cherokee 140	G-AVSI Flying Group	
G-AVSP	PA-28 Cherokee 180	Internet Search Services Ltd	
G-AVSR	Beagle D.5/180 Husky	G. R. Greenfield & S. D. J. Holwill	
G-AVTC	Slingsby Nipper T.66 RA.45 Srs 3	J. Crawford	
G-AVTP	Cessna F.172H	G. & N. Kieswetter	
G-AVTT	Ercoupe 415D	Wright's Farm Eggs Ltd	
G-AVUG	Cessna F.150H	Skyways Flying Group	
G-AVUH	Cessna F.150H	A. G. McLaren	
G-AVUO	Luton LA4 Minor	M. E. Vaisey	
G-AVUS	PA-28 Cherokee 140	P. K. Pemberton	
G-AVUT	PA-28 Cherokee 140	Bencray Ltd	
G-AVUZ	PA-32 Cherokee Six 300	Ceesix Ltd	
G-AVVC	Cessna F.172H	Babs Flying Group	
G-AVVO	Avro 652A Anson 19 (VL348)★	Newark Air Museum	
G-AVWA	PA-28 Cherokee 140	SFG Ltd	
G-AVWD	PA-28 Cherokee 140	M. Howells	
G-AVWI	PA-28 Cherokee 140	L. M. Veitch	
G-AVWL	PA-28 Cherokee 140	G-AVWL Group	
G-AVWM	PA-28 Cherokee 140	P. E. Preston & Partners	
G-AVWO	PA-28R Cherokee Arrow 180	Whiskey Oscar Group	
G-AVWR	PA-28R Cherokee Arrow 180	G-AVWR Flying Group	
G-AVWT	PA-28R Cherokee Arrow 180	O. D. Mihalop	
G-AVWU	PA-28R Cherokee Arrow 180	M. Ali & S. Din	
G-AVWV	PA-28R Cherokee Arrow 180	Strathtay Flying Group	
G-AVWY	Fournier RF-4D	J. P. Marriott	
G-AVXA	PA-25 Pawnee 235	S. Wales Gliding Club Ltd	
G-AVXD	Slingsby T.66 Nipper 3	J. A. Brompton	
G-AVXF	PA-28R Cherokee Arrow 180	G-AVXF Group	

Notes	Reg.	Type	Owner or Operator
	G-AVXW	D.62B Condor	C. Willmott
	G-AVXY	Auster AOP.9	G. J. Siddall
	G-AVXZ	PA-28 Cherokee 140 ★	ATC Hayle (instructional airframe)
	G-AVYB	HS.121 Trident 1E-140 ★	SAS training airframe/Hereford
	G-AVYK	Beagle A.61 Terrier 3	R. Burgun
	G-AVYL	PA-28 Cherokee 180	S. Collins
	G-AVYM	PA-28 Cherokee 180	C. D. London
	G-AVYS	PA-28R Cherokee Arrow 180	R. J. Schreiber
	G-AVYT	PA-28R Cherokee Arrow 180	M. Bonsall
	G-AVYV	Jodel D.120	R. Holt
	G-AVZB	Aero Z-37 Cmelak ★	Science Museum/Wroughton
	G-AVZI	Bölkow Bö.208C1 Junior	C. F. Rogers
	G-AVZP	Beagle B.121 Pup 1	T. A. White
	G-AVZR	PA-28 Cherokee 180	Lincoln Aero Club Ltd
	G-AVZU	Cessna F.150H	R. D. Forster
	G-AVZV	Cessna F.172H	A. D. Millington
	G-AVZW	EAA Biplane Model P	C. Edmondson
	G-AWAC	Gardan GY-80 Horizon 180	P. B. Hodgson
	G-AWAJ	Beech 95-D55 Baron	B. F. Whitworth
	G-AWAT	D.62B Condor	R. E. Matthews
	G-AWAU	Vickers FB.27A Vimy (replica) (F8614) ★	RAF Museum/Hendon
	G-AWAW	Cessna F.150F ★	Science Museum/South Kensington
	G-AWAX	Cessna 150D	G-AWAX Group
	G-AWAZ	PA-28R Cherokee Arrow 180	G-AWAZ Flying Group
	G-AWBB	PA-28R Cherokee Arrow 180	P. J. Young
	G-AWBC	PA-28R Cherokee Arrow 180	Anglo Aviation (UK) Ltd
	G-AWBE	PA-28 Cherokee 140	B. E. Boyle
	G-AWBG	PA-28 Cherokee 140	I. Herdis
	G-AWBJ	Fournier RF-4D	J. B. Giddins & D. M. Hook
	G-AWBM	D.31 Turbulent	D. E. Wood
	G-AWBN	PA-30 Twin Comanche 160B	Stourfield Investments Ltd
	G-AWBS	PA-28 Cherokee 140	R. A. Ballard
	G-AWBT	PA-30 Twin Comanche 160B ★	Instructional airframe/Cranfield
	G-AWBU	Morane-Saulnier N (replica) (MS824)	Flying Aces Movie Aircraft Collection
	G-AWBX	Cessna F.150H	R. Nightingale
	G-AWCM	Cessna F.150H	R. Garbett
	G-AWCN	Cessna FR.172E	B. & C. Stobart-Hook
	G-AWCP	Cessna F.150H (tailwheel)	C. E. Mason
	G-AWDA	Slingsby T.66 Nipper 3	J. A. Cheesebrough
	G-AWDO	D.31 Turbulent	R. N. Crosland
	G-AWDP	PA-28 Cherokee 180	B. H. & P. M. Illston
	G-AWDR	Cessna FR.172E	B. A. Wallace
	G-AWDU	Brantly B.2B	N. J. M. Freeman
	G-AWEA	Beagle B.121 Pup Srs.1	G. V. Crowe
	G-AWEF	SNCAN Stampe SV.4B	RAF Buchanan
	G-AWEI	D.62B Condor	P. A. Gange
	G-AWEK	Fournier RF-4D	M. P. J. Hill
	G-AWEL	Fournier RF-4D	A. B. Clymo
	G-AWEM	Fournier RF-4D	B. J. Griffin
	G-AWEP	Barritault JB-01 Minicab	R. K. Thomas
	G-AWES	Cessna 150H	D. W. Vincent
	G-AWEV	PA-28 Cherokee 140	Norflight Ltd
	G-AWEX	PA-28 Cherokee 140	RVL Aviation Ltd
	G-AWEZ	PA-28R Cherokee Arrow 180	R. G. E. Simpson
	G-AWFB	PA-28R Cherokee Arrow 180	J. C. Luke
	G-AWFC	PA-28R Cherokee Arrow 180	A. Simpson
	G-AWFD	PA-28R Cherokee Arrow 180	J. A. Canham
	G-AWFF	Cessna F.150H	R. A. Marven
	G-AWFJ	PA-28R Cherokee Arrow 180	Bavair Ltd
	G-AWFN	D.62B Condor	C. C. Bland
	G-AWFO	D.62B Condor	T. A. & R. E. Major
	G-AWFP	D.62B Condor	Blackbushe Flying Club
	G-AWFT	Jodel D.9 Bébé	W. H. Cole
	G-AWFW	Jodel D.117	C. J. Rodwell
	G-AWFZ	Beech A23 Musketeer	Bob Crowe Aircraft Sales Ltd
	G-AWGA	Beagle A.109 Airedale ★	(stored)
	G-AWGD	Cessna F.172H	Rutland Flying School
	G-AWGK	Cessna F.150H	G. E. Allen
	G-AWGN	Fournier RF-4D	R. J. Grimstead

Reg.	Type	Owner or Operator	Notes
G-AWGZ	Taylor JT.1 Monoplane	R. L. Sambell	
G-AWHB	CASA 2-111D (6J+PR) ★	Aces High Ltd/North Weald	
G-AWHE	Hispano HA.1112 M1L	Spitfire Ltd	
G-AWHX	Rollason Beta B.2	T. Jarvis	
G-AWHY	Falconar F.11-3	Why Fly Group (G-BDPB)	
G-AWIF	Brookland Mosquito 2	C. A. Reeves	
G-AWII	VS.349 Spitfire VC (AR501)	The Shuttleworth Collection	
G-AWIR	Midget Mustang	E. C. Murgatroyd	
G-AWIT	PA-28 Cherokee 180	G-AWIT Ltd	
G-AWIV	Airmark TSR.3	P. A. Gasson	
G-AWIW	SNCAN Stampe SV.4B	R. E. Mitchell	
G-AWJE	Slingsby T.66 Nipper 3	K G. G. Howe	
G-AWJV	DH.98 Mosquito TT Mk 35 (TA634) ★	De Havilland Heritage Museum/London Colney	
G-AWJX	Zlin Z.526 Trener Master	P. A. Colman	
G-AWKD	PA-17 Vagabond	C. C. & J. M. Lovell	
G-AWKO	Beagle B.121 Pup 1	J. Martin	
G-AWKP	Jodel DR.253	G-AWKP Group	
G-AWKX	Beech A65 Queen Air ★	(Instructional airframe)/Shoreham	
G-AWLF	Cessna F.172H	Gannet Aviation	
G-AWLG	SIPA 903	S. W. Markham	
G-AWLI	PA-22 Tri-Pacer 150	North Hangar Group	
G-AWLO	Boeing Stearman E75	N. D. Pickard	
G-AWLP	Mooney M.20F	I. C. Lomax	
G-AWLR	Slingsby T.66 Nipper 3	T. D. Reid	
G-AWLS	Slingsby T.66 Nipper 3	G. A. Dunster & B. Gallagher	
G-AWLX	Auster 5 J/2 Arrow	W. J. Taylor	
G-AWLZ	Fournier RF-4D	Nympsfield RF-4 Group	
G-AWMD	Jodel D.11	J. R. Cooper	
G-AWMF	PA-18 Super Cub 150 (modified)	Booker Gliding Club Ltd	
G-AWMN	Luton LA-4A Minor	S. Penfold	
G-AWMR	D.31 Turbulent	J. R. D. Bygraves	
G-AWMT	Cessna F.150H	Strategic Synergies Ltd	
G-AWNT	BN-2A Islander	Precision Terrain Surveys Ltd	
G-AWOE	Aero Commander 680E	J. M. Houlder	
G-AWOF	PA-15 Vagabond	N. G. Busschau	
G-AWOH	PA-17 Vagabond	A. Lovejoy & K. Downes	
G-AWOT	Cessna F.150H	D. I. Flory	
G-AWOU	Cessna 170B	S. Billington	
G-AWOX	Westland WS-58 Wessex 60 (150225) ★	Paintball Adventure West/Bristol	
G-AWPH	P.56 Provost T.1	J. A. D. Bradshaw	
G-AWPJ	Cessna F.150H	W. J. Greenfield	
G-AWPN	Shield Xyla	J. P. Gilbert	
G-AWPU	Cessna F.150J	LAC Flying School	
G-AWPW	PA-12 Super Cruiser	AK Leasing (Jersey) Ltd	
G-AWPZ	Andreasson BA-4B	J. M. Vening	
G-AWRP	Cierva Rotorcraft ★	IHM/Weston-super-Mare	
G-AWRS	Avro 19 Srs. 2 (TX213) ★	North East Aircraft Museum/Usworth	
G-AWRY	P.56 Provost T.1 (XF836)	A. J. House	
G-AWSA	Avro 652A Anson 19 (VL349) ★	Norfolk & Suffolk Aviation Museum/Flixton	
G-AWSH	Zlin Z.526 Trener Master	P. A. Colman	
G-AWSL	PA-28 Cherokee 180D	A. H. & A. H. Brown	
G-AWSM	PA-28 Cherokee 235	Aviation Projects Ltd	
G-AWSN	D.62B Condor	M. K. A. Blyth	
G-AWSP	D.62B Condor	R. Q. & A. S. Bond	
G-AWSS	D.62A Condor	N. J. & D. Butler	
G-AWST	D.62B Condor	J. R. Bell	
G-AWSV	Skeeter 12 (XM553)	Maj. M. Somerton-Rayner	
G-AWSW	Beagle D.5/180 Husky (XW635)	Windmill Aviation	
G-AWTL	PA-28 Cherokee 180D	G. B. Stevens	
G-AWTP	Schleicher Ka 6E	Papa Victor Syndicate	
G-AWTS	Beech A.23 Musketeer	J. G. Edwards & K. D. Maal	
G-AWTV	Beech 19A Musketeer Sport	J. Whittaker	
G-AWTX	Cessna F.150J	R. D. Forster	
G-AWUB	Gardan GY-201 Minicab	R. A. Hand	
G-AWUE	Jodel DR.1050	K. W. Wood & F. M. Watson	
G-AWUJ	Cessna F.150H	I. M. Ashpole & N. Sutton	
G-AWUL	Cessna F.150H	A. J. Baron	
G-AWUN	Cessna F.150H	G-AWUN Group	
G-AWUT	Cessna F.150J	Aerospace Resources Ltd	
G-AWUU	Cessna F.150J	D. P. Jones	
G-AWUX	Cessna F.172H	G-AWUX Group	

Notes	Reg.	Type	Owner or Operator
	G-AWUZ	Cessna F.172H	Five Percent Flying Group
	G-AWVA	Cessna F.172H	Barton Air Ltd
	G-AWVC	Beagle B.121 Pup 1	J. J. West & M. J. Applewhite
	G-AWVE	Jodel DR.1050/M1	E. A. Taylor
	G-AWVG	AESL Airtourer T.2	C. J. Schofield
	G-AWVN	Aeronca 7AC Champion	Champ Flying Group
	G-AWVY	BN-2A-26 Islander	Islander Aircraft Ltd
	G-AWVZ	Jodel D.112	D. C. Stokes
	G-AWWE	Beagle B.121 Pup 2	Pup Flyers
	G-AWWI	Jodel D.117	J. Pool
	G-AWWM	Gardan GY-201 Minicab	P. J. Brayshaw
	G-AWWN	Jodel DR.1050	The G-AWWN Group
	G-AWWO	Jodel DR.1050	W. G. Brooks
	G-AWWP	Aerosport Woody Pusher III	M. S. Bird & R. D. Bird
	G-AWWU	Cessna FR.172F	R. Henderson
	G-AWXR	PA-28 Cherokee 180D	Aero Clube da Costa Verde/Portugal
	G-AWXS	PA-28 Cherokee 180D	S. A. Hardiman
	G-AWXX	Westland Wessex 60 Srs 1	D. Brem-Wilson
	G-AWXY	MS.885 Super Rallye	K. Henderson
	G-AWXZ	SNCAN Stampe SV.4C	Bianchi Aviation Film Services Ltd
	G-AWYB	Cessna FR.172F	M.P. & S. T. Barnard & M. S. Macdonald
	G-AWYI	BE.2c replica (347)	M. C. Boddington & S. Slater
	G-AWYJ	Beagle B.121 Pup 2	H. C. Taylor
	G-AWYL	Jodel DR.253B	T. C. Van Lonkhuyzen
	G-AWYO	Beagle B.121 Pup 1	B. R. C. Wild
	G-AWYY	Slingsby T.57 Camel replica (B6401) ★	F.A.A. Museum/Yeovilton
	G-AWZI	HS.121 Trident 3B ★	A. Lee/FAST Museum (nose only)/Farnborough
	G-AWZJ	HS.121 Trident 3B ★	Dumfries & Galloway Museum
	G-AWZK	HS.121 Trident 3B ★	Trident Preservation Society/Manchester
	G-AWZM	HS.121 Trident 3B ★	Science Museum/Wroughton
	G-AWZP	HS.121 Trident 3B ★	Manchester Museum of Science & Industry (nose only)
	G-AWZX	HS.121 Trident 3B ★	BAA Airport Fire Services/Gatwick
	G-AXAB	PA-28 Cherokee 140	Bencray Ltd
	G-AXAN	DH.82A Tiger Moth (EM720)	D. & S. A. Firth
	G-AXAS	Wallis WA-116T	K. H. Wallis (G-AVDH)
	G-AXAT	Jodel D.117A	D. Evans
	G-AXBF	Beagle D.5/180 Husky	M. C. R. Wills
	G-AXBJ	Cessna F.172H	Atlantic Bridge Aviation Ltd
	G-AXBW	DH.82A Tiger Moth (T5879:RUC-W)	G-AXBW Ltd
	G-AXBZ	DH.82A Tiger Moth	W. J. de Jong Cleyndert
	G-AXCA	PA-28R Cherokee Arrow 200	W. H. Nelson
	G-AXCG	Jodel D.117	D. J. Millin
	G-AXCM	MS.880B Rallye Club	D. C. Manifold
	G-AXCX	Beagle B.121 Pup 2	L. A. Pink
	G-AXCY	Jodel D.117A	R. S. Marom
	G-AXDI	Cessna F.172H	M. F. & J. R. Leusby
	G-AXDK	Jodel DR.315	R. D. Bennett
	G-AXDN	BAC-Sud Concorde 01 ★	Duxford Aviation Society
	G-AXDV	Beagle B.121 Pup 1	T. A. White
	G-AXDZ	Cassutt Racer IIIM	A. Chadwick
	G-AXED	PA-25 Pawnee 235	Wolds Gliding Club Ltd
	G-AXEH	B.125 Bulldog 1 ★	Museum of Flight/East Fortune
	G-AXEI	Ward Gnome ★	Real Aeroplane Club/Breighton
	G-AXEO	Scheibe SF.25B Falke	P. F. Moffatt
	G-AXEV	Beagle B.121 Pup 2	D. S. Russell & D. G. Benson
	G-AXFG	Cessna 337D	County Garage (Cheltenham) Ltd
	G-AXFN	Jodel D.119	R. Manning & F. J. Wordsworth
	G-AXGE	MS.880B Rallye Club	R. P. Loxton
	G-AXGG	Cessna F.150J	A. J. Simpson
	G-AXGP	Piper J-3C-90 Cub	A. P. Acres
	G-AXGR	Luton LA-4A Minor	B. A. Schlussler
	G-AXGS	D.62B Condor	SAS Flying Group
	G-AXGV	D.62B Condor	Hawkaero Flying Group
	G-AXGZ	D.62B Condor	M. W. Richardson
	G-AXHC	SNCAN Stampe SV.4C	D. L. Webley
	G-AXHO	Beagle B.121 Pup 2	L. W. Grundy
	G-AXHP	Piper J-3C-65 Cub (480636:A-58)	Witham (Specialist) Vehicles Ltd
	G-AXHR	Piper J-3C-65 Cub (329601:D-44)	D. J. Dash
	G-AXHS	MS.880B Rallye Club	B. & A. Swales

Reg.	Type	Owner or Operator	Notes
G-AXHT	MS.880B Rallye Club	P. M. Murray	
G-AXHV	Jodel D.117A	Derwent Flying Group	
G-AXIA	Beagle B.121 Pup 1	C. K. Parsons	
G-AXIE	Beagle B.121 Pup 2	J. P. Thomas	
G-AXIO	PA-28 Cherokee 140B	A. D. Messenger	
G-AXIR	PA-28 Cherokee 140B	R. W. Howard	
G-AXIW	Scheibe SF.25B Falke	M. Pedley	
G-AXIX	Glos-Airtourer 150	S. Alexander	
G-AXJB	Omega 84 balloon	Southern Balloon Group	
G-AXJH	Beagle B.121 Pup 2	The Henry Flying Group	
G-AXJI	Beagle B.121 Pup 2	J. J. Sanders & J. A. Walley	
G-AXJJ	Beagle B.121 Pup 2	M. L. Jones & ptnrs	
G-AXJO	Beagle B.121 Pup 2	J. A. D. Bradshaw	
G-AXJR	Scheibe SF.25B Falke	Falke Syndicate	
G-AXJV	PA-28 Cherokee 140B	Seahawk Flying Group	
G-AXJX	PA-28 Cherokee 140B	Horizon Aviation Ltd	
G-AXKH	Luton LA-4A Minor	M. E. Vaisey	
G-AXKJ	Jodel D.9	Hinton D9 Group	
G-AXKO	Westland-Bell 47G-4A	M. Gallagher	
G-AXKS	Westland Bell 47G-4A ★	Museum of Army Flying/Middle Wallop	
G-AXKX	Westland Bell 47G-4A	R. A. Dale	
G-AXLI	Slingsby T.66 Nipper 3	D. & M. Shrimpton	
G-AXLS	Jodel DR.105A	Axle Flying Club	
G-AXLZ	PA-18 Super Cub 95	Perryair Ltd	
G-AXMA	PA-24 Comanche 180	B. C. Faulkner	
G-AXMD	Omega O-56 balloon ★	British Balloon Museum/Newbury	
G-AXMT	Bücker Bü 133 Jungmeister	C. Coltri	
G-AXMW	Beagle B.121 Pup 1	DJP Engineering (Knebworth) Ltd	
G-AXMX	Beagle B.121 Pup 2	Bob The Beagle Group	
G-AXNJ	Wassmer Jodel D.120	S. S. M. Turner	
G-AXNN	Beagle B.121 Pup 2	Gabrielle Aviation Ltd	
G-AXNP	Beagle B.121 Pup 2	J. W. Ellis & R. J. Hemmings	
G-AXNR	Beagle B.121 Pup 2	AXNR Group	
G-AXNS	Beagle B.121 Pup 2	Derwent Aero Group	
G-AXNW	SNCAN Stampe SV.4C	C. S. Grace	
G-AXNX	Cessna 182M	T. Latky & C.Csilla	
G-AXNZ	Pitts S.1C Special	November Zulu Group	
G-AXOG	PA-E23 Aztec 250D	G. H. Nolan	
G-AXOH	MS.894 Rallye Minerva	T. A. D. Crook	
G-AXOJ	Beagle B.121 Pup 2	Pup Flying Group	
G-AXOR	PA-28 Cherokee 180D	Oscar Romeo Aviation Ltd	
G-AXOS	MS.894A Rallye Minerva	R. S. M. Fendt	
G-AXOT	MS.893 Rallye Commodore 180	P. Evans	
G-AXOZ	Beagle B.121 Pup 1	R. J. Ogborn	
G-AXPA	Beagle B.121 Pup 1	C. B. Copsey	
G-AXPC	Beagle B.121 Pup 2	T. A. White	
G-AXPF	Cessna F.150K	D. R. Marks	
G-AXPG	Mignet HM.293	W. H. Cole (stored)	
G-AXPZ	Campbell Cricket	W. R. Partridge	
G-AXRC	Campbell Cricket	L. R. Morris	
G-AXRP	SNCAN Stampe SV-4C	C. C. Manning (G-BLOL)	
G-AXRR	Auster AOP.9 (XR241)	R. B. Webber	
G-AXRT	Cessna FA.150K (tailwheel)	C. C. Walley	
G-AXSF	Nash Petrel	Nash Aircraft Ltd	
G-AXSG	PA-28 Cherokee 180	The Tago Island Co Ltd	
G-AXSI	Cessna F.172H	J. B. Cutts (G-SNIP)	
G-AXSM	Jodel DR.1051	T. R. G. & M. S. Barnby	
G-AXSW	Cessna FA.150K	R. J. Whyham	
G-AXSZ	PA-28 Cherokee 140B	White Wings Flying Group	
G-AXTA	PA-28 Cherokee 140B	G-AXTA Aircraft Group	
G-AXTC	PA-28 Cherokee 140B	G-AXTC Group	
G-AXTJ	PA-28 Cherokee 140B	K. Patel	
G-AXTL	PA-28 Cherokee 140B	Bristol and West Aeroplane Club Ltd	
G-AXTO	PA-24 Comanche 260	J. L. Wright	
G-AXTX	Jodel D.112	C. Sawford	
G-AXUA	Beagle B.121 Pup 1	P. Wood	
G-AXUB	BN-2A Islander	Headcorn Parachute Club Ltd	
G-AXUC	PA-12 Super Cruiser	J. J. Bunton	
G-AXUF	Cessna FA.150K	R. Taggart	
G-AXUJ	Auster J/1 Autocrat	P. Gill (G-OSTA)	
G-AXUK	Jodel DR.1050	Downland Flying Group	

Notes	Reg.	Type	Owner or Operator
	G-AXUM	HP.137 Jetstream 1 ★	Sodeteg Formation/France
	G-AXVB	Cessna F.172H	R. & J. Turner
	G-AXVK	Campbell Cricket	B. Jones
	G-AXVM	Campbell Cricket	D. M. Organ
	G-AXVN	McCandless M.4	W. R. Partridge
	G-AXWA	Auster AOP.9 (XN437)	C. M. Edwards
	G-AXWT	Jodel D.11	C. S. Jackson
	G-AXWV	Jodel DR.253	R. Friedlander & D. C. Ray
	G-AXWZ	PA-28R Cherokee Arrow 200	Whisky Zulu Group
	G-AXXC	CP.301B Emeraude	J. C. & R. D. P. Cadle
	G-AXXV	DH.82A Tiger Moth (DE992)	R. B. Russell
	G-AXXW	Jodel D.117	R. K. G. Delve
	G-AXYK	Taylor JT.1 Monoplane	O. C. Pope
	G-AXYU	Jodel D.9 Bébé	P. Turton
	G-AXZD	PA-28 Cherokee 180E	Sirius Aviation Ltd
	G-AXZF	PA-28 Cherokee 180E	D. R. Clyde
	G-AXZH	Glasflugel H201B Standard Libelle	M. C. Gregorie
	G-AXZM	Slingsby T.66 Nipper 3	G. R. Harlow
	G-AXZP	PA-E23 Aztec 250D	D. M. Harbottle
	G-AXZT	Jodel D.117	P. Guest
	G-AXZU	Cessna 182N	W. Gollan
	G-AYAB	PA-28 Cherokee 180E	J. R. Green
	G-AYAC	PA-28R Cherokee Arrow 200	Fersfield Flying Group
	G-AYAJ	Cameron O-84 balloon	E. T. Hall
	G-AYAL	Omega 56 balloon ★	British Balloon Museum/Newbury
	G-AYAN	Slingsby Motor Cadet III	G. Hill & R. Moyse
	G-AYAR	PA-28 Cherokee 180E	A. Jahanfar
	G-AYAT	PA-28 Cherokee 180E	G-AYAT Flying Group
	G-AYAW	PA-28 Cherokee 180E	D. G., P. G. & R. J. Taylor
	G-AYBD	Cessna F.150K	Apollo Aviation Advisory Ltd
	G-AYBG	Scheibe SF.25B Falke	Anglia Sailplanes
	G-AYBO	PA-23 Aztec 250D	A. G. Gutknecht/Austria
	G-AYBP	Jodel D.112	G. J. Langston
	G-AYBR	Jodel D.112	I. S. Parker
	G-AYCC	Campbell Cricket	D. J. M. Charity
	G-AYCE	Scintex CP.301-C1 Emeraude	D. A. Healey
	G-AYCF	Cessna FA.150K	E. J. Atkins
	G-AYCG	SNCAN Stampe SV.4C	Tiger Airways
	G-AYCJ	Cessna TP.206D	A. Ahmed
	G-AYCK	AIA Stampe SV.4C	The Real Flying Co Ltd (G-BUNT)
	G-AYCN	Piper J-3C-65 Cub	W. R. & B. M. Young
	G-AYCO	CEA DR.360	J. D. Boyce & R. Underwood
	G-AYCP	Jodel D.112	J. A. Carey
	G-AYCT	Cessna F.172H	J. R. Benson
	G-AYDI	DH.82A Tiger Moth	E. G. & G. R. Woods
	G-AYDR	SNCAN Stampe SV.4C	D. J. Ashley
	G-AYDV	Coates Swalesong SA11	The Real Aeroplane Co.Ltd
	G-AYDW	Beagle A.61 Terrier 2	A. S. Topen
	G-AYDX	Beagle A.61 Terrier 2	T. S. Lee
	G-AYDY	Luton LA-4A Minor	J. Dible/Ireland
	G-AYDZ	Jodel DR.200	Zero One Group
	G-AYEB	Jodel D.112	Echo Bravo Partnership
	G-AYEE	PA-28 Cherokee 180E	Demero Ltd & Transcourt Ltd
	G-AYEF	PA-28 Cherokee 180E	Pegasus Flying Group
	G-AYEG	Falconar F-9	A. L. Smith
	G-AYEH	Jodel DR.1050	T. J. N. H. Palmer
	G-AYEJ	Jodel DR.1050	J. M. Newbold
	G-AYEN	Piper J-3C-65 Cub	P. Warde & C. F. Morris
	G-AYET	MS.892A Rallye Commodore 150	A. T. R. Bingley
	G-AYEW	Jodel DR.1051	J. R. Hope
	G-AYFC	D.62B Condor	A. R. Chadwick
	G-AYFD	D.62B Condor	B. G. Manning
	G-AYFE	D.62C Condor	M. Soulsby
	G-AYFF	D.62B Condor	H. Stuart
	G-AYFJ	MS.880B Rallye Club	Rallye FJ Group
	G-AYFV	Crosby BA-4B	D. W. Mathie
	G-AYGA	Jodel D.117	J. W. Bowes
	G-AYGB	Cessna 310Q ★	Instructional airframe/Perth
	G-AYGC	Cessna F.150K	Alpha Aviation Group

Reg.	Type	Owner or Operator	Notes
G-AYGD	Jodel DR.1051	J. F. M. Barlett & J. P. Liber	
G-AYGE	SNCAN Stampe SV.4C	L. J. Proudfoot & ptnrs	
G-AYGG	Jodel D.120	J. M. Dean	
G-AYGX	Cessna FR.172G	Reims Rocket Group	
G-AYHA	AA-1 Yankee	S. J. Carr	
G-AYHX	Jodel D.117A	A. P. Chapman & L. E. Cowling	
G-AYIA	Hughes 369HS ★	G. D. E. Bilton/Sywell	
G-AYIG	PA-28 Cherokee 140C	G. K. Clarkson	
G-AYII	PA-28R Cherokee Arrow 200	Double India Group	
G-AYIJ	SNCAN Stampe SV.4B	D. Savage	
G-AYJA	Jodel DR.1050	D. M. Blair	
G-AYJB	SNCAN Stampe SV.4C	F. J. M. & J. P. Esson	
G-AYJD	Alpavia-Fournier RF-3	Juliet Delta Group	
G-AYJP	PA-28 Cherokee 140C	Transcourt Ltd and Demero Ltd	
G-AYJR	PA-28 Cherokee 140C	Turweston Flying School	
G-AYJY	Isaacs Fury II	T. E. W. Terrell	
G-AYKD	Jodel DR.1050	L. S. Johnson	
G-AYKJ	Jodel D.117A	R. J. Hughes	
G-AYKK	Jodel D.117	J. M. Whitham	
G-AYKS	Leopoldoff L.7 Colibri	W. B. Cooper	
G-AYKT	Jodel D.117	D. I. Walker	
G-AYKW	PA-28 Cherokee 140C	Kilo Whiskey Group	
G-AYKZ	SAI KZ-8	R. E. Mitchell	
G-AYLA	Glos-Airtourer 115	C. P. L. Jenkins	
G-AYLC	Jodel DR.1051	G-AYLC Flying Group	
G-AYLF	Jodel DR.1051 (modified)	R. Twigg	
G-AYLL	Jodel DR.1050	C. Joly	
G-AYLP	AA-1 Yankee	D. Nairn	
G-AYLV	Jodel D.120	M. R. Henham	
G-AYME	Fournier RF-5	R. D. Goodger	
G-AYMK	PA-28 Cherokee 140C	R. Quinn	
G-AYMP	Currie Wot	R. C. Hibberd	
G-AYMR	Lederlin 380L	P. J. Brayshaw	
G-AYMU	Jodel D.112	M. R. Baker	
G-AYMV	Western 20 balloon	R. G. Turnbull	
G-AYNA	Phoenix Currie Wot	D. R. Partridge	
G-AYND	Cessna 310Q	Cotswold Aero Maintenance Ltd	
G-AYNF	PA-28 Cherokee 140C	BW Aviation Ltd	
G-AYNJ	PA-28 Cherokee 140C	A. Andreeva	
G-AYNN	Cessna 185B	Bencray Ltd	
G-AYNP	Westland WS-55 Whirlwind Srs 3 ★	IHM/Weston-super-Mare	
G-AYOW	Cessna 182N Skylane	I. F. Ellis, L. M. Hall & C. J. R. Vernon	
G-AYOZ	Cessna FA.150L	P. J. Worrall	
G-AYPE	MBB Bö.209 Monsun	Papa Echo Ltd	
G-AYPG	Cessna F.177RG	D. P. McDermott	
G-AYPH	Cessna F.177RG	M. L. & T. M. Jones	
G-AYPJ	PA-28 Cherokee 180	R. B. Petrie	
G-AYPM	PA-18 Super Cub 95 (115373)	A. N. R. Houghton & S. D. Barnard	
G-AYPO	PA-18 Super Cub 95	A. W. Knowles	
G-AYPS	PA-18 Super Cub 95	D. Racionzer	
G-AYPU	PA-28R Cherokee Arrow 200	Monalto Investments Ltd	
G-AYPV	PA-28 Cherokee 140D	Ashley Gardner Flying Club Ltd	
G-AYPZ	Campbell Cricket	A. Melody	
G-AYRG	Cessna F.172K	I. G. Harrison	
G-AYRI	PA-28R Cherokee Arrow 200	J. C. Houdret	
G-AYRM	PA-28 Cherokee 140D	M. J. Saggers	
G-AYRO	Cessna FA.150L Aerobat	Fat Boys Flying Club	
G-AYRS	Jodel D.120A	L. R. H. D'Eath	
G-AYRT	Cessna F.172K	S. Macfarlane	
G-AYRU	BN-2A-6 Islander	F. G. H. Jensen	
G-AYSB	PA-30 Twin Comanche 160C	M. J. Abbott	
G-AYSH	Taylor JT.1 Monoplane	C. J. Lodge	
G-AYSK	Luton LA-4A Minor	B. A. Schlussler & S. J. Rudkin	
G-AYSX	Cessna F.177RG	A. P. R. Dean	
G-AYSY	Cessna F.177RG	S. A. Tuer	
G-AYTA	SOCATA MS.880B Rallye Club ★	Manchester Museum of Science & Industry	
G-AYTR	CP.301A Emeraude	I. D. Worthington	
G-AYTT	Phoenix PM-3 Duet	R. B. Webber & J. K. Houlgrave	
G-AYTV	Jurca Tempete	C. W. Kirk	
G-AYUB	CEA DR.253B	P. J. Coward & E. D. Johnson	
G-AYUH	PA-28 Cherokee 180F	Broadland Flying Group Ltd	

Notes	Reg.	Type	Owner or Operator
	G-AYUJ	Evans VP-1	T. N. Howard
	G-AYUM	Slingsby T.61A Falke	M. H. Simms
	G-AYUN	Slingsby T.61A Falke	G-AYUN Group
	G-AYUP	Slingsby T.61A Falke	P. R. Williams
	G-AYUR	Slingsby T.61A Falke	R. Hanningan & R. Lingard
	G-AYUS	Taylor JT.1 Monoplane	J. G. W. Newton
	G-AYUT	Jodel DR.1050	G. Bell
	G-AYUV	Cessna F.172H	Justgold Ltd
	G-AYVO	Wallis WA-120 Srs 1	K. H. Wallis
	G-AYVP	Woody Pusher	J. R. Wraight
	G-AYWA	Avro 19 Srs 2 ★	N. K. Geddes
	G-AYWD	Cessna 182N	Wild Dreams Group
	G-AYWH	Jodel D.117A	D. Kynaston
	G-AYWM	Glos-Airtourer Super 150	Star Flying Group
	G-AYWT	AIA Stampe SV.4C	R. A. Palmer
	G-AYXP	Jodel D.117A	G. N. Davies
	G-AYXS	SIAI-Marchetti S205-18R	M. Llewellyn & B. Vincent
	G-AYXT	WS-55 Whirlwind Srs 2 (XK940:911) ★	IHM/Weston-super-Mare
	G-AYXU	Champion 7KCAB Citabria	E. V. Moffatt & J. S. Peplow
	G-AYYL	Slingsby T.61A Falke	Brightman Industries Ltd
	G-AYYO	Jodel DR.1050/M1	Bustard Flying Club Ltd
	G-AYYT	Jodel DR.1050/M1	R. Warner
	G-AYYU	Beech C23 Musketeer	G-AYYU Group
	G-AYZH	Taylor JT.2 Titch	T. Jarvis
	G-AYZI	SNCAN Stampe SV.4C	D. M. & P. A. Fenton
	G-AYZJ	Westland WS-55 Whirlwind HAS.7 ★	Newark Air Museum (XM685)
	G-AYZK	Jodel DR.1050/M1	D. G. Hesketh
	G-AYZS	D.62B Condor	M. N. Thrush
	G-AYZU	Slingsby T.61A Falke	A. J. Harpley
	G-AYZW	Slingsby T.61A Falke	Y-ZW Group
	G-AZAB	PA-30 Twin Comanche 160B	Bickertons Aerodromes Ltd
	G-AZAJ	PA-28R Cherokee Arrow 200B	P. Woulfe
	G-AZAW	Gardan GY-80 Horizon 160	J. W. Foley
	G-AZAZ	Bensen B.8M ★	F.A.A. Museum/Yeovilton
	G-AZBB	MBB Bö.209 Monsun 160FV	J. A. Webb
	G-AZBE	Glos-Airtourer Super 150	R. G. Vincent
	G-AZBI	Jodel 150	R. J. Wald
	G-AZBL	Jodel D.9 Bébé	J. Hill
	G-AZBN	Noorduyn AT-16 Harvard IIB (FT391)	Swaygate Ltd
	G-AZBU	Auster AOP.9 (XR246)	Auster Nine Group
	G-AZCB	SNCAN Stampe SV.4C	M. Coward
	G-AZCK	Beagle B.121 Pup 2	P. Crone
	G-AZCL	Beagle B.121 Pup 2	Flew LLP & J. M. Henry
	G-AZCN	Beagle B.121 Pup 2	P. Riley, E. J. Spencer & G. Wildgoose
	G-AZCP	Beagle B.121 Pup 1	A. C. Gunning
	G-AZCT	Beagle B.121 Pup 1	J. Coleman
	G-AZCU	Beagle B.121 Pup 1	D. W. Locke
	G-AZCV	Beagle B.121 Pup 2	N. R. W. Long
	G-AZCZ	Beagle B.121 Pup 2	L. & J. M. Northover
	G-AZDD	MBB Bö.209 Monsun 150FF	Double Delta Flying Group
	G-AZDE	PA-28R Cherokee Arrow 200B	London Elstree Aviation Ltd
	G-AZDG	Beagle B.121 Pup 2	T. W. Harris
	G-AZDJ	PA-32 Cherokee Six 300	K. J. Mansbridge & D. C. Gibbs
	G-AZDX	PA-28 Cherokee 180F	M. Cowan
	G-AZDY	DH.82A Tiger Moth	B. A. Mills
	G-AZEE	MS.880B Rallye Club	J. Shelton
	G-AZEF	Jodel D.120	P. R. Sears
	G-AZEG	PA-28 Cherokee 140D	Ashley Gardner Flying Club Ltd
	G-AZEU	Beagle B.121 Pup 2	G. M. Moir
	G-AZEV	Beagle B.121 Pup 2	G. H. Matthews
	G-AZEW	Beagle B.121 Pup 2	D. Ridley
	G-AZEY	Beagle B.121 Pup 2	B. K. & W. G. Ranger
	G-AZFA	Beagle B.121 Pup 2	J. Smith
	G-AZFC	PA-28 Cherokee 140D	WLS Flying Group
	G-AZFF	Jodel D.112	J. Bolger/Ireland
	G-AZFI	PA-28R Cherokee Arrow 200B	G-AZFI Ltd
	G-AZFM	PA-28R Cherokee Arrow 200B	P. J. Jenness
	G-AZGA	Jodel D.120	A. P. Hatton
	G-AZGC	SNCAN Stampe SV.4C	D. J. Ashley
	G-AZGE	SNCAN Stampe SV.4C	Tiger Airways

Reg.	Type	Owner or Operator	Notes
G-AZGF	Beagle B.121 Pup 2	K. Singh	
G-AZGL	MS.894A Rallye Minerva	The Cambridge Aero Club Ltd	
G-AZGY	CP.301B Emeraude	R. H. Braithwaite	
G-AZGZ	DH.82A Tiger Moth (NM181)	R. J. King	
G-AZHB	Robin HR.100/200B	J. F. Gould	
G-AZHC	Jodel D.112	Aerodel Flying Group	
G-AZHD	Slingsby T.61A Falke	R. J. Shallcrass	
G-AZHH	SA 102.5 Cavalier	D. W. Buckle	
G-AZHI	Glos-Airtourer Super 150	Flying Grasshoppers Ltd	
G-AZHK	Robin HR.100/200B	G. I. Applin (G-ILEG)	
G-AZHR	Piccard Ax6 balloon	C. Fisher	
G-AZHT	AESL Airtourer (modified)	Aviation West Ltd	
G-AZHU	Luton LA-4A Minor	C. C. Burton	
G-AZIB	ST-10 Diplomate	W. B. Bateson	
G-AZII	Jodel D.117A	J. S. Brayshaw	
G-AZIJ	Jodel DR.360	D. A. Gathercole	
G-AZIL	Slingsby T.61A Falke	D. W. Savage	
G-AZIP	Cameron O-65 balloon	Dante Balloon Group	
G-AZJC	Fournier RF-5	Seighford RF5 Group	
G-AZJE	Ord-Hume JB-01 Minicab	Kayee Flyers	
G-AZJN	Robin DR.300/140	C. P. Course	
G-AZJV	Cessna F.172L	G-AZJV Flying Group	
G-AZKE	MS.880B Rallye Club	D. A. Thompson & J. D. Headlam/Germany	
G-AZKO	Cessna F.337F	G. James	
G-AZKP	Jodel D.117	Moray Flying Group	
G-AZKR	PA-24 Comanche	S. J. McGovern	
G-AZKS	AA-1A Trainer	I. R. Matterface	
G-AZKW	Cessna F.172L	D. Stewart	
G-AZKZ	Cessna F.172L	R. D. & E. Forster	
G-AZLE	Boeing N2S-5 Kaydet (1102:102)	A. E. Paulson	
G-AZLF	Jodel D.120	M. S. C. Ball	
G-AZLH	Cessna F.150L	W. Ali	
G-AZLN	PA-28 Cherokee 180F	Enstone Sales & Services Ltd and J. Logan	
G-AZLV	Cessna 172K	G-AZLV Flying Group	
G-AZLY	Cessna F.150L	R. B. McLain	
G-AZMC	Slingsby T.61A Falke	P. J. R. White	
G-AZMD	Slingsby T.61C Falke	Tandem Gliding Syndicate	
G-AZMJ	AA-5 Traveler	W. R. Partridge	
G-AZMX	PA-28 Cherokee 140 ★	NE Wales Institute of Higher Education (Instructional airframe)/Flintshire	
G-AZMZ	MS.893A Rallye Commodore 150	J. Palethorpe	
G-AZNK	SNCAN Stampe SV.4A	November Kilo Group	
G-AZNL	PA-28R Cherokee Arrow 200D	B. P. Liversidge	
G-AZNO	Cessna 182P	M. S. Williams	
G-AZNT	Cameron O-84 balloon	P. Glydon	
G-AZOA	MBB Bö.209 Monsun 150FF	M. W. Hurst	
G-AZOB	MBB Bö.209 Monsun 150FF	J. A. Webb	
G-AZOE	Glos-Airtourer 115	G-AZOE 607 Group	
G-AZOF	Glos-Airtourer Super 150	R. C. Thursby & C. Goldsmith	
G-AZOG	PA-28R Cherokee Arrow 200D	Southend Flying Club	
G-AZOL	PA-34-200 Seneca II	Stapleford Flying Club Ltd	
G-AZOS	Jurca MJ.5-H1 Sirocco	P. J. Tanulak	
G-AZOU	Jodel DR.1050	Horsham Flying Group	
G-AZOZ	Cessna FRA.150L	J. E. Jones	
G-AZPA	PA-25 Pawnee 235	Black Mountains Gliding Club Ltd	
G-AZPC	Slingsby T.61C Falke	D. Heslop & J. R. Kimberley	
G-AZPF	Fournier RF-5	E. C. Mort	
G-AZPH	Craft-Pitts S-1S Special ★	Science Museum/South Kensington	
G-AZPX	Western O-31 balloon	Zebedee Balloon Service Ltd	
G-AZRA	MBB Bö.209 Monsun 150FF	Alpha Flying Ltd	
G-AZRH	PA-28 Cherokee 140D	Trust Flying Group	
G-AZRI	Payne Free Balloon	C. A. Butter & J. J. T. Cooke	
G-AZRK	Fournier RF-5	A. B. Clymo & J. F. Rogers	
G-AZRL	PA-18 Super Cub 95	I. Laws	
G-AZRM	Fournier RF-5	Romeo Mike Group	
G-AZRN	Cameron O-84 balloon	C. J. Desmet/Belgium	
G-AZRP	Glos-Airtourer 115	B. F. Strawford	
G-AZRS	PA-22 Tri-Pacer 150	R. H. Hulls	
G-AZRZ	Cessna U.206F	Cornish Parachute Club Ltd	
G-AZSA	Stampe et Renard SV.4B	M. R. Dolman	
G-AZSC	Noorduyn AT-16 Harvard IIB (43:SC)	Goodwood Road Racing Co Ltd	

Notes	Reg.	Type	Owner or Operator
	G-AZSF	PA-28R Cherokee Arrow 200D	Smart People Don't Buy Ltd
	G-AZTA	MBB Bö.209 Monsun 150FF	P. A. Grant & E. C. Dugard
	G-AZTF	Cessna F.177RG	R. Burgun
	G-AZTM	AESL Airtourer T2	Victa Restoration Group
	G-AZTS	Cessna F.172L	Eastern Air Executive Ltd
	G-AZTV	Stolp SA.500 Starlet	G. R. Rowland
	G-AZTW	Cessna F.177RG	I. M. Richmond & G. R. Waller
	G-AZUM	Cessna F.172L	Fowlmere Flyers
	G-AZUT	MS.893A Rallye Commodore 180	J. Palethorpe
	G-AZUY	Cessna E.310L	W. B. Bateson
	G-AZUZ	Cessna FRA.150L	D. J. Parker
	G-AZVA	MBB Bö.209 Monsun 150FF	M. P. Brinkmann
	G-AZVB	MBB Bö.209 Monsun 150FF	E. & P. M. L. Cliffe
	G-AZVF	MS.894A Rallye Minerva	Minerva Flying Group
	G-AZVG	AA-5 Traveler	M. A. Soakell
	G-AZVH	MS.894A Rallye Minerva	P. L. Jubb
	G-AZVI	MS.892A Rallye Commodore	G. C. Jarvis
	G-AZVL	Jodel D.119	A. K. & K. B. Raven
	G-AZVP	Cessna F.177RG	L. J. Klarenbeek
	G-AZWB	PA-28 Cherokee 140	G-AZWB Flying Group
	G-AZWF	SAN Jodel DR.1050	Cawdor Flying Group
	G-AZWS	PA-28R Cherokee Arrow 180	K. M. Turner
	G-AZWT	Westland Lysander IIIA (V9367)	The Shuttleworth Collection
	G-AZWY	PA-24 Comanche 260	Keymer Son & Co Ltd
	G-AZXB	Cameron O-65 balloon	R. J. Mitchener & P. F. Smart
	G-AZXD	Cessna F.172L	R. J. R. Williams & D. Palmer
	G-AZXG	PA-23 Aztec 250D ★	Instructional airframe/Cranfield
	G-AZYA	Gardan GY-80 Horizon 160	R. G. Whyte
	G-AZYB	Bell 47H-1 ★	IHM/Weston-super-Mare
	G-AZYD	MS.893A Rallye Commodore	Staffordshire Gliding Club Ltd
	G-AZYF	PA-28-180 Cherokee D	Airborne Adventures Ltd
	G-AZYS	CP.301C-1 Emeraude	C. G. Ferguson & D. Drew
	G-AZYU	PA-23 Aztec 250E	M. E. & M. H. Cromati & F. & N. P. Samuelson
	G-AZYY	Slingsby T.61A Falke	J. A. Towers
	G-AZYZ	Wassmer Wa.51A Pacific	M. P. Wiseman
	G-AZZR	Cessna F.150L	Zulu Romeo Group
	G-AZZV	Cessna F.172L	Zentelligence Ltd
	G-AZZZ	DH.82A Tiger Moth	S. W. McKay
	G-BAAD	Evans Super VP-1	Breighton VP-1 Group
	G-BAAF	Manning-Flanders MF1 (replica)	Aviation Film Services Ltd
	G-BAAI	MS.893A Rallye Commodore	R. D. Taylor
	G-BAAT	Cessna 182P	T. E. Earl
	G-BAAW	Jodel D.119	Alpha Whiskey Flying Group
	G-BABC	Cessna F.150L	B. B. Singh
	G-BABD	Cessna FRA.150L (modified)	BABD Group
	G-BABE	Taylor JT.2 Titch	T. A. Appleby
	G-BABG	PA-28 Cherokee 180	Mendip Flying Group
	G-BABK	PA-34-200 Seneca II	D. F. J. Flashman
	G-BACB	PA-34-200 Seneca II	Milbrooke Motors
	G-BACE	Fournier RF-5	G-BACE Fournier Group
	G-BACJ	Jodel D.120	Wearside Flying Association
	G-BACL	Jodel 150	E. Stokes & A. P. Hatton
	G-BACN	Cessna FRA.150L	F. Bundy
	G-BACO	Cessna FRA.150L	C. B. Harmer
	G-BADC	Rollason Beta B.2A	A. P. Grimley
	G-BADH	Slingsby T.61A Falke	M. J. Lake
	G-BADJ	PA-E23 Aztec 250E	C. Papadakis
	G-BADM	D.62B Condor	Delta Mike Condor Group
	G-BADV	Brochet MB50	W. B. Cooper
	G-BADW	Pitts S-2A Special	R. E. Mitchell
	G-BADZ	Aerotek Pitts S-2A Special	R. F. Warner
	G-BAEB	Robin DR.400/160	G. D. Jones
	G-BAEE	Jodel DR.1050/M1	R. Little
	G-BAEM	Robin DR.400/125	M. A. Webb
	G-BAEN	Robin DR.400/180	R. H. & C. R. Partington
	G-BAEO	Cessna F.172M	L. W. Scattergood
	G-BAEP	Cessna FRA.150L (modified)	A. M. Lynn
	G-BAER	Cosmic Wind	A. G. Truman
	G-BAET	Piper J-3C-65 Cub	C. J. Rees
	G-BAEU	Cessna F.150L	Advanced Flight Training Ltd

Reg.	Type	Owner or Operator	Notes
G-BAEV	Cessna FRA.L150L	Opex Ltd	
G-BAEW	Cessna F.172M ★	Westley Aircraft	
G-BAEY	Cessna F.172M	Skytrax Aviation Ltd	
G-BAEZ	Cessna FRA.150L	Donair Flying Club Ltd	
G-BAFA	AA-5 Traveler	C. F. Mackley	
G-BAFG	DH.82A Tiger Moth	Boultbee Vintage Ltd	
G-BAFL	Cessna 182P	R. B. Hopkinson & A. S. Pike	
G-BAFP	Robin DR.400/160	J. C. Bacon	
G-BAFT	PA-18 Super Cub 150	C. A. M. Neidt	
G-BAFU	PA-28 Cherokee 140	C. E. Taylor	
G-BAFV	PA-18 Super Cub 95	T. F. & S. J. Thorpe	
G-BAFW	PA-28 Cherokee 140	A. J. Peters	
G-BAFX	Robin DR.400/140	R. Foster	
G-BAGB	SIAI Marchetti SF.260	V. Balzer	
G-BAGC	Robin DR.400/140	G. Fox & J. R. Roberts	
G-BAGF	Jodel D.92 Bébé	J. Evans	
G-BAGG	PA-32 Cherokee Six 300E	A. D. Hoy	
G-BAGN	Cessna F.177RG	R. W. J. Andrews	
G-BAGR	Robin DR.400/140	J. D. Last	
G-BAGS	Robin DR.400/180 2+2	M. Whale & M. W. A. Lunn	
G-BAGT	Helio H.295 Courier	D. C. Hanss	
G-BAGX	PA-28 Cherokee 140	I. Lwanga	
G-BAGY	Cameron O-84 balloon	P. G. Dunnington	
G-BAHD	Cessna 182P Skylane	Lambley Flying Group	
G-BAHF	PA-28 Cherokee 140	Warwickshire Aviation Ltd	
G-BAHH	Wallis WA-121	K. H. Wallis	
G-BAHI	Cessna F.150H	MJP Aviation & Sales	
G-BAHJ	PA-24 Comanche 250	K. Cooper	
G-BAHL	Robin DR.400/160	J. B. McVeighty	
G-BAHP	Volmer VJ.22 Sportsman	Seaplane Group	
G-BAHS	PA-28R Cherokee Arrow 200-II	A. R. N. Morris	
G-BAHX	Cessna 182P	M. D. J. Moore	
G-BAIG	PA-34-200-2 Seneca	Mid-Anglia School of Flying	
G-BAIH	PA-28R Cherokee Arrow 200-II	M. G. West	
G-BAIK	Cessna F.150L	M. Sollitt	
G-BAIS	Cessna F.177RG	Cardinal Syndicate	
G-BAIW	Cessna F.172M	W. J. Greenfield	
G-BAIZ	Slingsby T.61A Falke	Falke Syndicate	
G-BAJA	Cessna F.177RG	M. J. J. Palmen	
G-BAJB	Cessna F.177RG	J. D. Loveridge	
G-BAJC	Evans VP-1	S. J. Greer	
G-BAJE	Cessna 177	Dynamic Aviation BV	
G-BAJN	AA-5 Traveler	P. J. Stead	
G-BAJO	AA-5 Traveler	Montgomery Aviation Ltd	
G-BAJR	PA-28 Cherokee 180	Spectrum Bravo Flying Group	
G-BAJZ	Robin DR.400/125	Rochester Aviation Ltd	
G-BAKH	PA-28 Cherokee 140	British NorthWest Airways Ltd	
G-BAKJ	PA-30 Twin Comanche 160B	Glareways (Neasden) Ltd	
G-BAKM	Robin DR.400/140	D. V. Pieri	
G-BAKN	SNCAN Stampe SV.4C	M. Holloway	
G-BAKR	Jodel D.117	R. W. Brown	
G-BAKV	PA-18 Super Cub 150	W. J. Murray	
G-BAKW	Beagle B.121 Pup 2	Cunning Stunts Flying Group	
G-BALD	Cameron O-84 balloon	C. A. Gould	
G-BALF	Robin DR.400/140	G. & D. A. Wasey	
G-BALG	Robin DR.400/180	S. G. Jones	
G-BALH	Robin DR.400/140B	G-BALH Flying Group	
G-BALJ	Robin DR.400/180	D. A. Batt & D. de Lacey-Rowe	
G-BALN	Cessna T.310Q	O'Brien Properties Ltd	
G-BALS	Tipsy Nipper T.66 Srs.3	N. C. Spooner	
G-BAMB	Slingsby T.61C Falke	H. J. Bradley	
G-BAMC	Cessna F.150L	R. J. Whyham	
G-BAML	Bell 206B Jet Ranger II ★	Aero Venture	
G-BAMR	PA-16 Clipper	G-BAMR Flying Group	
G-BAMU	Robin DR.400/160	The Alternative Flying Group	
G-BAMV	Robin DR.400/180	K. Jones & E. A. Anderson	
G-BAMY	PA-28R Cherokee Arrow 200-II	C. B. Clark	
G-BANA	Robin DR.221	G. T. Pryor	
G-BANB	Robin DR.400/180	M. Ingvarsden	
G-BANC	Gardan GY-201 Minicab	C. R. Shipley	
G-BANU	Wassmer Jodel D.120	C. H. Kilner	

Notes	Reg.	Type	Owner or Operator
	G-BANV	Phoenix Currie Wot	K. Knight
	G-BANW	CP.1330 Super Emeraude	P. S. Milner
	G-BANX	Cessna F.172M	Oakfleet 2000 Ltd
	G-BAOJ	MS.880B Rallye Club	R. E. Jones
	G-BAOM	MS.880B Rallye Club	P. J. D. Feehan
	G-BAOP	Cessna FRA.150L	R. D. Forster
	G-BAOS	Cessna F.172M	R. B. McLain
	G-BAOU	AA-5 Traveler	R. C. Mark
	G-BAPB	DHC.1 Chipmunk 22	R. C. P. Brookhouse
	G-BAPI	Cessna FRA.150L	Marketing Management Services International Ltd
	G-BAPJ	Cessna FRA.150L	M. D. Page
	G-BAPL	PA-23 Turbo Aztec 250E	Donington Aviation Ltd
	G-BAPP	Evans VP-1 Series 2	J. Ward
	G-BAPR	Jodel D.11	J. F. M. Bartlett
	G-BAPS	Campbell Cougar ★	IHM/Weston-super-Mare
	G-BAPV	Robin DR.400/160	J. D. & M. Millne
	G-BAPW	PA-28R Cherokee Arrow 180	A.G. Bourne & M. W. Freeman
	G-BAPX	Robin DR.400/160	White Rose Aviators
	G-BAPY	Robin HR.100/210	D. G. Doyle
	G-BARC	Cessna FR.172J	Severn Valley Aviation Group
	G-BARF	Jodel D.112 Club	R. N. Jones
	G-BARH	Beech C.23 Sundowner	G. Moorby & J. Hinchcliffe
	G-BARN	Taylor JT.2 Titch	R. G. W. Newton
	G-BARP	Bell 206B JetRanger 2	Helispares Ltd
	G-BARS	DHC.1 Chipmunk 22 (1377)	J. Beattie & R. M. Scarre
	G-BARZ	Scheibe SF.28A Tandem Falke	K. Kiely
	G-BASH	AA-5 Traveler	BASH Flying Group
	G-BASJ	PA-28-180 Cherokee	Bristol Aero Club
	G-BASL	PA-28-140 Cherokee	P. N. Clynes
	G-BASN	Beech C.23 Sundowner	Beech G-BASN Group Syndicate
	G-BASO	Lake LA-4 Amphibian	Uulster Seaplane Association Ltd
	G-BASP	Beagle B.121 Pup 1	B. J. Coutts
	G-BATC	MBB Bö.105D	South Georgia Heritage Trust
	G-BATJ	Jodel D.119	Clipgate TJ Group
	G-BATV	PA-28 Cherokee 180D	J. N. Rudsdale
	G-BATW	PA-28 Cherokee 140	C. D. Sainsbury
	G-BAUC	PA-25 Pawnee 235	Southdown Gliding Club Ltd
	G-BAUH	Jodel D.112	G. A. & D. Shepherd
	G-BAVB	Cessna F.172M	D. G. Smith
	G-BAVH	DHC.1 Chipmunk 22	Portsmouth Naval Gliding Club
	G-BAVL	PA-23 Aztec 250E	S. P. & A. V. Chillott
	G-BAVO	Boeing Stearman N2S (26)	R. C. McCarthy
	G-BAVR	AA-5 Traveler	A. J. McNeal
	G-BAWG	PA-28R Cherokee Arrow 200-II	Solent Air Ltd
	G-BAWK	PA-28 Cherokee 140	J. Stanley
	G-BAXD	BN-2A Mk.III-2 Trislander	Islander Aircraft Ltd (G-XTOR)
	G-BAXE	Hughes 269A	Reethorpe Engineering Ltd
	G-BAXK	Thunder Ax7-77 balloon ★	A. R. Snook
	G-BAXS	Bell 47G-5	C. R. Johnson
	G-BAXU	Cessna F.150L	M. W. Sheppardson
	G-BAXV	Cessna F.150L	CBM Associates Consulting Ltd
	G-BAXY	Cessna F.172M	Eaglesoar Ltd
	G-BAXZ	PA-28 Cherokee 140	G-BAXZ (87) Syndicate
	G-BAYL	SNCAN Nord 1101 Norecrin ★	(stored)/Chirk
	G-BAYO	Cessna 150L	J. A. & D. T. A. Rees
	G-BAYP	Cessna 150L	Yankee Papa Flying Group
	G-BAYR	Robin HR.100/210	P. D. Harries
	G-BAZC	Robin DR.400/160	S. G. Jones
	G-BAZM	Jodel D.11	A. F. Simpson
	G-BAZS	Cessna F.150L	L. W. Scattergood
	G-BAZT	Cessna F.172M	Teos BV
	G-BBAW	Robin HR.100/210	F. A. Purvis
	G-BBAX	Robin DR.400/140	G. J. Bissex & P. H. Garbutt
	G-BBAY	Robin DR.400/140	J. C. Stubbs
	G-BBBB	Taylor JT.1 Monoplane	M. C. Arnold
	G-BBBC	Cessna F.150L	S. Collins & C. A. Widdowson
	G-BBBI	AA-5 Traveler	Go Baby Aviation Group
	G-BBBN	PA-28 Cherokee 180	Estuary Aviation Ltd
	G-BBBW	FRED Srs 2	M. Palfreman
	G-BBBY	PA-28 Cherokee 140	N. G. Ogbourne

Reg.	Type	Owner or Operator	Notes
G-BBCH	Robin DR.400/2+2	The Cotswold Aero Club Ltd	
G-BBCI	Cessna 150H	A. M. & F. Alam	
G-BBCN	Robin HR.100/210	J. C. King	
G-BBCS	Robin DR.400/140	C. R. Brown	
G-BBCY	Luton LA-4A Minor	A. W. McBlain	
G-BBCZ	AA-5 Traveler	Mercantile Developments Ltd	
G-BBDC	PA-28-140 Cherokee	E. Ford	
G-BBDE	PA-28R Cherokee Arrow 200-II	R. L. Coleman, P. Knott & Istec Services Ltd	
G-BBDG	BAC-Aérospatiale Concorde 100 ★	Brooklands Museum	
G-BBDH	Cessna F.172M	J. D. Woodward	
G-BBDL	AA-5 Traveler	R. Nightingale	
G-BBDM	AA-5 Traveler	Jackeroo Aviation Group	
G-BBDO	PA-23 Turbo Aztec 250E	J. W. Anstee	
G-BBDP	Robin DR.400/160	Robin Lance Aviation Associates Ltd	
G-BBDT	Cessna 150H	Delta Tango Group	
G-BBDV	SIPA S.903	A. M. Partridge	
G-BBEA	Luton LA-4 Minor	D. S. Evans	
G-BBEB	PA-28R Cherokee Arrow 200-II	March Flying Group	
G-BBEC	PA-28 Cherokee 180	P. & M. Corrigan	
G-BBEN	Bellanca 7GCBC Citabria	C. A. G. Schofield	
G-BBFD	PA-28R Cherokee Arrow 200-II	C. H. Rose & M. J. Green	
G-BBFL	Gardan GY-201 Minicab	R. Smith	
G-BBFV	PA-32 Cherokee Six 260	Aviation Air Care Ltd	
G-BBGC	MS.893E Rallye 180GT	P. M. Nolan	
G-BBGI	Fuji FA.200-160	A and P West	
G-BBHF	PA-23 Aztec 250E	G. J. Williams	
G-BBHJ	Piper J-3C-65 Cub	Wellcross Flying Group	
G-BBHK	Noorduyn AT-16 Harvard IIB (FH153)	M. Kubrak	
G-BBHY	PA-28 Cherokee 180	Air Operations Ltd	
G-BBIF	PA-23 Aztec 250E	Marshall of Cambridge Aerospace Ltd	
G-BBIH	Enstrom F-28A-UK	Friebe France Aeronautique SARL	
G-BBII	Fiat G-46-3B (4-97/MM52801)	C. Coltri	
G-BBIL	PA-28 Cherokee 140	Saxondale Group	
G-BBIO	Robin HR.100/210	R. P. Caley	
G-BBIX	PA-28 Cherokee 140	Sterling Aviation Ltd	
G-BBJI	Isaacs Spitfire (RN218)	S. Vince	
G-BBJU	Robin DR.400/140	J. C. Lister	
G-BBJV	Cessna F.177RG	P. R. Powell	
G-BBJX	Cessna F.150L	L. W. Scattergood	
G-BBJY	Cessna F.172M	D. G. Wright	
G-BBJZ	Cessna F.172M	Group North Ltd	
G-BBKA	Cessna F.150L	G. Fox	
G-BBKB	Cessna F.150L	Justgold Ltd	
G-BBKG	Cessna FR.172J	R. Wright	
G-BBKI	Cessna F.172M	C. W. & S. A. Burman	
G-BBKL	CP.301A Emeraude	Piel G-BBKL	
G-BBKX	PA-28 Cherokee 180	DRA Flying Club Ltd	
G-BBKY	Cessna F.150L	F. W. Astbury	
G-BBKZ	Cessna 172M	KZ Flying Group	
G-BBLH	Piper J-3C-65 Cub (31145:G-26)	Shipping & Airlines Ltd	
G-BBLS	AA-5 Traveler	A. Grant	
G-BBLU	PA-34-200 Seneca II	R. H. R. Rue	
G-BBMB	Robin DR.400/180	Regent Flying Group	
G-BBMH	EAA. Sports Biplane Model P.1	G-BBMH Flying Group	
G-BBMJ	PA-23 Aztec 250E	Nationwide Caravan Rental Services Ltd	
G-BBMN	DHC.1 Chipmunk 22	R. Steiner	
G-BBMO	DHC.1 Chipmunk 22 (WK514)	Mike Oscar Group	
G-BBMR	DHC.1 Chipmunk 22 (WB763:14)	P. J. Wood	
G-BBMT	DHC.1 Chipmunk 22	MT Group	
G-BBMV	DHC.1 Chipmunk 22 (WG348)	Boultbee Vintage Ltd	
G-BBMW	DHC.1 Chipmunk 22 (WK628)	G. Fielder & A. Wilson	
G-BBMZ	DHC.1 Chipmunk 22	G-BBMZ Chipmunk Syndicate	
G-BBNA	DHC.1 Chipmunk 22 (Lycoming)	Coventry Gliding Club Ltd	
G-BBNC	DHC.1 Chipmunk T.10 (WP790) ★	De Havilland Heritage Museum/London Colney	
G-BBND	DHC.1 Chipmunk 22 (WD286)	Bernoulli Syndicate	
G-BBNH	PA-34-200 Seneca II	Airtime Aviation Holdings Ltd	
G-BBNI	PA-34-200 Seneca II	D. H. G. Penney	
G-BBNJ	Cessna F.150L	G-BBNJ Group	
G-BBNT	PA-31-350 Navajo Chieftain	Atlantic Bridge Aviation Ltd	
G-BBNZ	Cessna F.172M	J. H. Sandham Aviation	
G-BBOA	Cessna F.172M	J. D & A. M. Black	

Notes	Reg.	Type	Owner or Operator
	G-BBOH	Pitts S-1S Special	Venom Jet Promotions Ltd
	G-BBOL	PA-18 Super Cub 150	N. Moore
	G-BBOO	Thunder Ax6-56 balloon	K. Meehan Tigerjack
	G-BBOR	Bell 206B JetRanger 2	M. J. Easey
	G-BBPP	PA-28 Cherokee 180	Big Red Kite Ltd (G-WACP)
	G-BBPS	Jodel D.117	A. Appleby
	G-BBRA	PA-23 Aztec 250D	Aideen Ltd
	G-BBRB	DH.82A Tiger Moth (DF198)	R. Barham
	G-BBRC	Fuji FA.200-180	BBRC Ltd
	G-BBRI	Bell 47G-5A	Alan Mann Aviation Group Ltd
	G-BBRN	Procter Kittiwake 1 (XW784/VL)	H. M. Price
	G-BBRZ	AA-5 Traveler	B. McIntyre
	G-BBSA	AA-5 Traveler	Usworth 84 Flying Associates Ltd
	G-BBSS	DHC.1A Chipmunk 22	Coventry Gliding Club Ltd
	G-BBSW	Pietenpol Air Camper	J. K. S. Wills
	G-BBTB	Cessna FRA.150L	Solent School of Flying
	G-BBTG	Cessna F.172M	Jetstream Aero
	G-BBTH	Cessna F.172M	Tayside Aviation Ltd
	G-BBTJ	PA-23 Aztec 250E	J. A. & R. H. Cooper
	G-BBTK	Cessna FRA.150L	Cleveland Flying School Ltd
	G-BBTY	Beech C23 Sundowner	G-BBTY Group
	G-BBUJ	Cessna 421B	Aero VIP Companhia de Transportes & Servicios Aereos SA/Portugal
	G-BBUT	Western O-65 balloon	R. G. Turnbull
	G-BBUU	Piper J-3C-65 Cub	C. Stokes
	G-BBVF	SA Twin Pioneer Srs 3 ★	Museum of Flight/East Fortune
	G-BBVO	Isaacs Fury II (S1579)	W. Hinchcliffe
	G-BBXB	Cessna FRA.150L	D. C. Somerville
	G-BBXW	PA-28-151 Cherokee Warrior	Bristol Aero Club
	G-BBXY	Bellanca 7GCBC Citabria	R. R. L. Windus
	G-BBXZ	Evans VP-1	R. W. Burrows
	G-BBYB	PA-18 Super Cub 95	A. L. Walker
	G-BBYH	Cessna 182P	Ramco (UK) Ltd
	G-BBYM	HP.137 Jetstream 200 ★	Aerospace Museum/Cosford (G-AYWR)
	G-BBYP	PA-28 Cherokee 140	P. J. Terry
	G-BBYS	Cessna 182P	G-BBYS Group
	G-BBYU	Cameron O-56 balloon	British Balloon Museum
	G-BBZF	PA-28-140 Cherokee	D. Franzan
	G-BBZH	PA-28R Cherokee Arrow 200-II	G. Higgins, C. Harte and I. O'Brien
	G-BBZN	Fuji FA.200-180	D. Kynaston & ptnrs
	G-BBZV	PA-28R Cherokee Arrow 200-II	P. B. Mellor
	G-BCAH	DHC.1 Chipmunk 22 (WG316)	Century Aviation Ltd
	G-BCAP	Cameron O-56 balloon ★	Balloon Preservation Group/Lancing
	G-BCAR	Thunder Ax7-77 balloon ★	British Balloon Museum/Newbury
	G-BCAZ	PA-12 Super Cruiser	A. D. Williams
	G-BCBG	PA-23 Aztec 250E	M. J. L. Batt
	G-BCBH	Fairchild 24R-46A Argus III	Dreamticket Promotions Ltd
	G-BCBJ	PA-25 Pawnee 235	Deeside Gliding Club (Aberdeenshire) Ltd
	G-BCBL	Fairchild 24R-46A Argus III (HB751)	F. J. Cox
	G-BCBR	AJEP/Wittman W.8 Tailwind	D. P. Jones
	G-BCBX	Cessna F.150L	P. Lodge & J. G. McVey
	G-BCCC	Cessna F.150L	D. J. Parkinson
	G-BCCE	PA-23 Aztec 250E	Golf Charlie Echo Ltd
	G-BCCF	PA-28 Cherokee 180	Charlie Foxtrot Aviation
	G-BCCK	AA-5 Traveler	Prospect Air Ltd
	G-BCCR	CP.301A Emeraude (modified)	I. Taberer
	G-BCCX	DHC.1 Chipmunk 22 (Lycoming)	Charlie X-Ray Syndicate Ltd
	G-BCCY	Robin HR.200/100	M. E. Hicks
	G-BCDK	Partenavia P.68B	Mach 014 SAS Di Elstner Franziska Maria Helena & Co/Italy
	G-BCDL	Cameron O-42 balloon	D. P. & Mrs B. O. Turner Chums
	G-BCDN	F.27 Friendship Mk 200 ★	Instructional airframe/Norwich
	G-BCDY	Cessna FRA.150L	R. L. Nunn & T. R. Edwards
	G-BCEE	AA-5 Traveler	P. J. Marchant
	G-BCEF	AA-5 Traveler	G-BCEF Group
	G-BCEN	BN-2A-26 Islander	Reconnaissance Ventures Ltd
	G-BCEP	AA-5 Traveler	Sandown Aircraft Group G-BCEP
	G-BCER	Gardan GY-201 Minicab	D. Beaumont
	G-BCEU	Cameron O-42 balloon	P. Glydon
	G-BCEY	DHC.1 Chipmunk 22 (WG465)	Gopher Flying Group

Reg.	Type	Owner or Operator	Notes
G-BCFO	PA-18-150 Super Cub	D. J. Ashley	
G-BCFR	Cessna FRA.150L	Foxtrot Romeo Group	
G-BCFW	SAAB 91D Safir	D. R. Williams	
G-BCFY	Luton LA-4A Minor	M. P. Wiseman	
G-BCGB	Bensen B.8	A. Melody	
G-BCGC	DHC.1 Chipmunk 22 (WP903)	Henlow Chipmunk Group	
G-BCGH	SNCAN NC.854S	P. L. Lovegrove	
G-BCGI	PA-28 Cherokee 140	D. H. G. Penny	
G-BCGJ	PA-28 Cherokee 140	Demero Ltd & Transcourt Ltd	
G-BCGM	Jodel D.120	S. M. Kenyon-Roberts	
G-BCGN	PA-28 Cherokee 140	C. F. Hessey	
G-BCGS	PA-28R Cherokee Arrow 200	Arrow Aviation Group	
G-BCGW	Jodel D.11	G. H. Chittenden	
G-BCHL	DHC.1 Chipmunk 22A (WP788)	Shropshire Soaring Ltd	
G-BCHP	CP.1310-C3 Super Emeraude	G. Hughes & A. G. Just (G-JOSI)	
G-BCHT	Schleicher ASK.16	Dunstable K16 Group	
G-BCID	PA-34-200 Seneca II	Shenley Farms (Aviation) Ltd	
G-BCIH	DHC.1 Chipmunk 22 (WD363)	P. J. Richie	
G-BCIJ	AA-5 Traveler	S. D. Pryke	
G-BCIR	PA-28-151 Warrior	R. W. Harris	
G-BCJM	PA-28 Cherokee 140	Lomac Aviators Ltd	
G-BCJN	PA-28 Cherokee 140	Bristol and Wessex Aeroplane Club Ltd	
G-BCJO	PA-28R Cherokee Arrow 200	R. Ross	
G-BCJP	PA-28 Cherokee 140	J. Wilson	
G-BCKN	DHC.1A Chipmunk 22 (Lycoming)	The Royal Air Force Gliding and Soaring Association	
G-BCKS	Fuji FA.200-180AO	G. J. Ward	
G-BCKT	Fuji FA.200-180	A. G. Dobson	
G-BCKU	Cessna FRA.150L	Forge Consulting Ltd	
G-BCKV	Cessna FRA.150L	M. Bonsall	
G-BCLI	AA-5 Traveler	J. L. Hooker & S. Smith	
G-BCLL	PA-28 Cherokee 180	S. C. Hardman	
G-BCLS	Cessna 170B	M. J. Whiteman-Haywood	
G-BCLT	MS.894A Rallye Minerva 220	K. M. Bowen	
G-BCLU	Jodel D.117	N. E. Binner & J. Pawelec	
G-BCLW	AA-1B Trainer	South Yorkshire Aircraft Museum	
G-BCMD	PA-18 Super Cub 95	P. Stephenson	
G-BCMJ	Squarecraft Cavalier SA.102-5	N. F. Andrews	
G-BCMT	Isaacs Fury II	R.W. Burrows	
G-BCNC	Gardan GY-201 Minicab	J. R. Wraight	
G-BCNP	Cameron O-77 balloon	P. Spellward	
G-BCNX	Piper J-3C-65 Cub (540)	K. J. Lord	
G-BCNZ	Fuji FA.200-160	Y. A. Soojeri	
G-BCOB	Piper J-3C-65 Cub (329405:A-23)	C. Marklew-Brown	
G-BCOI	DHC.1 Chipmunk 22 (WP870:12)	M. J. Diggins	
G-BCOM	Piper J-3C-65 Cub	Dougal Flying Group	
G-BCOO	DHC.1 Chipmunk 22	Double Oscar Chipmunk Group	
G-BCOR	SOCATA Rallye 100ST	T. J. Horsley	
G-BCOU	DHC.1 Chipmunk 22 (WK522)	Loweth Flying Group	
G-BCOY	DHC.1 Chipmunk 22	Coventry Gliding Club Ltd	
G-BCPD	Gardan GY-201 Minicab	P. R. Cozens	
G-BCPG	PA-28R Cherokee Arrow 200-II	A. G. Antoniades	
G-BCPH	Piper J-3C-65 Cub (329934:B-72)	G. Earl	
G-BCPJ	Piper J-3C-65 Cub	J. W. Widdows	
G-BCPK	Cessna F.172M	D. C. C. Handley	
G-BCPN	AA-5 Traveler	G-BCPN Group	
G-BCPU	DHC.1 Chipmunk 22	P. Green	
G-BCRB	Cessna F.172M	Wingstask 1995Ltd	
G-BCRE	Cameron O-77 balloon ★	Balloon Preservation Group/Lancing	
G-BCRL	PA-28-151 Warrior	BCRL Ltd	
G-BCRR	AA-5B Tiger	S. Waite	
G-BCRX	DHC.1 Chipmunk 22 (WD292)	P. J. Tuplin & M. I. Robinson	
G-BCSA	DHC.1 Chipmunk 22 (Lycoming)	The Royal Air Force Gliding and Soaring Association	
G-BCSL	DHC.1 Chipmunk 22	Chipmunk Flyers Ltd	
G-BCTF	PA-28-151 Warrior	Durham Tees Flight Training Ltd	
G-BCTI	Schleicher ASK 16	Tango India Syndicate	
G-BCTK	Cessna FR.172J	M. G. E. Morton	
G-BCTT	Evans VP-1	E. R. G. Ludlow	
G-BCUB	Piper J-3C-65 Cub	A. L. Brown	
G-BCUF	Cessna F.172M	Howell Plant Hire & Construction	

BRITISH CIVIL REGISTRATIONS

Notes	Reg.	Type	Owner or Operator
	G-BCUH	Cessna F.150M	G-BCUH Group
	G-BCUJ	Cessna F.150M	Western Airways Ltd
	G-BCUL	SOCATA Rallye 100ST	C. A. Ussher & Fountain Estates Ltd
	G-BCUO	SA Bulldog Srs 120/122	Cranfield University
	G-BCUS	SA Bulldog Srs 120/122	Falcon Group
	G-BCUV	SA Bulldog Srs 120/122 (XX704)	Flew LLP
	G-BCUW	Cessna F.177RG	S. J. Westley
	G-BCUY	Cessna FRA.150M	J. C. Carpenter
	G-BCVB	PA-17 Vagabond	A. T. Nowak
	G-BCVC	SOCATA Rallye 100ST	W. Haddow
	G-BCVE	Evans VP-2	D. Masterson & D. B. Winstanley
	G-BCVF	Practavia Pilot Sprite	D. G. Hammersley
	G-BCVG	Cessna FRA.150L	G-BCVG Flying Group
	G-BCVH	Cessna FRA.150L	C. Quist
	G-BCVJ	Cessna F.172M	Rothland Ltd
	G-BCVY	PA-34-200T Seneca II	Oxford Aviation Academy (Oxford) Ltd
	G-BCWB	Cessna 182P	M. F. Oliver & A. J. Mew
	G-BCWH	Practavia Pilot Sprite	P. F. D. Waltham
	G-BCWK	Alpavia Fournier RF-3	T. J. Hartwell
	G-BCXB	SOCATA Rallye 100ST	The Rallye Group
	G-BCXE	Robin DR.400/2+2	Weald Air Services Ltd
	G-BCXJ	Piper L-4J Cub (480752:E-39)	W. Readman
	G-BCXN	DHC.1 Chipmunk 22 (WP800)	G. M. Turner
	G-BCYH	DAW Privateer Mk. 3	G-BCYH Group
	G-BCYK	Avro CF.100 Mk 4 Canuck (18393) ★	Imperial War Museum/Duxford
	G-BCYM	DHC.1 Chipmunk 22 (WK577)	G-BCYM Group
	G-BCYR	Cessna F.172M	G. Fox
	G-BCZM	Cessna F.172M	Cornwall Flying Club Ltd
	G-BDAD	Taylor JT.1 Monoplane	C. S. Whitwell
	G-BDAG	Taylor JT.1 Monoplane	N. R. Osborne
	G-BDAH	Evans VP-1	G. H. J. Geurts
	G-BDAI	Cessna FRA.150M	B. K. & W. G. Ranger
	G-BDAK	Rockwell Commander 112	M. C. Wilson
	G-BDAO	SIPA S.91	S. B. Churchill
	G-BDAP	AJEP Tailwind	D. G. Kelly
	G-BDAR	Evans VP-1	R. F. Powell
	G-BDAY	Thunder Ax5-42S1 balloon	T. M. Donnelly Meconium
	G-BDBF	FRED Srs 2	G. E. & R. E. Collins
	G-BDBH	Bellanca 7GCBC Citabria	C. J. Gray
	G-BDBI	Cameron O-77 balloon	C. Jones
	G-BDBS	Short SD3-30 ★	Ulster Aviation Society
	G-BDBU	Cessna F.150M	S. Collins
	G-BDBV	Jodel D.11A	Seething Jodel Group
	G-BDBZ	Westland WS-55 Whirlwind (XJ398) ★	Aeroventure/Doncaster
	G-BDCD	Piper J-3C-85 Cub (480133:B-44)	Cubby Cub Group
	G-BDCI	CP.301A Emeraude	D. L. Sentance
	G-BDDF	Jodel D.120	J. V. Thompson
	G-BDDG	Jodel D.112	J. Pool & D. G. Palmer
	G-BDDS	PA-25 Pawnee 235	Vale of Neath Gliding Club
	G-BDDX	Whittaker MW2B Excalibur ★	Cornwall Aero Park/Helston
	G-BDDZ	CP.301A Emeraude	E. C. Mort
	G-BDEC	SOCATA Rallye 100ST	J. Fingleton
	G-BDEH	Jodel D.120A	N. J. Cronin
	G-BDEI	Jodel D.9 Bébé	The Noddy Group
	G-BDEU	DHC.1 Chipmunk 22 (WP808)	Skylark Aviation Ltd
	G-BDEX	Cessna FRA.150M	A. P. F. Tucker
	G-BDEY	Piper J-3C-65 Cub	A. V. Williams
	G-BDEZ	Piper J-3C-65 Cub	F. Stoop
	G-BDFB	Currie Wot	J. Jennings
	G-BDFH	Auster AOP.9 (XR240)	R. B. Webber
	G-BDFR	Fuji FA.200-160	M. S. Bird
	G-BDFU	Dragonfly MPA Mk 1 ★	Museum of Flight/East Fortune
	G-BDFY	AA-5 Traveler	Grumman Group
	G-BDGB	Gardan GY-20 Minicab	T. W. Slater
	G-BDGH	Thunder Ax7-77 balloon	R. J. Mitchener & P. F. Smart
	G-BDGM	PA-28-151 Cherokee Warrior	J. Tonge
	G-BDHK	Piper J-3C-65 Cub (329417)	Knight Flying Group
	G-BDIE	Rockwell Commander 112	J. McAleer & R. J. Adams
	G-BDIG	Cessna 182P	A. J. Macdonald
	G-BDIH	Jodel D.117	N. D. H. Stokes

Reg.	Type	Owner or Operator	Notes
G-BDIX	DH.106 Comet 4C ★	Museum of Flight/East Fortune	
G-BDJD	Jodel D.112	J. E. Preston	
G-BDJG	Luton LA-4A Minor	Very Slow Flying Club	
G-BDJP	Piper J-3C-90 Cub	S. T. Gilbert	
G-BDJR	SNCAN Nord NC.858	R. F. M. Marson	
G-BDKC	Cessna A185F	Lude & Invergarry Farm Partnership	
G-BDKD	Enstrom F-28A	P. J. Price	
G-BDKH	CP.301A Emeraude	T. A. S. Rayner	
G-BDKJ	K & S SA.102.5 Cavalier	D. A. Garner	
G-BDKM	SIPA 903	S. W. Markham	
G-BDKW	Rockwell Commander 112A	N. J. Taaffe	
G-BDLO	AA-5A Cheetah	S. & J. Dolan	
G-BDLT	Rockwell Commander 112	M. R. Masters	
G-BDLY	K & S SA.102.5 Cavalier	P. R. Stevens	
G-BDMS	Piper J-3C-65 Cub (FR886)	A. T. H. Martin	
G-BDMW	Jodel DR.100A	Mike Whisky Group	
G-BDNC	Taylor JT.1 Monoplane	D. W. Mathie	
G-BDNG	Taylor JT.1 Monoplane	R. B. McComish	
G-BDNT	Jodel D.92 Bébé	R. J. Stobo	
G-BDNU	Cessna F.172M	J. & K. G. McVicar	
G-BDNW	AA-1B Trainer	N. A. Baxter	
G-BDNX	AA-1B Trainer	A. & N. Clark	
G-BDOD	Cessna F.150M	OD Group	
G-BDOG	SA Bulldog Srs 200	D. C. Bonsall	
G-BDOL	Piper J-3C-65 Cub	L. R. Balthazor	
G-BDPA	PA-28-151 Warrior	RAF Leuchars Flying Group	
G-BDPJ	PA-25 Pawnee 235B	Swift Aerobatic Display Team	
G-BDRD	Cessna FRA.150M	Aircraft Engineers Ltd	
G-BDRG	Taylor JT.2 Titch	D. R. Gray	
G-BDRJ	DHC.1 Chipmunk 22 (WP857)	WP857 Trust	
G-BDRK	Cameron O-65 balloon	R. J. Mitchener & P. F. Smart	
G-BDSB	PA-28-181 Archer II	Testair Ltd	
G-BDSF	Cameron O-56 balloon	J. H. Greensides	
G-BDSH	PA-28 Cherokee 140 (modified)	The Wright Brothers Flying Group	
G-BDSK	Cameron O-65 balloon	Southern Balloon Group Carousel II	
G-BDSM	Slingsby T.31B Cadet III	F. C. J. Wevers/Netherlands	
G-BDTB	Evans VP-1	P. W. Boyes	
G-BDTL	Evans VP-1 series 2	P. S. Gilmour	
G-BDTO	BN-2A Mk III-2 Trislander	Aurigny Air Services Ltd (G-RBSI/G-OTSB)	
G-BDTU	Omega III gas balloon	R. G. Turnbull	
G-BDTV	Mooney M.20F	S. Redfearn	
G-BDTX	Cessna F.150M	F. W. Ellis	
G-BDUI	Cameron V-56 balloon	D. J. W. Johnson	
G-BDUL	Evans VP-1 Srs.2	J. C. Lindsay	
G-BDUM	Cessna F.150M	P. B. Millington	
G-BDUN	PA-34-200T Seneca II	R. Paris	
G-BDUO	Cessna F.150M	D. J. Wood	
G-BDUY	Robin DR.400/140B	J. G. Anderson	
G-BDUZ	Cameron V-56 balloon	Zebedee Balloon Service	
G-BDVA	PA-17 Vagabond	I. M. Callier	
G-BDVB	PA-15 (PA-17) Vagabond	B. P. Gardner	
G-BDVC	PA-17 Vagabond	A. R. Caveen	
G-BDWE	Flaglor Scooter	P. King	
G-BDWH	SOCATA Rallye 150ST	M. A. Jones	
G-BDWJ	SE-5A (replica) (F8010:Z)	D. W. Linney	
G-BDWM	Mustang scale replica (FB226)	D. C. Bonsall	
G-BDWO	Howes Ax6 balloon	R. B. & C. Howes	
G-BDWP	PA-32R-300 Cherokee Lance	A. Belcastro & I. Bardelli/Italy	
G-BDWX	Jodel D.120A	R. P. Rochester	
G-BDWY	PA-28-140 Cherokee E	S. M. Pearce	
G-BDXX	SNCAN NC.858S	K. M. Davis	
G-BDYG	P.56 Provost T.1 (WV493) ★	Museum of Flight/East Fortune	
G-BDZA	Scheibe SF.25E Super Falke	Hereward Flying Group	
G-BDZC	Cessna F.150M	A. M. Lynn	
G-BDZD	Cessna F.172M	R. J. A. Durie	
G-BDZG	Slingsby T.59H Kestrel	R. E. Gretton	
G-BEAB	Jodel DR.1051	R. C. Hibberd	
G-BEAC	PA-28 Cherokee 140	R. Murray & A. Bagley-Murray	
G-BEAD	WG.13 Lynx ★	Instructional airframe/Middle Wallop	

Notes	Reg.	Type	Owner or Operator
	G-BEAG	PA-34-200T Seneca II	Oxford Aviation Academy (Oxford) Ltd
	G-BEAH	Auster J/2 Arrow	Bedwell Hey Flying Group
	G-BEBC	Westland WS-55 Whirlwind 3 (XP355) ★	Norwich Aviation Museum
	G-BEBN	Cessna 177B	P. A. Gray
	G-BEBR	GY-201 Minicab	A. R. Hawes
	G-BEBS	Andreasson BA-4B	N. J. W. Reid
	G-BEBU	Rockwell Commander 112A	I. Hunt
	G-BEBZ	PA-28-151 Warrior	Airways Flight Training (Exeter) Ltd
	G-BECA	SOCATA Rallye 100ST	N. G. Ogborne
	G-BECB	SOCATA Rallye 100ST	D. H. Tonkin
	G-BECK	Cameron V-56 balloon	N. H. & A. M. Ponsford
	G-BECN	Piper J-3C-65 Cub (480480:E-44)	CN Cub Group
	G-BECT	CASA 1.131E Jungmann 2000 (A-57)	Alpha 57 Group
	G-BECW	CASA 1.131E Jungmann 2000 (A-10)	C. M. Rampton
	G-BECZ	CAARP CAP-10B	C. M. Thompson
	G-BEDA	CASA 1-131E Jungmann Srs.2000	L. Atkin
	G-BEDB	Nord 1203 Norecrin ★	B. F. G. Lister (stored)/Chirk
	G-BEDD	Jodel D.117A	A. Boast
	G-BEDF	Boeing B-17G-105-VE (124485:DF-A)	B-17 Preservation Ltd
	G-BEDG	Rockwell Commander 112	G-BEDG Group
	G-BEDJ	Piper J-3C-65 Cub (44-80594)	R. Earl
	G-BEDV	V.668 Varsity T.1 (WJ945) ★	Duxford Aviation Society
	G-BEEE	Thunder Ax6-56A balloon ★	British Balloon Museum/Newbury
	G-BEEH	Cameron V-56 balloon	Sade Balloons Ltd
	G-BEEI	Cameron N-77 balloon	A. P. Griffiths
	G-BEER	Isaacs Fury II (K2075)	R. S. C. Andrews
	G-BEFA	PA-28-151 Warrior	K. T. Langstone
	G-BEFF	PA-28 Cherokee 140F	E. Merkado
	G-BEGG	Scheibe SF.25E Super Falke	G-BEGG Motorfalke
	G-BEHH	PA-32R Cherokee Lance 300	K. Swallow
	G-BEHU	PA-34-200T Seneca II	Pirin Aeronautical Ltd
	G-BEHV	Cessna F.172N	Edinburgh Air Centre Ltd
	G-BEIF	Cameron O-65 balloon	C. Vening
	G-BEIG	Cessna F.150M	R. D. Forster & M. S. B. Thorp
	G-BEII	PA-25 Pawnee 235D	Burn Gliding Club Ltd
	G-BEIP	PA-28-181 Archer II	S. Pope
	G-BEIS	Evans VP-1	D. L. Haines
	G-BEJK	Cameron S-31 balloon	Rango Balloon and Kite Company
	G-BEJV	PA-34-200T Seneca II	Oxford Aviation Academy (Oxford) Ltd
	G-BEKL	Bede BD-4E-150	F. E.Tofield
	G-BEKM	Evans VP-1	G. J. McDill
	G-BEKN	Cessna FRA.150M	T. J. Lynn
	G-BEKO	Cessna F.182Q	G. J. & F. J. Leese
	G-BELT	Cessna F.150J	A. Kumar (G-AWUV)
	G-BEMB	Cessna F.172M	Stocklaunch Ltd
	G-BEMM	Slingsby T.31B Motor Cadet III	E. and P. McEvoy
	G-BEMW	PA-28-181 Archer II	Touch & Go Ltd
	G-BEMY	Cessna FRA.150M	J. R. Power
	G-BEND	Cameron V-56 balloon	Dante Balloon Group
	G-BENJ	Rockwell Commander 112B	BENJ Flying Group
	G-BEOE	Cessna FRA.150M	W. J. Henderson
	G-BEOH	PA-28R-201T Turbo Arrow III	Gloucestershire Flying Club
	G-BEOI	PA-18 Super Cub 150	Southdown Gliding Club Ltd
	G-BEOK	Cessna F.150M	D. M. Cloke
	G-BEOL	Short SC.7 Skyvan 3 variant 100	Invicta Aviation Ltd
	G-BEOX	Lockheed 414 Hudson IV (A16-199) ★	RAF Museum/Hendon
	G-BEOY	Cessna FRA.150L	J. N. Ponsford
	G-BEOZ	A.W.650 Argosy 101 ★	Aeropark/East Midlands
	G-BEPF	SNCAN Stampe SV.4A	C. C. Rollings & F. J. Hodson
	G-BEPV	Fokker S.11-1 Instructor (174)	S. W. & M. Isbister & C. Tyers
	G-BEPY	Rockwell Commander 112B	T. L. Rippon
	G-BERA	SOCATA Rallye 150ST	A. C. Stamp
	G-BERC	SOCATA Rallye 150ST	Severn Valley Aero Group
	G-BERI	Rockwell Commander 114	K. B. Harper
	G-BERN	Saffrey S-330 balloon	B. Martin
	G-BERT	Cameron V-56 balloon	Southern Balloon Group Bert
	G-BERY	AA-1B Trainer	I. R. Matterface
	G-BETD	Robin HR.200/100	C. L. Wilsher
	G-BETE	Rollason B.2A Beta	T. M. Jones

Reg.	Type	Owner or Operator	Notes
G-BETF	Cameron 'Champion' SS balloon ★	British Balloon Museum/Newbury	
G-BETL	PA-25 Pawnee 235D	Cambridge University Gliding Trust Ltd	
G-BETM	PA-25 Pawnee 235D	Yorkshire Gliding Club (Pty) Ltd	
G-BEUA	PA-18 Super Cub 150	London Gliding Club (Pty) Ltd	
G-BEUD	Robin HR.100/285R	E. A. & L. M. C. Payton	
G-BEUI	Piper J-3C-65 Cub	M. C. Jordan	
G-BEUP	Robin DR.400/180	Samuels LLP	
G-BEUU	PA-18 Super Cub 95	F. Sharples	
G-BEUX	Cessna F.172N	Multiflight Ltd	
G-BEUY	Cameron N-31 balloon	J. J. Daly	
G-BEVB	SOCATA Rallye 150ST	M. Smullen	
G-BEVC	SOCATA Rallye 150ST	Wolds Flyers Syndicate	
G-BEVG	PA-34-200T-2 Seneca	Direct Aviation Management Ltd	
G-BEVO	Sportavia-Pützer RF-5	M. Hill	
G-BEVP	Evans VP-2	G. Moscrop & R. C. Crowley	
G-BEVS	Taylor JT.1 Monoplane	D. Hunter	
G-BEVT	BN-2A Mk III-2 Trislander	Aurigny Air Services Ltd	
G-BEVW	SOCATA Rallye 150ST	S. W. Brown	
G-BEWN	DH.82A Tiger Moth	H. D. Labouchere	
G-BEWO	Zlin Z.326 Trener Master	P. A. Colman	
G-BEWR	Cessna F.172N	P. Lodge & J. G. McVey	
G-BEWX	PA-28R-201 Arrow III	Three Greens Arrow Group	
G-BEWY	Bell 206B JetRanger 3	Polo Aviation Ltd (G-CULL)	
G-BEXN	AA-1C Lynx	XN Group	
G-BEXW	PA-28-181 Cherokee	J. O'Keeffe	
G-BEYA	Enstrom 280C	The Aviation Bureau	
G-BEYB	Fairey Flycatcher (replica) (S1287) ★	F.A.A. Museum/Yeovilton	
G-BEYF	HPR.7 Herald 401 ★	Jet Heritage Museum/Bournemouth	
G-BEYL	PA-28 Cherokee 180	Yankee Lima Group	
G-BEYT	PA-28 Cherokee 140	J. N. Plange	
G-BEYV	Cessna T.210M	P. Mason & R. Turnell	
G-BEYW	Taylor JT.1 Monoplane	R. A. Abrahams	
G-BEYZ	Jodel DR.1051/M1	M. L. Balding	
G-BEZC	AA-5 Traveler	C. M. O'Connell	
G-BEZE	Rutan Vari-Eze	S. K. Cockburn	
G-BEZF	AA-5 Traveler	The G-BEZF Flying Group	
G-BEZG	AA-5 Traveler	M. D. R. Harling	
G-BEZH	AA-5 Traveler	Zulu Hotel Group	
G-BEZI	AA-5 Traveler	C. J. & L. Campbell	
G-BEZK	Cessna F.172H	S. Jones	
G-BEZL	PA-31-310 Turbo Navajo C	2 Excel Aviation Ltd	
G-BEZO	Cessna F.172M	Staverton Flying School @ Skypark Ltd	
G-BEZP	PA-32 Cherokee Six 300D	T. P. McCormack & J. K. Zealley	
G-BEZR	Cessna F.172M	J. P. Birnie	
G-BEZV	Cessna F.172M	Insch Flying Group	
G-BEZY	Rutan Vari-Eze	I. J. Pountney	
G-BEZZ	Jodel D.112	G-BEZZ Jodel Group	
G-BFAF	Aeronca 7BCM (7797)	D. C. W. Harper	
G-BFAI	Rockwell Commander 114	P. Ellingford	
G-BFAK	GEMS MS.892A Rallye Commodore 150	J. M. Hedges	
G-BFAP	SIAI-Marchetti S.205-20R	A. O. Broin	
G-BFAS	Evans VP-1	A. I. Sutherland	
G-BFAW	DHC.1 Chipmunk 22	M. L. J. Goff	
G-BFAX	DHC.1 Chipmunk 22 (WG422)	M. F. Humphries	
G-BFBA	Jodel DR.100A	A. F. Vizoso	
G-BFBB	PA-23 Aztec 250E	D. Byrne	
G-BFBE	Robin HR.200/100	A. C. Pearson	
G-BFBM	Saffery S.330 balloon	B. Martin	
G-BFBR	PA-28-161 Warrior II	Phoenix Aviation	
G-BFBY	Piper J-3C-65 Cub	M. Shaw	
G-BFCT	Cessna Tu.206F	D. I. Schellingerhout	
G-BFDC	DHC.1 Chipmunk 22 (WG475)	N. F. O'Neill	
G-BFDE	Sopwith Tabloid (replica) (168) ★	RAF Museum/Hendon	
G-BFDF	SOCATA Rallye 235E	M. A. Wratten	
G-BFDI	PA-28-181 Archer II	Truman Aviation Ltd	
G-BFDK	PA-28-161 Warrior II	S. T. Gilbert	
G-BFDL	Piper J-3C-65 Cub (454537:J-04)	T. Holtbrook & B. A. Nicholson	
G-BFDO	PA-28R-201T Turbo Arrow III	J. Blackburn & J. Driver	
G-BFEB	Jodel 150	Jodel EB Group	
G-BFEF	Agusta-Bell 47G-3B1	I. F. Vaughan	

Notes	Reg.	Type	Owner or Operator
	G-BFEH	Jodel D.117A	M. D. Mold
	G-BFEK	Cessna F.152	Staverton Flying School @ Skypark Ltd
	G-BFEV	PA-25 Pawnee 235	Trent Valley Aerotowing Club Ltd
	G-BFFE	Cessna F.152-II	A. J. Hastings
	G-BFFJ	Sikorsky S-61N Mk II	Newquay Helicopters Ltd
	G-BFFP	PA-18 Super Cub 150 (modified)	East Sussex Gliding Club Ltd
	G-BFFT	Cameron V-56 balloon	R. I. M. Kerr & D. C. Boxall
	G-BFFW	Cessna F.152	Stapleford Flying Club Ltd
	G-BFGD	Cessna F.172N-II	Wannabe Flyers
	G-BFGG	Cessna FRA.150M	J. M. Machin
	G-BFGH	Cessna F.337G	S. Findlay
	G-BFGK	Jodel D.117	B. F. J. Hope
	G-BFGL	Cessna FA.152	E-Pane Ltd
	G-BFGS	MS.893E Rallye 180GT	Chiltern Flyers Ltd
	G-BFGZ	Cessna FRA.150M	C. M. Barnes
	G-BFHH	DH.82A Tiger Moth	P. Harrison & M. J. Gambrell
	G-BFHI	Piper J-3C-65 Cub	N. Glass & A. J. Richardson
	G-BFHP	Champion 7GCAA Citabria	Citabration Group
	G-BFHR	Jodel DR.220/2+2	J. E. Sweetman
	G-BFHU	Cessna F.152-II	M. Bonsall
	G-BFHX	Evans VP-1	D. A. Milstead
	G-BFIB	PA-31 Turbo Navajo	2 Excel Aviation Ltd
	G-BFID	Taylor JT.2 Titch Mk III	M. J. Wood
	G-BFIE	Cessna FRA.150M	J. P. A. Freeman
	G-BFIG	Cessna FR.172K XPII	M. Taylor
	G-BFIN	AA-5A Cheetah	Aircraft Engineers Ltd
	G-BFIP	Wallbro Monoplane 1909 (replica) ★	Norfolk & Suffolk Aviation Museum/Flixton
	G-BFIT	Thunder Ax6-56Z balloon	J. A. G. Tyson
	G-BFIU	Cessna FR.172K XP	R. Marsden
	G-BFIV	Cessna F.177RG	C. Fisher & M. L. Miller
	G-BFIX	Thunder Ax7-77A balloon	R. Owen
	G-BFIY	Cessna F.150M	R. J. Scott
	G-BFJR	Cessna F.337G	Teal Aviation
	G-BFJZ	Robin DR.400/140B	Weald Air Services Ltd
	G-BFKB	Cessna F.172N	Shropshire Flying Group
	G-BFKF	Cessna FA.152	Aerolease Ltd
	G-BFKL	Cameron N-56 balloon	Merrythought Toys Ltd *Merrythought*
	G-BFLU	Cessna F.152	Swiftair Maintenance Ltd
	G-BFLX	AA-5A Cheetah	A. M. Verdon
	G-BFLZ	Beech 95-A55 Baron	R. Tang
	G-BFMF	Cassutt Racer IIIM	T. D. Gardner
	G-BFMG	PA-28-161 Warrior II	J. G. Fricker & N. T. Oakman
	G-BFMH	Cessna 177B	Aerofoil Aviation Ltd
	G-BFMK	Cessna FA.152	The Leicestershire Aero Club Ltd
	G-BFMR	PA-20 Pacer 125	J. Knight
	G-BFMX	Cessna F.172N	M. Knowles
	G-BFNG	Jodel D.112	NG Group
	G-BFNI	PA-28-161 Warrior II	Lion Services
	G-BFNK	PA-28-161 Warrior II	Aviation Rentals
	G-BFNM	Globe GC-1B Swift	M. J. Butler
	G-BFOE	Cessna F.152	Redhill Air Services Ltd
	G-BFOF	Cessna F.152	ACS Engineering Ltd
	G-BFOG	Cessna 150M	C. R. Buckle
	G-BFOJ	AA-1 Yankee	D. D. Pharoah
	G-BFOP	Jodel D.120	R. J. Wesley & R. Lloyd
	G-BFOU	Taylor JT.1 Monoplane	G. Bee
	G-BFOV	Cessna F.172N	D. J. Walker
	G-BFPA	Scheibe SF.25B Falke	M. V. Hearns & P. Wigginton
	G-BFPH	Cessna F.172K	Linc-Air Flying Group
	G-BFPO	Rockwell Commander 112B	Doerr International Ltd
	G-BFPR	PA-25 Pawnee 235D	The Windrushers Gliding Club Ltd
	G-BFPS	PA-25 Pawnee 235D	Kent Gliding Club Ltd
	G-BFPZ	Cessna F.177RG Cardinal	O. C. Baars
	G-BFRI	Sikorsky S-61N	British International
	G-BFRR	Cessna FRA.150M	Romeo Romeo Flying Group
	G-BFRS	Cessna F.172N	Aerocomm Ltd
	G-BFRV	Cessna F.152	Cristal Air Ltd
	G-BFRY	PA-25 Pawnee 260	Yorkshire Gliding Club (Pty) Ltd
	G-BFSA	Cessna F.182Q	Colledge Redfern LLP
	G-BFSC	PA-25 Pawnee 235D	Essex Gliding Club Ltd
	G-BFSD	PA-25 Pawnee 235D	Deeside Gliding Club (Aberdeenshire) Ltd

Reg.	Type	Owner or Operator	Notes
G-BFSR	Cessna F.150J	W. Ali	
G-BFSS	Cessna FR.172G	Albedale Farms Ltd	
G-BFSY	PA-28-181 Archer II	Downland Aviation	
G-BFSZ	PA-28-161 Warrior II	R. J. Whyham (G-KBPI)	
G-BFTC	PA-28R-201T Turbo Arrow III	Top Cat Flying Group	
G-BFTF	AA-5B Tiger	F. C. Burrow Ltd	
G-BFTG	AA-5B Tiger	D. Hepburn & G. R. Montgomery	
G-BFTH	Cessna F.172N	T. W. Oakley	
G-BFTX	Cessna F.172N	Tri Society	
G-BFUB	PA-32RT-300 Lance II	Jolida Holdings Ltd	
G-BFUD	Scheibe SF.25E Super Falke	SF25E Syndicate	
G-BFVG	PA-28-181 Archer II	H. A. Schlosser	
G-BFVH	DH.2 (replica) (5964)	S. W. Turley	
G-BFVS	AA-5B Tiger	G-BFVS Flying Group	
G-BFVU	Cessna 150L	A. N. Mole	
G-BFWB	PA-28-161 Warrior II	Mid-Anglia School of Flying	
G-BFWD	Currie Wot (C3009)	D. Silsbury & B. Proctor	
G-BFXF	Andreasson BA.4B	P. N. Birch	
G-BFXG	D.31 Turbulent	XG Group	
G-BFXK	PA-28 Cherokee 140	G-BFXK Owners Ltd	
G-BFXL	Albatros D.5a replica (D5397/17) ★	F.A.A. Museum/Yeovilton	
G-BFXR	Jodel D.112	R. G. Marshall	
G-BFXS	Rockwell Commander 114	Romeo Whiskey Ltd	
G-BFXW	AA-5B Tiger	J. G. Bellerby	
G-BFXX	AA-5B Tiger	W. R. Gibson	
G-BFYA	MBB Bö.105DB	Alan Mann Aviation Group Ltd	
G-BFYI	Westland-Bell 47G-3B1	K. P. Mayes	
G-BFYK	Cameron V-77 balloon	L. E. Jones	
G-BFYL	Evans VP-2	F. C. Handy	
G-BFYM	PA-28-161 Warrior II	E. T. Hawkins	
G-BFYO	SPAD XIII (replica) (4513:1) ★	American Air Museum/Duxford	
G-BFYW	Slingsby T.65A Vega	S. A. Whitaker	
G-BFZB	Piper J-3C-85 Cub (480723:E5-J)	M. S. Pettit	
G-BFZD	Cessna FR.182RG	R. B. Lewis & Co	
G-BFZH	PA-28R Cherokee Arrow 200	Aircraft Engineers Ltd	
G-BFZM	Rockwell Commander 112TC	J. A. Hart & R. J. Lamplough	
G-BFZO	AA-5A Cheetah	J. W. Cross	
G-BFZU	Cessna FA.152	BJ Aviation Ltd	
G-BFZV	Cessna F.172M	The Army Flying Association	
G-BGAA	Cessna 152 II	PJC Leasing Ltd	
G-BGAB	Cessna F.152 II	TG Aviation Ltd	
G-BGAE	Cessna F.152 II	Aerolease Ltd	
G-BGAF	Cessna FA.152	G-BGAF Group	
G-BGAG	Cessna F.172N	S. J. Green	
G-BGAJ	Cessna F.182Q II	B. Blumberg	
G-BGAX	PA-28 Cherokee 140	G-BGAX Group	
G-BGAZ	Cameron V-77 balloon	C. J. Madigan & D. H. McGibbon	
G-BGBA	Robin R.2100A	Cotswold Aviation Services Ltd	
G-BGBE	Jodel DR.1050	J. A. & B. Mawby	
G-BGBF	Druine D.31 Turbulent	T. A. Stambach	
G-BGBG	PA-28-181 Archer II	Harlow Printing Ltd	
G-BGBI	Cessna F.150L	BI Flying Group	
G-BGBK	PA-38-112 Tomahawk	Truman Aviation Ltd	
G-BGBV	Slingsby T65A Vega	Vega Syndicate BGA2800	
G-BGBW	PA-38-112 Tomahawk	Truman Aviation Ltd	
G-BGCB	Slingsby T.65A Vega	T. E. J. Dutton & V. A. Watt	
G-BGCM	AA-5A Cheetah	G. & S. A. Jones	
G-BGCO	PA-44-180 Seminole	BAE Systems (Operations) Ltd	
G-BGCU	Slingsby T.65A Vega	K. Challinor	
G-BGCY	Taylor JT.1 Monoplane	A. T. Lane	
G-BGEF	Jodel D.112	G. G. Johnson	
G-BGEH	Monnett Sonerai II	E. C. Murgatroyd	
G-BGEI	Baby Great Lakes	M. Howells	
G-BGES	Phoenix Currie Super Wot	N. M. Bloom	
G-BGFC	Evans VP-2	S. W. C. Hollins	
G-BGFF	FRED Srs 2	I Pearson & P. C. Appleton	
G-BGFI	AA-5A Cheetah	D. Chowanietz & A. Necker	
G-BGFJ	Jodel D.9 Bébé	O. G. Jones	
G-BGFT	PA-34-200T Seneca II	Oxford Aviation Academy (Oxford) Ltd	
G-BGFX	Cessna F.152	Redhill Air Services Ltd	

Notes	Reg.	Type	Owner or Operator
	G-BGGA	Bellanca 7GCBC Citabria	L. A. King
	G-BGGB	Bellanca 7GCBC Citabria	D. A. Payne
	G-BGGC	Bellanca 7GCBC Citabria	G-BGGC RPA Memorial Group
	G-BGGD	Bellanca 8GCBC Scout	B. Walker & Co (Dursley) Ltd
	G-BGGE	PA-38-112 Tomahawk	Truman Aviation Ltd
	G-BGGI	PA-38-112 Tomahawk	Truman Aviation Ltd
	G-BGGM	PA-38-112 Tomahawk	E. Dohrn
	G-BGGO	Cessna F.152	East Midlands Flying School Ltd
	G-BGGP	Cessna F.152	East Midlands Flying School Ltd
	G-BGGU	Wallis WA-116/RR	K. H. Wallis
	G-BGGW	Wallis WA-112	K. H. Wallis
	G-BGHF	Westland WG.30 ★	IHM/Weston-super-Mare
	G-BGHI	Cessna F.152	V. R. McCready
	G-BGHJ	Cessna F.172N	Air Plane Ltd
	G-BGHM	Robin R.1180T	P. Price
	G-BGHP	Beech 76 Duchess	Magneta Ltd
	G-BGHS	Cameron N-31 balloon	G. Gray
	G-BGHT	Falconar F-12	C. R. Coates
	G-BGHU	NA T-6G Texan (115042:TA-042)	C. E. Bellhouse
	G-BGHY	Taylor JT.1 Monoplane	G. W. Hancox
	G-BGHZ	FRED Srs 2	A. J. Perry
	G-BGIB	Cessna 152 II	Redhill Air Services Ltd
	G-BGIG	PA-38-112 Tomahawk	Air Claire Ltd
	G-BGIU	Cessna F.172H	A. G. Arthur
	G-BGIY	Cessna F.172N	ACS Aviation Ltd
	G-BGKO	Gardan GY-20 Minicab	K. D. PEARCE
	G-BGKS	PA-28-161 Warrior II	Tayside Aviation Ltd
	G-BGKT	Auster AOP.9 (XN441)	Kilo Tango Group
	G-BGKU	PA-28R-201 Arrow III	Aerolease Ltd
	G-BGKV	PA-28R-201 Arrow III	R. Haverson & A. K. Lake
	G-BGKY	PA-38-112 Tomahawk	APB Leasing Ltd
	G-BGKZ	Auster J/5F Aiglet Trainer	R. B. Webber
	G-BGLA	PA-38-112 Tomahawk	J. T. Mountain
	G-BGLB	Bede BD-5B ★	Science Museum/Wroughton
	G-BGLF	Evans VP-1 Srs 2	B. A. Schlussler
	G-BGLG	Cessna 152	L. W. Scattergood
	G-BGLO	Cessna F.172N	J. R. Isabel
	G-BGLZ	Stits SA-3A Playboy	W. Hinchcliffe
	G-BGME	SIPA 903	M. Emery (G-BCML)
	G-BGMJ	Gardan GY-201 Minicab	G-BGMJ Group
	G-BGMP	Cessna F.172G	B. M. O'Brien
	G-BGMR	Gardan GY-20 Minicab	P. A. Hall
	G-BGMS	Taylor JT.2 Titch	M. A. J. Spice
	G-BGMT	SOCATA Rallye 235E	C. G. Wheeler & M. Faulkner
	G-BGMV	Scheibe SF.25B Falke	I. P. Manley
	G-BGND	Cessna F.172N	A. J. M. Freeman
	G-BGNT	Cessna F.152	Aerolease Ltd
	G-BGNV	GA-7 Cougar	G. J. Bissex & D. D. Saint
	G-BGOD	Colt 77A balloon	C. Allen & M. D. Steuer
	G-BGOG	PA-28-161 Warrior II	W. D. Moore & F. J. Morris
	G-BGOL	PA-28R-201T Turbo Arrow III	R. G. Jackson
	G-BGON	GA-7 Cougar	S. J. Green
	G-BGOR	AT-6D Harvard III (14863)	P. Meyrick
	G-BGPB	CCF T-6J Texan (1747)	Aircraft Spares & Materials Ltd
	G-BGPD	Piper J-3C-65 Cub (479744:M-49)	P. R. Whiteman
	G-BGPH	AA-5B Tiger	Shipping & Airlines Ltd
	G-BGPI	Plumb BGP-1	B. G. Plumb
	G-BGPJ	PA-28-161 Warrior II	W. Lancs Warrior Co Ltd
	G-BGPL	PA-28-161 Warrior II	Demero Ltd & Transcourt Ltd
	G-BGPM	Evans VP-2	N. D. Dykes
	G-BGPN	PA-18 Super Cub 150	A. R. Darke
	G-BGRE	Beech A200 Super King Air	Martin-Baker (Engineering) Ltd
	G-BGRI	Jodel DR.1051	R. G. Hallam
	G-BGRM	PA-38-112 Tomahawk	C. R. Salway
	G-BGRO	Cessna F.172M	Cammo Aviation
	G-BGRR	PA-38-112 Tomahawk	Hinton Pilot Flight Training Ltd
	G-BGRT	Steen Skybolt	O. Meier
	G-BGRX	PA-38-112 Tomahawk	A5E Ltd
	G-BGSA	Morane MS.892E-150	D. C. Tonkin
	G-BGSH	PA-38-112 Tomahawk	Lomac Aviators Ltd
	G-BGSJ	Piper J-3C-65 Cub	A. J. Higgins

Reg.	Type	Owner or Operator	Notes
G-BGSV	Cessna F.172N	Southwell Air Services Ltd	
G-BGSW	Beech F33 Debonair	J. J. Noakes	
G-BGSY	GA-7 Cougar	N. D. Anderson	
G-BGTC	Auster AOP.9 (XP282)	Terranne Auster Group	
G-BGTI	Piper J-3C-65 Cub	A. P. Broad	
G-BGUB	PA-32 Cherokee Six 300E	D. P. & E. A. Morris	
G-BGVB	Robin DR.315	P. J. Leggo	
G-BGVE	CP.1310-C3 Super Emeraude	R. Whitwell	
G-BGVH	Beech 76 Duchess	Velco Marketing	
G-BGVK	PA-28-161 Warrior II	Aviation South West Ltd	
G-BGVN	PA-28RT-201 Arrow IV	John Wailing Ltd	
G-BGVS	Cessna F.172M	Orkney Flying Club	
G-BGVV	AA-5A Cheetah	J. M. Currieie	
G-BGVY	AA-5B Tiger	R. J. C. Neal-Smith	
G-BGVZ	PA-28-181 Archer II	M. & W. Walsh	
G-BGWC	Robin DR.400/180	M. A. Newman	
G-BGWM	PA-28-181 Archer II	Thames Valley Flying Club Ltd	
G-BGWN	PA-38-112 Tomahawk	J. R. Davison	
G-BGWO	Jodel D.112	G-BGWO Group	
G-BGWZ	Eclipse Super Eagle ★	F.A.A. Museum/Yeovilton	
G-BGXA	Piper J-3C-65 Cub (329471:F-44)	P. King	
G-BGXC	SOCATA TB10 Tobago	M. H. & L. J. Cundey	
G-BGXD	SOCATA TB10 Tobago	D. F. P. Finan	
G-BGXO	PA-38-112 Tomahawk	Goodwood Terrena Ltd	
G-BGXR	Robin HR.200/100	J. R. Cross	
G-BGXS	PA-28-236 Dakota	G-BGXS Group	
G-BGXT	SOCATA TB10 Tobago	J. L. Alexander	
G-BGYH	PA-28-161 Warrior II	S. Collins	
G-BGYN	PA-18 Super Cub 150	B. J. Dunford	
G-BGZF	PA-38-112 Tomahawk	APB Leasing Ltd	
G-BHAA	Cessna 152 II	Herefordshire Aero Club Ltd	
G-BHAD	Cessna A.152	T. W. Gilbert	
G-BHAI	Cessna F.152	ACS Aviation Ltd	
G-BHAJ	Robin DR.400/160	Rowantask Ltd	
G-BHAV	Cessna F.152	T. M. & M. L. Jones	
G-BHAX	Enstrom F-28C-UK-2	PVS (Barnsley) Ltd	
G-BHAY	PA-28RT-201 Arrow IV	Alpha Yankee Ltd	
G-BHBA	Campbell Cricket	S. N. McGovern	
G-BHBE	Westland-Bell 47G-3B1 (Soloy)	T. R. Smith (Agricultural Machinery) Ltd	
G-BHBG	PA-32R Cherokee Lance 300	Teamtischer GmbH/Germany	
G-BHBT	Marquart MA.5 Charger	Bravo Tango Group	
G-BHCC	Cessna 172M	D. Wood-Jenkins	
G-BHCE	Jodel D.112	Charles Echo Group	
G-BHCM	Cessna F.172H	J. Dominic	
G-BHCP	Cessna F.152	Eastern Air Executive Ltd	
G-BHCZ	PA-38-112 Tomahawk	J. E. Abbott	
G-BHDD	V.668 Varsity T.1 (WL626:P) ★	Aeropark/East Midlands	
G-BHDE	SOCATA TB10 Tobago	Alpha-Alpha Ltd	
G-BHDK	Boeing B-29A-BN (461748:Y) ★	Imperial War Museum/Duxford	
G-BHDM	Cessna F.152 II	Big Red Kite Ltd	
G-BHDP	Cessna F.182Q II	Zone Travel Ltd	
G-BHDS	Cessna F.152 II	Redmosaic Formacao de Technicos de Aeronaves Unipessoal	
G-BHDV	Cameron V-77 balloon	P. Glydon	
G-BHDX	Cessna F.172N	GDX Ltd	
G-BHDZ	Cessna F.172N	Abbey Security Services Ltd	
G-BHEC	Cessna F.152 II	Stapleford Flying Club Ltd	
G-BHED	Cessna FA.152	TG Aviation Ltd	
G-BHEG	Jodel 150	D. M. Griffiths	
G-BHEK	CP.1315-C3 Super Emeraude	D. B. Winstanley	
G-BHEL	Jodel D.117	D. W. & S. J. McAllister	
G-BHEM	Bensen B.8M	G. C. Kerr	
G-BHEN	Cessna FA.152	Leicestershire Aero Club Ltd	
G-BHEU	Thunder Ax7-65 balloon	J. A. W. Dyer	
G-BHEV	PA-28R Cherokee Arrow 200	7-Up Group	
G-BHEX	Colt 56A balloon	A. S. Dear & ptnrs	
G-BHFC	Cessna F.152	JH Sandham Aviation	
G-BHFE	PA-44-180 Seminole	Transport Command Ltd	
G-BHFG	SNCAN Stampe SV.4C	A. D. R. Northeast & S. A. Cook	
G-BHFH	PA-34-200T Seneca II	Oxford Aviation Academy (Oxford) Ltd	
G-BHFI	Cessna F.152	BAe (Warton) Flying Club	

Notes	Reg.	Type	Owner or Operator
	G-BHFJ	PA-28RT-201T Turbo Arrow IV	S. A. Cook & D. R. Northeast
	G-BHFK	PA-28-151 Warrior	G-BHFK Warrior Group
	G-BHGC	PA-18 Super Cub 150	Vectis Gliding Club Ltd
	G-BHGF	Cameron V-56 balloon	P. Smallward
	G-BHGJ	Jodel D.120	Q. M. B. Oswell
	G-BHGO	PA-32 Cherokee Six 260	A. V. Harmer
	G-BHGY	PA-28R Cherokee Arrow 200	Truman Aviation Ltd
	G-BHHE	Jodel DR.1051/M1	P. Bridges & P. C. Matthews
	G-BHHG	Cessna F.152 II	TG Aviation Ltd
	G-BHHH	Thunder Ax7-65 balloon	J. M. J. Roberts
	G-BHHK	Cameron N-77 balloon ★	British Balloon Museum
	G-BHHN	Cameron V-77 balloon	Itchen Valley Balloon Group
	G-BHIB	Cessna F.182Q	The G-BHIB Flying Group
	G-BHII	Cameron V-77 balloon	R. V. Brown
	G-BHIJ	Eiri PIK-20E-1 (898)	P. M. Yeoman
	G-BHIN	Cessna F.152	Target Aviation Ltd
	G-BHIR	PA-28R Cherokee Arrow 200	Factorcore Ltd
	G-BHIS	Thunder Ax7-65 balloon	Hedgehoppers Balloon Group
	G-BHIY	Cessna F.150K	G. J. Ball
	G-BHJF	SOCATA TB10 Tobago	Tyas Aviation Ltd
	G-BHJI	Mooney M.20J	Otomed APS/Denmark
	G-BHJK	Maule M5-235C Lunar Rocket	M. K. H. Bell
	G-BHJN	Fournier RF-4D	RF-4 Group
	G-BHJO	PA-28-161 Warrior II	Brackla Flying Group
	G-BHJS	Partenavia P.68B	Flew LLP
	G-BHJU	Robin DR.400/2+2	Ageless Aeronautics
	G-BHKR	Colt 12A balloon ★	British Balloon Museum/Newbury
	G-BHKT	Jodel D.112	G. Dawes
	G-BHLE	Robin DR.400/180	A. V. Harmer
	G-BHLH	Robin DR.400/180	G-BHLH Group
	G-BHLJ	Saffery-Rigg S.200 balloon	I. A. Rigg
	G-BHLT	DH.82A Tiger Moth	R. C. P. Brookhouse
	G-BHLU	Fournier RF-3	A. C. Bell
	G-BHLW	Cessna 120	Moray Flying Group
	G-BHLX	AA-5B Tiger	M. D. McPherson
	G-BHMA	SIPA 903	H. J. Taggart
	G-BHMG	Cessna FA.152	R. J. Williamson
	G-BHMJ	Avenger T.200-2112 balloon	R. Light *Lord Anthony 1*
	G-BHMK	Avenger T.200-2112 balloon	P. Kinder *Lord Anthony 2*
	G-BHMT	Evans VP-1	R. T. Callow
	G-BHMY	F.27 Friendship Mk.200 ★	Norwich Aviation Museum
	G-BHNA	Cessna F.152 II	Eastern Air Executive Ltd
	G-BHNC	Cameron O-65 balloon	D. & C. Bareford
	G-BHNK	Jodel D.120A	K. R. Daly
	G-BHNO	PA-28-181 Archer II	B. J. Richardson
	G-BHNP	Eiri PIK-20E-1	D. A. Sutton
	G-BHNV	Westlan-Bell 47G-3B1	S. W. Hutchinson
	G-BHNX	Jodel D.117	M. J. A. Trudgill
	G-BHOA	Robin DR.400/160	T. L. Trott
	G-BHOL	Jodel DR.1050	S. J. Pearson
	G-BHOM	PA-18 Super Cub 95	Oscar Mike Flying Group
	G-BHOR	PA-28-161 Warrior II	Oscar Romeo Flying Group
	G-BHOT	Cameron V-65 balloon	Dante Balloon Group
	G-BHOZ	SOCATA TB9 Tampico	G-BHOZ Flying Group
	G-BHPK	Piper J-3C-65 Cub (238410:A-44)	L-4 Group
	G-BHPL	CASA 1.131E Jungmann 1000 (E3B-350:05-97) ★	A. Burroughes
	G-BHPS	Jodel D.120A	T. J. Price
	G-BHPZ	Cessna 172N	O'Brien Properties Ltd
	G-BHRC	PA-28-161 Warrior II	Sherwood Flying Club Ltd
	G-BHRH	Cessna FA.150K	Merlin Flying Club Ltd
	G-BHRO	Rockwell Commander 112	R. A. Blackwell
	G-BHRR	CP.301A Emeraude	T. W. Offen
	G-BHRW	Jodel DR.221	Dauphin Flying Club
	G-BHSB	Cessna 172N	J. W. Cope & M. P. Wimsey
	G-BHSD	Scheibe SF.25E Super Falke	Upwood Motorglider Group
	G-BHSE	Rockwell Commander 114	604 Sqdn Flying Group Ltd
	G-BHSN	Cameron N-56 balloon	I. Bentley
	G-BHSS	Pitts S-1S Special	N. Leis
	G-BHSY	Jodel DR.1050	T. R. Allebone
	G-BHTA	PA-28-236 Dakota	Dakota Ltd

Reg.	Type	Owner or Operator	Notes
G-BHTC	Jodel DR.1050/M1	G. Clark	
G-BHTG	Thunder Ax6-56 Bolt balloon	The British Balloon Museum & Library Ltd	
G-BHUB	Douglas C-47A (315509:W7-S) ★	Imperial War Museum/Duxford	
G-BHUE	Jodel DR.1050	M. J. Harris	
G-BHUG	Cessna 172N	L. Marriott, R. Wainwright & B. Wharton	
G-BHUI	Cessna 152	South Warwickshire School of Flying Ltd	
G-BHUJ	Cessna 172N	Uniform Juliet Group	
G-BHUM	DH.82A Tiger Moth	S. G. Towers	
G-BHUU	PA-25 Pawnee 235	Booker Gliding Club Ltd	
G-BHVF	Jodel 150A	Groupe Ariel	
G-BHVP	Cessna 182Q	G. S. Chapman	
G-BHVR	Cessna 172N	Victor Romeo Group	
G-BHVV	Piper J-3C-65 Cub	A. V. Williams	
G-BHWA	Cessna F.152	Lincoln Enterprises Ltd	
G-BHWB	Cessna F.152	Lincoln Enterprises Ltd	
G-BHWH	Weedhopper JC-24A	G. A. Clephane	
G-BHWK	MS.880B Rallye Club	D. F. Cumberlidge	
G-BHWY	PA-28R Cherokee Arrow 200-II	Kilo Foxtrot Flying Group	
G-BHWZ	PA-28-181 Archer II	M. A. Abbott	
G-BHXA	SA Bulldog Srs 120/1210	Air Plan Flight Equipment Ltd	
G-BHXD	Jodel D.120	D. A. Garner	
G-BHXK	PA-28 Cherokee 140	S. A. Finlay	
G-BHXS	Jodel D.120	Plymouth Jodel Group	
G-BHXY	Piper J-3C-65 Cub (44-79609:44-S)	F. W. Rogers	
G-BHYA	Cessna R.182RG II	J-P. Jarier	
G-BHYC	Cessna 172RG II	IB Aeroplanes Ltd	
G-BHYD	Cessna R.172K XP II	Sylmar Aviation Services Ltd	
G-BHYG	PA-34-200T Seneca II	Oxford Aviation Academy (Oxford) Ltd	
G-BHYI	SNCAN Stampe SV.4A	D. Hicklin	
G-BHYP	Cessna F.172M	Avior Ltd	
G-BHYR	Cessna F.172M	G-BHYR Group	
G-BHYV	Evans VP-1	I. P. Manley	
G-BHYX	Cessna 152 II	Stapleford Flying Club Ltd	
G-BHZE	PA-28-181 Archer II	Zegruppe Ltd	
G-BHZH	Cessna F.152	Fly NQY Pilot Training	
G-BHZK	AA-5B Tiger	ZK Group	
G-BHZO	AA-5A Cheetah	PG Air	
G-BHZR	SA Bulldog Srs 120/1210	White Knuckle Air Ltd	
G-BHZT	SA Bulldog Srs 120/1210	D. M. Curties	
G-BHZU	Piper J-3C-65 Cub	J. K. Tomkinson	
G-BHZV	Jodel D.120A	G-BHZV Group	
G-BIAC	SOCATA Rallye 235E	B. Brou	
G-BIAH	Jodel D.112	P. A. Gange	
G-BIAI	WMB.2 Windtracker balloon	I. Chadwick	
G-BIAP	PA-16 Clipper	G-BIAP Flying Group	
G-BIAR	Rigg Skyliner II balloon	I. A. Rigg	
G-BIAU	Sopwith Pup (replica) (N6452) ★	F.A.A. Museum/Yeovilton	
G-BIAX	Taylor JT.2 Titch	D. M. Bland	
G-BIAY	AA-5 Traveler	A. J. Black	
G-BIBA	SOCATA TB9 Tampico	TB Aviation Ltd	
G-BIBO	Cameron V-65 balloon	D. M. Hoddinott	
G-BIBS	Cameron P-20 balloon	Cameron Balloons Ltd	
G-BIBT	AA-5B Tiger	Bravo Tango Ltd	
G-BIBW	Cessna F.172N	Shields Estates Ltd	
G-BIBX	WMB.2 Windtracker balloon	I. A. Rigg	
G-BICD	Auster 5	T. R. Parsons	
G-BICE	NA AT-6C Harvard IIA (41-33275:CE)	C. M. L. Edwards	
G-BICG	Cessna F.152 II	Falcon Flying Services	
G-BICM	Colt 56A balloon	Avon Advertiser Balloon Club	
G-BICP	Robin DR.360	B. McVeighty	
G-BICR	Jodel D.120A	Beehive Flying Group	
G-BICS	Robin R.2100A	Chiltern Flying Group	
G-BICU	Cameron V-56 balloon	Black Pearl Balloons	
G-BICW	PA-28-161 Warrior II	Charlie Whisky Flying Group	
G-BIDD	Evans VP-1	J. Hodgkinson	
G-BIDG	Jodel 150A	D. R. Gray	
G-BIDH	Cessna 152 II	Hull Aero Club Ltd (G-DONA)	
G-BIDI	PA-28R-201 Arrow III	T. A. N. Brierley & A. Lidster	
G-BIDJ	PA-18A Super Cub 150	S. M. Hart	
G-BIDK	PA-18 Super Cub 150	Mapesbury Capital Partners Ltd	

Notes	Reg.	Type	Owner or Operator
	G-BIDO	CP.301A Emeraude	A. R. Plumb
	G-BIDV	Colt 14A balloon ★	British Balloon Museum/Newbury
	G-BIDW	Sopwith 1/2 Strutter (replica) (A8226) ★	RAF Museum/Hendon
	G-BIDX	Jodel D.112	P. Turton
	G-BIEN	Jodel D.120A	H. J. Morton/France
	G-BIEO	Jodel D.112	S. C. Solley
	G-BIES	Maule M5-235C Lunar Rocket	William Proctor Ltd
	G-BIET	Cameron O-77 balloon	G. M. Westley
	G-BIEY	PA-28-151 Warrior	M. J. Isaac
	G-BIFB	PA-28 Cherokee 150C	P. Coombs
	G-BIFO	Evans VP-1	J. R. Dunnett
	G-BIFP	Colt 56A balloon	J. W. Adkins
	G-BIFY	Cessna F.150L	Hope Aviation Ltd
	G-BIGJ	Cessna F.172M	Cirrus Aviation Ltd
	G-BIGK	Taylorcraft BC-12D	N. P. St. J. Ramsay
	G-BIGL	Cameron O-65 balloon	P. L. Mossman
	G-BIGR	Avenger T.200-2112 balloon	R. Light
	G-BIGX	Bensen B.8M	W. C. Turner
	G-BIHD	Robin DR.400/160	G. I. J. Thomson & R. A. Hawkins
	G-BIHF	SE-5A (replica) (F943)	C. J. Zeal
	G-BIHI	Cessna 172M	E-Plane Ltd
	G-BIHO	DHC.6 Twin Otter 310	Isles of Scilly Skybus Ltd
	G-BIHT	PA-17 Vagabond	B. Carter
	G-BIHU	Saffrey S.200 balloon	B. L. King
	G-BIHX	Bensen B.8M	P. P. Willmott
	G-BIIA	Fournier RF-3	C. J. Riley
	G-BIIB	Cessna F.172M	Civil Service Flying Club (Biggin Hill) Ltd
	G-BIID	PA-18 Super Cub 95	D. A. Lacey
	G-BIIF	Fournier RF-4D	A. Hoskins
	G-BIIK	MS.883 Rallye 115	N. J. Garbett
	G-BIIT	PA-28-161 Warrior II	Tayside Aviation Ltd
	G-BIIV	PA-28-181 Archer II	J. Thuret/France
	G-BIIZ	Great Lakes 2T-1A Sport Trainer	Circa 42 Ltd
	G-BIJB	PA-18 Super Cub 150	James Aero Ltd
	G-BIJD	Bölkow Bö.208C Junior	J. D. Day
	G-BIJE	Piper J-3C-65 Cub	R. L. Hayward & A. G. Scott
	G-BIJS	Luton LA-4A Minor	I. J. Smith
	G-BIJU	CP-301A Emeraude	Eastern Taildraggers Flying Group (G-BHTX)
	G-BIJV	Cessna F.152 II	Falcon Flying Services
	G-BIJW	Cessna F.152 II	Falcon Flying Services
	G-BIJX	Cessna F.152 II	Falcon Flying Services
	G-BIKC	Boeng 757-236F	DHL Air Ltd
	G-BIKE	PA-28R Cherokee Arrow 200	R. Taylor
	G-BIKF	Boeing 757-236F	DHL Air Ltd
	G-BIKG	Boeing 757-236F	DHL Air Ltd
	G-BIKI	Boeing 757-236F	DHL Air Ltd
	G-BIKJ	Boeing 757-236F	DHL Air Ltd
	G-BIKK	Boeing 757-236F	DHL Air Ltd
	G-BIKM	Boeing 757-236F	DHL Air Ltd
	G-BIKN	Boeing 757-236F	DHL Air Ltd
	G-BIKO	Boeing 757-236F	DHL Air Ltd
	G-BIKP	Boeing 757-236F	DHL Air Ltd
	G-BIKS	Boeing 757-236F	DHL Air Ltd
	G-BIKU	Boeing 757-236F	DHL Air Ltd
	G-BIKV	Boeing 757-236F	DHL Air Ltd
	G-BIKZ	Boeing 757-236F	DHL Air Ltd
	G-BILB	WMB.2 Windtracker balloon	B. L. King
	G-BILE	Scruggs BL.2B balloon	P. D. Ridout
	G-BILG	Scruggs BL.2B balloon	P. D. Ridout
	G-BILH	Slingsby T.65C Vega	G. L. Porter & A. I. Lambe
	G-BILI	Piper J-3C-65 Cub (454467:J-44)	G-BILI Flying Group
	G-BILL	PA-25 Pawnee 235	Pawnee Aviation
	G-BILR	Cessna 152 II	APB Leasing Ltd
	G-BILS	Cessna 152 II	Mona Flying Club
	G-BILU	Cessna 172RG	Full Sutton Flying Centre Ltd
	G-BILZ	Taylor JT.1 Monoplane	A. Petherbridge
	G-BIMK	Tiger T.200 Srs 1 balloon	M. K. Baron
	G-BIMM	PA-18 Super Cub 150	Spectrum Leisure Ltd
	G-BIMN	Steen Skybolt	R. J. Thomas
	G-BIMT	Cessna FA.152	Staverton Flying School @ Skypark Ltd

Reg.	Type	Owner or Operator	Notes
G-BIMU	Sikorsky S-61N	Bristow Helicopters Ltd	
G-BIMX	Rutan Vari-Eze	D. G. Crow	
G-BIMZ	Beech 76 Duchess	Firfax Aviation Ltd	
G-BINL	Scruggs BL.2B balloon	P. D. Ridout	
G-BINM	Scruggs BL.2B balloon	P. D. Ridout	
G-BINR	Unicorn UE.1A balloon	Unicorn Group	
G-BINS	Unicorn UE.2A balloon	Unicorn Group	
G-BINT	Unicorn UE.1A balloon	D. E. Bint	
G-BINX	Scruggs BL.2B balloon	P. D. Ridout	
G-BINY	Oriental balloon	J. L. Morton	
G-BIOA	Hughes 369D	AH Helicopter Services Ltd	
G-BIOB	Cessna F.172P	Network Mapping Ltd	
G-BIOC	Cessna F.150L	W. H. Milner	
G-BIOI	Jodel DR.1051/M	A. A. Alderdice	
G-BIOJ	Rockwell Commander 112TCA	A. T. Dalby	
G-BIOK	Cessna F.152	A. D. H. Macdonald	
G-BIOM	Cessna F.152	J. B. P. E. Fernandes	
G-BIOU	Jodel D.117A	M. R. Routh	
G-BIPA	AA-5B Tiger	Tri-Star Developments Ltd	
G-BIPH	Scruggs BL.2B balloon	C. M. Dewsnap	
G-BIPI	Everett gyroplane	J. G. Farina	
G-BIPN	Fournier RF-3	G-BIPN Group	
G-BIPT	Jodel D.112	C. R. Davies	
G-BIPV	AA-5B Tiger	Echo Echo Ltd	
G-BIPW	Avenger T.200-2112 balloon	B. L. King	
G-BIRD	Pitts S-1D Special	N. E. Smith	
G-BIRE	Colt 56 Bottle SS balloon	D. J. Stagg	
G-BIRH	PA-18 Super Cub 135 (R-163)	Banbury Gliding Club Ltd	
G-BIRI	CASA 1.131E Jungmann 1000	D. Watt	
G-BIRL	Avenger T.200-2112 balloon	R. Light	
G-BIRP	Arena Mk 17 Skyship balloon	A. S. Viel	
G-BIRT	Robin R.1180TD	W. D'A. Hall	
G-BIRW	MS.505 Criquet (F+IS) ★	Museum of Flight/East Fortune	
G-BISG	FRED Srs 3	T. Littlefair	
G-BISH	Cameron V-65 balloon	P. J. Bish	
G-BISL	Scruggs BL.2B balloon	P. D. Ridout	
G-BISM	Scruggs BL.2B balloon	P. D. Ridout	
G-BISS	Scruggs BL.2C balloon	P. D. Ridout	
G-BIST	Scruggs BL.2C balloon	P. D. Ridout	
G-BISX	Colt 56A balloon	C. D. Steel	
G-BITA	PA-18 Super Cub 150	Intrepid Aviation Co	
G-BITE	SOCATA TB10 Tobago	M. A. Smith	
G-BITF	Cessna F.152 II	G-BITF Owners Group	
G-BITH	Cessna F.152 II	J. R. Hyde (G-TFSA)	
G-BITK	FRED Srs 2	I. Pearson	
G-BITM	Cessna F.172P	Dreamtrade Ltd	
G-BITO	Jodel D.112D	A. Dunbar	
G-BITY	FD.31T balloon	A. J. Bell	
G-BIUM	Cessna F.152	Eastern Air Executive Ltd	
G-BIUP	SNCAN NC.854S	J. Greenaway & T. D. Cooper	
G-BIUY	PA-28-181 Archer II	J. S. Devlin & Z. Islam	
G-BIVA	Robin R.2112	D. M. Croucher	
G-BIVB	Jodel D.112	N. M. Harwood	
G-BIVC	Jodel D.112	T. D. Wood	
G-BIVF	CP.301C-3 Emeraude	W. C. Walters	
G-BIVK	Bensen B.8M	M. J. Atyeo	
G-BIWB	Scruggs RS.5000 balloon	P. D. Ridout	
G-BIWC	Scruggs RS.5000 balloon	P. D. Ridout	
G-BIWF	Warren balloon	P. D. Ridout	
G-BIWG	Zelenski Mk 2 balloon	P. D. Ridout	
G-BIWJ	Unicorn UE.1A balloon	B. L. King	
G-BIWN	Jodel D.112	C. R. Coates & P. K. Morley	
G-BIWR	Mooney M.20F	M. Broady	
G-BIWU	Cameron V-65 balloon	W. Rousell & J. Tyrrell	
G-BIWW	AA-5 Traveler	Dix-Sept Aviation Ltd	
G-BIWY	Westland WG.30 ★	Instructional airframe/Yeovil	
G-BIXA	SOCATA TB9 Tampico	W. Maxwell	
G-BIXB	SOCATA TB9 Tampico	B. G. Adams	
G-BIXH	Cessna F.152	Northumbria Flying School Ltd	
G-BIXL	P-51D Mustang (472216:HO-M)	R. Lamplough	
G-BIXN	Boeing Stearman A75N1 (FJ777)	V. S. E. Norman	

Notes	Reg.	Type	Owner or Operator
	G-BIXW	Colt 56B balloon	N. A. P. Bates
	G-BIXX	Pearson Srs 2 balloon	D. Pearson
	G-BIXZ	Grob G-109	Hinton Pilot Flight Training Ltd
	G-BIYI	Cameron V-65 balloon	Sarnia Balloon Group
	G-BIYJ	PA-18 Super Cub 95	S. Russell
	G-BIYK	Isaacs Fury II	S. M. Roberts
	G-BIYR	PA-18 Super Cub 150 (R-151)	Delta Foxtrot Flying Group
	G-BIYU	Fokker S.11.1 Instructor (E-15)	Fokker Syndicate
	G-BIYW	Jodel D.112	A. Appleby
	G-BIYX	PA-28 Cherokee 140	W. B. Bateson
	G-BIYY	PA-18 Super Cub 95	A. E. & W. J. Taylor
	G-BIZE	SOCATA TB9 Tampico	B. Higgins
	G-BIZF	Cessna F.172P	R. S. Bentley
	G-BIZG	Cessna F.152	M. A. Judge
	G-BIZI	Robin DR.400/120	Headcorn Flying School Ltd
	G-BIZK	Nord 3202 (78)	A. I. Milne
	G-BIZM	Nord 3202	Global Aviation Ltd
	G-BIZO	PA-28R Cherokee Arrow 200	Lemas Air
	G-BIZR	SOCATA TB9 Tampico	P. Marie (G-BSEC)
	G-BIZV	PA-18 Super Cub 95 (18-2001)	J. P. Nugent
	G-BIZW	Champion 7GCBC Citabria	G. Read & Sons
	G-BIZY	Jodel D.112	Wayland Tunley & Associates
	G-BJAD	FRED Srs 2 ★	Newark Air Museum
	G-BJAE	Lavadoux Starck AS.80 ★	D. J. & S. A. E. Phillips/Coventry
	G-BJAF	Piper J-3C-65 Cub	P. J. Cottle
	G-BJAG	PA-28-181 Archer II	C. R. Chubb
	G-BJAJ	AA-5B Tiger	Draycott Tiger Club
	G-BJAL	CASA 1.131E Jungmann 1000	G-BJAL Group
	G-BJAO	Bensen B.8M	A. P. Lay
	G-BJAP	DH.82A Tiger Moth (K2587)	K. Knight
	G-BJAS	Rango NA.9 balloon	A. Lindsay
	G-BJAV	Gardan GY-80 Horizon 160	W. R.Maloney
	G-BJAY	Piper J-3C-65 Cub	D. W. Finlay
	G-BJBK	PA-18 Super Cub 95	M. S. Bird
	G-BJBM	Monnett Sonerai I	I. Pearson
	G-BJBO	Jodel DR.250/160	Wiltshire Flying Group
	G-BJBW	PA-28-161 Warrior II	152 Group
	G-BJCA	PA-28-161 Warrior II	U. Kleinheyer
	G-BJCF	CP.1310-C3 Super Emeraude	K. M. Hodson & C. G. H. Gurney
	G-BJCI	PA-18 Super Cub 150 (modified)	The Borders (Milfield) Gliding Club Ltd
	G-BJCW	PA-32R-301 Saratoga SP	Golf Charlie Whisky Ltd
	G-BJDE	Cessna F.172M	J. K. P. Amor
	G-BJDF	MS.880B Rallye 100T	C. J. dos Santos Prado
	G-BJDJ	HS.125 Srs 700B	TAG Farnborough Engineering Ltd (G-RCDI)
	G-BJDK	European E.14 balloon	Aeroprint Tours
	G-BJDW	Cessna F.172M	J. Rae
	G-BJEE	BN-2T Turbine Islander	Cormack (Aircraft Services) Ltd
	G-BJEF	BN-2B-26 Islander	Cormack (Aircraft Services) Ltd
	G-BJEI	PA-18 Super Cub 95	H. J. Cox
	G-BJEJ	BN-2T Turbine Islander	Islander Aircraft Ltd
	G-BJEL	SNCAN NC.854	C. A. James
	G-BJEV	Aeronca 11AC Chief (897)	R. F. Willcox
	G-BJEX	Bölkow Bö.208C Junior	G. D. H. Crawford
	G-BJFC	European E.8 balloon	P. D. Ridout
	G-BJFE	PA-18 Super Cub 95	P. H. Wilmot-Allistone
	G-BJFM	Jodel D.120	J. V. George
	G-BJGM	Unicorn UE.1A balloon	D. Eaves & P. D. Ridout
	G-BJGY	Cessna F.172P	K. & S. Martin
	G-BJHB	Mooney M.20J	Zitair Flying Club Ltd
	G-BJHK	EAA Acro Sport	M. R. Holden
	G-BJHV	Voisin Replica ★	Brooklands Museum of Aviation/Weybridge
	G-BJIA	Allport balloon	D. J. Allport
	G-BJIC	Dodo 1A balloon	P. D. Ridout
	G-BJID	Osprey 1B balloon	P. D. Ridout
	G-BJIG	Slingsby T.67A	A. D. Hodgkinson
	G-BJIV	PA-18 Super Cub 180	Yorkshire Gliding Club (Pty) Ltd
	G-BJKF	SOCATA TB9 Tampico	G-BJKF Group
	G-BJKW	Wills Aera II	J. K. S. Wills
	G-BJLC	Monnett Sonerai IIL	P. O. Yeo
	G-BJLX	Cremer balloon	P. W. May

Reg.	Type	Owner or Operator	Notes
G-BJLY	Cremer balloon	P. Cannon	
G-BJML	Cessna 120	R. A. Smith	
G-BJMR	Cessna 310R	J. H. Sandham Aviation	
G-BJMW	Thunder Ax8-105 balloon	G. M. Westley	
G-BJMX	Jarre JR.3 balloon	P. D. Ridout	
G-BJMZ	European EA.8A balloon	P. D. Ridout	
G-BJNA	Arena Mk 117P balloon	P. D. Ridout	
G-BJND	Osprey Mk 1E balloon	A. Billington & D. Whitmore	
G-BJNG	Slingsby T.67AM	D. F. Hodgkinson	
G-BJNN	PA-38-112 Tomahawk	Carlisle Flight Training Ltd	
G-BJNY	Aeronca 11CC Super Chief	P. I. & D. M. Morgans	
G-BJNZ	PA-23 Aztec 250F	J. A. D. Richardson (G-FANZ)	
G-BJOB	Jodel D.140C	T. W. M. Beck & M. J. Smith	
G-BJOE	Jodel D.120A	H. Davies	
G-BJOT	Jodel D.117	R. A. Kilbride	
G-BJOV	Cessna F.150K	G-BJOV Flying Group	
G-BJPI	Bede BD-5G	M. D. McQueen	
G-BJRA	Osprey Mk 4B balloon	E. Osborn	
G-BJRG	Osprey Mk 4B balloon	A. E. de Gruchy	
G-BJRH	Rango NA.36 balloon	N. H. Ponsford	
G-BJRP	Cremer balloon	M. D. Williams	
G-BJRR	Cremer balloon	M. D. Williams	
G-BJRV	Cremer balloon	M. D. Williams	
G-BJSS	Allport balloon	D. J. Allport	
G-BJST	CCF T-6J Harvard IV (KF729)	M. F. Cuming, J. G. Fricker & N. T. Oakman	
G-BJSV	PA-28-161 Warrior II	Airways Flight Training (Exeter) Ltd	
G-BJSW	Thunder Ax7-65 balloon	J. Edwards	
G-BJSZ	Piper J-3C-65 Cub	K. Gilbert	
G-BJTB	Cessna A.150M	Cirrus Aviation Ltd	
G-BJTP	PA-18 Super Cub 95 (115302:TP)	P. J. Myers	
G-BJTY	Osprey Mk 4B balloon	A. E. de Gruchy	
G-BJUB	BVS Special 01 balloon	P. G. Wild	
G-BJUD	Robin DR.400/180R	Lasham Gliding Society Ltd	
G-BJUR	PA-38-112 Tomahawk	Truman Aviation Ltd	
G-BJUS	PA-38-112 Tomahawk	J. D. Williams	
G-BJUV	Cameron V-20 balloon	P. Spellward	
G-BJVC	Evans VP-2	S. J. Greer & S. E. Clarke	
G-BJVH	Cessna F.182Q	R. J. de Courcy Cuming	
G-BJVJ	Cessna F.152	Henlow Flying Club	
G-BJVK	Grob G-109	B. Kimberley	
G-BJVM	Cessna 172N	R. D. & M. S. B. Forster	
G-BJVS	CP.1310-C3 Super Emeraude	M. J. Hall	
G-BJVT	Cessna F.152	Northumbria Flying School Ltd	
G-BJVU	Thunder Ax6-56 Bolt balloon	N. R. Beckwith	
G-BJWH	Cessna F.152 II	J. D. Baines	
G-BJWI	Cessna F.172P	Flew LLP	
G-BJWT	Wittman W.10 Tailwind	Tailwind Group	
G-BJWV	Colt 17A balloon	D. T. Meyes	
G-BJWW	Cessna F.172N	Air Charter & Travel Ltd	
G-BJWX	PA-18 Super Cub 95	R. A. G. Lucas	
G-BJWY	S-55 Whirlwind HAR.21(WV198) ★	Solway Aviation Museum/Carlisle	
G-BJWZ	PA-18 Super Cub 95	G-BJWZ Syndicate	
G-BJXB	Slingsby T.67A	D. Pegley	
G-BJXK	Fournier RF-5	RF5 Syndicate	
G-BJXR	Auster AOP.9 (XR267)	I. Churm & J. Hanson	
G-BJXX	PA-23 Aztec 250E	V. Bojovic	
G-BJXZ	Cessna 172N	T. M. Jones	
G-BJYD	Cessna F.152 II	N. J. James	
G-BJYF	Colt 56A balloon	A. J. Moore	
G-BJYK	Jodel D.120A	M. R. Baker	
G-BJZB	Evans VP-2	R. B. McComish	
G-BJZF	DH.82A Tiger Moth	M. I. Lodge	
G-BJZN	Slingsby T.67A	ZN Group	
G-BJZR	Colt 42A balloon	Selfish Balloon Group	
G-BKAE	Jodel D.120	Bumble Bee Group	
G-BKAF	FRED Srs 2	N. Glass	
G-BKAM	Slingsby T.67M Firefly160	R. C. B. Brookhouse	
G-BKAO	Jodel D.112	H. Haigh	
G-BKAS	PA-38-112 Tomahawk	N. Z. Ali	
G-BKAY	Rockwell Commander 114	D. L. Bunning	

BRITISH CIVIL REGISTRATIONS

Notes	Reg.	Type	Owner or Operator
	G-BKAZ	Cessna 152	L. W. Scattergood
	G-BKBD	Thunder Ax3 balloon	P. Donkin
	G-BKBF	MS.894A Rallye Minerva 220	Bravo Foxtrot Group
	G-BKBN	SOCATA TB10 Tobago	P. M. Clayton & D. Turner
	G-BKBP	Bellanca 7GCBC Scout	M. G. & J. R. Jefferies
	G-BKBS	Bensen B8MV	L. Harrison
	G-BKBV	SOCATA TB10 Tobago	T. C. H. Wright
	G-BKBW	SOCATA TB10 Tobago	Merlin Aviation
	G-BKCC	PA-28 Cherokee 180	DR Flying Club Ltd
	G-BKCE	Cessna F.172P II	The Leicestershire Aero Club Ltd
	G-BKCI	Brügger MB.2 Colibri	M. R. Walters
	G-BKCN	Currie Wot	N. A. A. Podmore
	G-BKCV	EAA Acro Sport II	R. J. Bower
	G-BKCW	Jodel D.120	Dundee Flying Group (G-BMYF)
	G-BKCX	Mudry/CAARP CAP-10B	G. P. Gorvett
	G-BKCZ	Jodel D.120A	I. K. Ratcliffe
	G-BKDC	Monnett Sonerai II	K. J. Towell
	G-BKDH	Robin DR.400/120	Marine & Aviation Ltd
	G-BKDJ	Robin DR.400/120	S. Pritchard & I. C. Colwell
	G-BKDK	Thunder Ax7-77Z balloon	A. J. Byrne
	G-BKDP	FRED Srs 3	M. Whittaker
	G-BKDR	Pitts S-1S Special	L. E. Richardson
	G-BKDT	SE-5A (replica) (F943) ★	Yorkshire Air Museum/Elvington
	G-BKDX	Jodel DR.1050	D. G. T. & R. J. Ward
	G-BKEP	Cessna F.172M	R. M. Dalley
	G-BKER	SE-5A (replica) (F5447:N)	N. K. Geddes
	G-BKET	PA-18 Super Cub 95	H. M. MacKenzie
	G-BKEV	Cessna F.172M	Derby Arrows
	G-BKEW	Bell 206B JetRanger 3	N. R. Foster
	G-BKEY	FRED Srs 3	G. S. Taylor
	G-BKFC	Cessna F.152 II	C. Walton Ltd
	G-BKFG	Thunder Ax3 Maxi Sky Chariot balloon	S. G. Whatley
	G-BKFI	Evans VP-1	A. S. Watts
	G-BKFK	Isaacs Fury II	P. T. Catanach
	G-BKFL	Aerosport Scamp	J. Sherwood
	G-BKFM	QAC Quickie 1	G. E. Meakin
	G-BKFR	CP.301C Emeraude	Devonshire Flying Group
	G-BKFW	P.56 Provost T.1 (XF597)	Sylmar Aviation & Services Ltd
	G-BKGA	MS.892E Rallye 150GT	C. J. Spradbery
	G-BKGB	Jodel D.120	B. A. Ridgway
	G-BKGC	Maule M.6-235	The Vale of the White Horse Gliding Centre Ltd
	G-BKGD	Westland WG.30 Srs.100 ★	IHM/Weston-super-Mare
	G-BKGL	Beech D.18S (1164:64)	A. T. J. Darrah
	G-BKGM	Beech D.18S (HB275)	Skyblue Aero Services Ltd
	G-BKGR	Cameron O-65 balloon	K. Kidner & L. E. More
	G-BKGW	Cessna F.152-II	Leicestershire Aero Club Ltd
	G-BKHG	Piper J-3C-65 Cub (479766:D-63)	H. C. Cox
	G-BKHW	Stoddard-Hamilton Glasair IIRG	P. J. Mansfield
	G-BKHY	Taylor JT.1 Monoplane	B. C. J. O'Neill
	G-BKHZ	Cessna F.172P	L. R. Leader
	G-BKIB	SOCATA TB9 Tampico	G. A. Vickers
	G-BKIC	Cameron V-77 balloon	C. A. Butler
	G-BKIF	Fournier RF-6B	Tiger Airways
	G-BKII	Cessna F.172M	Sealand Aerial Photography Ltd
	G-BKIJ	Cessna F.172M	Cirrus Aviation Ltd
	G-BKIK	Cameron DG-19 airship ★	Balloon Preservation Group/Lancing
	G-BKIR	Jodel D.117	R. Shaw & D. M. Hardaker
	G-BKIS	SOCATA TB10 Tobago	Wessex Flying Group
	G-BKIT	SOCATA TB9 Tampico	Cavendish Aviation UK Ltd
	G-BKIU	Colt 17A Cloudhopper balloon	S. R. J. Pooley
	G-BKIX	Cameron V-31 Air Chair balloon	K. J. & M. E. Gregory
	G-BKIY	Thunder Ax3 balloon ★	Balloon Preservation Group/Lancing
	G-BKIZ	Cameron V-31 balloon	A. P. S. Cox
	G-BKJB	PA-18 Super Cub 135	W. S. Stanley
	G-BKJF	MS.880B Rallye 100T	R. Neeson
	G-BKJS	Jodel D.120A	B. F. Baldock & T. J. Nicholson
	G-BKJW	PA-23 Aztec 250E	Alan Williams Entertainments Ltd
	G-BKKN	Cessna 182R	R A. Marven
	G-BKKO	Cessna 182R	Just Plane Trading Ltd
	G-BKKZ	Pitts S-1D Special	P. G. Gabriele
	G-BKLO	Cessna F.172M	Stapleford Flying Club Ltd

Reg.	Type	Owner or Operator	Notes
G-BKMA	Mooney M.20J Srs 201	Foxtrot Whisky Aviation	
G-BKMB	Mooney M.20J Srs 201	G-BKMB Flying Group	
G-BKMG	Handley Page O/400 (replica)	The Paralyser Group	
G-BKMT	PA-32R-301 Saratoga SP	P. Ashworth	
G-BKNO	Monnett Sonerai IIL	S. Hardy	
G-BKNZ	CP.301A Emeraude	J. A. Thomas	
G-BKOA	SOCATA MS.893E Rallye 180GT	M. Jarrett	
G-BKOB	Z.326 Trener Master	A. L. Rae	
G-BKOK	BN-2B-26 Islander	Cormack (Aircraft Services) Ltd	
G-BKOT	Wassmer Wa.81 Piranha	B. N. Rolfe	
G-BKOU	P.84 Jet Provost T.3 (XN637)	G-BKOU/2 Ltd	
G-BKPA	Hoffmann H-36 Dimona	J. D. Hanton & R. Matthews	
G-BKPB	Aerosport Scamp	B. R. Thompson	
G-BKPC	Cessna A.185F	P. D. Cavanagh & R. J. Illidge	
G-BKPD	Viking Dragonfly	E. P. Browne & G. J. Sargent	
G-BKPE	Jodel DR.250/160	E. J. Jonker	
G-BKPS	AA-5B Tiger	A. E. T. Clarke	
G-BKPX	Jodel D.120A	D. M. Garrett & C. A. Jones	
G-BKPY	SAAB 91B/2 Safir (56321:U-AB) ★	Newark Air Museum	
G-BKPZ	Pitts S-1T Special	D. A. Slater	
G-BKRA	NA T-6G Texan (51-15227)	First Air Ltd	
G-BKRF	PA-18 Super Cub 95	R. Horner	
G-BKRH	Brügger MB.2 Colibri	T. C. Darters	
G-BKRK	SNCAN Stampe SV.4C	Strathgadie Stampe Group	
G-BKRL	Chichester-Miles Leopard ★	Bournemouth Aviation Museum	
G-BKRN	Beechcraft D.18S (43-35943)	A. A. Marshall & P. L. Turland	
G-BKRZ	Dragon G-77 balloon	J. R. Barber	
G-BKSC	Saro Skeeter AOP.12 (XN351) ★	R. A. L. Falconer	
G-BKSE	QAC Quickie Q.1	M. D. Burns	
G-BKST	Rutan Vari-Eze	R. Towle	
G-BKSX	SNCAN Stampe SV.4C	C. A. Bailey & J. A. Carr	
G-BKTA	PA-18 Super Cub 95	M. J. Dyson	
G-BKTH	CCF Hawker Sea Hurricane IB (Z7015)	The Shuttleworth Collection	
G-BKTM	PZL SZD-45A Ogar	Hinton Ogar Group	
G-BKTV	Cessna F.152	ACS Aviation Ltd	
G-BKTZ	Slingsby T.67M Firefly	P. R. Elvidge (G-SFTV)	
G-BKUE	SOCATA TB9 Tampico	Fife TB9ers	
G-BKUI	D.31 Turbulent	E. Shouler	
G-BKUR	CP.301A Emeraude	T. Harvey	
G-BKVA	SOCATA Rallye 180T	Norfolk Gliding Club Ltd	
G-BKVC	SOCATA TB9 Tampico	J. P. Gough	
G-BKVF	FRED Srs 3	G. E. & R. E. Collins	
G-BKVG	Scheibe SF.25E Super Falke	G-BKVG Ltd	
G-BKVK	Auster AOP.9 (WZ662)	J. K. Houlgrave	
G-BKVL	Robin DR.400/160	G. D. Jones	
G-BKVM	PA-18 Super Cub 150 (115684)	D. G. Caffrey	
G-BKVP	Pitts S-1D Special	S. A. Smith	
G-BKVW	Airtour 56 balloon	L. D. & H. Vaughan	
G-BKWD	Taylor JT.2 Titch	J. F. Sully	
G-BKWR	Cameron V-65 balloon	Window on the World Ltd	
G-BKWY	Cessna F.152	Northumbria Flying School Ltd	
G-BKXA	Robin R.2100	M. Wilson	
G-BKXF	PA-28R Cherokee Arrow 200	G. Booth	
G-BKXM	Colt 17A balloon	R. G. Turnbull	
G-BKXN	ICA-Brasov IS-28M2/80HP	R. J. S. Charnley	
G-BKXO	Rutan LongEz	M. G. Parsons	
G-BKXP	Auster AOP.6	B. J. Ellis	
G-BKXR	D.31A Turbulent	P. A. Gasson	
G-BKZE	AS.332L Super Puma	CHC Scotia Ltd	
G-BKZF	Cameron V-56 balloon	C. F. Sanger-Davies	
G-BKZI	Bell 206B JetRanger 2	Bucklefields Business Devlopments Ltd	
G-BKZT	FRED Srs 2	U. Chakravorty	
G-BKZV	Bede BD-4A	T. S. Smith	
G-BLAC	Cessna FA.152	W. Ali	
G-BLAF	Stolp SA.900 V-Star	A. T. Lane	
G-BLAH	Thunder Ax7-77-1 balloon	T. M. Donnelly	
G-BLAI	Monnett Sonerai 2L	T. Simpon	
G-BLAM	Jodel DR.360	J. S. Dalton	
G-BLAT	Jodel 150	G-BLAT Flying Group	
G-BLCC	Thunder Ax7-77Z balloon	W. J. Treacy & P. Murphy/Ireland	

BRITISH CIVIL REGISTRATIONS

Notes	Reg.	Type	Owner or Operator
	G-BLCH	Colt 65D balloon	S. Charlish
	G-BLCI	EAA Acro Sport	M. R. Holden
	G-BLCM	SOCATA TB9 Tampico	B. Smith
	G-BLCT	Jodel DR.220 2+2	F. N. P. Maurin
	G-BLCU	Scheibe SF.25B Falke	Charlie Uniform Syndicate
	G-BLCV	Hoffmann H-36 Dimona	R. & M. Weaver
	G-BLCW	Evans VP-1	K. Lewis
	G-BLDB	Taylor JT.1 Monoplane	J. P. J. Hefford
	G-BLDD	WAG-Aero CUBy AcroTrainer	M. P. Wiseman
	G-BLDG	PA-25 Pawnee 260C	Ouse Gliding Club Ltd
	G-BLDK	Robinson R22	Flight Academy (Gyrocopters) Ltd
	G-BLDN	Rand-Robinson KR-2	P. R. Diffey
	G-BLDV	BN-2B-26 Islander	Loganair Ltd
	G-BLES	Stolp SA.750 Acroduster Too	C. J. Kingswood
	G-BLFI	PA-28-181 Archer II	Aerospares 2000 Ltd
	G-BLFZ	PA-31-310 Turbo Navajo C	London Executive Aviation Ltd
	G-BLGH	Robin DR.300/180R	Booker Gliding Club Ltd
	G-BLGS	SOCATA Rallye 180T	A. Waters
	G-BLGV	Bell 206B JetRanger 3	Heliflight (UK) Ltd
	G-BLHH	Jodel DR.315	S. J. Luck
	G-BLHJ	Cessna F.172P	J. H. Sandham Aviation
	G-BLHM	PA-18 Super Cub 95	A. G. Edwards
	G-BLHN	Robin HR.100/285	K. A. & L. M. C. Payton
	G-BLHR	GA-7 Cougar	Advanced Aircraft Leasing Ltd
	G-BLHS	Bellanca 7ECA Citabria	A. J. Wilkins
	G-BLHW	Varga 2150A Kachina	Wilburton Flying Group
	G-BLID	DH.112 Venom FB.50 (J-1605) ★	P. G. Vallance Ltd
	G-BLIH	PA-18-135 Super Cub	A. S. Birrell & A. G. A. Obertelli
	G-BLIK	Wallis WA-116/F/S	K. H. Wallis
	G-BLIT	Thorp T-18 CW	A. P. Tyrwhitt-Drake
	G-BLIW	P.56 Provost T.51 (177)	A. D. M. & K. B. Edie
	G-BLIX	Saro Skeeter Mk 12 (XL809)	K. M. Scholes
	G-BLJM	Beech 95-B55 Baron	A. Nitsche/Germany
	G-BLJO	Cessna F.152	J. S. Develin & Z. Islam
	G-BLKA	DH.112 Venom FB.54 (WR410:N) ★	De Havilland Heritage Museum/London Colney
	G-BLKM	Jodel DR.1051	Kilo Mike Group
	G-BLKY	Beech 95-58 Baron	R. A. Perrot
	G-BLLA	Bensen B.8M	K. T. Donaghey
	G-BLLB	Bensen B.8M	D. H. Moss
	G-BLLD	Cameron O-77 balloon	G. Birchall
	G-BLLH	Jodel DR.220A 2+2	J. & J. K. Houlgrave
	G-BLLN	PA-18 Super Cub 95	Aeroclub du Bassin d'Arcachon/France
	G-BLLO	PA-18 Super Cub 95	D. G. Margetts
	G-BLLP	Slingsby T.67B	Air Navigation and Trading Co Ltd
	G-BLLR	Slingsby T.67B	R. L. Brinklow
	G-BLLS	Slingsby T.67B	D. McKendrick
	G-BLLW	Colt 56B balloon	G. Fordyce & ptnrs
	G-BLLZ	Rutan LongEz	R. S. Stoddart-Stones
	G-BLMA	Zlin 326 Trener Master	G. P. Northcott
	G-BLMC	Avro 698 Vulcan B.2A ★	Aeropark/East Midlands
	G-BLME	Robinson R22HP	Heli Air Ltd
	G-BLMG	Grob G.109B	Mike Golf Syndicate
	G-BLMI	PA-18-95 Super Cub (R-55)	T. F. F. Van Erck
	G-BLMN	Rutan LongEz	K. W. Scrivens
	G-BLMP	PA-17 Vagabond	D. & M. Shrimpton.
	G-BLMR	PA-18 Super Cub 150	M. Vickers
	G-BLMT	PA-18 Super Cub 135	I. S. Runnalls
	G-BLMW	T.66 Nipper 3	S. L. Millar
	G-BLMZ	Colt 105A balloon	M. D. Dickinson
	G-BLNO	FRED Srs 3	L. W. Smith
	G-BLOR	PA-30 Twin Comanche 160	M. C. Jordan
	G-BLOS	Cessna 185A (also flown with floats)	D. C. Minshaw
	G-BLOT	Colt Ax6-56B balloon	H. J. Anderson
	G-BLPA	Piper J-3C-65 Cub	I. Bazin
	G-BLPB	Turner TSW Hot Two Wot	Papa Bravo Group
	G-BLPE	PA-18 Super Cub 95	A. A. Haig-Thomas
	G-BLPF	Cessna FR.172G	S. Culpin
	G-BLPG	Auster J/1N Alpha (16693:693)	Annic Marketing (G-AIZH)
	G-BLPH	Cessna FRA.150L	J. D. Baines
	G-BLPI	Slingsby T.67B	RAF Wyton Flying Group Ltd
	G-BLPP	Cameron V-77 balloon	G. B. Davies

Reg.	Type	Owner or Operator	Notes
G-BLRC	PA-18 Super Cub 135	Supercub Group	
G-BLRF	Slingsby T.67C	R. C. Nicholls	
G-BLRL	CP.301C-1 Emeraude	A. M. Smith	
G-BLRM	Glaser-Dirks DG.400	J. A. & W. S. Y. Stephen	
G-BLSD	DH.112 Venom FB.54 (J-1758) ★	R. Lamplough/North Weald	
G-BLSX	Cameron O-105 balloon	B. J. Petteford	
G-BLTA	Thunder Ax7-77A	K. A. Schlussler	
G-BLTC	D.31A Turbulent	S. J. Butler	
G-BLTK	Rockwell Commander 112TC	Commander TC Group	
G-BLTM	Robin HR.200/100	Barton Robin Group	
G-BLTN	Thunder Ax7-65 balloon	V. Michel	
G-BLTR	Scheibe SF.25B Falke	V. Mallon/Germany	
G-BLTS	Rutan LongEz	R. W. Cutler	
G-BLTV	Slingsby T.67B	R. L. Brinklow	
G-BLTW	Slingsby T.67B	Cheshire Air Training Services Ltd	
G-BLTY	Westland WG.30 Srs 160	D. Brem-Wilson	
G-BLUE	Colt 77A balloon	D. P. Busby	
G-BLUV	Grob G.109B	109 Flying Group	
G-BLUX	Slingsby T.67M Firefly 200	R. L. Brinklow	
G-BLUZ	DH.82B Queen Bee (LF858)	The Bee Keepers Group	
G-BLVA	Airtour AH-31 balloon	D. L. Peltan & S. Church	
G-BLVB	Airtour AH-56 balloon	J. J. Daly	
G-BLVI	Slingsby T.67M Firefly Mk II	M. Power	
G-BLVK	CAARP CAP-10B	E. K. Coventry	
G-BLVL	PA-28-161 Warrior II	TG Aviation Ltd	
G-BLVS	Cessna 150M	D. H. G. Penney	
G-BLVW	Cessna F.172H	R. Holloway	
G-BLWD	PA-34-200T Seneca 2	Bencray Ltd	
G-BLWF	Robin HR.100/210	M. D. Parker	
G-BLWH	Fournier RF-6B-100	F. J. Hodson & C. C. Rollings	
G-BLWM	Bristol M.1C (replica) (C4994) ★	RAF Museum/Hendon	
G-BLWP	PA-38-112 Tomahawk	APB Leasing Ltd	
G-BLWT	Evans VP-1	M. W. Olliver	
G-BLWY	Robin R.2160D	Pure Aviation Support Services Ltd	
G-BLXA	SOCATA TB20 Trinidad	Trinidad Flyers Ltd	
G-BLXG	Colt 21A balloon	A. Walker	
G-BLXH	Fournier RF-3	R. H. W. A. Westerhuis	
G-BLXI	CP.1310-C3 Super Emeraude	R. Howard	
G-BLXO	Jodel 150	P. R. Powell	
G-BLXT	Eberhardt S.E.5E	R. S. Grace	
G-BLYD	SOCATA TB20 Trinidad	Yankee Delta Corporation Ltd	
G-BLYP	Robin 3000/120	Weald Air Services	
G-BLYT	Airtour AH-77 balloon	I. J. Taylor & R. C. Kincaid	
G-BLZA	Scheibe SF.25B Falke	Zulu Alpha Syndicate	
G-BLZH	Cessna F.152 II	P. D'Costa	
G-BLZJ	Aerospatiale AS.332L Super Puma	Bristow Helicopters Ltd (G-PUMJ)	
G-BLZP	Cessna F.152	East Midlands Flying School Ltd	
G-BMAD	Cameron V-77 balloon	M. A. Stelling	
G-BMAO	Taylor JT.1 Monoplane	S. J. Alston	
G-BMAX	FRED Srs 2	D. A. Arkley	
G-BMAY	PA-18 Super Cub 135	R. W. Davies	
G-BMBB	Cessna F.150L	S. Collins	
G-BMBJ	Schempp-Hirth Janus CM	BJ Flying Group	
G-BMBZ	Scheibe SF.25E Super Falke	K. E. Ballington	
G-BMCC	Thunder Ax7-77 balloon	A. K. & C. M. Russell	
G-BMCD	Cameron V-65 balloon	R. Lillyman	
G-BMCG	Grob G.109B	D. K. R. Draper	
G-BMCI	Cessna F.172H	A. B. Davis	
G-BMCN	Cessna F.152	Cristal Air Ltd	
G-BMCS	PA-22 Tri-Pacer 135	T. A. Hodges	
G-BMCX	Cessna F.152	Leicestershire Aero Club Ltd	
G-BMCX	AS.332L Super Puma	Bristow Southeast Asia Ltd	
G-BMDB	SE-5A (replica) (F235:B)	D. Biggs	
G-BMDE	Pietenpol AirCamper	P. B. Childs	
G-BMDJ	Price Ax7-77S balloon	R. A. Benham	
G-BMDK	PA-34-220T Seneca III	Air Medical Fleet Ltd	
G-BMDP	Partenavia P.64B Oscar 200	J. L. Sparks	
G-BMDS	Jodel D.120	J. V. Thompson	
G-BMEA	PA-18 Super Cub 95	M. J. Butler	
G-BMEH	Jodel 150 Special Super Mascaret	R. J. & C. J. Lewis	

Notes	Reg.	Type	Owner or Operator
	G-BMET	Taylor JT.1 Monoplane	M. K. A. Blyth
	G-BMEU	Isaacs Fury II	I. G. Harrison
	G-BMEX	Cessna A.150K	R. J. Grantham & D. Boatswain
	G-BMFD	PA-23 Aztec 250F	Giles Aviation Ltd (G-BGYY)
	G-BMFG	Dornier Do.27A-4	M. P. Wood
	G-BMFI	PZL SZD-45A Ogar	S. L. Morrey
	G-BMFP	PA-28-161 Warrior II	Bravo-Mike-Fox-Papa Group
	G-BMFU	Cameron N-90 balloon	J. J. Rudoni
	G-BMFY	Grob G.109B	P. J. Shearer
	G-BMGB	PA-28R Cherokee Arrow 200	Malmesbury Specialist Cars
	G-BMGC	Fairey Swordfish Mk II (W5856)	F.A.A. Museum/Yeovilton
	G-BMGG	Cessna 152 II	Falcon Flying Services
	G-BMGR	Grob G.109B	G-BMGR Group
	G-BMHA	Rutan LongEz	S. F. Elvins
	G-BMHC	Cessna U.206F	H. and R. Morley
	G-BMHL	Wittman W.8 Tailwind	H. J. Bennet
	G-BMHS	Cessna F.172M	Tango X-Ray Flying Group
	G-BMHT	PA-28RT-201T Turbo Arrow	G-BMHT Flying Group
	G-BMID	Jodel D.120	G-BMID Flying Group
	G-BMIG	Cessna 172N	BMIG Group
	G-BMIM	Rutan LongEz	R. M. Smith
	G-BMIO	Stoddard-Hamilton Glasair RG	P. Bint & L. McMahon
	G-BMIP	Jodel D.112	F. J. E. Brownsill
	G-BMIR	Westland Wasp HAS.1 (XT788) ★	Park Aviation Supply/Charlwood
	G-BMIS	Monnett Sonerai II	S. R. Edwards
	G-BMIV	PA-28R-201T Turbo Arrow III	Firmbeam Ltd
	G-BMIW	PA-28-181 Archer II	Oldbus Ltd
	G-BMIX	SOCATA TB20 Trinidad	Falcon Flying Group
	G-BMIY	Oldfield Baby Great Lakes	J. B. Scott (G-NOME)
	G-BMIZ	Robinson R22 Beta	Heli Air Ltd
	G-BMJA	PA-32R-301 Saratoga SP	H. Merkado
	G-BMJB	Cessna 152	Endrick Aviation LLP
	G-BMJC	Cessna 152 II	T. Brogden
	G-BMJD	Cessna 152 II	Donair Flying Club Ltd
	G-BMJJ	Cameron Watch 75 SS balloon	D. P. Busby
	G-BMJL	Rockwell Commander 114	D. J. & S. M. Hawkins
	G-BMJN	Cameron O-65 balloon	P. M. Traviss
	G-BMJO	PA-34-220T Seneca III	Fastnet Jet Alliance Ltd
	G-BMJX	Wallis WA-116X	K. H. Wallis
	G-BMJY	Yakovlev C18M (07)	W. A. E. Moore
	G-BMKB	PA-18 Super Cub 135	Cubair Flight Training Ltd
	G-BMKC	Piper J-3C-65 Cub (329854:R-44)	J. Hirst
	G-BMKD	Beech C90A King Air	ATC (Lasham) Ltd
	G-BMKF	Jodel DR.221	S. T. & L. A. Gilbert
	G-BMKG	PA-38-112 Tomahawk II	ACS Aviation Ltd
	G-BMKJ	Cameron V-77 balloon	R. C. Thursby
	G-BMKK	PA-28R-200 Cherokee Arrow II	P. M. Murray
	G-BMKP	Cameron V-77 balloon	R. Bayly
	G-BMKR	PA-28-161 Warrior II	Field Flying Group (G-BGKR)
	G-BMKY	Cameron O-65 balloon	A. R. Rich
	G-BMLJ	Cameron N-77 balloon	C. J. Dunkley
	G-BMLK	Grob G.109B	Brams Syndicate
	G-BMLL	Grob G.109B	G-BMLL Flying Group
	G-BMLM	Beech 95-58 Baron	Atlantic Bridge Aviation Ltd
	G-BMLS	PA-28R-201 Arrow III	R. M. Shorter
	G-BMLT	Pietenpol Air Camper	W. E. R. Jenkins
	G-BMLW	Cameron O-77 balloon	M. L. & L. P. Willoughby
	G-BMLX	Cessna F.150L	J. P. A. Freeman
	G-BMMF	FRED Srs 2	R. C. Thomas
	G-BMMI	Pazmany PL.4A	P. I. Morgans
	G-BMMK	Cessna 182P	G. G. Weston
	G-BMMM	Cessna 152 II	Falcon Flying Services Ltd
	G-BMGG	Grob G.109B	G-BMMP Ltd
	G-BMMV	ICA-Brasov IS-28M2A	C. D. King
	G-BMMW	Thunder Ax7-77 balloon	P. A. George
	G-BMNL	PA-28R Cherokee Arrow 200	Pearson Associates
	G-BMOE	PA-28R Cherokee Arrow 200	Piper Leasing Ltd
	G-BMOF	Cessna U206G	Wild Geese Skydiving Centre
	G-BMOG	Thunder Ax7-77 balloon	R. M. Boswell
	G-BMOH	Cameron N-77 balloon	P. J. Marshall & M. A. Clarke
	G-BMAD	ARV Super 2	R. E. Griffiths

Reg.	Type	Owner or Operator	Notes
G-BMOL	PA-23 Aztec 250D	LDL Enterprises (G-BBSR)	
G-BMOT	Bensen B.8M	M. Fontolan	
G-BMPC	PA-28-181 Archer II	C. J. & R. J. Barnes	
G-BMPD	Cameron V-65 balloon	R. P. E. Phillips	
G-BMPL	Optica Industries OA.7 Optica	J. K. Edgley	
G-BMPP	Cameron N-77 balloon	The Sarnia Balloon Group	
G-BMPR	PA-28R-201 Arrow III	T. J. Brammer & D. T. Colley	
G-BMPS	Strojnik S-2A	G. J. Green	
G-BMPY	DH.82A Tiger Moth	N. M. Eisenstein	
G-BMRA	Boeing 757-236F	DHL Air Ltd	
G-BMRB	Boeing 757-236F	DHL Air Ltd	
G-BMRC	Boeing 757-236F	DHL Air Ltd	
G-BMRD	Boeing 757-236F	DHL Air Ltd	
G-BMRE	Boeing 757-236F	DHL Air Ltd	
G-BMRF	Boeing 757-236F	DHL Air Ltd	
G-BMRH	Boeing 757-236F	DHL Air Ltd	
G-BMRJ	Boeing 757-236F	DHL Air Ltd	
G-BMSB	VS.509 Spitfire IX (MJ627:9G-P)	M. S. Bayliss (G-ASOZ)	
G-BMSC	Evans VP-2	R. S. Acreman	
G-BMSD	PA-28-181 Archer II	H. Merkado	
G-BMSE	Valentin Taifun 17E	D. O'Donnell	
G-BMSF	PA-38-112 Tomahawk	D. A. Whitmore	
G-BMSG	SAAB 32A Lansen ★	J. E. Wilkie/Cranfield	
G-BMSL	FRED Srs 3	T. C. Darters	
G-BMTA	Cessna 152 II	ACS Aviation Ltd	
G-BMTB	Cessna 152 II	Sky Leisure Aviation (Charters) Ltd	
G-BMTC	AS.355F1 Twin Squirrel	Cambridge & Essex Air Support Unit (G-SASU/ G-BSSM/G-BKUK/G-EPOL)	
G-BMTJ	Cessna 152 II	The Pilot Centre Ltd	
G-BMTO	PA-38-112 Tomahawk	A. Sanja	
G-BMTU	Pitts S-1E Special	N. A. A. Pogmore	
G-BMTX	Cameron V-77 balloon	J. A. Langley	
G-BMUD	Cessna 182P	C. Latky & K. T. Oszvald	
G-BMUG	Rutan LongEz	A. G. Sayers	
G-BMUJ	Colt Drachenfisch balloon	Virgin Airship & Balloon Co Ltd	
G-BMUO	Cessna A.152	Sky Leisure Aviation (Charters) Ltd	
G-BMUT	PA-34-200T Seneca II	BNTC Ltd	
G-BMUU	Thunder Ax7-77 balloon	A. R. Hill	
G-BMUZ	PA-28-161 Warrior II	Northumbria Flying School Ltd	
G-BMVA	Scheibe SF.25B Falke	Kent Gliding Club Ltd	
G-BMVB	Cessna F.152	W. Ali	
G-BMVG	QAC Quickie Q.1	N. Ciattoni	
G-BMVL	PA-38-112 Tomahawk	D. R. C. Bell	
G-BMVM	PA-38-112 Tomahawk	Brimpton Flying Group	
G-BMVT	Thunder Ax7-77A balloon	M. L. & L. P. Willoughby	
G-BMVU	Monnett Moni	Stacey Aviation Ltd	
G-BMWF	ARV Super 2	G. E. Collard	
G-BMWR	Rockwell Commander 112	M. & J. Edwards	
G-BMWU	Cameron N-42 balloon ★	I. Chadwick	
G-BMWV	Putzer Elster B	E. Foers	
G-BMXA	Cessna 152 II	ACS Aviation Ltd	
G-BMXB	Cessna 152 II	C. I. J. Young	
G-BMXC	Cessna 152 II	MK Aero Support Ltd	
G-BMYC	SOCATA TB10 Tobago	J. C. Woolard	
G-BMYG	Cessna FA.152	Greer Aviation Ltd	
G-BMYI	AA-5 Traveler	W. C. & S. C. Westran	
G-BMYU	Jodel D.120	N. C. Scanlan	
G-BMZF	WSK-Mielec LiM-2 (MiG-15bis) (01420) ★	F.A.A. Museum/Yeovilton	
G-BMZN	Everett gyroplane	T. A. Holmes	
G-BMZS	Everett gyroplane	L. W. Cload	
G-BMZW	Bensen B.8MR	P. D. Widdicombe	
G-BNAI	Wolf W-II Boredom Fighter (146-11083)	C. M. Bunn	
G-BNAJ	Cessna 152 II	Galair Ltd	
G-BNAN	Cameron V-65 balloon	Rango Balloon and Kite Company	
G-BNAW	Cameron V-65 balloon	A. Walker	
G-BNBW	Thunder Ax7-77 balloon	I. S. & S. W. Watthews	
G-BNBY	Beech 95-B55A Baron	P. Normand/France (G-AXXR)	
G-BNCB	Cameron V-77 balloon	C. W. Brown	
G-BNCM	Cameron N-77 balloon	C. A. Stone	

Notes	Reg.	Type	Owner or Operator
	G-BNCO	PA-38-112 Tomahawk	D. K. Walker
	G-BNCR	PA-28-161 Warrior II	Booker Aircraft Leasing Ltd
	G-BNCS	Cessna 180	C. Elwell Transport Ltd
	G-BNCX	Hawker Hunter T.7 (XL621) ★	Brooklands Museum of Aviation/Weybridge
	G-BNCZ	Rutan LongEz	D. G. Foreman
	G-BNDE	PA-38-112 Tomahawk	Airtime Aviation Holdings Ltd
	G-BNDG	Wallis WA-201/R Srs1	K. H. Wallis
	G-BNDN	Cameron V-77 balloon	A. Hornshaw
	G-BNDP	Brügger MB.2 Colibri	A. C. Barber
	G-BNDR	SOCATA TB10 Tobago	Monavion.fr
	G-BNDT	Brügger MB.2 Colibri	D. W. Rees
	G-BNDV	Cameron N-77 balloon	R. E. Jones
	G-BNEE	PA-28R-201 Arrow III	Britannic Management Aviation
	G-BNEL	PA-28-161 Warrior II	S. C. Westran
	G-BNEN	PA-34-200T Seneca II	CE Ventures Ltd
	G-BNEO	Cameron V-77 balloon	J. G. O'Connell
	G-BNEV	Viking Dragonfly	N. W. Eyre
	G-BNFG	Cameron O-77 balloon	Capital Balloon Club Ltd
	G-BNFO	Cameron V-77 balloon	M. B. Young
	G-BNFP	Cameron O-84 balloon	M. Clarke
	G-BNFR	Cessna 152 II	A. Jahanfar
	G-BNFV	Robin DR.400/120	J. P. A. Freeman
	G-BNGE	Auster AOP.6 (TW536)	K. A. Hale
	G-BNGJ	Cameron N-77 balloon	S. W. K. Smeeton
	G-BNGN	Cameron N-77 balloon	N. Dykes
	G-BNGO	Thunder Ax7-77 balloon	J. S. Finlan
	G-BNGT	PA-28-181 Archer II	Edinburgh Flying Club Ltd
	G-BNGV	ARV Super 2	N. A. Onions & L. J. Russell
	G-BNGW	ARV Super 2	Southern Gas Turbines Ltd
	G-BNGY	ARV Super 2	J. & P. Morris (G-BMWL)
	G-BNHB	ARV Super 2	C. J. Challener
	G-BNHG	PA-38-112 Tomahawk II	Highland Aviation Training Ltd
	G-BNHJ	Cessna 152 II	The Pilot Centre Ltd
	G-BNHK	Cessna 152 II	Wayfarers Flying Group
	G-BNHL	Colt beer glass SS balloon	J. A. Viner
	G-BNHN	Colt Ariel Bottle SS balloon ★	British Balloon Museum
	G-BNHT	Fournier RF-3	G-BNHT Group
	G-BNID	Cessna 152 II	MK Aero Support Ltd
	G-BNII	Cameron N-90 balloon	Topless Balloon Group
	G-BNIK	Robin HR.200/120	G-BNIK Group
	G-BNIM	PA-38-112 Tomahawk	Air Claire Ltd
	G-BNIN	Cameron V-77 balloon	Cloud Nine Balloon Group
	G-BNIO	Luscombe 8A Silvaire	India Oscar Group
	G-BNIP	Luscombe 8A Silvaire	M. J. Diggins
	G-BNIU	Cameron O-77 balloon	M. E. Dubois/France
	G-BNIV	Cessna 152 II	Cristal Air Ltd
	G-BNIW	Boeing Stearman PT-17	R. C. Goold
	G-BNJB	Cessna 152 II	Aerolease Ltd
	G-BNJC	Cessna 152 II	Stapleford Flying Club Ltd
	G-BNJH	Cessna 152 II	ACS Aviation Ltd
	G-BNJL	Bensen B.8MR	S. Ram
	G-BNJT	PA-28-161 Warrior II	Hawarden Flying Group
	G-BNJX	Cameron N-90 balloon	Mars UK Ltd
	G-BNKC	Cessna 152 II	Herefordshire Aero Club Ltd
	G-BNKD	Cessna 172N	R. Nightingale
	G-BNKE	Cessna 172N	Kilo Echo Flying Group
	G-BNKH	PA-38-112 Tomahawk	M. C. R. Sims
	G-BNKI	Cessna 152 II	RAF Halton Aeroplane Club Ltd
	G-BNKP	Cessna 152 II	Spectrum Leisure Ltd
	G-BNKR	Cessna 152 II	Flyglass Ltd
	G-BNKS	Cessna 152 II	APB Leasing Ltd
	G-BNKT	Cameron O-77 balloon	A. A. Brown
	G-BNKV	Cessna 152 II	Cristal Air Ltd
	G-BNLA	Boeing 747-436	British Airways
	G-BNLD	Boeing 747-436	British Airways
	G-BNLE	Boeing 747-436	British Airways
	G-BNLF	Boeing 747-436	British Airways
	G-BNLG	Boeing 747-436	British Airways
	G-BNLH	Boeing 747-436	British Airways
	G-BNLI	Boeing 747-436	British Airways
	G-BNLJ	Boeing 747-436	British Airways

Reg.	Type	Owner or Operator	Notes
G-BNLK	Boeing 747-436	British Airways	
G-BNLL	Boeing 747-436	British Airways	
G-BNLM	Boeing 747-436	British Airways	
G-BNLN	Boeing 747-436	British Airways	
G-BNLO	Boeing 747-436	British Airways	
G-BNLP	Boeing 747-436	British Airways	
G-BNLS	Boeing 747-436	British Airways	
G-BNLT	Boeing 747-436	British Airways	
G-BNLU	Boeing 747-436	British Airways	
G-BNLV	Boeing 747-436	British Airways	
G-BNLW	Boeing 747-436	British Airways	
G-BNLX	Boeing 747-436	British Airways	
G-BNLY	Boeing 747-436	British Airways	
G-BNLZ	Boeing 747-436	British Airways	
G-BNMB	PA-28-151 Warrior	Azure Flying Club Ltd	
G-BNMD	Cessna 152 II	T. M. Jones	
G-BNME	Cessna 152 II	M. Bonsall	
G-BNMF	Cessna 152 II	Redhill Air Services Ltd	
G-BNMH	Pietenpol Air Camper	N. M. Hitchman	
G-BNMI	Colt Flying Fantasy SS balloon	Air 2 Air Ltd	
G-BNML	Rand-Robinson KR-2	P. J. Brookman	
G-BNMO	Cessna TR.182RG	T. W. Gale & S. R. Whitling	
G-BNMX	Thunder Ax7-77 balloon	S. A. D. Beard	
G-BNNA	Stolp SA.300 Starduster Too	Banana Group	
G-BNNE	Cameron N-77 balloon	R. D. Allen, L. P. Hooper & M. J. Streat	
G-BNNO	PA-28-161 Warrior II	Premier Flight Training Ltd	
G-BNNT	PA-28-151 Warrior	S. T. Gilbert & D. J. Kirkwood	
G-BNNU	PA-38-112 Tomahawk	Lomac Aviators Ltd	
G-BNNX	PA-28R-201T Turbo Arrow III	Professional Flying Ltd	
G-BNNY	PA-28-161 Warrior II	Falcon Flying Services	
G-BNNZ	PA-28-161 Warrior II	R. West	
G-BNOB	Wittman W.8 Tailwind	D. G. Hammersley	
G-BNOF	PA-28-161 Warrior II	Tayside Aviation Ltd	
G-BNOH	PA-28-161 Warrior II	Sherburn Aero Club Ltd	
G-BNOJ	PA-28-161 Warrior II	BAE Systems (Warton) Flying Club Ltd	
G-BNOM	PA-28-161 Warrior II	J. H. Sandham Aviation	
G-BNON	PA-28-161 Warrior II	Tayside Aviation Ltd	
G-BNOP	PA-28-161 Warrior II	BAE Systems (Warton) Flying Club Ltd	
G-BNPE	Cameron N-77 balloon	R. N. Simpkins	
G-BNPF	Slingsby T.31M	S. Luck & ptnrs	
G-BNPH	P.66 Pembroke C.1 (WV740)	M. A. Stott	
G-BNPM	PA-38-112 Tomahawk	Papa Mike Aviation	
G-BNPO	PA-28-181 Archer II	NPAS Ltd	
G-BNPV	Bowers Fly-Baby 1B	A. Berry	
G-BNPY	Cessna 152 II	G. Tennant	
G-BNRA	SOCATA TB10 Tobago	Double D Airgroup	
G-BNRG	PA-28-161 Warrior II	Glenn Aviation Ltd	
G-BNRL	Cessna 152 II	Bulldog Aviation Ltd	
G-BNRP	PA-28-181 Archer II	PA-28 Warrior Ltd	
G-BNRR	Cessna 172P	Wentworth Productions	
G-BNRX	PA-34-200T Seneca II	Truman Aviation Ltd	
G-BNRY	Cessna 182Q	K. F. & S. J. Farey	
G-BNSG	PA-28R-201 Arrow III	The Leicestershire Aero Club Ltd	
G-BNSI	Cessna 152 II	Sky Leisure Aviation (Charters) Ltd	
G-BNSL	PA-38-112 Tomahawk II	Lomac Aviators Ltd	
G-BNSM	Cessna 152 II	Cornwall Flying Club Ltd	
G-BNSN	Cessna 152 II	The Pilot Centre Ltd	
G-BNSO	Slingsby T.67M Firefly Mk II	R. M. Rennoldson	
G-BNSP	Slingsby T.67M Firefly Mk II	N. J. Heard & M. R. Bromiley	
G-BNSR	Slingsby T.67M Firefly Mk II	Slingsby SR Group	
G-BNST	Cessna 172N	CSG Bodyshop	
G-BNSU	Cessna 152 II	Channel Aviation Ltd	
G-BNSV	Cessna 152 II	Channel Aviation Ltd	
G-BNSY	PA-28-161 Warrior II	R. A. Brown	
G-BNSZ	PA-28-161 Warrior II	H. Merkado	
G-BNTD	PA-28-161 Warrior II	M. N. Vance	
G-BNTP	Cessna 172N	Westnet Ltd	
G-BNTZ	Cameron N-77 balloon	Balloon Team	
G-BNUL	Cessna 152 II	Big Red Kite Ltd	
G-BNUN	Beech 95-58PA Baron	SMB Aviation Ltd	

Notes	Reg.	Type	Owner or Operator
	G-BNUO	Beech 76 Duchess	Pace Projects Ltd and Professional Flight Simulation Ltd
	G-BNUT	Cessna 152 Turbo	Stapleford Flying Club Ltd
	G-BNUX	Hoffmann H-36 Dimona	Buckminster Dimona Syndicate
	G-BNUY	PA-38-112 Tomahawk II	D. C. Storey
	G-BNVB	AA-5A Cheetah	Pelican Project Management Ltd
	G-BNVE	PA-28-181 Archer II	Take Flight Aviation Ltd
	G-BNVT	PA-28R-201T Turbo Arrow III	Victor Tango Group
	G-BNWA	Boeing 767-336ER	British Airways
	G-BNWB	Boeing 767-336ER	British Airways
	G-BNWC	Boeing 767-336ER	British Airways
	G-BNWD	Boeing 767-336ER	British Airways
	G-BNWH	Boeing 767-336ER	British Airways
	G-BNWI	Boeing 767-336ER	British Airways
	G-BNWM	Boeing 767-336ER	British Airways
	G-BNWN	Boeing 767-336ER	British Airways
	G-BNWO	Boeing 767-336ER	British Airways
	G-BNWR	Boeing 767-336ER	British Airways
	G-BNWS	Boeing 767-336ER	British Airways
	G-BNWT	Boeing 767-336ER	British Airways
	G-BNWU	Boeing 767-336ER	British Airways
	G-BNWV	Boeing 767-336ER	British Airways
	G-BNWW	Boeing 767-336ER	British Airways
	G-BNWX	Boeing 767-336ER	British Airways
	G-BNWY	Boeing 767-336ER	British Airways
	G-BNWZ	Boeing 767-336ER	British Airways
	G-BNXE	PA-28-161 Warrior II	M. S. Brown
	G-BNXK	Nott-Cameron ULD-3 balloon	J. R. P. Nott (G-BLJN)
	G-BNXL	Glaser-Dirks DG.400	M. Lee
	G-BNXM	PA-18 Super Cub 95	A. H. Soper
	G-BNXU	PA-28-161 Warrior II	Friendly Warrior Group
	G-BNXV	PA-38-112 Tomahawk	W. B. Bateson
	G-BNXX	SOCATA TB20 Trinidad	J. C. Taylor
	G-BNXZ	Thunder Ax7-77 balloon	Hale Hot Air Balloon Group
	G-BNYD	Bell 206B JetRanger 3	Aerospeed Ltd
	G-BNYK	PA-38-112 Tomahawk	Lomac Aviators Ltd
	G-BNYL	Cessna 152 II	V. J. Freeman
	G-BNYM	Cessna 172N	Kestrel Syndicate
	G-BNYO	Beech 76 Duchess	Multiflight Ltd
	G-BNYP	PA-28-181 Archer II	R. D. Cooper
	G-BNYZ	SNCAN Stampe SV.4E	Bianchi Film Aviation Services Ltd
	G-BNZB	PA-28-161 Warrior II	Falcon Flying Services Ltd
	G-BNZC	DHC.1 Chipmunk 22 (18671:671)	The Shuttleworth Collection
	G-BNZK	Thunder Ax7-77 balloon	T. D. Marsden
	G-BNZL	Rotorway Scorpion 133	J. R. Wraight
	G-BNZM	Cessna T.210N	A. J. M. Freeman
	G-BNZN	Cameron N-56 balloon	H. B. Pilo/Sweden
	G-BNZO	Rotorway Executive	J. S. David
	G-BNZV	PA-25 Pawnee 235	Aeroklub Alpski Letalski Center Lesce/Slovenia
	G-BNZZ	PA-28-161 Warrior II	Providence Aviation Ltd
	G-BOAA	BAC-Aérospatiale Concorde 102 ★	Museum Of Flight East Fortune (G-N94AA)
	G-BOAB	BAC-Aérospatiale Concorde 102 ★	Preserved at Heathrow (G-N94AB)
	G-BOAC	BAC-Aérospatiale Concorde 102 ★	Displayed in viewing area Manchester International (G-N81AC)
	G-BOAF	BAC-Aérospatiale Concorde 102 ★	Bristol Aero Collection/Filton (G-N94AF)
	G-BOAH	PA-28-161 Warrior II	Aircraft Engineers Ltd
	G-BOAI	Cessna 152 II	Aviation Spirit Ltd
	G-BOAL	Cameron V-65 balloon	N. H. & A. M. Ponsford
	G-BOAU	Cameron V-77 balloon	G. T. Barstow
	G-BOBA	PA-28R-201 Arrow III	Bravo Aviation Ltd
	G-BOBR	Cameron N-77 balloon	Trigger Concepts Ltd
	G-BOBT	Stolp SA.300 Starduster Too	G-BOBT Group
	G-BOBV	Cessna F.150M	M. Buxton
	G-BOBY	Monnett Sonerai II	R. G. Hallam
	G-BOCG	PA-34-200T Seneca II	Oxford Aviation Academy (Oxford) Ltd
	G-BOCI	Cessna 140A	Charlie India Aviators
	G-BOCK	Sopwith Triplane (replica) (N6290)	The Shuttleworth Collection
	G-BOCL	Slingsby T.67C	Richard Brinklow Aviation Ltd
	G-BOCM	Slingsby T.67C	Richard Brinklow Aviation Ltd
	G-BOCN	Robinson R22 Beta	Northmore Aviation Ltd

Reg.	Type	Owner or Operator	Notes
G-BODB	PA-28-161 Warrior II	Sherburn Aero Club Ltd	
G-BODD	PA-28-161 Warrior II	L. W. Scattergood	
G-BODE	PA-28-161 Warrior II	Sherburn Aero Club Ltd	
G-BODI	Glasair III Model SH-3R	A. P. Durston	
G-BODO	Cessna 152	Enstone Sales and Services Ltd	
G-BODR	PA-28-161 Warrior II	Booker Aircraft Leasing Ltd	
G-BODS	PA-38-112 Tomahawk	T. W. Gilbert	
G-BODT	Jodel D.18	L. D. McPhillips	
G-BODU	Scheibe SF.25C Falke	Hertfordshire County Scout Council	
G-BODY	Cessna 310R	Reconnaissance Ventures Ltd	
G-BODZ	Robinson R22 Beta	Langley Aviation Ltd	
G-BOEE	PA-28-181 Archer II	J. C. & G. M. Brinkley	
G-BOEH	Jodel DR.340	B. W. Griffiths	
G-BOEK	Cameron V-77 balloon	R. I. M. Kerr & ptnrs	
G-BOEM	Pitts S-2A	M. Murphy	
G-BOEN	Cessna 172M	G-BOEN Flying Group	
G-BOER	PA-28-161 Warrior II	B. Boult	
G-BOET	PA-28RT-201 Arrow IV	B. C. Chambers (G-IBEC)	
G-BOFC	Beech 76 Duchess	Magenta Ltd	
G-BOFF	Cameron N-77 balloon	R. S. McKibbin	
G-BOFL	Cessna 152 II	S. A. Abid	
G-BOFW	Cessna A.150M	P. J. Wagstaff	
G-BOFY	PA-28 Cherokee 140	R. A. Brown	
G-BOFZ	PA-28-161 Warrior II	Northumbria Flying School Ltd	
G-BOGI	Robin DR.400/180	A. L. M. Shepherd	
G-BOGK	ARV Super 2	M. K. Field	
G-BOGM	PA-28RT-201T Turbo Arrow IV	G. Marsango	
G-BOGO	PA-32R-301T Saratoga SP	Diff Air KFT	
G-BOGY	Cameron V-77 balloon	A. Reimann & P. Spellward	
G-BOHA	PA-28-161 Warrior II	Phoenix Aviation	
G-BOHD	Colt 77A balloon	D. B. Court	
G-BOHH	Cessna 172N	ASL Aviation	
G-BOHI	Cessna 152 II	Cirrus Aviation Ltd	
G-BOHJ	Cessna 152 II	Airlaunch	
G-BOHM	PA-28 Cherokee 180	B. F. Keogh & R. A. Scott	
G-BOHO	PA-28-161 Warrior II	Egressus Flying Group	
G-BOHR	PA-28-151 Warrior	R. M. E. Garforth	
G-BOHT	PA-38-112 Tomahawk	Durham Tees Flight Training Ltd	
G-BOHV	Wittman W.8 Tailwind	D. H. Greenwood	
G-BOHW	Van's RV-4	A. Mercy	
G-BOIB	Wittman W.10 Tailwind	C. R. Nash	
G-BOIC	PA-28R-201T Turbo Arrow III	M. J. Pearson	
G-BOID	Bellanca 7ECA Citabria	D. Mallinson	
G-BOIG	PA-28-161 Warrior II	The Flight Centre 2010 Ltd	
G-BOIK	Air Command 503 Commander	F. G. Shepherd	
G-BOIL	Cessna 172N	Upperstack Ltd	
G-BOIO	Cessna 152	Sandham Aviation	
G-BOIR	Cessna 152	APB Leasing Ltd	
G-BOIT	SOCATA TB10 Tobago	G-BOIT Flying Group	
G-BOIV	Cessna 150M	India Victor Group	
G-BOIX	Cessna 172N	J. W. N. Sharpe	
G-BOIY	Cessna 172N	L. W. Scattergood	
G-BOIZ	PA-34-200T Seneca II	S. F. Tebby & Son	
G-BOJB	Cameron V-77 balloon	I. M. & S. D. Warner	
G-BOJI	PA-28RT-201 Arrow IV	Arrow Two Group	
G-BOJK	PA-34-220T Seneca III	Omega Sky Taxi Ltd (G-BRUF)	
G-BOJM	PA-28-181 Archer II	R. P. Emms	
G-BOJS	Cessna 172P	Paul's Planes Ltd	
G-BOJW	PA-28-161 Warrior II	Phoenix Aviation	
G-BOJZ	PA-28-161 Warrior II	Falcon Flying Services	
G-BOKA	PA-28-201T Turbo Dakota	CBG Aviation Ltd	
G-BOKB	PA-28-161 Warrior II	Apollo Aviation Advisory Ltd	
G-BOKF	Air Command 532 Elite	J. K. Padden	
G-BOKH	Whittaker MW7	I. Pearson	
G-BOKW	Bolkow Bo.208C Junior	L. S. Johnson	
G-BOKX	PA-28-161 Warrior II	Shenley Farms (Aviation) Ltd	
G-BOKY	Cessna 152 II	D. F. F. & J. E. Poore	
G-BOLB	Taylorcraft BC-12-65	C. E. Tudor	
G-BOLC	Fournier RF-6B-100	J. D. Cohen	
G-BOLD	PA-38-112 Tomahawk	G-BOLD Group	
G-BOLE	PA-38-112 Tomahawk	Double S Group	

Notes	Reg.	Type	Owner or Operator
	G-BOLG	Bellanca 7KCAB Citabria	B. R. Pearson
	G-BOLI	Cessna 172P	Boli Flying Club
	G-BOLL	Lake LA-4 Skimmer	M. C. Holmes
	G-BOLN	Colt 21A balloon	G. Everett
	G-BOLO	Bell 206B JetRanger	Hargreaves Leasing Ltd
	G-BOLR	Colt 21A balloon	C. J. Sanger-Davies
	G-BOLS	FRED Srs 2	I. F. Vaughan
	G-BOLT	Rockwell Commander 114	I. R. Harnett
	G-BOLU	Robin R.3000/120	P. J. R. White & J. M. Smith
	G-BOLV	Cessna 152 II	Synergy Aircraft Leasing Ltd
	G-BOLW	Cessna 152 II	G-BOLW Flying Group
	G-BOLY	Cessna 172N	I. R. Chaplin
	G-BOMB	Cassutt Racer IIIM	D. Hart
	G-BOMN	Cessna 150F	P. A. Chamberlaine
	G-BOMO	PA-38-112 Tomahawk II	APB Leasing Ltd
	G-BOMP	PA-28-181 Archer II	H. Merkado
	G-BOMS	Cessna 172N	Penchant Ltd
	G-BOMU	PA-28-181 Archer II	J. Sawyer
	G-BOMY	PA-28-161 Warrior II	BOMY Group
	G-BOMZ	PA-38-112 Tomahawk	G-BOMZ Aviation
	G-BONC	PA-28RT-201 Arrow IV	G-BONC Holdings Group
	G-BONG	Enstrom F-28A-UK	Chobham Helicopters Ltd
	G-BONP	CFM Streak Shadow	G. J. Chater
	G-BONR	Cessna 172N	D. I. Craikl
	G-BONS	Cessna 172N	BONS Group
	G-BONT	Slingsby T.67M Mk II	Etico
	G-BONU	Slingsby T.67B	R. L. Brinklow
	G-BONW	Cessna 152 II	Lincoln Aero Club Ltd
	G-BONY	Denney Kitfox Model 1	R. Dunn & P. F. Hill
	G-BONZ	Beech V35B Bonanza	P. M. Coulten
	G-BOOB	Cameron N-65 balloon	P. J. Hooper
	G-BOOC	PA-18 Super Cub 150	S. A. C. Whitcombe
	G-BOOD	Slingsby T.31M Motor Tutor	J. D. C. Henslow
	G-BOOE	GA-7 Cougar	R. J. Moller
	G-BOOF	PA-28-181 Archer II	H. Merkado
	G-BOOG	PA-28RT-201T Turbo Arrow IV	Katheros Ltd
	G-BOOH	Jodel D.112	J. G. Bright
	G-BOOI	Cessna 152	Stapleford Flying Club Ltd
	G-BOOL	Cessna 172N	Wicklow Wings
	G-BOOW	Aerosport Scamp	D. A. Weldon/Ireland
	G-BOOX	Rutan LongEz	I. R. Wilde
	G-BOOZ	Cameron N-77 balloon	J. E. F. Kettlety
	G-BOPA	PA-28-181 Archer II	Flyco Ltd
	G-BOPC	PA-28-161 Warrior II	Aeros Ltd
	G-BOPD	Bede BD-4	S. T. Dauncey
	G-BOPH	Cessna TR.182RG	J. M. Mitchell
	G-BOPO	Brooklands OA.7 Optica	J. K. Edgley
	G-BOPR	Brooklands OA.7 Optica	Aeroelvira Ltd
	G-BOPT	Grob G.115	LAC Flying School
	G-BOPU	Grob G.115	LAC Flying School
	G-BORB	Cameron V-77 balloon	M. H. Wolff
	G-BORD	Thunder Ax7-77 balloon	Western Region British Balloon and Airship Club Ltd
	G-BORE	Colt 77A balloon	J. D. & C. J. Medcalf
	G-BORG	Campbell Cricket	R. L. Gilmore
	G-BORK	PA-28-161 Warrior II	Turweston Flying Club Ltd (G-IIIC)
	G-BORL	PA-28-161 Warrior II	Westair Flying School Ltd
	G-BORM	HS.748 Srs 2B ★	Airport Fire Service/Exeter
	G-BORN	Cameron N-77 balloon	I. Chadwick
	G-BORS	PA-28-181 Archer II	Aircraft Grouping Ltd
	G-BORW	Cessna 172P	Briter Aviation Ltd
	G-BORY	Cessna 150L	D. H. G. Penney
	G-BOSB	Thunder Ax7-77 balloon	G. Bann
	G-BOSE	PA-28-181 Archer II	G-BOSE Group
	G-BOSJ	Nord 3400 (124)	A. I. Milne
	G-BOSM	Jodel DR.253B	A. G. Stevens
	G-BOSN	AS.355F1 Twin Squirrel	Helicopter Services
	G-BOSO	Cessna A.152	J. S. Develin & Z. Islam
	G-BOTD	Cameron O-105 balloon	J. Taylor
	G-BOTF	PA-28-151 Warrior	G-BOTF Group
	G-BOTG	Cessna 152 II	Donington Aviation Ltd

Reg.	Type	Owner or Operator	Notes
G-BOTH	Cessna 182Q	P. E. Gethin	
G-BOTI	PA-28-151 Warrior	Falcon Flying Services	
G-BOTK	Cameron O-105 balloon	N. Woodham	
G-BOTN	PA-28-161 Warrior II	Apollo Aviation Advisory	
G-BOTO	Bellanca 7ECA Citabria	G-BOTO Group	
G-BOTP	Cessna 150J	R. F. Finnis & C. P. Williams	
G-BOTU	Piper J-3C-65 Cub	T. L. Giles	
G-BOTV	PA-32RT-300 Lance II	Robin Lance Aviation Association Ltd	
G-BOTW	Cameron V-77 balloon	M. R. Jeynes	
G-BOUE	Cessna 172N	P. Gray & G. N. R. Bradley	
G-BOUF	Cessna 172N	B. P. & M. I. Sneap	
G-BOUJ	Cessna 150M	The UJ Flying Group	
G-BOUK	PA-34-200T Seneca II	C. J. & R. J. Barnes	
G-BOUL	PA-34-200T Seneca II	Oxford Aviation Academy (Oxford) Ltd	
G-BOUM	PA-34-200T Seneca II	Oxford Aviation Academy (Oxford) Ltd	
G-BOUN	Rand-Robinson KR-2	P. J. Brookman	
G-BOUT	Colomban MC.12 Cri-Cri	C. K. Farley	
G-BOUV	Bensen B.8MR	L. R. Phillips	
G-BOUZ	Cessna 150G	Atlantic Bridge Aviation Ltd	
G-BOVB	PA-15 Vagabond	J. R. Kimberley	
G-BOVK	PA-28-161 Warrior II	Tayside Aviation Ltd	
G-BOVU	Stoddard-Hamilton Glasair III	B. R. Chaplin	
G-BOVX	Hughes 269C	Arrow Aviation Services Ltd	
G-BOWB	Cameron V-77 balloon	R. A. Benham	
G-BOWE	PA-34-200T Seneca II	Oxford Aviation Academy (Oxford) Ltd	
G-BOWM	Cameron V-56 balloon	R. S. Breakwell	
G-BOWN	PA-12 Super Cruiser	T. L. Giles	
G-BOWO	Cessna R.182	P. E. Crees (G-BOTR)	
G-BOWP	Jodel D.120A	T. E. Cummins	
G-BOWV	Cameron V-65 balloon	R. A. Harris	
G-BOWY	PA-28RT-201T Turbo Arrow IV	J. S. Develin & Z. Islam	
G-BOXA	PA-28-161 Warrior II	Channel Islands Aero Club (Jersey) Ltd	
G-BOXC	PA-28-161 Warrior II	Bravo Aviation Ltd	
G-BOXG	Cameron O-77 balloon	Associazione Sportiva Dilettantistica Billy Farm-Cico Farm	
G-BOXH	Pitts S-1S Special	G. R. Cotterell	
G-BOXJ	Piper J-3C-65 Cub (479897)	A. Bendkowski	
G-BOXR	GA-7 Cougar	London School of Flying Ltd	
G-BOXT	Hughes 269C	Goldenfly Ltd	
G-BOXU	AA-5B Tiger	A. Vaicvenas	
G-BOXV	Pitts S-1S Special	C. Waddington	
G-BOXW	Cassutt Racer Srs IIIM	D. I. Johnson	
G-BOYB	Cessna A.152	Modi Aviation Ltd	
G-BOYC	Robinson R22 Beta	Yorkshire Helicopters	
G-BOYF	Sikorsky S-76B	Darley Stud Management Co Ltd	
G-BOYH	PA-28-151 Warrior	R. Nightingale	
G-BOYI	PA-28-161 Warrior II	G-BOYI Group	
G-BOYL	Cessna 152 II	Redhill Air Services Ltd	
G-BOYM	Cameron O-84 balloon	M. P. Ryan	
G-BOYO	Cameron V-20 balloon	J. L. Hilditch & T. Ward	
G-BOYP	Cessna 172N	I. D. & D. Brierley	
G-BOYV	PA-28R-201T Turbo Arrow III	N. Halsall	
G-BOYX	Robinson R22 Beta	R. Towle	
G-BOZI	PA-28-161 Warrior II	Aerolease Ltd	
G-BOZN	Cameron N-77 balloon	Calarel Developments Ltd	
G-BOZO	AA-5B Tiger	J. Willis	
G-BOZR	Cessna 152 II	Adam Russell Ltd	
G-BOZS	Pitts S-1C Special	S. D. Blakey	
G-BOZV	CEA DR.340 Major	C. J. Turner & S. D. Kent	
G-BOZW	Bensen B.8M	M. E. Wills	
G-BOZY	Cameron RTW-120 balloon	Magical Adventures Ltd	
G-BOZZ	AA-5B Tiger	Dolphin Property (Management) Ltd	
G-BPAA	Acro Advanced	B. O. & F. A. Smith	
G-BPAB	Cessna 150M	A. Carter & S. Storry	
G-BPAF	PA-28-161 Warrior II	S. T. & T. W. Gilbert	
G-BPAJ	DH.82A Tiger Moth	P. A. Jackson (G-AOIX)	
G-BPAL	DHC.1 Chipmunk 22 (WG350)	K. F. & P. Tomsett (G-BCYE)	
G-BPAW	Cessna 150M	G-BPAW Group	
G-BPAY	PA-28-181 Archer II	H. Merkado	
G-BPBJ	Cessna 152 II	W. Shaw & P. G. Haines	

Notes	Reg.	Type	Owner or Operator
	G-BPBK	Cessna 152 II	Swiftair Maintenance Ltd
	G-BPBM	PA-28-161 Warrior II	Redhill Air Services Ltd
	G-BPBO	PA-28RT-201T Turbo Arrow IV	G. N. Broom & T. R. Lister
	G-BPBP	Brügger MB.2 Colibri	D. A. Preston
	G-BPCA	BN-2B-26 Islander	Loganair Ltd (G-BLNX)
	G-BPCF	Piper J-3C-65 Cub	B. M. O'Brien
	G-BPCI	Cessna R.172K	N. A. Bairstol
	G-BPCK	PA-28-161 Warrior II	Compton Abbas Airfield Ltd
	G-BPCL	SA Bulldog Srs 120/128 (HKG-6)	Isohigh Ltd
	G-BPCR	Mooney M.20K	T. & R. Harris
	G-BPCX	PA-28-236 Dakota	Blue Yonder Aviation Ltd
	G-BPDE	Colt 56A balloon	J. E. Weidema/Netherlands
	G-BPDJ	Chris Tena Mini Coupe	J. J. Morrissey
	G-BPDM	CASA 1.131E Jungmann 2000(781-32)	J. D. Haslam
	G-BPDT	PA-28-161 Warrior II	Channel Islands Aero Club (Jersey) Ltd
	G-BPDV	Pitts S-1S Special	G-BPDV Syndicate
	G-BPEM	Cessna 150K	D. Wright
	G-BPEO	Cessna 152 II	Swiftair Maintenance Ltd
	G-BPES	PA-38-112 Tomahawk II	Sherwood Flying Club Ltd
	G-BPEZ	Colt 77A balloon	J. W. Adkins
	G-BPFC	Mooney M.20C	MCT Agentur GmbH/Germany
	G-BPFD	Jodel D.112	M. & S. Mills
	G-BPFH	PA-28-161 Warrior II	M. H. Kleiser
	G-BPFI	PA-28-181 Archer II	F. Teagle
	G-BPFL	Davis DA-2	P. E. Barker
	G-BPFM	Aeronca 7AC Champion	D. Boyce
	G-BPFZ	Cessna 152 II	Devon and Somerset Flight Training Ltd
	G-BPGC	Air Command 532 Elite	A. G. W. Davis
	G-BPGD	Cameron V-65 balloon	Gone With The Wind Ltd
	G-BPGE	Cessna U.206C	Scottish Parachute Club
	G-BPGH	EAA Acro Sport II	R. Clark & A. C. May
	G-BPGK	Aeronca 7AC Champion	D. A. Crompton & G. C. Holmes
	G-BPGT	Colt AS-80 Mk II airship	P. Porati/Italy
	G-BPGU	PA-28-181 Archer II	G. Underwood
	G-BPGZ	Cessna 150G	J. B. Scott
	G-BPHG	Robin DR.400/180	B. Brenton
	G-BPHH	Cameron V-77 balloon	C. D. Aindow
	G-BPHI	PA-38-112 Tomahawk	Flying Fox Aviation
	G-BPHJ	Cameron V-77 balloon	C. W. Brown
	G-BPHK	Whittaker MW7	J. S. Shufflebottom
	G-BPHL	PA-28-161 Warrior II	J. D. Swales
	G-BPHO	Taylorcraft BC-12	P. A. Durrans
	G-BPHP	Taylorcraft BC-12-65	Bluebird Group
	G-BPHR	DH.82A Tiger Moth (A17-48)	N. Parry
	G-BPHU	Thunder Ax7-77 balloon	R. P. Waite
	G-BPHX	Cessna 140	M. J. Medland
	G-BPHZ	MS.505 Criquet (DM+BK)	Aero Vintage Ltd
	G-BPIF	Bensen-Parsons 2-place gyroplane	B. J. L. P. & W. J. A. L. de Saar
	G-BPII	Denney Kitfox	T. P. Lowe
	G-BPIK	PA-38-112 Tomahawk	Carlisle Flight Training Ltd
	G-BPIP	Slingsby T.31 Motor Cadet III	V. K. Meers
	G-BPIR	Scheibe SF.25E Super Falke	A. P. Askwith
	G-BPIT	Robinson R22 Beta	NA Air Ltd
	G-BPIU	PA-28-161 Warrior II	Golf India Uniform Group
	G-BPIV	B.149 Bolingbroke Mk IVT (R3821)	Blenheim (Duxford) Ltd
	G-BPIZ	AA-5B Tiger	D. A. Horsley
	G-BPJG	PA-18 Super Cub 150	M. W. Stein
	G-BPJK	Colt 77A balloon	P. Lavelle
	G-BPJS	PA-28-161 Cadet	Redhill Air Services Ltd
	G-BPJW	Cessna A.150K	G. Duck
	G-BPJZ	Cameron O-160 balloon	M. L. Gabb
	G-BPKF	Grob G.115	Swiftair Maintenance Ltd
	G-BPKK	Denney Kitfox Mk 1	D. Fahy
	G-BPKM	PA-28-161 Warrior II	Pure Aviation Support Services Ltd
	G-BPKT	Piper J.5A Cub Cruiser	A. J. Greenslade
	G-BPLH	Jodel DR.1051	C. K. Farley
	G-BPLM	AIA Stampe SV.4C	C. J. Jesson
	G-BPLO	BN-2T Turbine Islander	Islander Aircraft Ltd (G-CYPP)
	G-BPLV	Cameron V-77 balloon	V. Grenier/France
	G-BPLZ	Hughes 369HS	M. A. & R. J. Fawcett
	G-BPME	Cessna 152 II	Hinde Holdings Ltd

Reg.	Type	Owner or Operator	Notes
G-BPMF	PA-28-151 Warrior	Mike Foxtrot Group	
G-BPML	Cessna 172M	N. A. Bilton	
G-BPMM	Champion 7ECA Citabria	H. J. Taggart	
G-BPMU	Nord 3202B	E. C. Murgatroyd (G-BIZJ)	
G-BPMW	QAC Quickie Q.2	P. M. Wright (G-OICI/G-OGKN)	
G-BPMX	ARV Super 2	R. A. Collins	
G-BPNI	Robinson R22 Beta	Patriot Flight Training Ltd	
G-BPNO	Zlin Z.326 Trener Master	J. A. S. Bailey & S. T. Logan	
G-BPOA	Gloster Meteor T.7 (WF877) ★	39 Restoration Group	
G-BPOB	Sopwith Camel F.1 (replica) (B2458:R)	Flying Aces Movie Aircraft Collection	
G-BPOM	PA-28-161 Warrior II	POM Flying Group	
G-BPOS	Cessna 150M	Hull Aero Club Ltd	
G-BPOT	PA-28-181 Archer II	P. S. Simpson	
G-BPOU	Luscombe 8A Silvaire	J. L. Grayer	
G-BPPE	PA-38-112 Tomahawk	First Air Ltd	
G-BPPF	PA-38-112 Tomahawk	Bristol Strut Flying Group	
G-BPPJ	Cameron A-180 balloon	D. J. Farrar	
G-BPPK	PA-28-151 Warrior	Praxys Ltd	
G-BPPO	Luscombe 8A Silvaire	P. Dyer	
G-BPPP	Cameron V-77 balloon	Sarnia Balloon Group	
G-BPPZ	Taylorcraft BC-12D	G. C. Smith	
G-BPRA	Aeronca 11AC Chief	C. S. Tolchard	
G-BPRC	Cameron 77 Elephant SS balloon	A. Schneider/Germany	
G-BPRD	Pitts S-1C Special	Parrot Aerobatic Group	
G-BPRI	AS.355F1 Twin Squirrel	MW Helicopters Ltd (G-TVPA)	
G-BPRJ	AS.355F1 Twin Squirrel	PLM Dollar Group Ltd	
G-BPRL	AS.355F1 Twin Squirrel	MW Helicopters Ltd	
G-BPRM	Cessna F.172L	BJ Aviation Ltd (G-AZKG)	
G-BPRX	Aeronca 11AC Chief	J. E. S. Turner	
G-BPRY	PA-28-161 Warrior II	White Wings Aviation Ltd	
G-BPSH	Cameron V-77 balloon	P. G. Hossack	
G-BPSJ	Thunder Ax6-56 balloon	V. Hyland	
G-BPSL	Cessna 177	K. S. Herbert	
G-BPSO	Cameron N-90 balloon	J. Oberprieler/Germany	
G-BPSR	Cameron V-77 balloon	K. J. A. Maxwell	
G-BPTA	Stinson 108-2	M. L. Ryan	
G-BPTD	Cameron V-77 balloon	J. Lippett	
G-BPTE	PA-28-181 Archer II	J. S. Develin & Z. Islam	
G-BPTG	Rockwell Commander 112TC	B. Ogunyemi	
G-BPTI	SOCATA TB20 Trinidad	N. Davis	
G-BPTL	Cessna 172N	P. E. Smeeth	
G-BPTS	CASA 1.131E Jungmann 1000 (E3B-153:781-75)	E. P. Parkin	
G-BPTU	Cessna 152	A. M. Alam	
G-BPTV	Bensen B.8	C. Munro	
G-BPTZ	Robinson R22 Beta	Kuki Helicopter Sales Ltd and S. J. Nicholls	
G-BPUA	EAA Sport Biplane	E. J. & M. P. Hill	
G-BPUB	Cameron V-31 balloon	M. T. Evans	
G-BPUF	Thunder Ax6-56Z balloon	R. C. & M. A. Trimble (G-BHRL)	
G-BPUL	PA-18 Super Cub 150	C. D. Duthy-James & B. M. Reed	
G-BPUM	Cessna R.182RG	R. C. Chapman	
G-BPUP	Whittaker MW7	J. H. Beard	
G-BPUR	Piper J-3L-65 Cub (379994 52/J)	G. R. J. Caunter	
G-BPUU	Cessna 140	D. R. Speight	
G-BPUW	Colt 90A balloon	S. Sonnenberg/Germany	
G-BPVA	Cessna 172F	South Lancashire Flyers Group	
G-BPVE	Bleriot IX (replica) (1) ★	Bianchi Aviation Film Services Ltd/Booker	
G-BPVH	Cub Aircraft J-3C-65 Prospector	D. E. Cooper-Maguire	
G-BPVI	PA-32R-301 Saratoga SP	M. T. Coppen	
G-BPVK	Varga 2150A Kachina	D. W. Parfrey	
G-BPVM	Cameron V-77 balloon	J. Dyer	
G-BPVN	PA-32R-301T Turbo Saratoga SP	O. Green	
G-BPVO	Cassutt Racer IIIM	K. P. Rusling	
G-BPVW	CASA 1.131E Jungmann 2000	C. & J-W. Labeij/Netherlands	
G-BPVZ	Luscombe 8E Silvaire	S. M. Thomas & A. P. Wilkie	
G-BPWB	Sikorsky S-61N	Bristow Helicopters Ltd/HM Coastguard	
G-BPWC	Cameron V-77 balloon	R. F. Davey	
G-BPWE	PA-28-161 Warrior II	RPR Associates Ltd	
G-BPWG	Cessna 150M	GB Pilots Wilsford Group	
G-BPWI	Bell 206B JetRanger 3	Ridgway Aviation Ltd	
G-BPWK	Sportavia Fournier RF-5B	G-BPWK Flying Group	

Notes	Reg.	Type	Owner or Operator
	G-BPWL	PA-25 Pawnee 235	M. H. Sims
	G-BPWM	Cessna 150L	P. D. Button
	G-BPWN	Cessna 150L	A. J. & N. J. Bissex
	G-BPWP	Rutan LongEz (modified)	D. A. Field
	G-BPWR	Cessna R.172K	J. A. & D. T. A. Rees
	G-BPWS	Cessna 172P	Chartstone Ltd
	G-BPXA	PA-28-181 Archer II	Cherokee Flying Group
	G-BPXE	Enstrom 280C Shark	A. Healy
	G-BPXJ	PA-28RT-201T Turbo Arrow IV	J. & M. Holubecki-France
	G-BPXX	PA-34-200T Seneca II	Yorkshire Aviation Ltd
	G-BPYJ	Wittman W.8 Tailwind	J. P. & Y. Mills
	G-BPYK	Thunder Ax7-77 balloon	P. J. Waller
	G-BPYL	Hughes 369D	Morcorp (BVI) Ltd
	G-BPYN	Piper J-3C-65 Cub	The Aquila Group
	G-BPYR	PA-31-310 Turbo Navajo	Excel Aviation Ltd
	G-BPYS	Cameron O-77 balloon	D. J. Goldsmith
	G-BPYT	Cameron V-77 balloon	M. H. Redman
	G-BPYY	Cameron A-180 balloon	G. D. Fitzpatrick
	G-BPZA	Luscombe 8A Silvaire	M. J. Wright
	G-BPZB	Cessna 120	Cessna 120 Group
	G-BPZC	Luscombe 8A Silvaire	C. C. & J. M. Lovell
	G-BPZD	SNCAN NC.858S	Zula Delta Syndicate
	G-BPZE	Luscombe 8E Silvaire	M. A. Watts
	G-BPZM	PA-28RT-201 Arrow IV	Airways Flight Training (Exeter) Ltd (G-ROYW/G-CRTI)
	G-BPZY	Pitts S-1C Special	J. S. Mitchell
	G-BPZZ	Thunder Ax8-105 balloon	Capricorn Balloons Ltd
	G-BRAA	Pitts S-1C Special	R. J. Hodder
	G-BRAK	Cessna 172N	Falcon Flying Services Ltd
	G-BRAM	Mikoyan MiG-21PF (503) ★	FAST Museum/Farnborough
	G-BRAR	Aeronca 7AC Champion	R. B. Armitage
	G-BRBA	PA-28-161 Warrior II	C. Bonello & W. Richens
	G-BRBC	NA T-6G Texan	A. P. Murphy
	G-BRBD	PA-28-151 Warrior	G. Bowen
	G-BRBE	PA-28-161 Warrior II	KN Singles and Twins Aviation
	G-BRBG	PA-28 Cherokee 180	P. M. Carter
	G-BRBH	Cessna 150H	J. Maffia & H. Merkado
	G-BRBI	Cessna 172N	Skyhawk Flying Group
	G-BRBJ	Cessna 172M	N. Foster
	G-BRBK	Robin DR.400/180	A. Friday
	G-BRBL	Robin DR.400/180	Upavon Chipmunk Group
	G-BRBM	Robin DR.400/180	R. W. Davies
	G-BRBN	Pitts S-1S Special	G-BRBN Flying Group
	G-BRBO	Cameron V-77 balloon	M. B. Murby
	G-BRBP	Cessna 152	The Pilot Centre Ltd
	G-BRBV	Piper J-4A Cub Coupe	P. Clarke
	G-BRBW	PA-28 Cherokee 140	Air Navigation and Trading Co Ltd
	G-BRBX	PA-28-181 Archer II	Trent 199 Flying Group
	G-BRCA	Jodel D.112	R. C. Jordan
	G-BRCE	Pitts S-1C Special	M. P. & S. T. Barnard
	G-BRCJ	Cameron H-20 balloon	P. A. Sweatman
	G-BRCM	Cessna 172L	S. G. E. Plessis & D. C. C. Handley
	G-BRCO	Cameron H-20 balloon	P. Lawman
	G-BRCT	Denney Kitfox Mk 2	M. L. Roberts
	G-BRCV	Aeronca 7AC Champion	P. I. and D. M. Morgans
	G-BRCW	Aeronca 11AC Chief	R. B. Griffin
	G-BRDD	Avions Mudry CAP-10B	T. A. Smith
	G-BRDF	PA-28-161 Warrior II	White Waltham Airfield Ltd
	G-BRDG	PA-28-161 Warrior II	Falcon Flying Services
	G-BRDJ	Luscombe 8A Silvaire	G-BRDJ Group
	G-BRDM	PA-28-161 Warrior II	White Waltham Airfield Ltd
	G-BRDO	Cessna 177B	Cardinal Aviation
	G-BRDT	Cameron DP-70 airship	Balloon Promotion SAS
	G-BRDV	Viking Wood Products Spitfire Prototype replica (K5054) ★	Solent Sky, Southampton
	G-BRDW	PA-24 Comanche 180	I. P. Gibson
	G-BREA	Bensen B.8MR	D. J. Martin
	G-BREB	Piper J-3C-65 Cub	J. R. Wraight
	G-BREH	Cameron V-65 balloon	S. E. & V. D. Hurst
	G-BREL	Cameron O-77 balloon	R. A. Patey

Reg.	Type	Owner or Operator	Notes
G-BREP	PA-28RT-201 Arrow IV	Westbeach Aviation Ltd	
G-BRER	Aeronca 7AC Champion	R. N. R. Bellamy	
G-BREU	Montgomerie-Bensen B.8MR	J. S. Firth	
G-BREX	Cameron O-84 balloon	W. S. Calvert	
G-BREY	Taylorcraft BC-12D	BREY Group	
G-BREZ	Cessna 172M	L. A. Mills	
G-BRFB	Rutan LongEz	A. R. Oliver	
G-BRFC	Percival P.57 Sea Prince T.Mk.1 (WP321)	M. A. Stott	
G-BRFF	Colt 90A balloon	Amber Valley Aviation	
G-BRFI	Aeronca 7DC Champion	A. C. Lines	
G-BRFJ	Aeronca 11AC Chief	J. M. Mooney	
G-BRFL	PA-38-112 Tomahawk	A. D. Pocock	
G-BRFM	PA-28-161 Warrior II	Westbeach Aviation Ltd	
G-BRFO	Cameron V-77 balloon	Hedge Hoppers Balloon Group	
G-BRFW	Montgomerie-Bensen B.8 2-seat	A. J. Barker	
G-BRFX	Pazmany PL.4A	D. E. Hills	
G-BRGD	Cameron O-84 balloon	P. A. Davies	
G-BRGE	Cameron N-90 balloon	Oakfield Farm Products Ltd	
G-BRGF	Luscombe 8E Silvaire	Luscombe Flying Group	
G-BRGI	PA-28 Cherokee 180	R. A. Buckfield	
G-BRGT	PA-32 Cherokee Six 260	D. A. Hitchcock	
G-BRGW	Gardan GY-201 Minicab	R. G. White	
G-BRHA	PA-32RT-300 Lance II	Lance G-BRHA Group	
G-BRHO	PA-34-200 Seneca	Andrews Professional Colour Laboratories Ltd	
G-BRHP	Aeronca O-58B Grasshopper (31923)	R. B. McComish & C. J. Willis	
G-BRHR	PA-38-112 Tomahawk	D. C. Hanss	
G-BRHX	Luscombe 8E Silvaire	J. Lakin	
G-BRHY	Luscombe 8E Silvaire	R. A. Keech	
G-BRIE	Cameron N-77 balloon	S. F. Redman	
G-BRIH	Taylorcraft BC-12D	M. J. Medland	
G-BRIJ	Taylorcraft F-19	M. W. Oliver	
G-BRIK	T.66 Nipper 3	Clipgate Nipper Group	
G-BRIL	Piper J-5A Cub Cruiser	D. J. Bone	
G-BRIO	Turner Super T-40A	S. Bidwell	
G-BRIV	SOCATA TB9 Tampico Club	S. J. Taft	
G-BRIY	Taylorcraft DF-65 (42-58678:IY)	S. R. Potts	
G-BRJA	Luscombe 8A Silvaire	A. D. Keen	
G-BRJC	Cessna 120	C. R. White	
G-BRJK	Luscombe 8A Silvaire	C. J. L. Peat & M. Richardson	
G-BRJL	PA-15 Vagabond	A. R. Williams	
G-BRJN	Pitts S-1C Special	W. Chapel	
G-BRJX	PA-28-161 Cadet	Northumbria Flying School Ltd	
G-BRJX	Rand-Robinson KR-2	J. R. Bell	
G-BRJY	Rand-Robinson KR-2	R. E. Taylor	
G-BRKC	Auster J/1 Autocrat	J. W. Conlon	
G-BRKH	PA-28-236 Dakota	T. A. White	
G-BRKR	Cessna 182R	A. R. D. Brooker	
G-BRKW	Cameron V-77 balloon	T. J. Parker	
G-BRKY	Viking Dragonfly Mk II	G. D. Price	
G-BRLB	Air Command 532 Elite	F. G. Shepherd	
G-BRLF	Campbell Cricket (replica)	J. L. G. McLane	
G-BRLG	PA-28RT-201T Turbo Arrow IV	LG Group	
G-BRLI	Piper J-5A Cub Cruiser	D. J. M. Eardley	
G-BRLL	Cameron A-105 balloon	P. A. Sweatman	
G-BRLO	PA-38-112 Tomahawk	Durham Tees Flight Training Ltd	
G-BRLP	PA-38-112 Tomahawk	Highland Aviation Training Ltd	
G-BRLR	Cessna 150G	Blue Skys Aviation (NE) Ltd	
G-BRLS	Thunder Ax7-77 balloon	J. R. Palmer	
G-BRMA	WS-51 Dragonfly HR.5 (WG719) ★	IHM/Weston-super-Mare	
G-BRMB	B.192 Belvedere HC.1	IHM/Weston-super-Mare	
G-BRME	PA-28-181 Archer II	Blue Sky Investments Ltd	
G-BRML	PA-38-112 Tomahawk	J. S. Willcocks	
G-BRMT	Cameron V-31 balloon	B. Reed	
G-BRMU	Cameron V-77 balloon	A. P. Wallace	
G-BRMV	Cameron O-77 balloon	P. D. Griffiths	
G-BRNC	Cessna 150M	Penny Hydraulics Ltd	
G-BRND	Cessna 152 II	T. M. & M. L. Jones	
G-BRNE	Cessna 152 II	Redhill Air Services Ltd	
G-BRNK	Cessna 152 II	D. C. & M. Bonsall	
G-BRNN	Cessna 152 II	Eastern Air Executive Ltd	

Notes	Reg.	Type	Owner or Operator
	G-BRNT	Robin DR.400/180	C. E. Ponsford & ptnrs
	G-BRNU	Robin DR.400/180	November Uniform Travel Syndicate Ltd
	G-BRNV	PA-28-181 Archer II	J.J. Beall
	G-BRNW	Cameron V-77 balloon	N. Robertson & G. Smith
	G-BRNX	PA-22 Tri-Pacer 150	S. N. Askey
	G-BROE	Cameron N-65 balloon	A. I. Attwood
	G-BROG	Cameron V-65 balloon	R. Kunert
	G-BROJ	Colt 31A balloon	N. J. Langley
	G-BROO	Luscombe 8E Silvaire	P. R. Bush
	G-BROR	Piper J-3C-65 Cub	White Hart Flying Group
	G-BROX	Robinson R22 Beta	Pheonix Helicopter Academy Ltd
	G-BROY	Cameron V-77 balloon	J. Dyer
	G-BROZ	PA-18 Super Cub 150	P. G. Kynsey
	G-BRPE	Cessna 120	W. B. Bateson
	G-BRPF	Cessna 120	G. A. Robson
	G-BRPG	Cessna 120	I. C. Lomax
	G-BRPH	Cessna 120	J. A. Cook & C. J. Richardson
	G-BRPK	PA-28 Cherokee 140	G-BRPK Group
	G-BRPL	PA-28-140 Cherokee	British NorthWest Airways Ltd
	G-BRPM	T.66 Nipper 3	J. H. H. Turner
	G-BRPP	Brookland Hornet (modified)	B. J. L. P. & W. J. A. L. de Saar
	G-BRPR	Aeronca O-58B Grasshopper (31952)	A. F. Kutz
	G-BRPS	Cessna 177B	E. Janssen & A. Lietaert
	G-BRPT	Rans S.10 Sakota	J. A. Harris
	G-BRPV	Cessna 152	Eastern Air Executive Ltd
	G-BRPX	Taylorcraft BC-12D	G-BRPX Group
	G-BRPY	PA-15 Vagabond	J. & V. Hobday
	G-BRPZ	Luscombe 8A Silvaire	C. A. Flint
	G-BRRA	VS.361 Spitfire LF.IX	P. M. Andrews
	G-BRRB	Luscombe 8E Silvaire	J. Nicholls
	G-BRRF	Cameron O-77 balloon	K. P. & G. J. Storey
	G-BRRK	Cessna 182Q	Werewolf Aviation Ltd
	G-BRRR	Cameron V-77 balloon	K. P. & G. J. Storey
	G-BRRU	Colt 90A balloon	Reach For The Sky Ltd
	G-BRRY	Robinson R22 Beta	Swift Helicopter Services Ltd
	G-BRSA	Cameron N-56 balloon	O. J. Webb
	G-BRSD	Cameron V-77 balloon	M. E. Granger
	G-BRSF	VS.361 Spitfire HF.9c (RR232)	M. B. Phillips
	G-BRSL	Cameron N-56 balloon	S. Budd
	G-BRSP	Air Command 532 Elite	G. M. Hobman
	G-BRSW	Luscombe 8A Silvaire	Bloody Mary Aviation
	G-BRSX	PA-15 Vagabond	M. R. Holden
	G-BRSY	Hatz CB-1	Eaglescott Hatz Biplane Group
	G-BRTD	Cessna 152 II	152 Group
	G-BRTJ	Cessna 150F	A. Kinnaird
	G-BRTL	Hughes 369E	Road Tech Computer Systems Ltd
	G-BRTP	Cessna 152 II	R. Lee
	G-BRTT	Schweizer 269C	Fairthorpe Ltd
	G-BRTV	Cameron O-77 balloon	S. D. Wrighton
	G-BRTW	Glaser-Dirks DG.400	I. J. Carruthers
	G-BRTX	PA-28-151 Warrior	Brinkley (Meppershall) Ltd
	G-BRUB	PA-28-161 Warrior II	Flytrek Ltd
	G-BRUD	PA-28-181 Archer II	J. Frodsham
	G-BRUG	Luscombe 8E Silvaire	N. W. Barratt
	G-BRUJ	Boeing Stearman A.75N1 (6136:205)	Stamp Aviation Ltd
	G-BRUM	Cessna A.152	A. J. Gomes
	G-BRUN	Cessna 120	A. R. M. Eagle, J. A. Longworth & J. Peake (G-BRDH)
	G-BRUO	Taylor JT.1 Monoplane	S. T. S. Bygrave
	G-BRUV	Cameron V-77 balloon	T. W. & R. F. Benbrook
	G-BRUX	PA-44-180 Seminole	M. Ali
	G-BRVB	Stolp SA.300 Starduster Too	J. K. Cook
	G-BRVE	Beech D.17S	Patina Ltd
	G-BRVF	Colt 77A balloon	J. Adkins
	G-BRVG	NA SNJ-7 Texan (27)	D. Gilmour/Intrepid Aviation Co
	G-BRVH	Smyth Model S Sidewinder	B. D. Deleporte
	G-BRVI	Robinson R22 Beta	York Helicopters
	G-BRVJ	Slingsby T.31 Motor Cadet III	B. Outhwaite
	G-BRVL	Pitts S-1C Special	M. F. Pocock
	G-BRVN	Thunder Ax7-77 balloon	D. L. Beckwith
	G-BRVO	AS.350B Ecureuil	Rotorhire LLP

Reg.	Type	Owner or Operator	Notes
G-BRVZ	Jodel D.117	L. Holland	
G-BRWA	Aeronca 7AC Champion	J. R. Edwards	
G-BRWB	NA T-6G Texan (526)	R. Clifford	
G-BRWD	Robinson R22 Beta	Heli Air Ltd	
G-BRWP	CFM Streak Shadow	T. McDonald	
G-BRWR	Aeronca 11AC Chief	A. W. Crutcher	
G-BRWT	Scheibe SF.25C Falke	Booker Gliding Club Ltd	
G-BRWU	Luton LA-4A Minor	R. B. Webber	
G-BRWV	Brügger MB.2 Colibri	M. P. Wakem	
G-BRWX	Cessna 172P	R. A. Brown & A. C. Dove	
G-BRXA	Cameron O-120 balloon	R. J. Mansfield	
G-BRXD	PA-28-181 Archer II	R. C. G. Lywood	
G-BRXE	Taylorcraft BC-12D	B. T. Morgan & W. J. Durrad	
G-BRXF	Aeronca 11AC Chief	Aeronca Flying Group	
G-BRXG	Aeronca 7AC Champion	X-Ray Golf Flying Group	
G-BRXH	Cessna 120	BRXH Group	
G-BRXL	Aeronca 11AC Chief (42-78044)	P. L. Green	
G-BRXP	SNCAN Stampe SV.4C (modified)	T. Brown	
G-BRXS	Howard Special T Minus	F. A. Bakir	
G-BRXU	Aerospatiale AS.332L Super Puma	Bristow Helicopters Ltd	
G-BRXV	Robinson R22 Beta	Patriot Flight Taining Ltd	
G-BRXW	PA-24 Comanche 260	Oak Group	
G-BRXY	Pietenpol Air Camper	P. S. Ganczakowski	
G-BRZA	Cameron O-77 balloon	S. Nother	
G-BRZB	Cameron A-105 balloon	Headland Services Ltd	
G-BRZD	Hapi Cygnet SF-2A	C. I. Coghill	
G-BRZG	Enstrom F-28A	Duxburys Ltd	
G-BRZK	Stinson 108-2	Stunning Stinson	
G-BRZL	Pitts S-1D Special	T. R. G. Barnby	
G-BRZS	Cessna 172P	YP Flying Group	
G-BRZW	Rans S.10 Sakota	D. L. Davies	
G-BRZX	Pitts S-1S Special	Zulu Xray Group	
G-BRZZ	Streak Shadow	A. J. Thomas	
G-BSAI	Stoddard-Hamilton Glasair III	K. J. & P. J. Whitehead	
G-BSAJ	CASA 1.131E Jungmann 2000	P. G. Kynsey	
G-BSAK	Colt 21A balloon	M. D. Mitchell	
G-BSAS	Cameron V-65 balloon	P. Donkin	
G-BSAV	Thunder Ax7-77 balloon	I. G. & C. A. Lloyd	
G-BSAW	PA-28-161 Warrior II	Compton Abbas Airfield Ltd	
G-BSAZ	Denney Kitfox Mk 2	A. J. Lloyd	
G-BSBA	PA-28-161 Warrior II	Falcon Flying Services Ltd	
G-BSBG	CCF Harvard IV (20310:310)	A. P. St. John	
G-BSBI	Cameron O-77 balloon	D. M. Billing	
G-BSBM	Cameron N-77 balloon	K. F. Lowry	
G-BSBR	Cameron V-77 balloon	R. P. Wade	
G-BSBT	Piper J-3C-65 Cub	A. R. Elliott	
G-BSBV	Rans S.10 Sakota	S. Bain	
G-BSBW	Bell 206B JetRanger 3	Castle Air Ltd	
G-BSCC	Colt 105A balloon	A. F. Selby	
G-BSCE	Robinson R22 Beta	Carpets Direct (GB) Ltd	
G-BSCG	Denney Kitfox Mk 2	A. Levitt	
G-BSCH	Denney Kitfox Mk 2	G. R. Moore	
G-BSCI	Colt 77A balloon	S. C. Kinsey	
G-BSCK	Cameron H-24 balloon	J. D. Shapland	
G-BSCM	Denney Kitfox Mk 2	H. D. Colliver (G-MSCM)	
G-BSCN	SOCATA TB20 Trinidad	B. W. Dye	
G-BSCO	Thunder Ax7-77 balloon	F. J. Whalley	
G-BSCP	Cessna 152 II	Moray Flying Club (1990) Ltd	
G-BSCS	PA-28-181 Archer II	Wingtask 1995 Ltd	
G-BSCV	PA-28-161 Warrior II	Southwood Flying Group	
G-BSCW	Taylorcraft BC-65	G. Johnson	
G-BSCX	Thunder Ax8-105 balloon	S. Charlish	
G-BSCY	PA-28-151 Warrior	Take Flight Aviation Ltd	
G-BSCZ	Cessna 152 II	The RAF Halton Aeroplane Club Ltd	
G-BSDA	Taylorcraft BC-12D	A. D. Pearce	
G-BSDD	Denney Kitfox Mk 2	D. C. Crawley	
G-BSDH	Robin DR.400/180	G-BSDH Group	
G-BSDK	Piper J-5A Cub Cruiser	J. E. Mead	
G-BSDL	SOCATA TB10 Tobago	Delta Lima Flying Group	
G-BSDN	PA-34-200T Seneca II	S. J. Green	

Notes	Reg.	Type	Owner or Operator
	G-BSDO	Cessna 152 II	J. Vickers
	G-BSDP	Cessna 152 II	Paul's Planes Ltd
	G-BSDS	Boeing Stearman E75 (118)	L. W. Scattergood
	G-BSDW	Cessna 182P	Parker Diving Ltd
	G-BSDX	Cameron V-77 balloon	G. P. & S. J. Allen
	G-BSDZ	Enstrom 280FX	Rotormotive Ltd
	G-BSEA	Thunder Ax7-77 balloon	Zebedee Balloon Service Ltd
	G-BSED	PA-22 Tri-Pacer 160 (modified)	M. D. N. Fisher
	G-BSEE	Rans S.9	R. P. Hothersall
	G-BSEF	PA-28 Cherokee 180	I. D. Wakeling
	G-BSEJ	Cessna 150M	C. L. Day
	G-BSEL	Slingsby T.61G Super Falke	D. G. Holley
	G-BSER	PA-28 Cherokee 160	Yorkair Ltd
	G-BSEU	PA-28-181 Archer II	K. R. Taylor
	G-BSEV	Cameron O-77 balloon	P. B. Kenington
	G-BSEX	Cameron A-180 balloon	Heart of England Balloons
	G-BSEY	Beech A36 Bonanza	P. Malam-Wilson
	G-BSFA	Aero Designs Pulsar	P. F. Lorriman
	G-BSFD	Piper J-3C-65 Cub	P. E. S. Latham
	G-BSFE	PA-38-112 Tomahawk II	ACS Aviation Ltd
	G-BSFF	Robin DR.400/180R	Lasham Gliding Society Ltd
	G-BSFP	Cessna 152T	The Pilot Centre Ltd
	G-BSFR	Cessna 152 II	Galair Ltd
	G-BSFV	Woods Woody Pusher	W. J. Y. Ronge
	G-BSFW	PA-15 Vagabond	J. R. Kimberley
	G-BSFX	Denney Kitfox Mk 2	F. Colman
	G-BSGB	Gaertner Ax4 Skyranger balloon	B. Gaertner
	G-BSGD	PA-28 Cherokee 180	R. J. Cleverley
	G-BSGF	Robinson R22 Beta	Heliyorks Ltd
	G-BSGG	Denney Kitfox Mk 2	M. D. Gregory
	G-BSGH	Airtour AH-56B balloon	A. R. Hardwick
	G-BSGJ	Monnett Sonerai II	J. L. Loweth
	G-BSGL	PA-28-161 Warrior II	Keywest Air Charter Ltd
	G-BSGP	Cameron N-65 balloon	R. Leslie
	G-BSGS	Rans S.10 Sakota	M. R. Parr
	G-BSGT	Cessna T.210N	E. A. T. Brenninkmeyer
	G-BSHA	PA-34-200T Seneca II	Justgold Ltd
	G-BSHC	Colt 69A balloon	Magical Adventures Ltd
	G-BSHD	Colt 69A balloon	F. W. Ewer
	G-BSHH	Luscombe 8E Silvaire	S. L. Lewis
	G-BSHO	Cameron V-77 balloon	D. J. Duckworth & J. C. Stewart
	G-BSHP	PA-28-161 Warrior II	Multiflight Ltd
	G-BSHR	Cessna F.172N	Deep Cleavage Ltd (G-BFGE)
	G-BSHY	EAA Acro Sport I	R. J. Hodder
	G-BSIC	Cameron V-77 balloon	T. R. Tillson
	G-BSIF	Denney Kitfox Mk 2	S. M. Dougan
	G-BSIG	Colt 21A Cloudhopper balloon	C. J. Dunkley
	G-BSII	PA-34-200T Seneca II	R. L. Burt
	G-BSIJ	Cameron V-77 balloon	G. B. Davies
	G-BSIM	PA-28-181 Archer II	Falcon Flying Services Ltd
	G-BSIO	Cameron 80 Shed SS balloon	R. E. Jones
	G-BSIU	Colt 90A balloon	S. Travaglia/Italy
	G-BSIY	Schleicher ASK.14	P. W. Andrews
	G-BSIZ	PA-28-181 Archer II	P. J. Gerrard & M. J. Cunliffe
	G-BSJU	Cessna 150M	A. C. Williamson
	G-BSJX	PA-28-161 Warrior II	MK Aero Support Ltd
	G-BSJZ	Cessna 150J	M. H. Campbell
	G-BSKA	Cessna 150M	R. J. Cushing
	G-BSKG	Maule MX-7-180	A. J. Lewis
	G-BSKW	PA-28-181 Archer II	R. J. Whyham
	G-BSLA	Robin DR.400/180	A. B. McCoig
	G-BSLH	CASA 1.131E Jungmann 2000	M. A. Warden
	G-BSLK	PA-28-161 Warrior II	R. A. Rose
	G-BSLM	PA-28 Cherokee 160	Chester Flying Club Ltd
	G-BSLT	PA-28-161 Warrior II	L. W. Scattergood
	G-BSLU	PA-28 Cherokee 140	Merseyflight Air Training School
	G-BSLV	Enstrom 280FX	B. M. B Roumier
	G-BSLW	Bellanca 7ECA Citabria	J. S. Flavell
	G-BSLX	WAR Focke-Wulf Fw 190 (replica) (4+)	S. Freeman
	G-BSMD	Nord 1101 Noralpha (+14)	J. W. Hardie
	G-BSME	Bölkow Bö.208C1 Junior	D. J. Hampson

Reg.	Type	Owner or Operator	Notes
G-BSMG	Montgomerie-Bensen B.8M	A. C. Timperley	
G-BSMK	Cameron O-84 balloon	G-BSMK Shareholders	
G-BSMM	Colt 31A balloon	P. Spellward	
G-BSMN	CFM Streak Shadow	P. J. Porter	
G-BSMT	Rans S-10 Sakota	T. D. Wood	
G-BSMU	Rans S.6 Coyote II	W. Parker (G-MWJE)	
G-BSMV	PA-17 Vagabond (modified)	A. Cheriton	
G-BSNE	Luscombe 8E Silvaire	C. B. Buscombe, R. Goldsworthy & G. Vitta	
G-BSNF	Piper J-3C-65 Cub	D. A. Hammant	
G-BSNG	Cessna 172N	A. J. & P. C. MacDonald	
G-BSNJ	Cameron N-90 balloon	D. P. H. Smith/France	
G-BSNT	Luscombe 8A Silvaire	Luscombe Quartet	
G-BSNU	Colt 105A balloon	Gone Ballooning	
G-BSNX	PA-28-181 Archer II	Redhill Air Services Ltd	
G-BSOE	Luscombe 8A Silvaire	R. G. Downhill	
G-BSOF	Colt 25A balloon	J. M. Bailey	
G-BSOG	Cessna 172M	C. Shackleton	
G-BSOJ	Thunder Ax7-77 balloon	R. J. S. Jones	
G-BSOK	PA-28-161 Warrior II	A. Oxenham	
G-BSOM	Glaser-Dirks DG.400	G-BSOM Group	
G-BSON	Green S.25 balloon	J. J. Green	
G-BSOO	Cessna 172F	The Oscar Oscar Group	
G-BSOR	CFM Streak Shadow Srs SA	A. Parr	
G-BSOU	PA-38-112 Tomahawk II	D. J. Campbell	
G-BSOX	Luscombe 8AE Silvaire	B. A. Lanary	
G-BSOZ	PA-28-161 Warrior II	Highland Asset Management Ltd	
G-BSPA	QAC Quickie Q.2	G. V. McKirdy & B. K. Glover	
G-BSPC	Jodel D.140C	B. E. Cotton	
G-BSPE	Cessna F.172P	T. W. Williamson	
G-BSPG	PA-34-200T Seneca II	Andrews Professional Colour Laboratories Ltd	
G-BSPK	Cessna 195A	A. G. & D. L. Bompas	
G-BSPL	CFM Streak Shadow Srs SA	G. L. Turner	
G-BSPN	PA-28R-201T Turbo Arrow III	Wendex Vehicle Rental Ltd	
G-BSRD	Cameron N-105 balloon	A. Ockelmann	
G-BSRH	Pitts S-1C Special	C. D. Swift	
G-BSRI	Lancair 235	P. M. Harrison	
G-BSRK	ARV Super 2	D. Nieman	
G-BSRL	Campbell Cricket Mk.4 gyroplane	M. Brudnicki	
G-BSRP	Rotorway Executive	R. J. Baker	
G-BSRR	Cessna 182Q	C. M. Moore	
G-BSRT	Denney Kitfox Mk 2	M. J. Freeman	
G-BSRX	CFM Streak Shadow	C. M. Webb	
G-BSSA	Luscombe 8E Silvaire	Luscombe Flying Group	
G-BSSB	Cessna 150L	D. T. A. Rees	
G-BSSC	PA-28-161 Warrior II	Sky Blue Flight Training	
G-BSSF	Denney Kitfox Mk 2	F. W. Astbury	
G-BSSI	Rans S.6 Coyote II	J. Currell (G-MWJA)	
G-BSSK	QAC Quickie Q.2	R. Greatrex	
G-BSSP	Robin DR.400/180R	Soaring (Oxford) Ltd	
G-BSST	BAC-Sud Concorde 002 ★	F.A.A. Museum/Yeovilton	
G-BSSV	CFM Streak Shadow	R. W. Payne	
G-BSSW	PA-28-161 Warrior II	Hinton Pilot Flight Training Ltd	
G-BSSY	Polikarpov Po-2	Richard Shuttleworth Trustees	
G-BSTC	Aeronca 11AC Chief	J. Armstrong & D. Lamb	
G-BSTE	AS.355F2 Twin Squirrel	Oscar Mayer Ltd	
G-BSTH	PA-25 Pawnee 235	Scottish Gliding Union Ltd	
G-BSTI	Piper J-3C-65 Cub	J. A. Scott	
G-BSTK	Thunder Ax8-90 balloon	M. Williams	
G-BSTL	Rand-Robinson KR-2	C. S. Hales & N. Brauns	
G-BSTM	Cessna 172L	G-BSTM Group	
G-BSTO	Cessna 152 II	M. A. Stott & S. D. Baker	
G-BSTP	Cessna 152 II	LAC Aircraft Ltd	
G-BSTR	AA-5 Traveler	B. D. Jones	
G-BSTT	Rans S.6 Coyote II	D. G. Palmer	
G-BSTX	Luscombe 8A Silvaire	C. Chambers	
G-BSTZ	PA-28 Cherokee 140	Air Navigation & Trading Co Ltd	
G-BSUA	Rans S.6 Coyote II	A. J. Todd	
G-BSUB	Colt 77A balloon	F. W. Ewer	
G-BSUD	Luscombe 8A Silvaire	Luscombe Quartet	
G-BSUF	PA-32RT-300 Lance II	P. Muller	
G-BSUK	Colt 77A balloon	A. J. Moore	

Notes	Reg.	Type	Owner or Operator
	G-BSUO	Scheibe SF.25C Falke	Portmoak Falke Syndicate
	G-BSUU	Colt 180A balloon	British School of Ballooning
	G-BSUV	Cameron O-77 balloon	J. F. Trehern
	G-BSUW	PA-34-200T Seneca II	NPD Direct Ltd
	G-BSUX	Carlson Sparrow II	D. Harker
	G-BSUZ	Denney Kitfox Mk 3	C. G. Langham
	G-BSVB	PA-28-181 Archer II	Veebee Aviation Ltd
	G-BSVE	Binder CP.301S Smaragd	Smaragd Flying Group
	G-BSVG	PA-28-161 Warrior II	Booker Aircraft Leasing Ltd
	G-BSVH	Piper J-3C-65 Cub	C. R. & K. A. Maher
	G-BSVI	PA-16 Clipper	Clipper Aviation
	G-BSVK	Denney Kitfox Mk 2	C. Cox
	G-BSVM	PA-28-161 Warrior II	EFG Flying Services
	G-BSVN	Thorp T-18	D. H. Howell
	G-BSVP	PA-23-250 Aztec F	S. G. Spier
	G-BSVR	Schweizer 269C	M. K. E. Askham
	G-BSVS	Robin DR.400/100	D. McK. Chalmers
	G-BSWB	Rans S.10 Sakota	F. A. Hewitt
	G-BSWC	Boeing Stearman E75 (112)	Richard Thwaites Aviation Ltd
	G-BSWF	PA-16 Clipper	Durham Clipper Group
	G-BSWG	PA-17 Vagabond	P. E. J. Sturgeon
	G-BSWH	Cessna 152 II	Airspeed Aviation Ltd
	G-BSWI	Rans S.10 Sakota	J. M. Mooney
	G-BSWL	Slingsby T.61F Venture T.2	G-BSWL Group
	G-BSWM	Slingsby T.61F Venture T.2	Venture Gliding Group
	G-BSWR	BN-2T-26 Turbine Islander	Police Service of Northern Ireland
	G-BSWV	Cameron N-77 balloon	S. Charlish
	G-BSWX	Cameron V-90 balloon	B. J. Burrows
	G-BSWY	Cameron N-77 balloon	Nottingham Hot Air Balloon Club
	G-BSXA	PA-28-161 Warrior II	Falcon Flying Services
	G-BSXB	PA-28-161 Warrior II	S. R. Mendes
	G-BSXC	PA-28-161 Warrior II	Cristal Air Ltd
	G-BSXD	Soko P-2 Kraguj (30146)	S. M. Johnston
	G-BSXI	Mooney M.20E	D. H. G. Penney
	G-BSXM	Cameron V-77 balloon	C. A. Oxby
	G-BSXS	PA-28-181 Archer II	A. Klamke
	G-BSYA	Jodel D.18	K. Wright
	G-BSYF	Luscombe 8A Silvaire	V. R. Leggott
	G-BSYG	PA-12 Super Cruiser	Fat Cub Group
	G-BSYH	Luscombe 8A Silvaire	N. R. Osborne
	G-BSYJ	Cameron N-77 balloon	Chubb Fire Ltd
	G-BSYO	Piper J-3C-90 Cub	C. R. Reynolds (G-BSMJ/G-BRHE)
	G-BSYU	Robin DR.400/180	P. D. Smoothy
	G-BSYV	Cessna 150M	E-Plane Ltd
	G-BSYY	PA-28-161 Warrior II	Aerobility
	G-BSYZ	PA-28-161 Warrior II	F. C. P. Hood
	G-BSZB	Stolp SA.300 Starduster Too	D. T. Gethin
	G-BSZC	Beech C-45H (51-11701A:AF258)	K. A. O'Connor
	G-BSZD	Robin DR.400/180	Alfa Flight
	G-BSZF	Jodel DR.250/160	J. B. Randle
	G-BSZG	Stolp SA.100 Starduster	D. F. Chapman
	G-BSZH	Thunder Ax7-77 balloon	T. J. Wilkinson
	G-BSZJ	PA-28-181 Archer II	M. L. A. Pudney & R. D. Fuller
	G-BSZM	Montgomerie-Bensen B.8MR	A. McCredie
	G-BSZO	Cessna 152	A. Jahsanfar
	G-BSZT	PA-28-161 Warrior II	Golf Charlie Echo Ltd
	G-BSZV	Cessna 150F	C. A. Davis
	G-BSZW	Cessna 152	S. T. & T. W. Gilbert
	G-BTAK	EAA Acrosport II	J. Mann
	G-BTAL	Cessna F.152 II	Hertfordshire Aero Club Ltd
	G-BTAM	PA-28-181 Archer II	Tri-Star Farms Ltd
	G-BTAW	PA-28-161 Warrior II	Piper Flying Group
	G-BTAZ	Evans VP-2 ★	Norwich Aviation Museum
	G-BTBA	Robinson R22 Beta	Patriot Flight Training Ltd
	G-BTBB	Thunder Ax8-105 S2 balloon	G. J. Boulden
	G-BTBG	Denney Kitfox Mk 2	N. A. Woodward
	G-BTBH	Ryan ST3KR (854)	R. C. Piper
	G-BTBJ	Cessna 190	P. W. Moorcroft
	G-BTBL	Montgomerie-Bensen B.8MR	AES Radionic Surveillance Systems
	G-BTBU	PA-18 Super Cub 150	Betty Bu Syndicate

Reg.	Type	Owner or Operator	Notes
G-BTBV	Cessna 140	M. J. Medland	
G-BTBW	Cessna 120	C. O. P. Barth	
G-BTBY	PA-17 Vagabond	F. M. Ward	
G-BTCB	Air Command 582 Sport	G. Scurrah	
G-BTCC	Grumman F6F-3 Hellcat (40467:19)	Patina Ltd	
G-BTCD	P-51D-25-NA Mustang (413704:87-H)	Pelham Ltd	
G-BTCE	Cessna 152	S. T. Gilbert	
G-BTCH	Luscombe 8E Silvaire	G-BTCH Flying Group	
G-BTCI	PA-17 Vagabond	T. R. Whittome	
G-BTCJ	Luscombe 8E Silvaire	M. A. Watts	
G-BTCS	Colt 90A balloon	Branded Sky Ltd	
G-BTCZ	Cameron Chateau 84 balloon	Balleroy Developpement SAS	
G-BTDA	Slingsby T.61G Falke	G-BTDA Group	
G-BTDC	Denney Kitfox Mk 2	M. A. Potter	
G-BTDD	CFM Streak Shadow	S. H. Merrony	
G-BTDE	Cessna C-165 Airmaster	R. H. Screen	
G-BTDF	Luscombe 8A Silvaire	G. Johnson	
G-BTDI	Robinson R22	S. Klinge	
G-BTDN	Denney Kitfox Mk 2	M. G. Rummey	
G-BTDR	Aero Designs Pulsar	Screaming Eagles Flying Group	
G-BTDT	CASA 1.131E Jungmann 2000	T. A. Reed	
G-BTDV	PA-28-161 Warrior II	Falcon Flying Services Ltd	
G-BTDW	Cessna 152 II	J. H. Sandham Aviation	
G-BTDZ	CASA 1.131E Jungmann 2000	R. J. & M. Pickin	
G-BTEE	Cameron O-120 balloon	Floating Sensations	
G-BTEL	CFM Streak Shadow	J. E. Eatwell	
G-BTES	Cessna 150H	C. Burt-Brown & G. G. Saint	
G-BTET	Piper J-3C-65 Cub	City of Oxford Flying Group	
G-BTEU	SA.365N-2 Dauphin	Multiflight Ltd	
G-BTEW	Cessna 120	J. H. Milne & T. H. Bishop	
G-BTFA	Denney Kitfox Mk 2	K. R. Peek	
G-BTFC	Cessna F.152 II	Aircraft Engineers Ltd	
G-BTFE	Bensen-Parsons 2-seat gyroplane	D. C. Ellis	
G-BTFG	Boeing Stearman A75N1 (441)	TG Aviation Ltd	
G-BTFJ	PA-15 Vagabond	B. McCready	
G-BTFK	Taylorcraft BC-12D	M. J. Whitwell	
G-BTFL	Aeronca 11AC Chief	BTFL Group	
G-BTFM	Cameron O-105 balloon	Edinburgh University Hot Air Balloon Club	
G-BTFO	PA-28-161 Warrior II	Flyfar Ltd	
G-BTFP	PA-38-112 Tomahawk	Durham Tees Flight Training Ltd	
G-BTFT	Beech 58 Baron	Fastwing Air Charter Ltd	
G-BTFU	Cameron N-90 balloon	J. J. Rudoni & A. C. K. Rawson	
G-BTFV	Whittaker MW7	S. J. Luck	
G-BTFX	Bell 206B JetRanger 2	Amcay Ltd	
G-BTGD	Rand-Robinson KR-2 (modified)	B M. Neary	
G-BTGI	Rearwin 175 Skyranger	J. M. Fforde	
G-BTGJ	Smith DSA-1 Miniplane	G. J. Knowles	
G-BTGL	Light Aero Avid Flyer	J. S. Clair-Quentin	
G-BTGM	Aeronca 7AC Champion	A. J. McLuskie	
G-BTGO	PA-28 Cherokee 140	Demero Ltd & Transcourt Ltd	
G-BTGR	Cessna 152 II	A. J. Gomes	
G-BTGS	Stolp SA.300 Starduster Too	G. N. Elliott & ptnrs (G-AYMA)	
G-BTGT	CFM Streak Shadow	I. Heunis (G-MWPY)	
G-BTGW	Cessna 152 II	Stapleford Flying Club Ltd	
G-BTGX	Cessna 152 II	Stapleford Flying Club Ltd	
G-BTGY	PA-28-161 Warrior II	Stapleford Flying Club Ltd	
G-BTGZ	PA-28-181 Archer II	Nick Deyong Ltd	
G-BTHE	Cessna 150L	J. E. Preston	
G-BTHF	Cameron V-90 balloon	N. J. & S. J. Langley	
G-BTHK	Thunder Ax7-77 balloon	M. S.Trend	
G-BTHM	Thunder Ax8-105 balloon	Montgolfieres Club de L'Orme/France	
G-BTHP	Thorp T.211	M. Gardner	
G-BTHX	Colt 105A balloon	PSH Skypower Ltd	
G-BTHY	Bell 206B JetRanger 3	Suffolk Helicopters Ltd	
G-BTID	PA-28-161 Warrior II	Aviation South West Ltd	
G-BTIE	SOCATA TB10 Tobago	Aviation Spirit Ltd	
G-BTIF	Denney Kitfox Mk 3	D. S. Lally	
G-BTIG	Montgomerie-Bensen B.8MR	G. H. Leeming	
G-BTII	AA-5B Tiger	R. Clarke	
G-BTIJ	Luscombe 8E Silvaire	S. J. Hornsby	
G-BTIL	PA-38-112 Tomahawk	B. J. Pearson	

Notes	Reg.	Type	Owner or Operator
	G-BTIM	PA-28-161 Cadet	White Waltham Airfield Ltd
	G-BTIR	Denney Kitfox Mk 2	R. B. Wilson
	G-BTIV	PA-28-161 Warrior II	Warrior Group
	G-BTJA	Luscombe 8E Silvaire	S. R. Jones
	G-BTJB	Luscombe 8E Silvaire	M. Loxton
	G-BTJC	Luscombe 8F Silvaire	M. Colson
	G-BTJD	Thunder Ax8-90 S2 balloon	P. Richardson
	G-BTJF	Thunder Ax10-180 balloon	Airborne Adventures Ltd
	G-BTJH	Cameron O-77 balloon	M. Saveri
	G-BTJL	PA-38-112 Tomahawk	A5E Ltd
	G-BTJO	Thunder Ax9-140 balloon	G. P. Lane
	G-BTJS	Montgomerie-Bensen B.8MR	T. A. Holmes
	G-BTJU	Cameron V-90 balloon	Flambe Balloons Ltd
	G-BTJX	Rans S.10 Sakota	P. C. Avery
	G-BTKA	Piper J-5A Cub Cruiser	M. J. Walker
	G-BTKB	Renegade Spirit 912	P. J. Calvert
	G-BTKD	Denney Kitfox Mk 4	R. A. Hills
	G-BTKL	MBB Bö.105DB-4	Veritair Ltd
	G-BTKP	CFM Streak Shadow	S. L. Philp
	G-BTKT	PA-28-161 Warrior II	Biggin Hill Flying Club Ltd
	G-BTKV	PA-22 Tri-Pacer 160	R. A. Moore
	G-BTKX	PA-28-181 Archer II	D. J. Perkins
	G-BTLB	Wassmer Wa.52 Europa	The G-BTLB Group
	G-BTLG	PA-28R Cherokee Arrow 200	S. A. Thomas
	G-BTLL	Pilatus P.3-03	R. E. Dagless
	G-BTLM	PA-22 Tri-Pacer 160	F & H (Aircraft)
	G-BTLP	AA-1C Lynx	Partlease Ltd
	G-BTMA	Cessna 172N	Westbeach Aviation Ltd
	G-BTMK	Cessna R.172K XPII	K. E. Halford
	G-BTMO	Colt 69A balloon	Cameron Balloons Ltd
	G-BTMP	Campbell Cricket	P. W. McLaughlin
	G-BTMR	Cessna 172M	Linley Aviation Ltd
	G-BTMT	Denney Kitfox Mk 1	L. G. Horne
	G-BTMV	Everett Srs 2 gyroplane	L. Armes
	G-BTMW	Zenair CH.701 STOL	K. Thomas
	G-BTNA	Robinson R22 Beta	Attitude Arobatics Ltd
	G-BTNC	AS.365N-2 Dauphin 2	Multiflight Ltd
	G-BTNH	PA-28-161 Warrior II	Falcon Flying Services Ltd (G-DENH)
	G-BTNO	Aeronca 7AC Champion	J. M. Farquhar
	G-BTNR	Denney Kitfox Mk 3	High Notions Flying Group
	G-BTNT	PA-28-151 Warrior	Azure Flying Club Ltd
	G-BTNV	PA-28-161 Warrior II	B. Somerville & P. A. Teasdale
	G-BTNW	Rans S.6-ESA Coyote II	A. Cheshire
	G-BTOC	Robinson R22 Beta	Swift Helicopter Services Ltd
	G-BTOG	DH.82A Tiger Moth	TOG Group
	G-BTOL	Denney Kitfox Mk 3	P. J. Gibbs
	G-BTON	PA-28 Cherokee 140	Group G-BTON
	G-BTOO	Pitts S-1C Special	T. L. Davis
	G-BTOP	Cameron V-77 balloon	J. J. Winter
	G-BTOT	PA-15 Vagabond	Vagabond Flying Group
	G-BTOU	Cameron O-120 balloon	J. J. Daly
	G-BTOW	SOCATA Rallye 180GT	M. Jarrett
	G-BTOZ	Thunder Ax9-120 S2 balloon	H. G. Davies
	G-BTPA	BAe ATP	Atlantic Airlines Ltd
	G-BTPC	BAe ATP	Atlantic Airlines Ltd
	G-BTPE	BAe ATP	Atlantic Airlines Ltd
	G-BTPF	BAe ATP	Atlantic Airlines Ltd
	G-BTPG	BAe ATP	Atlantic Airlines Ltd
	G-BTPH	BAe ATP	Atlantic Airlines Ltd
	G-BTPJ	BAe ATP	European Turboprop Management AB
	G-BTPL	BAe ATP	European Turboprop Management AB
	G-BTPT	Cameron N-77 balloon	H. J. Andrews
	G-BTPV	Colt 90A balloon	C. J. Wootton & J. S. Russon
	G-BTPX	Thunder Ax8-90 BALLOON	B. J. Ross
	G-BTRC	Light Aero Avid Speedwing	Grangecote Ltd
	G-BTRF	Aero Designs Pulsar	P. F. Crosby & C. Smith
	G-BTRG	Aeronca 65C Super Chief	A. Welburn
	G-BTRI	Aeronca 11CC Super Chief	P. A. Wensak
	G-BTRK	PA-28-161 Warrior II	Stapleford Flying Club Ltd
	G-BTRL	Cameron N-105 balloon	J. Lippett
	G-BTRO	Thunder Ax8-90 balloon	Capital Balloon Club Ltd

Reg.	Type	Owner or Operator	Notes
G-BTRR	Thunder Ax7-77 balloon	P. J. Wentworth	
G-BTRS	PA-28-161 Warrior II	Airwise Flying Group	
G-BTRT	PA-28R Cherokee Arrow 200-II	Romeo Tango Group	
G-BTRU	Robin DR.400/180	R. H. Mackay	
G-BTRW	Slingsby T.61F Venture T.2	RW Group	
G-BTRY	PA-28-161 Warrior II	Oxford Aviation Academy (Oxford) Ltd	
G-BTRZ	Jodel D.18	A. P. Aspinall	
G-BTSJ	PA-28-161 Warrior II	Coastal Air (SW) Ltd	
G-BTSN	Cessna 150G	M. L. F. Langrick	
G-BTSP	Piper J-3C-65 Cub	A. Corcoran	
G-BTSR	Aeronca 11AC Chief	J. M. Miller	
G-BTSV	Denney Kitfox Mk 3	R. J. Folwell	
G-BTSW	Colt AS-80 Mk II airship	Gefa-Flug GmbH/Germany	
G-BTSX	Thunder Ax7-77 balloon	C. Moris-Gallimore/Portugal	
G-BTSY	EE Lightning F.6 (XR724) ★	Lightning Association	
G-BTSZ	Cessna 177A	Henlow Aviation Ltd	
G-BTTD	Montgomerie-Bensen B.8MR	A. J. P. Herculson	
G-BTTL	Cameron V-90 balloon	A. J. Baird	
G-BTTO	BAe ATP	Atlantic Airlines Ltd (G-OEDE)	
G-BTTR	Aerotek Pitts S-2A Special	Yellowbird Adventures	
G-BTTW	Thunder Ax7-77 balloon	J. Kenny	
G-BTTY	Denney Kitfox Mk 2	B. J. Clews	
G-BTTZ	Slingsby T.61F Venture T.2	G-BTTZ Group	
G-BTUA	Slingsby T.61F Venture T.2	Shenington Gliding Club	
G-BTUB	Yakovlev C.11	G. G. L. James	
G-BTUC	EMB-312 Tucano ★	Ulster Aviation Heritage	
G-BTUG	SOCATA Rallye 180T	Herefordshire Gliding Club Ltd	
G-BTUH	Cameron N-65 balloon	J. S. Russon	
G-BTUK	Aerotek Pitts S-2A Special	S. H. Elkington	
G-BTUL	Aerotek Pitts S-2A Special	Yakrobatics SCS	
G-BTUM	Piper J-3C-65 Cub	G-BTUM Syndicate	
G-BTUR	PA-18 Super Cub 95 (modified)	M. C. Curtis	
G-BTUS	Whittaker MW7	C. T. Bailey	
G-BTUW	PA-28-151 Warrior	T. S. Kemp	
G-BTUZ	American General AG-5B Tiger	R. V. Grocott	
G-BTVA	Thunder Ax7-77 balloon	C. M. Waters	
G-BTVC	Denney Kitfox Mk 2	M. J. Downes	
G-BTVE	Hawker Demon I (K8203)	Demon Displays Ltd	
G-BTVV	Cessna FA.337G	C. Keane	
G-BTVW	Cessna 152 II	Redmosaic Formacao de Technicos de Aeronaves/Portugal	
G-BTVX	Cessna 152 II	The Flight Centre 2010 Ltd	
G-BTWB	Denney Kitfox Mk 3	D. Doran (G-BTTM)	
G-BTWC	Slingsby T.61F Venture T.2	The Royal Air Force Gliding and Soaring Association	
G-BTWD	Slingsby T.61F Venture T.2	York Gliding Centre	
G-BTWE	Slingsby T.61F Venture T.2	Aston Down G-BTWE Syndicate	
G-BTWF	DHC.1 Chipmunk 22 (WK549)	G-BTWF Group	
G-BTWI	EAA Acro Sport I	J. O'Connell	
G-BTWJ	Cameron V-77 balloon	C. Gingell & M. Holden-Wadsworth	
G-BTWL	WAG-Aero Acro Sport Trainer	J. P. M. & P. White	
G-BTWX	SOCATA TB9 Tampico	T. I. Murtough	
G-BTWY	Aero Designs Pulsar	R. Bishop	
G-BTWZ	Rans S.10 Sakota	J. T. Phipps	
G-BTXD	Rans S.6-ESA Coyote II	A. I. Sutherland	
G-BTXF	Cameron V-90 balloon	G. Thompson	
G-BTXI	Noorduyn AT-16 Harvard IIB (FE695)	Patina Ltd	
G-BTXK	Thunder Ax7-65 balloon	A. F. Selby	
G-BTXM	Colt 21A Cloudhopper balloon	H. J. Andrews	
G-BTXT	Maule MXT-7-180 Star Rocket	B. de Greef & N. Lasnier	
G-BTXX	Bellanca 8KCAB Decathlon	Tatenhill Aviation Ltd	
G-BTXZ	Zenair CH.250	G-BTXZ Group	
G-BTYC	Cessna 150L	Polestar Aviation Ltd	
G-BTYH	Pottier P.80S	R. G. Marshall	
G-BTYI	PA-28-181 Archer II	S. W. Hedges	
G-BTYT	Cessna 152 II	Cristal Air Ltd	
G-BTYX	Cessna 140	R. F. Richards	
G-BTZA	Beech F33A Bonanza	G-BTZA Group	
G-BTZB	Yakovlev Yak-50 (10 yellow)	D. H. Boardman	
G-BTZD	Yakovlev Yak-1 (1342)	Historic Aircraft Collection Ltd	
G-BTZE	LET Yakovlev C.11	M. V. Rijkse	

Notes	Reg.	Type	Owner or Operator
	G-BTZO	SOCATA TB20 Trinidad	J. F. Busby
	G-BTZP	SOCATA TB9 Tampico	M. W. Orr
	G-BTZS	Colt 77A balloon	P. T. R. Ollivere
	G-BTZV	Cameron V-77 balloon	D. J. & H. M. Brown
	G-BTZX	Piper J-3C-65 Cub	ZX Cub Group
	G-BTZY	Colt 56A balloon	K. J. & M. E. Gregory
	G-BTZZ	CFM Streak Shadow	D. R. Stennett
	G-BUAB	Aeronca 11AC Chief	J. Reed
	G-BUAF	Cameron N-77 balloon	Zebedee Balloon Service Ltd
	G-BUAG	Jodel D.18	A. L. Silcox
	G-BUAI	Everett Srs 3 gyroplane	D. Stevenson
	G-BUAM	Cameron V-77 balloon	N. Florence
	G-BUAT	Thunder Ax9-120 balloon	S. W. K. Smeeton
	G-BUAV	Cameron O-105 balloon	D. & T. Dorrell
	G-BUAX	Rans S.10 Sakota	P. D. J. Brown
	G-BUBL	Thunder Ax8-105 balloon ★	British Balloon Museum/Newbury
	G-BUBN	BN-2B-26 Islander	Isles of Scilly Skybus Ltd
	G-BUBS	Lindstrand LBL-77B balloon	B. J. Bower
	G-BUBT	Stoddard Hamilton Glasair IIS RG	D. Bonucchi
	G-BUBU	PA-34-220T Seneca III	Brinor (Holdings) Ltd
	G-BUBW	Robinson R22 Beta	HQ Aviation Ltd
	G-BUCA	Cessna A.150K	BUCA Group
	G-BUCC	CASA 1.131E Jungmann 2000 (BU+CC)	P. L. Gaze (G-BUEM)
	G-BUCG	Schleicher ASW.20L (modified)	W. B. Andrews
	G-BUCH	Stinson V-77 Reliant	Gullwing Trading Ltd
	G-BUCI	Auster AOP.9 (XP242)	Historic Aircraft Flight Reserve Collectio
	G-BUCK	CASA 1.131E Jungmann 1000 (BU+CK)	Jungmann Flying Group
	G-BUCM	Hawker Sea Fury FB.11	Patina Ltd
	G-BUCO	Pietenpol Air Camper	A. James
	G-BUCT	Cessna 150L	Linking Partners BV/Nrtherlands
	G-BUDA	Slingsby T.61F Venture T.2	G-BUDA Syndicate
	G-BUDC	Slingsby T.61F Venture T.2 (ZA652)	G. Jones
	G-BUDE	PA-22 Tri-Pacer 135 (tailwheel)	P. Robinson
	G-BUDI	Aero Designs Pulsar	R. W. L. Oliver
	G-BUDK	Thunder Ax7-77 balloon	W. Evans
	G-BUDL	Auster 3 (NX534)	K. B. Owen
	G-BUDN	Cameron 90 Shoe SS balloon	Magical Adventures Ltd
	G-BUDO	PZL-110 Koliber 150	A. S. Vine
	G-BUDR	Denney Kitfox Mk 3	H. D. Colliver
	G-BUDS	Rand-Robinson KR-2	D. W. Munday
	G-BUDT	Slingsby T.61F Venture T.2	G-BUDT Group
	G-BUDU	Cameron V-77 balloon	T. M. G. Amery
	G-BUDW	Brügger MB.2 Colibri	S. P. Barrett (G-GODS)
	G-BUEC	Van's RV-6	A. H. Harper
	G-BUED	Slingsby T.61F Venture T.2	617 VGS Group
	G-BUEF	Cessna 152 II	Channel Aviation
	G-BUEG	Cessna 152 II	Aviation South West Ltd
	G-BUEI	Thunder Ax8-105 balloon	K. P. Barnes
	G-BUEK	Slingsby T.61F Venture T.2	G-BUEK Group
	G-BUEN	VPM M-14 Scout	C. R. Gordon
	G-BUEP	Maule MX-7-180	N. J. B. Bennett
	G-BUEW	Rans S-6 Coyote II	C. Cheeseman (G-MWYE)
	G-BUFG	Slingsby T.61F Venture T.2	K. E. Ballington
	G-BUFH	PA-28-161 Warrior II	Solent School of Flying
	G-BUFR	Slingsby T.61F Venture T.2	East Sussex Gliding Club Ltd
	G-BUFY	PA-28-161 Warrior II	Bickertons Aerodromes Ltd
	G-BUGE	Bellanca 7GCAA Citabria	V. Vaughan & N. O'Brien
	G-BUGG	Cessna 150F	C. P. J. Taylor & D. M. Forshaw
	G-BUGI	Evans VP-2	E. L. Periam
	G-BUGJ	Robin DR.400/180	W. E. R. Jenkins
	G-BUGL	Slingsby T.61F Venture T.2	VMG Group
	G-BUGP	Cameron V-77 balloon	R. Churcher
	G-BUGS	Cameron V-77 balloon	S. J. Dymond
	G-BUGT	Slingsby T.61F Venture T.2	Bambi Aircraft Group
	G-BUGV	Slingsby T.61F Venture T.2	Oxfordshire Sportflying Ltd
	G-BUGW	Slingsby T.61F Venture T.2	Holdcroft Aviatioin Services Ltd & Transcourt Ltd
	G-BUGY	Cameron V-90 balloon	Dante Balloon Group
	G-BUGZ	Slingsby T.61F Venture T.2	Dishforth Flying Group

Reg.	Type	Owner or Operator	Notes
G-BUHA	Slingsby T.61F Venture T.2 (ZA634:C)	Saltby Flying Group	
G-BUHM	Cameron V-77 balloon	L. A. Watts	
G-BUHO	Cessna 140	W. B. Bateson	
G-BUHR	Slingsby T.61F Venture T.2	The Northumbria Gliding Club Ltd	
G-BUHS	Stoddard-Hamilton Glasair SH TD-1	T. F. Horrocks	
G-BUHU	Cameron N-105 balloon	Unipart Balloon Club	
G-BUHZ	Cessna 120	The Cessna 120 Group	
G-BUIF	PA-28-161 Warrior II	Northumbria Flying School Ltd	
G-BUIG	Campbell Cricket (replica)	J. A. English	
G-BUIH	Slingsby T.61F Venture T.2	Falcon Gliding Group	
G-BUIJ	PA-28-161 Warrior II	D. J. Taplin	
G-BUIK	PA-28-161 Warrior II	S. M. Hart	
G-BUIL	CFM Streak Shadow	A. A. Castleton	
G-BUIN	Thunder Ax7-77 balloon	P. C. Johnson	
G-BUIP	Denney Kitfox Mk 2	Avcomm Developments Ltd	
G-BUIR	Light Aero Avid Speedwing Mk 4	S. J. Handley	
G-BUIZ	Cameron N-90 balloon	J. S. Russon	
G-BUJA	Slingsby T.61F Venture T.2	The Royal Air Force Gliding and Soaring Association	
G-BUJB	Slingsby T.61F Venture T.2	Falke Syndicate	
G-BUJE	Cessna 177B	FG93 Group	
G-BUJH	Colt 77B balloon	B. Fisher	
G-BUJI	Slingsby T.61F Venture T.2	Solent Venture Syndicate Ltd	
G-BUJJ	Avid Speedwing	T. M. Buick	
G-BUJK	Montgomerie-Bensen B.8MR	P. C. W. Raine	
G-BUJM	Cessna 120	Cessna 120 Flying Group	
G-BUJN	Cessna 172N	Warwickshire Aviation Ltd	
G-BUJO	PA-28-161 Warrior II	Falcon Flying Services	
G-BUJP	PA-28-161 Warrior II	Phoenix Aviation	
G-BUJV	Light Aero Avid Speedwing Mk 4	C. Thomas	
G-BUJX	Slingsby T.61F Venture T.2	The Burn Gliding Club Ltd	
G-BUJZ	Rotorway Executive 90 (modified)	M. P. Swoboda	
G-BUKB	Rans S.10 Sakota	M. K. Blatch	
G-BUKF	Denney Kitfox Mk 4	Kilo Foxtrot Group	
G-BUKH	D.31 Turbulent	J. G. Wilkins	
G-BUKI	Thunder Ax7-77 balloon	Virgin Balloon Flights	
G-BUKJ	BAe.ATP	PTB (Emerald) Pty.Ltd (G-OEDF)	
G-BUKK	Bücker Bü 133C Jungmeister (U-80)	E. J. F. McEntee	
G-BUKO	Cessna 120	Peregrine Flying Group	
G-BUKP	Denney Kitfox Mk 2	RNAV Europe Ltd	
G-BUKR	MS.880B Rallye Club 100T	G-BUKR Flying Group	
G-BUKU	Luscombe 8E Silvaire	Silvaire Flying Group	
G-BUKY	CCF Harvard 4M (52-8543)	N. T. Oakman	
G-BUKZ	Evans VP-2	P. R. Farnell	
G-BULB	Thunder Ax7-77 balloon	Ixion Group	
G-BULC	Light Aero Avid Flyer Mk 4	C. Nice	
G-BULG	Van's RV-4	V. D. Long	
G-BULH	Cessna 172N Skyhawk II	FlyBPL.com	
G-BULJ	CFM Streak Shadow	C. C. Brown	
G-BULL	SA Bulldog Srs 120/128 (HKG-5)	Bulldog Aeros Ltd	
G-BULN	Colt 210A balloon	H. G. Davies	
G-BULO	Luscombe 8A Silvaire	B. W. Foulds	
G-BULT	Campbell Cricket	A. T. Pocklington	
G-BULY	Light Aero Avid Flyer	J. M. Angiolini	
G-BULZ	Denney Kitfox Mk 2	T. G. F. Trenchard	
G-BUMP	PA-28-181 Archer II	G-BUMP Group	
G-BUNB	Slingsby T.61F Venture T.2	The Royal Air Force Gliding and Soaring Association	
G-BUNC	PZL-104 Wilga 35	R. F. Goodman	
G-BUND	PA-28RT-201T Turbo Arrow IV	E. Culot	
G-BUNG	Cameron N-77 balloon	A. Kaye	
G-BUNO	Lancair 320	J. Softley	
G-BUOA	Whittaker MW6-S Fatboy Flyer	H. N. Graham	
G-BUOB	CFM Streak Shadow	J. M. Hunter	
G-BUOD	SE-5A (replica) (B595:W)	M. D. Waldron/Belgium	
G-BUOE	Cameron V-90 balloon	A. Derbyshire	
G-BUOF	D.62B Condor	R. P. Loxton	
G-BUOI	PA-20-135 Pacer	S. S. Sellam	
G-BUOK	Rans S.6-ESA Coyote II	J. R. S. Heaton	
G-BUOL	Denney Kitfox Mk 3	M. P. Brigden-Gwinnutt	
G-BUON	Light Aero Avid Aerobat	I. A. J. Lappin	

Notes	Reg.	Type	Owner or Operator
	G-BUOR	CASA 1.131E Jungmann 2000	M. I. M. S. Voest/Netherlands
	G-BUOS	VS.394 Spitfire FR.XVIII	Spitfire Ltd
	G-BUOW	Aero Designs Pulsar XP	T. J. Hartwell
	G-BUPA	Rutan LongEz	N. G. Henry
	G-BUPB	Stolp SA.300 Starduster Too	J. R. Edwards & J. W. Widdows
	G-BUPC	Rollason Beta B.2	C. A. Rolph
	G-BUPF	Bensen B.8R	P. W. Hewitt-Dean
	G-BUPI	Cameron V-77 balloon	S. M. Sherwin (G-BOUC)
	G-BUPM	VPM M-16 Tandem Trainer	A. Kitson
	G-BUPP	Cameron V-42 balloon	C. L. Schoeman
	G-BUPR	Jodel D.18	R. W. Burrows
	G-BUPU	Thunder Ax7-77 balloon	R. C. Barkworth & D. G. Maguire/USA
	G-BUPV	Great Lakes 2T-1A	R. J. Fray
	G-BUPW	Denney Kitfox Mk 3	S. G. Metcalfe
	G-BURE	Jodel D.9	N. P. St.J. Ramsay
	G-BURG	Colt 77A balloon	P. A. & M. Still
	G-BURH	Cessna 150E	B. Russel
	G-BURI	Enstrom F-28C	D. W. C. Holmes
	G-BURJ	HS.748 Srs.2A	Clewer Aviation Ltd
	G-BURL	Colt 105A balloon	J. E. Rose
	G-BURN	Cameron O-120 balloon	G. Gray
	G-BURP	Rotorway Executive 90	N. K. Newman
	G-BURR	Auster AOP.9	Annic Aviation
	G-BURS	Sikorsky S-76A	Capital Air Services Ltd (G-OHTL)
	G-BURT	PA-28-161 Warrior II	Paul's Planes Ltd
	G-BURZ	Hawker Nimrod II (K3661:362)	Historic Aircraft Collection Ltd
	G-BUSH	Airbus A.320-211	SASOF TR-44 Aviation Ireland Ltd
	G-BUSI	Airbus A.320-211	SASOF TR-44 Aviation Ireland Ltd
	G-BUSN	Rotorway Executive 90	J. A. McGinley
	G-BUSR	Aero Designs Pulsar	S. S. Bateman & R. A. Watts
	G-BUSS	Cameron 90 Bus SS balloon	Magical Adventures Ltd
	G-BUSV	Colt 105A balloon	M. N. J. Kirby
	G-BUSW	Rockwell Commander 114	J. Vicoll
	G-BUTB	CFM Streak Shadow	H. O. Maclean
	G-BUTD	Van's RV-6	B. S. Carpenter
	G-BUTF	Aeronca 11AC Chief	G. A. McCarthy
	G-BUTG	Zenair CH.601HD	K. Thomas
	G-BUTH	CEA DR.220 2+2	Phoenix Flying Group
	G-BUTJ	Cameron O-77 balloon	D. Hoddinott
	G-BUTK	Murphy Rebel	A. J. Gibson
	G-BUTM	Rans S.6-116 Coyote II	J. D. Sinclair-Day
	G-BUTT	Cessna FA150K	Ag-Raum GmbH/Germany (G-AXSJ)
	G-BUTX	CASA 1.133C Jungmeister (ES.1-4)	Bucker Flying Group
	G-BUTY	Brügger MB.2 Colibri	R. M. Lawday
	G-BUTZ	PA-28 Cherokee 180C	M. H. Canning (G-DARL)
	G-BUUA	Slingsby T.67M Firefly Mk II	M. Geroschus
	G-BUUB	Slingsby T.67M Firefly Mk II	The Leicestershire Aero Club Ltd
	G-BUUC	Slingsby T.67M Firefly Mk II	Swiftair Maintenance Ltd
	G-BUUE	Slingsby T.67M Firefly Mk II	J. R. Bratty
	G-BUUF	Slingsby T.67M Firefly Mk II	Tiger Airways
	G-BUUI	Slingsby T.67M Firefly Mk II	Bustard Flying Club Ltd
	G-BUUJ	Slingsby T.67M Firefly Mk II	Durham Tees Flight Training Ltd
	G-BUUK	Slingsby T.67M Firefly Mk II	Avalanche Aviation Ltd
	G-BUUP	BAe ATP	Atlantic Airlines Ltd
	G-BUUR	BAe ATP	Atlantic Airlines Ltd
	G-BUUU	Cameron Bottle SS balloon ★	British Balloon Museum/Newbury
	G-BUUX	PA-28 Cherokee 180D	Aero Group 78
	G-BUVA	PA-22-135 Tri-Pacer	Oaksey VA Group
	G-BUVB	Colt 77A balloon	Zebedee Balloon Service Ltd
	G-BUVE	Colt 77B balloon	G. D. Philpot
	G-BUVL	Fisher Super Koala	A. D. Malcolm
	G-BUVM	CEA DR.250/160	G-BUVM Group
	G-BUVN	CASA 1.131E Jungmann 2000(BI-005)	W. Van Egmond/Netherlands
	G-BUVO	Cessna F.182P	Romeo Mike Flying Group (G-WTFA)
	G-BUVR	Christen A.1 Husky	A. E. Poulson
	G-BUVT	Colt 77A balloon	N. A. Carr
	G-BUVW	Cameron N-90 balloon	P. Spellward
	G-BUVX	CFM Streak Shadow	T. J. Shaw
	G-BUWE	SE-5A (replica) (C9533:M)	Airpark Flight Centre Ltd
	G-BUWF	Cameron N-105 balloon	R. E. Jones
	G-BUWH	Parsons 2-seat gyroplane	R. V. Brunskill

Reg.	Type	Owner or Operator	Notes
G-BUWI	Lindstrand LBL-77A balloon	Capital Balloon Club Ltd	
G-BUWJ	Pitts S-1C Special	M. A. Sims	
G-BUWK	Rans S.6-116 Coyote II	R. Warriner	
G-BUWL	Piper J-4A	M. L. Ryan	
G-BUWR	CFM Streak Shadow	T. Harvey	
G-BUWS	Denney Kitfox Mk 2	J. E. Brewis	
G-BUWT	Rand-Robinson KR-2	G. Bailey-Woods	
G-BUWU	Cameron V-77 balloon	T. R. Dews	
G-BUXA	Colt 210A balloon	Balloon School International Ltd	
G-BUXC	CFM Streak Shadow	N. R. Beale	
G-BUXD	Maule MXT-7-160	I. D. McClelland	
G-BUXI	Steen Skybolt	BUXI Group	
G-BUXK	Pietenpol Air Camper	B. M. D. Nelson	
G-BUXL	Taylor JT.1 Monoplane	P. J. Hebdon	
G-BUXN	Beech C23 Sundowner	Private Pilots Syndicate	
G-BUXS	MBB Bö.105DBS/4	Bond Air Services (G-PASA/G-BGWP)	
G-BUXW	Thunder Ax8-90 S2 balloon	N. T. Parry	
G-BUXX	PA-17 Vagabond	R. H. Hunt	
G-BUXY	PA-25 Pawnee 235	Bath, Wilts & North Dorset Gliding Club Ltd	
G-BUYB	Aero Designs Pulsar	P. Robichaud	
G-BUYC	Cameron 80 Concept balloon	R. P. Cross	
G-BUYD	Thunder Ax8-90 balloon	S. McGuigan	
G-BUYF	Falcon XP	M. J. Hadland	
G-BUYK	Denney Kitfox Mk 4	M. S. Shelton	
G-BUYL	RAF 2000GT gyroplane	M. H. J. Goldring	
G-BUYO	Colt 77A balloon	S. F. Burden/Netherlands	
G-BUYS	Robin DR.400/180	G-BUYS Flying Group	
G-BUYU	Bowers Fly-Baby 1A	R. C. Piper	
G-BUYY	PA-28 Cherokee 180	G-BUYY Group	
G-BUZA	Denney Kitfox Mk 3	A. O'Brien/Ireland	
G-BUZB	Aero Designs Pulsar XP	S. M. Macintyre	
G-BUZC	Everett Srs 3A gyroplane	M. P. L'Hermette	
G-BUZE	Avid Speed Wing	F. Sayyah	
G-BUZG	Zenair CH.601HD	A. R. Whyte	
G-BUZH	Aero Designs Star-Lite SL-1	C. A. McDowall	
G-BUZK	Cameron V-77 balloon	Zebedee Balloon Service Ltd	
G-BUZM	Light Aero Avid Flyer Mk 3	R. McLuckie & O. G. Jones	
G-BUZO	Pietenpol Air Camper	D. A. Jones	
G-BUZR	Lindstrand LBL-77A balloon	Lindstrand Technologies Ltd	
G-BUZT	Kolb Twinstar Mk 3	J. A. G. Robb	
G-BUZZ	Agusta-Bell 206B JetRanger 2	Rivermead Aviation Ltd	
G-BVAB	Zenair CH.601HDS	B. N. Rides	
G-BVAC	Zenair CH.601HD	J. A. Tyndall & S. Wisedale	
G-BVAF	Piper J-3C-65 Cub	G-BVAF Group	
G-BVAH	Denney Kitfox Mk.3	S. Allinson	
G-BVAI	PZL-110 Koliber 150	B. G. Ell	
G-BVAM	Evans VP-1	Breighton VP-1 Group	
G-BVAO	Colt 25A balloon	M. E. Dworski	
G-BVAW	Staaken Z-1 Flitzer (D-692)	L. R. Williams	
G-BVAY	Rutan Vari-Eze	D. A. Young	
G-BVBF	PA-28-151 Warrior	R. K. Spence	
G-BVBK	Colt Flying Coffe Jar SS balloon	M. E. White	
G-BVBS	Cameron N-77 balloon	S. M. Gabb	
G-BVCA	Cameron N-105 balloon	Kent Ballooning	
G-BVCG	Van's RV-6	A. W. Shellis	
G-BVCL	Rans S.6-116 Coyote II	A. M. Colman	
G-BVCN	Colt 56A balloon	G. A. & I. Chadwick & S. Richards	
G-BVCO	FRED Srs 2	I. W. Bremner	
G-BVCP	Piper CP.1 Metisse	B. M. Diggins	
G-BVCS	Aeronca 7BCM Champion	A. C. Lines	
G-BVCT	Denney Kitfox Mk 4	A. F. Reid	
G-BVCY	Cameron H-24 balloon	A. C. K. Rawson & J. J. Rudoni	
G-BVDB	Thunder Ax7-77 balloon	S. J. Hollingsworth & M. K. Bellamy (G-ORDY)	
G-BVDC	Van's RV-3	R. S. Hatwell	
G-BVDF	Cameron Doll 105 SS balloon	A. Kaye & K-H Gruenauer	
G-BVDH	PA-28RT-201 Arrow IV	P. J. Dalton	
G-BVDI	Van's RV-4	J. G. Gorman & H. Tallini	
G-BVDJ	Campbell Cricket (replica)	S. Jennings	
G-BVDM	Cameron 60 Concept balloon	M. P. Young	
G-BVDO	Lindstrand LBL-105A balloon	K. Graham	

Notes	Reg.	Type	Owner or Operator
	G-BVDP	Sequoia F.8L Falco	N. M. Turner
	G-BVDR	Cameron O-77 balloon	M. D. Sullivan-Gould
	G-BVDS	Lindstrand LBL-69A balloon	Lindstrand Hot-Air Balloons Ltd
	G-BVDT	CFM Streak Shadow	A. Harner
	G-BVDW	Thunder Ax8-90 balloon	S. C. Vora
	G-BVDX	Cameron V-90 balloon	R. K. Scott
	G-BVDY	Cameron 60 Concept balloon	P. Baker/Ireland
	G-BVDZ	Taylorcraft BC-12D	N. Rushen
	G-BVEA	Mosler Motors N.3 Pup	D. A. Porter (G-MWEA)
	G-BVEH	Jodel D.112	M. L. Copland
	G-BVEL	Evans VP-1 Srs.2	M. J. & S. J. Quinn
	G-BVEN	Cameron 80 Concept balloon	R. M. Powell
	G-BVEP	Luscombe 8A Master	B. H. Austen
	G-BVER	DHC.2 Beaver 1 (XV268)	Seaflite Ltd (G-BTDM)
	G-BVEV	PA-34-200 Seneca	G-BVEV Flying Group
	G-BVEW	Lindstrand LBL-150A balloon	S. J. Colin
	G-BVEY	Denney Kitfox Mk 4-1200	J. H. H. Turner
	G-BVEZ	P.84 Jet Provost T.3A (XM479)	Newcastle Jet Provost Co Ltd
	G-BVFA	Rans S.10 Sakota	D. S. Wilkinson
	G-BVFB	Cameron N-31 balloon	P. Lawman
	G-BVFF	Cameron V-77 balloon	R. J. Kerr & G. P. Allen
	G-BVFM	Rans S.6-116 Coyote II	F. B. C. de Beer
	G-BVFO	Light Aero Avid Speedwing	T. G. Solomon
	G-BVFR	CFM Streak Shadow	J. H. Pope
	G-BVFS	Slingsby T.31M	S. R. Williams
	G-BVFU	Cameron 105 Sphere SS balloon	Stichting Phoenix/Netherlands
	G-BVFZ	Maule M5-180C Lunar Rocket	R. C. Robinson
	G-BVGA	Bell 206B JetRanger3	Findon Air Services
	G-BVGB	Thunder Ax8-105 S2 balloon	E. K. Read
	G-BVGE	WS-55 Whirlwind HAR.10 (XJ729)	A. D. Whitehouse
	G-BVGF	Shaw Europa	T. C. Hyde
	G-BVGH	Hawker Hunter T.7 (XL573)	M. Stott
	G-BVGI	Pereira Osprey II	D. Westoby
	G-BVGJ	Cameron C-80 balloon	J. M. J. & V. F. Roberts
	G-BVGK	Lindstrand LBL Newspaper SS balloon	H. Holmqvist
	G-BVGO	Denney Kitfox Mk 4-1200	P. Madden
	G-BVGP	Bücker Bü 133 Jungmeister (U-95)	M. V. Rijkse
	G-BVGT	Auster J/1 (modified)	K. D. & C. S. Rhodes
	G-BVGW	Luscombe 8A Silvaire	J. Smith
	G-BVGX	Thunder Ax8-90 S2 balloon	G-BVGX Group/New Zealand
	G-BVGY	Luscombe 8E Silvaire	Torquil Aviation Ltd
	G-BVGZ	Fokker Dr.1 (replica) (450/17) ★	R. A. Fleming
	G-BVHC	Grob G.115D-2 Heron	Tayside Aviation Ltd
	G-BVHD	Grob G.115D-2 Heron	Tayside Aviation Ltd
	G-BVHE	Grob G.115D-2 Heron	Tayside Aviation Ltd
	G-BVHF	Grob G.115D-2 Heron	Tayside Aviation Ltd
	G-BVHG	Grob G.115D-2 Heron	Tayside Aviation Ltd
	G-BVHI	Rans S.10 Sakota	J. D. Amos
	G-BVHJ	Cameron A-180 balloon	S. J. Boxall
	G-BVHK	Cameron V-77 balloon	A. R. Rich
	G-BVHL	Nicollier HN.700 Menestrel II	W. Dobinson & D. Hawkins
	G-BVHM	PA-38-112 Tomahawk	Hinton Pilot Flight Training Ltd (G-DCAN)
	G-BVHO	Cameron V-90 balloon	N. W. B. Bews
	G-BVHR	Cameron V-90 balloon	G. P. Walton
	G-BVHS	Murphy Rebel	S. T. Raby
	G-BVIA	Rand-Robinson KR-2	M. T. Taylor
	G-BVIE	PA-18 Super Cub 95 (modified)	J. C. Best (G-CLIK/G-BLMB)
	G-BVIF	Montgomerie-Bensen B.8MR	R. M. & D. Mann
	G-BVIK	Maule MXT-7-180 Star Rocket	Graveley Flying Group
	G-BVIL	Maule MXT-7-180 Star Rocket	K. & S. C. Knight
	G-BVIN	Rans S-6-ESA Coyote II	J. Broome
	G-BVIS	Brügger MB.2 Colibri	B. H. Shaw
	G-BVIV	Light Aero Avid Speedwing	S. Styles
	G-BVIW	PA-18-Super Cub 150	I. H. Logan
	G-BVIZ	Shaw Europa	J. E. Lipman
	G-BVJF	Montgomerie-Bensen B.8MR	D. M. F. Harvey
	G-BVJG	Cyclone AX3/K	J. Gilroy (G-MYOP)
	G-BVJK	Glaser-Dirks DG.800A	J. S. Forster
	G-BVJN	Shaw Europa	JN Europa Group
	G-BVJT	Cessna F.406	Nor Leasing
	G-BVJU	Evans VP-1	BVJU Flying Club & Associates

Reg.	Type	Owner or Operator	Notes
G-BVJX	Marquart MA.5 Charger	A. E. Cox	
G-BVKF	Shaw Europa	J. R. F. Bennett	
G-BVKG	Colt Flying Hot Dog SS balloon	Longbreak Ltd/USA	
G-BVKK	Slingsby T.61F Venture T.2	Buckminster Gliding Club Ltd	
G-BVKL	Cameron A-180 balloon	Dragon Balloon Co Ltd	
G-BVKM	Rutan Vari-Eze	J. P. G. Lindquist/Switzerland	
G-BVKU	Slingsby T.61F Venture T.2	G-BVKU Syndicate	
G-BVLA	Lancair 320	Eaglescott Lancair Group	
G-BVLD	Campbell Cricket (replica)	C. Berry	
G-BVLF	CFM Starstreak Shadow SS-D	J. C. Pratelli	
G-BVLG	AS.355F1 Twin Squirrel	PLM Dollar Group PLC	
G-BVLH	Shaw Europa	D. Barraclough	
G-BVLL	Lindstrand LBL-210A balloon	Airborne Balloon Flights Ltd	
G-BVLN	Aero Designs Pulsar XP	D. A. Campbell	
G-BVLP	PA-38-112 Tomahawk	J. Hornby	
G-BVLR	Van's RV-4	RV4 Group	
G-BVLT	Bellanca 7GCBC Citabria	Slade Associates	
G-BVLU	D.31 Turbulent	C. D. Bancroft	
G-BVLV	Shaw Europa	Euro 39 Group	
G-BVLX	Slingsby T.61F Venture T.2	The Royal Air Force Gliding and Soaring Association	
G-BVMA	Beech 200 Super King Air	Dragonfly Aviation Services Ltd (G-VPLC)	
G-BVMH	WAG-Aero Sport Trainer (39624:D-39)	J. Mathews	
G-BVMJ	Cameron 95 Eagle SS balloon	R. D. Sargeant	
G-BVMM	Robin HR.200/100	Gloster Aero Group	
G-BVMN	Ken Brock KB-2 gyroplane	G-BVMN Group	
G-BVMR	Cameron V-90 balloon	I. R. Comley	
G-BVMU	Yakovlev Yak-52 (09 yellow)	M. Bockemuhl & F. Loock	
G-BVNG	DH.60G-III Moth Major	P. & G. Groves	
G-BVNI	Taylor JT-2 Titch	G. de Halle	
G-BVNS	PA-28-181 Archer II	Scottish Airways Flyers (Prestwick) Ltd	
G-BVNU	FLS Aerospace Sprint Club	M. D. R. Elmes	
G-BVNY	Rans S.7 Courier	S. Hazleden	
G-BVOC	Cameron V-90 balloon	A. R. Hardwick	
G-BVOH	Campbell Cricket (replica)	A. Kitson	
G-BVOI	Rans S.6-116 Coyote II	S. J. Taft	
G-BVOK	Yakovlev Yak-52 (55 grey)	Trans Holdings Ltd	
G-BVOP	Cameron N-90 balloon	October Gold Ballooning Ltd	
G-BVOR	CFM Streak Shadow	J. M. Chandler	
G-BVOS	Shaw Europa	Durham Europa Group	
G-BVOW	Shaw Europa	H. P. Brooks	
G-BVOY	Rotorway Executive 90	C. H. Drake	
G-BVOZ	Colt 56A balloon	British School of Ballooning	
G-BVPA	Thunder Ax8-105 S2 balloon	Firefly Balloon Promotions	
G-BVPD	CASA 1.131E Jungmann 2000	D. Bruton	
G-BVPM	Evans VP-2 Coupé	P. Marigold	
G-BVPN	Piper J-3C-65 Cub	C. Sarcelet (G-TAFY)	
G-BVPS	Jodel D.112	BAT Group	
G-BVPV	Lindstrand LBL-77B balloon	P. G. Hill	
G-BVPW	Rans S.6-116 Coyote II	T. B. Woolley	
G-BVPX	Bensen B.8 (modified) Tyro Gyro	A. W. Harvey	
G-BVPY	CFM Streak Shadow	A. J. Grant	
G-BVRA	Shaw Europa	N. E. Stokes	
G-BVRH	Taylorcraft BL.65	M. J. Kirk	
G-BVRJ	Avro RJ-70	QinetiQ Ltd	
G-BVRL	Lindstrand LBL-21A balloon	T. J. Orchard & M. E. Banks	
G-BVRU	Lindstrand LBL-105A balloon	C & R Jemmett	
G-BVRV	Van's RV-4	A. Troughton	
G-BVRZ	PA-18 Super Cub 95	R. W. Davison	
G-BVSB	TEAM mini-MAX	D. G. Palmer	
G-BVSD	SE.3130 Alouette II (V-54)	M. J. Cuttell	
G-BVSF	Aero Designs Pulsar	R. J. & J. A. Freestone	
G-BVSN	Light Aero Avid Speedwing	R. C. Bowley	
G-BVSP	P.84 Jet Provost T.3A (XM370)	H. G. Hodges & Son Ltd	
G-BVSS	Jodel D.150	D. H. Pattison	
G-BVST	Jodel D.150	A. Shipp/Breighton	
G-BVSX	TEAM mini-MAX 91	J. A. Clark	
G-BVSZ	Pitts S-1E (S) Special	H. J. Morton	
G-BVTA	Tri-R Kis	A. F. Prosser	
G-BVTC	P.84 Jet Provost T.5A (XW333)	Global Aviation Ltd	
G-BVTL	Colt 31A balloon	A. Lindsay	

Notes	Reg.	Type	Owner or Operator
	G-BVTM	Cessna F.152 II	RAF Halton Aeroplane Club (G-WACS)
	G-BVTV	Rotorway Executive 90	P. M. Scheiwiller
	G-BVTW	Aero Designs Pulsar	R. J. Panther
	G-BVTX	DHC.1 Chipmunk 22A (WP809)	TX Flying Group
	G-BVUA	Cameron O-105 balloon	Wickers World Ltd
	G-BVUC	Colt 56A balloon	J. F. Till
	G-BVUG	Betts TB.1 (Stampe SV.4C)	H. F. Fekete (G-BEUS)
	G-BVUH	Thunder Ax6-65B balloon	H. J. M. Lacoste
	G-BVUI	Lindstrand LBL-25A balloon	J. W. Hole
	G-BVUK	Cameron V-77 balloon	H. G. Griffiths & W. A. Steel
	G-BVUM	Rans S.6-116 Coyote II	M. A. Abbott
	G-BVUN	Van's RV-4	D. J. Harvey
	G-BVUT	Evans VP-1 Srs. 2	M. J. Barnett
	G-BVUU	Cameron C-80 balloon	T. M. C. McCoy
	G-BVUV	Shaw Europa	R. J. Mills
	G-BVUZ	Cessna 120	T. K. Duffy
	G-BVVB	Carlson Sparrow II	L. M. McCullen
	G-BVVE	Jodel D.112	M. Balls
	G-BVVG	Nanchang CJ-6A (68)	Nanchang CJ6A Group
	G-BVVH	Shaw Europa	T. G. Hoult
	G-BVVI	Hawker Audax I (K5600)	Aero Vintage Ltd
	G-BVVK	DHC.6 Twin Otter 310	Loganair Ltd/Flybe
	G-BVVL	EAA Acro Sport II	G-BVVL Syndicate
	G-BVVM	Zenair CH.601HD	D. Macdonald
	G-BVVN	Brügger MB.2 Colibri	N. F. Andrews
	G-BVVP	Shaw Europa	I. Mansfield
	G-BVVR	Stits SA-3A Playboy	P. Burton
	G-BVVS	Van's RV-4	E. G. & N. S. C. English
	G-BVVU	Lindstrand LBL Four SS balloon	Magical Adventures Ltd/USA
	G-BVVW	Yakovlev Yak-52	M. Blackman
	G-BVVZ	Corby CJ-1 Starlet	P. V. Flack
	G-BVWB	Thunder Ax8-90 S2 balloon	M. A. Stelling & K. C. Tanner
	G-BVWC	EE Canberra B.6 (WK163)	Classic Aviation Projects Ltd
	G-BVWD	Avro RJ85	Trident Aviation Leasing Services (Jersey) Ltd
	G-BVWI	Cameron light bulb SS balloon	Mobberley Balloon Collection
	G-BVWM	Shaw Europa	A. Head
	G-BVWW	Lindstrand LBL-90A balloon	J. D. A. Shields
	G-BVWZ	PA-32-301 Saratoga	The Saratoga (WZ) Group
	G-BVXA	Cameron N-105 balloon	R. E. Jones
	G-BVXC	EE Canberra B.6 (WT333) ★	Classic Aviation Projects Ltd/Bruntingthorpe
	G-BVXD	Cameron O-84 balloon	Hedge Hoppers Balloon Group
	G-BVXE	Steen Skybolt	J. Buglass (G-LISA)
	G-BVXJ	CASA 1.133 Jungmeister	C. Butler & G. G. Ferriman
	G-BVXK	Yakovlev Yak-52 (26 grey)	Yak UK Ltd
	G-BVXM	AS.350B Ecureuil	The Berkeley Leisure Group Ltd
	G-BVXR	DH.104 Devon C.2 (XA880)	M. Whale & M. W. A. Lunn
	G-BVYF	PA-31-350 Navajo Chieftain	J. A. Rees & D. T. Rees (G-SAVE)
	G-BVYG	CEA DR.300/180	Ulster Gliding Club Ltd
	G-BVYK	TEAM mini-MAX	A. G. Ward
	G-BVYM	CEA DR.300/180	London Gliding Club (Pty) Ltd
	G-BVYO	Robin R.2160	D. J. S. McClean
	G-BVYP	PA-25 Pawnee 235B	Bidford Gliding & Flying Club Ltd
	G-BVYU	Cameron A-140 balloon	S. Charlish
	G-BVYX	Light Aero Avid Speedwing Mk 4	O. P. Sparrow
	G-BVYY	Pietenpol Air Camper	Pietenpol G-BVYY Group
	G-BVYZ	Stemme S.10V	L. Gubbay
	G-BVZJ	Rand-Robinson KR-2	G. M. Rundle
	G-BVZN	Cameron C-80 balloon	S. J. Clarke
	G-BVZO	Rans S.6-116 Coyote II	P. J. Brion
	G-BVZR	Zenair CH.601HD	R. A. Perkins
	G-BVZT	Lindstrand LBL-90A balloon	J. Edwards
	G-BVZV	Rans S.6-116 Coyote II	A. H. & F. A. Macaskill
	G-BVZX	Cameron H-34 balloon	R. H. Etherington
	G-BVZZ	DHC.1 Chipmunk 22 (WP795)	Portsmouth Naval Gliding Club
	G-BWAB	Jodel D.14	R. G. Fairall
	G-BWAC	Waco YKS-7	D. N. Peters
	G-BWAD	RAF 2000GT gyroplane	A. Melody
	G-BWAF	Hawker Hunter F.6A (XG160:U) ★	Bournemouth Aviation Museum/Bournemouth
	G-BWAG	Cameron O-120 balloon	P. M. Skinner
	G-BWAH	Montgomerie-Bensen B.8MR	J. B. Allan

Reg.	Type	Owner or Operator	Notes
G-BWAI	CFM Streak Shadow	C. M. James	
G-BWAJ	Cameron V-77 balloon	B. Mead	
G-BWAN	Cameron N-77 balloon	I. Chadwick	
G-BWAO	Cameron C-80 balloon	M. D. Freeston & S. Mitchell	
G-BWAP	FRED Srs 3	G. A. Shepherd	
G-BWAR	Denney Kitfox Mk 3	I. Wightman	
G-BWAT	Pietenpol Air Camper	P. W. Aitchison	
G-BWAU	Cameron V-90 balloon	K. M. & A. M. F. Hall	
G-BWAV	Schweizer 269C	Helihire	
G-BWAW	Lindstrand LBL-77A balloon	D. Bareford	
G-BWBI	Taylorcraft F-22A	R. T. G. Preston	
G-BWBT	Lindstrand LBL-90A balloon	British Telecommunications PLC	
G-BWBZ	ARV-1 Super 2	M. P. Holdstock	
G-BWCA	CFM Streak Shadow	I. C. Pearson	
G-BWCK	Everett Srs 2 gyroplane	B. F. Pearson	
G-BWCS	P.84 Jet Provost T.5 (XW293:Z)	J. H. Ashcroft	
G-BWCT	Tipsy T.66 Nipper 1	J. S. Hemmings & C. R. Steer	
G-BWCV	Shaw Europa	G. C. McKirdy	
G-BWCY	Murphy Rebel	S. Burrow	
G-BWDB	ATR-72-202	Aurigny Air Services Ltd	
G-BWDH	Cameron N-105 balloon	M. A. Scholes	
G-BWDP	Shaw Europa	S. Attubato	
G-BWDS	P.84 Jet Provost T.3A (XM424)	Aviation Heritage Ltd	
G-BWDT	PA-34-220T Seneca III	H. R. Chambers (G-BKHS)	
G-BWDX	Shaw Europa	J. Robson	
G-BWDZ	Sky 105-24 balloon	M. T. Wiltshire	
G-BWEA	Lindstrand LBL-120A balloon	S. R. Seager	
G-BWEB	P.84 Jet Provost T.5A (XW422:3)	J. Miller	
G-BWEE	Cameron V-42 balloon	A. J. Davey & C. Muth/Germany	
G-BWEF	SNCAN Stampe SV.4C	Acebell G-BWEF Syndicate (G-BOVL)	
G-BWEG	Shaw Europa	J. W. Kelly	
G-BWEM	VS.358 Seafire L.IIIC (RX168)	Mark One Partners LLC	
G-BWEN	Macair Merlin GT	D. A. Hill	
G-BWEU	Cessna F.152 II	Eastern Air Executive Ltd	
G-BWEW	Cameron N-105 balloon	Unipart Balloon Club	
G-BWEY	Bensen B.8	F. G. Shepherd	
G-BWEZ	Piper J-3C-65 Cub (436021)	J. G. McTaggart	
G-BWFG	Robin HR.200/120B	Air Atlantique Ltd	
G-BWFH	Shaw Europa	G. C. Grant	
G-BWFJ	Evans VP-1	G. Robson	
G-BWFK	Lindstrand LBL-77A balloon	C. J. Wootton & J. S. Russon	
G-BWFM	Yakovlev Yak-50	Fox Mike Group	
G-BWFN	Hapi Cygnet SF-2A	G-BWFN Group	
G-BWFO	Colomban MC.15 Cri-Cri	K. D. & C. S. Rhodes	
G-BWFT	Hawker Hunter T.8M (XL602)	G. I. Begg	
G-BWFX	Shaw Europa	A. D. Stewart	
G-BWFZ	Murphy Rebel	J. E. Lipman (G-SAVS)	
G-BWGA	Lindstrand LBL-105A balloon	R. Thompson	
G-BWGF	P.84 Jet Provost T.5A (XW325)	Viper Jet Provost Group Ltd	
G-BWGJ	Chilton DW.1A	T. J. Harrison	
G-BWGL	Hawker Hunter T.8C (XJ615)	Stichting Hawker Hunter Foundation/Netherlands	
G-BWGO	Slingsby T.67M Firefly 200	R. Gray	
G-BWGS	BAC.145 Jet Provost T.5A (XW310)	M. P. Grimshaw	
G-BWGU	Cessna 150F	Goodair Leasing Ltd	
G-BWGY	HOAC Katana DV.20	JL Flying Ltd	
G-BWHA	Hawker Hurricane IIB (Z5252)	Historic Flying Ltd	
G-BWHD	Lindstrand LBL-31A balloon	M. R. Noyce & R. P. E. Phillips	
G-BWHI	DHC.1 Chipmunk 22A (WK624)	N. E. M. Clare	
G-BWHK	Rans S.6-116 Coyote II	S. J. Wakeling	
G-BWHM	Sky 140-24 balloon	C. J. S. Limon	
G-BWHP	CASA 1.131E Jungmann (S4+A07)	J. F. Hopkins	
G-BWHR	Tipsy Nipper T.66 Srs 1	L. R. Marnef	
G-BWHS	RAF 2000 gyroplane	B. J. Payne	
G-BWHU	Westland Scout AH.1 (XR595)	N. J. F. Boston	
G-BWIA	Rans S.10 Sakota	A. C. G. T. da Costa, J. A. F. Monteiro & R. M. M. Moura	
G-BWID	D.31 Turbulent	N. Huxtable	
G-BWII	Cessna 150G	J. D. G. Hicks (G-BSKB)	
G-BWIJ	Shaw Europa	R. Lloyd	
G-BWIK	DH.82A Tiger Moth (NL985)	P. J. Lawton	

Notes	Reg.	Type	Owner or Operator
	G-BWIL	Rans S-10	G. Forde
	G-BWIP	Cameron N-90 balloon	K. C. Tanner
	G-BWIR	Dornier 328-100	Loganair Ltd
	G-BWIV	Shaw Europa	T. G. Ledbury
	G-BWIW	Sky 180-24 balloon	T. M. Donnelly
	G-BWIX	Sky 120-24 balloon	J. M. Percival
	G-BWIZ	QAC Quickie Tri-Q 200	M. C. Davies
	G-BWJB	Thunder Ax8-105 balloon	Justerini & Brooks Ltd
	G-BWJG	Mooney M.20J	S. Nahum
	G-BWJH	Shaw Europa	I. R. Willis
	G-BWJM	Bristol M.1C (replica) (C4918)	The Shuttleworth Collection
	G-BWJY	DHC.1 Chipmunk 22 (WG469)	K. J. Thompson
	G-BWKK	Auster A.O.P.9 (XP279)	C. A. Davis & D. R. White
	G-BWKT	Stephens Akro Laser	P. D. Begley
	G-BWKU	Cameron A-250 balloon	British School of Ballooning
	G-BWKV	Cameron V-77 balloon	A. P. Wallace
	G-BWKW	Thunder Ax8-90 balloon	Gone With The Wind Ltd
	G-BWKZ	Lindstrand LBL-77A balloon	J. H. Dobson
	G-BWLD	Cameron O-120 balloon	D. Pedri/Italy
	G-BWLF	Cessna 404	Reconnaisance Ventures Ltd (G-BNXS)
	G-BWLJ	Taylorcraft DCO-65 (42-35870/129)	B. J. Robe
	G-BWLL	Murphy Rebel	F. W. Parker
	G-BWLM	Sky 65-24 balloon	W. J. Brogan
	G-BWLY	Rotorway Executive 90	P. W. & I. P. Bewley
	G-BWMB	Jodel D.119	C. Hughes
	G-BWMC	Cessna 182P	Iscavia Ltd
	G-BWMF	Gloster Meteor T.7 (WA591)	Aviation Heritage Ltd
	G-BWMH	Lindstrand LBL-77B balloon	A. P. Jay
	G-BWMI	PA-28RT-201T Turbo Arrow IV	R. W. Pascoe
	G-BWMJ	Nieuport 17/2B (replica) (N1977:8)	R. Gauld-Galliers & M. R. Lancombe
	G-BWMK	DH.82A Tiger Moth (T8191)	K. F. Crumplin
	G-BWMN	Rans S.7 Courier	P. J. Tyler
	G-BWMO	Oldfield Baby Lakes	D. Maddocks (G-CIII)
	G-BWMS	DH.82A Tiger Moth	Stichting Vroege Vogels/Netherlands
	G-BWMU	Cameron 105 Monster Truck SS balloon	Magical Adventures Ltd/Canada
	G-BWMV	Colt AS-105 Mk II airship	D. Stuber/Germany
	G-BWMX	DHC.1 Chipmunk 22 (WG407:67)	407th Flying Group
	G-BWMY	Cameron Bradford & Bingley SS balloon	Magical Adventures Ltd/USA
	G-BWNB	Cessna 152 II	South Warwickshire School of Flying
	G-BWNC	Cessna 152 II	South Warwickshire School of Flying
	G-BWND	Cessna 152 II	South Warwickshire School of Flying Ltd & G. Davies
	G-BWNI	PA-24 Comanche 180	B. V. & J. B. Haslam
	G-BWNJ	Hughes 269C	L. R. Fenwick
	G-BWNK	D,H,C,1 Chipmunk 22 (WD390)	WD390 Group
	G-BWNM	PA-28R Cherokee Arrow 180	M. & R. C. Ramnial
	G-BWNO	Cameron O-90 balloon	T. Knight
	G-BWNP	Cameron 90 Club SS balloon	H. Cusden & J. Edwards
	G-BWNS	Cameron O-90 balloon	I. C. Steward
	G-BWNT	DHC.1 Chipmunk 22 (WP901)	P. G. D. Bell & A. Stafford
	G-BWNU	PA-38-112 Tomahawk	Kemble Aero Club Ltd
	G-BWNY	Aeromot AMT-200 Super Ximango	Powell-Brett Associates Ltd
	G-BWNZ	Agusta A109C	Anglo Beef Processors Ltd
	G-BWOB	Luscombe 8F Silvaire	S. R. H. Martin
	G-BWOF	P.84 Jet Provost T.5	Techair London Ltd
	G-BWOH	PA-28-161 Cadet	Redhill Air Services Ltd
	G-BWOI	PA-28-161 Cadet	Aviation Rentals
	G-BWOJ	PA-28-161 Cadet	Aviation Rentals
	G-BWOK	Lindstrand LBL-105G balloon	Lindstrand Hot Air Balloons Ltd
	G-BWOR	PA-18 Super Cub 135	G. Cormack
	G-BWOV	Enstrom F-28A	P. A. Goss
	G-BWOW	Cameron N-105 balloon	Skybus Ballooning
	G-BWOY	Sky 31-24 balloon	C. Wolstenholme
	G-BWOZ	CFM Streak Shadow SA	J. A. Lord
	G-BWPC	Cameron V-77 balloon	H. Vaughan
	G-BWPE	Murphy Renegade Spirit UK	J. Hatswell/France
	G-BWPF	Sky 120-24 balloon	J. Francis
	G-BWPH	PA-28-181 Archer II	H. Merkado
	G-BWPJ	Steen Skybolt	D. Houghton

Reg.	Type	Owner or Operator	Notes
G-BWPP	Sky 105-24 balloon	The Sarnia Balloon Group	
G-BWPS	CFM Streak Shadow SA	P. J. Mogg	
G-BWPT	Cameron N-90 balloon	G.Everett	
G-BWPZ	Cameron N-105 balloon	D. M. Moffat	
G-BWRA	Sopwith LC-1T Triplane (replica) (N500)	J. G. Brander (G-PENY)	
G-BWRC	Light Aero Avid Speedwing	C. G. Thompson	
G-BWRO	Shaw Europa	G-BWRO Europa Group	
G-BWRR	Cessna 182Q	A. & R. Reid	
G-BWRS	SNCAN Stampe SV.4C	G. P. J. M. Valvekens/Belgium	
G-BWRT	Cameron 60 Concept balloon	Zebedee Balloon Service Ltd	
G-BWSB	Lindstrand LBL-105A balloon	R. Calvert-Fisher	
G-BWSC	PA-38-112 Tomahawk II	The Hawstead Flying Group	
G-BWSD	Campbell Cricket	R. F. G. Moyle	
G-BWSG	P.84 Jet Provost T.5 (XW324/K)	J. Bell	
G-BWSH	P.84 Jet Provost T.3A (XN498)	Global Aviation Ltd	
G-BWSI	K & S SA.102.5 Cavalier	B. W. Shaw	
G-BWSJ	Denney Kitfox Mk 3	J. M. Miller	
G-BWSL	Sky 77-24 balloon	E. J. Briggs	
G-BWSN	Denney Kitfox Mk 3	M. J. Laundy	
G-BWSU	Cameron N-105 balloon	A. M. Marten	
G-BWSV	Yakovlev Yak-52	M. W. Fitch	
G-BWTB	Lindstrand LBL-105A balloon	Servatruc Ltd	
G-BWTC	Zlin Z.242L	S. W. Turley	
G-BWTE	Cameron O-140 balloon	T. G. Church	
G-BWTG	DHC.1 Chipmunk 22 (WB671:910)	R. G. T. de Man/Netherlands	
G-BWTH	Robinson R22 Beta	Helicopter Services	
G-BWTJ	Cameron V-77 balloon	A. J. Montgomery	
G-BWTK	RAF 2000 GTX-SE gyroplane	L. P. Rolfe	
G-BWTN	Lindstrand LBL-90A balloon	J. A. Lomas	
G-BWTO	DHC.1 Chipmunk 22 (WP984)	Skycraft Services Ltd	
G-BWTW	Mooney M.20C	T. J. Berry	
G-BWUA	Campbell Cricket	N. J. Orchard	
G-BWUE	Hispano HA.1112M1L	Historic Flying Ltd (G-AWHK)	
G-BWUH	PA-28-181 Archer III	A. Davis	
G-BWUJ	Rotorway Executive 162F	Southern Helicopters Ltd	
G-BWUL	Noorduyn AT-16 Harvard IIB	G-BWUL Flying Group	
G-BWUN	DHC.1 Chipmunk 22 (WD310)	T. Henderson	
G-BWUP	Shaw Europa	V. Goddard	
G-BWUS	Sky 65-24 balloon	N. A. P. Bates	
G-BWUT	DHC.1 Chipmunk 22 (WZ879)	Herbert Aviation Ltd	
G-BWUU	Cameron N-90 balloon	Bailey Balloons Ltd	
G-BWUV	DHC.1 Chipmunk 22A (WK640)	A. C. Darby	
G-BWUZ	Campbell Cricket (replica)	K. A. Touhey	
G-BWVB	Pietenpol Air Camper	E. B. Toulson	
G-BWVC	Jodel D.18	R. W. J. Cripps	
G-BWVF	Pietenpol Air Camper	N. Clark	
G-BWVI	Stern ST.80	I. Pearson	
G-BWVM	Colt AA-1050 balloon	B. B. Baxter Ltd	
G-BWVN	Whittaker MW7	S. T. G. Ingram	
G-BWVR	Yakovlev Yak-52 (52 yellow)	I. Parkinson	
G-BWVS	Shaw Europa	D. R. Bishop	
G-BWVT	DHA.82A Tiger Moth	R. Jewitt	
G-BWVU	Cameron O-90 balloon	J. Atkinson	
G-BWVY	DHC.1 Chipmunk 22 (WP896)	N. Gardner	
G-BWVZ	DHC.1 Chipmunk 22A (WK590)	D. Campion/Belgium	
G-BWWA	Ultravia Pelican Club GS	J. S. Aplin	
G-BWWB	Shaw Europa	P. Levi	
G-BWWC	DH.104 Dove 7 (XM223)	Air Atlantique Ltd	
G-BWWE	Lindstrand LBL-90A balloon	B. J. Newman	
G-BWWF	Cessna 185A	T. N. Bartlett & S. M. C. Harvey	
G-BWWG	SOCATA Rallye 235E	J. J. Frew	
G-BWWJ	Hughes 269C	R. J. Scott (G-BMYZ)	
G-BWWK	Hawker Nimrod I (S1581)	Patina Ltd	
G-BWWL	Colt Flying Egg SS balloon	Magical Adventures Ltd/USA	
G-BWWN	Isaacs Fury II (K8303:D)	J. S. Marten-Hale	
G-BWWT	Dornier 328-100	Loganair Ltd	
G-BWWU	PA-22 Tri-Pacer 150	K. M. Bowen	
G-BWWW	BAe Jetstream 3102	British Aerospace PLC	
G-BWWX	Yakovlev Yak-50	D. P. McCoy/Ireland	
G-BWWY	Lindstrand LBL-105A balloon	M. J. Smith	

Notes	Reg.	Type	Owner or Operator
	G-BWXA	Slingsby T.67M Firefly 260	Swift Aircraft Ltd
	G-BWXB	Slingsby T.67M Firefly 260	Redline Aviation Security Ltd
	G-BWXC	Slingsby T.67M Firefly 260	Swift Aircraft Ltd
	G-BWXD	Slingsby T.67M Firefly 260	Swift Aircraft Ltd
	G-BWXE	Slingsby T.67M Firefly 260	Swift Aircraft Ltd
	G-BWXF	Slingsby T.67M Firefly 260	Swift Aircraft Ltd
	G-BWXG	Slingsby T.67M Firefly 260	Swift Aircraft Ltd
	G-BWXH	Slingsby T.67M Firefly 260	Swift Aircraft Ltd
	G-BWXI	Slingsby T.67M Firefly 260	Swift Aircraft Ltd
	G-BWXJ	Slingsby T.67M Firefly 260	D. I. Stanbridge
	G-BWXK	Slingsby T.67M Firefly 260	Swift Aircraft Ltd
	G-BWXL	Slingsby T.67M Firefly 260	Airspeed BVBA/Belgium
	G-BWXN	Slingsby T.67M Firefly 260	Swift Aircraft Ltd
	G-BWXP	Slingsby T.67M Firefly 260	D. S. McGregor
	G-BWXR	Slingsby T.67M Firefly 260	Swift Aircraft Ltd
	G-BWXS	Slingsby T.67M Firefly 260	Swift Aircraft Ltd
	G-BWXT	Slingsby T.67M Firefly 260	Cranfield University
	G-BWXU	Slingsby T.67M Firefly 260	Swift Aircraft Ltd
	G-BWXV	Slingsby T.67M Firefly 260	TC Trading & Consulting SPRL/BVBA
	G-BWXX	Slingsby T.67M Firefly 260	Swift Aircraft Ltd
	G-BWXY	Slingsby T.67M Firefly 260	Swift Aircraft Ltd
	G-BWXZ	Slingsby T.67M Firefly 260	Swift Aircraft Ltd
	G-BWYB	PA-28 Cherokee 160	A. J. Peters
	G-BWYD	Shaw Europa	F. H. Mycroft
	G-BWYI	Denney Kitfox Mk3	A. J. Glading
	G-BWYK	Yakovlev Yak-50	Foley Farm Flying Group
	G-BWYN	Cameron O-77 balloon	W. H. Morgan (G-ODER)
	G-BWYO	Sequoia F.8L Falco	M. C. R. Sims
	G-BWYR	Rans S.6-116 Coyote II	D. A. Lord
	G-BWYU	Sky 120-24 balloon	Aerosauras Balloons Ltd
	G-BWZA	Shaw Europa	T. G. Cowlishaw
	G-BWZG	Robin R.2160	Sherburn Aero Club Ltd
	G-BWZJ	Cameron A-250 balloon	Balloon Club of Great Britain
	G-BWZU	Lindstrand LBL-90B balloon	K. D. Pierce
	G-BWZY	Hughes 269A	Reeve Newfields Ltd (G-FSDT)
	G-BXAB	PA-28-161 Warrior II	TG Aviation Ltd (G-BTGK)
	G-BXAC	RAF 2000 GTX-SE gyroplane	J. A. Robinson
	G-BXAF	Pitts S-1D Special	N. J. Watson
	G-BXAJ	Lindstrand LBL-14A balloon	Oscair Project AB/Sweden
	G-BXAK	Yakovlev Yak-52 (44 black)	J. Calverley
	G-BXAN	Scheibe SF-25C Falke	C. Falke Syndicate
	G-BXAO	Avtech Jabiru SK	P. J. Thompson
	G-BXAU	Pitts S-1 Special	L. Westnage
	G-BXAX	Cameron N-77 balloon ★	Balloon Preservation Group
	G-BXAY	Bell 206B JetRanger 3	Viewdart Ltd
	G-BXBB	PA-20 Pacer 150	M. E. R. Coghlan
	G-BXBK	Avions Mudry CAP-10B	S. Skipworth
	G-BXBL	Lindstrand LBL-240A balloon	Firefly Balloon Promotions
	G-BXBM	Cameron O-105 balloon	Bristol University Hot Air Ballooning Society
	G-BXBU	Avions Mudry CAP-10B	J. F. Cosgrave & H. R. Pearson
	G-BXBZ	PZL-104 Wilga 80	J. H. Sandham Aviation
	G-BXCA	Hapi Cygnet SF-2A	J. D. C. Henslow
	G-BXCC	PA-28-201T Turbo Dakota	Greer Aviation Ltd
	G-BXCD	TEAM mini-MAX 91A	A. Maltby
	G-BXCG	Jodel DR.250/160	CG Group
	G-BXCJ	Campbell Cricket (replica)	A. G. Peel
	G-BXCN	Sky 105-24 balloon	Nottingham Hot-Air Balloon Club
	G-BXCO	Colt 120A balloon	J. R. Lawson
	G-BXCP	DHC.1 Chipmunk 22 (WP859)	M. P. O'Connor
	G-BXCT	DHC.1 Chipmunk 22 (WB697)	Wickenby Aviation
	G-BXCU	Rans S.6-116 Coyote II	S. C. Ord
	G-BXCV	DHC.1 Chipmunk 22 (WP929)	Ardmore Aviation Services Ltd/Hong Kong
	G-BXCW	Denney Kitfox Mk 3	M. J. Blanchard
	G-BXDA	DHC.1 Chipmunk 22 (WP860)	D. C. Mowat
	G-BXDB	Cessna U.206F	D. A. Howard (G-BMNZ)
	G-BXDE	RAF 2000GTX-SE gyroplane	B. Jones
	G-BXDG	DHC.1 Chipmunk 22 (WK630)	Felthorpe Flying Group
	G-BXDH	DHC.1 Chipmunk 22 (WD331)	Royal Aircraft Establishment Aero Club Ltd
	G-BXDI	DHC.1 Chipmunk 22 (WD373)	Sunrise Global Aviation Ltd
	G-BXDN	DHC.1 Chipmunk 22 (WK609)	W. D. Lowe, G. James & L. A. Edwards

Reg.	Type	Owner or Operator	Notes
G-BXDO	Rutan Cozy	Cozy Group	
G-BXDP	DHC.1 Chupmunk 22 (WK642)	Gipsy Captains	
G-BXDR	Lindstrand LBL-77A balloon	A. J. & A. R. Brown	
G-BXDS	Bell 206B JetRanger III	Aerospeed Limited (G-TAMF/G-OVBJ)	
G-BXDU	Aero Designs Pulsar	K. P. Rusling	
G-BXDV	Sky 105-24 balloon	N. A. Carr	
G-BXDY	Shaw Europa	S. Attubato & D. G. Watts	
G-BXDZ	Lindstrand LBL-105A balloon	D. J. & A. D. Sutcliffe	
G-BXEC	DHC.1 Chipmunk 22 (WK633)	A. J. Robinson & M. J. Miller	
G-BXEJ	VPM M-16 Tandem Trainer	AES Radionic Surveillance Systems	
G-BXEN	Cameron N-105 balloon	E. Ghio/Italy	
G-BXES	P.66 Pembroke C.1 (XL954)	Air Atlantique Ltd	
G-BXEX	PA-28-181 Archer II	R. Mayle	
G-BXEZ	Cessna 182P	Forhawk Ltd	
G-BXFB	Pitts S-1 Special	J. F. Dowe	
G-BXFC	Jodel D.18	B. S. Godbold	
G-BXFE	Avions Mudry CAP-10B	Avion Aerobatic Ltd	
G-BXFG	Shaw Europa	A. Rawicz-Szczerbo	
G-BXFI	Hawker Hunter T.7 (WV372)	Canfield Hunter Ltd	
G-BXFK	CFM Streak Shadow	A. G. Sindrey	
G-BXFN	Colt 77A balloon	Charter Ballooning Ltd	
G-BXGA	AS.350B2 Ecureuil	PLM Dollar Group Ltd	
G-BXGD	Sky 90-24 balloon	Servo & Electronic Sales Ltd	
G-BXGG	Shaw Europa	D. J. Joyce	
G-BXGH	Diamond Katana DA20-A1	M. Dorrian	
G-BXGL	DHC.1 Chipmunk 22	N. P. Marriott	
G-BXGM	DHC.1 Chipmunk 22 (WP928:D)	Chipmunk G-BXGM Group	
G-BXGO	DHC.1 Chipmunk 22 (WB654:U)	Trees Group	
G-BXGP	DHC.1 Chipmunk 22 (WZ882)	Eaglescott Chipmunk Group	
G-BXGS	RAF 2000 gyroplane	D. W. Howell	
G-BXGT	I.I.I. Sky Arrow 650T	J. S. C. Goodale	
G-BXGV	Cessna 172R	G-BXGV Skyhawk Group	
G-BXGX	DHC.1 Chipmunk 22 (WK586:V)	The Real Flying Co.Ltd	
G-BXGY	Cameron V-65 balloon	Dante Balloon Group	
G-BXGZ	Stemme S.10V	G. S. Craven & A. J. Garner	
G-BXHA	DHC.1 Chipmunk 22 (WP925)	H. M. & S. Roberts	
G-BXHE	Lindstrand LBL-105A balloon	L. H. Ellis	
G-BXHF	DHC.1 Chipmunk 22 (WP930:J)	Hotel Fox Syndicate	
G-BXHH	AA-5A Cheetah	A. W. Daffin	
G-BXHJ	Hapi Cygnet SF-2A	I. J. Smith	
G-BXHL	Sky 77-24 balloon	C. D. Monk	
G-BXHO	Lindstrand Telewest Sphere SS balloon	Magical Adventures Ltd	
G-BXHR	Stemme S.10V	J. H. Rutherford	
G-BXHT	Bushby-Long Midget Mustang	K. Manley	
G-BXHU	Campbell Cricket Mk 6	P. J. Began	
G-BXHY	Shaw Europa	Jupiter Flying Group	
G-BXIA	DHC.1 Chipmunk 22 (WB615)	Dales Aviation	
G-BXIC	Cameron A-275 balloon	Aerosaurus Balloons LLP	
G-BXIE	Colt 77B balloon	I. R. Warrington	
G-BXIF	PA-28-161 Warrior II	Piper Flight Ltd	
G-BXIG	Zenair CH.701 STOL	B. McFadden	
G-BXIH	Sky 200-24 balloon	Kent Ballooning	
G-BXII	Shaw Europa	D. A. McFadyean	
G-BXIJ	Shaw Europa	R. James	
G-BXIM	DHC.1 Chipmunk 22 (WK512)	A. B. Ashcroft & P. R. Joshua	
G-BXIO	Jodel DR.1050M	B. N. Stevens	
G-BXIT	Zebedee V-31 balloon	Zebedee Balloon Service Ltd	
G-BXIX	VPM M-16 Tandem Trainer	P. P. Willmott	
G-BXIY	Blake Bluetit (BAPC37)	M. J. Aubrey	
G-BXIZ	Lindstrand LBL-31A balloon	J. S. Russon	
G-BXJB	Yakovlev Yak-52	Yak Display Group	
G-BXJC	Cameron A-210 balloon	British School of Ballooning	
G-BXJD	PA-28-180C Cherokee	S. Atherton	
G-BXJG	Lindstrand LBL-105B balloon	C. E. Wood	
G-BXJH	Cameron N-42 balloon	D. M. Hoddinott	
G-BXJJ	PA-28-161 Cadet	White Waltham Airfield Ltd	
G-BXJM	Cessna 152	ACS Aviation Ltd	
G-BXJO	Cameron O-90 balloon	Dragon Balloon Co Ltd	
G-BXJP	Cameron C-80 balloon	A. Sarrasin	
G-BXJS	Schempp-Hirth Janus CM	Janus Syndicate	
G-BXJT	Sky 90-24 balloon	J. G. O'Connell	

Notes	Reg.	Type	Owner or Operator
	G-BXJY	Van's RV-6	J. P. Kynaston
	G-BXJZ	Cameron C-60 balloon	N. J. & S. J. Bettin
	G-BXKF	Hawker Hunter T.7(XL577/V)	R. F. Harvey
	G-BXKL	Bell 206B JetRanger 3	Swattons Aviation Ltd
	G-BXKM	RAF 2000 GTX-SE gyroplane	A. H. Goddard
	G-BXKU	Colt AS-120 Mk II airship	D. C. Chipping/Portugal
	G-BXKW	Slingsby T.67M Firefly 200	J-F Jansen & A. Huygens
	G-BXKX	Auster V	J. A. Clark
	G-BXLF	Lindstrand LBL-90A balloon	W. Rousell & J. Tyrrell
	G-BXLG	Cameron C-80 balloon	S. M. Anthony
	G-BXLK	Shaw Europa	R. G. Fairall
	G-BXLN	Fournier RF-4D	P. W. Cooper & M. R. Fox
	G-BXLO	P.84 Jet Provost T.4 (XR673/L)	Century Aviation Ltd
	G-BXLP	Sky 90-24 balloon	D. Bedford & J. Edwards
	G-BXLS	PZL-110 Koliber 160A	D. C. Bayes
	G-BXLT	SOCATA TB200 Tobago XL	C., G. & J. Fisher & D. Fitton
	G-BXLW	Enstrom F.28F	Rhoburt Ltd
	G-BXLY	PA-28-151 Warrior	Multiflight Ltd (G-WATZ)
	G-BXMG	RAF 2000 GTX gyroplane	J. S. Wright
	G-BXMM	Cameron A-180 balloon	High Road Balloons
	G-BXMV	Scheibe SF.25C Falke 1700	K. E. Ballington
	G-BXMX	Currie Wot	R. B. Griffin
	G-BXMY	Hughes 269C	R. J. Scott
	G-BXNA	Light Aero Avid Flyer	A. P. Daines
	G-BXNC	Shaw Europa	J. K. Cantwell
	G-BXNN	DHC.1 Chipmunk 22 (WP983/B)	E. N. Skinner
	G-BXNS	Bell 206B JetRanger 3	Sterling Helicopters Ltd
	G-BXNT	Bell 206B JetRanger 3	Sterling Helicopters Ltd
	G-BXOA	Robinson R22 Beta	MG Group Ltd
	G-BXOC	Evans VP-2	M. P. Wiseman
	G-BXOF	Diamond Katana DA20-A1	Aircraft Engineers Ltd
	G-BXOI	Cessna 172R	E. J. Watts
	G-BXOJ	PA-28-161 Warrior III	Tayside Aviation Ltd
	G-BXOM	Isaacs Spitfire	S. Vince
	G-BXON	Auster AOP.9	C. J. & D. J. Baker
	G-BXOT	Cameron C-70 balloon	Dante Balloon Group
	G-BXOU	CEA DR.360	J. A. Lofthouse
	G-BXOX	AA-5A Cheetah	R. L. Carter & P. J. Large
	G-BXOY	QAC Quickie Q.235	C. C. Clapham
	G-BXOZ	PA-28-181 Archer II	Spritetone Ltd
	G-BXPC	Diamond Katana DA20-A1	Cubair Flight Training Ltd
	G-BXPD	Diamond Katana DA20-A1	Cubair Flight Training Ltd
	G-BXPI	Van's RV-4	B. M. Diggins
	G-BXPK	Cameron A-250 balloon	Alba Ballooning Ltd
	G-BXPM	Beech 58 Baron	Whitehouse Retail Ltd
	G-BXPP	Sky 90-24 balloon	S. A. Nother
	G-BXPR	Colt 110 Can SS balloon	P. O. Wagner/Germany
	G-BXPT	Ultramagic H-77 balloon	Aerobility
	G-BXRA	Avions Mudry CAP-10B	J. W. Scott
	G-BXRB	Avions Mudry CAP-10B	T. T. Duhig
	G-BXRC	Avions Mudry CAP-10B	Group Alpha
	G-BXRF	CP.1310-C3 Super Emeraude	D. T. Gethin
	G-BXRO	Cessna U.206G	M. Penny
	G-BXRP	Schweizer 269C	AH Helicopter Services Ltd
	G-BXRR	Westland Scout AH.1 (XW612)	M. Soor
	G-BXRS	Westland Scout AH.1 (XW613)	B-N Group Ltd
	G-BXRT	Robin DR.400-180	T. P. Usborne
	G-BXRV	Van's RV-4	Cleeve Flying Grouip
	G-BXRY	Bell 206B JetRanger	Corbett Holdings Ltd
	G-BXRZ	Rans S.6-116 Coyote II	M. P. Hallam
	G-BXSC	Cameron C-80 balloon	N. A. Apsey
	G-BXSD	Cessna 172R	R. Paston
	G-BXSE	Cessna 172R	MK Aero Support Ltd
	G-BXSG	Robinson R22 Beta II	Rivermead Aviation Ltd
	G-BXSH	Glaser-Dirks DG.800B	R. O'Conor
	G-BXSI	Avtech Jabiru SK	P. F. Gandy
	G-BXSP	Grob G.109B	Deeside Grob Group
	G-BXSR	Cessna F172N	N. C. K. G. Copeman
	G-BXST	PA-25 Pawnee 235C	The Northumbria Gliding Club Ltd
	G-BXSU	TEAM mini-MAX 91A	I. Pearson (G-MYGL)
	G-BXSV	SNCAN Stampe SV.4C	P. A. Greenhalgh

Reg.	Type	Owner or Operator	Notes
G-BXSX	Cameron V-77 balloon	D. R. Medcalf	
G-BXSY	Robinson R22 Beta II	N. M. G. Pearson	
G-BXTB	Cessna 152	Durham Tees Flight Training Ltd	
G-BXTD	Shaw Europa	P. R. Anderson	
G-BXTE	Cameron A-275 balloon	D. S. Messmer	
G-BXTF	Cameron N-105 balloon	C. J. Dunkley	
G-BXTG	Cameron N-42 balloon	P. M. Watkins & S. M. M. Carden	
G-BXTH	Westland Gazelle HT.1 (XW866)	Armstrong Aviation Ltd	
G-BXTI	Pitts S-1S Special	Fly Hire Ltd	
G-BXTJ	Cameron N-77 balloon	Chubb Fire Ltd Chubb	
G-BXTO	Hindustan HAL-6 Pushpak	P. Q. Benn	
G-BXTS	Diamond Katana DA20-A1	I. M. Armitage & D. J. Short	
G-BXTT	AA-5B Tiger	J. Ducray	
G-BXTV	Bug Mk.4 helicopter	B. R. Cope	
G-BXTW	PA-28-181 Archer III	Davison Plant Hire	
G-BXTY	PA-28-161 Cadet	Flew LLP	
G-BXTZ	PA-28-161 Cadet	Flew LLP	
G-BXUA	Campbell Cricket Mk.5	A. W. Harvey	
G-BXUC	Robinson R22 Beta	Rivermead Aviation Ltd/Switzerland	
G-BXUF	Agusta-Bell 206B JetRanger 3	SJ Contracting Services Ltd	
G-BXUG	Lindstrand Baby Bel SS balloon	K-H. Gruenauer/Germany	
G-BXUH	Lindstrand LBL-31A balloon	K. Gruenauer	
G-BXUI	Glaser-Dirks DG.800B	J. Le Coyte	
G-BXUM	Shaw Europa	D. Bosomworth	
G-BXUO	Lindstrand LBL-105A balloon	Lindstrand Technologies Ltd	
G-BXUS	Sky 65-24 balloon	PSH Skypower Ltd	
G-BXUU	Cameron V-65 balloon	M. D. Freeston & S. Mitchell	
G-BXUW	Cameron Colt 90A balloon	V. Beardall	
G-BXUX	Brandli Cherry BX-2	M. F. Fountain	
G-BXUY	Cessna 310Q	G. A. Vickers	
G-BXVA	SOCATA TB200 Tobago XL	M. Goehen	
G-BXVB	Cessna 152 II	PJC (Leasing) Ltd	
G-BXVD	CFM Streak Shadow SA	I. J. C. Burman	
G-BXVG	Sky 77-24 balloon	M. Wolf	
G-BXVK	Robin HR.200/120B	Modi Aviation Ltd	
G-BXVM	Van's RV-6A	J. C. Lomax	
G-BXVO	Van's RV-6A	B. R. Hunter	
G-BXVP	Sky 31-24 balloon	T. Dudman	
G-BXVR	Sky 90-24 balloon	P. Hegarty	
G-BXVS	Brügger MB.2 Colibri	G. T. Snoddon	
G-BXVT	Cameron O-77 balloon	R. P. Wade	
G-BXVU	PA-28-161 Warrior II	Jet Connections Ltd	
G-BXVV	Cameron V-90 balloon	Adeilad Cladding	
G-BXVX	Rutan Cozy	G. E. Murray	
G-BXVY	Cessna 152	Stapleford Flying Club Ltd	
G-BXWA	Beech 76 Duchess	Aviation South West Ltd	
G-BXWB	Robin HR.100/200B	Yorkshire Land Ltd	
G-BXWG	Sky 120-24 balloon	M. E. White	
G-BXWH	Denney Kitfox Mk.4-1200	M. G. Porter	
G-BXWK	Rans S.6-ESA Coyote II	P. B. Davey	
G-BXWL	Sky 90-24 balloon	E. J. Briggs	
G-BXWO	PA-28-181 Archer II	J. S. Develin & Z. Islam	
G-BXWP	PA-32 Cherokee Six 300	R. J. Sharpe	
G-BXWR	CFM Streak Shadow	M. A. Hayward (G-MZMI)	
G-BXWT	Van's RV-6	R. C. Owen	
G-BXWU	FLS Aerospace Sprint 160	Aeroelvia Ltd	
G-BXWV	FLS Aerospace Sprint 160	Aeroelvia Ltd	
G-BXWX	Sky 25-16 balloon	C. O'Neill & G. Davis	
G-BXXG	Cameron N-105 balloon	R. N. Simpkins	
G-BXXH	Hatz CB-1	R. D. Shingler	
G-BXXI	Grob G.109B	M. N. Martin	
G-BXXJ	Colt Flying Yacht SS balloon	Magical Adventures Ltd/USA	
G-BXXK	Cessna FR.172N	P. Porter	
G-BXXL	Cameron N-105 balloon	C. J. Dunkley	
G-BXXN	Robinson R22 Beta	Helicopter Services	
G-BXXO	Lindstrand LBL-90B balloon	G. P. Walton	
G-BXXP	Sky 77-24 balloon	T. R. Wood	
G-BXXS	Sky 105-24 balloon	Flying Pictures Ltd	
G-BXXT	Beech 76 Duchess	Pridenote Ltd	
G-BXXU	Colt 31A balloon	Sade Balloons Ltd	
G-BXXW	Enstrom F-28F	D. A. Marks (G-SCOX)	

Notes	Reg.	Type	Owner or Operator
	G-BXYE	CP.301-C1 Emeraude	D. T. Gethin
	G-BXYF	Colt AS-105 GD airship	LN Flying Ltd
	G-BXYI	Cameron H-34 balloon	S. P. Harrowing
	G-BXYJ	Jodel DR.1050	G-BXYJ Group
	G-BXYM	PA-28 Cherokee 235	Redfly Aviation Ltd
	G-BXYO	PA-28RT-201 Arrow IV	S. Viner
	G-BXYP	PA-28RT-201 Arrow IV	G. I. Cooper
	G-BXYT	PA-28RT-201 Arrow IV	Falcon Flying Services Ltd
	G-BXZA	PA-38-112 Tomahawk	Aviatlantic
	G-BXZB	Nanchang CJ-6A (2632019)	R. Davy & J. L. Swallow
	G-BXZF	Lindstrand LBL-90A balloon	B. T. Harris
	G-BXZI	Lindstrand LBL-90A balloon	J. A. Viner
	G-BXZK	MDH MD-900 Explorer	Police & Crime Commissioner for West Yorkshire
	G-BXZO	Pietenpol Air Camper	P. J. Cooke
	G-BXZU	Micro Aviation Bantam B.22-S	M. E. Whapham & R. W. Hollamby
	G-BXZV	CFM Streak Shadow	M. D. O'Brien
	G-BXZY	CFM Streak Shadow Srs DD	G. T. Webster
	G-BYAT	Boeing 757-204ER	Thomson Airways Ltd
	G-BYAV	Taylor JT.1 Monoplane	D. M. Lockley
	G-BYAW	Boeing 757-204ER	Thomson Airways Ltd
	G-BYAX	Boeing 757-204ER	Thomson Airways Ltd
	G-BYAY	Boeing 757-204ER	Thomson Airways Ltd
	G-BYAZ	CFM Streak Shadow	A. G. Wright
	G-BYBC	Agusta-Bell 206B JetRanger 2	Sky Charter UK Ltd (G-BTWW)
	G-BYBD	Cessna F.172H	S. Cooke (G-OBHX/G-AWMU)
	G-BYBE	Jodel D.120A	J. M. Alexander
	G-BYBF	Robin R.2160i	D. J. R. Lloyd-Evans
	G-BYBH	PA-34-200T Seneca II	Goldspear (UK) Ltd
	G-BYBI	Bell 206B JetRanger 3	Castle Air Ltd
	G-BYBJ	Medway Hybred 44XLR	M. Gardner
	G-BYBK	Murphy Rebel	J. R. Howard
	G-BYBL	Gardan GY-80 Horizon 160D	M. J. Sutton
	G-BYBM	Avtech Jabiru SK	P. J. Hatton
	G-BYBN	Cameron N-77 balloon	M. G. Howard
	G-BYBO	Medway Hybred 44XLR Eclipser	C. Hershaw
	G-BYBP	Cessna A.185F	G. M. S. Scott
	G-BYBR	Rans S.6-116 Coyote II	S. & A. F. Williams
	G-BYBS	Sky 80-16 balloon	B. K. Rippon
	G-BYBU	Renegade Spirit UK	R. L. Williams
	G-BYBV	Mainair Rapier	M. W. Robson
	G-BYBX	Slingsby T.67M Firefly 260	Slingsby Advanced Composites Ltd
	G-BYBY	Thorp T.18C Tiger	P. G. Mair
	G-BYBZ	Jabiru SK	D. Licheri
	G-BYCA	PA-28 Cherokee 140D	R. Steptoe
	G-BYCD	Cessna 140 (modified)	D. J. Whittaker
	G-BYCF	Robinson R22 Beta II	Heliservices
	G-BYCJ	CFM Shadow Srs DD	P. I. Hodgson
	G-BYCM	Rans S.6-ES Coyote II	E. W. McMullan
	G-BYCN	Rans S.6-ES Coyote II	T. J. Croskery
	G-BYCP	Beech B200 Super King Air	London Executive Aviation Ltd
	G-BYCS	Jodel DR.1051	G. A. Stops
	G-BYCT	Aero L-29A Delfin	M. P. Grimshaw & M. C. Hall
	G-BYCV	Meridian Maverick 430	A. Vaughan
	G-BYCW	Mainair Blade 912	P. C. Watson
	G-BYCX	Westland Wasp HAS.1	C. J. Marsden
	G-BYCY	I.I.I. Sky Arrow 650T	K. A. Daniels
	G-BYCZ	Avtech Jabiru SK	T. Herbert
	G-BYDB	Grob G.115B	J. B. Baker
	G-BYDE	VS.361 Spitfire LF. IX (PT879)	P. A. Teichman
	G-BYDF	Sikorsky S-76A	Brecqhou Development Ltd
	G-BYDG	Beech C24R Sierra	Professional Flight Simulation Ltd
	G-BYDJ	Colt 120A balloon	D. K. Hempleman-Adams
	G-BYDK	SNCAN Stampe SV.4C	Bianchi Aviation Film Services Ltd
	G-BYDL	Hawker Hurricane IIB (Z5207)	P. J. Lawton
	G-BYDT	Cameron N-90 balloon	R. M. Stanley
	G-BYDV	Van's RV-6	B. F. Hill
	G-BYDY	Beech 58 Baron	Pilot Services Flying Group Ltd
	G-BYDZ	Pegasus Quantum 15-912	A. Beatty
	G-BYEA	Cessna 172P	M. Gates
	G-BYEC	Glaser-Dirks DG.800B	The 23 Syndicate

Reg.	Type	Owner or Operator	Notes
G-BYEE	Mooney M.20K	Double Echo Flying Group	
G-BYEH	CEA Jodel DR.250	S. T. Scully	
G-BYEJ	Scheibe SF-28A Tandem Falke	D. Shrimpton	
G-BYEK	Stoddard Hamilton Glastar	M. W. Meynell	
G-BYEL	Van's RV-6	D. Millar	
G-BYEM	Cessna R.182 RG	Bickertons Aerodromes Ltd	
G-BYEO	Zenair CH.601HDS	J. R. Clarke	
G-BYER	Cameron C-80 balloon	J. M. Langley	
G-BYES	Cessna 172P	Surrey Aviation Ltd	
G-BYEW	Pegasus Quantum 15-912	W. B. J. Davis	
G-BYEY	Lindstrand LBL-21 Silver Dream balloon	Oscair Project Ltd/Sweden	
G-BYFA	Cessna F.152 II	Redhill Air Services Ltd (G-WACA)	
G-BYFC	Avtech Jabiru SK	M. Flint	
G-BYFF	Pegasus Quantum 15-912	T. A. Willcox	
G-BYFI	CFM Starstreak Shadow SA	J. A. Cook	
G-BYFJ	Cameron N-105 balloon	R. J. Mercer	
G-BYFK	Cameron Printer 105 SS balloon	Mobberley Balloon Collection	
G-BYFL	Diamond HK.36 TTS	Seahawk Gliding Club	
G-BYFM	Jodel DR.1050M-1 (replica)	A. J. Roxburgh	
G-BYFR	PA-32R-301 Saratoga II HP	ATT Aviation Holding Ltd	
G-BYFT	Pietenpol Air Camper	G. Everett	
G-BYFV	TEAM mini-MAX 91	W. E. Gillham	
G-BYFX	Colt 77A balloon	Wye Valley Aviation Ltd	
G-BYFY	Avions Mudry CAP-10B	R. N. Crosland	
G-BYGA	Boeing 747-436	British Airways	
G-BYGB	Boeing 747-436	British Airways	
G-BYGC	Boeing 747-436	British Airways	
G-BYGD	Boeing 747-436	British Airways	
G-BYGE	Boeing 747-436	British Airways	
G-BYGF	Boeing 747-436	British Airways	
G-BYGG	Boeing 747-436	British Airways	
G-BYHC	Cameron Z-90 balloon	T. J. Wilkinson	
G-BYHE	Robinson R22 Beta	Helicopter Services Ltd	
G-BYHG	Dornier 328-100	Loganair Ltd	
G-BYHH	PA-28-161 Warrior III	Stapleford Flying Club Ltd	
G-BYHI	PA-28-161 Warrior II	T. W. & W. S. Gilbert	
G-BYHJ	PA-28R-201 Arrow	Flew LLP	
G-BYHK	PA-28-181 Archer III	T-Air Services	
G-BYHL	DHC.1 Chipmunk 22 (WG308)	M. R. & I. D. Higgins	
G-BYHO	Mainair Blade 912	T. Porter & D. Whiteley	
G-BYHP	CEA DR.253B	HP Flying Group	
G-BYHR	Pegasus Quantum 15-912	I. D. Chantler	
G-BYHS	Mainair Blade 912	Telzor Group	
G-BYHT	Robin DR.400/180R	Deeside Robin Group	
G-BYHU	Cameron N-105 balloon	ABC Flights Ltd	
G-BYHV	Raj Hamsa X'Air 582	M. G. Adams	
G-BYHY	Cameron V-77 balloon	P. Spellward	
G-BYIA	Avtech Jabiru SK	M. D. Doyle	
G-BYIB	Rans S.6-ES Coyote II	W. Anderson	
G-BYID	Rans S.6-ES Coyote II	R. M. Watson	
G-BYIE	Robinson R22 Beta II	G. R. S. Harrison	
G-BYII	TEAM mini-MAX	G. Wilkinson	
G-BYIJ	CASA 1.131E Jungmann 2000	R. N. Crosland	
G-BYIK	Shaw Europa	P. M. Davis	
G-BYIL	Cameron N-105 balloon	N. W. N. Townshend	
G-BYIM	Avtech Jabiru UL	A. & J. McVey	
G-BYIN	RAF 2000 gyroplane	J. R. Legge	
G-BYIO	Colt 105A balloon	N. Charbonnier/Italy	
G-BYIP	Aerotek Pitts S-2A Special	D. P. Heather-Hayes	
G-BYIR	Aerotek Pitts S-1S Special	S. Kramer	
G-BYIS	Pegasus Quantum 15-912	D. J. Ramsden	
G-BYIU	Cameron V-90 balloon	H. Micketeit/Germany	
G-BYIV	Cameron PM-80 balloon	A. Schneider/Germany	
G-BYIW	Cameron PM-80 balloon	Team Ballooning/Germany	
G-BYIX	Cameron PM-80 balloon	A. Schneider/Germany	
G-BYIY	Lindstrand LBL-105B balloon	J. H. Dobson	
G-BYJA	RAF 2000 GTX-SE	C. R. W. Lyne	
G-BYJB	Mainair Blade 912	P. C. Terry	
G-BYJC	Cameron N-90 balloon	A. G. Merry	
G-BYJD	Avtech Jabiru UL	M. W. Knights	

Notes	Reg.	Type	Owner or Operator
	G-BYJE	TEAM Mini-MAX 91	T. A. Willcox
	G-BYJF	Thorpe T.211	AD Aviation Ltd
	G-BYJH	Grob G.109B	A. J. Buchanan
	G-BYJI	Shaw Europa	M. Gibson (G-ODTI)
	G-BYJK	Pegasus Quantum 15-912	C. Yaxley
	G-BYJL	Aero Designs Pulsar	F. A. H. Ashmead
	G-BYJM	Cyclone AX2000	I. Miles
	G-BYJN	Lindstrand LBL-105A balloon	B. Meeson
	G-BYJO	Rans S.6-ES Coyote II	D. J. Warren
	G-BYJP	Aerotek Pitts S-1S Special	Eaglescott Pitts Group
	G-BYJR	Lindstrand LBL-77B balloon	B. M. Reed
	G-BYJS	SOCATA TB20 Trinidad	A. P. Bedford
	G-BYJT	Zenair CH.601HD	J. D. T. Tannock
	G-BYJW	Cameron Sphere 105 balloon	Balleroy Developpement SAS
	G-BYJX	Cameron C-70 balloon	B. Perona
	G-BYKA	Lindstrand LBL-69A balloon	B. Meeson
	G-BYKB	Rockwell Commander 114	Hayling Island Safety Consultancy Ltd
	G-BYKC	Mainair Blade 912	A. Williams
	G-BYKD	Mainair Blade 912	D. C. Boyle
	G-BYKF	Enstrom F-28F	S. C. Severeyns & G. T. Williams
	G-BYKG	Pietenpol Air Camper	K. B. Hodge
	G-BYKI	Cameron N-105 balloon	J. A. Leahy/Ireland
	G-BYKJ	Westland Scout AH.1	Austen Associates
	G-BYKK	Robinson R44	Dragonfly Aviation
	G-BYKL	PA-28-181 Archer II	Transport Command Ltd
	G-BYKP	PA-28R-201T Turbo Arrow IV	D. W. Knox & D. L. Grimes
	G-BYKT	Pegasus Quantum 15-912	N. J. Howarth
	G-BYKU	BFC Challenger II	P. A. Tarplee
	G-BYKW	Lindstrand LBL-77B balloon	K. Allemand/France
	G-BYKX	Cameron N-90 balloon	C. O'N. Davis
	G-BYLB	D. H. 82A Tiger Moth	P. A. Layzell
	G-BYLC	Pegasus Quantum 15-912	T. J. C. Horne
	G-BYLD	Pietenpol Air Camper	S. Bryan
	G-BYLF	Zenair CH.601HDS Zodiac	S. Plater
	G-BYLI	Nova Vertex 22 hang glider	M. Hay
	G-BYLJ	Letov LK-2M Sluka	W. J. McCarroll
	G-BYLL	Sequoia F.8L Falco	N. J. Langrick
	G-BYLO	T.66 Nipper Srs 1	M. J. A. Trudgill
	G-BYLP	Rand-Robinson KR-2	C. S. Hales
	G-BYLS	Bede BD-4	P. J. Greenrod
	G-BYLT	Raj Hamsa X'Air 582	T. W. Phipps
	G-BYLV	Thunder Ax8-105 S2 balloon	kb Voli Di Chiozzi Bartolomeo EC SAS/Italy
	G-BYLW	Lindstrand LBL-77A balloon	Associazione Gran Premio Italiano
	G-BYLX	Lindstrand LBL-105A balloon	Italiana Aeronavi/Italy
	G-BYLY	Cameron V-77 balloon (1)	R. Bayly/Italy (G-ULIA)
	G-BYLZ	Rutan Cozy	W. S. Allen
	G-BYMB	Diamond Katana DA20-C1	S. Staniulis & A. Zakaras
	G-BYMD	PA-38-112 Tomahawk II	M. A. Petrie
	G-BYMF	Pegasus Quantum 15-912	G. R. Stockdale
	G-BYMG	Cameron A-210 balloon	Cloud Nine Balloon Co
	G-BYMH	Cessna 152	PJC (Leasing) Ltd
	G-BYMI	Pegasus Quantum 15	N. C. Grayson
	G-BYMJ	Cessna 152	PJC (Leasing) Ltd
	G-BYMK	Dornier 328-100	Loganair Ltd
	G-BYMN	Rans S.6-ESA Coyote II	R. J. P. Herivel
	G-BYMP	Campbell Cricket Mk 1	J. J. Fitzgerald
	G-BYMR	Raj Hamsa X'Air R100(3)	W. Drury
	G-BYMU	Rans S.6-ES Coyote II	I. R. Russell
	G-BYMV	Rans S.6-ES Coyote II	R. M. Moulton
	G-BYMW	Boland 52-12 balloon	C. Jones
	G-BYMX	Cameron A-105 balloon	H. Reis/Germany
	G-BYMY	Cameron N-90 balloon	A. Cakss
	G-BYNA	Cessna F.172H	D. M. White (G-AWTH)
	G-BYND	Pegasus Quantum 15	W. J. Upton
	G-BYNE	Pilatus PC-6/B2-H4 Turbo Porter	D. M. Penny
	G-BYNF	NA-64 Yale I (3349)	R. S. Van Dijk
	G-BYNI	Rotorway Exec 90	M. Bunn
	G-BYNK	Robin HR.200/160	Penguin Flight Group
	G-BYNM	Mainair Blade 912	J. P. Hanlon & A. C. McAllister
	G-BYNN	Cameron V-90 balloon	Cloud Nine Balloon Group
	G-BYNP	Rans S.6-ES Coyote II	R. J. Lines

Reg.	Type	Owner or Operator	Notes
G-BYNS	Avtech Jabiru SK	D. K. Lawry	
G-BYNU	Cameron Thunder Ax7-77 balloon	B. Fisher	
G-BYNW	Cameron H-34 balloon	I. M. Ashpole	
G-BYNX	Cameron RX-105 balloon	Cameron Balloons Ltd	
G-BYNY	Beech 76 Duchess	Magenta Ltd	
G-BYOB	Slingsby T.67M Firefly 260	Stapleford Flying Club Ltd	
G-BYOD	Slingsby T.67C	D. I. Stanbridge	
G-BYOG	Pegasus Quantum 15-912	M. D. Hinge	
G-BYOH	Raj Hamsa X'Air 582 (5)	J. Owen	
G-BYOI	Sky 80-16 balloon	D. J. Tofton	
G-BYOJ	Raj Hamsa X'Air 582 (1)	T. C. Ellison	
G-BYOK	Cameron V-90 balloon	D. S. Wilson	
G-BYON	Mainair Blade	R. Campbell-Moore	
G-BYOO	CFM Streak Shadow	G. R. Eastwood	
G-BYOR	Raj Hamsa X'Air 582(7)	R. Dilkes	
G-BYOT	Rans S.6-ES Coyote II	G. Shaw	
G-BYOU	Rans S.6-ES Coyote II	P. G. Bright & G. Thompson	
G-BYOV	Pegasus Quantum 15-912	M. Howland	
G-BYOW	Mainair Blade	J. Stobie & I. Bryden	
G-BYOX	Cameron Z-90 balloon	D. R. Rawlings	
G-BYOZ	Mainair Rapier	A. G. Lomas	
G-BYPB	Pegasus Quantum 15-912	Cleaprop Microlight School Ltd	
G-BYPD	Cameron A-105 balloon	Headland Hotel Ltd	
G-BYPE	Gardan GY-80 Horizon 160D	P. B. Hodgson	
G-BYPF	Thruster T.600N	M. A. Beadman	
G-BYPG	Thruster T.600N	M. A. Roxburgh	
G-BYPH	Thruster T.600N	D. M. Canham	
G-BYPJ	Pegasus Quantum 15-912	M. Watson	
G-BYPL	Pegasus Quantum 15-912	N. J. Evison	
G-BYPM	Shaw Europa XS	G. F.Stratton	
G-BYPN	MS.880B Rallye Club	R. Edwards and D. & S. A. Bell	
G-BYPO	Raj Hamsa X'Air 582 (1)	D. W. Willis	
G-BYPR	Zenair CH.601HD Zodiac	R. Line	
G-BYPT	Rans S.6-ES Coyote II	G. P. & P. T. Willcox	
G-BYPU	PA-32R-301 Saratoga SP	AM Blatch Electrical Contractors Ltd	
G-BYPW	Raj Hamsa X'Air 583 (3)	K. J. Kimpton	
G-BYPY	Ryan ST3KR (001)	T. Curtis-Taylor	
G-BYPZ	Rans S.6-116 Super 6	R. A. Blackbourne	
G-BYRC	Westland WS-58 Wessex HC.2 (XT671)	D. Brem-Wilson	
G-BYRG	Rans S.6-ES Coyote II	S. J. Macmillan	
G-BYRJ	Pegasus Quantum 15-912	R. W. Taplin	
G-BYRK	Cameron V-42 balloon	R. Kunert	
G-BYRO	Mainair Blade	P. W. F. Coleman	
G-BYRR	Mainair Blade 912	G. R. Sharples	
G-BYRU	Pegasus Quantum 15-912	L. M. Westwood	
G-BYRV	Raj Hamsa X'Air 582 (1)	A. D. Russell	
G-BYRX	Westland Scout AH.1 (XT634)	Edwalton Aviation Ltd	
G-BYRY	Slingsby T.67M Firefly 200	PI Air Services SPRL/Belgium	
G-BYSA	Shaw Europa XS	R. L. Hitchcock	
G-BYSE	Agusta-Bell 206B JetRanger 2	C. I. Motors Ltd (G-BFND)	
G-BYSF	Avtech Jabiru UL	P. F. Morgan	
G-BYSG	Robin HR.200/120B	Modi Aviation Ltd	
G-BYSI	WSK-PZL Koliber 160A	J. & D. F. Evans	
G-BYSJ	DHC.1 Chipmunk 22 (WB569:R)	Propshop Ltd	
G-BYSK	Cameron A-275 balloon	Balloon School (International) Ltd	
G-BYSM	Cameron A-210 balloon	Balloon School (International) Ltd	
G-BYSN	Rans S.6-ES Coyote II	M. Salisbury	
G-BYSP	PA-28-181 Archer II	Take Flight Aviation Ltd	
G-BYSS	Medway Rebel SS	K. A. Sutton	
G-BYSV	Cameron N-120 balloon	S. Simmington	
G-BYSX	Pegasus Quantum 15-912	P. Simpson	
G-BYSY	Raj Hamsa X'Air 582 (1)	I. D. Mallinson	
G-BYTB	SOCATA TB20 Trinidad	Watchman Aircraft Ltd	
G-BYTC	Pegasus Quantum 15-912	P. J. Ensinger	
G-BYTI	PA-24 Comanche 250	M. Carruthers & G. Auchterlonie	
G-BYTJ	Cameron C-80 balloon	R. A. Vale	
G-BYTK	Avtech Jabiru UL	G. R. Phillips	
G-BYTL	Mainair Blade 912	D. A. Meek & T.J. Burrow	
G-BYTM	Dyn' Aero MCR-01	I. Lang & E. J. Clarke	
G-BYTN	DH.82A Tiger Moth (N6720:VX)	R. Merewood & J. W. Freckington	
G-BYTR	Raj Hamsa X'Air 582 (1)	P. R. Howson	

Notes	Reg.	Type	Owner or Operator
	G-BYTS	Montgomerie-Bensen B.8MR gyroplane	C. Seaman
	G-BYTU	Mainair Blade 912	G-BYTES
	G-BYTV	Avtech Jabiru UK	M. W. T. Wilson
	G-BYTW	Cameron O-90 balloon	Sade Balloons Ltd
	G-BYTZ	Raj Hamsa X'Air 582 (1)	R. Armstrong
	G-BYUA	Grob G.115E Tutor	Babcock Aerospace Ltd
	G-BYUB	Grob G.115E Tutor	Babcock Aerospace Ltd
	G-BYUC	Grob G.115E Tutor	Babcock Aerospace Ltd
	G-BYUD	Grob G.115E Tutor	Babcock Aerospace Ltd
	G-BYUE	Grob G.115E Tutor	Babcock Aerospace Ltd
	G-BYUF	Grob G.115E Tutor	Babcock Aerospace Ltd
	G-BYUG	Grob G.115E Tutor	Babcock Aerospace Ltd
	G-BYUH	Grob G.115E Tutor	Babcock Aerospace Ltd
	G-BYUI	Grob G.115E Tutor	Babcock Aerospace Ltd
	G-BYUJ	Grob G.115E Tutor	Babcock Aerospace Ltd
	G-BYUK	Grob G.115E Tutor	Babcock Aerospace Ltd
	G-BYUL	Grob G.115E Tutor	Babcock Aerospace Ltd
	G-BYUM	Grob G.115E Tutor	Babcock Aerospace Ltd
	G-BYUN	Grob G.115E Tutor	Babcock Aerospace Ltd
	G-BYUO	Grob G.115E Tutor	Babcock Aerospace Ltd
	G-BYUP	Grob G.115E Tutor	Babcock Aerospace Ltd
	G-BYUR	Grob G.115E Tutor	Babcock Aerospace Ltd
	G-BYUS	Grob G.115E Tutor	Babcock Aerospace Ltd
	G-BYUU	Grob G.115E Tutor	Babcock Aerospace Ltd
	G-BYUV	Grob G.115E Tutor	Babcock Aerospace Ltd
	G-BYUW	Grob G.115E Tutor	Babcock Aerospace Ltd
	G-BYUX	Grob G.115E Tutor	Babcock Aerospace Ltd
	G-BYUY	Grob.G.115E Tutor	Babcock Aerospace Ltd
	G-BYUZ	Grob G.115E Tutor	Babcock Aerospace Ltd
	G-BYVA	Grob G.115E Tutor	Babcock Aerospace Ltd
	G-BYVB	Grob G.115E Tutor	Babcock Aerospace Ltd
	G-BYVC	Grob G.115E Tutor	Babcock Aerospace Ltd
	G-BYVD	Grob G.115E Tutor	Babcock Aerospace Ltd
	G-BYVE	Grob G.115E Tutor	Babcock Aerospace Ltd
	G-BYVF	Grob G.115E Tutor	Babcock Aerospace Ltd
	G-BYVG	Grob G.115E Tutor	Babcock Aerospace Ltd
	G-BYVH	Grob G.115E Tutor	Babcock Aerospace Ltd
	G-BYVI	Grob G.115E Tutor	Babcock Aerospace Ltd
	G-BYVJ	Grob G.115E Tutor	Babcock Aerospace Ltd
	G-BYVK	Grob G.115E Tutor	Babcock Aerospace Ltd
	G-BYVL	Grob G.115E Tutor	Babcock Aerospace Ltd
	G-BYVM	Grob G.115E Tutor	Babcock Aerospace Ltd
	G-BYVO	Grob G.115E Tutor	Babcock Aerospace Ltd
	G-BYVP	Grob G.115E Tutor	Babcock Aerospace Ltd
	G-BYVR	Grob G.115E Tutor	Babcock Aerospace Ltd
	G-BYVS	Grob G.115E Tutor	Babcock Aerospace Ltd
	G-BYVT	Grob G.115E Tutor	Babcock Aerospace Ltd
	G-BYVU	Grob G.115E Tutor	Babcock Aerospace Ltd
	G-BYVV	Grob G.115E Tutor	Babcock Aerospace Ltd
	G-BYVW	Grob G.115E Tutor	Babcock Aerospace Ltd
	G-BYVX	Grob G.115E Tutor	Babcock Aerospace Ltd
	G-BYVY	Grob G.115E Tutor	Babcock Aerospace Ltd
	G-BYVZ	Grob G.115E Tutor	Babcock Aerospace Ltd
	G-BYWA	Grob G.115E Tutor	Babcock Aerospace Ltd
	G-BYWB	Grob G.115E Tutor	Babcock Aerospace Ltd
	G-BYWC	Grob G.115E Tutor	Babcock Aerospace Ltd
	G-BYWD	Grob G.115E Tutor	Babcock Aerospace Ltd
	G-BYWE	Grob G.115E Tutor	Babcock Aerospace Ltd
	G-BYWF	Grob G.115E Tutor	Babcock Aerospace Ltd
	G-BYWG	Grob G.115E Tutor	Babcock Aerospace Ltd
	G-BYWH	Grob G.115E Tutor	Babcock Aerospace Ltd
	G-BYWI	Grob G.115E Tutor	Babcock Aerospace Ltd
	G-BYWJ	Grob G.115E Tutor	Babcock Aerospace Ltd
	G-BYWK	Grob G.115E Tutor	Babcock Aerospace Ltd
	G-BYWL	Grob G.115E Tutor	Babcock Aerospace Ltd
	G-BYWM	Grob G.115E Tutor	Babcock Aerospace Ltd
	G-BYWN	Grob G.115E Tutor	Babcock Aerospace Ltd
	G-BYWO	Grob G.115E Tutor	Babcock Aerospace Ltd
	G-BYWP	Grob G.115E Tutor	Babcock Aerospace Ltd
	G-BYWR	Grob G.115E Tutor	Babcock Aerospace Ltd
	G-BYWS	Grob G.115E Tutor	Babcock Aerospace Ltd

Reg.	Type	Owner or Operator	Notes
G-BYWT	Grob G-115E Tutor	Babcock Aerospace Ltd	
G-BYWU	Grob G.115E Tutor	Babcock Aerospace Ltd	
G-BYWV	Grob G.115E Tutor	Babcock Aerospace Ltd	
G-BYWW	Grob G.115E Tutor	Babcock Aerospace Ltd	
G-BYWX	Grob G.115E Tutor	Babcock Aerospace Ltd	
G-BYWY	Grob G.115E Tutor	Babcock Aerospace Ltd	
G-BYWZ	Grob G.115E Tutor	Babcock Aerospace Ltd	
G-BYXA	Grob G.115E Tutor	Babcock Aerospace Ltd	
G-BYXB	Grob G.115E Tutor	Babcock Aerospace Ltd	
G-BYXC	Grob G.115E Tutor	Babcock Aerospace Ltd	
G-BYXD	Grob G.115E Tutor	Babcock Aerospace Ltd	
G-BYXE	Grob G.115E Tutor	Babcock Aerospace Ltd	
G-BYXF	Grob G.115E Tutor	Babcock Aerospace Ltd	
G-BYXG	Grob G.115E Tutor	Babcock Aerospace Ltd	
G-BYXH	Grob G.115E Tutor	Babcock Aerospace Ltd	
G-BYXI	Grob G.115E Tutor	Babcock Aerospace Ltd	
G-BYXJ	Grob G.115E Tutor	Babcock Aerospace Ltd	
G-BYXK	Grob G.115E Tutor	Babcock Aerospace Ltd	
G-BYXL	Grob G.115E Tutor	Babcock Aerospace Ltd	
G-BYXM	Grob G.115E Tutor	Babcock Aerospace Ltd	
G-BYXN	Grob G.115E Tutor	Babcock Aerospace Ltd	
G-BYXO	Grob G.115E Tutor	Babcock Aerospace Ltd	
G-BYXP	Grob G.115E Tutor	Babcock Aerospace Ltd	
G-BYXS	Grob G.115E Tutor	Babcock Aerospace Ltd	
G-BYXT	Grob G.115E Tutor	Babcock Aerospace Ltd	
G-BYXW	Medway Eclipser	G. A. Hazell	
G-BYXX	Grob G.115E Tutor	Babcock Aerospace Ltd	
G-BYXY	Grob G.115E Tutor	Babcock Aerospace Ltd	
G-BYXZ	Grob G.115E Tutor	Babcock Aerospace Ltd	
G-BYYA	Grob G.115E Tutor	Babcock Aerospace Ltd	
G-BYYB	Grob G.115E Tutor	Babcock Aerospace Ltd	
G-BYYC	Hapi Cygnet SF-2A	G. H. Smith	
G-BYYE	Lindstrand LBL-77A balloon	Virgin Balloon Flights	
G-BYYG	Slingsby T.67C	The Pathfinder Flying Club Ltd	
G-BYYL	Avtech Jabiru SPL-450	S. Langley	
G-BYYM	Raj Hamsa X'Air 582 (1)	S. M. S. Smith	
G-BYYN	Pegasus Quantum 15-912	R. J. Bullock	
G-BYYO	PA-28R -201 Arrow III	Stapleford Flying Club Ltd	
G-BYYP	Pegasus Quantum 15	D. A. Linsey-Bloom	
G-BYYR	Raj Hamsa X'Air 582 (4)	T. D. Bawden	
G-BYYT	Avtech Jabiru UL 450	A. C. Cale and A. J. Young.	
G-BYYX	TEAM mini-MAX 91	P. S. Lewinton	
G-BYYY	Pegasus Quantum 15-912	Clearprop Microlight School Ltd	
G-BYYZ	Staaken Z-21A Flitzer	T. White	
G-BYZA	AS.355F2 Twin Squirrel	MMAir Ltd	
G-BYZB	Mainair Blade	A. M. Thornley	
G-BYZF	Raj Hamsa X'Air 582 (1)	R. P. Davies	
G-BYZG	Cameron A-275 balloon	A. M. Holly	
G-BYZL	Cameron GP-65 balloon	P. Thibo	
G-BYZO	Rans S.6-ES Coyote II	Golf Zulu Oscar Group	
G-BYZP	Robinson R22 Beta	Aero-Heli Ltd	
G-BYZR	I.I.I. Sky Arrow 650TC	G-BYZR Flying Group	
G-BYZS	Avtech Jabiru UL-450	D. P. Pearson	
G-BYZT	Nova Vertex 26	M. Hay	
G-BYZU	Pegasus Quantum 15	N. I. Clifton	
G-BYZV	Sky 90-24 balloon	P. Farmer	
G-BYZW	Raj Hamsa X'Air 582 (2)	H. C. Lowther	
G-BYZX	Cameron R-90 balloon	D. K. Hempleman-Adams	
G-BYZY	Pietenpol Aircamper	D. M. Hanchett	
G-BZAE	Cessna 152	Tatenhill Aviation Ltd	
G-BZAI	Pegasus Quantum 15	K. M. Sullivan	
G-BZAK	Raj Hamsa X'Air 582 (1)	G. L. Daniels	
G-BZAL	Mainair Blade 912	J. Potts	
G-BZAM	Europa	K. N. Cobb	
G-BZAP	Avtech Jabiru UL-450	I. J. Grindley & D. R. Griffiths	
G-BZAR	Denney Kitfox 4-1200 Speedster	N. J. France (G-LEZJ)	
G-BZAS	Isaacs Fury II (K5673)	N. C. Stone	
G-BZBC	Rans S.6-ES Coyote II	A. J. Baldwin	
G-BZBE	Cameron A-210 balloon	L. J. M. Muir	
G-BZBF	Cessna 172M	L. W. Scattergood	

Notes	Reg.	Type	Owner or Operator
	G-BZBH	Thunder Ax6-65 balloon	P. J. Hebdon & A. C. Fraser
	G-BZBI	Cameron V-77 balloon	C. & A. I. Gibson
	G-BZBJ	Lindstrand LBL-77A balloon	P. T. R. Ollivere
	G-BZBL	Lindstrand LBL-120A balloon	East Coast Balloons Ltd
	G-BZBO	Stoddard-Hamilton Glasair III	M. B. Hamlett/France
	G-BZBP	Raj Hamsa X'Air 582 (1)	J. L. B. Roy
	G-BZBR	Pegasus Quantum 15-912	P. D. Neilson
	G-BZBS	PA-28-161 Warrior III	White Waltham Airfield Ltd
	G-BZBT	Cameron H-34 Hopper balloon	T. J. Wilkinson
	G-BZBU	Robinson R22	I. C. Macdonald
	G-BZBW	Rotorway Executive 162F	G-BZBW Group
	G-BZBX	Rans S.6-ES Coyote II	P. J. Taylor
	G-BZBZ	Jodel D.9	D. C. Unwin
	G-BZDA	PA-28-161 Warrior III	White Waltham Airfield Ltd
	G-BZDC	Mainair Blade	E. J. Wells & P. J. Smith
	G-BZDD	Mainair Blade 912	G. E. L. Philp
	G-BZDE	Lindstrand LBL-210A balloon	Toucan Travel Ltd
	G-BZDF	CFM Streak Shadow SA	W. M. Moylan
	G-BZDH	PA-28R Cherokee Arrow 200-II	G-BZDH Ltd
	G-BZDJ	Cameron Z-105 balloon	BWS Security Systems Ltd
	G-BZDK	X'Air 582(2)	G. W. Perry
	G-BZDM	Stoddard-Hamilton Glastar	F. G. Miskelly
	G-BZDN	Cameron N-105 balloon	I. R. Warrington & P. A. Foot
	G-BZDP	SA Bulldog Srs 120/121 (XX551:E)	R. M. Raikes
	G-BZDR	Tri-R Kis	D. F. Sutherland
	G-BZDS	Pegasus Quantum 15-912	K. C. Yeates
	G-BZDT	Maule MXT-7-180	Strongcrew Ltd
	G-BZDV	Westland Gazelle HT.2	D. A. Gregory
	G-BZEA	Cessna A.152	Sky Leisure Aviation (Charters) Ltd
	G-BZEB	Cessna 152	Sky Leisure Aviation (Charters) Ltd
	G-BZEC	Cessna 152	Sky Leisure Aviation (Charters) Ltd
	G-BZED	Pegasus Quantum 15-912	D. Crozier
	G-BZEG	Mainair Blade	R. P. Cookson
	G-BZEJ	Raj Hamsa X'Air 582 (7)	H-Flight X'Air Flying Group
	G-BZEL	Mainair Blade 912	E. Kelly & M. Neild
	G-BZEN	Avtech Jabiru UL-450	C. A. Gryniewicz
	G-BZEP	SA Bulldog Srs 120/121 (XX561:7)	R. C. Skinner
	G-BZER	Raj Hamsa X'Air R100 (1)	N. P. Lloyd & H. Lloyd-Jones
	G-BZES	Rotorway Executive 90	Southern Helicopters Ltd (G-LUFF)
	G-BZEU	Raj Hamsa X'Air 582 (2)	R. Marrs
	G-BZEW	Rans S.6-ES Coyote II	M. J. Wooldridge
	G-BZEY	Cameron N-90 balloon	Northants Auto Parts and Service Ltd
	G-BZEZ	CFM Streak Shadow	G. J. Pearce
	G-BZFB	Robin R.2112A	J. T. Britcher
	G-BZFC	Pegasus Quantum 15-912	G. Addison
	G-BZFD	Cameron N-90 balloon	C. D. & E. Gingell
	G-BZFG	Sky 105 balloon	Virgin Airship & Balloon Co Ltd
	G-BZFH	Pegasus Quantum 15-912	D. W. Adams
	G-BZFI	Avtech Jabiru UL	Group Family
	G-BZFN	SA Bulldog Srs 120/121 (XX667:16)	Risk Logical Ltd
	G-BZFP	DHC.6 Twin Otter 310	Loganair Ltd/Flybe.com
	G-BZFR	Extra EA.300/L	T. C. Beadle
	G-BZFS	Mainair Blade 912	N. R. Stockton
	G-BZFT	Murphy Rebel	R. Dixon
	G-BZFU	Lindstrand LBL HS-110 HA Airship	Lindstrand Hot Air Balloons Ltd
	G-BZFV	Zenair CH.601UL	M. E. Caton
	G-BZGA	DHC.1 Chipmunk 22 (WK585)	The Real Flying Co Ltd
	G-BZGB	DHC.1 Chipmunk 22 (WZ872:E)	G. Briggs
	G-BZGF	Rans S.6-ES Coyote II	C. A. Purvis & D. F. Castle
	G-BZGH	Cessna F.172N	Wicklow Wings
	G-BZGJ	Thunder Ax10-180 S2 balloon	Merlin Balloons
	G-BZGL	NA OV-10B Bronco (99+26)	Aircraft Restoration Co Ltd
	G-BZGM	Mainair Blade 912	D. Avery
	G-BZGO	Robinson R44	Flight Academy (Gyrocopters) Ltd
	G-BZGR	Rans S.6-ES Coyote II	J. M. Benton
	G-BZGS	Mainair Blade 912	M. J. Holmes
	G-BZGT	Avtech Jabiru SPL-450	P. J. Swain
	G-BZGV	Lindstrand LBL-77A balloon	J. H. Dryden
	G-BZGW	Mainair Blade	M. Liptrot
	G-BZGX	Raj Hamsa X'Air 582 (6)	P. J. Gleeson
	G-BZGY	Dyn'Aéro CR.100	B. Appleby

Reg.	Type	Owner or Operator	Notes
G-BZGZ	Pegasus Quantum 15-912	D. W. Beech	
G-BZHA	Boeing 767-336ER	British Airways	
G-BZHB	Boeing 767-336ER	British Airways	
G-BZHC	Boeing 767-336ER	British Airways	
G-BZHE	Cessna 152	International Artists Sports Management Ltd	
G-BZHF	Cessna 152	Modi Aviation Ltd	
G-BZHG	Tecnam P92 Echo	R. W. F. Boarder	
G-BZHJ	Raj Hamsa X'Air 582 (7)	S. Hardy	
G-BZHL	Noorduyn AT-16 Harvard IIB	R. H. Cooper & S. Swallow	
G-BZHN	Pegasus Quantum 15-912	A. M. Sirant	
G-BZHO	Pegasus Quantum 15	A. C. Brown & D. Reston	
G-BZHR	Avtech Jabiru UL-450	G. W. Rowbotham & W. Turner	
G-BZHT	PA-18A Super Cub 150	Lakes Gliding Club Ltd	
G-BZHU	Wag-Aero Sport Trainer	Teddy Boys Flying Group	
G-BZHV	PA-28-181 Archer III	R. M. & T. A. Limb	
G-BZHX	Thunder Ax11-250 S2 balloon	Wizard Balloons Ltd	
G-BZHY	Mainair Blade 912	R. F. Rankine	
G-BZIA	Raj Hamsa X'Air 700 (1)	J. L. Pritchett	
G-BZIC	Lindstrand LBL Sun SS balloon	Ballongaventyr 1 Sakne AB/Sweden	
G-BZID	Montgomerie-Bensen B.8MR	A. Gault	
G-BZIG	Thruster T.600N	K. M. Jones	
G-BZIH	Lindstrand LBL-31A balloon	H. & L. D. Vaughan	
G-BZII	Extra EA.300/1	D. Hayes	
G-BZIJ	Robin DR.400/500	Rob Airways Ltd	
G-BZIK	Cameron A-250 balloon	K. R. Karlstrom	
G-BZIL	Colt 120A balloon	Champagne Flights	
G-BZIM	Pegasus Quantum 15-912	M. J. Stalker	
G-BZIO	PA-28-161 Warrior III	White Waltham Airfield Ltd	
G-BZIP	Montgomerie-Bensen B.8MR	C. D. Prebble	
G-BZIS	Raj Hamsa X'Air 582 (2)	A. J. Spary	
G-BZIT	Beech 95-B55 Baron	Propellorhead Aviation Ltd	
G-BZIV	Avtech Jabiru UL-450	A. Parr	
G-BZIW	Pegasus Quantum 15-912	J. M. Hodgson	
G-BZIX	Cameron N-90 balloon	M. Stefanini & P. Marmugi/Italy	
G-BZIY	Raj Hamsa X'Air 582 (2)	A. L. A. Gill	
G-BZIZ	Ultramagic H-31 balloon	P. Spellward	
G-BZJB	Yakovlev Yak-52	L. V. Mougel	
G-BZJC	Thruster T.600N	M. H. Moulai	
G-BZJD	Thruster T.600T	C. C. Belcher	
G-BZJG	Cameron A-400 balloon	Cameron Balloons Ltd	
G-BZJH	Cameron Z-90 balloon	Balloon SpA	
G-BZJI	Nova X-Large 37 paraplane	M. Hay	
G-BZJM	VPM M-16 Tandem Trainer	D. Wood	
G-BZJN	Mainair Blade 912	K. Roberts	
G-BZJO	Pegasus Quantum 15	W. C. Bryan	
G-BZJP	Zenair CH.701UL	B. J. Fallows	
G-BZJR	Montgomerie-Bensen B.8MR	G. Golding (G-IPFM)	
G-BZJV	CASA 1-131E Jungmann 1000	R. A. Cumming	
G-BZJW	Cessna 150F	P. Ligertwood	
G-BZJZ	Pegasus Quantum 15	S. Baker	
G-BZKC	Raj Hamsa X'Air 582 (11)	J. E. Evans	
G-BZKD	Stolp Starduster Too	P. & C. Edmunds	
G-BZKE	Lindstrand LBL-77B balloon	H. Cresswell	
G-BZKF	Rans S.6-ES Coyote II	A. W. Lowrie	
G-BZKL	PA-28R-201 Arrow III	M. A. & M. H. Cromati	
G-BZKO	Rans S-6-ES Coyote II	G. Millar	
G-BZKU	Cameron Z-105 balloon	N. A. Fishlock	
G-BZKV	Cameron Sky 90-24 balloon	Omega Selction Services Ltd	
G-BZKW	Ultramagic M-77 balloon	Slowfly Montgolfiere SNC/Italy	
G-BZLC	WSK-PZL Koliber 160A	G. F. Smith	
G-BZLE	Rans S.6-ES Coyote II	B. M. Davis	
G-BZLF	CFM Shadow Srs CD	D. W. Stacey	
G-BZLG	Robin HR.200/120B	Flew LLP	
G-BZLH	PA-28-161 Warrior II	Multiflight Ltd	
G-BZLK	Slingsby T.31M Motor Tutor	G. Smith	
G-BZLL	Pegasus Quantum 15-912	R. Torrie	
G-BZLP	Robinson R44	Polar Helicopters Ltd	
G-BZLS	Cameron Sky 77-24 balloon	D. W. Young	
G-BZLU	Lindstrand LBL-90A balloon	A. E. Lusty	
G-BZLV	Avtech Jabiru UL-450	G. Dalton	
G-BZLX	Pegasus Quantum 15-912	D. McCabe & M. Harris	

Notes	Reg.	Type	Owner or Operator
	G-BZLY	Grob G.109B	R. W. Hegmann
	G-BZLZ	Pegasus Quantum 15-912	A. S. Martin
	G-BZMB	PA-28R-201 Arrow III	Thurrock Arrow Group
	G-BZMC	Avtech Jabiru UL	D. Maddison
	G-BZMD	SA Bulldog Srs 120/121 (XX554)	Mad Dog Flying Group
	G-BZME	SA Bulldog Srs 120/121 (XX698:9)	S. J. Whitworth
	G-BZMF	Rutan LongEz	Go-Ez Group
	G-BZMG	Robinson R44	G. Martinelli/Italy
	G-BZMH	SA Bulldog Srs 120/121 (XX692:A)	M. E. J. Hingley
	G-BZMJ	Rans S-6-ES Coyote II	R. J. G. Clark
	G-BZML	SA Bulldog Srs 120/121 (XX693:07)	I. D. Anderson
	G-BZMM	Robin DR.400/180R	Cairngorm Gliding Club
	G-BZMO	Robinson R22 Beta	Polar Helicopters Ltd
	G-BZMS	Mainair Blade	T. R. Villa
	G-BZMT	PA-28-161 Warrior III	White Waltham Airfield Ltd
	G-BZMW	Pegasus Quantum 15-912	A. W. Micklem
	G-BZMY	SPP Yakovlev Yak C-11	A. M. Holman-West
	G-BZMZ	CFM Streak Shadow	J. F. F. Fouche
	G-BZNC	Pegasus Quantum 15-912	D. E. Wall
	G-BZND	Sopwith Pup Replica	M. J. Goddard
	G-BZNE	Beech B300 Super King Air	Skyhopper LLP
	G-BZNF	Colt 120A balloon	N. Charbonnier/Italy
	G-BZNH	Rans S.6-ES Coyote II	S. R. A. Brierley
	G-BZNJ	Rans S.6-ES Coyote II	R. A. McKee
	G-BZNK	Morane Saulnier MS.315-D2 (354)	R. H. Cooper & S. Swallow
	G-BZNM	Pegasus Quantum 15	J. T. Davies
	G-BZNN	Beech 76 Duchess	Flew LLP
	G-BZNP	Thruster T.600N	J. D. Gibbons
	G-BZNS	Mainair Blade	A. G. Laycock
	G-BZNT	Aero L-29 Delfin	S. M. Norman
	G-BZNU	Cameron A-300 balloon	Balloon School (International) Ltd
	G-BZNV	Lindstrand LBL-31A balloon	G. R. Down
	G-BZNW	Isaacs Fury II (K2048)	S. M. Johnston
	G-BZNX	SOCATA MS.880B Rallye Club	Air & Ground Aviation Ltd
	G-BZNY	Shaw Europa XS	W. J. Harrison
	G-BZOB	Slepcev Storch (6G-ED)	P. J. Clegg
	G-BZOE	Pegasus Quantum 15	G. Rokita
	G-BZOF	Montgomerie-Bensen B.8MR gyroplane	S. J. M. Ledingham
	G-BZOG	Dornier 328-100	Loganair Ltd
	G-BZOI	Nicollier HN.700 Menestrel II	S. J. McCollum
	G-BZOL	Robin R.3000/140	S. D. Baker & M. A. Stott
	G-BZON	SA Bulldog Srs 120/121 (XX528:D)	D. J. Critchley
	G-BZOO	Pegasus Quantum 15-912	A. J. Maxfield
	G-BZOR	TEAM mini-MAX 91	T. P. V. Sheppard
	G-BZOU	Pegasus Quantum 15-912	M. A. Bradford
	G-BZOV	Pegasus Quantum 15-912	D. Turner
	G-BZOW	Whittaker MW7	G. W. Peacock
	G-BZOX	Cameron Colt 90B balloon	D. J. Head
	G-BZOZ	Van's RV-6	M. & S. Sheppard
	G-BZPA	Mainair Blade 912S	J. McGoldrick
	G-BZPD	Cameron V-65 balloon	P. Spellward
	G-BZPF	Scheibe SF-24B Motorspatz	D. & M. Shrimpton
	G-BZPG	Beech C24R Sierra 200	Wycombe Air Centre Ltd
	G-BZPH	Van's RV-4	G-BZPH RV-4 Group
	G-BZPI	SOCATA TB20 Trinidad	A. Setterfield
	G-BZPK	Cameron C-80 balloon	D. L. Homer
	G-BZPN	Mainair Blade 912S	G. R. Barker
	G-BZPR	Ultramagic N-210 balloon	A. M. Holly
	G-BZPS	SA Bulldog Srs 120/121 (XX658:07)	A. J. Robinson & M. J. Miller
	G-BZPT	Ultramagic N-210 balloon	South Downs Ballooning Ltd
	G-BZPW	Cameron V-77 balloon	J. Vonka
	G-BZPX	Ultramagic S-105 balloon	Scotair Balloons
	G-BZPY	Ultramagic H-31 balloon	Scotair Balloons
	G-BZPZ	Mainair Blade	D. & M. Bailey
	G-BZRA	Rans S.6-ES Coyote II	M. Allen
	G-BZRB	Mainair Blade	K. J. Barnard
	G-BZRJ	Pegasus Quantum 15-912	G-BZRJ Group
	G-BZRO	PA-30 Twin Comanche C	Gloucester Comanche Group
	G-BZRP	Pegasus Quantum 15-912	M. Tomlinson
	G-BZRR	Pegasus Quantum 15-912	G. Clark
	G-BZRS	Eurocopter EC 135T2	Bond Air Services Ltd

Reg.	Type	Owner or Operator	Notes
G-BZRV	Van's RV-6	N. M. Hitchman	
G-BZRW	Mainair Blade 912S	G. J. E. Alcorn	
G-BZRY	Rans S.6-ES Coyote II	A. G. Smith	
G-BZRZ	Thunder Ax11-250 S2 balloon	A. C. K. Rawson & J. J. Rudoni	
G-BZSB	Pitts S-1S Special	A. D. Ingold	
G-BZSC	Sopwith Camel F.1 (replica)	The Shuttleworth Collection	
G-BZSE	Hawker Hunter T.8B (WV322:Y)	Canfield Hunter Ltd	
G-BZSG	Pegasus Quantum 15-912	S. Andrews	
G-BZSH	Ultramagic H-77 balloon	P. M. G. Vale	
G-BZSI	Pegasus Quantum 15	D. G. Cull	
G-BZSM	Pegasus Quantum 15	K. J. Bradley	
G-BZSO	Ultramagic M-77C balloon	C. C. Duppa-Miller	
G-BZSP	Stemme S.10	A. Flewelling & L. Bleaken	
G-BZSS	Pegasus Quantum 15-912	BZSS Group	
G-BZST	Jabiru SPL-450	D. J and L. Rhys	
G-BZSX	Pegasus Quantum 15-912	J. P. Neilan	
G-BZSY	SNCAN Stampe SV.4A	G. J. N. Valvekens/Belgium	
G-BZSZ	Avtech Jabiru UL-450	T. J. Heaton	
G-BZTA	Robinson R44	Jarretts Motors Ltd	
G-BZTC	TEAM mini-MAX 91	G. G. Clayton	
G-BZTD	Thruster T.600T 450 JAB	B. O. McCartan	
G-BZTF	Yakovlev Yak-52	M. Marziali	
G-BZTH	Shaw Europa	T. J. Houlihan	
G-BZTJ	CASA Bü 133C Jungmeister	R. A. Seeley	
G-BZTK	Cameron V-90 balloon	E. Appollodorus	
G-BZTM	Mainair Blade	P. A. Houston	
G-BZTN	Europa XS	R. S. Gent	
G-BZTR	Mainair Blade	A. R. Lynn	
G-BZTS	Cameron 90 Bertie Bassett SS balloon	Trebor Bassett Ltd	
G-BZTT	Cameron A-275 balloon	A. M. Holly	
G-BZTU	Mainair Blade 912	C. T. Halliday	
G-BZTV	Mainair Blade 912S	R. D. McManus	
G-BZTW	Hunt Wing Avon 582 (1)	T. S. Walker	
G-BZTX	Mainair Blade 912	K. A. Ingham	
G-BZTY	Avtech Jabiru UL	R. P. Lewis	
G-BZUB	Mainair Blade	J. Campbell	
G-BZUC	Pegasus Quantum 15-912	G. Breen/Portugal	
G-BZUD	Lindstrand LBL-105A balloon	A. Nimmo	
G-BZUE	Pagasus Quantum 15-912	M. J. Jones	
G-BZUF	Mainair Rapier	B. Craig	
G-BZUG	RL.7A XP Sherwood Ranger	J. G. Boxall	
G-BZUH	Rans S.6-ES Coyote II	B. E. Toulson	
G-BZUI	Pegasus Quantum 15-912	A. P. Slade	
G-BZUL	Avtech Jabiru UL	J. G. Campbell	
G-BZUP	Raj Hamsa X'Air Jabiru(3)	M. T. Sheelan	
G-BZUU	Cameron C-90 balloon	D. C. Ball	
G-BZUV	Cameron H-24 balloon	J. N. Race	
G-BZUX	Pegasus Quantum 15	C. Gorvett	
G-BZUY	Van's RV-6	T. W. Wielkopolski	
G-BZUZ	Hunt Avon-Blade R.100 (1)	C. F. Janes	
G-BZVA	Zenair CH.701UL	M. W. Taylor	
G-BZVB	Cessna FR.172H	Victor Bravo Group (G-BLMX)	
G-BZVI	Nova Vertex 24 hang glider	M. Hay	
G-BZVJ	Pegasus Quantum 15	R. Blackhall	
G-BZVK	Raj Hamsa X'Air 582 (2)	J. Breslin	
G-BZVM	Rans S.6-ES Coyote II	D. P. Sudworth	
G-BZVN	Van's RV-6	Syndicate RV6 G-BZVN	
G-BZVR	Raj Hamsa X'Air 582 (4)	R. F. E. Berry	
G-BZVT	I.I.I. Sky Arrow 650T	D. J. Goldsmith	
G-BZVU	Cameron Z-105 balloon	Ballooning Network Ltd	
G-BZVV	Pegasus Quantum 15-912	S. Runcie & C. A. Brock	
G-BZVW	Ilyushin IL-2 Stormovik	S. Swallow & R. H. Cooper	
G-BZVX	Ilyushin IL-2 Stormovik	S. Swallow & R. H. Cooper	
G-BZWB	Mainair Blade 912	E. Avery & O. S. Blythin	
G-BZWC	Raj Hamsa X'Air Falcon 912 (1)	G. Hayes	
G-BZWG	PA-28 Cherokee 140	H. Merkado	
G-BZWH	Cessna 152	ACS Engineering Ltd	
G-BZWJ	CFM Streak Shadow	T. A. Morgan	
G-BZWK	Avtech Jabiru SK	M. Dovey	
G-BZWM	Pegasus XL-Q	D. T. Evans	
G-BZWN	Van's RV-8	A. J. Symms & R. D. Harper	

Notes	Reg.	Type	Owner or Operator
	G-BZWR	Mainair Rapier	M. A. Steele
	G-BZWS	Pegasus Quantum 15-912	G-BZWS Syndicate
	G-BZWT	Technam P.92-EM Echo	R. F. Cooper
	G-BZWU	Pegasus Quantum 15-912	C. A. Reynolds
	G-BZWV	Steen Skybolt	D. E. Blaxland
	G-BZWX	Whittaker MW5D Sorcerer	J. Bate
	G-BZWZ	Van's RV-6	A. P. Mardlin & K. Banks
	G-BZXA	Raj Hamsa X'Air V2 (1)	J. Bulpin
	G-BZXB	Van's RV-6	B. J. King-Smith & D. J. Akerman
	G-BZXC	SA Bulldog Srs 120/121 (XX612:A, 03)★	Carnegie College
	G-BZXI	Nova Philou 26 hang glider	M. Hay
	G-BZXK	Robin HR.200/120B	Flew LLP
	G-BZXM	Mainair Blade 912	B. Birtle
	G-BZXN	Avtech Jabiru UL-450	D. A. Hall & A. G. Sparshott
	G-BZXO	Cameron Z-105 balloon	D. K. Jones & K. D. Thomas
	G-BZXP	Kiss 400-582 (1)	A. Fairbrother
	G-BZXR	Cameron N-90 balloon	F. R. Battersby
	G-BZXS	SA Bulldog Srs 120/121 (XX631:W)	K. J. Thompson
	G-BZXT	Mainair Blade 912	J. Wood & D. J. Gillott
	G-BZXV	Pegasus Quantum 15-912	P. I. Oliver
	G-BZXW	VPM M-16 Tandem Trainer	P. J. Troy-Davies (G-NANA)
	G-BZXX	Pegasus Quantum 15-912	D. J. Johnston & D. Ostle
	G-BZXY	Robinson R44	Helicopter Services Ltd
	G-BZXZ	SA Bulldog Srs 120/121 (XX629:V)	C. M. Fopp
	G-BZYA	Rans S.6-ES Coyote II	M. R. Osbourn
	G-BZYD	Westland Gazelle AH.1 (XZ239)	Aerocars Ltd
	G-BZYG	Glaser-Dirks DG.500MB	R. C. Bromwich
	G-BZYI	Nova Phocus 123 hang glider	M. Hay
	G-BZYK	Avtech Jabiru UL	Cloudbase Aviation G-BZYK
	G-BZYN	Pegasus Quantum 15-912	J. Cannon
	G-BZYR	Cameron N-31 balloon	C. J. Sanger-Davies
	G-BZYS	Micro Aviation Bantam B.22-S	D. L. Howell
	G-BZYU	Whittaker MW6 Merlin	K. J. Cole
	G-BZYV	Snowbird Mk.V 582 (1)	M. A. Oakley
	G-BZYX	Raj Hamsa X'Air 700 (1A)	A. M. Sutton
	G-BZYY	Cameron N-90 balloon	M. E. Mason
	G-BZZD	Cessna F.172M	R. H. M. Richardson-Bunbury (G-BDPF)
	G-CAHA	PA-34-200T Seneca II	TGD Leasing Ltd
	G-CALL	PA-23 Aztec 250F	J. D. Moon
	G-CAMM	Hawker Cygnet (replica)	Richard Shuttleworth Trustees
	G-CAMR	BFC Challenger II	P. R. A. Walker
	G-CAPI	Mudry/CAARP CAP-10B	PI Group (G-BEXR)
	G-CAPX	Avions Mudry CAP-10B	H. J. Pessall
	G-CARS†	Pitts S-2A Special (replica)★	Toyota Ltd
	G-CBAB	SA Bulldog Srs 120/121 (XX543:F)	J. N. R. Davidson, L. C. T. George & P. J. R. Hill
	G-CBAD	Mainair Blade 912	J. Stocking
	G-CBAF	Lancair 320	L. H. & M. van Cleeff
	G-CBAK	Robinson R44	D. Copley
	G-CBAL	PA-28-161 Warrior II	Azure Flying Club Ltd
	G-CBAN	SA Bulldog Srs 120/121 (XX668:1)	C. Hilliker
	G-CBAP	Zenair CH.601UL	I. J. M. Donnelly
	G-CBAR	Stoddard-Hamilton Glastar	Fishburn Flyers
	G-CBAS	Rans S.6-ES Coyote II	S. Stockill
	G-CBAT	Cameron Z-90 balloon	British Telecommunications PLC
	G-CBAU	Rand-Robinson KR-2	C. B. Copsey
	G-CBAV	Raj Hamsa X'Air V.2 (1)	D. W. Stamp & G. J. Lampitt
	G-CBAW	Cameron A-300 balloon	D. K. Hempleman-Adams
	G-CBAX	Tecnam P92-EA Echo	L. Collier
	G-CBAZ	Rans S.6-ES Coyote II	E. S. Wills
	G-CBBB	Pegasus Quantum 15-912	F. A. Dimmock
	G-CBBC	SA Bulldog Srs 120/121 (XX515:4)	Bulldog Support Ltd
	G-CBBF	Beech 76 Duchess	Flew LLP
	G-CBBG	Mainair Blade	G-CBBG Flying Group
	G-CBBH	Raj Hamsa X'Air 582 (11)	D. J. Lewis
	G-CBBK	Robinson R22	R. J. Everett
	G-CBBL	SA Bulldog Srs 120/121 (XX550:Z)	A. Cunningham
	G-CBBM	Savannah VG Jabiru (1)	J. Pavelin
	G-CBBN	Pegasus Quantum 15-912	G-CBBN Flying Group
	G-CBBO	Whittaker MW5D Sorcerer	P. J. Gripton

Reg.	Type	Owner or Operator	Notes
G-CBBP	Pegasus Quantum 15-912	C. E. Thompson	
G-CBBS	SA Bulldog Srs 120/121 (XX694:E)	Newcastle Aerobatic Academy Ltd	
G-CBBT	SA Bulldog Srs 120/121 (XX695:3)	K. A. Johnston	
G-CBBW	SA Bulldog Srs 120/121 (XX619:T)	S. E. Robottom-Scott	
G-CBCB	SA Bulldog Srs 120/121 (XX537:C)	M. W. Minary The General Aviation Trading Co Ltd	
G-CBCD	Pegasus Quantum 15	I. A. Lumley	
G-CBCF	Pegasus Quantum 15-912	P. A. Bromley	
G-CBCH	Zenair CH.701UL	K. Kerr	
G-CBCI	Raj Hamsa X'Air 582 (2)	C. P. Lincoln	
G-CBCK	Tipsy T.66 Nipper Srs 3	N. M. Bloom (G-TEDZ)	
G-CBCL	Stoddard-Hamilton Glastar	D. W. Parfrey	
G-CBCM	Raj Hamsa X'Air 700 (1A)	M. Ellis	
G-CBCP	Van's RV-6A	G-CBCP Group	
G-CBCR	SA Bulldog Srs 120/121 (XX702:P)	D. Wells	
G-CBCX	Pegasus Quantum 15	The Microlight School (Lichfield) Ltd	
G-CBCY	Beech C24R Sierra Super	Wycombe Air Centre Ltd	
G-CBCZ	CFM Streak Shadow SLA	J. O'Malley-Kane	
G-CBDC	Thruster T.600N 450-JAB	P. M. Yeoman	
G-CBDD	Mainair Blade 912	G. Hird	
G-CBDG	Zenair CH.601HD	R. E. Lasnier	
G-CBDH	Flight Design CT2K	K. Tuck	
G-CBDI	Denney Kitfox Mk.2	J. G. D. Barbour	
G-CBDJ	Flight Design CT2K	P. J. Walker	
G-CBDK	SA Bulldog Srs 120/121 (XX611:7)	J. N. Randle	
G-CBDL	Mainair Blade	M. D. Howe	
G-CBDM	Tecnam P92-EM Echo	J. J. Cozens	
G-CBDN	Mainair Blade	T. Peckham	
G-CBDP	Mainair Blade 912	R. J. Roberts	
G-CBDS	SA Bulldog Srs 120/121 (XX707:4)	J. R. Parry	
G-CBDU	Quad City Challenger II	E. J. Brooks	
G-CBDV	Raj Hamsa X'Air 582	Delta Victor Group	
G-CBDX	Pegasus Quantum 15	P. Sinkler	
G-CBDZ	Pegasus Quantum 15-912	I. Fernihough	
G-CBEB	Kiss 400-582 (1)	M. Harris	
G-CBEC	Cameron Z-105 balloon	A. L. Ballarino/Italy	
G-CBED	Cameron Z-90 balloon	John Aimo Balloons SAS/Italy	
G-CBEE	PA-28R Cherokee Arrow 200	IHC Ltd	
G-CBEF	SA Bulldog Srs 120/121 (XX621:H)	A. L. Butcher & F. W. Sandwell	
G-CBEH	SA Bulldog Srs 120/121 (XX521:H)	J. E. Lewis	
G-CBEI	PA-22 Colt 108	D. Sharp	
G-CBEJ	Colt 120A balloon	The Cotswold Balloon Co. Ltd	
G-CBEK	SA Bulldog Srs 120/121 (XX700:17)	B. P. Robinson	
G-CBEM	Mainair Blade	K. W. Bodley	
G-CBEN	Pegasus Quantum 15-912	A. T. Cook	
G-CBES	Shaw Europa XS	M. R. Hexley	
G-CBEU	Pegasus Quantum 15-912	S. D. Cox	
G-CBEV	Pegasus Quantum 15-912	K. Wilson	
G-CBEW	Flight Design CT2K	Shy Talk Group	
G-CBEX	Flight Design CT2K	A. G. Quinn	
G-CBEY	Cameron C-80 balloon	M. N. Hume	
G-CBEZ	Robin DR.400/180	K. V. Field	
G-CBFA	Diamond DA40 Star	Lyrastar Ltd	
G-CBFE	Raj Hamsa X'Air V.2 (1)	T. D. Wolstenholme	
G-CBFJ	Robinson R44	F. Klinge	
G-CBFK	Murphy Rebel	P. J. Gibbs	
G-CBFM	SOCATA TB21 Trinidad	Exec Flight Ltd	
G-CBFN	Robin DR.100/200B	Foxtrot November Group	
G-CBFO	Cessna 172S	P. Gray	
G-CBFP	SA Bulldog Srs 120/121 (XX636:Y)	R. Nisbet & A. R. Dix	
G-CBFU	SA Bulldog Srs 120/121 (XX628:9)	J. R. & S. J. Huggins	
G-CBFW	Bensen B.8	A. J. Thomas	
G-CBFX	Rans S.6-ES Coyote II	D. R. Burridge	
G-CBFY	Cameron Z-250 balloon	M. L. Gabb	
G-CBGB	Zenair CH.601UL	J. F. Woodham	
G-CBGC	SOCATA TB10 Tobago	Tobago Aviation Ltd	
G-CBGD	Zenair CH.701UL	I. S. Walsh	
G-CBGE	Tecnam P92-EM Echo	J. P. Spiteri	
G-CBGG	Pegasus Quantum 15	T. E. Davies	
G-CBGH	Teverson Bisport	M. J. Larroucau	
G-CBGJ	Aeroprakt A.22 Foxbat	E. Smyth & T. G. Fitzpatrick	

Notes	Reg.	Type	Owner or Operator
	G-CBGL	MH.1521M Broussard	MAXB Group
	G-CBGO	Murphy Maverick 430	K. J. Miles & R. Withall
	G-CBGP	Ikarus C.42 FB UK	C. F. Welby
	G-CBGR	Avtech Jabiru UL-450	R. G. Kirkland
	G-CBGS	Cyclone AX2000	North East Flight Training Ltd
	G-CBGU	Thruster T.600N 450-JAB	B. R. Cardosi
	G-CBGV	Thruster T.600N 450	West Flight Aviators
	G-CBGW	Thruster T.600N 450-JAB	A. R. Pluck
	G-CBGX	SA Bulldog Srs 120/121 (XX622:B)	Henfield Lodge Ltd
	G-CBGZ	Westland Gazelle HT.2 (ZB646:59/CU)	D. Weatherhead Ltd
	G-CBHA	SOCATA TB10 Tobago	Oscar Romeo Aviation Ltd
	G-CBHB	Raj Hamsa X'Air 582 (5)	J. E. Merriman
	G-CBHC	RAF 2000 GTX-SE gyroplane	A. J. Thomas
	G-CBHG	Mainair Blade 912S	A. W. Ambrose
	G-CBHI	Shaw Europa XS	Active Aviation Ltd
	G-CBHJ	Mainair Blade 912	B. C. Jones
	G-CBHK	Pegasus Quantum 15 (HKS)	B. Dossett
	G-CBHM	Mainair Blade 912	F. J. Thorne
	G-CBHN	Pegasus Quantum 15-912	G. G. Cook
	G-CBHO	Gloster Gladiator II (N5719)	Retro Track & Air (UK) Ltd
	G-CBHP	Corby CJ-1 Starlet	D. H. Barker
	G-CBHR	Lazer Z200	A. Windel
	G-CBHU	RL.5A Sherwood Ranger	G-CBHU Group
	G-CBHW	Cameron Z-105 balloon	Bristol Chamber of Commerce, Industry & Shipping
	G-CBHX	Cameron V-77 balloon	N. A. Apsey
	G-CBHY	Pegasus Quantum 15-912	D. W. Allen
	G-CBHZ	RAF 2000 GTX-SE gyroplane	M. P. Donnelly
	G-CBIB	Flight Design CT2K	T. R. Villa
	G-CBIC	Raj Hamsa X'Air V2 (2)	J. T. Blackburn & D. R. Sutton
	G-CBID	SA Bulldog Srs 120/121(XX549:6)	Red Dog Group/Bulldog Group
	G-CBIE	Flight Design CT2K	B. M. Jones & S. R. McKiernan
	G-CBIF	Avtech Jabiru SPL-450	S. N. J. Huxtable
	G-CBIH	Cameron Z-31 balloon	Gone With The Wind Ltd
	G-CBIJ	Ikarus C.42 FB UK Cyclone	J. A. Smith
	G-CBIL	Cessna 182K	E. Bannister (G-BFZZ)
	G-CBIM	Lindstrand LBL-90A balloon	R. K. Parsons
	G-CBIN	TEAM mini-MAX 91	A. R. Mikolaczyk
	G-CBIP	Thruster T.600N 450-JAB	D. R. Seabrook
	G-CBIR	Thruster T.600N 450-JAB	C. E. Walsh
	G-CBIS	Raj Hamsa X'Air 582 (2)	P. T. W. T. Derges
	G-CBIT	RAF 2000 GTX-SE gyroplane	Terrafirma Services Ltd
	G-CBIU	Cameron 95 Flame SS balloon	PSH Skypower Ltd
	G-CBIV	Skyranger 912 (1)	J. N. Whelan
	G-CBIX	Zenair CH.601UL	R. A. & B. M. Roberts
	G-CBIY	Aerotechnik EV-97 Eurostar	S. J. Smith
	G-CBIZ	Pegasus Quantum 15-912	B. Cook
	G-CBJD	Stoddard-Hamilton Glastar	K. F. Farey
	G-CBJE	RAF 2000 GTX-SE gyroplane	V. G. Freke
	G-CBJG	DHC.1 Chipmunk 20 (1373)	C. J. Rees
	G-CBJH	Aeroprakt A.22 Foxbat	H. Smith
	G-CBJL	Kiss 400-582 (1)	R. E. Morris
	G-CBJM	Avtech Jabiru SP-470	G. R. T. Elliott
	G-BCJN	RAF 2000 GTX-SE	M. P. Lhermette
	G-CBJO	Pegasus Quantum 15-912	A. E. Kemp
	G-CBJP	Zenair CH.601UL	R. E. Peirse
	G-CBJR	Aerotechnik EV-97A Eurostar	Madley Flying Group
	G-CBJS	Cameron C-60 balloon	N. Ivison
	G-CBJT	Mainair Blade	P. T. Flanagan
	G-CBJV	Rotorway Executive 162F	P. W. Vaughan
	G-CBJW	Ikarus C.42 Cyclone FB UK	E. Foster & J. H. Peet
	G-CBJX	Raj Hamsa X'Air Falcon J22	N. & E. Hart
	G-CBJY	Jabiru UL-450	M. A. Gould
	G-CBJZ	Westland Gazelle HT.3	K. G. Theurer/Germany
	G-CBKA	Westland Gazelle HT.3 (XZ937:Y)	J. Windmill
	G-CBKB	Bücker Bü 181C Bestmann	W. R. & G. D. Snadden
	G-CBKD	Westland Gazelle HT.2	Flying Scout Ltd
	G-CBKF	Easy Raider J2.2 (1)	B. S. Carpenter
	G-CBKG	Thruster T.600N 450 JAB	Silver Shadow Group
	G-CBKK	Ultramagic S-130 balloon	Hayrick Ltd
	G-CBKL	Raj Hamsa X'Air Jabiru(2)	Caithness X-Air Group
	G-CBKM	Mainair Blade 912	Grampian Microlight Flying Club

Reg.	Type	Owner or Operator	Notes
G-CBKN	Mainair Blade 912	D. S. Clews	
G-CBKO	Mainair Blade 912S	S. J. Taft	
G-CBKR	PA-28-161 Warrior III	Yeovil Auto Tuning	
G-CBKU	Ikarus C.42 Cyclone FB UK	C. Blackburn	
G-CBKW	Pegasus Quantum 15-912	W. G. Coulter	
G-CBKY	Avtech Jabiru SP-470	P. R. Sistern	
G-CBLA	Aero Designs Pulsar XP	J. P. Kynaston	
G-CBLB	Technam P.92-EM Echo	R. Lewis-Evans	
G-CBLD	Mainair Blade 912S	N. E. King	
G-CBLE	Robin R.2120U	Flew LLP	
G-CBLF	Raj Hamsa X'Air 582 (11)	B. J. Harper & P. J. Soukup	
G-CBLK	Hawker Hind	Aero Vintage Ltd	
G-CBLL	Pegasus Quantum 15-912	G. J. McNally	
G-CBLM	Mainair Blade 912	A. S. Saunders	
G-CBLN	Cameron Z-31 balloon	P. M. Oggioni	
G-CBLO	Lindstrand LBL-42A balloon	R. J. Clements	
G-CBLP	Raj Hamsa X'Air Falcon	A. C. Parsons	
G-CBLS	Fiat CR.42	Fighter Collection Ltd	
G-CBLT	Mainair Blade 912	B. J. Bader	
G-CBLU	Cameron C-90 balloon	A. G. Martin	
G-CBLW	Raj Hamsa X'Air Falcon 582(3)	R. G. Halliwell	
G-CBLX	Kiss 400-582 (1)	A. Campbell	
G-CBLY	Grob G.109B	G-CBLY Syndicate	
G-CBLZ	Rutan LongEz	S. K. Cockburn	
G-CBMA	Raj Hamsa X'Air 582 (10)	O. C. Rash	
G-CBMB	Cyclone Ax2000	T. H. Chadwick	
G-CBMC	Cameron Z-105 balloon	B. R. Whatley	
G-CBMD	IDA Bacau Yakovlev Yak-52 (10 yellow)	R. J. Hunter	
G-CBME	Cessna F.172M	Skytrax Aviation Ltd	
G-CBMI	Yakovlev Yak-52	I. A. Harding	
G-CBMK	Cameron Z-120 balloon	G. Davies	
G-CBML	DHC.6 Twin Otter 310	Isles of Scilly Skybus Ltd	
G-CBMM	Mainair Blade 912	W. L. Millar	
G-CBMO	PA-28 Cherokee 180	T. Rawlings	
G-CBMP	Cessna R.182	Orman (Carrolls Farm) Ltd	
G-CBMR	Medway Eclipser	D. S. Blofeld	
G-CBMT	Robin DR.400/180	A. C. Williamson	
G-CBMU	Whittaker MW6-S Fat Boy Flyer	A. M. Witt	
G-CBMV	Pegasus Quantum 15	G. Poulett	
G-CBMW	Zenair CH.701 UL	Forge consulting Ltd	
G-CBMZ	Aerotechnik EV-97 Eurostar	J. C. O'Donnell	
G-CBNB	Eurocopter EC 120B	Arenbosch Consultadoria E Servicos LDA/Madeira	
G-CBNC	Mainair Blade 912	K. L. Smith	
G-CBNF	Rans S.7 Courier	M. Henderson	
G-CBNG	Robin R.2112	R. K. Galbally & E. W. Russell	
G-CBNI	Lindstrand LBL-180A balloon	K. W. Scott	
G-CBNJ	Raj Hamsa X'Air 912 (1)	N. C. Marciano	
G-CBNL	Dyn'Aéro MCR-01 Club	D. H. Wilson	
G-CBNO	CFM Streak Shadow	D. J. Goldsmith	
G-CBNT	Pegasus Quantum 15-912	B. H. Goldsmith	
G-CBNV	Rans S.6-ES Coyote II	M. R. Garland	
G-CBNW	Cameron N-105 balloon	Bailey Balloons	
G-CBNX	Mongomerie-Bensen B.8MR	A. C. S. M. Hart	
G-CBNZ	TEAM hi-MAX 1700R	A. P. S. John	
G-CBOA	Auster B.8 Agricola Srs 1	C. J. Baker	
G-CBOC	Raj Hamsa X'Air 582 (5)	A. J. McAleer	
G-CBOE	Hawker Hurricane IIB	P. J. Lawton	
G-CBOF	Shaw Europa XS	I. W. Ligertwood	
G-CBOG	Mainair Blade 912S	OG Group	
G-CBOM	Mainair Blade 912	G. Suckling	
G-CBOO	Mainair Blade 912S	H. Moore	
G-CBOP	Avtech Jabiru UL-450	D. W. Batchelor	
G-CBOR	Cessna F.172N	Vetsonic LLP	
G-CBOS	Rans S.6-ES Coyote II	J. T. Athulathmudali	
G-CBOW	Cameron Z-120 balloon	Turner Balloons Ltd	
G-CBOY	Pegasus Quantum 15-912	Charlie Boy Syndicate	
G-CBOZ	IDA Bacau Yakovlev Yak-52	M. J. Babbage	
G-CBPC	Sportavia-Putzer RF-5B Sperber	Lee RF-5B Group	
G-CBPD	Ikarus C.42 Cyclone FB UK	Waxwing Group	
G-CBPE	SOCATA TB10 Tobago	A. F. Welch	

Notes	Reg.	Type	Owner or Operator
	G-CBPI	PA-28R-201 Arrow III	M. J. Richardson
	G-CBPM	Yakovlev Yak-50 (50 black)	P. W. Ansell
	G-CBPP	Avtech Jabiru UL-450	P. R. Houckman
	G-CBPR	Avtech Jabiru UL-450	S. I. Laurence
	G-CBPU	Raj Hamsa X'Air R100(3)	R. Power
	G-CBPV	Zenair CH.601UL	R. D. Barnard
	G-CBPW	Lindstrand LBL-105A balloon	A. C. Elson
	G-CBRB	Ultramagic S-105 balloon	I. S. Bridge
	G-CBRC	Jodel D.18	B. W. Shaw
	G-CBRD	Jodel D.18	J. D. Haslam
	G-CBRE	Mainair Blade 912	J. Jones
	G-CBRG	Cessna 560XL Citation Excel	Eurojet Aviation Ltd
	G-CBRJ	Mainair Blade 912S	R. W. Janion
	G-CBRK	Ultramagic M-77 balloon	Hampshire Balloons Ltd
	G-CBRM	Mainair Blade	M. H. Levy
	G-CBRO	Robinson R44	R. D. Jordan
	G-CBRR	Aerotechnik EV-97A Eurostar	T. O. Powley & M. S. Turner
	G-CBRT	Murphy Elite	T. W. Baylie
	G-CBRV	Cameron C-90 balloon	C. J. Teall
	G-CBRW	Aerostar Yakovlev Yak-52 (50 grey)	Max-Alpha Aviation GmbH/Germany
	G-CBRX	Zenair CH.601UL Zodiac	C. J. Meadows
	G-CBRZ	Kiss 400-582(1)	J. J. Ryan/Ireland
	G-CBSF	Westland Gazelle HT.2	Falcon Aviation Ltd
	G-CBSH	Westland Gazelle HT.3 (XX406:P)	Alltask Ltd
	G-CBSI	Westland Gazelle HT.3 (XZ934:U)	P. S. Unwin
	G-CBSK	Westland Gazelle HT.3 (ZB627:A)	Falcon Flying Group
	G-CBSL	IDA Bacau Yakovlev Yak-52 (67 red)	N. & A. D. Barton
	G-CBSO	PA-28-181 Archer II	Archer One Ltd
	G-CBSP	Pegasus Quantum 15-912	J. S. Jarvis
	G-CBSR	Yakovlev Yak-52	Grovinvest Srl
	G-CBSS	IDA Bacau Yakovlev Yak-52	E. J. F. Verhellen/Belgium
	G-CBSU	Avtech Jabiru UL	K. R. Crawley
	G-CBSV	Montgomerie-Bensen B.8MR	J. A. McGill
	G-CBSZ	Mainair Blade 912S	P. J. Nolan
	G-CBTB	I.I.I. Sky Arrow 650TS	J. S. Hudson
	G-CBTD	Pegasus Quantum 15-912	D. Baillie
	G-CBTE	Mainair Blade 912|S	M. T. Dawson
	G-CBTG	Ikarus C42 FB UK Cyclone	G-CBTG Flying Group
	G-CBTK	Raj Hamsa X'Air 582 (5)	M. Shaw
	G-CBTL	Monnett Moni	P. N. Stacey
	G-CBTM	Mainair Blade	D. A. A. Hewitt
	G-CBTN	PA-31 Navajo C	Durban Aviation Services Ltd
	G-CBTO	Rans S.6-ES Coyote II	D. Wakefield
	G-CBTR	Lindstrand LBL-120A balloon	R. H. Etherington
	G-CBTS	Gloster Gamecock (replica)	Retro Track & Air (UK) Ltd
	G-CBTT	PA-28-181 Archer II	Cedar Aviation Ltd (G-BFMM)
	G-CBTW	Mainair Blade 912	J. R. Davis
	G-CBTX	Denney Kitfox Mk.2	G. I. Doake
	G-CBUA	Extra EA.230	G-CBUA Group
	G-CBUC	Raj Hamsa X'Air 582 (5)	R. S. Noremberg
	G-CBUD	Pegasus Quantum 15-912	G. N. S. Farrant
	G-CBUF	Flight Design CT2K	N. A. Thomas
	G-CBUG	Technam P.92-EM Echo	J. J. Bodnarec
	G-CBUI	Westland Wasp HAS.1 (XT420:606)	The Helicopter Squadron Ltd
	G-CBUJ	Raj Hamsa X'Air 582 (10)	M. W. & P. A. Aston
	G-CBUK	Van's RV-6A	P. G. Greenslade
	G-CBUN	Barker Charade	D. R. Wilkinson & T. Coldwell
	G-CBUO	Cameron O-90 balloon	W. J. Treacy & P. M. Smith
	G-CBUP	VPM M-16 Tandem Trainer	J. S. Firth
	G-CBUR	Zenair CH.601UL	R. Simpson
	G-CBUS	Pegasus Quantum 15	J. Liddiard
	G-CBUU	Pegasus Quantum 15-912	D. & P. Allman
	G-CBUW	Cameron Z-133 balloon	Balloon School (International) Ltd
	G-CBUX	Cyclone AX2000	I. R. M. Scott
	G-CBUY	Rans S.6-ES Coyote II	I. L. Johnson
	G-CBUZ	Pegasus Quantum 15	D. G. Seymour
	G-CBVA	Thruster T.600N 450	D. J. Clingan
	G-CBVB	Robin R.2120U	Flew LLP
	G-CBVC	Raj Hamsa X'Air 582 (5)	G. & J. Weir & P. Higgins
	G-CBVD	Cameron C-60 balloon	Phoenix Balloons Ltd
	G-CBVF	Murphy Maverick	H. A. Leek

Reg.	Type	Owner or Operator	Notes
G-CBVG	Mainair Blade 912S	A. M. Buchanan	
G-CBVH	Lindstrand LBL-120A balloon	G. R. Down	
G-CBVM	Aerotechnik EV-97 Eurostar	M. Sharpe	
G-CBVN	Pegasus Quik	C. Kearney	
G-CBVR	Best Off Skyranger 912 (2)	S. H. Lunney	
G-CBVS	Best Off Skyranger 912 (1)	S. C. Cornock	
G-CBVT	Yakovlev Yak-52	M. A. G. Lopez	
G-CBVU	PA-28R Cherokee Arrow 200-II	S. Crowley	
G-CBVV	Cameron N-120 balloon	John Aimo Balloons SAS/Italy	
G-CBVX	Cessna 182P	P. & A. de Weerdt	
G-CBVY	Ikarus C.42 Cyclone FB UK	D. Jessop	
G-CBVZ	Flight Design CT2K	A. N. D. Arthur	
G-CBWA	Flight Design CT2K	Sun Fun Luxury Travel	
G-CBWB	PA-34-200T Seneca II	Gama Engineering Ltd	
G-CBWD	PA-28-161 Warrior III	J. Wright	
G-CBWE	Aerotechnik EV-97 Eurostar	J. & C. W. Hood	
G-CBWG	Aerotechnik EV-97 Eurostar	C. Long & M. P. & T. Middleton	
G-CBWI	Thruster T. 600N 450	P. L. Jarvis	
G-CBWJ	Thruster T. 600N 450	Voliamo Group	
G-CBWK	Ultramagic H-77 balloon	H. C. Peel	
G-CBWN	Campbell Cricket Mk.6	P. J. Croft	
G-CBWO	Rotorway Executive 162F	N. T. Oakman	
G-CBWP	Shaw Europa	T. W. Greaves	
G-CBWS	Whittaker MW6 Merlin	W. Turner	
G-CBWU	Rotorway Executive 162F	F. A. Cavaciuti	
G-CBWV	Falconar F-12A Cruiser	A. Ackland	
G-CBWW	Skyranger 912 (2)	N. S. Wellsl	
G-CBWY	Raj Hamsa X'Air 582 (6)	J. C. Rose	
G-CBWZ	Robinson R22 Beta	Carrdoon Ltd	
G-CBXB	Lindstrand LBL-150A balloon	M. A. Webb	
G-CBXC	Ikarus C.42 Cyclone FB UK	J. A. Robinson	
G-CBXE	Easy Raider J2.2 (3)	A. K. Day	
G-CBXF	Easy Raider J2.2 (2)	M. R. Grunwell	
G-CBXG	Thruster T.600N 450	Newtownards Microlight Group	
G-CBXJ	Cessna 172S	Steptoe and Sons Properties Ltd	
G-CBXK	Robinson R22 Mariner	Kington Building Supplies Ltd	
G-CBXM	Mainair Blade	B. A. Coombe	
G-CBXN	Robinson R22 Beta II	N. M. G. Pearson	
G-CBXR	Raj Hamsa X-Air Falcon 582 (1)	J. F. Heath	
G-CBXS	Skyranger J2.2 (1)	The Ince Skyranger Group	
G-CBXU	TEAM mini-MAX 91A	C. D. Hatcher	
G-CBXW	Shaw Europa XS	R. G. Fairall	
G-CBXZ	Rans S.6-ES Coyote II	D. Tole	
G-CBYB	Rotorway Executive 162F	Clark Contracting	
G-CBYC	Cameron Z-275 balloon	Virgin Balloon Flights	
G-CBYD	Rans S.6-ES Coyote II	R. Burland	
G-CBYE	Pegasus Quik	C. E. Morris	
G-CBYF	Mainair Blade	J. Ayre	
G-CBYH	Aeroprakt A.22 Foxbat	G. C. Moore	
G-CBYI	Pegasus Quantum 15-503	The G-BCYI Group	
G-CBYJ	Steen Skybolt	The Skybolt Group	
G-CBYM	Mainair Blade	D. Reid	
G-CBYN	Shaw Europa XS	G. M. Tagg	
G-CBYO	Pegasus Quik	G-CBYO Syndicate	
G-CBYP	Whittaker MW6-S Fat Boy Flyer	R. J. Grainger	
G-CBYS	Lindstrand LBL-21 balloon France	B. M. Reed/France	
G-CBYT	Thruster T.600N 450	T. G. V. Oyston	
G-CBYU	PA-28-161 Warrior II	Stapleford Flying Club Ltd	
G-CBYV	Pegasus Quantum 15-912	G-CBYV Syndicate	
G-CBYW	Hatz CB-1	T. A. Hinton	
G-CBYZ	Tecnam P92-EM Echo-Super	B. Weaver	
G-CBZA	Mainair Blade	M. Lowe	
G-CBZD	Mainair Blade	G. F. Jones	
G-CBZE	Robinson R44	Alps (Scotland) Ltd	
G-CBZG	Rans S.6-ES Coyote II	W. Chang	
G-CBZH	Pegasus Quik	B. D. Searle	
G-CBZJ	Lindstrand LBL-25A balloon	Pegasus Ballooning	
G-CBZK	Robin DR.400/180	R. A. Fleming	
G-CBZL	Westland Gazelle HT.3	Armstrong Aviation Ltd	
G-CBZM	Avtech Jabiru SPL-450	M. E. Ledward	
G-CBZN	Rans S.6-ES Coyote II	R. G. Morris	

Notes	Reg.	Type	Owner or Operator
	G-CBZP	Hawker Fury 1 (K5674)	Historic Aircraft Collection
	G-CBZR	PA-28R-201 Arrow III	Folada Aero & Technical Services Ltd
	G-CBZS	Aurora	J. Lynden
	G-CBZT	Pegasus Quik	A. P. Portsmouth
	G-CBZU	Lindstrand LBL-180A balloon	Adventure Balloons Ltd
	G-CBZW	Zenair CH.701UL	T. M. Siles
	G-CBZX	Dyn' Aero MCR-01 ULC	A. C. N. Freeman & M. P. Wilson
	G-CBZZ	Cameron Z-275 balloon	A. C. K. Rawson & J. J. Rudoni
	G-CCAB	Mainair Blade	A. J. Morris
	G-CCAC	Aerotech EV-97 Eurostar	D. C. Lugg
	G-CCAD	Mainair Pegasus Quik	L. A. Hosegood & M. J. Mawle
	G-CCAE	Avtech Jabiru UL-450	D. Logan
	G-CCAF	Skyranger 912 (1)	D. W. & M. L. Squire
	G-CCAG	Mainair Blade 912	A. Robinson
	G-CCAK	Zenair CN.601HD	A. Kimmond
	G-CCAL	Technam P.92-EA Echo	M. Rudd
	G-CCAP	Robinson R22 Beta II	D. Baker, M. Healer & H. Price
	G-CCAR	Cameron N-77 balloon	D. P. Turner
	G-CCAS	Pegasus Quik	Caunton Alpha Syndicate
	G-CCAT	AA-55A Cheetah	A. Ohringer (G-OAJH/G-KILT/G-BJFA)
	G-CCAV	PA-28-181 Archer II	Archer II Ltd
	G-CCAW	Mainair Blade 912	A. D. Carr
	G-CCAY	Cameron Z-42 balloon	P. Stern
	G-CCAZ	Mainair Pegasus Quik	J. P. Floyd
	G-CCBB	Skyranger R.100	Fourstrokes Group
	G-CCBB	Cameron N-90 balloon	S. C. A. & L. D. Craze
	G-CCBC	Thruster T.600N 450	E. J. Girling & J. A. E. Bowen
	G-CCBF	Maule M.5-235C	C. G. Sims (G-NHVH)
	G-CCBG	Skyranger V.2 + (1)	P. R. Mailer & F. Stannard
	G-CCBH	PA-28 Cherokee 236	J. R. Hunt & M. Kenny
	G-CCBI	Raj Hamsa X'Air 582(11)	O. Sanda
	G-CCBJ	Skyranger 912 (2)	J. d'Rozario
	G-CCBK	Aerotechnik EV-97 Eurostar	B. S. Waycott
	G-CCBL	Agusta-Bell 206B JetRanger 3	Formula Karting Ltd
	G-CCBM	Aerotechnik EV-97 Eurostar	W. Graves
	G-CCBN	Scale Replica SE-5a (80105/19)	V. C. Lockwood
	G-CCBR	Jodel D.120	A. Dunne & M. Munnelly
	G-CCBT	Cameron Z-90 balloon	I. J. Sharpe
	G-CCBV	Cameron Z-225 balloon	New Spirit Baloons ASBL, Luxembourg
	G-CCBW	Sherwood Ranger	A. L. Virgoe
	G-CCBX	Raj Hamsa X'Air 133 (2)	P. D. Hadley
	G-CCBY	Avtech Jabiru UL-450	D. M. Goodman
	G-CCBZ	Aero Designs Pulsar	J. M. Keane
	G-CCCA	VS.509 Spitfire Tr.IX	Historic Flying Ltd (G-BHRH/G-TRIX)
	G-CCCB	Thruster T.600N 450	G-CCCB Flying Group
	G-CCCD	Mainair Pegasus Quantum 15	R. N. Gamble
	G-CCCE	Aeroprakt A.22 Foxbat	P. Sykes
	G-CCCF	Thruster T.600N 450	P. R. Norman
	G-CCCG	Mainair Pegasus Quik	J. W. Sandars
	G-CCCH	Thruster T600N 450	G. Scullion
	G-CCCI	Medway Eclipse R	C. Dunford
	G-CCCJ	Nicollier HN.700 Menestrel II	G. A. Rodmell
	G-CCCK	Skyranger 912 (2)	P. L. Braniff
	G-CCCM	Skyranger 912 (2)	Connel Gliding Group
	G-CCCN	Robin R.3000/160	DR Flyers 2
	G-CCCO	Aerotechnik EV-97A Eurostar	D. R. G. Whitelaw
	G-CCCR	Best Off Sky Ranger 912(2)	S. R. McKiernan
	G-CCCU	Thruster T.600N 450	A. F. Cashin
	G-CCCV	Raj Hamsa X'Air Falcon 133 (1)	G. J. Boyer
	G-CCCW	Pereira Osprey 2	D. J. Southward
	G-CCCY	Skyranger 912 (2)	A. Watson
	G-CCDB	Mainair Pegasus Quik	A. Pritchard
	G-CCDD	Mainair Pegasus Quik	M. P. Hadden & M. H. Rollins
	G-CCDF	Mainair Pegasus Quik	R. P. McGann
	G-CCDG	Skyranger 912 (1)	Freebird Group
	G-CCDH	Skyranger 912 (2)	M. L. Willmington
	G-CCDJ	Raj Hamsa X'Air Falcon 582 (2)	P. White
	G-CCDK	Pegasus Quantum 15-912	G. Charman
	G-CCDL	Raj Hamsa X'Air Falcon 582 (2)	P. J. Disley
	G-CCDM	Mainair Blade	P. R. G. Morley

Reg.	Type	Owner or Operator	Notes
G-CCDO	Mainair Pegasus Quik	S. T. Welsh	
G-CCDP	Raj Hamsa X'Air R.100 (3)	F. J. McGuigan	
G-CCDR	Raj Hamsa X'Air Falcon Jabiru	F. Overall	
G-CCDS	Nicollier HN.700 Menestrel II	B. W. Gowland	
G-CCDU	Tecnam P92-EM Echo	D. J. Gardner	
G-CCDV	Thruster T.600N 450	G. C. Hobson	
G-CCDW	Skyranger 582 (1)	Debts R Us Family Group	
G-CCDX	Aerotechnik EV-97 Eurostar	G-CCDX Syndicate 2013	
G-CCDY	Skyranger 912 (2)	I. Brumpton	
G-CCDZ	Pegasus Quantum 15-912	R. D. Leigh	
G-CCEA	Mainair Pegasus Quik	G. D. Ritchie	
G-CCEB	Thruster T.600N 450	Thruster Air Services Ltd	
G-CCED	Zenair CH.601UL	R. P. Reynolds	
G-CCEE	PA-15 Vagabond	I. M. Callier (G-VAGA)	
G-CCEF	Shaw Europa	C. P. Garner	
G-CCEH	Skyranger 912 (2)	ZC Owners	
G-CCEJ	Aerotechnik EV-97 Eurostar	J. R. Iveson & M. D. S. Williams	
G-CCEK	Kiss 400-582 (1)	R. C. Hinkins & M. Thurlbourn	
G-CCEL	Avtech Jabiru UL	S. K. Armstrong	
G-CCEM	Aerotechnik EV-97 Eurostar	Oxenhope Flying Group	
G-CCEN	Cameron Z-120 balloon	R. Hunt	
G-CCEO	Thunder Ax10-180 S2 balloon	P. Heitzeneder/Austria	
G-CCEP	Raj Hamsa X'Air Falcon Jabiru	G-CCEP Flying Group	
G-CCES	Raj Hamsa X'Air 3203(1)	G. V. McCloskey	
G-CCET	Nova Vertex 28 hang glider	M. Hay	
G-CCEU	RAF 2000 GTX-SE gyroplane	N. G. Dovaston	
G-CCEW	Mainair Pegasus Quik	N. F. Mackenzie	
G-CCEY	Raj Hamsa X'582 (11)	Thorley Motors Ltd	
G-CCEZ	Easy Raider J2.2	P. J Clegg	
G-CCFB	Mainair Pegasus Quik	P. Bailey	
G-CCFC	Robinson R44 II	H. J. Walters	
G-CCFD	BFC Challenger II	W. Oswald	
G-CCFE	Tipsy Nipper T.66 Srs 2	S. Eustace	
G-CCFG	Dyn'Aéro MCR-01 Club	P. H. Milward	
G-CCFI	PA-32 Cherokee Six 260	McManus Truck & Trailer Spares Ltd	
G-CCFJ	Kolb Twinstar Mk.3	S. Buckland	
G-CCFK	Shaw Europa	C. R. Knapton	
G-CCFL	Mainair Pegasus Quik	P. G. Mallon	
G-CCFO	Pitts S-1S Special	R. J. Anderson	
G-CCFS	Diamond DA40D Star	R. H. Butterfield	
G-CCFT	Mainair Pegasus Quantum 15-912	D. A. Bannister	
G-CCFU	Diamond DA40D Star	Jetstream Aviation Academy/Greece	
G-CCFV	Lindstrand LBL-77A balloon	Alton Aviation Ltd	
G-CCFW	WAR Focke-Wulf Fw.190	D. B. Conway	
G-CCFX	EAA Acrosport 2	C. D. Ward	
G-CCFY	Rotorway Executive 162F	Southern Helicopters Ltd	
G-CCFZ	Ikarus C.42 FB UK	B. W. Drake	
G-CCGB	TEAM mini-MAX	A. D, Pentland	
G-CCGC	Mainair Pegasus Quik	R. W. Street	
G-CCGE	Robinson R22 Beta	Patriot Aviation Ltd	
G-CCGF	Robinson R22 Beta	Multiflight Ltd	
G-CCGG	Jabiru Aircraft Jabiru J400	R. Haverson	
G-CCGH	Supermarine Aircraft Spitfire Mk.26 (AB196)	Cokebusters Ltd	
G-CCGK	Mainair Blade	C. M. Babiy & M. Hurn	
G-CCGM	Kiss 450-582 (1)	M. Nazm	
G-CCGO	Medway Raven X	D. A. Coupland	
G-CCGP	Bristol Type 200	R. L. Holman	
G-CCGR	Raj Hamsa X'Air 133 (1)	J. E. Merriman	
G-CCGS	Dornier 328-100	Loganair Ltd	
G-CCGU	Van's RV-9A	B. J. Main & ptnrs	
G-CCGW	Shaw Europa	D. Buckley	
G-CCGY	Cameron Z-105 balloon	Cameron Balloons Ltd	
G-CCHD	Diamond DA40D Star	Flying Time Ltd	
G-CCHH	Pegasus Quik	C. A. Green	
G-CCHI	Mainair Pegasus Quik	M. R. Starling	
G-CCHL	PA-28-181 Archer iii	Archer Three Ltd	
G-CCHM	Kiss 450	M. J. Jessup	
G-CCHN	Corby CJ.1 Starlet	N. S. Dell	
G-CCHO	Mainair Pegasus Quik	M. Allan	
G-CCHP	Cameron Z-31 balloon	M. H. Redman	

Notes	Reg.	Type	Owner or Operator
	G-CCHR	Easy Raider 583 (1)	M. P. Wiseman
	G-CCHS	Raj Hamsa X'Air 582	N. H. Gokul
	G-CCHT	Cessna 152	J. S. Devlin & Z. Islam
	G-CCHV	Mainair Rapier	B. J. Wesley
	G-CCHW	Cameron Z-77 balloon	M. A. Scholes & D. J. Day
	G-CCHX	Scheibe SF.25C Falke	Lasham Gliding Society Ltd
	G-CCID	Jabiru Aircraft Jabiru J400	G-CCID Syndicate
	G-CCIF	Mainair Blade	S. P. Moores
	G-CCIG	Aero Designs Pulsar	P. Maguire
	G-CCIH	Mainair Pegasus Quantum 15	T. Smith
	G-CCII	ICP Savannah Jabiru (3)	D. Chaloner
	G-CCIJ	PA-28R Cherokee Arrow 180	S. A. Hughes
	G-CCIK	Skyranger 912 (2)	M. D. Kirby
	G-CCIR	Van's RV-8	N. W. Charles
	G-CCIS	Scheibe SF.28A Tandem Falke	The Tandem-Falke Syndicate
	G-CCIT	Zenair CH.701UL	J. A. R. Hughes
	G-CCIU	Cameron N-105 balloon	W. W. Leitlein
	G-CCIV	Mainair Pegasus Quik	G. H. Ousby
	G-CCIW	Raj Hamsa X'Air 582 (2)	N. Watts
	G-CCIY	Skyranger 912 (2)	L. F. Tanner
	G-CCIZ	PZL-110 Koliber 160A	J. P. Nugent
	G-CCJA	Skyranger 912 (2)	C. Day
	G-CCJB	Zenair CH.701 STOL	E. G. Brown
	G-CCJD	Mainair Pegasus Quantum 15	P. Clark
	G-CCJF	Cameron C-90 balloon	Balloon School International Ltd
	G-CCJH	Lindstrand LBL-90A balloon	J. R. Hoare
	G-CCJI	Van's RV-6	A. Jenkins
	G-CCJJ	Medway Pirana	P. K. Bennett
	G-CCJK	Aerostar Yakovlev Yak-52	G-CCJK Group
	G-CCJL	Supermarine Spitfire XXVI (PV303)	M. W. Hanley & P. M. Whitaker
	G-CCJM	Mainair Pegasus Quik	S. R. Smyth
	G-CCJN	Rans S.6ES Coyote II	J. Murphy
	G-CCJO	ICP-740 Savannah Jabiru 4	R. & I. Fletcher
	G-CCJT	Skyranger 912 (2)	Juliet Tango Group
	G-CCJU	ICP MXP-740 Savannah Jabiru (4)	A. R. & M. A. Baxter
	G-CCJV	Aeroprakt A.22 Foxbat	Foxbat UK015 Syndicate
	G-CCJW	Skyranger 912 (2)	J. R. Walter
	G-CCJX	Shaw Europa XS	J. S. Baranski
	G-CCJY	Cameron Z-42 balloon	D. J. Griffin
	G-CCKF	Skyranger 912 (2)	D. McCabe & M. Harris
	G-CCKG	Skyranger 912 (2)	C. E. Penny
	G-CCKH	Diamond DA40D Star	Flying Time Ltd
	G-CCKI	Diamond DA40D Star	S. C. Horwood
	G-CCKJ	Raj Hamsa X'Air 133 (3)	G. A. Davidson
	G-CCKL	Aerotechnik EV-97A Eurostar	G-CCKL Group
	G-CCKM	Mainair Pegasus Quik	W. T. Milburn & P. A. Kershaw
	G-CCKN	Nicollier HN.700 Menestrel II	C. R. Partington
	G-CCKO	Mainair Pegasus Quik	T. H. Beales & M. D. Howe
	G-CCKP	Robin DR.400/120	Duxford Flying Group
	G-CCKR	Pietenpol Air Camper	C. R. Thompson
	G-CCKT	Hapi Cygnet SF-2	P. W. Abraham
	G-CCKV	Isaacs Fury II	G. Smith
	G-CCKW	PA-18 Super Cub 135	P. A. Layzell (G-GDAM)
	G-CCKX	Lindstrand LBL-210A balloon	Alba Ballooning Ltd
	G-CCKZ	Customcraft A-25 balloon	P. A. George
	G-CCLF	Best Off Skyranger 912 (2)	J. Bannister & N. J. Sutherland
	G-CCLG	Lindstrand LBL-105A balloon	M. A. Derbyshire
	G-CCLH	Rans S.6-ES Coyote II	K. R. Browne
	G-CCLM	Mainair Pegasus Quik	D. J. Shippen & C. C. Colclough
	G-CCLO	Ultramagic H-77 balloon-	S. J. M. Hornsby
	G-CCLP	ICP MXP-740 Savannah	C. J. Powell & A. H. Watkins
	G-CCLR	Schleicher Ash 26E	M. T. Burton & A. Darby
	G-CCLS	Comco Ikarus C.42 FB UK	B. D. Wykes
	G-CCLU	Best Off Skyranger 912	C. M. Babiy
	G-CCLW	Diamond DA40D Star	Shacklewell Diamond Group
	G-CCLX	Mainair Pegasus Quik	J. W. Edwards
	G-CCMC	Jabiru Aircraft Jabiru UL 450	K. J. Simpson
	G-CCMD	Mainair Pegasus Quik	J. T. McCormack
	G-CCME	Mainair Pegasus Quik	Caunton Graphites Syndicate
	G-CCMH	M.2H Hawk Major	J. A. Pothecary

Reg.	Type	Owner or Operator	Notes
G-CCMI	SA Bulldog Srs 120/121 (XX513:10)	XX513 Bulldog Group (G-KKKK)	
G-CCMJ	Easy Raider J2.2 (1)	G. F. Clews	
G-CCMK	Raj Hamsa X'Air Falcon	G. J. Digby	
G-CCML	Mainair Pegasus Quik	D. Renton	
G-CCMM	Dyn'Aéro MCR-01 ULC Banbi	J. D. Harris	
G-CCMN	Cameron C-90 balloon	A.E. Austin	
G-CCMO	Aerotechnik EV-97 Eurostar	G. Hardman	
G-CCMP	Aerotechnik EV-97A Eurostar	E. K. McAlinden	
G-CCMR	Robinson R22 Beta	G. F. Smith	
G-CCMS	Mainair Pegasus Quik	Barton Charlie Charlie Group	
G-CCMT	Thruster T.600N 450	G. L. Logan	
G-CCMU	Rotorway Executive 162F	D. J. Fravigar & J. Smith	
G-CCMW	CFM Shadow Srs.DD	M. Wilkinson	
G-CCMX	Skyranger 912 (2)	K. J. Cole	
G-CCMZ	Best Off Skyranger 912 (2)	D. D. Appleford	
G-CCNA	Jodel DR.100A (Replica)	R. Everitt	
G-CCNC	Cameron Z-275 balloon	J. D. & K. Griffiths	
G-CCND	Van's RV-9A	K. S. Woodard	
G-CCNE	Mainair Pegasus Quantum 15	G. D. Barker	
G-CCNF	Raj Hamsa X'Air 582 Falcon 133	R. E. Williams	
G-CCNG	Flight Design CT2K	S. C. Reeve	
G-CCNH	Rans S.6ES Coyote II	J. E. Howard	
G-CCNJ	Skyranger 912 (2)	J. D. Buchanan	
G-CCNL	Raj Hamsa X'Air Falcon 133(1)	S. E. Vallance	
G-CCNM	Mainair Pegasus Quik	J. G. McMinn	
G-CCNP	Flight Design CT2K	M. J. Hawkins	
G-CCNR	Skyranger 912 (2)	K. Washbourne	
G-CCNS	Skyranger 912 (2)	A. Kennedy, D. Murdoch & S. Hanssen	
G-CCNT	Ikarus C.42 FB80	November Tango Group	
G-CCNU	Skyranger J2.2 (2)	P. D. Priestley	
G-CCNW	Mainair Pegasus Quantum Lite	J. Childs	
G-CCNX	CAB CAP-10B	Arc Input Ltd	
G-CCNY	Robinson R44	J. & S. J. Strange	
G-CCNZ	Raj Hamsa X'Air 133 (1)	J. F. Heath	
G-CCOB	Aero C.104 Jungmann	C. W. Tomkins	
G-CCOC	Mainair Pegasus Quantum 15	C. M. Ayres	
G-CCOF	Rans S.6-ESA Coyote II	A. J. Wright & M. Govan	
G-CCOG	Mainair Pegasus Quik	A. O. Sutherland	
G-CCOK	Mainair Pegasus Quik	C. Curtin	
G-CCOM	Westland Lysander IIIA (V9312)	Propshop Ltd	
G-CCOP	Ultramagic M-105 balloon	M. E. J. Whitewood	
G-CCOR	Sequoia F.8L Falco	D. J. Thoma	
G-CCOS	Cameron Z-350 balloon	Wickers World Ltd	
G-CCOT	Cameron Z-105 balloon	Airborne Adventures Ltd	
G-CCOU	Mainair Pegasus Quik	D. E. J. McVicker	
G-CCOV	Shaw Europa XS	B. C. Barton	
G-CCOW	Mainair Pegasus Quik	J. R. Houston	
G-CCOY	NA AT-6D Harvard II	Classic Flying Machine Collection Ltd	
G-CCOZ	Monnett Sonerai II	W. H. Cole	
G-CCPA	Kiss 400-582(1)	C.P. Astridge	
G-CCPC	Mainair Pegasus Quik	S. M. Oliver	
G-CCPD	Campbell Cricket Mk.4	T. H. Geake	
G-CCPE	Steen Skybolt	C. Moore	
G-CCPF	Skyranger 912 (2)	R. S. Oliver	
G-CCPG	Mainair Pegasus Quik	A.W. Lowrie	
G-CCPH	EV-97 TeamEurostar UK	A. H. Woolley	
G-CCPJ	EV-97 TeamEurostar UK	J. S. Webb	
G-CCPK	Murphy Rebel	B. A. W. Bridgewater	
G-CCPL	Skyranger 912 (2)	G-CCPL Group	
G-CCPM	Mainair Blade 912	P. S. Davies	
G-CCPN	Dyn'Aéro MCR-01 Club	M. Sibson	
G-CCPO	Cameron N-77 balloon	A. M. Daniels (G-MITS)	
G-CCPP	Cameron 70 Concept balloon	Sarnia Balloon Group	
G-CCPS	Ikarus C.42 FB100 VLA	H. Cullens	
G-CCPT	Cameron Z-90 balloon	Charter Ballooning Ltd	
G-CCPV	Jabiru J400	J. R. Lawrence & M. J. Worrall	
G-CCPY	Hughes 369D	Alpha Properties (London) Ltd	
G-CCRA	Glaser-Dirks DG-800B	R. Fischer	
G-CCRB	Kolb Twinstar Mk.3 (modified)	M. Daly	
G-CCRC	Cessna Tu.206G	D. M. Penny	
G-CCRF	Mainair Pegasus Quantum 15	N. F. Taylor	

BRITISH CIVIL REGISTRATIONS

Notes	Reg.	Type	Owner or Operator
	G-CCRG	Ultramagic M-77 balloon	M. Cowling
	G-CCRI	Raj Hamsa X'Air 582 (5)	R. W. Wallace
	G-CCRJ	Shaw Europa	J. F. Cliff
	G-CCRK	Luscombe 8A Silvaire	J. R. Kimberley
	G-CCRN	Thruster T.600N 450	R. A. Wright
	G-CCRP	Thruster T.600N 450	M. M. Lane (G-ULLY)
	G-CCRR	Skyranger 912 (1)	M. Cheetham
	G-CCRS	Lindstrand LBL-210A balloon	Aerosaurus Ballooning Ltd
	G-CCRT	Mainair Pegasus Quantum 15	N. Mitchell
	G-CCRV	Skyranger 912 (1)	R. O'Malley-White
	G-CCRW	Mainair Pegasus Quik	S. O. Hutchinson
	G-CCRX	Jabiru UL-450	M. Everest
	G-CCSD	Mainair Pegasus Quik	S. J. M. Morling
	G-CCSF	Mainair Pegasus Quik	D. G. Barnes & A. Sorah
	G-CCSG	Cameron Z-275 balloon	Wickers World Ltd
	G-CCSH	Mainair Pegasus Quik	N. C. Milnes
	G-CCSI	Cameron Z-42 balloon	IKEA Ltd
	G-CCSJ	Cameron A-275 balloon	D. S. Messmer
	G-CCSL	Mainair Pegasus Quik	A. J. Harper
	G-CCSN	Cessna U.206G	K. Brady
	G-CCSO	Raj Hamsa X'Air Falcon	D. J. Brightman
	G-CCSP	Cameron N-77 balloon	Ballongforeningen Oscair I Goteberg/Sweden
	G-CCSR	Aerotechnik EV-97A Eurostar	Sierra Romeo Flying Group
	G-CCSS	Lindstrand LBL-90A balloon	British Telecom
	G-CCST	PA-32R-301 Saratoga	G. G. L. James
	G-CCSU	IDA Bacau Yakovlev Yak-52	S. Ullrich/Germany
	G-CCSV	ICP MXP-740 Savannah Jabiru (1)	R. D. Wood
	G-CCSW	Nott PA balloon	J. R. P.Nott
	G-CCSX	Best Off Skyranger 912(1)	T. Jackson
	G-CCSY	Mainair Pegasus Quik	G. J. Gibson
	G-CCTA	Zenair CH.601UL Zodiac	G. E. Reynolds
	G-CCTC	Mainair Pegasus Quik	D. R. Purslow
	G-CCTD	Mainair Pegasus Quik	R. N. S. Taylor
	G-CCTE	Dyn'Aéro MCR-01 Banbi	C. J. McInnes
	G-CCTF	Aerotek Pitts S-2A Special	Stampe and Pitts Flying Group
	G-CCTG	Van's RV-3B	A. Donald
	G-CCTH	Aerotechnik EV-97 TeamEurostar UK	M. W. Fitch
	G-CCTI	Aerotechnik EV-97 Teameurostar	Flylight Airsports Ltd
	G-CCTL	Robinson R44 II	B. Daly
	G-CCTM	Mainair Blade	J. N. Hanso
	G-CCTO	Aerotechnik EV-97 Eurostar	A. J. Bolton
	G-CCTP	Aerotechnik EV-97 Eurostar	P. E. Rose
	G-CCTR	Skyranger 912	G. Lampit & D. W. Stamp
	G-CCTS	Cameron Z-120 balloon	F. R. Hart
	G-CCTT	Cessna 172S	ACS Engineering Ltd
	G-CCTU	Mainair Pegasus Quik	J. J. C. Parrish & I. D. Smart
	G-CCTV	Rans S.6ESA Coyote II	G. & S. Simons
	G-CCTW	Cessna 152	R. J. Dempsey
	G-CCTX	Rans S.8ES Coyote II	N. Blair
	G-CCTZ	Mainair Pegasus Quik 912S	S. Baker
	G-CCUA	Mainair Pegasus Quik	J. B. Crawford
	G-CCUB	Piper J-3C-65 Cub	G. Cormack
	G-CCUC	Best Off Skyranger J2.2(1)	N. C. Vining
	G-CCUE	Ultramagic T-180 balloon	M. Cowling
	G-CCUF	Skyranger 912(2)	R. E. Parker
	G-CCUH	RAF 2000 GTX-SE gyroplane	J. H. Haverhals
	G-CCUI	Dyn'Aéro MCR-01 Banbi	J. T. Morgan
	G-CCUK	Agusta A109-II	Eastern Atlantic Helicopters Ltd
	G-CCUL	Shaw Europa XS	Europa 6
	G-CCUO	Hughes 369D	Claremont Air Services
	G-CCUR	Mainair Pegasus Quantum 15-912	D. W. Power & D. James
	G-CCUT	Aerotechnik EV-97 Eurostar	Doctor and the Medics
	G-CCUY	Shaw Europa	N. Evans
	G-CCUZ	Thruster T.600N 450	Fly 365 Ltd
	G-CCVA	Aerotechnik EV-97 Eurostar	K. J. Scott
	G-CCVF	Lindstrand LBL-105 balloon	Alan Patterson Design
	G-CCVH	Curtiss H-75A-1 (82:8)	The Fighter Collection
	G-CCVI	Zenair CH.701 SP	The 701 Group
	G-CCVJ	Raj Hamsa X'Air Falcon 133	I. S. Doig
	G-CCVK	Aerotechnik EV-97 TeamEurostar UK	J. Holditch
	G-CCVL	Zenair CH.601XL Zodiac	A. Y.-T. Leungr & G. Constantine

Reg.	Type	Owner or Operator	Notes
G-CCVM	Van's RV-7A	J. G. Small	
G-CCVN	Jabiru SP-470	Teesside Aviators Group	
G-CCVP	Beech 58	Richard Nash Cars Ltd	
G-CCVR	Skyranger 912(2)	M. J. Batchelor	
G-CCVS	Van's RV-6A	J. Edgeworth (G-CCVC)	
G-CCVT	Zenair CH.601UL Zodiac	P. Millar	
G-CCVU	Robinson R22 Beta II	J. H. P. S. Sargent	
G-CCVW	Nicollier HN.700 Menestrel II	B. F. Enock	
G-CCVX	Mainair Tri Flyer 330	J. A. Shufflebotham	
G-CCVZ	Cameron O-120 balloon	T. M. C. McCoy	
G-CCWC	Skyranger 912	W. Goldsmith	
G-CCWE	Lindstrand LBL-330A balloon	Adventure Balloons Ltd	
G-CCWF	Raj Hamsa X'Air 133	F. Loughran	
G-CCWH	Dyn'Aéro MCR-01 Bambi	B. J. Mills & N. J. Mines	
G-CCWL	Mainair Blade	M. E. Rushworth	
G-CCWM	Robin DR.400/180	D. M. Scorer	
G-CCWO	Mainair Pegasus Quantum 15-912	R. Fitzgerald	
G-CCWP	Aerotechnik EV-97 TeamEurostar UK	G. Finney	
G-CCWR	Mainair Pegasus Quik	A. Harding	
G-CCWU	Skyranger 912	W. J. Byrd	
G-CCWV	Mainair Pegasus Quik	C. Buttery	
G-CCWW	Mainair Pegasus Quantum 15-912	I. W. Barlow	
G-CCWZ	Raj Hamsa X'Air Falcon 133	M. R. Wyatt	
G-CCXA	Boeing Stearman A75N-1 Kaydet (669)	Skymax (Aviation) Ltd	
G-CCXB	Boeing Stearman B75N1	C. D. Walker	
G-CCXC	Avion Mudry CAP-10B	Skymax (Aviation) Ltd	
G-CCXD	Lindstrand LBL-105B balloon	Silver Ghost Balloon Club	
G-CCXF	Cameron Z-90 balloon	Turner Balloons Ltd	
G-CCXG	SE-5A (replica) (C5430)	C. Morris	
G-CCXH	Skyranger J2.2	M. J. O'Connor	
G-CCXK	Pitts S-1S Special	P. G. Bond	
G-CCXM	Skyranger 912(1)	C. J. Finnigan	
G-CCXN	Skyranger 912(1)	S. E. Garner & G. P. Martin	
G-CCXO	Corgy CJ-1 Starlet	S. C. Ord	
G-CCXP	ICP Savannah Jabiru	B. J. Harper	
G-CCXR	Mainair Pegasus Blade	P. L. Owen	
G-CCXS	Montgomerie-Bensen B.8MR	A. Morgan	
G-CCXT	Mainair Pegasus Quik	C. Turner	
G-CCXU	Diamond DA40D Star	R. J. & L. Hole	
G-CCXV	Thruster T.600N 450	T. N. Farley	
G-CCXW	Thruster T.600N 450	G-CCXW Syndicate	
G-CCXX	AG-5B Tiger	P. D. Lock	
G-CCXZ	Mainair Pegasus Quik	K. J. Sene	
G-CCYB	Escapade 912(1)	B. E. & S. M. Renehan	
G-CCYC	Robinson R44 II	Derg Developments Ltd/Ireland	
G-CCYE	Mainair Pegasus Quik	P. M. Scrivener	
G-CCYG	Robinson R44	Moorland Windows	
G-CCYI	Cameron O-105 balloon	S. Bitti/Italy	
G-CCYJ	Mainair Pegasus Quik	YJ Syndicate	
G-CCYL	MainairPegasus Quantum 15	A. M. Goulden	
G-CCYM	Skyranger 912	I. Pilton	
G-CCYO	Christen Eagle II	P. C. Woolley	
G-CCYP	Colt 56A balloon	Magical Adventures Ltd	
G-CCYR	Ikarus C.42 FB80	Airbourne Aviation Ltd	
G-CCYS	Cessna F.182Q	S. Dyson	
G-CCYU	Ultramagic S-90 balloon	A. R. Craze	
G-CCYX	Bell 412	RCR Aviation Ltd	
G-CCYY	PA-28-161 Warrior II	Flightcontrol Ltd	
G-CCYZ	Dornier EKW C3605	CW Tomkins Ltd	
G-CCZA	SOCATA MS.894A Rallye Minerva 220	R. N. Aylett	
G-CCZB	Mainair Pegasus Quantum 15	A. Johnson	
G-CCZD	Van's RV-7	D. Powell	
G-CCZI	Cameron A-275 balloon	Balloon School (International) Ltd	
G-CCZJ	Raj Hamsa X' Air Falcon 582	P. A. Lindford	
G-CCZK	Zenair CH.601 UL Zodiac	R. J. Hopkins & J. Lonergan	
G-CCZL	Ikarus C-42 FB80	Shadow Aviation Ltd	
G-CCZM	Skyranger 912S	D. Woodward	
G-CCZN	Rans S.6-ES Coyote II	R. D. Proctor	
G-CCZO	Mainair Pegasus Quik	P. G. Penhaligon	
G-CCZR	Medway Raven Eclipse R	K. A. Sutton	
G-CCZS	Raj Hamsa X'Air Falcon 582	A. T. Kilpatrick	

Notes	Reg.	Type	Owner or Operator
	G-CCZT	Van's RV-9A	Zulu Tango Flying Group
	G-CCZV	PA-28-151 Warrior	London School of Flying Ltd
	G-CCZW	Mainair Pegasus Blade	A. F. & M. S. Foster
	G-CCZX	Robin DR.400/180	Exeter Aviation Ltd
	G-CCZY	Van's RV-9A	CCZY Syndicate
	G-CCZZ	Aerotechnik EV-97 Eurostar	B. M Starck & J. P. Aitken
	G-CDAA	Mainair Pegasus Quantum 15-912	I. A. Macadam
	G-CDAB	Glasair Super IISRG	W. L. Hitchins
	G-GDAC	Aerotechnik EV-97 TeamEurostar	Nene Valley Microlights Ltd
	G-CDAD	Lindstrand LBL-25A balloon	G. J. Madelin
	G-CDAE	Van's RV-6A	K. J. Fleming
	G-CDAG	Mainair Blade	K. I. Making
	G-CDAI	Robin DR.400/140B	D. Hardy & J. Sambrook
	G-CDAK	Zenair CH.601 UK Zodiac	W. K. Evans
	G-CDAL	Zenair CH.601UL Zodiac	R. J. Howell
	G-CDAO	Mainair Pegasus Quantum 15 -912	J. C. Duncan
	G-CDAP	Aerotechnik EV-97 TeamEurostar UK	Mainair Microlight School Ltd
	G-CDAR	Mainair Pegasus Quik	A. R. Pitcher
	G-CDAT	ICP MXP-740 Savannah Jabiru	G. M. Railson
	G-CDAX	Mainair Pegasus Quik	L. Hurman
	G-CDAY	Skyranger 912	P. Vicary
	G-CDAZ	Aerotechnik EV-97 Eurostar	M. C. J. Ludlow
	G-CDBA	Skyranger 912(S)	P. J. Brennan
	G-CDBB	Mainair Pegasus Quik	G. Hall
	G-CDBD	Jabiru J400	I. D. Rutherford
	G-CDBE	Montgomerie-Bensen B.8M	P. Harwood
	G-CDBG	Robinson R22 Beta	Jepar Rotorcraft
	G-CDBJ	Yakovlev Yak-3	C. E. Bellhouse
	G-CDBK	Rotorway Executive 162F	N. K. Foreman
	G-CDBM	Robin DR.400/180	C. M. Simmonds
	G-CDBO	Skyranger 912	G-CDBO Flying Group
	G-CDBR	Stolp SA.300 Starduster Too	R. J. Warren
	G-CDBS	MBB Bö.105DBS-4	Bond Air Services Ltd
	G-CDBU	Ikarus C.42 FB100	S. E. Meehan
	G-CDBV	Skyranger 912S	K. Hall
	G-CDBX	Shaw Europa XS	R. Marston
	G-CDBY	Dyn'Aero MCR-01 ULC	A. Thornton
	G-CDBZ	Thruster T.600N 450	BZ Flying Group
	G-CDCB	Robinson R44 II	L. Paarsch
	G-CDCC	Aerotechnik EV-97A Eurostar	R. E. & & N. G. Nicholson
	G-CDCD	Van's RVF-9A	RV9ers
	G-CDCE	Avions Mudry CAP-10B	The Tiger Club (1990) Ltd
	G-CDCF	Mainair Pegasus Quik	T. J. Gayton-Polley
	G-CDCG	Ikarus C.42 FB UK	N. E. Ashton
	G-CDCH	Skyranger 912(2)	G-CDCH Group
	G-CDCI	Pegasus Quik	R. J. Allarton
	G-CDCK	Mainair Pegasus Quik	R. Solomons
	G-CDCM	Ikarus C.42 FB UK	S. T. Allen
	G-CDCO	Ikarus C.42 FB UK	G. S. Gee-Carter & R. Urquhart
	G-CDCP	Avtech Jabiru J400	J. Cherry
	G-CDCR	Savannah Jabiru(1)	T. Davidson
	G-CDCS	PA-12 Super Cruiser	D. Todorovic
	G-CDCT	Aerotechnik EV-97 TeamEurostar UK	G. R. Nicholson
	G-CDCU	Mainair Pegasus Blade	W. S. Clare
	G-CDCV	Robinson R44 II	3GR Comm Ltd
	G-CDCW	Escapade 912 (1)	P. Nicholls
	G-CDDA	SOCATA TB20 Trinidad	Z. Clean
	G-CDDB	Grob/Schemmp-Hirth CS-11	K. D. Barber/France
	G-CDDF	Mainair Pegasus Quantum 15-912	B. C. Blackburn & J. L. Dalgetty
	G-CDDG	PA-26-161 Warrior II	Smart People Don't Buy Ltd
	G-CDDH	Raj Hamsa X'Air Falcon	G. Loosley
	G-CDDI	Thruster T.600N 450	R. Nayak
	G-CDDK	Cessna 172M	M. H. & P. R. Kavern
	G-CDDL	Cameron Z-350 balloon	Balloon School (International) Ltd
	G-CDDM	Lindstrand LBL 90A balloon	A. M. Holly
	G-CDDN	Lindstrand LBL 90A balloon	Flying Enterprises
	G-CDDO	Raj Hamsa X'Air 133(2)	S. Bain
	G-CDDP	Lazer Z.230	D. E. H. Nichols
	G-CDDR	Skyranger 582(1)	A. Greenwell & A. Carver
	G-CDDS	Zenair CH.601HD	S. Foreman
	G-CDDU	Skyranger 912(2)	R. Newton & P. A. Burton

Reg.	Type	Owner or Operator	Notes
G-CDDV	Cameron Z-250 balloon	Alba Ballooning Ltd	
G-CDDW	Aeroprakt A.22 Foxbat	W. E. Kyle	
G-CDDX	Thruster T.600N 450	B. S. P. Finch	
G-CDDY	Van's RV-8	The AV8ors	
G-CDEA	SAAB 2000	Eastern Airways	
G-CDEB	SAAB 2000	Eastern Airways	
G-CDEF	PA-28-161 Cadet	Western Air (Thruxton) Ltd	
G-CDEH	ICP MXP-740 Savannah	D. C. Crawley	
G-CDEM	Raj Hamsa X'Air 133	R. J. Froud	
G-CDEN	Mainair Pegasus Quantum 15 912	J. D. J. Spragg	
G-CDEO	PA-28 Cherokee 180	Hinde Holdings Ltd	
G-CDEP	Aerotechnik EV-97 TeamEurostar	Echo Papa Group	
G-CDER	PA-28-161 Warrior II	Archer Five Ltd	
G-CDET	Culver LCA Cadet	J. Gregson	
G-CDEU	Lindstrand LBL-90B balloon	N. Florence & P. J. Marshall	
G-CDEV	Escapade 912 (1)	M. B. Devenport	
G-CDEW	Pegasus Quik	K. M. Sullivan	
G-CDEX	Shaw Europa	K. Martindale	
G-CDEZ	Robinson R44 II	Heli Air Ltd	
G-CDFA	Kolb Twinstar Mk3 Extra	I. C. Lewis	
G-CDFD	Scheibe SF.25C Falke	The Royal Air Force Gliding and Soaring Association	
G-CDFG	Mainair Pegasus Quik	D. Gabbott	
G-CDFJ	Skyranger 912	L. A. Hosegood	
G-CDFK	Jabiru UL-450	J. A. Ellis	
G-CDFL	Zenair CH.601UL	Caunton Zodiac Group	
G-CDFM	Raj Hamsa X'Air 582 (5)	W. A. Keel-Stocker	
G-CDFN	Thunder Ax7-77 balloon	E. Rullo/Italy	
G-CDFO	Pegasus Quik	The Foxtrot Oscars	
G-CDFP	Skyranger 912 (1)	J. M. Gammidge	
G-CDFR	Mainair Pegasus Quantum 15	A. Jopp	
G-CDFU	Rans S.6-ES Coyote II	J. A. & M. K. Ashmore	
G-CDGA	Taylor JT.1 Monoplane	R. M. Larimore	
G-CDGB	Rans S.6-116 Coyote	S. Penoyre	
G-CDGC	Pegasus Quik	A. T. K. Crozier	
G-CDGD	Pegasus Quik	I. D. & V. A. Milne	
G-CDGE	Edge XT912-IIIB	M. R. Leyshon	
G-CDGF	Ultramagic S-105 balloon	D. & K. Bareford	
G-CDGG	Dyn'Aéro MCR-01 Club	N. Rollins	
G-CDGH	Rans S.6-ES Coyote	G-CDGH Group	
G-CDGI	Thruster T600N 450	R. North	
G-CDGN	Cameron C-90 balloon	M. C. Gibbons	
G-CDGO	Pegasus Quik	J. C. Townsend	
G-CDGP	Zenair CH 601XL	B. & P. J. Chandler	
G-CDGR	Zenair CH 701UL	I. A. R. Sim	
G-CDGS	AG-5B Tiger	M. R. O'B. Thompson	
G-CDGT	Montgomerie-Parsons Two Place g/p	J. B. Allan	
G-CDGU	VS.300 Spitfire I (X4276)	Peter Monk Ltd	
G-CDGW	PA-28-181 Archer III	Rutland Flying Group	
G-CDGX	Pegasus Quantum 15-912	S. R. Green	
G-CDGY	VS.349 Spitfire Mk VC	Aero Vintage Ltd	
G-CDHA	Skyranger 912S(1)	A. T. Cameron	
G-CDHC	Slingsby T67C	N. J. Morgan	
G-CDHE	Skyranger 912(2)	R. G. Jeffrey	
G-CDHF	PA-30 Twin Comanche B	Reid International (Guernsey) Ltd	
G-CDHG	Mainair Pegasus Quik	T. W. Pelan	
G-CDHH	Robinson R44 II	Abwood Homes/Ireland	
G-CDHJ	Lindstrand LBL-90B balloon	Lindstrand Hot Air Balloons Ltd	
G-CDHM	Pegasus Quantum 15	M. R. Smith	
G-CDHN	Lindstrand LBL-317A balloon	Aerosaurus Balloons Ltd	
G-CDHO	Raj Hamsa X'Air 133 (1)	S. B. Walters & P. Osborne	
G-CDHR	Ikarus C.42 FB80	M. D. J. Drake	
G-CDHU	Skyranger 912 (2)	G-CDHU Group	
G-CDHX	Aeroprakt A.22 Foxbat	N. E. Stokes	
G-CDHY	Cameron Z-90 balloon	D. M. Roberts	
G-CDHZ	Nicollier HN.700 Menestrel II	G. E. Whittaker	
G-CDIA	Thruster T.600N 450	T. Davidson	
G-CDIB	Cameron Z-350Z balloon	Ballooning Network Ltd	
G-CDIF	Mudry CAP-10B	J. D. Gordon	
G-CDIG	Aerotechnik EV-97 Eurostar	P. D. Brisco & J. Young	
G-CDIH	Cameron Z-275 balloon	Bailey Balloons Ltd	

Notes	Reg.	Type	Owner or Operator
	G-CDIJ	Skyranger 912 (2)	G. J. Chapman & K. C. Yeates
	G-CDIL	Pegasus Quantum 15-912	G. J. Prisk
	G-CDIO	Cameron Z-90 balloon	Slowfly Montgolfiere SNC/Italy
	G-CDIP	Skyranger 912S(1)	A. Ryan
	G-CDIR	Mainair Pegasus Quantum 15-912	M. Crane
	G-CDIS	Cessna 150F	S. P. Fox
	G-CDIT	Cameron Z-105 balloon	Bailey Balloons Ltd
	G-CDIU	Skyranger 912S(1)	Darley Moor Flyers Club
	G-CDIX	Ikarus C.42 FB.100	T. G. Greenhill & J. G. Spinks
	G-CDIY	Aerotechnik EV-97A Eurostar	R. E. Woolsey
	G-CDIZ	Escapade 912(3)	E. G. Bishop & E. N. Dunn
	G-CDJB	Van's RV-4	J. Mann
	G-CDJD	ICP MXP-740 Savannah Jabiru (4)	D. W. Mullin
	G-CDJE	Thruster T.600N 450	C. H. Ford
	G-CDJF	Flight Design CT2K	P. A. James
	G-CDJG	Zenair 601UL Zodiac	D. Garcia
	G-CDJI	UltraMagic M-120 balloon	Zebedee Balloon Service Ltd
	G-CDJJ	IAV Yakovlev Yak-52	J. J. Miles
	G-CDJK	Ikarus C.42 FB 80	Cornish Aviation Ltd
	G-CDJL	Avtech Jabiru J400	J. Gardiner
	G-CDJN	RAF 2000 GTX-SE gyroplane	D. J. North
	G-CDJO	DH.82A Tiger Moth	D. Dal Bon
	G-CDJP	Skyranger 912(2)	I. A. Cunningham
	G-CDJR	Aerotechnik EV-97 TeamEurostar	K. C. Lye & M. D. White
	G-CDJU	CASA 1.131E Jungmann Srs.1000	P. Gaskell
	G-CDJV	Beech A.36 Bonanza	Atlantic Bridge Aviation Ltd
	G-CDJX	Cameron N-56 balloon	Cameron Balloons Ltd
	G-CDJY	Cameron C-80 balloon	British Airways PLC
	G-CDKA	SAAB 2000	Eastern Airways
	G-CDKB	SAAB 2000	Eastern Airways
	G-CDKE	Rans S6-ES Coyote II	J. E. Holloway
	G-CDKF	Escapade 912 (1)	K. R. Butcher
	G-CDKH	Skyranger 912S (1)	C. Lenaghan
	G-CDKI	Skyranger 912S (1)	J. M. Hucker
	G-CDKJ	Silence Twister	A. H. R. Stansfield
	G-CDKK	Mainair Pegasus Quik	P. M. Knight
	G-CDKL	Escapade 912 (2)	M. A. Hodgson & D. Maidment
	G-CDKM	Pegasus Quik	P. Lister
	G-CDKN	ICP MXP-740 Savannah Jabiru (4)	T. Wicks
	G-CDKO	ICP MXP-740 Savannah Jabiru (4)	C. Jones & B. Hunter
	G-CDKP	Avtech Jabiru UL-D Calypso	Rochester Microlights Ltd
	G-CDKX	Skyranger J.2 .2 (1)	E. Lewis
	G-CDKY	Robinson R44	Specialist Technical Solutions Ltd
	G-CDKZ	Thunder Ax10-160 S2 balloon	Cameron Flights Southern Ltd
	G-CDLA	Mainair Pegasus Quik	C. R. Stevens
	G-CDLB	Cameron Z-120 balloon	J. A. Hibberd and Tchemma Products
	G-CDLC	CASA 1.131E Jungmann 2000	R. D. Loder
	G-CDLD	Mainair Pegasus Quik 912S	W. Williams
	G-CDLG	Skyranger 912 (2)	M. R. Foreman
	G-CDLI	Airco DH.9 (E8894)	Aero Vintage Ltd
	G-CDLJ	Mainair Pegasus Quik	J. S. James & R. S. Keyser
	G-CDLK	Skyranger 912S	L. E. Cowling
	G-CDLL	Dyn'Aéro MCR-01 ULC	R. F. Connell
	G-CDLR	ICP MXP / 740 Savannah Jabiru (4)	A. J. Burton & P. Read
	G-CDLS	Jabiru Aircrraft Jabiru J400	Kestrel Group
	G-CDLT	Raytheon Hawker 800XP	Tesco Stores Ltd
	G-CDLW	Zenair ZH.601UL Zodiac	W. A. Stphen
	G-CDLY	Cirrus SR20	JSC Aidarsa
	G-CDLZ	Mainair Pegasus Quantum 15-912	C. M. Jeffrey & J. L. Dalgetty
	G-CDMA	PA-28-151 Warrior	Wingtask 1995 Ltd
	G-CDMC	Cameron Z-105 balloon	First Flight
	G-CDMD	Robin DR.400/500	P. R. Liddle
	G-CDME	Van's RV-7	M. W. Elliott
	G-CDMF	Van's RV-9A	J. R. Bowden
	G-CDMG	Robinson R22 Beta	Polar Helicopters Ltd
	G-CDMH	Cessna P.210N	J. G. Hinley
	G-CDMJ	Mainair Pegasus Quik	M. J. R. Dean
	G-CDMK	Montgomerie-Bensen B8MR	P. Rentell
	G-CDML	Mainair Pegasus Quik	P. O'Rourke
	G-CDMN	Van's RV-9	G. J. Smith
	G-CDMO	Cameron S Can-100 balloon	A. Schneider/Germany

Reg.	Type	Owner or Operator	Notes
G-CDMP	Best Off Skyranger 912(1)	J. A. Charlton	
G-CDMS	Ikarus C,42 FB 80	Airbourne Aviation Ltd	
G-CDMT	Zenair CH.601XL Zodiac	B. A. Ritchie	
G-CDMU	Mainair Pegasus Quik	T. M. Bolton & S. D. Jones	
G-CDMV	Best Off Skyranger 912S(1)	D. O'Keeffe & K. E. Rutter	
G-CDMX	PA-28-161 Warrior II	S. Collins	
G-CDMY	PA-28-161 Warrior II	Redhill Air Services Ltd	
G-CDNA	Grob G.109A	Army Gliding Association	
G-CDND	GA-7 Cougar	C. J. Chaplin	
G-CDNE	Best Off Skyranger 912S(1)	G-CDNE Syndicate	
G-CDNF	Aero Design Pulsar 3	D. Ringer	
G-CDNG	Aerotechnik EV-97 TeamEurostar UK	G-CDNG Syndicate	
G-CDNH	Mainair Pegasus Quik	T. P. R. Wright	
G-CDNI	Aerotechnik EV-97 TeamEurostar UK	G-CDNI Group	
G-CDNJ	Colomban MC-15 Cri Cri	Cri Cri Group	
G-CDNM	Aerotechnik EV-97 TeamEurostar UK	H. C. Lowther	
G-CDNO	Westland Gazelle AH.1 (XX432)	CJ Helicopters	
G-CDNP	Aerotechnik EV-97 TeamEurostar UK	Eaglescott Eurostar Group	
G-CDNR	Ikarus C.42 FB1000	G. P. Burns	
G-CDNS	Westland Gazelle AH.1 (XZ321)	Falcon Aviation Ltd	
G-CDNT	Zenair CH.601XL Zodiac	W. McCormack	
G-CDNW	Ikarus C.42 FB UK	W. Gabbott	
G-CDNY	Jabiru SP-470	G. Lucey	
G-CDNZ	Ultramagic M-120 balloon	R. H. Etherington/Italy	
G-CDOA	EV-97 TeamEurostar UK	A. Costello & J. Cunliffe	
G-CDOB	Cameron C-90 balloon	G. D. & S. M. Philpot	
G-CDOC	Mainair Quik GT450	D. M. Broom	
G-CDOE	Avro 146 RJ70	Trident Turboprop (Dublin) Ltd	
G-CDOG	Lindstrand LBL-Dog SS balloon	ABC Flights Ltd	
G-CDOK	Ikarus C.42 FB 100	M Aviation Ltd	
G-CDOM	Mainair Pegasus Quik	G-CDOM Flying Group	
G-CDON	PA-28-161 Warrior II	G-CDON Group	
G-CDOO	Mainair Pegasus Quantum 15-912	O. C. Harding	
G-CDOP	Mainair Pegasus Quik	H. A. Duthie & R. C. Tadman	
G-CDOR	Mainair Blade	J. D. Otter	
G-CDOT	Ikarus C.42 FB 100	A. C. Anderson	
G-CDOV	Skyranger 912(2)	B. Richardson	
G-CDOY	Robin DR.400/180R	Lasham Gliding Society Ltd	
G-CDOZ	EV-97 TeamEurostar UK	L. Campbell	
G-CDPA	Alpi Pioneer 300	N. D. White	
G-CDPB	Skyranger 982(1)	N. S. Bishop	
G-CDPD	Mainair Pegasus Quik	M. D. Vearncombe	
G-CDPE	Skyranger 912(2)	M. J. Morson	
G-CDPG	Crofton Auster J1-A	G-CDPG Group	
G-CDPH	Tiger Cub RL5A LW Sherwood Ranger ST	K. F. Crumplin	
G-CDPJ	Van's RV-8	P. Johnson	
G-CDPL	EV-97 TeamEurostar UK	C. I. D. H Garrison	
G-CDPN	Ultramagic S-105	D. J. MacInnes	
G-CDPP	Ikarus C42 FB UK	H. M. Owen	
G-CDPS	Raj Hamsa X'Air 133	S. I. Hatherall	
G-CDPV	PA-34-200T Seneca II	Globebrow Ltd	
G-CDPW	Mainair Pegasus Quantum 15-912	T. D. Welburn	
G-CDPY	Shaw Europa	A. Burrill	
G-CDPZ	Flight Design CT2K	M. E. Henwick	
G-CDRC	Cessna 182Q Skylane	Heriot Capital	
G-CDRD	AirBorne XT912-B Edge/Streak III-B	Fly NI Ltd	
G-CDRF	Cameron Z-90 balloon	Chalmers Ballong Corps	
G-CDRG	Mainair Pegasus Quik	R. J. Gabriel	
G-CDRH	Thruster T.600N	Carlisle Thruster Group	
G-CDRI	Cameron O-105 balloon	Snapdragon Balloon Group	
G-CDRJ	Tanarg/Ixess 15 912S(1)	M. Delves-Yates	
G-CDRN	Cameron Z-225 balloon	Balloon School (International) Ltd	
G-CDRO	Ikarus C42 F880	Airbourne Aviation Ltd	
G-CDRP	Ikarus C42 FB80	D. S. Parker	
G-CDRR	Mainair Pegasus Quantum 15-912	M. I. White	
G-CDRS	Rotorway Executive 162F	R. C. Swann	
G-CDRT	Mainair Pegasus Quik	R. Tetlow	
G-CDRU	CASA 1.131E Jungmann 2000	P. Cunniff	
G-CDRV	Van's RV-9A	R. J. Woodford	
G-CDRW	Mainair Pegasus Quik	G. L. Fearon	

Notes	Reg.	Type	Owner or Operator
	G-CDRX	Cameron Z-225 balloon	Balloon School (International) Ltd
	G-CDRY	Ikarus C42 FB100 VLA	R. J. Mitchell
	G-CDRZ	Balóny Kubicek BB22 balloon	Club Amatori Del Volo In Montgolfiera
	G-CDSA	Mainair Pegasus Quik	G-CDSA Group
	G-CDSB	Alpi Pioneer 200	T. A. & P. M. Pugh
	G-CDSC	Scheibe SF.25C Rotax-Falke	Devon & Somerset Motorglider Group
	G-CDSD	Alpi Pioneer 300	J. A. Ball
	G-CDSF	Diamond DA40D Star	Flying Time Ltd
	G-CDSH	ICP MXP-740 Savannah Jabiru(5)	T. N. Huggins-Haig
	G-CDSK	Reality Escapade Jabiru(3)	R. H. Sear
	G-CDSM	P & M Aviation Quik GT450	S. L. Cogger
	G-CDSN	Raj Hamsa X'Air Jabiru(3)	S. P. Heard
	G-CDSS	Mainair Pegasus Quik	P. A. Bass
	G-CDST	Ultramagic N-250 balloon	Adventure Balloons Ltd
	G-CDSW	Ikarus C.42 FB UK	R. W. Skelton & J. Toner
	G-CDSX	EE Canberra T.Mk.4 (VN799)	Aviation Heritage Ltd
	G-CDSY	Robinson R44	D. Romagnoli
	G-CDTA	EV-97 TeamEurostar UK	R. D. Stein
	G-CDTB	Mainair Pegasus Quantum 15-912	D. W. Corbett
	G-CDTG	Diamond DA.42 Twin Star	CTC Aviation Group Ltd
	G-CDTH	Schempp-Hirth Nimbus 4DM	M. A. V. Gatehouse
	G-CDTI	Messerschmitt Bf.109E (4034)	Rare Aero Ltd
	G-CDTJ	Escapade Jabiru(1)	R. N. R. Bellamy
	G-CDTL	Avtech Jabiru J-400	M. I. Sistern
	G-CDTO	P & M Quik GT450	A. R. Watt
	G-CDTP	Skyranger 912S (1)	P. M. Whitaker
	G-CDTR	P & M Quik GT450	M. G. Freeman
	G-CDTT	Savannah Jabiru(4)	M. J. Day
	G-CDTU	EV-97 TeamEurostar UK	G-CDTU Group
	G-CDTV	Tecnam P2002 EA Sierra	S. A. Noble
	G-CDTX	Cessna F.152	J. S. Develin & Z. Islam
	G-CDTY	Savannah Jabiru (5)	A. J. Ferguson & T. W. Pawson
	G-CDTZ	Aeroprakt A.22 Foxbat	Colditz Group
	G-CDUE	Robinson R44	P. L. Hynds
	G-CDUH	P & M Quik GT450	A. P. & P. R. Santus
	G-CDUJ	Lindstrand LBL 31A balloon	J. M. Frazer
	G-CDUK	Ikarus C.42 FB UK	J. Molinari
	G-CDUL	Skyranger 912S (2)	T. W. Thiele & C. D. Hogbourne
	G-CDUS	Skyranger 912S (1)	G. Devlin & J. Northage
	G-CDUT	Jabiru J400	T. W. & A. Pullin.
	G-CDUU	P & M Quik GT450	Caunton Charlie Delta Group
	G-CDUV	Savannah Jabiru(5)	D. M. Blackman
	G-CDUW	Aeronca C3	N. K. Geddes
	G-CDUX	PA-32 Cherokee Six 300	D. J. Mason
	G-CDUY	Thunder & Colt 77A balloon	G. Birchall
	G-CDVA	Skyranger 912 (2)	S. J. Dovey
	G-CDVB	Agusta A.109E Power	Agusta Westland Ltd
	G-CDVD	Aerotechnik EV-97A Eurostar	P. Ritchie
	G-CDVE	Agusta A.109E Power	Agusta Westland Ltd
	G-CDVF	Rans S.6-ES Coyote II	B. J. Mould
	G-CDVG	Pegasus Quik	C. M. Lewis
	G-CDVH	Pegasus Quantum 15	D. J. Gaunt
	G-CDVI	Ikarus C42 FB80	Airbourne Aviation Ltd
	G-CDVJ	Montgomerie-Bensen B8MR	D. J. Martin
	G-CDVK	Savannah Jabiru (5)	M. Peters
	G-CDVL	Alpi Pioneer 300	J. D. Clabon
	G-CDVN	P & M Quik GT450	P. Warrener
	G-CDVO	P & M Quik	D. Sykes
	G-CDVR	P & M Quik GT450	Flying Group G-CDVR
	G-CDVS	Europa XS	J. F. Lawn
	G-CDVT	Van's RV-6	P. J. Wood
	G-CDVU	Aerotechnik EV-97 TeamEurostar	W. D. Kyle & T. J. Dowling
	G-CDVV	SA Bulldog Srs. 120/121 (XX626:02, W)	W. H. M. Mott
	G-CDVZ	P & M Quik GT450	S. M. Green & M. D. Peacock
	G-CDWB	Skyranger 912(2)	T. Collins
	G-CDWD	Cameron Z-105 balloon	Bristol University Ballooning Society
	G-CDWE	Nord NC.856 Norvigie	R. H. & J. A. Cooper
	G-CDWG	Dyn'Aéro MCR-01 Club	S. E. Gribble
	G-CDWI	Ikarus C42 FB80	The Scottish Flying Club
	G-CDWJ	Flight Design CTSW	G. P. Rood
	G-CDWK	Robinson R44	B. Morgan

Reg.	Type	Owner or Operator	Notes
G-CDWL	Raj Hamsa X'Air 582 (5)	The CDWL Flying Group	
G-CDWM	Skyranger 912S (1)	R. W. Marshall	
G-CDWN	Ultramagic N-210 balloon	S. R. Seager	
G-CDWO	P & M Quik GT450	G. W. Carwardine	
G-CDWP	P & M Quik GT450	R. W. Thornborough	
G-CDWR	P & M Quik GT450	G-CDWR Group	
G-CDWT	Flight Design CTSW	R. Scammell	
G-CDWU	Zenair CH.601UL Zodiac	A. D. Worrall	
G-CDWW	P & M Quik GT450	J. H. Bradbury	
G-CDWX	Lindstrand LBL 77A balloon	LSB Public Relations Ltd	
G-CDWZ	P & M Quik GT450	B. J. Holloway	
G-CDXA	Robinson R44 Raven	Northumbria Helicopters Ltd	
G-CDXD	Medway SLA100 Executive	A. J. Baker & G. Withers	
G-CDXF	Lindstrand LBL 31A balloon	R. S. Mohr	
G-CDXG	P & M Pegasus Quantum 15-912	A. P. Fox	
G-CDXH	Avro RJ100	Trident Jet Leasing (Ireland) Ltd	
G-CDXI	Cessna 182P	B. G. McBeath	
G-CDXJ	Jabiru J400	J. C. Collingwood	
G-CDXK	Diamond DA42 Twin Star	A. M. Healy	
G-CDXL	Flight Design CTSW	A. K. Paterson	
G-CDXN	P & M Quik GT450	D. J. Brookfield	
G-CDXP	Aerotechnik EV-97 Eurostar	R. J. Crockett	
G-CDXR	Replica Fokker DR.1	P. B. Dickinson	
G-CDXS	Aerotechnik EV-97 Eurostar	J. C. Rose	
G-CDXT	Van's RV-9	T. M. Storey	
G-CDXU	Chilton DW.1A	M. Gibbs	
G-CDXW	Cameron Orange 120 SS balloon	You've Been Tangoed	
G-CDXX	Robinson R44 Raven II	Nedroc Aviation Services Ltd	
G-CDXY	Skystar Kitfox Mk.7	D. E. Steade	
G-CDYB	Rans S.6-ES Coyote II	D. E. Rubery	
G-CDYD	Ikarus C42 FB80	C42 Group	
G-CDYI	BAe Jetstream 4100	Eastern Airways	
G-CDYL	Lindstrand LBL-77A balloon	J. H. Dobson	
G-CDYM	Murphy Maverick 430	M. R. Cann	
G-CDYO	Ikarus C42 FB80	A. R. Hughes	
G-CDYP	Aerotechnik EV-97 TeamEurostar UK	R. V. Buxton & R. Cranborne	
G-CDYR	Bell 206L-3 LongRanger III	Yorkshire Helicopters	
G-CDYT	Ikarus C42 FB80	A. & J. McVey	
G-CDYU	Zenair CH.701UL	A. Gannon	
G-CDYX	Lindstrand LBL-77B balloon	H. M. Savage	
G-CDYY	Alpi Pioneer 300	B. Williams	
G-CDYZ	Van's RV-7	Holden Group Ltd	
G-CDZA	Alpi Pioneer 300	J. F. Dowe	
G-CDZB	Zenair CH.601UL Zodiac	L. J. Dutch	
G-CDZD	Van's RV-9A	D. King	
G-CDZG	Ikarus C42-FB80	Mainair Microlight School Ltd	
G-CDZO	Lindstrand LBL-60X balloon	R. D. Parry	
G-CDZR	Nicollier HN.700 Menestrel II	M. P. Smith	
G-CDZS	Kolb Twinstar Mk.3 Extra	P. W. Heywood	
G-CDZU	ICP MXP-740 Savannah Jabiru (5)	P. J. Cheney	
G-CDZW	Cameron N-105 balloon	Backetorp Byggconsult AB	
G-CDZY	Medway SLA 80 Executive	Medway Microlights	
G-CDZZ	Rotorsport UK MT-03	H. E. Simons	
G-CEAK	Ikarus C42 FB80	Barton Heritage Flying Group	
G-CEAM	Aerotechnik EV-97 TeamEurostar UK	Flylight Airsports Ltd	
G-CEAN	Ikarus C42 FB80	T. Penn & C. P. Roche	
G-CEAO	Jurca MJ.5 Sirocco	P. S. Watts	
G-CEAR	Alpi Pioneer 300	W. C. Walters & D. K. Gibson	
G-CEAT	Zenair CH.601HDS Zodiac	T. B. Smith	
G-CEAU	Robinson R44	Mullahead Property Co Ltd	
G-CEAX	Ultramagic S-130 balloon	T. J. Parker	
G-CEAY	Ultramagic H-42 balloon	J. D. A. Shields	
G-CEBA	Zenair CH.601XL Zodiac	P. G. Morris	
G-CEBC	ICP MXP-740 Savannah Jabiru (5)	R. Duckett	
G-CEBE	Schweizer 269C-1	Millburn World Travel Services Ltd	
G-CEBF	Aerotechnik EV-97A Eurostar	M. Lang	
G-CEBG	Balóny Kubícek BB26 balloon	P. M. Smith	
G-CEBH	Tanarg 912S/Bionix 15	D. A. Chamberlain	
G-CEBI	Kolb Twinstar Mk.3	R. W. Livingstone	

Notes	Reg.	Type	Owner or Operator
	G-CEBL	Balóny Kubícek BB20GP balloon	Associazione Sportiva Aerostatica Lombada/Italy
	G-CEBM	P & M Quik GT450	S. P. Jones
	G-CEBN	Avro RJ100	Trident Jet Leasing (Ireland) Ltd
	G-CEBO	Ultramagic M-65C balloon	M. J. Woodcock
	G-CEBP	EV-97 TeamEurostar UK	T. R. Southall
	G-CEBT	P & M Quik GT450	A. J. Riddell
	G-CEBW	P-51D Mustang	Dental Insurance Solutions Ltd
	G-CEBZ	Zenair CH.601UL Zodiac	I. M. Ross & A Watt
	G-CECA	P & M Quik GT450	A. Weatherall
	G-CECC	Ikarus C42 FB80	G-CECC Group
	G-CECD	Cameron C-90 balloon	S. P. Harrowing
	G-CECE	Jabiru UL-D	ST Aviation Ltd
	G-CECF	Just/Reality Escapade Jabiru (3)	M. M. Hamer
	G-CECG	Jabiru UL-D	S. M. Spencer
	G-CECH	Jodel D.150	W. R. Prescott
	G-CECI	Pilatus PC-6/B2-H4 Turbo Porter	D. M. Penny
	G-CECJ	Aeromot AMT-200S Super Ximango	G-CECJ Syndicate
	G-CECK	ICP MXP-740 Savannah Jabiru (5)	B. L. Prime
	G-CECL	Ikarus C42 FB80	C. Lee
	G-CECO	Hughes 269C	H. Larcombe
	G-CECP	Best Off Skyranger 912(2)	A. Asslanian
	G-CECS	Lindstrand LBL-105A balloon	R. P. Ashford
	G-CECV	Van's RV-7	D. M. Stevens
	G-CECX	Robinson R44	Dolphin Property (Management) Ltd
	G-CECY	EV-97 Eurostar	M. R. M. Welch
	G-CECZ	Zenair CH.601XL Zodiac	Bluebird Aviation
	G-CEDB	Reality Escapade Jabiru (3)	R. F. Morton
	G-CEDC	Ikarus C42 FB100	L. M. Call
	G-CEDE	Flight Design CTSW	F. Williams & J. A. R. Hartley
	G-CEDF	Cameron N-105 balloon	Bailey Balloons Ltd
	G-CEDG	Robinson R44	P. J. Barnes
	G-CEDI	Best Off Skyranger 912(2)	S. E. Bettley
	G-CEDJ	Aero Designs Pulsar XP	P. F. Lorriman
	G-CEDK	Cessna 750 Citation X	The Duke of Westminster
	G-CEDL	TEAM Minimax 91	A. J. Weir
	G-CEDN	Pegasus Quik	Microlight Flight Lessons
	G-CEDO	Raj Hamsa X'Air Falcon 133(2)	OCTN Trust
	G-CEDR	Ikarus C42 FB80	Newtownards Microlight Group
	G-CEDT	Tanarg/Ixess 15 912S(1)	N. S. Brayn
	G-CEDV	Evektor EV-97 TeamEurostar UK	Airbourne Aviation Ltd
	G-CEDW	TEAM Minimax 91	J. K. Buckingham
	G-CEDX	Evektor EV-97 TeamEurostar UK	Delta X-Ray Group
	G-CEDZ	Best Off Skyranger 912(2)	J. E. Walendowski & I. Bell
	G-CEEB	Cameron C-80 balloon	Cameron Balloons Ltd
	G-CEEC	Raj Hamsa X'Air Hawk	P. J. Callis & B. G. King
	G-CEED	ICP MXP-740 Savannah Jabiru(5)	A. C. Thompson
	G-CEEE	Robinson R44	C. R. Caswell
	G-CEEG	Alpi Pioneer 300	D. McCormack
	G-CEEI	P & M Quik GT450	G. L. Hall
	G-CEEJ	Rans S-7S Courier	J. M. Lister
	G-CEEK	Cameron Z-105 balloon	PSH Skypower Ltd
	G-CEEL	Ultramagic S-90 balloon	San Paolo Company SRL
	G-CEEM	P & M Quik GT450	D. P. Sayer
	G-CEEN	PA-28-161 Cadet	Cristal Air Ltd
	G-CEEO	Flight Design CTSW	E. McCallum
	G-CEEP	Van's RV-9A	B. M. Jones
	G-CEER	ELA 07R	F. G. Shepherd
	G-CEES	Cameron C-90 balloon	P. C. May
	G-CEEU	PA-28-161 Cadet	White Waltham Airfield Ltd
	G-CEEV	PA-28-161 Warrior III	Best Fly KFT
	G-CEEW	Ikarus C42 FB100	C-More Flying School Ltd
	G-CEEX	ICP MXP-740 Savannah Jabiru(5)	G. M. Teasdale
	G-CEEZ	PA-28-161 Warrior III	Best Fly KFT
	G-CEFA	Ikarus C42 FB100 VLA	Ultimate Plant Exporter Ltd
	G-CEFB	Ultramagic H-31 balloon	J. L. Guy
	G-CEFC	Super Marine Spitfire 26	D. R. Bishop
	G-CEFJ	Sonex	R. W. Chatterton
	G-CEFK	Evektor EV-97 TeamEurostar UK	P. Morgan
	G-CEFM	Cessna 152	Cristal Air Ltd
	G-CEFP	Jabiru J430	G. Hammond

Reg.	Type	Owner or Operator	Notes
G-CEFS	Cameron C-100 balloon	Gone With The Wind Ltd	
G-CEFT	Whittaker MW5-D Sorcerer	W. Bruce	
G-CEFV	Cessna 182T Skylane	G. H. Smith and Son	
G-CEFY	ICP MXP-740 Savannah Jabiru(4)	B. Hartley	
G-CEFZ	Evektor EV-97 TeamEurostar UK	Robo Flying Group	
G-CEGE	Fairchild SA.226TC Metro II	BCA Charters Ltd	
G-CEGG	Lindstrand LBL-25A Cloudhopper balloon	C. G. Dobson	
G-CEGH	Van's RV-9A	M. E. Creasey	
G-CEGI	Van's RV-8	D. R. Fraser & R. Tye	
G-CEGJ	P & M Quik GT450	Flylight Airsports Ltd	
G-CEGK	ICP MXP-740 Savannah VG Jabiru(1)	A. & C. Kimpton	
G-CEGL	Ikarus C42 FB100	M. A. McLoughlin	
G-CEGO	Evektor EV-97A Eurostar	N. J. Keeling, R. F. McLachlan & J. A. Charlton	
G-CEGP	Beech 200 Super King Air	Cega Air Ambulance UK Ltd (G-BXMA)	
G-CEGR	Beech 200 Super King Air	Henfield Lodge Ltd	
G-CEGS	PA-28-161 Warrior II	Aviation Rentals	
G-CEGT	P & M Quik GT450	S. J. Fisher	
G-CEGU	PA-28-151 Warrior	White Waltham Airfield Ltd	
G-CEGV	P & M Quik GT450	S. P. A. Morris	
G-CEGW	P & M Quik GT450	P. Barrow	
G-CEGZ	Ikarus C42 FB80	C42 Swift Instruction Group	
G-CEHC	P & M Quik GT450	G-CEHC Syndicate	
G-CEHD	Best Off Skyranger 912(2)	A. W. Martin	
G-CEHE	Medway SLA 100 Executive	R. P. Stoner	
G-CEHG	Ikarus C42 FB100	C. J. Hayward & C. Walters	
G-CEHI	P & M Quik GT450	A. Costello	
G-CEHL	EV-97 TeamEurostar UK	Poet Pilot (UK) Ltd	
G-CEHM	Rotorsport UK MT-03	K. B. Laskowski	
G-CEHN	Rotorsport UK MT-03	P. A. Harwood	
G-CEHR	Auster AOP.9	J. Cooke & R. B. Webber	
G-CEHS	CAP.10B	M. D. Wynne	
G-CEHT	Rand KR-2	P. P. Geoghegan	
G-CEHV	Ikarus C42 FB80	Mainair Microlight School Ltd	
G-CEHW	P & M Quik GT450	G-CEHW Group	
G-CEHX	Lindstrand LBL-9A balloon	P. Baker	
G-CEHZ	Edge XT912-B/Streak III-B	J. Daly	
G-CEIA	Rotorsport UK MT-03	M. P Chetwynd-Talbot	
G-CEIB	Yakovlev Yak-18A	R. A. Fleming	
G-CEID	Van's RV-7	A. Moyce	
G-CEIE	Flight Design CTSW	D. K. Ross	
G-CEIG	Van's RV-7	W. K. Wilkie	
G-CEII	Medway SLA80 Executive	F. J. Clarehugh	
G-CEIK	Ultramagic M-90 ballon	M. R. W. Steyaert	
G-CEIL	Reality Escapade 912(2)	C. D. Pidler	
G-CEIS	Jodel DR.1050	G. R. Richardson	
G-CEIT	Van's RV-7	S. S. Gould	
G-CEIV	Tanarg/Ixess 15 912S(2)	W. O. Fogden	
G-CEIW	Europa	R. Scanlan	
G-CEIX	Alpi Pioneer 300	R. S. C. Andrews	
G-CEIY	Ultramagic M-120 balloon	A. Cesarano/Italy	
G-CEIZ	PA-28-161 Warrior II	IZ Aviation	
G-CEJA	Cameron V-77 balloon	G. Gray (G-BTOF)	
G-CEJC	Cameron N-77 balloon	I. Welsford	
G-CEJD	PA-28-161 Warrior III	Western Air (Thruxton) Ltd	
G-CEJE	Wittman W.10 Tailwind	R. A. Povall	
G-CEJG	Ultramagic M-56 balloon	Dragon Balloon Co.Ltd	
G-CEJI	Lindstrand LBL-105A balloon	Richard Nash Cars Ltd	
G-CEJJ	P & M Quik GT450	Juliet Juliet Group	
G-CEJL	Ultramagic H-31 balloon	Robert Wiseman Dairies PLC	
G-CEJN	Mooney M.20F	G. R. Wakeley	
G-CEJW	Ikarus C42 FB80	M. I. Deeley	
G-CEJX	P & M Quik GT450	P. Stewart & A. J. Huntly	
G-CEJY	Aerospool Dynamic WT9 UK	R. G. Bennett	
G-CEJZ	Cameron C-90 balloon	M. J. Woodcock	
G-CEKA	Robinson R-44 II	N. J. Whittingham	
G-CEKC	Medway SLA100 Executive	B. W. Webb	
G-CEKD	Flight Design CTSW	M. K. Arora	
G-CEKE	Robin DR400/180	M. F. Cuming	
G-CEKG	P & M Quik GT450	G-CEKG Flying Group	
G-CEKI	Cessna 172P	N. Houghton	

BRITISH CIVIL REGISTRATIONS

Notes	Reg.	Type	Owner or Operator
	G-CEKJ	Evektor EV-97A Eurostar	C. W. J. Vershoyle-Greene
	G-CEKK	Best Off Sky Ranger Swift 912S(1)	M. S. Schofield & B. W. G. Stanbridge
	G-CEKO	Robin DR400/100	Exeter Aviation Ltd
	G-CEKS	Cameron Z-105 balloon	Phoenix Balloons Ltd
	G-CEKT	Flight Design CTSW	Charlie Tango Group
	G-CEKV	Europa	K. Atkinson
	G-CEKW	Jabiru J430	J430 Syndicate
	G-CELA	Boeing 737-377	Jet 2
	G-CELB	Boeing 737-377	Jet 2
	G-CELC	Boeing 737-377	Jet 2 (G-OBMA)
	G-CELD	Boeing 737-377	Jet 2 (G-OBMB)
	G-CELE	Boeing 737-377	Jet 2 (G-MONN)
	G-CELF	Boeing 737-377	Jet 2
	G-CELG	Boeing 737-377	Jet 2
	G-CELH	Boeing 737-330	Jet 2
	G-CELI	Boeing 737-330	Jet 2
	G-CELJ	Boeing 737-330	Jet 2
	G-CELK	Boeing 737-330	Jet 2
	G-CELM	Cameron C-80 balloon	L. Greaves
	G-CELO	Boeing 737-33AQC	Jet 2
	G-CELP	Boeing 737-330QC	Jet 2
	G-CELR	Boeing 737-330QC	Jet 2
	G-CELS	Boeing 737-377	Jet 2
	G-CELU	Boeing 737-377	Jet 2
	G-CELV	Boeing 737-377	Jet 2
	G-CELW	Boeing 737-377	Jet 2
	G-CELX	Boeing 737-377	Jet 2
	G-CELY	Boeing 737-377	Jet 2
	G-CELZ	Boeing 737-377	Jet 2
	G-CEMA	Alpi Pioneer 200	D. M. Bracken
	G-CEMB	P & M Quik GT450	D. W. Logue
	G-CEMC	Robinson R44 Raven II	Castle Air Ltd
	G-CEME	Evektor EV-97 Eurostar	F. W. McCann
	G-CEMF	Cameron C-80 balloon	Linear Communications Consultants Ltd
	G-CEMG	Ultramagic M-105 balloon	Comunicazione In Volo SRL/Italy
	G-CEMI	Europa XS	B. D. A. Morris
	G-CEMM	P & M Quik GT450	M. A. Rhodes
	G-CEMO	P & M Quik GT450	T. D. Stock
	G-CEMR	Mainair Blade 912	J. A. Sweeney
	G-CEMS	MDH MD900 Explorer	Yorkshire Air Ambulance Ltd.
	G-CEMT	P & M Quik GT450	M. Tautz
	G-CEMU	Cameron C-80 balloon	J. G. O'Connell
	G-CEMV	Lindstrand LBL-105A balloon	R. G. Turnbull
	G-CEMW	Lindstrand LBL Bananas balloon	P. Baker (G-OCAW)
	G-CEMX	P & M Pegasus Quik	S. J. Meehan
	G-CEMY	Alpi Pioneer 300	J. C. A. Garland & P. F. Salter
	G-CEMZ	Pegasus Quik	P. G. Eastlake
	G-CENA	Dyn'Aero MCR-01 ULC Banbi	I. N. Drury & D. Goodman
	G-CENB	Evektor EV-97 TeamEurostar UK	K. J. Gay
	G-CEND	Evektor EV-97 TeamEurostar UK	Flylight Airsports Ltd
	G-CENE	Flight Design CTSW	The CT Flying Group
	G-CENG	SkyRanger 912(2)	R. A. Knight
	G-CENH	Tecnam P2002-EA Sierra	M. W. Taylor
	G-CENI	Supermarine Spitfire Mk.26(W3257:FY-E)	R. Ellingworth & A. G. Thomas
	G-CENJ	Medway SLA 951	M. Ingleton
	G-CENK	Schempp-Hirth Nimbus 4DT	R. A. Christie
	G-CENL	P & M Quik GT450	P. Von Sydow & S. Baker
	G-CENM	Evektor EV-97 Eurostar	N. D. Meer
	G-CENN	Cameron C-60 balloon	Stonebee Ltd
	G-CENO	Aerospool Dynamic WT9 UK	R. O. Lewthwaite
	G-CENP	Ace Magic Laser	A. G. Curtis
	G-CENR	ELA 07S	M. S. Gough
	G-CENS	SkyRanger Swift 912S(1)	G. C. Long
	G-CENV	P & M Quik GT450	RAF Microlight Flying Association
	G-CENW	Evektor EV-97A Eurostar	Southside Flyers
	G-CENX	Lindstrand LBL-360A	Wickers World Ltd
	G-CENZ	Aeros Discus/Alize	J. D. Buchanan
	G-CEOB	Pitts S-1 Special	N. J. Radford
	G-CEOC	Tecnam P2002-EA Sierra	M. A. Lomas
	G-CEOF	PA-28R-201 Arrow	J. H. Sandham Aviation
	G-CEOG	PA-28R-201 Arrow	A. J. Gardiner

Reg.	Type	Owner or Operator	Notes
G-CEOH	Raj Hamsa X'Air Falcon ULP(1)	J. C. Miles	
G-CEOI	Cameron C-60 balloon	M. E. White	
G-CEOJ	Eurocopter EC 155B	Starspeed Ltd	
G-CEOL	Flylight Lightfly-Discus	A. Bill	
G-CEOM	Jabiru UL-450	J. R. Caylow	
G-CEON	Raj Hamsa X'Air Hawk	K. S. Campbell	
G-CEOO	P & M Quik GT450	S. Moran	
G-CEOP	Aeroprakt A22-L Foxbat	G. F. Elvis	
G-CEOS	Cameron C-90 balloon	British School of Ballooning	
G-CEOT	Dudek ReAction Sport/Bailey Quattro 175	J. Kelly	
G-CEOU	Lindstrand LBL-31A balloon	Lindstrand Hot Air Balloons Ltd	
G-CEOV	Lindstrand LBL-120A balloon	Lindstrand Hot Air Balloons Ltd	
G-CEOW	Europa XS	R. W. Wood	
G-CEOX	Rotorsport UK MT-03	A. J. Saunders	
G-CEOY	Schweizer 269C-1	Helitrex Aviation Services	
G-CEOZ	Paramania Action GT26/PAP Chariot Z	A. M. Shepherd	
G-CEPL	Super Marine Spitfire Mk.26 (P9398)	S. R. Marsh	
G-CEPM	Jabiru J430	T. R. Sinclair	
G-CEPN	Kolb Firefly	I. Brewster	
G-CEPP	P & M Quik GT450	W. M. Studley	
G-CEPR	Cameron Z-90 balloon	Sport Promotion SRL/Italy	
G-CEPU	Cameron Z-77 balloon	G. Forgione/Italy	
G-CEPV	Cameron Z-77 balloon	John Aimo Balloons SAS/Italy	
G-CEPW	Alpi Pioneer 300	N. K. Spedding	
G-CEPX	Cessna 152	Cristal Air Ltd	
G-CEPY	Ikarus C42 FB80	L. Lay	
G-CEPZ	DR.107 One Design	CEPZ Flying Group	
G-CERB	SkyRanger Swift 912S(1)	J. J. Littler	
G-CERC	Cameron Z-350 balloon	Ballooning Network Ltd	
G-CERD	D.H.C.1 Chipmunk 22	A. C. Darby	
G-CERE	Evektor EV-97 TeamEurostar UK	Airborne Aviation Ltd	
G-CERF	Rotorsport UK MT-03	P. J. Robinson	
G-CERH	Cameron C-90 balloon	A. Walker	
G-CERI	Shaw Europa XS	S. J. M. Shepherd	
G-CERK	Van's RV-9A	P. E. Brown	
G-CERL	Ultramagic M-77 balloon	A. M. Holly	
G-CERN	P & M Quik GT450	P. M. Jackson	
G-CERO	Agusta A109C	Castle Air Ltd (G-OBEK/G-CDDJ)	
G-CERP	P & M Quik GT450	G. R. Cassie, A. J. L. Coulson, D. A. Howe & S. O. Kennedy	
G-CERT	Mooney M.20K	M. Simon	
G-CERV	P & M Quik GT450	East Fortune Flyers	
G-CERW	P & M Pegasus Quik	D. J. Cornelius	
G-CERX	Hawker 850XP	Hangar 8 Management Ltd	
G-CERY	SAAB 2000	Eastern Airways	
G-CERZ	SAAB 2000	Eastern Airways	
G-CESA	Replica Jodel DR.1050	T. J. Bates	
G-CESD	SkyRanger Swift 912S(1)	S. E. Dancaster	
G-CESH	Cameron Z-90 balloon	M. Rowlands	
G-CESI	Aeroprakt A22-L Foxbat	D. N. L. Howell	
G-CESJ	Raj Hamsa X'Air Hawk	J. Bolton & R. Shewan	
G-CESM	TL2000UK Sting Carbon	E. Stephenson	
G-CESR	P & M Quik GT450	G. Kerr	
G-CEST	Robinson R44	Startrade Heli Gmbh & Co KG/Germany	
G-CESU	Robinson R22 Beta	M. Boni	
G-CESV	EV-97 TeamEurostar UK	N. Jones	
G-CESW	Flight Design CTSW	J. Whiting	
G-CESZ	CZAW Sportcruiser	J. F. Macknay	
G-CETB	Robin DR.400/180	QR Flying Club	
G-CETD	PA-28-161 Warrior III	Aviation Maintenance Ltd	
G-CETE	PA-28-161 Warrior III	Aviation Maintenance Ltd	
G-CETF	Flight Design CTSW	I. Epton	
G-CETK	Cameron Z-145 balloon	R. H. Etherington	
G-CETL	P & M Quik GT450	J. I. Greenshields	
G-CETM	P & M Quik GT450	I. Burnside	
G-CETN	Hummel Bird	A. A. Haseldine	
G-CETO	Best Off Sky Ranger Swift 912S(1)	S. C. Stoodley	
G-CETP	Van's RV-9A	D. Boxall & S. Hill	
G-CETR	Ikarus C42 FB100	A. E. Lacy-Hulbert	
G-CETS	Van's RV-7	TS Group	

Notes	Reg.	Type	Owner or Operator
	G-CETT	Evektor EV-97 TeamEurostar UK	Tango Tango Group
	G-CETU	Best Off Sky Ranger Swift 912S(1)	A. Raithby & N. McCusker
	G-CETV	Best Off Sky Ranger Swift 912S(1)	C. J. Johnson
	G-CETX	Alpi Pioneer 300	J. M. P. Ree
	G-CETY	Rans S-6-ES Coyote II	J. North
	G-CETZ	Ikarus C42 FB100	Airways Airsports Ltd
	G-CEUE	BN-2T Islander	Britten-Norman Aircraft Ltd
	G-CEUF	P & M Quik GT450	G. T. Snoddon
	G-CEUH	P & M Quik GT450	G. J. McNally
	G-CEUJ	SkyRanger Swift 912S(1)	J. P. Batty & J. R. C. Brightman
	G-CEUL	Ultramagic M-105 balloon	R. A. Vale
	G-CEUM	Ultramagic M-120 balloon	Bridges Van Hire Ltd
	G-CEUN	Orlican Discus CS	The Royal Air Force Gliding and Soaring Association
	G-CEUT	Hoffman H-36 Dimona II	A. L. D. Munro & M. Tolson
	G-CEUU	Robinson R44 II	A. Stafford-Jones
	G-CEUV	Cameron C-90 balloon	I. Parsons
	G-CEUW	Zenair CH.601XL Zodiac	J. S. Griffiths
	G-CEUZ	P & M Quik GT450	B. S. Smy
	G-CEVA	Ikarus C42 FB80	The Scottish Flying Group
	G-CEVB	P & M Quik GT450	S. Jeffrey
	G-CEVC	Van's RV-4	P. A. Brook
	G-CEVD	Rolladen-Schneider LS3	Victor Delta Syndicate
	G-CEVE	Centrair 101A	T. P. Newham
	G-CEVG	P & M Pegasus Quik	Bartn Quik Group
	G-CEVH	Cameron V-65 balloon	J. A. Atkinson
	G-CEVJ	Alpi Pioneer 200-M	K. Worthington
	G-CEVK	Schleicher Ka 6CR	K. E. & O. J. Wilson
	G-CEVL	Fairchild M-62A-4 Cornell	UK Cornell Group
	G-CEVM	Tecnam P2002-EA Sierra	R. C. Mincik
	G-CEVN	Rolladen-Schneider LS7	N. Gaunt & B. C. Toon
	G-CEVO	Grob G.109B	T.J. Wilkinson
	G-CEVP	P & M Quik GT450	P. J. Lowe
	G-CEVS	EV-97 TeamEurostar UK	Hotel Victor Flying Group
	G-CEVT	Dudek Reaction 27/Bailey Quattro 175	J. Kelly
	G-CEVU	Savannah VG Jabiru(4)	I. C. May
	G-CEVV	Rolladen-Schneider LS3	LS3 307 Syndicate
	G-CEVW	P & M Quik GT450	R. W. Sutherland
	G-CEVX	Aeriane Swift Light PAS	P. Trueman
	G-CEVY	Rotorsport UK MT-03	P. Robinson
	G-CEVZ	Centrair ASW-20FL	B. Watkins
	G-CEWC	Schleicher ASK-21	London Gliding Club Proprietary Ltd
	G-CEWD	P & M Quik GT450	S. C. Key
	G-CEWE	Schempp-Hirth Nimbus 2	T. Clark
	G-CEWF	Jacobs V35 Airchair balloon	G. F. & I. Chadwick & M. G. Roberts
	G-CEWG	Aerola Alatus-M	Flylight Airsports Ltd
	G-CEWH	P & M Quik GT450	B. W. Hunter
	G-CEWI	Schleicher ASW-19B	S. R. Edwards
	G-CEWK	Cessna 172S	S. Howe
	G-CEWL	Alpi Pioneer 200	G-CEWL Ltd
	G-CEWM	DHC.6 Twin Otter 300	Isles of Scilly Skybus Ltd
	G-CEWN	Diamond DA-42 Twin Star	Halsbury Travel Ltd
	G-CEWO	Schleicher Ka 6CR	DQS Group
	G-CEWP	Grob G.102 Astir CS	G-CEWP Flying Group
	G-CEWR	Aeroprakt A22-L Foxbat	C. S. Bourne & G. P. Wiley
	G-CEWS	Zenair CH.701SP	D. L. Aspinall & G. E. MacCuish
	G-CEWT	Flight Design CTSW	A and R. W. Osborne
	G-CEWU	Ultramagic H-77 balloon	P. C. Waterhouse
	G-CEWW	Grob G.102 Astir CS	G. J. Walker
	G-CEWX	Cameron Z-350 balloon	Original Bristol FM Ltd
	G-CEWY	Quicksilver GT500	R. J. Scott
	G-CEWZ	Schempp-Hirth Discus bT	J. F. Goudie
	G-CEXL	Ikarus C42 FB80	Syndicate C42-1
	G-CEXM	Best Off Sky Ranger Swift 912S(1)	A. F. Batchelor
	G-CEXN	Cameron A-120 balloon	Dragon Balloon Company Ltd
	G-CEXO	PA-28-161 Warrior III	Durham Tees Flight Training Ltd
	G-CEXP	HPR.7 Herald 209 ★	Towing and rescue trainer/Gatwick
	G-CEXX	Rotorsport UK MT-03	D. B. Roberts
	G-CEYC	DG Flugzeugbau DG-505 Elan Orion	Scottish Gliding Union Ltd
	G-CEYD	Cameron N-31 balloon	J. C. Harris (G-LLYD)
	G-CEYE	PA-32R-300 Cherokee Lance	D. C. McH. Wilson

Reg.	Type	Owner or Operator	Notes
G-CEYF	Eurocopter EC135 T1	Lynx-Heli Ltd (G-HARP)	
G-CEYG	Cessna 152	Usefly EG/Germany	
G-CEYH	Cessna 152	Cornwall Flying Club Ltd	
G-CEYK	Europa XS	A. B. Milne	
G-CEYL	Bombardier BD-700-1A10 Global Express	Aravco Ltd	
G-CEYM	Van's RV-6	R. B. Skinner	
G-CEYN	Grob G.109B	G-CEYN Flying Group	
G-CEYO	Aerospatiale AS.350B2 Ecureuil	FB Heliservices Ltd	
G-CEYP	North Wing Design Stratus/ATF	J. S. James	
G-CEYR	Rotorsport UK MT-03	S. R. Voller	
G-CEYU	SA.365N1 Dauphin 2	Multiflight Ltd	
G-CEYX	Rotorsport UK MT-03	N. Creveul	
G-CEYY	EV-97 TeamEurostar UK	N. J. James	
G-CEYZ	Sikorsky S-76C	Bristow Helicoipters Ltd	
G-CEZA	Ikarus C42 FB80	P. Harper & P. J. Morton	
G-CEZB	Savannah VG Jabiru(1)	J. Finch	
G-CEZD	EV-97 TeamEurostar	G. P. Jones	
G-CEZE	Best Off Sky Ranger Swift 912S	G-CEZE Group	
G-CEZF	EV-97 TeamEurostar UK	D. J. Dick	
G-CEZH	Aerochute Dual	G. Stokes	
G-CEZI	PA-28-161 Cadet	Redhill Air Services Ltd	
G-CEZK	Stolp S.750 Acroduster Too	R. I. M. Hague	
G-CEZL	PA-28-161 Cadet	Chalrey Ltd	
G-CEZM	Cessna 152	Cristal Air Ltd	
G-CEZN	Pacific Airwave Pulse 2/Skycycle	G. W. Cameron	
G-CEZO	PA-28-161 Cadet	Redhill Air Services Ltd	
G-CEZR	Diamond DA.40D Star	Flying Time Ltd	
G-CEZS	Zenair CH.601HDS Zodiac	R. Wyness	
G-CEZT	P & M Aviation Quik GT450	B. C. Blackburn	
G-CEZU	CFM Streak Shadow SA	D. E. Foster	
G-CEZV	Zenair CH.601HDS Zodiac	H. R. Carey	
G-CEZW	Jodel D.150 Mascaret	N. J. Kilford	
G-CEZX	P & M Aviation Quik GT450	D. J. Haycocks & R. Patwardhan	
G-CEZZ	Flight Design CTSW	J. A. Lynch	
G-CFAG	Rotorsport UK MT-03	M. D. Cole	
G-CFAJ	DG-300 Elan	S. Marriott	
G-CFAK	Rotorsport UK MT-03	R. M. Savage	
G-CFAM	Schempp-Hirth Nimbus 3/24.5	Nimbus III Syndicate J15	
G-CFAO	Rolladen-Schneider LS4	V. R. Roberts	
G-CFAP	Interplane ZJ-Viera	Flylight Airsports Ltd	
G-CFAR	Rotorsport UK MT-03	P. M. Twose	
G-CFAS	Escapade Jabiru(3)	C. G. N. Boyd	
G-CFAT	P & M Aviation Quik GT450	T. G. Jackson	
G-CFAU	Cameron Z-105 balloon	High On Adventure Balloons Ltd	
G-CFAV	Ikarus C42 FB80	P. E. Scopes	
G-CFAW	Lindstrand LBL-35A Cloudhopper balloon	A. Walker	
G-CFAX	Ikarus C42 FB80	R. E. Parker & B. Cook	
G-CFAY	Sky 120-24 balloon	G. B. Lescott	
G-CFBA	Schleicher ASW-20BL	C. R. Little	
G-CFBB	Schempp-Hirth Standard Cirrus	L. Dale	
G-CFBC	Schleicher ASW-15B	CFBC Group	
G-CFBE	Ikarus C42 FB80	C. A. Hasell	
G-CFBF	Lindstrand LBL 203T gas balloon	S and D Leisure (Europe) Ltd	
G-CFBH	Glaser-Dirks DG-100G Elan	IBM Gliding Club	
G-CFBJ	Rotorsport UK MT-03	C-More Flying School Ltd	
G-CFBK	BAC 167 Strikemaster Mk.80A (1125)	Everett Aerospace	
G-CFBL	Best Off Sky Ranger Swift 912S(1)	D. Hemmings	
G-CFBM	P & M Quantum 15-912	G-CFBM Flying Group	
G-CFBN	Glasflugel Mosquito B	S. R. & J. Nash	
G-CFBO	Reality Escapade Jabiru(3)	Hangar 1 Ltd	
G-CFBS	Best Off Sky Ranger Swift 912S(1)	A. J. Tyler	
G-CFBT	Schempp-Hirth Ventus bT	488 (Gransden) Group	
G-CFBV	Schleicher ASK-21	London Gliding Club Proprietary Ltd	
G-CFBW	DG-100G Elan	G-CFBW Syndicate	
G-CFBX	Beech C90GTI King Air	J. M. Lynch	
G-CFBY	Best Off Sky Ranger Swift 912S(1)	J. A. Armin	
G-CFBZ	Schleicher Ka 6CR	R. H. W. Martyn	
G-CFCA	Schempp-Hirth Discus b	M. R. Hayden	

Notes	Reg.	Type	Owner or Operator
	G-CFCB	Centrair 101	T. J. Berriman & M. Phillimore
	G-CFCC	Cameron Z-275 balloon	Ballooning Network Ltd
	G-CFCD	SkyRanger Swift 912S(1)	D. & L. Payn
	G-CFCE	Raj Hamsa X'Air Hawk	B. M. Tibenham
	G-CFCF	Aerochute Dual	C. J. Kendal & S. G. Smith
	G-CFCH	Campbell Cricket Mk.4	E. J. Barton
	G-CFCI	Cessna F.172N	J. Blacklock
	G-CFCJ	Grob G.102 Astir CS	A. J. C. Beaumont & P. Hardwick
	G-CFCK	Best Off Sky Ranger 912S(1)	C. M. Sperring
	G-CFCL	Rotorsport UK MT-03	Rotary Wing Adventures Ltd
	G-CFCM	Robinson R44	Newmarket Plant Hire Ltd
	G-CFCN	Schempp-Hirth Standard Cirrus	P. C. Bunniss
	G-CFCP	Rolladen-Schneider LS6-a	R. E. Robertson
	G-CFCR	Schleicher Ka-6E	R. F. Whittaker
	G-CFCS	Schempp-Hirth Nimbus 2C	J. Luck & P. Dolling
	G-CFCT	EV-97 TeamEurostar UK	Sutton Eurostar Group
	G-CFCU	Lindstrand LBL-203T gas balloon	Lindstrand Aeroplatforms Ltd
	G-CFCV	Schleicher ASW-20	M. J. Davis
	G-CFCW	Rotorsport UK MT-03	C. M. Jones
	G-CFCX	Rans S-6-ES Coyote II	D. & S. Morrison
	G-CFCY	Best Off Sky Ranger Swift 912S(1)	M. E. & T. E. Simpson
	G-CFCZ	P & M Quik GT450	P. K. Dale
	G-CFDA	Schleicher ASW-15	N. B. Coggins
	G-CFDC	P & M Aviation Quik GT450	P. R. Davies
	G-CFDE	Schempp-Hirth Ventus bT	P. Clay
	G-CFDF	Ultramagic S-90 balloon	Edinburgh University Hot Air Balloon Club
	G-CFDG	Schleicher Ka 6CR	Delta-Golf Group
	G-CFDI	Van's RV-6	M. D. Challoner
	G-CFDJ	EV-97 TeamEurostar UK	J. D. J. Spragg & M. Jones
	G-CFDK	Rans S-6-ES Coyote II	Conair Sports Ltd
	G-CFDL	P & M QuikR	C. E. O. Hopkins
	G-CFDM	Schempp-Hirth Discus b	J. L. & T. G. M. Whiting
	G-CFDN	Best Off Sky Ranger Swift 912S(1)	A. C. Richards
	G-CFDO	Flight Design CTSW	D. I. Waller
	G-CFDP	Flight Design CTSW	N. Fielding
	G-CFDS	TL2000UK Sting Carbon	TL Sting G-CFDS Group
	G-CFDT	Aerola Alatus-M	R. J. Marshall
	G-CFDU	BB03 Trya/BB103	J. M. Macleod
	G-CFDV	Sikorsky S-76C	Bristow Helicopters Ltd
	G-CFDX	PZL-Bielsko SZD-48-1 Jantar Standard 2	A. Phillips
	G-CFDY	P &M Quik GT450	C. N. Thornton
	G-CFDZ	Flight Design Exxtacy/Alize	N. C. O. Watney
	G-CFEA	Cameron C-90 balloon	A. M. Holly
	G-CFEB	Cameron C-80 balloon	N. Edmunds
	G-CFED	Van's RV-9	E. W. Taylor
	G-CFEE	Evektor EV-97 Eurostar	G.CFEE Flying Group
	G-CFEF	Grob G.102 Astir CS	Oxford University Gliding Club
	G-CFEG	Schempp-Hirth Ventus b/16.6	P. Ottomaniello
	G-CFEH	Centrair 101 Pegase	Booker Gliding Club Ltd
	G-CFEJ	Schempp-Hirth Discus b	Lima Charlie Syndicate
	G-CFEK	Cameron Z-105 balloon	R. M. Penny (Plant Hire and Demolition) Ltd
	G-CFEL	EV-97 Eurostar	S. R. Green
	G-CFEI	RAF 2000 GTX-SE	A. M. Wells
	G-CFEM	P & M Aviation Quik GT450	A. M. King
	G-CFEN	PZL-Bielsko SZD-50-3 Puchacz	The Northumbria Gliding Club Ltd
	G-CFEO	EV-97 Eurostar	J. B. Binks
	G-CFER	Schempp-Hirth Discus b	S. R. Westlake
	G-CFES	Schempp-Hirth Discus b	M. J. Spittal
	G-CFET	Van's RV-7	J. Astor
	G-CFEV	P & M Pegasus Quik	W. T. Davis
	G-CFEX	P & M Quik GT450	H. Wilson
	G-CFEY	Aerola Alatus-M	M. S. Hayman
	G-CFEZ	CZAW Sportcruiser	J. F. Barber & J. R. Large
	G-CFFA	Ultramagic M-90 balloon	Proxim SPA/Italy
	G-CFFB	Grob G.102 Astir CS	M. H. Simms
	G-CFFC	Centrair 101A	P. Lazenby
	G-CFFE	EV-97 TeamEurostar UK	M. Lawton
	G-CFFF	Pitts S-1S Special	P. J. Roy
	G-CFFG	Aerochute Dual	G. J. Pemberton
	G-CFFH	Aeros Discus 15T Dragonfly	D. Wilson

Reg.	Type	Owner or Operator	Notes
G-CFFJ	Flight Design CTSW	R. Germany	
G-CFFL	Lindstrand LBL-317A balloon	Aerosarus Balloons Ltd	
G-CFFN	P & M Quik GT450	Kent County Scout Council	
G-CFFO	P & M Quik GT450	D. E. McGauley & J. R. North	
G-CFFS	Centrair 101A	W. Murray	
G-CFFT	Schempp-Hirth Discus b	P. R. Wilson	
G-CFFU	Glaser-Dirks DG-101G Elan	FFU Group	
G-CFFV	PZL-Bielsko SZD-51-1 Junior	Herefordshire Gliding Club Ltd	
G-CFFX	Schempp-Hirth Discus b	P. J. Richards	
G-CFFY	PZL-Bielsko SZD-51-1 Junior	Scottish Gliding Union Ltd	
G-CFGA	VS Spitfire VIII	The Pembrokeshire Spitfire Aeroplane Company Ltd	
G-CFGB	Cessna 680 Citation Sovereign	Keepflying LLP	
G-CFGC	Demoiselle	R. B. Hewing	
G-CFGD	P & M Quik GT450	D. J. Revell	
G-CFGE	Stinson 108-1 Voyager	M. J. Medland	
G-CFGF	Schempp-Hirth Nimbus 3T	R. E. Cross	
G-CFGG	Rotorsport UK MT-03	G-CFGG Flying Group	
G-CFGH	Jabiru J160	D. F. Sargant	
G-CFGI	VS.358 Seafire Mk.II (MB293)	Mark One Partners LLC	
G-CFGJ	VS.300 Spitfire I (N3200)	Mark One Partners LLC	
G-CFGK	Grob G.102 Astir CS	P. Allingham	
G-CFGM	Ikarus C42	R. S. O'Carroll	
G-CFGN	VS.300 Spitfire IA	Mark One Partners LLC	
G-CFGO	Best Off Sky Ranger Swift 912S	R. G. Hearsey & C. Lamb	
G-CFGP	Schleicher ASW-19	A. E. Prime	
G-CFGR	Schleicher ASK-13	Portsmouth Naval Gliding Centre	
G-CFGT	P & M Aviation Quik GT450	C. W. Thompson	
G-CFGU	Schempp-Hirth Standard Cirrus	D. Higginbottom	
G-CFGV	P & M Quik GT450	R. Bennett	
G-CFGX	EV-97 TeamEurostar UK	Golf XRay Group	
G-CFGY	Rotorsport UK MT-03	G. J. Slater & N. D. Leak	
G-CFGW	Centrair 101A	L. P. Smith	
G-CFGZ	Flight Design CTSW	B. Gorvett	
G-CFHB	Micro Aviation B.22J Bantam	P. Rayson	
G-CFHC	Micro Aviation B.22J Bantam	D. J. Vickery	
G-CFHD	Schleicher ASW-20 BL	196 Syndicate	
G-CFHF	PZL-Bielsko SZD-51-1	Black Mountains Gliding Club	
G-CFHG	Schempp-Hirth Mini Nimbus C	R. W. & M. P. Weaver	
G-CFHI	Van's RV-9	J. R. Dawe	
G-CFHJ	Centrair 101A Pegase	Booker Gliding Club Ltd	
G-CFHK	Aeroprakt A22-L Foxbat	R. Bellew	
G-CFHL	Rolladen-Schneider LS4	N. Craig & M. C. Jenkins	
G-CFHM	Schleicher ASK-13	Lasham Gliding Society Ltd	
G-CFHN	Schleicher K 8B	The Nene Valley Gliding Club Ltd	
G-CFHO	Grob G.103 Twin Astir II	The Surrey Hills Gliding Club Ltd	
G-CFHP	Ikarus C42 FB80	Airbourne Aviation Ltd	
G-CFHR	Schempp-Hirth Discus b	M. Fursedon, J. Jervis & T. Turner	
G-CFHS	Tchemma T01/77 balloon	D. J. Farrar	
G-CFHU	Robinson R22 Beta	Cameron and Brown Partnership	
G-CFHW	Grob G.102 Astir CS	D. J. Wedlock & D. Brown	
G-CFHX	Schroeder Fire Balloons G22/24 balloon	T. J. Ellenrieder	
G-CFHY	Fokker Dr.1 Triplane replica	P. G. Bond	
G-CFHZ	Schleicher Ka 6CR	G. D. Leatherland	
G-CFIA	Best Off Sky Ranger Swift 912S(1)	D. I. Hall	
G-CFIC	Jodel DR.1050/M1	J. H. & P. I. Kempton	
G-CFID	Tanarg/Ixess 15 912S	D. Smith	
G-CFIE	Rotorsport UK MT-03	A. McCredie	
G-CFIF	Christen Eagle II	CFG Flying Group	
G-CFIG	P & M Aviation Quik GT450	J. Whitfield	
G-CFIH	Piel CP.1320	I. W. L. Aikman	
G-CFII	DH.82A Tiger Moth	Motair LLP	
G-CFIJ	Christen Eagle II	A. P. Shoobert	
G-CFIK	Lindstrand LBL-60X balloon	L. Sambrook	
G-CFIL	P & M Aviation Quik GT450	S. N. Catchpole	
G-CFIM	P & M Aviation Quik GT450	A. Szczepanek	
G-CFIO	Cessna 172S	Skytrek Air Services	
G-CFIT	Ikarus C42 FB100	G-CFIT Group	
G-CFIU	CZAW Sportcruiser	G. Everett & D. Smith	
G-CFIW	Balony Kubicek BB20XR balloon	H. C. J. Williams	
G-CFIZ	Best Off Sky Ranger 912(2)	J. A. Hartshorne	

Notes	Reg.	Type	Owner or Operator
	G-CFJB	Rotorsport UK MT-03	N. J. Hargreaves
	G-CFJF	Schempp-Hirth SHK-1	J. F. Mills
	G-CFJG	Best Off Sky Ranger Swift 912S(1)	C. M. Gray
	G-CFJH	Grob G.102 Astir CS77	P. Hardman
	G-CFJI	Ultramagic M-105 balloon	Club Aerostatico Wind & Fire/Italy
	G-CFJJ	Best Off Sky Ranger Swift 912S(1)	J. J. Ewing
	G-CFJK	Centrair 101A	D. Lewis
	G-CFJL	Raj Hamsa X'Air Hawk	G. L. Craig
	G-CFJM	Rolladen-Schneider LS4-a	K. Woods & S. Hill
	G-CFJN	Diamond DA.40D Star	Atlantic Flight Training Ltd
	G-CFJO	Diamond DA.40D Star	Atlantic Flight Training Ltd
	G-CFJP	Cameron N-56 balloon	V. J. M. L de Gail
	G-CFJR	Glaser-Dirks DG-300 Club Elan	W. Palmer & H. Smith
	G-CFJS	Glaser-Dirks DG-300 Club Elan	K. L. Goldsmith
	G-CFJU	Raj Hamsa X'Air Hawk	R. J. Minns & H. M. Wooldridge
	G-CFJV	Schleicher ASW-15	R. Abercrombie
	G-CFJW	Schleicher K7	K7 Group
	G-CFJX	DG-300 Elan	Crown Service Gliding Club
	G-CFJZ	Schempp-Hirth SHK-1	B. C. Irwin & R. H. Hanna
	G-CFKA	Rotorsport UK MT-03	M. J. L. Carter
	G-CFKB	CZAW Sportcruiser	KB Flying Group
	G-CFKD	Raj Hamsa X'Air Falcon Jabiru(2)	A. M. Fawthrop
	G-CFKE	Raj Hamsa X'Air Hawk	S. Rance
	G-CFKG	Rolladen-Schneider LS4-a	G-CFKG Group
	G-CFKH	Zenair CH.601XL Zodiac	R. Hingley & C. Prince
	G-CFKJ	P & M Aviation Quik GT450	B. Geary
	G-CFKK	Flylight Dragonfly	R. A. Taylor
	G-CFKL	Schleicher ASW-20 BL	J. Ley
	G-CFKM	Schempp-Hirth Discus b	Lasham Gliding Society Ltd
	G-CFKN	Lindstrand GA22 Mk.II airship	Lindstrand Technologies Ltd
	G-CFKO	P & M Aviation Quik GT450	D. W. C. Beer
	G-CFKP	Performance Designs Barnstormer/ Voyager	G. A. Dobson
	G-CFKR	P & M Aviation Pegasus Quik	R. D. Ballard
	G-CFKS	Flight Design CTSW	D. J. M. Williams
	G-CFKT	Schleicher K 8B	FKT Group
	G-CFKU	P & M Aviation Quik GT450	C. A. Hasell
	G-CFKW	Alpi Pioneer 200	A. A. Mortimer
	G-CFKX	Cameron Z-160 balloon	K. R. Karlstrom
	G-CFKY	Schleicher Ka 6CR	J. A. Timmis
	G-CFKZ	Europa XS	P. I. Morgans
	G-CFLA	P & M Aviation Quik GT450	P. H. Woodward
	G-CFLC	Glaser-Dirks DG-300 Club Elan	J. L.Hey
	G-CFLD	Ikarus C42 FB80	L. McWilliams
	G-CFLE	Schempp-Hirth Discus b	D. A. Humphreys & S. J. A. McCracken
	G-CFLF	Rolladen-Schneider LS4-a	D. Lamb
	G-CFLG	CZAW Sportcruiser	D. A. Buttress
	G-CFLH	Schleicher K8B	The South Wales Gliding Club Ltd
	G-CFLI	Europa Aviation Europa	A. & E. Bennett
	G-CFLK	Cameron C-90 balloon	J. R. Rivers-Scott
	G-CFLL	EV-97 Eurostar	D. R. Lewis
	G-CFLM	P & M Pegasus Quik	The JAG Flyers
	G-CFLN	Best Off Sky Ranger Swift 912S(1)	D. Bletcher
	G-CFLO	Rotorsport UK MT-03	R. G. Mulford
	G-CFLP	D.31 Turbulent	Eaglescott Turbulent Group
	G-CFLR	P & M Aviation Quik GT450	S. J. Baker
	G-CFLS	Schleicher Ka 6CR	University College London Union
	G-CFLU	SAAB 2000	Eastern Airways
	G-CFLV	SAAB 2000	Eastern Airways
	G-CFLW	Schempp-Hirth Standard Cirrus 75	J. Pack
	G-CFLX	DG-300 Club Elan	R. Emms
	G-CFLZ	Scheibe SF-27A Zugvogel V	SF Group
	G-CFMA	BB03 Trya/BB103	D. Sykes
	G-CFMB	P & M Aviation Quik GT450	Countermine Technologies PLC
	G-CFMC	Van's RV-9A	G-CFMC Flying Group
	G-CFMD	P & M Aviation Quik GT450	Wilson G. Jamieson Ltd
	G-CFME	SOCATA TB10 Tobago	G. M. Paeckmeyer & B. B. Singh
	G-CFMH	Schleicher ASK-13	Lasham Gliding Society Ltd
	G-CFMI	Best Off Sky Ranger 912(1)	P. Shelton
	G-CFMM	Cessna 172S	Cristal Air Ltd
	G-CFMN	Schempp-Hirth Ventus cT	FMN Glider Syndicate

Reg.	Type	Owner or Operator	Notes
G-CFMO	Schempp-Hirth Discus b	P. D. Bagnall	
G-CFMP	Europa XS	M. P. Gamble	
G-CFMR	Ultramagic V-14 balloon	P. Baker	
G-CFMS	Schleicher ASW-15	Loughborough Students Union Gliding Club	
G-CFMT	Schempp-Hirth Standard Cirrus	J. M. Brooke	
G-CFMU	Schempp-Hirth Standard Cirrus	P. S. Carder	
G-CFMV	Aerola Alatus-M	P. J. Wood	
G-CFMW	Scheibe SF-25C	The Windrushers Gliding Club Ltd	
G-CFMX	PA-28-161 Warrior II	Stapleford Flying Club Ltd	
G-CFMY	Rolladen-Schneider LS7	G-CFMY Group	
G-CFNB	Cameron TR-70 balloon	Balslooning Team BVBA/Belgium	
G-CFNC	Flylight Dragonfly	W. G. Minns	
G-CFND	Schleicher Ka 6E	C. Scutt	
G-CFNE	PZL-Bielsko SZD-38A Jantar 1	T. Robson, J. Murray & I. Gordon	
G-CFNF	Robinson R44 II	S. G. Dykes	
G-CFNG	Schleicher ASW-24	M. D. Wright	
G-CFNH	Schleicher ASW-19	S. N. & P. E. S. Longland	
G-CFNI	Airborne Edge XT912-B/Streak III-B	Fly NI Ltd	
G-CFNK	Slingsby T.65A Vega	I. P. Goldstraw	
G-CFNL	Schempp-Hirth Discus b	A. S. Ramsay & P. P. Musto	
G-CFNM	Centrair 101B Pegase	D. T. Hartley	
G-CFNO	Best Off Sky Ranger Swift 912S(1)	P. R. Hanman	
G-CFNP	Schleicher Ka 6CR	P. Pollard-Wilkins	
G-CFNR	Schempp-Hirth Discus b	D. A. Hope	
G-CFNS	Glaser-Dirks DG-300 Club Elan	P. E. Williams, K. F. Byrne & J. M. Price	
G-CFNT	Glaser-Dirks DG-600	G-CFNT Group	
G-CFNU	Rolladen Schneider LS4-a	R. J. Simpson	
G-CFNV	CZAW Sportcruiser	N. D. McAllister & M. Owen	
G-CFNW	EV-97 TeamEurostar UK	The Scottish Aero Club Ltd	
G-CFNX	ixess 13 (modified/Buggy 582 Trike)	A. E. Barron	
G-CFNY	Flylight Dragonfly	M. J. Jessop	
G-CFNZ	Airborne Edge XT912-B/Streak III-B	P. Walton	
G-CFOB	Schleicher ASW-15B	G. J. Chisholm	
G-CFOC	Glaser-Dirks DG200/17	DG202 Flying Syndicate	
G-CFOF	Scheibe SF-27A Zugvogel V	S. Maddex	
G-CFOG	Ikarus C42 FB UK	P. D. Coppin	
G-CFOI	Cessna 172N	P. Fearon	
G-CFOJ	Eurocopter EC.155 B1	Starspeed Ltd	
G-CFOM	Scheibe SF27A	K. A. Ford & R. D. Noon	
G-CFON	Wittman W8 Tailwind	C. F. O'Neill	
G-CFOO	P & M Aviation Quik R	Microavionics	
G-CFOP	Cameron Hopping Bag 120 SS balloon	J. Ravibalan	
G-CFOR	Schleicher K 8B	Dorset Gliding Club Ltd	
G-CFOS	Flylight Dragonfly	P. S. Bendall	
G-CFOT	PZL-Bielsko SZD-48-3 Jantar Standard 3	T. Greenwood	
G-CFOU	Schleicher K7	Vectis Gliding Club Ltd	
G-CFOV	CZAW Sportcruiser	J. G. Murphy	
G-CFOW	Best Off Sky Ranger Swift 912S(1)	Oscar Whiskey Syndicate	
G-CFOX	Marganski MDM-1	Fox Syndicate	
G-CFOY	Schempp-Hirth Discus b	B. W. Mills, J. W. Slater & R. F. Dowty	
G-CFOZ	Rolladen-Schneider LS1-f	L51 Group	
G-CFPA	CZAW Sportcruiser	T. W. Lorimer	
G-CFPB	Schleicher ASW-15B	G-CFPB Syndicate	
G-CFPD	Rolladen-Schneider LS7	LS7 Group	
G-CFPE	Schempp-Hirth Ventus cT	R. Palmer	
G-CFPF	Scheibe L-Spatz 55	N. C. Stone	
G-CFPG	AMS-Flight Carat A	B. J. L. Bollen	
G-CFPH	Centrair ASW-20F	A. L. D. Munro & J. R. King	
G-CFPI	P & M Aviation Quik GT450	G-CFPI Group	
G-CFPJ	CZAW Sportcruiser	S. R. Winter	
G-CFPL	Schempp-Hirth Ventus c	R. V. Barrett	
G-CFPM	PZL-Bielsko SZD-51-1 Junior	Kent Gliding Club Ltd	
G-CFPN	Schleicher ASW-20	M. Rayner	
G-CFPP	Schempp-Hirth Nimbus 2B	R. Jones & R. Murfitt	
G-CFPR	P & M Aviation Quik R	D. Seiler	
G-CFPS	Sky 25-16 balloon	G. B. Lescott	
G-CFPT	Schleicher ASW-20	L. Hornsey and L. Weeks Syndicate	
G-CFPW	Glaser-Dirks DG-600	P. B. Gray	
G-CFRC	Schempp-Hirth Nimbus 2B	Tim and Martin Nimbus 2B Group	
G-CFRE	Schleicher Ka 6E	K6-FRE Syndicate	
G-CFRF	Lindstrand LBL-31A	RAF Halton Hot Air Balloon Club	

Notes	Reg.	Type	Owner or Operator
	G-CFRH	Schleicher ASW-20CL	J. N. Wilton
	G-CFRI	Ultramagic N-355 balloon	Kent Ballooning
	G-CFRJ	Schempp-Hirth Standard Cirrus	J. Francis & P. Gould
	G-CFRK	Schleicher ASW-15B	P. R. Boet
	G-CFRL	Grob G.102 Astir CS	The South Wales Gliding Club Ltd
	G-CFRM	SkyRanger Swift 912S(1)	R. K. & T. A. Willcox
	G-CFRN	Rotorsport UK MTO Sport	R. Marks
	G-CFRP	Centrair 101A Pegase	G. D. Rogers
	G-CFRR	Centrair 101A	G-CFRR Syndicate
	G-CFRS	Scheibe Zugvogel IIIB	G-CFRS Flying Group
	G-CFRT	EV-97 TeamEurostar UK	G. J. Slater & N. D. Leak
	G-CFRV	Centrair 101A	P. J. Britten
	G-CFRW	Schleicher ASW-20L	R. M. Green
	G-CFRX	Centrair 101A	S. Woolrich
	G-CFRY	Zenair CH 601UL	C. K. Fry
	G-CFRZ	Schempp-Hirth Standard Cirrus	S. G. Lapworth
	G-CFSB	Tecnam P2002-RG Sierra	W. J. Gale and Son
	G-CFSD	Schleicher ASK-13	Portsmouth Naval Gliding Centre
	G-CFSE	Cameron H-340HL balloon	Balloon School (International) Ltd
	G-CFSF	P & M Aviation QuikR	C. J. Gordon
	G-CFSG	Van's RV-9	R. A. L. Hubbard
	G-CFSH	Grob G.102 Astir CS Jeans	Buckminster Gliding Club Ltd
	G-CFSI	Aerola Alatus-M	T. J. Birkbeck
	G-CFSJ	Jabiru J160	T. J. Adams-Lewis
	G-CFSK	Dyn'Aero MCR-01 VLA Sportster	S. Collins
	G-CFSL	Kubicek BB-26Z balloon	M. R. Jeynes
	G-CFSM	Cessna 172Q	Zentelligence Ltd
	G-CFSO	Flylight Dragonfly/Aeros Discus 15T	J. G. McMinn
	G-CFSR	DG-300 Elan	A. P. Montague
	G-CFSS	Schleicher Ka 6E	FSS Syndicate
	G-CFST	Schleicher ASH-25E	D. Tucker & K. H. Lloyd
	G-CFSW	Skyranger Swift 912S(1)	S. B. & L. S. Williams
	G-CFSX	Savannah VG Jabiru(1)	J. P. Swadling
	G-CFTA	Ace Magic Laser	P and M Aviation Ltd
	G-CFTB	Schleicher Ka 6CR	D. A. Parker
	G-CFTC	PZL-Bielsko SZD-51-1 Junior	Seahawk Gliding Club
	G-CFTD	Schleicher ASW-15B	G-CFTD Flying Group
	G-CFTF	Roe 1 Triplane Replica	E. A. Verdon-Roe
	G-CFTG	P & M Aviation Quik R	A. V. Cosser
	G-CFTH	PZL-Bielsko SZD-50-3 Puchacz	Buckminster Gliding Club Ltd
	G-CFTI	Evektor EV-97A Eurostar	R. J. Dance
	G-CFTJ	Aerotechnik EV-97A Eurostar	C. B. Flood
	G-CFTK	Grob G.102 Astir CS Jeans	Ulster Gliding Club Ltd
	G-CFTL	Schleicher ASW-20CL	J. S. & S. V. Shaw
	G-CFTM	Cameron C-80 balloon	P. A. Meecham
	G-CFTN	Schleicher K 8B	Mendip Gliding Club Ltd
	G-CFTO	Ikarus C42 FB80	Fly Hire Ltd
	G-CFTP	Schleicher ASW-20CL	D. J. Pengilley
	G-CFTR	Grob G.102 Astir CS77	The University of Nottingham Students Union
	G-CFTS	Glaser-Dirks DG-300 Club Elan	FTS Syndicate
	G-CFTT	Van's RV-7	R. I. & D. J. Blain
	C-CFTU	Flylight Dragonfly	R. J. Cook
	G-CFTV	Rolladen-Schneider LS7-WL	D. Hilton
	G-CFTW	Schempp-Hirth Discus b	230 Syndicate
	G-CFTX	Jabiru J160	R. K. Creasey
	G-CFTY	Rolladen-Schneider LS7-WL	J. A. Thomson & A. Burgess
	G-CFTZ	Evektor EV-97 Eurostar	G. G. Bevis
	G-CFUA	Van's RV-9A	I. M. Macleod
	G-CFUB	Schleicher Ka 6CR	C. Boyd
	G-CFUD	Skyranger Swift 912S(1)	G-CFUD Group
	G-CFUE	Alpi Pioneer 300 Hawk	A. Dayani
	G-CFUF	Ultramagic N-300 balloon	Merlin Balloons
	G-CFUG	Grob G.109B	Portsmouth Naval Gliding Centre
	G-CFUH	Schempp-Hirth Ventus c	C. G. T. Huck
	G-CFUI	Hunt Wing/Avon 503(4)	R. F. G. Moyle
	G-CFUJ	Glaser-Dirks DG-300 Elan	Foxtrot Uniform Juliet Group
	G-CFUL	Schempp-Hirth Discus b	Discus 803 Syndicate
	G-CFUN	Schleicher ASW-20CL	D. C. W. Sanders
	G-CFUP	Schempp-Hirth Discus b	Lasham Gliding Society Ltd
	G-CFUR	Schempp-Hirth Ventus cT	A. P. Carpenter
	G-CFUS	PZL-Bielsko SZD-51-1 Junior	Scottish Gliding Union Ltd

Reg.	Type	Owner or Operator	Notes
G-CFUT	Glaser-Dirks DG-300 Club Elan	M. J. Barnett	
G-CFUU	DG-300 Club Elan	S. K. Ruffell	
G-CFUV	Rolladen-Schneider LS7-WL	G. J. Hoile	
G-CFUW	Rotorsport UK MTO Sport	D. A. Robertson	
G-CFUX	Cameron C-80 balloon	B. D. Close	
G-CFUY	PZL-Bielsko SZD-50-3 Puchacz	The Bath, Wilts and North Dorset Gliding Club	
G-CFUZ	CZAW Sportcruiser	M. W. Bush	
G-CFVA	P & M Quik GT450	Countermine Technologies PLC	
G-CFVC	Schleicher ASK-13	Mendip Gliding Club Ltd	
G-CFVE	Schempp-Hirth Nimbus 2	L. Mitchell	
G-CFVF	Kiss 400-582(1)	J. D. Pinkney	
G-CFVG	Rotorsport UK MTO Sport	J. B. R. Eliot	
G-CFVH	Rolladen-Schneider LS7	C. C. & J. C. Marshall	
G-CFVI	Evektor EV-97 TeamEurostar	Nene Valley Microlights Ltd	
G-CFVJ	Cvjetkovic CA-65 Skyfly	D. Hunter	
G-CFVK	Skyranger HKS(1)	Flylight Airsports Ltd	
G-CFVL	Scheibe Zugvogel IIIB	The G-CFVL Flying Group	
G-CFVM	Centrair 101A Pegase	S. H. North	
G-CFVN	Centrair 101A Pegase	G-CFVN Group	
G-CFVP	Centrair 101A Pegase	Foxtrot Victor Papa Group	
G-CFVR	Europa XS	K. A. O'Neill	
G-CFVT	Schempp-Hirth Nimbus 2	I. Dunkley	
G-CFVU	Schleicher ASK-13	The Vale of the White Horse Gliding Centre Ltd	
G-CFVV	Centrair 101A Pegase	Cambridge Gliding Club Ltd	
G-CFVW	Schempp-Hirth Ventus bT	A. D. Johnson	
G-CFVX	Cameron C-80 balloon	A. Hornshaw	
G-CFVY	Cameron A-120 balloon	Rocket M edia (UK) Ltd	
G-CFVZ	Schleicher Ka 6E	N. R. Bowers	
G-CFWA	Schleicher Ka 6CR	C. C. Walley	
G-CFWB	Schleicher ASK-13	Cotswold Gliding Club	
G-CFWC	Grob G.103C Twin III Acro	The South Wales Gliding Club Ltd	
G-CFWD	Rotorsport UK MTO Sport	Gower Gyronautics	
G-CFWE	PZL-Bielsko SZD-50-3 Puchacz	Deeside Gliding Club (Aberdeenshire) Ltd	
G-CFWF	Rolladen-Schneider LS7	G. B. Hibberd	
G-CFWH	Scheibe SF27A	A. S. Carter	
G-CFWI	Kubicek BB-22Z balloon	V. Gounon	
G-CFWJ	P & M Quik GT450	H. C. Jones	
G-CFWK	Schempp-Hirth Nimbus-3DT	29 Syndicate	
G-CFWL	Schleicher K8B	A. S. Burton	
G-CFWM	Glaser-Dirks DG-300 Club Elan	FWM Group	
G-CFWN	P & M Quik GT450	G-CFWN Group	
G-CFWO	Murphy Maverick 430	A. Vaughan	
G-CFWP	Schleicher ASW-19B	980 Syndicate	
G-CFWR	Best Off Sky Ranger 912(2)	J. Mills & A. M. Wood	
G-CFWS	Schleicher ASW-20C	662 Syndicate	
G-CFWT	PZL-Bielsko SZD-50-3 Puchacz	Coventry Gliding Club Ltd	
G-CFWU	Rolladen-Schneider LS7-WL	H. Macdonald & R. Kern	
G-CFWV	Van's RV-7	S. J. Carr & D. K. Sington	
G-CFWW	Schleicher ASH-25E	G-CFWW Syndicate	
G-CFWY	Centrair 101A Pegase	G. M. Dodwell & J. Randall	
G-CFWZ	Schleicher ASW-19B	Whiskey Zulu Gliding Group	
G-CFXA	Grob G.104 Speed Astir IIB	A. V. Jupp & D. C. White	
G-CFXB	Schleicher K 8B	R. Sansom & M. A. Keller	
G-CFXC	Schleicher Ka 6E	G. E. Pook & C. J. Basham	
G-CFXD	Centrair 101A Pegase	D. G. England & R. Banks	
G-CFXF	Magni M-16C Tandem Trainer	M. W. King	
G-CFXG	Flylight Dragonfly	N. L. Stammers	
G-CFXH	Schleicher K 7	P. Fabian	
G-CFXI	Lindstrand LBL Box balloon	A. M. Holly	
G-CFXK	Flylight Dragonfly	M. J. Pollard	
G-CFXL	Lindstrand LBL-90A balloon	A. M. Holly	
G-CFXM	Schempp-Hirth Discus bT	G. R. E. Bottomley	
G-CFXN	CZAW Sportcruiser	R. D. Masters	
G-CFXO	PZL-Bielsko SZD-50-3 Puchacz	Coventry Gliding Club Ltd	
G-CFXP	Lindstrand LBL-105A balloon	Shaun Bradley Project Services Ltd	
G-CFXR	Lindstrand LBL-105A balloon	Lindstrand Hot Air Balloons Ltd	
G-CFXS	Schleicher Ka 6E	J. A. Loveland	
G-CFXT	Naval Aircraft Factory N3N-3	R. H. & J. A. Cooper	
G-CFXU	Schleicher Ka-6E	FXU Syndicate	
G-CFXW	Schleicher K8B	The South Wales Gliding Club Ltd	
G-CFXX	P & M Quik R	M. C. Shortman	

Notes	Reg.	Type	Owner or Operator
	G-CFXY	Schleicher ASW-15B	E. L. Youle
	G-CFXZ	P & M Quik R	T. Smith & M. Naylor
	G-CFYA	PZL-Bielsko SZD-50-3 Puchacz	Cairngorm Gliding Club
	G-CFYB	Rolladen-Schneider LS7	A. T. Macdonald & V. P. Haley
	G-CFYC	Schempp-Hirth Ventus b	G. Smith
	G-CFYD	Aeroprakt A22-L Foxbat	A. P. Fenn
	G-CFYE	Scheibe Zugvogel IIIB	P. G. H. Purdie
	G-CFYF	Schleicher ASK-21	London Gliding Club Proprietary Ltd
	G-CFYG	Glasflugel Club Libelle 205	FYG Syndicate
	G-CFYH	Rolladen-Schneider LS4-a	G. W. & C. A. Craig
	G-CFYI	Grob G.102 Astir CS	S. R. Hill, A. H. Kay & D. A. Spencer
	G-CFYJ	Schempp-Hirth Standard Cirrus	FYJ Syndicate
	G-CFYK	Rolladen-Schneider LS7-WL	R. R. Ward
	G-CFYL	PZL-Bielsko SZD-50-3 Puchacz	Deesside Gliding Club (Aberdeenshire) Ltd
	G-CFYM	Schempp-Hirth Discus bT	B. F. Laverick-Smith
	G-CFYN	Schempp-Hirth Discus b	N. White & P. R. Foulger
	G-CFYO	P & M Quik R	S. Webb & G. R. Homan
	G-CFYP	FBM & W Silex M/Flyke/Monster	A. J. R. Carver
	G-CFYR	LET L-23 Super Blanik	G-CFYR Group
	G-CFYS	Dynamic WT9 UK	E. M. Middleton
	G-CFYU	Glaser-Dirks DG-100 Elan	I. M. & C. Shepherd
	G-CFYV	Schleicher ASK-21	The Bristol Gliding Club Proprietary Ltd
	G-CFYW	Rolladen-Schneider LS7	C. Bessant
	G-CFYX	Schempp-Hirth Discus b	Discus FYX Group
	G-CFYY	Schleicher ASK-13	Lasham Gliding Society Ltd
	G-CFYZ	Schleicher ASH-25	171 Syndicate
	G-CFZA	PZL-Bielsko SZD-51-1	Booker Gliding Club Ltd
	G-CFZB	Glasflugel H201B Standard Libelle	J. C. Meyer
	G-CFZD	Jabiru J430	C. J. Judd & A. Macknish
	G-CFZF	PZL-Bielsko SZD-51-1 Junior	Devon and Somerset Gliding Club Ltd
	G-CFZH	Schempp-Hirth Ventus c	FZH Group
	G-CFZI	Savannah Jabiru (5)	J. T., A. L. & O. D. Lewis
	G-CFZJ	VS.388 Seafire F.46	C. T. Charleston
	G-CFZK	Schempp-Hirth Standard Cirrus	S. Lucas & R. Burgoyne
	G-CFZL	Schleicher ASW-20 CL	A. L. & R. M. Housden
	G-CFZM	Avro RJ85	Triangle Regional Aircraft Leasing Ltd
	G-CFZO	Schempp-Hirth Nimbus 3	954 Syndicate
	G-CFZR	Schleicher Ka 6CR	J. Vickers
	G-CFZT	Ace Magic Laser	J. M. Breaks
	G-CFZV	Rolladen-Schneider LS7	W. M. Davies
	G-CFZW	Glaser-Dirks DG-300 Club Elan	D. O'Flanagan & G. Stilgoe
	G-CFZX	Rotorsport UK MTO Sport	Gyro-I Ltd
	G-CFZZ	LET L-33 Solo	The Andreas L33 Group
	G-CGAA	Flylight Dragonfly	G. Adkins
	G-CGAB	AB Sportine LAK-12 Lietuva	W. T. Emery
	G-CGAC	P & M Quik GT450	A. Gillett
	G-CGAD	Rolladen-Schneider LS3	P. B. Turner
	G-CGAF	Schleicher ASK-21	Lasham Gliding Society Ltd
	G-CGAG	Scleicher ASK-21	Stratford on Avon Gliding Club Ltd
	G-CGAH	Schempp-Hirth Standard Cirrus	J. W. Williams
	G-CGAI	Raj Hamsa X'Air Hawk	P. J. Kilshaw
	G-CGAJ	Alpi Pioneer 400	C. Rusalen
	G-CGAK	Acrosport II	P. D. Sibbons
	G-CGAL	P & M Quik R	R. A. Keene
	G-CGAM	Schleicher ASK-21	Oxford University Gliding Club
	G-CGAN	Glasflugel H301 Libelle	M. D. Butcher
	G-CGAO	DHC.1 Chipmunk 22	P. Jeffery
	G-CGAP	Schempp-Hirth Ventus bT	J. R. Greenwell
	G-CGAR	Rolladen-Schneider LS6-c	A. Warbrick
	G-CGAS	Schempp-Hirth Ventus cT	G. M. J. Monaghan
	G-CGAT	Grob G.102 Astir CS	N. J. Hooper & S. J. Chapman
	G-CGAU	Glasflugel H201B Standard Libelle	G-CGAU Group
	G-CGAV	Scheibe SF-27A Zugvogel V	GAV Syndicate
	G-CGAW	Beech 200 Super King Air	Aerodynamics Ltd
	G-CGAX	PZL-Bielsko SZD-55-1 Promyk	I. D. Macro & P. Gold
	G-CGAZ	P & M Aviation Quik R	E. J. Douglas
	G-CGBA	Schleicher ASK-13	Edensoaring Ltd
	G-CGBB	Schleicher ASK-21	University of Edinburgh Sports Union
	G-CGBD	PZL-Bielsko SZD-50-3	The Northumbria Gliding Club Ltd
	G-CGBF	Schleicher ASK-21	London Gliding Club Pty Ltd

Reg.	Type	Owner or Operator	Notes
G-CGBG	Rolladen-Schneider LS6-18w	C. Villa	
G-CGBH	Raj Hamsa X'Air Hawk	S. E. McEwen	
G-CGBJ	Grob G.102 Astir CS	Banbury Gliding Club Ltd	
G-CGBK	Grob G.102 Astir CS	Yorkshire Gliding Club (Pty) Ltd	
G-CGBL	Rolladen-Schneider LS7-WL	P. A. Roche	
G-CGBM	Flight Design CTSW	Stardust Aviation Ltd	
G-CGBN	Schleicher ASK-21	Essex and Suffolk Gliding Club Ltd	
G-CGBO	Rolladen-Schneider LS6	G-CGBO Syndicate	
G-CGBR	Rolladen-Schneider LS6-c	V. L. Brown	
G-CGBS	Glaser-Dirks DG-300 Club Elan	A. Gillanders & M. C. Chalmers	
G-CGBU	Centrair 101A Pegase	D. J. Arblaster & R. M. Rowland	
G-CGBV	Schleicher ASK-21	Wolds Gliding Club Ltd	
G-CGBX	Schleicher ASW-22	D. A. Ashby	
G-CGBY	Rolladen-Schneider LS7-WL	I. Ashdown	
G-CGBZ	Glaser-Dirks DG-500 Elan Trainer	G. N. Turner	
G-CGCA	Schleicher ASW-19B	Deeside Gliding Club (Aberdeenshire) Ltd	
G-CGCC	PZL-Bielsko SZD-51-1 Junior	Coventry Gliding Club Ltd	
G-CGCD	Schempp-Hirth Standard Cirrus	Cirrus Syndicate	
G-CGCE	Magni M16C Tandem Trainer	A. J. A. Fowler	
G-CGCF	Schleicher ASK-23	Needwood Forest Gliding Club Ltd	
G-CGCH	CZAW Sportcruiser	C. Harrison	
G-CGCK	PZL-Bielsko SZD-50-3 Puchacz	Kent Gliding Club Ltd (G-BTJV)	
G-CGCL	Grob G.102 Astir CS	Southdown Gliding Club Ltd	
G-CGCM	Rolladen-Schneider LS6-c	G. R. Glazebrook	
G-CGCN	MCR-01 Club	D. J. Smith	
G-CGCO	Schempp-Hirth Cirrus VTC	TP. Wilcox & P. W. Brown	
G-CGCP	Schleicher Ka-6CR	D. & B. Clarke	
G-CGCR	Schleicher ASW-15B	ASW15B 748 Group	
G-CGCS	Glasflugel Club Libelle 205	D. G. Coats	
G-CGCT	Schempp-Hirth Discus b	P. J. Brown	
G-CGCU	PZL-Bielsko SZD-50-3 Puchacz	Buckminster Gliding Club Ltd	
G-CGCV	Raj Hamsa X'Air Hawk	W. J. Whyte	
G-CGCW	Skyranger Swift 912(1)	C. M. Wilkes	
G-CGCX	Schleicher ASW-15	C. D. Bingham	
G-BGCY	Centrair 101A Pegase	GCY Group	
G-CGDA	Rolladen-Schneider LS3-17	A. R. Fish	
G-CGDB	Schleicher K 8B	The Welland Gliding Club Ltd	
G-CGDC	Rotorsport UK MTO Sport	R. E. Derham & T. R. Kingsley	
G-CGDD	Bolkow Phoebus C	G. C. Kench	
G-CGDE	Schleicher Ka 6CR	K6 Syndicate	
G-CGDF	Schleicher Ka 6BR	H. Marshall & D. Pask	
G-CGDG	Cameron C-80 balloon	Atlantic Balooning BVBA/Belgium	
G-CGDH	Europa XS	G-CGDH Group	
G-CGDI	EV-97A Eurostar	D. Street	
G-CGDJ	PA-28-161 Warrior II	C. G. D. Jones (G-ETDA)	
G-CGDK	Schleicher K 8B	Dartmoor Gliding Society	
G-CGDL	P & M Quik R	S. J. Bunce	
G-CGDM	Sonex Sonex	D. Scott	
G-CGDN	Rolladen-Schneider LS3-17	S. J. Pepler	
G-CGDO	Grob G.102 Astir CS	P. Lowe & R. Bostock	
G-CGDR	Schempp-Hirth Discus CS	J. H. C. Friend	
G-CGDS	Schleicher ASW-15B	B. Birk & P. A. Crouch	
G-CGDT	Schleicher ASW-24	Tango 54 Syndicate	
G-CGDV	CSA Sportcruiser	Delta Victor Group	
G-CGDW	CSA PS-28 Sportcruiser	Onega Ltd	
G-CGDX	Orlican Discus CS	D. Bieniasz	
G-CGDY	Schleicher ASW-15B	Cloud Nine Syndicate	
G-CGDZ	Schleicher ASW-24	J. M. Norman	
G-CGEA	Schleicher Ka 6CR	R. C. Sharman	
G-CGEB	Grob G.102 Astir CS77	T. R. Dews	
G-CGEC	Flight Design CTLS	S. Munday	
G-CGEE	Glasflugel H201B Standard Libelle	C. Metcalfe & J. Kelsey	
G-CGEG	Schleicher K 8B	Darlton Gliding Club Ltd	
G-CGEH	Schleicher ASW-15B	P. Nayeri	
G-CGEI	Cessna 550 Citation Bravo	S. W. Bond	
G-CGEJ	Alpi Pioneer 200-M	P. S. & N. Bewley	
G-CGEL	PZL-Bielsko SZD-50-3	The Northumbria Gliding Club Ltd	
G-CGEM	Schleicher Ka 6CR	GEM Syndicate	
G-CGEN	RAF 2000	D. E. Worley	
G-CGEO	CSA Sportcruiser	The Jester Flying Group	
G-CGEP	Schempp-Hirth Standard Cirrus	D. J. Bundock	

BRITISH CIVIL REGISTRATIONS

Notes	Reg.	Type	Owner or Operator
	G-CGER	Cameron Z-105 balloon	M. Casaburo/Italy
	G-CGEU	Flylight Dragonfly	M. G. Preston
	G-CGEV	Heliopolis Gomhouria Mk.6	A. Brier
	G-CGEW	Rotorsport UK MTO Sport	G. W. Libby & C. W. Rose
	G-CGEX	P & M Quik GT450	D. L. Clark
	G-CGEY	Julian CD Dingbat	G. Carr
	G-CGEZ	Raj Hamsa X'Air Hawk	M. Howes & B. J. Ellis
	G-CGFB	BB03 Trya/BB103	B. J. Fallows
	G-CGFG	Cessna 152	Cristal Air Ltd
	G-CGFH	Cessna T182T Turbo Skylane	H. Riffkin
	G-CGFJ	Cessna 172M	T. I. Murtough
	G-CGFK	Ace Magic Laser	F. McDonagh
	G-CGFN	Cameron C-60 balloon	R. S. Mohr
	G-CGFO	Ultramagic H-42 balloon	J. A. W. Dyer
	G-CGFP	Pietenpol Aircamper	D. Hetherington
	G-CGFR	Lindstrand LBL HS-120 Airship	Lindstrand Hot Air Balloons Ltd
	G-CGFS	Nanchang CJ-6A	B. Blanchard
	G-CGFU	Schempp-Hirth Mini-Nimbus C	S. Foster
	G-CGFY	Lindstrand LBL-105A balloon	G. J. Grimes
	G-CGFZ	Thruster T.600N 450	K. J. Crompton
	G-CGGD	Eurocopter AS365N2 Dauphin 2	Multiflight Ltd
	G-CGGE	Cameron Z-275 balloon	Wickers World Ltd
	G-CGGF	Robinson R44 II	Sky Helicopteros SA/Spain
	G-CGGG	Robinson R44	K. Hayes (G-SJDI)
	G-CGGH	Sky 220-24 balloon	Zebedee Balloon Service Ltd
	G-CGGJ	Schweizer 269C-1	Patriot Aviation Ltd
	G-CGGK	Westland Wasp HAS Mk.1	The Real Aeroplane Co.Ltd
	G-CGGL	Rotorsport UK MTOSport	A. D. Lysser
	G-CGGM	EV-97 TeamEurostar UK	GM Group
	G-CGGO	Robin DR.400-180 Regent	AWE Holdings Ltd
	G-CGGP	Autogyro MTOSport	N. Cowley
	G-CGGS	Robinson R44 II	Oakfield Investments Ltd
	G-CGGT	P & M Quik GT450	M. Earp
	G-CGGV	Rotorsport UK MTO Sport	S. Morris
	G-CGGW	Rotorsport UK MTO Sport	P. Adams
	G-CGGX	TEAM Minimax 91	P. D. Parry
	G-CGGY	UltraMagic N-425 balloon	Adventure Balloons Ltd
	G-CGGZ	UltraMagic S-90 balloon	P. Lawman
	G-CGHA	P & M Quik R	K. M. Hughes
	G-CGHB	NAMC CJ-6A	M. J. Harvey
	G-CGHC	Pioneer 300 Hawk	M. Bettaglio
	G-CGHD	Cessna 172S	Steptoe & Son Properties Ltd
	G-CGHG	P & M Quik GT450	J. & K. D. McAlpine
	G-CGHH	P & M Quik R	C. Pyle & N. Richardson
	G-CGHJ	Staaken Z-21A Flitzer	D. J. Ashley
	G-CGHK	Alpi Pioneer 300 Hawk	D. J. Ashley
	G-CGHL	Rotorsport UK MTOSport	C. S. Mackenzie
	G-CGHM	PA-28 Cherokee 140	North Wales Air Academy Ltd
	G-CGHN	Aeros Discus/Alize	R. Simpson & N. Sutton
	G-CGHO	P & M Quik R	N. Creveau
	G-CGHR	Magic Laser	N. P. Power
	G-CGHS	DG Flugzeugbau DG-808C	M. A. V. Gatehouse
	G-CGHT	Dyn'Aero MCR-01 Banbi	J. F. McAulay (G-POOP)
	G-CGHU	Hawker Hunter T.Mk.8C	Hawker Hunter Aviation Ltd
	G-CGHV	Raj Hamsa X'Air Hawk SW	G. A. J. Salter
	G-CGHW	Czech Sport Aircraft Sportcruiser	Sport Cruiser 290 Group
	G-CGHZ	P & M Quik R	J. Rockey
	G-CGIA	Paramania Action/Adventure	A. E. C. Phillips
	G-CGIB	Magic Cyclone	S. J. Oxnard
	G-CGIC	Rotorsport MTO Sport	J. Harmon & K. Snell
	G-CGID	PA-31-350 Navajo Chieftain	T. Michaels
	G-CGIE	Flylight Dragonfly	N. S. Brayn
	G-CGIF	Flylight Dragonfly	G. Nicholas
	G-CGIG	Lindstrand LBL-90A balloon	M. R. Stokoe
	G-CGIH	Cameron C-90 balloon	W. Bracken
	G-CGIJ	Agusta Westland AW139	HM Coastguard
	G-CGIK	Isaacs Spitfire	A. J. Harpley
	G-CGIL	CZAW Sportcruiser	G-CGIL Group
	G-CGIM	Ace Aviation Magic Laser	C. Royle
	G-CGIN	Paramania Action GT/Adventure	A. E. C. Phillips
	G-CGIO	Medway SLA100 Executive	K. J. Draper

Reg.	Type	Owner or Operator	Notes
G-CGIP	CZAW Sportcruiser	P. N. Davis	
G-CGIR	Remos GX	L. R. Marks & J. A. Pereira	
G-CGIS	Cameron Parachutist 110 SS balloon	K-H. Gruenauer (G-RIPS)	
G-CGIU	AX1 balloon	M. W. A. Shemilt	
G-CGIV	Kolb Firefly	W. A. Emmerson	
G-CGIW	Sikorsky S-76C-2	Bristow Helicopters (International) Ltd	
G-CGIX	Rotorsport UK MTO Sport	J. K. Houldcroft	
G-CGIY	Piper J3C-65	R. C. Cummings	
G-CGIZ	Flight Design CTSW	J. Hilton	
G-CGJB	Schempp-Hirth Duo Discus T	G. J. Basey	
G-CGJC	Rotorsport UK MTO Sport	J. C. Collingwood	
G-CGJD	Rotorsport UK Calidus	C. Collins	
G-CGJE	VS.361 Spitfire IX	Historic Flight Ltd	
G-CGJF	Fokker E.111 Replica	I. Brewster	
G-CGJH	P & M Quik GT450	B. Montila	
G-CGJI	Best Off Skyranger 912S(1)	Flylight Airsports Ltd	
G-CGJJ	P & M Quik R	A. J. Hubbard	
G-CGJL	CZAW Sportcruiser	G-CGJL Flying Group	
G-CGJM	Skyranger Swift 912S(1)	J. P. Metcalfe	
G-CGJN	Van's RV-7	E. K. Coventry	
G-CGJO	P & M Quik R	D. E. Lord	
G-CGJP	Van's RV-10	G-CGIP Group	
G-CGJS	CZAW Sportcruiser	J. M. Tiley	
G-CGJT	CZAW Sportcruiser	D. F. Toller	
G-CGJV	Lindstrand LBL Motorbike SS balloon	Lindstrand Hot Air Balloons Ltd	
G-CGJW	RAF 2000 GTX-SE	J. J. Wollen	
G-CGJX	SA.341B Gazelle AH Mk.1	B. W. Stuart	
G-CGJZ	SA.341D Gazelle HT Mk.3	A. W. J. Stuart	
G-CGKA	Grob G115E Tutor	Babcock Aerospace Ltd	
G-CGKB	Grob G115E Tutor	Babcock Aerospace Ltd	
G-CGKC	Grob G115E Tutor	Babcock Aerospace Ltd	
G-CGKD	Grob G115E Tutor	Babcock Aerospace Ltd	
G-CGKE	Grob G115E Tutor	Babcock Aerospace Ltd	
G-CGKF	Grob G115E Tutor	Babcock Aerospace Ltd	
G-CGKG	Grob G115E Tutor	Babcock Aerospace Ltd	
G-CGKH	Grob G115E Tutor	Babcock Aerospace Ltd	
G-CGKI	Grob G115E Tutor	Babcock Aerospace Ltd	
G-CGKJ	Grob G115E Tutor	Babcock Aerospace Ltd	
G-CGKK	Grob G115E Tutor	Babcock Aerospace Ltd	
G-CGKL	Grob G115E Tutor	Babcock Aerospace Ltd	
G-CGKM	Grob G115E Tutor	Babcock Aerospace Ltd	
G-CGKN	Grob G115E Tutor	Babcock Aerospace Ltd	
G-CGKO	Grob G115E Tutor	Babcock Aerospace Ltd	
G-CGKP	Grob G115E Tutor	Babcock Aerospace Ltd	
G-CGKR	Grob G115E Tutor	Babcock Aerospace Ltd	
G-CGKS	Grob G115E Tutor	Babcock Aerospace Ltd	
G-CGKT	Grob G115E Tutor	Babcock Aerospace Ltd	
G-CGKU	Grob G115E Tutor	Babcock Aerospace Ltd	
G-CGKV	Grob G115E Tutor	Babcock Aerospace Ltd	
G-CGKW	Grob G115E Tutor	Babcock Aerospace Ltd	
G-CGKX	Grob G115E Tutor	Babcock Aerospace Ltd	
G-CGKY	Cessna 182T	T. A. E. Dobell	
G-CGKZ	Best Off Sky Ranger Swift 912S(1)	A. Worthington	
G-CGLB	Airdrome Dream Classic	S. J. Ball	
G-CGLC	Czech Sport Aircraft Sportcruiser	P. Taylor	
G-CGLE	Flylight Dragonfly	B. Skelding	
G-CGLF	Magni M-16C Tandem Trainer	J. S. Walton	
G-CGLG	P & M Quik GT450	P. H. Evans	
G-CGLI	Alpi Pioneer 200M	B. A. Lyford	
G-CGLJ	TL 2000UK Sting Carbon	L. A. James	
G-CGLK	Magni M-16C Tandem Trainer	R. M. Savage	
G-CGLM	Rotorsport UK MTO Sport	J. Owen	
G-CGLN	Jabiru J430	J. R. Frohnsdorff	
G-CGLO	P & M Quik R	R. H. Lowndes	
G-CGLP	CZAW Sportcruiser	P. S. Tanner	
G-CGLR	Czech Sport Aircraft Sportcruiser	G-CGLR Group	
G-CGLT	Czech Sport Aircraft Sportcruiser	P. J. V. Dibble	
G-CGLW	P & M Pegasus Quik	S. Dixon	
G-CGLY	Rotorsport UK Calidus	R. J. Steel	
G-CGLZ	TL 2000UK Sting Carbon	T. Booth	
G-CGMA	Ace Magic Laser	J. N. Hanson	

Notes	Reg.	Type	Owner or Operator
	G-CGMB	Embraer EMB-135ER	Eastern Airways
	G-CGMC	Embraer EMB-135ER	Eastern Airways
	G-CGMD	Rotorsport UK Calidus	W. H. Morgan
	G-CGME	Ellipse Fuji/Pulma 2000	I. M. Vass
	G-CGMF	Cessna 560XL Citation XLS	Multiflight Charter Services LLP
	G-CGMG	Van's RV-9	D. J. Bone
	G-CGMH	Jodel D150A Mascaret	G. S. Jackson
	G-CGMI	P & M Quik GT450	W. G. Reynolds
	G-CGMK	Best Off Sky Ranger 582(1)	G. J. Burley
	G-CGML	TL 2000UK Sting Carbon	G. T. Leedham
	G-CGMM	CZAW Sportcruiser	TAF and Co
	G-CGMN	Best Off Sky Ranger Swift 912S	D. E. Bassett
	G-CGMO	Ace Magic Laser	G. J. Latham
	G-CGMP	CZAW Sportcruiser	R. Hasler
	G-CGMR	Colt Bibendum-110 balloon	Mobberley Balloon Collection (G-GRIP)
	G-CGMS	Sutton/Aquilair KID 1	K. A. Sutton
	G-CGMV	Roko Aero NG 4HD	Eshott NG4 Group
	G-CGMW	Alpi Pioneer 200M	M. S. McCrudden
	G-CGMZ	P & M Quik R	M. J. Hyde
	G-CGNA	Cameron Super FMG-100 balloon	Cameron Balloons Ltd
	G-CGNC	Rotorsport UK MTO Sport	Comedy South West Ltd
	G-CGND	Robinson R44 II	Ajax Machinery
	G-CGNE	Robinson R44 II	Heli Air Ltd
	G-CGNG	CZAW Sportcruiser	T. Dounias
	G-CGNH	Reality Escapade Jabiru(3)	A. H. Paul
	G-CGNI	Ikarus C42 FB80	A. G. Cummings
	G-CGNJ	Cameron Z-105 balloon	Loughborough Students Union Hot Air Balloon Club
	G-CGNK	P & M Quik GT450	G. W. Hillidge
	G-CGNL	Cameron Z-90 balloon	A. M. Holly
	G-CGNM	Magni M-16C Tandem Trainer	Evolo Ltd
	G-CGNN	Montgomerie-Bensen B.8MR	P. M. Ryder
	G-CGNO	P & M Quik GT450	A. Fern
	G-CGNS	Sky 65-24 balloon	R. L. Bovell
	G-CGNV	Reality Escapade	P. M. Noonan
	G-CGNW	Scheibe SF-25C Falke	The Royal Air Force Gliding and Soaring Association
	G-CGNX	Rotorsport UK MTO Sport	L. McCallum
	G-CGNY	Cessna 340A	P. W. J. Sharpe-Brash
	G-CGNZ	Europa XS	R. Vianello
	G-CGOA	Cessna 550 Citation II	Xclusive Jet Charter Ltd (G-JMDW)
	G-CGOB	P & M Quik R	P & M Aviation Ltd
	G-CGOD	Cameron N-77 balloon	G. P. Lane
	G-CGOG	Evektor EV-97A Eurostar	J. S. Holden
	G-CGOH	Cameron C-80 balloon	Lindstrand Hot Air Balloons Ltd
	G-CGOI	Stewart S-51 Mustang (413926 E2-S)	K. E. Armstrong
	G-CGOJ	Jodel D.11	J. A. Macleod
	G-CGOK	Ace Magic Cyclone	V. Grayson
	G-CGOL	Jabiru J430	J. F. Woodham
	G-CGOM	Flight Design MC	P and M Aviation Ltd
	G-CGOO	Sorrell SNS-8 Hyperlight	W. F. Hayward
	G-CGOR	Jodel D.18	R. D. Cook
	G-CGOS	PA-28-161 Warrior III	S. H. B. Smith
	G-CGOT	Rotorsport UK Calidus	P. Slater
	G-CGOU	Sikorsky S-76C	Bristow Helicopters Ltd
	G-CGOV	Raj Hamsa X'Air Falcon 582(2)	Rhubarb Flying Group
	G-CGOW	Cameron Z-77 balloon	J. F. Till
	G-CGOX	Raj Hamsa X'Air Hawk	Oscar Xray Group
	G-CGOZ	Cameron GB-1000 free gas balloon	Cameron Balloons Ltd
	G-CGPA	Ace Magic Cyclone	A. Williams
	G-CGPB	Magni M-24C	D. Beevers
	G-CGPC	P & M Pegasus Quik	A. C. Barnes & D. W. Watson
	G-CGPD	Ultramagic S-90 balloon	S. J. Farrant
	G-CGPE	P & M Quik GT450	E. H. Gatehouse
	G-CGPF	Flylight Dragonfly	K. T. Vinning
	G-CGPG	Rotosport UK MTO Sport	H. A. Batchelor
	G-CGPH	Ultramagic S-50 balloon	The Packhouse Ltd
	G-CGPI	Eurocopter EC135 T2+	Bond Air Services Ltd (G-TAGG)
	G-CGPJ	Robin DR.400-140	W. H. Cole & P. Dass
	G-CGPK	Rotorsport UK MT-03	Ellis Flying Group (G-RIFS)
	G-CGPL	Sonex Sonex	P. C. Askew
	G-CGPN	SOCATA MS.880B Rallye Club	J. Fingleton

Reg.	Type	Owner or Operator	Notes
G-CGPO	TL2000UK Sting Carbon	G. A. Squires	
G-CGPR	Czech Sport Aircraft Pipersport	J. T. Langford	
G-CGPS	EV-97 Eurostar SL	P. R. Jenson & R. A. Morris	
G-CGPV	Cameron C-80 balloon	D. G. Such & M. Tomlin	
G-CGPW	Raj Hamsa X'Air Hawk	C. Parkinson	
G-CGPX	Zenair CH.601XL Zodiac	A. James	
G-CGPY	Boeing A75L 300 Stearman	M. P. Dentith	
G-CGPZ	Rans S-4 Coyote	I. C. Lewis	
G-CGRB	Flight Design CTLS	I. R. Jones	
G-CGRC	P & M Quik R	R. J. Cook	
G-CGRD	Cirrus SR22	Craigard Property Trading Ltd	
G-CGRE	Cessna F.172H	Parachuting Aircraft Ltd	
G-CGRJ	Carnet Paramotor	M. Carnet	
G-CGRL	Robinson R44	Difuria Contractors Ltd	
G-CGRM	VS.329 Spitfire Mk.IIA	M. R. Oliver	
G-CGRN	Pazmany PL-4A	G. Hudson	
G-CGRO	Robin DR.400/140B	R. J. Hopkins	
G-CGRR	P & M Quik	A. W. Buchan	
G-CGRS	P & M Quik	J. Crosby	
G-CGRV	DG Flugzeugbau DG-1000M	BR Aviation Ltd	
G-CGRW	P & M Quik	P. M. Coppola	
G-CGRX	Cessna F.172N	S. J. Burke	
G-CGRY	Magni M-24C	K. Herbert	
G-CGRZ	Magni M-24C	R. S. B. O'Kane	
G-CGSA	Flylight Dragonfly	G. Sykes	
G-CGSB	Cessna 525A Citationjet CJ2	Sol Aviation Companhia de Aviaco Lda/Portugal	
G-CGSC	Quad City Challenger II	L. Gregory	
G-CGSD	Magni M-16C	The Gyrocopter Company UK Ltd	
G-CGSG	Cessna 421C	J. R. Shannon	
G-CGSH	Evektor EV-97 TeamEurostar UK	D. B. Medland	
G-CGSI	Zenair CH.601HDS Zodiac	E. McHugh	
G-CGSJ	Bombardier BD700-1A10 Global Express	Abbeville Holdings Ltd	
G-CGSO	P & M Quik GT450	Light Vending Ltd	
G-CGSP	Cessna 152	C. M. de CamposCosta Cabral	
G-CGSU	Cassutt Racer IIIM	D. J. Howell	
G-CGSW	Flylight Motorfloater	M. P. Wimsey	
G-CGSX	Aeroprakt A22-L Foxbat	P. J. Trimble	
G-CGSY	Stemme S6-RT	D. B. Smith	
G-CGSZ	Schempp-Hirth Ventus 2CM	D. B. Smith	
G-CGTA	Taylorcraft BC-12-65	D. P. Busby	
G-CGTB	Taylorcraft BC-12D	D. P. & D. S. Busby	
G-CGTC	BN-2T-4S Islander	Police Service of Northern Ireland	
G-CGTD	EV-97 TeamEurostar UK	R. J. Butler	
G-CGTE	Cherry BX-2	D.Roberts	
G-CGTF	AutoGyro MT-03	N. R. Osborne	
G-CGTG	Skyranger 912S(1)	B. A. McMahon	
G-CGTK	Magni M-24C	S. Brogden	
G-CGTL	Alpi Pioneer 300	M. S. Ashby	
G-CGTM	Cessna 172S	Skytrek Air Services	
G-CGTR	Best Off Sky Ranger Nynja 912S(1)	M. Jenvey	
G-CGTS	Cameron A-140 balloon	A. A. Brown	
G-CGTT	EV-97 Eurostar SL	D. L. Walker	
G-CGTU	P & M Quik GT450	I. G. R. Christie	
G-CGTV	MXP-740 Savannah VG Jabiru(1)	B. L. Cook & P. Etherington	
G-CGTW	Flylight MotorFloater	S. J. Varden	
G-CGTX	CASA 1-131E Jungmann Srs 2000	G. Hunter & T. A. S. Rayner	
G-CGTY	Cameron Z-250 balloon	The Cotswold Balloon Co.Ltd	
G-CGTZ	Reality Escapade Kid	E. O. Otun	
G-CGUA	Eurocopter EC.225LP Super Puma	Bristow Helicopters Ltd	
G-CGUB	Eurocopter EC.225LP Super Puma	Bristow Helicopters Ltd	
G-CGUD	Lindstrand LBL-77A balloon	I. J. Sharpe	
G-CGUE	Aroprakt A-22-L Foxbat	A. T. Hayward	
G-CGUG	P & M Quik R	J. D. Lawrance	
G-CGUI	Clutton FRED Srs.II	I. Pearson	
G-CGUK	VS.300 Spitfire 1A (X4650)	Comanche Warbirds Ltd	
G-CGUL	Gulfstream V-SP	Tesco Stores Ltd	
G-CGUN	Alpha R2160	S. Birt	
G-CGUO	DH.83C Fox Moth	R. I. Souch	
G-CGUP	P & M Quik GT450	D. J. Allen	
G-CGUR	P & M QuikR	M. J. Williams	

Notes	Reg.	Type	Owner or Operator
	G-CGUS	Embraer ERJ-145MP	ECC Leasing Co.Ltd
	G-CGUT	Balloon Works Firefly 9B-15	J. N. Uhrmann
	G-CGUU	Sky Ranger Nynja 912S(1)	J. A. Hunt
	G-CGUV	Balloon Works Firefly 9B-15	J. N. Uhrmann
	G-CGUW	Tecnam P2002-EA Sierra	D. J. Burton
	G-CGUY	Rotorsport UK Calidus	R. F. Harrison
	G-CGUZ	Cessna 525A CitationJet CJ2	Tesco Stores Ltd
	G-CGVA	Aeroprakt A-22-L Foxbat	T. R. C. Griffin
	G-CGVC	PA-28-181 Archer III	Western Air (Thruxton) Ltd
	G-CGVD	Van's RV-12	RV12 Flying Group
	G-CGVE	Raj Hamsa X'Air Hawk	P. Millership
	G-CGVG	Flight Design CTSW	J. T. James
	G-CGVH	Flylight Motorfloater	P. F. Mayes
	G-CGVJ	Europa XS	D. Glowa
	G-CGVK	Autogyro UK Calidus	B & H Mouldings Ltd
	G-CGVM	Lindstrand LBL-35A Cloudhopper balloon	Airship and Balloon Co.Ltd
	G-CGVO	Alpi Pioneer 400	F. A. Cavaciuti
	G-CGVP	EV-97 Eurstar	G. R. Pritchard
	G-CGVS	Raj Hamsa X'Air Hawk	J. Anderson
	G-CGVT	EV-97 TeamEurostar UK	Mainair Microlight School Ltd
	G-CGVU	Avro RJ85	Trident Turboprop (Dublin) Ltd
	G-CGVV	Cameron Z-90 Balloon	Cameron Balloons Ltd
	G-CGVX	Europa	M. P. Sambrook
	G-CGVY	Cameron Z-77 balloon	M. P. Hill
	G-CGVZ	Zenair CH.601XL Zodiac	K. A. Dilks
	G-CGWA	Ikarus C42 FB80 Bravo	M. A. Bull
	G-CGWB	Agusta AW139	CHC Scotia Ltd/HM Coastguard
	G-CGWC	Ultramagic H-31 balloon	G. Everett
	G-CGWD	Robinson R-44	J. M. Henderson
	G-CGWE	EV-97A Eurostar	W. S. Long
	G-CGWF	Van's RV-7	M. S. Hill
	G-CGWG	Van's RV-7	G. Waters
	G-CGWH	CZAW Sportcruiser	P. J. F. Spedding
	G-CGWI	Supermarine Aircraft Spitfire Mk.26	Bertha Property LLP
	G-CGWK	Ikarus C42 FB80	GS Aviation (Europe) Ltd
	G-CGWL	Sky Ranger Nynja 912S(1)	Exodus Airsports Ltd
	G-CGWM	Dragonfly Lite	P. A. Gardner
	G-CGWN	Dragonfly Lite	P. M. Finlay
	G-CGWO	Tecnam P2002-JF Sierra	Shropshire Aero Club Ltd
	G-CGWP	Aeroprakt A22-L Foxbat	P. K. Goff
	G-CGWR	Nord NC.856A Norvigie	R. B. McLain
	G-CGWS	Raj Hamsa X'Air Hawk	I. S. McNulty
	G-CGWT	Best Off Sky Ranger Swift 912(1)	N. A. & P. A. Allwood
	G-CGWU	UltraMagic S-90 balloon	K. Graham
	G-CGWV	Embraer EMB-145MP	Eastern Airways
	G-CGWX	Cameron C-90 balloon	J. D. A. Shields
	G-CGWZ	P & M QuikR	N. D. Leak
	G-CGXB	Glasair Super IIS RG	P. J. Brion
	G-CGXC	Flylight Dragonfly	W. Lofts
	G-CGXE	P & M Quik GT450	C. D. Waldron
	G-CGXF	North Wing Stratus/Skycycle	G. W. Cameron
	G-CGXG	Yakovlev Yak-3M	Chameleon Technologies Ltd
	G-CGXI	Ikarus C42 FB80	G. V. Aggett
	G-CGXJ	Schweizer 269C-1	Milford Aviation
	G-CGXL	Robin DR.400/180	SPH Groundworks Ltd (G-GLKE)
	G-CGXN	American Legend Cub	Beaver (UK) Ltd
	G-CGXO	Lindstrand LBL-105A balloon	Aerosaurus Balloons Ltd
	G-CGXP	Grob G.109B	Gransden Grob XP
	G-CGXR	Van's RV-9A	Solway Flyers 2010 Ltd
	G-CGXS	Avro RJ-85	Trident Aviation Leasing Services (Jersey) Ltd (G-JAYV)
	G-CGXT	Kowacs Midgie	J. P. Kovacs
	G-CGXV	P & M Quik R	D. W. Allen
	G-CGXW	Grob G.109B	I. B. Kennedy
	G-CGXX	ICP MXP-740 Savannah HKS(1)	P. Hayward
	G-CGXY	Flylight Dragonfly	A. I. Lea
	G-CGXZ	AutoGyro MTO Sport	G-CGXZ Flying Group
	G-CGYA	Stoddard-Hamilton Glasair III	Aerocars Ltd
	G-CGYB	EV-97 TeamEurostar UK	J. Waite
	G-CGYC	Aeropro Eurofox 912(S)	D. C. Fairbrass

Reg.	Type	Owner or Operator	Notes
G-CGYD	Fairey Firefly TT.1	Propshop Ltd	
G-CGYE	Schroeder Fire Balloons G balloon	M. Cutraro	
G-CGYF	Gloster Gamecock II	Retro Track & Air (UK) Ltd	
G-CGYG	Aeropro Eurofox 912(S)	Highland Gliding Club Ltd	
G-CGYH	Magni M-24C	J. L. Ward	
G-CGYI	Van's RV-12	R. A. Smith	
G-CGYJ	VS.361 Spitfire HF.IX (TD314:FX-P)	K. M. Perkins	
G-CGYM	AT-16 Harvard IIB	Reflight Airworks Ltd	
G-CGYO	Van's RV-6A	F. D. Cowan	
G-CGYP	Best Off Sky Ranger 912(2)	Yankee Papa Group	
G-CGYR	Avro RJ-85	Trident Turboprop (Dublin) Ltd	
G-CGYS	Avro RJ-85	Trident Aviation Leasing Services (Jersey) Ltd	
G-CGYT	Flylight Dragonfly	G-CGYT Syndicate	
G-CGYU	Avro RJ-85	Trident Turboprop (Dublin) Ltd	
G-CGYV	Avro RJ-85	Trident Turboprop (Dublin) Ltd	
G-CGYW	Sikorsky S-92A	Bristow Helicopters Ltd	
G-CGYY	MXP-740 Savannah VG Jabiru(1)	Carlisle Skyrangers	
G-CGYZ	P & M Quik GT450	M. Florence	
G-CGZA	Kolb Twinstar Mk.3 Xtra	A. Wilson	
G-CGZB	Avro RJ-85	Trident Aviation Leasing Services (Jersey) Ltd	
G-CGZD	Eurocopter EC135 P2	Bond Air Services Ltd	
G-CGZE	Rotorsport UK MTO Sport	The Gyrocopter Company UK Ltd	
G-CGZF	EV-97 TeamEurostar UK	24/7 Rescue and Recovery (Membury) Ltd	
G-CGZG	AutoGyro MTO Sport	D. C. Dewey	
G-CGZI	SOCATA TB-21 Trinidad TC	K. B. Hallam	
G-CGZJ	ITV Dakota XL	C. J. Lines	
G-CGZL	Flylight Motor Floater Fox 16T	Flylight Airsports Ltd	
G-CGZM	AutoGyro MTO Sport	A. K. & J. A. Hughes	
G-CGZN	Dudek Synthesis 31/Nirvana Carbon	M. J. Parker	
G-CGZO	Avro RJ-85	Trident Aviation Leasing Services (Jersey) Ltd	
G-CGZP	Curtiss P-40F Kittyhawk (41-19841 X-17)	The Fighter Collection	
G-CGZR	Cameron Z-350 balloon	Ballooning Network Ltd	
G-CGZT	Aeroprakt A22-L Foxbat	R. J. Davey	
G-CGZU	VS.361 Spitfire F.IXc (LZ842:EF-F)	M. A. Bennett	
G-CGZV	Europa XS	R. W. Collings	
G-CGZW	Scheibe SF-25C Falke	Glidesport UK Ltd	
G-CGZY	EV-97 TeamEurostar UK	Exodus Airsports Ltd	
G-CGZZ	Kubicek BB22E balloon	A. M. Holly	
G-CHAB	Schleicher Ka 6CR	G-CHAB Group	
G-CHAC	PZL-Bielsko SZD-50-3 Puchacz	Peterborough and Spalding Gliding Club Ltd	
G-CHAD	Aeroprakt A.22 Foxbat	DJB Foxbat	
G-CHAE	Glasflugel H205 Club Libelle	J. C. Cavill & R. S. Hanslip	
G-CHAF	PZL-Bielsko SZD-50-3 Puchacz	Seahawk Gliding Club	
G-CHAG	Guimbal Cabri G2	European Helicopter Importers Ltd	
G-CHAH	Shaw Europa	T. Higgins	
G-CHAI	Bombardier CL.601-3R	Mercury Air Ltd (G-FBFI)	
G-CHAJ	Cirrus SR22	S. R. Kay	
G-CHAK	Boeing 737-505	European Aviation Ltd	
G-CHAM	Cameron 90 Pot SS balloon	Pendle Balloon Company	
G-CHAN	Robinson R22 Beta	Aztec Aviators Ltd	
G-CHAO	Rolladen-Schneider LS6-b	A. R. J. Hughes	
G-CHAP	Robinson R44	Brierley Lifting Tackle Co Ltd	
G-CHAR	Grob G.109B	The Royal Air Force Gliding and Soaring Association	
G-CHAS	PA-28-181 Archer II	G-CHAS Flying Group	
G-CHAU	Cameron C-80 balloon	G. G. Cannon & P. Haworth	
G-CHAW	Replica Fokker EIII	S. W. C. Duckworth	
G-CHAX	Schempp-Hirth Standard Cirrus	C. Keating & R. Jarvis	
G-CHAY	Rolladen-Schneider LS7	N. J. Leaton	
G-CHBA	Rolladen-Schneider LS7	C. J. Davison	
G-CHBB	Schleicher ASW-24	London Gliding Club Propietary Ltd	
G-CHBC	Rolladen-Schneider LS6-c	A. Crowden	
G-CHBD	Glaser-Dirks DG-200	Bravo Delta Group	
G-CHBE	Glaser-Dirks DG-300 Club Elan	DG 356 Group	
G-CHBF	Schempp-Hirth Nimbus 2C	J. A. Clark	
G-CHBG	Schleicher ASW-24	Imperial College of Science, Technology and Medicine	
G-CHBH	Grob G.103C Twin III Acro	Imperial College of Science, Technology and Medicine	
G-CHBJ	Westland Gazelle AH.Mk.1	MW Helicopters Ltd	

Notes	Reg.	Type	Owner or Operator
	G-CHBK	Grob G.103 Twin Astir II	S. Naylor
	G-CHBL	Grob G.102 Astir CS77	C. Morris
	G-CHBM	Grob G.102 Astir CS77	P. W. Brown
	G-CHBN	Westland Gazelle AH Mk.1	MW Helicopters Ltd
	G-CHBO	Schleicher Ka 6CR	C. J. Sturdy
	G-CHBP	Glaser-Dirks DG-500	A. Taverna
	G-CHBS	PZL-Bielsko SZD-41A Jantar Standard 1	P. J. Chaisty & D. Hendry
	G-CHBT	Grob G.102 Astir CS Jeans	Astir Syndicate
	G-CHBU	Centrair ASW-20F	M. Staljan, S. Brogger & C. Behrendt
	G-CHBV	Schempp-Hirth Nimbus 2B	G. J. Evison, J. Lynas & R. Strarup
	G-CHBW	Jurca Spitfire	T. A. Major
	G-CHBX	Lindstrand LBL-77A balloon	Lindstrand Hot Air Balloons Ltd
	G-CHBY	Agusta AW.139	Bristow Helicopters Ltd
	G-CHBZ	TL2000UK Sting Carbon	C. R. Ashley
	G-CHCF	AS.332L-2 Super Puma	CHC Scotia Ltd
	G-CHCG	AS.332L-2 Super Puma	CHC Scotia Ltd
	G-CHCH	AS.332L-2 Super Puma	CHC Scotia Ltd
	G-CHCI	AS.332L-2 Super Puma	CHC Scotia Ltd
	G-CHCJ	EC.225LP Super Puma	CHC Scotia Ltd
	G-CHCK	Sikorsky S-92A	CHC Scotia Ltd
	G-CHCL	EC.225LP Super Puma	CHC Scotia Ltd
	G-CHCM	EC.225LP Super Puma	CHC Scotia Ltd
	G-CHCP	Agusta AB.139	CHC Scotia Ltd
	G-CHCS	Sikorsky S-92A	CHC Scotia Ltd
	G-CHCT	Agusta AB.139	CHC Scotia Ltd
	G-CHCU	AS.332L2 Super Puma II	CHC Scotia Ltd
	G-CHCV	Agusta AW.139	CHC Scotia Ltd
	G-CHCX	EC.225LP Super Puma	CHC Scotia Ltd
	G-CHDA	Pilatus B4-PC11AF	HDA Syndicate
	G-CHDB	PZL-Bielsko SZD-51-1 Junior	Stratford on Avon Gliding Club Ltd
	G-CHDD	Centrair 101B Pegase 90	591 Glider Syndicate
	G-CHDE	Pilatus B4-PC11AF	A. A. Jenkins
	G-CHDH	Lindstrand LBL-77A balloon	Lindstrand Hot Air Balloons Ltd
	G-CHDJ	Schleicher ASW-20CL	G. E. G. Lambert & L. M. M. Sebreights
	G-CHDK	Magni M-16C Tandem Trainer	Gyromania Ltd
	G-CHDL	Schleicher ASW-20	137 Syndicate
	G-CHDM	P & M QuikR	A. Sheveleu
	G-CHDN	Schleicher K 8B	Upward Bound Trust
	G-CHDP	PZL-Bielsko SZD-50-3 Puchacz	Heron Gliding Club
	G-CHDR	DG-300 Elan	R. Robins
	G-CHDS	Rans S-6-ES Coyote II	M. Bradley
	G-CHDT	Avro RJ-85	Trident Aviation Leasing Services (Ireland) Ltd
	G-CHDU	PZL-Bielsko SZD-51-1 Junior	Cambridge Gliding Club Ltd
	G-CHDV	Schleicher ASW-19B	ASW Aviation
	G-CHDW	Pilatus B4-PC11AF	D. Poll
	G-CHDX	Rolladen-Schneider LS7-WL	D. Holborn & R. T. Halliburton
	G-CHDY	Schleicher K 8B	V. Mallon
	G-CHDZ	Cameron O-120 balloon	R. J. Mansfield
	G-CHEB	Shaw Europa	I. C. Smit & P. Whittingham
	G-CHEC	PZL-Bielsko SZD-55-1	D. Pye
	G-CHED	Flylight Dragonfly	J. D. Ellis
	G-CHEE	Schempp-Hirth Discus b	A. Henderson
	G-CHEF	Glaser-Dirks DG-500 Elan Trainer	Yorkshire Gliding Club (Proprietary) Ltd
	G-CHEG	AB Sportine Aviacija LAK-12	Z. Kmita, R. Hannigan & S. Grant
	G-CHEH	Rolladen-Schneider LS7-WL	P. Candler
	G-CHEI	Cameron Z-275 balloon	Airborne Balloon Flights Ltd
	G-CHEJ	Schleicher ASW-15B	A. F. F. Webb
	G-CHEK	PZL-Bielsko SZD-51-1	Cambridge Gliding Club Ltd
	G-CHEL	Colt 77B balloon	Chelsea Financial Services PLC
	G-CHEM	PA-34-200T Seneca II	London Executive Aviation Ltd
	G-CHEN	Schempp-Hirth Discus b	G-CHEN Group
	G-CHEO	Schleicher ASW-20	The Eleven Group
	G-CHEP	PZL-Bielsko SZD-50-3 Puchacz	Peterborough and Spalding Gliding Club Ltd
	G-CHER	PA-38-112 Tomahawk II	Carlisle Flight Training Ltd
	G-CHEW	Rolladen-Schneider LS6-c18	D. N. Tew
	G-CHEX	Aero Designs Pulsar	D. R. Piercey
	G-CHFA	Schempp-Hirth Ventus b/16.6	A. K. Lincoln
	G-CHFB	Schleicher Ka-6CR	P. J. Galloway
	G-CHFC	P & M Quik GTR	A. Niarchos
	G-CHFD	Agusta AW.109SP	Flight Charter Services Pty Ltd
	G-CHFE	Avro RJ-85	Trident Aviation Leasing Services (Ireland) Ltd

Reg.	Type	Owner or Operator	Notes
G-CHFF	Schempp-Hirth Standard Cirrus	Foxtrot 2 Group	
G-CHFG	Van's RV-6	RV Flying Group	
G-CHFH	PZL-Bielsko SZD-50-3	Trent Valley Aerotowing Club Ltd	
G-CHFI	Ibis Magic GS700 LSA	Nilsoft Ltd	
G-CHFK	PA-32-360 Cherokee Six	Aerobility	
G-CHFL	Scheibe SF-25C Falke	Glidesport UK Ltd	
G-CHFM	Cameron Z-120 balloon	David Hathaway Transport Ltd	
G-CHFN	Aerodyne Jumbe L/Trike Buggy	D. Newton	
G-CHFO	P & M Quik GTR	G. J. Slater	
G-CHFP	Hawker Sea Fury T.Mk.20 (WG655)	N. Grey	
G-CHFR	Avro RJ-85	Trident Turboprop (Dublin) Ltd	
G-CHFT	Tanarg Bionix 15 912S(1)	N. C. Stubbs	
G-CHFU	P & M Quik GTR	W. K. C. Davies	
G-CHFV	Schempp-Hirth Ventus B/16.6	A. Cliffe & B. Pearson	
G-CHFW	Schleicher K 8B	Oxford Gliding Co.Ltd	
G-CHFX	Schempp-Hirth Nimbus 4T	B. Flewett & A. I. Perley	
G-CHFZ	Best Off Sky Ranger Nynja 912S(1)	G-CHFZ Group	
G-CHGA	P & M Quik GTR	Flying for Freedom Ltd	
G-CHGB	Grob G.102 Astir CS	G. Jaques, P. Hollamby & G. Clark	
G-CHGD	Lindstrand LBL-69X balloon	P. Burrows	
G-CHGE	EV-97 TeamEurostar UK	I. C. Tandy	
G-CHGF	Schleicher ASW-15B	HGF Flying Group	
G-CHGG	Schempp-Hirth Standard Cirrus	HGG Flying Group	
G-CHGI	Beech A.36 Bonanza	Atlantic Bridge Aviation Ltd	
G-CHGJ	Flylight MotorFloater Fox 16T	A. Brooks	
G-CHGK	Schempp-Hirth Discus bT	P. W. Berridge	
G-CHGL	Bell 206B JetRanger II	Vantage Aviation Ltd (G-BPNG/G-ORTC)	
G-CHGM	Groppo Trail	D. Cassidy	
G-CHGN	Ace Aviation Easy Riser Spirit	Airways Airsports Ltd	
G-CHGO	AB Sportine Aviacija LAK-12	P. Raymond & J-M Peuffier	
G-CHGP	Rolladen-Schneider LS6-c	D. J. Miller	
G-CHGR	AB Sportline Aviacija LAK-12	M. R. Garwood	
G-CHGS	Schempp-Hirth Discus b	G-CHGS Syndicate	
G-CHGT	FFA Diamant 16.5	T. E. Lynch	
G-CHGU	Ace Aviation Easy Riser Touch	T. A. Dobbins	
G-CHGV	Glaser-Dirks DG500/22 Elan	Hotel Golf Victor Syndicate	
G-CHGW	Centrair ASW-20F	S. C. Moss	
G-CHGX	AB Sportine LAK-12 Lietuva	M. Jenks	
G-CHGY	Schleicher ASW-27-18	G-CHGY Flying Group	
G-CHGZ	Schempp-Hirth Discus bT	G-CHGZ Syndicate	
G-CHHA	Avro RJ-85	Trident Turboprop (Dublin) Ltd	
G-CHHB	Aeroprakt A22-LS Foxbat	A. J. L. Gordon	
G-CHHC	Cameron A-300 balloon	Wickers World Ltd	
G-CHHD	RL7A XP Sherwood Ranger	M. Taylor	
G-CHHF	Sikorsky S-92A	Bristow Helicopters Ltd	
G-CHHG	Dudek Synthesis	R. W. Houldsworth	
G-CHHH	Rolladen-Schneider LS6-c	P. H. Rackham	
G-CHHI	Van's RV-7	M. G. Jefferies	
G-CHHJ	Aeropro Eurofox 912(1)	K. J. Watt	
G-CHHK	Schleicher ASW-19B	M. Walker	
G-CHHL	Cameron C-80 balloon	H. G. Griffiths & W. A. Steel	
G-CHHM	AB Sportline LAK-12 Lietuva	D. Martin	
G-CHHN	Schempp-Hirth Ventus b/16.6	N. A. C. Norman & R. K. Forrest	
G-CHHO	Schempp-Hirth Discus bT	97Z Syndicate	
G-CHHP	Schempp-Hirth Discus b	F. R. Knowles	
G-CHHR	PZL-Bielsko SZD-55-1 Promyk	R. T. & G. Starling	
G-CHHS	Schleicher ASW-20	P.J. Rocks & D. Britt	
G-CHHT	Rolladen-Schneider LS6-c	F. Roles	
G-CHHU	Rolladen-Schneider LS6-c	J. M. Hall & P. Shuttleworth	
G-CHHV	Junqua Ibis RJ.03	J. J. R. Joubert	
G-CHHW	AB Sportine LAK-12	A. J. Dibdin	
G-CHHX	Wassmer WA.26P Squale	M. H. Gagg	
G-CHHY	Ace Magic Laser	S. W. Walker	
G-CHHZ	Schempp-Hirth Cirrus	B. J. Dawson & S. E. Richardson	
G-CHIA	North American SNJ-5 Texan	The Warplane Flying Company Ltd	
G-CHIB	Lindstrand LBL-77A balloon	Lindstrand Hot Air Balloons Ltd	
G-CHID	Eurofox 912	J. W. Taylor	
G-CHIE	Dudek Nucleon 34/Flymecc Mini Trike	J. M. Keen	
G-CHIF	Ozone Power Speedster/Bailey Quattro	T. A. Dobbins	
G-CHIG	Grob G.109B	Southdown Gliding Club Ltd	
G-CHIH	Aeropro Eurofox 912(S)	Banbury Gliding Club Ltd	

Notes	Reg.	Type	Owner or Operator
	G-CHII	CASA 1-131E Jungmann Srs 1000	J. A. Sykes
	G-CHIJ	Ikarus C42 FB80	G. E. Cole
	G-CHIK	Cessna F.152	Stapleford Flying Club Ltd (G-BHAZ)
	G-CHIM	Ultramagic H-31 balloon	G. B. Lescott
	G-CHIN	Avro RJ-85	Trident Turboprop (Dublin) Ltd
	G-CHIO	Cameron Z-120 balloon	Cameron Balloons Ltd
	G-CHIP	PA-28-181 Archer II	J. A. Divis
	G-CHIR	Van's RV-7	F. Sharples
	G-CHIS	Robinson R22 Beta	Staffordshire Helicopters Training Ltd
	G-CHIT	AutoGyro MTO Sport	N. G. H. Staunton
	G-CHIV	P & M Quik R	G. H. Sharwood-Smith
	G-CHIW	Raj Hamsa X'Air Hawk	M. D. Boley
	G-CHIX	Robin DR.400/500	P. A. & R. Stephens
	G-CHIY	Flylight MotorFloater	W. Seal
	G-CHIZ	Flylight Dragonfly	J. Paterson
	G-CHJB	Flylight Dragonfly	Celtic Solutions Ltd
	G-CHJC	Rolladen-Schneider LS6-c	F. J. Davies
	G-CHJD	Schleicher Ka 6E	The Ruby Syndicate
	G-CHJE	Schleicher K 8B	M. P. Webb
	G-CHJF	Rolladen-Schneider LS6-c	J. L. Bridge
	G-CHJG	Evektor EV-97 TeamEurostar UK	S. Hoyle
	G-CHJH	Schempp-Hirth Discus bT	Hotel Juliet Hotel Group
	G-CHJJ	Medway Clipper-80	J. C. Kitchen
	G-CHJK	Cessna T.206H Turbo Stationair	G. G. Weston
	G-CHJL	Schempp-Hirth Discus bT	Discus JL Group
	G-CHJM	Cameron C-80 balloon	C. L. Smith
	G-CHJN	Schempp-Hirth Standard Cirrus	P. M. Hardingham
	G-CHJO	Bushby-Long Midget Mustang M-1	R. J. Hodder
	G-CHJP	Schleicher Ka-6CR	D. M. Cornelius
	G-CHJR	Glasflugel H201B Standard Libelle	B. O. Marcham & B. Magnani
	G-CHJS	Schleicher ASW-27-18E	J. D. Spencer
	G-CHJT	Centrair ASW-20F	R. J. Pirie & M. S. R. Broadway
	G-CHJV	Grob G.102 Astir CS	Cotswold Gliding Club
	G-CHJW	P & M Quik GTR	A. C. Rowlands
	G-CHJX	Rolladen-Schneider LS6-c	M. R. Haynes & P. Robinson
	G-CHJY	Schempp-Hirth Standard Cirrus	R. S. Rose
	G-CHJZ	Luscombe 8E Silvaire Deluxe	P. Durdey
	G-CHKA	Orlican Discus CS	R. W. & M. P. Weaver
	G-CHKB	Grob G.102 Astir CS77	G-CHKB Group
	G-CHKC	Schempp-Hirth Standard Cirrus	A. Taylor
	G-CHKD	Schempp-Hirth Standard Cirrus	R. Jeffcoate
	G-CHKF	Grob G.109B	T. R. Dews
	G-CHKG	Best Off Skyranger Nynja 912S(1)	S. Worthington
	G-CHKH	Schleicher ASW-28	D. Bradley
	G-CHKI	Sikorsky S-92A	Bristow Helicopters Ltd
	G-CHKK	Schleicher K8B	Tweeetie Bird
	G-CHKL	Cameron 120 Kookaburra SS balloon	Eagle Ltd/Australia
	G-CHKM	Grob G.102 Astir CS Jeans	Essex and Suffolk Gliding Club Ltd
	G-CHKN	Kiss 400-582(1)	P. J. Higgins
	G-CHKO	Best Off Skyranger Swift 912S(1)	J. V. Clewer & A. A. Howland
	G-CHKP	Avro RJ85	Trident Turboprop (Dublin) Ltd
	G-CHKR	Jastreb Standard Cirrus G/81	N. A. White
	G-CHKS	Jastreb Standard Cirrus G/81	G. G. Butler
	G-CHKT	Balony Kubicek BB22E balloon	D. L. Beckwith
	G-CHKU	Schempp-Hirth Standard Cirrus	T. J. Wheeler & T. M. O'Sullivan
	G-CHKV	Scheibe Zugvogel IIIA	Dartmoor Gliding Society Ltd
	G-CHKW	Robinson R44	Simple Technical Solutions Ltd
	G-CHKX	Rolladen-Schneider LS4-B	J. McMackin
	G-CHKY	Schempp-Hirth Discus b	M. T. Davis
	G-CHKZ	CARMAM JP 15-36AR Aiglon	T. A. & A. J. Hollings
	G-CHLB	Rolladen-Schneider LS4-b	E. G. Leach & K. F. Rogers
	G-CHLC	Pilatus B4-PC11AF	E. Lockhart
	G-CHLD	AutoGyro MTO Sport	A. D. Lysser
	G-CHLE	Cameron A-160 balloon	Virgin Baloon Flights
	G-CHLH	Schleicher K 8B	Shenington Gliding Club
	G-CHLI	Cosmik Aviation Superchaser	Cosmik Aviation Ltd
	G-CHLK	Glasflugel H.301 Libelle	G. L. J. Barrett
	G-CHLM	Schleicher ASW-19B	R. A. Colbeck
	G-CHLN	Schempp-Hirth Discus CS	Portsmouth Naval Gliding Centre
	G-CHLO	Grob G.109B	F. Waller
	G-CHLP	Schleicher ASK-21	Southdown Gliding Club Ltd

Reg.	Type	Owner or Operator	Notes
G-CHLR	Embraer EMB-135BJ Legacy	ECC Leasing Co.Ltd	
G-CHLS	Schempp-Hirth Discus b	R. A. Lennard	
G-CHLU	Westland WA.341B Gazelle AH.Mk.1	Kemet Global Ltd	
G-CHLV	Schleicher ASW-19B	P. J. Belcher & R. I. Brickwood	
G-CHLW	Westland WA.341B Gazelle AH.Mk.1	Kemet Global Ltd	
G-CHLX	Schleicher ASH-25	A. di Stasi	
G-CHLY	Schempp-Hirth Discus CS	S. J. Pearce	
G-CHLZ	Best Off Skyranger 582(1)	S. K. Ridge	
G-CHMA	PZL-Bielsko SZD-51-1 Junior	The Welland Gliding Club Ltd	
G-CHMB	Glaser-Dirks DG-300 Elan	A. D. & P. Langlands	
G-CHMC	Ozone Power Speedster/Bailey Quattro	D. J. Piper	
G-CHMD	DG Flugzeugbau LS8-T	G. B. Monslow & A. P. Balkwill	
G-CHME	Glaser-Dirks DG-300 Elan	D. J. Baldwin & J. Stiles	
G-CHMF	Westland WA.341B Gazelle AH.Mk.1	Paramount Logistics Corporation Ltd	
G-CHMG	ICA IS-28B2	A. Sutton, R. Maksymowicz & A. J. Palfreyman	
G-CHMH	Schleicher K8B	Shenington Gliding Club	
G-CHMI	Lindstrand LBL-105A balloon	J. A. Lawton	
G-CHMJ	Sikorsky S-92A	Bristow Helicopters Ltd	
G-CHMK	Rolladen-Schneider LS6-18W	R. C. Hodge	
G-CHML	Schempp-Hirth Discus CS	I. D. Bateman	
G-CHMM	Glasflugel 304B	Delta 19 Group	
G-CHMN	Raj Hamsa X'Air Falcon Jabiru(1)	F. C. Claydon	
G-CHMO	Orlican Discus CS	S. Barter	
G-CHMP	Bellanca 7ACA Champ	I. J. Langley	
G-CHMR	Embraer EMB-145MP	Eastern Airways	
G-CHMS	Glaser-Dirks DG-100	J. D. Blaskett	
G-CHMT	Glasflugel Mosquito B	J. Taberham	
G-CHMU	CARMAM JP-15/36AR Aiglon	G-CHMU Group	
G-CHMV	Schleicher ASK-13	The Windrushers Gliding Club Ltd	
G-CHMW	Evektor EV-97 Eurostar SL	N. R. Beale	
G-CHMX	Rolladen-Schneider LS4-a	K. P. Nakhla & L Couval	
G-CHMY	Schempp-Hirth Standard Cirrus	HMY Syndicate	
G-CHMZ	Fedorov ME7 Mechta	R. Andrews	
G-CHNA	Glaser-Dirks DG-500/20 Elan	G-CHNA Group	
G-CHNB	Scheibe SF-28A	S. E. Abbott	
G-CHNC	Schleicher ASK-19B	T. J. Highton	
G-CHND	Ultramagic H-65	N. Dykes	
G-CHNF	Schempp-Hirth Duo Discus	Booker Gliding Club Ltd	
G-CHNH	Schempp-Hirth Nimbus 2C	C. J. Pollard	
G-CHNI	Magni M-24C	A. Smith	
G-CHNJ	Eurocopter AS.365N3 Dauphin 2	Ministry of Defence	
G-CHNK	PZL-Bielsko SZD-51-1 Junior	Booker Gliding Club Ltd	
G-CHNM	Standard Cirrus G/81	Bicester Cirrus Crew	
G-CHNO	Cameron C-60 balloon	J. F. Till	
G-CHNP	Dragon Chaser	Flylight Airsports Ltd	
G-CHNR	P & M Quik GTR	S. J. Sheppard	
G-CHNS	Agusta AW.139	Bristow Helicopters Ltd	
G-CHNT	Schleicher ASW-15	S. J. Lintott & I. Dawkins	
G-CHNU	Schempp-Hirth Nimbus 4DT	D. E. Findon	
G-CHNV	Rolladen-Schneider LS4-b	S. K. Armstrong & P. H. Dixon	
G-CHNW	Schempp-Hirth Duo Discus	G-CHNW Group	
G-CHNY	Centrair 101A Pegase	M. O. Breen	
G-CHNZ	Centrair 101A Pegase	R. H. Partington	
G-CHOA	Bell 206B-3 JetRanger III	Haverholme Farm Partnership	
G-CHOD	Schleicher ASW-20	S. E. Archer-Jones & A. Duerden	
G-CHOE	Robin DR400/140B	Exavia Ltd	
G-CHOF	CARMAM M100S	M. A. Farrelly	
G-CHOG	AB Sportine LAK-12	J. M. Pursey	
G-CHOI	ReplicaWhite Monoplane 1912 Canard Pusher	J. Aubert	
G-CHOJ	Cameron A-375 balloon	K. R. Karlstrom	
G-CHOO	Ikarus C42 FB80	GS Aviation (Europe) Ltd	
G-CHOP	Westland-Bell 47G-3B1	Leamington Hobby Centre Ltd	
G-CHOR	Schempp-Hirth Discus b	The Windrushers Gliding Club Ltd	
G-CHOT	Grob G.102 Astir CS77	Southdown Gliding Club Ltd	
G-CHOU	EV-97 TeamEurostar UK	R. A. Betts	
G-CHOX	Shaw Europa XS	Chocs Away Ltd	
G-CHOY	Schempp-Hirth Mini Nimbus C	A. H. Sparrow	
G-CHOZ	Rolladen-Schneider LS6-18W	R. E. Scott	
G-CHPA	Robinson R22 Beta	Rivermead Aviation Ltd/Switzerland	
G-CHPC	Schleicher ASW-20 CL	B. L. Liddard & P. J. Williams	

Notes	Reg.	Type	Owner or Operator
	G-CHPD	Rolladen-Schneider LS6-c18	C. J. & K. A. Teagle
	G-CHPE	Schleicher ASK-13	Dumfries and District Gliding Club
	G-CHPG	Cirrus SR-20	S. G. Jones
	G-CHPH	Schempp-Hirth Discus CS	I. N & S. G. Hunt
	G-CHPI	DHC.1 Chipmunk Mk.22	G-CHPI Group
	G-CHPJ	Embraer EMB-135BJ Legacy 600	ECC Leasing Co.Ltd
	G-CHPK	Van's RV-8	Viscount A. C. Andover (G-JILS)
	G-CHPL	Rolladen-Schneider LS4-b	Southdown Gliding Club Ltd
	G-CHPM	DHC.1 Chipmunk Mk.22	J. A. & R. H. Cooper
	G-CHPN	Grumman FM-2 Wildcat	Richard Shuttleworth Trustees
	G-CHPO	Schleicher Ka-6CR	N. Robinson
	G-CHPP	Dudek Nucleon Cabrio 42/Paratrike	B. G. Hackman
	G-CHPR	Robinson R22 Beta	C. Gozzi
	G-CHPS	Best Off SkyRanger 582(1)	J. A. Gregorig
	G-CHPT	Federov ME7 Mechta	Midland Gliding Club Ltd
	G-CHPU	Powerplay Sting 250/Albatros	A. Kulpa
	G-CHPV	Schleicher ASK-21	Scottish Gliding Union Ltd
	G-CHPW	Schleicher ASK-21	Scottish Gliding Union Ltd
	G-CHPX	Schempp-Hirth Discus CS	G-CHRS Group
	G-CHPY	DHC.1 Chipmunk 22 (WB652:V)	Devonair Executive Business Travel Ltd
	G-CHPZ	P & M Aviation Quik GT450	S. Cooke
	G-CHRC	Glaser-Dirks DG500/20 Elan	DG500-390 Syndicate
	G-CHRD	Flylight Dragonlite	I. A. Barclay
	G-CHRE	Nicollier HN.700 Menestrel II	B. S. Godbold
	G-CHRF	Avro RJ85	Trident Aviation Leasing Services (Ireland) Ltd
	G-CHRG	PZL-Bielsko SZD-51-1 Junior	Scottish Gliding Union Ltd
	G-CHRH	Schempp-Hirth Discus 2cT	C. Hyett
	G-CHRJ	Schleicher K 8B	Shenington Gliding Club
	G-CHRK	Centrair 101 Pegase	P. T. Bushill & M. Morris
	G-CHRL	Schempp-Hirth Standard Cirrus	B. L. C. Gordon
	G-CHRM	Ikarus C42 FB80 Bravo	D. R. Stevens
	G-CHRN	Schleicher ASK-18	Stratford on Avon Gliding Club Ltd
	G-CHRS	Schempp-Hirth Discus CS	M. Santopinto
	G-CHRT	EV-97 TeamEurostar UK	A. Parker
	G-CHRU	Flylight Dragonlite Fox	J. R. Kendall
	G-CHRV	Van's RV-7	R. E. Tyers
	G-CHRW	Schempp-Hirth Duo Discus	802 Syndicate
	G-CHRX	Schempp-Hirth Discus a	D. S. Lodge
	G-CHRY	Medway EclipseR	S. D. McLaughlin
	G-CHRZ	Avro RJ85	Triangle Regional Aircraft Leasing Ltd
	G-CHSB	Glaser-Dirks DG-303 Elan	C. M. Hawkes & J. Weddell
	G-CHSD	Schempp-Hirth Discus b	G-CHSD Group
	G-CHSE	Grob G.102 Astir CS77	G. J. Armes
	G-CHSF	Avro RJ85	Triangle Regional Aircraft Leasing Ltd
	G-CHSG	Scheibe SF27A	HSG Syndicate
	G-CHSH	Scheibe Zugvogel IIIB	R. D. Newton
	G-CHSI	Ellipse Fuji/Pulma 2000	H. J. Mayer
	G-CHSK	Schleicher ASW-20CL	A. J. Watson & C. C. Ramshorn
	G-CHSM	Schleicher ASK-13	Stratford on Avon Gliding Club Ltd
	G-CHSN	Schleicher Ka-6CR	Needwood Forest Gliding Club Ltd
	G-CHSO	Schempp-Hirth Discus b	Midland Gliding Club Ltd
	G-CHSP	UltraMagic M-65C balloon	S. Bareford
	G-CHSS	Ikarus C42 FB80 Bravo	J. Noel
	G-CHST	Van's RV-9A	R. J. Charles
	G-CHSU	Eurocopter EC 135T1	Eurocopter UK Ltd
	G-CHSX	Scheibe SF-27A	Essex & Suffolk Gliding Club Ltd
	G-CHSY	Aeroprakt A22-LS Foxbat	A. Everitt
	G-CHSZ	Rolladen-Schneider LS8-a	I. G. Garden
	G-CHTA	AA-5A Cheetah	C. A. Johnson & K. T. Pierce (G-BFRC)
	G-CHTB	Schempp-Hirth Janus	Janus G-CHTB Syndicate
	G-CHTC	Schleicher ASW-15B	G-CHTC Group
	G-CHTD	Grob G.102 Astir CS	S. Waldie
	G-CHTE	Grob G.102 Astir CS77	HTE Group
	G-CHTF	AB Sportline LAK-12	M. Tolson
	G-CHTH	Zenair CH.701SP	S. C. Richards & R. E. Lasnier
	G-CHTI	Van's RV-12	Paludis Ltd
	G-CHTJ	Schleicher ASK-13	Queen's University Gliding Club
	G-CHTK	Hawker Sea Hurricane 1B (P3886)	P. R. Monk (G-TWTD)
	G-CHTL	Schempp-Hirth Arcus T	38 Syndicate
	G-CHTM	Rolladen-Schneider LS8-18	M. J. Chapman
	G-CHTO	Rans S-7S	J. D. Llewellyn

Reg.	Type	Owner or Operator	Notes
G-CHTR	Grob G.102 Astir CS	I. P. & D. M. Wright	
G-CHTS	Rolladen-Schneider LS8-18	P. T. Cunnison	
G-CHTU	Schempp-Hirth Cirrus	Open Cirrus Group	
G-CHTV	Schleicher ASK-21	Cambridge Gliding Club Ltd	
G-CHTW	Grob G.109	M. Pettican	
G-CHTX	Voltair 86	D. R. Skill	
G-CHTZ	Airbus A.330-243	Thomas Cook Airlines Ltd (G-WWBM)	
G-CHUA	Schleicher ASW-19B	G. D. Vaughan	
G-CHUC	Denney Kitfox Model 2	Silver Fox Group	
G-CHUD	Schleicher ASK-13	London Gliding Club Propietary Ltd	
G-CHUE	Schleicher ASW-27	M. J. Smith	
G-CHUF	Schleicher ASK-13	The Welland Gliding Club Ltd	
G-CHUG	Shaw Europa	C. M. Washington	
G-CHUH	Schempp-Hirth Janus	Janus D31 Syndicate	
G-CHUI	Cessna 560XL Citation XLS	Eurojet Aviation Ltd	
G-CHUJ	Centrair ASW-20F	P. D. Ruskin	
G-CHUK	Cameron O-77 balloon	R. P. E. Phillips	
G-CHUL	Schempp-Hirth Cirrus	Cirrus CHUL Group	
G-CHUN	Grob G.102 Astir CS Jeans	Staffordshire Gliding Club Ltd	
G-CHUO	Federov ME7 Mechta	J. D. A. Cooper & W. H. Ollis	
G-CHUP	Aeropro Eurofox 912(S)	B Walker & Co (Dursley) Ltd	
G-CHUR	Schempp-Hirth Cirrus	M. Rossiter & A. G. Thomas	
G-CHUS	Scheibe SF27A Zugvogel V	SF27 HUS Syndicate	
G-CHUT	Centrair ASW-20F	S. R. Phelps	
G-CHUU	Schleicher ASK-13	Upward Bound Trust	
G-CHUX	P & M Aviation QuikR	R. G. Beecham	
G-CHUY	Schempp-Hirth Ventus cT	M. A. & M. N. Challans	
G-CHUZ	Schempp-Hirth Discus bT	P. A. Gelsthorpe	
G-CHVB	P & M Aviation Quik R	Victor Bravo Group	
G-CHVC	Cameron C-60 balloon	Breitling UK Ltd	
G-CHVF	Rolladen-Schneider LS8-18	J. Haigh	
G-CHVG	Schleicher ASK-21	Rattlesden Gliding Club Ltd	
G-CHVH	Pilatus B4-PC11AF	London Gliding Club Proprietary Ltd	
G-CHVI	Cameron Z-210 balloon	First Flight	
G-CHVJ	VS.349 Spitfire Vb	G. N. S. Farrant	
G-CHVK	Grob G.102 Astir CS	P. G. Goulding	
G-CHVL	Rolladen-Schneider LS8-18	Cumulus Gliding Syndicate	
G-CHVM	Glaser-Dirks DG-300	Glider Syndicate 303	
G-CHVO	Schleicher ASK-13	R. Brown	
G-CHVP	Schleicher ASW-20	P. J. Williams & G. P. Northcott	
G-CHVR	Schempp-Hirth Discus b	Yorkshire Gliding Club (Proprietary) Ltd	
G-CHVS	ICP MXP-740 Savannah VG Jabiru(1)	Sandtoft Ultralights	
G-CHVT	Schempp-Hirth Ventus 2b	Victor Tango Group	
G-CHVU	Rolladen-Schneider LS8-a	European Soaring Club	
G-CHVV	Rolladen-Schneider LS4-b	A. J. Bardgett	
G-CHVY	Ikarus C42 FB80	G-CHVY Syndicate	
G-CHUW	Rolladen-Schneider LS8-18	S8 Group	
G-CHVX	Centrair ASW-20F	D. Coker	
G-CHVW	Scleicher ASK-13	Rattlesden Gliding Club Ltd	
G-CHVZ	Schempp-Hirth Standard Cirrus	ABC Soaring	
G-CHWA	Schempp-Hirth Ventus 2c	C. Garton	
G-CHWB	Schempp-Hirth Duo Discus	Lasham Gliding Society Ltd	
G-CHWC	Glasflugel Standard Libelle 201B	Whiskey Charlie Group	
G-CHWD	Schempp-Hirth Standard Cirrus	M. R. Hoskins	
G-CHWE	Lindstrand LBL-77A balloon	B. P. Witter	
G-CHWF	Jastreb Standard Cirrus G/81	G. McCann	
G-CHWG	Glasflugel Standard Libelle 201B	M. Kalweit	
G-CHWH	Schempp-Hirth Ventus cT	M. J. Philpott	
G-CHWI	APEV Demoichelle	G. R. Moore	
G-CHWJ	Guimbal Cabri G2	European Helicopter Importers Ltd	
G-CHWK	Aerochute Dual	W. A. Kimberlin	
G-CHWL	Rolladen-Schneider LS8-a	W. M. Coffee	
G-CHWM	AutoGyro Cavalon	Devon Autogyro Ltd	
G-CHWN	Ikarus C42 FB100 Bravo	P. D. Ashley	
G-CHWO	P & M Aviation Quik GTR	E. K. Jupp	
G-CHWP	Glaser-Dirks DG-100G Elan	K. H. Bates	
G-CHWS	Rolladen-Schneider LS8-18	G. E. & H. B. Chalmers	
G-CHWT	Schleicher K 8B	Shenington Gliding Club	
G-CHWV	Baldwin Quad	P. I. Baldwin	
G-CHWW	Grob G.103A Twin II Acro	Crown Service Gliding Club	
G-CHXA	Scheibe Zugvogel IIIB	G-CHXA Group	

Notes	Reg.	Type	Owner or Operator
	G-CHXB	Grob G.102 Astir CS77	T. S. Miller
	G-CHXD	Schleicher ASW-27	J. Quartermaine & M. Jerman
	G-CHXE	Schleicher ASW-19B	M. J. Hargreaves
	G-CHXF	Cameron A-140 balloon	Gone With The Wind Ltd
	G-CHXG	CZAW Sportcruiser	R. J. Warne
	G-CHXH	Schempp-Hirth Discus b	Deeside Gliding Club (Aberdeenshire) Ltd
	G-CHXJ	Schleicher ASK-13	Cotswold Gliding Club
	G-CHXK	Scheibe SF-25A Falke 2000	Stratford on Avon Gliding Club Ltd
	G-CHXM	Grob G.102 Astir CS	University of Bristol Students Union
	G-CHXN	Balony Kubicek BB20GP balloon	D. R. Medcalf
	G-CHXO	Schleicher ASH-25	The Eleven Group
	G-CHXP	Schleicher ASK-13	The Vale of the White Horse Gliding Centre Ltd
	G-CHXR	Schempp-Hirth Ventus cT	560 Group
	G-CHXS	Cameron C-90 balloon	Dribuild Ltd
	G-CHXT	Rolladen-Schneider LS-4a	H. Hingley
	G-CHXU	Schleicher ASW-19B	UCLU
	G-CHXV	Schleicher ASK-13	Aquila Gliding Club Ltd
	G-CHXW	Rolladen-Schneider LS8-18	W. Aspland
	G-CHXX	Schempp-Hirth Standard Cirrus	A. Coatsworth & R. M. Wootten
	G-CHXZ	Rolladen-Schneider LS4	G-CHXZ Group
	G-CHYA	Rolladen-Schneider LS6c-18	Y. Melou
	G-CHYB	Grob G.109B	Morgan Airborne LLP
	G-CHYC	Westlake Altair AX4-31/12 balloon	D. W. Westlake
	G-CHYD	Schleicher ASW-24	E. S. Adlard
	G-CHYE	DG-505 Elan Orion	The Bristol Gliding Club Proprietary Ltd
	G-CHYF	Rolladen-Schneider LS8-18	R. E. Francis
	G-CHYG	Sikorsky S-92A	Bristow Helicopters Ltd
	G-CHYH	Rolladen-Schneider LS3-17	B. Silke
	G-CHYI	Sikorsky S-92A	Bristow Helicopters Ltd
	G-CHYJ	Schleicher ASK-21	Highland Gliding Club Ltd
	G-CHYK	Centrair ASW-20FL	K. H. Bates
	G-CHYN	CCF Harvard 4	M. J. M. Edwards & R. F. Warner
	G-CHYO	Ace Magic Laser	J. Lane
	G-CHYP	PZL-Bielsko SZD-50-3 Puchacz	Rattlesden Gliding Club Ltd
	G-CHYR	Schleicher ASW-27	A. J. Manwaring & A. R. Hutchings
	G-CHYS	Schleicher ASK-21	Army Gliding Association
	G-CHYT	Schleicher ASK-21	Army Gliding Association
	G-CHYU	Schempp-Hirth Discus CS	Army Gliding Association
	G-CHYV	Westland SA.341B Gazelle AH.1	Kemet Global Ltd
	G-CHYX	Schleicher K 8B	Oxford University Gliding Club
	G-CHYY	Schempp-Hirth Nimbus 3DT	G-CHYY Syndicate
	G-CHYZ	Skystar Vixen	M. J. Turner
	G-CHZB	PZL-Swidnik PW-5 Smyk	The Burn Gliding Club Ltd
	G-CHZD	Schleicher ASW-15B	C. P. Ellison & S. Barber
	G-CHZE	Schempp-Hirth Discus CS	HZE Glider Syndicate
	G-CHZF	Westland S..341B Gazelle AH.1	Kemet Global Ltd
	G-CHZG	Rolladen-Schneider LS8-18	M. J. & T. J. Webb
	G-CHZH	Schleicher Ka 6CR	C. Hankinson
	G-CHZI	Cessna 172RG	Aeroplano-Planeamento Exploracao e Manutencao de Aeronaves Lda/Portugal
	G-CHZJ	Schempp-Hirth Standard Cirrus	P. Mucha
	G-CHZK	Europa XS	P. J. Harrod
	G-CHZL	Zenair CH.601XL Zodiac	R. J. Clarke
	G-CHZM	Rolladen-Schneider LS4-a	J. M. Bevan
	G-CHZO	Schleicher ASW-27	A. A. Gilmore
	G-CHZP	Cessna 152	Aeroplano-Planeamento Exploracao e Manutencao de Aeronaves Lda/Portugal
	G-CHZR	Schleicher ASK-21	K21 HZR Group
	G-CHZS	Zenair CH.601HDS	G. Addison
	G-CHZT	Groppo Trail	A. Strachan & B. J. Main
	G-CHZU	Schempp-Hirth Standard Cirrus	S. A. W. Becker
	G-CHZV	Schempp-Hirth Standard Cirrus	S. M. Sheard
	G-CHZW	P & M Aviation Quik GTR	N. J. Braund
	G-CHZX	Schleicher K 8B	S. M. Chapman & S. Potter
	G-CHZY	Rolladen-Schneider LS4-a	N. P. Wedi
	G-CHZZ	Schleicher ASW-20L	LD Syndicate
	G-CIAA	Mitchinson Safari	C. W. Mitchinson
	G-CIAB	Avion Riot/Samba	Avian Ltd
	G-CIAC	HOAC DV.20 Katana	M. Anasi
	G-CIAE	Cameron TR-70 balloon	Cameron Balloons Ltd

Reg.	Type	Owner or Operator	Notes
G-CIAF	TL3000 Sirius	P. H. Ronfell	
G-CIAG	Diamond DA.20-A1 Katana	M. Anasi	
G-CIAH	Ultramagic S-70 balloon	A. M. Holly	
G-CIAI	Schempp-Hirth Arcus T	G-CIAI Group	
G-CIAK	Groppo Trail	I. Markham	
G-CIAL	Cameron Z-77 balloon	A. A. Osman	
G-CIAM	PA-28-181 Archer III	J. Mendonca-Caridad	
G-CIAN	Unicorn Ax6 balloon	G. A. & I. Chadwick	
G-CIAO	I.I.I. Sky Arrow 1450-L	G. Arscott	
G-CIAP	Cameron Z-77 balloon	A. A. Osman	
G-CIAR	P & M Aviation Quik GTR	C. R. Paterson	
G-CIAS	BN-2B-21 Islander	Channel Island Air Search Ltd (G-BKJM)	
G-CIAU	Bombardier CL600-1A11 Challenger 600	Inflite Aviation (IOM) Ltd	
G-CIAV	Ace Magic Cyclone	W. T. Davis	
G-CIAW	Ikarus C42 FB80	GS Aviation (Europe) Ltd	
G-CIAX	CZAW Sportcruiser	A. G. Higgins	
G-CIAY	Cameron C-70 balloon	R. L. Wright	
G-CIAZ	Aeropro Eurofox 912(1)	M. W. Houghton	
G-CIBA	Cameron N-145 balloon	J. D. Smith	
G-CIBB	Cessna F.172H	Aviation Air Care Ltd	
G-CIBC	Aeropro Eurofox 912(S)	M. P. Brockington	
G-CIBD	Cessna 172S	Air-Unlimited Sweden AB/Sweden	
G-CIBE	Boeing 737-4Q8	International Student Recruit	
G-CIBF	Aeropro Eurofox 912(S)	The Borders (Milfield) Gliding Club Ltd	
G-CIBG	Rolladen-Schneider LS4	GIA Syndicate	
G-CIBH	Van's RV-8A	W. B. Blair-Hickman	
G-CIBI	Lindstrand LBL-90A balloon	A. J. & S. J. M. Boyle	
G-CIBJ	Colomban MC-30 Luciole	R. A. Gardiner	
G-CIBL	AutoGyro Cavalon	M. J. Taylor	
G-CIBM	Van's RV-8	G. P. Williams & S. J. Wood	
G-CIBN	Cameron Z-90 balloon	B. J. Newman	
G-CIBO	Cessna 180K	CIBO Ops Ltd	
G-CIBP	Cameron Z-77 balloon	A. A. Osman	
G-CIBR	P & M Quik GT450	K. D. Smith	
G-CIBT	P & M Quik R	G-CIBT Syndicate	
G-CIBU	Jabiru J160	M. Flint	
G-CIBV	Best Off Skyranger Swift 912S(1)	H. Cooke & B. Robertson	
G-CIBW	Westland Scout AH.1 (XT626)	Ministry of Defence (Army Historic Aircraft Flight)	
G-CIBX	Cameron Z-31 balloon	Cameron Balloons Ltd	
G-CIBZ	Aeropro Eurofox 912(S1)	K. N. Rigley & D. Thorpe	
G-CICA	Europa Aviation Europa XS	J. R. Lambert	
G-CICB	Cessna 172S	Air-Unlimited Sweden AB/Sweden	
G-CICC	Cessna 152	The Pilot Centre Ltd	
G-CICD	Colt 105A balloon	N. Smith	
G-CICE	Paramania Revo 2/Bailey Quattro Plus	P. D. Johnson	
G-CICF	Ikarus C42 FB80	D. Durrans	
G-CICG	Ikarus C42 FB80	G-CICG Group	
G-CICH	Sikorsky S-92A	Bristow Helicopters Ltd	
G-CICJ	Sikorsky S-92A	Bristow Helicopters Ltd	
G-CICL	Boeing 737-7JW	Strategic Aircraft Leasing Ltd	
G-CICM	Rotorsport UK Calidus	F. Hammond	
G-CICN	Agusta-Bell Sioux H. Mk.1	Ministry of Defence (Army Historic Aircraft Flight)	
G-CICO	UltraMagic H-42 balloon	A. M. Holly	
G-CICP	de Havilland DHC-2 Beaver AL.Mk.1	Ministry of Defence (Army Historic Aircraft Flight)	
G-CICR	Auster AOP.Mk.9	Ministry of Defence (Army Historic Aircraft Flight)	
G-CICS	Sud SE.3130 Alouette AH.Mk.2	Ministry of Defence (Army Historic Aircraft Flight)	
G-CICT	Schempp-Hirth Ventus 2cT	S. G. Jones (G-ZENN)	
G-CICU	Raj Hamsa X'Air Hawk	H. Quinn & M. Donnelly	
G-CICV	Rotorsport UK MTO Sport	J. Owen	
G-CICX	Aeropro Eurofox 912(S)	L. J. Kaye	
G-CICY	PZL-Bielsko SZD-50-3 Puchasz	Deeside Gliding Club (Aberdeenshire) Ltd	
G-CICZ	Eurocopter AS.350B3 Ecureuil	Eurocopter UK Ltd	
G-CIDB	Flylight Dragon Chaser	D. M. Broom	
G-CIDD	Bellanca 7ECA Citabria	M. J. Medland	
G-CIDE	Paramania Revolution 26M	G. M. Fowler	
G-CIDF	Rotorsport UK MTOSport	K. J. Whitehead	

Notes	Reg.	Type	Owner or Operator
	G-CIDG	P & M Aviation Quik GTR	P and M Aviation Ltd
	G-CIDI	Embraer ERJ190-100LR	CIT Aerospace International
	G-CIDK	Eurocopter EC.225LP Super Puma	Wilmington Trust SP Services (Dublin) Ltd
	G-CIDL	Cameron A-300 balloon	High Road Balloons (G-LIDL)
	G-CIDM	Eurocopter EC.225LP Super Puma	Wilmington Trust SP Services (Dublin) Ltd
	G-CIDO	Glaser-Dirks DG-600/18M	S. S. M. Turner
	G-CIDP	Sonex	C. C. Miller
	G-CIDS	Ikarus C42 FB100	Ludham Airfield Ltd
	G-CIDT	Schleicher ASH-25E	S. G. Jones (G-KIGR)
	G-CIDV	Magic Laser	P. F. Brightmore
	G-CIDW	Aerotechnik EV-97 Eurostar	D. Workman
	G-CIDX	Sonex Sonex	J. P. Dilks
	G-CIDY	P&M Quik GTR	G. P. Wade
	G-CIED	Aeros Ltd Fox 16T/RIP1	P.J. Ripley
	G-CIEE	Ikarus C42 FB100	Hadair
	G-CIEI	Lindstrand CBL HS110 Airship	Lindstrand Asia Ltd (G-TRIB)
	G-CIEL	Cessna 560XL Citation Excel	Enerway Ltd
	G-CIET	Lindstrand LBL-31A balloon	C. A. Butter
	G-CIFI	Cameron Z-77 balloon	A. M. Holly (G-UKFT)
	G-CIFO	Eurofox 912(S)	Herefordshire Gliding Club Ltd
	G-CIFZ	Ikarus C42 FB80	GS Aviation (Europe) Ltd
	G-CIGS	Rotorsport UK MTOSport	G. J. Slater
	G-CIGY	Westland-Bell 47G-3B1	M. L. Romeling (G-BGXP)
	G-CIRI	Cirrus SR20	Cirrus Flyers Group
	G-CIRU	Cirrus SR20	Cirrent BV/Netherlands
	G-CITR	Cameron Z-105 balloon	A. Kaye
	G-CITY	PA-31-350 Navajo Chieftain	Blue Sky Investments Ltd
	G-CIVA	Boeing 747-436	British Airways
	G-CIVB	Boeing 747-436	British Airways
	G-CIVC	Boeing 747-436	British Airways
	G-CIVD	Boeing 747-436	British Airways
	G-CIVE	Boeing 747-436	British Airways
	G-CIVF	Boeing 747-436	British Airways
	G-CIVG	Boeing 747-436	British Airways
	G-CIVH	Boeing 747-436	British Airways
	G-CIVI	Boeing 747-436	British Airways
	G-CIVJ	Boeing 747-436	British Airways
	G-CIVK	Boeing 747-436	British Airways
	G-CIVL	Boeing 747-436	British Airways
	G-CIVM	Boeing 747-436	British Airways
	G-CIVN	Boeing 747-436	British Airways
	G-CIVO	Boeing 747-436	British Airways
	G-CIVP	Boeing 747-436	British Airways
	G-CIVR	Boeing 747-436	British Airways
	G-CIVS	Boeing 747-436	British Airways
	G-CIVT	Boeing 747-436	British Airways
	G-CIVU	Boeing 747-436	British Airways
	G-CIVV	Boeing 747-436	British Airways
	G-CIVW	Boeing 747-436	British Airways
	G-CIVX	Boeing 747-436	British Airways
	G-CIVY	Boeing 747-436	British Airways
	G-CIVZ	Boeing 747-436	British Airways
	G-CIXB	Grob G.109B	G-CIXB Syndicate
	G-CJAI	P & M Quik GT450	J. C. Kitchen
	G-CJAL	Schleicher Ka 6E	JAL Syndicate
	G-CJAO	Schempp-Hirth Discus b	O. Kahn
	G-CJAP	Ikarus C42 FB80	J. A. Paley
	G-CJAR	Schempp-Hirth Discus bT	C. J. H Donnelly
	G-CJAS	Glasflugel Standard Libelle 201B	M. J. Collett
	G-CJAT	Schleicher K8B	Wolds Gliding Club Ltd
	G-CJAV	Schleicher ASK-21	Wolds Gliding Club Ltd
	G-CJAW	Glaser-Dirks DG-200/17	P. D. Harvey
	G-CJAX	Schleicher ASK-21	Wolds Gliding Club Ltd
	G-CJAY	Mainair Pegasus Quik GT450	J. C. Kitchen
	G-CJAZ	Grob G.102 Astir CS Jeans	The Bath, Wilts and North Dorset Gliding Club
	G-CJBB	Rolladen-Schneider LS8-a	H. A. Brunt
	G-CJBC	PA-28 Cherokee 180	J. B. Cave
	G-CJBH	Eiriavion PIK-20D	537 Syndicate
	G-CJBJ	Schempp-Hirth Standard Cirrus	S. T. Dutton
	G-CJBK	Schleicher ASW-19B	D. Caielli, P. Deane & G. Nixon
	G-CJBM	Schleicher ASK-21	The Burn Gliding Club Ltd

Reg.	Type	Owner or Operator	Notes
G-CJBO	Rolladen-Schneider LS8-18	L7 Syndicate	
G-CJBR	Schempp-Hirth Discus b	G-CJBR Group	
G-CJBT	Schleicher ASW-19B	G. Dennis	
G-CJBW	Schempp-Hirth Discus bT	G-CJBW Syndicate	
G-CJBX	Rolladen-Schneider LS4-a	P. W. Lee	
G-CJBY	AB Sportine LAK-12	P. G. Steggles & N. Clarke	
G-CJBZ	Grob G.102 Astir CS	The Royal Air Force Gliding Association	
G-CJCA	Schleicher ASW-15B	S. Briggs	
G-CJCD	Schleicher ASW-24	M. D. Evershed	
G-CJCF	Grob G.102 Astir CS77	The Northumbria Gliding Club Ltd	
G-CJCG	PZL-Swidnik PW-5 Smyk	M. Evans & T. J Wallace	
G-CJCJ	Schempp-Hirth Standard Cirrus	G-CJCJ Syndicate	
G-CJCK	Schempp-Hirth Discus bT	T. Wright	
G-CJCM	Schleicher ASW-27	J. R. Klunder & K. E. Singer	
G-CJCN	Schempp-Hirth Standard Cirrus 75	F. J. Bradley	
G-CJCT	Schempp-Hirth Nimbus 4T	E. W. Richards	
G-CJCU	Schempp-Hirth Standard Cirrus B	R. A. Davenport	
G-CJCW	Grob G.102 Astir CS77	G. E. Iles & N. G. Smith	
G-CJCX	Schempp-Hirth Discus bT	C. W. M. Claxton	
G-CJCY	Rolladen-Schneider LS8-18	R. Visona & R. Zaccour	
G-CJCZ	Schleicher Ka 6CR	N. Barnes	
G-CJDB	Cessna 525 Citationjet	Breed Aircraft Ltd	
G-CJDC	Schleicher ASW-27	T. A. Sage	
G-CJDD	Glaser-Dirks DG-200/17	M. Bond	
G-CJDE	Rolladen-Schneider LS8-18	Army Gliding Association	
G-CJDG	Rolladen-Schneider LS6-b	R. H. & A. Moss	
G-CJDJ	Rolladen-Schneider LS3	J. C. Burdett	
G-CJDK	Rolladen-Schneider LS8-18	B. Bredenbeck	
G-CJDM	Schleicher ASW-15B	C. J. H. Donnelly	
G-CJDN	Cameron C-90 balloon	N. Ivison	
G-CJDP	Glaser-Dirks DG-200/17	The Owners of JDP	
G-CJDR	Schleicher ASW-15	A. K. Holden	
G-CJDS	Schempp-Hirth Standard Cirrus 75	P. Nicholls	
G-CJDT	Rolladen-Schneider LS8-a	J. N. & L. Rebbeck	
G-CJDV	DG Flugzeugbau DG-300 Elan Acro	J. M. Gilbey & B. D. Michael	
G-CJDX	Wassmer WA-28	R. Hutchinson	
G-CJEA	Rolladen-Schneider LS8-18	P. Morgan	
G-CJEB	Schleicher ASW-24	P. C. Scholz	
G-CJEC	PZL-Bielsko SZD-50-3 Puchasz	Cambridge Gliding Club Ltd	
G-CJED	Schempp-Hirth Nimbus 3/24.5	J. Edyvean	
G-CJEE	Schleicher ASW-20L	B. Pridgeon	
G-CJEH	Glasflugel Mosquito B	M. J. Vickery	
G-CJEL	Schleicher ASW-24	S. M. Chapman	
G-CJEM	Schempp-Hirth Duo Discus	Duo Discus 572 Flying Group	
G-CJEP	Rolladen-Schneider LS4-b	C. F. Carter & N. Backes	
G-CJER	Schempp-Hirth Standard Cirrus 75	Cirrus Group	
G-CJEU	Glasflugel Standard Libelle	D. B. Johns	
G-CJEV	Schempp-Hirth Standard Cirrus	R. P. Hypher & E. M. Morris	
G-CJEW	Schleicher Ka 6CR	W. J. Prince	
G-CJEX	Schempp-Hirth Ventus 2a	D. S. Watt	
G-CJEZ	Glaser-Dirks DG-100	R. Kehr	
G-CJFA	Schempp-Hirth Standard Cirrus	P. M. Sheahan	
G-CJFC	Schempp-Hirth Discus CS	The Royal Air Force Gliding and Soaring Association	
G-CJFE	Schempp-Hirth Janus CE	A. Cordonnier	
G-CJFH	Schempp-Hirth Duo Discus	The Royal Air Force Gliding and Soaring Association	
G-CJFJ	Schleicher ASW-20CL	R. J. Stirk	
G-CJFM	Schleicher ASK-13	Darlton Gliding Club Ltd	
G-CJFR	Schempp-Hirth Ventus cT	L. Rayment, D. Ryall & D. W. Smith	
G-CJFT	Schleicher K-8B	The Surrey Hills Gliding Club Ltd	
G-CJFU	Schleicher ASW-19B	M. T. Stanley	
G-CJFX	Rolladen-Schneider LS8-a	P. E. Baker	
G-CJFZ	Fedorov ME7 Mechta	R. J. Colbourne	
G-CJGB	Schleicher K 8B	Edensoaring Ltd	
G-CJGD	Scleicher K 8B	R. E. Pettifer & C. A. McLay	
G-CJGE	Schleicher ASK-21	M. R. Wall	
G-CJGF	Schempp-Hirth Ventus c	R. D. Slater	
G-CJGG	P & M Quik GT450	J. M. Pearce	
G-CJGH	Schempp-Hirth Nimbus 2C	G-CJGH Syndicate	
G-CJGJ	Schleicher ASK-21	Midland Gliding Club Ltd	

Notes	Reg.	Type	Owner or Operator
	G-CJGK	Eiri PIL-200	The Four Aces
	G-CJGL	Schempp-Hirth Discus CS	The Royal Air Force Gliding and Soaring Association
	G-CJGM	Schempp-Hirth Discus CS	The Royal Air Force Gliding and Soaring Association
	G-CJGN	Schempp-Hirth Standard Cirrus	P. A. Shuttleworth
	G-CJGR	Schempp-Hirth Discus bT	S. P. Wareham & G. W. Kemp
	G-CJGS	Rolladen-Schneider LS8-18	T. Stupnik
	G-CJGU	Schempp-Hirth Mini-Nimbus B	N. D. Ashton
	G-CJGW	Schleicher ASK-13	Darlton Gliding Club Ltd
	G-CJGX	Schleicher K 8B	Andreas K8 Group
	G-CJGY	Schempp-Hirth Standard Cirrus	P. J. Shout
	G-CJGZ	Glasflugel Standard Libelle 201B	A. & D. M. Cornish
	G-CJHD	Schleicher Ka 6E	The Royal Air Force Gliding and Soaring Association
	G-CJHE	Astir CS77	Aero Club de Portugal
	G-CJHG	Grob G.102 Astir CS	P. L. E. Zelazowski
	G-CJHJ	Glasflugel Standard Libelle 201B	N. P. Marriott
	G-CJHK	Schleicher K8B	K. J. Sturt
	G-CJHL	Schleicher Ka 6E	J. R. Gilbert
	G-CJHM	Schempp-Hirth Discus b	J. C. Thwaites
	G-CJHN	Grob G.102 Astir CS Jeans	J. C. Hurne
	G-CJHO	Schleicher ASK-18	RAF Gliding and Soaring Association
	G-CJHP	Flight Design CTSW	S. J. Reader
	G-CJHR	Centrair SNC34C Alliance	The Borders (Milfield) Gliding Club Ltd
	G-CJHS	Schleicher ASW-19B	JHS Syndicate
	G-CJHW	Glaser-Dirks DG-200	A. W. Thornhill & S. Webster
	G-CJHX	Bolkow Phoebus C	J. Hewitt
	G-CJHY	Rolladen-Schneider LS8-18	A. J. Rees & N. Wall
	G-CJHZ	Schleicher ASW-20	T. J. Stanley
	G-CJJB	Rolladen-Schneider LS4	M. Tomlinson
	G-CJJD	Schempp-Hirth Discus bT	C. E. Turner & D. Wilson
	G-CJJE	Schempp-Hirth Discus a	A. Soffici
	G-CJJH	DG Flugzeugbau DG-800S	J. S. Weston
	G-CJJJ	Schempp-Hirth Standard Cirrus	R. McLuckie
	G-CJJK	Rolladen-Schneider LS8-18	A. D. Roch
	G-CJJL	Schleicher ASW-19B	G-CJJL Group
	G-CJJP	Schempp-Hirth Duo Discus	N. Clements
	G-CJJT	Schleicher ASW-27	Portsmouth Naval Gliding Centre
	G-CJJU	Rolladen-Schneider LS8-a	A. J. French & M. N. Marshall
	G-CJJX	Schleicher ASW-15B	J. J. Sconce
	G-CJJZ	Schempp-Hirth Discus bT	S. J. C. Parker
	G-CJKA	Schleicher ASK-21	East Sussex Gliding Club Ltd
	G-CJKB	PZL-Swidnik PW-5 Smyk	A. J. Spray
	G-CJKD	Rolladen-Schneider LS8-18	D. G. Glover & A. Cockerell
	G-CJKE	PZL-Swidnik PW-5 Smyk	The Burn Gliding Club Ltd
	G-CJKF	Glaser-Dirks DG-200	D. O. Sandells & R. K. Stafford
	G-CJKG	Schleicher ASK-18	The Royal Air Force Gliding and Soaring Association
	G-CJKJ	Schleicher ASK-21	The Royal Air Force Gliding and Soaring Association
	G-CJKK	Schleicher ASK-21	Army Gliding Association
	G-CJKM	Glaser-Dirks DG200/17	G. F. Coles & E. W. Russell
	G-CJKN	Rolladen-Schneider LS8-18	G. C. Lewis
	G-CJKO	Schleicher ASK-21	The Royal Air Force Gliding and Soaring Association
	G-CJKP	Rolladen-Schneider LS4-b	D. M. Hope
	G-CJKS	Schleicher ASW-19B	R. J. P. Lancaster
	G-CJKT	Schleicher ASK-13	The Royal Air Force Gliding and Soaring Association
	G-CJKU	Schleicher ASK-18	Derbyshire & Lancashire Gliding Club Ltd
	G-CJKV	Grob G.103A Twin II Acro	The Welland Gliding Club Ltd
	G-CJKW	Grob G.102 Astir CS77	The Bath, Wilts and North Dorset Gliding Club Ltd
	G-CJKY	Schempp-Hirth Ventus cT	G. V. Matthews & M. P. Osborn
	G-CJKZ	Schleicher ASK-21	The Royal Air Force Gliding and Soaring Association
	G-CJLA	Schempp-Hirth Ventus 2cT	S. G. Jones
	G-CJLC	Schempp-Hirth Discus CS	The Royal Air Force Gliding and Soaring Association
	G-CJLF	Schleicher ASK-13	V. Mallon
	G-CJLH	Rolladen-Schneider LS4	JLH Syndicate

Reg.	Type	Owner or Operator	Notes
G-CJLJ	Rolladen-Schneider LS4-b	Army Gliding Association	
G-CJLK	Rolladen-Schneider LS7	D. N. Munro & J. P. W. Roche-Kelly	
G-CJLL	Robinson R44 II	AT and P Rentals Ltd	
G-CJLN	Rolladen-Schneider LS8-18	The Royal Air Force Gliding and Soaring Association	
G-CJLO	Schleicher ASK-13	Bowland Forest Gliding Club Ltd	
G-CJLP	Schempp-Hirth Discus CS	The Royal Air Force Gliding and Soaring Association	
G-CJLS	Schleicher K-8B	E. Ustenler	
G-CJLV	Schleicher Ka 6E	J. M. & J. C. Cooper	
G-CJLW	Schempp-Hirth Discus CS	The Royal Air Force Gliding and Soaring Association	
G-CJLX	Schempp-Hirth Standard Cirrus	L. C. Clark	
G-CJLY	Schleicher ASW-27	L. M. Astle & P. C. Piggott	
G-CJLZ	Grob G.103A Twin II Acro	21 Syndicate	
G-CJMA	Schleicher ASK-18	The Royal Air Force Gliding and Soaring Association	
G-CJMD	Embraer RJ135BJ	Hangar * AOC Ltd	
G-CJMG	PZL-Bielsko SZD-51-1 Junior	Kent Gliding Club Ltd	
G-CJMJ	Schleicher ASK-13	The Royal Air Force Gliding and Soaring Association	
G-CJMK	Schleicher ASK-18	The Royal Air Force Gliding and Soaring Association	
G-CJML	Grob G.102 Astir CS77	The Royal Air Force Gliding and Soaring Association	
G-CJMN	Schempp-Hirth Nimbus 2	R. A. Holroyd	
G-CJMO	Rolladen-Schneider LS8-18	D. J. Langrick	
G-CJMP	Schleicher ASK-13	East Sussex Gliding Club Ltd	
G-CJMS	Schleicher ASK-21	The Royal Air Force Gliding and Soaring Association	
G-CJMT	Rolladen-Schneider LS8-18	D. P. & K. M. Draper	
G-CJMU	Rolladen-Schneider LS8-18	302 Flying Group	
G-CJMV	Schempp-Hirth Nimbus-2C	G. Tucker & K. R. Walton	
G-CJMW	Schleicher ASK-13	The Royal Air Force Gliding and Soaring Association	
G-CJMX	Schleicher ASK-13	Shalbourne Soaring Society Ltd	
G-CJMY	PZL-Bielsko SZD-51-1 Junior	Highland Gliding Club Ltd	
G-CJMZ	Schleicher ASK-13	Devon & Somerset Gliding Club Ltd	
G-CJNA	Grob G.102 Astir CS Jeans	Shenington Gliding Club	
G-CJNB	Rolladen-Schneider LS8-18	Tatenhill Aviation Ltd	
G-CJNE	Schempp-Hirth Discus 2a	R. Priest	
G-CJNF	Schempp-Hirth Discus 2a	M. Scutter	
G-CJNG	Glasflugel Standard Libelle 201B	C. A. Willson	
G-CJNJ	Rolladen-Schneider LS8-18	A. B. Laws	
G-CJNK	Rolladen-Schneider LS8-18	Army Gliding Association	
G-CJNN	Schleicher K 8B	Buckminster Gliding Club Ltd	
G-CJNO	Glaser-Dirks DG-300 Elan	Yankee Kilo Group	
G-CJNP	Rolladen-Schneider LS6-b	E. & P. S. Fink	
G-CJNR	Glasflugel Mosquito B	S. L. Barnes & C. R. North	
G-CJNT	Schleicher ASW-19B	M. D. Borrowdale	
G-CJNZ	Glaser-Dirks DG-100	T. Tordoff & R. Jones	
G-CJOA	Schempp-Hirth Discus b	The Royal Air Force Gliding and Soaring Association	
G-CJOB	Schleicher K 8B	JQB Syndicate	
G-CJOC	Schempp-Hirth Discus bT	287 Syndicate	
G-CJOD	Rolladen-Schneider LS8-18	The Royal Air Force Gliding and Soaring Association	
G-CJOE	Schempp-Hirth Standard Cirrus	D. I. Bolsdon & P. T. Johnson	
G-CJOG	Grob G.103A Twin II Acro	Acro Syundicate	
G-CJOJ	Schleicher K 8B	H. Reeves	
G-CJON	Grob G.102 Astir CS77	The Royal Air Force Gliding and Soaring Association	
G-CJOO	Schempp-Hirth Duo Discus	185 Syndicate	
G-CJOP	Centrair 101A Pegase	P. A. Woodcock	
G-CJOR	Schempp-Hirth Ventus 2cT	A. M. George & N. A. Maclean	
G-CJOS	Schempp-Hirth Standard Cirrus	G-CJOS Group	
G-CJOU	AB Sportline Aviacija LAK-17A	B. Dorozko	
G-CJOV	Schleicher ASW-27	J. W. White	
G-CJOW	Schempp-Hirth Cirrus VTC	North Wales Gliding Club Ltd	
G-CJOX	Schleicher ASK-21	Southdown Gliding Club Ltd	
G-CJOZ	Schleicher K 8B	Derbyshire and Lancashire Gliding Club Ltd	

Notes	Reg.	Type	Owner or Operator
	G-CJPA	Schempp-Hirth Duo Discus	Coventry Gliding Club Ltd
	G-CJPC	Schleicher ASK-13	Shalbourne Soaring Society Ltd
	G-CJPJ	Grob G.104 Speed Astir IIB	R. J. L. Maisonpierre
	G-CJPL	Rolladen-Schneider LS8-18	I. A. Reekie
	G-CJPM	Grob G.102 Astir CS Jeans	G-CJPM Syndicate
	G-CJPO	Schleicher ASK-18	The Royal Air Force Gliding and Soaring Association
	G-CJPP	Schempp-Hirth Discus b	S. R. Thompson
	G-CJPR	Rolladen-Schneider LS8-18	D. M. Byass & J. A. McCoshim
	G-CJPT	Schleicher ASW-27	R. C. Willis-Fleming
	G-CJPV	Schleicher ASK-13	Cyprus Gliding Group/Cyprus
	G-CJPW	Glaser-Dirks DG-200	A. Brownbridge & A. Kitchen
	G-CJPX	Schleicher ASW-15	R. Hayden & P. Daly
	G-CJPY	Schleicher ASK-13	The Royal Air Force Gliding and Soaring Association
	G-CJPZ	Schleicher ASK-18	The Royal Air Force Gliding and Soaring Association
	G-CJRA	Rolladen-Schneider LS8-18	J. Williams
	G-CJRB	Schleicher ASW-19B	J. W. Baxter
	G-CJRC	Glaser-Dirks DG-300 Elan	P. J. Sillett
	G-CJRD	Grob G.102 Astir CS	A. J. Hadwin
	G-CJRE	Scleicher ASW-15	R. A. Starling
	G-CJRF	PZL-Bielsko SZD-50-3 Puchacz	Wolds Gliding Club Ltd
	G-CJRG	Schempp-Hirth Standard Cirrus	N. J. Laux
	G-CJRH	Schleicher ASW-27	C. Jackson & P. C. Jarvis
	G-CJRJ	PZL-Bielsko SZD-50-3 Puchacz	Derbyshire & Lancashire Gliding Club Ltd
	G-CJRL	Glaser-Dirks DG-100G Elan	P. Lazenby
	G-CJRM	Grob G.102 Astir CS	M. P. Webb
	G-CJRN	Glaser-Dirks DG-200/17	T. G. Roberts
	G-CJRR	Schempp-Hirth Discus bT	N. A. Hays
	G-CJRT	Schempp-Hirth Standard Cirrus	N. G. Henry
	G-CJRU	Schleicher ASW-24	S. A. Kerby
	G-CJRV	Schleicher ASW-19B	M. Roome & R. Taylor
	G-CJRX	Schleicher ASK-13	The Royal Air Force Gliding and Soaring Association
	G-CJSA	Nanchang NAMC CJ-6A	Fordaire Aviation Ltd
	G-CJSC	Schempp-Hirth Nimbus-3DT	S. G. Jones
	G-CJSD	Grob G.102 Astir CS	The Royal Air Force Gliding and Soaring Association
	G-CJSE	Schempp-Hirth Discus b	Imperial College of Science, Technology and Medicine
	G-CJSG	Schleicher Ka 6E	A. J. Emck
	G-CJSH	Grob G.102 Club Astir IIIB	Lasham Gliding Society Ltd
	G-CJSJ	Rolladen-Schneider LS7-WL	S. P. Woolcock
	G-CJSK	Grob G.102 Astir CS	Sierra Kilo Group
	G-CJSL	Schempp-Hirth Ventus cT	D. Latimer
	G-CJSN	Schleicher K 8B	Cotswold Gliding Club
	G-CJSS	Schleicher ASW-27	G. K. & S. R. Drury
	G-CJST	Rolladen-Schneider LS1-c	W. A. Bowness & E. Richar
	G-CJSU	Rolladen-Schneider LS8-18	J. G. Bell
	G-CJSV	Schleicher ASK-13	The Royal Air Force Gliding and Soaring Association
	G-CJSW	Rolladen-Schneider LS4-a	C. Benoit
	G-CJSX	AMS-Flight DG-500	Oxford Gliding Company Ltd
	G-CJSZ	Schleicher ASK-18	C. Weston
	G-CJTB	Schleicher ASW-24	V17 Syndicate
	G-CJTH	Schleicher ASW-24	R. J. & J. E. Lodge
	G-CJTJ	Schempp-Hirth Mini-Nimbus B	R. A. Bowker
	G-CJTK	DG Flugzeugbau DG-300 Elan Acro	D. G. Pask
	G-CJTL	Rolladen-Schneider LS8-18	J. M. & R. S. Hood
	G-CJTM	Rolladen-Schneider LS8-18	A. D. Holmes
	G-CJTN	Glaser-Dirks DG-300 Elan	A. D. Noble & P. W. Schartau
	G-CJTO	Glasflugel H303A Mosquito	Tango Oscar Group
	G-CJTP	Schleicher ASW-20L	C. A. Sheldon
	G-CJTR	Rolladen-Schneider LS7-WL	D53 Syndicate
	G-CJTS	Schempp-Hirth Cirrus VTC	G-CJTS Cirrus Group
	G-CJTU	Schempp-Hirth Duo Discus T	JTU Syndicate
	G-CJTV	Cessna 525A Citationjet CJ2	Arena Aviation (G-EDCL)
	G-CJTW	Glasflugel Mosquito B	S. Urry
	G-CJTY	Rolladen-Schneider LS8-a	BBC (London) Club
	G-CJUB	Schempp-Hirth Discus CS	Coventry Gliding Club Ltd

Reg.	Type	Owner or Operator	Notes
G-CJUD	Denney Kitfox Mk 3	D. Joy	
G-CJUF	Schempp-Hirth Ventus 2cT	M. H. B. Pope	
G-CJUJ	Schleicher ASW-27	P. A. Ivens	
G-CJUK	Grob G.102 Astir CS	P. Freer & S. J. Calvert	
G-CJUM	Schempp-Hirth Duo Discus T	2 UP Group	
G-CJUN	Schleicher ASW-19B	M. P. S. Roberts	
G-CJUP	Schempp-Hirth Discus 2b	The Discuss 2 Uniform Papa Group	
G-CJUR	Valentin Mistral C	M. J. W. Harris	
G-CJUS	Grob G.102 Astir CS	East Sussex Gliding Club Ltd	
G-CJUU	Schempp-Hirth Standard Cirrus	H. R. Fraser	
G-CJUV	Schempp-Hirth Discus b	Lasham Gliding Society Ltd	
G-CJUX	Aviastroitel AC-4C	R. J. Walton	
G-CJUZ	Schleicher ASW-19B	K. W. Clarke	
G-CJVA	Schempp-Hirth Ventus 2cT	M. S. Armstrong	
G-CJVB	Schempp-Hirth Discus bT	C. J. Edwards	
G-CJVC	PZL-Bielsko SZD-51-1 Junior	York Gliding Centre Ltd	
G-CJVE	Eiriavion PIK-20D	S. R. Wilkinson	
G-CJVF	Schempp-Hirth Discus CS	J. Hodgson	
G-CJVG	Schempp-Hirth Discus bT	S. J. Bryan & P. J. Bramley	
G-CJVJ	AB Sportine LAK-17A	J. A. Sutton	
G-CJVL	DG-300 Elan	A. T. Vidion & A. Griffiths	
G-CJVM	Schleicher ASW-27	G. K. Payne	
G-CJVP	Glaser-Dirks DG-200	M. S. Howey & S. Leadbeater	
G-CJVS	Schleicher ASW-28	A. & G. S. J. Bambrook	
G-CJVU	Standard Cirrus CS-11-75L	Cirrus 75 Syndicate	
G-CJVV	Schempp-Hirth Janus C	J50 Syndicate	
G-CJVW	Schleicher ASW-15	Victor Whiskey Group	
G-CJVX	Schempp-Hirth Discus CS	G-CJVX Syndicate	
G-CJVZ	Schleicher ASK-21	Yorkshire Gliding Club (Proprietary) Ltd	
G-CJWA	Schleicher ASW-28	P. R. Porter & M. J. Taylor	
G-CJWB	Schleicher ASK-13	East Sussex Gliding Club Ltd	
G-CJWD	Schleicher ASK-21	London Gliding Club Proprietary Ltd	
G-CJWF	Schleicher ASW-27	B. A. Fairston & A. Stotter	
G-CJWG	Schempp-Hirth Nimbus 3	880 Group	
G-CJWJ	Schleicher ASK-13	The Royal Air Force Gliding and Soaring Association	
G-CJWK	Schempp-Hirth Discus bT	722 Syndicate	
G-CJWM	Grob G.103 Twin Astir II	Norfolk Gliding Club Ltd	
G-CJWP	Bolkow Phoebus B1	A. Fidler	
G-CJWR	Grob G.102 Astir CS	Cairngorm Gliding Club	
G-CJWT	Glaser-Dirks DG-200	K. R. Nash	
G-CJWU	Schempp-Hirth Ventus bT	B. C. P. & C. Crook	
G-CJWX	Schempp-Hirth Ventus 2cT	M. M. A. Lipperheide & S. G. Olender	
G-CJXA	Schempp-Hirth Nimbus 3	Y44 Syndicate	
G-CJXB	Centrair 201B Marianne	A. C. Cherry	
G-CJXC	Wassmer WA28	A. P. Montague	
G-CJXG	Eiriavion PIK-20D	W5 Group	
G-CJXL	Schempp-Hirth Discus CS	J. Hall & M. J. Hasluck	
G-CJXM	Schleicher ASK-13	The Windrushers Gliding Club	
G-CJXN	Centrair 201B	R. D. Trussell	
G-CJXP	Glaser-Dirks DG-100	N. L. Morris	
G-CJXR	Schempp-Hirth Discus b	Cambridge Gliding Club Ltd	
G-CJXT	Schleicher ASW-24B	P. McAuley	
G-CJXW	Schempp-Hirth Duo Discus T	R. A. Beatty	
G-CJXX	Pilatus B4-PC11AF	N. H. Buckenham	
G-CJXY	Neukom Elfe S4A	J. Hunt	
G-CJYC	Grob G.102 Astir CS	R. A. Christie	
G-CJYD	Schleicher ASW-27	J. E. Gatfield	
G-CJYE	Schleicher ASK-13	North Wales Gliding Club Ltd	
G-CJYF	Schempp Hirth Discus CS	C. D. Sword	
G-CJYL	AB Sportine Aviacija LAK-12	A. Camerotto	
G-CJYO	Glaser-Dirks DG-100G Elan	A. M. Booth	
G-CJYP	Grob G.102 Club Astir II	M. D. Vanston	
G-CJYR	Schempp-Hirth Duo Discus T	CJYR Flying Group	
G-CJYS	Schempp-Hirth Mini Nimbus C	A. Jenkins	
G-CJYU	Schempp-Hirth Ventus 2cT	The Royal Air Force Gliding and Soaring Association	
G-CJYV	Schleicher K8B	Club Agrupacion de Pilotos del Sureste/Spain	
G-CJYW	Schleicher K8B	Club Agrupacion de Pilotos del Sureste/Spain	
G-CJYX	Rolladen-Schneider LS3-17	D. Meyer-Beeck & V. G. Diaz	
G-CJZB	DG-500 Elan Orion	Bicester JZB Syndicate	

Notes	Reg.	Type	Owner or Operator
	G-CJZE	Schleicher ASK-13	Needwood Forest Gliding Club Ltd
	G-CJZG	Schempp-Hirth Discus bT	I. K. G. Mitchell
	G-CJZH	Schleicher ASW-20 CL	C. P. Gibson & C. A. Hunt
	G-CJZK	DG-505 Elan Orion	Devon and Somerset Gliding Club Ltd
	G-CJZL	Schempp-Hirth Mini Nimbus B	P. A. Dunthorne
	G-CJZM	Schempp-Hirth Ventus 2a	S. Crabb
	G-CJZN	Schleicher ASW-28	P. J. Coward
	G-CJZY	Grob G.102 Standard Astir III	Lasham Gliding Society Ltd
	G-CJZZ	Rolladen-Schneider LS7	Birkett Air Services Ltd
	G-CKAC	Glaser-Dirks DG-200	M. G. Stringer
	G-CKAE	Centrair 101A Pegase	M. Manning & C. Martin-Pitt
	G-CKAK	Schleicher ASW-28	S. J. Kelman
	G-CKAL	Schleicher ASW-28	D. A. Smith
	G-CKAM	Glasflugel Club Libelle 205	P. A. Cronk & R. C. Tallowin
	G-CKAN	PZL-Bielsko SZD-50-3 Puchacz	The Bath Wilts and North Dorset Gliding Club Ltd
	G-CKAP	Schempp-Hirth Discus CS	H. A. Johnston & R. Gollings
	G-CKAR	Schempp-Hirth Duo Discus T	977 Syndicate
	G-CKAS	Schempp-Hirth Ventus 2cT	KAS Club
	G-CKAU	DG Flugzeugbau DG-303 Elan Acro	G. Earle
	G-CKAX	AMS-Flight DG-500 Elan Orion	York Gliding Centre Ltd
	G-CKAY	Grob G.102 Astir CS	D. J. Ryder
	G-CKBA	Centrair 101A Pegase	KBA Pegase 101A Syndicate
	G-CKBC	Rolladen-Schneider LS6-c18	A. W. Lyth
	G-CKBD	Grob G.102 Astir CS	Astir KBD Syndicate
	G-CKBF	AMS-Flight DG-303 Elan	A. L. Garfield
	G-CKBG	Schempp-Hirth Ventus 2cT	D. Martin& R. Bollom
	G-CKBH	Rolladen-Schneider LS6	F. C. Ballard & P. Walker
	G-CKBK	Schempp-Hirth Ventus 2cT	D. Rhys-Jones
	G-CKBL	Grob G.102 Astir CS	Norfolk Gliding Club Ltd
	G-CKBM	Schleicher ASW-28	C. S. & M. E. Newland-Smith
	G-CKBN	PZL-Bielsko SZD-55-1 Promyk	N. D. Pearson
	G-CKBT	Schempp-Hirth Standard Cirrus	P. R. Johnson
	G-CKBU	Schleicher ASW-28	G. C. Metcalfe
	G-CKBV	Schleicher ASW-28	P. Whipp
	G-CKBX	Schleicher ASW-27	M. Wright
	G-CKCB	Rolladen-Schneider LS4-a	The Bristol Gliding Club Proprietary Ltd
	G-CKCD	Schempp-Hirth Ventus 2cT	R. S. Jobar & S. G. Jones
	G-CKCE	Schempp-Hirth Ventus 2cT	M. W. Cater & J. P. Walker
	G-CKCH	Schempp-Hirth Ventus 2cT	J. J. Pridal & L. R. Marks
	G-CKCJ	Schleicher ASW-28	S. L. Withall
	G-CKCK	Enstrom 280FX	Rhoburt Ltd
	G-CKCM	Glasflugel Standard Libelle 201B	G. A. Cox
	G-CKCN	Schleicher ASW-27	W. J. Head
	G-CKCP	Grob G.102 Astir CS	Norfolk Gliding Club Ltd
	G-CKCR	AB Sportine Aviacija LAK-17A	M. Kessler/Italy
	G-CKCT	Schleicher ASK-21	Kent Gliding Club Aircraft Ltd
	G-CKCV	Schempp-Hirth Duo Discus T	WE4 Group
	G-CKCY	Schleicher ASW-20	J. Sugden
	G-CKCZ	Schleicher ASK-21	Booker Gliding Club Ltd
	G-CKDA	Schempp-Hirth Ventus 2B	D. J. Eade
	G-CKDB	Schleicher Ka 6CR	Banbury Gliding Club Ltd
	G-CKDC	Centrair ASW-20F	M. Staljan, S. Brogger & C. Behrendt
	G-CKDF	Schleicher ASK-21	Portsmouth Naval Gliding Centre
	G-CKDK	Rolladen-Schneider LS4-a	M. C. & P. A. Ridger
	G-CKDN	Schleicher ASW-27B	J. S. McCullagh
	G-CKDO	Schempp-Hirth Ventus 2cT	M. W. Edwards
	G-CKDP	Schleicher ASK-21	Kent Gliding Club Aircraft Ltd
	G-CKDR	PZL-Bielsko SZD-48-3 Jantar Standard 3	G. Hyrkowski
	G-CKDS	Schleicher ASW-27	A. W. Gillett & G. D. Morris
	G-CKDU	Glaser-Dirks DG-200/17	P. G. Noonan
	G-CKDV	Schempp-Hirth Ventus B/16.6	M. A. Codd
	G-CKDW	Schleicher ASW-27	C. Colton
	G-CKDX	Glaser-Dirks DG-200	Delta X Ray Group
	G-CKDY	Glaser-Dirks DG-100	503 Syndicate
	G-CKDZ	Schempp-Hirth Standard Cirrus 75	Charlie 75
	G-CKEA	Schempp-Hirth Cirrus 18	C. M. Reed
	G-CKEB	Schempp-Hirth Standard Cirrus	A. J. Mugleston
	G-CKED	Schleicher ASW-27B	A. & R. Maskell
	G-CKEE	Grob G.102 Astir CS	Essex and Suffolk Gliding Club Ltd
	G-CKEJ	Schleicher ASK-21	London Gliding Club Proprietary Ltd

Reg.	Type	Owner or Operator	Notes
G-CKEK	Schleicher ASK-21	Devon and Somerset Gliding Club Ltd	
G-CKEP	Rolladen-Schneider LS6-b	G-CKEP Group	
G-CKER	Schleicher ASW-19B	W. A. Bowness & E. Richards	
G-CKES	Schempp-Hirth Cirrus 18	D. Judd & N. Hawley	
G-CKET	Rolladen-Schneider LS8-8	M. B. Jefferyes & J. C. Taylor	
G-CKEV	Schempp-Hirth Duo Discus	The Royal Air Force Gliding and Soaring Association	
G-CKEY	PA-28-161 Warrior II	Warwickshire Aviation Ltd	
G-CKEZ	DG Flugzeugbau LS8	D. A. Jesty	
G-CKFA	Schempp-Hirth Standard Cirrus 75	G. C. Bell	
G-CKFB	Schempp-Hirth Discus-2T	P. L. & P. A. G. Holland	
G-CKFC	Schempp-Hirth Ventus 2cT	P. Lecci	
G-CKFD	Schleicher ASW-27B	W. T. Craig	
G-CKFE	Eiriavion PIK-20D	O. Houlihan	
G-CKFG	Grob G.103A Twin II Acro	The Surrey Hills Gliding Club Ltd	
G-CKFH	Schempp-Hirth Mini Nimbus	G-CKFH Flying Group	
G-CKFJ	Schleicher ASK-13	York Gliding Centre Ltd	
G-CKFK	Schempp-Hirth Standard Cirrus 75	P. R. Wilkinson	
G-CKFL	Rolladen-Schneider LS4	D. O'Brien & D. R. Taylor	
G-CKFN	DG Flugzeugbau DG1000	Yorkshire Gliding Club (Proprietary) Ltd	
G-CKFP	Schempp-Hirth Ventus 2cxT	C. R. Sutton	
G-CKFR	Schleicher ASK-13	Club Acrupacion de Pilotos del Sureste/Spain	
G-CKFT	Schempp-Hirth Duo Discus T	Duo Discus Syndicate	
G-CKFV	DG Flugzeugbau LS8-t	G. A. Rowden & K. I. Arkley	
G-CKFX	Centrair 101AP	G_CKFX Flying Group	
G-CKFY	Schleicher ASK.21	Cambridge Gliding Club	
G-CKGA	Schempp-Hirth Ventus 2cxT	D. R. Campbell	
G-CKGC	Schempp-Hirth Ventus 2cxT	C. P. A. Jeffery	
G-CKGD	Schempp-Hirth Ventus 2cxT	C. Morris	
G-CKGF	Schempp-Hirth Duo Discus T	Duo 233 Group	
G-CKGH	Grob G.102 Club Astir II	I. M. Gavan	
G-CKGK	Schleicher ASK-21	The Royal Air Force Gliding & Soaring Association	
G-CKGL	Schempp-Hirth Ventus 2cT	Kilo Golf Lima Syndicate	
G-CKGM	Centrair 101A Pegase	S. France	
G-CKGU	Schleicher ASW-19B	ASW 19 KGU Group	
G-CKGV	Schleicher ASW-20	A. H. Reynolds	
G-CKGX	Schleicher ASK-21	Coventry Gliding Club Ltd	
G-CKGY	Scheibe Bergfalke IV	B. R. Pearson	
G-CKHA	PZL SZD-51-1 Junior	Devon & Somerset Gliding Club Ltd	
G-CKHB	Rolladen-Schneider LS3	C. J. Cole	
G-CKHC	DG Flugzeugbau DG.505	G-CKHC Group	
G-CKHD	Schleicher ASW-27B	N. D Tillett	
G-CKHE	AB Sportine Aviacija LAK-17AT	N. J. Gough & A. J. Garrity	
G-CKHG	Schleicher ASW-27B	R. A. F. King	
G-CKHH	Schleicher ASK-13	The South Wales Gliding Club Ltd	
G-CKHK	Schempp-Hirth Duo Discus T	Duo Discus Syndicate	
G-CKHM	Centrair 101A Pegase 90	J. Randall & J. A. Tipler	
G-CKHN	PZL SZD-51-1 Junior	The Nene Valley Gliding Club Ltd	
G-CKHR	PZL-Bielsko SZD-51-1 Junior	Wolds Gliding Club Ltd	
G-CKHS	Rolladen-Schneider LS7-WL	M. Lawson & D. Wallis	
G-CKHV	Glaser-Dirks DG-100	G-CKHV Trust	
G-CKHW	PZL SZD-50-3 Puchacz	Derbyshire and Lancashire Gliding Club Ltd	
G-CKJB	Schempp-Hirth Ventus bT	J. R. Matthews & J. R. Rayner	
G-CKJC	Schempp-Hirth Nimbus 3T	A. C. Wright	
G-CKJD	Schempp-Hirth Cirrus 75-VTC	P. J. P. Vanden Boer	
G-CKJE	DG Flugzeugbau LS8-18	M. D. Wells	
G-CKJF	Schempp-Hirth Standard Cirrus	L. A. Lawes	
G-CKJG	Schempp-Hirth Cirrus VTC	S. J. Wright	
G-CKJH	Glaser-Dirks DG.300 Elan	Yorkshire Gliding Club	
G-CKJJ	DG Flugzeugbau DG-500 Elan Orion	Ulster Gliding Club Ltd	
G-CKJL	Scleicher ASK-13	Lincolnshire Gliding Club Ltd	
G-CKJM	Schempp-Hirth Ventus cT	G-CKJM Group	
G-CKJN	Schleicher ASW-20	R. Logan	
G-CKJP	Schleicher ASK-21	The Royal Air Force Gliding and Soaring Association	
G-CKJS	Schleicher ASW-28-18E	G-CKJS Syndicate	
G-CKJV	Schleicher ASW-28-18E	A. C. Price	
G-CKJZ	Schempp-Hirth Discus bT	G-CKJZ Group	
G-CKKB	Centrair 101A Pegase	D. M. Rushton	
G-CKKC	DG Flugzeugbau DG-300 Elan Acro	Charlie Kilo Kilo Charlie Syndicate	

Notes	Reg.	Type	Owner or Operator
	G-CKKE	Schempp-Hirth Duo Discus T	The Foxtrot Group
	G-CKKF	Schempp-Hirth Ventus 2cT	A. R. MacGregor
	G-CKKH	Schleicher ASW-27	P. L. Hurd
	G-CKKK	AB Sportine Aviacija LAK-17A	C. J. Nicolas
	G-CKKP	Schleicher ASK-21	Bowland Forest Gliding Club Ltd
	G-CKKR	Schleicher ASK-13	The Windrushers Gliding Club Ltd
	G-CKKV	DG Flugzeugbau DG-1000S	Lasham Gliding Society Ltd
	G-CKKX	Rolladen-Schneider LS4-A	B. W. Svenson
	G-CKKY	Schempp-Hirth Duo Discus T	P. D. Duffin
	G-CKLA	Schleicher ASK-13	Booker Gliding Club Ltd
	G-CKLC	Glasflugel H206 Hornet	W. Ellis
	G-CKLD	Schempp-Hirth Discus 2cT	797 Syndicate
	G-CKLF	Schempp-Hirth Janus	Kilo Lima Foxtrot
	G-CKLG	Rolladen-Schneider LS4	P. M. Scheiwiller
	G-CKLN	Rolladen-Schneider LS4-A	Army Gliding Association
	G-CKLP	Scleicher ASW-28-18	J. T. Birch
	G-CKLR	Pezetel SZD-55-1	Zulu Five Gliding Group (G-CKLM)
	G-CKLS	Rolladen-Schneider LS4	Wolds Gliding Club Ltd
	G-CKLT	Schempp-Hirth Nimbus 3/24.5	G. N. Thomas
	G-CKLV	Schempp-Hirth Discus 2cT	S. Baker
	G-CKLW	Schleicher ASK-21	Yorkshire Gliding Club
	G-CKLY	DG Flugzeugbau DG-1000T	G-CKLY Flying Group
	G-CKMA	DG Flugzeugbau LS8-T	W. J. Morecraft
	G-CKMB	AB Sportline Aviacija LAK-19T	D. J. McKenzie
	G-CKMD	Schempp-Hirth Standard Cirrus	S. A. Crabb
	G-CKME	DG Flugzeugbau LS8-T	S. M. Smith
	G-CKMF	Centrair 101A Pegase	D. L. M. Jamin
	G-CKMG	Glaser-Dirks DG-101G Elan	R. A. Johnson
	G-CKMI	Schleicher K8C	V. Mallon
	G-CKMJ	Schleicher Ka 6CR	V. Mallon
	G-CKML	Schempp-Hirth Duo Discus T	G-CKML Group
	G-CKMM	Schleicher ASW-28-18E	R. G. Munro
	G-CKMO	Rolladen-Schneider LS7-WL	G. E. M. Turpin
	G-CKMP	AB Sportine Aviacija LAK-17A	J. L. McIver
	G-CKMT	Grob G103C	Essex & Suffolk Gliding Club Ltd
	G-CKMV	Rolladen-Schneider LS3-17	S. Procter & M. P. Woolmer
	G-CKMW	Schleicher ASK-21	The Royal Air Force Gliding & Soaring Association
	G-CKMZ	Schleicher ASW-28-18	G. A. Marshall & G. N. Fraser
	G-CKNB	Schempp-Hirth Standard Cirrus	A. Booker
	G-CKNC	Caproni Calif A21S	J. J. & M. E. Pritchard
	G-CKND	DG Flugzeugbau DG-1000T	KND Group
	G-CKNE	Schempp-Hirth Standard Cirrus 75-VTC	G. D. E. Macdonald
	G-CKNF	DG Flugzeugbau DG-1000T	Six November Fox
	G-CKNG	Schleicher ASW-28-18E	M. P. Brockinhton
	G-CKNK	Glaser-Dirks DG.500	Cotswold Gliding Club
	G-CKNL	Schleicher ASK-21	Buckminster Gliding Club Ltd
	G-CKNM	Scleicher ASK-18	I. L. Pattingale
	G-CKNO	Schempp-Hirth Ventus 2cxT	R. T. Starling
	G-CKNR	Schempp-Hirth Ventus 2cxT	R. J. Nicholls
	G-CKNS	Rolladen-Schneider LS4-A	I. R. Willows
	G-CKNV	Schleicher ASW-28-18E	The KNV Group
	G-CKOD	Schempp-Hirth Discus BT	A. L. Harris & M. W. Talbot
	G-CKOE	Schleicher ASW-27-18	R. C. Bromwich
	G-CKOH	DG Flugzeugbau DG-1000T	Oscar Hotel Group
	G-CKOI	AB Sportine Aviacija LAK-17AT	C. G. Corbett
	G-CKOK	Schempp-Hirth Discus 2cT	P. Topping
	G-CKOL	Schempp-Hirth Duo Discus T	Oscar Lima Syndicate
	G-CKOM	Schleicher ASW-27-18	L. M. P. Wells
	G-CKON	Schleicher ASW-27-18E	J. P. Gorringe
	G-CKOO	Schleicher ASW-27-18E	A. Darlington, J. P. Lewis & C. T. P. Williams
	G-CKOR	Glaser-Dirks DG-300 Elan	J. A. Sparrow
	G-CKOT	Schleicher ASK-21	Ulster Gliding Club Ltd
	G-CKOU	AB Sportine Aviacija LAK-19T	PAC LAK Syndicate
	G-CKOW	DG-505 Elan Orion	Southdown Gliding Club Ltd
	G-CKOX	AMS-Flight DG-505 Elan Orion	Seahawk Gliding Club
	G-CKOY	Schleicher ASW-27-18E	G-CKOY Group
	G-CKOZ	Schleicher ASW-27-18E	E. W. Johnston
	G-CKPA	AB Sportline Aviacija LAK-19T	O. R. Momege
	G-CKPE	Schempp-Hirth Duo Discus	Portsmouth Naval Gliding Centre
	G-CKPG	Schempp-Hirth Discus 2cT	G. Knight & P. Rowden
	G-CKPJ	Neukom S-4D Elfe	S. Szladowski

Reg.	Type	Owner or Operator	Notes
G-CKPK	Schempp-Hirth Ventus 2cxT	I. C. Lees	
G-CKPM	DG Flugzeugbau LS8-T	8T Soaring	
G-CKPN	PZL-Bielsko SZD-51-1 Junior	Rattlesden Gliding Club Ltd	
G-CKPO	Schempp-Hirth Duo Discus xT	KPO Syndicate	
G-CKPP	Schleicher ASK-21	The Gliding Centre	
G-CKPU	Schleicher ASW-27-18E	A. J. Kellerman	
G-CKPV	Schempp-Hirth HS.7 Mini-Nimbus B	D. K. McCarthy	
G-CKPX	ZS Jezow PW-6U	North Wales Gliding Club Ltd	
G-CKPY	Schempp-Hirth Duo Discus xT	Duo-Discus Syndicate	
G-CKPZ	Schleicher ASW-20	T. Davies	
G-CKRB	Schleicher ASK-13	Derbyshire and Lancashire Gliding Club Ltd	
G-CKRC	Schleicher ASW-28-18E	M. Woodcock	
G-CKRD	Schleicher ASW-27-18E	R. F. Thirkell	
G-CKRF	DG-300 Elan	G. A. King	
G-CKRH	Grob G.103 Twin Astir II	Staffordshire Gliding Club Ltd	
G-CKRI	Schleicher ASK-21	Kent Gliding Club Aircraft Ltd	
G-CKRJ	Schleicher ASW-27-18E	J. J. Marshall	
G-CKRN	Grob G.102 Astir CS	Yorkshire Gliding Club (Proprietary) Ltd	
G-CKRO	Schempp-Hirth Duo Discus T	Duo Discus Syndicate KRO	
G-CKRR	Schleicher ASW-15B	C. D. Ellis	
G-CKRS	FFA Diamant 16.5	R. J. Aylesbury & J. Young	
G-CKRU	ZS Jezow PW-6U	Cotswold Gliding Club	
G-CKRV	Schleicher ASW-27-18E	Z. Marczynski	
G-CKRW	Schleicher ASK-21	The Royal Air Force Gliding and Soaring Association	
G-CKRX	Jezow PW-6U	Cotswold Gliding Club	
G-CKSC	Czech Sport Aircraft Sportcruiser	Czechmate Syndicate	
G-CKSD	Rolladen-Schneider LS8-a	J. H. Cox & K. A. Fox	
G-CKSK	Pilatus B4-PC11	K. Steinmair	
G-CKSL	Schleicher ASW-15B	Sierra Lima Group	
G-CKSM	Schempp-Hirth Duo Discus T	J. H. May & S. P. Ball	
G-CKSX	Schleicher ASW-27-18E	M. C. Foreman	
G-CKSY	Rolladen-Schneider LS-7-WL	C. M. Lewis	
G-CKTB	Schempp-Hirth Ventus 2cT	M. H. Player	
G-CKTC	Schleicher Ka 6CR	Tango Charlie Group	
G-CKZT	PA-28-235 Cherokee Pathfinder	U. Chakravorty	
G-CLAC	PA-28-161 Warrior II	G-CLAC Group	
G-CLAD	Cameron V-90 balloon	Adeilad Cladding	
G-CLAR	EC.225LP Super Puma	CHC Scotia Ltd	
G-CLAV	Shaw Europa	G. Laverty	
G-CLAY	Bell 206B JetRanger 3	Claygate Distribution Ltd (G-DENN)	
G-CLDS	Rotorsport UK Calidus	T. R. Galloway	
G-CLEA	PA-28-161 Warrior II	Freedom Aviation Ltd	
G-CLEE	Rans S.6-ES Coyote II	P. S. Chapman	
G-CLEG	Flight Design CTSW	C. A. S. Powell	
G-CLEM	Bölkow Bö.208A2 Junior	G-CLEM Group (G-ASWE)	
G-CLEO	Zenair CH.601HD	K. M. Bowen	
G-CLES	Schleicher ASW-27-18E	A. P. Brown & N. D. Tillett	
G-CLEU	Glaser-Dirks DG-200	S. F. Tape	
G-CLFB	Rolladen-Schneider LS4-A	K2 Syndicate	
G-CLFC	Mainair Blade	G. N. Cliffe & G. Marshall	
G-CLFH	Schleicher ASW-20C	T. Fordwich-Gorefly & P. Armstrong	
G-CLFX	Schempp-Hirth Duo Discus T	A. L. Baillie	
G-CLFZ	Schleicher ASW-18E	C. F. Cownden & J. P. Davies	
G-CLGC	Schempp-Hirth Duo Discus	London Gliding Club Proprietary Ltd	
G-CLGL	Schempp-Hirth Ventus 2c	M. J. Collett and A. Hegner	
G-CLGR	Glasflugel Club Libelle 205	A. A. Gillon	
G-CLGT	Rolladen-Schneider LS4	C. B. & N. M. Hill	
G-CLGU	Schleicher ASW-27-18	T. J. Scott	
G-CLGW	Centrair 101A Pegase	M. White	
G-CLGZ	Schempp-Hirth Duo Discus T	D. R. Irving	
G-CLHF	Scheibe Bergfalke IV	Andreas Gliding Club Ltd	
G-CLHG	Schempp-Hirth Discus b	S. J. Edinborough	
G-CLIC	Cameron A-105 balloon	R. S. Mohr	
G-CLIF	Ikarus C42 FB UK	E. R. Sims	
G-CLIN	Ikarus C42 FB100	J. O'Halloran	
G-CLJE	Schleicher ASH-25M	G. F. Mann	
G-CLJK	PZL-Bielsko SZD-51-1 Junior	Coventry Gliding Club Ltd	
G-CLJZ	Schleicher ASH-31Mi	J. C. Thompson	
G-CLKF	Schempp-Hirth Cirrus VTC	E. C. Wright	

Notes	Reg.	Type	Owner or Operator
	G-CLKG	Schempp-Hirth Janus CM	Lakes Janus Group
	G-CLKK	Schleicher ASH-31 Mi	Bailey Aviation
	G-CLKU	Schleicher Ka 6E	K. Richards
	G-CLLB	Schempp-Hirth Discus 2cT	R. P. Das
	G-CLLC	HpH Glasflugel 304 Shark	F16 Group
	G-CLLH	HpH Glasflugel 304 Shark	J. Haigh
	G-CLLT	Grob G.102 Standard Astir II	B. T. & R. M. Green
	G-CLLY	Rolladen-Schneider LS6-C18	D. H. Smith
	G-CLME	Schempp-Hirth Ventus 2cT	S. H. Gibson
	G-CLMF	Glaser-Dirks DG-200	P.J. Whitehouse
	G-CLOE	Sky 90-24 balloon	J. Skinner
	G-CLOS	PA-34-200 Seneca II	R. A. Doherty
	G-CLOW	Beech 200 Super King Air	Clowes (Estates) Ltd
	G-CLRK	Sky 77-24 balloon	William Clark & Son (Parkgate) Ltd
	G-CLUE	PA-34-200T Seneca II	P. Pigg
	G-CLUX	Cessna F.172N	G. Fox
	G-CLWN	Cameron Clown SS balloon	Magical Adventures Ltd (G-UBBE)
	G-CMAS	Embraer EMB-135BJ Legacy	Execujet (UK) Ltd
	G-CMBR	Cessna 172S	C. M. B. Reid
	G-CMBS	MDH MD-900 Explorer	Police & Crime Commissioner for West Yorkshire
	G-CMED	SOCATA TB9 Tampico	D. Primorac
	G-CMEW	Aerospool Dynamic WT9 UK	M. W. Frost
	G-CMGC	PA-25 Pawnee 235	G. G. L. James (G-BFEX)
	G-CMOR	Skyranger 912(2)	M. C. McCart
	G-CMOS	Cessna T.303 Crusader	C. J. Moss
	G-CMPC	Titan T-51 Mustang	J. A. Carey
	G-CMSN	Robinson R22 Beta	Kuki Helicopter Sales Ltd (G-MGEE//G-RUMP)
	G-CMWK	Grob G.102 Astir CS	J. Schaper
	G-CMXX	Robinson R44 II	Northern Excavators Ltd
	G-CNAB	Avtech Jabiru UL	E. M. Christoffersen
	G-CNCN	Rockwell Commander 112CA	G. R. Frost
	G-CNHB	Van's RV-7	M. E. Wood
	G-COAI	Cranfield A.1	Cranfield University (G-BCIT)
	G-COBI	Beech 300 Super King Air	Cobham Flight Inspection Ltd
	G-COBM	Beech 300 Super King Air	Cobham Flight Inspection Ltd
	G-COBO	ATR-72-212A	Aurigny Air Services Ltd
	G-COBS	Diamond DA.42 M-NG	Cobham Flight Inspection Ltd
	G-COCO	Cessna F.172M	P. C. Sheard & R. C. Larder
	G-CODY	Kolb Twinstar Mk.3 Extra	J. W. Codd
	G-COIN	Bell 206B JetRanger 2	J. P. Niehorster
	G-COLA	Beech F33C Bonanza	Airport Direction Ltd (G-BUAZ)
	G-COLH	PA-28 Cherokee 140	Full Sutton Flying Centre Ltd (G-AVRT)
	G-COLI	Rotorsport UK MT-03	J. L. Chappell
	G-COLR	Colt 69A balloon ★	British School of Ballooning/Lancing
	G-COLS	Van's RV-7A	C. Terry
	G-COLY	Aeropro Eurofox 912(S)	C. J. Norman
	G-COMB	PA-30 Twin Comanche 160B	Comanche Court Flyers (G-AVBL)
	G-COML	Eurocopter EC120B	Combilift
	G-COMP	Cameron N-90 balloon	Computacenter Ltd
	G-CONA	Flight Design CTLS	S. Connah (G-CGED)
	G-CONB	Robin DR.400/180	M. D. Souster (G-BUPX)
	G-CONC	Cameron N-90 balloon	A. A. Brown
	G-CONL	SOCATA TB10 Tobago	J. M. Huntington
	G-CONN	Eurocopter EC.120B Colibri	M. J. Connors (G-BZMK)
	G-CONR	Champion 7GCBC Scout	Aerofoyle Group
	G-CONV	Convair CV-440-54 ★	Reynard Nursery/Carluke
	G-CONY	BAe Jetstream 3101	Linksair Ltd
	G-COOK	Cameron N-77 balloon	IAZ (International) Ltd
	G-COOT	Taylor Coot A	P. M. Napp
	G-COPP	Scheücher ASW 27-18E	G. D. Coppin
	G-COPS	Piper J-3C-65 Cub	R. W. Sproat
	G-CORA	Shaw Europa XS	A. P. Gardner (G-ILUM)
	G-CORB	SOCATA TB20 Trinidad	Corvid Aviation Ltd
	G-CORD	Slingsby T.66 Nipper 3	P. S. Gilmour (G-AVTB)
	G-CORL	AS.350B3 Ecureuil	Abbeyflight Ltd
	G-CORW	PA-28-180 Cherokee C	R. P. Osborne & C. A. Wilson (G-AVRY)
	G-COSF	PA-28-161 Warrior II	PA-28 Warrior Ltd
	G-COSY	Lindstrand LBL-56A balloon	M. H. Read & J. E. Wetters

Reg.	Type	Owner or Operator	Notes
G-COTH	MD-900 Explorer	Police Aviation Services Ltd	
G-COTT	Cameron 60 Cottage SS balloon	Dragon Balloon Co Ltd	
G-COUZ	X'Air 582(2)	D. J. Couzens	
G-COVA	PA-26-161 Warrior III	Coventry (Civil) Aviation Ltd (G-CDCL)	
G-COVB	PA-28-161 Warror III	Coventry (Civil) Aviation Ltd	
G-COVE	Avtech Jabiru UL	A. A. Rowson	
G-COVZ	Cessna F.150M	R. A. Doherty (G-BCRT)	
G-COWN	P & M Quik GTR	S. Turnbull	
G-COXS	Aeroprakt A.22 Foxbat	S. Cox	
G-COZI	Rutan Cozy III	R. Machin	
G-CPAO	Eurocopter EC.135P2+	Police & Crime Commissioner for West Yorkshire	
G-CPAS	Eurocopter EC.135P2+	Police & Crime Commissioner for West Yorkshire	
G-CPCD	CEA DR.221	P. J. Taylor	
G-CPDA	DH.106 Comet 4C (XS235) ★	C. Walton Ltd/Bruntingthorpe	
G-CPDW	Avions Mudry CAP.10B	Hilfa Ltd	
G-CPEU	Boeing 757-236	Thomson Airways Ltd	
G-CPEV	Boeing 757-236	Thomson Airways Ltd	
G-CPFC	Cessna F.152 II	Falcon Flying Services Ltd	
G-CPFM	PA-28-161 Warrior II	M. O'Rourke (G-BNNS)	
G-CPII	Avions Mudry CAP-231	A. D. Hoy	
G-CPMK	DHC.1 Chipmunk 22 (WZ847)	P. A. Walley	
G-CPMS	SOCATA TB20 Trinidad	Charlotte Park Management Services Ltd	
G-CPOL	AS.355F1 Twin Squirrel	MW Helicopters Ltd	
G-CPPG	Alpi Pioneer 400	P. B. Godfrey	
G-CPPM	North American Harvard II	S. D. Wilch	
G-CPRR	Cessna 680 Citation Sovereign	Bookajet Aircraft Management Ltd	
G-CPSH	Eurocopter EC 135T1	West Yorkshire Police Authority	
G-CPSS	Cessna 208B Grand Caravan	Army Parachute Association	
G-CPTM	PA-28-151 Warrior	T. J. & C. Mackay (G-BTOE)	
G-CPTR	Rotorsport UK Calidus	A. Marshall (G-CGLH)	
G-CPXC	Avions Mudry CAP-10C	JRW Aerobatics Ltd	
G-CRAB	Skyranger 912 (1)	J. O. Williams	
G-CRAR	CZAW Sportcruiser	J. S. Kinsey	
G-CRBV	Balóny Kubiček BB26 balloon	Charter Ballooning Ltd	
G-CRES	Denney Kitfox Mk 3	J. McGoldrick	
G-CREY	SeaRey Amphibian	K. M. & M. Gallagher & A. F. Reid	
G-CRIC	Colomban MC.15 Cri-Cri	R. S. Stoddart-Stones	
G-CRIK	Colomban MC.15 Cri-Cri	C. R. Harrison	
G-CRIL	Rockwell Commander 112B	Rockwell Aviation Group	
G-CRIS	Taylor JT.1 Monoplane	C. R. Steer	
G-CRJW	Schleicher ASW-27-18	R. J. Welford	
G-CRLA	Cirrus SR20	Aero Club Heidelberg EV/Germany	
G-CROB	Shaw Europa XS T-G	R. G. Hallam	
G-CROL	Maule MXT-7-180	J. R. Pratt	
G-CROP	Cameron Z-105 balloon	PSH Skypower Ltd	
G-CROW	Robinson R44	Longmoore Ltd	
G-CROY	Shaw Europa	M. T. Austin	
G-CRSR	Czech Sport Aircraft Sportcruiser	G-CRSR Flying Group	
G-CRUI	CZAW Sportcruiser	J. Massey	
G-CRUM	Westland Scout AH.1 (XV137)	G-CRUM Group	
G-CRUZ	Cessna T.303	J. R. Tubb	
G-CRWZ	CZAW Sportcruiser	P. B. Lowry	
G-CRZA	CZAW Sportcruiser	A. J. Radford	
G-CSAM	Van's RV-9A	B. G. Murray	
G-CSAV	Thruster T.600N 450	D. J. N. Brown	
G-CSAW	CZAW Sportcruiser	B. C. Fitzgerald-O'Connor	
G-CSBD	PA-28-236 Dakota	I. J. Harper (G-CSBO)	
G-CSBM	Cessna F.150M	M. Howells	
G-CSCS	Cessna F.172N	C.Sullivan	
G-CSDJ	Avtech Jabiru UL	M. Smith	
G-CSDR	Corvus CA22	Crusader Syndicate	
G-CSFC	Cessna 150L	Foxtrot Charlie Flying Group	
G-CSFT	PA-23 Aztec 250D ★	Aces High Ltd (G-AYKU)	
G-CSGT	PA-28-161 Warrior II	C. P. Awdry (G-BPHB)	
G-CSIX	PA-32 Cherokee Six 300	A. J. Hodge	
G-CSKW	Van's RV-7	G-CSKW Group (G-CDJW)	

Notes	Reg.	Type	Owner or Operator
	G-CSMK	Aerotechnik EV-97 Eurostar	R. Frey
	G-CSPR	Van's RV-6A	P. J. Pengilly
	G-CSUE	ICP MXP-740 Savannah Jabiru (5)	J. R. Stratton
	G-CSUT	Cassutt Racer IIIM	Hunter Flight Academy & C. V. J. Heames (G-BXMF)
	G-CSZM	Zenair CH.601XL Zodiac	C. Budd
	G-CTAG	Rolladen-Schneider LS8-18	C. D. R. Tagg
	G-CTAM	Cirrus SR22	M. R. Munn
	G-CTAV	Aerotechnik EV-97 Eurostar	P. Simpson
	G-CTCB	Diamond DA42 Twin Star	CTC Aviation Group Ltd (G-CDTG)
	G-CTCC	Diamond DA42 Twin Star	CTC Aviation Group Ltd (G-OCCZ)
	G-CTCD	Diamond DA42 Twin Star	CTC Aviation Group Ltd
	G-CTCE	Diamond DA42 Twin Star	CTC Aviation Group Ltd
	G-CTCF	Diamond DA42 Twin Star	CTC Aviation Group Ltd
	G-CTCG	Diamond DA42 Twin Star	I. Annenskiy
	G-CTCH	Diamond DA42 Twin Star	CTC Aviation Group Ltd
	G-CTCL	SOCATA TB10 Tobago	Gift Aviation Club (G-BSIV)
	G-CTDH	Flight Design CT2K	A. D. Thelwall
	G-CTDW	Flight Design CTSW	B. S. Keene
	G-CTED	Van's RV-7A	E. W. Lyon
	G-CTEL	Cameron N-90 balloon	M. R. Noyce
	G-CTFL	Robinson R44	T. G. Tunnelling Ltd (G-CLOT)
	G-CTIO	SOCATA TB20 Trinidad	I. R. Hunt
	G-CTIX	VS.509 Spitfire T.IX (PT462)	A. A. Hodgson
	G-CTKL	Noorduyn AT-16 Harvard IIB (54137)	M. R. Simpson
	G-CTLS	Flight Design CTLS	D. J. Haygreen
	G-CTNG	Cirrus SR20	K. S. Mitchell & J. Crackett
	G-CTOY	Denney Kitfox Mk 3	J. I. V. Hill
	G-CTPW	Bell 206B JetRanger 3	Aviation Rentals
	G-CTRL	Robinson R22 Beta	Central Helicopters Ltd
	G-CTUG	PA-25 Pawnee 235	The Borders (Milfield) Gliding Club Ltd
	G-CTWO	Schempp-Hirth Standard Cirrus	R. J. Griffin
	G-CTZO	SOCATA TB20 Trinidad GT	G-CTZO Group
	G-CUBA	PA-32R-301T Turbo Saratoge	M. Atlass
	G-CUBB	PA-18 Super Cub 180	Bidford Gliding Ltd
	G-CUBE	Skyranger 912 (2)	A. I. Medler
	G-CUBI	PA-18 Super Cub 125	G. T. Fisher
	G-CUBJ	PA-18 Super Cub 150 (18-5395:CDG)	A. L. Grisay
	G-CUBN	PA-18 Super Cub 150	N. J. R. Minchin
	G-CUBP	PA-18 Super Cub 150	D. W. Berger
	G-CUBS	Piper J-3C-65 Cub	S. M. Rolfe (G-BHPT)
	G-CUBW	WAG-Aero Acro Trainer	B. G. Plumb & ptnrs
	G-CUBY	Piper J-3C-65 Cub	D. Vignal (G-BTZW)
	G-CUCP	Cessna P337H Pressurized Skymaster	Oscar Lopes Cardozo Beheer BV/Netherlands
	G-CUCU	Colt 180A balloon	S. R. Seage
	G-CUDY	Enstrom 480B	D'Arcy Holdings Ltd (G-REAN)
	G-CUGC	Schleicher ASW-19B	Cambridge University Gliding Club (G-CKEX)
	G-CUIK	QAC Quickie Q.200	C. S. Rayner
	G-CUMU	Schempp-Hirth Discus b	C. E. Fernando
	G-CUPP	Pitts S-2A	Avmarine Ltd
	G-CURV	Avid Speedwing	K. S. Kelso
	G-CUTE	Dyn'Aéro MCR-01	E. G. Shimmin
	G-CUTH	P & M Quik R	A. R. & S. Cuthbertson
	G-CVAL	Ikarus C42 FB100	G. W. F. Morton
	G-CVBA	Rolladen-Schneider LS6-18W	A. J. H. Munro
	G-CVBF	Cameron A-210 balloon	Virgin Balloon Flights Ltd
	G-CVET	Flight Design CTLS	AAA Dev LLP (G-CGVR)
	G-CVII	Dan Rihn DR.107 One Design	One Design Group
	G-CVIX	DH.110 Sea Vixen D.3 (XP924)	DS Aviation (UK) Ltd
	G-CVLN	Autogyro Cavalon	P. G. Farmiloe (G-CIAT)
	G-CVMI	PA-18-150 Super Cub	D. Heslop & J. R. Kemberley
	G-CVST	Jodel D.140E	D. Runnalls & R. Sheridan
	G-CVXN	Cessna F.406 Caravan	Caledonian Airborne Systems Ltd (G-SFPA)
	G-CVZT	Schempp-Hirth Ventus 2cT	C. D. Sterritt & M. W. Conboy
	G-CWAG	Sequoia F. 8L Falco	D. R. Austin
	G-CWAL	Raj Hamsa X'Air 133	L. R. Morris
	G-CWAY	Ikarus C42 FB100	M. Conway

Reg.	Type	Owner or Operator	Notes
G-CWBM	Phoenix Currie Wot	G-CWBM Group (G-BTVP)	
G-CWEB	P & M Quik GT450	K. A. Forsyth	
G-CWFA	PA-38-112 Tomahawk	T. Mikschaitis (G-BTGC)	
G-CWFC	PA-38-112 Tomahawk ★	Cardiff-Wales Flying Club Ltd (G-BRTA)	
G-CWFS	Tecnam P2002-JF Sierra	VLA Management Ltd	
G-CWIC	Mainair Pegasus Quik	G-CWIC Group	
G-CWIS	Diamond DA.20 Star	R. A. Eve	
G-CWLC	Schleicher ASH-25	G-CWLC Group	
G-CWMC	P & M Quik GT450	A. R. Hughes	
G-CWMT	Dyn'Aéro MCR-01 Bambi	J. Jones	
G-CWOW	Balony Kubicek BB45Z balloon	Skybus Ballooning	
G-CWTD	Aeroprakt A22 Foxbat	E. Fogarty	
G-CWVY	Mainair Pegasus Quik	G-CWVY Group	
G-CXCX	Cameron N-90 balloon	Cathay Pacific Airways (London) Ltd	
G-CXDZ	Cassutt Speed Two	J. A. H. Chadwick	
G-CXIP	Thruster T.600N	R. J. Howells	
G-CXIV	Thatcher CX4	I. B. Melville	
G-CXLS	Cessna 560 XL Citation XLS	Aviation Beauport Ltd (G-PKRG)	
G-CXSM	Cessna 172R	S. Eustathiou (G-BXSM)	
G-CYGI	HAPI Cygnet SF-2A	B. Brown	
G-CYLL	Sequoia F.8L Falco	N. J. Langrick & A. J. Newall	
G-CYMA	GA-7 Cougar	Cyma Petroleum (UK) Ltd (G-BKOM)	
G-CYPM	Cirrus SR22	R. M. Steeves	
G-CYRA	Kolb Twinstar Mk. 3 (Modified)	S. J. Fox (G-MYRA)	
G-CYRL	Cessna 182T	D. R. Rayne	
G-CYRS	Bell 206L Long Ranger	HJS Helicopters Ltd	
G-CZAC	Zenair CH.601XL	K. W. Eskins	
G-CZAG	Sky 90-24 balloon	S. Paszkowicz	
G-CZAW	CZAW Sportcruiser	Sprite Aviation Services Ltd	
G-CZCZ	Avions Mudry CAP-10B	M. Farmer	
G-CZMI	Best Off Skyranger Swift 912(1)	L. M. Bassett	
G-CZNE	BN-2B-20 Islander	Skyhopper LLP (G-BWZF)	
G-CZOS	Cirrus SR20	H. G. Dilloway	
G-CZSC	CZAW Sportcruiser	F. J. Wadia	
G-DAAN	Eurocopter EC 135P2+	Devon Air Ambulance Trading Co.Ltd	
G-DAAZ	PA-28RT-201T Turbo Arrow IV	Calais Ltd	
G-DABS	Robinson R22 Beta II	Helicom Ltd	
G-DACA	P.57 Sea Prince T.1 (WF118) ★	P. G. Vallance Ltd/Charlwood	
G-DACE	Corben Baby Ace D	G. N. Holland (G-BTSB)	
G-DACF	Cessna 152 II	T. M. & M. L. Jones (G-BURY)	
G-DADA	Rotorsport UK MT-03	J. C. Hilton-Johnson	
G-DADD	Reality Escapade	P. S. Balmer	
G-DADG	PA-18-150 Super Cub	F. J. Cox	
G-DADJ	Glaser-Dirks DG-200	M. Roberts	
G-DADZ	CZAW Sportcruiser	Meon Flying Group	
G-DAGF	EAA Acrosport II	D. A. G. Fraser	
G-DAGJ	Zenair CH.601HD Zodiac	D. A. G. Johnson	
G-DAGS	Cessna 525A Citationjet CJ2	Air Charter Scotland Ltd	
G-DAIR	Luscombe 8A Silvaire	D. F. Soul (G-BURK)	
G-DAIV	Ultramagic H-77 balloon	D. Harrison-Morris	
G-DAJB	Boeing 757-2T7	Monarch Airlines Ltd	
G-DAJC	Boeing 757-31K	Thomas Cook Airlines Ltd	
G-DAKK	Douglas C-47A	General Technics Ltd	
G-DAKM	Diamond DA40D Star	K. MacDonald	
G-DAKO	PA-28-236 Dakota	Methods Consulting Ltd	
G-DAME	Vans RV-7	H. Manners	
G-DAMY	Shaw Europa	U. A. Schliessler & R. J. Kelly	
G-DANA	Jodel DR.200 (replica)	Cheshire Eagles (G-DAST)	
G-DAND	SOCATA TB10 Tobago	S. Gledden & L. Hopwood-Robinson	
G-DANY	Avtech Jabiru UL	D. A. Crosbie	
G-DASG	Schleicher ASW-27-18E	E. Alston	
G-DASH	Rockwell Commander 112	M. J. P. Lynch (G-BDAJ)	
G-DASS	Ikarus C.42 FB100	D. D. J. Rossdale	
G-DATG	Cessna F.182P	Oxford Aeroplane Co Ltd	
G-DAVB	Aerosport Scamp	D. R. Burns	
G-DAVD	Cessna FR.172K	D. M. Driver & S. Copeland	
G-DAVE	Jodel D.112	I. D. Worthington	

Notes	Reg.	Type	Owner or Operator
	G-DAVG	Robinson R44 II	AG Aviation Ltd (G-WOWW)
	G-DAVM	Akrotech Europe CAP.10B	D. Moorman
	G-DAVS	AB Sportine Aviacija LAK-17AT	G-DAVS Syndicate
	G-DAVZ	Cessna 182T Skylane	D. J. Lawrence
	G-DAWG	SA Bulldog Srs 120/121 (XX522)	S. J. Wood
	G-DAWZ	Glasflugel 304 CZ	B. Vikstrom
	G-DAYI	Europa	A. F. Day
	G-DAYS	Europa	D. A. Gittins
	G-DAYZ	Pietenpol Air Camper	A. M. Silsbury
	G-DAZZ	Van's RV-8	Wishanger RV8
	G-DBCA	Airbus A.319-131	British Airways plc
	G-DBCB	Airbus A.319-131	British Airways plc
	G-DBCC	Airbus A.319-131	British Airways plc
	G-DBCD	Airbus A.319-131	British Airways plc
	G-DBCE	Airbus A.319-131	British Airways plc
	G-DBCF	Airbus A.319-131	British Airways plc
	G-DBCG	Airbus A.319-131	British Airways plc
	G-DBCH	Airbus A.319-131	British Airways plc
	G-DBCI	Airbus A.319-131	British Airways plc
	G-DBCJ	Airbus A.319-131	British Airways plc
	G-DBCK	Airbus A.319-131	British Airways plc
	G-DBDB	VPM M-16 Tandem Trainer	D. R. Bolsover (G-IROW)
	G-DBIN	Medway SLA 80 Executive	S. P. Hoskins
	G-DBJD	PZL-Bielsko SZD-9BIS Bocian 1D	Bertie the Bocian Glider Syndicate
	G-DBKL	VS.379 Spitfire F.Mk.XIV	P. M. Andrews
	G-DBND	Schleicher Ka 6CR	Lincolnshire Gliding Club Ltd
	G-DBNH	Schleicher Ka 6CR	The Bath, Wilts and North Dorset Gliding Club Ltd
	G-DBNP	Slingsby T.50 Skylark 4	D. H. Smith
	G-DBOD	Cessna 172S	Goodwood Road Racing Co Ltd
	G-DBOL	Schleicher Ka 6CR	A. C. Thorne
	G-DBRT	Slingsby T.51 Dart	C. W. Logue
	G-DBRU	Slingsby T.51 Dart	P. S. Whitehead
	G-DBRY	Slingsby T.51 Dart	D. J. Knights
	G-DBSA	Slingsby T.51 Dart	G. K. Stanford
	G-DBSL	Slingsby T.51 Dart	G-DBSL Group
	G-DBSR	Kubicek BB26Z balloon	G. J. Bell
	G-DBTF	Schleicher Ka 6CR	T. Fletcher
	G-DBTJ	Schleicher Ka 6CR	I. G. Robinson
	G-BDTM	Schleicher Ka 6CR	The Nene Valley Gliding Club Ltd
	G-DBUZ	Schleicher Ka 6CR	J. J. Hartwell
	G-DBVB	Schleicher K7	Dartmoor Gliding Society Ltd
	G-DBVH	Slingsby T.51 Dart 17R	P. G. Addy
	G-DBVR	Schleicher Ka 6CR	J. M. Brooke
	G-DBVX	Schleicher Ka 6CR	R. Lynch
	G-DBVY	LET L-13 Blanik	Victor Yankee Group
	G-DBVZ	Schleicher Ka 6CR	G-DBVZ Group
	G-DBWC	Schleicher Ka 6CR	Stratford on Avon Gliding Club Ltd
	G-DBWJ	Slingsby T.51 Dart 17R	M. F. Defendi
	G-DBWM	Slingsby T.51 Dart 17R	P. L. Poole
	G-DBWO	Slingsby T.51 Dart	C. R. Stacey
	G-DBWP	Slingsby T.51 Dart 17R	R. Johnson
	G-DBWS	Slingsby T.51 Dart 17R	R. D. Broome
	G-DBXE	Slingsby T.51 Dart	Group G-DBXE
	G-DBXG	Slingsby T.51 Dart 17R	J. M. Whelan
	G-DBXT	Schleicher Ka 6CR	C. I. Knowles
	G-DBYC	Slingsby T.51 Dart 17R	R. L. Horsnell & N. A. Jaffray
	G-DBYG	Slingsby T.51 Dart 17R	W. T. Emery
	G-DBYL	Schleicher Ka 6CR	Channel Gliding Club Ltd
	G-DBYM	Schleicher Ka 6CR	K. S. Smith
	G-DBYU	Schleicher Ka-6CR	G. B. Sutton
	G-DBYX	Schleicher Ka-6E	J. R. Dent
	G-DBZF	Slingsby T.51 Dart 17R	S. Rhenius & D. Charles
	G-DBZJ	Slingsby T.51 Dart 17R	S. Foster
	G-DBZX	Schleicher Ka 6CR	J. Brattle
	G-DCAE	Schleicher Ka 6E	J. R. & P. R. Larner
	G-DCAG	Schleicher Ka 6E	715 Syndicate
	G-DCAM	Eurocopter AS.355NP Ecureuil 2	Cameron Charters LLP
	G-DCAO	Schempp-Hirth SHK-1	M. G. Entwisle & A. K. Bartlett
	G-DCAS	Schleicher Ka 6E	R. F. Tindall
	G-DCAZ	Slingsby T-51 Dart 17R	D. A. Bullock & Man L. C.

Reg.	Type	Owner or Operator	Notes
G-DCBA	Slingsby T.51 Dart 17R	K. T. Kreis	
G-DCBI	Schweizer 269C-1	N. Colclough	
G-DCBM	Schleicher Ka 6CR	R. J. Shepherd	
G-DCBW	Schleicher ASK-13	Stratford on Avon Gliding Club Ltd	
G-DCBY	Schleicher Ka 6CR	R. G. Appleboom	
G-DCCA	Schleicher Ka 6E	R. K. Forrest	
G-DCCB	Schempp-Hirth SHK-1	CCB Syndicate	
G-DCCD	Schleicher Ka 6E	Charlie Charlie Delta Group	
G-DCCE	Schleicher ASK-13	Oxford Gliding Co.Ltd	
G-DCCF	Schleicher ASK-13	Norfolk Gliding Club Ltd	
G-DCCG	Schleicher Ka 6E	R. J. Playle	
G-DCCL	Schleicher Ka 6E	G-DCCL Group	
G-DCCM	Schleicher ASK-13	The Burn Gliding Club Ltd	
G-DCCP	Schleicher ASK-13	Lima 99 Syndicate	
G-DCCR	Schleicher Ka 6E	A. Shaw	
G-DCCT	Schleicher ASK-13	Stratford on Avon Gliding Club Ltd	
G-DCCU	Schleicher Ka 6E	J. L. Hasker	
G-DCCV	Schleicher Ka 6E	C. H. Page	
G-DCCW	Schleicher ASK-13	Needwood Forest Gliding Club Ltd	
G-DCCX	Schleicher ASK-13	Trent Valley Gliding Club Ltd	
G-DCCY	Schleicher ASK-13	Devon and Somerset Gliding Club Ltd	
G-DCCZ	Schleicher ASK-13	The Windrushers Gliding Club Ltd	
G-DCDA	Schleicher Ka 6E	R. E. Musselwhite & D. C. Kirby-Smith	
G-DCDC	Lange E1 Antares	J. D. Williams	
G-DCDF	Schleicher Ka 6E	CDF Syndicate	
G-DCDG	FFA Diamant 18	J. Cashin & D. McCarty	
G-DCDO	Ikarus C42 FB80	C42 Dodo Syndicate	
G-DCDW	Diamant 18	D. R. Chapman	
G-DCDZ	Schleicher Ka 6E	J. R. J. Minns	
G-DCEB	PZL-Bielsko SZD-9BIS Bocian 1E	G-DCEB Syndicate	
G-DCEC	Schempp-Hirth Cirrus	Cirrus 18 Group	
G-DCEM	Schleicher Ka 6E	A. J. Harris	
G-DCEN	PZL-Bielsko SZD-30 Pirat	Essex & Suffolk Gliding Club Ltd	
G-DCEO	Schleicher Ka 6E	C. L. Lagden & J. C. Green	
G-DCEW	Schleicher Ka 6E	J. W. Richardson and Partners Group	
G-DCEX	Schleicher ASK-13	R. B. Walker	
G-DCFA	Schleicher ASK-13	Booker Gliding Club Ltd	
G-DCFE	Schleicher ASK-13	Loughborough Students Union Gliding Club	
G-DCFF	Schleicher K 8B	Derbyshire and Lancashire Gliding Club Ltd	
G-DCFG	Schleicher ASK-13	The Nene Valley Gliding Club Ltd	
G-DCFK	Schempp-Hirth Cirrus	P. D. Whitters	
G-DCFL	Schleicher Ka 6E	M. B. Pridal	
G-DCFS	Glasflugel Standard Libelle 201B	P. J. Flack	
G-DCFW	Glasflugel Standard Libelle 201B	D. J. Edwardes & T. J. Price	
G-DCFX	Glasflugel Standard Libelle 201B	K. D. Fishenden	
G-DCFY	Glasflugel Standard Libelle 201B	C. W. Stevens	
G-DCGB	Schleicher Ka 6E	P. M. Turner & S. C. Male	
G-DCGD	Schleicher Ka 6E	Charlie Golf Delta Group	
G-DCGE	Schleicher Ka 6E	C. V. Hill & P. C. Hazlehurst	
G-DCGH	Schleicher K 8B	K7 (1971) Syndicate	
G-DCGM	FFA Diamant 18	J. G. Batch	
G-DCGO	Schleicher ASK-13	Oxford Gliding Company Ltd	
G-DCGY	Schempp-Hirth Cirrus	M. P. Gadd & G. Nevisky	
G-DCHB	Schleicher Ka 6E	D. L. Jones	
G-DCHC	Bolkow Phoebus C	H. Nolz	
G-DCHJ	Bolkow Phoebus C	D. C. Austin	
G-DCHL	PZL-Bielsko SZD-30	A. P. P. Scorer & A. Stocks	
G-DCHT	Schleicher ASW-15	P. G. Roberts & J. M. Verrill	
G-DCHU	Schleicher K 8B	Highland Gliding Club K8 Syndicate	
G-DCHW	Schleicher ASK-13	Dorset Gliding Club Ltd	
G-DCHZ	Schleicher Ka 6E	B. L. Cooper	
G-DCJB	Bolkow Phoebus C	R. Idle	
G-DCJF	Schleicher K-8B	G. Smith	
G-DCJJ	Bolkow Phoebus C	P. N. Maddocks	
G-DCJK	Schempp-Hirth SHK-1	R. H. Short	
G-DCJM	Schleicher K-8B	Midland Gliding Club Ltd	
G-DCJN	Schempp-Hirth SHK-1	R. J. Makin	
G-DCJR	Schempp-Hirth Cirrus	J. C. K. Brown	
G-DCJY	Schleicher Ka 6CR	CJY Syndicate	
G-DCKD	PZL-Bielsko SZD-30	Dartmoor Gliding Society Ltd	
G-DCKK	Cessna F.172N	KK Group	

Notes	Reg.	Type	Owner or Operator
	G-DCKL	Schleicher Ka 6E	BGA1603 Owners Syndicate
	G-DCKN	PZL-Bielsko SZD-9bis Bocian 1E	Dartmoor Gliding Society Ltd
	G-DCKP	Schleicher ASW-15	ASW 15-BGA1606 Partnership
	G-DCKR	Schleicher ASK-13	Midland Gliding Club Ltd
	G-DCKV	Schleicher ASK-13	Black Mountains Gliding Club
	G-DCKY	Glasflugel Standard Libelle 201B	G. Herbert
	G-DCKZ	Schempp-Hirth Standard Cirrus	G. I. Bustin
	G-DCLA	Schempp-Hirth Standard Cirrus	S. A. Lees
	G-DCLM	Glasflugel Standard Libelle 201B	C. J. Heide & R. Smith
	G-DCLO	Schempp-Hirth Cirrus	Bravo Delta Group
	G-DCLP	Glasflugel Standard Libelle 201B	D. Heaton
	G-DCLT	Schleicher K7	Dartmoor Gliding Society
	G-DCLV	Glasflugel Standard Libelle 201B	K. Vanderputten
	G-DCLZ	Schleicher Ka 6E	G-DCLZ Flying Group
	G-DCMG	Schleicher K7	B. Czerwinski, M. Norbert, M. Oleksiewicz & K. Pindral
	G-DCMI	Mainair Pegasus Quik	T. F. Fitzsimons
	G-DCMK	Schleicher ASK-13	The South Wales Gliding Club Ltd
	G-DCMN	Schleicher K 8B	The Bristol Gliding Club Proprietary Ltd
	G-DCMO	Glasflugel Standard Libelle 201B	M. E. Wolff & L. C. Wood
	G-DCMR	Glasflugel Standard Libelle 201B	N. D. A. Graham
	G-DCMS	Glasflugel Standard Libelle 201B	Libelle 602 Syndicate
	G-DCMV	Glasflugel Standard Libelle 201B	M. Izdorczak
	G-DCMW	Glasflugel Standard Libelle 201B	T. Rose
	G-DCNC	Schempp-Hirth Standard Cirrus	Cirrus 273 Syndicate
	G-DCND	PZL-Bielsko SZD-9bis Bocian 1E	Angus Gliding Club Ltd
	G-DCNE	Glasflugel Standard Libelle 201B	25 Syndicate
	G-DCNG	Glasflugel Standard Libelle 201B	M. C. J. Gardner
	G-DCNJ	Glasflugel Standard Libelle 201B	R. Thornley
	G-DCNM	PZL-Bielsko SZD-9bis Bocian 1E	Bocian Syndicate
	G-DCNP	Glasflugel Standard Libelle 201B	I. G. Carrick & D. J. Miles
	G-DCNS	Slingsby T.59A Kestrel	J. R. Greenwell
	G-DCNW	Slingsby T.59F Kestrel	S. R. Watson
	G-DCNX	Slingsby T.59F Kestrel	M. Boxall
	G-DCOI	Agusta Westland AW.139	Profred Partners LLP
	G-DCOJ	Slingsby T.59A Kestrel	T. W. Treadaway
	G-DCOR	Schempp-Hirth Standard Cirrus	H. R. Ford
	G-DCOY	Schempp-Hirth Standard Cirrus	A. D. Walsh & M. R. Latham
	G-DCPA	MBB BK.117C-1C	Veritair Aviation Ltd (G-LFBA)
	G-DCPB	Eurocopter MBB-BK 117C-2	Police & Crime Commissioner for West Yorkshire
	G-DCPD	Schleicher ASW-17	A. J. Hewitt
	G-DCPF	Glasflugel Standard Libelle 201B	S. Coveney
	G-DCPG	Schleicher K7	T. A. Crawford
	G-DCPJ	Schleicher KA6E	G-DCPJ Group
	G-DCPM	Glasflugel Standard Libelle 201B	N. Godson & P. E. Jessop
	G-DCPU	Schempp-Hirth Standard Cirrus	P. J. Ketelaar
	G-DCPV	PZL-Bielsko SZD-30 Pirat	CPV Group
	G-DCRB	Glasflugel Standard Libelle 201B	A. I. Mawer
	G-DCRH	Schempp-Hirth Standard Cirrus	P. E. Thelwall
	G-DCRN	Schempp-Hirth Standard Cirrus	J. Craig & L. Runhaar
	G-DCRO	Glasflugel Standard Libelle 201B	G-DCRO Group
	G-DCRS	Glasflugel standard Libelle 201B	J. R. Hiley & M. W. Fisher
	G-DCRT	Schleicher ASK-13	Bowland Forest Gliding Club Ltd
	G-DCRV	Glasflugel Standard Libelle 201B	G. G. Dale
	G-DCRW	Glasflugel Standard Libelle 201B	T. Fletcher
	G-DCSB	Slingsby T.59F Kestrel	W. Fischer
	G-DCSD	Slingsby T.59D Kestrel	L. P. Davidson
	G-DCSE	Robinson R44	Heli Air Ltd
	G-DCSF	Slingsby T.59F Kestrel 19	R. Birch & S. Glassett
	G-DCSI	Robinson R44 II	Enable International Ltd (G-TGDL)
	G-DCSJ	Glasflugel Standard Libelle 201B	P. J. Gill
	G-DCSK	Slingsby T.59D Kestrel	Kestrel CSK Group
	G-DCSN	Pilatus B4-PC11AF	J. S. Firth
	G-DCSP	Pilatus B4-PC11	G-DCSP Group
	G-DCSR	Glasflugel Standard Libelle 201B	Glasgow and West of Scotland Gliding Club
	G-DCTB	Schempp-Hirth Standard Cirrus	S. E. McCurdy
	G-DCTJ	Slingsby T.59D Kestrel	J. Young & R. J. Aylesbury
	G-DCTL	Slingsby T.59D Kestrel	E. S. E. Hibbard
	G-DCTM	Slingsby T.59D Kestrel	C. Roney
	G-DCTO	Slingsby T.59D Kestrel	G-DCTO Gliding Syndicate
	G-DCTP	Slingsby T.59D Kestrel	D. C. Austin

Reg.	Type	Owner or Operator	Notes
G-DCTR	Slingsby T.59D Kestrel	M. W. Hands	
G-DCTT	Schempp-Hirth Standard Cirrus	E. Sparrow	
G-DCTU	Glasflugel Standard Libelle 201B	F. K. Hutchinson & P. M. Davies	
G-DCTV	PZL-Bielsko SZD-30	Black Mountains Gliding Club	
G-DCTX	PZL-Bielsko SZD-30	J. R. Sniadowski	
G-DCUB	Pilatus B4-PC11	Staffordshire Gliding Club Ltd	
G-DCUC	Pilatus B4-PC11	G. M. Cumner	
G-DCUD	Yorkshire Sailplanes YS53 Sovereign	T. J. Wilkinson	
G-DCUJ	Glasflugel Standard Libelle 201B	T. G. B. Hobbis	
G-DCUO	Pilatus B4-PC11	R. J. A. Colenso	
G-DCUS	Schempp-Hirth Cirrus VTC	R. C. Graham	
G-DCUT	Pilatus B4 PC11AF	A. L. Walker	
G-DCVE	Schempp-Hirth Cirrus VTC	H. Whybrow	
G-DCVG	Pilatus B4 PC11AF	M. Kempf	
G-DCVK	Pilatus B4-PC11AF	J. P. Marriott	
G-DCVL	Glasflugel Standard Libelle 201B	J. Williams	
G-DCVP	PZL-Bielsko SZD-9bis Bocian 1E	Portmoak CVP Group	
G-DCVR	PZL-Bielsko SZD-30 Pirat	M. T. Pitorak	
G-DCVS	PZL-Bielsko SZD-36A	I. A. Burgin	
G-DCVV	Pilatus B4-PC11AF	Syndicate CVV	
G-DCVW	Slingsby T.59D Kestrel	J. J. Green	
G-DCVY	Slingsby T.59D Kestrel	N. Dickenson	
G-DCWA	Slingsby T.59D Kestrel	D. J. Jeffries	
G-DCWB	Slingsby T.59D Kestrel	Kestrel 677 Syndicate	
G-DCWD	Slingsby T.59D Kestrel	Deeside Kestrel Group	
G-DCWE	Glasflugel Standard Libelle 201B	T. W. J. Stoker	
G-DCWF	Slingsby T.59D Kestrel	P. F. Nicholson	
G-DCWG	Glasflugel Standard Libelle 201B	Libelle 322 Group	
G-DCWH	Schleicher ASK-13	York Gliding Centre Ltd	
G-DCWJ	Schleicher K7	Angus Gliding Club K7 Syndicate	
G-DCWP	PZL-Bielsko SZD-36A Cobra 15	D. Poll	
G-DCWR	Schempp-Hirth Cirrus VTC	CWR Group	
G-DCWS	Schempp-Hirth Cirrus VTC	Cirrus G-DCWS Syndicate	
G-DCWT	Glasflugel Standard Libelle 201B	B. J. Darton	
G-DCWX	Glasflugel Standard Libelle	C. A. Weyman	
G-DCWY	Glasflugel Standard Libelle 201B	S. J. Taylor	
G-DCWZ	Glasflugel Standard Libelle 201B	C. Maul	
G-DCXH	PZL-Bielsko SZD-36A Cobra 15	C. Street	
G-DCXI	Slingsby T.61F Venture T.2	611 Vintage Flight (G-BUDB)	
G-DCXK	Glasflugel Standard Libelle 201B	J. M. Whelan	
G-DCXM	Slingsby T.59D Kestrel	W. H. Dyozinski	
G-DCXV	Yorkshire Sailplanes YS-53 Sovereign	T53 Syndicate	
G-DCYA	Pilatus B4 PC-11	B4-072 Group	
G-DCYD	PZL-Bielsko SZD-30 Pirat	G-DCYD First Group	
G-DCYG	Glasflugel H201B Standard Libelle	R. Barsby & A. C. S. Lintott	
G-DCYM	Schempp-Hirth Standard Cirrus	K. M. Fisher	
G-DCYO	Schempp-Hirth Standard Cirrus	G. M. Maguire, P. Summers & M. Layton	
G-DCYP	Schempp-Hirth Standard Cirrus	A. F. Scott	
G-DCYT	Schempp-Hirth Standard Cirrus	R. Robertson	
G-DCYZ	Schleicher K 8B	Oxford Gliding Co.Ltd	
G-DCZD	Pilatus B4 PC-11AF	T. Dale	
G-DCZE	PZL-Bielsko SZD-30	L. A. Bean	
G-DCZG	PZL-Bielsko SZD-30	J. T. Pajdak	
G-DCZJ	PZL-Bielsko SZD-30	B. L. C. Gordon	
G-DCZN	Schleicher ASW-15B	G-DCZN Group	
G-DCZR	Slingsby T.59D Kestrel	R. P. Brisbourne	
G-DCZU	Slingsby T.59D Kestrel	Kestrel 826 Syndicate	
G-DCZZ	Slingsby T.59D Kestrel	C. J. Lowrie	
G-DDAC	PZL-Bielsko SZD-36A	R. J. A. Colenso	
G-DDAJ	Shempp-Hirth Nimbus 2	North Devon Gliding Club Nimbus Group	
G-DDAK	Schleicher K-7 Rhonadler	Dartmoor Gliding Society	
G-DDAN	PZL-Bielsko SZD-30	J. M. A. Shannon	
G-DDAP	SZL-Bielsko SZD-30	Delta Alpha Papa Group	
G-DDAS	Schempp-Hirth Standard Cirrus	G. Goodenough	
G-DDAU	PZL-Bielsko SZD-30	Buckminster Gliding Club Ltd	
G-DDAV	Robinson R44 II	Aviobox SRL/Italy	
G-DDAW	Schleicher Ka 6CR	R. G. Charlesson	
G-DDAY	PA-28R-201T Turbo Arrow III	G-DDAY Group (G-BPDO)	
G-DDBB	Slingsby T.51 Dart 17R	S. Foster	
G-DDBC	Pilatus B4-PC11	J. H. France & G. R. Harris	

Notes	Reg.	Type	Owner or Operator
	G-DDBD	Shaw Europa XS	B. Davies
	G-DDBG	ICA IS-29D	P. S. Whitehead
	G-DDBK	Slingsby T.59D Kestrel	523 Syndicate
	G-DDBN	Slingsby T.59D Kestrel	G. K. HutchinsonI
	G-DDBP	Glasflugel Club Libelle 205	J. P. Beach
	G-DDBS	Slingsby T.59D Kestrel	K. Millar
	G-DDBV	PZL-Bielsko SZD-30	L. Clarke
	G-DDCA	PZL-Bielsko SZD-36A Cobra 15	J. Young & J. R. Aylesbury
	G-DDCC	Glasflugel Standard Libelle 201B	G-DDCC Syndicate
	G-DDCW	Schleicher Ka 6CR	B. W. Rendall
	G-DDDA	Schempp-Hirth Standard Cirrus	A. J. Davis
	G-DDDB	Schleicher ASK-13	Shenington Gliding Club
	G-DDDE	PZL-Bielsko SZD-38A Jantar 1	Jantar One Syndicate
	G-DDDJ	Learjet 45	RCS Trading Corporation Ltd
	G-DDDK	PZL-Bielsko SZD-30	Buckminster Gliding Club Ltd
	G-DDDL	Schleicher K8B	G-DDDL Group
	G-DDDM	Schempp-Hirth Cirrus	DDM Syndicate
	G-DDDR	Schempp-Hirth Standard Cirrus	J. D. Ewence
	G-DDDY	P & M Quik GT450	J. W. Dodson
	G-DDEA	Slingsby T.59D Kestrel	A. Pickles
	G-DDEB	Slingsby T.59D Kestrel	J. L. Smoker
	G-DDEG	ICA IS-28B2	P. S. Whitehead
	G-DDEO	Glasflugel H205 Club Libelle	R. M. Theil
	G-DDEP	Schleicher Ka-6CR	M. D. Brooks
	G-DDEV	Schleicher Ka-6CR	DEV Group
	G-DDEW	ICA-Brasov IS-29D	G. V. Prater
	G-DDEX	LET-13 Blanik	Blanik DEX Group
	G-DDFC	Schempp-Hirth Standard Cirrus	C. E. Fisher & I. Helme
	G-DDFE	Molino PIK-20B	M. A. Roff-Jarrett
	G-DDFK	Molino PIK-20B	B. H. & M. J. Fairclough
	G-DDFL	PZL-Bielsko SZD-38A Jantar 1	G-DDFL Group
	G-DDFR	Grob G.102 Astir CS	The Windrushers Gliding Club Ltd
	G-DDGA	Schleicher K-8B	The Welland Gliding Club Ltd
	G-DDGE	Schempp-Hirth Standard Cirrus	A. S. Cobbett
	G-DDGG	Schleicher Ka 6E	N. F. Holmes & F. D. Platt
	G-DDGJ	Champion 8KCAB	Western Air (Thruxton) Ltd
	G-DDGK	Schleicher Ka 6CR	R. G. Olsen
	G-DDGV	Breguet 905S Fauvette	J. N. Lee
	G-DDGX	Schempp-Hirth Standard Cirrus 75	USKGC Group
	G-DDGY	Schempp-Hirth Nimbus 2	Nimbus 195 Group
	G-DDHA	Schleicher K 8B	Shalborne Soaring Society Ltd
	G-DDHC	PZL-Bielsko SZD-41A	P. J. Kelly
	G-DDHE	Slingsby T.53B	Aviation Preservation Society of Scotland
	G-DDHG	Schleicher Ka 6CR	Angus Gliding Club Ltd
	G-DDHH	Eiriavion PIK-20B	D. M. Steed
	G-DDHJ	Glaser-Dirks DG-100	G. E. McLaughlin
	G-DDHK	Glaser-Dirks DG-100	B. J. & C. M. Griffin
	G-DDHL	Glaser-Dirks DG-100	DHL Syndicate
	G-DDHT	Schleicher Ka 6E	I. Deans & N. Worrell
	G-DDHW	Schempp-Hirth Nimbus 2	M. J. Carruthers & D. Thompson
	G-DDHX	Schempp-Hirth Standard Cirrus B	J. Franke
	G-DDHZ	PZL-Bielsko SZD-30	Peterborough and Spalding Gliding Club
	G-DDIG	Rockwell Commander 114	Daedalus Flying Group (G-CCDT)
	G-DDJB	Schleicher K-8B	Portsmouth Naval Gliding Centre
	G-DDJD	Grob G.102 Astir CS	P. E. Gascoigne
	G-DDJF	Schempp-Hirth Duo Discus T	R. J. H. Fack
	G-DDJK	Schleicher ASK-18	Booker Gliding Club Ltd
	G-DDJN	Eiriavion PIK-20B	M. Ireland & S. Lambourne
	G-DDJR	Schleicher Ka 6CR	Syndicate K6
	G-DDJX	Grob G.102 Astir CS	Trent Valley Gliding Club Ltd
	G-DDKC	Schleicher K 8B	Yorkshire Gliding Club (Proprietary) Ltd
	G-DDKD	Glasflugel Hornet	Hornet Syndicate
	G-DDKE	Schleicher ASK-13	The South Wales Gliding Club Ltd
	G-DDKG	Schleicher Ka 6CR	C. B. Woolf
	G-DDKL	Schempp-Hirth Nimbus 2	G. J. Croll
	G-DDKM	Glasflugel Hornet	R. S. Lee
	G-DDKR	Grob G.102 Astir CS	Oxford Gliding Co.Ltd
	G-DDKS	Grob G.102 Astir CS	Oxford Gliding Co.Ltd
	G-DDKT	Eiriavion PIK-20B	A. Robinson
	G-DDKU	Grob G.102 Astir CS	Delta Kilo Uniform Syndicate
	G-DDKV	Grob G.102 Astir CS	T. J. Ireson

Reg.	Type	Owner or Operator	Notes
G-DDKW	Grob G.102 Astir CS	M. A. Sandwith	
G-DDKX	Grob G.102 Astir CS	L. R. Bennett	
G-DDLA	Pilatus B4 PC-11	P. R. Seddon	
G-DDLB	Schleicher ASK-18	The Vale of the White Horse Gliding Centre Ltd	
G-DDLC	Schleicher ASK-13	Lasham Gliding Society Ltd	
G-DDLE	Schleicher Ka 6E	P. J. Abbott & J. Banks	
G-DDLG	Schempp-Hirth Standard Cirrus 75	S. Naylor	
G-DDLH	Grob G.102 Astir CS77	M. D. & M. E. Saunders	
G-DDLJ	Eiriavion PIK-20B	M. S. Parkes	
G-DDLM	Grob G.102 Astir CS	P. W. McEnery	
G-DDLP	Schleicher Ka 6CR	J. R. Crosse	
G-DDLS	Schleicher K 8B	North Devon Gliding Club	
G-DDLT	ICA IS-28B2	P. S. Whitehead	
G-DDLY	Eiriavion PIK-20D	M. Conrad	
G-DDMB	Schleicher K 8B	Crown Service Gliding Club	
G-DDMD	Glaser-Dirks DG-100	K. G. Guest	
G-DDMG	Schleicher K 8B	Dorset Gliding Club Ltd	
G-DDMH	Grob G.102 Astir CS	C. K. Lewis	
G-DDMK	Schempp-Hirth SHK-1	D. Breeze	
G-DDML	Schleicher K-7	Dumfries and District Gliding Club	
G-DDMM	Schempp-Hirth Nimbus 2	T. Linee	
G-DDMN	Glasflugel Mosquito	DMN Group	
G-DDMO	Schleicher Ka 6E	S. D. Hawkin	
G-DDMP	Grob G.102 Astir CS	Kingswood Syndicate	
G-DDMR	Grob G.102 Astir CS	Mendip Gliding Club Ltd	
G-DDMS	Glasflugel Standard Libelle 201B	G-DDMS Group	
G-DDMU	Eiriavion PIK-20D	J. Mjels	
G-DDMV	NA T-6G Texan (493209)	C. Dabin	
G-DDMX	Schleicher ASK-13	Dartmoor Gliding Society Ltd	
G-DDNC	Grob G.102 Astir CS	W. J. Veitch	
G-DDND	Pilatus B4-PC11AF	DND Group	
G-DDNE	Grob G.102 Astir CS77	621 Astir Syndicate	
G-DDNG	Schempp-Hirth Nimbus 2	Nimbus 265 Syndicate	
G-DDNK	Grob G.102 Astir CS	G-DDNK Group	
G-DDNT	PZL-Bielsko SZD-30	W. Rossmann	
G-DDNU	PZL-Bielsko SZD-42-1 Jantar 2	C. D. Rowland & D. Chalmers-Brown	
G-DDNV	Schleicher ASK-13	Channel Gliding Club Ltd	
G-DDNW	Schleicher Ks 6CR	C. Styles & L. Wootton	
G-DDNX	Schleicher Ka 6CR	Black Mountains Gliding Club	
G-DDNZ	Schleicher K 8B	Southampton University Gliding Club	
G-DDOA	Schleicher ASK-13	Essex and Suffolk Gliding Club Ltd	
G-DDOB	Grob G.102 Astir CS77	C. E. Hutson	
G-DDOC	Schleicher Ka 6CR	W. St. G. V. Stoney	
G-DDOE	Grob G.102 Astir CS77	Heron Gliding Club	
G-DDOF	Schleicher Ka 6CR	A. J. Watson	
G-DDOG	SA Bulldog Srs 120/121 (XX524:04)	Deltaero Ltd	
G-DDOK	Schleicher Ka 6E	R. S. Hawley & S. Y. Duxbury	
G-DDOU	Eiriavion PIK-20D	J. M. A. Shannon	
G-DDOX	Schleicher K-7	The Nene Valley Gliding Club Ltd	
G-DDPA	Schleicher ASK-18	J. P. Kirby	
G-DDPH	Schempp-Hirth Mini-Nimbus B	J. W. Murdoch	
G-DDPK	Glasflugel H303A Mosquito	G. Lawley	
G-DDPL	Eiriavion PIK-20D	437 Syndicate	
G-DDPO	Grob G.102 Astrir CS77	Dorset Gliding Club Ltd	
G-DDPY	Grob G.102 Astir CS77	C. A. Bailey	
G-DDRA	Schleicher Ka 6CR	K6CR Group Shobdon	
G-DDRB	Glaser-Dirks DG-100	DRB Syndicate	
G-DDRD	Schleicher Ka 6CR	Essex and Suffolk Gliding Club Ltd	
G-DDRE	Schleicher Ka 6CR	I. D. King	
G-DDRJ	Schleicher ASK-13	Lasham Gliding Society Ltd	
G-DDRL	Scheibe SF26A	T. A. Lipinski	
G-DDRM	Schleicher K 7	K7 DRM Syndicate	
G-DDRN	Glasflugel H303A Mosquito	A. & V. R. Roberts	
G-DDRO	Grob G.103 Twin Astir	Astir 258 Syndicate	
G-DDRP	Pilatus B4-PC11	DRP Syndicate	
G-DDRT	Eiriavion PIK-20D	PIK 688 Syndicate	
G-DDRV	Schleicher K 8B	DRV Syndicate	
G-DDRW	Grob G.102 Astir CS	The Royal Air Force Gliding & Soaring Associationl	
G-DDRY	Schleicher Ka 6CR	M. K. Bradford	
G-DDRZ	Schleicher K-8B	East Sussex Gliding Club Ltd	

Notes	Reg.	Type	Owner or Operator
	G-DDSB	Schleicher Ka-6E	G. B. Griffiths
	G-DDSF	Schleicher K-8B	University of Edinburgh Sports Union
	G-DDSG	Schleicher Ka 6CR	P. S. Whitehead
	G-DDSH	Grob G.102 Astir CS77	Astir 648 Syndicate
	G-DDSJ	Grob G.103 Twin Astir II	Herefordshire Gliding Club Ltd
	G-DDSL	Grob G.103 Twin Astir	DSL Group
	G-DDSP	Schempp-Hirth Mini Nimbus B	270 Syndicate
	G-DDST	Schleicher ASW-20L	A. Delaney & J. Innes
	G-DDSU	Grob G.102 Astir CS77	Bowland Forest Gliding Club Ltd
	G-DDSV	Pilatus B4-PC11AF	G. M. Drinkell & S. J. Brenton
	G-DDSX	Schleicher ASW-19B	T. Johns, J. F. L. Scaife & J. F. Stoneman
	G-DDSY	Schleicher Ka-6CR	G. Jones & P. J. Shuff
	G-DDTA	Glaser-Dirks DG-200	G. A. Nash
	G-DDTC	Schempp-Hirth Janus B	Darlton Gliding Club Ltd
	G-DDTE	Schleicher ASW-19B	G. R. Purcell
	G-DDTG	Schempp-Hirth SHK-1	A. P. Benbow
	G-DDTK	Glasflugel Mosquito B	P. France
	G-DDTM	Glaser-Dirks DG-200	R. S. Skinner
	G-DDTN	Schleicher K 8B	C. G. & G. N. Thomas
	G-DDTP	Schleicher ASW-20	T. S. & S. M. Hills
	G-DDTS	CARMAM M-100S	I. A. Macadam
	G-DDTU	Schempp-Hirth Nimbus 2B	Nimbus Syndicate
	G-DDTV	Glasflugel Mosquito B	S. R. Evans
	G-DDTW	PZL-Bielsko SZD-30 Pirat	NDGC Pirat Syndicate
	G-DDTX	Glasflugel Mosquito B	P. T. S. Nash
	G-DDTY	Glasflugel H303 Mosquito B	W. H. L. Bullimore
	G-DDUB	Glasflugel H303 Mosquito B	M. W. Cartney
	G-DDUE	Schleicher ASK-13	Norfolk Gliding Club Ltd
	G-DDUF	Schleicher K 8B	M. Staljan
	G-DDUH	Scheibe L-Spatz 55	R. J. Aylesbury & J. Young
	G-DDUK	Schleicher K-8B	The Bristol Gliding Club Propietary Ltd
	G-DDUL	Grob G.102 Astir CS77	W. I. H. Hall
	G-DDUR	Schleicher Ka 6CR	B. N. Bromley & M. Witthread
	G-DDUS	Schleicher Ka 6 E	W. Ellis
	G-DDUT	Schleicher ASW-20	M. E. Doig & E. T. J. Murphy
	G-DDUY	Glaser-Dirks DG-100	R. L. & K. P. McLean
	G-DDVB	Schleicher ASK-13	Essex and Suffolk Gliding Club Ltd
	G-DDVC	Schleicher ASK-13	Staffordshire Gliding Club Ltd
	G-DDVG	Schleicher Ka-6CR	G-DDVG Banana Group
	G-DDVH	Schleicher Ka 6 E	M. A. K. Cropper
	G-DDVK	PZL-Bielsko SZD-48 Jantar Standard 2	D. S. Sigournay
	G-DDVL	Schleicher ASW-19	X96 Syndicate
	G-DDVM	Glasflugel H205 Club Libelle	M. A. Field
	G-DDVN	Eiriavion PIL-20D-78	T. P. Bassett & A. D. Butler
	G-DDVP	Schleicher ASW-19	VP Syndicate
	G-DDVS	Schempp-Hirth Standard Cirrus	J. C. & T. J. Milner
	G-DDVV	Schleicher ASW-20L	A. M. Hooper
	G-DDVX	Schleicher ASK-13	Shenington Gliding Club
	G-DDVY	Schempp-Hirth Cirrus	M. G. Ashton & G. Martin
	G-DDVZ	Glasflugel H303 Mosquito B	B. H. Shaw & R. Spreckley
	G-DDWB	Glasflugel H303 Mosquito B	D. T. Edwards
	G-DDWC	Schleicher Ka 6 E	D. E. Jones
	G-DDWJ	Glaser-Dirks DG-200	A. P. Kamp & P. R. Desmond
	G-DDWL	Glasflugel Mosquito B	H. A. Stanford
	G-DDWN	Schleicher K7 Rhonadler	L. R. & J. E. Merritt
	G-DDWP	Glasflugel Mosquito B	I. H. Murdoch
	G-DDWR	Glasflugel Mosquito B	C. D. Lovell
	G-DDWS	Eiriavion PIK-20D	D. G. Slocombe
	G-DDWT	Slingsby T.65C Vega	A. P. Grimley
	G-DDWU	Grob G.102 Astir CS	G-DDWU Syndicate
	G-DDWW	Slingsby T.65A Vega	M. Finnie & B. Grice
	G-DDWZ	Schleicher ASW-19B	P. Woodcock
	G-DDXA	Glasflugel H303 Mosquito B	G-DDXA Group
	G-DDXB	Schleicher ASW-20	81 Syndicate
	G-DDXD	Slingsby T.65A Vega	G-DDXD Flying Group
	G-DDXE	Slingsby T.65A Vega	H. K. Rattray
	G-DDXF	Slingsby T.65A Vega	B. A. Walker
	G-DDXG	Slingsby T.65A Vega	DXG Group
	G-DDXH	Schleicher Ka 6 E	D. E. Findon
	G-DDXJ	Grob G.102 Astir CS77	M. T. Stickland
	G-DDXK	Centrair ASW-20F	E. & A. Townsend

Reg.	Type	Owner or Operator	Notes
G-DDXL	Schempp-Hirth Standard Cirrus	A. C. Bridges	
G-DDXN	Glaser-Dirks DG-200	J. A. Johnston	
G-DDXT	Schempp-Hirth Mini-Nimbus C	S. E. Evans	
G-DDXW	Glasflugel Mosquito B	I. W. Myles & J. E. Shaw	
G-DDXX	Schleicher ASW-19B	Cotswold Gliding Club	
G-DDYC	Schleicher Ka 6CR	F. J. Bradley	
G-DDYE	Schleicher ASW-20L	P. J. L. Howell	
G-DDYF	Grob G.102 Astir CS77	York Gliding Centre Ltd	
G-DDYH	Glaser-Dirks DG-200	P. Johnson	
G-DDYJ	Schleicher Ka 6CR	Upward Bound Trust	
G-DDYL	CARMAM JP 15-36AR	P. A. Pickering	
G-DDYR	Schleicher K7	University of the West of England Gliding Club	
G-DDYU	Schempp-Hirth Nimbus -2C	C. B. Shepperd	
G-DDZA	Slingsby T.65A Vega	K-H. Kuntze	
G-DDZB	Slingsby T.65A Vega	A. A. Black	
G-DDZF	Schempp-Hirth Standard Cirrus	G-DDZF Group	
G-DDZG	Schleicher ASW-19B	D. Burton	
G-DDZJ	Grob G.102 Astir CS Jeans	Mendip Astir Syndicate	
G-DDZM	Slingsby T.65A Vega	A. Mattano	
G-DDZN	Slingsby T.65A Vega	D. A. White	
G-DDZP	Slingsby T.65A Vega	M. T. Crews	
G-DDZR	IS-28B2	Lakes Gliding Club Ltd	
G-DDZT	Eiriavion PIK-20D	PIK-20D 106 Group	
G-DDZU	Grob G.102 Astir CS	P. Clarke	
G-DDZV	Scheibe SF-27A	N. Newham	
G-DDZW	Schleicher Ka 6CR	S. W. Naylor	
G-DDZY	Schleicher ASW-19B	M. C. Fairman	
G-DEAE	Schleicher ASW-20L	R. Burghall	
G-DEAF	Grob G.102 Astir CS77	The Borders (Milfield) Gliding Club Ltd	
G-DEAG	Slingsby T.65A Vega	G-DEAG Group	
G-DEAH	Schleicher Ka 6E	ESGC K6 Syndicate	
G-DEAJ	Schempp-Hirth Nimbus 2	R. M. Crockett	
G-DEAK	Glasflugel H303 Mosquito B	T. A. L. Barnes	
G-DEAM	Schempp-Hirth Nimbus 2B	Alpha Mike Syndicate	
G-DEAN	Solar Wings Pegasus XL-Q	Y. G. Richardson (G-MVJV)	
G-DEAR	Eiriavion PIK-20D	G-DEAR Group	
G-DEAT	Eiriavion PIK-20D	A. Spencer & D. Bieniasz	
G-DEAU	Schleicher K7	The Welland Gliding Club Ltd	
G-DEAV	Schempp-Hirth Mini-Nimbus C	G. D. H. Crawford	
G-DEAW	Grob G.102 Astir CS77	EAW Group	
G-DEBR	Shaw Europa	P. Curley	
G-DEBT	Pioneer 300	N. J. T. Tonks	
G-DEBX	Schleicher ASW-20	S. M. Economou & R. M Harris	
G-DECC	Schleicher Ka 6CR	Redwing	
G-DECF	Schleicher Ka 6CR	ECF Group	
G-DECJ	Slingsby T.65A Vega	J. E. B. Hart	
G-DECL	Slingsby T.65A Vega	J. M. Sherman	
G-DECM	Slingsby T.65A Vega	F. Wilson	
G-DECO	Dyn'Aéro MCR-01 Club	G-DECO Flying Group	
G-DECP	Rolladen-Schneider LS3-17	M. H. Ewer	
G-DECR	P & M Quik R	D. V. Lawrence	
G-DECS	Glasflugel H303 Mosquito B	S. Briggs & G. Richardson	
G-DECW	Schleicher ASK-21	Norfolk Gliding Club Ltd	
G-DECZ	Schleicher ASK-21	Booker Gliding Club Ltd	
G-DEDG	Schleicher Ka 6CR	S. J. Wood	
G-DEDH	Glasflugel H303 Mosquito B	B. L. Liddiard	
G-DEDJ	Glasflugel H303 Mosquito B	D. M. Ward	
G-DEDK	Schleicher K7 Rhonadler	North Wales Gliding Club Ltd	
G-DEDM	Glaser-Dirks DG-200	A. H. G. St.Pierre	
G-DEDN	Glaser-Dirks DG-100G	DG 280 Syndicate	
G-DEDU	Schleicher ASK-13	Channel Gliding Club Ltd	
G-DEDX	Slingsby T.65D Vega	G. Kirkham	
G-DEDY	Slingsby T.65D Vega	T. McKinley	
G-DEDZ	Slingsby T.65C Vega	R. C. R. Copley	
G-DEEA	Slingsby T.65C Vega	Borders Sports Vega Syndicate (337)	
G-DEEC	Schleicher ASW-20L	D. Beams	
G-DEED	Schleicher K-8B	The Windrushers Gliding Club Ltd	
G-DEEF	Rolladen-Schneider LS3-17	Echo Echo Foxtrot Group	
G-DEEG	Slingsby T.65C Vega	Vega Syndicate	
G-DEEO	Schleicher ASW-19	K. Kiely	

Notes	Reg.	Type	Owner or Operator
	G-DEEJ	Schleicher ASW-20L	G-DEEJ Group
	G-DEEK	Schempp-Hirth Nimbus 2C	W. P. Stephen
	G-DEEM	Schleicher K-8	The South Wales Gliding Club Ltd
	G-DEEN	Schempp-Hirth Standard Cirrus 75	G-DEEN Flying Group
	G-DEEO	Grob G.102 Club Astir II	G-DEEO Group
	G-DEEP	Wassmer WA.26P Squale	B. J. Key & A. S. Jones
	G-DEES	Rolladen-Schneider LS3-17	J. B. Illidge
	G-DEEW	Schleicher Ka 6CR	S. M. Dodds
	G-DEEX	Rolladen-Schneider LS3-17	The LS3 Flyers
	G-DEEZ	Denney Kitfox Mk.3	J. D. & D. Cheesman
	G-DEFA	Schleicher ASW-20L	Eight Eighties Syndicate
	G-DEFB	Schempp-Hirth Nimbus 2C	N. Revell
	G-DEFE	Centrair ASW-20F	W. A. Horne & D. A. Mackenzie
	G-DEFF	Schempp-Hirth Nimbus 2C	J. W. L. Clarke and P. J. D. Smith
	G-DEFN	Scheibe L-Spatz 55	P. L. E. Duguay
	G-DEFS	Rolladen-Schneider LS3	P. R. Thomas
	G-DEFT	Flight Design CTSW	M. & N. D. Stannard
	G-DEFV	Schleicher ASW-20	A. R. McKillen
	G-DEFW	Slingsby T.65C Sport Vega	Darlton Gliding Club Ltd
	G-DEFZ	Rolladen-Schneider LS3-a	EFZ Syndicate
	G-DEGE	Rolladen-Schneider LS3-a	EGE Glider Syndicate
	G-DEGF	Slingsby T.65D Vega	Shalbourne Soaring Society Ltd
	G-DEGH	Slingsby T.65C Vega	K. Dykes, M. J. Davies & R. A. Starling
	G-DEGJ	Slingsby T.65C Vega	Cotswold Vega Syndicate
	G-DEGK	Schempp-Hirth Standard Cirrus	G. Deane
	G-DEGN	Grob G.103 Twin Astir II	Staffordshire Gliding Club Ltd
	G-DEGP	Schleicher ASW-20L	S. Pozerskis
	G-DEGS	Schempp-Hirth Nimbus 2CS	R. C. Nichols
	G-DEGT	Slingsby T.65D Vega	G-DEGT Group
	G-DEGW	Schempp-Hirth Mini-Nimbus C	I. F. Barnes and Partners
	G-DEGX	Slingsby T.65C Vega	Haddenham Vega Syndicate
	G-DEGZ	Schleicher ASK-21	Black Mountains Gliding Club
	G-DEHC	Eichelsdorfer SB-5B	J. A. Castle
	G-DEHG	Slingsby T.65C Vega	Vega Syndicate
	G-DEHH	Schempp-Hirth Ventus a	J. A. White
	G-DEHK	Rolladen-Schneider LS4	S. Eyles
	G-DEHM	Schleicher Ka 6E	J. B. Symonds
	G-DEHO	Schleicher ASK-21	Lasham Gliding Society Ltd
	G-DEHP	Schempp-Hirth Nimbus 2C	D. J. King
	G-DEHT	Schempp-Hirth Nimbus 2C	Nimbus 2C Syndicate
	G-DEHU	Glasflugel 304	F. Townsend
	G-DEHV	Schleicher ASW-20L	G-DEHV Soaring Group
	G-DEHY	Slingsby T.65D Vega	Vega Syndicate
	G-DEHZ	Schleicher ASW-20L	D. Crimmins
	G-DEIA	Cessna 560XL Citation XLS	Jaymax Jersey Ltd
	G-DEJA	ICA IS-28B2	M. H. Simms
	G-DEJB	Slingsby T.65C Vega	D. Tait & I. G. Walker
	G-DEJC	Slingsby T.65C Vega	I. Powis
	G-DEJD	Slingsby T.65D Vega	R. L. & K. P. McLean
	G-DEJE	Slingsby T.65C Vega	Crown Service Gliding Club
	G-DEJF	Schleicher K 8B	Cotswold Gliding Club
	G-DEJH	Eichelsdorfer SB-5E	I. R. Campbell
	G-DEJR	Schleicher ASW-19B	J. C. M. Docherty
	G-DEJY	PZL-Bielsko SZD-9bis Bocian 1D	G-DEJY Group
	G-DEJZ	Scheibe SF26A	J. M. Collin
	G-DEKA	Cameron Z-90 balloon	P. G. Bogliaccino
	G-DEKC	Schleicher Ka 6E	S. L. Benn
	G-DEKF	Grob G.102 Club Astir III	The Bristol Gliding Club Proprietary Ltd
	G-DEKG	Schleicher ASK-21	Army Gliding Association
	G-DEKJ	Schempp-Hirth Ventus b	I. J. Metcalfe
	G-DEKS	Scheibe SF27A Zugvogel V	R. Trickey
	G-DEKU	Schleicher ASW-20L	A. J. Gillson
	G-DEKV	Rolladen-Schneider LS4	S. L. Helstrip
	G-DEKW	Schempp-Hirth Nimbus 2B	V. Luscombe-Mahoney
	G-DELA	Schleicher ASW-19B	S. G. Jones
	G-DELB	Robinson R-22 Beta ★	Aero Venture
	G-DELD	Slingsby T65C Vega	ELD Syndicate
	G-DELF	Aero L-29A Delfin	Komo-Sky KFT/Hungary
	G-DELG	Schempp-Hirth Ventus b/16.6	A. G. Machin
	G-DELN	Grob G.102 Astir CS Jeans	Bowland Forest Gliding Club Ltd
	G-DELO	Slingsby T.65D Vega	I. Sim

Reg.	Type	Owner or Operator	Notes
G-DELR	Schempp-Hirth Ventus b	I. D. Smith	
G-DELU	Schleicher ASW-20L	V. Derrick	
G-DELZ	Schleicher ASW-20L	D. A. Fogden	
G-DEME	Glaser-Dirks DG-200/17	E. D. Casagrande	
G-DEMF	Rolladen-Schneider LS4	R. N. Johnston & M. C. Oggelsby	
G-DEMG	Rolladen-Schneider LS4	R. C. Bowsfield	
G-DEMH	Cessna F.172M (modified)	M. Hammond (G-BFLO)	
G-DEMJ	Slingsby T65C Sport Vega	Vega G-DEMJ Syndicate	
G-DEMM	AS.350B2 Ecureuil	Three Counties Helicopter Co.Ltd	
G-DEMN	Slingsby T.65D Vega	C. D. Sword	
G-DEMP	Slingsby T.65C Vega	The Surrey Hills Gliding Club Ltd	
G-DEMR	Slingsby T.65C Vega	J. C. Jenks	
G-DEMT	Rolladen-Schneider LS4	M. R. Fox	
G-DEMU	Glaser-Dirks DG-202/17	A. Butterfield & N. Swinton	
G-DEMZ	Slingsby T65A Vega	Vega Syndicate (G-BGCA)	
G-DENB	Cessna F.150G	T. M. Williams (G-ATZZ)	
G-DENC	Cessna F.150G	G-DENC Cessna Group (G-AVAP)	
G-DEND	Cessna F.150M	R. N. Tate (G-WAFC/G-BDFI)	
G-DENE	PA-28-140 Cherokee	DSC Ltd (G-ATOS)	
G-DENI	PA-32-300 Cherokee Six	A. Bendkowski (G-BAIA)	
G-DENJ	Schempp-Hirth Ventus b/16.6	S. Boyden	
G-DENO	Glasflugel Standard Libelle 201B	D. M. Bland	
G-DENS	Binder CP.301S Smaragd	Garston Smaragd Group	
G-DENT	Cameron N-145 balloon	T. G. Church	
G-DENU	Glaser-Dirks DG-100G	435 Syndicate	
G-DENV	Schleicher ASW-20L	R. D. Hone	
G-DENX	PZL-Bielsko SZD-48 Jantar Standard 2	J. M. Hire	
G-DEOA	Rolladen-Schneider LS4	A. A. Jenkins & R. L. Smith	
G-DEOB	PZL-Bielsko SZD-30	R. M. Golding	
G-DEOD	Grob G.102 Astir CS77	D. S. Fenton	
G-DEOE	Schleicher ASK-13	Essex Gliding Club Ltd	
G-DEOF	Schleicher ASK-13	Essex Gliding Club Ltd	
G-DEOJ	Centrair ASW-20FL	J. E. Gatfield	
G-DEOK	Centrair 101A Pegase	J. V. D. Hoek & J. Hunt	
G-DEOM	Carman M100S	S. W. Hutchinson	
G-DEON	Schempp-Hirth Nimbus 3	117 Syndicate	
G-DEOT	Grob G.103A Twin II Acro	R. Tyrrell	
G-DEOU	Pilatus B4-PC11	D. J. Blackman	
G-DEOV	Schempp-Hirth Janus C	Burn Gliding Club Ltd	
G-DEOW	Schempp-Hirth Janus C	383 Syndicate	
G-DEOX	Carmam M-200 Foehn	B. S. Goodspeed	
G-DEOZ	Schleicher K 8B	Cotswold Gliding Club	
G-DEPD	Schleicher ASK-13	EPD Glider Syndicate	
G-DEPE	Schleicher ASW-19B	P. A. Goulding	
G-DEPF	Centrair ASW-20FL	323 Syndicate	
G-DEPG	CARMAM M100S	J. D. Owen	
G-DEPP	Schleicher ASK-13	Mendip Gliding Club Ltd	
G-DEPS	Schleicher ASW-20L	C. Beveridge	
G-DEPT	Schleicher K-8B	R. McEvoy	
G-DEPU	Glaser-Dirks DG-101G Elan	J. F. Rogers	
G-DEPX	Schempp-Hirth Ventus b/16.6	M. E. S. Thomas	
G-DERA	Centrair ASW-20FL	R. J. Lockett	
G-DERH	Schleicher ASK-21	The Burn Gliding Club Ltd	
G-DERJ	Schleicher ASK-21	The Royal Air Force Gliding and Soaring Association	
G-DERR	Schleicher ASW-19B	D. Clarke	
G-DERS	Schleicher ASW-19B	V. J. R. Day & J. Hubberstey	
G-DERU	Schempp-Hirth Nimbus 3/25.5	Verein fur Streckenegelflug Leipzig/Roitzshjora EV/Germany	
G-DERV	Cameron Truck SS balloon	J. M. Percival	
G-DERX	Centrair 101A Pegase	Pegasus Aviators	
G-DESB	Schleicher ASK-21	The Windrushers Gliding Club Ltd	
G-DESC	Rolladen-Schneider LS4	J. Crawford & J. M. Staley	
G-DESH	Centrair 101A	J. E. Moore	
G-DESJ	Schleicher K8B	Bowland Forest Gliding Club Ltd	
G-DESO	Glaser-Dirks DG-300 Elan	G. R. P. Brown	
G-DESU	Schleicher ASK-21	Banbury Gliding Club Ltd	
G-DETA	Schleicher ASK-21	P. Hawkins	
G-DETD	Schleicher K8B	Cotswold Gliding Club	
G-DETG	Rolladen-Schneider LS4	K. J. Woods	
G-DETJ	Centrair 101A	S. C. Phillips	

Notes	Reg.	Type	Owner or Operator
	G-DETM	Centrair 101A	D. Bowden
	G-DETV	Rolladen-Schneider LS4	P. Fabian
	G-DETY	Rolladen-Schneider LS4	D. T. Staff
	G-DETZ	Schleicher ASW-20CL	The 20 Syndicate
	G-DEUC	Schleicher ASK-13	The Bristol Gliding Club Proprietary Ltd
	G-DEUD	Schleicher ASW-20C	R. Tietema
	G-DEUF	PZL-Bielsko SZD-50-3	Puchacz Group
	G-DEUH	Rolladen-Schneider LS4	F. J. Parkinson
	G-DEUJ	Schempp-Hirth Ventus b/16.6	S. C. Renfrew
	G-DEUK	Centrair ASW-20FL	P. A. Clark
	G-DEUS	Schempp-Hirth Ventus b/16.6	R. J. Whitaker
	G-DEUV	PZL-Bielsko SZD-42-2 Jantar 2B	G. V. McKirdy
	G-DEUX	AS.355F Ecureuil 2	Elmridge Ltd
	G-DEUY	Schleicher ASW-20BL	ASW20BL-G-DUEY Group
	G-DEVF	Schempp-Hirth Nimbus 3T	A. G. Leach
	G-DEVH	Schleicher Ka 10	C. W. & K. T. Matten
	G-DEVJ	Schleicher ASK-13	Lasham Gliding Society Ltd
	G-DEVK	Grob G.102 Astir CS	Peterborough and Spalding Gliding Club Ltd
	G-DEVL	Eurocopter EC 120B	Saxon Logistics Ltd
	G-DEVM	Centrair 101A	Seahawk Gliding Club
	G-DEVO	Centrair 101A	G-DEVO Pegase Glider
	G-DEVP	Schleicher ASK-13	Lasham Gliding Society Ltd
	G-DEVS	PA-28 Cherokee 180	180 Group/Blackbushe (G-BGVJ)
	G-DEVV	Schleicher ASK-23	Midland Gliding Club Ltd
	G-DEVW	Schleicher ASK-23	London Gliding Club Proprietary Ltd
	G-DEVX	Schleicher ASK-23	London Gliding Club Proprietary Ltd
	G-DEVY	Schleicher ASK-23	London Gliding Club Proprietary Ltd
	G-DEWD	Pitts Model 12	J. Miller (G-CGRP)
	G-DEWE	P & M Flight Design CTSW	Comunica Industries International Ltd
	G-DEWG	Grob G.103A Twin II Acro	Herefordshire Gliding Club Ltd
	G-DEWI	Rotorsport UK MTO Sport	D. V. Nockels
	G-DEWP	Grob G.103A Twin II Acro	Cambridge Gliding Club Ltd
	G-DEWR	Grob G.103A Twin II Acro	The Bristol Gliding Club Proprietary Ltd
	G-DEWY	Alpi Pioneer 300	W. D. Dewey (G-SRAW)
	G-DEWZ	Grob G.103A Twin II Acro	T. R. Dews
	G-DEXA	Grob G.103A Twin II Acro	Trent Valley Aerotowing Club Ltd
	G-DEXP	ARV Super 2	R. W. Clarke
	G-DEXT	Robinson R44 II	Berkley Properties Ltd
	G-DFAF	Schleicher ASW-20L	A. S. Miller
	G-DFAR	Glasflugel H205 Club Libelle	Alpha Romeo Syndicate
	G-DFAT	Schleicher ASK-13	Dorset Gliding Club Ltd
	G-DFAV	ICA IS-32A	Ibis 32 Syndicate
	G-DFAW	Schempp-Hirth Ventus b/16.6	P. R. Stafford-Allen
	G-DFBD	Schleicher ASW-15B	D. A. Wilson
	G-DFBE	Rolladen-Schneider LS6	J. B. Van Woerden
	G-DFBJ	Schleicher K 8B	Bidford Gliding & Flying Club Ltd
	G-DFBM	Schempp-Hirth Nimbus 3/24.5	D. Gardiner
	G-DFBO	Schleicher ASW-20BL	454 Syndicate
	G-DFBR	Grob G.102 Astir CS77	773 Syndicate
	G-DFBY	Schempp-Hirth Discus b	D. Latimer
	G-DFCD	Centrair 101A	G. J. Bass
	G-DFCK	Schempp-Hirth Ventus b	S. A. Adlard
	G-DFCL	Schleicher K 8B	Bidford Gliding Ltd
	G-DFCM	Glaser-Dirks DG-300	A. Davis & I. D. Roberts
	G-DFCW	Schleicher ASK-13	Lasham Gliding Society Ltd
	G-DFCY	Schleicher ASW-15	M. R. Shaw
	G-DFDF	Grob G.102 Astir CS	The Bristol Gliding Club Proprietary Ltd
	G-DFDP	ICA IS-30	IS-30 Group
	G-DFDW	Glaser-Dirks DG-300	C. M. Hadley
	G-DFEB	Grob G.102 Club Astir III	Lasham Gliding Society Ltd
	G-DFEO	Schleicher ASK-13	Lasham Gliding Society Ltd
	G-DFEX	Grob G.102 Astir CS77	J. Taylor
	G-DFFP	Schleicher ASW-19B	Foxtrot Papa Group
	G-DFGJ	Schleicher Ka 6CR	K6 Syndicate
	G-DFGT	Glaser-Dirks DG-300 Elan	T. J. Gray
	G-DFHS	Schempp-Hirth Ventus cT	154 Group
	G-DFHY	Scheibe SF-27A	J. M. Pursey
	G-DFJJ	Schempp-Hirth Ventus cT	S. G. Jones
	G-DFJO	Schempp-Hirth Ventus cT	FJO Syndicate
	G-DFKH	Schleicher Ka 6CR	I. A. Megarry

Reg.	Type	Owner or Operator	Notes
G-DFKI	Westland Gazelle HT.2	Bourne Park Aviation Group (G-BZOT)	
G-DFKX	Schleicher Ka 6CR	J. E. Herring	
G-DFMG	Schempp-Hirth Discus b	M. T. Davis & J. Melvin	
G-DFOG	Rolladen-Schneider LS7	J. J. Shaw	
G-DFOX	AS.355F1 Twin Squirrel	Potter Aviation Ltd (G-NAAS/G-BPRG/G-NWPA)	
G-DFRA	Rolladen-Schneider LS6-b	79 Syndicate	
G-DFSA	Grob G.102 Astir CS	Astir 498 Syndicate	
G-DFTF	Schleicher Ka 6CR	B. P. Soanes	
G-DFTJ	PZL-Bielsko SZD-48-1 Jantar Standard 2	P. Nock	
G-DFUN	Van's RV-6	G-DFUN Flying Group	
G-DFWJ	Rolladen-Schneider LS7-WL	G-DFWJ Group	
G-DFXR	Sportine Aviacija LAK-12	M. C. Bailey	
G-DGAL	Ikarus C42 FB80 Bravo	D. & P. A. Gall	
G-DGAW	Schleicher Ka 6CR	H. C. Yorke & D. Searle	
G-DGBE	Schleicher Ka-6CR-P	L. Ferguson-Dalling	
G-DGCL	Glaser-Dirks DG.800B	C. J. Lowrie	
G-DGDJ	Rolladen-Schneider LS4-a	450 Syndicate	
G-DGDW	Scheibe SF-27A Zugvogel V	M. W. Hands	
G-DGFD	Robinson R44 II	Macrae Aviation Ltd (G-CGNF)	
G-DGFY	Flylight Dragonfly	M. R. Sands	
G-DGHI	Dyn'Aéro MCR-01 Club	D. G. Hall	
G-DGIO	Glaser-Dirks DG-100G Elan	DG1 Group	
G-DGIV	Glaser-Dirks DG.800B	S. M. Tilling & J. Vella-Grech	
G-DGKB	Centrair ASW-20F	E. Dillon	
G-DGMT	III Sky Arrow 650 T	A. Powell	
G-DGPS	Diamond DA-42 Twin Star	Flight Calibration Services Ltd	
G-DGSC	CZAW Sportcruiser	D. J. Gunn	
G-DGSM	Glaser-Dirks DG-400-17	T. E. Snoddy & L. J. McKelvie	
G-DGST	Beech 95-B55 Baron	CE Ventures Ltd (G-BXDF)	
G-DHAA	Glasflugel H201B Standard Libelle	D. J. Jones & R. N. Turner	
G-DHAD	Glasflugel H201B Standard Libelle	R. Hines	
G-DHAH	Aeronca 7BCM Champion	Alpha Hotel Group (G-JTYE)	
G-DHAL	Schleicher ASK-13	The Windrushers Gliding Club Ltd	
G-DHAP	Schleicher Ka 6E	M.Fursedon & T. Turner	
G-DHAT	Glaser-Dirks DG-200/17	G-DHAT Group	
G-DHCA	Grob G.103 Twin Astir	Midland Gliding Club Ltd	
G-DHCC	DHC.1 Chipmunk 22 (WG321:G)	Eureka Aviation BVBA/Belgium	
G-DHCE	Schleicher ASW-19B	A. M. Wilmot	
G-DHCF	PZL-Bielsko SZD-50-3	Shalbourne Soaring Society Ltd	
G-DHCJ	Grob G.103A Twin II Acro	Peterborough and Spalding Gliding Club Ltd	
G-DHCL	Schempp-Hirth Discus b	C. E. Broom & L. Chicot	
G-DHCO	Glasflugel Standard Libelle 201B	M. J. Birch	
G-DHCR	PZL-Bielsko SZD-51-1	East Sussex Gliding Club Ltd	
G-DHCU	DG-300 Club Elan	R. B. Hankey & M. S. Smith	
G-DHCV	Schleicher ASW-19B	J. E. G. Savage	
G-DHCW	PZL-Bielsko SZD-51-1	Deeside Gliding Club (Aberdeenshire) Ltd	
G-DHCX	Schleicher ASK-21	Devon and Somerset Gliding Club Ltd	
G-DHCZ	DHC.2 Beaver 1	Propshop Ltd (G-BUCJ)	
G-DHDH	Glaser-Dirks DG-200	J. T. Newbery	
G-DHDV	DH.104 Dove 8 (VP981)	Air Atlantique Ltd	
G-DHEB	Schleicher Ka 6CR	J. Burrow	
G-DHEM	Schempp-Hirth Discus CS	473 Syndicate	
G-DHER	Schleicher ASW-19B	R. R. Bryan	
G-DHES	Centrair 101A	C. J. Cole & D. R. Bennett	
G-DHET	Rolladen-Schneider LS6-c18	M. P. Brooks	
G-DHEV	Schempp-Hirth Cirrus	HEV Group	
G-DHGL	Schempp-Hirth Discus b	R. G. Corbin & S. E. Buckley	
G-DHGS	Robinson R22 Beta	Fly Executive Ltd	
G-DHGY	SZD-24C Foka	A. B. Clarke & G. J. Furniss	
G-DHJH	Airbus A.321-211	Thomas Cook Airlines Ltd	
G-DHKL	Schempp-Hirth Discus bT	M. A. Thorne	
G-DHLE	Boeing 767-3JHF	DHL Air Ltd	
G-DHLF	Boeing 767-3JHF	DHL Air Ltd	
G-DHLG	Boeing 767-3JHF	DHL Air Ltd	
G-DHLH	Boeing 767-3JHF	DHL Air Ltd	
G-DHMP	Schempp-Hirth Discus b	HMP Discus Syndicate	
G-DHNX	Rolladen-Schneider LS4-b	M. B. Margetson	
G-DHOC	Scheibe Bergfalke II-55	R. Karch	
G-DHOK	Schleicher ASW-20CL	S. D. Minson	

Notes	Reg.	Type	Owner or Operator
	G-DHOP	Van's RV-9A	A. S. Orme
	G-DHOX	Schleicher ASW-15B	P. Ridgill & A. Griffiths
	G-DHPA	Issoire E-78 Silene	P. Woodcock
	G-DHPM	OGMA DHC.1 Chipmunk 20 (1365)	P. Meyrick
	G-DHPR	Schempp-Hirth Discus b	G. J. Bowser
	G-DHRR	Schleicher ASK-21	Lakes Gliding Club Ltd
	G-DHSJ	Schempp-Hirth Discus b	D. Byrne
	G-DHSR	AB Sportine LAK-12 Lietuva	G. Forster
	G-DHTG	Grob G.102 Astir CS	Trent Valley Gliding Club Ltd
	G-DHUB	PZL-Bielsko SZD-48-3	P. Maxwell
	G-DHUK	Schleicher Ka 6CR	Essex Gliding Club Ltd
	G-DHVM	DH.112 Venom FB.50 (WR470)	Air Atlantique Ltd/Coventry (G-GONE)
	G-DHYL	Schempp-Hirth Ventus 2a	M. J. Cook
	G-DHZF	DH.82A Tiger Moth (N9192)	C. A.Parker & M. R. Johnson (G-BSTJ)
	G-DIAT	PA-28 Cherokee 140	Cloud Global Ltd (G-BCGK)
	G-DICK	Thunder Ax6-56Z balloon	R. D. Sargeant
	G-DIDG	Van's RV-7	E. T. & D. K. Steele
	G-DIDY	Thruster T600T 450	D. R. Sims
	G-DIGG	Robinson R44 II	Thames Materials Ltd
	G-DIGI	PA-32 Cherokee Six 300	D. Stokes
	G-DIGS	Hughes 369HE	Mackinnon Construction Ltd (G-DIZZ)
	G-DIII	Pitts S-2B Special	J. A. Coutts (G-STUB)
	G-DIKY	Murphy Rebel	Stoke Golding Flyers
	G-DIME	Rockwell Commander 114	H. B. Richardson
	G-DINA	AA-5B Tiger	Portway Aviation Ltd
	G-DINO	Pegasus Quantum 15	R. D. J. Buchanan (G-MGMT)
	G-DIPI	Cameron 80 Tub SS balloon	C. G. Dobson
	G-DIPM	PA-46-350P Malibu Mirage	MAS Mix Ltd
	G-DIPZ	Colt 17A Cloudhopper balloon	C. G. Dobson
	G-DIRK	Glaser-Dirks DG.400	P. W. McEnery
	G-DISA	SA Bulldog Srs 120/125	I. W. Whiting
	G-DISK	PA-24 Comanche 250	Kenya Air Services Ltd (G-APZG)
	G-DISO	Jodel 150	P. F. Craven
	G-DIWY	PA-32 Cherokee Six 300	IFS Chemicals Ltd
	G-DIXY	PA-28-181 Archer III	Modern Air (UK) Ltd
	G-DIZI	Reality Escapade 912(2)	I. Johnson
	G-DIZO	Jodel D.120A	D. Aldersea (G-EMKM)
	G-DIZY	PA-28R-201T Turbo Arrow III	Dizy Aviation Ltd
	G-DJAA	Schempp-Hirth Janus B	Bidford Gliding & Flying Club Ltd
	G-DJAB	Glaser-Dirks DG-300 Elan	I. G. Johnston
	G-DJAC	Schempp-Hirth Duo Discus	G-DJAC Group
	G-DJAD	Schleicher ASK-21	The Borders (Milfield) Gliding Club Ltd
	G-DJAE	Cessna 500 Citation	R. C. Lyne (G-JEAN)
	G-DJAH	Schempp-Hirth Discus b	K. Neave & C. F. M. Smith
	G-DJAN	Schempp-Hirth Discus b	N. F. Perren
	G-DJAY	Avtech Jabiru UL-450	G. S. Stokes
	G-DJBC	Ikarus C42 FB100	Bluecool Water Dispensers
	G-DJCR	Varga 2150A Kachina	D. J. C. Robertson (G-BLWG)
	G-DJET	Diamond DA42 Twin Star	Diamond Executive Aviation Ltd
	G-DJGG	Schleicher ASW-15B	A. A. Cole
	G-DJHP	Valentin Mistral C	P. B. Higgs
	G-DJJA	PA-28-181 Archer II	Interactive Aviation Ltd
	G-DJLL	Schleicher ASK-13	Bidford Gliding & Flying Club Ltd
	G-DJMC	Schleicher ASK-21	The Royal Air Force Gliding and Soaring Association
	G-DJMD	Schempp-Hirth Discus b	M. Dixon
	G-DJMM	Cessna 172S	J. Browne & M. Manston
	G-DJNC	ICA-Brasov IS-28B2	Delta Juliet November Group
	G-DJNE	DG Flugzeugbau DG-808C	J. N. Ellis (G-DGRA)
	G-DJNH	Denney Kitfox Mk 3	N. S. Lomax
	G-DJST	Ixess 912(1)	K. Buckley
	G-DJVY	Scintex CP.1315-C3 Super Emeraude	A. P. Goodwin
	G-DJWS	Schleicher ASW-15B	C. Harkness
	G-DKBA	DKBA AT 0301-0 balloon	I. Chadwick
	G-DKDP	Grob G.109	Grob 4
	G-DKEM	Bell 407	True Course Helicopter Ltd
	G-DKEN	Rolladen-Schneider LS4-a	K. L. Sangster and B. Lytollis
	G-DKEY	PA-28-161 Warrior II	PA-28 Warrior Ltd

Reg.	Type	Owner or Operator	Notes
G-DKFU	Schempp-Hirth Ventus 2cxT	R. L. Watson (G-CKFU)	
G-DKGF	Viking Dragonfly ★	(stored)/Enstone	
G-DKNY	Robinson R44 II	Williamair Ltd	
G-DKTA	PA-28-236 Dakota	G. Beattie & C. J. T. Kitchen	
G-DLAA	Cessna 208 Caravan 1	Aerodynamics Ltd	
G-DLAB	Beech 99	Aerodynamics Ltd	
G-DLAF	Bristell NG5 Speed Wing	A. French & G. Dangerfield	
G-DLAK	Cessna 208 Caravan 1	Aerodynamics Ltd	
G-DLAL	Beech E90 King Air	Aerodynamics Ltd	
G-DLCB	Shaw Europa	K. Richards	
G-DLDL	Robinson R22 Beta	Cambridge Aviation Ltd	
G-DLEE	SOCATA TB9 Tampico Club	D. A. Lee (G-BPGX)	
G-DLFN	Aero L-29 Delfin	J. A. Southern	
G-DLOM	SOCATA TB20 Trinidad	J. N. A. Adderley	
G-DLTR	PA-28 Cherokee 180E	R. A. Brown (G-AYAV)	
G-DMAC	Avtech Jabiru SP-430	C. J. Pratt	
G-DMAH	SOCATA TB20 Trinidad	William Cook Aviation Ltd	
G-DMBO	Van's RV-7	C. J. Goodwin	
G-DMCA	Douglas DC-10-30 ★	Forward fuselage/Manchester Airport Viewing Park	
G-DMCI	Ikarus C42 FB100	C-More Flying School Ltd	
G-DMCS	PA-28R Cherokee Arrow 200-II	Arrow Associates (G-CPAC)	
G-DMCT	Flight Design CT2K	A. M. Sirant	
G-DMCW	Magni M-24C	B. A. Carnegie (G-CGVF)	
G-DMEE	Cameron Z-105 balloon	Airship & Balloon Company Ltd	
G-DMES	Cameron Minion 105 SS balloon	Airship & Balloon Company Ltd	
G-DMEV	Cameron Z-105 balloon	Airship & Balloon Company Ltd	
G-DMEZ	Cameron Minion 105 SS balloon	Airship & Balloon Company Ltd	
G-DMND	Diamond DA42 Twin Star	MC Air Ltd	
G-DMON	Xtremeair XA-42 Sbach 342	P. F. Brice & R. M. Hockey	
G-DMPP	Diamond DA42 Twin Star	Diamond Executive Aviation Ltd	
G-DMRS	Robinson R44 II	Nottinghamshire Helicopters (2004) Ltd	
G-DMSS	Westland Gazelle HT.3 (XW858:C)	G. Wood	
G-DMWW	CFM Shadow Srs DD	G-DMWW Flying Group	
G-DNBH	Raj Hamsa X'Air Hawk	D. N. B. Hearn	
G-DNGA	Balóny Kubíček BB.20	G. J. Bell	
G-DNGR	Colt 31A balloon	G. J. Bell	
G-DKNY	Ikarus C42 FB80	D. N. K. & M. A. Symon	
G-DNOP	PA-46-350P Malibu Mirage	Campbell Aviation Ltd	
G-DOBS	Van's RV-8	R. G. Dobney	
G-DOCA	Boeing 737-436	British Airways	
G-DOCB	Boeing 737-436	British Airways	
G-DOCE	Boeing 737-436	British Airways	
G-DOCF	Boeing 737-436	British Airways	
G-DOCG	Boeing 737-436	British Airways	
G-DOCH	Boeing 737-436	British Airways	
G-DOCL	Boeing 737-436	British Airways	
G-DOCN	Boeing 737-436	British Airways	
G-DOCO	Boeing 737-436	British Airways	
G-DOCS	Boeing 737-436	British Airways	
G-DOCT	Boeing 737-436	British Airways	
G-DOCU	Boeing 737-436	British Airways	
G-DOCV	Boeing 737-436	British Airways	
G-DOCW	Boeing 737-436	British Airways	
G-DOCX	Boeing 737-436	British Airways	
G-DOCY	Boeing 737-436	British Airways (G-BVBY)	
G-DOCZ	Boeing 737-436	British Airways (G-BVBZ)	
G-DODB	Robinson R22 Beta	Heliyorks Ltd	
G-DODD	Cessna F.172P-II	K. Watts	
G-DODG	Aerotechnik EV-97A Eurostar	K. G. Vaughan	
G-DOEA	AA-5A Cheetah	B. J. Green (G-RJMI)	
G-DOFY	Bell 206B JetRanger 3	Castle Air Ltd	
G-DOGE	SA Bulldog Srs 100/101	Mid America (UK) Ltd (G-AZHX)	
G-DOGG	SA Bulldog Srs 120/121 (XX638)	P. Sengupta	
G-DOGI	Robinson R22 Beta	Southern Heliservices Ltd (G-BVGS)	
G-DOGZ	Horizon 1	M. J. Nolan	
G-DOIG	CZAW Sportcruiser	J. H. Doyle	

Notes	Reg.	Type	Owner or Operator
	G-DOIN	Skyranger 912(S)1	A. G. Borer
	G-DOIT	AS.350B1 Ecureuil	FB Heliservices Ltd
	G-DOLF	AS.365N3 Dauphin II	Profred Partners LLP
	G-DOLI	Cirrus SR20	Furness Asset Management Ltd
	G-DOLY	Cessna T.303	KW Aviation Ltd (G-BJZK)
	G-DOME	PA-28-161 Warrior III	Target Aviation Ltd
	G-DOMS	Aerotechnik EV-97A Eurostar	R. K. & C. A. Stewart
	G-DONI	AA-5B Tiger	W. P. Moritz (G-BLLT)
	G-DONS	PA-28RT-201T Turbo Arrow IV	C. E. Griffiths
	G-DONT	Xenair CH.601XL Zodiac	J. A. Kentzer
	G-DOOM	Cameron Z-105 balloon	C. L. Thompson
	G-DORM	Robinson R44 II	TSL Contractors Ltd
	G-DORN	EKW C-3605	R. G. Gray
	G-DORS	Eurocopter EC 135T2+	Premier Fund Leasing
	G-DORY	Cameron Z-315 balloon	P. Baker
	G-DOSA	Diamond DA42 Twin Star	DO Systems Ltd
	G-DOSB	Diamond DA42 Twin Star	DO Systems Ltd
	G-DOSC	Diamond DA42 Twin Star	DO Systems Ltd
	G-DOTT	CFM Streak Shadow	R. J. Bell
	G-DOTW	Savannah VG Jabiru(1)	I. S. Wright
	G-DOTY	Van's RV-7	H. A. Daines
	G-DOVE	Cessna 182Q	G. Wills
	G-DOVE†	D. H. 104 Devon C.2 (VP967)★	E. Surrey College/Gatton Point, Redhill (G-KOOL)
	G-DOVS	Robinson R44 II	D. B. Hamilton
	G-DOWN	Colt 31A balloon	M. Williams
	G-DOZI	Ikarus C.42 FB100	D. A. Izod
	G-DOZZ	Best Off Sky Ranger Swift 912S(1)	J. P. Doswell
	G-DPEP	Aero AT-3 R100	Ormand Flying Club Ltd
	G-DPJR	Sikorsky S-76B	Blackbird Logistics Ltd (G-JCBA)
	G-DPPF	Augusta A.109E Power	Dyfed-Powys Police Authority
	G-DPYE	Robin DR400/500	C. R. J. Walker
	G-DRAM	Cessna FR.172F (floatplane)	H. R. Mitchell
	G-DRAT	Slingsby T.51 Dart 17R	W. R. Longstaff
	G-DRAW	Colt 77A balloon	A. G. Odell
	G-DRCS	Schleicher ASH-25E	C. R. Smithers
	G-DREG	Superchaser	N. R. Beale
	G-DREI	Fokker DR.1 Triplane Replica	P. M. Brueggemann
	G-DRGC	P & M Quik GT450	D. R. G. Cornwell
	G-DRGS	Cessna 182S	Walter Scott & Partners Ltd
	G-DRIL	Pilatus PC-12/47E	Drilling Systems Ltd
	G-DRIV	Robinson R44 II	MFH Helicopters Ltd
	G-DRMM	Shaw Europa	T. J. Harrison
	G-DROL	Robinson R44 II	M. R. Lord (G-OPDG)
	G-DROP	Cessna U.206C	K. Brady (G-UKNO/G-BAMN)
	G-DRPK	Reality Escapade	P. A. Kirkham
	G-DRRT	Slingsby T.51 Dart 17R	L. W. Whittington (G-DBXH)
	G-DRSV	CEA DR.315 (modified)	R. S. Voice
	G-DRYS	Cameron N-90 balloon	C. A. Butter
	G-DRZF	CEA DR.360	P. K. Kaufeler
	G-DSFT	PA-28R Cherokee Arrow 200-II	J. Jones (G-LFSE/G-BAXT)
	G-DSGC	PA-25 Pawnee 235C	Devon & Somerset Gliding Club Ltd
	G-DSID	PA-34-220T Seneca III	I. S. Gillbe
	G-DSKI	Aerotechnik EV-97 Eurostar	G-DSKI Group
	G-DSKY	Diamond DA.42 Twin Star	Diamond Executive Aviation Ltd (G-CDSZ)
	G-DSLL	Pegasus Quantum 15-912	D. T. Evans
	G-DSMA	P & M Aviation Quik R	IP Rights Ltd
	G-DSPK	Cameron Z-140	Bailey Balloons Ltd
	G-DSPL	Diamond DA40 Star	Dynamic Signal Processing Ltd (G-GBOS)
	G-DSPY	Diamond D42M Twin Star	Diamond Executive Aviation Ltd
	G-DSPZ	Robinson R44 II	Focal Point Communications Ltd
	G-DSVN	Rolladen-Schneider LS8-18	A. R. Paul
	G-DTAR	P & M Aviation Quik GT450	D. Tarvit
	G-DTCP	PA-32R-300 Cherokee Lance	R. S. Cook (G-TEEM)
	G-DTFF	Cessna T.182T Turbo Skylane	Ridgway Aviation Ltd
	G-DTFL	PA-46-500TP Malibu Meridian	Tyrone Fabrication Ltd
	G-DTOY	Ikarus C.42.FB100	C. W. Laske

Reg.	Type	Owner or Operator	Notes
G-DTSM	EV-97 TeamEurostar UK	J. R. Stothart	
G-DTUG	Wag-Aero Super Sport	D. A. Bullock	
G-DTWO	Schempp-Hirth Discus 2A	O. M. McCormack	
G-DUBI	Lindstrans LBL-120A balloon	A. Nimmo	
G-DUDE	Van's RV-8	P. J. & W. M. Hodgkins	
G-DUDI	Rotorsport UK MTO Sport	Cloud 9 Gyro Flight Ltd	
G-DUDZ	Robin DR.400/180	W. J. Lee (G-BXNK)	
G-DUFF	Rand Robinson KR-2	J. I. B. Duff	
G-DUGE	Ikarus C42 FB UK	D. Stevenson	
G-DUGI	Lindstrand LBL-90A balloon	R. P. Waite	
G-DUKY	Robinson R44	English Braids Ltd	
G-DUNK	Cessna F172M Skyhawk	Devon and Somerset Flight Training Ltd	
G-DUNS	Lindstrand LBL-90A balloon	A. Murphy	
G-DUOT	Schempp-Hirth Duo Discus T	G-DUOT Soaring Group	
G-DURO	Shaw Europa	W. R. C. Williams-Wynne	
G-DURX	Thunder 77A balloon	R. C. and M. A. Trimble	
G-DUSK	DH.115 Vampire T.11 (XE856) ★	Bournemouth Aviation Museum	
G-DUST	Stolp SA.300 Starduster Too	N. M. Robinson	
G-DUVL	Cessna F.172N	G-DUVL Flying Group	
G-DVAA	Eurocopter EC135 T2+	Devon Air Ambulance Trading Co.Ltd	
G-DVBF	Lindstrand LBL-210A balloon	Virgin Balloon Flights	
G-DVIP	Agusta A.109E Power	Castle Air Ltd	
G-DVMI	Van's RV-7	G-DVMI Group	
G-DVON	DH.104 Devon C.2 (VP955)	C. L. Thatcher	
G-DWCE	Robinson R44 II	Jim Davies Civil Engineering Ltd	
G-DWEM	Eurocopter EC135 T2	Bond Air Services Ltd (G-SSXX/G-SSSX)	
G-DWIA	Chilton D.W.1A	D. Elliott	
G-DWIB	Chilton D.W.1B (replica)	J. Jennings	
G-DWJM	Cessna 550 Citation II	TL Aviation Instrad LLP (G-BJIR)	
G-DWMS	Avtech Jabiru UL-450	B. J. Weighell	
G-DWPH	Ultramagic M-77 balloon	Ultramagic SA/Spain	
G-DXLT	Schempp-Hirth Duo Discus xLT	G-DXLT Group	
G-DYCE	Robinson R44 II	Moorland Windows	
G-DYKE	Dyke JD.2 Delta	M. S. Bird	
G-DYMC	Aerospool Dynamic WT9 UK	S. Hoyle	
G-DYNA	Dynamic WT9 UK	Yeoman Light Aircraft Co.Ltd	
G-DYNM	Aerospool Dynamic WT9 UK	November Mike Group	
G-DZDZ	Rolladen-Schneider LS4	I. MacArthur	
G-DZKY	Diamond DA.40D Star	L. K. Horobin (G-CEZP)	
G-DZZY	Champion 8KCAB	Paul's Planes Ltd	
G-EAGA	Sopwith Dove (replica)	A. Wood	
G-EAOU†	Vickers Vimy (replica)(NX71MY)	Greenco (UK) Ltd	
G-EASD	Avro 504L	G. M. New	
G-EASQ†	Bristol Babe (replica) (BAPC87) ★	Bristol Aero Collection (stored)/Kemble	
G-EAVX	Sopwith Pup (B1807)	K. A. M. Baker	
G-EBED†	Vickers 60 Viking (replica) (BAPC114)★	Brooklands Museum of Aviation/Weybridge	
G-EBHB	Avro 504K	T. W. Harris	
G-EBHX	DH.53 Humming Bird	The Shuttleworth Collection	
G-EBIA	RAF SE-5A (F904)	The Shuttleworth Collection	
G-EBIB	RAF SE-5A ★	Science Museum/South Kensington	
G-EBIC	RAF SE-5A (F938) ★	RAF Museum/Hendon	
G-EBIR	DH.51	The Shuttleworth Collection	
G-EBJE	Avro 504K (E449) ★	RAF Museum/Hendon	
G-EBJG	Parnall Pixie IIIH	Midland Aircraft Preservation Society	
G-EBJI	Hawker Cygnet (replica)	C. J. Essex	
G-EBJO	ANEC IIH	The Shuttleworth Collection	
G-EBKY	Sopwith Pup (9917)	The Shuttleworth Collection	
G-EBLV	DH.60 Cirrus Moth	British Aerospace PLC	
G-EBMB	Hawker Cygnet I ★	RAF Museum/Cosford	
G-EBNV	English Electric Wren	The Shuttleworth Collection	
G-EBQP	DH.53 Humming Bird (J7326) ★	P. L. Kirk & T. G. Pankhurst	
G-EBWD	DH.60X Hermes Moth	The Shuttleworth Collection	

Notes	Reg.	Type	Owner or Operator
	G-EBZM	Avro 594 Avian IIIA ★	Manchester Museum of Science & Industry
	G-EBZN	DH.60X Moth	J. Hodgkinson (G-UAAP)
	G-ECAC	Alpha R21620U	Bulldog Aviation Ltd
	G-ECAD	Cessna FA.152	Bulldog Aviation Ltd (G-JEET/G-BHMF)
	G-ECAE	Royal Aircraft Factory SE.5A	H. A. D. Monro
	G-ECAF	Robin HR.200-120B	Bulldog Aviation Ltd (G-BZET)
	G-ECAI	Cessna 560XL Citation XLS	London Executive Aviation Ltd
	G-ECAK	Cessna F.172M	Bulldog Aviation Ltd (G-BENK)
	G-ECAM	EAA Acrosport II	C. England
	G-ECAN	DH.84 Dragon	Norman Aeroplane Trust
	G-ECBH	Cessna F.150K	ECBH Flying Group
	G-ECBI	Schweizer 269C-1	Iris Aviation Ltd
	G-ECDB	Schleicher Ka 6E	C. W. R. Neve
	G-ECDS	DH.82A Tiger Moth	N. C. Wilson
	G-ECDX	DH.71 Tiger Moth (replica)	M. D. Souch
	G-ECEA	Schempp-Hirth Cirrus	CEA Group
	G-ECGC	Cessna F.172N	S. Din
	G-ECGO	Bölkow Bö.208C1 Junior	P. Norman
	G-ECHB	Dassault Falcon 900DX	TAG Aviation (UK) Ltd
	G-ECJM	PA-28R-201T Turbo Arrow III	Regishire Ltd (G-FESL/G-BNRN)
	G-ECKB	Escapade 912(2)	C. M. & C. P. Bradford
	G-ECLW	Glasflugel Standard Libelle 201B	R. G. Parker
	G-ECMC	Robinson R22 Beta	Bulldog Aviation Ltd (G-LSWL)
	G-ECMK	PA-18-150 Super Cub	Shacklewell Super Cub Group
	G-ECOA	DHC.8-402 Dash Eight	Flybe.com
	G-ECOB	DHC.8-402 Dash Eight	Flybe.com
	G-ECOC	DHC.8-402 Dash Eight	Flybe.com
	G-ECOD	DHC.8-402 Dash Eight	Flybe.com
	G-ECOE	DHC.8-402 Dash Eight	Flybe.com
	G-ECOF	DHC.8-402 Dash Eight	Flybe.com
	G-ECOG	DHC.8-402 Dash Eight	Flybe.com
	G-ECOH	DHC.8-402 Dash Eight	Flybe.com
	G-ECOI	DHC.8-402 Dash Eight	Flybe.com
	G-ECOJ	DHC.8-402 Dash Eight	Flybe.com
	G-ECOK	DHC.8-402 Dash Eight	Flybe.com
	G-ECOL	Schempp-Hirth Nimbus 2	M. Upex & L. I. Rigby
	G-ECOM	DHC.8-402 Dash Eight	Flybe.com
	G-ECOO	DHC.8-402 Dash Eight	Flybe.com
	G-ECOP	DHC.8-402 Dash Eight	Flybe.com
	G-ECOR	DHC.8-402 Dash Eight	Flybe.com
	G-ECOT	DHC.8-402 Dash Eight	Flybe.com
	G-ECOX	Grega GN.1 Air Camper	H. C. Cox
	G-ECPA	Glasflugel H201B Standard Libelle	M. J. Witton
	G-ECTF	Comper CLA.7 Swift Replica	P. R. Cozens
	G-ECUB	PA-18 Super Cub 150	G-ECUB Flying Group (G-CBFI)
	G-ECVB	Pietenpol Air Camper	N. A. Constantine
	G-ECVZ	Staaken Z-1S Flitzer	V. D. Long
	G-ECXL	PZL-Bielsko SZD-30 Pirat	Charlie X-Ray Lima Group
	G-EDAV	SA Bulldog Srs 120/121 (XX534:B)	Edwalton Aviation Ltd
	G-EDAY	BAe Jetstream 3101	Skylease Sweden AB
	G-EDBD	PZL-Bielsko SZD-30 Pirat	S. P. Burgess
	G-EDCJ	Cessna 525 CitationJet	A. Ringland
	G-EDDD	Schempp-Hirth Nimbus 2	C. A. Mansfield (G-BKPM)
	G-EDDS	CZAW Sportcruiser	C. P. Davis
	G-EDDV	PZL-Bielsko SZD-38A Jantar 1	S. R. Bruce
	G-EDEE	Comco Ikarus C.42 FB100	C. L. & D. Godfrey
	G-EDEL	PA-32-300 Cherokee Six D	I. Blamire
	G-EDEN	SOCATA TB10 Tobago	Group Eden
	G-EDEO	Beech B.24R Sierra 200	G-EDEO Group
	G-EDFS	Pietenpol Air Camper	J. V. Comfort
	G-EDGA	PA-28-161 Warrior II	The RAF Halton Aeroplane Club Ltd
	G-EDGE	Jodel 150	A. D. Edge
	G-EDGI	PA-28-161 Warrior II	Medcentres Property Portfolio Ltd
	G-EDGJ	Zivko Edge 360	D. G. Jenkins
	G-EDGY	Flight Test Edge 540	C. R. A. Scrope
	G-EDLY	Airborne Edge 912/Streak IIIB	M. & P. L. Eardley
	G-EDMC	Pegasus Quantum 15-912	A. Taylor & D. Coppin
	G-EDNA	PA-38-112 Tomahawk	Pure Aviation Support Services Ltd

Reg.	Type	Owner or Operator	Notes
G-EDRE	Lindstrand LBL 90A balloon	Edren Homes Ltd	
G-EDRV	Van's RV-6A	G-EDRV Flying Group	
G-EDTO	Cessna FR.172F	N. G. Hopkinson	
G-EDVK	RH78 Tiger Light	M. Peters (G-MZGT)	
G-EDVL	PA-28R Cherokee Arrow 200-II	J. S. Devlin & Z. Islam (G-BXIN)	
G-EDYO	PA-32-260 Cherokee Six	R. A. Sargent & A. D. Paton	
G-EDZZ	Ikarus C42 FB100 Bravo	Microavionics UK Ltd	
G-EEAD	Slingsby T.65A Vega	D. S. Smith	
G-EEBA	Slingsby T.65A Vega	J. A. Cowie & K. Robertson	
G-EEBD	Scheibe Bergfalke IV	F. A. P. M. Otten	
G-EEBF	Schempp-Hirth Mini Nimbus C	M. Pingel	
G-EEBK	Schempp-Hirth Mini Nimbus C	G. S. Bell	
G-EEBL	Schleicher ASK-13	Derbyshire and Lancashire Gliding Club Ltd	
G-EEBN	Centrair ASW-20FL	S. MacArthur & R. Carlisle	
G-EEBR	Glaser-Dirks DG200/17	P. W. Roberts	
G-EEBS	Scheibe Zugvogel IIIA	J. A. Stockford	
G-EEBZ	Schleicher ASK-13	Booker Gliding Club Ltd	
G-EECC	Aerospool Dynamic WT9 UK	C. V. Ellingworth	
G-EECK	Slingsby T65A Vega	The ECK Syndicate	
G-EECO	Lindstrand LBL-25A balloon	A. Jay	
G-EEDE	Centrair ASW-20F	G. M. Cumner	
G-EEEK	Extra EA.300/200	A. R. Willis	
G-EEER	Schempp-Hirth Mini Nimbus C	D. J. Uren	
G-EEEZ	Champion 8KCAB	P. J. Webb	
G-EEFA	Cameron Z-90 balloon	A. Murphy	
G-EEFK	Centrair ASW-20FL	J. Gale & A. Donaldson	
G-EEFT	Schempp-Hirth Nimbus 2B	S. A. Adlard	
G-EEGL	Christen Eagle II	M. P. Swoboda & S. L. Nicholson	
G-EEGU	PA-28-161 Warrior II	Premier Flight Training Ltd	
G-EEJE	PA-31 Navajo B	Geeje Ltd	
G-EEKA	Glaser-Dirks DG-202/17	M. J. R. Lindsay & P. Hayward	
G-EEKK	Cessna 152	M. Richards (G-BNSW)	
G-EEKS	Pegasus Quantum 15-912	D. Subhani (G-BYIZ)	
G-EEKX	P & M Aviation Quik	D. Subhani	
G-EEKY	PA-28 Cherokee 140B	Cherokee Aviation Ltd	
G-EELS	Cessna 208B Caravan 1	Glass Eels Ltd	
G-EELT	Rolladen-Schneider LS4	ELT Syndicate	
G-EELY	Schleicher Ka 6CR	K6 ELY Syndicate	
G-EENE	Rolladen-Schneider LS4	R. A. Hine	
G-EENI	Shaw Europa	M. P. Grimshaw	
G-EENK	Schleicher ASK-21	Essex Gliding Club Ltd	
G-EENT	Glasflugel 304	M. Hastings & P. D. Morrison	
G-EENW	Schleicher ASW-20L	G-EENW Group	
G-EENZ	Schleicher ASW-19B	O. L. Pugh	
G-EEPJ	Pitts S-1S Special	P. Westerby-Jones	
G-EERV	Van's RV-6	M. Crunden & C. B. Stirling	
G-EERY	Robinson R22	EGB (Helicopters) Ltd	
G-EESA	Shaw Europa	C. Deith (G-HIIL)	
G-EESY	Rolladen-Schneider LS4	G. S. Morley	
G-EETG	Cessna 172Q Cutlass	Tango Golf Flying Group	
G-EETH	Schleicher K.8B	Bowland Forest Gliding Club Ltd	
G-EEUP	SNCAN Stampe SV.4C	A. M. Wajih	
G-EEVL	Grob G.102 Astir CS77	G. D. E. Macdonald	
G-EEWS	Cessna T.210N	G. W. Mountford	
G-EEWZ	Mainair Pegasus Quik	A. J. Roche	
G-EEYE	Mainair Blade 912	B. J. Egerton	
G-EEZO	DG Flugzeugbau DG-808C	G-ZO Syndicate	
G-EEZR	Robinson R44	Geezer Aviation LLP	
G-EEZS	Cessna 182P	D. A. G. Johnson	
G-EEZZ	Zenair CH.601XL Zodiac	K. W. Allan	
G-EFAM	Cessna 182S Skylane	G-EFAM Flying Group	
G-EFAT	Robinson R44 II	U. Momberg	
G-EFBP	Cessna FR.172K	B. & R. J. Howard	
G-EFCG	Aeropro Eurofox 912(S)	C. A. White	
G-EFCM	PA-28-180 Cherokee D	ATC Trading Ltd	
G-EFGH	Robinson R22 Beta	Ryvoan Aviation Ltd	
G-EFJD	MBB Bo.209 Monsun	E. J. Smith	
G-EFLT	Glasflugel Standard Libelle 201B	P. A. Tietema	
G-EFLY	Centrair ASW-20FL	I. D. & J. H. Atherton	

Notes	Reg.	Type	Owner or Operator
	G-EFOF	Robinson R22 Beta	NT Burton Aviation
	G-EFOX	Eurofox 912(2)	A. R. Grist
	G-EFRP	Bower Fly Baby 1A	R. A. Phillips (G-BFRD)
	G-EFSF	Cessna FR.172K	A. Vaughan
	G-EFSM	Slingsby T.67M Firefly 260	A. J. Macdonald (G-BPLK)
	G-EFTE	Bölkow Bö.207	B. Morris & R. L. Earl
	G-EFTF	AS.350B Ecureuil	T French & Son (G-CWIZ/G-DJEM/G-ZBAC/
			G-SEBI/G-BMCU)
	G-EFUN	Bishop & Castelli E-Go	E-Go Aeroplanes Ltd
	G-EFVS	Wassmer WA.52 Europa	D. F. Hurn
	G-EGAG	SOCATA TB20 Trinidad	D. & E. Booth
	G-EGAL	Christen Eagle II	Eagle Partners
	G-EGBS	Van's RV-9A	Shobdon RV-9A Group
	G-EGEG	Cessna 172R	C. D. Lever
	G-EGES	Lindstrand LBL Triangle balloon	Lighter Than Air Ltd
	G-EGEL	Christen Eagle II	G-EGEL Flying Group
	G-EGGI	Ikarus C.42FB UK	A. G. & G. J. Higgins
	G-EGGS	Robin DR.400/180	G-EGGS Syndicate
	G-EGGZ	Best Off Sky Ranger Swift 912S(1)	J. C. Sheardown
	G-EGHA	Czech Sport PS-28 Cruiser	Compton Abbas Airfield Ltd
	G-EGHH	Hawker Hunter F.58 (J-4083)	Heritage Aviation Developments Ltd
	G-EGIA	UltraMagic M-65C balloon	Balloon Promotion SAS/Italy
	G-EGIL	Christen Eagle II	Smoke On Go Ltd
	G-EGJA	SOCATA TB20 Trinidad	Mesogeion Aeroclub
	G-EGLE	Christen Eagle II	D. Thorpe
	G-EGLG	PA-31 Turbo Navajo C	H. Merkado (G-OATC/G-OJPW/G-BGCC)
	G-EGLL	PA-28-161 Warrior II	Booker Aircraft Leasing Ltd (G-BLEJ)
	G-EGLS	PA-28-181 Archer III	M. Wallace
	G-EGLT	Cessna 310R	RVL Aviation Ltd (G-BHTV)
	G-EGPG	PA-18-135 Super Cub	G. Cormack (G-BWUC)
	G-EGRV	Van's RV-8	B. M. Gwynnett (G-PHMG)
	G-EGSJ	Jabiru J400	C. N. & K. J. Stephen (G-MGRK)
	G-EGSR	Van's RV-7A	L. J. Merritt
	G-EGTB	PA-28-161 Warrior II	Tayside Aviation Ltd (G-BPWA)
	G-EGTC	Robinson R44	MFH Helicopters Ltd (G-CCNK)
	G-EGUR	Jodel D.140B	S. H. Williams
	G-EGVA	PA-28R-200 Cherokee Arrow	M. Williams
	G-EGVO	Dassault Falcon 900EX	TAG Aviation (UK) Ltd
	G-EGWN	American Champion 7ECA	The Royal Air Force Halton Aeroplane Club Ltd
	G-EHAA	MDH MD.900 Explorer	Police Aviation Services Ltd (G-GNAA)
	G-EHAV	Glasflugel Standard Libelle 201B	A. Liran & M. Truelove
	G-EHAZ	PA-28-161 Warrior III	Freedom Aviation Ltd (G-CEEY)
	G-EHBJ	CASA 1.131E Jungmann 2000	E. P. Howard
	G-EHCB	Schempp-Hirth Nimbus 3DT	G-EHCB Group
	G-EHCC	PZL-Bielsko SZD-50-3 Puchacz	Heron Gliding Club
	G-EHCZ	Schleicher K8B	The Surrey Hills Gliding Club Ltd
	G-EHDS	CASA 1.131E Jungmann 2000	C. W. N. & A. A. M. Huke (G-DUDS)
	G-EHGF	PA-28-181 Archer II	G. P. Robinson
	G-EHGW	Cessna 550 Citation Bravo	Eurojet Aviation Ltd (G-FCDB)
	G-EHIC	Jodel D.140B	G-EHIC Group
	G-EHLX	PA-28-181 Archer II	ASG Leasing Ltd
	G-EHMF	Isaacs Fury II	M. W. Bodger
	G-EHMJ	Beech S35 Bonanza	A. J. Daley
	G-EHMM	Robin DR.400/180R	Booker Gliding Club Ltd
	G-EHMS	MD Helicopters MD-900	London's Air Ambulance Ltd
	G-EHTT	Schleicher ASW-20CL	HTT Syndicate
	G-EHUP	Aérospatiale SA.341G Gazelle 1	MW Helicopters Ltd
	G-EHXP	Rockwell Commander 112A	A. L. Stewart
	G-EIBM	Robinson R22 Beta	HJS Helicopters Ltd (G-BUCL)
	G-EICK	Cessna 172S	Centenary Flying Group
	G-EIKY	Shaw Europa	J. D. Milbank
	G-EINI	Europa XS	K. J. Burns (G-KDCC)
	G-EIRE	Cessna T.182T	J. Byrne
	G-EISG	Beech A36 Bonanza	R. J. & B. Howard
	G-EISO	SOCATA MS.892A Rallye	EISO Group
		Commodore 150	
	G-EITE	Luscombe 8F Silvaire	C. P. Davey
	G-EIWT	Cessna FR.182RG	J. R. Pybus

Reg.	Type	Owner or Operator	Notes
G-EIZO	Eurocopter EC 120B	R. M. Bailey	
G-EJAC	Mudry CAP.232	G. C. J. Cooper, P. Varinot & E. Vazeille (G-OGBR)	
G-EJAE	GlaserDirks DG-200	D. L. P. H. Waller	
G-EJAR	Airbus A.319-111	EasyJet Airline Co Ltd	
G-EJBI	Bolkow Bo.207	J. O'Donnell & J. L. Bone	
G-EJEL	Cessna 550 Citation II	Futura Trading SAS	
G-EJGO	Z.226HE Trener	S. K. T. & C. M. Neofytou	
G-EJHH	Schempp-Hirth Standard Cirrus	D. M. Cornelius	
G-EJIM	Schempp-Hirth Discus 2cT	J. Lynchehaun	
G-EJOC	AS.350B Ecureuil	Air and Ground Aviation Ltd (G-GEDS/G-HMAN/G-SKIM/G-BIVP)	
G-EJRC	Robinson R44 II	Perry Farming Co.	
G-EJRS	PA-28-161 Cadet	Carlisle Flight Traing Ltd	
G-EJTC	Robinson R44	N. Parkhouse	
G-EJWI	Flight Design CTLS	E. Wright	
G-EKEY	Schleicher ASW-20 CL	A. P. Nisbet	
G-EKIM	Alpi Pioneer 300	Targett Aviation Ltd	
G-EKIR	PA-28-262 Cadet	Aeros Leasing Ltd	
G-EKKL	PA-28-161 Warrior II	Apollo Aviation Advisory Ltd	
G-EKOS	Cessna FR.182 RG	S. Charlton	
G-ELAM	PA-30 Twin Comanche160B	Hangar 39 Ltd (G-BAWU/G-BAWV)	
G-ELDR	PA-32 Cherokee Six 260	Demero Ltd	
G-ELEE	Cameron Z-105 balloon	M. A. Stelling	
G-ELEN	Robin DR.400/180	Foster ELEN Group	
G-ELIS	PA-34-200T Seneca II	Global Aviation SA (G-BOPV)	
G-ELIZ	Denney Kitfox Mk 2	A. J. Ellis	
G-ELKA	Christen Eagle II	J. T. Matthews	
G-ELKS	Avid Speedwing Mk 4	J. C. Thompson	
G-ELLA	PA-32R-301 Saratoga IIHP	C. C. W. Hart	
G-ELLE	Cameron N-90 balloon	D. J. Stagg	
G-ELLI	Bell 206B JetRanger 3	A. Chatham	
G-ELMH	NA AT-6D Harvard III (42-84555:EP-H)	M. Hammond	
G-ELSE	Diamond DA42 Twin Star	R. Swann	
G-ELSI	Tanarg/Ixess 15 912S(1)	D. Daniel	
G-ELUE	PA-28-161 Warrior II	Freedom Aviation Ltd	
G-ELUN	Robin DR.400/180R	Cotswold DR.400 Syndicate	
G-ELUT	PA-28R Cherokee Arrow 200-II	Green Arrow Europe Ltd	
G-ELVN	Van's RV-7A	G. P. Elvin	
G-ELWK	Van's RV-12	J. Devlin	
G-ELYS	Cessna FA.150K	Skyworthy Hire (G-BIBN)	
G-ELZN	PA-28-161 Warrior II	ZN Flying Group	
G-ELZY	PA-28-161 Warrior II	Redhill Air Services Ltd	
G-EMAA	Eurocopter EC 135T2	Bond Air Services Ltd	
G-EMAC	Robinson R22 Beta	Unique Helicopters (NI) Ltd (G-CBDB)	
G-EMAX	PA-31-350 Navajo Chieftain	Atlantic Bridge Aviation Ltd	
G-EMBC	Embraer RJ145EP	ECC Leasing Co.Ltd	
G-EMBH	Embraer RJ145EU	Aircraft Solutions ERJ-145 LLC	
G-EMBI	Embraer RJ145EP	bmi regional	
G-EMBJ	Embraer RJ145EP	bmi regional	
G-EMBM	Embraer RJ145EU	Aircraft Solutions Lux II SARL	
G-EMBN	Embraer RJ145EP	bmi regional	
G-EMBO	Embraer RJ145EP	Aircraft Solutions ERJ-145 LLC	
G-EMBP	Embraer RJ145EU	Aircraft Solutions ERJ-145 LLC	
G-EMCA	Commander Aircraft 114B	S. Roberts	
G-EMDM	Diamond DA40-P9 Star	D. J. Munson	
G-EMHC	Agusta A109E Power	NT Burton Aviation	
G-EMHK	MBB Bö.209 Monsun 150FV	T. A. Crone (G-BLRD)	
G-EMID	Eurocopter EC 135P2	Police & Crime Commissioner for West Yorkshire	
G-EMIN	Shaw Europa	S. A. Lamb	
G-EMJA	CASA 1.131E Jungmann 2000	C. R. Maher	
G-EMLE	Aerotechnik EV-97 Eurostar	A. R. White	
G-EMLS	Cessna T210L Turbo Centurion	I. K. F. Simcock	
G-EMLY	Pegasus Quantum 15	S. J. Reid	
G-EMMM	Diamond DA40 Star	A. J. Leigh	
G-EMMS	PA-38-112 Tomahawk	Ravenair Aircraft Ltd/Liverpool	

Notes	Reg.	Type	Owner or Operator
	G-EMMY	Rutan Vari-Eze	M. J. Tooze
	G-EMOL	Schweizer 269C-1	Bournemouth Helicopters Ltd
	G-EMSA	Czech Sport Aircraft Sportcruiser	A. C. & M. A. Naylor
	G-EMSI	Shaw Europa	P. W. L. Thomas
	G-EMSY	DH.82A Tiger Moth	G-EMSY Group (G-ASPZ)
	G-ENAA	Supermarine Spitfire Mk.26B	G-ENAA Syndicate
	G-ENBD	Lindstrand LBL-120A balloon	A. Nimmo
	G-ENBW	Robin DR.400-180R	P. S. Carder & B. Elliott
	G-ENCE	Partenavia P.68B	Exeter Flights Ltd (G-OROY/G-BFSU)
	G-ENEA	Cessna 182P	Air Ads Ltd
	G-ENEE	CFM Streak Shadow SA	A. L. & S. Roberts
	G-ENES	Bell 206B JetRanger III	Celtic Energy Ltd
	G-ENGO	Steen Skybolt	R. G. Fulton
	G-ENGR	Head AX8-105 balloon	Royal Engineers Balloon Club
	G-ENHP	Enstrom 480B	H. J. Pelham
	G-ENIA	Staaken Z-21 Flitzer	A. F. Wankowski
	G-ENID	Reality Escapade	Q. Irving
	G-ENIE	Tipsy T.66 Nipper 3	R. J. Ripley
	G-ENII	Cessna F.172M	J. Howley
	G-ENIO	Pitts S-2C Special	Advanced Flying (London) Ltd
	G-ENMY	Baloney Kubicek BB SS baloon	A. M. Holly
	G-ENNA	PA-28-161 Warrior II	Falcon Flying Serices Ltd (G-ESFT)
	G-ENNI	Robin R.3000/180	W. Schmidt
	G-ENNK	Cessna 172S	Pooler-LMT Ltd
	G-ENNY	Cameron V-77 balloon	J. H. Dobson
	G-ENOA	Cessna F.172F	M. K. Acors (G-ASZW)
	G-ENRE	Avtech Jabiru UL	P. R. Turton
	G-ENRI	Lindstrand LBL-105A balloon	P. G. Hall
	G-ENST	CZAW Sportcruiser	Enstone Flyers
	G-ENTL	P & M Quik R	A. Kurt-Elli
	G-ENTS	Van's RV-9A	L. G. Johnson
	G-ENTT	Cessna F.152 II	C. & A. R. Hyett (G-BHHI)
	G-ENTW	Cessna F.152 II	Aldenham Aviation LLP (G-BFLK)
	G-ENVO	MBB Bo.105CBS-4	F. C. Owen
	G-ENVR	Dornier 228-201	National Environment Research Council
	G-ENXA	Falcon 900EX	Execujet (UK) Ltd
	G-ENZO	Cameron Z-105 balloon	Garelli VI SPA
	G-EOFW	Pegasus Quantum 15-912	G-EOFW Microlight Group
	G-EOGE	Gefa-Flug AS105GD airship (hot air)	George Brazil Airship Ltd
	G-EOHL	Cessna 182L	G. P. James
	G-EOID	Aeroprakt A22-L Foxbat	M. D. Northwood
	G-EOIN	Zenair CH.701UL	G. D. Summers & T. Clyde
	G-EOJB	Robinson R44 II	G. J. Braithwaite (G-EDES)
	G-EOLD	PA-28-161 Warrior II	Fly Welle Ltd
	G-EOLX	Cessna 172N	Westward Airways (Lands End) Ltd
	G-EOMA	Airbus A.330-243	Monarch Airlines Ltd
	G-EOMI	Robin HR.200/120B	LAC Aircraft Ltd
	G-EOMK	Robin DR400/180	MK Group
	G-EOPH	Cameron C-90 balloon	A. J. Cherrett
	G-EORG	PA-38-112 Tomahawk	Control Developments (UK) Ltd
	G-EORJ	Shaw Europa	P. E. George
	G-EPAR	Robinson R22 Beta II	Jepar Rotorcraft
	G-EPDI	Cameron N-77 balloon	R. Moss
	G-EPGI	Cessna 560 Citation XLS	GEPGI Aviation Ltd
	G-EPIC	Jabiru UL-450	T. Chadwick
	G-EPOC	Jabiru UL-450	S. Cope
	G-EPSN	Ultramagic M-105 balloon	G. Everett
	G-EPTR	PA-28R Cherokee Arrow 200-II	ACS Aviation Ltd
	G-ERCO	Ercoupe 415D	A. R. & M. V. Tapp
	G-ERDA	Staaken Z-21A Flitzer	J. Cresswell
	G-ERDS	DH.82A Tiger Moth	W. A. Gerdes
	G-ERDW	Enstrom F-28F Falcon	G. Wolfshohl/Germany
	G-ERED	Beech C.90GTI King Air	G. R. Kinally (G-WLLM)
	G-ERFS	PA-28-161 Warrior II	Medcentres Property Portfolio Ltd
	G-ERIC	Rockwell Commander 112TC	G. R. Frost
	G-ERIE	Raytheon Beech 400A	Platinum Executive Aviation Ltd
	G-ERIK	Cameron N-77 balloon	T. M. Donnelly

Reg.	Type	Owner or Operator	Notes
G-ERIW	Staaken Z-21 Flitzer	R. I. Wasey	
G-ERJA	Embraer RJ145EP	Falak Fin Nine Ltd	
G-ERJC	Embraer RJ145EP	Falak Fin Ten Ltd	
G-ERKN	Eurocopter EC.350B3 Ecureuil	Jet Helicopters Ltd (G-ORKI)	
G-ERMO	ARV Super 2	S. Vince (G-BMWK)	
G-ERNI	PA-28-181 Archer II	J. Gardener & N. F. P. Hopwood (G-OSSY)	
G-EROB	Europa XS	R. J. Bull (G-RBJW)	
G-EROL	Westland SA.341G Gazelle 1	MW Helicopters Ltd (G-NONA/G-FDAV/G-RIFA/ G-ORGE/G-BBHU)	
G-EROM	Robinson R22 Beta	EBG (Helicopters) Ltd	
G-EROS	Cameron H-34 balloon	Evening Standard Co Ltd	
G-ERRY	AA-5B Tiger	The GERRY Group (G-BFMJ)	
G-ERTE	Skyranger 912S (1)	A. P. Trumper	
G-ERTI	Staaken Z-21A Flitzer	A. M. Wyndham	
G-ERYR	P & M Aviation Quik GT450	R. D. Ellis	
G-ESCA	Escapade Jabiru (1)	G. W. E. & R. H. May	
G-ESCC	Escapade 912	G. & S. Simons	
G-ESCP	Escapade 912(1)	M. J. Bromley	
G-ESET	Eurocopter EC.130B4 Ecureuil	Cyclix LLP	
G-ESEX	Eurocopter EC 135T2	Police & Crime Commissioner for West Yorkshire	
G-ESGA	Reality Escapade	I. Bamford	
G-ESKA	Escapade 912	Wessex Microlight Flying Club	
G-ESME	Cessna R.182 II (15211)	G. C. Cherrington (G-BNOX)	
G-ESSL	Cessna 182R Skylane II	Euro Seaplane Services Ltd	
G-ESTA	Cessna 550 Citation II	Executive Aviation Services Ltd (G-GAUL)	
G-ESTR	Van's RV-6	S. D. Glover	
G-ESUS	Rotorway Executive 162F	Southern Helicopters Ltd	
G-ETAT	Cessna 172S Skyhawk	Fredair Ltd	
G-ETBY	PA-32 Cherokee Six 260	G-ETBY Group (G-AWCY)	
G-ETDC	Cessna 172P	The Moray Flying Club	
G-ETHY	Cessna 208	N. A. Moore	
G-ETIM	Eurocopter EC 120B	Tenterfield (Holdings) Ltd	
G-ETIN	Robinson R22 Beta	HQ Aviation Ltd	
G-ETIV	Robin DR.400/180	L. A. Seers	
G-ETME	Nord 1002 Pingouin (KG+EM)	108 Flying Group	
G-ETNT	Robinson R44	Irwin Plant Hire	
G-ETUG	Aeropro Eurofox 912(S)	R. M. Cornwell	
G-ETVS	Alpi Pioneer 300 Hawk	V. Serazzi	
G-EUAB	Europa XS	A. D. Stephens	
G-EUAN	Jabiru UL-D	M. Wade & M. Lusted	
G-EUFO	Rolladen-Schneider LS7-WL	G. D. Alcock & M. J. Mingay	
G-EUJG	Avro 594 Avian IIIA	R. I. & D. E. Souch	
G-EUKS	Westland Widgeon III	R. I. Souch	
G-EUNA	Airbus A.318-112	British Airways	
G-EUNB	Airbus A.318-112	British Airways	
G-EUNG	Europa NG	D. I. Stanbridge	
G-EUNI	Beech B200 Super King Air	Universita Telematica E-Campus (G-TAGH)	
G-EUOA	Airbus A.319-131	British Airways	
G-EUOB	Airbus A.319-131	British Airways	
G-EUOC	Airbus A.319-131	British Airways	
G-EUOD	Airbus A.319-131	British Airways	
G-EUOE	Airbus A.319-131	British Airways	
G-EUOF	Airbus A.319-131	British Airways	
G-EUOG	Airbus A.319-131	British Airways	
G-EUOH	Airbus A.319-131	British Airways	
G-EUOI	Airbus A.319-131	British Airways	
G-EUOJ	Airbus A.319-131	British Airways	
G-EUOK	Airbus A.319-131	British Airways	
G-EUOL	Airbus A.319-131	British Airways	
G-EUPA	Airbus A.319-131	British Airways	
G-EUPB	Airbus A.319-131	British Airways	
G-EUPC	Airbus A.319-131	British Airways	
G-EUPD	Airbus A.319-131	British Airways	
G-EUPE	Airbus A.319-131	British Airways	
G-EUPF	Airbus A.319-131	British Airways	
G-EUPG	Airbus A.319-131	British Airways	
G-EUPH	Airbus A.319-131	British Airways	

Notes	Reg.	Type	Owner or Operator
	G-EUPJ	Airbus A.319-131	British Airways
	G-EUPK	Airbus A.319-131	British Airways
	G-EUPL	Airbus A.319-131	British Airways
	G-EUPM	Airbus A.319-131	British Airways
	G-EUPN	Airbus A.319-131	British Airways
	G-EUPO	Airbus A.319-131	British Airways
	G-EUPP	Airbus A.319-131	British Airways
	G-EUPR	Airbus A.319-131	British Airways
	G-EUPS	Airbus A.319-131	British Airways
	G-EUPT	Airbus A.319-131	British Airways
	G-EUPU	Airbus A.319-131	British Airways
	G-EUPV	Airbus A.319-131	British Airways
	G-EUPW	Airbus A.319-131	British Airways
	G-EUPX	Airbus A.319-131	British Airways
	G-EUPY	Airbus A.319-131	British Airways
	G-EUPZ	Airbus A.319-131	British Airways
	G-EUSO	Robin DR.400/140 Major	Weald Air Services Ltd
	G-EUUA	Airbus A.320-232	British Airways
	G-EUUB	Airbus A.320-232	British Airways
	G-EUUC	Airbus A.320-232	British Airways
	G-EUUD	Airbus A.320-232	British Airways
	G-EUUE	Airbus A.320-232	British Airways
	G-EUUF	Airbus A.320-232	British Airways
	G-EUUG	Airbus A.320-232	British Airways
	G-EUUH	Airbus A.320-232	British Airways
	G-EUUI	Airbus A.320-232	British Airways
	G-EUUJ	Airbus A.320-232	British Airways
	G-EUUK	Airbus A.320-232	British Airways
	G-EUUL	Airbus A.320-232	British Airways
	G-EUUM	Airbus A.320-232	British Airways
	G-EUUN	Airbus A.320-232	British Airways
	G-EUUO	Airbus A.320-232	British Airways
	G-EUUP	Airbus A.320-232	British Airways
	G-EUUR	Airbus A.320-232	British Airways
	G-EUUS	Airbus A.320-232	British Airways
	G-EUUT	Airbus A.320-232	British Airways
	G-EUUU	Airbus A.320-232	British Airways
	G-EUUV	Airbus A.320-232	British Airways
	G-EUUW	Airbus A.320-232	British Airways
	G-EUUX	Airbus A.320-232	British Airways
	G-EUUY	Airbus A.320-232	British Airways
	G-EUUZ	Airbus A.320-232	British Airways
	G-EUXC	Airbus A.321-231	British Airways
	G-EUXD	Airbus A.321-231	British Airways
	G-EUXE	Airbus A.321-231	British Airways
	G-EUXF	Airbus A.321-231	British Airways
	G-EUXG	Airbus A.321-231	British Airways
	G-EUXH	Airbus A.321-231	British Airways
	G-EUXI	Airbus A.321-231	British Airways
	G-EUXJ	Airbus A.321-231	British Airways
	G-EUXK	Airbus A.321-231	British Airways
	G-EUXL	Airbus A.321-231	British Airways
	G-EUXM	Airbus A.321-231	British Airways
	G-EUYA	Airbus A.320-232	British Airways
	G-EUYB	Airbus A.320-232	British Airways
	G-EUYC	Airbus A.320-232	British Airways
	G-EUYD	Airbus A.320-232	British Airways
	G-EUYE	Airbus A.320-232	British Airways
	G-EUYF	Airbus A.320-232	British Airways
	G-EUYG	Airbus A.320-232	British Airways
	G-EUYH	Airbus A.320-232	British Airways
	G-EUYI	Airbus A.320-232	British Airways
	G-EUYJ	Airbus A.320-232	British Airways
	G-EUYK	Airbus A.320-232	British Airways
	G-EUYL	Airbus A.320-232	British Airways
	G-EUYM	Airbus A.320-232	British Airways
	G-EUYN	Airbus A.320-232	British Airways
	G-EUYO	Airbus A.320-232	British Airways
	G-EUYP	Airbus A.320-232	British Airways
	G-EUYR	Airbus A.320-232	British Airways
	G-EUYS	Airbus A.320-232	British Airways

Reg.	Type	Owner or Operator	Notes
G-EUYT	Airbus A.320-232	British Airways	
G-EVAJ	Best Off Skyranger 912S(1)	A. B. Gridley	
G-EVBF	Cameron Z-350 balloon	Virgin Balloon Flights	
G-EVET	Cameron 80 Concept balloon	L. O. & H. Vaughan	
G-EVEY	Thruster T.600N 450-JAB	The G-EVEY Flying Group	
G-EVIE	PA-28-181 Warrior II	Tayside Aviation Ltd (G-ZULU)	
G-EVIG	Evektor EV-97 TeamEurostar UK	A. S. Mitchell	
G-EVII	Schempp-Hirth Ventus 2cT	Ventus G-EVII Syndicate	
G-EVIL	Xtremeair XA-41	Unlimited Aerobatics Ltd	
G-EVLE	Rearwin 8125 Cloudster	M. C. Hiscock (G-BVLK)	
G-EVPH	Aerotechnik EV-97 Eurostar	A. H. Woolley	
G-EVPI	Evans VP-1 Srs 2	C. P. Martyr	
G-EVRO	Aerotechnik EV-97 Eurostar	Newtownards Microlight Group	
G-EVSL	Aerotechnik EV-97 Eurostar SL	M. Vouros	
G-EVSW	Evektor EV-97 Sportstar	Cosmik Aviation Ltd	
G-EVTO	PA-28-161 Warrior II	Redhill Air Services Ltd	
G-EWAD	Robinson R44 II	Excel Law Ltd	
G-EWAN	Prostar PT-2C	C. G. Shaw	
G-EWBC	Avtec Jabiru SK	E. W. B. Comber	
G-EWEN	Aeropro Eurofox 912(S)	M. H. Talbot	
G-EWES	Pioneer 300	D. A. Ions	
G-EWEW	AB Sportine Aviacija LAK-19T	J. B. Strzebrakowski	
G-EWIZ	Pitts S-2E Special	R. S. Goodwin	
G-EWME	PA-28 Cherokee 235	R. J. Clarke	
G-EWZZ	CZAW Sportcruiser	K. Dickinson	
G-EXAM	PA-28RT-201T Turbo Arrow IV	RR. S. Urquhart & A. Cameron	
G-EXEC	PA-34-200 Seneca	Sky Air Travel Ltd	
G-EXES	Shaw Europa XS	D. Barraclough	
G-EXEX	Cessna 404	Reconnaissance Ventures Ltd	
G-EXGC	Extra EA.300/200	P. J. Bull	
G-EXHL	Cameron C-70 balloon	R. K. Gyselynck	
G-EXII	Extra EA.300	A. D. Hoy	
G-EXIL	Extra EA.300/S	C. W. Burkett & S. French	
G-EXIT	MS.893E Rallye 180GT	G-EXIT Group	
G-EXLL	Zenair CH.601	J. L. Adams	
G-EXLT	Extra EA.300/LT	J. W. Marshall	
G-EXPL	Champion 7GCBC Citabria	P. Koehmann	
G-EXTR	Extra EA.260	S. J. Carver	
G-EXXL	Zenair CH.601XL Zodiac	J. P. Ashford	
G-EYAK	Yakovlev Yak-50 (50 yellow)	P. N. A. Whitehead	
G-EYAS	Denney Kitfox Mk 2	R. E. Hughes	
G-EYCO	Robin DR.400/180	M. J. Hanlon	
G-EYNL	MBB Bö.105DBS/5	Alan Mann Aviation Group Ltd	
G-EYOR	Van's RV-6	S. I. Fraser	
G-EYUP	Cessna 560XL Citation XLS	Harrock Aviation Ltd	
G-EZAA	Airbus A.319-111	easyJet Airline Co Ltd	
G-EZAB	Airbus A.319-111	easyJet Airline Co Ltd	
G-EZAC	Airbus A.319-111	easyJet Airline Co Ltd	
G-EZAD	Airbus A.319-111	easyJet Airline Co Ltd	
G-EZAF	Airbus A.319-111	easyJet Airline Co Ltd	
G-EZAG	Airbus A.319-111	easyJet Airline Co Ltd	
G-EZAI	Airbus A.319-111	easyJet Airline Co Ltd	
G-EZAJ	Airbus A.319-111	easyJet Airline Co Ltd	
G-EZAK	Airbus A.319-111	easyJet Airline Co Ltd	
G-EZAL	Airbus A.319-111	easyJet Airline Co Ltd	
G-EZAM	Airbus A.319-111	easyJet Airline Co Ltd (G-CCKA)	
G-EZAN	Airbus A.319-111	easyJet Airline Co Ltd	
G-EZAO	Airbus A.319-111	easyJet Airline Co Ltd	
G-EZAP	Airbus A.319-111	easyJet Airline Co Ltd	
G-EZAR	Pegasus Quik	D. McCormack	
G-EZAS	Airbus A.319-111	easyJet Airline Co Ltd	
G-EZAT	Airbus A.319-111	easyJet Airline Co Ltd	
G-EZAU	Airbus A.319-111	easyJet Airline Co Ltd	
G-EZAV	Airbus A.319-111	easyJet Airline Co Ltd	
G-EZAW	Airbus A.319-111	easyJet Airline Co Ltd	
G-EZAX	Airbus A.319-111	easyJet Airline Co Ltd	

Notes	Reg.	Type	Owner or Operator
	G-EZAY	Airbus A.319-111	easyJet Airline Co Ltd
	G-EZAZ	Airbus A.319-111	easyJet Airline Co Ltd
	G-EZBA	Airbus A.319-111	easyJet Airline Co Ltd
	G-EZBB	Airbus A.319-111	easyJet Airline Co Ltd
	G-EZBC	Airbus A.319-111	easyJet Airline Co Ltd
	G-EZBD	Airbus A.319-111	easyJet Airline Co Ltd
	G-EZBE	Airbus A.319-111	easyJet Airline Co Ltd
	G-EZBF	Airbus A.319-111	easyJet Airline Co Ltd
	G-EZBG	Airbus A.319-111	easyJet Airline Co Ltd
	G-EZBH	Airbus A.319-111	easyJet Airline Co Ltd
	G-EZBI	Airbus A.319-111	easyJet Airline Co Ltd
	G-EZBJ	Airbus A.319-111	easyJet Airline Co Ltd
	G-EZBK	Airbus A.319-111	easyJet Airline Co Ltd
	G-EZBL	Airbus A.319-111	easyJet Airline Co Ltd
	G-EZBM	Airbus A.319-111	easyJet Airline Co Ltd
	G-EZBN	Airbus A.319-111	easyJet Airline Co Ltd
	G-EZBO	Airbus A.319-111	easyJet Airline Co Ltd
	G-EZBR	Airbus A.319-111	easyJet Airline Co Ltd
	G-EZBT	Airbus A.319-111	easyJet Airline Co.Ltd
	G-EZBU	Airbus A.319-111	easyJet Airline Co.Ltd
	G-EZBV	Airbus A.319-111	easyJet Airline Co.Ltd
	G-EZBW	Airbus A.319-111	easyJet Airline.Co.Ltd
	G-EZBX	Airbus A.319-111	easyJet Airline Co.Ltd
	G-EZBY	Airbus A.319-111	easyJet Airline Co.Ltd
	G-EZBZ	Airbus A.319-111	easyJet Airline Co.Ltd
	G-EZDA	Airbus A.319-111	easyJet Airline Co.Ltd
	G-EZDB	Airbus A.319-111	easyJet Airline Co.Ltd
	G-EZDC	Airbus A.319-111	easyJet Airline Co Ltd (G-CCKB)
	G-EZDD	Airbus A.319-111	easyJet Airline Co.Ltd
	G-EZDE	Airbus A.319-111	easyJet Airline Co.Ltd
	G-EZDF	Airbus A.319-111	easyJet Airline Co.Ltd
	G-EZDG	Rutan Vari-Eze	L. Bayes (G-EZOS)
	G-EZDH	Airbus A.319-111	easyJet Airline Co.Ltd
	G-EZDI	Airbus A.319-111	easyJet Airline Co.Ltd
	G-EZDJ	Airbus A.319-111	easyJet Airline Co.Ltd
	G-EZDK	Airbus A.319-111	easyJet Airline Co.Ltd
	G-EZDL	Airbus A.319-111	easyJet Airline Co.Ltd
	G-EZDM	Airbus A.319-111	easyJet Airline Co.Ltd
	G-EZDN	Airbus A.319-111	easyJet Airline Co.Ltd
	G-EZDO	Airbus A.319-111	easyJet Airline Co.Ltd
	G-EZDP	Airbus A.319-111	easyJet Airline Co.Ltd
	G-EZDR	Airbus A.319-111	easyJet Airline Co.Ltd
	G-EZDS	Airbus A.319-111	easyJet Airline Co.Ltd
	G-EZDT	Airbus A.319-111	easyJet Airline Co.Ltd
	G-EZDU	Airbus A.319-111	easyJet Airline Co.Ltd
	G-EZDV	Airbus A.319-111	easyJet Airline Co.Ltd
	G-EZDW	Airbus A.319-111	easyJet Airline Co.Ltd
	G-EZDX	Airbus A.319-111	easyJet Airline Co.Ltd
	G-EZDY	Airbus A.319-111	easyJet Airline Co.Ltd
	G-EZDZ	Airbus A.319-111	easyJet Airline Co.Ltd
	G-EZEB	Airbus A.319-111	easyJet Airline Co.Ltd
	G-EZED	Airbus A.319-111	easyJet Airline Co.Ltd
	G-EZEG	Airbus A.319-111	easyJet Airline Co Ltd
	G-EZEL	Westland SA.341G Gazelle 1	W. R. Pitcher (G-BAZL)
	G-EZES	Airbus A.319-111	easyJet Airline Co Ltd
	G-EZET	Airbus A.319-111	easyJet Airline Co Ltd
	G-EZEV	Airbus A.319-111	easyJet Airline Co Ltd
	G-EZEW	Airbus A.319-111	easyJet Airline Co Ltd
	G-EZEZ	Airbus A.319-111	easyJet Airline Co Ltd
	G-EZFA	Airbus A.319-111	easyJet Airline Co.Ltd
	G-EZFB	Airbus A.319-111	easyJet Airline Co.Ltd
	G-EZFC	Airbus A.319-111	easyJet Airline Co.Ltd
	G-EZFD	Airbus A.319-111	easyJet Airline Co.Ltd
	G-EZFE	Airbus A.319-111	easyJet Airline Co.Ltd
	G-EZFF	Airbus A.319-111	easyJet Airline Co.Ltd
	G-EZFG	Airbus A.319-111	easyJet Airline Co.Ltd
	G-EZFH	Airbus A.319-111	easyJet Airline Co.Ltd
	G-EZFI	Airbus A.319-111	easyJet Airline Co.Ltd
	G-EZFJ	Airbus A.319-111	easyJet Airline Co.Ltd
	G-EZFK	Airbus A.319-111	easyJet Airline Co.Ltd
	G-EZFL	Airbus A.319-111	easyJet Airline Co.Ltd

Reg.	Type	Owner or Operator	Notes
G-EZFM	Airbus A.319-111	easyJet Airline Co.Ltd	
G-EZFN	Airbus A.319-111	easyJet Airline Co.Ltd	
G-EZFO	Airbus A.319-111	easyJet Airline Co.Ltd	
G-EZFP	Airbus A.319-111	easyJet Airline Co.Ltd	
G-EZFR	Airbus A.319-111	easyJet Airline Co.Ltd	
G-EZFS	Airbus A.319-111	easyJet Airline Co.Ltd	
G-EZFT	Airbus A.319-111	easyJet Airline Co.Ltd	
G-EZFU	Airbus A.319-111	easyJet Airline Co.Ltd	
G-EZFV	Airbus A.319-111	easyJet Airline Co.Ltd	
G-EZFW	Airbus A.319-111	easyJet Airline Co.Ltd	
G-EZFX	Airbus A.319-111	easyJet Airline Co.Ltd	
G-EZFY	Airbus A.319-111	easyJet Airline Co.Ltd	
G-EZFZ	Airbus A.319-111	easyJet Airline Co.Ltd	
G-EZGA	Airbus A.319-111	easyJet Airline Co.Ltd	
G-EZGB	Airbus A.319-111	easyJet Airline Co.Ltd	
G-EZGC	Airbus A.319-111	easyJet Airline Co.Ltd	
G-EZGD	Airbus A.319-111	easyJet Airline Co.Ltd	
G-EZGE	Airbus A.319-111	easyJet Airline Co.Ltd	
G-EZGF	Airbus A.319-111	easyJet Airline Co.Ltd	
G-EZGG	Airbus A.319-111	easyJet Airline Co.Ltd	
G-EZGH	Airbus A.319-111	easyJet Airline Co.Ltd	
G-EZGI	Airbus A.319-111	easyJet Airline Co.Ltd	
G-EZGJ	Airbus A.319-111	easyJet Airline Co.Ltd	
G-EZGK	Airbus A.319-111	easyJet Airline Co.Ltd	
G-EZGL	Airbus A.319-111	easyJet Airline Co.Ltd	
G-EZGM	Airbus A.319-111	easyJet Airline Co.Ltd	
G-EZGN	Airbus A.319-111	easyJet Airline Co.Ltd	
G-EZGP	Airbus A.319-111	easyJet Airline Co.Ltd	
G-EZIH	Airbus A.319-111	easyJet Airline Co Ltd	
G-EZII	Airbus A.319-111	easyJet Airline Co Ltd	
G-EZIJ	Airbus A.319-111	easyJet Airline Co Ltd	
G-EZIK	Airbus A.319-111	easyJet Airline Co Ltd	
G-EZIL	Airbus A.319-111	easyJet Airline Co Ltd	
G-EZIM	Airbus A.319-111	easyJet Airline Co Ltd	
G-EZIN	Airbus A.319-111	easyJet Airline Co Ltd	
G-EZIO	Airbus A.319-111	easyJet Airline Co Ltd	
G-EZIP	Airbus A.319-111	easyJet Airline Co Ltd	
G-EZIR	Airbus A.319-111	easyJet Airline Co Ltd	
G-EZIS	Airbus A.319-111	easyJet Airline Co Ltd	
G-EZIT	Airbus A.319-111	easyJet Airline Co Ltd	
G-EZIV	Airbus A.319-111	easyJet Airline Co Ltd	
G-EZIW	Airbus A.319-111	easyJet Airline Co Ltd	
G-EZIX	Airbus A.319-111	easyJet Airline Co Ltd	
G-EZIY	Airbus A.319-111	easyJet Airline Co Ltd	
G-EZIZ	Airbus A.319-111	easyJet Airline Co Ltd	
G-EZMH	Airbus A.319-111	easyJet Airline Co Ltd (G-CCKD)	
G-EZNC	Airbus A.319-111	easyJet Airline Co Ltd (G-CCKC)	
G-EZPG	Airbus A.319-111	easyJet Airline Co Ltd	
G-EZSM	Airbus A.319-111	easyJet Airline Co Ltd (G-CCKE)	
G-EZTA	Airbus A.320-214	easyJet Airline Co.Ltd	
G-EZTB	Airbus A.320-214	easyJet Airline Co.Ltd	
G-EZTC	Airbus A.320-214	easyJet Airline Co.Ltd	
G-EZTD	Airbus A.320-214	easyJet Airline Co.Ltd	
G-EZTE	Airbus A.320-214	easyJet Airline Co.Ltd	
G-EZTF	Airbus A.320-214	easyJet Airline Co.Ltd	
G-EZTG	Airbus A.320-214	easyJet Airline Co.Ltd	
G-EZTH	Airbus A.320-214	easyJet Airline Co.Ltd	
G-EZTI	Airbus A.320-214	easyJet Airline Co.Ltd	
G-EZTJ	Airbus A.320-214	easyJet Airline Co.Ltd	
G-EZTK	Airbus A.320-214	easyJet Airline Co.Ltd	
G-EZTL	Airbus A.320-214	easyJet Airline Co.Ltd	
G-EZTM	Airbus A.320-214	easyJet Airline Co.Ltd	
G-EZTR	Airbus A.320-214	easyJet Airline Co.Ltd	
G-EZTT	Airbus A.320-214	easyJet Airline Co.Ltd	
G-EZTV	Airbus A.320-214	easyJet Airline Co.Ltd	
G-EZTX	Airbus A.320-214	easyJet Airline Co.Ltd	
G-EZTY	Airbus A.320-214	easyJet Airline Co.Ltd	
G-EZTZ	Airbus A.320-214	easyJet Airline Co.Ltd	
G-EZUA	Airbus A.320-214	easyJet Airline Co.Ltd	
G-EZUB	Zenair CH.601HD Zodiac	R. A. C. Stephens	
G-EZUC	Airbus A.320-214	easyJet Airline Co.Ltd	

Notes	Reg.	Type	Owner or Operator
	G-EZUD	Airbus A.320-214	easyJet Airline Co.Ltd
	G-EZUF	Airbus A.320-214	easyJet Airline Co.Ltd
	G-EZUG	Airbus A.320-214	easyJet Airline Co.Ltd
	G-EZUH	Airbus A.320-214	easyJet Airline Co.Ltd
	G-EZUI	Airbus A.320-214	easyJet Airline Co.Ltd
	G-EZUJ	Airbus A.320-214	easyJet Airline Co.Ltd
	G-EZUK	Airbus A.320-214	easyJet Airline Co.Ltd
	G-EZUL	Airbus A.320-214	easyJet Airline Co.Ltd
	G-EZUM	Airbus A.320-214	easyJet Airline Co.Ltd
	G-EZUN	Airbus A.320-214	easyJet Airline Co.Ltd
	G-EZUO	Airbus A.320-214	easyJet Airline Co.Ltd
	G-EZUP	Airbus A.320-214	easyJet Airline Co.Ltd
	G-EZUR	Airbus A.320-214	easyJet Airline Co.Ltd
	G-EZUS	Airbus A.320-214	easyJet Airline Co.Ltd
	G-EZUT	Airbus A.320-214	easyJet Airline Co.Ltd
	G-EZUU	Airbus A.320-214	easyJet Airline Co.Ltd
	G-EZUV	Airbus A.320-214	easyJet Airline Co.Ltd
	G-EZUW	Airbus A.320-214	easyJet Airline Co.Ltd
	G-EZUY	Airbus A.320-214	easyJet Airline Co.Ltd
	G-EZUZ	Airbus A.320-214	easyJet Airline Co.Ltd
	G-EZVS	Colt 77B balloon	A. J. Lovell
	G-EZWA	Airbus A.320-214	easyJet Airline Co.Ltd
	G-EZWB	Airbus A.320-214	easyJet Airline Co.Ltd
	G-EZWC	Airbus A.320-214	easyJet Airline Co.Ltd
	G-EZWD	Airbus A.320-214	easyJet Airline Co.Ltd
	G-EZWE	Airbus A.320-214	easyJet Airline Co.Ltd
	G-EZWF	Airbus A.320-214	easyJet Airline Co.Ltd
	G-EZWG	Airbus A.320-214	easyJet Airline Co.Ltd
	G-EZWH	Airbus A.320-214	easyJet Airline Co.Ltd
	G-EZWI	Airbus A.320-214	easyJet Airline Co.Ltd
	G-EZWJ	Airbus A.320-214	easyJet Airline Co.Ltd
	G-EZWK	Airbus A.320-214	easyJet Airline Co.Ltd
	G-EZWL	Airbus A.320-214	easyJet Airline Co.Ltd
	G-EZWM	Airbus A.320-214	easyJet Airline Co.Ltd
	G-EZWN	Airbus A.320-214	easyJet Airline Co.Ltd
	G-EZWO	Airbus A.320-214	easyJet Airline Co.Ltd
	G-EZWP	Airbus A.320-214	easyJet Airline Co.Ltd
	G-EZWR	Airbus A.320-214	easyJet Airline Co.Ltd
	G-EZWS	Airbus A.320-214	easyJet Airline Co.Ltd
	G-EZXO	Colt 56A balloon	I. Lilja
	G-EZZA	Shaw Europa XS	J. C. R. Davey
	G-EZZE	CZAW Sportcruiser	G. Verity
	G-EZZL	Westland Gazelle HT.3	Regal Group UK (G-CBKC)
	G-EZZY	Evektor EV-97 Eurostar	D. P. Creedy
	G-FABO	Bombardier CL600-2B16 Challenger 604	Hangar 8 Management Ltd
	G-FACE	Cessna 172S	Oxford Aviation Services Ltd
	G-FADF	PA-18-150 Super Cub	A. J. Neale
	G-FAIR	SOCATA TB10 Tobago	Fairwings Ltd
	G-FAJC	Alpi Pioneer 300 Hawk	M. Clare
	G-FAJM	Robinson R44 II	Ryvoan Aviation Ltd
	G-FALC	Aeromere F.8L Falco	D. M. Burbridge (G-AROT)
	G-FAME	Starstreak Shadow SA-II	S. R. Whitehead
	G-FAMH	Zenair CH.701	F. Omaraie-Hamdanie
	G-FANC	Fairchild 24R-46 Argus III	A. T. Fines
	G-FANL	Cessna FR.172K XP-II	J. A. Rees
	G-FAOH	Zenair CH.601UL Zodiac	F. Omaraie-Hamdanie (G-CDPI)
	G-FARE	Robinson R44 II	Toriamos Ltd/Ireland
	G-FARL	Pitts S-1E Special	T. I. Williams
	G-FARO	Aero Designs Star-Lite SL.1	S. C. Goozee
	G-FARR	Jodel 150	G. H. Farr
	G-FARY	QAC Quickie Tri-Q	A. Bloomfield and A. Underwood
	G-FATB	Rockwell Commander 114B	James D. Pearce & Co
	G-FATE	Falco F8L	G-FATE Flying Group
	G-FAVS	PA-32-300 Cherokee Six	Cool Flourish Ltd (G-BKEK)
	G-FBAT	Aeroprakt A.22 Foxbat	J. Jordan
	G-FBEA	Embraer ERJ190-200LR	Flybe.com
	G-FBEB	Embraer ERJ190-200LR	Flybe.com
	G-FBEC	Embraer ERJ190-200LR	Flybe.com

Reg.	Type	Owner or Operator	Notes
G-FBED	Embraer ERJ190-200LR	Flybe.com	
G-FBEE	Embraer ERJ190-200LR	Flybe.com	
G-FBEF	Embraer ERJ190-200LR	Flybe.com	
G-FBEG	Embraer ERJ190-200LR	Flybe.com	
G-FBEH	Embraer ERJ190-200LR	Flybe.com	
G-FBEI	Embraer ERJ190-200LR	Flybe.com	
G-FBEJ	Embraer ERJ190-200LR	Flybe.com	
G-FBEK	Embraer ERJ190-200LR	Flybe.com	
G-FBEL	Embraer ERJ190-200LR	Flybe.com	
G-FBEM	Embraer ERJ190-200LR	Flybe.com	
G-FBEN	Embraer ERJ190-200LR	Flybe.com	
G-FBII	Ikarus C.42 FB100	F. Beeson	
G-FBJA	Embraer ERJ170-200STD	Flybe.com	
G-FBJB	Embraer ERJ170-200STD	Flybe.com	
G-FBJC	Embraer ERJ170-200STD	Flybe.com	
G-FBJD	Embraer ERJ170-200STD	Flybe.com	
G-FBJE	Embraer ERJ170-200STD	Flybe.com	
G-FBJF	Embraer ERJ170-200STD	Flybe.com	
G-FBJG	Embraer ERJ170-200STD	Flybe.com	
G-FBJH	Embraer ERJ170-200STD	Flybe.com	
G-FBJI	Embraer ERJ170-200STD	Flybe.com	
G-FBJJ	Embraer ERJ170-200STD	Flybe.com	
G-FBJK	Embraer ERJ170-200STD	Flybe.com	
G-FBJL	Dassault Falcon 2000	TAG Aviation (UK) Ltd	
G-FBKB	Cessna 510 Citation Mustang	Blink Ltd	
G-FBKC	Cessna 510 Citation Mustang	Blink Ltd	
G-FBLK	Cessna 510 Citation Mustang	Blink Ltd	
G-FBNK	Cessna 510 Citation Mustang	Blink Ltd	
G-FBOY	Skystar Kitfox Mk 7	A. Bray	
G-FBPL	PA-34-200 Seneca	Purple Horse Sales and Hire Ltd (G-BBXK)	
G-FBRN	PA-28-181 Archer II	Herefordshire Aero Club Ltd	
G-FBSS	Aeroprakt A22-LS Foxbat	A. K. & L. Lynn	
G-FBTT	Aeroprakt A22-L Foxbat	A. W. Leadley	
G-FBWH	PA-28R Cherokee Arrow 180	F. A. Short	
G-FCAV	Schleicher ASK-13	M. F. Cuming	
G-FCBI	Schweizer 269C-1	Lift West Ltd	
G-FCCC	Schleicher ASK-13	Shenington Gliding Club	
G-FCED	PA-31T2 Cheyenne IIXL	Provident Partners Ltd	
G-FCKD	Eurocopter EC 120B	Red Dragon Management LLP	
G-FCLA	Boeing 757-28A	Thomas Cook Airlines Ltd	
G-FCLD	Boeing 757-25F	Thomas Cook Airlines Ltd	
G-FCLE	Boeing 757-28A	Thomas Cook Airlines Ltd	
G-FCLI	Boeing 757-28A	Thomas Cook Airlines Ltd	
G-FCLJ	Boeing 757-2Y0	Thomas Cook Airlines Ltd	
G-FCLK	Boeing 757-2Y0	Thomas Cook Airlines Ltd	
G-FCOM	Slingsby T.59F Kestrel	P. A. C. Wheatcroft & A. G. Truman	
G-FCSL	PA-32-350 Navajo Chieftain	Culross Aerospace Ltd (G-CLAN)	
G-FCSP	Robin DR.400/180	P. G. Hayward	
G-FCUK	Pitts S-1C Special	H. C. Luck	
G-FCUM	Robinson R44 II	The Grange Country Club Ltd	
G-FDDY	Schleicher Ka 6CR	M. D. Brooks	
G-FDPS	Aviat Pitts S-2C Special	Flights and Dreams Ltd	
G-FDZA	Boeing 737-8K5	Thomson Airways Ltd	
G-FDZB	Boeing 737-8K5	Thomson Airways Ltd	
G-FDZD	Boeing 737-8K5	Thomson Airways Ltd	
G-FDZE	Boeing 737-8K5	Thomson Airways Ltd	
G-FDZF	Boeing 737-8K5	Thomson Airways Ltd	
G-FDZG	Boeing 737-8K5	Thomson Airways Ltd	
G-FDZJ	Boeing 737-8K5	Thomson Airways Ltd	
G-FDZR	Boeing 737-8K5	Thomson Airways Ltd	
G-FDZS	Boeing 737-8K5	Thomson Airways Ltd	
G-FDZT	Boeing 737-8K5	Thomson Airways Ltd	
G-FDZU	Boeing 737-8K5	Thomson Airways Ltd	
G-FDZW	Boeing 737-8K5	Thomson Airways Ltd	
G-FDZX	Boeing 737-8K5	Thomson Airways Ltd	
G-FDZY	Boeing 737-8K5	Thomson Airways Ltd	
G-FDZZ	Boeing 737-8K5	Thomson Airways Ltd	
G-FEAB	PA-28-181 Archer III	Feabrex Ltd	

Notes	Reg.	Type	Owner or Operator
	G-FEBB	Grob G.104 Speed Astir IIB	M. Ogbe
	G-FEBJ	Schleicher ASW-19B	A. P. Hatton
	G-FECO	Grob G.102 Astir CS77	Eco Warriors
	G-FEEF	Jodel DR.220-2 + 2	A. C. Walker
	G-FEET	Mainair Pegasus Quik	M. P. Duckett
	G-FELC	Cirrus SR22	F. Rossello
	G-FELD	Rotorsport UK MTO Sport	S. Pearce
	G-FELL	Shaw Europa	M. C. Costin & J. A. Inglis
	G-FELM	PA-28-180 Cherokee C	F. P. M. Vaille
	G-FELT	Cameron N-77 balloon	Allan Industries Ltd
	G-FELX	CZAW Sportcruiser	T. F. Smith
	G-FERN	Mainair Blade 912	M. H. Moulai
	G-FERV	Rolladen-Schneider LS4	R. J. J. Bennett
	G-FESS	Pegasus Quantum 15-912	P. M. Fessi (G-CBBZ)
	G-FEVS	PZL-Bielsko SZD-50-3 Puchacz	The Borders (Milfield) Gliding Club Ltd
	G-FEWG	Fuji FA.200-160	Caseright Ltd (G-BBNV)
	G-FEZZ	Bell 206B JetRanger II	R. J. Myram
	G-FFAB	Cameron N-105 balloon	B. J. Hammond
	G-FFAF	Cessna F.150L	B. M. & T. F. Freake
	G-FFBG	Cessna F.182Q	W. G. E. James
	G-FFEN	Cessna F.150M	B. Emerson & J. Tuckwell
	G-FFFA	P&M Pulsr	Flying for Freedom Ltd
	G-FFFT	Lindstrand LBL-31A balloon	W. Rousell & J. Tyrrell
	G-FFIT	Pegasus Quik	R. G. G. Pinder
	G-FFMV	Diamond DA.42 M-NG Twin Star	Diamond Airborne Sensing GmbH
	G-FFOX	Hawker Hunter T.7B (WV318:D)	Hunter Flight Academy and C. V. J. Heames
	G-FFRA	Dassault Falcon 20DC	FR Aviation Ltd
	G-FFRI	AS.355F1 Twin Squirrel	Sterling Helicopters Ltd (G-GLOW/G-PAPA/ G-CNET/G-MCAH)
	G-FFTI	SOCATA TB20 Trinidad	R. Lenk
	G-FFUN	Pegasus Quantum 15	J. R. F. Hollingshead
	G-FFWD	Cessna 310R	T. S. Courtman (G-TVKE/G-EURO)
	G-FGAZ	Schleicher Ka 6E	C. M. Billings, B. A. & M. A. Roberts
	G-FGID	Vought FG-1D Corsair (KD345:130-A)	Patina Ltd
	G-FGSI	Montgomerie-Bensen B8MR	F. G. Shepherd
	G-FHAS	Scheibe SF.25E Super Falke	D. C. Mason
	G-FIAT	PA-28 Cherokee 140	Demero Ltd & Transcourt Ltd (G-BBYW)
	G-FIBS	AS.350BA Ecureuil	G. Mazza/Italy
	G-FICS	Flight Design CTSW	J. I. Spring & A. Harris
	G-FIDL	Thruster T.600N 450	T. A. Colman (G-CBIO)
	G-FIFA	Cessna 404 Titan	RVL Aviation Ltd (G-TVIP/G-KIWI/G-BHNI)
	G-FIFE	Cessna FA.152	The Moray Flying Club (1990) (G-BFYN)
	G-FIFI	SOCATA TB20 Trinidad	A. T. Paton (G-BMWS)
	G-FIFT	Ikarus C.42 FB 100	A. R. Jones
	G-FIFY	Colomban MC-30 Luciole	D. R. Hall
	G-FIGA	Cessna 152	Bowen-Air Ltd
	G-FIGB	Cessna 152	A. J. Gomes
	G-FIII	Extra EA.300/L	J. S. Allison (G-RGEE)
	G-FIJJ	Cessna F.177RG	D. R. Vale (G-AZFP)
	G-FIJV	Lockheed L.188CF Electra	Atlantic Airlines Ltd
	G-FILE	PA-34-200T Seneca	Bristol & Wessex Aeroplane Club Ltd
	G-FINA	Cessna F.150L	A. Boyd (G-BIFT)
	G-FIND	Cessna F.406	Reconnaissance Ventures Ltd
	G-FINT	Piper L-4B Grasshopper	G. & H. M. Picarella
	G-FINZ	I.I.I Sky Arrow 650T	C. A. Bloom
	G-FIRM	Cessna 550 Citation Bravo	The Cambridge Aero Club Ltd
	G-FIRZ	Murphy Renegade Spirit UK	S. Koutsoukos
	G-FITY	Europa XS	D. C. A. Moore & M. Fielder
	G-FIXX	Van's RV-7	Hambilton Engineering Ltd
	G-FIZU	Lockheed L.188CF Electra	Atlantic Airlines Ltd
	G-FIZY	Shaw Europa XS	J. S. Davis (G-DDSC)
	G-FIZZ	PA-28-161 Warrior II	G-FIZZ Group
	G-FJET	Cessna 550 Citation II	London Executive Aviation Ltd (G-DCFR/ G-WYLX/G-JETD)
	G-FJMS	Partenavia P.68B	J. B. Randle (G-SVHA)
	G-FJTH	Aeroprakt A.22 Foxbat	B. Gurling

Reg.	Type	Owner or Operator	Notes
G-FKNH	PA-15 Vagabond	M. J. Mothershaw	
G-FKOS	PA-28-181 Archer II	M. K. Johnson	
G-FLAG	Colt 77A balloon	B. A. Williams	
G-FLAV	PA-28-161 Warrior II	The Crew Flying Group	
G-FLBA	DHC.8-402 Dash Eight	Flybe.com	
G-FLBB	DHC.8-402 Dash Eight	Flybe.com	
G-FLBC	DHC.8-402 Dash Eight	Flybe.com	
G-FLBD	DHC.8-402 Dash Eight	Flybe.com	
G-FLBE	DHC.8-402 Dash Eight	Flybe.com	
G-FLBK	Cessna 510 Citation Mustang	Blink Ltd	
G-FLBY	Ikarus C42 FB100 Bravo	42 Fly	
G-FLCA	Fleet Model 80 Canuck	E. C. Taylor	
G-FLCN	Dassault Falcon 900B	Xclusive Jet Charter Ltd	
G-FLCT	Hallam Fleche	R. G. Hallam	
G-FLDG	Skyranger 912	A. J. Gay	
G-FLEA	SOCATA TB10 Tobago	P. Mather	
G-FLEE	ZJ-Viera	P. C. Piggott	
G-FLEX	Mainair Pegasus Quik	L. A. Read	
G-FLGT	Lindstrand LBL-105A balloon	Ballongaventyr I. Skane AB/Sweden	
G-FLIK	Pitts S-1S Special	R. P. Millinship	
G-FLIP	Cessna FA.152	South East Area Flying Section (G-BOES)	
G-FLIS	Magni M.16C	M. L. L. Temple	
G-FLIT	Rotorway Executive 162F	R. S. Snell	
G-FLIZ	Staaken Z-21 Flitzer	M. J. Clark	
G-FLKE	Scheibe SF.25C Falke	The Royal Air Force Gliding & Soaring Association	
G-FLKS	Scheibe SF.25C Falke	London Gliding Club Propietary Ltd	
G-FLKY	Cessna 172S	M. E. Falkingham	
G-FLOR	Shaw Europa	A. F. C. van Eldik	
G-FLOW	Cessna 172N	P. H. Archard	
G-FLOX	Shaw Europa	DPT Group	
G-FLPI	Rockwell Commander 112	J. B. Thompson	
G-FLTC	BAe 146-300	E3205 Trading Ltd (G-JEBH/G-BVTO/G-NJID)	
G-FLUZ	Rolladen-Schneider LS8-18	D. M. King	
G-FLYA	Mooney M.20J	B. Willis	
G-FLYB	Ikarus C.42 FB100	Red-Air UK	
G-FLYC	Ikarus C.42 FB100	Solent Flight Ltd	
G-FLYF	Mainair Blade 912	D. G. Adley	
G-FLYG	Slingsby T.67C	G. Laden	
G-FLYI	PA-34-200 Seneca II	Falcon Flying Services Ltd (G-BHVO)	
G-FLYM	Ikarus C42 FB100	R. S. O'Carroll	
G-FLYP	Beagle B.206 Srs 2	Key Publishing Ltd (G-AVHO)	
G-FLYT	Shaw Europa	K. F. & R. Richardson	
G-FLYW	Beech B.200 Super King Air	J. A. Rees (G-LIVY/G-PSTR)	
G-FLYX	Robinson R44 II	R. D. Hagger	
G-FLYY	BAC.167 Strikemaster 80A	G-FLYY Strikemaster Ltd	
G-FLZR	Staaken Z-21 Flitzer	I. V. Staines	
G-FMAM	PA-28-151 Warrior (modified)	Airtime Aviation Holdings Ltd (G-BBXV)	
G-FMBS	Inverted US 12	W. P. Wright	
G-FMGB	Cameron Z-90 balloon	A. M. Holly	
G-FMGG	Maule M5-235C Lunar Rocket	S. Bierbaum (G-RAGG)	
G-FMKA	Diamond HK.36TC Super Dimona	G. P. Davis	
G-FMLY	Commander 114B	PNG Air Ltd (G-VICS)	
G-FMSG	Cessna FA.150K	G. Owen/Gamston (G-POTS/G-AYUY)	
G-FNAV	PA-31-350 Navajo Chieftain	Flight Calibration Services Ltd (G-BFFR)	
G-FNEY	Cessna F.177RG	F. Ney	
G-FNLD	Cessna 172N	Papa Hotel Flying Group	
G-FOFO	Robinson R44 II	Kuki Helicopter Sales Ltd	
G-FOGG	Cameron N-90 balloon	J. P. E. Money-Kyrle	
G-FOGI	Shaw Europa XS	B. Fogg	
G-FOKK	Fokker DR1 (replica)	P. D. & S. E. Ford	
G-FOKR	Fokker E.III Replica	Eshott Eindecker Group	
G-FOLD	Light Aero Avid Speedwing	B. W. & G. Evans	
G-FOLI	Robinson R22 Beta II	G. M. Duckworth	
G-FOLY	Aerotek Pitts S-2A Modified	C. T. Charleston	
G-FOPP	Lancair 320	Great Circle Design Ltd	
G-FORA	Schempp-Hirth Ventus cT	G. Bailey & J. D. Sorrell	

Notes	Reg.	Type	Owner or Operator
	G-FORC	SNCAN Stampe SV.4C	C. C. Rollings & F. J. Hodson
	G-FORD	SNCAN Stampe SV.4C	P. H. Meeson
	G-FORM	Learjet 45	Broomco 3598 Ltd
	G-FORZ	Pitts S-1S Special	N. W. Parkinson
	G-FOSY	MS.880B Rallye Club	A. G. Foster (G-AXAK)
	G-FOWL	Colt 90A balloon	M. R. Stokoe
	G-FOWS	Cameron N-105 balloon	Ezmerelda Balloon Syndicate
	G-FOXA	PA-28-161 Cadet	Leicestershire Aero Club Ltd
	G-FOXB	Aeroprakt A.22 Foxbat	G. D. McCullough
	G-FOXC	Denney Kitfox Mk 3	T. Willford
	G-FOXD	Denney Kitfox Mk 2	P. P. Trangmar
	G-FOXE	Denney Kitfox Mk 2	K. M. Pinkar
	G-FOXF	Denney Kitfox Mk 4	M. S. Goodwin
	G-FOXG	Denney Kitfox Mk 2	J. U. McKercher
	G-FOXI	Denney Kitfox	I. M. Walton
	G-FOXL	Zenair CH.601XL Zodiac	R. W. Taylor
	G-FOXM	Bell 206B JetRanger 2	Tyringham Charter & Group Services (G-STAK/G-BNIS)
	G-FOXO	Aeropro Eurofox 912(S)	S. E. Coles
	G-FOXS	Denney Kitfox Mk 2	M. A. Baker
	G-FOXX	Denney Kitfox	A. W. Hodder
	G-FOXZ	Denney Kitfox	S. C. Goozee
	G-FOZY	Van's RV-7	M. G. Forrest (G-COPZ)
	G-FOZZ	Beech A36 Bonanza	Go To Air Ltd
	G-FPIG	PA-28-151 Warrior	G. F. Strain (G-BSSR)
	G-FPLD	Beech 200 Super King Air	Cobham Flight Inspection Ltd
	G-FPLE	Beech 200 Super King Air	Cobham Flight Inspection Ltd
	G-FPSA	PA-28-161 Warrior II	Falcon Flying Services (G-RSFT/G-WARI)
	G-FRAD	Dassault Falcon 20E	Cobham Leasing Ltd (G-BCYF)
	G-FRAF	Dassault Falcon 20E	FR Aviation Ltd
	G-FRAG	PA-32 Cherokee Six 300E	T. A. Houghton
	G-FRAH	Dassault Falcon 20DC	FR Aviation Ltd
	G-FRAI	Dassault Falcon 20E	FR Aviation Ltd
	G-FRAJ	Dassault Falcon 20E	FR Aviation Ltd
	G-FRAK	Dassault Falcon 20DC	FR Aviation Ltd
	G-FRAL	Dassault Falcon 20DC	FR Aviation Ltd
	G-FRAN	Piper J-3C-90 Cub(480321:H-44)	Essex L-4 Group (G-BIXY)
	G-FRAO	Dassault Falcon 20DC	FR Aviation Ltd
	G-FRAP	Dassault Falcon 20DC	FR Aviation Ltd
	G-FRAR	Dassault Falcon 20DC	FR Aviation Ltd
	G-FRAS	Dassault Falcon 20C	FR Aviation Ltd
	G-FRAT	Dassault Falcon 20C	FR Aviation Ltd
	G-FRAU	Dassault Falcon 20C	FR Aviation Ltd
	G-FRAW	Dassault Falcon 20ECM	FR Aviation Ltd
	G-FRAY	Cassutt IIIM (modified)	C. I. Fray
	G-FRCE	Folland Gnat T.Mk.1 (XS104)	Red Gnat Ltd
	G-FRDY	Dynamic WT9 UK	Peter Dodd Consultants
	G-FRGN	PA-28-236 Dakota	P. J. Vacher
	G-FRGT	P & M Quik GT450	G-FRGT Group
	G-FRIK	P & M Quik GT450	G-FRIK Group
	G-FRIL	Lindstrand LBL-105A balloon	K. R. Karlstrom
	G-FRJB	Britten Sheriff SA-1 ★	Aeropark
	G-FRNK	Skyranger 912(2)	D. L. Foxley & G. Lace
	G-FROM	Ikarus C.42 FB100	G-FROM Group
	G-FRSX	VS.388 Seafire F.46 (LA564)	Seafire Displays Ltd
	G-FRYI	Beech 200 Super King Air	London Executive Aviation Ltd (G-OAVX/ G-IBCA/G-BMCA)
	G-FRYL	Beech 390 Premier 1	Hawk Air Ltd
	G-FRZN	Agusta A109S Grand	Iceland Foods Ltd
	G-FSEU	Beech 200 Super King Air	Air Mercia Ltd
	G-FSHA	Denney Kitfox Mk 2	F. Jorgensen
	G-FSZY	TB-10 Tobago	P. J. Bentley
	G-FTAX	Cessna 421C	Gold Air International Ltd (G-BFFM)
	G-FTIL	Robin DR.400/180R	RAF Wyton Flying Club Ltd
	G-FTIN	Robin DR.400/100	YP Flying Group
	G-FTOM	Agusta Westland AW.139	CHC Scotia Ltd
	G-FTSE	BN-2A Mk.III-2 Trislander	Aurigny Air Services Ltd (G-BEPI)

Reg.	Type	Owner or Operator	Notes
G-FTUS	Ultramagic F-12 Paquete balloon	A. M. Holly	
G-FUEL	Robin DR.400/180	R. Darch	
G-FUFU	Agusta A.109 Grand	Air Harrods Ltd	
G-FUKM	Westland Gazelle AH.1 (ZA730)	Falcon Aviation Ltd	
G-FULL	PA-28R Cherokee Arrow 200-II	Stapleford Flying Club Ltd (G-HWAY/G-JULI)	
G-FULM	Sikorsky S-76C	Air Harrods Ltd	
G-FUND	Thunder Ax7-65Z balloon	G. B. Davies	
G-FUNK	Yakovlev Yak-50	Redstar Aero Services Ltd	
G-FUNN	Plumb BGP-1	J. Riley	
G-FURI	Isaacs Fury II	S. M. Johnston	
G-FURZ	Best Off Sky Ranger Nynja 912S(1)	S. R. Swift	
G-FUSE	Cameron N-105 balloon	S. A. Lacey	
G-FUUN	Silence SA.180 Twister	A. W. McKee	
G-FUZZ	PA-18 Super Cub 95 (51-15319)	G. W. Cline	
G-FVEE	Monnett Sonerai 1	J. S. Baldwin	
G-FVEL	Cameron Z-90 balloon	Fort Vale Engineering Ltd	
G-FVIP	Agustas A.109E Power	Castle Air Ltd (G-HCFC)	
G-FWAY	Lindstrand LBL-90A balloon	H. W. R. Stewart	
G-FWJR	Ultramagic M-56 balloon	Harding and Sons Ltd	
G-FWKS	Tanarg/Ixess 15 912S(1)	M. A. Coffin (G-SYUT)	
G-FWPW	PA-28-236 Dakota	P. A. & F. C. Winters	
G-FXBT	Aeroprakt A.22 Foxbat	R. H. Jago	
G-FXII	VS.366 Spitfire F.XII (EN224)	Air Leasing Ltd	
G-FYAN	Williams Westwind MLB	M. D. Williams	
G-FYAO	Williams Westwind MLB	M. D. Williams	
G-FYAU	Williams Westwind Mk 2 MLB	M. D. Williams	
G-FYAV	Osprey Mk 4E2 MLB	C. D. Egan & C. Stiles	
G-FYBX	Portswood Mk XVI MLB	I. Chadwick	
G-FYCL	Osprey Mk 4G MLB	P. J. Rogers	
G-FYCV	Osprey Mk 4D MLB	M. Thomson	
G-FYDF	Osprey Mk 4DV	K. A. Jones	
G-FYDI	Williams Westwind Two MLB	M. D. Williams	
G-FYDN	European 8C MLB	P. D. Ridout	
G-FYDO	Osprey Mk 4D MLB	N. L. Scallan	
G-FYDP	Williams Westwind Three MLB	M. D. Williams	
G-FYDS	Osprey Mk 4D MLB	N. L. Scallan	
G-FYEK	Unicorn UE.1C MLB	D. & D. Eaves	
G-FYEO	Eagle Mk 1 MLB	M. E. Scallan	
G-FYEV	Osprey Mk 1C MLB	M. E. Scallan	
G-FYEZ	Firefly Mk 1 MLB	M. E. & N. L. Scallan	
G-FYFI	European E.84DS MLB	M. Stelling	
G-FYFJ	Williams Westland 2 MLB	M. D. Williams	
G-FYFN	Osprey Saturn 2 MLB	J. & M. Woods	
G-FYFW	Rango NA-55 MLB	Rango Balloon and Kite Company	
G-FYFY	Rango NA-55RC MLB	Rango Balloon and Kite Company	
G-FYGC	Rango NA-42B MLB	L. J. Wardle	
G-FYGJ	Airspeed 300 MLB	N. Wells	
G-FYGM	Saffrey/Smith Princess MLB	A. Smith	
G-FZZA	General Avia F22-A	P. J. Tanulak	
G-FZZI	Cameron H-34 balloon	Magical Adventures Ltd	
G-GABI	Lindstrand LBL-35A Cloudhopper balloon	R. D. Sargeant	
G-GABS	Cameron TR-70 balloon	N. M. Gabriel	
G-GABY	Bombardier BD-700-1A10 Global Express	Bookajet Ltd	
G-GACA	P.57 Sea Prince T.1 (WP308:572CU) ★	P. G. Vallance Ltd/Charlwood	
G-GACB	Robinson R44 II	A. C. Barker	
G-GAEA	Aquila AT01	Khair BV/Netherlands	
G-GAEC	Aquila AT01	Khair BV/Netherlands	
G-GAFA	PA-34-200T Seneca II	Oxford Aviation Academy (Oxford) Ltd	
G-GAFT	PA-44-180 Seminole	Bravo Aviation Ltd	
G-GAII	Hawker Hunter GA.11 (XE685)	Hawker Hunter Aviation Ltd	
G-GAJB	AA-5B Tiger	G-GAJB Group (G-BHZN)	
G-GALA	PA-28 Cherokee 180E	FlyBPL.com	
G-GALB	PA-28-161 Warrior II	LB Aviation Ltd	

Notes	Reg.	Type	Owner or Operator
	G-GALC	Sikorsky S-92A	Bristow Helicopters Ltd
	G-GAMA	Beech 58 Baron	Gama Aviation Ltd (G-WWIZ/G-BBSD)
	G-GAME	Cessna T.303	J. & R. K. Hyatt
	G-GAND	Agusta-Bell 206B Jet Ranger	The Henderson Group (G-AWMK)
	G-GANE	Sequoia F.8L Falco	F. M. Magnat
	G-GAOH	Robin DR.400 / 2 +2.	S. D. Baker & M. Stott
	G-GAOM	Robin DR.400 / 2+2	P. M. & P. A. Chapman
	G-GARB	EV-97 Team Eurostar	R. J. Garbutt
	G-GARI	Ace Aviation Touch/Buzz	G. B. Shaw
	G-GASP	PA-28-181 Archer II	G-GASP Flying Group
	G-GASS	Thunder Ax7-77 balloon	Servowarm Balloon Syndicate
	G-GAST	Van's RV-8	G. M. R. Abrey
	G-GATE	Robinson R44 II	J. W. Gate
	G-GATT	Robinson R44 II	B. W. Faulkner
	G-GAVA	BAe Jetstream 3102	A C Aviation Wales Ltd (G-CCPW)
	G-GAVH	P & M Quik	N. H. Taylor
	G-GAWA	Cessna 140	C140 Group (G-BRSM)
	G-GAZA	Aérospatiale SA.341G Gazelle 1	The Auster Aircraft Co Ltd (G-RALE/G-SFTG)
	G-GAZN	P & M Quik GT450	C. Hughes
	G-GAZO	Ace Magic Cyclone	G. J. Pearce
	G-GAZZ	Aérospatiale SA.341G Gazelle 1	Cheqair Ltd
	G-GBAO	Robin R1180TD	J. Toulorge
	G-GBBB	Schleicher ASH-25	ASH25 BB Glider Syndicate
	G-GBBT	Ultramagic M-90 balloon	British Telecommunications PLC
	G-GBCC	Ikarus C42 FB100	I. R. Westrope
	G-GBEE	Mainair Pegasus Quik	M. G. Evans
	G-GBET	Ikarus C42 FB UK	Olympic Flying Club (G-BDBMK/G-MROY)
	G-GBFF	Cessna F.172N	Aviation Rentals
	G-GBFR	Cessna F.177RG	Airspeed Aviation Ltd
	G-GBGA	Scheibe SF.25C Falke	The Royal Air Force Gliding and Soaring Association
	G-GBGB	Ultramagic M.105 balloon	Universal Car Services Ltd
	G-GBGF	Cameron Dragon SS balloon	Magical Adventures Ltd (G-BUVH)
	G-GBHI	SOCATA TB10 Tobago	J. Watt
	G-GBJP	Mainair Pegasus Quantum 15	M. P. Chew
	G-GBLP	Cessna F.172M	Aviate Scotland Ltd (G-GWEN)
	G-GBMR	Beech B200 Super King Air	M and R Aviation LLP
	G-GBOB	Alpi Pioneer 300 Hawk	R. E. Burgess
	G-GBPP	Rolladen-Schneider LS6-c18	G. J. Lyons & R. Sinden
	G-GBRB	PA-28 Cherokee 180C	Bravo Romeo Group
	G-GBRU	Bell 206B JetRanger 3	R. A. Fleming Ltd (G-CDGV)
	G-GBRV	Van's RV-9A	G. Carter & K. L. Chorley (G-THMB)
	G-GBSL	Beech 76 Duchess	M. H. Cundsy (G-BGVG)
	G-GBTA	Boeing 737-436	British Airways (G-BVHA)
	G-GBTB	Boeing 737-436	British Airways (G-BVHB)
	G-GBTL	Cessna 172S	Bohana Technology Ltd
	G-GBUE	Robin DR.400/120A	J. A. Kane (G-BPXD)
	G-GBUN	Cessna 182T	G. M. Bunn
	G-GBVX	Robin DR400/120A	The Leuchars Flying Company
	G-GBXF	Robin HR200/120	B. A. Mills
	G-GCAC	Europa XS T-G	J. L. Gunn
	G-GCAT	PA-28 Cherokee 140B	Group Cat (G-BFRH)
	G-GCCL	Beech 76 Duchess	Aerolease Ltd
	G-GCDA	Cirrus SR20	Friends Aloft Ltd
	G-GCDB	Cirrus SR20	Friends Aloft Ltd
	G-GCDC	Cirrus SR20	RPR Associates Ltd
	G-GCDD	Cirrus SR20	Daedalus Aviation (Services) Ltd
	G-GCEA	Pegasus Quik	A. P. Douglas-Dixon
	G-GCFM	Diamond DA.40D Star	VifoGmbhsrl/Germany
	G-GCIY	Robin DR.400-140B	M. S. Lonsdale
	G-GCJA	Rolladen-Schneider LS8-18	N. T. Mallender
	G-GCJH	Aerospool Dynamic WT9 UK	Yeoman Light Aircraft Co.Ltd
	G-GCKI	Mooney M.20K	B. Barr
	G-GCMM	Agusta A109E	Hadleigh Partners
	G-GCMW	Grob G.102 Astir CS	M. S. F. Wood
	G-GCUF	Robin DR400/160	Exeter Aviation Ltd
	G-GCYC	Cessna F.182Q	The Cessna 180 Group
	G-GDEF	Robin DR.400/120	J. M. Shackleton
	G-GDER	Robin R.1180TD	Berkshire Aviation Services Ltd

Reg.	Type	Owner or Operator	Notes
G-GDEZ	BAe 125 Srs.100B	Frewton Ltd	
G-GDFB	Boeing 737-33A	Jet 2	
G-GDFC	Boeing 737-8K2	Jet 2	
G-GDFD	Boeing 737-8K5	Jet 2	
G-GDFE	Boeing 737-3Q8	Jet 2	
G-GDFF	Boeing 737-85P	Jet 2	
G-GDFG	Boeing 737-36Q	Jet 2	
G-GDFH	Boeing 737-3Y5	Jet 2	
G-GDFJ	Boeing 737-804	Jet 2 (G-CDZI)	
G-GDFK	Boeing 737-36N	Jet 2 (G-STRE/G-XBHX)	
G-GDFL	Boeing 737-36N	Jet 2	
G-GDFM	Boeing 737-36N	Jet 2	
G-GDFN	Boeing 737-33V	Jet 2 (G-EZYH)	
G-GDFO	Boeing 737-3U3	Jet 2 (G-THOP)	
G-GDFP	Boeing 737-8Z9	Jet 2	
G-GDFR	Boeing 737-8Z9	Jet 2	
G-GDFT	Boeing 737-36Q	Jet 2 (G-TOYM/G-OHAJ)	
G-GDFT	Boeing 737-86N	Jet 2	
G-GDFV	Boeing 737-85F	Jet 2	
G-GDJF	Robinson R44 II	Berkley Properties Ltd (G-DEXT)	
G-GDKR	Robin DR400/140B	Popham Flying Group	
G-GDMW	Beech 76 Duchess	Flew LLP	
G-GDOG	PA-28R Cherokee Arrow 200-II	The Mutley Crew Group (G-BDXW)	
G-GDSG	Agusta A109E Power	Pendley Farm	
G-GDRV	Van's RV-6	J. R. S. Heaton & R. Feather	
G-GDTL	Airbus A.320-231	MyTravel Airways	
G-GDTU	Avions Mudry CAP-10B	D. C. Cooper & A. L. Farr	
G-GECO	Hughes 369HS	N. Duggan (G-ATVEE/G-GCXK)	
G-GEEP	Robin R.1180TD	The Aiglon Flying Group	
G-GEHL	Cessna 172S	Ebryl Ltd	
G-GEHP	PA-28RT-201 Arrow IV	Aeros Leasing Ltd	
G-GEKO	Parmania Revolution/Kobra Kilo (modified)	D. J. Eldridge	
G-GELI	Colt 31A balloon	S. F. Burden (G-CDFI)	
G-GEMM	Cirrus SR20	Schmolke Grosskuechensysteme GmbH	
G-GEMS	Thunder Ax8-90 Srs 2 balloon	Kraft Bauprojekt GmbH/Germany	
G-GEOF	Pereira Osprey 2	G. Crossley	
G-GEOS	Diamond HK.36 TTC-ECO	University Court (School of Geosciences) of the Super Dimona University of Edinburgh	
G-GERS	Robinson R44 II	M. Virdee	
G-GERT	Van's RV-7	Barnstormers	
G-GERY	Stoddard-Hamilton Glastar	S. G. Brown	
G-GEZZ	Bell 206B JetRanger II	Rivermead Aviation Ltd	
G-GFAA	Slingsby T.67A	Slingsby Flying Group (G-BJXA)	
G-GFCA	PA-28-161 Cadet	Aeros Leasing Ltd	
G-GFCB	PA-28-161 Cadet	South West Air Ltd	
G-GFEY	PA-34-200T Seneca II	The G-GFEY Owners Group	
G-GFIA	Cessna 152	Aircraft Grouping Ltd	
G-GFIB	Cessna F.152	B. Somerville (G-BPIO)	
G-GFID	Cessna 152 II	Pure Aviation Support Services Ltd (G-BORJ)	
G-GFIE	Cessna 152	Aircraft Grouping Ltd (G-CEUS)	
G-GFIG	Cessna 152	Westbeach Aviation Ltd (G-BNOZ)	
G-GFKY	Zenair CH.250	R. G. Kelsall	
G-GFLY	Cessna F.150L	Hangar 1 Ltd	
G-GFNO	Robin ATL	B. F. Walker	
G-GFOX	Aeroprakt A.22 Foxbat	G. F. Elvis	
G-GFRA	PA-28RT-201T Turbo Arrow IV	NSP Ltd (G-LROY/G-BNTS)	
G-GFRO	Robin ATL	B. F. Walker	
G-GFSA	Cessna 172R Skyhawk	M. Casey	
G-GFTA	PA-28-161 Warrior III	One Zero Three Ltd	
G-GGDV	Schleicher Ka 6E	H. J. Fox	
G-GGGG	Thunder Ax7-77A balloon	T. A. Gilmour	
G-GGHZ	Robin ATL	Box MR Ltd	
G-GGJK	Robin DR.400/140B	Headcorn Jodelers	
G-GGLA	Cessna 560XL Citation XLS+	E and A Aviation Ltd	
G-GGOW	Colt 77A balloon	T. W. Blunt, T. J. Gouder & N. R. P. Wren	
G-GGRR	SA Bulldog Srs 120/121 (XX614:V)	D. J. Sharp (G-CBAM)	
G-GGTT	Agusta-Bell 47G-4A	P. R. Smith	

Notes	Reg.	Type	Owner or Operator
	G-GHEE	Aerotechnik EV-97 Eurostar	C. J. Ball
	G-GHER	AS.355N Ecureuil II	Gallagher Air LLP
	G-GHKX	PA-28-161 Warrior II	Multiflight Ltd
	G-GHOP	Cameron Z-77 balloon	Lakeside Lodge Golf Centre
	G-GHOW	Cessna F.182Q	Oscar Whiskey Flying Group
	G-GHRW	PA-28RT-201 Arrow IV	P. Cowley (G-ONAB/G-BHAK)
	G-GHZJ	SOCATA TB9 Tampico	P. K. Hayward
	G-GIBB	Robinson R44 II	Tingdene Aviation Ltd
	G-GIBP	Moravan Zlin Z.526 Trener Master	D. G. Cowden
	G-GIDY	Shaw Europa XS	Gidy Group
	G-GIFF	Balony Kubicek BB26XR balloon	A. M. Holly
	G-GIGA	Vulcanair P68C	Apem Aviation Ltd
	G-GIGZ	Van's RV-8	N. G. Rhind & K. A. A. McDonald
	G-GILI	Robinson R44	Twylight Management Ltd
	G-GIPC	PA-32R-301 Saratoga SP	S. Empson
	G-GIRY	AG-5B Tiger	Romeo Yankee Flying Group
	G-GIVE	Cameron A-300 balloon	Wickers World Ltd
	G-GIWT	Shaw Europa XS	A. Twigg
	G-GJCD	Robinson R22 Beta	J. C. Lane
	G-GJMB	Bombardier CL-600-2B19 Challenger 850	Corporate Jet Management Ltd (G-CJMB)
	G-GKAT	Enstrom 280C	D. G. Allsop & A. J. Clark
	G-GKEV	Alpi Pioneer 300	A. P. Sellars
	G-GKFC	RL-5A LW Sherwood Ranger	W. A. Douthwaite (G-MYZI)
	G-GKKI	Avions Mudry CAP 231EX	L. Love
	G-GKRC	Cessna 180K	S. J. Beaty
	G-GKUE	SOCATA TB-9 Tampico Club	E. Pavanello & D. Peverley
	G-GLAD	Gloster G.37 Gladiator II (N5903:H)	Patina Ltd
	G-GLAK	AB Sportine LAK-12	C. Roney
	G-GLAW	Cameron N-90 balloon	R. A. Vale
	G-GLBX	Bombardier BD700-1A10 Global Express	Finesse Executive Ltd
	G-GLED	Cessna 150M	Aldenham Aviation LLP
	G-GLHI	Skyranger 912	S. F. Winter
	G-GLID	Schleicher ASW-28-18E	S. Bovin and Compagnie Belge d'Assurances Aviation
	G-GLII	Great Lakes 2T-1A-2	T. J. Richardson
	G-GLOC	Extra EA.300/200	The Cambridge Aero Club Ltd
	G-GLST	Great Lakes Sport Trainer	D. A. Graham
	G-GLTT	PA-31-350 Navajo Chieftain	Blue Sky Investments Ltd
	G-GLUC	Van's RV-6	P. Shoesmith & J. M. Whitham
	G-GLUE	Cameron N-65 balloon	L. J. M. Muir & G. D. Hallett
	G-GMAA	Learjet 45	Gama Aviation Ltd
	G-GMAB	BAe 125 Srs 1000A	Gama Aviation Ltd (G-BUWX)
	G-GMAC	Gulfstream G-IVSP	Gama Aviation Ltd
	G-GMAD	Beech B.300C Super King Air 350C	Gama Aviation Ltd
	G-GMAX	SNCAN Stampe SV.4C	G. H. Stinnes (G-BXNW)
	G-GMCM	AS.350B3 Ecureuil	T. J. Morris Ltd
	G-GMED	PA-42-720 Cheyenne IIA	Air Medical Fleet Ltd
	G-GMIB	Robin DR400/500	St. David's Farm & Equine Practice
	G-GMKD	Robin HR200/120B	J. Owens
	G-GMKE	Robin HR200/120B	Pilot Flying Group
	G-GMPB	BN-2T-4S Defender 4000	Greater Manchester Police Authority (G-BWPU)
	G-GMPX	MDH MD-900 Explorer	Police & Crime Commissioner for West Yorkshire
	G-GMSI	SOCATA TB9 Tampico	M. L. Rhodes
	G-GNJW	Ikarus C.42	N. C. Pearse
	G-GNRV	Van's RV-9A	N. K. Beavins
	G-GNTB	SAAB SF.340A	Loganair Ltd
	G-GNTF	SAAB SF.340A	Loganair Ltd
	G-GOAC	PA-34-200T Seneca II	Oxford Aviation Academy (Oxford) Ltd
	G-GOAL	Lindstrand LBL-105A balloon	I. Chadwick
	G-GOBD	PA-32R-301 Saratoga IIHP	F. & M. Garventa (G-OARW)
	G-GOBT	Colt 77A balloon	British Telecom PLC
	G-GOCX	Cameron N-90 balloon	R. D. Parry/Hong Kong

Reg.	Type	Owner or Operator	Notes
G-GOER	Bushby-Long Midget Mustang	J. M. Keane	
G-GOES	Robinson R44-II	Fordville Ltd	
G-GOFF	Extra EA.300/LC	George J. Goff Ltd	
G-GOGB	Lindstrand LBL ,90A	J. Dyer (G-CDFX)	
G-GOGW	Cameron N-90 balloon	S. E. Carroll	
G-GOHI	Cessna 208 Caravan 1 amphibian	S. Ulrich	
G-GOLF	SOCATA TB10 Tobago	B. Lee	
G-GOOF	Flylight Dragonfly	J. L. Guy	
G-GORE	CFM Streak Shadow	M. S. Clinton	
G-GORV	Van's RV-8	G-GORV Group	
G-GOSL	Robin DR.400/180	R. M. Gosling (G-BSDG)	
G-GOSS	Jodel DR.221	Avon Flying Group	
G-GOTC	GA-7 Cougar	Western Air (Thruxton) Ltd	
G-GOTH	PA-28-161 Warrior III	Stamp Aviation Ltd	
G-GOUP	Robinson R22 Beta	M. A. Bennett (G-DIRE)	
G-GOWF	Eurocopter EC.135 T2+	Bond Air Services Ltd	
G-GOYA	Bombardier BD700-1A10 Global Express	TAG Aviation (UK) Ltd	
G-GPAG	Van's RV-6	P. A. Green	
G-GPAT	Beech 76 Duchess	Folada Aero & Technical Services Ltd	
G-GPEG	Sky 90-24 balloon	R. Cains-Collinson	
G-GPMW	PA-28RT-201T Turbo Arrow IV	Calverton Flying Group Ltd	
G-GPPN	Cameron TR-70 balloon	Backetorp Byggconsult AB	
G-GPSF	Jabiru J430	P. S. Furlow	
G-GPSI	Grob G.115	Westbeach Aviation Ltd	
G-GPSR	Grob G.115	Westbeach Aviation Ltd	
G-GPSX	Grob G.115A	Westbeach Aviation Ltd	
G-GREY	PA-46-350P Malibu Mirage	S. T. Day & S. C. Askham	
G-GRIN	Van's RV-6	R. J. Tobin	
G-GRIZ	PA-18-135 Super Cub (modified)	P. N. Elkington (G-BSHV)	
G-GRMN	Aerospool Dynamic WT9 UK	R. M. North	
G-GRND	Agusta A109S	Galegrove 2 LBG	
G-GROE	Grob G.115A	H. Merkado	
G-GROL	Maule MXT-7-180	D. C. Croll & ptnrs	
G-GROW	Cameron N-77 balloon	Derbyshire Building Society	
G-GRPA	Ikarus C.42 FB100	R. Wood	
G-GGRH	Robinson R44	Heli Air Ltd	
G-GRRR	SA Bulldog Srs 120/122	Horizons Europe Ltd (G-BXGU)	
G-GRSR	Schempp-Hirth Discus bT	SR Group	
G-GRVE	Van's RV-6	G-GRVE Group	
G-GRVY	Van's RV-8	P. H. Yarrow	
G-GRWL	Lilliput Type 4 balloon	A. E. & D. E. Thomas	
G-GRWW	Robinson R44 II	G. R. Williams (G-HEEL)	
G-GRYN	Rotorsport UK Calidus	K. Hedger	
G-GRYZ	Beech F33A Bonanza	J. Kawadri & M. Kaveh	
G-GRZD	Gulfstream V-SP	TAG Aviation (UK) Ltd	
G-GRZZ	Robinson R44 II	GGR Group Ltd	
G-GSAL	Fokker E.III Reolica	Grass Strip Aviation Ltd	
G-GSCV	Ikarus C42 FB UK	D. E. Talbot	
G-GSMT	Rotorsport UK MTOSport	C. D. Jackson	
G-GSPY	Robinson R44 II	Percy Wood Leisure Ltd	
G-GSSD	Boeing 747-87UF	Global Supply Systems Ltd/British Airways Cargo	
G-GSSE	Boeing 747-87UF	Global Supply Systems Ltd/British Airways Cargo	
G-GSSF	Boeing 747-87UF	Global Supply Systems Ltd/British Airways Cargo	
G-GSST	Grob G.102 Astir CS77	770 Group	
G-GSYJ	Diamond DA42 Twin Star	Crosby Aviation (Jersey) Ltd	
G-GSYL	PA-28RT-201T Turbo Arrow IV	S. J. Sylvester (G-DAAH)	
G-GSYS	PA-34-220T Seneca V	SYS (Scaffolding Contractors) Ltd	
G-GTAX	PA-31-350 Navajo Chieftain	Hadagain Investments Ltd (G-OIAS)	
G-GTFC	P & M Quik	A. J. Fell	
G-GTGT	P & M Quik GT.450	D. J. Gavan	
G-GTHM	PA-38-112 Tomahawk	R. J. Grainger	
G-GTJD	P & M Quik GT450	P. Craigie	
G-GTJM	Eurocopter EC 120B Colibri	D. Robson	

Notes	Reg.	Type	Owner or Operator
	G-GTOM	Alpi Pioneer 300	S. C. Oliphant
	G-GTRE	PrM Quik GTR	M. J. Austin
	G-GTRR	P & M Quik GTR	Fly Hire Ltd
	G-GTRX	P & M Quik GTR	J. A. Lockert
	G-GTSO	P & M Quik GT450	C. Bayliss
	G-GTTP	P & M Quik GT450	S. E. Powell
	G-GTVM	Beech 58 Baron	Baron Flying Club Ltd
	G-GTWO	Schleicher ASW-15	J. M. G. Carlton & R. Jackson
	G-GUCK	Beech C23 Sundowner 180	G-GUCK Flying Group (G-BPYG)
	G-GULP	I.I.I. Sky Arrow 650T	S. Marriott
	G-GULZ	Christen Eagle II	T. N. Jinks
	G-GUMS	Cessna 182P	L. W. Scattergood (G-CBMN)
	G-GUNS	Cameron V-77 balloon	V. Grenier
	G-GUNZ	Van's RV-8	Bibielle UK Ltd
	G-GURN	PA-31 Navajo C	Batair Ltd (G-BHGA)
	G-GURU	PA-28-161 Warrior II	P. J. Wiseman
	G-GUSS	PA-28-151 Warrior	The Sierra Flying Group (G-BJRY)
	G-GVPI	Evans VP-1 srs.2	G. Martin
	G-GWIZ	Colt Clown SS balloon	Magical Adventures Ltd
	G-GWYN	Cessna F.172M	Magic Carpet Flying Co
	G-GYAK	Yakovlev Yak-50	M. W. Levy & M. V. Rijske
	G-GYAT	Gardan GY-80 Horizon 180	Rochester GYAT Flying Group Club
	G-GYAV	Cessna 172N	Southport & Merseyside Aero Club (1979) Ltd
	G-GYRO	Campbell Cricket	J. W. Pavitt
	G-GYTO	PA-28-161 Warrior III	Smart People Don't Buy Ltd
	G-GZDO	Cessna 172N	Cambridge Hall Aviation
	G-GZIP	Rolladen-Schneider LS8-18	D. S. S. Haughton
	G-GZOO	Gulfstream G200	NAL Asset Management Ltd
	G-GZRP	PA-42-720 Cheyenne IIIA	Air Medical Fleet Ltd
	G-HAAH	Schempp-Hirth Ventus 2cT	The V66 Syndicate
	G-HAAT	MDH MD.900 Explorer	Police Aviation Services Ltd (G-GMPS)
	G-HABI	Best Off SkyRanger 912S(1)	J. Habicht
	G-HABS	Cessna 172S	Apem Aviation Ltd (G-RGAP)
	G-HABT	Supermarine Aircraft Spitfire Mk.26	Wright Grumman Aviation Ltd
	G-HACE	Van's RV-6A	D. C. McElroy
	G-HACK	PA-18 Super Cub 150	Intrepid Aviation Co
	G-HACS	Tecnam P2002-JF	The RAF Halton Aeroplane Club Ltd
	G-HADD	P & M Quik R	T. J. Barker
	G-HAEF	EV-97 TeamEurostar UK	RAF Microlight Flying Association
	G-HAFG	Cessna 340A	Pavilion Aviation Ltd
	G-HAFT	Diamond DA42 Twin Star	Atlantic Flight Training Ltd
	G-HAGL	Robinson R44 II	HQ Aviation Ltd
	G-HAHU	Yakovlev Yak-18T	A. Leftwich
	G-HAIB	Aviat A-1B Husky	H. Brockmueller
	G-HAIG	Rutan LongEz	X. Le Donne
	G-HAIR	Robin DR.400/180	S. P. Copson
	G-HAJJ	Glaser-Dirks DG.400	W. G. Upton & J. G. Kosak
	G-HALC	PA-28R Cherokee Arrow 200	Halcyon Aviation Ltd
	G-HALI	Eurocopter EC.225LP Super Puma	CHC Scotia Ltd
	G-HALJ	Cessna 140	A. P. Shoobert & A. Wills
	G-HALL	PA-22 Tri-Pacer 160	F. P. Hall (G-ARAH)
	G-HALT	Mainair Pegasus Quik	J. McGrath
	G-HAMI	Fuji FA.200-180	HAMI Group (G-OISF/G-BAPT)
	G-HAMM	Yakovlev Yak-50	Propeller Studios Ltd
	G-HAMP	Bellanca 7ACA Champ	R. J. Grimstead
	G-HAMR	PA-28-161 Warrior II	Electric Scribe 2000 Ltd
	G-HAMS	Pegasus Quik	D. R. Morton
	G-HANA	Westland WS-58 Wessex HC.2	R. A. Fidler
	G-HANG	Diamond DA42 Twin Star	Atlantic Flight Training Ltd
	G-HANS	Robin DR.400 2+2	J. S. Russell
	G-HANY	Agusta-Bell 206B JetRanger 3	Beech Holdings Ltd (G-ESAL/G-BHXW/ G-JEKP)
	G-HAPE	Pietenpol Aircamper	J. P. Chape
	G-HAPI	Lindstrand LBL-105A balloon	Adventure Balloons Ltd
	G-HAPY	DHC.1 Chipmunk 22A (WP803)	Astrojet Ltd

Reg.	Type	Owner or Operator	Notes
G-HARA	Sikorsky S-76C	Air Harrods Ltd	
G-HARD	Dyn'Aéro MCR-01 ULC	N. A. Burnet	
G-HARE	Cameron N-77 balloon	D. H. Sheryn & C. A. Buck	
G-HARI	Raj Hamsa X'Air V2 (2)	J. Blackburn	
G-HARN	PA-28-181 Archer II	K. Saxton (G-DENK/G-BXRJ)	
G-HARR	Robinson R22 Beta	Unique Helicopters Ltd	
G-HART	Cessna 152 (tailwheel)	Air Atlantique Ltd (G-BPBF)	
G-HARY	Alon A-2 Aircoupe	M. B. Willis (G-ATWP)	
G-HATD	DH.115 Vampire T.55	Aviation Heritage Ltd	
G-HATF	Thorp T-18CW	A. T. Fraser	
G-HATZ	Hatz CB-1	S. P. Rollason	
G-HAUL	Westland WG.30 Srs 300 ★	IHM/Weston-super-Mare	
G-HAUT	Schempp-Hirth Mini Nimbus C	530 Syndicate	
G-HAVI	Eurocopter EC.130B4	J. & J. Havakin	
G-HAYY	Czech Sport Aircraft Sportcruiser	B. R. W. Hay	
G-HAZE	Thunder Ax8-90 balloon	T. G. Church	
G-HBBC	DH.104 Dove 8	Roger Gawn 2007 Family Trust (G-ALFM)	
G-HBBH	Ikarus C42 FB100	Golf Bravo Hotel Group	
G-HBEK	Agusta A109C	HPM Investments Ltd (G-RNLD/G-DATE)	
G-HBJT	Eurocopter EC.155B1	Starspeed Ltd	
G-HBMW	Robinson R22	Durham Flying Syndicate (G-BOFA)	
G-HBOB	Eurocopter EC135 T2+	Bond Air Services Ltd/Thames Valley Air Ambulance	
G-HBOS	Scheibe SF-25C Rotax-Falke	Coventry Gliding Club Ltd	
G-HBUG	Cameron N-90 balloon	Black Horse Ballooning Club (G-BRCN)	
G-HCAC	Schleicher Ka 6E	Ka 6E 994 Group	
G-HCAT	Sindlinger Hawker Hurricane	G. S. Jones & A. Hoskins	
G-HCCF	Vans RV-8A	S. M. E. Solomon	
G-HCCL	Beech B200GT Super King Air	J. M. Lynch	
G-HCGD	Learjet 45	TAG Aviation (UK) Ltd	
G-HCPD	Cameron C-80 balloon	H. Crawley& P. Dopson	
G-HCSA	Cessna 525A CJ2	Bookajet Aircraft Management Ltd	
G-HDAE	DHC.1 Chipmunk 22	Airborne Classics Ltd	
G-HDEF	Robinson R44 II	Arena Aviation Ltd (G-LOCO/G-TEMM)	
G-HDEW	PA-32R-301 Saratoga SP	A. H. Biddulph & P. Wood	
G-HDIX	Enstrom 280FX	Clovetree Ltd	
G-HDTV	Agusta A109A-II	Castle Air Ltd (G-BXWD)	
G-HEAD	Colt Flying Head SS balloon	Ikeair	
G-HEAN	AS.355NP Ecureuil 2	Brookview Developments Ltd	
G-HEBB	Schleicher ASW-27-18E	E. Y. Heinonen	
G-HEBO	BN-2B-20 Islander	Hebridean Air Services Ltd (G-BUBK)	
G-HEBS	BN-2B-26 Islander	Hebridean Air Services Ltd (G-BUBJ)	
G-HEBZ	BN-2A-26 Islander	Cormack (Aircraft Services) Ltd (G-BELF)	
G-HECB	Fuji FA.200-160	H. E. W. E. Bailey (G-BBZO)	
G-HECK	Robinson R44 II	Helivation Aviation Ltd (G-ILLG)	
G-HEHE	Eurocopter EC.120B Colibri	HE Group Ltd	
G-HEKK	RAF 2000 GTX-SE gyroplane	C. J. Watkinson (G-BXEB)	
G-HEKL	Percival Mew Gull Replica	D. Beale	
G-HELA	SOCATA TB10 Tobago	M. A. Soakell	
G-HELE	Bell 206B JetRanger 3	B. E. E. Smith (G-OJFR)	
G-HELN	Piper PA-18-95 Super Cub	Helen Group	
G-HELV	DH.115 Vampire T.55 (XJ771)	Aviation Heritage Ltd	
G-HEMN	Eurocopter EC135 T2+	Bond Air Services Ltd	
G-HEMZ	Agusta A109S Grand	Sloane Helicopters Ltd	
G-HENT	SOCATA Rallye 110ST	F. Monds	
G-HENY	Cameron V-77 balloon	R. S. D'Alton	
G-HEOI	Eurocopter EC135 P2+	Police & Crime Commisioner for West Yorkshire	
G-HERC	Cessna 172S	Cambridge Aero Club Ltd	
G-HERD	Lindstrand LBL-77B balloon	S. W. Herd	
G-HERT	BAE Herti	BAe Systems (Operations) Ltd	
G-HEWI	Piper J-3C-90 Cub	Denham Grasshopper Group (G-BLEN)	
G-HEWS	Hughes 369D ★	Spares' use	
G-HEXE	Colr 17A balloon	A. Dunnington	
G-HEYY	Cameron 72 Bear SS balloon	Magical Adventures Ltd	
G-HFBM	Curtiss Robin C-2	D. M. Forshaw	
G-HFCB	Cessna F.150L	G-HFCB Flying Group	

Notes	Reg.	Type	Owner or Operator
	G-HFCL	Cessna F.152	MK Aero Support Ltd (G-BGLR)
	G-HFCT	Cessna F.152	Stapleford Flying Club Ltd
	G-HFLY	Robinson R44 II	Helifly (UK) Ltd
	G-HFRH	DHC-1 Chipmunk 22	Sunrise Global Aviation Ltd
	G-HGAS	Cameron N-77 balloon	N. J. Tovey
	G-HGPI	SOCATA TB20 Trinidad	M. J. Jackson
	G-HGRB	Robinson R44	Heli Air Scotland Ltd (G-BZIN)
	G-HHAA	HS. Buccaneer S.2B (XX885)	Hawker Hunter Aviation Ltd
	G-HHAC	Hawker Hunter F.58 (J-4021)	Hawker Hunter Aviation Ltd (G-BWIU)
	G-HHDR	Cessna 182T	D. R. & H. Howell
	G-HHII	Hawker Hurricane 2B (BE505: XP-L)	Hangar 11 Collection (G-HRLO)
	G-HHPM	Cameron Z-105 balloon	J. Armstrong
	G-HIBM	Cameron N-145 balloon	Alba Ballooning Ltd
	G-HICU	Schleicher ASW-27-18E	N. Hoare
	G-HIEL	Robinson R22 Beta	Crown Helicopters Ltd
	G-HIJK	Cessna 421C	DO Systems Ltd (G-OSAL)
	G-HIJN	Ikarus C.42 FB80	M. A. Hanson
	G-HILI	Van's RV-3B	A. G. & E. A. Hill
	G-HILO	Rockwell Commander 114	Alpha Golf Flying Group
	G-HILS	Cessna F.172H	LS Flying Group (G-AWCH)
	G-HILT	SOCATA TB10 Tobago	S. Harrison
	G-HILY	Zenair CH.600 Zodiac	K. V. Hill & D. Woolliscroft (G-BRII)
	G-HILZ	Van's RV-8	A. G. & E. A. Hill
	G-HIMM	Cameron Z-105 balloon	C. M. D. Haynes
	G-HIND	Maule MT-7-235	M. A. Ashmole
	G-HINZ	Avtec Jabiru SK	P. J. Jackson
	G-HIPO	Robinson R22 Beta	SI Plan Electronics (Research) Ltd (G-BTGB)
	G-HIRE	GA-7 Cougar	London Aerial Tours Ltd (G-BGSZ)
	G-HITM	Raj Hamsa X'Air 582 (1)	I. Johnson & J. Hennegan
	G-HITT	Hawker Hurricane 1 (P3717:SW-P)	H. Taylor
	G-HIUP	Cameron A-250 balloon	J. D. & K. Griffiths
	G-HIVA	Cessna 337A	G. J. Banfield (G-BAES)
	G-HIVE	Cessna F.150M	M. P. Lynn (G-BCXT)
	G-HIYA	Best Off Skyranger 912(2)	R. D. & C. M. Parkinson
	G-HIZZ	Robinson R22 II	Flyfare (G-CNDY/G-BXEW)
	G-HJSM	Schempp-Hirth Nimbus 4DM	G. Paul (G-ROAM)
	G-HJSS	AIA Stampe SV.4C (modified)	H. J. Smith (G-AZNF)
	G-HKAA	Schempp-Hirth Duo Discus T	A. Aveling
	G-HKCF	Enstrom 280C-UK	HKC Helicopter Services (G-MHCF/G-GSML/ G-BNNV)
	G-HKHM	Hughes 369B	Heli Air Ltd
	G-HLCF	Starstreak Shadow SA-II	F. E. Tofield
	G-HLEE	Best Off Sky Ranger J2.2(1)	P. G. Hill
	G-HLOB	Cessna 172S	Goodwood Road Racing Co.Ltd
	G-HMBJ	Rockwell Commander 114B	D. W. R. Best
	G-HMCA	EV-97 TeamEurostar UK	RAF Microlight Flying Association
	G-HMCB	Skyranger Swift 912S(1)	R. W. Goddin
	G-HMCD	Ikarus C42 FB80	RAF Microlight Flying Association
	G-HMCE	Ikarus C42 FB80	RAF Microlight Flying Association
	G-HMDX	MDH MD-900 Explorer	Police Aviation Services Ltd
	G-HMED	PA-28-161 Warrior III	Eglinton Flying Club Ltd
	G-HMEI	Dassault Falcon 900	Executive Jet Group Ltd
	G-HMHM	Rotorsport UK MTO Sport	R. M. Kimbell
	G-HMJB	PA-34-220T Seneca III	W. B. Bateson
	G-HMKA	Gefa-Flug AS105GD	Llego Papa/UK LLC Ltd
	G-HMPS	CZAW Sportcruiser	H. & P. Shedden
	G-HMPT	Agusta-Bell 206B JetRanger 2	Yorkshire Helicopters
	G-HNGE	Ikarus C42 FB100	Compton Abbas Airfield Ltd
	G-HNTR	Hawker Hunter T.7 (XL571:V) ★	Yorkshire Air Museum/Elvington
	G-HOBO	Denney Kitfox Mk 4	J. P. Donovan
	G-HOCA	Robinson R44 II	JRS Aviation Ltd
	G-HOCK	PA-28 Cherokee 180	G-HOCK Flying Club (G-AVSH)

Reg.	Type	Owner or Operator	Notes
G-HOFF	P & M Aviation Quik GT450	L. Mazurek	
G-HOFM	Cameron N-56 balloon	Magical Adventures Ltd	
G-HOGS	Cameron 90 Pig SS balloon	Magical Adventures Ltd	
G-HOJO	Schempp-Hirth Discus 2a	S. G. Jones	
G-HOLA	PA-28-201T Turbo Dakota	Curtis Moore Aviation Ltd (G-BNYB)	
G-HOLD	Robinson R44 II	Mignini and Petrini Spa/Italy	
G-HOLE	P & M Quik GT450	C. J. R. Hardman (G-CEBD)	
G-HOLI	Ultramagic M-77 balloon	G. Everett	
G-HOLM	Eurocopter EC.120B Colibri	Oxford Air Services Ltd	
G-HOLY	ST.10 Diplomate	M. K. Barsham	
G-HONG	Slingsby T.67M Firefly 200	Jewel Aviation and Technology Ltd	
G-HONI	Robinson R22 Beta	Patriot Aviation Ltd (G-SEGO)	
G-HONK	Cameron O-105 balloon	M. A. Green	
G-HONY	Lilliput Type 1 Srs A balloon	A. E. & D. E. Thomas	
G-HOOD	SOCATA TB20 Trinidad GT	M. J. Hoodless	
G-HOPA	Lindstrand LBL-35A balloon	S. F. Burden/Netherlands	
G-HOPE	Beech F33A Bonanza	Hope Aviation Ltd	
G-HOPR	Lindstrand LBL-25A balloon	K. C. Tanner	
G-HOPY	Van's RV-6A	R. C. Hopkinson	
G-HORK	Pioneer 300 Hawk	R. Y. Kendal	
G-HOSS	Beech F33A	T. D. Broadhurst	
G-HOTA	EV-97 TeamEurostar UK	W. Chang	
G-HOTB	Eurocopter EC155 B1	Noirmont (EC155) Ltd (G-CEXZ)	
G-HOTM	Cameron C-80 balloon	A. M. Holly	
G-HOTR	P & M Quik GTR	M. E. Fowler	
G-HOTZ	Colt 77B balloon	C. J. & S. M. Davies	
G-HOUS	Colt 31A balloon ★	The British Balloon Museum and Library	
G-HOWE	Thunder Ax7-77 balloon	C. Suggitt	
G-HOWI	Cessna F.182Q	H. Poulson	
G-HOWL	RAF 2000 GTX-SE gyroplane	C. J. Watkinson	
G-HOXN	Van's RV-9	XRay November Flying Club	
G-HPAD	Bell 206B JetRanger 2	Helipad Ltd (G-CITZ/G-BRTB)	
G-HPEN	Ultramagic M-120 balloon	G. Holtam	
G-HPJT	HpH Glasflugel 304S	JT Group	
G-HPOL	MDH MD-902 Explorer	Humberside Police Authority	
G-HPSF	Rockwell Commander 114B	R. W. Scandrett	
G-HPSL	Rockwell Commander 114B	M. B. Endean	
G-HPUX	Hawker Hunter T.7 (XL587)	Hawker Hunter Aviation Ltd	
G-HPWA	Van's RV-8	M. de Ferranti	
G-HRAF	Schleicher ASK-13	Upward Bound Trust (G-DETS)	
G-HRCC	Robin HR200/100	P. R and J. S. Johnson	
G-HRHE	Robinson R22 Beta	J. Porter (G-BTWP)	
G-HRIO	Robin HR.100/120	R. Mullender	
G-HRLI	Hawker Hurricane 1 (V7497)	Hawker Restorations Ltd	
G-HRLK	SAAB 91D/2 Safir	Sylmar Aviation & Services Ltd (G-BRZY)	
G-HRLM	Brügger MB.2 Colibri	N. M. Booth	
G-HRND	Cessna 182T	H. B. Gregorian	
G-HROI	Rockwell Commander RC.112	Intereuropean Aviation Ltd	
G-HRPN	Robinson R44 II	M. Lazzari	
G-HRVD	CCF Harvard IV	P. Earthy (G-BSBC)	
G-HRVS	Van's RV-8	D. J. Harvey	
G-HRYZ	PA-28-180 Cherokee Archer	Gama Engineering Ltd (G-WACR/G-BCZF)	
G-HSAR	Agusta A.109E Power	Caste Air Ltd	
G-HSBC	Lindstrand LBL-69X balloon	A. Nimmo	
G-HSEB	Pegasus Quantum 15-912	D. Gwyther (G-BYNO)	
G-HSKE	Aviat A-18 Husky	R. B. Armitage & S. L. Davis	
G-HSKI	Aviat A-1B	C. J. R. Flint	
G-HSOO	Hughes 369HE	A. Shade Greener (F1) Ltd (G-BFYJ)	
G-HSTH	Lindstrand LBL. HS-110 balloon	Lindstrand Hot Air Balloons Ltd	
G-HSXP	Raytheon Hawker 850XP	Fowey Services Ltd	
G-HTAX	PA-31-350 Navajo Chieftain	Hadagain Investments Ltd	
G-HTEL	Robinson R44	Henley Aviation Ltd	
G-HTFU	Gippsland GA8-TC 320 Airvan	Skydive London Ltd	
G-HTML	P & M Aviation Quik R	A. P. Whitmarsh	
G-HTRL	PA-34-220T Seneca III	Techtest Ltd (G-BXXY)	
G-HTWE	Rans S6-116	H. C. C. Coleridge	

Notes	Reg.	Type	Owner or Operator
	G-HUBB	Partenavia P.68B	Ravenair Aircraft Ltd
	G-HUBY	Embraer EMB-135BJ Legacy	London Executive Aviation Ltd
	G-HUCH	Cameron 80 Carrots SS balloon	Magical Adventures Ltd (G-BYPS)
	G-HUDS	P & M Quik GTR	C. Hudson
	G-HUES	Hughes 369HS	P. F. Ressle (G-GASC/ G-WELD/G-FROG)
	G-HUEW	Shaw Europa XS	C. R. Wright
	G-HUEY	Bell UH-1H	MX Jets Ltd
	G-HUFF	Cessna 182P	Highfine Ltd
	G-HUKA	MDH Hughes 369E	B. P. Stein (G-OSOO)
	G-HULK	Skyranger 912(2)	L. C. Stockman
	G-HULL	Cessna F.150M	Hull Aero Club Ltd
	G-HUMH	Van's RV-9A	G-HUMH Group
	G-HUND	Aviat A-1B Husky	U Ladurner
	G-HUNI	Bellanca 7GCBC Scout	R. G. Munro
	G-HUPW	Hawker Hurricane 1 (R4118:UP-W)	Minmere Farm Partnership
	G-HURI	CCF Hawker Hurricane XIIA (Z5140/HA-C)	Historic Aircraft Collection Ltd
	G-HURN	Robinson R22 Beta	CMT Aviation Partnership
	G-HUSK	Aviat A-1B	G. D. Ettlmayr
	G-HUTE	Aerochute Dual	W. A. Kimberlin
	G-HUTT	Denney Kitfox Mk.2	H. D. Colliver
	G-HUTY	Van's RV-7	S. A. Hutt
	G-HVAN	RL-5A LW Sherwood Ranger ST	P. S. Taylor
	G-HVBF	Lindstrand LBL-210A balloon	Virgin Balloon Flights
	G-HVER	Robinson R44 II	Equation Associates Ltd
	G-HVRZ	Eurocopter EC 120B	EDM Helicopters Ltd
	G-HWAA	Eurocopter EC 135T2	Bond Air Services Ltd
	G-HWKS	Robinson R44	Hawk Site Facilities Ltd (G-ETFF/G-HSLJ)
	G-HXTD	Robin DR.400/180	P. Malone
	G-HYBD	Gramex Song	University of Cambridge
	G-HYLL	Robinson R44	Holbeck GHYLL Country House Hotel Ltd (G-KLAS)
	G-HYLT	PA-32R-301 Saratoga SP	T. G. Gordon
	G-HYST	Enstrom 280FX Shark	M. Jop
	G-IACA	Sikorsky S-92A	Bristow Helicopters Ltd
	G-IACB	Sikorsky S-92A	Bristow Helicopters Ltd
	G-IACC	Sikorsky S-92A	Bristow Helicopters Ltd
	G-IACD	Sikorsky S-92A	Bristow Helicopters Ltd
	G-IACE	Sikorsky S-92A	Bristow Helicopters Ltd
	G-IACF	Sikorsky S-92A	Bristow Helicopters Ltd
	G-IAGL	Eurocopter EC.120B Colibri	AGL Helicopters (G-UYFI)
	G-IAHS	EV-97 TeamEurostar UK	I. A. Holden
	G-IAJJ	Robinson R44 II	O'Connor Utilities Ltd
	G-IAJS	Ikarus C.42 FB UK	A. J. Slater
	G-IAMP	Cameron H-34 balloon	W. D. Mackinnon
	G-IANB	Glaser-Dirks DG-800B	I. S. Bullous
	G-IANC	SOCATA TB10 Tobago	General Aero Equipment Ltd (G-BIAK)
	G-IANH	SOCATA TB10 Tobago	R. J. Wright
	G-IANI	Shaw Europa XS T-G	I. F. Rickard & I. A. Watson
	G-IANJ	Cessna F.150K	J. A. & D. T. A. Rees (G-AXVW)
	G-IANN	Kolb Twinstar Mk 3	I. Newman
	G-IANW	AS.350B3 Ecureuil	Milford Aviation Services Ltd
	G-IANZ	P & M Quik GT450	Forward Agronomy Ltd
	G-IARC	Stoddard-Hamilton Glastar	A. A. Craig
	G-IASA	Beech B.200 Super King Air	IAS Medical Ltd
	G-IASM	Beech B.200 Super King Air	MIAW LLP (G-OEAS)
	G-IBAZ	Ikarus C.42 FB100	B. R. Underwood
	G-IBBS	Shaw Europa	R. H. Gibbs
	G-IBCF	Cameron Z-105 balloon	Cash 4 Cars
	G-IBED	Robinson R22A	Brian Seedle Helicopters Blackpool (G-BMHN)
	G-IBFC	BFC Challenger II	K. J. Underwood
	G-IBFF	Beech A23-24 Musketeer Super	J. Lankfer (G-AXCJ)
	G-IBFP	VPM .M.16 Tandem Trainer	B. F. Pearson
	G-IBFW	PA-28R-201 Arrow III	Archer Four Ltd
	G-IBHH	Hughes 269C	Alpha Properties (London) Ltd (G-BSCD)

Reg.	Type	Owner or Operator	Notes
G-IBIG	Bell 206B JetRanger 3	Big Heli-Charter Ltd (G-BORV)	
G-IBII	Pitts S-2A Special	Aerobatic Displays Ltd (G-XATS)	
G-IBLP	P & M Quik GT450	C. Zizzo	
G-IBME	SA.342J Gazelle	Gazelle Management Services LLP	
G-IBMS	Robinson R44	Beoley Mill Software Ltd	
G-IBNH	Westland Gazelle HT Mk.2 (XW853)	Buckland Newton Hire Ltd (G-SWWM)	
G-IBSY	VS.349 Spitfire Mk.VC	Fairfax Spitfires LLP (G-VMIJ)	
G-IBUZ	CZAW Sportcruiser	G. L. Fearon	
G-IBZA	Cessna 550 Citation II	International Flight Referral BVBA/Belgium (G-OTIS)	
G-ICAS	Pitts S-2B Special	J. C. Smith	
G-ICBM	Stoddard-Hamilton Glasair III Turbine	G. V. Walters & D. N. Brown	
G-ICDM	Jabiru UL-450	D. J. R. Wenham (G-CEKM)	
G-ICES	Thunder Ax6-56 balloon ★	British Balloon Museum & Library Ltd	
G-ICGA	PA-28-140 Cherokee E	28-7225317H-Douwes/Netherlands	
G-ICKY	Lindstrand LBL-77A balloon	P. & S. J. Donkin	
G-ICLC	Cessna 150L	Cooperatief Air Waterland UA/Netherlands	
G-ICMT	Evektor EV-97 Eurostar	R. Haslam	
G-ICOM	Cessna F.172M	C. G. Elesmore (G-BFXI)	
G-ICON	Rutan LongEz	S. J. & M. A. Carradice	
G-ICRS	Ikarus C.42 FB UK Cyclone	Ikarus Flying Group Ltd	
G-ICSG	AS.355F1 Twin Squirrel	RCR Aviation Ltd (G-PAMI/G-BUSA)	
G-ICUT	Maule MX-7-180A Super Rocket	S. D. Evans	
G-ICWT	Pegasus Quantum 15-912	M. E. Rees	
G-IDAY	Skyfox CA-25N Gazelle	G. G. Johnstone	
G-IDEB	AS.355F1 Ecureuil 2	MW Helicopters Ltd (G-ORMA/G-SITE/ G-BPHC)	
G-IDER	Orlican Discus CS	A. J. Preston & D. B. Keith	
G-IDII	Dan Rihn DR.107 One Design	C. Darlow	
G-IDOL	Evektor EV-97 Eurostar	K. Handley	
G-IDRO	Bombardier BD700-1A10 Global Express	Corporate Jet Management Ltd	
G-IDUP	Enstrom 280C Shark	Antique Buildings Ltd (G-BRZF)	
G-IEEF	Raj Hamsa X'Air Hawk	P. J. Sheehy	
G-IEIO	PA-34-200T Seneca II	Sky Zone Servicos Aereos Lda	
G-IEJH	Jodel 150A	A. Turner & D. Worth (G-BPAM)	
G-IENN	Cirrus SR20	Renneta Ltd (G-TSGE)	
G-IFAB	Cessna F.182Q	Bristol & West Aeroplane Club Ltd	
G-IFBP	AS.350B2 Ecureuil	Frank Bird Aviation	
G-IFFR	PA-32 Cherokee Six 300	Brendair (G-BWVO)	
G-IFFY	Flylight Dragonfly	R. D. Leigh	
G-IFIF	Cameron TR-60 balloon	M. G. Howard	
G-IFIT	PA-31-350 Navajo Chieftain	Dart Group PLC (G-NABI/G-MARG)	
G-IFLE	Aerotechnik EV-97 TeamEurostar UK	M. R. Smith	
G-IFLI	AA-5A Cheetah	C. M. Petherbridge	
G-IFLP	PA-34-200T Seneca II	ACS Aviation Ltd	
G-IFRH	Agusta A109C	Helicopter Services Ltd	
G-IFTE	HS.125 Srs 700B	Albion Aviation Management Ltd (G-BFVI)	
G-IFTF	BAe 125 Srs 800B	Albion Aviation Management Ltd (G-RCEJ/ G-GEIL)	
G-IFWD	Schempp-Hirth Ventus cT	J. C. Ferguson & C. J. Hamilton	
G-IGEL	Cameron N-90 balloon	Computacenter Ltd	
G-IGGL	SOCATA TB10 Tobago	G-IGGL Flying Group (G-BYDC)	
G-IGHH	Enstrom 480	Raw Sports Ltd	
G-IGHT	Van's RV-8	E. A. Yates	
G-IGIA	AS.350B3 Ecureuil	Faloria Ltd	
G-IGIE	SIAI Marchetti SF.260	Flew LLP	
G-IGII	Shaw Europa	C. D. Peacock	
G-IGLE	Cameron V-90 balloon	G-IGLE Group	
G-IGLI	Schempp-Hirth Duo Discus T	C. Fox	
G-IGLL	AutoGyro MTO Sport	I. M. Donnellan	
G-IGLY	P & M Aviation Quik GT450	K. G. Grayson & R. D. Leigh	
G-IGLZ	Champion 8KCAB	Woodgate Aviation (IOM) Ltd	
G-IGPW	Eurocopter EC 120B	PDQ Rotor Ltd (G-CBRI)	
G-IGTE	SIAI Marchetti F.260	D. Fletcher & J. J. Watts	
G-IGWT	Bombardier CL600-2B19	Skywings Ltd	

Notes	Reg.	Type	Owner or Operator
	G-IGZZ	Robinson R44 II	Rivermead Aviation Ltd
	G-IHOP	Cameron Z-31 balloon	N. W. Roberts
	G-IHOT	Aerotechnik EV-97 Eurostar UK	Exodos Airsports Ltd
	G-IIAC	Aeronca 11AC Chief	Fox Flying Group (G-BTPY)
	G-IIAI	Mudry CAP.232	J. Bennett
	G-IIAN	Aero Designs Pulsar	I. G. Harrison
	G-IICC	Van's RV-4	R. H. Clifton (G-MARX)
	G-IICT	Schempp-Hirth Ventus 2Ct	P. McLean
	G-IICX	Schempp-Hirth Ventus 2cxT	T. P. Jenkinson
	G-IIDC	Midget Mustang	D. Cooke (G-IIMT/G-BDGA)
	G-IIDI	Extra EA.300/L	Power Aerobatics Ltd (G-XTRS)
	G-IIDR	Ikarus C42 FB100	D. M. Richards
	G-IIDY	Aerotek Pitts S-2B Special	The S-2B Group (G-BPVP)
	G-IIEX	Extra EA.300/L	S. G. Jones
	G-IIFM	Edge 360	F. L. McGee
	G-IIFX	Marganski MDM-1	Swift Aerobatic Display Team
	G-IIGI	Van's RV-4	T. D. R. Hardy
	G-IIHI	Extra 300/SC	YAK UK Ltd
	G-IIHX	Bushby-Long Midget Mustang	M. C. Huxtable
	G-IIHZ	Avions Murdy CAP 231	Hard Zero Flying (G-OZZO)
	G-IIID	Dan Rihn DR.107 One Design	D. A. Kean
	G-IIIE	Aerotek Pitts S-2B Special	Dianagomesdasilva Aerobatics
	G-IIIG	Boeing Stearman A75N1	Stearman G-IIIG Group /Belgium (G-BSDR)
	G-IIII	Aerotek Pitts S-2B Special	Aerospace Optics Ltd
	G-IIIK	Extra EA.300/SC	Extra 300SC LLP
	G-IIIL	Pitts S-1T Special	Empyreal Airways Ltd
	G-IIIM	Stolp SA.100 Starduster	H. Mackintosh
	G-IIIO	Schempp-Hirth Ventus 2CM	S. J. Clark
	G-IIIP	Pitts S-1D Special	R. S. Grace (G-BLAG)
	G-IIIR	Pitts S-1S Special	R. O. Rogers
	G-IIIT	Aerotek Pitts S-2A Special	Aerobatic Displays Ltd
	G-IIIV	Pitts Super Stinker 11-260	S. D. Barnard & A. N. R. Houghton
	G-IIIX	Pitts S-1S Special	D. S. T. Eggleton (G-LBAT/G-UCCI/G-BIYN)
	G-IIIZ	Sukhoi Su-26M	P. M. M. Bonhommy
	G-IIJC	Midget Mustang	Iconic Aviation Ltd (G-CEKU)
	G-IIJI	Xtremeair XA-42 Sbach 342	G. H. Willson
	G-IILL	Vans RV-7	D. G. Cowden
	G-IILY	Robinson R44 I	Twylight Management Ltd (G-DCSG/G-TRYG)
	G-IIMI	Extra EA.300/L	Firebird Aerobatics Ltd
	G-IINI	Van's RV-9A	N. W. Thomas
	G-IIOO	Schleicher ASW-27-18E	M. Clarke
	G-IIPB	DR.107 One Design	P. D. Baisden
	G-IIPT	Robinson R22 Beta	W. M. Gray (G-FUSI)
	G-IIPZ	Mudry CAP.232	S. P. R. Madle & J. Murfitt
	G-IIRG	Stoddard-Hamilton Glasair IIS RG	A. C. Lang
	G-IIRI	Xtreme Air Sbach 300	One Sky Aviation LLP
	G-IIRP	Mudry CAP.232	R. J. Pickin
	G-IIRV	Van's RV-7	D. S. Watson
	G-IIRW	Van's RV-8	R. Winward
	G-IITC	Mudry CAP.232	T. W. Cassells
	G-IIXF	Van's RV-7	C. A. & S. Noujaim
	G-IIXI	Extra EA.300/L	B. Nielsen
	G-IIXX	Parsons 2-seat gyroplane	J. M. Montgomerie
	G-IIYK	Yakovlev Yak-50	Eaglescott Yak 50 Group
	G-IIZI	Extra EA.300	Power Aerobatics Ltd
	G-IJAC	Light Aero Avid Speedwing Mk 4	I. J. A. Charlton
	G-IJAG	Cessna 182T Skylane	AG Group
	G-IJBB	Enstrom 480	R. P. Bateman (G-LIVA/G-PBTT)
	G-IJMC	Magni M-16 Tandem Trainer	R. F. G. Moyle (G-POSA/G-BVJM)
	G-IJOE	PA-28RT-201T Turbo Arrow IV	J. H. Bailey
	G-IKAH	Slingsby T.51 Dart 17R	K. A. Hale
	G-IKBP	PA-28-161 Warrior II	F. J. Page
	G-IKEA	Cameron 120 Ikea SS balloon	IKEA Ltd
	G-IKES	Stoddard-Hamilton GlaStar	M. Stow
	G-IKEV	Jabiru UL-450	D. I. Taylor & A. J. Sharratt
	G-IKON	Van's RV-4	S. Sampson
	G-IKOS	Cessna 550 Citation Bravo	Medox Enterprises Ltd

Reg.	Type	Owner or Operator	Notes
G-IKRK	Shaw Europa	K. R. Kesterton	
G-IKRS	Ikarus C.42 FK UK Cyclone	K. J. Warburton	
G-IKUS	Ikarus C.42 FB UK Cyclone	C. I. Law	
G-ILBO	Rolladen-Schneider LS3-A	J. P. Gilbert	
G-ILBT	Cessna 182T	G. E. Gilbert	
G-ILDA	VS.361 Spitfire HF.IX (SM520 : KJ-1)	Boultbee Vintage LLP (G-BXHZ)	
G-ILEE	Colt 56A balloon	Two's Company	
G-ILES	Cameron O-90 balloon	G. N. Lantos	
G-ILIB	PZL-Bielsko SZD-36A	D. Poll	
G-ILLE	Boeing Stearman A75L3 (379)	M. Minkler	
G-ILLY	PA-28-181 Archer II	R. A. & G. M. Spiers	
G-ILPD	SIAI Marchetti F.260C	M. Mignini/Italy	
G-ILRS	Ikarus C.42 FB UK Cyclone	J. J. Oliver	
G-ILSE	Corby CJ-1 Starlet	S. Stride	
G-ILTS	PA-32 Cherokee Six 300	P. G. Teasdale & Foremans Aviation Ltd (G-CVOK)	
G-ILUA	Alpha R2160I	A. R. Haynes	
G-ILYA	Agusta-Bell 206B Jet Ranger II	Elmdawn Ltd (G-MHMH/G-HOLZ/G-CDBT)	
G-IMAB	Europa XS	T. J. Price	
G-IMAC	Canadair CL-600-2A12 Challenger	Gama Aviation Ltd	
G-IMAD	Cessna 172P	Leus Aviation Ltd	
G-IMAG	Colt 77A balloon ★	Balloon Preservation Group	
G-IMBI	QAC Quickie 1	J. D. King (G-BWIT)	
G-IMBL	Bell 407	Northern Flights Ltd	
G-IMBY	Pietenpol AirCamper	C. Brockis	
G-IMCD	Van's RV-7	I. G. McDowell	
G-IMEA	Beech 200 Super King Air	2 Excel Aviation Ltd (G-OWAX)	
G-IMEC	PA-31 Navajo C	Planeco Ltd (G-BFOM)	
G-IMED	Cessna 550 Citation II	Xclusive Jet Charter Ltd	
G-IMEL	Rotary Air Force RAF 2000 GTX-SE	N. A. Smith	
G-IMHK	P & M Quik R	J. Waite	
G-IMME	Zenair CH.701SP	T. R. Sinclair	
G-IMMI	Escapade Kid	J. Pearce	
G-IMMY	Robinson R44	Dielle SRL/Italy	
G-IMNY	Escapade 912	D. S. Bremner	
G-IMOK	Hoffmann HK-36R Super Dimona	A. L. Garfield	
G-IMPS	Skyranger Nynja 912S	B. J. Killick	
G-IMPX	Rockwell Commander 112B	Impatex Computer Systems Ltd	
G-IMPY	Light Aero Avid Flyer C	T. R. C. Griffin	
G-IMUP	Tanarg/Ixess 15 912S (1)	A. Wakeham	
G-INCA	Glaser-Dirks DG.400	K. D. Hook	
G-INCE	Skyranger 912(2)	N.P. Sleigh	
G-INDC	Cessna T.303	J-Ross Developments Ltd	
G-INDI	Pitts S-2C Special	L. Coesens	
G-INDX	Robinson R44	Kinetic Computers Ltd	
G-INDY	Robinson R44	Lincoln Aviation	
G-INGA	Thunder Ax8-84 balloon	M. L. J. Ritchie	
G-INGS	American Champion 8KCAB	Scotflight Ltd	
G-INII	Pitts S-1 Special	C. Davidson (G-BTEF)	
G-INJA	Ikarus C42 FB UK	C. E. Walls	
G-INNI	Jodel D.112	Clipgate Group	
G-INNY	SE-5A (replica) (F5459:Y)	M. J. Speakman	
G-INSR	Cameron N-90 balloon	P. J. Waller	
G-INTS	Van's RV-4	N. J. F. Campbell	
G-INTV	AS.355F2 Ecureuil 2	Arena Aviation Ltd (G-JETU)	
G-IOFR	Lindstrand LBL-105A balloon	RAF Halton Hot Air Balloon Club	
G-IOIA	I.I.I. Sky Arrow 650T	P.J. Lynch, P.G. Ward, N.J.C. Ray	
G-IOMC	Raytheon RB390 Premier 1	RB209 IoM Ltd	
G-IOMI	Cameron Z-105 balloon	Elgas SRL/Italy	
G-IONX	Dassault Falcon 7X	TAG Aviation (UK) Ltd	
G-IOOI	Robin DR.400/160	N. B. Mason	
G-IOOP	Christen Eagle II	A. P. S. Maynard	
G-IOOZ	Agusta A109S Grand	Hundred Percent Aviation Ltd	
G-IOPT	Cessna 182P	Indy Oscar Group	
G-IORG	Robinson R22 Beta	Staffordshire Helicopters Training Ltd	
G-IORV	Van's RV-10	A. F. S. & B. L. Caldecourt	
G-IOSI	Jodel DR.1051	D. C. & M. Brooks	

Notes	Reg.	Type	Owner or Operator
	G-IOSL	Van's RV-9	S. Leach (G-CFIX)
	G-IOSO	Jodel DR.1050	A. E. Jackson
	G-IOWE	Shaw Europa XS	P. G. & S. J. Jeffers
	G-IPAT	Jabiru SP	H. Adams
	G-IPAX	Cessna 560XL Citation Excel	Pacific Aviation Ltd
	G-IPEP	Beech 95-B55 Baron	P. E. T. Price (G-FABM)
	G-IPJF	Robinson R44 II	Specialist Group International Ltd (G-RGNT/ G-DMCG)
	G-IPKA	Alpi Pioneer 300	M. E. Hughes
	G-IPOD	Europa XS	J. Wighton (G-CEBV)
	G-IPSI	Grob G.109B	D. G. Margetts (G-BMLO)
	G-IPUP	Beagle B.121 Pup 2	Swift Flying Group
	G-IRAF	RAF 2000 GTX-SE gyroplane	M. P. Wiseman
	G-IRAK	SOCATA TB-10 Tobago	Flying Feather Ltd
	G-IRAL	Thruster T600N 450	J. Giraldez
	G-IRAP	Bombardier BD-700-1A10 Global Express	TAG Aviation (UK) Ltd (G-CJME)
	G-IRAR	Van's RV-9	J. Maplethorpe
	G-IRED	Ikarus C42 FB100	Red-Air UK
	G-IREN	SOCATA TB-20 Trinidad GT	Chios Aeroclub
	G-IRGJ	Champion 7ECA Citabria Aurora	B. T. Meese
	G-IRIS	AA-5B Tiger	J. L. Yourell & M. R. Cavinder (G-BIXU)
	G-IRJX	Avro RJX-100 ★	Manchester Heritage Museum
	G-IRKB	PA-28R-201 Arrow III	M. G. A. Hussein
	G-IRLE	Schempp-Hirth Ventus cT	D. J. Scholey
	G-IRLI	P & M Quik GTR	A. S. Markey
	G-IRLY	Colt 90A balloon	C. E. R. Smart
	G-IRLZ	Lindstrand LBL-60X balloon	A. M. Holly
	G-IROE	Flight Design CTSW	S. Roe
	G-IRON	Shaw Europa XS	T. M. Clark
	G-IROS	Rotorsport UK Calidus	JB Aviation Ltd
	G-IRPC	Cessna 182Q	A. T. Jeans (G-BSKM)
	G-IRPW	Europa XS	R. P. Wheelwright
	G-IRTM	DG Flugzeugbau DG-1000M	ATSl Ltd
	G-IRYC	Schweizer 269-1	Virage Helicopter Acadewmy LLP
	G-ISAN	Bombardier BD700-1A11 Global 5000	Aravco Ltd
	G-ISAR	Cessna 421C	Rescue Global Management Services Ltd (G-BHKJ)
	G-ISAX	PA-28-181 Archer III	Spectrum Flying Group
	G-ISBD	Alpi Pioneer 300 Hawk	B. Davies
	G-ISCD	Czech Sport Aircraft Sportcruiser	P. W. Shepherd
	G-ISDB	PA-28-161 Warrior II	Action Air Services Ltd (G-BWET)
	G-ISDN	Boeing Stearman A75N1	D. R. L. Jones
	G-ISEH	Cessna 182R	S. J. Nash (G-BIWS)
	G-ISEL	Best Off Skyranger 912 (2)	P. A. Robertson
	G-ISEW	P & M Quik GT450	S. P. McVeigh
	G-ISHA	PA-28-161 Warrior III	LAC Flying School
	G-ISHK	Cessna 172S	E. A. Poore
	G-ISLB	BAe Jetstream 3201	Blue Islands Ltd
	G-ISLC	BAe Jetstream 3202	Blue Islands Ltd
	G-ISLD	BAe Jetstream 3202	Blue Islands Ltd
	G-ISLF	Aerospatiale ATR-42-500	Blue Islands Ltd
	G-ISLG	Aerospatiale ATR-42-300	Blue Islands Ltd
	G-ISLH	Aerospatiale ATR-42-320	Blue Islands Ltd
	G-ISLI	Aerospatiale ATR-72-212A	Blue Islands Ltd
	G-ISMA	Van's RV-7	S. Marriott (G-STAF)
	G-ISMO	Robinson R22 Beta	Moy Motorsport Ltd
	G-ISMS	Sorrell SNS-7 Hyperbipe	D. G. Curran (G-HIPE)
	G-ISON	AirBike UK Elite	AirBike UK Ltd
	G-ISPH	Bell 206B JetRanger 2	Blades Aviation (UK) LLP (G-OPJM)
	G-ISSG	DHC.6-310 Twin Otter	Isles of Scilly Skybus Ltd
	G-ISSV	Eurocopter EC 155B1	Bristow Helicopters Ltd
	G-ISSY	Eurocopter EC 120B	D. R. Williams (G-CBCG)
	G-ISZA	Aerotek Pitts S-2A Special	F. L. McGee (G-HISS/G-BLVU)
	G-ITAF	SIAI-Marchetti SF.260AM	N. A. Whatling
	G-ITAR	Magni M-16C Tandem Trainer	B. Lesslie
	G-ITBT	Alpi Pioneer 300 Hawk	F. Paolini

Reg.	Type	Owner or Operator	Notes
G-ITII	Aerotech Pitts S-2A Special	P. J. Kirkpatrick	
G-ITOI	Cameron N-90 balloon	Flying Pictures Ltd	
G-ITPH	Robinson R44 II	Helicopter Services Europe Ltd	
G-ITSU	Embraer EMB-500 Phenom 100	Flairjet Ltd (G-RUBO)	
G-ITVM	Lindstrand LBL-105A balloon	Elmer Balloon Team	
G-ITWB	DHC.1 Chipmunk 22	I. T. Whitaker-Bethe	
G-IUAN	Cessna 525 CitationJet	Premium Jet SRL/Italy	
G-IUII	Aerostar Yakovlev Yak-52	A. L. Grisay	
G-IUMB	Schleicher ASW-20L	M. S. Szymkowicz	
G-IVAC	Airtour AH-77B balloon	T. D. Gibbs	
G-IVAL	CAB CAP-10B	H. Thomas	
G-IVAN	Shaw TwinEze	A. M. Aldridge	
G-IVAR	Yakovlev Yak-50	A. H. Soper	
G-IVEN	Robinson R44 II	OKR Group/Ireland	
G-IVER	Shaw Europa XS	I. Phillips	
G-IVES	Shaw Europa	M. W. Olliver (G-JOST)	
G-IVET	Shaw Europa	K. J. Fraser	
G-IVII	Van's RV-7	M. A. N. Newall	
G-IVIP	Agusta A109E Power	Castle Air Ltd (G-VIRU)	
G-IVIV	Robinson R44	D. Brown	
G-IVJM	Agusta A109E Power	Air Harrods Ltd (G-MOMO)	
G-IVOR	Aeronca 11AC Chief	South Western Aeronca Group	
G-IWIN	Raj Hamsa X'Air Hawk	J. R. Gardiner	
G-IWIZ	Flylight Dragonfly	S. Wilson	
G-IWON	Cameron V-90 balloon	D. P. P. Jenkinson (G-BTCV)	
G-IWRB	Agusta A109A-II	Maison Air Ltd (G-VIPT)	
G-IXII	Christen Eagle II	Eagle Flying Group (G-BPZI)	
G-IXXI	Schleicher ASW-27-18E	G. P. Stingemore	
G-IYRO	RAF2000 GTX-SE	R. Boese (G-BXDD)	
G-IZIT	Rans S.6-116 Coyote II	D. J. Flower	
G-IZOB	Eurocopter EC.120B Colibri	D. M. McGarrity	
G-IZZI	Cessna T.182T	D. J. & E-S Lucey	
G-IZZS	Cessna 172S	Air Claire Ltd	
G-IZZZ	Champion 8KCAB	Phoenix Flyers Ltd	
G-JAAB	Avtech Jabiru UL	J. White	
G-JABB	Avtech Jabiru UL	R. J. Sutherland	
G-JABE	Jabiru Aircraft Jabiru UL-D	H. M. Manning and P. M. Jones	
G-JABI	Jabiru Aircraft Jabiru J400	K. & M. A. Payne	
G-JABJ	Jabiru Aircraft Jabiru J400	South East Flying Group	
G-JABS	Avtech Jabiru UL-450	Jabiru Flying Group	
G-JABU	Jabiru J430	S. D. Miller	
G-JABY	Avtech Jabiru UL-450	F. Patterson & B. J. Robe	
G-JABZ	Avtech Jabiru UL-450	G-JABZ Group	
G-JACA	PA-28-161 Warrior II	The Pilot Centre Ltd	
G-JACB	PA-28-181 Archer III	P. R. Coe (G-PNNI)	
G-JACH	PA-28-181 Archer III	Alderney Flight Training Ltd (G-IDPH)	
G-JACI	Bell 206L-4 LongRanger IV	Morgan Airborne LLP	
G-JACK	Cessna 421C	JCT 600 Ltd	
G-JACO	Avtech Jabiru UL	C. D. Matthews/Ireland	
G-JACS	PA-28-181 Archer III	Modern Air (UK) Ltd	
G-JADJ	PA-28-181 Archer III	S. A. Spevack	
G-JADW	Ikarus C42 FB80	J. W. & D. A. Wilding	
G-JAEE	Van's RV-6A	J. A. E. Edser	
G-JAES	Bell 206B JetRanger 3	Helicom Ltd (G-STOX/G-BNIR)	
G-JAFT	Diamond DA.42 Twin Star	Atlantic Flight Training Ltd	
G-JAGA	Embraer EMB-505 Phenom 300	London Executive Aviation Ltd	
G-JAGS	Cessna FRA.150L	RAF Marham Flying Club (G-BAUY)	
G-JAGY	Europa XS	J. S. Chaggar	
G-JAIR	Mainair Blade	G. Spittlehouse	
G-JAJA	Robinson R44 II	J. D. Richardson	
G-JAJB	AA-5A Cheetah	Active Aviation Ltd	
G-JAJK	PA-31-350 Navajo Chieftain	Blue Sky Investments Ltd (G-OLDB/G-DIXI)	
G-JAJP	Avtech Jabiru UL	J. Anderson	
G-JAKF	Robinson R44 Raven II	J. G. Froggatt	
G-JAKI	Mooney M.20R	J. M. Moss & D. M. Abrahamson	

Notes	Reg.	Type	Owner or Operator
	G-JAKS	PA-28 Cherokee 160	K. Harper (G-ARVS)
	G-JAMA	Schweizer 269C-1	R. J. Scott
	G-JAME	Zenair CH 601UL	A. Batters (G-CDFZ)
	G-JAMP	PA-28-151 Warrior	Lapwing Flying Group Ltd (G-BRJU)
	G-JAMY	Shaw Europa XS	J. P. Sharp
	G-JAMZ	P & M QuikR	S. Cuthbertson
	G-JANA	PA-28-181 Archer II	S. Hoo-Hing
	G-JANB	Colt Flying Bottle SS balloon	Justerini & Brooks Ltd
	G-JANI	Robinson R44	JT Helicopters Ltd
	G-JANN	PA-34-220T Seneca III	D. J. Whitcombe
	G-JANS	Cessna FR.172J	S. F. Scott
	G-JANT	PA-28-181 Archer II	Janair Aviation Ltd
	G-JAOC	Best Off Sky Ranger Swift 912S(1)	M. J. Stolworthy & K. G. Winter
	G-JAPK	Grob G.130A Twin II Acro	Cairngorm Gliding Club
	G-JARM	Robinson R44	J. Armstrong
	G-JASE	PA-28-161 Warrior II	Mid-Anglia School of Flying
	G-JASS	Beech B200 Super King Air	Platinum Executive Aviation LLP
	G-JAVO	PA-28-161 Warrior II	Victor Oscar Ltd (G-BSXW)
	G-JAWC	Pegasus Quantum 15-912	M. J. Robbins
	G-JAWZ	Pitts S-1S Special	A. R. Harding
	G-JAXS	Avtech Jabiru UL	J. P. Pullin
	G-JAYI	Auster J/1 Autocrat	Aviation Heritage Ltd
	G-JAYS	Skyranger 912S(1)	R. A. Green
	G-JAYZ	CZAW Sportcruiser	J. Williams
	G-JBAN	P & M Quik GT450	J. Bond & A. Nourse
	G-JBAS	Neico Lancair 200	A. Slater
	G-JBBZ	AS.350B3 Ecureuil	BZ Air Ltd
	G-JBDB	Agusta-Bell 206B JetRanger	Dicksons Van World Ltd (G-OOPS/G-BNRD)
	G-JBDH	Robin DR.400/180	W. A. Clark
	G-JBEN	Mainair Blade 912	G. J. Bentley
	G-JBII	Robinson R22 Beta	Startrade Heli GmbH & Co.KG/Germany (G-BXLA)
	G-JBIS	Cessna 550 Citation II	247 Jet Ltd
	G-JBIZ	Cessna 550 Citation II	247 Jet Ltd
	G-JBKA	Robinson R44	J. G. Harrison
	G-JBLZ	Cessna 550 Citation Bravo	247 Jet Ltd
	G-JBRE	Rotorsport UK MT-03	P. A. Remfry
	G-JBRG	Agusta A109A II	Jetworx Ltd (G-TMUR/G-CEPO)
	G-JBRN	Cessna 182S	Ngaio Aviation (G-RITZ)
	G-JBRS	Van's RV-8	C. Jobling
	G-JBSP	Avtech Jabiru SP-470	C. R. James
	G-JBTR	Van's RV-8	R. A. Ellis
	G-JBUL	Best Off Skyranger 912(2)	J. Bulpin (G-CDJC)
	G-JBUZ	Robin DR400/180R Remorqueur	D. A. Saywell
	G-JCBB	Gulfstream V-SP	J. C. Bamford Excavators Ltd
	G-JCBX	Dassault Falcon 900EX	J. C. Bamford Excavators Ltd
	G-JCJC	Colt Flying Jeans SS balloon	Magical Adventures Ltd
	G-JCKT	Stemme S.10VT	J. C. Taylor
	G-JCMW	Rand KR-2	S. H. Leahy
	G-JCOP	Eurocopter AS.350B3 Ecureuil	Optimum Ltd
	G-JCUB	PA-18 Super Cub 135	Vintage Aircraft Flying Group
	G-JCWM	Robinson R44 II	M. L. J. Goff
	G-JCWS	Reality Escapade 912(2)	J. C. W. Seward
	G-JDBC	PA-34-200T Seneca II	JD Aviation Ltd (G-BDEF)
	G-JDEE	SOCATA TB20 Trinidad	JDEE Group
	G-JDEL	Jodel 150	K. F. & R. Richardson (G-JDLI)
	G-JDPB	PA-28R-201T Turbo Arrow III	BC Arrow Ltd (G-DNCS)
	G-JDRD	Alpi Pioneer 300	Anvilles Flying Group
	G-JEAJ	BAe 146-200	Trident Aviation Leasing Services (Jersey) Ltd (G-OLCA)
	G-JEBS	Cessna 172S	Integrated Hi-Tech Ltd
	G-JECE	DHC.8-402 Dash Eight	Flybe.com
	G-JECF	DHC.8-402 Dash Eight	Flybe.com
	G-JECG	DHC.8-402 Dash Eight	Flybe.com
	G-JECH	DHC.8-402 Dash Eight	Flybe.com
	G-JECI	DHC.8-402 Dash Eight	Flybe.com
	G-JECJ	DHC.8-402 Dash Eight	Flybe.com

Reg.	Type	Owner or Operator	Notes
G-JECK	DHC.8-402 Dash Eight	Flybe.com	
G-JECL	DHC.8-402 Dash Eight	Flybe.com	
G-JECM	DHC.8-402 Dash Eight	Flybe.com	
G-JECN	DHC.8-402 Dash Eight	Flybe.com	
G-JECO	DHC.8-402 Dash Eight	Flybe.com	
G-JECP	DHC.8-402 Dash Eight	Flybe.com	
G-JECR	DHC.8-402 Dash Eight	Flybe.com	
G-JECX	DHC.8-402 Dash Eight	Flybe.com	
G-JECY	DHC.8-402 Dash Eight	Flybe.com	
G-JECZ	DHC.8-402 Dash Eight	Flybe.com	
G-JEDH	Robin DR.400/180	J. B. Hoolahan	
G-JEDK	DHC.8-402 Dash Eight	Amra Leasing Ltd	
G-JEDM	DHC.8-402 Dash Eight	Flybe.com	
G-JEDP	DHC.8-402 Dash Eight	Flybe com	
G-JEDR	DHC.8-402 Dash Eight	Flybe com	
G-JEDS	Andreasson BA-4B	S. B. Jedburgh (G-BEBT)	
G-JEDT	DHC.8-402 Dash Eight	Flybe com	
G-JEDU	DHC.8-402 Dash Eight	Flybe com	
G-JEDV	DHC.8-402 Dash Eight	Flybe.com	
G-JEDW	DHC.8-402 Dash Eight	Flybe.com	
G-JEEP	Evektor EV-97 Eurostar	G-JEEP Group (G-CBNK)	
G-JEFA	Robinson R44	Simlot Ltd	
G-JEJE	RAF 2000 GTX-SE gyroplane	A. F. Smallacombe	
G-JEJH	Jodel DR.1050 Ambassadeur	Bredon Hill Flying Group	
G-JEMA	BAe ATP	PTB (Emerald) Pty Ltd	
G-JEMC	BAe ATP	PTB (Emerald) Pty Ltd	
G-JEMI	Lindstrand LBL-90A balloon	J. A. Lawton	
G-JEMM	Jodel DR.1050	D. W. Garbe	
G-JENA	Mooney M.20K	Jena Air Force	
G-JENI	Cessna R.182	R. A. Bentley	
G-JENK	Ikarus C42 FB80	P. J. Oakey	
G-JENZ	Eurocopter EC.225LP Super Puma	CHC Scotia Ltd	
G-JERO	Shaw Europa XS	P. Jenkinson and N. Robshaw	
G-JESE	AS.355F2 Ecureuil 2	Arena Aviation Ltd (G-EMHH/G-BYKH)	
G-JESI	AS.350B Ecureuil	Staske Construction Ltd (G-JOSS/G-WILX/ G-RAHM/G-UNIC/G-COLN/G-BHIV)	
G-JESP	Eurocopter MBB BK-117C-2	Eurocopter UK Ltd	
G-JESS	PA-28R-201T Turbo Arrow III	R. E. Trawicki (G-REIS)	
G-JETA	Cessna 550 Citation II	Icon Two Ltd (G-RDBS)	
G-JETH	Hawker Sea Hawk FGA.6 (XE489) ★	P. G. Vallance Ltd/Charlwood	
G-JETM	Gloster Meteor T.7 (VZ638) ★	P. G. Vallance Ltd/Charlwood	
G-JETX	Bell 206B JetRanger 3	Morgan Airborne LLP	
G-JETZ	Hughes 369E	GJP Helicopters Ltd	
G-JEWL	Van's RV-7	H. A. & J. S. Jewell	
G-JEZA	Agusta AW.139	CHC Scotia Ltd	
G-JEZZ	Skyranger 912S(1)	N. J. Brownlow & P. W. Day	
G-JFAN	P & M Quik R	P. R. Brooker & G. R. Hall	
G-JFDI	Dynamic WT9 UK	M. S. Gregory	
G-JFER	Rockwell Commander 114B	P. S. Jones (G-HPSE)	
G-JFLO	Aerospool Dynamic WT9 UK	J. Flood	
G-JFLY	Schleicher ASW-24	Cambridge Gliding Club Ltd	
G-JFMK	Zenair CH.701SP	J. D. Pearson	
G-JFRV	Van's RV-7A	J. H. Fisher	
G-JFWI	Cessna F.172N	Staryear Ltd	
G-JGBI	Bell 206L-4 LongRanger	Dorbcrest Homes Ltd	
G-JGCA	VS.361 Spitfire LF.IXe (TE517)	P. M. Andrews (G-CCIX/G-BIXP)	
G-JGMN	CASA 1.131E Jungmann 2000	P. D. Scandrett	
G-JGSI	Pegasus Quantum 15-912	Airways Airsports Ltd	
G-JHAA	Csameron Z-90 balloon	C. L. Thompson	
G-JHAC	Cessna FRA.150L	J. H. A. Clarke (G-BACM)	
G-JHDD	Czech Sport Aircraft Sportcruiser	D. Draper & J. W. Hagley	
G-JHEW	Robinson R22 Beta	Heli Air Ltd	
G-JHKP	Shaw Europa XS	J. D. Heykoop	
G-JHNY	Cameron A.210 balloon	Floarting Sensations Ltd	
G-JHPC	Cessna 182T	J. R. Turner	
G-JHYS	Shaw Europa	G-JHYS Group	
G-JIBO	BAe Jetstream 3102	AC Aviation Wales Ltd (G-OJSA/G-BTYG)	

Notes	Reg.	Type	Owner or Operator
	G-JIFI	Schempp-Hirth Duo Discus T	620 Syndicate
	G-JIII	Stolp SA.300 Starduster Too	VTIO Co
	G-JIIL	Pitts S-2AE Special	A. M. Southwell
	G-JIMB	Beagle B.121 Pup 1	K. D. H. Gray & P. G. Fowler (G-AWWF)
	G-JIMC	Van's RV-7	J. Chapman
	G-JIMH	Cessna F.152 II	D. J. Howell (G-SHAH)
	G-JIMM	Shaw Europa XS	J. Riley
	G-JIMP	Messerschmitt Bf 109G-2	M. R. Oliver
	G-JIMZ	Van's RV-4	J.W.Hale
	G-JINI	Cameron V-77 balloon	I. R. Warrington
	G-JINX	Silence SA.180 Twister	P. M. Wells
	G-JJAB	Jabiru J400	K. Ingebrigsten
	G-JJAN	PA-28-181 Archer II	J. S. Develin & Z. Islam
	G-JJEN	PA-28-181 Archer III	K. M. R. Jenkins
	G-JJFB	Eurocopter EC.120B Colibri	J. G. Rhoden
	G-JJIL	Extra EA.300/L	Link Goals SP ZOO
	G-JJSI	BAe 125 Srs 800B	Gama Leasing Ltd (G-OMGG)
	G-JJWL	Robinson R44	Willbeth Ltd
	G-JKAY	Robinson R44	Jamiroquai Ltd
	G-JKEL	Van's RV-7	J. D. Kelsall (G-LNNE)
	G-JKKK	Cessna 172S	P. Eaton
	G-JKMH	Diamond DA42 Twin Star	ADR Aviation
	G-JKMI	Diamond DA42 Twin Star	Flying Time Ltd (G-KELV/G-CTCH)
	G-JKMJ	Diamond DA42 Twin Star	Medox Enterprises Ltd
	G-JKRV	Schempp-Hirth Arcus T	G-JKRV Syndicate
	G-JLAT	Aerotechnik EV-97 Eurostar	J. Latimer
	G-JLCA	PA-34-200T Seneca II	Tayside Aviation Ltd (G-BOKE)
	G-JLEE	Agusta-Bell 206B JetRanger 3	Leamington Hobby Centre Ltd (G-JOKE/ G-CSKY/G-TALY)
	G-JLHS	Beech A36 Bonanza	I. G. Meredith
	G-JLIN	PA-28-161 Cadet	JH Sandham Aviation
	G-JLLT	Aerotechnik EV-97 Eurostar	J. Latimer
	G-JLRW	Beech 76 Duchess	Airways Flight Training
	G-JMAA	Boeing 757-3CQ	Thomas Cook Airlines Ltd
	G-JMAB	Boeing 757-3CQ	Thomas Cook Airlines Ltd
	G-JMAC	BAe Jetstream 4100 ★	Jetstream Club, Liverpool Marriott Hotel South, Speke (G-JAMD/G-JXLI)
	G-JMAL	Jabiru UL-D	A. D. Sutton
	G-JMCD	Boeing 757-25F	Thomas Cook Airlines Ltd
	G-JMCE	Boeing 757-25F	Thomas Cook Airlines Ltd
	G-JMCG	Boeing 757-2G5	Thomas Cook Airlines Ltd
	G-JMCL	Boeing 737-322	Atlantic Airlines Ltd
	G-JMCM	Boeing 737-3YO	Atlantic Airlines Ltd
	G-JMCO	Boeing 737-3TOF	Atlantic Airlines Ltd
	G-JMCP	Boeing 737-3TO	Atlantic Airlines Ltd
	G-JMCR	Boeing 737-4YO	Atlantic Airlines Ltd
	G-JMCT	Boeing 737-3YO	Atlantic Airlines Ltd (G-ZAPV/G-IGOC)
	G-JMDI	Schweizer 269C	D. A. Sempers (G-FLAT)
	G-JMED	Learjet 35A	Air Medical Fleet Ltd, Argyll Ltd & Provident Partners Ltd
	G-JMJR	Cameron Z-90	J. M. Reck/France
	G-JMKE	Cessna 172S	M. C. Plomer-Roberts
	G-JMKM	AutoGyro MTO Sport	K. O. Maurer
	G-JMMY	PA-28R-200 Cherokee Arrow B	JMMY Ltd (G-GYMM/G-AYWW)
	G-JMON	Agusta A109A-II	Falcon Aviation Ltd (G-RFDS/G-BOLA)
	G-JMOS	PA-34-220T Seneca V	Moss Aviation LLP
	G-JMRV	Van's RV-7	J. W. Marshall
	G-JMTS	Robin DR.400/180	G-JMTS Group
	G-JNAS	AA-5A Cheetah	C. J. Williams
	G-JNET	Robinson R22 Beta	R. L. Hartshorn
	G-JNMA	VS.379 Spitfire FR.Mk.XIVe	P. M. Andrews
	G-JNNB	Colt 90A balloon	N. A. P. Godfrey
	G-JNSC	Schempp-Hirth Janus CT	D. S. Bramwell
	G-JNUS	Schempp-Hirth Janus C	N. A. Peatfield
	G-JOAL	Beech B200 Super King Air	South Coast Air Charter LLP

Reg.	Type	Owner or Operator	Notes
G-JOBA	P & M Quik GT450	B. Hall	
G-JOBS	Cessna T182T	Tech Travel Ltd (G-BZVF)	
G-JODE	Jodel D.150	B. R. Vickers	
G-JODL	Jodel D.1050/M	R. J. D. Mellor	
G-JOED	Lindstrand LBL-77A balloon	G. R. Down	
G-JOEY	BN-2A Mk III-2 Trislander	Aurigny Air Services (G-BDGG)	
G-JOHA	Cirrus SR20	N. Harris	
G-JOID	Cirrus SR20	I. F. Doubtfire	
G-JOJO	Cameron A-210 balloon	A. C. Rawson & J. J. Rudoni	
G-JOKR	Extra EA.300/L	C. Jefferies	
G-JOLY	Cessna 120	B. V. Meade	
G-JONB	Robinson R22 Beta	J. Bignall	
G-JONG	Rotorway Executive 162F	J. V. George	
G-JONL	CZAW Sportcruiser	J. R. Linford	
G-JONM	PA-28-181 Archer III	J. H. Massey	
G-JONO	Colt 77A balloon★	British Balloon Museum and Library	
G-JONT	Cirrus SR22	J. A. Green	
G-JONX	Aeropro Eurofox 912(1)	A. J. South	
G-JONY	Cyclone AX2000 HKS	K. R. Matheson	
G-JONZ	Cessna 172P	Truman Aviation Ltd	
G-JONT	Cirrus SR22	J. A. Green	
G-JOOL	Mainair Blade 912	P. C. Collins	
G-JORD	Robinson R44 II	Overby Ltd	
G-JOTA	Beech B.90 King Air	Jota Aircraft Leasing Ltd (G-OJRO)	
G-JOTB	Beech C.90 King Air	Jota Aircraft Leasing Ltd	
G-JOYT	PA-28-181 Archer II	John K. Cathcart Ltd (G-BOVO)	
G-JOYZ	PA-28-181 Archer III	S. Wilson	
G-JOZI	AS.350BA Ecureuil	Aero Maintenance Ltd	
G-JPAT	Robin HR.200/100	L. Girardier	
G-JPBA	Van's RV-6	S. B. Austin	
G-JPEG	BN-2A-20 Islander	Apem Aviation Ltd (G-BEDW)	
G-JPIP	Schempp-Hirth Discus bT	S. Cervantes	
G-JPJR	Robinson R44 II	Longstop Investments Ltd	
G-JPMA	Avtech Jabiru UL	A. J. Thomas	
G-JPOT	PA-32R-301 Saratoga SP	P.J.Wolstencroft (G-BIYM)	
G-JPRO	P.84 Jet Provost T.5A (XW433)	Air Atlantique Ltd	
G-JPTV	P.84 Jet Provost T.5A (XW354)	Century Aviation Ltd	
G-JPVA	P.84 Jet Provost T.5A (XW289)	H. Cooke (G-BVXT)	
G-JPWM	Skyranger 912 (2)	R. S. Waters & M. Pittock	
G-JRCR	Bell 206L-1 LongRanger II	Commercial Legal Ltd (G-EYRE/G-STVI)	
G-JRED	Robinson R44	J. Reddington Ltd	
G-JREE	Maule MX-7-180	C. R. P. Briand	
G-JRME	Jodel D.140E	J. E. & L. L. Rex	
G-JROO	Agusta-Bell 206B JetRanger II	Rooney Air Ltd (G-VJMJ/G-PEAK/G-BLJE)	
G-JRSL	Agusta A109E Power	Perment Ltd	
G-JRVB	Van's RV-8	J. W. Salter	
G-JSAK	Robinson R22 Beta II	Tukair Aircraft Charter	
G-JSAT	BN-2T Turbine Islander	MV Capital Ltd (G-BVFK)	
G-JSCA	PA-28RT-201 Arrow IV	I. P. Haddon (G-ICSA)	
G-JSEY	Bollonbau Worner NL-STU/1000	M. Leblanc	
G-JSKY	Ikarus C42 FB80	M. S. Westman	
G-JSON	Cameron N-105 balloon	Up and Away Ballooning Ltd	
G-JSPL	Avtech Jabiru SPL-450	A. E. Stowe	
G-JSRV	Van's RV-6	J. Stringer	
G-JSSD	HP.137 Jetstream 3001 ★	Museum of Flight/East Fortune	
G-JTBX	Bell 206B Jet Ranger III	J. Tobias (G-EWAW/G-DORB)	
G-JTEM	Van's RV-7	J. C. Bacon	
G-JTHU	Agusta AW.109SP	Jetheli Ltd	
G-JTJT	Robinson R44	Skyrunner Aviation Ltd	
G-JTNC	Cessna 500 Citation	Eurojet Aviation Ltd (G-OEJA/G-BWFL)	
G-JTPC	Aeromot AMT-200 Super Ximango	G. J. & J. T. Potter	
G-JTSA	Robinson R44 II	S. Novotny	
G-JUDD	Avtech Jabiru UL-450H	G. S. Elder	
G-JUDE	Robin DR.400/180	Bravo India Flying Group Ltd	
G-JUDY	AA-5A Cheetah	Gray Hooper Holt LLP	
G-JUGE	Aerotechnik EV-97 TeamEurostar UK	L. J. Appleby	

Notes	Reg.	Type	Owner or Operator
	G-JUGS	Autogyro MTOSport	S. J. M. Hornsby
	G-JULE	P & M Quik GT450	G. Almond
	G-JULL	Stemme S.10VT	J. P. C. Fuchs
	G-JULU	Cameron V-90 balloon	J. M. Searle
	G-JULZ	Shaw Europa	J. S. Firth
	G-JUNG	CASA 1.131E Jungmann 1000 (E3B-143)	A. Burroughes
	G-JUNO	Fokker D.VII Replica	D. A. Graham
	G-JURG	Rockwell Commander 114A	Wright Aviation Dunchurch Ltd
	G-JUST	Beech F33A Bonanza	L. J. Macpherson
	G-JVBF	Lindstrand LBL-210A balloon	Virgin Balloon Flights
	G-JVBP	Aerotechnik EV-97 Team Eurostar UK	B. J. Partridge & J. A. Valentine
	G-JWBI	Agusta-Bell 206B JetRanger 2	J. W. Bonser (G-RODS/G-NOEL/G-BCWN)
	G-JWCM	SA Bulldog Srs 120/1210	N. Cooper
	G-JWDB	Ikarus C.42 FB80	A. R. Hughes
	G-JWDS	Cessna F.150G	G. Sayer (G-AVNB)
	G-JWEB	Robinson R44	P. T. Birdsall
	G-JWIV	Jodel DR.1051	C. M. Fitton
	G-JWJW	CASA 1-131E Jungmann Srs.2000	J. W. & J. T. Whicher
	G-JWNW	Magni M-16C Tandem Trainer	A. G. Jones
	G-JWXS	Shaw Europa XS T-G	J. Wishart
	G-JXTA	BAe Jetstream 3103	Skybird SP Ltd
	G-JXTC	BAe Jetstream 3108★	University of Glamorgan instructional airframe (G-LOGT/G-BSFH)
	G-JYAK	Yakovlev Yak-50 (93 white outline)	J. W. Stow & A. P. Wilson
	G-JYRO	Rotorsport UK MT-03	A. Richards
	G-KAAT	MDH MD-902 Explorer	Police Aviation Services Ltd (G-PASS)
	G-KAAZ	Eurocopter EC.130 B4	Falcon Group Europe Ltd
	G-KAEW	Fairey Gannet AEW Mk.3	M. Stott
	G-KAFT	Diamond DA40D Star	Atlantic Flight Training Ltd
	G-KAIR	PA-28-181 Archer II	G. Fox
	G-KALS	Bombardier BD-100-1A10	Air Charter Scotland Ltd
	G-KAMP	PA-18 Super Cub 135	G. Cormack
	G-KAMY	AT-6D Harvard III	Orion Enterprises Ltd
	G-KANE	Aerospatiale SA.341G Gazelle 1	MW Helicopters Ltd (G-GAZI)
	G-KANZ	Westland Wasp HAS.1 (NZ3909)	T. J. Manna
	G-KAOM	Scheibe SF.25C Falke	Falke G-KAOM Syndicate
	G-KAOS	Van's RV-7	J. L. Miles
	G-KAPW	P.56 Provost T.1 (XF603)	The Shuttleworth Collection
	G-KARA	Brügger MB.2 Colibri	C. L. Hill (G-BMUI)
	G-KARI	Fuji FA.200-160	C. P. Rowley
	G-KARK	Dyn'Aéro MCR-01 Club	R. Bailes-Brown
	G-KARN	Rotorway Executive 90	I. R. Brown (G-VART/G-BSUR)
	G-KART	PA-28-161 Warrior II	Romeo Tango Aviation Ltd
	G-KASW	Rotorsport UK Calidus	K. C. Wigley
	G-KASX	VS.384 Seafire Mk.XVII (SX336)	T. J. Manna (G-BRMG)
	G-KATE	Westland WG.30 Srs 100 ★	(stored)/Yeovil
	G-KATI	Rans S.7 Courier	T. S. D. Lyle
	G-KATT	Cessna 152 II	Best Fly KFT (G-BMTK)
	G-KATZ	Flight Design CT2K	A. N. D. Arthur
	G-KAWA	Denney Kitfox Mk 2	J. K. Ewing
	G-KAXF	Hawker Hunter F.6A (N-294)	Stichting Dutch Hawker Hunter Foundation/Netherlands
	G-KAXT	Westland Wasp HAS.1 (XT787)	T. E. Martin
	G-KAXW	Westland Scout AH-1 (XW612)	Orion Enterprise Ltd (G-BXRR)
	G-KAYH	Extra EA.300/L	Faralley Beheer en Management BV/Netherlands
	G-KAYI	Cameron Z-90 balloon	Snow Business International Ltd
	G-KAZA	Sikorsky S-76C	Bristow Helicopters Ltd
	G-KAZB	Sikorsky S-76C	Bristow Helicopters Ltd
	G-KAZI	Mainair Pegasus Quantum 15-912	Fairlight Engineering Ltd
	G-KBOJ	Autogyro MTOSport	K. M. G. Barnett
	G-KBOX	Flight Design CTSW	C. R. Mason
	G-KBWP	Schempp-Hirth Arcus T	B. F. & P. Walker
	G-KCHG	Schempp-Hirth Ventus Ct	Ventus KJW Syndicate

Reg.	Type	Owner or Operator	Notes
G-KCIG	Sportavia RF-5B	Deeside Fournier Group	
G-KCIN	PA-28-161 Cadet	S. J. Green (G-CDOX)	
G-KCWJ	Schempp-Hirth Duo Discus T	G-KCWJ Group	
G-KDCD	Thruster T.600N 450	M. N. Watson	
G-KDEY	Scheibe SF.25E Super Falke	Falke Syndicate	
G-KDIX	Jodel D.9 Bébé	J. A. Sykes	
G-KDMA	Cessna 560 Citation V	Gamston Aviation Ltd	
G-KDOG	SA Bulldog Srs 120/121 (XX624:E)	M. van den Broeck	
G-KEAM	Schleicher ASH 26E	I. W. Paterson	
G-KEAY	AutoGyro MTO Sport	R. Keay	
G-KEDK	Schempp-Hirth Discus bT	S. G. Vardigans	
G-KEEF	Commander Aircraft 112A	K. D. Pearse	
G-KEEN	Stolp SA.300 Starduster Too	Sharp Aerobatics Ltd/Netherlands	
G-KEES	PA-28 Cherokee 180	C. N. Ellerbrook	
G-KEJY	Aerotechnik EV-97 TeamEurostar UK	Kemble Eurostar 1	
G-KELI	Robinson R44 Raven II	KN Network Services Ltd	
G-KELL	Van's RV-6	K A Keigher/Ireland	
G-KELS	Van's RV-7	F. W. Hardiman	
G-KELX	Van's RV-6	P. J. McMahon (G-HAMY)	
G-KELZ	Van's RV-8	B. F. Hill (G-DJRV)	
G-KEMC	Grob G.109	Norfolk Gliding Club Ltd	
G-KEMI	PA-28-181 Archer III	Modern Air (UK) Ltd	
G-KENB	Air Command 503 Commander	K. Brogden	
G-KENG	Rotorsport UK MT-03	K. A. Graham	
G-KENI	Rotorway Executive	P. A. Taylor	
G-KENM	Luscombe 8EF Silvaire	M. G. Waters	
G-KENW	Robin DR400/500	K. J. White	
G-KENZ	Rutan Vari-Eze	K. M. McConnel I (G-BNUI)	
G-KEPE	Schempp-Hirth Nimbus 3DT	G-KEPE Group	
G-KEPP	Rans S.6-ES Coyote II	R. G. Johnston	
G-KESS	Glaser-Dirks DG-400	M. T. Collins & T. Flude	
G-KEST	Steen Skybolt	G-KEST Syndicate	
G-KESY	Slingsby T.59D Kestrel	A. J. Whiteman & P. J. R. Hogarth	
G-KETH	Agusta-Bell 206B JetRanger 2	DAC Leasing Ltd	
G-KEVA	Ace Magic Cyclone	K. A. Armstrong	
G-KEVB	PA-28-181 Archer III	Palmair Ltd	
G-KEVG	Rotorsport UK MT-03	K. J. Robinson & R. N. Bodley	
G-KEVI	Jabiru J400	P. Horth & P. G. Macintosh	
G-KEVK	Flight Design CTSW	K. Kirby	
G-KEVL	Rotorway Executive 162F	K. D. Longhurst (G-CBIK)	
G-KEVS	P 7 M Quik GT450	I. A. Macadam	
G-KEVZ	P & M Quik R	K. Mallin	
G-KEWT	Ultramagic M.90 balloon	R. D. Parry	
G-KEYS	PA-23 Aztec 250F	Giles Aviation Ltd	
G-KEYY	Cameron N-77 balloon	B. N. Trowbridge (G-BORZ)	
G-KFAN	Scheibe SF.25B Falke	R. G. & J. A. Boyes	
G-KFCA	Ikarus C42 FB80	C42A Group	
G-KFLY	Flight Design CTSW	G. WF. Morton & J. J. Brutnell (G-LFLY)	
G-KFOX	Denney Kitfox	I. R. Lawrence & R. Hampshire	
G-KFZI	KFZ-1 Tigerfalck	L. R. Williams	
G-KGAO	Scheibe SF.25C Falke 1700	Falke 2000 Group	
G-KGAW	Scheibe SF-25C	The Windrushers Gliding Club Ltd	
G-KHCC	Schempp-Hirth Ventus Bt	J. L. G. McLane	
G-KHCG	AS.355F2 Ecureuil II	CE Aviation UK Ltd (G-SDAY/G-SYPA/G-BPRE)	
G-KHEA	Scheibe SF-25B Falke	A. R. Thorpe & R. W. J. Raynsford	
G-KHEH	Grob G.109B	N. A. Tziros	
G-KHOP	Zenair CH.601HDS Zodiac	K. Hopkins	
G-KHRE	MS.893E Rallye 150SV	Kingsmuir Group	
G-KICK	Pegasus Quantum 15-912	G. van der Gaag	
G-KIDD	Jabiru J430	R. L. Lidd (G-CEBB)	
G-KIEV	DKBA AT 0300-0 balloon	The Volga Balloon Team	
G-KIII	Extra EA.300/L	Extra 200 Ltd	
G-KIMA	Zenair CH.601XL Zodiac	H. R. Carey	
G-KIMB	Robin DR.340/140	R. M. Kimbell	
G-KIMH	Rotorsport UK MTO Sport	P. B. Harrison	

Notes	Reg.	Type	Owner or Operator
	G-KIMK	Partenavia P.68B	M. Konstantinovic (G-BCPO)
	G-KIMM	Shaw Europa XS	R. A. Collins
	G-KIMY	Robin DR.400/140B	M. N. King
	G-KIRB	Europa XS	P. Handford (G-OIZI)
	G-KIRC	Pietenpol Air Camper	M. Kirk (G-BSVZ)
	G-KIRT	Stoddard-Hamilton GlaStar	K. Luby
	G-KISS	Rand-Robinson KR-2	E. A. Rooney
	G-KITH	Alpi Pioneer 300	K. G. Atkinson
	G-KITI	Pitts S-2E Special	The Roland Pitch Group
	G-KITS	Shaw Europa	J. R. Evernden
	G-KITT	Curtiss P-40M Kittyhawk (42-10855)	P.A. Teichman
	G-KITY	Denney Kitfox Mk 2	Kitfox KFM Group
	G-KIZZ	Kiss 450-582	D. L. Price
	G-KJBS	CSA Sportcruiser	S. M. Lowe
	G-KJJR	Schempp-Hirth Ventus 2cT	M. P. Clark
	G-KKAM	Schleicher ASW-22BLE	D. P. Taylor
	G-KKER	Avtech Jabiru SPL-450	M. A. Coffin
	G-KKEV	DHC.8-402 Dash Eight	Flybe.com
	G-KLAW	Christen Eagle II	R. S. Goodwin & B. Lovering
	G-KLNB	Beech 300 Super King Air	Saxonair Charter Ltd
	G-KLNE	Hawker 900XP	Saxonair Charter Ltd
	G-KLNP	Eurocopter EC120B Colibri	Saxonair Charter Ltd
	G-KLNR	Hawker 400A	Saxonair Charter Ltd
	G-KLNS	Beech G.58 Baron	Klyne Air Ltd
	G-KLNW	Cessna 510 Citation Mustang	Saxonair Charter Ltd
	G-KLOE	Raytheon Hawker 800XP	Gama Aviation Ltd (G-OJWB)
	G-KLYE	Best Off Sky Ranger Swift 912S(1)	J. F. Murphy
	G-KMBB	Scheibe SF-25D Falke	Hinton Pilot Flight Training Ltd
	G-KMFW	Glaser-Dirks DG-800B	F. Pilkington & S. S. M. Turner
	G-KMKM	AutoGyro MTO Sport	O. & T. Brooking
	G-KMRV	Van-s RV-9A	G. K. Mutch
	G-KNCG	PA-32-301FT 6X	MJC Aviation Ltd
	G-KNEE	Ultramagic M-77C balloon	M. A.Green
	G-KNEK	Grob G.109B	Syndicate 109
	G-KNIB	Robinson R22 Beta II	C. G. Knibb
	G-KNOW	PA-32 Cherokee Six 300	Nationwide Logistical Solutions Ltd
	G-KNYA	PA-32R-301T Saratoga II TC	C. Sharp
	G-KNYT	Robinson R44	Aircol
	G-KOBH	Schempp-Hirth Discus bT	C. F. M. Smith & K. Neave
	G-KOCO	Cirrus SR22	R. Fitzgerald
	G-KODA	Cameron O-77 balloon	K. Stamurs
	G-KOFM	Glaser-Dirks DG.600/18M	A. Mossman
	G-KOKL	Hoffmann H-36 Dimona	Dimona Group
	G-KOLB	Kolb Twinstar Mk 3A	M. P. Wiseman
	G-KOLI	WSK PZL-110 Koliber 150	J. R. Powell
	G-KONG	Slingsby T.67M Firefly 200	W. Hillick
	G-KORE	Sportavia SFS31 Milan	J. R. Edyvean
	G-KOTA	PA-28-236 Dakota	M. D. Rush
	G-KOYY	Schempp-Hirth Nimbus 4T	R. Kalin
	G-KPLG	Schempp-Hirth Ventus 2cM	M. F. Lassan & A. C. Broadbridge
	G-KPTN	Dassault Falcon 50	Tri-Leg Leasing Ltd
	G-KRES	Stoddard-Hamilton Glasair IIS RG	A. D. Murray
	G-KRIB	Robinson R44 II	Cribarth Helicopters
	G-KRII	Rand-Robinson KR-2	M. R. Cleveley
	G-KRMA	Cessna 425 Corsair	Speedstar Holdings Ltd
	G-KRNW	Eurocopter EC 135T2	Bond Air Services Ltd
	G-KRUZ	CZAW Sportcruiser	A. W. Shellis & P. Whittingham
	G-KSFR	Bombardier BD-100-1A10 Challenger	The Lily Partnership LLP
	G-KSHI	Beech A36 Bonanza	Hangar 11 Collection
	G-KSIR	Stoddard-Hamilton Glasair IIS RG	K. M. Bowen
	G-KSIX	Schleicher Ka 6E	C. D. Sterritt
	G-KSKS	Cameron N-105 balloon	Kiss the Sky Ballooning

Reg.	Type	Owner or Operator	Notes
G-KSKY	Sky 77-24 balloon	J. W. Dale	
G-KSSA	MDH MD-900 Explorer	Police Aviation Services Ltd	
G-KSSH	MDH MD-900 Explorer	Police Aviation Services Ltd (G-WMID)	
G-KSVB	PA-24 Comanche 260	Knockin Flying Club Ltd	
G-KTEE	Cameron V-77 balloon	A. Ruitenburg	
G-KTIA	Hawker 900XP	TAG Aviation (UK) Ltd	
G-KTKT	Sky 260-24 balloon	Adventure Balloons Ltd	
G-KTOW	Ikarus C42 FB100	Mayfly G-KTOW Ltd	
G-KTTY	Denney Kitfox Model 3	S. D. Morris (G-LESJ)	
G-KTWO	Cessna 182T	S. J. G. Mole	
G-KUGG	Schleicher ASW-27-18E	J. W. L. Otty	
G-KUIK	Mainair Pegasus Quik	P. Nugent	
G-KUIP	CZAW Sportcruiser	A. J. Kuipers	
G-KULA	Best Off Skyranger 912ULS	G. S. Cridland	
G-KUPP	Flight Design CTSW	S. J. Peet	
G-KURK	J-3C-65 Cub	M. J. Kirk	
G-KURT	Jurca MJ.8 Fw190	S. D. Howes	
G-KUTI	Flight Design CTSW	D. F. & S. M. Kenny	
G-KUTU	Quickie Q.2	R. Nash & J. Parkinson	
G-KUUI	J-3C-65 Cub	V. S. E. Norman	
G-KVBF	Cameron A-340HL balloon	Virgin Balloon Flights	
G-KVIP	Beech 200 Super King Air	Capital Air Charter Ltd	
G-KWAK	Scheibe SF.25C	Mendip Gliding Club Ltd	
G-KWKI	QAC Quickie Q.200	R. Greatrex	
G-KWKR	P and M Aviation QuikR	L. G. White	
G-KXXI	Schleicher ASK-21	C. G. Bell	
G-KYLE	Thruster T600N 450	J. M. English	
G-KYTE	Piper PA-28-161 Warrior II	G. Whitlow (G-BRRN)	
G-LABS	Shaw Europa	C. T. H. Pattinson	
G-LACA	PA-28-161 Warrior II	J. H. Mitchell	
G-LACB	PA-28-161 Warrior II	LAC Flying School	
G-LACC	Cameron C-90 balloon	Directorate Army Aviation	
G-LACD	PA-28-181 Archer III	Target Aviation Ltd (G-BYBG)	
G-LACI	Cessna 172S Skyhawk	D. C. & J. Taylor	
G-LACR	Denney Kitfox	C. M. Rose	
G-LADD	Enstrom 480	Foscombe Transport LLP	
G-LADS	Rockwell Commander 114	D. F. Soul	
G-LAFF	Cameron TR-84 Srs.2 balloon	Balloonists Supporting Barretstown	
G-LAFT	Diamond DA40D Star	Atlantic Flight Training Ltd	
G-LAGR	Cameron N-90 balloon	J. R. Clifton	
G-LAIN	Robinson R22 Beta	Patriot Aviation Ltd	
G-LAIR	Stoddard-Hamilton Glasair IIS FT	A. I.O'Broin & S. T. Raby	
G-LAKE	Lake LA-250 Renegade	Lake Aviation Ltd	
G-LAKI	Jodel DR.1050	G. Cameron (G-JWBB)	
G-LALE	Embraer EMB-135BJ Legacy	London Executive Aviation Ltd	
G-LAMM	Shaw Europa	S. A. Lamb	
G-LAMP	Cameron 110 Lampbulb SS balloon	S. A. Lacey	
G-LAMS	Cessna F.152 II	Lomac Aviators Ltd	
G-LANC	Avro 683 Lancaster X (KB889) ★	Imperial War Museum/Duxford	
G-LAND	Robinson R22 Beta	Heli Air Ltd	
G-LANE	Cessna F.172N	A. Holmes	
G-LANS	Cessna 182T	AK Enterprises Ltd	
G-LAOL	PA-28RT-201 Arrow IV	Arrow Flying Group	
G-LARA	Robin DR.400/180	K. D. & C. A. Brackwell	
G-LARE	PA-39 Twin Comanche 160 C/R	Glareways (Neasden) Ltd	
G-LARK	Helton Lark 95	N. Huxtable & K Keen	
G-LARR	AS.350B3 Squirrel	Larsen Manufacturing Ltd	
G-LASN	Skyranger J2.2(1)	A. J. Coote	
G-LASR	Stoddard-Hamilton Glasair II	G. Lewis	
G-LASS	Rutan Vari-Eze	J. Mellor	
G-LASU	Eurocopter EC 135T2	Police & Crime Commissioner for West Yorkshire	
G-LATE	Falcon 2000EX	Hangar 8 Management Ltd	
G-LAVE	Cessna 172R	M. L. Roland (G-BYEV)	

Notes	Reg.	Type	Owner or Operator
	G-LAWX	Sikorsky S-92A	Air Harrods Ltd
	G-LAZL	PA-28-161 Warrior II	Highland Aviation Training Ltd
	G-LAZR	Cameron O-77 balloon	Wickers World Ltd
	G-LAZZ	Stoddard-Hamilton Glastar	A. N. Evans
	G-LBAC	Evektor EV-97 TeamEurostar UK	G. Burder & A. Cox
	G-LBAL	Agusta AW139	Haughey Air Ltd
	G-LBDC	Bell 206B JetRanger III	Fresh Direct Travel Ltd
	G-LBMM	PA-28-161 Warrior II	M. A. Jones
	G-LBRC	PA-28RT-201 Arrow IV	D. J. V. Morgan
	G-LBSB	Beech B.300C King Air	Gama Support Services Ltd
	G-LBUK	Lindstrand LBL-77A balloon	Morrison Design Ltd
	G-LBUZ	Aerotechnick EV-97A Eurostar	D. P. Tassart
	G-LCDH	Bombardier CL600-2B16 Challenger	TAG Aviation (UK) Ltd
	G-LCGL	Comper CLA.7 Swift (replica)	R. A. Fleming
	G-LCKY	Flight Design CTSW	G. D. Honey
	G-LCLE	Colomban MC-30 Luciole	J. A. Harris
	G-LCMW	TL 2000UK Sting Carbon	B. J. Tyre
	G-LCOK	Colt 69A balloon	Hot-Air Balloon Co Ltd (G-BLWI)
	G-LCPL	AS.365N-2 Dauphin 2	Charterstyle Ltd
	G-LCUB	PA-18 Super Cub 95	The Tiger Club 1990 Ltd (G-AYPR)
	G-LCYD	Embraer ERJ170-100STD	BA Cityflyer Ltd
	G-LCYE	Embraer ERJ170-100STD	BA Cityflyer Ltd
	G-LCYF	Embraer ERJ170-100STD	BA Cityflyer Ltd
	G-LCYG	Embraer ERJ170-100STD	BA Cityflyer Ltd
	G-LCYH	Embraer ERJ170-100STD	BA Cityflyer Ltd
	G-LCYI	Embraer ERJ170-100STD	BA Cityflyer Ltd
	G-LCYJ	Embraer ERJ190-100SR	BA Cityflyer Ltd
	G-LCYK	Embraer ERJ190-100SR	BA Cityflyer Ltd
	G-LCYL	Embraer ERJ190-100SR	BA Cityflyer Ltd
	G-LCYM	Embraer ERJ190-100SR	BA Cityflyer Ltd
	G-LCYN	Embraer ERJ190-100SR	BA Cityflyer Ltd
	G-LCYO	Embraer ERJ190-100SR	BA Cityflyer Ltd
	G-LCYP	Embraer ERJ190-100SR	BA Cityflyer Ltd
	G-LCYR	Embraer ERJ190-100SR	BA Cityflyer Ltd
	G-LDAH	Skyranger 912 (2)	P. D. Brookes & L. Dickinson
	G-LDER	Schleicher ASW-22	P. Shrosbree & D. Starer
	G-LDVO	Europa Aviation Europa XS	D. J. Park
	G-LDWS	Jodel D.150	A. L. Hall-Carpenter (G-BKSS)
	G-LDYS	Colt 56A balloon	M. J. Myddelton
	G-LEAA	Cessna 510 Citation Mustang	London Executive Aviation Ltd
	G-LEAB	Cessna 510 Citation Mustang	London Executive Aviation Ltd
	G-LEAC	Cessna 510 Citation Mustang	London Executive Aviation Ltd
	G-LEAF	Cessna F.406	Reconnaisance Ventures Ltd
	G-LEAH	Alpi Pioneer 300	A. Bortolan
	G-LEAI	Cessna 510	London Executive Aviation Ltd
	G-LEAM	PA-28-236 Dakota	G-LEAM Group (G-BHLS)
	G-LEAS	Sky 90-24 balloon	C. I. Humphrey
	G-LEAU	Cameron N-31 balloon	P. L. Mossman
	G-LEAX	Cessna 560XL Citation XLS	London Executive Aviation Ltd
	G-LEAZ	Bombardier BD700-1A10 Challenger 300	London Executive Aviation Ltd
	G-LEBE	Shaw Europa	J. E. Fallis
	G-LECA	AS.355F1 Twin Squirrel	HFS (Aviation) Ltd (G-BNBK)
	G-LEDE	Zenair CH.601UL Zodiac	P. Boyle
	G-LEDR	Westland Gazelle HT.2	R. D. Leader (G-CBSB)
	G-LEED	Denney Kitfox Mk 2	P. Newman
	G-LEEE	Avtech Jabiru SPL-450	J. P. Mimnagh
	G-LEEH	Ultramagic M-90 balloon	Sport Promotion SRL/Italy
	G-LEEJ	Hughes 369HS	S. J. Halliwell
	G-LEEK	Reality Escapade	G-LEEK Phoenix Flying Group
	G-LEEN	Aero Designs Pulsar XP	R. B. Hemsworth (G-BZMP/G-DESI)
	G-LEES	Glaser-Dirks DG.400 (800)	Active Aviation Ltd
	G-LEEZ	Bell 206L-1 LongRanger 2	Pennine Helicopters Ltd (G-BPCT)
	G-LEGC	Embraer EMB-135BJ Legacy	Delos Engineering Corporation
	G-LEGG	Cessna F.182Q	W. A. L. Mitchell (G-GOOS)
	G-LEGO	Cameron O-77 balloon	P. M. Traviss
	G-LEGY	Flight Design CTLS	P. J. Clegg
	G-LELE	Lindstrand LBL-31A balloon	D. S. Wilson

Reg.	Type	Owner or Operator	Notes
G-LEMI	Van's RV-8	The Lord Rotherwick	
G-LEMM	Ultramagic Z-90 balloon	M. Maranoni/Italy	
G-LENF	Mainair Blade 912S	G. D. Fuller	
G-LENI	AS.355F1 Twin Squirrel	Grid Defence Systems Ltd (G-ZFDB/G-BLEV)	
G-LENM	Avro RJ-85	Cello Aviation Ltd	
G-LENN	Cameron V-56 balloon	D. J. Groombridge	
G-LENX	Cessna 172N	November XRay Ltd	
G-LEOD	Pietenpol Aircamper	I. D. McCleod	
G-LEOS	Robin DR.400/120	R. J. O. Walker	
G-LESH	BB Microlight BB03 Trya/Alien	L. R. Hodgson	
G-LESZ	Denney Kitfox Mk 5	G. M. Park	
G-LETS	Van's RV-7	M. O'Hearne	
G-LEVI	Aeronca 7AC Champion	G-LEVI Group	
G-LEXX	Van's RV-8	S. Emery	
G-LEXY	Van's RV-8	R. McCarthy	
G-LEZE	Rutan LongEz	Bill Allen's Autos Ltd	
G-LFES	AB Sportine LAK-17B FES	P. C. Piggott	
G-LFEZ	AB Sportine LAK-17B FES	Baltic Sailplanes Ltd	
G-LFIX	VS.509 Spitfire T.IX (ML407)	C. S. Grace	
G-LFSA	PA-38-112 Tomahawk	Liverpool Flying School Ltd (G-BSFC)	
G-LFSB	PA-38-112 Tomahawk	J. D. Burford	
G-LFSC	PA-28 Cherokee 140	P. G. Smith (G-BGTR)	
G-LFSG	PA-28 Cherokee 180E	Liverpool Flying School Ltd (G-AYAA)	
G-LFSH	PA-38-112 Tomahawk	Liverpool Flying School Ltd (G-BOZM)	
G-LFSI	PA-28 Cherokee 140	Flying Group G-LFSI (G-AYKV)	
G-LFSJ	PA-28-161 Warrior II	FlyBPL.com	
G-LFSM	PA-38-112 Tomahawk	Liverpool Flying School Ltd (G-BWNR)	
G-LFSN	PA-38-112 Tomahawk	Liverpool Flying School Ltd (G-BNYV)	
G-LFSR	PA-28RT-201 Arrow IV	Liverpool Flying School Ltd (G-JANO)	
G-LFVB	VS.349 Spitfire LF.Vb (EP120)	Patina Ltd	
G-LGAR	Learjet 60	TAG Aviation (UK) Ltd	
G-LGCA	Robin DR.400/180R	London Gliding Club Proprietary Ltd	
G-LGCB	Robin DR.400/180R	London Gliding Club Proprietary Ltd	
G-LGCC	Robin DR 400/180R	London Gliding Club Proprietary Ltd (G-BNXI)	
G-LGEZ	Rutan Long-EZ	P. C. Elliott	
G-LGKD	Gulfstream 550	TAG Aviation (UK) Ltd	
G-LGLG	Cameron Z-210 balloon	Flying Circus SRL/Spain	
G-LGMG	Embraer EMB-500 Phenom 100	Aviogreen SRL	
G-LGNA	SAAB SF.340B	Loganair Ltd/Flybe.com	
G-LGNB	SAAB SF.340B	Loganair Ltd/Flybe.com	
G-LGNC	SAAB SF.340B	Loganair Ltd/Flybe.com	
G-LGND	SAAB SF.340B	Loganair Ltd/Flybe.com (G-GNTH)	
G-LGNE	SAAB SF.340B	Loganair Ltd/Flybe.com (G-GNTI)	
G-LGNF	SAAB SF.340B	Loganair Ltd/Flybe.com (G-GNTJ)	
G-LGNG	SAAB SF.340B	Loganair Ltd/Flybe.com	
G-LGNH	SAAB SF.340B	Loganair Ltd/Flybe.com	
G-LGNI	SAAB SF.340B	Loganair Ltd/Flybe.com	
G-LGNJ	SAAB SF.340B	Loganair Ltd/Flybe.com	
G-LGNK	SAAB SF.340B	Loganair Ltd/Flybe.com	
G-LGNL	SAAB SF.340B	Loganair Ltd/Flybe.com	
G-LGNM	SAAB SF.340B	Loganair Ltd/Flybe.com	
G-LGNN	SAAB SF.340B	Loganair Ltd/Flybe.com	
G-LGOC	Aero AT-3 R100	Propeller Film SP ZOO	
G-LHCA	Robinson R22 Beta	London Helicopter Centres Ltd	
G-LHCB	Robinson R22 Beta	London Helicopter Centres Ltd (G-SIVX)	
G-LHCD	Robinson R22 Beta	London Helicopter Centres Ltd (G-CDED)	
G-LHCI	Bell 47G-5	Heli-Highland Ltd (G-SOLH/G-AZMB)	
G-LHEL	AS.355F2 Twin Squirrel	Beechview Aviation Ltd	
G-LHER	Czech Sport Aircraft Piper Sport	M. P. Lhermette	
G-LHTB	Eurocopter AS.350B2 Ecureuil	Jet Helicopters Ltd	
G-LHXL	Robinson R44	Phoenix Helicopter Academy Ltd	
G-LIBB	Cameron V-77 balloon	R. J. Mercer	
G-LIBI	Glasflugel Standard Libelle 201B	G. Spreckley	
G-LIBS	Hughes 369HS	R. J. H. Strong	
G-LIBY	Glasflugel Standard Libelle 201B	R. P. Hardcastle	
G-LICK	Cessna 172N II	Sky Back Ltd (G-BNTR)	
G-LIDA	Hoffmann H36 Dimona	Bidford Airfield Ltd	

Notes	Reg.	Type	Owner or Operator
	G-LIDE	PA-31-350 Navajo Chieftain	Blue Sky Investments Ltd
	G-LIDY	Schleicher ASW-27B	T. Stuart
	G-LIGA	Kubicek BB-S/Fish balloon	I. Charbonnier
	G-LIKE	Europa	N. G. Henry (G-CHAV)
	G-LILY	Bell 206B JetRanger 3	T. S. Brown (G-NTBI)
	G-LIMO	Bell 206L-1 LongRanger	Heliplayer Ltd
	G-LIMP	Cameron C-80 balloon	T. & B. Chamberlain
	G-LINE	AS.355N Twin Squirrel	National Grid Electricity Transmission PLC
	G-LINN	Shaw Europa XS	T. Pond
	G-LINS	Robinson R22 Beta	Heli Air Ltd (G-DMCD/G-OOLI)
	G-LIOA	Lockheed 10A ElectraH (NC5171N) ★	Science Museum/South Kensington
	G-LION	PA-18 Super Cub 135 (R-167)	JG Jones Haulage Ltd
	G-LIOT	Cameron O-77 balloon	N. D. Eliot
	G-LIPE	Robinson R22 Beta	Heliservices (G-BTXJ)
	G-LIPS	Cameron 90 Lips SS balloon	Reach For The Sky Ltd (G-BZBV)
	G-LISS	AutogGyro UK Calidus	J. M. & M. J. Newman
	G-LITE	Rockwell Commander 112A	B. G. Rhodes
	G-LITS	P & M Quik R	A. Dixon
	G-LITZ	Pitts S-1E Special	H. J. Morton
	G-LIVH	Piper J-3C-65 Cub (330238:A-24)	U. E. Allman
	G-LIVS	Schleicher ASH-26E	P. O. Sturley
	G-LIZI	PA-28 Cherokee 160	G-LIZI Group (G-ARRP)
	G-LIZY	Westland Lysander III (V9673) ★	G. A. Warner/Duxford
	G-LIZZ	PA-E23 Aztec 250E	I. Kazi & T. J. Nathan (G-BBWM)
	G-LJCC	Murphy Rebel	P. H. Hyde
	G-LKTB	PA-28-181 Archer III	L. D. Charles & J. J. Kennedy
	G-LLCH	Cessna 172S	K. Neilson (G-PLBI)
	G-LLEW	Aeromot AMT-200S Super Ximango	Echo Whiskey Ximango Syndicate
	G-LLGE	Lindstrand LBL-360A balloon	Adventure Balloons Ltd
	G-LLIZ	Robinson R44 II	HQ Aviation Ltd
	G-LLLL	Rolladen-Schneider LS8-18	P. C. Fritche
	G-LLMW	Diamond DA42 Twin Star	Ming W. L.
	G-LLOV	Agusta AW.139	CHC Scotia Ltd
	G-LLOY	Alpi Pioneer 300	A. R. Lloyd
	G-LMAO	Cessna F.172N	Skyview R Us Ltd
	G-LMBO	Robinson R44	Thurston Helicopters Ltd
	G-LMCB	Raj Hamsa X'Air Hawk	B. N. Thresher
	G-LMLV	Dyn'Aéro MCR-01	G-LMLV Flying Group
	G-LNAA	MDH MD-900 Explorer	Police Aviation Services Ltd
	G-LNCT	MDH MD-900 Explorer	Police Aviation Services Ltd
	G-LNDS	Robinson R44	MC Air Ltd
	G-LNIG	Flylight Dragonfly	P. J. Cheyney
	G-LNKS	BAe Jestream 3102	Linksair Ltd (G-JURA)
	G-LOAD	Dan Rihn DR.107 One Design	M. J. Clark
	G-LOAM	Flylight MotorFloater	A. W. Nancarrow
	G-LOAN	Cameron N-77 balloon	P. Lawman
	G-LOBO	Cameron O-120 balloon	Solo Aerostatics
	G-LOCH	Piper J-3C-65 Cub	M. C. & M. R. Greenland
	G-LOFB	Lockheed L.188CF Electra	Atlantic Airlines Ltd
	G-LOFM	Maule MX-7-180A	Air Atlantique Ltd
	G-LOFT	Cessna 500 Citation I	Fox Tango (Jersey) Ltd
	G-LOIS	Avtech Jabiru UL	B. O Harvey
	G-LOKI	Ultramagic M-77C balloon	L. J. M. Muir & G. D. Hallett
	G-LOLA	Beech A36 Bonanza	AJW Construction Ltd
	G-LOLL	Cameron V-77 balloon	R. K. McCulloch
	G-LONE	Bell 206L-1 LongRanger	Central Helicopters Ltd
	G-LOOC	Cessna 172S	Goodwood Road Racing Co Ltd
	G-LOON	Cameron C-60 balloon	Atlantic Ballooning BVBA/Belgium
	G-LOOP	Pitts S-1C Special	D. Shutter
	G-LORC	PA-28-161 Cadet	Sherburn Aero Club Ltd
	G-LORD	PA-34-200T Seneca II	H. E. Held-Ruf
	G-LORN	Avions Mudry CAP-10B	D. G. R. & P. M. Wansbrough
	G-LORR	PA-28-181 Archer III	Shropshire Aero Club Ltd
	G-LORY	Thunder Ax4-31Z balloon	A. J. Moore
	G-LOSI	Cameron Z-105 balloon	Aeropubblicita Vicenza SRL/Italy

Reg.	Type	Owner or Operator	Notes
G-LOSM	Gloster Meteor NF.11 (WM167)	Aviation Heritage Ltd	
G-LOST	Denney Kitfox Mk 3	J. H. S. Booth	
G-LOSY	Aerotechnik EV-97 Eurostar	C. D. Reeves	
G-LOTA	Robinson R44	Rahtol Ltd	
G-LOTI	Bleriot XI (replica) ★	Brooklands Museum Trust Ltd	
G-LOTY	P & M Aviation Pegasus Quik	S. J. Sherriff	
G-LOWE	Monett Sonerai I	P. A. Hall & A. R. Lewis	
G-LOWS	Sky 77-24 balloon	A. J. Byrne & D. J. Bellinger	
G-LOWZ	P & M Quik GT450	P. R. Biggs	
G-LOYA	Cessna FR.172J	Mid America (UK) Ltd (G-BLVT)	
G-LOYD	Aérospatiale SA.341G Gazelle 1	S. Atherton (G-SFTC)	
G-LOYN	Robinson R44 II	C. J. Siva-Jothy	
G-LPAD	Lindstrand LBL-105A balloon	G. R. Down	
G-LPIN	P & M Aviation Quik R	Arnold Gilpin Associates Ltd	
G-LREE	Grob G.109B	G-LREE Group	
G-LRGE	Lindstrand LBL-330A balloon	Adventure Balloons Ltd	
G-LSAA	Boeing 757-236	Jet 2 (G-BNSF)	
G-LSAB	Boeing 757-27B	Jet 2 (G-OAHF)	
G-LSAC	Boeing 757-23A	Jet 2	
G-LSAD	Boeing 757-236	Jet 2 (G-OOOS/G-BRJD)	
G-LSAE	Boeing 757-27B	Jet 2	
G-LSAG	Boeing 757-21B	Jet 2	
G-LSAH	Boeing 757-21B	Jet 2	
G-LSAI	Boeing 757-21B	Jet 2	
G-LSAJ	Boeing 757-236	Jet 2 (G-CDUP/G-OOOT/G-BRJJ)	
G-LSAK	Boeing 757-23N	Jet 2	
G-LSAN	Boeing 757-2K2	Jet 2	
G-LSCM	Cessna 172S	G. A. Luscombe	
G-LSCP	Rolladen-Schneider LS6-18W	M. F. Collins	
G-LSED	Rolladen-Schneider LS6-c	McKnight/Baker Syndicate	
G-LSFB	Rolladen-Schneider LS7-WL	P. Thomson	
G-LSFI	AA-5A Cheetah	J. Ibbotson (G-BGSK)	
G-LSFR	Rolladen-Schneider LS4	A. Mulder	
G-LSFT	PA-28-161 Warrior II	Biggin Hill Flying Club Ltd (G-BXTX)	
G-LSGB	Rolladen-Schneider LS6-b	T. J. Brenton	
G-LSGM	Rolladen-Schneider LS3-17	M. R. W. Crook	
G-LSHI	Colt 77A balloon	J. H. Dobson	
G-LSIF	Rolladen-Schneider LS1-f	R. C. Godden	
G-LSIV	Rolladen-Schneider LS4	264 Syndicate	
G-LSIX	Rolladen-Schneider LS6-18W	D. P. Masson & A. V. W. Nunn	
G-LSJE	Escapade Jabiru(1)	L. S. J. Webb	
G-LSKV	Rolladen-Schneider LS8-18	J. R. W. Luxton & S. C. Williams	
G-LSKY	Mainair Pegasus Quik	I. T. Carlse	
G-LSLS	Rolladen-Schneider LS4	288 Syndicate	
G-LSMB	Dassault Falcon 2000EX	Aviation Beauport Ltd	
G-LSPH	Van's RV-8	R. S. Partridge-Hicks	
G-LSTR	Stoddard-Hamilton Glastar	A. Vaughan	
G-LSVI	Rolladen-Schneider LS6-c18	R. Hanks	
G-LTEE	Cessna F.172N	A. S. Bamrah (G-BGBR)	
G-LTFB	PA-28 Cherokee 140	Polishing Consulting Ltd (G-AVLU)	
G-LTRF	Sportavia Fournier RF-7	D. Radewald (G-EHAP)	
G-LTSB	Cameron LTSB-90 balloon	ABC Flights Ltd	
G-LTSK	Bombardier CL600-2B16 Challenger	TAG Aviation (UK) Ltd	
G-LTWA	Robinson R44	L. T. W. Alderman	
G-LUBB	Cessna 525 Citationjet	Centreline Air Charter Ltd	
G-LUBE	Cameron N-77 balloon	A. C. K. Rawson	
G-LUBY	Jabiru J430	K. Luby	
G-LUCK	Cessna F.150M	A. W. C. Knight	
G-LUCL	Colomban MC-30 Luciole	R. C. Teverson	
G-LUDM	Van's RV-8	S. J. Perkins	
G-LUED	Aero Designs Pulsar	J. C. Anderson	
G-LUEK	Cessna 182T	D. J. Medcraft	
G-LUEY	Rans S-7S Courier	S. Garfield	
G-LUKA	Beech G.58 Baron	Bentley O-S Ltd	
G-LUKE	Rutan LongEz	R. A. Pearson	
G-LULA	Cameron C-90 balloon	S. D. Davis	

Notes	Reg.	Type	Owner or Operator
	G-LULU	Grob G.109	A. P. Bowden
	G-LULV	Diamond DA-42 Twin Star	Deltabond Ltd
	G-LUNE	Mainair Pegasus Quik	D. Muir
	G-LUNG	Rotorsport UK MT-03	P. Krysiak
	G-LUNY	Pitts S-1S Special	G-LUNY Group
	G-LUON	Schleicher ASW-27-18E	P. C. Naegeli
	G-LUPY	Marganski Swift S-1	G. S. S. Rizk
	G-LUSC	Luscombe 8E Silvaire	M. Fowler
	G-LUSH	PA-28-151 Warrior	S. S. Bamrah
	G-LUSI	Luscombe 8F Silvaire	P. H. Isherwood
	G-LUSK	Luscombe 8F Silvaire	M. A. Lamprell & P. J. Laycock (G-BRGG)
	G-LUST	Luscombe 8E Silvaire	C. J. Watson & M. R. Griffiths
	G-LUUP	Pilatus B4-PC11AF	B. L. Coopere (G-ECSW)
	G-LUXE	BAe 146-301	BAE Systems (Operations) Ltd (G-SSSH)
	G-LUXY	Cessna 551 Citation IISP	Longhan Ltd
	G-LVCY	Colomban MC-30 Luciole	C. Wright
	G-LVDC	Bell 206L Long Ranger III	Freshair UK Ltd (G-OFST/G-BXIB)
	G-LVES	Cessna 182S	R. W. & A. M. Glaves (G-ELIE)
	G-LVPL	Edge XT912 B/Streak III/B	C. D. Connor
	G-LWDC	Canadair CL600-2A12 Challenger	African Petroleum Ltd
	G-LWLW	Diamond DA.40D Star	M. P. Wilkinson (G-CCLV)
	G-LWNG	Aero Designs Pulsar	A. B. Wood (G-OMKF)
	G-LXUS	Alpi Pioneer 300	A. & J. Oswald
	G-LYDA	Hoffmann H-36 Dimona	G-LYDA Flying Group
	G-LYDF	PA-31-350 Navajo Chieftain	Atlantic Bridge Aviation Ltd
	G-LYFA	IDABacau Yakovlev Yak-52	Fox Alpha Group
	G-LYNC	Robinson R22 Beta II	Subacoustech Ltd
	G-LYND	PA-25 Pawnee 235	York Gliding Centre Ltd (G-ASFX/G-BSFZ)
	G-LYNI	Aerotechnik EV-97 Eurostar	M. W. Holmes & A. C. Thomson
	G-LYNK	CFM Shadow Srs DD	B. A. Richards
	G-LYNX	Westland WG.13 Lynx (ZB500)	IHM/Weston-super-Mare
	G-LYPG	Avtech Jabiru UL	A. J. Geary
	G-LYPH	Rolladen-Schneider LS8-18-st	S. & S. Barter
	G-LYSA	Schleicher ASW-20L	L. A. Humphries
	G-LYTE	Thunder Ax7-77 balloon	G. M. Bulme
	G-LZED	AutoGyro MTO Sport	L. Zivanovic
	G-LZII	Laser Z200	K. G. Begley
	G-LZZY	PA-28RT-201T Turbo Arrow IV	S. P. Rawlinson & S. J. Newham (G-BMHZ)
	G-MAAM	CFM Shadow Srs.C	S. J. Halliwell (G-MTCA)
	G-MAAN	Shaw Europa XS	P. S. Mann
	G-MABE	Cessna F.150L	I. D. McClelland (G-BLJP)
	G-MABL	Quik GTR	S. J. Reid
	G-MACA	Robinson R22 Beta	Jepar Rotorcraft
	G-MACH	SIAI-Marchetti SF.260	Cheyne Motors Ltd
	G-MACI	Van's RV-7	N. J. F. Campbell
	G-MACN	Cirrus SR22	J. D. M. Tickell
	G-MACO	Bombardier CL600-2B16 Challenger	Zenith Aviation Ltd (G-MACP/G-CGFF/G-OCSF)
	G-MACU	Robinson R44 II	HQ Aviation Ltd (G-SEFI)
	G-MADV	P & M Quik GT450	D. A. Valentine
	G-MAFA	Cessna F.406	Directflight Ltd (G-DFLT)
	G-MAFB	Cessna F.406	Directflight Ltd
	G-MAFF	BN-2T Turbine Islander	FR Aviation Ltd (G-BJEO)
	G-MAFI	Dornier 228-202K	FR Aviation Ltd
	G-MAFT	Diamond DA.40 Star	Atlantic Flight Training Ltd
	G-MAGC	Cameron Grand Illusion SS balloon	Magical Adventures Ltd
	G-MAGG	Pitts S-1SE Special	R. G. Gee
	G-MAGK	Schleicher ASW-20L	A. G. K. Mackenzie
	G-MAGL	Sky 77-24 balloon	RCM SRL/Luxembourg
	G-MAGN	Magni M-24C	Net2Net IPS Ltd
	G-MAGZ	Robin DR.400/500	T. J. Thomas
	G-MAIE	PA-32RT-301T Turbo Saratoga II TC	Sub Marine Services Ltd
	G-MAIN	Mainair Blade 912	G. L. Logan & R. Wells
	G-MAIR	PA-34-200T Seneca II	Ravenair Aircraft Ltd
	G-MAJA	BAe Jetstream 4102	Eastern Airways
	G-MAJB	BAe Jetstream 4102	Eastern Airways (G-BVKT)

Reg.	Type	Owner or Operator	Notes
G-MAJC	BAe Jetstream 4102	Eastern Airways (G-LOGJ)	
G-MAJD	BAe Jetstream 4102	Eastern Airways (G-WAWR)	
G-MAJE	BAe Jetstream 4102	Eastern Airways (G-LOGK)	
G-MAJF	BAe Jetstream 4102	Eastern Airways (G-WAWL)	
G-MAJG	BAe Jetstream 4102	Eastern Airways (G-LOGL)	
G-MAJH	BAe Jetstream 4102	Eastern Airways (G-WAYR)	
G-MAJI	BAe Jetstream 4102	Eastern Airways (G-WAND)	
G-MAJJ	BAe Jetstream 4102	Eastern Airways (G-WAFT)	
G-MAJK	BAe Jetstream 4102	Eastern Airways	
G-MAJL	BAe Jetstream 4102	Eastern Airways	
G-MAJR	DHC.1 Chipmunk 22 (WP805)	C. Adams	
G-MAJS	Airbus A.300B4-605R	Monarch Airlines Ltd	
G-MAJT	BAe Jetstream 4100	Eastern Airways	
G-MAJU	BAe Jetstream 4100	Eastern Airways	
G-MAJW	BAe Jetstream 4100	Eastern Airways	
G-MAJY	BAe Jetstream 4100	Eastern Airways	
G-MAJZ	BAe Jetstream 4100	Eastern Airways	
G-MAKE	Rotorsport UK Calidus	P. M. Ford	
G-MAKI	Robinson R44	Hoe Leasing Ltd	
G-MAKK	Aeroprakt A22-L Foxbat	M. A. McKillop	
G-MAKS	Cirrus SR22	Amey Aviation LLP	
G-MALA	PA-28-181 Archer II	Energies Ltd (G-BIIU)	
G-MALC	AA-5 Traveler	B. P. Hogan (G-BCPM)	
G-MALS	Mooney M.20K-231	P. Mouterde	
G-MALT	Colt Flying Hop SS balloon	P. J. Stapley	
G-MANC	BAe ATP	European Turboprop Management AB (G-LOGF)	
G-MANH	BAe ATP	Atlantic Airlines Ltd (G-LOGC/G-OLCC)	
G-MANM	BAe ATP	Atlantic Airlines Ltd (G-BZWW/G-OATP)	
G-MANN	Aérospatiale SA.341G Gazelle 1	MW Helicopters Ltd	
G-MANO	BAe ATP	Atlantic Airlines Ltd (G-UIET)	
G-MANW	Tri-R Kis	M. T. Manwaring	
G-MANX	FRED Srs 2	S. Styles	
G-MANZ	Robinson R44 II	Steve Hill Ltd	
G-MAOL	Agusta AW109SP Grand New	Mash Aviation Ltd	
G-MAPP	Cessna 402B	Reconnaisance Ventures Ltd	
G-MAPR	Beech A36 Bonanza	M. J. B. Cozens	
G-MAPS	Sky Flying Map balloon	C. G. Dobson	
G-MARA	Airbus A.321-231	Monarch Airlines Ltd	
G-MARE	Schweizer 269C	The Earl of Caledon	
G-MARF	Robinson R44 II	Marfleet Civil Engineering Ltd (G-OSJL)	
G-MARO	Skyranger J2.2 (2)	P. Marks	
G-MARZ	Thruster T.600N 450	S. W. Plume	
G-MASC	Jodel 150A	K. F. & R. Richardson	
G-MASF	PA-28-181 Archer II	Mid-Anglia School of Flying	
G-MASH	Westland-Bell 47G-4A	Kinetic Avionics Ltd (G-AXKU)	
G-MASS	Cessna 152 II	MK Aero Support Ltd (G-BSHN)	
G-MATE	Moravan Zlin Z.50LX	C. Doury & M. Fromager	
G-MATS	Colt GA-42 airship	P. A. Lindstrand	
G-MATT	Robin R.2160	Flew LLP (G-BKRC)	
G-MATZ	PA-28 Cherokee 140	Midland Air Training School (G-BASI)	
G-MAUK	Colt 77A balloon	B. Meeson	
G-MAUS	Shaw Europa XS	A. P. Ringrose	
G-MAUX	Raj Hamsa X'Air Hawk	M. A. Urch	
G-MAVI	Robinson R22 Beta	Northumbria Helicopters Ltd	
G-MAVV	Aero AT-3 R100	Medcentres Property Portfolio Ltd	
G-MAXG	Pitts S-1S Special	The Assets of G-MAXG Group	
G-MAXI	PA-34-200T Seneca II	Draycott Seneca Syndicate Ltd	
G-MAXP	Raytheon Hawker 800XP	Xclusive Jet Charter Ltd (G-CGHY)	
G-MAXS	Mainair Pegasus Quik 912S	W. J. Walker	
G-MAXV	Van's RV-4	R. S. Partridge-Hicks	
G-MAYE	Bell 407	M. Maye	
G-MAZA	Rotorsport UK MT-03	N. Crownshaw & M. Manson	
G-MAZY†	DH.82A Tiger Moth ★	Newark Air Museum	
G-MBAA	Hiway Skytrike Mk 2	M. J. Aubrey	
G-MBAB	Hovey Whing-Ding II	M. J. Aubrey	
G-MBAD	Weedhopper JC-24A	M. Stott	
G-MBAF	R. J. Swift 3	C. G. Wrzesien	
G-MBAW	Pterodactyl Ptraveller	J. C. K. Scardifield	
G-MBBB	Skycraft Scout 2	A. J. & B. Chalkley	

Notes	Reg.	Type	Owner or Operator
	G-MBBJ	Hiway Demon	M. J. Aubrey
	G-MBCJ	Mainair Sports Tri-Flyer	R. A. Smith
	G-MBCK	Eipper Quicksilver MX	P. Rowbotham
	G-MBCL	Sky-Trike/Typhoon	P. J. Callis
	G-MBCX	Airwave Nimrod 165	M. Maylor
	G-MBDG	Eurowing Goldwing	A. J. Glynn
	G-MBDL	AES Lone Ranger ★	North East Aircraft Museum
	G-MBDM	Southdown Sigma Trike	A. R. Prentice
	G-MBET	MEA Mistral Trainer	B. H. Stephens
	G-MBGF	Twamley Trike	T. B. Woolley
	G-MBHE	American Aerolights Eagle	R. J. Osborne
	G-MBHK	Flexiform Skytrike	K. T. Vinning
	G-MBHZ	Pterodactyl Ptraveller	J. C. K. Scardifield
	G-MBIT	Hiway Demon Skytrike	K. S. Hodgson
	G-MBIZ	Mainair Tri-Flyer	D. M. A. Templeman/E. F. C. Clapham/
			S. P. Slade/W. B. S. Dobie
	G-MBJF	Hiway Skytrike Mk II	C. H. Bestwick
	G-MBJK	American Aerolights Eagle	B. W. Olley
	G-MBJM	Striplin Lone Ranger	C. K. Brown
	G-MBKY	American Aerolight Eagle	M. J. Aubrey
	G-MBKZ	Hiway Skytrike	S. I. Harding
	G-MBLU	Southdown Lightning L.195	C. R. Franklin
	G-MBMG	Rotec Rally 2B	J. R. Pyper
	G-MBOF	Pakes Jackdaw	L. G. Pakes
	G-MBOH	Microlight Engineering Mistral	N. A. Bell
	G-MBPB	Pterodactyl Ptraveller	N. A. Bell
	G-MBPJ	Moto-Delta	J. B. Jackson
	G-MBPX	Eurowing Goldwing	A. R. Channon
	G-MBRB	Electraflyer Eagle 1	R. C. Bott
	G-MBRD	American Aerolights Eagle	R. J. Osborne
	G-MBRH	Ultraflight Mirage Mk II	R. W. F. Boarder
	G-MBSJ	American Aerolights Eagle 215B	T. J. Gayton-Polley
	G-MBSX	Ultraflight Mirage II	C. J. Draper
	G-MBTJ	Solar Wings Microlight	H. A. Comber
	G-MBTW	Raven Vector 600	W. A. Fuller
	G-MBYM	Eipper Quicksilver MX	M. P. Harper & L. L. Perry
	G-MBZO	Tri-Pacer 330	A. N. Burrows
	G-MBZV	American Aerolights Eagle	M. J. Aubrey
	G-MCAB	Gardan GY-201 Minicab	P. G. Hooper
	G-MCAI	Robinson R44 II	M. C. Allen
	G-MCAN	Agusta A109S Grand	Cannon Air LLP
	G-MCAP	Cameron C-80 balloon	L. D. Pickup
	G-MCCF	Thruster T.600N	C. C. F. Fuller
	G-MCCY	IDA Bacau Yakolev Yak-52	D. P. McCoy/Ireland
	G-MCDB	VS.361 Spitfire LF.IX	M. Collenette
	G-MCEL	Pegasus Quantum 15-912	F. Hodgson
	G-MCGA	Sikorsky S-92A	Bristow Helicopters Ltd
	G-MCGB	Sikorsky S-92A	Bristow Helicopters Ltd
	G-MCGC	Sikorsky S-92A	Bristow Helicopters Ltd
	G-MCGD	Sikorsky S-92A	Bristow Helicopters Ltd
	G-MCJL	Pegasus Quantum 15-912	RM Aviation Ltd
	G-MCLK	Van's RV-10	M. W. Clarke
	G-MCLY	Cessna 172P	McAully Flying Group Ltd
	G-MCMC	SOCATA TBM-700	SogestaoAdministraca Gerencia SA
	G-MCMS	Aero Designs Pulsar	R. J. Bost
	G-MCOW	Lindstrand LBL-77A balloon	S. & S. Villiers
	G-MCOX	Fuji FA.200-180AO	W. Surrey Engineering (Shepperton) Ltd
	G-MCPI	Bell 206B JetRanger 3	Castle Air Charters Ltd (G-ONTB)
	G-MCPR	PA-32-301T Turbo Saratoga	M. C. Plomer-Roberts (G-MOLL)
	G-MCRO	Dyn'Aero MCR-01	J. M. Keane
	G-MCUB	Escapade	W. H. Bliss
	G-MCVY	Flight Design CT2K	J. McVey (G-CBNA)
	G-MCXV	Colomban MC.15 Cri-Cri	P. C. Appleton
	G-MDAC	PA-28-181 Archer II	S. A. Nicklen
	G-MDAY	Cessna 170B	M. Day
	G-MDBC	Pegasus Quantum 15-912	J. H. Bradbury
	G-MDBD	Airbus A.330-243	Thomas Cook Airlines Ltd
	G-MDDT	Robinson R44 II	M. D. Tracey
	G-MDGE	Robinson R22 Beta	C. J. Siva-Jothy (G-OGOG/G-TILL)

Reg.	Type	Owner or Operator	Notes
G-MDJE	Cessna 208 Caravan 1 (amphibian)	Aerodynamics Ltd	
G-MDJN	Beech 95-B55 Baron	WAFO Schnecken und Zylinder GmbH (G-SUZI/G-BAXR)	
G-MDKD	Robinson R22 Beta	M. A. & M. L. Mulcahy	
G-MDPI	Agusta A109A-II	Langfast Ltd (G-PERI/G-EXEK/G-SLNE/ G-EEVS/G-OTSL)	
G-MEDF	Airbus A.321-231	British Airways PLC	
G-MEDG	Airbus A.321-231	British Airways PLC	
G-MEDJ	Airbus A.321-232	British Airways PLC	
G-MEDK	Airbus A.320-232	British Airways PLC	
G-MEDL	Airbus A.321-231	British Airways PLC	
G-MEDM	Airbus A.321-231	British Airways PLC	
G-MEDN	Airbus A.321-231	British Airways PLC	
G-MEDU	Airbus A.321-231	British Airways PLC	
G-MEDX	Agusta A109E Power	Sloane Helicopters Ltd	
G-MEEE	Schleicher ASW-20L	T. E. Macfadyen	
G-MEGG	Shaw Europa XS	M. E. Mavers	
G-MEGN	Beech B200 Super King Air	Dragonfly Aviation Services Ltd	
G-MEGS	Cessna 172S	The Cambridge Aero Club Ltd	
G-MEGZ	Ikarus C42 FB100	J. M. Mooney	
G-MELL	CZAW Sportcruiser	G. A. & J. A. Mellins	
G-MELS	PA-28-181 Archer III	P. J. Sowood	
G-MELT	Cessna F.172H	Falcon Aviation Ltd (G-AWTI)	
G-MEME	PA-28R-201 Arrow III	Henry J. Clare Ltd	
G-MENU	Robinson R44 II	Eagles in Flight Ltd	
G-MEOW	CFM Streak Shadow	G. J. Moor	
G-MEPU	Rotorsport UK MT-03	M. C. Elliott	
G-MERC	Colt 56A balloon	A. F. & C. D. Selby	
G-MERE	Lindstrand LBL-77A balloon	R. D. Baker	
G-MERF	Grob G.115A	G-MERF Group	
G-MERL	PA-28RT-201 Arrow IV	W. T. Jenkins	
G-MESH	CZAW Sportcruiser	M. E. S. Heaton	
G-METH	Cameron C-90 balloon	A. & D. Methley	
G-MEUP	Cameron A-120 balloon	J. M. Woodhouse	
G-MFAC	Cessna F.172H	Cezzy Flying Group (G-AVGZ)	
G-MFEF	Cessna FR.172J	E. N. Ford	
G-MFHI	Shaw Europa	Hi Fliers	
G-MFLA	Robin HR200/120B	Multiflight Ltd (G-HHUK)	
G-MFLB	Robin HR200/120B	Multiflight Ltd (G-BXOR)	
G-MFLC	Robin HR200/120B	Multiflight Ltd (G-BXGW)	
G-MFLD	Robin HR200/120B	Multiflight Ltd (G-BXDT)	
G-MFLE	Robin HR200/120B	Multiflight Ltd (G-BYLH)	
G-MFLI	Cameron V-90 balloon	J. M. Percival	
G-MFLJ	P & M Quik GT450	M. F. Jakeman	
G-MFLM	Cessna F.152 II	Multiflight Ltd (G-BFFC)	
G-MFLY	Mainair Rapier	J. J. Tierney	
G-MFMF	Bell 206B JetRanger 3	Lomas Helicopters (G-BJNJ)	
G-MFMM	Scheibe SF.25C Falke	J. E. Selman	
G-MFOX	Aeropro Eurofox 912(1)	R. M. Cornwell	
G-MGAG	Aviasud Mistral 532GB	S. B. Love	
G-MGAN	Robinson R44	FlyBPL.com	
G-MGCA	Jabiru Aircraft Jabiru UL	K. D. Pearce	
G-MGCB	Pegasus XL-Q	M. G. Gomez	
G-MGCK	Whittaker MW6-S FT	A. Chidlow & M. W. J. Whittaker	
G-MGDL	Pegasus Quantum 15	M. J. Buchanan	
G-MGEC	Rans S.6-ESD-XL Coyote II	M. Lowe & D. Williams	
G-MGEF	Pegasus Quantum 15	M. A. Steadman	
G-MGFC	Aeropro Eurofox 912(1)	M. G. F. Cawson	
G-MGFK	Pegasus Quantum 15	F. A. A. Kay	
G-MGGG	Pegasus Quantum 15	R. A. Beauchamp	
G-MGGT	CFM Streak Shadow SAM	D. R. Stansfield	
G-MGGV	Pegasus Quantum 15-912	K. Loder	
G-MGIC	Ace Magic Cyclone	I. J. Richardson	
G-MGMM	PA-18 Super Cub 150	Alice's Flying Group	
G-MGOD	Medway Raven	A. Wherrett/N. R. Andrew/D. J. Millward	
G-MGOO	Renegade Spirit UK Ltd	J. Aley	
G-MGPA	Ikarus C42 FB100	S. Ashley	
G-MGPD	Pegasus XL-R	H. T. Mounfield	

Notes	Reg.	Type	Owner or Operator
	G-MGPH	CFM Streak Shadow	V. C. Readhead (G-RSPH)
	G-MGPX	Kolb Twinstar Mk.3 Extra	S. P. Garton
	G-MGRH	Quad City Challenger II	A. Hepburn
	G-MGTG	Pegasus Quantum 15	R. B. Milton (G-MZIO)
	G-MGTR	Hunt Wing	A. C. Ryall
	G-MGTV	Thruster T.600N 450	R. Bingham
	G-MGTW	CFM Shadow Srs DD	G. T. Webster
	G-MGUN	Cyclone AX2000	M. A. Boffin
	G-MGUY	CFM Shadow Srs BD	Shadow Flight Centre Ltd
	G-MGWH	Thruster T.300	J. J. Hill
	G-MGWI	Robinson R44	Ed Murray and Sons Ltd (G-BZEF)
	G-MHAR	PA-42-720 Cheyenne IIIA	BAE Systems (Operations) Ltd
	G-MHCE	Enstrom F-28A	C. Roumet (G-BBHD)
	G-MHCM	Enstrom 280FX	Kingswood Bank LLP (G-IBWF/G-ZZWW/G-BSIE)
	G-MHGS	Stoddard-Hamilton Glastar	H. D. Jones
	G-MHIS	Cessna 550 Citation Bravo	Mail Handling International Ltd (G-IDAB)
	G-MHJK	Diamond DA42 Twin Star	Plane Talking Ltd
	G-MHMR	Pegasus Quantum 15-912	Hadair
	G-MHRV	Van's RV-6A	M. R. Harris
	G-MICE	Cessna 510 Citation Mustang	Fteron Ltd
	G-MICH	Robinson R22 Beta	Tiger Helicopters Ltd (G-BNKY)
	G-MICI	Cessna 182S	Steve Parrish Racing (G-WARF)
	G-MICK	Cessna F.172N	Branscombe Airfield Ltd
	G-MICR	Cameron Z-120 balloon	Avio San Michele SRL/Italy
	G-MICU	Cameron TR-77 balloon	Avio San Michele SRL/Italy
	G-MICY	Everett Srs 1 gyroplane	D. M. Hughes
	G-MIDD	PA-28 Cherokee 140	Midland Air Training School (G-BBDD)
	G-MIDG	Midget Mustang	C. E. Bellhouse
	G-MIDO	Airbus A.320-232	British Airways PLC
	G-MIDS	Airbus A.320-232	British Airways PLC
	G-MIDT	Airbus A.320-232	British Airways PLC
	G-MIDX	Airbus A.320-232	British Airways PLC
	G-MIDY	Airbus A.320-232	British Airways PLC
	G-MIFF	Robin DR.400/180	G. E. Snushall
	G-MIGG	WSK-Mielec LiM-5 (1211) ★	D. Miles (G-BWUF)
	G-MIII	Extra EA.300/L	Angels High Ltd
	G-MIKE	Brookland Hornet	M. H. J. Goldring
	G-MIKI	Rans S.6-ESA Coyote II	S. P. Slade
	G-MILA	Cessna F.172N	P. J. Miller
	G-MILD	Scheibe SF.25C Falke	P. G. Marks
	G-MILE	Cameron N-77 balloon	Miles Air Ltd
	G-MILF	Harmon Rocket II	E. Stinton
	G-MILN	Cessna 182Q	G-MILN Group
	G-MIME	Shaw Europa	P. Lewis & N. G. Ley
	G-MIND	Cessna 404	Reconnaissance Ventures Ltd
	G-MINN	Lindstrand LBL-90A balloon	S. M. & D. Johnson (G-SKKC/G-OHUB)
	G-MINS	Nicollier HN.700 Menestrel II	R. Fenion
	G-MINT	Pitts S-1S Special	T. R. G. Barnby
	G-MIOO	M.100 Student ★	Museum of Berkshire Aviation/Woodley (G-APLK)
	G-MIRA	Jabiru SP-340	C. P. L. Helson/Belgium (G-LUMA)
	G-MIRM	Stinson HW-75 Voyager	J. M. & S. Bain (G-BMSA/G-BCUM)
	G-MIRN	Remos GX	M. Kurkic
	G-MISH	Cessna 182R	Graham Churchill Plant Ltd (G-RFAB/G-BIXT)
	G-MISJ	CZAW Sportcruiser	S. J. Aviators Ltd
	G-MISK	Robinson R44	C. A. Rosenberg (G-BYCE)
	G-MISS	Taylor JT.2 Titch	D. Beale
	G-MITE	Raj Hamsa X'Air Falcon	G-MITE Flying Group
	G-MITY	Mole Mite	R. H. Mole
	G-MITZ	Cameron N-77 balloon	Colt Car Co Ltd
	G-MJAD	Eipper Quicksilver MX	J. McCullough
	G-MJAE	American Aerolights Eagle	T. B. Woolley
	G-MJAJ	Eurowing Goldwing	M. J. Aubrey
	G-MJAM	Eipper Quicksilver MX	J. C. Larkin
	G-MJAN	Hiway Skytrike	G. M. Sutcliffe
	G-MJBL	American Aerolights Eagle	B. W. Olley
	G-MJCU	Tarjani	J. K. Ewing
	G-MJDE	Huntair Pathfinder	P. Rayson

Reg.	Type	Owner or Operator	Notes
G-MJDJ	Hiway Skytrike Demon	A. J. Cowan	
G-MJEO	American Aerolights Eagle	A. M. Shaw	
G-MJER	Flexiform Striker	D. S. Simpson	
G-MJFM	Huntair Pathfinder	M. J. Aubrey	
G-MJFX	Skyhook TR-1	M. R. Dean	
G-MJFZ	Hiway Demon/Tri-flyer	A. W. Lowrie	
G-MJHC	Ultrasports Tripacer 330	P. L. Wilkinson	
G-MJHR	Southdown Lightning	B. R. Barnes	
G-MJHV	Hiway Demon 250	A. G. Griffiths	
G-MJIR	Eipper Quicksilver MX	H. Feeney	
G-MJJA	Huntair Pathfinder	J. M. Watkins & R. D. Bateman	
G-MJJK	Eipper Quicksilver MXII	J. McCullough	
G-MJKB	Striplin Skyranger	A. P. Booth	
G-MJKO	Goldmarque 250 Skytrike	M. J. Barry	
G-MJKP	Super Scorpion/Sky-Trike ★	Aero Venture	
G-MJKX	Ultralight Skyrider Phantom	L. R. Graham	
G-MJMN	Mainair Tri-Flyer 330/Flexiform Striker	A. Bishop	
G-MJMR	Solar Wings Typhoon	J. C. S. Jones	
G-MJOC	Huntair Pathfinder	A. J. Glynn	
G-MJOE	Eurowing Goldwing	R. J. Osborne	
G-MJPE	Hiway Demon Skytrike	T. G. Elmhirst	
G-MJPV	Eipper Quicksilver MX	F. W. Ellis	
G-MJRL	Eurowing Goldwing	M. Daniels	
G-MJSF	Skyrider Airsports Phantom	B. J. Towers	
G-MJSL	Dragon 200	M. J. Aubrey	
G-MJSO	Hiway Skytrike	D. C. Read	
G-MJSP	Romain Tiger Cub 440	A. R. Sunley	
G-MJST	Pterodactyl Ptraveller	B. W. Olley	
G-MJSY	Eurowing Goldwing	A. J. Rex	
G-MJSZ	DH Wasp	J. J. Hill	
G-MJTM	Aerostructure Pipistrelle 2B	A. M. Sirant	
G-MJTX	Skyrider Airsports Phantom	P. D. Coppin	
G-MJTY	Huntair Pathfinder Mk.1	A. S. Macdonald	
G-MJTZ	Skyrider Airsports Phantom	B. J. Towers	
G-MJUR	Skyrider Aviation Phantom	M. J. Whiteman-Haywood	
G-MJUW	MBA Tiger Cub 440	D. G. Palmer	
G-MJUX	Skyrider Airsports Phantom	T. J. Searle	
G-MJVF	CFM Shadow	J. A. Cook	
G-MJVN	Ultrasports Puma 440	R. McGookin	
G-MJVP	Eipper Quicksilver MX II	G. J. Ward	
G-MJVU	Eipper Quicksilver MX II	F. J. Griffith	
G-MJVY	Dragon Srs 150	J. C. Craddock	
G-MJWB	Eurowing Goldwing	D. G. Palmer	
G-MJWF	Tiger Cub 440	R. A. & T. Maycock	
G-MJYV	Mainair Triflyer 2 Seat	H. L. Phillips	
G-MJYW	Wasp Gryphon III	P. D. Lawrence	
G-MJYX	Mainair Tri-Flyer/Hiway Demon	K. G. Grayson & R. D. Leigh	
G-MJZK	Southdown Puma Sprint 440	R. J. Osborne	
G-MJZX	Hummer TX	M. J. Aubrey	
G-MKAA	Boeing 747-2S4F	Transatlantic Aviation Ltd	
G-MKAK	Colt 77A balloon	A. C. Ritchie	
G-MKAS	PA-28 Cherokee 140	3G's Flying Group (G-BKVR)	
G-MKCA	Boeing 747-2B5B	Transatlantic Aviation Ltd	
G-MKDA	Boeing 747-2B5F	Transatlantic Aviation Ltd	
G-MKER	P & M QuikR	M. C. Kerr	
G-MKEV	EV-96 Eurostar	K. Laud	
G-MKGA	Boeing 747-2R7F	Transatlantic Aviation Ltd	
G-MKIA	VS.300 Spitfire Mk.1A (P9374)	Mark One Partners LLC	
G-MKKA	Boeing 747-219B	European Aviation Ltd	
G-MKVB	VS.349 Spitfire LF.VB (BM597)	Historic Aircraft Collection	
G-MKXI	VS.365 Spitfire PR.XI (PL624:R)	P. A. Teichman	
G-MLAL	Jabiru J400	J. M. Pipping	
G-MLAS	Cessna 182E ★	Parachute jump trainer/St. Merryn	
G-MLAW	P & M Quik GT450	J. R. Payne	
G-MLHI	Maule MX-7-180 Star Rocket	Maulehigh (G-BTMJ)	
G-MLJL	Airbus A.330-243	Thomas Cook Airlines Ltd	
G-MLKE	P & M Aviation Quik R	G. Oliver	
G-MLLE	CEA DR.200A-B	A. D. Evans	
G-MLLI	PA-32RT-300 Lance II	Evans Aircraft Ltd (G-JUPP/G-BNJF)	

Notes	Reg.	Type	Owner or Operator
	G-MLWI	Thunder Ax7-77 balloon	C. A. Butter
	G-MLXP	Europa	M. Davies
	G-MLZZ	Best Off Sky Ranger Swift 912S(1)	I. D. Grossart
	G-MMAC	Dragon Srs.200	J. F. Ashton & J. P. Kirwan
	G-MMAG	MBA Tiger Cub 440	M. J. Aubrey
	G-MMAR	Mainair Gemini/Southdown Puma Sprint	B. A. Fawkes
	G-MMBE	MBA Tiger Cub 440	A. Gannon
	G-MMBL	Southdown Puma	B. J. Farrell
	G-MMBU	Eipper Quicksilver MX II	D. A. Norwood
	G-MMCV	Solar Wings Typhoon III	G. Addison
	G-MMDN	Flexiform Striker	M. G. Griffiths
	G-MMDP	Southdown Sprint X	M. Bryan
	G-MMEK	Medway Hybred 44XL	M. G. J. Bridges
	G-MMFE	Flexiform Striker	W. Camm
	G-MMFV	Flexiform Striker	R. A. Walton
	G-MMGF	MBA Tiger Cub 440	I. J. Webb
	G-MMGL	MBA Tiger Cub 440	H. E. Dunning
	G-MMGS	Solar Wings Panther XL	G. C. Read
	G-MMGT	Solar Wings Typhoon	H. Cook
	G-MMGV	Whittaker MW5 Sorcerer	M. W. J. Whittaker & G. N. Haffey
	G-MMHE	Gemini Sprint	N. L. Zaman
	G-MMHN	MBA Tiger Cub 440	M. J. Aubrey
	G-MMHS	SMD Viper	C. J. Meadows
	G-MMIE	MBA Tiger Cub 440	B. M. Olliver
	G-MMIZ	Lightning MkII	D. Coging
	G-MMJD	Southdown Puma Sprint	M. P. Robertshaw
	G-MMJF	Ultrasports Panther Dual 440	I. A. Macadam
	G-MMJV	MBA Tiger Cub 440	D. G. Palmer
	G-MMKA	Ultrasports Panther Dual	R. S. Wood
	G-MMKM	Flexiform Dual Striker	S. W. Hutchinson
	G-MMKP	MBA Tiger Cub 440	J. W. Beaty
	G-MMKR	Southdown Lightning DS	C. R. Madden
	G-MMKX	Skyrider Phantom 330	G. J. Lampitt
	G-MMLE	Eurowing Goldwing SP	M. J. Aubrey
	G-MMMG	Eipper Quicksilver MXL	J. G. Campbell
	G-MMMH	Hadland Willow	M. J. Hadland
	G-MMML	Dragon 150	M. J. Aubrey
	G-MMMN	Ultrasports Panther Dual 440	C. Downton
	G-MMNB	Eipper Quicksilver MX	M. J. Lindop
	G-MMNC	Eipper Quicksilver MX	W. S. Toulmin
	G-MMNH	Dragon 150	T. J. Barlow
	G-MMNN	Buzzard	E. W. Sherry
	G-MMOB	Southdown Sprint	D. Woolcock
	G-MMOK	Solar Wings Panther XL	R. F. & A. J. Foster
	G-MMPH	Southdown Puma Sprint	J. Siddle
	G-MMPL	Flexiform Dual Striker	P. D. Lawrence
	G-MMPO	Mainair Gemini/Flash	M.A Feber
	G-MMPZ	Teman Mono-Fly	H. Smith
	G-MMRH	Highway Skytrike	A. M. Sirant
	G-MMRL	Solar Wings Panther XL	R. J. Hood
	G-MMRN	Southdown Puma Sprint	D. C. Read
	G-MMRP	Mainair Gemini	J. C. S. Jones
	G-MMRW	Flexiform Dual Striker	M. D. Hinge
	G-MMSA	Ultrasports Panther XL	T. W. Thiele & G. Savage
	G-MMSG	Solar Wings Panther XL-S	R. W. McKee
	G-MMSH	Solar Wings Panther XL	I. J. Drake
	G-MMSP	Mainair Gemini/Flash	J. Whiteford
	G-MMSS	Lightning/Tri-Pacer	C. Parkinson
	G-MMSZ	Medway Half Pint/Aerial Arts 130SX	D. M. Pecheur
	G-MMTD	Mainair Tri-Flyer 330	W. E. Teare
	G-MMTL	Mainair Gemini	K. Birkett
	G-MMTR	Ultrasports Panther	P. M. Kelsey
	G-MMTY	Fisher FP.202U	M. A. Welch
	G-MMUA	Southdown Puma Sprint	M. R. Crowhurst
	G-MMUO	Mainair Gemini/Flash	D. R. Howells & B. D. Bastin
	G-MMUV	Southdown Puma Sprint	D. C. Read
	G-MMUW	Mainair Gemini/Flash	J. C. K. Scardifield
	G-MMUX	Gemini Sprint	D. R. Gregson
	G-MMVA	Southdown Puma Sprint	C. E. Tomkins
	G-MMVH	Southdown Raven	G. W. & K. M. Carwardine

Reg.	Type	Owner or Operator	Notes
G-MMVI	Southdown Puma Sprint	G. R. Williams	
G-MMVS	Skyhook Pixie	B. W. Olley	
G-MMWG	Greenslade Mono-Trike	G-MMWG Group	
G-MMWS	Mainair Tri-Flyer	P. H. Risdale	
G-MMWX	Southdown Puma Sprint	G. A. Webb	
G-MMXL	Mainair Gemini Flash	G. W. Warner	
G-MMXO	Southdown Puma Sprint	D. J. Tasker	
G-MMXU	Mainair Gemini/Flash	T. J. Franklin	
G-MMXV	Mainair Gemini/Flash	M. A. Boffin	
G-MMZA	Mainair Gemini/Flash	G. T. Johnston	
G-MMZD	Mainair Gemini/Flash	S. McDonnell	
G-MMZK	Mainair Gemini/Flash	G. Jones & B. Lee	
G-MMZV	Mainair Gemini/Flash	N. M. Toulson	
G-MMZW	Southdown Puma Sprint	M. G. Ashbee	
G-MNAE	Mainair Gemini/Flash	G. C. luddington	
G-MNAI	Ultrasports Panther XL-S	R. G. Cameron	
G-MNAZ	Solar Wings Pegasus XL-R	R. W. houldsworth	
G-MNBA	Solar Wings Pegasus XL-R	L. Hughes	
G-MNBB	Solar Wings Pegasus XL-R	M. F. P. Pettipher	
G-MNBC	Solar Wings Pegasus XL-R	R. T. Parry	
G-MNBI	Solar Wings Panther XL-S	M. O'Connell	
G-MNBM	Southdown Puma Sprint	C. Hall-Gardiner	
G-MNBN	Mainair Gemini/Flash	I. Bond	
G-MNBP	Mainair Gemini/Flash	B. J. James	
G-MNBS	Mainair Gemini/Flash	P. A. Comins	
G-MNBT	Mainair Gemini/Flash	R. R. A. Dean	
G-MNCA	Hiway Demon 175	M. A. Sirant	
G-MNCF	Mainair Gemini/Flash	C. F. Janes	
G-MNCG	Mainair Gemini/Flash	T. Lynch	
G-MNCM	CFM Shadow Srs B	K. G. D. Macrae	
G-MNCO	Eipper Quicksilver MXII	S. Lawton	
G-MNCP	Southdown Puma Sprint	D. A. Payne	
G-MNCS	Skyrider Airsports Phantom	K. J. Underwood	
G-MNCU	Medway Hybred 44XL	J. E. Evans	
G-MNCV	Medway Hybred 44XL	M. J. Turland	
G-MNDD	Mainair Scorcher Solo	L. Hurman	
G-MNDE	Medway Half Pint	Delta Echo Half Pint Group	
G-MNDM	Mainair Gemini/Flash	J. C. Birkbeck	
G-MNDU	Midland Sirocco 377GB	M. A. Collins	
G-MNDY	Southdown Puma Sprint	A. M. Coupland	
G-MNEG	Mainair Gemini/Flash	A. Sexton/Ireland	
G-MNEH	Mainair Gemini/Flash	I. Rawson	
G-MNER	CFM Shadow Srs B	P. A. Taylor	
G-MNET	Mainair Gemini/Flash	I. P. Stubbins	
G-MNEY	Mainair Gemini/Flash	D. A. Spiers	
G-MNFB	Southdown Puma Sprint	C. Lawrence	
G-MNFF	Mainair Gemini/Flash	C. H. Spencer & R. P. Cook	
G-MNFG	Southdown Puma Sprint	M. Ingleton	
G-MNFL	AMF Chevvron	S. S. M. Turner	
G-MNFM	Mainair Gemini/Flash	P. M. Fidell	
G-MNFN	Mainair Gemini/Flash	J. R. Martin	
G-MNGD	Solar Wings Typhoon/Tri-Pacer	I. White	
G-MNGG	Solar Wings Pegasus XL-R	W. Healy	
G-MNGK	Mainair Gemini/Flash	G. P. Warnes	
G-MNGM	Mainair Gemini/Flash	R. J. Webb	
G-MNGW	Mainair Gemini/Flash	F. R. Stephens	
G-MNHD	Solar Wings Pegasus XL-R	A. Evans	
G-MNHH	Solar Wings Panther XL-S	F. J. Williams	
G-MNHI	Solar Wings Pegasus XL-R	R. W. Matthews	
G-MNHJ	Solar Wings Pegasus XL-R	C. Council	
G-MNHK	Solar Wings Pegasus XL-R	G. J. Eaton	
G-MNHL	Solar Wings Pegasus XL-R	The Microlight School (Lichfield) Ltd	
G-MNHM	Solar Wings Pegasus XL-R	P. A. Howell	
G-MNHR	Solar Wings Pegasus XL-R	B. D. Jackson	
G-MNHZ	Mainair Gemini/Flash	I. O. S. Ross	
G-MNIA	Mainair Gemini/Flash	A. E. Dix	
G-MNID	Mainair Gemini/Flash	M. I. Potts	
G-MNIG	Mainair Gemini/Flash	A. B. Woods	
G-MNII	Mainair Gemini/Flash	R. F. Finnis	
G-MNIK	Pegasus Photon	M. Belemet	

Notes	Reg.	Type	Owner or Operator
	G-MNIM	Maxair Hummer	K. Wood
	G-MNIW	Airwave Nimrod/Tri-Flyer	C. Murphy
	G-MNIZ	Mainair Gemini/Flash	A. G. Power
	G-MNJB	Southdown Raven	W. Flood
	G-MNJD	Southdown Puma Sprint	S. D. Smith
	G-MNJJ	Solar Wings Pegasus Flash	P. A. Shelley
	G-MNJL	Solar Wings Pegasus Flash	S. D. Thomas
	G-MNJN	Solar Wings Pegasus Flash	P. Ayres
	G-MNJR	Solar Wings Pegasus Flash	M. G. Ashbee
	G-MNJS	Southdown Puma Sprint	E. A. Frost
	G-MNJX	Medway Hybred 44XL	H. A. Stewart
	G-MNKB	Solar Wings Pegasus Photon	M. E. Gilbert
	G-MNKC	Solar Wings Pegasus Photon	K. B. Woods
	G-MNKD	Solar Wings Pegasus Photon	A. M. Sirant
	G-MNKE	Solar Wings Pegasus Photon	H. C. Lowther
	G-MNKG	Solar Wings Pegasus Photon	S. N. Robson
	G-MNKK	Solar Wings Pegasus Photon	M. E. Gilbert
	G-MNKM	MBA Tiger Cub 440	A. R. Sunley
	G-MNKN	Skycraft Scout Mk.3-3R	M. A. Aubrey
	G-MNKO	Solar Wings Pegasus Flash	T. A. Goundry
	G-MNKP	Solar Wings Pegasus Flash	I. N. Miller
	G-MNKU	Southdown Puma Sprint	S. P. O'Hannrachain
	G-MNKW	Solar Wings Pegasus Flash	G. J. Eaton
	G-MNKX	Solar Wings Pegasus Flash	T. A. Newton
	G-MNKZ	Southdown Raven	D. M. Pecheur
	G-MNLT	Southdown Raven	J. L. Stachini
	G-MNMC	Mainair Gemini Sprint	J. C. Peat
	G-MNMG	Mainair Gemini/Flash	N. A. M. Beyer-Kay
	G-MNMK	Solar Wings Pegasus XL-R	A. F. Smallacombe
	G-MNMM	Aerotech MW5 Sorcerer	S. F. N. Warnell
	G-MNMU	Southdown Raven	M. J. Curley
	G-MNMV	Mainair Gemini/Flash	S. Staig
	G-MNMW	Aerotech MW6 Merlin	E. F. Clapham
	G-MNMY	Cyclone 70	N. R. Beale
	G-MNNA	Southdown Raven	D. & G. D. Palfrey
	G-MNNF	Mainair Gemini/Flash	W. J. Gunn
	G-MNNG	Solar Wings Photon	K. B. Woods
	G-MNNL	Mainair Gemini/Flash II	C. L. Rumney
	G-MNNM	Mainair Scorcher Solo	L. L. Perry & S. R. Leeper
	G-MNNO	Southdown Raven	M. J. Robbins
	G-MNNS	Eurowing Goldwing	B. K. Harrison & F. W. McCann
	G-MNNY	Solar Wings Pegasus Flash	C. W. Payne
	G-MNPC	Mainair Gemini/Flash	M. S. McGimpsey
	G-MNPY	Mainair Scorcher Solo	R. D. Leigh
	G-MNPZ	Mainair Scorcher Solo	S. Stevens
	G-MNRD	Ultraflight Lazair IIIE	Sywell Lazair Group
	G-MNRE	Mainair Scorcher Solo	R. D. Leigh
	G-MNRI	Hornet Dual Trainer	R. H. Goll
	G-MNRM	Hornet Dual Trainer	I. C. Cannan
	G-MNRS	Southdown Raven	M. C. Newman
	G-MNRT	Midland Ultralights Sirocco	R. F. Hinton
	G-MNRX	Mainair Gemini/Flash II	R. Downham
	G-MNRZ	Mainair Scorcher Solo	A. Costello
	G-MNSJ	Mainair Gemini/Flash	P. Cooney
	G-MNSL	Southdown Raven X	P. B. Robinson
	G-MNSY	Southdown Raven X	L. A. Hosegood
	G-MNTD	Aerial Arts Chaser 110SX	B. Richardson
	G-MNTE	Southdown Raven X	E. Foster
	G-MNTK	CFM Shadow Srs B	K. Davies
	G-MNTP	CFM Shadow Srs B	C. Lockwood
	G-MNTV	Mainair Gemini/Flash II	A.M. Sirant
	G-MNUF	Mainair Gemini/Flash II	K. Jones
	G-MNUI	Skyhook Cutlass Dual	M. Holling
	G-MNUR	Mainair Gemini/Flash II	J. S. Hawkins
	G-MNUX	Solar Wings Pegasus XL-R	M. Devlin
	G-MNVB	Solar Wings Pegasus XL-R	M. Cairns
	G-MNVE	Solar Wings Pegasus XL-R	M. P. Aris
	G-MNVG	Solar Wings Pegasus Flash II	D. J. Ward
	G-MNVI	CFM Shadow Srs B	D. R. C. Pugh
	G-MNVJ	CFM Shadow Srs CD	G. Mudd
	G-MNVK	CFM Shadow Srs B	A. K. Atwell

Reg.	Type	Owner or Operator	Notes
G-MNVO	Hovey Whing-Ding II	C. Wilson	
G-MNVT	Mainair Gemini/Flash II	ACB Hydraulics	
G-MNVV	Mainair Gemini/Flash II	T. Wilbor	
G-MNVW	Mainair Gemini/Flash II	J. C. Munro-Hunt	
G-MNVZ	Solar Wings Pegasus Photon	J. J. Russ	
G-MNWG	Southdown Raven X	D. Murray	
G-MNWI	Mainair Gemini/Flash II	P. Dickinson	
G-MNWL	Aerial Arts 130SX	E. H. Snook	
G-MNWO	Mainair Gemini/Flash II	P. Burgess	
G-MNWY	CFM Shadow Srs C	R. R. L. & S. R. Potts	
G-MNXE	Southdown Raven X	A. E. Silvey	
G-MNXF	Southdown Raven X	D. E. Gwenin	
G-MNXG	Southdown Raven X	E. M. & M. A. Williams	
G-MNXO	Medway Hybred 44XLR	R. P. Taylor	
G-MNXU	Mainair Gemini/Flash II	J. M. Hucker	
G-MNXX	CFM Shadow Srs BD	M. Nazm	
G-MNXZ	Whittaker MW5 Sorcerer	A. J. Glynn	
G-MNYA	Solar Wings Pegasus Flash II	C. Trollope	
G-MNYC	Solar Wings Pegasus XL-R	J. S. Hawkins	
G-MNYD	Aerial Arts 110SX Chaser	B. Richardson	
G-MNYF	Aerial Arts 110SX Chaser	R. W. Twamley	
G-MNYM	Southdown Raven X	R. L. Davis	
G-MNYP	Southdown Raven X	A. G. Davies	
G-MNYU	Pegasus XL-R	G. L. Turner	
G-MNYW	Solar Wings Pegasus XL-R	M. P. Waldock	
G-MNYX	Solar Wings Pegasus XL-R	P. F. Mayes	
G-MNZC	Mainair Gemini/Flash II	C. J. Whittaker	
G-MNZD	Mainair Gemini/Flash II	N. D. Carter	
G-MNZJ	CFM Shadow Srs BD	E. W. Laidlaw	
G-MNZK	Solar Wings Pegasus XL-R	P. J. Appleby	
G-MNZP	CFM Shadow Srs B	J. G. Wakeford	
G-MNZS	Aerial Arts 130SX	N. R. Beale	
G-MNZU	Eurowing Goldwing	P. D. Coppin & P. R. Millen	
G-MNZW	Southdown Raven X	T. A. Willcox	
G-MNZZ	CFM Shadow Srs B	Shadow Aviation Ltd	
G-MOAC	Beech F33A Bonanza	R. M. Camrass	
G-MOAN	Aeromot AMT-200S Super Ximango	A. E. Mayhew	
G-MODE	Eurocopter EC 120B	HE Group Ltd	
G-MOFB	Cameron O-120 balloon	D. M. Moffat	
G-MOFZ	Cameron O-90 balloon	D. M. Moffat	
G-MOGI	AA-5A Cheetah	Octopus GmbH/Germany (G-BFMU)	
G-MOGS	CZAW Sportcruiser	J. M. Oliver	
G-MOGY	Robinson R22 Beta	Northumbria Helicopters Ltd	
G-MOKE	Cameron V-77 balloon	G-MOKE ASBC/Luxembourg	
G-MOLA	Evektor EV-97 TeamEurostar UK	J. Bate	
G-MOMA	Thruster T.600N 450	Compton Abbas Microlight Group (G-CCIB)	
G-MONI	Monnett Moni	P. N. Stacey	
G-MONJ	Boeing 757-2T7	Monarch Airlines Ltd	
G-MONK	Boeing 757-2T7	Monarch Airlines Ltd	
G-MONS	Airbus A.300-605R	Monarch Airlines Ltd	
G-MONX	Airbus A.320-212	Monarch Airlines Ltd	
G-MOOR	SOCATA TB10 Tobago	P. D. Kirkham (G-MILK)	
G-MOOS	P.56 Provost T.1 (XF690)	H. Cooke (G-BGKA)	
G-MOOV	CZAW Sportcruiser	G-MOOV Syndicate	
G-MOPS	Best Off Sky Ranger Swift 912S	P. Stretton	
G-MORG	Balony Kubicek BB-SS balloon	A. M. Holly	
G-MOSA	Morane Saulnier MS317	A. C. Whitehead	
G-MOSJ	Beech C.90GTi King Air	Moss Aviation LLP	
G-MOSS	Beech D55 Baron	D. J. da Costa Marques (G-AWAD)	
G-MOSY	Cameron O-84 balloon	P. L. Mossman	
G-MOTA	Bell 206B JetRanger 3	J. W. Sandle	
G-MOTH	DH.82A Tiger Moth (K2567)	P. T. Szluha	
G-MOTI	Robin DR.400/500	Tango India Flying Group	
G-MOTO	PA-24 Comanche 180	S. M. R. Hickman (G-EDHE/G-ASFH)	
G-MOTW	Meyers OTW-145	J. K. Padden	
G-MOUL	Maule M6-235	M. Klinge	
G-MOUR	HS. Gnat T.1 (XR991)	Heritage Aircraft Ltd	
G-MOUT	Cessna 182T	C. Mountain	
G-MOVI	PA-32R-301 Saratoga SP	G-BOON Ltd (G-MARI)	
G-MOWG	Aeroprakt A22-L Foxbat	J. Smith	

Notes	Reg.	Type	Owner or Operator
	G-MOYR	Aeropro Eurofox 912(S)	Yorkshire Gliding Club (Proprietary) Ltd
	G-MOZE	P & M Quik GTR	M. R. Mosley
	G-MOZI	Glasflugel Mosquito	J. Christensen & P. Smith
	G-MOZZ	Avions Mudry CAP-10B	N. Skipworth & P. M. Wells
	G-MPAA	PA-28-181 Archer III	Shropshire Aero Club Ltd
	G-MPAC	Ultravia Pelican PL	J. H. Leigh t/a The Clipgate Flying Grp
	G-MPAT	EV-97 TeamEurostar UK	P. J. Dale
	G-MPFC	Grumman AA-5B	MPFC Ltd (G-ZARI/G-BHVY)
	G-MPHY	Ikarus C42 FB100	P. Murphy
	G-MPIT	CFM Shadow Srs DD	P. Cicconetti (G-MZOM)
	G-MPLA	Cessna 182T	Oxford Aviation Academy (Oxford) Ltd
	G-MPLB	Cessna 182T	Oxford Aviation Academy (Oxford) Ltd
	G-MPLC	Cessna 182T	Oxford Aviation Academy (Oxford) Ltd
	G-MPLD	Cessna 182T	Oxford Aviation Academy (Oxford) Ltd
	G-MPLE	Cessna 182T	Oxford Aviation Academy (Oxford) Ltd
	G-MPLF	Cessna 182T	Oxford Aviation Academy (Oxford) Ltd
	G-MPMP	Bombardier CL600-2B16 Challenger	TAG Aviation (UK) Ltd (G-JMMP)
	G-MPRL	Cessna 210M	Mike Stapleton & Co.Ltd
	G-MPSA	Eurocopter MBB BK-117C-2	The Mayor's Office for Policing & Crime
	G-MPSB	Eurocopter MBB BK-117C-2	The Mayor's Office for Policing & Crime
	G-MPSC	Eurocopter MBB BK-117C-2	The Mayor's Office for Policing & Crime
	G-MPWI	Robin HR.100/210	P. G. Clarkson & S. King
	G-MRAJ	Hughes 369E	A. Jardine
	G-MRAM	Mignet HM.1000 Balerit	R. A. Marven
	G-MRAP	Bombardier BD100-1A10 Challenger 300	Ability Air Charter LLP
	G-MRDS	CZAW Sportcruiser	P. Wood
	G-MRED	Christavia Mk 1	The Barton Group
	G-MRGT	Skyranger Swift 912(1)	G. I. Taylor
	G-MRJC	AutoGyro Cavalon	Tipjets UK Ltd
	G-MRJJ	Mainair Pegasus Quik	J.H. Sparks
	G-MRJK	Airbus A.320-214	Monarch Airlines Ltd
	G-MRJP	Silence Twister	M. D. Carruthers
	G-MRKS	Robinson R44	TJD Trade Ltd (G-RAYC)
	G-MRKT	Lindstrand LBL-90A balloon	Marketplace Public Relations (London) Ltd
	G-MRLL	NA P-51D Mustang (413521:5Q-B)	M. Hammond
	G-MRLN	Sky 240-24 balloon	Merlin Balloons
	G-MRLS	AutoGyro Calidus	M. R. Love
	G-MRLX	Gulfstream 550	Gama Aviation Ltd
	G-MRME	Gefa-Flug AS 105 GD airship	Airship Over Atlanta Ltd
	G-MRMJ	Eurocopter AS.365N3 Dauphin 2	Whirligig Ltd
	G-MROC	Pegasus Quantum 15-912	P. Hill & M. A. Metzler
	G-MROD	Van's RV-7A	K. R. Emery
	G-MRPH	Murphy Rebel	P. & B. S. Metson
	G-MRPT	Cessna 172S	Kuki Helicopter Sales Ltd (G-UFCC)
	G-MRRR	Hughes 369E	J. Paxton
	G-MRRY	Robinson R44 II	MRRY Flying Group
	G-MRSN	Robinson R22 Beta	Yorkshire Helicopters Ltd
	G-MRSS	Ikarus C42 FB80	Purple Aviation Ltd
	G-MRST	PA-28 RT-201 Arrow IV	G. de Beaufort/France
	G-MRSW	Lindstrand LBL-90A balloon	D. S. Wilson (G-CHWU)
	G-MRTN	SOCATA TB10 Tobago	G. C. Jarvis (G-BHET)
	G-MRTY	Cameron N-77 balloon	R. A. Vale & ptnrs
	G-MRVK	Czech Sport Aircraft Pipersport	M. Farrugia
	G-MRVL	Van's RV-7	L. W. Taylor
	G-MRVN	PZL-Bielsko SZD-50-3	The Bath, Wilts and North Dorset Gliding Club Ltd
	G-MSAL	MS.733 Alcyon (143)	M. Isbister t/a Alcyon Flying Group
	G-MSFC	PA-38-112 Tomahawk	Sherwood Flying Club Ltd
	G-MSFT	PA-28-161 Warrior II	Western Air (Thruxton) Ltd (G-MUMS)
	G-MSIX	Glaser-Dirks DG.800B	G-MSIX Group
	G-MSKY	Ikarus C.42 FB100 VLA	MSKY Group
	G-MSON	Cameron Z-90 balloon	Regional Property Services Ltd
	G-MSOO	Revolution Mini 500 helicopter	R. H. Ryan
	G-MSPT	Eurocopter EC 135T2	M Sport Ltd
	G-MSPY	Pegasus Quantum 15-912	B. E. Wagenhauser
	G-MSTG	NA P-51D Mustang (414419:LH-F)	M. Hammond
	G-MSTR	Cameron 110 Monster SS Balloon	Monster Syndicate (G-OJOB)
	G-MSVI	Agusta A.109S Grand	JPM Ltd (G-ETOU)

Reg.	Type	Owner or Operator	Notes
G-MTAB	Mainair Gemini/Flash II	L. Clarkson	
G-MTAC	Mainair Gemini/Flash II	R. Massey	
G-MTAF	Mainair Gemini/Flash II	A. G. Lister	
G-MTAG	Mainair Gemini/Flash II	M. J. Cowie & J. P. Hardy	
G-MTAH	Mainair Gemini/Flash II	A. J. Rowe	
G-MTAI	Solar Wings Pegasus XL-R	S. T. Elkington	
G-MTAL	Solar Wings Pegasus Photon	I. T. Callaghan	
G-MTAP	Southdown Raven X	M. C. Newman	
G-MTAS	Whittaker MW5 Sorcerer	R. J. Scott	
G-MTAV	Solar Wings Pegasus XL-R	S. Fairweather	
G-MTAW	Solar Wings Pegasus XL-R	M. G. Ralph	
G-MTAX	Solar Wings Pegasus XL-R	L. J. Tonkinson	
G-MTAY	Solar Wings Pegasus XL-R	S. A. McLatchie	
G-MTAZ	Solar Wings Pegasus XL-R	M. O'Connell	
G-MTBB	Southdown Raven X	A. Miller	
G-MTBD	Mainair Gemini/Flash II	J. G. Jones	
G-MTBE	CFM Shadow Srs BD	S. K. Brown	
G-MTBH	Mainair Gemini/Flash II	P. & T. Sludds	
G-MTBJ	Mainair Gemini/Flash II	P. J. & R. M. Perry	
G-MTBL	Solar Wings Pegasus XL-R	R. N. Whiting	
G-MTBN	Southdown Raven X	A. J. & S. E. Crosby-Jones	
G-MTBO	Southdown Raven X	J. Liversuch	
G-MTBR	Aerotech MW5 Sorcerer	R. Poulter	
G-MTBS	Aerotech MW5 Sorcerer	D. J. Pike	
G-MTCK	SW Pegasus Flash	A. M. Chilingirov	
G-MTCM	Southdown Raven X	J. C. Rose	
G-MTCP	Aerial Arts Chaser 110SX	B. Richardson	
G-MTCU	Mainair Gemini/Flash II	T. J. Philip	
G-MTDD	Aerial Arts Chaser 110SX	B. Richardson	
G-MTDE	American Aerolights 110SX	J. T. Meager	
G-MTDF	Mainair Gemini/Flash II	P. G. Barnes	
G-MTDK	Aerotech MW-5B Sorcerer	C. C. Wright	
G-MTDO	Eipper Quicksilver MXII	D. L. Ham	
G-MTDR	Mainair Gemini/Flash II	D. J. Morriss	
G-MTDU	CFM Shadow Srs BD	A. G. Vallis	
G-MTDW	Mainair Gemini/Flash II	S. R. Leeper	
G-MTDY	Mainair Gemini/Flash II	S. Penoyre	
G-MTEC	Solar Wings Pegasus XL-R	R. W. Glover	
G-MTEE	Solar Wings Pegasus XL-R	The Microlight School (Lichfield) Ltd	
G-MTEK	Mainair Gemini/Flash II	G. M. Wrigley & M. O'Hearne	
G-MTER	Solar Wings Pegasus XL-R	G. Carr	
G-MTES	Solar Wings Pegasus XL-R	N. P. Read	
G-MTET	Solar Wings Pegasus XL-R	K. Gilsenan	
G-MTEU	Solar Wings Pegasus XL-R	T. E. Thomas	
G-MTEY	Mainair Gemini/Flash II	A. Wells	
G-MTFB	Solar Wings Pegasus XL-R	K. P. Smith	
G-MTFC	Medway Hybred 44XLR	J. K. Masters	
G-MTFG	AMF Chevvron 232	J. Batchelor	
G-MTFM	Solar Wings Pegasus XL-R	P. R. G. Morley	
G-MTFN	Aerotech MW5 Sorcerer	S. M. King	
G-MTFT	Solar Wings Pegasus XL-R	S. J. Ward	
G-MTFU	CFM Shadow Srs CD	G. J. Jones & D. C. Lees	
G-MTGA	Mainair Gemini/Flash	Microbus	
G-MTGB	Thruster TST Mk 1	M. J. Aubrey	
G-MTGC	Thruster TST Mk 1	G. M. Cruise-Smith	
G-MTGD	Thruster TST Mk 1	B. A. Janaway	
G-MTGF	Thruster TST Mk 1	B. Swindon	
G-MTGL	Solar Wings Pegasus XL-R	R. & P. J. Openshaw	
G-MTGM	Solar Wings Pegasus XL-R	G. D. Sanders	
G-MTGO	Mainair Gemini/Flash	J. Ouru	
G-MTGR	Thruster TST Mk 1	M. R. Grunwell	
G-MTGS	Thruster TST Mk 1	R. J. Nelson	
G-MTGV	CFM Shadow Srs BD	V. R. Riley	
G-MTGW	CFM Shadow Srs BD	N. Hart	
G-MTHH	Solar Wings Pegasus XL-R	J. Palmer	
G-MTHJ	Solar Wings Pegasus XL-R	M. R. Harrison	
G-MTHN	Solar Wings Pegasus XL-R	M. T. Seal	
G-MTHT	CFM Shadow Srs BD	A. P. Jones	
G-MTHV	CFM Shadow Srs BD	S. J. Ellis	
G-MTIA	Mainair Gemini/Flash IIA	M. & T. R. Parsons	
G-MTIB	Mainair Gemini/Flash IIA	M. D. Maclagan	

Notes	Reg.	Type	Owner or Operator
	G-MTIE	Solar Wings Pegasus XL-R	P. Wibberley
	G-MTIH	Solar Wings Pegasus XL-R	R. J. Turner
	G-MTIJ	Solar Wings Pegasus XL-R	M. J. F. Gilbody
	G-MTIK	Southdown Raven X	G. A. Oldershaw
	G-MTIL	Mainair GemIni/Flash IIA	M. Ward
	G-MTIM	Mainair Gemini/Flash IIA	T. M. Swan
	G-MTIR	Solar Wings Pegasus XL-R	P. Jolley
	G-MTIS	Solar Wings Pegasus XL-R	Upottery Aerotow Club
	G-MTIW	Solar Wings Pegasus XL-R	G. S. Francis
	G-MTIX	Solar Wings Pegasus XL-R	S. Pickering
	G-MTIZ	Solar Wings Pegasus XL-R	S. L. Blount
	G-MTJB	Mainair Gemini/Flash IIA	B. Skidmore
	G-MTJC	Mainair Gemini/Flash IIA	T. A. Dockrell
	G-MTJE	Mainair Gemini/Flash IIA	S. R. Eskins
	G-MTJG	Medway Hybred 44XLR	M. A. Trodden
	G-MTJH	SW Pegasus Flash	C. G. Ludgate
	G-MTJL	Mainair Gemini/Flash IIA	P. Smith
	G-MTJT	Mainair Gemini/Flash IIA	D. Sisson
	G-MTJV	Mainair Gemini/Flash IIA	R. W. Hocking
	G-MTJX	Hornet Dual Trainer/Raven	J. P. Kirwan
	G-MTKA	Thruster TST Mk 1	M. J. Coles & S. R. Williams
	G-MTKB	Thruster TST Mk 1	M. Hanna
	G-MTKD	Thruster TST Mk 1	E. Spain/Ireland
	G-MTKG	Solar Wings Pegasus XL-R	S. J. Halliwell
	G-MTKH	Solar Wings Pegasus XL-R	B. P. Hoare
	G-MTKI	Solar Wings Pegasus XL-R	M. Wady
	G-MTKR	CFM Shadow Srs BD	D. P. Eichhorn
	G-MTKW	Mainair Gemini/Flash IIA	J. H. McIvor
	G-MTKZ	Mainair Gemini/Flash IIA	G-MTKZ Syndicate
	G-MTLB	Mainair Gemini/Flash IIA	J. S. Garrett
	G-MTLC	Mainair Gemini/Flash IIA	R. J. Alston
	G-MTLG	Solar Wings Pegasus XL-R	PFT (Cotswolds)
	G-MTLL	Mainair Gemini/Flash IIA	M. S. Lawrence
	G-MTLM	Thruster TST Mk 1	R.J. Nelson
	G-MTLN	Thruster TST Mk 1	P. W. Taylor
	G-MTLT	Solar Wings Pegasus XL-R	K. M. Mayling
	G-MTLV	Solar Wings Pegasus XL-R	P. Cave
	G-MTLX	Medway Hybred 44XLR	D. A. Coupland
	G-MTLY	Solar Wings Pegasus XL-R	I. Johnston
	G-MTLZ	Whittaker MW5 Sorceror	J. O'Keeffe
	G-MTMA	Mainair Gemini/Flash IIA	G-MTMA Flying Group
	G-MTMC	Mainair Gemini/Flash IIA	Rovogate Ltd
	G-MTMF	Solar Wings Pegasus XL-R	H. T. M. Smith
	G-MTMG	Solar Wings Pegasus XL-R	C. W. & P. E. F. Suckling
	G-MTML	Mainair Gemini/Flash IIA	J. F. Ashton
	G-MTMR	Hornet Dual Trainer/Raven	D. J. Smith
	G-MTMT	Mainair Gemini/Flash IIA	C. Pickvance
	G-MTMV	Mainair Gemini/Flash IIA	G. J. Small
	G-MTMW	Mainair Gemini/Flash IIA	D. J. Boulton
	G-MTMX	CFM Shadow Srs BD	D. R. White
	G-MTNC	Mainair Gemini/Flash IIA	M. G. Titmus & M. E. Cook
	G-MTND	Medway Hybred 44XLR	Butty Boys Flying Group
	G-MTNE	Medway Hybred 44XLR	A. G. Rodenburg
	G-MTNF	Medway Hybred 44XLR	P. A. Bedford
	G-MTNG	Mainair Gemini/Flash IIA	A. N. Bellis
	G-MTNI	Mainair Gemini/Flash IIA	F. J. Clarehugh
	G-MTNK	Weedhopper JC-24B	G. R. Moore
	G-MTNM	Mainair Gemini/Flash IIA	P. M. Cary
	G-MTNO	Solar Wings Pegasus XL-Q	P. J. Knibb & G. J. Rowe
	G-MTNR	Thruster TST Mk 1	A. M. Sirant
	G-MTNU	Thruster TST Mk 1	T. H. Brearley
	G-MTNV	Thruster TST Mk 1	J. B. Russell
	G-MTOA	Solar Wings Pegasus XL-R	R. A. Bird
	G-MTOH	Solar Wings Pegasus XL-R	H. Cook
	G-MTON	Solar Wings Pegasus XL-R	D. J. Willett
	G-MTOY	Solar Wings Pegasus XL-R	G-MTOY Group
	G-MTOZ	Solar Wings Pegasus XL-R	C. P. Davies
	G-MTPB	Mainair Gemini/Flash IIA	C. P. Whitwell
	G-MTPE	Solar Wings Pegasus XL-R	J. Bassett
	G-MTPF	Solar Wings Pegasus XL-R	P. M. Watts & A. S. Mitchel
	G-MTPH	Solar Wings Pegasus XL-R	G. Barker & L. Blight

Reg.	Type	Owner or Operator	Notes
G-MTPJ	Solar Wings Pegasus XL-R	D. Lockwood	
G-MTPL	Solar Wings Pegasus XL-R	C. J. Jones	
G-MTPM	Solar Wings Pegasus XL-R	D. K. Seal	
G-MTPR	Solar Wings Pegasus XL-R	T. Kenny	
G-MTPU	Thruster TST Mk 1	N. Hay	
G-MTPW	Thruster TST Mk 1	K. Hawthorne	
G-MTPX	Thruster TST Mk 1	T. Snook	
G-MTRA	Mainair Gemini/Flash IIA	A. Davis	
G-MTRC	Midlands Ultralights Sirocco 377G	D. Thorpe	
G-MTRM	Solar Wings Pegasus XL-R	M. Morris	
G-MTRS	Solar Wings Pegasus XL-R	W. R. Edwards	
G-MTRX	Whittaker MW5 Sorceror	W. Turner	
G-MTRZ	Mainair Gemini/Flash IIA	D. S. Lally	
G-MTSC	Mainair Gemini/Flash IIA	J. Kilpatrick	
G-MTSH	Thruster TST Mk 1	R. R. Orr	
G-MTSJ	Thruster TST Mk 1	S. R. Cockram	
G-MTSK	Thruster TST Mk 1	J. S. Pyke	
G-MTSM	Thruster TST Mk 1	R. J. Webb	
G-MTSS	Solar Wings Pegasus XL-R	V. Marchant	
G-MTSZ	Solar Wings Pegasus XL-R	D. L. Pickover	
G-MTTA	Solar Wings Pegasus XL-R	J. P. Anderson	
G-MTTE	Solar Wings Pegasus XL-R	C. F. Barnard	
G-MTTF	Aerotech MW6 Merlin	P. Cotton	
G-MTTI	Mainair Gemini/Flash IIA	G-MTTI Flying Group	
G-MTTM	Mainair Gemini/Flash IIA	M. Anderson	
G-MTTN	Ultralight Flight Phantom	F. P. Welsh	
G-MTTP	Mainair Gemini/Flash IIA	A. Ormson	
G-MTTU	Solar Wings Pegasus XL-R	A. Friend	
G-MTTY	Solar Wings Pegasus XL-Q	N. A. Perry	
G-MTTZ	Solar Wings Pegasus XL-Q	M. O. Bloy	
G-MTUA	Solar Wings Pegasus XL-R	Fly Hire Ltd	
G-MTUC	Thruster TST Mk 1	N. S. Chittenden	
G-MTUD	Thruster TST Mk 1	S. Cooper & J. Parker	
G-MTUK	Solar Wings Pegasus XL-R	G. McLaughlin	
G-MTUN	Solar Wings Pegasus XL-Q	M. J. O'Connor	
G-MTUP	Solar Wings Pegasus XL-Q	B. P. Vinall	
G-MTUR	Solar Wings Pegasus XL-Q	G. Ball	
G-MTUS	Solar Wings Pegasus XL-Q	G. Nicol	
G-MTUT	Solar Wings Pegasus XL-Q	R. E. Bull	
G-MTUU	Mainair Gemini/Flash IIA	L. E. Donaldson	
G-MTUV	Mainair Gemini/Flash IIA	M. Parsons	
G-MTUY	Solar Wings Pegasus XL-Q	H. C. Lowther	
G-MTVH	Mainair Gemini/Flash IIA	P. H. Statham	
G-MTVI	Mainair Gemini/Flash IIA	R. A. McDowell	
G-MTVJ	Mainair Gemini/Flash IIA	I. Callaghan	
G-MTVP	Thruster TST Mk 1	J. M. Evans	
G-MTVR	Thruster TST Mk 1	D. R. Lucas	
G-MTVT	Thruster TST Mk 1	W. H. J. Knowles	
G-MTVV	Thruster TST Mk 1	P. Timothy	
G-MTVX	Solar Wings Pegasus XL-Q	D. A. Foster	
G-MTWG	Mainair Gemini/Flash IIA	N. Mackenzie & P. S. Bunting	
G-MTWH	CFM Shadow Srs BD	I. W. Hogg	
G-MTWK	CFM Shadow Srs BD	M. Cooper	
G-MTWR	Mainair Gemini/Flash IIA	J. B. Hodson	
G-MTWS	Mainair Gemini/Flash IIA	M. P. Duncan & C. R. Stewart	
G-MTWX	Mainair Gemini/Flash IIA	J. Donley	
G-MTWY	Thruster TST Mk 1	J. F. Gardner	
G-MTWZ	Thruster TST Mk 1	M. J. Aubrey	
G-MTXA	Thruster TST Mk 1	B. Dennis	
G-MTXB	Thruster TST Mk 1	J. J. Hill	
G-MTXC	Thruster TST Mk.1	W. Macleod	
G-MTXD	Thruster TST Mk 1	D. Newton	
G-MTXJ	Solar Wings Pegasus XL-Q	E. W. Laidlaw	
G-MTXK	Solar Wings Pegasus XL-Q	D. R. G. Whitelaw	
G-MTXL	Noble Hardman Snowbird Mk IV	P. J. Collins	
G-MTXM	Mainair Gemini/Flash IIA	H. J. Vinning	
G-MTXO	Whittaker MW6	T. L. Dean	
G-MTXR	CFM Shadow Srs BD	S. A. O'Neill	
G-MTXU	Snowbird Mk.IV	M. A. Oakley	
G-MTXZ	Mainair Gemini/Flash IIA	J. S. Hawkins	
G-MTYC	Solar Wings Pegasus XL-Q	C. I. D. H. Garrison	

Notes	Reg.	Type	Owner or Operator
	G-MTYD	Solar Wings Pegasus XL-Q	K. H. Almond
	G-MTYF	Solar Wings Pegasus XL-Q	D. J. Hineson
	G-MTYI	Solar Wings Pegasus XL-Q	I. D. Edwards
	G-MTYL	Solar Wings Pegasus XL-Q	N. A. Perry
	G-MTYR	Solar Wings Pegasus XL-Q	D. T. Evans
	G-MTYS	Solar Wings Pegasus XL-Q	R. G. Wall
	G-MTYV	Southdown Raven X	S. R. Jones
	G-MTYW	Raven X	R. Solomons
	G-MTYY	Solar Wings Pegasus XL-R	L. A. Hosegood
	G-MTZA	Thruster TST Mk 1	J. F. Gallagher
	G-MTZB	Thruster TST Mk 1	J. E. Davies
	G-MTZC	Thruster TST Mk 1	B. McCann
	G-MTZE	Thruster TST Mk 1	B. S. P. Finch
	G-MTZF	Thruster TST Mk 1	J. M. English
	G-MTZG	Mainair Gemini/Flash IIA	A. P. Fenn
	G-MTZH	Mainair Gemini/Flash IIA	D. C. Hughes
	G-MTZL	Mainair Gemini/Flash IIA	N. S. Brayn
	G-MTZM	Mainair Gemini/Flash IIA	W. Anderson
	G-MTZO	Mainair Gemini/Flash IIA	R. C. Hinds
	G-MTZR	Solar Wings Pegasus XL-Q	P. J. Hatchett
	G-MTZV	Mainair Gemini/Flash IIA	D. J. Horton
	G-MTZW	Mainair Gemini/Flash IIA	M. Kalausis
	G-MTZX	Mainair Gemini/Flash IIA	R. G. Cuckow
	G-MTZY	Mainair Gemini/Flash IIA	K. M. Gough & R. Dunn
	G-MTZZ	Mainair Gemini/Flash IIA	G. J. Cadden
	G-MUCK	Lindstrand LBL 77A	C. J. Wootton
	G-MUDD	Hughes 369E	Derwen Plant Co.Ltd
	G-MUDI	PA-18-150 Super Cub	R. S. Grace (G-BCFO)
	G-MUDY	PA-18-150 Super Cub	C. S. Grace (G-OTUG)
	G-MUIR	Cameron V-65 balloon	L. C. M. Muir
	G-MUJD	Van's RV-12	M. F. El-Deen
	G-MUKY	Van's RV-8	I. E. K. Mackay
	G-MULT	Beech 76 Duchess	Folada Aero & Technical Services Ltd
	G-MUMM	Colt 180A balloon	D. K. Hempleman-Davis
	G-MUMY	Vans RV-4	S. D. Howes
	G-MUNI	Mooney M.20J	P. R. Williams
	G-MUPP	Lindstrand LBL-90A balloon	J. A. Viner
	G-MURG	Van's RV-6	Cadmium Lake Ltd
	G-MUSH	Robinson R44 II	Heli Air Ltd
	G-MUSO	Rutan LongEz	N. M. Robbins
	G-MUTT	CZAW Sportcruiser	W. Gillam
	G-MUTS	Jurca MJ.100 Spitfire	S. M. Johnston & J. E. D. Rogerson (G-CDPM)
	G-MUTZ	Avtech Jabiru J430	N. C. Dean
	G-MUZY	Titan T-51 Mustang	R. McCarthy
	G-MUZZ	Agusta AW.109SP Grand	Hagondale Ltd
	G-MVAC	CFM Shadow Srs BD	R. G. Place
	G-MVAH	Thruster TST Mk 1	M. W. H. Henton
	G-MVAI	Thruster TST Mk 1	P. J. Houtman
	G-MVAJ	Thruster TST Mk 1	D. Watson
	G-MVAM	CFM Shadow Srs BD	C. P. Barber
	G-MVAN	CFM Shadow Srs BD	R. W. Frost
	G-MVAO	Mainair Gemini/Flash IIA	S. W. Grainger
	G-MVAP	Mainair Gemini/Flash IIA	B. D. Pettit
	G-MVAR	Solar Wings Pegasus XL-R	A. J. Thomas
	G-MVAV	Solar Wings Pegasus XL-R	D. J. Utting
	G-MVAX	Solar Wings Pegasus XL-Q	N. M. Cuthbertson
	G-MVAY	Solar Wings Pegasus XL-Q	V. O. Morris
	G-MVBC	Aerial Arts Tri-Flyer 130SX	D. Beer
	G-MVBF	Mainair Gemini/Flash IIA	P. H. Norman
	G-MVBJ	Solar Wings Pegasus XL-R	M. Sims
	G-MVBK	Mainair Gemini/Flash IIA	B. R. McLoughlin
	G-MVBL	Mainair Gemini/Flash IIA	S. T. Cain
	G-MVBN	Mainair Gemini/Flash IIA	N. C. Stone
	G-MVBO	Mainair Gemini/Flash IIA	M. Bailey
	G-MVBT	Thruster TST Mk 1	TST Group Flying
	G-MVBZ	Solar Wings Pegasus XL-R	A. G. Butler
	G-MVCA	Solar Wings Pegasus XL-R	R. Walker
	G-MVCC	CFM Shadow Srs BD	Shadow Group
	G-MVCD	Medway Hybred 44XLR	V. W. Beynon

Reg.	Type	Owner or Operator	Notes
G-MVCF	Mainair Gemini/Flash IIA	M. W. Luke	
G-MVCL	Solar Wings Pegasus XL-Q	T. E. Robinson	
G-MVCM	Solar Wings Pegasus XL-Q	P. J. Croney	
G-MVCR	Solar Wings Pegasus XL-Q	P. Hoeft	
G-MVCS	Solar Wings Pegasus XL-Q	J. J. Sparrow	
G-MVCT	Solar Wings Pegasus XL-Q	G. S. Lampitt	
G-MVCV	Solar Wings Pegasus XL-Q	G. Stewart	
G-MVCW	CFM Shadow Srs BD	D. A. Coupland	
G-MVCY	Mainair Gemini/Flash IIA	A. M. Smith	
G-MVCZ	Mainair Gemini/Flash IIA	P. J. Devine	
G-MVDA	Mainair Gemini/Flash IIA	C. Tweedley	
G-MVDE	Thruster TST Mk 1	T. S. Walker	
G-MVDF	Thruster TST Mk 1	G-MVDF Syndicate	
G-MVDH	Thruster TST Mk 1	T. W. Davis	
G-MVDJ	Medway Hybred 44XLR	W. D. Hutchins	
G-MVDK	Aerial Arts Chaser S	S. Adams	
G-MVDL	Aerial Arts Chaser S	N. P. Lloyd	
G-MVDP	Aerial Arts Chaser S	R. G. Mason	
G-MVDT	Mainair Gemini/Flash IIA	D. C. Stephens	
G-MVDV	Solar Wings Pegasus XL-R	K. Mudra	
G-MVDY	Solar Wings Pegasus XL-R	C. G. Murphy	
G-MVDZ	Solar Wings Pegasus XL-R	A. K. Pickering	
G-MVEG	Solar Wings Pegasus XL-R	A. M. Shaw	
G-MVEH	Mainair Gemini/Flash IIA	R. A. Needham	
G-MVEI	CFM Shadow Srs BD	R. L. Morgan	
G-MVEL	Mainair Gemini/Flash IIA	M. R. Starling	
G-MVEN	CFM Shadow Srs BD	M. R. Garwood	
G-MVER	Mainair Gemini/Flash IIA	J. R. Davis	
G-MVES	Mainair Gemini/Flash IIA	J. Helm	
G-MVET	Mainair Gemini/Flash IIA	N. J. Case & D. P. Turner	
G-MVEV	Mainair Gemini/Flash IIA	K. Davies	
G-MVFA	Solar Wings Pegasus XL-Q	D. J. Bromley	
G-MVFB	Solar Wings Pegasus XL-Q	M. O. Bloy	
G-MVFC	Solar Wings Pegasus XL-Q	J. K. Ewing	
G-MVFD	Solar Wings Pegasus XL-Q	C. D. Humphries	
G-MVFE	Solar Wings Pegasus XL-Q	S. J. Weeks	
G-MVFF	Solar Wings Pegasus XL-Q	A. Makepiece	
G-MVFH	CFM Shadow Srs BD	M. D. Goad	
G-MVFJ	Thruster TST Mk 1	B. E. Reneham	
G-MVFL	Thruster TST Mk 1	E. J. Wallington	
G-MVFM	Thruster TST Mk 1	G. J. Boyer	
G-MVFO	Thruster TST Mk 1	M. D. Harris	
G-MVFT	Solar Wings Pegasus XL-R	J. Bohea	
G-MVFX	Thruster TST Mk 1	A. M. Dalgetty	
G-MVFZ	Solar Wings Pegasus XL-R	R. K. Johnson	
G-MVGA	Aerial Arts Chaser S	N. R. Beale	
G-MVGC	AMF Chevvron 2-32	W. Fletcher	
G-MVGD	AMF Chevvron 2-32	T. R. James	
G-MVGF	Aerial Arts Chaser S	P. J. Higgins	
G-MVGG	Aerial Arts Chaser S	J. A. Horn	
G-MVGH	Aerial Arts Chaser S	J. A. Horn	
G-MVGI	Aerial Arts Chaser S	J. E. Orbell	
G-MVGK	Aerial Arts Chaser S	D. J. Smith	
G-MVGM	Mainair Gemini/Flash IIA	J. K. Clayton	
G-MVGN	Solar Wings Pegasus XL-R	M. J. Smith	
G-MVGO	Solar Wings Pegasus XL-R	J. B. Peacock	
G-MVGY	Medway Hybred 44XL	M. Vines	
G-MVGZ	Ultraflight Lazair IIIE	D. M. Broom	
G-MVHD	CFM Shadow Srs BD	F. McManus	
G-MVHE	Mainair Gemini/Flash IIA	T. J. McMenamin	
G-MVHG	Mainair Gemini/Flash II	C. A. J. Elder	
G-MVHH	Mainair Gemini/Flash IIA	A. M. Lynch	
G-MVHI	Thruster TST Mk 1	G. L. Roberts	
G-MVHJ	Thruster TST Mk 1	T. Welch	
G-MVHK	Thruster TST Mk 1	D. J. Gordon	
G-MVHL	Thruster TST Mk 1	G. Jones	
G-MVHP	Solar Wings Pegasus XL-Q	J. B. Gasson	
G-MVHR	Solar Wings Pegasus XL-Q	J. M. Hucker	
G-MVHS	Solar Wings Pegasus XL-Q	A. P. Clarke	
G-MVIB	Mainair Gemini/Flash IIA	LSA Systems	
G-MVIE	Aerial Arts Chaser S	T. M. Stiles	

Notes	Reg.	Type	Owner or Operator
	G-MVIF	Medway Raven X	G. Cousins
	G-MVIG	CFM Shadow Srs BD	M. J. Green
	G-MVIH	Mainair Gemini IIA	T. M. Gilesnan
	G-MVIL	Noble Hardman Snowbird Mk IV	S. J. Reid
	G-MVIN	Noble Hardman Snowbird Mk.IV	C. P. Dawes
	G-MVIO	Noble Hardman Snowbird Mk.IV	C. R. Taylor
	G-MVIP	AMF Chevvron 232	M. S. Westman
	G-MVIR	Thruster TST Mk 1	T. Dziadkiewicz
	G-MVIU	Thruster TST Mk 1	Anglesey Thrusters Syndicate
	G-MVIV	Thruster TST Mk 1	G. Rainey
	G-MVIX	Mainair Gemini/Flash IIA	S. G. A. Milburn
	G-MVJC	Mainair Gemini/Flash IIA	B. Temple
	G-MVJD	Solar Wings Pegasus XL-R	P. E. Woodhead
	G-MVJE	Mainair Gemini FlashIIA	M. D. Payne
	G-MVJF	Aerial Arts Chaser S	V. S. Rudham
	G-MVJG	Aerial Arts Chaser S	T. H. Scott
	G-MVJJ	Aerial Arts Chaser S	C. W. Potts
	G-MVJK	Aerial Arts Chaser S	S. P. Maher
	G-MVJN	Solar Wings Pegasus XL-Q	J. B. Allan
	G-MVJP	Solar Wings Pegasus XL-Q	S. H. Bakowski
	G-MVJU	Solar Wings Pegasus XL-Q	J. C. Sutton
	G-MVKB	Medway Hybred 44XLR	J. Newby
	G-MVKC	Mainair Gemini/Flash IIA	A. Hazelwood
	G-MVKH	Solar Wings Pegasus XL-R	K. M. Elson
	G-MVKJ	Solar Wings Pegasus XL-R	G. V. Warner
	G-MVKK	Solar Wings Pegasus XL-R	G. P. Burns
	G-MVKL	Solar Wings Pegasus XL-R	J. Powell-Tuck
	G-MVKN	Solar Wings Pegasus XL-Q	A. S. Wason
	G-MVKO	Solar Wings Pegasus XL-Q	A. R. Hughes
	G-MVKP	Solar Wings Pegasus XL-Q	J. Williams
	G-MVKS	Solar Wings Pegasus XL-Q	K. S. Wright
	G-MVKT	Solar Wings Pegasus XL-Q	P. Roberts
	G-MVKU	Solar Wings Pegasus XL-Q	I. K. Priestley
	G-MVKV	Solar Wings Pegasus XL-Q	D. R. Stansfield
	G-MVKW	Solar Wings Pegasus XL-Q	A. T. Scott
	G-MVKZ	Aerial Arts Chaser S	K. P. Smith
	G-MVLA	Aerial Arts Chaser S	K. R. Emery
	G-MVLB	Aerial Arts Chaser S	R. P. Wilkinson
	G-MVLC	Aerial Arts Chaser S	B. R. Barnes
	G-MVLD	Aerial Arts Chaser S	J. D. Doran
	G-MVLE	Aerial Arts Chaser S	R. G. hooker
	G-MVLJ	CFM Shadow Srs B	R. S. Cochrane
	G-MVLL	Mainair Gemeni/Flash IIA	W. R. Furness
	G-MVLS	Aerial Arts Chaser S	R. J. Turner
	G-MVLT	Aerial Arts Chaser S	P. H. Newson
	G-MVLX	Solar Wings Pegasus XL-Q	J. F. Smith
	G-MVLY	Solar Wings Pegasus XL-Q	I. B. Osborn
	G-MVMA	Solar Wings Pegasus XL-Q	G. C. Winter-Goodwin
	G-MVMC	Solar Wings Pegasus XL-Q	N. J. Humberstone
	G-MVMG	Thruster TST Mk 1	A. D. McCaldin
	G-MVMI	Thruster TST Mk 1	S. J. Westgate
	G-MVMK	Medway Hybred 44XLR	D. J. Lewis
	G-MVML	Aerial Arts Chaser S	G. C. Luddington
	G-MVMM	Aerial Arts Chaser S	D. Margereson
	G-MVMO	Mainair Gemini/Flash IIA	G. Shimmin
	G-MVMR	Mainair Gemini/Flash IIA	P. W. Ramage
	G-MVMT	Mainair Gemini/Flash IIA	R. F. Sanders
	G-MVMW	Mainair Gemini/Flash IIA	G. Jones
	G-MVMX	Mainair Gemini/Flash IIA	E. A. Dygutowicz
	G-MVNA	Powerchute Raider	J. McGoldrick
	G-MVNC	Powerchute Raider	S. T. P. Askew
	G-MVNE	Powerchute Raider	A. E. Askew
	G-MVNK	Powerchute Raider	A. E. Askew
	G-MVNL	Powerchute Raider	E. C. Rhodes
	G-MVNM	Gemini/Flash IIA	C. D. Phillips
	G-MVNP	Aerotech MW5 (K) Sorcerer	A. M. Edwards
	G-MVNR	Aerotech MW5 (K) Sorcerer	E. I. Rowlands-Jones
	G-MVNS	Aerotech MW5 (K) Sorcerer	A. M. Sirant
	G-MVNW	Mainair Gemini/Flash IIA	D. Furey & D. W. Robinson
	G-MVNX	Mainair Gemini/Flash IIA	A. R. Lynn
	G-MVNY	Mainair Gemini/Flash IIA	M. K. Buckland

Reg.	Type	Owner or Operator	Notes
G-MVNZ	Mainair Gemini/Flash IIA	A. C. Hodges	
G-MVOB	Mainair Gemini/Flash IIA	M. Bailey	
G-MVOD	Aerial Arts Chaser 110SX	N. R. Beale	
G-MVOF	Mainair Gemini/Flash IIA	J. H. Brooks	
G-MVOJ	Noble Hardman Snowbird Mk IV	C. D. Beetham	
G-MVON	Mainair Gemini/Flash IIA	D. S. Lally	
G-MVOO	AMF Chevvron 2-32	M. K. Field	
G-MVOP	Aerial Arts Chaser S	D. Thorpe	
G-MVOR	Mainair Gemini/Flash IIA	P. T. & R. M. Jenkins	
G-MVOT	Thruster TST Mk 1	Doyt Ltd	
G-MVOV	Thruster TST Mk 1	G-MVOV Group	
G-MVPA	Mainair Gemini/Flash IIA	J. E. Milburn	
G-MVPB	Mainair Gemini/Flash IIA	G. A. Harper	
G-MVPC	Mainair Gemini/Flash IIA	W. O. Flannery	
G-MVPD	Mainair Gemini/Flash IIA	P. Thelwel	
G-MVPF	Medway Hybred 44XLR	G. H. Crick	
G-MVPH	Whittaker MW6 Merlin	A. K. Mascord	
G-MVPI	Mainair Gemini/Flash IIA	R. Guild	
G-MVPK	CFM Shadow Srs B	P. Sarfas	
G-MVPM	Whittaker MW6 Merlin	K. W. Curry	
G-MVPN	Whittaker MW6 Merlin	A. M. Field	
G-MVPR	Solar Wings Pegasus XL-Q	C. R. Grainger	
G-MVPS	Solar Wings Pegasus XL-Q	R. J. Hood	
G-MVPW	Solar Wings Pegasus XL-R	C. A. Mitchell	
G-MVPX	Solar Wings Pegasus XL-Q	J. R. Appleton	
G-MVPY	Solar Wings Pegasus XL-Q	G. H. Dawson	
G-MVRA	Mainair Gemini/Flash IIA	F. Flood	
G-MVRB	Mainair Gemini/Flash	G. Callaghan	
G-MVRD	Mainair Gemini/Flash IIA	A. R. Helm	
G-MVRG	Aerial Arts Chaser S	F. S. Ogden	
G-MVRH	Solar Wings Pegasus XL-Q	K. Farr	
G-MVRI	Solar Wings Pegasus XL-Q	P. Martin	
G-MVRM	Mainair Gemini/Flash IIA	R. A. Gardiner	
G-MVRO	CFM Shadow Srs CD	K. H. Creed	
G-MVRR	CFM Shadow Srs BD	S. P. Christian	
G-MVRS	CFM Shadow Srs BD ★	Aero Venture	
G-MVRT	CFM Shadow Srs BD	J. C. Butterfield	
G-MVRW	Solar Wings Pegasus XL-Q	F. Gardner & C. A. Hamps	
G-MVRZ	Medway Hybred 44XLR	I. Oswald	
G-MVSE	Solar Wings Pegasus XL-Q	T. Wilbor	
G-MVSG	Aerial Arts Chaser S	M. Roberts	
G-MVSI	Medway Hybred 44XLR	C. T. H. Tenison	
G-MVSJ	Aviasud Mistral 532	D. W. Curtis	
G-MVSM	Midland Ultralights Sirocco	C. G. Benham	
G-MVSO	Mainair Gemini/Flash IIA	A. B. Shayes	
G-MVSP	Mainair Gemini/Flash IIA	D. R. Buchanan	
G-MVST	Mainair Gemini/Flash IIA	S. R. Stockley	
G-MVSX	Solar Wings Pegasus XL-Q	A. R. Law	
G-MVTD	Whittaker MW6 Merlin	G. R. Reynolds	
G-MVTF	Aerial Arts Chaser S 447	D. A. Morgan	
G-MVTI	Solar Wings Pegasus XL-Q	P. J. Taylor	
G-MVTJ	Solar Wings Pegasus XL-Q	M. P. & R. A. Wells	
G-MVTL	Aerial Arts Chaser S	N. D. Meer	
G-MVTM	Aerial Arts Chaser S	G. L. Davies	
G-MVUA	Mainair Gemini/Flash IIA	E. W. Hughes	
G-MVUB	Thruster T.300	A. K. Grayson	
G-MVUC	Medway Hybred 44XLR	B. Pounder	
G-MVUF	Solar Wings Pegasus XL-Q	G. P. Blakemore	
G-MVUG	Solar Wings Pegasus XL-Q	J. M. N. Oud	
G-MVUI	Solar Wings Pegasus XL-Q	J. K. Edgecombe & P. E. Hadley	
G-MVUJ	Solar Wings Pegasus XL-Q	J. H. Cooper	
G-MVUO	AMF Chevvron 2-32	W. D. M. Turtle	
G-MVUP	Aviasud Mistral 532GB	L. S. Bailey	
G-MVUS	Aerial Arts Chaser S	H. Poyzer	
G-MVUU	Hornet ZA	K. W. Warn	
G-MVVI	Medway Hybred 44XLR	C. J. Turner	
G-MVVK	Solar Wings Pegasus XL-R	A. J. Weir	
G-MVVO	Solar Wings Pegasus XL-Q	A. L. Scarlett	
G-MVVP	Solar Wings Pegasus XL-Q	I. Pite	
G-MVVT	CFM Shadow Srs BD	W. F. Hayward	
G-MVVV	AMF Chevvron 2-32	J. S. Firth	

Notes	Reg.	Type	Owner or Operator
	G-MVVZ	Powerchute Raider	G. A. Marples
	G-MVWJ	Powerchute Raider	N. J. Doubek
	G-MVWN	Thruster T.300	R. D. Leigh
	G-MVWR	Thruster T.300	G. Rainey
	G-MVWS	Thruster T.300	R. J. Hunphries
	G-MVWW	Aviasud Mistral	Golf Whisky Whisky Group
	G-MVWZ	Aviasud Mistral	C. Buckley
	G-MVXA	Brewster I MW6	J. C. Gates
	G-MVXB	Mainair Gemini/Flash IIA	P. A. Henderson
	G-MVXC	Mainair Gemini/Flash IIA	A. Worthington
	G-MVXJ	Medway Hybred 44XLR	P. J. Wilks
	G-MVXN	Aviasud Mistral	P. W. Cade
	G-MVXP	Aerial Arts Chaser S	P. Blackbourn & S. T. Hayes
	G-MVXR	Mainair Gemini/Flash IIA	D. M. Bayne
	G-MVXV	Aviasud Mistral	D. L. Chalk & G. S. Jefferies
	G-MVXX	AMF Chevron 232	T. R. James
	G-MVYC	Solar Wings Pegasus XL-Q	P. E. L. Street
	G-MVYD	Solar Wings Pegasus XL-Q	J. S. Hawkins
	G-MVYE	Thruster TST Mk 1	M. J. Aubrey
	G-MVYI	Hornet R-ZA	K. W. Warn
	G-MVYN	Hornet RS-ZA	M. J. Olsen
	G-MVYS	Mainair Gemini/Flash IIA	P. D. Finch
	G-MVYT	Noble Hardman Snowbird Mk IV	M. A. Oakley
	G-MVYV	Noble Hardman Snowbird Mk IV	D. W. Hayden
	G-MVYW	Noble Hardman Snowbird Mk IV	T. J. Harrison
	G-MVYX	Noble Hardman Snowbird Mk IV	R. McBlain
	G-MVYY	Aerial Arts Chaser S508	R. G. Mason
	G-MVZA	Thruster T.300	H. M. Chase
	G-MVZC	Thruster T.300	S. Dougan
	G-MVZD	Thruster T.300	G-MVZD Syndicate
	G-MVZE	Thruster T.300	T. L. Davis
	G-MVZI	Thruster T.300	R. R. R. Whittern
	G-MVZJ	Solar Wings Pegasus XL-Q	G. P. Burns
	G-MVZL	Solar Wings Pegasus XL-Q	P. R. Dobson
	G-MVZM	Aerial Arts Chaser S	R. Cotterell
	G-MVZO	Medway Hybred 44XLR	S. J. Taft
	G-MVZP	Murphy Renegade Spirit UK	The North American Syndicate
	G-MVZS	Mainair Gemini/Flash IIA	R. L. Beese
	G-MVZT	Solar Wings Pegasus XL-Q	C. J. Meadows
	G-MVZU	Solar Wings Pegasus XL-Q	M. G. McMurray
	G-MVZV	Solar Wings Pegasus XL-Q	K. D. Masters
	G-MVZX	Renegade Spirit UK	G. Holmes
	G-MVZZ	AMF Chevron 232	W. A. L. Mitchell
	G-MWAB	Mainair Gemini/Flash IIA	J. E. Buckley
	G-MWAC	Solar Wings Pegasus XL-Q	H. Lloyd-Hughes
	G-MWAE	CFM Shadow Srs BD	M. D. Brown
	G-MWAF	Solar Wings Pegasus XL-R	R. Horner
	G-MWAN	Thruster T.300	E. J. Girling
	G-MWAP	Thruster T.300	The Wanda Flying Group
	G-MWAT	Solar Wings Pegasus XL-Q	D. G. Seymour
	G-MWAV	Solar Wings Pegasus XL-R	T. Woodward
	G-MWBI	Medway Hybred 44XLR	G. E. Coates
	G-MWBJ	Medway Sprint	C. C. Strong
	G-MWBK	Solar Wings Pegasus XL-Q	A. W. Jarvis
	G-MWBL	Solar Wings Pegasus XL-R	J. C. Ring
	G-MWBR	Hornet RS-ZA	M. R. Gregory
	G-MWBS	Hornet RS-ZA	P. D. Jaques
	G-MWBW	Hornet RS-ZA	C. G. Bentley
	G-MWBY	Hornet RS-ZA	IP Rights Ltd
	G-MWCC	Solar Wings Pegasus XL-R	I. K. Priestley
	G-MWCE	Mainair Gemini/Flash IIA	B. A. Tooze
	G-MWCF	Solar Wings Pegasus XL-R	S. P. Tkaczyk
	G-MWCG	Microflight Spectrum	C. Ricketts
	G-MWCH	Rans S.6 Coyote	G-MWCH Group
	G-MWCK	Powerchute Kestrel	A. E. Askew
	G-MWCL	Powerchute Kestrel	R. W. Twamley
	G-MWCM	Powerchute Kestrel	J. R. Hewitt
	G-MWCN	Powerchute Kestrel	A. E. Askew
	G-MWCO	Powerchute Kestrel	J. R. E. Gladstone
	G-MWCP	Powerchute Kestrel	R. S. McFadyen
	G-MWCS	Powerchute Kestrel	S. T. P. Askew

Reg.	Type	Owner or Operator	Notes
G-MWCY	Medway Hybred 44XLR	J. K. Masters	
G-MWDB	CFM Shadow Srs BD	M. D. Meade	
G-MWDC	Solar Wings Pegasus XL-R	R. Littler	
G-MWDE	Hornet RS-ZA	H. G. Reid	
G-MWDI	Hornet RS-ZA	R. J. Perrin	
G-MWDK	Solar Wings Pegasus XL-R	R. J. Dolby	
G-MWDL	Solar Wings Pegasus XL-R	D. J. Windsor	
G-MWDN	CFM Shadow Srs BD	N. R. Henry	
G-MWDS	Thruster T.300	A. W. Nancarrow	
G-MWDZ	Eipper Quicksilver MXL II	S. Cooper & J. Parker	
G-MWEG	Solar Wings Pegasus XL-Q	S. P. Michlig	
G-MWEH	Solar Wings Pegasus XL-Q	K. A. Davidson	
G-MWEK	Whittaker MW5 Sorcerer	D. W. & M. L. Squire	
G-MWEL	Mainair Gemini/Flash IIA	E. St John-Foti	
G-MWEN	CFM Shadow Srs BD	C. Dawn	
G-MWEO	Whittaker MW5 Sorcerer	J. Morton	
G-MWEP	Rans S.4 Coyote	E. J. Wallington	
G-MWER	Solar Wings Pegasus XL-Q	J. A. O'Neill	
G-MWES	Rans S.4 Coyote	A. P. Love	
G-MWEZ	CFM Shadow Srs CD	G-MWEZ Group	
G-MWFC	TEAM mini-MAX (G-BTXC)	P. C. C. H. Crossley	
G-MWFD	TEAM mini-MAX	J. T. Blackburn	
G-MWFF	Rans S.4 Coyote	P. J. Greenrod	
G-MWFG	Powerchute Kestrel	R. I. Simpson	
G-MWFL	Powerchute Kestrel	M. A. Stevenson	
G-MWFT	MBA Tiger Cub 440	J. R. Ravenhill	
G-MWFU	Quad City Challenger II UK	C. J. Whittaker	
G-MWFV	Quad City Challenger II UK	M. Liptrot	
G-MWFW	Rans S.4 Coyote	M. P. Hallam	
G-MWFX	Quad City Challenger II UK	I. M. Walton	
G-MWFY	Quad City Challenger II UK	C. C. B. Soden	
G-MWFZ	Quad City Challenger II UK	A. Slade	
G-MWGA	Rans S.5 Coyote	P. C. Burns	
G-MWGI	Whittaker MW5 (K) Sorcerer	J. Aley	
G-MWGJ	Whittaker MW5 (K) Sorcerer	I. Pearson	
G-MWGK	Whittaker MW5 (K) Sorcerer	R. J. Cook	
G-MWGL	Solar Wings Pegasus XL-Q	F. McGlynn	
G-MWGM	Solar Wings Pegasus XL-Q	I. Davis	
G-MWGN	Rans S.4 Coyote II	V. Hallam	
G-MWGR	Solar Wings Pegasus XL-Q	M. Jady	
G-MWGU	Powerchute Kestrel	M. Pandolfino	
G-MWGZ	Powerchute Kestrel	J. L. Lynch	
G-MWHC	Solar Wings Pegasus XL-Q	P. J. Lowery	
G-MWHF	Solar Wings Pegasus XL-Q	N. J. Troke	
G-MWHG	Solar Wings Pegasus XL-Q	M. D. Morris	
G-MWHH	TEAM mini-MAX	I. D. Worthington	
G-MWHI	Mainair Gemini/Flash	P. Harwood	
G-MWHL	Solar Wings Pegasus XL-Q	S. J. Reader	
G-MWHO	Mainair Gemini/Flash IIA	T. G. Carter	
G-MWHP	Rans S.6-ESD Coyote	J. F. Bickerstaffe	
G-MWHR	Mainair Gemini/Flash IIA	B. Brazier	
G-MWHX	Solar Wings Pegasus XL-Q	N. P. Kelly	
G-MWIA	Mainair Gemini/Flash IIA	A. Evans	
G-MWIB	Aviasud Mistral	P. Brady	
G-MWIE	Solar Wings Pegasus XL-Q	X. S. Norman	
G-MWIF	Rans S.6-ESD Coyote II	K. Kelly	
G-MWIG	Mainair Gemini/Flash IIA	A. P. Purbrick	
G-MWIM	Solar Wings Pegasus Quasar	M. C. Keeley	
G-MWIO	Rans S.4 Coyote	K. T. Short	
G-MWIP	Whittaker MW6 Merlin	B. J. Merret & D. Beer	
G-MWIS	Solar Wings Pegasus XL-Q	P. G. Strangward	
G-MWIU	Pegasus Quasar TC	W. Hepburn	
G-MWIW	Solar Wings Pegasus Quasar	W. R. Furness	
G-MWIX	Solar Wings Pegasus Quasar	G. Hawes	
G-MWIZ	CFM Shadow Srs BD	T. P. Ryan	
G-MWJF	CFM Shadow Srs BD	T. de B. Gardner	
G-MWJH	Solar Wings Pegasus Quasar	L. A. Hosegood	
G-MWJI	Solar Wings Pegasus Quasar	L. Luscombe	
G-MWJJ	Solar Wings Pegasus Quasar	A. J. Harris	
G-MWJN	Solar Wings Pegasus XL-Q	J. C. Corrall	
G-MWJP	Medway Hybred 44XLR	C. D. Simmons	

Notes	Reg.	Type	Owner or Operator
	G-MWJR	Medway Hybred 44XLR	T. G. Almond
	G-MWJT	Solar Wings Pegasus Quasar	D. L. Mitchell
	G-MWKE	Hornet R-ZA	D. R. Stapleton
	G-MWKO	Solar Wings Pegasus XL-Q	P. M. Golden
	G-MWKX	Microflight Spectrum	C. R. Ions
	G-MWKZ	Solar Wings Pegasus XL-Q	G. K. Wilderspin
	G-MWLB	Medway Hybred 44XLR	G. P. D. Coan
	G-MWLD	CFM Shadow Srs BD	J. J. Hansen
	G-MWLE	Solar Wings Pegasus XL-R	D. Stevenson
	G-MWLG	Solar Wings Pegasus XL-R	C. Cohen
	G-MWLJ	Solar Wings Pegasus Quasar	N. D. Dykes
	G-MWLK	Solar Wings Pegasus Quasar	D. J. Shippen
	G-MWLL	Solar Wings Pegasus XL-Q	A. J. Bacon
	G-MWLM	Solar Wings Pegasus XL-Q	M. C. Wright
	G-MWLN	Whittaker MW6-S Fatboy Flyer	S. J. Field
	G-MWLO	Whittaker MW6 Merlin	G-MWLO Flying Group
	G-MWLP	Mainair Gemini/Flash IIA	K. M. Husecken
	G-MWLS	Medway Hybred 44XLR	M. A. Oliver
	G-MWLU	Solar Wings Pegasus XL-R	T. P. G. Ward
	G-MWLW	TEAM mini-MAX	E. J. Oteng
	G-MWLX	Mainair Gemini/Flash IIA	J. K. Kerr, B. O. Lyell & P. A. Smith
	G-MWLZ	Rans S.4 Coyote	B. J. Hewitt
	G-MWMB	Powerchute Kestrel	S. T. P. Askew
	G-MWMC	Powerchute Kestrel	Talgarreg Flying Club
	G-MWMD	Powerchute Kestrel	D. J. Jackson
	G-MWMF	Powerchute Kestrel	P. J. Blundell
	G-MWMG	Powerchute Kestrel	M. D. Walton
	G-MWMH	Powerchute Kestrel	E. W. Potts
	G-MWMI	SolarWings Pegasus Quasar	R. G. Wyatt
	G-MWML	SolarWings Pegasus Quasar	F. A. Collar
	G-MWMM	Mainair Gemini/Flash IIA	W. Brownlie
	G-MWMN	Solar Wings Pegasus XL-Q	P. A. Arnold & N. A. Rathbone
	G-MWMO	Solar Wings Pegasus XL-Q	D. S. F. McNair
	G-MWMV	Solar Wings Pegasus XL-R	M. Nutting
	G-MWMW	Renegade Spirit UK	P. Wise
	G-MWMX	Mainair Gemini/Flash IIA	P. G. Hughes/Ireland
	G-MWMY	Mainair Gemini/Flash IIA	G. W. Bright
	G-MWNB	Solar Wings Pegasus XL-Q	P. F. J. Rogers
	G-MWND	Tiger Cub Developments RL.5A	D. A. Pike
	G-MWNE	Mainair Gemini/Flash IIA	D. Matthews
	G-MWNF	Renegade Spirit UK	R. Haslam
	G-MWNK	Solar Wings Pegasus Quasar	G. S. Lynn
	G-MWNL	Solar Wings Pegasus Quasar	N. H. S. Install
	G-MWNO	AMF Chevvron 232	I. K. Hogg
	G-MWNP	AMF Chevvron 232	M. K. Field
	G-MWNR	Renegade Spirit UK	RJR Flying Group
	G-MWNS	Mainair Gemini/Flash IIA	J. G. Hilliard
	G-MWNT	Mainair Gemini/Flash IIA	November Tango Group
	G-MWNU	Mainair Gemini/Flash IIA	C. C. Muir
	G-MWNX	Powerchute Kestrel	J. H. Greenroyd
	G-MWOC	Powerchute Kestrel	D. M. F. Harvey
	G-MWOD	Powerchute Kestrel	T. Morgan
	G-MWOE	Powerchute Raider	S. T. P. Askew
	G-MWOI	Solar Wings Pegasus XL-R	B. T. Geoghegan
	G-MWOJ	Mainair Gemini/Flash IIA	C. J. Pryce
	G-MWOO	Renegade Spirit UK	R. C. Wood
	G-MWOV	Whittaker MW6 Merlin	S. Jeffs
	G-MWOY	Solar Wings Pegasus XL-Q	S. P. Griffin
	G-MWPB	Mainair Gemini/Flash IIA	J. Fenton & S. G. Roberts
	G-MWPC	Mainair Gemini/Flash IIA	M. A. Pantling
	G-MWPD	Mainair Gemini/Flash IIA	S. M. Oliver
	G-MWPE	Solar Wings Pegasus XL-Q	E. C. R. Hudson
	G-MWPF	Mainair Gemini/Flash IIA	G. P. Taggart
	G-MWPG	Microflight Spectrum	D. Brunton
	G-MWPH	Microflight Spectrum	A. Whittaker
	G-MWPN	CFM Shadow Srs CD	W. R. H. Thomas
	G-MWPO	Mainair Gemini/Flash IIA	W. Anderson
	G-MWPP	CFM Streak Shadow	A. J. Price
	G-MWPR	Whittaker MW6 Merlin	S. F. N. Warnell
	G-MWPS	Renegade Spirit UK	M. D. Stewart
	G-MWPU	Solar Wings Pegasus Quasar TC	P. R. Murdock

Reg.	Type	Owner or Operator	Notes
G-MWPW	AMF Chevvron 2-32C	M. S. Westman	
G-MWPX	Solar Wings Pegasus XL-R	R. J. Wheeler	
G-MWPZ	Renegade Spirit UK	J. Ievers	
G-MWRC	Mainair Gemini/Flash IIA	T. Karczewski	
G-MWRD	Mainair Gemini/Flash IIA	D. Morton	
G-MWRE	Mainair Gemini/Flash IIA	J. Davies	
G-MWRF	Mainair Gemini/Flash IIA	N. Hay	
G-MWRH	Mainair Gemini/Flash IIA	D. Ben-Lamri	
G-MWRJ	Mainair Gemini/Flash IIA	P. F. Brightmore	
G-MWRL	CFM Shadow Srs.CD	I. W. Hogg	
G-MWRN	Solar Wings Pegasus XL-R	Malvern Aerotow Club	
G-MWRR	Mainair Gemini/Flash IIA	J. Clark t/a G-MWRR Group	
G-MWRS	Ultravia Super Pelican	T. B. Woolley	
G-MWRT	Solar Wings Pegasus XL-R	G. L. Gunnell	
G-MWRU	Solar Wings Pegasus XL-R	M. Corcoran	
G-MWRY	CFM Shadow Srs CD	A. T. Armstrong	
G-MWSA	TEAM mini-MAX	G. J. Jones	
G-MWSB	Mainair Gemini/Flash IIA	P. J. Bosworth	
G-MWSC	Rans S.6-ESD Coyote II	D. G. Fisher	
G-MWSD	Solar Wings Pegasus XL-Q	A. M. Harley	
G-MWSF	Solar Wings Pegasus XL-R	J. J. Freeman	
G-MWSI	Solar Wings Pegasus Quasar TC	K. C. Noakes	
G-MWSJ	Solar Wings Pegasus XL-Q	R. J. Collison	
G-MWSK	Solar Wings Pegasus XL-Q	J. Doogan	
G-MWSL	Mainair Gemini/Flash IIA	C. W. Frost	
G-MWSM	Mainair Gemini/Flash IIA	R. M. Wall	
G-MWSO	Solar Wings Pegasus XL-R	M. A. Clayton	
G-MWSP	Solar Wings Pegasus XL-R	S. I. Hatherall	
G-MWST	Medway Hybred 44XLR	A. Ferguson	
G-MWSU	Medway Hybred 44XLR	T. De Landro	
G-MWSW	Whittaker MW6 Merlin	S. F. N. Warnell	
G-MWSX	Whittaker MW5 Sorcerer	A. T. Armstrong	
G-MWSY	Whittaker MW5 Sorcerer	J. E. Holloway	
G-MWSZ	CFM Shadow Srs CD	M. W. W. Clotworthy	
G-MWTC	Solar Wings Pegasus XL-Q	M. M. Chittenden	
G-MWTI	Solar Wings Pegasus XL-Q	H. R. Bethune	
G-MWTJ	CFM Shadow Srs CD	Shadow Tango Juliet Group	
G-MWTL	Solar Wings Pegasus XL-R	B. Lindsay	
G-MWTN	CFM Shadow Srs CD	M. J. Broom	
G-MWTO	Mainair Gemini/Flash IIA	E. Beckett	
G-MWTP	CFM Shadow Srs CD	R. E. M. Gibson-Bevan	
G-MWTT	Rans S.6-ESD Coyote II	L. E. Duffin	
G-MWTZ	Mainair Gemini/Flash IIA	C. W. R. Felce	
G-MWUA	CFM Shadow Srs CD	P. A. James	
G-MWUB	Solar Wings Pegasus XL-R	A. C. Green	
G-MWUD	Solar Wings Pegasus XL-R	A. J. Weir	
G-MWUI	AMF Chevvron 2-32C	Group G-MWUI	
G-MWUK	Rans S.6-ESD Coyote II	G. K. Hoult	
G-MWUL	Rans S.6-ESD Coyote II	D. M. Bayne	
G-MWUN	Rans S.6-ESD Coyote II	J. Parke	
G-MWUO	Solar Wings Pegasus XL-Q	A. P. Slade	
G-MWUR	Solar Wings Pegasus XL-R	Nottingham Aerotow Club	
G-MWUS	Solar Wings Pegasus XL-R	H. R. Loxton	
G-MWUU	Solar Wings Pegasus XL-R	B. R. Underwood	
G-MWUV	Solar Wings Pegasus XL-R	XL Group	
G-MWUW	Solar Wings Pegasus XL-R	Ultraflight Microlights Ltd	
G-MWUX	Solar Wings Pegasus XL-Q	B. D. Attwell	
G-MWUZ	Solar Wings Pegasus XL-Q	S. R. Nanson	
G-MWVA	Solar Wings Pegasus XL-Q	D. P. Henderson	
G-MWVE	Solar Wings Pegasus XL-R	W. A. Keel-Stocker	
G-MWVF	Solar Wings Pegasus XL-R	J. B. Wright	
G-MWVG	CFM Shadow Srs CD	Shadow Aviation Ltd	
G-MWVH	CFM Shadow Srs CD	M. McKenzie	
G-MWVL	Rans S.6-ESD Coyote II	J. C. Gates	
G-MWVM	Solar Wings Pegasus Quasar II	A. A. Edmonds	
G-MWVN	Mainair Gemini/Flash IIA	J. McCafferty	
G-MWVO	Mainair Gemini/Flash IIA	I. B. Plested	
G-MWVP	Renegade Spirit UK	P. D. Mickleburgh	
G-MWVT	Mainair Gemini/Flash IIA	P. J. Newman	
G-MWVY	Mainair Gemini/Flash IIA	S. F. Kennedy	
G-MWVZ	Mainair Gemini/Flash IIA	R. W. Twamley	

Notes	Reg.	Type	Owner or Operator
	G-MWWB	Mainair Gemini/Flash IIA	W. P. Seward
	G-MWWC	Mainair Gemini/Flash IIA	D. & A. Margereson
	G-MWWD	Renegade Spirit	R. A. Arrowsmith
	G-MWWH	Solar Wings Pegasus XL-Q	R. G. Wall
	G-MWWI	Mainair Gemini/Flash IIA	M. A. S. Nesbitt
	G-MWWK	Mainair Gemini/Flash IIA	S. D. Puddle
	G-MWWN	Mainair Gemini/Flash IIA	P. Thaxter
	G-MWWS	Thruster T.300	Galaxy Microlights
	G-MWWV	Solar Wings Pegasus XL-Q	R. W. Livingstone
	G-MWWZ	Cyclone Chaser S	P. K. Dale
	G-MWXF	Mainair Mercury	D. McAuley
	G-MWXH	Solar Wings Pegasus Quasar IITC	R. P. Wilkinson
	G-MWXJ	Mainair Mercury	P. J. Taylor
	G-MWXK	Mainair Mercury	M. P. Wilkinson
	G-MWXP	Solar Wings Pegasus XL-Q	A. P. Attfield
	G-MWXV	Mainair Gemini/Flash IIA	T. A. Daniel
	G-MWXW	Cyclone Chaser S	D. Darcy-Ewing
	G-MWXX	Cyclone Chaser S 447	P. I. Frost
	G-MWXY	Cyclone Chaser S 447	D. Curtis
	G-MWXZ	Cyclone Chaser S 508	D. L. Hadley
	G-MWYA	Mainair Gemini/Flash IIA	R. F. Hunt
	G-MWYC	Solar Wings Pegasus XL-Q	R. M. Jarvis
	G-MWYD	CFM Shadow Srs C	F. E. Greenfield
	G-MWYE	Rans S.6-ESD Coyote II	G. A. M. Moffat
	G-MWYG	Mainair Gemini/Flash IIA	N. Fitzmaurice
	G-MWYI	Solar Wings Pegasus Quasar II	T. S. Chadfield
	G-MWYJ	Solar Wings Pegasus Quasar II	A. Clarke & L. B. Hughes
	G-MWYL	Mainair Gemini/Flash IIA	A. J. Hinks
	G-MWYM	Cyclone Chaser S 1000	C. J. Meadows
	G-MWYS	CGS Hawk 1 Arrow	Civilair
	G-MWYT	Mainair Gemini/Flash IIA	J. R. Kendall
	G-MWYU	Solar Wings Pegasus XL-Q	L. A. Dotchin
	G-MWYV	Mainair Gemini/Flash IIA	R. Bricknell
	G-MWYY	Mainair Gemini/Flash IIA	R. D. Allard
	G-MWYZ	Solar Wings Pegasus XL-Q	D. R. Williams
	G-MWZA	Mainair Mercury	A. J. Malham
	G-MWZB	AMF Microlight Chevvron 2-32C	E. Ratcliffe
	G-MWZD	Solar Wings Pegasus Quasar IITC	N. W. Mallen
	G-MWZF	Solar Wings Pegasus Quasar IITC	R. G. T. Corney
	G-MWZJ	Solar Wings Pegasus XL-R	P. Kitchen
	G-MWZL	Mainair Gemini/Flash IIA	D. Renton
	G-MWZO	Solar Wings Pegasus Quasar IITC	A. Robinson
	G-MWZP	Solar Wings Pegasus Quasar IITC	C. Garton
	G-MWZR	Solar Wings Pegasus Quasar IITC	R. Veart
	G-MWZS	Solar Wings Pegasus Quasar IITC	G. Bennett
	G-MWZU	Solar Wings Pegasus XL-R	A. D. Winebloom
	G-MWZV	Solar Wings Pegasus XL-R	D. J. Newby
	G-MWZY	Solar Wings Pegasus XL-R	Darley Moor Airsports Club Ltd
	G-MWZZ	Solar Wings Pegasus XL-R	The Microlight School (Lichfield) Ltd
	G-MXII	Pitts Model 12	P. T. Borchert
	G-MXMX	PA-46R-350T Malibu Matrix	Feabrex Ltd
	G-MXPH	BAC.167 Strikemaster Mk 84 (311)	R. S. Partridge-Hicks (G-SARK)
	G-MXVI	VS.361 Spitfire LF.XVIe (TE184:D)	S. R. Stead
	G-MYAB	Solar Wings Pegasus XL-R	A. N. F. Stewart
	G-MYAC	Solar Wings Pegasus XL-Q	M. E. Gilman
	G-MYAE	Solar Wings Pegasus XL-Q	C. R. Bunce
	G-MYAF	Solar Wings Pegasus XL-Q	K. H. Almond
	G-MYAG	Quad City Challenger II	I. Ciziks
	G-MYAH	Whittaker MW5 Sorcerer	I. D. Worthington
	G-MYAI	Mainair Mercury	J. Ellerton
	G-MYAJ	Rans S.6-ESD Coyote II	J. Beattie
	G-MYAN	Whittaker MW5 (K) Sorcerer	A. F. Reid
	G-MYAO	Mainair Gemini/Flash IIA	R. A. Chapman
	G-MYAR	Thruster T.300	G. Hawkins
	G-MYAS	Mainair Gemini/Flash IIA	J. R. Davis
	G-MYAT	TEAM mini-MAX	M. W. Hands
	G-MYAZ	Renegade Spirit UK	R. Smith
	G-MYBA	Rans S.6-ESD Coyote II	A. M. Hughes
	G-MYBB	Maxair Drifter	M. Ingleton

Reg.	Type	Owner or Operator	Notes
G-MYBC	CFM Shadow Srs CD	P. C. H. Clarke	
G-MYBE	Solar Wings Pegasus Quasar IITC	G. Bullock & A. Turner	
G-MYBF	Solar Wings Pegasus XL-Q	K. H. Pead	
G-MYBI	Rans S.6-ESD Coyote II	D. Wilkinson	
G-MYBJ	Mainair Gemini/Flash IIA	G. C. Bowers	
G-MYBM	TEAM mini-MAX	B. Hunter	
G-MYBR	Solar Wings Pegasus XL-Q	M. J. Larbey & G. T. Hunt	
G-MYBT	Solar Wings Pegasus Quasar IITC	G. A. Rainbow-Ockwell	
G-MYBU	Cyclone Chaser S 447	R. L. Arscott	
G-MYBV	Solar Wings Pegasus XL-Q	L. R. Hodgson	
G-MYBW	Solar Wings Pegasus XL-Q	J. S. Chapman	
G-MYCA	Whittaker MW6 Merlin	R. A. L-V. Harris	
G-MYCB	Cyclone Chaser S 447	N. I. Garland	
G-MYCE	Solar Wings Pegasus Quasar IITC	S. W. Barker	
G-MYCJ	Mainair Mercury	C. A. McLean	
G-MYCK	Mainair Gemini/Flash IIA	T. Kelly	
G-MYCL	Mainair Mercury	P. B. Cole	
G-MYCM	CFM Shadow Srs CD	C. I. Chegwen	
G-MYCN	Mainair Mercury	P. Lowham	
G-MYCO	Renegade Spirit UK	T. P. Williams	
G-MYCP	Whittaker MW6 Merlin	W. Turner	
G-MYCR	Mainair Gemini/Flash IIA	A. P. King	
G-MYCS	Mainair Gemini/Flash IIA	S. L. Parkinson	
G-MYCT	TEAM Mini-MAX 91	R. Smith	
G-MYCX	Powerchute Kestrel	S. J. Pugh-Jones	
G-MYDA	Powerchute Kestrel	K. J. Greatrix	
G-MYDC	Mainair Mercury	K. M. C. Littlefair	
G-MYDD	CFM Shadow Srs CD	C. H. Gem/Spain	
G-MYDE	CFM Shadow Srs CD	D. N. L. Howell	
G-MYDF	TEAM mini-MAX	J. G. Bright	
G-MYDJ	Solar Wings Pegasus XL-R	Cambridgeshire Aerotow Club	
G-MYDK	Rans S.6-ESD Coyote II	J. W. Caush & W. Doyle	
G-MYDN	Quad City Challenger II	J. E. Barlow	
G-MYDP	Kolb Twinstar Mk 3	Norberts Flying Group	
G-MYDR	Thruster Tn.300	H. G. Soper	
G-MYDT	Thruster T.300	J. B. Grotrian	
G-MYDU	Thruster T.300	S. Collins	
G-MYDV	Mainair Gemini /Flash IIA	S. J. Mazilis	
G-MYDX	Rans S.6-ESD Coyote II	J. R. Tomlin	
G-MYDZ	Mignet HM.1000 Balerit	D. S. Simpson	
G-MYEA	Solar Wings Pegasus XL-Q	A. M. Taylor	
G-MYED	Solar Wings Pegasus XL-R	G-MYED Group	
G-MYEH	Solar Wings Pegasus XL-R	J. Spuffard	
G-MYEI	Cyclone Chaser S447	D. J. Hyatt	
G-MYEJ	Cyclone Chaser S447	A. W. Lowrie	
G-MYEK	Solar Wings Pegasus Quasar IITC	The Microlight School (Lichfield) Ltd	
G-MYEM	Solar Wings Pegasus Quasar IITC	D. J. Moore	
G-MYEN	Solar Wings Pegasus Quasar IITC	T. J. Feeney	
G-MYEO	Solar Wings Pegasus Quasar IITC	A. K. Robinson	
G-MYEP	CFM Shadow Srs. CD	S. A. Taylor	
G-MYER	Cyclone AX3/503	T. F. Horrocks	
G-MYES	Rans S.6-ESD Coyote II	S. J. Mathison	
G-MYET	Whittaker MW6 Merlin	G. Campbell	
G-MYEX	Powerchute Kestrel	R. J. Watkin	
G-MYFA	Powerchute Kestrel	M. Phillips	
G-MYFH	Quad City Challenger II	C. Lockwood	
G-MYFK	Solar Wings Pegasus Quasar IITC	P. T. M. Kroef	
G-MYFL	Solar Wings Pegasus Quasar IITC	C. C. Wright	
G-MYFO	Cyclone Airsports Chaser S	J. G. Hilliard	
G-MYFP	Mainair Gemini/Flash IIA	A. Brier & M. P. Lomax	
G-MYFR	Mainair Gemini/Flash IIA	J. R. Hairsine	
G-MYFT	Mainair Scorcher	M. R. Kirby	
G-MYFV	Cyclone AX3/503	J. K. Sargent	
G-MYFW	Cyclone AX3/503	Microlight School (Lichfield) Ltd	
G-MYGD	Cyclone AX3/503	G. M. R. Keenan	
G-MYGF	TEAM mini-MAX	R. D. Barnard	
G-MYGK	Cyclone Chaser S 508	P. C. Collins	
G-MYGM	Quad City Challenger II	P. K. Jenkins	
G-MYGN	AMF Chevvron 2-32C	P. J. Huston	
G-MYGO	CFM ShadowSrs CD	Thorley Motors Ltd	
G-MYGP	Rans S.6-ESD Coyote II	R. H. Y. Farrer	

Notes	Reg.	Type	Owner or Operator
	G-MYGR	Rans S.6-ESD Coyote II	W. Scott
	G-MYGT	Solar Wings Pegasus XL-R	Condors Aerotow Syndicate
	G-MYGU	Solar Wings Pegasus XL-R	J. A. Sims
	G-MYGV	Solar Wings Pegasus XL-R	J. A. Crofts & G. M. Birkett
	G-MYGZ	Mainair Gemini/Flash IIA	G. J. Molloy
	G-MYHG	Cyclone AX/503	N. P. Thomson & C. Alsop
	G-MYHH	Cyclone AX/503	D. J. Harber
	G-MYHI	Rans S.6-ESD Coyote II	I. J. Steele
	G-MYHJ	Cyclone AX3/503	B. J. Palfreyman
	G-MYHK	Rans S.6-ESD Coyote II	M. R. Williamson
	G-MYHL	Mainair Gemini/Flash IIA	M. Coates & H. B. Blackwell
	G-MYHM	Cyclone AX3/503	G-MYHM Group
	G-MYHN	Mainair Gemini/Flash IIA	H. J. Timms
	G-MYHP	Rans S.6-ESD Coyote II	K. E. Gair & D. M. Smith
	G-MYHR	Cyclone AX3/503	C. W. Williams
	G-MYIA	Quad City Challenger II	I. Pearson
	G-MYIF	CFM Shadow Srs CD	P. J. Edwards
	G-MYIH	Mainair Gemini/Flash IIA	A. N. Huddart
	G-MYII	TEAM mini-MAX	G. H. Crick
	G-MYIK	Kolb Twinstar Mk 3	B. A. Janaway
	G-MYIL	Cyclone Chaser S 508	R. A. Rawes
	G-MYIN	Solar Wings Pegasus Quasar IITC	W. P. Hughes
	G-MYIP	CFM Shadow Srs CD	T. Bailey
	G-MYIR	Rans S.6-ESD Coyote II	P. D. Smalley
	G-MYIS	Rans S.6-ESD Coyote II	I. S. Everett & M. Stott
	G-MYIT	Cyclone Chaser S 508	R. Barringer
	G-MYIV	Mainair Gemini/Flash IIA	P. Norton & T. Williams
	G-MYIX	Quad City Challenger II	R. Sinclair-Brown
	G-MYIY	Mainair Gemini/Flash IIA	D. Jackson
	G-MYIZ	TEAM mini-MAX 2	J. C. Longmore
	G-MYJC	Mainair Gemini/Flash IIA	M. N. Irven
	G-MYJD	Rans S.6-ESD Coyote II	A. A. Ross
	G-MYJF	Thruster T.300	P. F. McConville
	G-MYJG	Thruster T.300	J. W. Rice
	G-MYJJ	Solar Wings Pegasus Quasar IITC	T. A. Willcox
	G-MYJK	Solar Wings Pegasus Quasar IITC	The Microlight School (Lichfield) Ltd
	G-MYJM	Mainair Gemini/Flash IIA	J. G. Treanor
	G-MYJO	Cyclone Chaser S 508	A. W. Rawlings
	G-MYJS	Solar Wings Pegasus Quasar IITC	J. P. Rooms
	G-MYJT	Solar Wings Pegasus Quasar IITC	S. Ferguson
	G-MYJU	Solar Wings Pegasus Quasar IITC	D. Al-Bassam
	G-MYJZ	Whittaker MW5D Sorcerer	My Jazz Group
	G-MYKA	Cyclone AX3/503	T. Whittall
	G-MYKB	Kolb Twinstar Mk 3	T. Antell
	G-MYKE	CFM Shadow Srs BD	MKH Engineering
	G-MYKF	Cyclone AX3/503	M. A. Collins
	G-MYKG	Mainair Gemini/Flash IIA	B. D. Walker
	G-MYKH	Mainair Gemini/Flash IIA	A. W. Leadley
	G-MYKJ	TEAM mini-MAX	T. de Breffe Gardner
	G-MYKO	Whittaker MW6-S Fat Boy Flyer	J. A. Weston
	G-MYKR	Solar Wings Pegasus Quasar IITC	C. Stallard
	G-MYKS	Solar Wings Pegasus Quasar IITC	D. J. Oskis
	G-MYKV	Mainair Gemini/Flash IIA	P. J. Gulliver
	G-MYKX	Mainair Mercury	D. T. McAfee
	G-MYKY	Mainair Mercury	E. Ibanez
	G-MYKZ	TEAM mini-MAX	J. H. Richardson
	G-MYLB	TEAM mini-MAX	J. G. Burns
	G-MYLC	Solar Wings Pegasus Quantum 15	C. McKay
	G-MYLD	Rans S.6-ESD Coyote II	E. Kaplan
	G-MYLE	Solar Wings Pegasus Quantum 15	Quantum Quartet
	G-MYLF	Rans S.6-ESD Coyote II	A. J. Spencer
	G-MYLG	Mainair Gemini/Flash IIA	N. J. Axworthy
	G-MYLH	Solar Wings Pegasus Quantum 15	G. Carr
	G-MYLI	Solar Wings Pegasus Quantum 15	A. M. Keyte
	G-MYLK	Solar Wings Pegasus Quantum 15	G-MYLK Group
	G-MYLL	Solar Wings Pegasus Quantum 15	M. P. Bawden
	G-MYLM	Solar Wings Pegasus Quasar IITC	M. W. Scott
	G-MYLN	Kolb Twinstar Mk 3	J. F. Joyes
	G-MYLO	Rans S.6-ESD Coyote II	P. Bowers
	G-MYLP	Kolb Twinstar Mk 3	R. Thompson (G-BVCR)
	G-MYLR	Mainair Gemini/Flash IIA	A. L. Lyall

Reg.	Type	Owner or Operator	Notes
G-MYLS	Mainair Mercury	W. K. C. Davies	
G-MYLT	Mainair Blade	T. D. Hall	
G-MYLV	CFM Shadow Srs CD	Aviation for Paraplegics and Tetraplegics Trust	
G-MYLW	Rans S6-ESD	A. D. Dias	
G-MYLX	Medway Raven	K. Hayley	
G-MYMB	Solar Wings Pegasus Quantum 15	D. B. Jones	
G-MYMC	Solar Wings Pegasus Quantum 15	I. A. Macadam	
G-MYMH	Rans S.6-ESD Coyote II	P. V. Stevens	
G-MYMI	Kolb Twinstar Mk.3	F. J. Brown	
G-MYMJ	Medway Raven	N. Brigginshaw	
G-MYMK	Mainair Gemini/Flash IIA	A. Britton	
G-MYML	Mainair Mercury	D. J. Dalley	
G-MYMM	Ultraflight Fun 18S	N. P. Power	
G-MYMN	Whittaker MW6 Merlin	K. J. Cole	
G-MYMP	Rans S.6-ESD Coyote II	D. V. Magee (G-CHAZ)	
G-MYMS	Rans S.6-ESD Coyote II	P. G. Briscoe	
G-MYMV	Mainair Gemini/Flash IIA	A. J. Evans	
G-MYMW	Cyclone AX3/503	L. J. Perring	
G-MYMX	Solar Wings Pegasus Quantum 15	I. A. Thomson	
G-MYMZ	Cyclone AX3/503	Microlight School (Lichfield) Ltd	
G-MYNB	Solar Wings Pegasus Quantum 15	J. A. Gregorig	
G-MYND	Mainair Gemini/Flash IIA	M. I. Weatherly	
G-MYNE	Rans S.6-ESD Coyote II	J. L. Smoker	
G-MYNF	Mainair Mercury	C. I. Hemingway	
G-MYNH	Rans S.6-ESD Coyote II	E. F. & V. M. Clapham	
G-MYNI	TEAM mini-MAX	I. Pearson	
G-MYNK	Solar Wings Pegasus Quantum 15	M. R. Wallis	
G-MYNL	Solar Wings Pegasus Quantum 15	S. J. Whalley	
G-MYNN	Solar Wings Pegasus Quantum 15	V. Loy	
G-MYNP	Solar Wings Pegasus Quantum 15	K. A. Davidson	
G-MYNR	Solar Wings Pegasus Quantum 15	C. A. Reynolds	
G-MYNS	Solar Wings Pegasus Quantum 15	F. J. McVey	
G-MYNT	Solar Wings Pegasus Quantum 15	C. D. Arnold	
G-MYNV	Solar Wings Pegasus Quantum 15	J. Goldsmith-Ryan	
G-MYNX	CFM Streak Shadow SA	S. P. Fletcher	
G-MYNY	Kolb Twinstar Mk 3	I. F. Hill	
G-MYNZ	Solar Wings Pegasus Quantum 15	P. W. Rogers	
G-MYOA	Rans S6-ESD Coyote II	N. S. M. Day	
G-MYOG	Kolb Twinstar Mk 3	T. A. Womersley	
G-MYOH	CFM Shadow Srs CD	D. R. Sutton	
G-MYOL	Air Creation Fun 18S GTBIS	S. N. Bond	
G-MYON	CFM Shadow Srs CD	A. Munro	
G-MYOO	Kolb Twinstar Mk 3	P. D. Coppin	
G-MYOS	CFM Shadow Srs CD	C. A. & E. J. Bowles	
G-MYOT	Rans S.6-ESD Coyote II	D. E. Wilson	
G-MYOU	Solar Wings Pegasus Quantum 15	D. J. Tasker	
G-MYOV	Mainair Mercury	P. Newton	
G-MYOX	Mainair Mercury	K. Driver	
G-MYPA	Rans S.6-ESD Coyote II	G. J. Jones	
G-MYPC	Kolb Twinstar Mk 3	S. J. Ball	
G-MYPE	Mainair Gemini/Flash IIA	C. A. Carstairs	
G-MYPG	Solar Wings Pegasus XL-Q	V. Ashwell	
G-MYPH	Solar Wings Pegasus Quantum 15	I. E. Chapman	
G-MYPI	Solar Wings Pegasus Quantum 15	P. L. Jarvis	
G-MYPJ	Rans S.6-ESD Coyote II	K. A. Eden	
G-MYPL	CFM Shadow Srs CD	G. I. Madden	
G-MYPN	Solar Wings Pegasus Quantum 15	D. P. Graham	
G-MYPP	Whittaker MW6-S Fat Boy Flyer	G. Everett & D. Smith	
G-MYPS	Whittaker MW6 Merlin	I. S. Bishop	
G-MYPT	CFM Shadow Srs CD	R. Gray	
G-MYPV	Mainair Mercury	B. Donnan	
G-MYPW	Mainair Gemini/Flash IIA	P. Lacon & K. Tunnicliff	
G-MYPX	Solar Wings Pegasus Quantum 15	C. Cleveland & M. M. P. Evans	
G-MYPY	Solar Wings Pegasus Quantum 15	E. C. Rhodes	
G-MYPZ	Quad City Challenger II	J. McCullough	
G-MYRD	Mainair Blade	D. R. Slater	
G-MYRE	Cyclone Chaser S	S. W. Barker	
G-MYRF	Solar Wings Pegasus Quantum 15	P. D. Gregory	
G-MYRG	TEAM mini-MAX	J. Jones	
G-MYRH	Quad City Challenger II	M. A. Manning	
G-MYRK	Renegade Spirit UK	D. J. Newton	

Notes	Reg.	Type	Owner or Operator
	G-MYRL	TEAM mini-MAX	J. N. Hanson
	G-MYRN	Solar Wings Pegasus Quantum 15	I. L. Waghorn
	G-MYRP	Letov LK-2M Sluka	R. M. C. Hunter
	G-MYRS	Solar Wings Pegasus Quantum 15	I. G. Poutney
	G-MYRT	Solar Wings Pegasus Quantum 15	G. P. Preston
	G-MYRV	Cyclone AX3/503	M. Gardiner
	G-MYRW	Mainair Mercury	G. C. Hobson
	G-MYRY	Solar Wings Pegasus Quantum 15	N. J. Lindsay
	G-MYRZ	Solar Wings Pegasus Quantum 15	R. E. Forbes
	G-MYSB	Solar Wings Pegasus Quantum 15	H. G. Reid
	G-MYSC	Solar Wings Pegasus Quantum 15	K. R. White
	G-MYSD	BFC Challlenger II	C. W. Udale
	G-MYSG	Mainair Mercury	P. A. Parry
	G-MYSI	HM14/93	A. R. D. Seaman
	G-MYSJ	Mainair Gemini/Flash IIA	A. Warnock
	G-MYSK	Team Minimax 91	T. D. Wolstenholme
	G-MYSL	Aviasud Mistral	P. Smith
	G-MYSO	Cyclone AX3/50	R. Bowden
	G-MYSP	Rans S.6-ESD Coyote II	Wez Group
	G-MYSR	Solar Wings Pegasus Quatum 15	W. G. Craig
	G-MYSU	Rans S.6-ESD Coyote II	C. N. Nairn
	G-MYSV	Aerial Arts Chaser	G. S. Highley
	G-MYSW	Solar Wings Pegasus Quantum 1	I. A. Macadam
	G-MYSX	Solar Wings Pegasus Quantum 1	L. E. Lesurf
	G-MYSY	Solar Wings Pegasus Quantum 15	B. D. S. Vere
	G-MYSZ	Mainair Mercury	W. Fletcher & R. J. Coppin
	G-MYTB	Mainair Mercur	P. J. Higgins
	G-MYTD	Mainair Blade	B. E. Warburton & D. B. Meades
	G-MYTE	Rans S.6-ESD Coyote II	S. P. Jarvis
	G-MYTH	CFM Shadow Srs CD	S. G. Smith
	G-MYTI	Solar Wings Pegasus Quantum 15	K. M. Gaffney
	G-MYTJ	Solar Wings Pegasus Quantum 15	L. Blight
	G-MYTK	Mainair Mercury	D. A. Holroyd
	G-MYTL	Mainair Blade	S. W. Tallamy
	G-MYTN	Solar Wings Pegasus Quantum 15	M. Humphries
	G-MYTO	Quad City Challenger II	A. Studley
	G-MYTP	Arrowflight Hawk II	R. J. Turner
	G-MYTT	Quad City Challenger II	D. M. Lockley
	G-MYTU	Mainair Blade	A. Worthington
	G-MYTY	CFM Streak Shadow Srs M	D. A. Daniel
	G-MYUA	Air Creation Fun 18S GTBIS	Darley Moor Airsports Club Ltd
	G-MYUC	Mainair Blade	A. D. Clayton
	G-MYUD	Mainair Mercury	P. W. Margetson
	G-MYUF	Renegade Spirit	P. J. Watson
	G-MYUH	Solar Wings Pegasus XL-Q	K. S. Daniels
	G-MYUI	Cyclone AX3/503	T. Crocombe
	G-MYUL	Quad City Challenger II UK	N. V. & B. M. R. Van Cleve
	G-MYUN	Mainair Blade	G. A. Barratt
	G-MYUO	Solar Wings Pegasus Quantum 15	E. J. Hughes
	G-MYUP	Letov LK-2M Sluka	F. Overall
	G-MYUU	Pegasus Quantum 15	J. L. Parker
	G-MYUV	Pegasus Quantum 15	Group Uniform Victor
	G-MYUW	Mainair Mercury	G. C. Hobson
	G-MYVA	Kolb Twinstar Mk 3	E. Bayliss
	G-MYVB	Mainair Blade	P. Mountain
	G-MYVC	Pegasus Quantum 15	D. P. Clarke
	G-MYVE	Mainair Blade	C. R. Buckle
	G-MYVG	Letov LK-2M Sluka	S. P. Halford
	G-MYVH	Mainair Mercury	R. H. de C. Ribeiro
	G-MYVI	Air Creation Fun 18S GTBIS	Flylight Airsports Ltd
	G-MYVJ	Pegasus Quantum 15	A. I. McPherson & P. W. Davidson
	G-MYVK	Pegasus Quantum 15	T. P. C. Hague
	G-MYVL	Mainair Mercury	P. J. Judge
	G-MYVM	Pegasus Quantum 15	G. J. Gibson
	G-MYVN	Cyclone AX3/503	F. Watt
	G-MYVO	Mainair Blade	Victor Oscar Group
	G-MYVP	Rans S.6-ESD Coyote II	K. J. Legg
	G-MYVR	Pegasus Quantum 15	J. M. Webster & M. Winwood
	G-MYVV	Medway Hybred 44XLR	S. Perity
	G-MYVY	Mainair Blade	G. Heeks
	G-MYVZ	Mainair Blade	R. Llewellyn

Reg.	Type	Owner or Operator	Notes
G-MYWC	Hunt Wing	M. A. Coffin	
G-MYWE	Thruster T.600	W. A. Stephenson	
G-MYWG	Pegasus Quantum 15	S. L. Greene	
G-MYWH	Hunt Wing/Experience	G. N. Hatchett	
G-MYWI	Pegasus Quantum 15	C. Elliott	
G-MYWJ	Pegasus Quantum 15	L. M. Sams & I. Clarkson	
G-MYWK	Pegasus Quantum 15	M. Garvey	
G-MYWL	Pegasus Quantum 15	S. J. Prouse	
G-MYWM	CFM Shadow Srs CD	N. McKinley	
G-MYWN	Cyclone Chaser S 508	R. A. Rawes	
G-MYWO	Pegasus Quantum 15	J. Featherstone	
G-MYWP	Kolb Twinstar Mk 3	P. R. Day	
G-MYWR	Pegasus Quantum 15	R. Horton	
G-MYWS	Cyclone Chaser S 447	M. H. Broadbent	
G-MYWT	Pegasus Quantum 15	P. B. J. Eveleigh	
G-MYWU	Pegasus Quantum 15	C. Trickett & S. McAleer	
G-MYWV	Rans S.4C Coyote	P. G. Anthony & D. A. Crouchman	
G-MYWW	Pegasus Quantum 15	C. W. Bailie	
G-MYWY	Pegasus Quantum 15	P. Byrne	
G-MYXA	TEAM mini-MAX 91	D. C. Marsh	
G-MYXB	Rans S.6-ESD Coyote II	M. Gaffney	
G-MYXC	Quad City Challenger II	Intelisen Ltd	
G-MYXD	Pegasus Quasar IITC	A. Cochrane	
G-MYXE	Pegasus Quantum 15	J. F. Bolton	
G-MYXF	Air Creation Fun GT503	D. J. N. Brown	
G-MYXH	Cyclone AX3/503	S. C. B. Bruton	
G-MYXI	Aries 1	H. Cook	
G-MYXJ	Mainair Blade	S. N. Robson	
G-MYXL	Mignet HM.1000 Baleri	R. W. Hollamby	
G-MYXM	Mainair Blade	S. C. Hodgson	
G-MYXN	Mainair Blade	P. K. Dale	
G-MYXO	Letov LK-2M Sluka	E. Bentley	
G-MYXP	Rans S.6-ESD Coyote II	R. S. Amor	
G-MYXT	Pegasus Quantum 15	L. A. Washer	
G-MYXU	Thruster T.300	D. W. Wilson	
G-MYXV	Quad City Challenger II	T. S. Savage	
G-MYXW	Pegasus Quantum 15	J. Uttley	
G-MYXX	Pegasus Quantum 15	G. Fish	
G-MYXY	CFM Shadow Srs CD	B. P. Cater	
G-MYXZ	Pegasus Quantum 15	A. K. Hole	
G-MYYA	Mainair Blade	D. N. Ward	
G-MYYB	Pegasus Quantum 15	A. L. Johnson & D. S. Ross	
G-MYYC	Pegasus Quantum 15	S. B. Cooper	
G-MYYD	Cyclone Chaser S 447	P. J. Hopkins	
G-MYYF	Quad City Challenger II	J. G. & J. A. Smith	
G-MYYH	Mainair Blade	D. J. Dodd	
G-MYYI	Pegasus Quantum 15	C. M. Day	
G-MYYJ	Hunt Wing	R. M. Jarvis	
G-MYYK	Pegasus Quantum 15	N. Ionita	
G-MYYL	Cyclone AX3/503	R. Ferguson	
G-MYYP	AMF Chevvron 2-45CS	J. Cook	
G-MYYR	TEAM mini-MAX 91	M. A. Field	
G-MYYS	TEAM mini-MAX	G. L. Campbell	
G-MYYV	Rans S.6-ESD Coyote IIXL	J. Rochead	
G-MYYW	Mainair Blade	M. D. Kirby	
G-MYYX	Pegasus Quantum 15	B. J. Chapman	
G-MYYY	Mainair Blade	E. D. Lockie	
G-MYYZ	Medway Raven X	J. W. Leaper	
G-MYZB	Pegasus Quantum 15	M. A. Lovatt	
G-MYZC	Cyclone AX3/503	P. E. Owen	
G-MYZE	TEAM mini-MAX	J. Broome	
G-MYZF	Cyclone AX3/503	Microflight (Ireland) Ltd	
G-MYZG	Cyclone AX3/503	I. A. Holden	
G-MYZH	Chargus Titan 38	T. J. Gayton-Polley	
G-MYZJ	Pegasus Quantum 15	P. A. M. Henderson	
G-MYZK	Pegasus Quantum 15	G. G. Wilson	
G-MYZL	Pegasus Quantum 15	A. D. Jackson	
G-MYZM	Pegasus Quantum 15	J. V. Clewer	
G-MYZP	CFM Shadow Srs DD	A. C. Holmes	
G-MYZR	Rans S.6-ESD Coyote II	Rans Clan	
G-MYZV	Rans S.6-ESD Coyote II	B. W. Savory	

Notes	Reg.	Type	Owner or Operator
	G-MYZY	Pegasus Quantum 15	C. Chapman
	G-MZAA	Mainair Blade	A. G. Butler
	G-MZAB	Mainair Blade	D. Brennan
	G-MZAC	Quad City Challenger II	T. R. Gregory
	G-MZAE	Mainair Blade	A. P. Finn
	G-MZAF	Mainair Blade	P. F. Mayes
	G-MZAG	Mainair Blade	M. J. P. Sanderson
	G-MZAJ	Mainair Blade	M. P. Daley
	G-MZAK	Mainair Mercury	I. Rawson
	G-MZAM	Mainair Blade	G-MZAM Syndicate
	G-MZAN	Pegasus Quantum 15	P. M. Leahy
	G-MZAP	Mainair Blade	K. D. Adams
	G-MZAR	Mainair Blade	P. Bowden
	G-MZAS	Mainair Blade	T. Carter
	G-MZAT	Mainair Blade	M. J. Moulton
	G-MZAU	Mainair Blade	A. F. Glover
	G-MZAV	Mainair Blade	S. M. Clarke
	G-MZAW	Pegasus Quantum 15	C. A. Mackenzie
	G-MZAZ	Mainair Blade	P. J. Pickering
	G-MZBC	Pegasus Quantum 15	B. M. Quinn
	G-MZBD	Rans S-6-ESD-XL Coyote II	J. P. & M. P. Tilzey
	G-MZBF	Letov LK-2M Sluka	V. Simpson
	G-MZBG	Hodder MW6-A	E. I. Rowlands-Jons & M. W. Kilvert
	G-MZBH	Rans S.6-ESD Coyote II	D. Sutherland
	G-MZBK	Letov LK-2M Sluka	R. M. C. Hunter
	G-MZBL	Mainair Blade	C. J. Rubery
	G-MZBN	CFM Shadow Srs B	W. J. Buskell
	G-MZBS	CFM Shadow Srs D	S. K. Ryan
	G-MZBT	Pegasus Quantum 15	A. C. Barlow
	G-MZBU	Rans S.6-ESD Coyote II	R. S. Marriott
	G-MZBV	Rans S.6-ESD Coyote II	R. I. Cannan & C. N. Carine
	G-MZBW	Quad City Challenger II UK	R. M. C. Hunter
	G-MZBY	Pegasus Quantum 15	I. J. Rawlingson
	G-MZBZ	Quad City Challenger II UK	T. R. Gregory
	G-MZCA	Rans S.6-ESD Coyote II	W. Scott
	G-MZCB	Cyclone Chaser S 447	R. W. Keene
	G-MZCC	Mainair Blade 912	K. S. Rissmann
	G-MZCD	Mainair Blade	S. P. Maxwell
	G-MZCE	Mainair Blade	I. C. Hindle
	G-MZCF	Mainair Blade	C. Hannanby
	G-MZCH	Whittaker MW6-S Fatboy Flyer	J. A. Weston
	G-MZCI	Pegasus Quantum 15	P. H. Risdale
	G-MZCJ	Pegasus Quantum 15	C. R. Madden
	G-MZCK	AMF Chevvron 2-32C	M. Daly
	G-MZCM	Pegasus Quantum 15	J. E. Bullock
	G-MZCN	Mainair Blade	A. N. Jones
	G-MZCR	Pegasus Quantum 15	J. E. P. Stubberfield
	G-MZCS	TEAM mini-MAX	J. Aley
	G-MZCT	CFM Shadow Srs CD	W. G. Gill
	G-MZCU	Mainair Blade	C. E. Pearce
	G-MZCV	Pegasus Quantum 15	I. Davidson
	G-MZCW	Pegasus Quantum 15	K. L. Baldwin
	G-MZCX	Huntwing Avon Skytrike	Easter Airfield Microlight Flying Group
	G-MZCY	Pegasus Quantum 15	G. Murphy
	G-MZDA	Rans S.6-ESD Coyote IIXL	R. Plummer
	G-MZDB	Pegasus Quantum 15	Scottish Aerotow Club
	G-MZDC	Pegasus Quantum 15	A. Cordes
	G-MZDD	Pegasus Quantum 15	A. J. Todd
	G-MZDE	Pegasus Quantum 15	R. G. Hedley
	G-MZDF	Mainair Blade	M. Liptrot
	G-MZDG	Rans S.6-ESD Coyote IIXL	P. Coates
	G-MZDH	Pegasus Quantum 15	A. T. Willis
	G-MZDJ	Medway Raven X	R. Bryan & S. Digby
	G-MZDK	Mainair Blade	P. Combellack
	G-MZDL	Whittaker MW6-S Fatboy Flyer	N. Hogarth
	G-MZDM	Rans S.6-ESD Coyote II	M. E. Nicholas
	G-MZDN	Pegasus Quantum 15	P. G. Ford
	G-MZDP	AMF Chevvron 2-32	J. Pool
	G-MZDT	Mainair Blade	G. A. Davidson & I. Lee
	G-MZDU	Pegasus Quantum 15	G. Breen/Portugal

Reg.	Type	Owner or Operator	Notes
G-MZDV	Pegasus Quantum 15	S. A. Mallett	
G-MZDX	Letov LK-2M Sluka	J. L. Barker	
G-MZDY	Pegasus Quantum 15	M. J. King	
G-MZDZ	Hunt Wing	E. W. Laidlaw	
G-MZEA	BFC Challenger II	G. S. Cridland	
G-MZEB	Mainair Blade	R. A. Campbell	
G-MZEC	Pegasus Quantum 15	A. B. Godber	
G-MZEE	Pegasus Quantum 15	J. L. Brogan	
G-MZEG	Mainair Blade	K. Grimley	
G-MZEH	Pegasus Quantum 15	P. S. Hall	
G-MZEJ	Mainair Blade	P. G. Thomas	
G-MZEK	Mainair Mercury	G. Crane	
G-MZEL	Cyclone Airsports AX3/503	L. M. Jackson & R. I. Simpson	
G-MZEM	Pegasus Quantum 15	L. H. Black	
G-MZEN	Rans S.6-ESD Coyote II	P. R. Hutty	
G-MZEO	Rans S.6-ESD Coyote IIXL	A. Higgins	
G-MZEP	Mainair Rapier	A. G. Bird	
G-MZES	Letov LK-2N Sluka	J. L. Self	
G-MZEU	Rans S.6-ESD Coyote IIXL	N. Grugan	
G-MZEV	Mainair Rapier	W. T. Gardner	
G-MZEW	Mainair Blade	T. D. Holder	
G-MZEX	Pegasus Quantum 15	J. P. Quinlan	
G-MZEZ	Pegasus Quantum 15	M. J. Ing	
G-MZFA	Cyclone AX2000	G. S. Highley	
G-MZFB	Mainair Blade	A. J. Plant	
G-MZFC	Letov LK-2M Sluka	F. Overall	
G-MZFD	Mainair Rapier	C. J. Kew	
G-MZFE	Hunt Wing	G. J. Latham	
G-MZFF	Hunt Wing	B. J. Adamson	
G-MZFG	Pegasus Quantum 15	A. M. Prentice	
G-MZFH	AMF Chevvron 2-32C	Eagle Flying Group	
G-MZFL	Rans S.6-ESD Coyote IIXL	H. Adams	
G-MZFM	Pegasus Quantum 15	M. Devlin	
G-MZFN	Rans S.6.ESD Coyote IIXL	C. J. & W. R. Wallbank	
G-MZFO	Thruster T.600N	S. J. P. Stevenson	
G-MZFS	Mainair Blade	P. L. E. Zelazowski	
G-MZFT	Pegasus Quantum 15	C. Childs	
G-MZFU	Thruster T.600N	J. R. Wilkinson	
G-MZFX	Cyclone AX2000	AX Group	
G-MZFY	Rans S.6-ESD Coyote IIXL	L. G. Tserkezos	
G-MZFZ	Mainair Blade	D. J. Bateman	
G-MZGA	Cyclone AX2000	R. D. Leigh	
G-MZGB	Cyclone AX2000	P. Hegarty	
G-MZGC	Cyclone AX2000	C. E. Walls	
G-MZGD	Rans S.5 Coyote II	P. J. Greenrod	
G-MZGF	Letov LK-2M Sluka	G. Lombardi	
G-MZGG	Pegasus Quantum 15	J. Drewe	
G-MZGH	Hunt Wing/Avon 462	J. H. Cole	
G-MZGI	Mainair Blade 912	H. M. Roberts	
G-MZGJ	Kolb Twinstar Mk 1	L. G. G. Faulkner	
G-MZGK	Pegasus Quantum 15	C. D. Cross & S. H. Moss	
G-MZGL	Mainair Rapier	D. Thrower	
G-MZGM	Cyclone AX2000	A. F. Smallacombe	
G-MZGN	Pegasus Quantum 15	B. J. Youngs	
G-MZGO	Pegasus Quantum 15	S. F. G. Allen	
G-MZGP	Cyclone AX2000	Buchan Light Aeroplane Club	
G-MZGR	TEAM mini-MAX	K. G. Seeley	
G-MZGS	CFM Shadow Srs BD	C. S. Nagy	
G-MZGU	Arrowflight Hawk II (UK)	J. N. Holden	
G-MZGV	Pegasus Quantum 15	B. A. & D. K. Janaway	
G-MZGW	Mainair Blade	R. Almond	
G-MZGX	Thruster T.600N	Fen Tiger Flying Group	
G-MZGY	Thruster T.600N 450	S. J. Miles	
G-MZHA	Thruster T.600N	P. Stark	
G-MZHB	Mainair Blade	P. J. Glover	
G-MZHD	Thruster T.600N	B. E. Foster	
G-MZHF	Thruster T.600N	C. Carmichael	
G-MZHG	Whittaker MW6-T Merlin	D. R. Thompson	
G-MZHI	Pegasus Quantum 15	F. R. Macdonald	
G-MZHJ	Mainair Rapier	G. Standish & R. Jones	
G-MZHK	Pegasus Quantum 15	R. Hussain	

BRITISH CIVIL REGISTRATIONS

Notes	Reg.	Type	Owner or Operator
	G-MZHM	Team Himax 1700R	M. H. McKeown
	G-MZHN	Pegasus Quantum 15	F. W. Ferichs
	G-MZHO	Quad City Challenger II	J. Pavelin
	G-MZHP	Pegasus Quantum 15	W. J. Flood
	G-MZHR	Cyclone AX2000	D. K. Wedge
	G-MZHS	Thruster T.600T	J. R. Davis
	G-MZHT	Whittaker MW6 Merlin	G. J. Chadwick
	G-MZHV	Thruster T.600T	H. G. Denton
	G-MZHW	Thruster T.600N	A. J. Glynn
	G-MZHY	Thruster T.600N	B. W. Webster
	G-MZIB	Pegasus Quantum 15	S. Murphy
	G-MZID	Whittaker MW6 Merlin	C. P. F. Sheppard
	G-MZIE	Pegasus Quantum 15	Flylight Airsports Ltd
	G-MZIF	Pegasus Quantum 15	D. Parsons
	G-MZIH	Mainair Blade	N. J. Waller
	G-MZIJ	Pegasus Quantum 15	D. L. Wright
	G-MZIK	Pegasus Quantum 15	C. M. Wilkinson
	G-MZIL	Mainair Rapier	A. J. Owen & J. C. Price
	G-MZIM	Mainair Rapier	M. J. McKegney
	G-MZIR	Mainair Blade	S. Connor
	G-MZIS	Mainair Blade	M. K. Richings
	G-MZIT	Mainair Blade 912	P. M. Horn
	G-MZIU	Pegasus Quantum 15-912	A. P. Douglas-Dixon
	G-MZIV	Cyclone AX2000	A. I. Rotaru
	G-MZIW	Mainair Blade	S. R. Pickering
	G-MZIY	Rans S.6-ESD Coyote II	G. Munro
	G-MZIZ	Renegade Spirit UK (G-MWGP)	B. L. R. J. Keeping
	G-MZJA	Mainair Blade	P. L. Dowd
	G-MZJD	Mainair Blade	M. Howard
	G-MZJE	Mainair Rapier	G. Ramsay & G. Shand
	G-MZJF	Cyclone AX2000	D. J. Lewis & V. E. Booth
	G-MZJG	Pegasus Quantum 15	K. M. C. Compton
	G-MZJH	Pegasus Quantum 15	P. Copping
	G-MZJJ	Murphy Maverick	M. F. Farrer
	G-MZJK	Mainair Blade	P. G. Angus
	G-MZJL	Cyclone AX2000	M. H. Owen
	G-MZJM	Rans S.6-ESD Coyote IIXL	K. A. Hastie
	G-MZJO	Pegasus Quantum 15	D. J. Cook
	G-MZJP	Whittaker MW6-S Fatboy Flyer	R. C. Funnell & D. J. Burton
	G-MZJR	Cyclone AX2000	N. A. Martin
	G-MZJT	Pegasus Quantum 15	N. Hammerton
	G-MZJV	Mainair Blade 912	M. A. Roberts
	G-MZJW	Pegasus Quantum 15	M. J. J. Clutterbuck
	G-MZJX	Mainair Blade	N. Cowell & D. Nicholls
	G-MZJY	Pegasus Quantum 15	D. C. Peto
	G-MZJZ	Mainair Blade	I. J. Richardson
	G-MZKA	Pegasus Quantum 15	S. P. Tkaczyk
	G-MZKC	Cyclone AX2000	D. J. Pike
	G-MZKD	Pegasus Quantum 15	T. M. Frost
	G-MZKE	Rans S.6-ESD Coyote IIXL	P. A. Flaherty
	G-MZKF	Pegasus Quantum 15	R. E. J. Pattenden
	G-MZKG	Mainair Blade	N. S. Rigby
	G-MZKH	CFM Shadow Srs DD	S. P. H. Calvert
	G-MZKI	Mainair Rapier	D. L. Aspinall
	G-MZKJ	Mainair Blade	The G-MZKJ Group
	G-MZKL	Pegasus Quantum 15	G. Williams
	G-MZKN	Mainair Rapier	O. P. Farrell
	G-MZKR	Thruster T.600N	R. J. Arnett
	G-MZKS	Thruster T.600N	P. J. Hepburn
	G-MZKT	Thruster T.600N	Great Thornes Flying Group
	G-MZKU	Thruster T.600N	A. S. Day
	G-MZKV	Mainair Blade 912	J. D. Harriman
	G-MZKW	Quad City Challenger II	K. W. Warn
	G-MZKY	Pegasus Quantum 15	P. S. Constable
	G-MZKZ	Mainair Blade	R. P. Wolstenholme
	G-MZLA	Pegasus Quantum 15	S. P. McVeigh
	G-MZLC	Mainair Blade 912	N. R. Pettigrew
	G-MZLD	Pegasus Quantum 15	D. Hamilton
	G-MZLE	Maverick (G-BXSZ)	J. S. Hill
	G-MZLF	Pegasus Quantum 15	S. Seymour
	G-MZLG	Rans S.6-ESD Coyote IIXL	F. Y. Allery

Reg.	Type	Owner or Operator	Notes
G-MZLI	Mignet HM.1000 Balerit	A. G. Barr	
G-MZLJ	Pegasus Quantum 15	R. M. Williams	
G-MZLL	Rans S.6-ESD Coyote II	J. A. Willats & G. W. Champion	
G-MZLM	Cyclone AX2000	P. E. Hadley	
G-MZLN	Pegasus Quantum 15	P. A. Greening	
G-MZLP	CFM Shadow Srs D	D. J. Gordon	
G-MZLR	Solar Wings Pegasus XL-Q	B. Lorraine	
G-MZLT	Pegasus Quantum 15	B. Jackson	
G-MZLV	Pegasus Quantum 15	A. Armsby	
G-MZLW	Pegasus Quantum 15	R. W. R. Crevel & D. P. Hampson	
G-MZLX	Micro Aviation B.22S Bantam	V. J. Vaughan	
G-MZLY	Letov LK-2M Sluka	W. McCarthy	
G-MZLZ	Mainair Blade	W. Biddulph	
G-MZMA	Solar Wings Pegasus Quasar IITC	M. L. Pardoe	
G-MZMC	Pegasus Quantum 15	J. J. Baker	
G-MZME	Medway Eclipser	P. A. Wenham	
G-MZMF	Pegasus Quantum 15	A. J. Tranter	
G-MZMG	Pegasus Quantum 15	A. G. Kemp	
G-MZMH	Pegasus Quantum 15	L. Hogan & W. Gray	
G-MZMJ	Mainair Blade	D. Wilson	
G-MZMK	Chevvron 2-32C	A. J. Doyle	
G-MZML	Mainair Blade 912	T. C. Edwards	
G-MZMM	Mainair Blade 912	J. Lynch	
G-MZMN	Pegasus Quantum 912	R. H. Cheesley	
G-MZMO	TEAM mini-MAX 91	I. Whetton	
G-MZMT	Pegasus Quantum 15	J. A. Davies	
G-MZMU	Rans S.6-ESD Coyote II	P. F. Berry & T. D. Wood	
G-MZMV	Mainair Blade	P. B. Smith	
G-MZMW	Mignet HM.1000 Balerit	M. E. Whapham	
G-MZMX	Cyclone AX2000	L. A. Lacy	
G-MZMY	Mainair Blade	C. J. Millership	
G-MZMZ	Mainair Blade	W. A. Stacey	
G-MZNA	Quad City Challenger II UK	S. Hennessy	
G-MZNB	Pegasus Quantum 15	F. Gorse	
G-MZNC	Mainair Blade 912	A. J. Harrison	
G-MZND	Mainair Rapier	D. W. Stamp	
G-MZNG	Pegasus Quantum 15	The Scottish Flying Club	
G-MZNH	CFM Shadow Srs DD	P. A. James	
G-MZNJ	Mainair Blade	R. A. Hardy	
G-MZNM	TEAM mini-MAX	S. M. Williams	
G-MZNN	TEAM mini-MAX	P. J. Bishop	
G-MZNO	Mainair Blade	P. J. Lomax	
G-MZNR	Pegasus Quantum 15	E. S. Wills	
G-MZNS	Pegasus Quantum 15	S. Uzochukwu	
G-MZNT	Pegasus Quantum 15-912	N. W. Barnett	
G-MZNU	Mainair Rapier	B. Johnson	
G-MZNV	Rans S.6-ESD Coyote II	A. P. Thomas	
G-MZNX	Thruster T.600N	B. Rogan	
G-MZNY	Thruster T.600N	G. Price	
G-MZNZ	Letov LK-2M Sluka	B. F. Crick	
G-MZOC	Mainair Blade	A. S. Davies	
G-MZOD	Pegasus Quantum 15	E. Schoonbrood	
G-MZOE	Cyclone AX2000	G-MZOE Flying Group	
G-MZOF	Mainair Blade	R. M. Ellis	
G-MZOG	Pegasus Quantum 15-912	D. Smith	
G-MZOH	Whittaker MW5D Sorcerer	I. Pearson	
G-MZOI	Letov LK-2M Sluka	E. Bentley	
G-MZOJ	Pegasus Quantum 15	G. P. Church	
G-MZOK	Whittaker MW6 Merlin	G-MZOK Syndicate	
G-MZOP	Mainair Blade 912	K. M. Thorogood	
G-MZOS	Pegasus Quantum 15-912	J. R. Moore	
G-MZOV	Pegasus Quantum 15	Pegasus XL Group	
G-MZOW	Pegasus Quantum 15-912	G. P. Burns	
G-MZOX	Letov LK-2M Sluka	D. L. Hadley	
G-MZOY	TEAM Mini-MAX 91	P. R. & S. E. Whitehouse	
G-MZOZ	Rans S.6-ESD Coyote IIXL	S. G. & D. C. Emmons	
G-MZPH	Mainair Blade	Chilbolton Flexwing Syndicate	
G-MZPJ	TEAM mini-MAX	S. I. Hatherall	
G-MZPW	Pegasus Quasar IITC	R. J. Coppin	
G-MZRC	Pegasus Quantum 15	M. Hopkins	
G-MZRM	Pegasus Quantum 15	R. Milwain	

Notes	Reg.	Type	Owner or Operator
	G-MZRS	CFM Shadow Srs CD	R. Barton
	G-MZTS	Aerial Arts Chaser S	D. G. Ellis (G-MVDM)
	G-MZUB	Rans S.6-ESD Coyote IIXL	R. E. Main
	G-MZZT	Kolb Twinstar Mk 3	D. E. Martin
	G-MZZY	Mainair Blade 912	A. Mucznik
	G-NAAL	Bombardier CL600-2B16 Challenger	Maleth-Aero AOC Ltd
	G-NACA	Norman NAC-2 Freelance 180	A. R. Norman
	G-NACI	Norman NAC-1 Srs 100	L. J. Martin (G-AXFB)
	G-NACL	Norman NAC-6 Fieldmaster	EPA Aircraft Co Ltd (G-BNEG)
	G-NACO	Norman NAC-6 Fieldmaster	EPA Aircraft Co Ltd
	G-NACP	Norman NAC-6 Fieldmaster	EPA Aircraft Co Ltd
	G-NADO	Titan Tornado SS	Euro Aviation LLP
	G-NADS	TEAM mini-MAX 91	R. L. Williams
	G-NADZ	Van's RV-4	R. A. Pritchard (G-BROP)
	G-NAGG	Rotorsport UK MT-03	C. A. Clements
	G-NALA	Cessna 172S	NAL Asset Management Ltd (G-GFEA/G-CEDY)
	G-NANI	Robinson R44 II	MOS Gmbh
	G-NANO	Avid Speed Wing	T. M. C. Handley
	G-NAPO	Pegasus Quantum 15-912	J. M. Brigham
	G-NAPP	Van's RV-7	R. C. Meek
	G-NARG	Tanarg/Ixess 15 912S (1)	K. Kirby
	G-NARO	Cassutt Racer	C. Ball & R. Supply (G-BTXR)
	G-NARR	Stolp SA300 Starduster Too	G. J. D. Thomson
	G-NATI	Corby CJ-1 Starlet	S. P. Evans
	G-NATT	Rockwell Commander 114A	Northgleam Ltd
	G-NATY	HS. Gnat T.1 (XR537) ★	DS Aviation (UK) Ltd
	G-NBDD	Robin DR.400/180	B. & S. E. Chambers
	G-NBEL	AS.355F1 Ecureuil 2	Latitude Aviation Ltd (G-SKYW/G-TBIS/G-TALI)
	G-NBSI	Cameron N-77 balloon	Nottingham Hot-Air Balloon Club
	G-NCCC	Bombardier CL600-2B16	TAG Aviation (UK) Ltd
	G-NCFC	PA-38-112 Tomahawk II	A. M. Heynen
	G-NCUB	Piper J-3C-65 Cub	R. J. Willies (G-BGXV)
	G-NDAA	MBB Bö.105DBS-4	Bond Air Services Ltd (G-WMAA/G-PASB/G-BDMC)
	G-NDAD	Medway SLA100 Executive	K. Angel
	G-NDOL	Europa	S. Longstaff
	G-NDOT	Thruster T.600N	P. C. Bailey
	G-NDPA	Ikarus C42 FB UK	Grandpa's Flying Group
	G-NEAL	PA-32-260 Cherokee Six	I. Parkinson (G-BFPY)
	G-NEAT	Europa	P. F. D. Foden
	G-NEAU	Eurocopter EC 135T2	Police & Crime Commissioner for West Yorkshire
	G-NEDS	Skyranger Nynja 912S(1)	H. Van Allen
	G-NEEL	Rotorway Executive 90	I. C. Bedford
	G-NEIL	Thunder Ax3 balloon	R. M. Powell
	G-NELI	PA-28R Cherokee Arrow 180	MK Aero Support Ltd
	G-NEMO	Raj Hamsa X'Air Jabiru (4)	G. F. Allen
	G-NEON	PA-32 Cherokee Six 300B	P. J. P. Coutney
	G-NEPB	Cameron N-77 balloon	The Post Office
	G-NESA	Shaw Europa XS	A. M. Kay
	G-NESE	Tecnam P2002-JF	N. & S. Easton
	G-NESH	Robinson R44 II	M. Tancock
	G-NEST	Christen Eagle II	P. J. Nonat
	G-NESV	Eurocopter EC 135T1	Eurocopter UK Ltd
	G-NESW	PA-34-220T Seneca III	G. C. U. Guida
	G-NESY	PA-18 Super Cub 95	V. Featherstone
	G-NETR	AS.355F1 Twin Squirrel	PLM Dollar Group Ltd (G-JARV/G-OGHL)
	G-NETT	Cessna 172S	Aero-Club Rhein-Nahe EV
	G-NETY	PA-18 Super Cub 150	N. B. Mason
	G-NEWT	Beech 35 Bonanza	J. S. Allison (G-APVW)
	G-NEWZ	Bell 206B JetRanger 3	Guay Tulliemet Aviation Ltd
	G-NFLA	BAe Jetstream 3102	Cranfield University (G-BRGN/G-BLHC)
	G-NFLC	HP.137 Jetstream 1H (G-AXUI) ★	Instructional airframe/Perth
	G-NFLY	Tecnam P2002-EA Sierra	C. N. Hodgson
	G-NFNF	Robin DR.400/180	M. Child, W. Cobb & J. Archer
	G-NFON	Van's RV-8	N. F. O'Neill

Reg.	Type	Owner or Operator	Notes
G-NGLS	Aerospool Dynamic WT9 UK	The Nigels Ltd	
G-NHAA	AS.365N-2 Dauphin 2	The Great North Air Ambulance Service (G-MLTY)	
G-NHAB	AS.365N-2 Dauphin 2	The Great North Air Ambulance Service (G-DAUF)	
G-NHAC	AS.365N-2 Dauphin 2	The Great North Air Ambulance Service	
G-NHRH	PA-28 Cherokee 140	C. J. Milsom	
G-NHRJ	Shaw Europa XS	D. A. Lowe	
G-NICC	Aerotechnik EV-97 Team Eurostar UK	Pickup and Son Ltd	
G-NICI	Robinson R44	David Fishwick Vehicles Sales Ltd	
G-NICK	PA-18 Super Cub	M. W. Zipfell	
G-NICS	Best Off Sky Ranger Swift 912S(1)	I. A. Forrest & C. K. Richardson	
G-NIDG	Aerotechnik EV-97 Eurostar	Skydrive Ltd	
G-NIEN	Van's RV-9A	NIEN Group	
G-NIFE	SNCAN Stampe SV.4A (156)	Tiger Airways	
G-NIGC	Avtech Jabiru UL-450	C. K. Fry	
G-NIGE	Luscombe 8E Silvaire	Garden Party Ltd (G-BSHG)	
G-NIGL	Shaw Europa	N. M. Graham	
G-NIGS	Thunder Ax7-65 balloon	S. D. Annett	
G-NIKE	PA-28-181 Archer II	Key Properties Ltd	
G-NIKK	Diamond Katana DA20-C1	Cubair Flight Training Ltd	
G-NIKO	Airbus A.321-211	Thomas Cook Airlines Ltd	
G-NIKS	Aeropro Eurofox 912(1)	N. G. Heywood	
G-NIKX	Robinson R-44 II	P. R. Holloway	
G-NIMA	Balóny Kubíček BB30Z balloon	C. Williamson	
G-NIMB	Schempp-Hirth Nimbus 2C	G. S. S. Rizk	
G-NIME	Cessna T.206H Turbo Stationair	Whitby Seafoods Ltd	
G-NINA	PA-28-161 Warrior II	A. P. Gorrod (G-BEUC)	
G-NINC	PA-28-180 Cherokee	Flintshire Flying School Ltd	
G-NIND	PA-28-180 Cherokee	Aquarelle Investments Ltd	
G-NINE	Murphy Renegade 912	R. C. McCarthy	
G-NIOG	Robinson R44 II	Helicopter Sharing Ltd	
G-NIOS	PA-32R-301 Saratoga SP	Plant Aviation	
G-NIPA	Slingsby T.66 Nipper 3	R. J. O. Walker (G-AWDD)	
G-NIPL	Eurocopter AS.350B3 Ecureuil	Pacific Helicopters Ltd	
G-NIPP	Slingsby T.66 Nipper 3	R. J. Porter (G-AVKJ)	
G-NIPR	Slingsby T.66 Nipper 3	P. A. Gibbs (G-AVXC)	
G-NIPS	Tipsy T.66 Nipper 2	B. W. Faulkner	
G-NIPY	Hughes 369HS	Jet Aviation (Northwest) Ltd	
G-NISA	Robinson R44 II	G. P. Jones (G-HTMT)	
G-NISH	Van's RV-8	N. H. F. Hampton & S. R. Whitling	
G-NITA	PA-28 Cherokee 180	T. Clifford (G-AVVG)	
G-NIVA	Eurocopter EC 155B1	Lanthwaite Aviation Ltd	
G-NIXX	Best Off Skyranger 912(1)	N. A. Thomas (G-CDYJ)	
G-NJBA	Rotorway Executive 162F	British Waterproofing Ltd	
G-NJET	Schempp-Hirth Ventus cT	V. S. Bettle	
G-NJPG	Best Off Skyranger Nynja 912S(1)	P. Gibbs	
G-NJPW	P & M Quik GT450	N. J. P. West	
G-NJSH	Robinson R22 Beta	ATN Farms	
G-NJSP	Jabiru J430	N. J. S. Pitman	
G-NJTC	Aeroprakt A22-L Foxbat	B. Jackson & T. F. Casey	
G-NLCH	Lindstrand LBL-35A balloon	S. A. Lacey	
G-NLDR	AS.355F2 Ecureuil 2	PDG Helicopters (G-PDGS)	
G-NLEE	Cessna 182Q	C. G. D. Jones (G-TLTD)	
G-NLMB	Zenair CH.601UL Zodiac	N. Lamb	
G-NLPA	Hawker 750	Hangar 8 Management Ltd	
G-NLSE	AS.355F2 Ecureuil 2	PLM Dollar Group Ltd (G-ULES/G-OBHL/ G-HARO/G-DAFT/G-BNNN)	
G-NLYB	Cameron N-105 balloon	P. H. E. Van Overwalle/Belgium	
G-NMAK	Airbus A.319-115	Twinjet Aircraft Sales Ltd	
G-NMBG	Jabiru J400	P. R. Hendry-Smith & H. I. Smith	
G-NMCL	Eurofox 912(S)	N. R. McLeod	
G-NMID	Eurocopter EC 135T2	Police & Crime Commissioner for West Yorkshire	
G-NMOS	Cameron C-80 balloon	C. J. Thomas & M. C. East	
G-NMRV	Van's RV-6	R. L. N. & S. C. Lucey	

Notes	Reg.	Type	Owner or Operator
	G-NNAC	PA-18 Super Cub 135	PAW Flying Services Ltd
	G-NNON	Mainair Blade	D. R. Kennedy
	G-NOAH	Airbus A.319-115CJ	Acropolis Aviation Ltd
	G-NOCK	Cessna FR.182RG II	M. K. Aves (G-BGTK)
	G-NODE	AA-5B Tiger	Ultranomad Sro
	G-NOIL	BN-2A-26 Islander	Diamond Executive Aviation Ltd (G-BJWO/ G-BAXC)
	G-NOMO	Cameron O-31 balloon	Balloon Promotion SAS/Italy
	G-NOMZ	Balony Kubicek BB-S Gnome SS balloon	A. M. Holly
	G-NONE	Dyn'Aéro MCR-01 ULC	M. A. Collins
	G-NONI	AA-5 Traveler	November India Group (G-BBDA)
	G-NOOR	Commander 114B	As-Al Ltd
	G-NORA	Ikarus C.42 FB UK	N. A. Rathbone
	G-NORB	Saturne S110K hang glider	R. N. Pearce
	G-NORD	SNCAN NC.854	A. D. Pearce
	G-NORK	Bell 206B-3 JetRanger III	R. S. Forsyth
	G-NOSE	Cessna 402B	Reconnaissance Ventures Ltd (G-MPCU)
	G-NOTE	PA-28-181 Archer III	J. Beach
	G-NOTS	Skyranger 912S(1)	S. F. N. Warnell
	G-NOTT	Nott ULD-2 balloon	J. R. P. Nott
	G-NOUS	Cessna 172S	Flyglass Ltd
	G-NOWW	Mainair Blade 912	R. S. Sanby
	G-NOXY	Robinson R44	S. A. Knox (G-VALV)
	G-NOYA	Gulfstream 550	TAG Aviation (UK) LTD
	G-NPKJ	Van's RV-6	M. R. Turner
	G-NPPL	Comco Ikarus C.42 FB.100	Papa Lima Group
	G-NREG	Bombardier CL600-2B16 Challenger	Skymiddleeast UK Ltd
	G-NRFK	Van's RV-8	C. N. Harper & P. G. Peal
	G-NRIA	Beech 23 Musketeer	Respondmatte Flugeliclub
	G-NRMA	Dan Rihn DR.107 One Design	A. W. Brown
	G-NROY	PA-32RT-300 Lance II	B. Nedjati-Gilani (G-LYNN/G-BGNY)
	G-NRRA	SIAI-Marchetti SF.260 ★	G. Boot
	G-NSBB	Ikarus C.42 FB-100 VLA	M. Pratt
	G-NSEW	Robinson R44	G-NSEW Ltd
	G-NSKB	Aeroprakt A22-L Foxbat	N. F. Smith
	G-NSOF	Robin HR.200/120B	Grosvenor Aircraft Ltd
	G-NSTG	Cessna F.150F	Westair Flying Services Ltd (G-ATNI)
	G-NTVE	Beagle A-61 Terrier 3	R. E. Dagless (G-ASIE)
	G-NTWK	AS.355F2 Twin Squirrel	PLM Dollar Group (G-FTWO/G-OJOR/G-BMUS)
	G-NUDE	Robinson R44	The Last Great Journey Ltd (G-NSYT)
	G-NUFC	Best Off Skyranger 912S(1)	C. R. Rosby
	G-NUGC	Grob G.103A Twin II Acro	The University of Nottingham Students Union
	G-NUKA	PA-28-181 Archer II	N. Ibrahim
	G-NULA	Flight Design CT2K	L. I. Bailey
	G-NUNI	Lindstrand LBL-77A balloon	The University of Nottingham
	G-NUTA	Christen Eagle II	C. Butler & G. G. Ferriman
	G-NUTT	Mainair Pegasus Quik	NUTT Syndicate
	G-NVBF	Lindstrand LBL-210A balloon	Virgin Balloon Flights
	G-NWAA	Eurocopter EC.135T2	Bond Air Services Ltd
	G-NWAE	Eurocopter EC.135T2	Bond Air Services Ltd (G-DAAT)
	G-NWFA	Cessna 150M	North Weald Flying Group Ltd (G-CFBD)
	G-NWFC	Cessna 172P	North Weald Flying Group Ltd
	G-NWFG	Cessna 172P	North Weald Flying Group Ltd
	G-NWFS	Cessna 172P	North Weald Flying Group Ltd (G-TYMS)
	G-NWFT	Cessna F.172N	North Weald Flying Group Ltd (G-BURD)
	G-NWOI	Eurocopter EC135 P2+	Police & Crime Commissioner for West Yorkshire
	G-NWPR	Cameron N-77 balloon	D. B. Court
	G-NWPS	Eurocopter EC 135T1	Veritair Aviation Ltd
	G-NXOE	Cessna 172S	Goodwood Road Racing Co.Ltd
	G-NXUS	Nexus Mustang	G. W. Miller
	G-NYKS	Cessna 182T	N. B. Le-Grys

Reg.	Type	Owner or Operator	Notes
G-NYMB	Schempp-Hirth Nimbus 3	Nimbus Syndicate	
G-NYMF	PA-25 Pawnee 235D	Bristol Gliding Club Pty Ltd	
G-NYNA	Van's RV-9A	B. Greathead & S. Hiscox	
G-NYNE	Schleicher ASW-27-18E	R. C. W. Ellis	
G-NYNJ	Best Off Skyranger Nynja 912S)1)	N. J. Sutherland	
G-NZGL	Cameron O-105 balloon	R. A. Vale & ptnrs	
G-NZSS	Boeing Stearman N2S-5 (343251:27)	R. W. Davies	
G-OAAA	PA-28-161 Warrior II	Red Hill Air Services Ltd	
G-OAAF	BAe ATP	PTB (Emerald) Pty.Ltd (G-JEMB)	
G-OAAM	Cameron C-90 balloon	A. M. Holly	
G-OABB	Jodel D.150	K. Manley	
G-OABC	Colt 69A balloon	P. A. C. Stuart-Kregor	
G-OABO	Enstrom F-28A	C. R. Taylor (G-BAIB)	
G-OABR	AG-5B Tiger	A. J. Neale	
G-OACA	PA-44-180 Seminole	H. Merkado (G-GSFT)	
G-OACE	Valentin Taifun 17E	I. F. Wells	
G-OACF	Robin DR.400/180	A. C. Fletcher	
G-OACI	MS.893E Rallye 180GT	Full Sutton Flying Centre Ltd	
G-OADY	Beech 76 Duchess	Multiflight Ltd	
G-OAGA	Eurocopter EC.225LP Super Puma	CHC Scotia Ltd	
G-OAER	Lindstrand LBL-105A balloon	M. P. Rowley	
G-OAFF	Cessna 208 Caravan 1	Army Parachute Association	
G-OAFR	Cameron Z-105 balloon	PSH Skypower Ltd	
G-OAGB	Agusta Westland AW.139	CHC Scotia Ltd	
G-OAGC	Eurocopter EC.225LP Super Puma	CHC Scotia Ltd	
G-OAGI	FLS Aerospace Sprint 160	A. L. Breckell (G-FLSI)	
G-OAGL	Bell 206B JetRanger 3	Ridgway Aviation Ltd (G-CORN/G-BHTR)	
G-OAHC	Beech F33C Bonanza	Cirrus Aviation Ltd (G-BTTF)	
G-OAJC	Robinson R44	Adare International Transport Ltd	
G-OAJL	Ikarus C.42 FB100	G. D. M. McCullogh	
G-OAJS	PA-39 Twin Comanche 160 C/R	S. Vansteenkiste (G-BCIO)	
G-OALD	SOCATA TB20 Trinidad	Gold Aviation	
G-OALH	Tecnam P92-EA Echo	K. D. Pearce	
G-OAMF	Pegasus Quantum 15-912	G. A. Viquerat	
G-OAMI	Bell 206B JetRanger 2	Leamington Hobby Centre Ltd (G-BAUN)	
G-OAML	Cameron AML-105 balloon	Stratton Motor Co (Norfolk) Ltd	
G-OAMP	Cessna F.177RG	P. Denegre (G-AYPF)	
G-OANI	PA-28-161 Warrior II	J. F. Mitchell	
G-OANN	Zenair CH.601HD	Zodiac Group Mona	
G-OAPR	Brantly B.2B	Helicopter International Magazine	
G-OAPW	Glaser-Dirks DG.400	P. L. Poole	
G-OARA	PA-28R-201 Arrow III	Obmit Ltd	
G-OARC	PA-28RT-201 Arrow IV	J. E. Bray (G-BMVE)	
G-OARI	PA-28R-201 Arrow III	Flew LLP	
G-OARO	PA-28R-201 Arrow III	Booker Aircraft Leasing Ltd	
G-OARS	Cessna 172S	Air-Unlimited Sweden AB/Sweden	
G-OART	PA-23 Aztec 250D	Prescribing Services Ltd (G-AXKD)	
G-OARU	PA-28R-201 Arrow III	S. J. Green	
G-OARV	ARV Super 2	I. F. Davidson	
G-OASA	Flight Design CTSW	O. EW. & S. M. Achurch (G-CGHE)	
G-OASH	Robinson R22 Beta	J. C. Lane	
G-OASJ	Thruster T.600N 450	T. Harrison-Smith	
G-OASP	AS.355F2 Twin Squirrel	Helicopter Services Ltd	
G-OASW	Schleicher ASW-27	M. P. W. Mee	
G-OATE	Mainair Pegasus Quantum 15-912	A. Roberts	
G-OATV	Cameron V-77 balloon	A. W. & E. P. Braund-Smith	
G-OAUD	Robinson R44	A. Giles (G-CDHV)	
G-OATZ	Van's RV-12	J. Jones & J. W. Armstrong	
G-OAVA	Robinson R22 Beta	Phoenix Helicopter Academy Ltd	
G-OAWL	Agusta AW.139	Profred Partners LLP	
G-OAWS	Colt 77A balloon	P. Lawman	
G-OBAB	Lindstrand LBL-35A Cloudhopper balloon	B. A. Bower	
G-OBAK	PA-28R-201T Turbo Arrow III	G-OBAK Group Aviation	
G-OBAL	Mooney M.20J	G-OBAL Group	
G-OBAN	Jodel D.140B	S. R. Cameron (G-ATSU)	
G-OBAX	Thruster T.600N 450-JAB	G. B. Denton	
G-OBAZ	Best Off Skyranger 912(2)	B. J. Marsh	

Notes	Reg.	Type	Owner or Operator
	G-OBBO	Cessna 182S	A. E. Kedros
	G-OBDA	Diamond Katana DA20-A1	Oscar Papa Ltd
	G-OBDN	PA-28-161 Warrior II	R. M. Bennett
	G-OBEE	Boeing Stearman A75N-1 (3397:174)	P. G. Smith
	G-OBEI	SOCATA TB200 Tobago XL	K. Stoter
	G-OBEN	Cessna 152 II	Globibussola Lda (G-NALI/G-BHVM)
	G-OBET	Sky 77-24 balloon	P. M. Watkins & S. M. Carden
	G-OBFE	Sky 120-24 balloon	J. Sonnabend
	G-OBFS	PA-28-161 Warrior III	Claris Aviation Ltd
	G-OBIB	Colt 120A balloon	M. B. Vennard
	G-OBIL	Robinson R22 Beta	Helicopter Services Ltd
	G-OBIO	Robinson R22 Beta	Burbage Farms Ltd
	G-OBJB	Lindstrand LBL-90A balloon	B. J. Bower
	G-OBJH	Colt 77A balloon	Hayrick Ltd
	G-OBJM	Taylor JT.1 Monoplane	R. K. Thomas
	G-OBJP	Pegasus Quantum 15-912	G. I. Somers
	G-OBJT	Shaw Europa	A. Burill (G-MUZO)
	G-OBLC	Beech 76 Duchess	Pridenote Ltd
	G-OBLU	Cameron H-34 balloon	John Aimo Balloons SAS/Italy
	G-OBMI	Mainair Blade	S. R. Kirkham & D. F. Reeves
	G-OBMP	Boeing 737-3Q8	KLM UK Engineering Ltd
	G-OBMS	Cessna F.172N	Mike Sierra Group
	G-OBNA	PA-34-220T Seneca V	Palmair Ltd
	G-OBNC	BN-2B-20 Islander	Britten-Norman Aircraft Ltd
	G-OBOF	Remos GX	D. Hawkins
	G-OBPP	Schleicher ASG-29E	M. H. Patel
	G-OBRO	Alpi Pioneer 200M	A. Brown
	G-OBRY	Cameron N-180 balloon	A. C. K. Rawson & J. J. Rudoni
	G-OBSM	Robinson R44 Raven	Patriot Aviation Ltd (G-CDSE)
	G-OBSR	Partenavia P68	Ravenair Aircraft Ltd
	G-OBTS	Cameron C-90 balloon	D. G. Such
	G-OBUP	DG Flugzeugbau DG-808C	R. A. Roberts
	G-OBUU	Replica Comper CLA Swift	J. A. Pothecary & R. H. Hunt
	G-OBUY	Colt 69A balloon	T. G. Read
	G-OBUZ	Van's RV-6	A. F. Hall
	G-OBWP	BAe ATP	European Turboprop Management AB (G-BTPO)
	G-OBYF	Boeing 767-304ER	Thomsonfly Ltd
	G-OBYG	Boeing 767-3Q8ER	Thomsonfly Ltd
	G-OBYH	Boeing 767-304ER	Thomsonfly Ltd
	G-OBYT	Agusta-Bell 206A JetRanger	R. J. Everett (G-BNRC)
	G-OBZR	Aerostyle Breezer LSA	D. Curtin & S. Greenall
	G-OCAC	Robin R-2112	The Cotswold Aero Club Ltd (G-EWHT)
	G-OCAD	Sequoia F.8L Falco	D. R. Vale
	G-OCAM	AA-5A Cheetah	R. E. Dagless (G-BLHO)
	G-OCBI	Schweizer 269C-1	Alpha Properties (London) Ltd
	G-OCBT	IDA Bacau Yakovlev Yak-52	Cambridge Business Travel
	G-OCCF	Diamond DA40D Star	Flying Time Ltd
	G-OCCG	Diamond DA40D Star	Flying Time Ltd
	G-OCCH	Diamond DA40D Star	Innovative Aviation (Leeds) Ltd
	G-OCCK	Diamond DA40D Star	Westbeach Aviation Ltd
	G-OCCL	Diamond DA40D Star	Westbeach Aviation Ltd
	G-OCCN	Diamond DA40D Star	Flying Time Ltd
	G-OCCU	Diamond DA40D Star	Chalrey Ltd
	G-OCCX	Diamond DA42 Twin Star	Westbeach Aviation Ltd
	G-OCDC	Best Off Sky Ranger Nynja 912S(1)	C. D. Church
	G-OCDP	Flight Design CTSW	M. A. Beadman
	G-OCDW	Jabiru UL-450	H. T. Willingham
	G-OCEG	Beech B.200 Super King Air	Cega Aviation Ambulance UK Ltd.
	G-OCFC	Robin R.2160	Cornwall Flying Club Ltd
	G-OCFD	Bell 206B JetRanger 3	Rushmere Helicopters LLP (G-WGAL/G-OICS)
	G-OCFM	PA-34-200 Seneca II	Stapleford Flying Club Ltd (G-ELBC/G-BANS)
	G-OCFT	Bombasrdier CL600-2B16 Challenger	Hangar 8 Management Ltd
	G-OCGC	Robin DR.400-180R	Cambridge Gliding Club Ltd
	G-OCHM	Robinson R44	Westleigh Developments Ltd
	G-OCJZ	Cessna 525A Citationjet CJ2	Centreline Air Charter Ltd
	G-OCLC	Aviat A-1B Husky	U. Heissel
	G-OCLH	Avro RJ-85	Trident Aviation Leasing Services (Jersey) Ltd
	G-OCMM	Agusta A109A II	Castle Air Ltd (G-BXCB/G-ISEB/G-IADT/G-HBCA)
	G-OCMS	EV-97 TeamEurostar UK	C. M. Saysell
	G-OCMT	EV-97 TeamEurostar UK	P. Crowhurst

Reg.	Type	Owner or Operator	Notes
G-OCOD	Bombardier CL600-2B16 Challenger	Hangar 8 Management Ltd	
G-OCOK	American Champion 8KCAB Super Decathlon	L. Levinson	
G-OCOM	Bombardier CL600-2B16 Challenger	TAG Aviation (UK) Ltd (G-PRKR)	
G-OCON	Robinson R44	P. Kelly	
G-OCOV	Robinson R22 Beta	Heli Air Ltd	
G-OCPC	Cessna FA.152	E. & M. O'Toole	
G-OCRI	Colomban MC.15 Cri-Cri	M. J. J. Dunning	
G-OCRL	Europa	R. J. Lewis (G-OBEV)	
G-OCRZ	CZAW Sportcruiser	P. Marsden	
G-OCST	Agusta-Bell 206B JetRanger 3	Lift West Ltd (G-BMKM)	
G-OCTI	PA-32 Cherokee Six 260	D. G. Williams (G-BGZX)	
G-OCTS	Cameron Z-90 balloon	Collett Transport Services Ltd	
G-OCTU	PA-28-161 Cadet	Glenn Aviation Ltd	
G-OCUB	Piper J-3C-90 Cub	Zebedee Flying Group	
G-OCZA	CZAW Sportcruiser	S. M. Dawson	
G-ODAC	Cessna F.152 II	T. M. Jones (G-BITG)	
G-ODAD	Colt 77A balloon	J. H. Dobson	
G-ODAF	Lindstrand LBL-105A balloon	T. J. Horne	
G-ODAK	PA-28-236 Dakota	Flydak LLP	
G-ODAY	Cameron N-56 balloon	British Balloon Museum & Library	
G-ODAZ	Robinson R44 II	S. L. Walton	
G-ODBN	Lindstrand LBL Flowers SS balloon	Magical Adventures Ltd	
G-ODCH	Schleicher ASW-20L	P. J. Stratten	
G-ODCR	Robinson R44 II	D. Lynn	
G-ODDF	Siren PIK-30	G. F. Bailey, J. D. Sorrell & D. M. Thomas	
G-ODDS	Aerotek Pitts S-2A	A. C. Cassidy	
G-ODDY	Lindstrand LBL-105A balloon	P. & T. Huckle	
G-ODDZ	Schempp-Hirth Duo Discus T	P. A. King	
G-ODEB	Cameron A-250 balloon	A. Derbyshire	
G-ODEE	Van's RV-6	D. Cook	
G-ODEL	Falconar F-11-3	G. F. Brummell	
G-ODGS	Avtech Jabiru UL-450	S. R. Eskins	
G-ODHB	Robinson R44	A. J. Mossop	
G-ODHL	Cameron N-77 balloon	DHL International (UK) Ltd	
G-ODIN	Avions Mudry CAP-10B	CAP Ten	
G-ODIZ	AutoGyro Cavalon	P. Williams	
G-ODJD	Raj Hamsa X'Air 582 (7)	S. Richens	
G-ODJF	Lindstrand LBL-90B balloon	Helena Dos Santos SA/Portugal	
G-ODJG	Shaw Europa	K. R. Challis & C. S. Andersson	
G-ODJH	Mooney M.20C	R. M. Schweitzer/Netherlands (G-BMLH)	
G-ODOC	Robinson R44	A. Bristow	
G-ODOG	PA-28R Cherokee Arrow 200-II	M. Brancart (G-BAAR)	
G-ODPJ	VPM M-16 Tandem Trainer	K. J. Robinson & S. Palmer (G-BVWX)	
G-ODRD	PA-32R-301T Saratoga II	Interceptor Properties Ltd	
G-ODRT	Cameron Z-105 balloon	N. W. N. Townshend	
G-ODSA	Bell 429	Starspeed Ltd	
G-ODTW	Shaw Europa	D. T. Walters	
G-ODUD	PA-28-181 Archer II	S. Barlow, R. N. Ingle & R. J. Murray (G-IBBO)	
G-ODUO	Schempp-Hirth Duo Discus	3D Syndicate	
G-ODUR	Raytheon Hawker 900XP	Hangar 8 Ltd	
G-ODVB	CFM Shadow Srs DD	L. J. E. Moss	
G-ODWS	Silence Twister	T. R. Dews	
G-ODXB	Lindstrand LBL-120A balloon	A. Nimmo	
G-OEAC	Mooney M.20J	S. Lovatt	
G-OEAT	Robinson R22 Beta	C. Y. O. Seeds Ltd (G-RACH)	
G-OECM	Commander 114B	ECM (Vehicle Delivery Service) Ltd	
G-OECO	Flylight Dragonfly	P. A. & M. W. Aston	
G-OEDB	PA-38-112 Tomahawk	M. A. Petrie (G-BGGJ)	
G-OEDP	Cameron N-77 balloon	M. J. Betts	
G-OEGG	Cameron Egg-65 SS balloon	Mobberley Balloon Collection	
G-OEGL	Christen Eagle II	Smart People UK Ltd	
G-OEKS	Ikarus C42 FB80	J. D. Smith	
G-OELD	Pegasus Quantum 15-912	R. P. Butler	
G-OELZ	Wassmer WA.52 Europa	G-OELZ Group	
G-OEMT	MBB BK-117 C-1	Sterling Helicopters Ltd	
G-OERR	Lindstrand LBL-60A balloon	P. C. Gooch	
G-OERS	Cessna 172N	N. J. Smith & A. Stevens (G-SSRS)	
G-OESY	Easy Raider J2.2 (1)	J. Gray	

Notes	Reg.	Type	Owner or Operator
	G-OETI	Bell 206B JetRanger 3	T. A. Wells (G-RMIE/G-BPIE)
	G-OETV	PA-31-350 Navajo Chieftain	Hinde Holdings Ltd
	G-OEVA	PA-32-260 Cherokee Six	M. G. Cookson & G. A. Thornton (G-FLJA/G-AVTJ)
	G-OEWD	Raytheon 390 Premier 1	Wolfe Securities Ltd
	G-OEZI	Easy Raider J2.2(2)	M. Housley
	G-OEZY	Shaw Europa	A. W. Wakefield
	G-OFAA	Cameron Z-105 balloon	R. A. Schwab
	G-OFAL	Ozone Roadster/Bailey Quattro	Malcolm Roberts Heating, Plumbing and Electrical Ltd
	G-OFAS	Robinson R22 Beta	Advance Helicopters Ltd
	G-OFBU	Ikarus C.42 FB UK	Old Sarum C42 Group
	G-OFCM	Cessna F.172L	Sirius Aviation Ltd (G-AZUN)
	G-OFDT	Mainair Pegasus Quik	J. Smith
	G-OFER	PA-18 Super Cub 150	White Watham Airfield Ltd
	G-OFFA	Pietenpol Air Camper	OFFA Group
	G-OFFO	Extra EA.300/L	2 Excel Aviation Ltd
	G-OFGC	Aeroprakt A22-L Foxbat	J. M. Fearn
	G-OFIT	SOCATA TB10 Tobago	GFI Aviation Group (G-BRIU)
	G-OFIX	Grob G.109B	T. R. Dews
	G-OFJC	Eiriavion PIK-20E	G. Bailey, J. D. Sorrell & D. Thomas
	G-OFLI	Colt 105A balloon	Virgin Airship & Balloon Co Ltd
	G-OFLT	EMB-110P1 Bandeirante ★	Rescue trainer/Aveley, Essex (G-MOBL/G-BGCS)
	G-OFLY	Cessna 210M	A. P. Mothew
	G-OFMC	Avro RJ100	Trident Jet (Dublin) Ltd (G-CDUI)
	G-OFNC	Balony Kubicek BB17XR balloon	M. R. Jeynes
	G-OFOA	BAe 146-100	Formula One Administration Ltd (G-BKMN/G-ODAN)
	G-OFOM	BAe 146-100	Formula One Management Ltd (G-BSLP/G-BRLM)
	G-OFOX	Denney Kitfox	P. R. Skeels
	G-OFRB	Everett gyroplane	T. N. Holcroft-Smith
	G-OFRY	Cessna 152	Devon and Somerset Flight Training Ltd
	G-OFSP	CZAW Sportcruiser	F. S. Pullman
	G-OFTC	Agusta A109E Power	Castle Air Ltd
	G-OFTI	PA-28 Cherokee 140	G-OFTI Group
	G-OGAR	PZL SZD-45A Ogar	P. Rasmussen t/a Perranporth Ogar Flying Group
	G-OGAS	Westland WG.30 Srs 100 ★	(stored)/Yeovil (G-BKNW)
	G-OGAY	Baloney Kubicek BB-26 balloon	J. W. Soukup
	G-OGAZ	Aérospatiale SA.341G Gazelle 1	Killochries Fold (G-OCJR/G-BRGS)
	G-OGCA	PA-28-161 Warrior II	Cardiff-Wales Aviation Services Ltd
	G-OGEM	PA-28-181 Archer II	GEM Integrated Solutions Ltd
	G-OGEO	Aérospatiale SA.341G Gazelle 1	George Steel Contract Services (G-BXJK)
	G-OGES	Enstrom 280FX	G. E. Werkle (G-CBYL)
	G-OGET	PA-39 Twin Comanche	D. Saxton (G-AYXY)
	G-OGFS	BAe.125 Srs 800B	Sadoc Ltd (G-GRGA/G-DCTA/G-OSPG/G-ETOM/G-BVFC/G-TPHK/G-FDSL)
	G-OGGB	Grob G.102 Astir CS	Golf Brave Group
	G-OGGM	Cirrus SR22	Morson Human Resources Ltd
	G-OGGS	Thunder Ax8-84 balloon	G. Gamble & Sons (Quorn) Ltd
	G-OGGY	Aviat A.1B	Shropshire Aero Club Ltd
	G-OGIL	Short SD3-30 Variant 100 ★	North East Aircraft Museum/Usworth (G-BITV)
	G-OGJC	Robinson R44 II	Telecom Advertising & Promotions Ltd
	G-OGJM	Cameron C-80 balloon	G. F. Madelin
	G-OGJP	Commander 114B	M. J. Church
	G-OGJS	Puffer Cozy	G. J. Stamper
	G-OGKB	Sequoia Falco F8L	S. O. Foxlee
	G-OGLY	Cameron Z-105 balloon	H. M. Ogston
	G-OGOD	P & M Quik GT450	C. M. Theakstone
	G-OGOS	Everett gyroplane	N. A. Seymour
	G-OGSA	Avtech Jabiru SPL-450	G-OGSA Group
	G-OGSK	Embraer EMB-135BJ Legacy	TAG Aviation (UK) Ltd
	G-OGTR	P & M Quik GTR	K. J. Bowles
	G-OGTS	Air Command 532 Elite	GTS Engineering (Coventry) Ltd
	G-OHAC	Cessna F.182Q	Maguirelzatt LLP
	G-OHAL	Pietenpol Air Camper	UK Pietenpol Club
	G-OHAM	Robinson R44 II	Hamsters Wheel Productions Ltd (G-GBEN/G-CDJZ)
	G-OHAV	ATG Ltd HAV-3	Hybrid Air Vehicles Ltd

Reg.	Type	Owner or Operator	Notes
G-OHCP	AS.355F1 Twin Squirrel	Staske Construction Ltd (G-BTVS/G-STVE/ G-TOFF/G-BKJX)	
G-OHDC	Colt Film Cassette SS balloon ★	Balloon Preservation Group	
G-OHGA	Hughes O-6A (69-16011)	MSS Holdings (UK) Ltd	
G-OHGC	Scheibe SF.25C Falke	Heron Gliding Club	
G-OHIG	EMB-110P1 Bandeirante ★	Air Salvage International/Alton (G-OPPP)	
G-OHIO	Dyn'Aero MCR-01	J. M. Keane	
G-OHIY	Van's RV-10	M. A. Hutton	
G-OHJE	Alpi Pioneer 300 Hawk	F. A. Cavaciuti	
G-OHJV	Robinson R44	I. Taylor	
G-OHKS	Pegasus Quantum 15-912	J. L. Jordan	
G-OHLI	Robinson R44 II	NCS Partnership	
G-OHMS	AS.355F1 Twin Squirrel	HFS (Aviation) Ltd	
G-OHNO	Yakovlev Yak-55	J. Fesl	
G-OHOV	Rotorway Executive 162F	M. G. Bird	
G-OHPC	Cessna 208 Caravan 1	S. Ulrich	
G-OHPH	HpH Glasflugel 304MS	G-OHPH Group	
G-OHWV	Raj Hamsa X'Air 582(6)	P. B. Readings	
G-OHYE	Thruster T.600N 450	A. P. W. O'Brien (G-CCRO)	
G-OIBO	PA-28 Cherokee 180	Azure Flying Club Ltd (G-AVAZ)	
G-OIFM	Cameron 90 Dude SS balloon	Magical Adventures Ltd	
G-OIHC	PA-32R-301 Saratoga IIHP	N. J. Lipczynski (G-PUSK)	
G-OIIO	Robinson R22 Beta	Whizzard Helicopters (G-ULAB)	
G-OIMC	Cessna 152 II	East Midlands Flying School Ltd	
G-OINN	UltraMagic H-31 balloon	G. Everett	
G-OINT	Balony Kubicek BB20XR balloon	M. A. Green	
G-OIOB	Mudry CAP.10B	J. Ceotto	
G-OIOZ	Thunder Ax9-120 S2 balloon	R. H. Etherington	
G-OIRP	Gulfstream G200	Air Charter Scotland Ltd	
G-OITV	Enstrom 280C-UK-2	C. W. Brierley Jones (G-HRVY/G-DUGY/ G-BEEL)	
G-OIVN	Liberty XL-2	I. Shaw	
G-OJAB	Avtech Jabiru SK	Flying Spanners Group	
G-OJAC	Mooney M.20J	Hornet Engineering Ltd	
G-OJAG	Cessna 172S	Valhalla Aviation LLP	
G-OJAN	Robinson R22 Beta	J. C. Lane (G-SANS/G-BUHX)	
G-OJAS	Auster J/1U Workmaster	D. S. Hunt	
G-OJAZ	Robinson R44 II	A. J. Berwick	
G-OJBB	Enstrom 280FX	C. A. Reed	
G-OJBM	Cameron N-90 balloon	P. Spinlove	
G-OJBS	Cameron N-105A balloon	Up & Away Ballooning Ltd	
G-OJBW	Lindstrand LBL J & B Bottle SS balloon	N. A. P. Godfrey	
G-OJCW	PA-32RT-300 Lance II	P. G. Dobson	
G-OJDA	EAA Acrosport II	D. B. Almey	
G-OJDC	Thunder Ax7-77 balloon	A. Heginbottom	
G-OJDS	Ikarus C.42 FB 80	The Rans Group	
G-OJEG	Airbus A.321-231	Monarch Airlines Ltd	
G-OJEH	PA-28-181 Archer II	P. C. & M. A. Greenaway	
G-OJEN	Cameron V-77 balloon	C. & C. Westwood	
G-OJER	Cessna 560XL Citation XLS	Aviation Beauport Ltd	
G-OJGC	Van's RV-4	J. G. Claridge	
G-OJGT	Maule M.5-235C	Newnham Joint Flying Syndicate	
G-OJHC	Cessna 182P	Stapleford Flying Club Ltd	
G-OJHL	Shaw Europa	M. D. Burns & G. Rainey	
G-OJIL	PA-31-350 Navajo Chieftain	Redhill Aviation Ltd	
G-OJIM	PA-28R-201T Turbo Arrow III	G-OJIM Flyers Ltd	
G-OJJV	P & M Pegasus Quik	J. J. Valentine	
G-OJKM	Rans S.7 Courier	A. J. Gibney	
G-OJLD	Van's RV-7	J. L. Dixon	
G-OJLH	TEAM mini-MAX 91	B. Plunkett (G-MYAW)	
G-OJMB	Airbus A.330-243	Thomas Cook Airlines Ltd	
G-OJMF	Enstrom 280FX	Reidinger Helicopter GmbH/Austria (G-DDOD)	
G-OJMR	Airbus A.300B4-605R	Monarch Airlines Ltd	
G-OJMS	Cameron Z-90 balloon	Joinerysoft Ltd	
G-OJNB	Linsdstrand LBL-21A balloon	N. A. P. Godfrey	
G-OJNE	Schempp-Hirth Nimbus 3T	J. N. Ellis	
G-OJON	Taylor JT.2 Titch	Freelance Aviation Ltd	
G-OJPS	Bell 206B JetRanger 2	Milford Aviation (G-UEST/G-ROYB/G-BLWU)	
G-OJRH	Robinson R44	J. R. Holgate	

Notes	Reg.	Type	Owner or Operator
	G-OJRM	Cessna T.182T	Colne Airways Ltd
	G-OJSA	BAe Jetstream 3102	Diamond Air Charter Ltd
	G-OJSF	PA-23 Aztec 250F	Comed Aviation Ltd (G-SFHR/G-BHSO)
	G-OJSH	Thruster T.600N 450 JAB	G-OJSH Group
	G-OJVA	Van's RV-6	J. A. Village
	G-OJVH	Cessna F.150H	G. H. Tempest-Hay (G-AWJZ)
	G-OJVL	Van's RV-6	S. E. Tomlinson
	G-OJWB	Hawker 800XP	Langford Lane Ltd
	G-OJWS	PA-28-161 Warrior II	P. J. Ward
	G-OKAY	Pitts S-1E Special	S. R. S. Evans
	G-OKBT	Colt 25A Mk II balloon	British Telecommunications PLC
	G-OKCC	Cameron N-90 balloon	D. J. Head
	G-OKCP	Lindstrand LBL Battery SS balloon	D. Bedford & J. Edwards (G-MAXX)
	G-OKED	Cessna 150L	L. J. Pluck
	G-OKEM	Mainair Pegasus Quik	W. J. Hardy
	G-OKEN	PA-28R-201T Turbo Arrow III	K. Woodcock
	G-OKER	Van's RV-7	R. M. Johnson
	G-OKEV	Shaw Europa	K. A. Kedward
	G-OKEW	UltraMagic M-65C balloon	Hampshire Balloons Ltd
	G-OKEY	Robinson R22 Beta	Recovair Ltd
	G-OKID	Reality Escapade Kid	V. H. Hallam
	G-OKIM	Best Off Sykyranger 912 (2)	K. P. Taylor
	G-OKIS	Tri-R Kis	M. R. Cleveley
	G-OKMA	Tri-R Kis	K. Miller
	G-OKPW	Tri-R Kis	P. J. Reilly
	G-OKTA	Ikarus C42 FB80	Avion Training & Consultancy Ltd
	G-OKTI	Aquila AT01	P. H. Ferdinand
	G-OKYA	Cameron V-77 balloon	R. J. Pearce
	G-OKYM	PA-28 Cherokee 140	North Wales Air Academy Ltd (G-AVLS)
	G-OLAA	Alpi Pioneer 300 Hawk	G. G. Hammond
	G-OLAU	Robinson R22 Beta	MPW Aviation Ltd
	G-OLAW	Lindstrand LBL-25A balloon	George Law Plant Ltd
	G-OLCP	AS.355N Twin Squirrel	Charterstyle Ltd (G-CLIP)
	G-OLDG	Cessna T.182T	Gold Aviation Ltd (G-CBTJ)
	G-OLDH	Aérospatiale SA.341G Gazelle 1	MW Helicopters Ltd (G-UTZY/G-BKLV)
	G-OLDM	Pegasus Quantum 15-912	J. W. Holme
	G-OLDO	Eurocopter EC.120B Colibri	Gold Aviation Ltd (G-HIGI)
	G-OLDP	Mainair Pegasus Quik	A. G. Woodward
	G-OLDT	Learjet 45	Gold Aviation Ltd
	G-OLDX	Cessna 182T	Gold Air International Ltd (G-IBZT)
	G-OLEE	Cessna F.152	Redhill Air Services Ltd
	G-OLEM	Jodel D.18	G. E. Roe (G-BSBP)
	G-OLEW	Vans RV-7A	A. Burani
	G-OLEZ	Piper J-3C-65 Cub	L. Powell (G-BSAX)
	G-OLFA	AS.350B3 Ecureuil	Heliaviation Ltd
	G-OLFB	Pegasus Quantum 15-912	M. S. McGimpsey
	G-OLFF	Cameron Z-120 balloon	A. Nimmo
	G-OLFT	Rockwell Commander 114	D. A. Tubby (G-WJMN)
	G-OLFZ	P & M Quik GT450	A. J. Boyd
	G-OLGA	Starstreak Shadow SA-II	G. L. Turner
	G-OLHR	Cassutt Racer IIIM	P. A. Hall & A. R. Lewis (G-BNJZ)
	G-OLJT	Mainair Gemini Flash IIA	M. H. Moulai
	G-OLLI	Cameron O-31 SS balloon	The British Balloon Museum & Library Ltd
	G-OLLS	Cessna U.206H Floatplane	Loch Lomond Seaplanes Ltd
	G-OLNT	SA.365N1 Dauphin 2	LNT Aviation Ltd (G-POAV/G-BOPI)
	G-OLOW	Robinson R44	C. O. Semik
	G-OLPM	P & M Quik R	T. J. Billingham
	G-OLRT	Robinson R22 Beta	Swift Helicopter Services Ltd
	G-OLSA	Breezer LSA	RGV Aviation Ltd
	G-OLSF	PA-28-161 Cadet	Flew LLP (G-OTYJ)
	G-OLUG	Cameron Z-120 balloon	K. H. Gruenauer
	G-OMAA	Eurocopter EC.135 T2+	Bond Air Services Ltd
	G-OMAF	Dornier 228-200	FR Aviation Ltd
	G-OMAG	Cessna 182B	Bodmin Light Aeroplane Services Ltd
	G-OMAL	Thruster T.600N 450	M. Howland
	G-OMAO	SOCATA TB-20 Trinidad	Alpha Oscar Group (G-GDGR)
	G-OMAS	Cessna A.150M	M. A. Segar (G-BTFS)
	G-OMAT	PA-28 Cherokee 140	Midland Air Training School (G-JIMY/G-AYUG)

Reg.	Type	Owner or Operator	Notes
G-OMBI	Cessna 525B Citationjet CJ3	Ravenheat Manufacturing Ltd	
G-OMCC	AS.350B Ecureuil	MJH Capital Ltd (G-JTCM/G-HLEN/G-LOLY)	
G-OMCH	PA-28-161 Warrior III	Chalrey Ltd	
G-OMDB	Van's V-6A	D. A. Roseblade	
G-OMDD	Thunder Ax8-90 S2 balloon	M. D. Dickinson	
G-OMDH	Hughes 369E	Stilgate Ltd	
G-OMDR	Agusta-Bell 206B JetRanger 3	Castle Air Ltd (G-HRAY/G-VANG/G-BIZA)	
G-OMEA	Cessna 560XL Citation XLS	Marshall Executive Aviation	
G-OMEL	Robinson R44	J. M. & L. Prowse (G-BVPB)	
G-OMEM	Eurocopter EC 120B	BC Helicopter Services LLP (G-BXYD)	
G-OMEN	Cameron Z-90 balloon	M. G. Howard	
G-OMER	Avtech Jabiru UL-450	G. D. Omer (G-GPAS)	
G-OMEX	Zenair CH.701 UL	C. R. Buckle	
G-OMEZ	Zenair CH.601HDS	GOMEZ Group	
G-OMGH	Robinson R44 II	True Gas Ltd	
G-OMGR	Cameron Z-105 balloon	Omega Resource Group PLC	
G-OMHC	PA-28RT-201 Arrow IV	Fly BPL.com	
G-OMHD	EE Canberra PR.Mk.9 (XH134)	Canberra 134 Ltd	
G-OMHI	Mills MH-1	J. P. Mills	
G-OMHP	Avtech Jabiru UL	J. Livingstone	
G-OMIA	MS.893A Rallye Commodore 180	L. Perryman	
G-OMIK	Shaw Europa	M. J. Clews	
G-OMIW	Pegasus Quik	G. P. Masters	
G-OMJA	PA-28-181 Archer II	R. D. Masters & S. Walker	
G-OMJT	Rutan LongEz	M. J. Timmons	
G-OMMG	Robinson R22 Beta	CDS Aviation Ltd (G-BPYX)	
G-OMMM	Colt 90A balloon	A. & M. Frayling	
G-OMNI	PA-28R Cherokee Arrow 200D	Cotswold Aviation Services Ltd (G-BAWA)	
G-OMOO	Ultramagic T-150 balloon	Robert Wiseman Dairies PLC	
G-OMPW	Mainair Pegasus Quik	M. P. Wimsey	
G-OMRB	Cameron V-77 balloon	I. J. Jevons	
G-OMRC	Van's RV-10	A. W. Collett	
G-OMRH	Cessna 550 Citation Bravo	McAir Services LLP	
G-OMRP	Flight Design CTSW	M. E. Parker	
G-OMSA	Flight Design CTSW	Microlight Sport Aviation Ltd	
G-OMST	PA-28-161 Warrior III	Mid-Sussex Timber Co Ltd (G-BZUA)	
G-OMSV	Beech B.200GT King Air	JPM Ltd	
G-OMUM	Rockwell Commander 114	Thessaly Air Club	
G-OMYJ	Airbus A.321-211	Thomas Cook Airlines Ltd (G-OOAF/G-UNID/ G-UKLO)	
G-OMYT	Airbus A.330-243	Thomas Cook Airlines Ltd (G-MOJO)	
G-ONAA	North American Rockwell OV-10B Bravo	Invicta Aviation Ltd	
G-ONAF	Naval Aircraft Factory N3N-3 (4406:12)	J. P. Birnie	
G-ONAT	Grob G.102 Astir CS77	N. A. Toogood	
G-ONAV	PA-31-310 Turbo Navajo C	Panther Aviation Ltd (G-IGAR)	
G-ONCB	Lindstrand LBL-31A balloon	M. D. Freeston & S. Mitchell	
G-ONCS	Slingsby T.66 Nipper 3	Ardleigh Flying Group (G-AZBA)	
G-ONEP	Robinson R44 II	Neptune Property Developments Ltd	
G-ONES	Slingsby T.67M Firefly 200	Aquaman Aviation Ltd	
G-ONET	PA-28 Cherokee 180E	Hatfield Flying Club Ltd (G-AYAU)	
G-ONEZ	Glaser-Dirks DG-200/17	One Zulu Group	
G-ONFL	Murphy Maverick 430	G. J. Johnson (G-MYUJ)	
G-ONGC	Robin DR.400/180R	Norfolk Gliding Club Ltd	
G-ONHH	Forney F-1A Aircoupe	R. D. I. Tarry (G-ARHA)	
G-ONIC	Evektor EV-97 Sportstar Max	D. M. Jack	
G-ONIG	Murphy Elite	N. S. Smith	
G-ONIX	Cameron C-80 balloon	Above All Services Ltd	
G-ONKA	Aeronca K	N. J. R. Minchin	
G-ONNE	Westland Gazelle HT.3 (XW858:C)	A. M. Parkes (G-DMSS)	
G-ONON	RAF 2000 GTX-SE gyroplane	M. P. Lhermette	
G-ONPA	PA-31-350 Navajo Chieftain	Synergy Aircraft Leasing Ltd	
G-ONSO	Pitts S-1C Special	S. H. Brun (G-BRRS)	
G-ONSW	Skyranger Swift 9128(1)	N. S. Wells	
G-ONTV	Agusta-Bell 206B-3 JetRanger III	Castle Air Ltd (G-GOUL)	
G-ONUN	Van's RV-6A	K. R. H. Wingate	
G-OOBA	Boeing 757-26N	Thomson Airways Ltd	
G-OOBB	Boeing 757-28A	Thomson Airways Ltd	
G-OOBC	Boeing 757-28A	Thomson Airways Ltd	
G-OOBD	Boeing 757-28A	Thomson Airways Ltd	

Notes	Reg.	Type	Owner or Operator
	G-OOBE	Boeing 757-28A	Thomson Airways Ltd
	G-OOBF	Boeing 757-28A	Thomson Airways Ltd
	G-OOBG	Boeing 757-236	Thomson Airways Ltd
	G-OOBH	Boeing 757-236	Thomson Airways Ltd
	G-OOBK	Boeing 767-324ER	Thomson AirwaysLtd
	G-OOBL	Boeing 767-324ER	Thomson Airways Ltd
	G-OOBM	Boeing 767-324ER	Thomson Airways Ltd
	G-OOBN	Boeing 757-2G5	Thomson Airways Ltd
	G-OOBP	Boeing 757-2G5	Thomson Airways Ltd
	G-OOCH	Ultramagic H-42 balloon	D. G. Such
	G-OODE	SNCAN Stampe SV.4C (modified)	G-OODE Flying Group (G-AZNN)
	G-OODI	Pitts S-1D Special	C. Hutson & R. S. Wood (G-BBBU)
	G-OODW	PA-28-181 Archer II	Redhill Air Services Ltd
	G-OOER	Lindstrand LBL-25A balloon	Airborne Adventures Ltd
	G-OOEX	Cirrus SR22T	Data Interchange PLC
	G-OOEY	Balony Kubicek BB-222 balloon	A. W. Holly
	G-OOFE	Thruster T.600N 450	R. P. Tribe
	G-OOFT	PA-28-161 Warrior III	Aviation Maintenance Ltd
	G-OOGO	GA-7 Cougar	M. M. Naviede
	G-OOGS	GA-7 Cougar	P. Wilkinson (G-BGJW)
	G-OOGY	P & M Quik R	Cambridge Road Professional Services Ltd
	G-OOIO	AS.350B3 Ecureuil	Hovering Ltd
	G-OOJP	Commander 114B	R. J. Rother
	G-OOLE	Cessna 172M	P. S. Eccersley (G-BOSI)
	G-OOMA	PA-28-161 Warrior II	Aviation Advice and Consulting Ltd (G-BRBB)
	G-OOMC	Raytheon 390 Premier 1°	RB209 IOM Ltd
	G-OOMF	PA-18-150 Super Cub	C. G. Bell
	G-OONA	Robinson R44 II	Malaika Developments LLP
	G-OONE	Mooney M.20J	Go One Aviation Ltd
	G-OONK	Cirrus SR22	N. P. Kingdon
	G-OONY	PA-28-161 Warrior II	J. R. Golding
	G-OONZ	P & M Aviation Quik	A. P. Burch
	G-OOON	PA-34-220T Seneca III	Pelican Air Ltd
	G-OORV	Van's RV-6	T. I. Williams
	G-OOSE	Rutan Vari-Eze	B. O. Smith & J. A. Towers
	G-OOSH	Zenair CH.601UL Zodiac	A. G. Ransom
	G-OOSY	DH.82A Tiger Moth	G. Berryman
	G-OOTC	PA-28R-201T Turbo Arrow III	D. G. & C. M. King (G-CLIV)
	G-OOTT	Eurocopter AS.350B3 Ecureuil	R. J. Green
	G-OOUK	Cirrus SR22	R. S. Tomlinson
	G-OOWS	Eurocopter AS.350B3 Ecureuil	Millburn World Travel Services Ltd
	G-OOXP	Aero Designs Pulsar XP	P. C. Avery
	G-OPAG	PA-34-200 Seneca II	A. H. Lavender (G-BNGB)
	G-OPAH	Eurocopter EC135 T2 +	VLL Ltd (G-RWLA)
	G-OPAM	Cessna F.152 II (tailwheel)	PJC Leasing Ltd (G-BFZS)
	G-OPAR	Van's RV-6	R. Parr (G-CGNR)
	G-OPAT	Beech 76 Duchess	R. D. J. Axford (G-BHAO)
	G-OPAZ	Pazmany PL.2	A. D. Wood
	G-OPCG	Cessna 182T	S. K. Pomfret
	G-OPEJ	TEAM Minimax 91A	P. E. Jackson
	G-OPEM	Cessna 550 Citation Bravo	International Plywood (Aviation) Ltd
	G-OPEN	Bell 206B	Gazelle Aviation LLP
	G-OPEP	PA-28RT-201T Turbo Arrow IV	SAM Ltd
	G-OPET	PA-28-181 Archer II	Cambrian Flying Group Ltd
	G-OPFA	Pioneer 300	S. Eddison & R. Minett
	G-OPFR	Diamond DA.42 Twin Star	P. F. Rothwell
	G-OPHT	Schleicher ASH-26E	J. S. Wand
	G-OPIC	Cessna FRA.150L	A. V. Harmer (G-BGNZ)
	G-OPIK	Eiri PIK-20E	G-OPIK Syndicate
	G-OPIT	CFM Streak Shadow Srs SA	I. J. Guy
	G-OPJD	PA-28RT-201T Turbo Arrow IV	J. M. McMillan
	G-OPJK	Shaw Europa	P. J. Kember
	G-OPJS	Pietenpol Air Camper	P. J. Shenton
	G-OPKF	Cameron 90 Bowler SS balloon	D. K. Fish
	G-OPLC	DH.104 Dove 8	Columba Aviation Ltd (G-BLRB)
	G-OPME	PA-23 Aztec 250D	A. A. Mattacks & R. G. Pardo (G-ODIR/G-AZGB)
	G-OPMP	Robinson R44 II	E. K. Richardson (G-HHHH)
	G-OPMT	Lindstrand LBL-105A balloon	K. R. Karlstrom
	G-OPNH	Stoddard-Hamilton Glasair IIRG	A. E. Korhonen (G-CINY)
	G-OPPO	Groppo Trail	A. C. Hampson

Reg.	Type	Owner or Operator	Notes
G-OPRC	Shaw Europa XS	M. J. Ashby-Arnold	
G-OPRM	Bombardier CL600-2B16 Challenger	Oryx Jet Ltd	
G-OPSF	PA-38-112 Tomahawk	P. I. Higham (G-BGZI)	
G-OPSG	Aeropro Eurofox 912(S)	P. S. Gregory	
G-OPSL	PA-32R-301 Saratoga SP	Defence Vision Systems Pte Ltd (G-IMPW)	
G-OPSP	Diamond DA.40D Star	P. Plaisted (G-OCCR)	
G-OPSS	Cirrus SR20	Clifton Aviation Ltd	
G-OPST	Cessna 182S	M. J. G. Wellings & Welmacs Ltd	
G-OPTC	PA-44-180 Seminole	M. J. Edgeworth (G-BGTF)	
G-OPTF	Robinson R44 II	D. Fahy	
G-OPTI	PA-28-161 Warrior II	A. K. Hulme	
G-OPUB	Slingsby T.67M Firefly 160	A. L. Waller (G-DLTA/G-SFTX)	
G-OPUK	PA-28-161 Warrior III	I. J. Flitcroft	
G-OPUP	Beagle B.121 Pup 2	F. A. Zubiel (G-AXEU)	
G-OPUS	Avtech Jabiru SK	K. W. Whistance	
G-OPVM	Van's RV-9A	J. A. & J. C. Ferguson	
G-OPWS	Mooney M.20K	D. S. Overton	
G-OPYE	Cessna 172S	Far North Aviation	
G-OPYO	Alpi Pioneer 300 Hawk	T. J. Franklin & D. S. Simpson	
G-ORAC	Cameron 110 Van SS balloon	A. G. Kennedy	
G-ORAE	Van's RV-7	R. W. Eaton	
G-ORAF	CFM Streak Shadow	A. P. Hunn	
G-ORAM	Thruster T600N 450	D. W. Wilson	
G-ORAR	PA-28-181 Archer III	P. N. & S. M. Thornton	
G-ORAS	Clutton FRED Srs 2	A. I. Sutherland	
G-ORAU	Evektor EV-97A Eurostar	W. R. C. Williams-Wynne	
G-ORAY	Cessna F.182Q II	Unicorn Consultants Ltd (G-BHDN)	
G-ORBK	Robinson R44 II	T2 Technology Ltd (G-CCNO)	
G-ORBS	Mainair Blade	J. W. Dodson	
G-ORCA	Van's RV-4	I. A. Harding	
G-ORCC	AutoGyro Calidus	R. P. Churchill-Coleman	
G-ORCW	Schempp-Hirth Ventus 2cT	J. C. A. Garland & M. S. Hawkins	
G-ORDB	Cessna 550 Citation Bravo	Equipe Air Ltd	
G-ORDH	AS.355N Twin Squirrel	Harpin Ltd	
G-ORDM	Cessna 182T	The Cambridge Aero Club Ltd (G-KEMY)	
G-ORDS	Thruster T.600N 450	G. J. Pill	
G-ORED	BN-2T Turbine Islander	B-N Group Ltd (G-BJYW)	
G-ORIG	Glaser-Dirks DG.800A	P. Crawley	
G-ORIX	ARV K1 Super 2	T. M. Lyons (G-BUXH/G-BNVK)	
G-ORJW	Laverda F.8L Falco Srs 4	Viking BV/Netherlands	
G-ORKY	AS.350B2 Ecureuil	PLM Dollar Group Ltd	
G-ORLA	P & M Pegasus Quik	J. Summers	
G-ORMB	Robinson R22 Beta	Heli Air Scotland Ltd	
G-ORMW	Ikarus C.42 FB100	B. J. Jenkins	
G-OROD	PA-18 Super Cub 150	B. W. Faulkner	
G-OROS	Ikarus C.42 FB80	R. I. Simpson	
G-ORPC	Shaw Europa XS	P. W. Churms	
G-ORPR	Cameron O-77 balloon	S. R. Vining	
G-ORRG	Robin DR.400-180 Regent	Radley Robin Group	
G-ORTH	Beech E90 King Air	Gorthair Ltd	
G-ORUG	Thruster T.600N 450	D. J. N. Brown	
G-ORVE	Van's RV-6	R. J. F. Swain & F. M. Sperryn	
G-ORVG	Van's RV-6	RV Group	
G-ORVI	Van's RV-6	J. D. N. Cooke	
G-ORVR	Partenavia P.68B	Ravenair Aircraft Ltd (G-BFBD)	
G-ORVS	Van's RV-9	C. J. Marsh	
G-ORZA	Diamond DA42 Twin Star	Aviation Maintenance Ltd (G-FCAC)	
G-OSAT	Cameron Z-105 balloon	A. V. & M. R. Noyce	
G-OSAW	QAC Quickie Q.2	S. A. Wilson (G-BVYT)	
G-OSAZ	Robinson R22	Hi-Air (Redditch) Ltd (G-DERB/G-BPYH)	
G-OSCC	PA-32 Cherokee Six 300	BG & G Airlines Ltd (G-BGFD)	
G-OSCO	TEAM mini-MAX 91	V. Grayson	
G-OSDF	Schempp-Hirth Ventus a	S. D. Foster	
G-OSEA	BN-2B-26 Islander	W. T. Johnson & Sons (Huddersfield) Ltd (G-BKOL)	
G-OSEP	Mainair Blade 912	J. D. Smith	
G-OSFB	Diamond HK.36TTC Super Dimona	Oxfordshire Sportflying Ltd	
G-OSFS	Cessan F.177RG	D. G. Wright	
G-OSHK	Schempp-Hirth SHK-1	P. B. Hibbard	

Notes	Reg.	Type	Owner or Operator
	G-OSHL	Robinson R22 Beta	Sloane Helicopters Ltd
	G-OSIC	Pitts S-1C Special	J. A. Dodd (G-BUAW)
	G-OSII	Cessna 172N	India India Flying Group (G-BIVY)
	G-OSIS	Pitts S-1S Special	P. J. Burgess
	G-OSIT	Pitts S-1T Special	C. J. J. Robertson
	G-OSJF	PA-23-250 Aztec F	R. Tang (G-SFHR/G-BHSO)
	G-OSJN	Shaw Europa XS	P. Potuzak
	G-OSKR	Skyranger 912 (2)	K. Clark
	G-OSKY	Cessna 172M	Skyhawk Leasing Ltd
	G-OSLD	Shaw Europa XS	S. Percy & C. Davies
	G-OSLO	Schweizer 269C	A. H. Helicopter Services Ltd
	G-OSMD	Bell 206B JetRanger 2	TR Aviation Services Ltd (G-LTEK/G-BMIB)
	G-OSND	Cessna FRA.150M	Group G-OSND (G-BDOU)
	G-OSOD	P & M Quik GTR	J. R. Elcocks
	G-OSOE	HS.748 Srs 2A	PTB (Emerald) Pty Ltd (G-AYYG)
	G-OSON	P & M QuikR	R. Parr
	G-OSPD	Aerotechnik EV-97 TeamEurostar UK	R. A. Stewart-Jones
	G-OSPH	Ikarus C42 FB100	SPH Groundworks Ltd
	G-OSPK	Cessna 172S	Air-Unlimited Sweden/Sweden
	G-OSPS	PA-18 Super Cub 95	R. C. Lough
	G-OSPY	Cirrus SR20	Cambridge Guarantee Ltd
	G-OSRA	Boeing 727-2S2F	T2 Aviation Ltd
	G-OSRL	Learjet 45	S. R. Lloyd
	G-OSRS	Cameron A-375 balloon	Wickers World Ltd
	G-OSSA	Cessna Tu.206B	Skydive St.Andrews Ltd
	G-OSST	Colt 77A balloon	A. A. Brown
	G-OSTC	AA-5A Cheetah	5th Generation Designs Ltd
	G-OSTL	Ikarus C.42 FB 100	G-OSTL Syndicate
	G-OSTY	Cessna F.150G	Prospects Learning Foundation Ltd (G-AVCU)
	G-OSUP	Lindstrand LBL-90A balloon	M. E. Banks
	G-OSUS	Mooney M.20K	J. B. King
	G-OSUT	Scheibe SF-25C Rotax-Falke	Yorkshire Gliding Club (Pty.) Ltd
	G-OSVN	AutoGyro Cavalon	S. P. Pearce
	G-OSVY	Sky 31-24 balloon	C. G. Dobson
	G-OSZA	Aerotek Pitts S-2A	Septieme Ciel
	G-OSZB	Christen Pitts S-2B Special	K. A. Fitton & A. M. Gent (G-OGEE)
	G-OSZS	Pitts S-2S Special	L. V. Nieuwenhove
	G-OTAL	ARV Super 2	J. M. Cullen (G-BNGZ)
	G-OTAM	Cessna 172M	G. V. White
	G-OTAN	PA-18 Super Cub 135 (54-2445)	A. & J. D. Owen
	G-OTAZ	Hawker 900XP	Hangar 8 Management Ltd
	G-OTCH	Streak Shadow	R. M. M. & A. G. Moura
	G-OTCV	Skyranger 912S (1)	T. C. Viner
	G-OTCZ	Schempp-Hirth Ventus 2cT	D. H. Conway t/a CZ Group
	G-OTEC	Tecnam P2002 Sierra Deluxe	C. W. Thirtle
	G-OTEL	Thunder Ax8-90 balloon	J. W. Adkins
	G-OTFL	Eurocopter EC 120B	J. Henshall (G-IBRI)
	G-OTFT	PA-38-112 Tomahawk	P. Tribble (G-BNKW)
	G-OTGA	PA-28R-201 Arrow III	TG Aviation Ltd
	G-OTGL	Embraer EMB-135BJ Legacy 650	Aravco Ltd
	G-OTHE	Enstrom 280C-UK Shark	G. E. Heritage (G-OPJT/G-BKCO)
	G-OTIB	Robin DR.400/180R	The Windrushers Gliding Club Ltd
	G-OTIG	AA-5B Tiger	L. Burke (G-PENN)
	G-OTIM	Bensen B.8MV	T. J. Deane
	G-OTIV	Aerospool Dynamic WT9 UK	D. N. E. d'Ath
	G-OTJH	Pegasus Quantum 15-912	L. R. Gartside
	G-OTJS	Robinson R44 II	Kuki Helicopter Sales Ltd
	G-OTJT	Glasflugel 304SJ Shark	N. J. L. Busvine
	G-OTLC	Grumman AA-5 Traveller	Total Logistics Concepts Ltd (G-BBUF)
	G-OTNA	Robinson R44 Raven II	Abel Developments Ltd
	G-OTOE	Aeronca 7AC Champion	D. Cheney (G-BRWW)
	G-OTOO	Stolp SA.300 Starduster Too	I. M. Castle
	G-OTOP	P & M Quik R	S. D. Pain
	G-OTRV	Van's RV-6	E. N. Burnett
	G-OTRY	Schleicher ASW-24	L. R. Roberts
	G-OTSP	AS.355F1 Twin Squirrel	MW Helicopters Ltd (G-XPOL/G-BPRF)
	G-OTTY	Rotorsport UK Calidus	J. M. Giles
	G-OTUI	SOCATA TB20 Trinidad	H. Graff (G-KKDL/G-BSHU)
	G-OTUN	Aerotechnik EV-97 Eurostar	S. P. Slater
	G-OTVI	Robinson R44 II	Summit Media Ltd

Reg.	Type	Owner or Operator	Notes
G-OTVR	PA-34-220T Seneca V	IAS Medical Ltd	
G-OTYE	Aerotechnik EV-97 Eurostar	A. B. Godber & J. Tye	
G-OTYP	PA-28 Cherokee 180	T. C. Lewis	
G-OUCH	Cameron N-105 balloon	A. C. Elson	
G-OUDA	Aeroprakt A22-L Foxbat	A. R. Cattell	
G-OUGH	Yakovlev Yak-52	I. M. Gough (G-LAOK)	
G-OUHI	Shaw Europa XS	N. M. Graham	
G-OUIK	Mainair Pegasus Quik	D. G. Baker	
G-OUMC	Lindstrand LBL-105A balloon	J. Francis	
G-OUNI	Cirrus SR20	Schonborn Park Baubetreuunh GmbH/ (G-TABI)	
G-OURO	Shaw Europa	I. M. Mackay	
G-OURS	Sky 120-24 balloon	S. Sevrin	
G-OUVI	Cameron O-105 balloon	Bristol University Hot Air Ballooning Society	
G-OVAL	Ikarus C.42 FB100	N. G. Tomes	
G-OVBF	Cameron A-250 balloon	Virgin Balloon Flights	
G-OVBL	Lindstrand LBL-150A balloon	R. J. Henderson	
G-OVET	Cameron O-56 balloon	B. D. Close	
G-OVFM	Cessna 120	T. B. Parmenter	
G-OVFR	Cessna F.172N	Marine and Aviation Ltd	
G-OVIA	Lindstrand LBL-105A balloon	N. C. Lindsey	
G-OVII	Van's RV-7	T. J. Richardson	
G-OVIN	Rockwell Commander 112TC	G. Vekaria	
G-OVIV	Aerostyle Breezer LSA	P. & V. Lynch	
G-OVLA	Ikarus C.42 FB	Webb Plant Sales	
G-OVMC	Cessna F.152 II	Swiftair Maintenance Ltd	
G-OVNE	Cessna 401A H	Norwich Aviation Museum	
G-OVNR	Robinson R22 Beta	Glenntrade Ltd	
G-OVOL	Skyranger 912S(1)	A. S. Docherty	
G-OVON	PA-18-95 Super Cub	V. F. A. Stanley	
G-OWAI	Schleicher ASK-21	Scottish Gliding Union	
G-OWAL	PA-34-220T Seneca III	R. G. & W. Allison	
G-OWAN	Cessna 210D Centurion	G. Owen	
G-OWAP	PA-28-161 Cherokee Warrior II	Tayside Aviation Ltd (G-BXNH)	
G-OWAR	PA-28-161 Warrior II	Bickertons Aerodromes Ltd	
G-OWAY	Bombardier CL600-2B16 Challenger 601	Air Charter Scotland Ltd	
G-OWAZ	Pitts S-1C Special	P. E. S. Latham (G-BRPI)	
G-OWBA	Alpi Pioneer 300 Hawk	L. J. Tonkinson	
G-OWBR	Tipsy Nipper T.66 series 2	W. J. Y. Ronge	
G-OWEL	Colt 105A balloon	S. R. Seager	
G-OWEN	K & S Jungster	R. C. Owen	
G-OWET	Thurston TSC-1A2 Teal	A. R. Wyatt	
G-OWFS	Cessna A.152	Westair Flying Services Ltd (G-DESY/G-BNJE)	
G-OWGC	Slingsby T.61F Venture T.2	Wolds Gliding Club Ltd	
G-OWLC	PA-31 Turbo Navajo	Channel Airways Ltd (G-AYFZ)	
G-OWMC	Thruster T.600N	Wilts Microlight Centre	
G-OWOW	Cessna 152 II	T. W. Gilbert (G-BMSZ)	
G-OWRC	Cessna F.152 II	Unimat SA/France	
G-OWRT	Cessna 182G	W. B. Bateson (G-ASUL)	
G-OWTN	Embraer EMB-145EP	BAE Systems (Corporate Air Travel) Ltd	
G-OWWW	Shaw Europa	R. F. W. Holder	
G-OWYN	Aviamilano F.14 Nibbio	Karpol Sp zoo/Poland	
G-OXBA	Cameron Z-160 balloon	J. E. Rose	
G-OXBC	Cameron A-140 balloon	J. E. Rose	
G-OXBY	Cameron N-90 balloon	C. A. Oxby	
G-OXII	Van's RV-12	J. A. King	
G-OXKB	Cameron 110 Sports Car SS balloon	D. M. Moffat	
G-OXLS	Cessna 560XL Citation XLS	Go XLS Ltd	
G-OXOM	PA-28-161 Cadet	Aviation Rentals (G-BRSG)	
G-OXPS	Falcon XPS	J. C. Greenslade (G-BUXP)	
G-OXRS	Bombardier BD700 1A10 Global Express	Profred Partners LLP	
G-OXVI	VS.361 Spitfire LF.XVIe (TD248:CR-S)	Spitfire Ltd	
G-OYAK	Yakovlev C-11 (9 white)	A. H. Soper	
G-OYES	Mainair Blade 912	B. McAdam & A. Hatton	
G-OYIO	Robin DR.400/120	Exeter Aviation Ltd	

Notes	Reg.	Type	Owner or Operator
	G-OYST	Agusta-Bell 206B JetRanger 2	L. E. V. Knifton (G-JIMW/G-UNIK/G-TPPH/ G-BCYP)
	G-OYTE	Rans S.6ES Coyote II	C. W. Brady
	G-OZAR	Enstrom 480	Benham Helicopters Ltd (G-BWFF)
	G-OZBB	Airbus A.320-212	Monarch Airlines Ltd
	G-OZBE	Airbus A.321-231	Monarch Airlines Ltd
	G-OZBF	Airbus A.321-231	Monarch Airlines Ltd
	G-OZBG	Airbus A.321-231	Monarch Airlines Ltd
	G-OZBH	Airbus A.321-231	Monarch Airlines Ltd
	G-OZBI	Airbus A.321-231	Monarch Airlines Ltd
	G-OZBK	Airbus A.320-214	Monarch Airlines Ltd
	G-OZBL	Airbus A.321-231	Monarch Airlines Ltd (G-MIDE)
	G-OZBM	Airbus A.321-231	Monarch Airlines Ltd (G-MIDJ)
	G-OZBN	Airbus A.321-231	Monarch Airlines Ltd (G-MIDK)
	G-OZBO	Airbus A.321-231	Monarch Airlines Ltd (G-MIDM)
	G-OZBP	Airbus A.321-231	Monarch Airlines Ltd (G-TTIB)
	G-OZBR	Airbus A.321-231	Monarch Airlines Ltd
	G-OZBS	Airbus A.321-231	Monarch Airlines Ltd (G-TTIA)
	G-OZBT	Airbus A.321-231	Monarch Airlines Ltd (G-TTIH)
	G-OZBU	Airbus A.321-231	Monarch Airlines Ltd (G-TTII)
	G-OZBW	Airbus A.320-214	Monarch Airlines Ltd (G-OOPP/G-OOAS)
	G-OZBX	Airbus A.320-214	Monarch Airlines Ltd (G-OOPU/G-OOAU)
	G-OZBY	Airbus A.320-214	Monarch Airlines Ltd (G-OOAR)
	G-OZBZ	Airbus A.321-231	Monarch Airlines Ltd
	G-OZEE	Light Aero Avid Speedwing Mk 4	G. D. Bailey
	G-OZEF	Shaw Europa XS	Z. M. Ahmad
	G-OZIE	Jabiru J400	Teoa BV/Netherlands
	G-OZIO	Aquila AT01	G. W. Brown
	G-OZOI	Cessna R.182	J. R. G. & F. L. G. Fleming (G-ROBK)
	G-OZOO	Cessna 172N	R. A. Brown (G-BWEI)
	G-OZOZ	Schempp-Hirth Nimbus 3DT	G-OZOZ Syndicate
	G-OZZE	Lambert Mission M108	A. & J. Oswald
	G-OZZI	Jabiru SK	A. H. Godfrey
	G-PABL	Cessna 550 Citation Bravo	E & A Aviation Ltd
	G-PACE	Robin R.1180T	M. T. Fitzpatrick & T. C. Wise
	G-PACL	Robinson R22 Beta	Whizzard Helicopters
	G-PACO	Sikorsky S-76C	Cardinal Helicopter Services
	G-PACT	PA-28-181 Archer III	A. Parsons
	G-PADE	Escapade Jabiru(3)	C. L. G. Innocent
	G-PADI	Cameron V-77 balloon	C. Chardon
	G-PAFC	Cameron C-70 balloon	D. R. Rawlings
	G-PAFF	AutoGyro MTO Sport	S. R. Paffett
	G-PAFR	Glaser-Dirks DG-300 Elan	Y. G. J-P. Clave
	G-PAIG	Grob G.109B	M. E. Baker
	G-PAIZ	PA-12 Super Cruiser	B. R. Pearson
	G-PALI	Czech Sport Aircraft Piper Sport	P. A. Langley
	G-PAMY	Robinson R44 II	Batchelor Aviation Ltd
	G-PAOL	Cessna 525B Citationjet CJ3	Blu Halkin Ltd
	G-PAPE	Diamond DA42 Twin Star	Diamond Executive Aviation Ltd
	G-PARG	Pitts S-1C Special	M. Kotsageridis
	G-PARI	Cessna 172RG Cutlass	V. A. Holliday
	G-PASH	AS.355F1 Twin Squirrel	MW Helicopters Ltd
	G-PASN	Enstrom F-28F	Passion 4 Health International Ltd (G-BSHZ)
	G-PATF	Shaw Europa	E. P. Farrell
	G-PATG	Cameron O-90 balloon	S. Neighbour & N. Symonds
	G-PATI	Cessna F.172M	Nigel Kenny Aviation Ltd (G-WACZ/G-BCUK)
	G-PATN	SOCATA TB10 Tobago	J. D. C. Pritchard (G-LUAR)
	G-PATO	Zenair CH.601UL Zodiac	N. D. Townend
	G-PATP	Lindstrand LBL-77A balloon	P. Pruchnickyj
	G-PATS	Shaw Europa	G-PATS Flying Group
	G-PATX	Lindstrand LBL-90A balloon	M. R. Noyce & R. P. E. Phillips
	G-PATZ	Shaw Europa	H. P. H. Griffin
	G-PAVL	Robin R.3000/120	MintLPG Ltd
	G-PAWL	PA-28 Cherokee 140	Skyferry & BFR Holdings (G-AWEU)
	G-PAWN	PA-25 Pawnee 260C	A. P. Meredith (G-BEHS)
	G-PAWS	AA-5A Cheetah	M. J. Patrick
	G-PAWZ	Best Off Sky Ranger Swift 912S(1)	G-PAWZ Syndicate
	G-PAXX	PA-20 Pacer 135 (modified)	C. W. Monsell
	G-PAYD	Robin DR.400/180	M. J. Bennett

Reg.	Type	Owner or Operator	Notes
G-PAZY	Pazmany PL.4A	M. Richardson (G-BLAJ)	
G-PBAT	Czech Sport Aircraft Sportcruiser	P. M. W. Bath	
G-PBCL	Cessna 182P	Kammon BV/Netherlands	
G-PBEC	Van's RV-7	P. G. Reid	
G-PBEE	Robinson R44	Echo Echo Syndicate	
G-PBEL	CFM Shadow Srs DD	S. Fairweather	
G-PBIX	VS.361 Spitfire LF XVI E	Pemberton-Billing LLP (G-XVIA)	
G-PBRL	Robinson R22	Com2Com (UK) Ltd	
G-PBWR	Agusta A109S Grand	Helix Helicopters Ltd	
G-PBWS	Schleicher ASH-31MI	P. B. Walker	
G-PBYA	Consolidated PBY-5A Catalina (433915)	Catalina Aircraft Ltd	
G-PBYY	Enstrom 280FX	S. Craske (G-BXKV)	
G-PBZN	AS.350B Ecureuil	Quarry and Mining Equipment Ltd (G-MURP)	
G-PCAT	SOCATA TB10 Tobago	G-PCAT Group (G-BHER)	
G-PCCC	Alpi Pioneer 300	R. Pidcock	
G-PCDP	Zlin Z.526F Trener Master	P. A. Colman	
G-PCMC	P & M Quik R	M. J. & P. J. Canty	
G-PCOP	Beech B200 Super King Air	Albert Batlett and Sons (Airdrie) Ltd	
G-PDAY	Augusta A109S Grand	Sky Border Logistics Ltd (G-CDWY)	
G-PDGE	Eurocopter EC 120B	D. M. McGarrity	
G-PDGF	AS.350B2 Ecureuil	PLM Dollar Group Ltd (G-FROH)	
G-PDGG	Aeromere F.8L Falco Srs 3	P. J. Beeson	
G-PDGI	AS.350B1 Ecureuil	PLM Dollar Group Ltd (G-BVJE)	
G-PDGK	SA.365N Dauphin 2	PLM Dollar Group Ltd (G-HEMS)	
G-PDGN	SA.365N Dauphin 2	PLM Dollar Group Ltd (G-TRAF/G-BLDR)	
G-PDGR	AS.350B2 Ecureuil	PLM Dollar Group Ltd (G-RICC/G-BTXA)	
G-PDGT	AS.355F2 Ecureuil 2	PLM Dollar Group Ltd (G-BOOV)	
G-PDHJ	Cessna T.182R	P. G. Vallance Ltd	
G-PDOC	PA-44-180 Seminole	Medicare (G-PVAF)	
G-PDOG	Cessna O-1E Bird Dog (24550)	J. D. Needham	
G-PDSI	Cessna 172N	DA Flying Group	
G-PEAR	P &M Pegasus Quik	N. D. Major	
G-PECK	PA-32-300 Cherokee Six D	The Big Six Flyers Ltd (G-ETAV/G-MCAR/ G-LADA/G-AYWK)	
G-PEEK	Diamond DA.42M-NG Twin Star	Diamond Executive Aviation Ltd	
G-PEER	Cessna 525A Citationjet CJ2	Air Charter Scotland (Holdings) Ltd (G-SYGC/ G-HGRC)	
G-PEGA	Pegasus Quantum 15-912	M. Konisti	
G-PEGE	Skyranger 912	A. N. Hughes	
G-PEGI	PA-34-200T Seneca II	ACS Aviation Ltd	
G-PEGY	Shaw Europa	A. Carter	
G-PEGZ	Centrair 101A Pegase	G-PEGZ Group	
G-PEJM	PA-28-181 Archer III	S. J. Clark	
G-PEKT	SOCATA TB20 Trinidad	The WEY Flying Group	
G-PENH	Ultramagic M-90 balloon	G. Holtam	
G-PEPE	Cessna 560XL Citation XLS	Fram Partners LLP	
G-PEPI	Embraer EMB-135BJ Legacy	London Executive Aviation Ltd	
G-PERB	Agusta AW.139	Bond Offshore Helicopters Ltd	
G-PERC	Cameron N-90 balloon	I. R. Warrington	
G-PERD	Agusta Westland AW.139	Bond Offshore Helicopters Ltd	
G-PERE	Robinson R22 Beta	R. F. McLachlan	
G-PERF	Eurocopter EC.120B Colibri	M. Munson	
G-PERR	Cameron 60 Bottle SS balloon ★	British Balloon Museum/Newbury	
G-PEST	Hawker Tempest II (MW401)	Tempest Two Ltd	
G-PETH	PA-24-260C Comanche	J. V. Hutchinson	
G-PETO	Hughes 369HM	P. E. Tornberg (G-HAUS/G-KBOT/G-RAMM)	
G-PETR	PA-28-140 Cherokee	A. A. Gardner (G-BCJL)	
G-PETS	Diamond DA42NG Twin Star	Diamond Executive Aviation Ltd	
G-PEYO	Gefa-Flug AS 105 GD airship	International Merchandising Promotion and Services SA	
G-PFAA	EAA Biplane Model P	T. A. Fulcher	
G-PFAF	FRED Srs 2	M. S. Perkins	
G-PFAH	Evans VP-1	J. A. Scott	
G-PFAP	Currie Wot/SE-5A (C1904:Z)	J. H. Seed	
G-PFAR	Isaacs Fury II (K2059)	M. A. Watts	

BRITISH CIVIL REGISTRATIONS

Notes	Reg.	Type	Owner or Operator
	G-PFAT	Monnett Sonerai II	H. B. Carter
	G-PFAW	Evans VP-1	R. F. Shingler
	G-PFCL	Cessna 172S	C. H. S. Carpenter
	G-PFCT	Learjet 45	Jet Aircraft Ltd (G-GOMO/G-OLDF/G-JRJR)
	G-PFKD	Yakovlev Yak-12M	R. D. Bade
	G-PFFN	Beech 200 Super King Air	The Puffin Club Ltd
	G-PFSL	Cessna F.152	P. A. Simon
	G-PGAC	MCR-01	G. A. Coatesworth
	G-PGBR	Vulcanair P-68R	Airborne Technologies GmbH/Austria
	G-PGFG	Tecnam P92-EM Echo	P. G. Fitzgerald
	G-PGGY	Robinson R44	J. Henshall
	G-PGHM	Air Creation 582(2)/Kiss 450	R. P. McGuffie
	G-PGSA	Thruster T.600N	B. S. Davis
	G-PGSI	Pierre Robin R2160	M. A. Spencer
	G-PHAA	Cessna F.150M	J. T. Yousaf (G-BCPE)
	G-PHAB	Cirrus SR22	G3 Aviation Ltd (G-MACL)
	G-PHAT	Cirrus SR20	Hetherington Properties Ltd
	G-PHCJ	Vol Mediterrani VM-1 Esqual C	C. R. James
	G-PHNM	Embraer EMB-500 Phenom 100	YC Investments
	G-PHNX	Schempp-Hirth Duo Discus Xt	J. L. Birch & R. Maskell
	G-PHOR	Cessna FRA.150L Aerobat	M. Bonsall (G-BACC)
	G-PHOX	Aeroprakt A22-L Foxbat	J. D. Webb
	G-PHSE	Balony Kubicek BB26Z balloon	The Packhouse Ltd
	G-PHSI	Colt 90A balloon	P. H. Strickland
	G-PHTG	SOCATA TB10 Tobago	A. J. Baggarley
	G-PHUN	Cessna FRA.150L Aerobat	M. Bonsall (G-BAIN)
	G-PHVM	Van's RV-8	G. Howes & V. Millard
	G-PHYL	Denney Kitfox Mk 4	G-PHYL Group
	G-PHYS	Jabiru SP-470	C. Mayer
	G-PHYZ	Jabiru J430	P. C. Knight
	G-PIAF	Thunder Ax7-65 balloon	L. Battersley
	G-PICX	P & M Aviation QuikR	C. J. Meadows
	G-PIEL	CP.301A Emeraude	P. R. Thorne (G-BARY)
	G-PIES	Thunder Ax7-77Z balloon	S. J. Hollingsworth & M. K. Bellamy
	G-PIET	Pietenpol Air Camper	A. R. Wyatt
	G-PIGI	Aerotechnik EV-97 Eurostar	Pigs Might Fly Group
	G-PIGS	SOCATA Rallye 150ST	Boonhill Flying Group (G-BDWB)
	G-PIGY	Short SC.7 Skyvan Srs 3A Variant 100	Invicta Aviation Ltd
	G-PIII	Pitts S-1D Special	On A Roll Aerobatics Group (G-BETI)
	G-PIIT	Pitts S-2 Special	R. Reid
	G-PIKD	Eiriavion PIK-20D-78	M. C. Hayes
	G-PIKE	Robinson R22 Mariner	Sloane Helicopters Ltd
	G-PIKK	PA-28 Cherokee 140	Coventry Aviators Flying Group (G-AVLA)
	G-PILE	Rotorway Executive 90	J. B. Russell
	G-PILL	Light Aero Avid Flyer Mk 4	D. R. Meston
	G-PILY	Pilatus B4 PC-11	N. Frost & K. E. Fox
	G-PILZ	AutoGyro MT-03	G. Millward
	G-PIMM	Ultramagic M-77 balloon	G. Everett
	G-PIMP	Robinson R44	Maxim Gestioni SRL
	G-PINC	Cameron Z-90 balloon	C. W. Clarke
	G-PING	AA-5A Cheetah	D. C. Hanss
	G-PINO	AutoGyro MTO Sport	P. A. Tolman
	G-PINT	Cameron 65 Barrel SS balloon	D. K. Fish
	G-PINX	Lindstrand Pink Panther SS balloon	Magical Adventures Ltd/USA
	G-PION	Alpi Pioneer 300	P. F. J. Burton
	G-PIPI	Mainair Pegasus Quik	N. R. Williams
	G-PIPR	PA-18 Super Cub 95	R. Forfitt & A. J. J. Sproule (G-BCDC)
	G-PIPS	Van's RV-4	P.N. Davis
	G-PIPY	Cameron 105 Pipe SS balloon	D. M. Moffat
	G-PITS	Pitts S-2AE Special	P. N. A. & S. N. Whithead
	G-PITT	Pitts S-2 Special	Mansfield Property Consultancy Ltd
	G-PITZ	Pitts S-2A Special	M. J. Wood
	G-PIXE	Colt 31A balloon	J. F. Trehern
	G-PIXI	Pegasus Quantum 15-912	K. J. Rexter
	G-PIXL	Robinson R44 II	Flying TV Ltd
	G-PIXX	Robinson R44 II	Flying TV Ltd
	G-PIXY	Supermarine Aircraft Spitfire Mk.26 (RK855)	R. Collenette
	G-PJMT	Lancair 320	V. Hatton & P. Gilroy

Reg.	Type	Owner or Operator	Notes
G-PJPJ	Boeing 737-5H6	Celestrial Aviation Trading Ltd (G-GFFJ)	
G-PJSY	Van's RV-6	P. J. York	
G-PJTM	Cessna FR.172K II	R. & J. R. Emery (G-BFIF)	
G-PKPK	Schweizer 269C	C. H. Dobson & M. R. Golden	
G-PLAD	Kolb Twinstar Mk.III Extra	A. Young	
G-PLAJ	BAe Jetstream 3102	Skybird SP Ltd	
G-PLAN	Cessna F.150L	G-PLAN Flying Group	
G-PLAR	Vans RV-9A	M. P. Board	
G-PLAY	Robin R.2112	S. J. Wilson	
G-PLAZ	Rockwell Commander 112	I. Hunt (G-RDCI/G-BFWG)	
G-PLEE	Cessna 182Q	Peterlee Parachute Centre	
G-PLIP	Diamond DA.40D Star	C. A. & D. R. Ho	
G-PLLT	Lindstrand Box SS balloon	Lindstrand Hot Air Balloons Ltd	
G-PLMH	AS.350B2 Ecureuil	PLM Dollar Group Ltd	
G-PLMI	SA.365C-1 Dauphin	PLM Dollar Group Ltd	
G-PLOP	Magni M-24C	C. A. Ho	
G-PLOW	Hughes 269B	C. Walton Ltd (G-AVUM)	
G-PLPC	Schweizer Hughes 269C	A. R. Baker	
G-PLPL	Agusta A109E Power	Iceland Foods Ltd (G-TMWC)	
G-PLPM	Shaw Europa XS	P. L. P. Mansfield	
G-PLSA	Aero Designs Pulsar XP	J. L. A. Campbell (G-NEVS)	
G-PLSR	P & M PulsR	P and M Aviation Ltd	
G-PMAM	Cameron V-65 balloon	P. A. Meecham	
G-PMGG	Agusta-Bell 206A JetRanger	P. M. Gallagher (G-EEGO/G-PELS/G-DNCN)	
G-PMHT	SOCATA TBM850	Ewan Air	
G-PMNF	VS.361 Spitfire HF.IX (TA805:FX-M)	P. R. Monk	
G-PMSL	UltraMagic M-120 balloon	High Road Adventures Ltd	
G-PNEU	Colt 110 Bibendum SS balloon	P. A. Rowley	
G-PNGC	Schleicher ASK-21	Portsmouth Naval Gliding Centre	
G-PNIX	Cessna FRA.150L	Dukeries Aviation (G-BBEO)	
G-PNTA	Eurocopter EC.135 T2+	Abbey International Finance Ltd	
G-PNTB	Eurocopter EC.135 T2+	Abbey International Finance Ltd	
G-POET	Robinson R44 II	GP Owen Ltd	
G-POGO	Flight Design CT2K	L. I. Bailey	
G-POLA	Eurocopter EC 135 P2+	Police & Crime Commissioner for West Yorkshire	
G-POLI	Robinson R44 II	Luxtronic Ltd	
G-POLL	Skyranger 912 (1)	D. A. Perkins	
G-POLY	Cameron N-77 balloon	S. Church & S. Jenkins	
G-POND	Oldfield Baby Lakes	U. Reichert/Germany	
G-POOH	Piper J-3C-65 Cub	P. L. Beckwith	
G-POOL	ARV Super 2	E. Stinton (G-BNHA)	
G-POPA	Beech A36 Bonanza	C. J. O'Sullivan	
G-POPE	Eiri PIK-20E-1	G-POPE Syndicate	
G-POPI	SOCATA TB10 Tobago	I. S. Hacon & C. J. Earle (G-BKEN)	
G-POPW	Cessna 182S	D. L. Price	
G-POPY	Best Off Sky Ranger Swift 912S(1)	S. G. Penk	
G-PORK	AA-5B Tiger	R. A. Lambert (G-BFHS)	
G-POSH	Colt 56A balloon	B. K. Rippon (G-BMPT)	
G-POUX	Pou du Ciel-Bifly	G. D. Priest	
G-POWC	Boeing 737-33A	Titan Airways Ltd	
G-POWD	Boeing 767-36N	Titan Airways Ltd	
G-POWF	Avro RJ100	North Cariboo Flying Service Ltd/Canada (G-CFAA)	
G-POWG	Cessna 525A Citationjet CJ2	Hagondale Ltd	
G-POWH	Boeing 757-256	Titan Airways Ltd	
G-POWI	Airbus A.320-233	Titan Airways Ltd	
G-POWJ	Boeing 757-256	Titan Airways Ltd	
G-POWL	Cessna 182R	Myriad Public Relations Ltd	
G-POZA	Escapade Jabiru ULP (1)	M. R. Jones	
G-PPFS	Cessna FRA.150L	M. Bonsall (G-AZJY)	
G-PPIO	Cameron C-90 balloon	A. G. Martin	
G-PPLG	Rotorsport UK MT-03	J. E. Butler	
G-PPLL	Van's RV-7A	D. Bull	
G-PPOD	Europa Aviation Europa XS	S. Easom	

Notes	Reg.	Type	Owner or Operator
	G-PPPP	Denney Kitfox Mk 3	R. Powers
	G-PRAG	Brügger MB.2 Colibri	Colibri Flying Group
	G-PRAH	Flight Design CT2K	G. N. S. Farrant
	G-PRDH	AS.355F2 Ecureuil 2	EZ-Int Ltd
	G-PRET	Robinson R44	Heliservices
	G-PREY	Pereira Osprey II	A. L. I. Barron (G-BEPB)
	G-PRFI	Agusta-Bell 206B Jet Ranger II	Topex Ltd (G-CPTS)
	G-PRII	Hawker Hunter PR.11 (XG194)	Interactive Dynamics Ltd
	G-PRIM	PA-38-112 Tomahawk	Braddock Ltd
	G-PRIV	VS.353 Spitfire PR.IV	P. R. Arnold
	G-PRLY	Avtech Jabiru SK	J. McVey (G-BYKY)
	G-PROJ	Robinson R44 II	Project Racing Team Ltd
	G-PROO	Hawker 4000 Horizon	TAG Aviation (UK) Ltd
	G-PROS	Van's RV-7A	A. J. & S. A. Sutcliffe
	G-PROV	P.84 Jet Provost T.52A (T.4)	Provost Group
	G-PROW	Aerotechnik EV-97A Eurostar	Nene Valley Microlights Ltd
	G-PRTT	Cameron N-31 balloon	A. Kaye
	G-PRXI	VS.365 Spitfire PR.XI (PL983)	Propshop Ltd
	G-PSAX	Lindstrand LBL-77B balloon	M. V. Farrant & I. Risbridger
	G-PSFG	Robin R.21601	Mardenair Ltd (G-COVD/G-BYOF)
	G-PSGC	PA-25 Pawnee 260C (modified)	Peterborough & Spalding Gliding Club Ltd (G-BDDT)
	G-PSHK	Schempp-Hirth SHK-1	P. Gentil
	G-PSIR	Jurca MJ.77 Gnatsum (474008 'VF-R')	P. W. Carlton & D. F. P. Finan
	G-PSKY	Skyranger 912S(1)	P. W. Curnock & J. W. Wilcox
	G-PSMS	Eurofox 912(1)	P. V. Stevens
	G-PSNI	Eurocopter EC 135T2	Police Service of Northern Ireland
	G-PSNO	Eurocopter MBB BK-117C-2	Police Service of Northern Ireland
	G-PSNR	MBB-BK 117 C-2	Police Service of Northern Ireland (G-LFRS)
	G-PSRT	PA-28-151 Warrior	R. W. Nash (G-BSGN)
	G-PSST	Hunter F.58A	Heritage Aviation Developments Ltd
	G-PSUE	CFM Shadow Srs CD	D. A. Crosbie (G-MYAA)
	G-PSUK	Thruster T.600N 450	Thruster Syndicate
	G-PTAG	Shaw Europa	R. C. Harrison
	G-PTAR	Best Off Skyranger 912S(1)	P. Vergette
	G-PTCA	Cessna F.172P	Shernburn Ltd
	G-PTCC	PA-28RT-201 ArrowIV	Shernburn Ltd (G-BXYS)
	G-PTDD	Bücker Bü133C Jungmeister	T. J. Reeve & M. S. Pettit (G-AEZX)
	G-PTEA	PA-46-350P Malibu Mirage	P. J. Caiger
	G-PTFL	Eurocopter AS.350BA Ecureuil	Tyrone Fabrication Ltd
	G-PTOO	Bell 206L-4 LongRanger 4	P2 Air Ltd
	G-PTRE	SOCATA TB20 Trinidad	Trantshore Ltd (G-BNKU)
	G-PTRI	Cessna 182T	G-PTRI LLP
	G-PTTS	Aerotek Pitts S-2A	P. & J. Voce
	G-PUDL	PA-18 Super Cub 150	C. M. Edwards
	G-PUDS	Shaw Europa	C. R. A. Spirit
	G-PUFF	Thunder Ax7-77A balloon	Intervarsity Balloon Club
	G-PUGS	Cessna 182H	M. D. Joyce
	G-PUGZ	P & M Aviation Quik GT450	A. E. Hill
	G-PUKA	Jabiru Aircraft Jabiru J400	D. P. Harris
	G-PULR	Pitts S-2AE	A. Ayre
	G-PUMB	AS.332L Super Puma	CHC Scotia Ltd
	G-PUMM	AS.332L Super Puma	CHC Scotia Ltd
	G-PUMN	AS.332L Super Puma	CHC Scotia Ltd
	G-PUMO	AS.332L-2 Super Puma	CHC Scotia Ltd
	G-PUMS	AS.332L-2 Super Puma	CHC Scotia Ltd
	G-PUNK	Thunder Ax8-105 balloon	S. C. Kinsey
	G-PUNT	Robinson R44 II	R. D. Cameron
	G-PUPP	Beagle B.121 Pup 2	M. R. Badminton (G-BASD)
	G-PUPS	Cameron Z-210 balloon	High On Adventure Balloons Ltd
	G-PUPY	Shaw Europa XS	D. A. Cameron
	G-PURE	Cameron can 70 SS balloon	Mobberley Balloon Collection
	G-PURL	PA-32R-301 Saratoga II	A. P.H. & E. Hay
	G-PURP	Lindstrand LBL-90° balloon	C. & P. Mackley
	G-PURR	AA-5A Cheetah	D. H. Green (G-BJDN)
	G-PURS	Rotorway Executive	J. E. Houseman
	G-PUSA	Gefa-Flug AS105GD Hot Air Airship	Skyking Aviation Ltd

Reg.	Type	Owner or Operator	Notes
G-PUSI	Cessna T.303	Crusader Craft	
G-PUSS	Cameron N-77 balloon	B. D. Close	
G-PUTT	Cameron Golfball 76 SS balloon	Lakeside Lodge Golf Centre	
G-PVBF	Lindstrand LBL-260S balloon	Virgin Balloon Flights	
G-PVCV	Robin DR400/140	Bustard Flying Club Ltd	
G-PVET	DHC.1 Chipmunk 22 (WB565)	Connect Properties Ltd	
G-PVHT	Dassault Falcon 7X	TAG Aviation (UK) Ltd	
G-PVML	Robin DR400/140B	Weald Air Services Ltd	
G-PVSS	P & M Quik GT450	K. & L. Ramsay	
G-PWAD	Eurocopter EC.120B Colibri	Bapchild Motoring World (Kent) Ltd	
G-PWBE	DH.82A Tiger Moth	M. F. Newman	
G-PWIT	Bell 206L-1 LongRanger	Formal Holdings Ltd (G-DWMI)	
G-PWNS	Cessna 525 Citationjet	Hangar 8 Management Ltd	
G-PWUL	Van's RV-6	D. C. Arnold	
G-PYNE	Thruster T.600N 450	R. Dereham	
G-PYPE	Van's RV-7	R. & L. Pyper	
G-PYRO	Cameron N-65 balloon	A. C. Booth	
G-PZAS	Schleicher ASW-27-18	A. P. C. Sampson	
G-PZPZ	P & M Aviation Pegasus Quantum 15-912	J. Urrutia	
G-RAAA	Bombardier BD700-1A10 Global Express	TAG Aviation (UK) Ltd	
G-RAAF	VS.359 Spitfire VIII	Composite Mast Engineering and Technology Ltd	
G-RAAM	PA-28-161 Warrior II	Falcon Flying Services Ltd (G-BRSE)	
G-RAAY	Taylor JT.1 Monoplane	R. Bowden (G-BEHM)	
G-RABS	Alpi Pioneer 300	J. Mullen	
G-RACA	P.57 Sea Prince T.1 (571/CU) ★	(stored)/Long Marston	
G-RACK	Ikarus C42 FB80	R. W. Rackstraw (G-CFIY)	
G-RACO	PA-28R Cherokee Arrow 200-II	Graco Group Ltd	
G-RACR	Ultramagic M-65C balloon	R. A. Vale	
G-RACY	Cessna 182S	N. J. Fuller	
G-RADA	Soko P-2 Kraguj	S. M. Johnston	
G-RADI	PA-28-181 Archer II	I. Davidson	
G-RADR	Douglas AD-4NA Skyraider (126922:503)	Orion Enterprises Ltd (G-RAID)	
G-RADY	Bombardier CL600-2B19 Challenger 850	TAG Aviation (UK) Ltd	
G-RAEF	Schempp-Hirth SHK-1	R. A. Earnshaw-Fretwell	
G-RAEM	Rutan LongEz	Cambridge Business Travel	
G-RAES	Boeing 777-236	British Airways	
G-RAFA	Grob G.115	RAF College Flying Club Ltd	
G-RAFB	Grob G.115	RAF College Flying Club Ltd	
G-RAFC	Robin R.2112	RAF Charlie Group	
G-RAFE	Thunder Ax7-77 balloon	Giraffe Balloon Syndicate	
G-RAFG	Slingsby T.67C Firefly	Aeros Holdings Ltd	
G-RAFH	Thruster T.600N 450	G-RAFH Group	
G-RAFR	Skyranger J2.2(1)	A. M. Hemmings	
G-RAFS	Thruster T.600N 450	Caunton GRAFS Syndicate	
G-RAFT	Rutan LongEz	W. S. Allen	
G-RAFV	Avid Speedwing	Fox Victor Group (G-MOTT)	
G-RAFW	Mooney M.20E	Vinola (Knitwear) Manufacturing Co Ltd (G-ATHW)	
G-RAFY	Best Off Sky Ranger Swift 912S(1)	M. A. Evans & C. R. Cawley	
G-RAFZ	RAF 2000 GTX-SE	John Pavitt (Engineers) Ltd	
G-RAGE	Wilson Cassutt IIIM	R. S. Grace (G-BEUN)	
G-RAGS	Pietenpol Air Camper	S. H. Leonard	
G-RAGT	PA-32-301FT Cherokee Six	Oxhill Aviation	
G-RAIG	SA Bulldog Srs 100/101	Power Aerobatics Ltd (G-AZMR)	
G-RAIR	Schleicher ASH-25	P. T. Reading	
G-RAIX	CCF AT-16 Harvard 4 (KF584)	M. R. Paul (G-BIWX)	
G-RAJA	Raj Hamsa X'Air 582 (2)	C. Roadnight	
G-RAJJ	BAe 146-200	Cello Aviation Ltd (G-CFDH)	
G-RALA	Robinson R44 Clipper II	HQ Aviation Ltd	
G-RALF	Rotorway Executive 162F	I. C. Bedford (G-BZOM)	
G-RAMA	Cameron C-70 balloon	Poppies (UK) Ltd	

BRITISH CIVIL REGISTRATIONS

Notes	Reg.	Type	Owner or Operator
	G-RAMI	Bell 206B JetRanger 3	Yorkshire Helicopters
	G-RAMP	Piper J-3C-65 Cub	J. A. Holman & T. A. Hinton
	G-RAMS	PA-32R-301 Saratoga SP	Mike Sierra LLP
	G-RAMY	Bell 206B JetRanger 2	Lincair Ltd
	G-RAPD	Hughes 369E	FS Aviation LLP
	G-RAPH	Cameron O-77 balloon	P. A. Sweatman
	G-RAPI	Lindstrand LBL-105A balloon	P. A. Foot
	G-RARA	AutoGyro MTO Sport	K. O. Maurer
	G-RARB	Cessna 172N	Prior Group Holdings Ltd
	G-RARE	Thunder Ax5-42 SS balloon ★	Balloon Preservation Group
	G-RASA	Diamond DA42 Twin Star	C. D. Hill
	G-RASC	Evans VP-2	R. F. Powell
	G-RASH	Grob G.109E	G-RASH Syndicate
	G-RATC	Van's RV-4	A. F. Ratcliffe
	G-RATD	Van's RV-8	J. R. Pike
	G-RATE	AA-5A Cheetah	G-RATE Flying Group (G-BIFF)
	G-RATH	Rotorway Executive 162F	W. H. Cole
	G-RATI	Cessna F.172M	D. Daniel (G-PATI/G-WACZ/G-BCUK)
	G-RATT	Aeropro Eurofox 912(S)	Rattlesden Gliding Club Ltd
	G-RATV	PA-28RT-201T Turbo Arrow IV	Tango Victor Ltd (G-WILS)
	G-RATZ	Shaw Europa	W. Goldsmith
	G-RAVE	Southdown Raven X	M. J. Robbins (G-MNZV)
	G-RAVN	Robinson R44	Brambledown Aircraft Hire
	G-RAWB	P & M Quik GT450	R. Blatchford
	G-RAWS	Rotorway Executive 162F	R. P. Robinson & D. D. Saint
	G-RAXA	Hawker Hunter T.Mk.7	Canberra 134 Ltd (G-VETA/G-BVWN)
	G-RAYB	P & M Quik GT450	R. Blatchford
	G-RAYH	Zenair CH.701UL	R. Horner
	G-RAYO	Lindstrand LBL-90A balloon	R. Owen
	G-RAYY	Cirrus SR22	Alquiler de Veleros SL/Spain
	G-RAYZ	Tecnam P2002-EA Sierra	R. Wells
	G-RAZY	PA-28-181 Archer II	T. H. Pemberton (G-REXS)
	G-RAZZ	Maule MX-7-180	C. S. Baird
	G-RBBB	Shaw Europa	T. J. Hartwell
	G-RBCA	Agusta A109A II	G-RBCA Ltd (G-TBGL/G-VJCB/G-BOUA)
	G-RBCI	BN-2A Mk.III-2 Trislander	Aurigny Air Services Ltd (G-BDWV)
	G-RBCT	Schempp-Hirth Ventus 2Ct	M. J. Weston & J. D. Huband
	G-RBIL	SA.341D Gazelle HT Mk.3	P. J. Whitaker (G-CGJY)
	G-RBMV	Cameron O-31 balloon	P. D. Griffiths
	G-RBNS	Embraer EMB-135BJ Legacy 650	Portrack Global Ltd
	G-RBOS	Colt AS-105 airship ★	Science Museum/Wroughton
	G-RBOW	Thunder Ax-7-65 balloon	R. S. McDonald
	G-RBSN	Ikarus C.42 FB80	P. B. & M. Robinson
	G-RCAV	Bombardier CL600-2B16 Challenger	Hangar 8 Management Ltd
	G-RCED	Rockwell Commander 114	D. J. and D. Pitman
	G-RCHL	P & M Quik GT450	R. M. Broughton
	G-RCHY	Aerotechnik EV-97 Eurostar	N. McKenzie
	G-RCKT	Harmon Rocket II	K. E. Armstrong
	G-RCMC	Murphy Renegade 912	J. Matcham
	G-RCMF	Cameron V-77 balloon	J. M. Percival
	G-RCML	Sky 77-24 balloon	R. C. M. Sarl/Luxembourg
	G-RCNB	Eurocopter EC.120B	C. B. Ellis
	G-RCOH	Cameron Cube 105 SS balloon	A. M. Holly
	G-RCOM	Bell 206L-3 LongRanger 3	G. R. S. Harrison
	G-RCRC	P & M Quik	R. M. Brown
	G-RCSR	Replica de Havilland DH.88 Comet	K. Fern
	G-RCST	Jabiru J430	G. R. Cotterell
	G-RCUB	Piper L-18C (modified)	N. F. O'Neill
	G-RCUS	Schempp-Hirth Arcus T	Lleweni Parc Ltd
	G-RDAD	Reality Escapade ULP(1)	R. W. Burge
	G-RDAY	Van's RV-9	R. M. Day
	G-RDCO	Avtech Jabiru J430	J. M. Record
	G-RDFX	Aero AT-3	B. Wilson
	G-RDHS	Shaw Europa XS	R. D. H. Spencer
	G-RDNS	Rans S.6-S Super Coyote	P. G. Cowling & J. S. Crofts
	G-RDNY	AutoGyro Cavalon	C. Rodney
	G-RDPH	P & M Quik R	R. S. Partridge-Hicks

Reg.	Type	Owner or Operator	Notes
G-READ	Colt 77A balloon	Intervarsity Balloon Club	
G-REAF	Jabiru J400	R. E. Afia	
G-REAH	PA-32R-301 Saratoga SP	M. Q. Tolbod & S. J. Rogers (G-CELL)	
G-REAR	Lindstrand LBL-69X balloon	A. M. Holly	
G-REAS	Van's RV-6A	T. J. Smith	
G-REBB	Murphy Rebel	M. Stow	
G-RECO	Jurca MJ-5L Sirocco	J. D. Tseliki	
G-REDC	Pegasus Quantum 15-912	S. Houghton	
G-REDF	Eurocopter AS.365N3 Dauphin 2	Bond Offshore Helicopters Ltd	
G-REDG	Eurocopter AS.365N3 Dauphin 2	Bond Offshore Helicopters Ltd	
G-REDH	Eurocopter AS.365N3 Dauphin 2	Bond Offshore Helicopters Ltd	
G-REDJ	Eurocopter AS.332L-2 Super Puma	International Aviation Leasing Ltd	
G-REDK	Eurocopter AS.332L-2 Super Puma	International Aviation Leasing Ltd	
G-REDM	Eurocopter AS.332L-2 Super Puma	International Aviation Leasing Ltd	
G-REDN	Eurocopter AS.332L-2 Super Puma	International Aviation Leasing Ltd	
G-REDO	Eurocopter AS.332L-2 Super Puma	International Aviation Leasing Ltd	
G-REDP	Eurocopter AS.332L-2 Super Puma	International Aviation Leasing Ltd	
G-REDR	Eurocopter AS.225LP Super Puma	International Aviation Leasing Ltd	
G-REDT	Eurocopter EC.225LP Super Puma	International Aviation Leasing LLP	
G-REDV	Eurocopter EC.225LP Super Puma	Bond Offshore Helicopters Ltd	
G-REDW	Eurocopter EC.225LP Super Puma	Bond Offshore Helicopters Ltd	
G-REDX	Experimental Aviation Berkut	G. V. Waters	
G-REDY	Robinson R22 Beta	L. Iampieri	
G-REDZ	Thruster T.600T 450	N. S. Dell	
G-REEC	Sequoia F.8L Falco	J. D. Tseliki	
G-REED	Mainair Blade 912S	I. C. Macbeth	
G-REEF	Mainair Blade 912S	G. Mowll	
G-REEM	AS.355F1 Twin Squirrel	Heliking Ltd (G-EMAN/G-WEKR/G-CHLA)	
G-REER	Centrair 101A Pegase	R. L. Howorth & G. C. Stinchcombe	
G-REES	Jodel D.140C	G-REES Flying Group	
G-REGC	Zenair CH.601XL Zodiac	G. P. Coutie	
G-REGE	Robinson R44	Rotorvale Helicopters	
G-REGI	Cyclone Chaser S508	G. S. Stokes (G-MYZW)	
G-REGS	Thunder Ax7-77 balloon	D. R. Rawlings	
G-REGZ	Aeroprakt A-22L Foxbat	M. D. Northwood	
G-REJP	Europa XS	A. Milner	
G-REKO	Pegasus Quasar IITC	M. Carter (G-MWWA)	
G-RELL	D.62B Condor	M. J. Golder (G-OPJH/G-AVDW)	
G-REMH	Bell 206B-3 JetRanger III	Flightpath Ltd	
G-RENI	Balony Kubicek BB-30Z balloon	A. M. Holly	
G-RENO	SOCATA TB10 Tobago	V. W. Ood	
G-RESC	MBB BK.117C-1	Veritair ASviation Ltd	
G-RESG	Dyn'Aéro MCR-01 Club	R. E. S. Greenwood	
G-REST	Beech P35 Bonanza	C. R. Taylor (G-ASFJ)	
G-RETA	CASA 1.131 Jungmann 2000	Richard Shuttleworth Trustees (G-BGZC)	
G-REVE	Van's RV-6	J. D. Winder	
G-REVO	Skyranger 912(2)	H. Murray	
G-REYS	Canadair CL600-2B16 Challenger 604	TAG Aviation	
G-RFIO	Aeromot AMT-200 Super Ximango	M. D. Evans	
G-RFLY	Extra EA.300/L	H. B. Sauer	
G-RFOX	Denney Kitfox Mk 3	J. R. Chapman & G. Harrington	
G-RFSB	Sportavia RF-5B	G-RFSB Group	
G-RFUN	Robinson R44	Brooklands Developments Ltd	
G-RGSG	Raytheon Hawker 900XP	Hangar 8 Management Ltd	
G-RGTS	Schempp-Hirth Discus b	G. R. & L. R. Green	
G-RGUS	Fairchild 24A-46A Argus III (44-83184)	T. R. Coulton & J. L. Bryan	
G-RGZT	Cirrus SR20	M. Presenti	
G-RHAM	Skyranger 582(1)	I. Smart & T. Driffield	
G-RHCB	Schweizer 269C-1	Lift West Ltd	
G-RHMS	Embraer EMB-135BJ Legacy	TAG Aviation (UK) Ltd	
G-RHOS	ICP MXP-740 Savannah VG Jabiru(1)	J. C. Munro-Hunt	
G-RHYM	PA-31-310 Turbo Navajo B	2 Excel Aviation Ltd (G-BJLO)	
G-RHYS	Rotorway Executive 90	A. K. Voase	
G-RIAM	SOCATA TB10 Tobago	H. Varia	
G-RIBA	P & M Quik GT450	R. J. Murphy	
G-RICK	Beech 95-B55 Baron	J. Jack (G-BAAG)	
G-RICO	AG-5B Tiger	Delta Lima Flying Group	

Notes	Reg.	Type	Owner or Operator
	G-RICS	Shaw Europa	The Flying Property Doctor
	G-RIDA	Eurocopter AS.355NP Ecureuil 2	National Grid Electricity Transmission PLC
	G-RIDB	Bell 429	National Grid Electricity Transmission PLC
	G-RIDE	Stephens Akro	R. Mitchell
	G-RIDG	Van's RV-7	C. Heathcote
	G-RIEF	DG Flugzeugbau DG-1000T	EF Gliding Group
	G-RIET	Hoffmann H.36 Dimona	Dimona Gliding Group
	G-RIEV	Rolladen-Schneider LS8-18	R. D. Grieve
	G-RIFB	Hughes 269C	AA Consultants Ltd
	G-RIFN	Avion Mudry CAP-10B	D. E. Starkey & R. A. J. Spurrell
	G-RIFO	Schempp-Hirth Standard Cirrus 75-VTC	A. Mura (G-CKGT)
	G-RIFY	Christen Eagle II	C. I. D. H. Garrison
	G-RIGB	Thunder Ax7-77 balloon	N. J. Bettin
	G-RIGH	PA-32R-301 Saratoga IIHP	G. M. R. Graham
	G-RIGS	PA-60 Aerostar 601P	G. G. Caravatti & P. G. Penati/Italy
	G-RIHN	Dan Rihn DR.107 One Design	P. J. Burgess
	G-RIII	Vans RV-3B	R. S. Grace & D. H. Burge
	G-RIIV	Van's RV-4	M. R. Overall
	G-RIKI	Mainair Blade 912	RIKI Group
	G-RIKS	Shaw Europa XS	R. A. & W. R. Davies
	G-RIKY	Mainair Pegasus Quik	S. Clarke
	G-RILA	Flight Design CTSW	P. A. Mahony
	G-RILY	Monnett Sonnerai 2L	A Sharp
	G-RIMB	Lindstrand LBL-105A balloon	D. Grimshaw
	G-RIME	Lindstrand LBL-25A balloon	N. Ivison
	G-RIMM	Westland Wasp HAS.1 (XT435:430)	G. P. Hinkley
	G-RINN	Mainair Blade	P. Hind
	G-RINO	Thunder Ax7-77 balloon	D. J. Head
	G-RINS	Rans S.6-ESA Coyote II	R. W. Hocking
	G-RINT	CFM Streak Shadow	D. Grint
	G-RINZ	Van's RV-7	P. Chaplin (G-UZZL)
	G-RIPA	Partenavia P68 Observer 2	Apem Ltd
	G-RIPH	VS.384 Seafire F.XVII	Seafire Displays Ltd (G-CDTM)
	G-RISA	PA-28-180 Cherokee C	D. B. Riseborough (G-ATZK)
	G-RISE	Cameron V-77 balloon	D. L. Smith
	G-RISH	Rotorway Exeecutive 162F	C. S. Rische
	G-RISK	Hughes 369E	Wavendon Social Housing Ltd
	G-RISY	Van's RV-7	G-RISY Group
	G-RITT	P & M Quik	T. H. Parr
	G-RIVA	SOCATA TBM-700N	Airpark One Ltd
	G-RIVE	Jodel D.153	P. Fines
	G-RIVR	Thruster T.600N 450	Thruster Air Services Ltd
	G-RIVT	Van's RV-6	N. Reddish
	G-RIXA	J-3C-65 Cub	J. J. Rix
	G-RIXS	Shaw Europa XS	R. Iddon
	G-RIXY	Cameron Z-77 balloon	Rix Petroleum (Hull) Ltd
	G-RIZE	Cameron O-90 balloon	S. F. Burden/Netherlands
	G-RIZI	Cameron N-90 balloon	R. Wiles
	G-RIZZ	PA-28-161 Warrior II	Modi Aviation Ltd
	G-RJAH	Boeing Stearman A75N1 (44)	R. J. Horne
	G-RJAM	Sequoia F.8L Falco	D. G. Drew
	G-RJCC	Cessna 172S	R. J. Chapman
	G-RJCP	Rockwell Commander 114B	Heltor Ltd
	G-RJMS	PA-28R-201 Arrow III	M. G. Hill
	G-RJRJ	Evektor EV-97A Eurostar	D. P. Myatt
	G-RJWW	Maule M5-235C Lunar Rocket	D. E. Priest (G-BRWG)
	G-RJWX	Shaw Europa XS	D. S. P. Disney
	G-RJXA	Embraer RJ145EP	bmi regional
	G-RJXB	Embraer RJ145EP	bmi regional
	G-RJXC	Embraer RJ145EP	bmi regional
	G-RJXD	Embraer RJ145EP	bmi regional
	G-RJXE	Embraer RJ145EP	bmi regional
	G-RJXF	Embraer RJ145EP	bmi regional
	G-RJXG	Embraer RJ145EP	bmi regional
	G-RJXH	Embraer RJ145EP	bmi regional
	G-RJXI	Embraer RJ145EP	bmi regional
	G-RJXJ	Embraer RJ135LR	bmi regional
	G-RJXK	Embraer RJ135LR	bmi regional
	G-RJXL	Embraer RJ135LR	bmi regional
	G-RJXM	Embraer RJ145MP	bmi regional

Reg.	Type	Owner or Operator	Notes
G-RJXP	Embraer RJ135ER	bmi regional (G-CDFS)	
G-RJXR	Embraer RJ145EP	bmi regional (G-CCYH)	
G-RKEL	Agusta-Bell 206B JetRanger 3	Nunkeeling Ltd	
G-RKKT	Cessna FR.172G	K. L. Irvine (G-AYJW)	
G-RLEF	Hawker Hurricane XII	P. J. Lawton	
G-RLMW	Tecnam P2002-EA Sierra	G. J. Slater	
G-RLON	BN-2A Mk III-2 Trislander	Aurigny Air Services Ltd (G-ITEX/G-OCTA/ G-BCXW)	
G-RLWG	Ryan ST3KR	R. A. Fleming	
G-RMAC	Shaw Europa	P. J. Lawless	
G-RMAN	Aero Designs Pulsar	G. Hawkins	
G-RMAX	Cameron C-80 balloon	J. Kenny	
G-RMCS	Cessna 182R	R. W. C. Sears	
G-RMHE	Aerospool Dynamic WT9 UK	R. M. Hughes-Ellis	
G-RMIT	Van's RV-4	J. P. Kloos	
G-RMMA	Dassault Falcon 900EX	TAG Aviation (UK) Ltd	
G-RMMT	Europa XS	N. Schmitt	
G-RMPI	Whittaker MW5D Sorcerer	N. R. Beale	
G-RMPS	Van's RV-12	K. D. Boardman	
G-RMPY	Aerotechnik EV-97 Eurostar	N. R. Beale	
G-RMRV	Van's RV-7A	R. Morris	
G-RMTO	Rotorsport UK MTO Sport	J. R. S. Heaton	
G-RMUG	Cameron Nescafe Mug 90 SS balloon	The British Balloon Museum & Library Ltd	
G-RNAC	IDA Bacau Yakovlev Yak-52	RNAEC Group	
G-RNAS	DH.104 Sea Devon C.20 (XK896) ★	Airport Fire Service/Filton	
G-RNBW	Bell 206B JetRanger 2	Rainbow Helicopters Ltd	
G-RNCH	PA-28-181 Archer II	Carlisle Flight Training Ltd	
G-RNDD	Robin DR.400/500	Witham (Specialist Vehicles) Ltd	
G-RNER	Cessna 510 Citation Mustang	S. J. Davies	
G-RNGO	Robinson R22 II	Elisemroma SRL/Italy	
G-RNHF	Hawker Sea Fury T.Mk.20 (VX281)	Naval Aviation Ltd (G-BCOW)	
G-RNIE	Cameron 70 Ball SS balloon	N. J. Bland	
G-RNLI	VS.236 Walrus I (W2718) ★	Walrus Aviation Ltd	
G-RNRM	Cessna A.185F	Skydive St. Andrews Ltd	
G-RNRS	SA Bulldog Srs.100/101	Power Aerobatics Ltd (G-AZIT)	
G-ROAD	Robinson R44 II	Aztec Aviators Ltd	
G-ROBD	Shaw Europa	M. P. Wiseman	
G-ROBG	P & M Quik GT450	Exodus Airsports Ltd	
G-ROBJ	Robin DR.500/200i	D. R. L. Jones	
G-ROBN	Pierre Robin R1180T	N. D. Anderson	
G-ROBT	Hawker Hurricane I (P2902:DX-X)	R. A. Roberts	
G-ROBY	Colt 17A balloon	Virgin Airship & Balloon Co Ltd	
G-ROBZ	Grob G109B	Bravo Zulu Group	
G-ROCH	Cessna T.303	R. S. Bentley	
G-ROCK	Thunder Ax7-77 balloon	M. A. Green	
G-ROCO	ACLA Sirocco	D. C. Arnold	
G-ROCR	Schweizer 269C	Hayles Aviation	
G-ROCT	Robinson R44 II	A. von Liechtenstein	
G-RODC	Steen Skybolt	D. G. Girling	
G-RODD	Cessna 310R II	R. J. Herbert Engineering Ltd (G-TEDD/ G-MADI)	
G-RODG	Avtech Jabiru UL	G-RODG Group	
G-RODI	Isaacs Fury (K3731)	M. J. Bond	
G-RODJ	Ikarus C42 FB80	T. J. Hyde	
G-RODO	Shaw Europa XS	R. M. Carson (G-ROWI)	
G-RODZ	Van's RV-3A	M. J. Wood	
G-ROEI	Avro Roe 1 Replica	Brooklands Museum Trust Ltd	
G-ROEN	Cameron C-70 balloon	R. M. W. Romans	
G-ROFS	Groppo Trail	R. F. Bond	
G-ROGY	Cameron 60 Concept balloon	S. A. Laing	
G-ROKO	Roko-Aero NG-4HD	K. D. Taylor	
G-ROKS	Robinson R44 II	R. Starling (G-WEGO)	
G-ROKT	Cessna FR.172E	G-ROKT Flying Club Ltd	
G-ROKY	Gruppo Trail	Skyview Systems Ltd	
G-ROLF	PA-32R-301 Saratoga SP	P. F. Larkins	
G-ROLL	Pitts S-2A Special	Aerobatic Displays Ltd	

Notes	Reg.	Type	Owner or Operator
	G-ROLY	Cessna F.172N	M. Bonsall (G-BHIH)
	G-ROME	I.I.I. Sky Arrow 650TC	Sky Arrow (Kits) UK Ltd
	G-ROMP	Extra 230H	D. G. Cowden & S. C. Hipwell
	G-ROMW	Cyclone AX2000	K. V. Falvey
	G-RONA	Shaw Europa	C. M. Noakes
	G-RONG	PA-28R Cherokee Arrow 200-II	D. Griffiths & S. P. Rooney
	G-RONI	Cameron V-77 balloon	R. E. Simpson
	G-RONS	Robin DR.400/180	R. & K. Baker
	G-RONW	FRED Srs 2	F. J. Keitch
	G-RONZ	Ikarus C42 FB80 Bravo	R. F. Dean
	G-ROOK	Cessna F.172P	Rolim Ltd
	G-ROOO	Jabiru J430	H. S. A. Brewis (G-HJZN)
	G-ROOV	Shaw Europa XS	P. W. Hawkins & K. Siggery
	G-ROPO	Groppo Trail	R. D. P. Cadle
	G-ROPP	Groppo Trail	P. T. Price
	G-RORB	Spitfire Mk.26	Bertha Property LLP
	G-RORI	Folland Gnat T.1 (XR538)	Heritage Aircraft Ltd
	G-RORY	Piaggio FWP.149D	M. Edwards (G-TOWN)
	G-ROSI	Thunder Ax7-77 balloon	J. E. Rose
	G-ROTS	CFM Streak Shadow Srs SA	J. Edwards
	G-ROUS	PA-34-200T Seneca II	Oxford Aviation Training Ltd
	G-ROVE	PA-18 Super Cub 135 (R-156)	S. J. Gaveston
	G-ROVY	Robinson R22 Beta	Fly Executive Ltd
	G-ROWA	Aquila AT01	R. Simpson
	G-ROWE	Cessna F.182P	D. Rowe
	G-ROWL	AA-5B Tiger	T. A. Timms
	G-ROWS	PA-28-151 Warrior	Air Academy
	G-ROXI	Cameron C-90 balloon	N. R. Beckwith
	G-ROYC	Avtech Jabiru UL450	R. L. Flowerday
	G-ROYM	Robinson R44 II	HQ Aviation Ltd
	G-ROYN	Robinson R44	Napier Helicopters Ltd (G-DCON)
	G-ROZE	Magni M-24C	R. I. Simpson
	G-ROZI	Robinson R44	Rotormotive Ltd
	G-ROZZ	Ikarus C.42 FB 80	A. J. Blackwell
	G-RPAF	Europa XS	G-RPAF Group
	G-RPAX	CASA 1-133 Jungmeister	A. J. E. Smith
	G-RPCC	Europa XS	R. P. Churchill-Coleman
	G-RPEZ	Rutan LongEz	M. P. Dunlop
	G-RPPO	Groppo Trail	G. N. Smith
	G-RPRV	Van's RV-9A	M. G. Titmus
	G-RRAK	Enstrom 480B	A. Fawsitt (G-RIBZ)
	G-RRAT	CZAW Sportcruiser	G. Sipson
	G-RRCU	CEA DR.221B Dauphin	Merlin Flying Club Ltd
	G-RRED	PA-28-181 Archer II	J. P. Reddington
	G-RRFC	SOCATA TB20 Trinidad GT	C. A. Hawkins
	G-RRFF	VS.329 Spitfire Mk.IIB	Retro Track & Air (UK) Ltd
	G-RRGN	VS.390 Spitfire PR.XIX (PS853)	Rolls-Royce PLC (G-MXIX)
	G-RROB	Robinson R44 II	R. S. Rai
	G-RRRV	Van's RV-6A	C. St. J. Hall
	G-RRRZ	Van's RV-8	D. J. C. Davidson
	G-RRSR	Piper J-3C-65 Cub (480173:57-H)	R. W. Roberts
	G-RRVV	Van's RV-8	The Victor Victor Flying Group
	G-RRVX	Van's RV-10	R. D. Mastersd
	G-RSAF	BAC.167 Strikemaster 80A	Viper Classics Ltd
	G-RSAM	P & M Quik GTR	S. F. Beardsell
	G-RSCU	Agusta A.109E	Sloane Helicopters Ltd
	G-RSHI	PA-34-220T Seneca V	R. S. Hill and Sons
	G-RSKR	PA-28-161 Warrior II	ACS Engineering Ltd (G-BOJY)
	G-RSKY	Skyranger 912(2)	C. G. Benham & C. H. Tregonning
	G-RSMC	Medway SLA 100 Executive	W. S. C. Toulmin
	G-RSSF	Denney Kitfox Mk 2	R. W. Somerville
	G-RSWO	Cessna 172R	G. Fischer
	G-RSWW	Robinson R22 Beta	Kington building Supplies Ltd
	G-RSXL	Cessna 560 Citation XLS	Aircraft Leasing Overseas Ltd
	G-RTBI	Thunder Ax6-56 balloon	D. J. Stagg
	G-RTFM	Jabiru J400	I. A. Macphee
	G-RTHS	Rans S-6-ES Coyote II	R. G. Hughes

Reg.	Type	Owner or Operator	Notes
G-RTIN	Rotorsport UK MT-03	G. McAleer	
G-RTMS	Rans S.6 ES Coyote II	C. J. Arthur	
G-RTMY	Ikarus C.42 FB 100	Mike Yankee Group	
G-RTRV	V an's RV-9A	R. Taylor	
G-RUBB	AA-5B Tiger	D. E. Gee	
G-RUBY	PA-28RT-201T Turbo Arrow IV	Arrow Aircraft Group (G-BROU)	
G-RUCK	Bell 206B-3 JetRanger III	J. A. Ruck	
G-RUES	Robin HR.100/210	R. H. R. Rue	
G-RUFF	Mainair Blade 912	P. Mulvey	
G-RUFS	Avtech Jabiru UL	M. Bastin	
G-RUGS	Campbell Cricket Mk 4 gyroplane	J. L. G. McLane	
G-RUIA	Cessna F.172N	D. C. Parry	
G-RULE	Robinson R44 Raven II	Huckair	
G-RUMI	Noble Harman Snowbird Mk.IV	G. Crossley (G-MVOI)	
G-RUMM	Grumman F8F-2P Bearcat (121714:201B)	Patina Ltd	
G-RUMN	AA-1A Trainer	M. T. Manwaring	
G-RUMW	Grumman FM-2 Wildcat (JV579:F)	Patina Ltd	
G-RUNS	P & M Quik GT450	S. Nicol	
G-RUNT	Cassutt Racer IIIM	D. P. Lightfoot	
G-RUPS	Cameron TR-70 balloon	R. M. Stanley	
G-RUSL	Van's RV-6A	G. R. Russell	
G-RUSO	Robinson R22 Beta	R. M. Barnes-Gorell	
G-RUSS	Cessna 172N ★	Leisure Lease (stored)/Southend	
G-RUVE	Van's RV-8	J. P. Brady & D. J. Taylor	
G-RUVI	Zenair CH.601UL	P. G. Depper	
G-RUVY	Van's RV-9A	R. D. Taylor	
G-RVAB	Van's RV-7	I. M. Belmore & A. T. Banks	
G-RVAC	Van's RV-7	A. F. S. & B. Caldecourt	
G-RVAH	Van's RV-7	R. C. W. King	
G-RVAL	Van's RV-8	R. N. York	
G-RVAN	Van's RV-6	D. Broom	
G-RVAT	Van's RV-8	T. R. Grief	
G-RVAW	Van's RV-6	C. Rawlings & R. J. Tomlinson	
G-RVBA	Van's RV-8A	D. P. Richard	
G-RVBC	Van's RV-6A	B. J. Clifford	
G-RVBF	Cameron A-340 balloon	Virgin Balloon Flights	
G-RVBI	Van's RV-8	M. A. N. Newall	
G-RVCE	Van's RV-6A	C. & M. D. Barnard	
G-RVCH	Van's RV-8A	R. J. Birt	
G-RVCL	Van's RV-6	M. A. Wyer	
G-RVDG	Van's RV-9	D. M. Gill	
G-RVDH	Van's RV-8	D. J. Harrison (G-ONER)	
G-RVDJ	Van's RV-6	J. D. Jewitt	
G-RVDP	Van's RV-4	O. Florin	
G-RVDR	Van's RV-6A	P. R. Redfern	
G-RVDX	Van's RV-4	P. J. Scullion (G-FTUO)	
G-RVEE	Van's RV-6	J. C. A. Wheeler	
G-RVEI	Van's RV-8	D. Stephens	
G-RVEM	Van's RV-7A	N. A. Quintin (G-CBJU)	
G-RVER	Van's RV-4	R. D. E. Holah	
G-RVET	Van's RV-6	D. R. Coleman	
G-RVGA	Van's RV-6A	R. Emery	
G-RVGO	Van's RV-10	D. C. Arnold	
G-RVIA	Van's RV-6A	K. R. W. Scull & J. Watkins	
G-RVIB	Van's RV-6	P. D. Gorman	
G-RVIC	Van's RV-6A	I. T. Corse	
G-RVII	Van's RV-7	P. H. C. Hall	
G-RVIN	Van's RV-6	N. Reddish	
G-RVIO	Van's RV-10	G-RVIO Group	
G-RVIS	Van's RV-8	I. V. Sharman	
G-RVIT	Van's RV-6	P. J. Shotbolt	
G-RVIV	Van's RV-4	S. B. Robson	
G-RVIW	Van's RV-9	G. S. Scott	
G-RVIX	Van's RV-9A	J. R. Holt & C. S. Simmons	
G-RVIZ	Van's RV-12	J. E. Singleton	
G-RVJM	Van's RV-6	M. D. Challoner	
G-RVJO	Van's RV-9A	P. D. Chandler	
G-RVJP	Van's RV-9A	R. M. Palmer	

Notes	Reg.	Type	Owner or Operator
	G-RVJW	Van's RV-4	J. M. Williams
	G-RVLC	Van's RV-9A	L. J. Clark
	G-RVMB	Van's RV-9A	M. James & R. W. Littledale
	G-RVMT	Van's RV-6	M. J. Aldridge
	G-RVMZ	Van's RV-8	A. E. Kay
	G-RVNA	PA-38-112 Tomahawk	Ravenair Aircraft Ltd (G-DFLY)
	G-RVNB	PA-38-112 Tomahawk	NPA Aviation (G-SUKI/G-BPNV)
	G-RVNC	PA-38-112 Tomahawk	Ravenair Aircraft Ltd (G-BTJK)
	G-RVND	PA-38-112 Tomahawk	NPA Aviation (G-BTAS)
	G-RVNE	Partenavia P.68B	Ravenair Aircraft Ltd (G-SAMJ)
	G-RVNG	Partenavia P.68B	Ravenair Aircraft Ltd (G-BMOI)
	G-RVNH	Van's RV-9A	N. R. Haines
	G-RVNI	Van's RV-6A	G-RVNI Group
	G-RVNJ	Partenavia P.68B	Ravenair Aircraft Ltd
	G-RVNK	Partenavia P.68B	Ravenair Aircraft Ltd (G-BHBZ)
	G-RVNM	Partenavia P.68B	Ravenair Aircraft Ltd (G-BFBU)
	G-RVNP	Partenavia P.68B	Ravenair Aircraft Ltd
	G-RVNS	Van's RV-4	P. I. Lewis (G-CBGN)
	G-RVOM	Van's RV-8	O. D. Mihalop
	G-RVPH	Van's RV-8	J. C. P. Herbert
	G-RVPL	Van's RV-8	B. J. Summers
	G-RVPM	Van's RV-4	D. P. Lightfoot (G-RVDS)
	G-RVPW	Van's RV-6A	C. G. Deeley
	G-RVRA	PA-28 Cherokee 140	Par Contractors Ltd (G-OWVA)
	G-RVRB	PA-34-200T Seneca II	Ravenair Aircraft Ltd (G-BTAJ)
	G-RVRC	PA-23 Aztec 250E	B. J. Green (G-BNPD)
	G-RVRD	PA-23 Aztec 250E	Ravenair Aircraft Ltd (G-BRAV/G-BBCM)
	G-RVRE	Partenavia P.68B	Ravenair Aircraft Ltd
	G-RVRI	Cessna 172H Skyhawk	L. Kelly (G-CCCC)
	G-RVRJ	PA-E23 Aztec 250E	Ravenair Aircraft Ltd (G-BBGB)
	G-RVRK	PA-38-112 Tomahawk	Ravenair Aircraft Ltd (G-BGZW)
	G-RVRL	PA-38-112 Tomahawk	Ravenair Aircraft Ltd (G-BGZW/G-BGBY)
	G-RVRM	PA-38-112 Tomahawk	Ravenair Aircraft Ltd (G-BGEK)
	G-RVRN	PA-28-161 Warrior II	Ravenair Aircraft Ltd (G-BPID)
	G-RVRO	PA-38-112 Tomahawk II	Ravenair Aircraft Ltd (G-BOUD)
	G-RVRP	Van's RV-7	R. C. Parris
	G-RVRR	PA-38-112 Tomahawk	Ravenair Aircraft Ltd (G-BRHT)
	G-RVRT	PA-28-140 Cherokee C	Ravenair Aircraft Ltd (G-AYKX)
	G-RVRU	PA-38-112 Tomahawk	Ravenair Aircraft Ltd (G-NCFE/G-BKMK)
	G-RVRV	Van's RV-4	P. Jenkins
	G-RVRW	PA-23 Aztec 250E	Ravenair Aircraft Ltd (G-BAVZ)
	G-RVRX	Partenavia P.68B	Ravenair Aircraft Ltd (G-PART)
	G-RVRY	PA-38-112 Tomahawk	Ravenair Aircraft Ltd (G-BTND)
	G-RVRZ	PA-23-250 Aztec E	Ravenair Aircraft Ltd (G-NRSC/G-BSFL)
	G-RVSA	Van's RV-6A	W. H. Knott
	G-RVSD	Van's RV-9A	S. W. Damarell
	G-RVSG	Van's RV-9A	S. Gerrish
	G-RVSH	Van's RV-6A	S. J. D. Hall
	G-RVSR	Van's RV-8	R. K. & S. W. Elders
	G-RVST	Van's RV-6	J. D. Rooney (G-BXYX)
	G-RVSX	Van's RV-6	R. L. & V. A. West
	G-RVTE	Van's RV-6	E. McShane & T. Feeny
	G-RVTN	Van's RV-10	C. I. Law
	G-RVTT	Van's RV-7	R. L. Mitcham
	G-RVTW	Van's RV-12	A. P. Watkins
	G-RVUK	Van's RV-7	P. D. G. Grist
	G-RVVI	Van's RV-6	G. G. Ferriman
	G-RVVY	Van's RV-10	P. R. Marskell
	G-RVWJ	Van's RV-9A	N. J. Williams-Jones
	G-RVXP	Van's RV-3B	A. N. Buchan
	G-RWAY	Rotorway Executive 162F	C. R. Johnson (G-URCH)
	G-RWEW	Robinson R44	Northern Heli Charters
	G-RWGS	Robinson R44 II	R. W. G. Simpson
	G-RWIA	Robinson R22 Beta	GPS Fabrications Ltd (G-BOEZ)
	G-RWIN	Rearwin 175	A. B. Bourne & N. D. Battye
	G-RWLY	Shaw Europa XS	Active Aviation Ltd
	G-RWMW	Zenair CH.601XL Zodiac	R. W. H. Watson (G-DROO)
	G-RWOD	Dan Rihn DR.107 One Design	R. S. Wood
	G-RWSS	Denney Kitfox Mk 2	R. W. Somerville

Reg.	Type	Owner or Operator	Notes
G-RWWW	WS-55 Whirlwind HCC.12 (XR486)★	IHM/Weston-super-Mare	
G-RXUK	Lindstrand LBL-105A balloon	C. C. & R. K. Scott	
G-RYAL	Avtech Jabiru UL	S. A. Ivell	
G-RYDR	Rotorsport UK MT-03	H. W. Parsons & U. Junger	
G-RYNS	PA-32-301FT Cherokee Six	D. A. Earle	
G-RYPE	DG Flugzeugbau DG-1000T	DG-1000T Partners	
G-RYPH	Mainair Blade 912	I. A. Cunningham	
G-RYZZ	Robinson R44 II	Rivermead Aviation Ltd	
G-RZEE	Schleicher ASW-19B	D. I. Wadsworth & J. M. Anderson	
G-RZLY	Flight Design CTSW	J. D. Macnamara	
G-SAAA	Flight Design CTSW	Comunica Industries International Ltd	
G-SABA	PA-28R-201T Turbo Arrow III	C. A. Burton (G-BFEN)	
G-SABB	Eurocopter EC 135T1	Bond Air Services Ltd	
G-SABR	NA F-86A Sabre (8178:FU-178)	Golden Apple Operations Ltd	
G-SACH	Stoddard-Hamilton Glastar	R. S. Holt	
G-SACI	PA-28-161 Warrior II	PJC (Leasing) Ltd	
G-SACM	TL2000UK Sting Carbon	M. Clare	
G-SACO	PA-28-161 Warrior II	Stapleford Flying Club Ltd	
G-SACR	PA-28-161 Cadet	Sherburn Aero Club Ltd	
G-SACS	PA-28-161 Cadet	Sherburn Aero Club Ltd	
G-SACT	PA-28-161 Cadet	Sherburn Aero Club Ltd	
G-SACW	Aero AT-3 R100	Sherburn Aero Club Ltd	
G-SACX	Aero AT-3 R100	Sherburn Aero Club Ltd	
G-SACY	Aero AT-3 R100	Sherburn Aero Club Ltd	
G-SAFE	Cameron N-77 balloon	P. J. Waller	
G-SAFI	CP.1320 Super Emeraude	C. S. Carleton-Smith	
G-SAFR	SAAB 91D Safir	Sylmar Aviation & Services Ltd	
G-SAGA	Grob G.109B	G-GROB Ltd/Booker	
G-SAGE	Luscombe 8A Silvaire	C. Howell (G-AKTL)	
G-SAHI	Trago Mills SAH-1	Hotel India Group	
G-SAIG	Robinson R44 II	Torfield Aviation Ltd	
G-SAIR	Cessna 421C	Air Support Aviation Services Ltd (G-OBCA)	
G-SAJA	Schempp-Hirth Discus 2	J. G. Arnold	
G-SALA	PA-32 Cherokee Six 300E	R. M. J. Harrison & J. W. A. Portch	
G-SALE	Cameron Z-90 balloon	R. D. Baker	
G-SAMC	Ikarus C42 FB80	G. Cooper	
G-SAMG	Grob G.109B	The Royal Air Force Gliding and Soaring Association	
G-SAMY	Shaw Europa	K. R. Tallent	
G-SAMZ	Cessna 150D	Fly More Aviation Ltd (G-ASSO)	
G-SANL	Bombardier BD700-1A10 Global Express	Sanctuary Aviation LLP	
G-SAOC	Schempp-Hirth Discus 2cT	The Royal Air Force Gliding and Soaring Association	
G-SAPM	SOCATA TB20 Trinidad	G-SAPM Ltd (G-EWFN)	
G-SARA	PA-28-181 Archer II	Apollo Aviation Advisory Ltd	
G-SARD	Agusta Westland AW139	CHC Scotia Ltd (HM Coastguard)	
G-SARJ	P & M Quik GT450	A. R. Jones	
G-SARM	Ikarus C.42 FB80	G-SARM Group	
G-SARV	Van's RV-4	Hinton Flying Group	
G-SASA	Eurocopter EC 135T1	Bond Air Services Ltd	
G-SASB	Eurocopter EC 135T2+	Bond Air Services Ltd	
G-SASC	Beech B200C Super King Air	Gama Aviation Ltd	
G-SASD	Beech B200C Super King Air	Gama Aviation Ltd	
G-SASG	Schleicher ASW-27-18E	F. B. Jeynes	
G-SASH	MDH MD.900 Explorer	Yorkshire Air Ambulance Ltd	
G-SASI	CZAW Sportcruiser	A. S. Arundell	
G-SASK	PA-31P Pressurised Navajo	Middle East Business Club Ltd (G-BFAM)	
G-SASM	Westland Scout AH.Mk.1 (XV138)	C. J. Marsden	
G-SASY	Eurocopter EC.130 B4	R. J. H. Smith	
G-SATN	PA-25-260 Pawnee C	The Royal Gliding and Soaring Association	
G-SAUO	Cessna A.185F	T. G. Lloyd	
G-SAUK	Rans S6-ES	M. D. Tulloch	
G-SAVY	Savannah VG Jabiru(1)	C. S. Hollingworth & S. P. Yardley	
G-SAWI	PA-32RT-300T Turbo Lance II	Regularity Ltd	

Notes	Reg.	Type	Owner or Operator
	G-SAXL	Schempp-Hirth Duo Discus T	The Royal Air Force Gliding and Soaring Association
	G-SAXT	Schempp-Hirth Duo Discus Xt	The Royal Air Force Gliding and Soaring Association
	G-SAYS	RAF 2000 GTX-SE gyroplane	K. J. Whitehead
	G-SAZM	Piper J-3C-65 Cub	I. E. M. J. Van Vuuren
	G-SAZY	Avtech Jabiru J400	S.M. Pink
	G-SAZZ	CP.328 Super Emeraude	D. J. Long
	G-SBAE	Cessna F.172P	BAe (Warton) Flying Club
	G-SBAG	Phoenix Currie Wot	R. W. Clarke (G-BFAH)
	G-SBAP	Rans S-6 ES Coyote II	Royal Aeronautical Society
	G-SBDB	Remos GX	G-SBDB Group
	G-SBIZ	Cameron Z-90 balloon	Snow Business International Ltd
	G-SBKR	SOCATA TB10 Tobago	S. C. M. Bagley
	G-SBLT	Steen Skybolt	Skybolt Group
	G-SBOL	Steen Skybolt	M. P. Barley
	G-SBRK	Aero AT-3 R100	Sywell Aerodrome Ltd
	G-SBUS	BN-2A-26 Islander	Isles of Scilly Skybus Ltd (G-BMMH)
	G-SCAN	Vinten-Wallis WA-116/100	K. H. Wallis
	G-SCBI	SOCATA TB20 Trinidad	G. & J. Steven
	G-SCCZ	CZAW Sportcruiser	J. W. Ellis
	G-SCHI	AS.350B2 Ecureuil	Patriot Aviation Ltd
	G-SCHO	Robinson R22 Beta	Blades Aviation (UK) LLP
	G-SCHZ	Eurocopter AS.355N Ecureuil 2	Veritair Aviation Ltd (G-STON)
	G-SCII	Agusta A109C	Plattreid Ltd (G-JONA)
	G-SCIP	SOCATA TB20 Trinidad GT	The Studio People Ltd
	G-SCLX	FLS Aerospace Sprint 160	E. J. F. McEntee (G-PLYM)
	G-SCNN	Schempp-Hirth Standard Cirrus	G. C. Short
	G-SCOL	Gippsland GA-8 Airvan	Parachuting Aircraft Ltd
	G-SCPD	Escapade 912 (1)	R. K. W. Moss
	G-SCPI	CZAW Sportcruiser	I. M. Speight & P. R. W. Goslin
	G-SCPL	PA-28 Cherokee 140	Aeros Leasing Ltd (G-BPVL)
	G-SCRZ	CZAW Sportcruiser	P. H. Grant
	G-SCSC	CZAW Sportcruiser	G-SCSC Group
	G-SCTA	Westland Scout AH.1	G. R. Harrison
	G-SCUB	PA-18 Super Cub 135 (542447)	M. E. Needham
	G-SCUL	Rutan Cozy	K. R. W. Scull
	G-SCVF	Czech Sprt Aircraft Sportcruiser	V. Flintham
	G-SCZR	CZAW Sportcruiser	R. Manning
	G-SDAT	Flight Design CTSW	CTSW Alfa Tango Group
	G-SDCI	Bell 206B JetRanger 2	S. D. Coomes (G-GHCL/G-SHVV)
	G-SDEC	American Champion 8KCAB	D. Boag
	G-SDEV	DH. 104 Sea Devon C.20 (XK895)	Aviation Heritage Ltd
	G-SDFM	Aerotechnik EV-97 Eurostar	G-SDFM Group
	G-SDNI	VS.361 Spitfire LF.IX E	P. M. Andrews
	G-SDOB	Tecnam P2002-EA Sierra	S. P. S. Dornan
	G-SDOI	Aeroprakt A.22 Foxbat	S. A. Owen
	G-SDOZ	Tecnam P92-EA Echo Super	Cumbernauld Flyers G-SDOZ
	G-SDRY	Cessna 525C CitationJet CJ4	Dowdeswell Aviation LLP
	G-SEAI	Cessna U.206G (amphibian)	K. O'Conner
	G-SEAL	Robinson R44 II	London Helicopter Centres Ltd (G-KLNJ)
	G-SEAT	Colt 42A balloon	Virgin Balloon Flights
	G-SEBN	Skyranger 912S(1)	C. M. James
	G-SEDO	Cameron N-105 balloon	Wye Valley Aviation Ltd
	G-SEED	Piper J-3C-65 Cub	J. H. Seed
	G-SEEE	Pegasus Quik GT450	I. M. Spence
	G-SEEK	Cessna T.210N	A. Hopper
	G-SEHK	Cessna 182T	Golf HK Ltd
	G-SEJW	PA-28-161 Warrior II	Premier Flight Training Ltd
	G-SELA	Cessna 152	L. W. Scattergood (G-FLOP)
	G-SELB	PA-28-161 Warrior II	L. W. Scattergood (G-LFSK)
	G-SELC	Diamond DA42 Twin Star	Stapleford Flying Club Ltd
	G-SELF	Shaw Europa	N. D. Crisp & ptnrs
	G-SELL	Robin DR.400/180	C. R. Beard Farmers Ltd
	G-SELY	Agusta-Bell 206B JetRanger 3	DSC North Ltd
	G-SEMI	PA-44-180 Seminole	J. Benfell & M. Djukic (G-DENW)
	G-SEMR	Cessna T206H Turbo Stationair	Semer LLP

Reg.	Type	Owner or Operator	Notes
G-SENA	Rutan LongEz	G. Bennett	
G-SEND	Colt 90A balloon	Air du Vent/France	
G-SENE	PA-34-200T Seneca II	M. O'Hara	
G-SENS	Eurocopter EC.135T2+	Saville Air Services	
G-SENT	Bombardier BD700-1A10 Global Express	Africa Energy SA Nigeria Ltd	
G-SENX	PA-34-200T Seneca II	First Air Ltd (G-DARE/G-WOTS/G-SEVL)	
G-SEPT	Cameron N-105 balloon	A. G. Merry	
G-SERE	Diamond DA42 Twin Star	Sere Ltd	
G-SERL	SOCATA TB10 Tobago	D. J. Hawes (G-LANA)	
G-SERV	Cameron N-105 balloon	Servo & Electronic Sales Ltd	
G-SESA	RAF SE.5A 75 replica	D. J. Calvert	
G-SETI	Cameron Sky 80-16 balloon	R. P. Allan	
G-SEUK	Cameron TV-80 ss balloon	Mobberley Balloon Collection	
G-SEVA	SE-5A (replica) (F141:G)	G-SEVA Trust	
G-SEVE	Cessna 172N	MK Aero Support Ltd	
G-SEVN	Van's RV-7	N. Reddish	
G-SEXE	Scheibe SF.25C Falke	SF25C G-SESE Syndicate	
G-SEXX	PA-28-161 Warrior II	Weald Air Services Ltd	
G-SEXY	AA-1 Yankee ★	Jetstream Club, Liverpool Marriott Hotel South, Speke (G-AYLM)	
G-SFAR	Ikarus C42 FB100	Hadair	
G-SFLA	Ikarus C42 FB80	Solent Flight Ltd	
G-SFLB	Ikarus C42 FB80	Solent Flight Ltd	
G-SFLY	Diamond DA40 Star	L. & N. P. L. Turner	
G-SFPB	Cessna F.406	Reims Aviation Industries SA/France	
G-SFRY	Thunder Ax7-77 balloon	M. Rowlands	
G-SFSL	Cameron Z-105 balloon	A. J. Gregory	
G-SFTZ	Slingsby T.67M Firefly 160	Slingsby T.67M Group	
G-SGEN	Ikarus C.42 FB 80	G. A. Arturi	
G-SGRP	Agusta AW.109SP Grand New	WA Developments International Ltd	
G-SGSE	PA-28-181 Archer II	U. Patel (G-BOJX)	
G-SHAA	Enstrom 280-UK	C. J. Vincent	
G-SHAF	Robinson R44 II	Tresillian Leisure Ltd	
G-SHAK	Cameron Cabin SS balloon	Magical Adventures Ltd (G-ODIS)	
G-SHAL	Bombardier CL-600-2B19	TAG Aviation (UK) Ltd	
G-SHAN	Robinson R44 II	M. Herzog	
G-SHAR	Cessna 182T Skylane	G. N. Clarkson	
G-SHAY	PA-28R-201T Turbo Arrow III	Alpha Yankee Flying Group (G-BFDG/G-JEFS)	
G-SHBA	Cessna F.152	Paul's Planes Ltd	
G-SHED	PA-28-181 Archer II	G-SHED Flying Group (G-BRAU)	
G-SHEE	P & M Quik GT450	L. Cottle	
G-SHEZ	Mainair Pegasus Quik	R. Wells	
G-SHHH	Glaser-Dirks DG-100G	P. J. Masson	
G-SHIM	CFM Streak Shadow	K. R. Anderson	
G-SHIP	PA-23 Aztec 250F ★	Midland Air Museum/Coventry	
G-SHKI	Ikarus C42 FB80	Poet Pilot (UK) Ltd	
G-SHMI	Evektor EV-97 Team EuroStar UK	Poet Pilot (UK) Ltd	
G-SHMK	Cirrus SR22T	Avicon	
G-SHOG	Colomban MC.15 Cri-Cri	K. D. & C. S. Rhodes (G-PFAB)	
G-SHOW	MS.733 Alycon	J. Wesson	
G-SHRK	Enstrom 280C-UK	Flighthire Ltd/Belgium (G-BGMX)	
G-SHRN	Schweizer 269C-1	CSL Industrial Ltd	
G-SHRT	Robinson R44 II	Staverton Flying School @ Skypark Ltd	
G-SHSH	Shaw Europa	S. G. Hayman & J. Price	
G-SHSP	Cessna 172S	Shropshire Aero Club Ltd	
G-SHUC	Rans S-6-ESD Coyote II	T. A. England (G-MYKN)	
G-SHUF	Mainair Blade	G. Holdcroft	
G-SHUG	PA-28R-201T Turbo Arrow III	G-SHUG Ltd	
G-SHUU	Enstrom 280C-UK-2	Startrade Heli GmbH & Co AG/Germany (G-OMCP/G-KENY/G-BJFG)	
G-SHUV	Aerosport Woody Pusher	J. R. Wraigh	
G-SHWK	Cessna 172S	Cambridge Aero Club Ltd	
G-SIAI	SIAI-Marchetti SF.260W	Air Training Services	
G-SIBK	Raytheon Beech A36 Bonanza	B. & S. J. Shaw	
G-SICA	BN-2B-20 Islander	Shetland Leasing and Property Development Ltd (G-SLAP)	

BRITISH CIVIL REGISTRATIONS

Notes	Reg.	Type	Owner or Operator
	G-SICB	BN-2B-20 Islander	Shetlands Islands Council (G-NESU/G-BTVN)
	G-SIGN	PA-39 Twin Comanche 160 C/R	D. Buttle
	G-SIIE	Christen Pitts S-2B Special	Wild Thing (G-SKYD)
	G-SIII	Extra EA.300	Owners of G-SIII
	G-SIIS	Pitts S-1S Special	R. P. Marks (G-RIPE)
	G-SIJJ	North American P-51D-NA Mustang (472035)	P. A. Teichman
	G-SIJW	SA Bulldog Srs 120/121 (XX630:5)	M. Miles
	G-SILS	Pietenpol Skyscout	D. Silsbury
	G-SILY	Pegasus Quantum 15	S. D. Sparrow
	G-SIMI	Cameron A-315 balloon	Balloon Safaris
	G-SIMM	Ikarus C.42 FB 100 VLA	D. Simmons
	G-SIMS	Robinson R22 Beta	Heli Air Ltd
	G-SIMY	PA-32-300 Cherokee Six	I. Simpson (G-OCPF/G-BOCH)
	G-SINK	Schleicher ASH-25	G-SINK Group
	G-SIPA	SIPA 903	A. C. Leak & G. S. Dilland (G-BGBM)
	G-SIPP	Lindstrand lbl-35a Cloudhopper balloon	N. Bourke
	G-SIRD	Robinson R44 II	Peglington Productions Ltd
	G-SIRE	Best Off Sky Ranger Swift 912S(1)	D. S. Murrell
	G-SIRO	Dassault Falcon 900EX	Condor Aviation LLP
	G-SIRS	Cessna 560XL Citation Excel	London Executive Aviation Ltd
	G-SISI	Schempp-Hirth Duo Discus	Glider Sierra India
	G-SISU	P & M Quik GT450	Executive and Business Aviation Support Ltd
	G-SITA	Pegasus Quantum 15-912	A. F. S. McDougall
	G-SIVJ	Westland Gazelle HT.2	Skytrace (UK) Ltd (G-CBSG)
	G-SIVK	MBB Bolkow Bo.105DBS-4	C. J. Siva-Jothy (G-PASX)
	G-SIVR	MDH MD.900 Explorer	Police Aviation Services Ltd
	G-SIVW	Lake LA-250 Renegade	C. J. Siva-Jothy
	G-SIXC	Douglas DC-6B★	The DC-6 Diner/Coventry
	G-SIXD	PA-32 Cherokee Six 300D	M. B. Paine & I. Gordon
	G-SIXG	AutoGyro MTO Sport	G. R. Lynch
	G-SIXT	PA-28-161 Warrior II	Booker Aircraft Leasing Ltd (G-BSSX)
	G-SIXX	Colt 77A balloon	S. Drawbridge
	G-SIXY	Van's RV-6	C. J. Hall & C. R. P. Hamlett
	G-SIZZ	Jabiru J400	K. J. Betteley
	G-SJBI	Pitts S-2C Special	S. L. Walton
	G-SJES	Evektor EV-97 TeamEurostar UK	Purple Aviation Ltd
	G-SJKR	Lindstrand LBL-90A balloon	S. J. Roake
	G-SJMH	Robin DR.400-140B	C. S. & J. A. Bailey
	G-SJPI	Dynamic WT9 UK	S. J. Phillips
	G-SJSS	Bombardier CL600-2B16	TAG Aviation (UK) Ltd
	G-SKAN	Cessna F.172M	M. Richardson & J. Williams (G-BFKT)
	G-SKAZ	Aero AT-3 r100	G-SKAZ Flying Group
	G-SKCI	Rutan Vari-Eze	C. Hannan
	G-SKEN	Cessna 182T	Kenward Orthopaedic Ltd
	G-SKEW	Mudry CAP-232	J. H. Askew
	G-SKIE	Steen Skybolt	K. G. G. Howe and M. J. Coles
	G-SKKY	Cessna 172S Skyhawk	J. Herbert & G. P. Turner
	G-SKNT	Pitts S-2A	First Light Aviation Ltd (G-PEAL)
	G-SKOT	Cameron V-42 balloon	S. A. Laing
	G-SKPG	Best Off Skyranger 912 (2)	T. Farncombe
	G-SKPH	Yakovlev Yak-50	R. S. Partridge-Hicks & I. C. Austin (G-BWWH)
	G-SKPP	Eurocopter EC.120B Colbri	Bournemouth Helicopters Ltd (G-MKII)
	G-SKRA	Best Off Skyranger 912S (1)	P. A. Banks
	G-SKRG	Best Off Skyranger 912 (2)	I. D. Town
	G-SKSW	Best Off Sky Ranger Swift 912S	M. D. & S. M. North
	G-SKTN	Avro 696 Shackleton MR.Mk.2 (WR963)	Shackleton Preservation Trust
	G-SKUA	Stoddard-Hamilton Glastar	F. P. Smiddy (G-LEZZ/G-BYCR)
	G-SKYC	Slingsby T.67M Firefly	T. W. Cassells (G-BLDP)
	G-SKYE	Cessna TU.206G	RAF Sport Parachute Association
	G-SKYF	SOCATA TB10 Tobago	W. L. McNeil
	G-SKYJ	Cameron Z-315 balloon	Aerosaurus Balloons Ltd
	G-SKYK	Cameron A-275 balloon	A. M. Holly
	G-SKYL	Cessna 182S	G. A. Gee
	G-SKYO	AS.355F1 Twin Squirrel	Arena Aviation Ltd (G-OGRK/G-BWZC/G-MODZ)
	G-SKYO	Slingsby T.67M-200	R. H. Evelyn
	G-SKYT	I.I.I. Sky Arrow 650TC	W. M. Bell & S. J. Brooks
	G-SKYV	PA-28RT-201T Turbo Arrow IV	North Yorks Properties Ltd (G-BNZG)
	G-SKYW	AS355F1	Skywalker Aviation Ltd (G-BTIS/G-TALI)

Reg.	Type	Owner or Operator	Notes
G-SLAC	Cameron N-77 balloon	A. Barnes	
G-SLAK	Thruster T.600N 450	M. P. Williams (G-CBXH)	
G-SLAR	Agusta A109C	MW Helicopters Ltd (G-OWRD/G-USTC/G-LAXO)	
G-SLCE	Cameron C-80 balloon	A. M. Holly	
G-SLCT	Diamond DA42NG Twin Star	Stapleford Flying Club Ltd	
G-SLEA	Mudry/CAARP CAP-10B	M. J. M. Jenkins & N. R. Thorburn	
G-SLII	Cameron O-90 balloon	J. Edwards	
G-SLIP	Easy Raider	D. R. Squires	
G-SLMG	Diamond HK.36 TTC Super Dimona	G-SLMG Syndicate	
G-SLNM	EV-97 TeamEurostar UK	N. W. Mayes	
G-SLNT	Flight Design CTSW	K. Kirby	
G-SLNW	Robinson R22 Beta	Heli-4 Charter LLP (G-LNIC)	
G-SLYN	PA-28-161 Warrior II	Flew LLP	
G-SMAN	Airbus A.330-243	Monarch Airlines Ltd	
G-SMAR	Schempp-Hirth Arcus M	Alpha Syndicate	
G-SMAS	BAC.167 Strikemaster 80A (1104)	M. A. Petrie	
G-SMBM	Pegasus Quantum 15-912	P. A. Henretty	
G-SMDH	Shaw Europa XS	S. W. Pitt	
G-SMDJ	AS.350B2 Ecureuil	Denis Ferranti Hoverknights Ltd	
G-SMIG	Cameron O-65 balloon	R. D. Parry	
G-SMIL	Lindstrand LBL-105A balloon	A. L. Wade	
G-SMLI	Groppo Trail	A. M. Wilson	
G-SMMA	Cessna F.406 Caravan II	Secretary of State for Scotland per Environmental and Rural Affairs Department	
G-SMMB	Cessna F.406 Caravan II	Secretary of State for Scotland per Environmental and Rural Affairs Department	
G-SMRS	Cessna 172F	M. R. Sarling	
G-SMRT	Lindstrand LBL-260A balloon	A. M. Holly	
G-SMTD	Eurocopter AS.350B3 Ecureuil	Bournemouth Helicopters Ltd	
G-SMTH	PA-28 Cherokee 140	R. W. Harris & A. Jahanfar (G-AYJS)	
G-SMYK	PZL-Swidnik PW-5 Smyk	PW-5 Syndicate	
G-SNAL	Cessna 182T	N. S. Lyndhurst	
G-SNCA	PA-34-200T Seneca II	Social Infrastructure Ltd	
G-SNEV	CFM Streak Shadow SA	J. D. Reed	
G-SNIF	Cameron A-300 balloon	A. C. K. Rowson & Sudoni	
G-SNOG	Kiss 400-582 (1)	B. H. Ashman	
G-SNOP	Shaw Europa	V. F. Flett (G-DESL/G-WWWG)	
G-SNOW	Cameron V-77 balloon	I. Welsford	
G-SNOZ	Shaw Europa	P. O. Bayliss (G-DONZ)	
G-SNSA	Agusta AW139	CHC Scotia Ltd	
G-SNSB	Agusta AW139	CHC Scotia Ltd	
G-SNUZ	PA-28-161 Warrior II	Freedom Aviation Ltd	
G-SNZY	Learjet 45	European Skyjets Ltd	
G-SOAF	BAC.167 Strikemaster Mk. 82A (425)	Strikemaster Flying Club	
G-SOAR	Eiri PIK-20E	L. J. Kaye	
G-SOAY	Cessna T.303	Wrekin Construction Co Ltd	
G-SOBI	PA-28-181 Archer II	G-SOBI Flying Group	
G-SOCK	Mainair Pegasus Quik	K. R. McCartney	
G-SOCT	Yakovlev Yak-50 (AR-B)	C. R. Turton	
G-SOHO	Diamond DA40D Star	Soho Aviation Ltd	
G-SOKO	Soko P-2 Kraguj (30149)	P. C. Avery (G-BRXK)	
G-SOLA	Aero Designs Star-Lite SL.1	G. P. Thomas	
G-SONA	SOCATA TB10 Tobago	J. Freeman (G-BIBI)	
G-SONE	Cessna 525A Citationjet	Centreline Air Charter	
G-SONX	Sonex	M. Chambers	
G-SOOA	Cessna172S	Goodwood Road Racing Co.Ltd	
G-SOOC	Hughes 369HS	R.J.H. Strong (G-BRRX)	
G-SOOS	Colt 21A balloon	P. J. Stapley	
G-SOOT	PA-28 Cherokee 180	R. J. Hunter (G-AVNM)	
G-SOPH	Skyranger 912(2)	S. Marathe	
G-SORA	Glaser-Dirks DG.500/22	C. A. Boyle, C. P. Arthur, B. Douglas & R. Jackson	
G-SOUL	Cessna 310R	Reconnaissance Ventures Ltd	
G-SOVB	Learjet 45	Zenith Aviation Ltd (G-OLDJ)	
G-SPAM	Avid Aerobat (modified)	M. Durcan	
G-SPAO	Eurocopter EC135	Bond Air Services Ltd	

Notes	Reg.	Type	Owner or Operator
	G-SPAT	Aero AT-3 R100	S2T Aero Ltd
	G-SPCZ	CZAW Sportcruiser	R. J. Robinson
	G-SPDR	DH.115 Sea Vampire T.22 (N6-766)	M. J. Cobb
	G-SPDY	Raj Hamsa X'Air Hawk	G. H. Gilmour-White
	G-SPED	Alpi Pioneer 300	C. F. Garrod
	G-SPEE	Robinson R22 Beta	Heliclub de laValle du Loing (G-BPJC)
	G-SPEL	Sky 220-24 balloon	Khaos Ballooning
	G-SPEY	Agusta-Bell 206B JetRanger 3	Castle Air Ltd (G-BIGO)
	G-SPFX	Rutan Cozy	B. D. Tutty
	G-SPHU	Eurocopter EC 135T2+	Bond Air Services Ltd
	G-SPID	Ultramagic S-90 balloon	A. Fawcett
	G-SPIN	Pitts S-2A Special	P. Avery
	G-SPIP	SNCAN Stampe SV.4C	A. G. & P. M. Solleveld (G-BTIO)
	G-SPIT	VS.379 Spitfire FR.XIV (MV268)	Patina Ltd (G-BGHB)
	G-SPJE	Robinson R44 II	Abel Alarm Co.Ltd
	G-SPMM	Best Off Sky Ranger Swift 912S(1)	L. Chesworth & M. L. Sumner
	G-SPOG	Jodel DR.1050	G-SPOG Group (G-AXVS)
	G-SPRE	Cessna 550 Citation Bravo	Xclusive Jet Charter Ltd
	G-SPTR	Robinson R44 II	Heli Air Ltd
	G-SPTT	Diamond DA.40D Star	C. J. King (G-OCCS)
	G-SPUR	Cessna 550 Citation II	London Executive Aviation Ltd
	G-SPUT	Yakovlev Yak-52	N. J. Stillwell (G-BXAV)
	G-SPVK	AS.350B3 Ecureuil	Stratos Aviation LLP (G-CERU)
	G-SPXX	VS.356 Spitfire F.22	P. R. Arnold
	G-SPYS	Robinson R44 II	SKB Partners LLP
	G-SRAH	Schempp-Hirth Mini-Nimbus C	P. Hawkins
	G-SRDG	Dassault Falcon 7X	Triair (Bermuda) Ltd
	G-SRII	Easy Raider 503	K. Myles
	G-SROE	Westland Scout AH.1 (XP907)	Saunders-Roe Helicopter Ltd
	G-SRRA	Tecnam P2002-EA Sierra	J. Dunn
	G-SRTT	Cirrus SR22	S. A. Breslaw
	G-SRVO	Cameron N-90 balloon	Servo & Electronic Sales Ltd
	G-SRVY	Partenavia P.68 Observer 2	Vulcanair SpA/Italy
	G-SRWN	PA-28-161 Warrior II	Bluewing Flight Services Ltd (G-MAND/G-BRKT)
	G-SRYY	Shaw Europa XS	I. O'Brien
	G-SRZZ	Cirrus SR22	M. P. Bowcock
	G-SSCL	MDH Hughes 369E	Shaun Stevens Contractors Ltd
	G-SSDR	Scooter	J. Attard
	G-SSIX	Rans S.6-116 Coyote II	R. I. Kelly
	G-SSKY	BN-2B-26 Islander	Isles of Scilly Skybus Ltd (G-BSWT)
	G-SSLM	Cessna 510 Citation Mustang	M. Richardson
	G-SSRD	Balony Kubicek BB17XR balloon	A. M. Holly
	G-SSTI	Cameron N-105 balloon	A. A. Brown
	G-SSVB	VS.349 Spitfire LF.Vb	I. D. Ward (G-CGBI)
	G-SSWV	Sportavia Fournier RF-5B	Fournier Flying Group
	G-STAV	Cameron O-84 balloon	A. Pollock
	G-STAY	Cessna FR.172K	J. M. Wilkins
	G-STBA	Boeing 777-336ER	British Airways
	G-STBB	Boeing 777-36NER	British Airways
	G-STBC	Boeing 777-36NER	British Airways
	G-STBD	Boeing 777-36NER	British Airways
	G-STBE	Boeing 777-36NER	British Airways
	G-STBF	Boeing 777-336ER	British Airways
	G-STBG	Boeing 777-336ER	British Airways
	G-STBH	Boeing 777-336ER	British Airways
	G-STBI	Boeing 777-336ER	British Airways
	G-STBT	Cameron N-42 balloon	D. Sjokvist (G-BVLC)
	G-STBY	Flylight MotorFloater	A. G. Bramley
	G-STCH	Fiesler Fi 156A-1 Storch (GM+AI)	P. R. Holloway
	G-STDL	Phillips ST.2 Speedtwin	Speedtwin Developments Ltd (G-DPST)
	G-STEA	PA-28R Cherokee Arrow 200	D. W. Breden
	G-STEE	EV-97 Eurostar	S. G. Beeson
	G-STEL	BRM Aero Bristell NG5	A. J. Palmer & F. Sayyah
	G-STEM	Stemme S.10V	A. M. Booth
	G-STEN	Stemme S.10 (4)	G-STEN Syndicate
	G-STEP	Schweizer 269C	Sor Air-Sociedade de Aero/Portugal
	G-STEU	Rolladen-Schneider LS6-18W	F. K. Russell
	G-STEV	Jodel DR.221	S. W. Talbot

Reg.	Type	Owner or Operator	Notes
G-STGR	Agusta 109S Grand	A. W. Jenkinson	
G-STHA	PA-31-350 Navajo Chieftain	Hinde Holdings Ltd (G-GLUG/G-BLOE/G-NITE)	
G-STIN	TL 2000UK Sting Carbon	N. A. Smith	
G-STIR	UltraMagic M-105 balloon	A. M. Holly	
G-STIX	Van's RV-7	R. D. S. Jackson	
G-STLL	BRM Aero Bristell NG5 Speed Wing	A. Palmer & F. Sayyah	
G-STME	Stemme S 10-VT	R. A. Roberts	
G-STMP	SNCAN Stampe SV.4A	A. C. Thorne	
G-STMT	Dassault Falcon 7X	TAG Aviation (UK) Ltd	
G-STNG	TL2000UK Sting Carbon	Geesting 3 Syndicate	
G-STNR	IDA Bacau Yakovlev Yak-52	S. M. Norman (G-BWOD)	
G-STNS	Agusta A109A-II	Patriot Flight Training Ltd	
G-STOD	ICP MXP-740 Savannah VG Jabiru(1)	M. P. Avison & L. J. Boardman	
G-STOK	Colt 77B balloon	A. C. Booth	
G-STOO	Stolp Starduster Too	K. F. Crumplin	
G-STOP	Robinson R44 Raven II	HLQ Services Ltd/Ireland	
G-STOW	Cameron 90 Wine Box SS balloon	Flying Enterprises	
G-STPK	Lambert Mission M108	S. T. P. Kember	
G-STRG	Cyclone AX2000	Pegasus Flight Training (Cotswolds)	
G-STRK	CFM Streak Shadow SA	E. J. Hadley	
G-STRL	AS.355N Twin Squirrel	Harrier Enterprises Ltd	
G-STSN	Stinson 108-3 Voyager	M. S. Colebrook (G-BHMR)	
G-STUA	Aerotek Pitts S-2A Special (modified)	G-STUA Group	
G-STUI	Pitts S-2AE	S. L. Goldspink	
G-STUN	TL2000UK Sting Carbon	D. Russell (G-KEVT)	
G-STUY	Robinson R44 II	Central Helicopters Ltd	
G-STVT	CZAW Sportcruiser	S. Taylor	
G-STWO	ARV Super 2	P. M. Paul	
G-STZZ	TL2000UK Sting Carbon	Dorset Aviation Group	
G-SUAU	Cameron C-90 balloon	A. Heginbottom	
G-SUCH	Cameron V-77 balloon	D. G. Such (G-BIGD)	
G-SUCK	Cameron Z-105 balloon	R. P. Wade	
G-SUCT	Robinson R22	Irwin Plant Sales	
G-SUEB	PA-28-181 Archer III	Curtis Moore Aviation Ltd	
G-SUED	Thunder Ax8-90 balloon	E. C. Lubbock & S. A. Kidd (G-PINE)	
G-SUEI	Diamond DA.42 Twin Star	Sue Air	
G-SUEL	P & M Quik GT450	J. M. Ingram	
G-SUEO	Diamond DA.40NG Star	Sue Air	
G-SUER	Bell 206B JetRanger	Aerospeed Ltd (G-CBYX)	
G-SUET	Bell 206B JetRanger	Aerospeed Ltd (G-BLZN)	
G-SUEW	Airbus A.320-214	Thomas Cook Airlines Ltd	
G-SUEX	Agusta-Bell 206B JetRanger 2	Aerospeed Ltd (G-AYBC/G-BTWW)	
G-SUEY	Bell 206L-1 Long Ranger	Aerospeed Ltd	
G-SUEZ	Agusta-Bell 206B JetRanger 2	Aerospeed Ltd	
G-SUFK	Eurocopter EC 135P2+	Police & Crime Commissioner for West Yorkshire	
G-SUGA	Embraer EMB-135BJ Legacy 650	Amsair Aircraft Ltd	
G-SUMX	Robinson R22 Beta	Beeston Manor Ltd	
G-SUMZ	Robinson R44 II	Frankham Bros Ltd	
G-SUNN	Robinson R44	R. Purchase	
G-SUPA	PA-18 Super Cub 150	S. E. Leach	
G-SURG	PA-30 Twin Comanche 160B	A. R. Taylor (G-VIST/G-AVHG)	
G-SURY	Eurocopter EC 135T2	Police & Crime Commissioner for West Yorkshire	
G-SUSE	Shaw Europa XS	P. R. Tunney	
G-SUSI	Cameron V-77 balloon	J. H. Dryden	
G-SUSX	MDH MD-902 Explorer	Police & Crime Commissioner for West Yorkshire	
G-SUTD	Jabiru UL-D	W. J. Lister	
G-SUTN	I.I.I. Sky Arrow 650TC	D. J. Goldsmith	
G-SUZN	PA-28-161 Warrior II	Durham Tees Flight Training Ltd	
G-SVAS	PA-18-150 Super Cub	Richard Shuttleworth Trustees	
G-SVDG	Jabiru SK	R. Tellegen	
G-SVEA	PA-28-161 Warrior II	G-SVEA Group	
G-SVEN	Centrair 101A Pegase	G7 Group	
G-SVET	Yakovlev Yak-50	The Assets of the Svetlana Group	
G-SVEY	Vulcanair P-68TC Observer 2	C Aviation Ltd	
G-SVIP	Cessna 421B Golden Eagle II	R. P. Bateman	
G-SVIV	SNCAN Stampe SV.4C	J. E. Keighley	

Notes	Reg.	Type	Owner or Operator
	G-SVNC	Rolladen-Schneider LS4	M. C. Jenkins
	G-SVNH	Savannah VG Jabiru(1)	K. Harmston (G-CFKV)
	G-SVNX	Dassault Falcon 7X	Executive Jet Charter Ltd
	G-SVPN	PA-32R-301T Turbo Saratoga	LAC Marine Ltd
	G-SWAK	Oldfield Baby Lakes	A. G. Fowles
	G-SWAT	Robinson R44 II	Unique Helicopters (NI) Ltd
	G-SWAY	PA-18-150 Super Cub	R. Lillywhite
	G-SWCT	Flight Design CTSW	J. A. Shufflebotham
	G-SWEE	Beech 95-B55 Baron	Orman (Carrolls Farm) Ltd (G-AZDK)
	G-SWEL	Hughes 369HS	M. A. Crook & A. E. Wright (G-RBUT)
	G-SWIF	VS.541 Swift F.7 (XF114) ★	Solent Sky, Southampton
	G-SWIG	Robinson R44	S. Goddard
	G-SWIP	Silence Twister	Zulu Glasstek Ltd (G-RIOT)
	G-SWLL	Aero AT-3 R100	Sywell Aerodrome Ltd
	G-SWON	Pitts S-1S Special	S. L. Goldspink
	G-SWOT	Currie Wot (C3011:S)	P. N. Davis
	G-SWSW	Schempp-Hirth Ventus bT	R. Kalin
	G-SWYM	CZAW Sportcruiser	R. W. Beal
	G-SXIX	Rans S.19	J. L. Almey
	G-SXTY	Learjet 60	TAG Aviation (UK) Ltd
	G-SYEL	Aero AT-3 R100	Sywell Aerodrome Ltd
	G-SYFW	Focke-Wulf Fw.190 replica (2+1)	J. C. Metcalf
	G-SYGA	Beech B200 Super King Air	Synergy Aircraft Leasing Ltd (G-BPPM)
	G-SYLJ	Embraer RJ135BJ	TAG Aviation (UK) Ltd
	G-SYLV	Cessna 208B Grand Caravan	WAS Aircraft Leasing Ltd
	G-SYNA	Embraer EMB-135BJ Legacy 650	Etlagh Aviation Ltd (G-VILP)
	G-SYPS	MDH MD.900 Explorer	Police & Crime Commissioner for West Yorkshire
	G-SYWL	Aero AT-3 R100	Sywell Aerodrome Ltd
	G-TAAB	Cirrus SR22	TAA UK Ltd
	G-TAAC	Cirrus SR20	TAA UK Ltd
	G-TAAS	Agusta AW.109SP Grand New	Sloane Helicopters Ltd
	G-TABB	Schempp-Hirth Ventus 2cT	G. Tabbner
	G-TABS	EMB-110P1 Bandeirante	Alan Mann Aviation Group Ltd (G-PBAC)
	G-TACK	Grob G.109B	A. P. Mayne
	G-TAFF	CASA 1.131E Jungmann 1000	R. A. Fleming (G-BFNE)
	G-TAFI	Bücker Bü 133C Jungmeister	R. P. Lamplough
	G-TAGE	Bombardier CL600-2B16 Challenger	Aviation (UK) Ltd
	G-TAGF	Dassault Falcon 900DX	TAG Aviation (UK) Ltd
	G-TAGK	Dassault Falcon 900DX	TAG Aviation (UK) Ltd
	G-TAGR	Europa	C. G. Sutton
	G-TAJF	Lindstrand LBL-77A balloon	T. A. J. Fowles
	G-TAKE	AS.355F1 Ecureuil II	Arena Aviation Ltd (G-OITN)
	G-TALA	Cessna 152 II	Tatenhill Aviation Ltd (G-BNPZ)
	G-TALB	Cessna 152 II	Tatenhill Aviation Ltd (G-BORO)
	G-TALC	Cessna 152	Tatenhill Aviation Ltd (G-BPBG)
	G-TALD	Cessna F.152	Tatenhill Aviation Ltd (G-BHRM)
	G-TALE	PA-28-181 Archer II	Tatenhill Aviation Ltd (G-BJOA)
	G-TALF	PA-24-250 Comanche	Tatenhill Aviation Ltd (G-APUZ)
	G-TALG	PA-28-151 Warrior	Tatenhill Aviation Ltd (G-BELP)
	G-TALH	PA-28-181 Archer II	Tatenhill Aviation Ltd (G-CIFR)
	G-TALJ	Grumman AA-5 Traveler	Tatenhill Aviation Ltd (G-BBUE)
	G-TALN	Rotorway A600 Talon	Southern Helicopters Ltd
	G-TAMC	Schweizer 269D	Alan Mann Aviation Group Ltd
	G-TAMR	Cessna 172S	Caledonian Air Surveys Ltd
	G-TAMS	Beech A23-24 Musketeer Super	M. Lewis & M. B. Blackmore
	G-TANA	Tanarg 912S(2)/Ixess 15	A. P. Marks
	G-TANG	Tanarg 912S(2)/Ixess 15	N. L. Stammers
	G-TANJ	Raj Hamsa X'Air 582(5)	M. M. & P. M. Stoney
	G-TANK	Cameron N-90 balloon	D. J., A. H. & A. M. Mercer
	G-TANS	SOCATA TB20 Trinidad	B. J. Ryan
	G-TANY	EAA Acrosport 2	P. J. Tanulak
	G-TAPS	PA-28RT-201T Turbo Arrow IV	P. G. Doble
	G-TARN	Pietenpol Air Camper	P. J. Heilbron
	G-TARR	P & M Quik	A. Edwards
	G-TART	PA-28-236 Dakota	N. K. G. Prescot
	G-TASH	Cessna 172N (modified)	N. Pletl
	G-TASK	Cessna 404	Reconnaissance Ventures Ltd

Reg.	Type	Owner or Operator	Notes
G-TATO	Robinson R22	A. E. Wright	
G-TATR	Replica Travelair R Type	R. A. Seeley	
G-TATS	AS.350BA Ecureuil	T. J. Hoare	
G-TATT	Gardan GY-20 Minicab	Tatt's Group	
G-TAWA	Boeing 737-8K5	Thomson Airways Ltd	
G-TAWB	Boeing 737-8K5	Thomson Airways Ltd	
G-TAWC	Boeing 737-8K5	Thomson Airways Ltd	
G-TAWD	Boeing 737-8K5	Thomson Airways Ltd	
G-TAWF	Boeing 737-8K5	Thomson Airways Ltd	
G-TAWG	Boeing 737-8K5	Thomson Airways Ltd	
G-TAWH	Boeing 737-8K5	Thomson Airways Ltd	
G-TAWI	Boeing 737-8K5	Thomson Airways Ltd	
G-TAWJ	Boeing 737-8K5	Thomson Airways Ltd	
G-TAWK	Boeing 737-8K5	Thomson Airways Ltd	
G-TAWL	Boeing 737-8K5	Thomson Airways Ltd	
G-TAWM	Boeing 737-8K5	Thomson Airways Ltd	
G-TAWN	Boeing 737-8K5	Thomson Airways Ltd	
G-TAWO	Boeing 737-8K5	Thomson Airways Ltd	
G-TAWP	Boeing 737-8K5	Thomson Airways Ltd	
G-TAWR	Boeing 737-8K5	Thomson Airways Ltd	
G-TAYC	Gulfstream G450	TAG Aviation (UK) Ltd	
G-TAYI	Grob G.115	K. P. Widdowson & K. Hackshall (G-DODO)	
G-TAYL	Pitts S-1S Special	R. S. Taylor	
G-TAZZ	Dan Rihn DR.107 One Design	N. J. Riddin	
G-TBAE	BAe 146-200	Tronosjet Mintenance Inc (G-HWPB/G-BSRU/ G-OSKI/G-JEAR)	
G-TBAG	Murphy Renegade II	M. R. Tetley	
G-TBBC	Pegasus Quantum 15-912	J. Horn	
G-TBEA	Cessna 525A Citation CJ2	Centreline Air Charter Ltd	
G-TBGT	SOCATA TB10 Tobago GT	P. G. Sherry & A. J. Simmonds	
G-TBHH	AS355F2 Twin Squirrel	Alpha Properties (London) Ltd (G-HOOT/ G-SCOW/G-POON/G-MCAL)	
G-TBIO	SOCATA TB10 Tobago	R. G. L. Solomon and J. S. Ritchie	
G-TBJP	Mainair Pegasus Quik	R. J. Price	
G-TBLB	P & M Quik GT450	B. L. Benson	
G-TBLY	Eurocopter EC 120B	AD Bly Aircraft Leasing Ltd	
G-TBMR	P & M Aviation Quik GT450	B. Robertson	
G-TBMW	Murphy Renegade Spirit	S. J. & M. J. Spavins (G-MYIG)	
G-TBOK	SOCATA TB10 Tobago	TB10 Ltd	
G-TBSV	SOCATA TB20 Trinidad GT	Condron Concrete Ltd	
G-TBTB	Robinson R44	D. M. McGarrity (G-CDUN)	
G-TBTN	SOCATA TB10 Tobago	Airways International Ltd (G-BKIA)	
G-TBUK	AA-5A Cheetah	T. M. Buick (G-PADD/G-ESTE/G-GHNC)	
G-TBXX	SOCATA TB20 Trinidad	Aeroplane Ltd	
G-TBYD	Raj Hamsa X'Air Falcon D(1)	T. Ansari	
G-TBZO	SOCATA TB20 Trinidad	R. P. Lewis	
G-TCAC	Airbus A.320-232	Thomas Cook Airlines Ltd (G-ERAA)	
G-TCAD	Airbus A.320-214	Thomas Cook Airlines Ltd	
G-TCAL	Robinson R44 II	C. M. Gough-Cooper	
G-TCAN	Colt 69A balloon	H. C. J. Williams	
G-TCBB	Boeing 757-236	Thomas Cook Airlines Ltd	
G-TCBC	Boeing 757-236	Thomas Cook Airlines Ltd	
G-TCCA	Boeing 767-31K	Thomas Cook Airlines Ltd (G-SJMC)	
G-TCCB	Boeing 767-31KER	Thomas Cook Airlines Ltd (G-DIMB)	
G-TCDA	Airbus A.321-211	Thomas Cook Airlines Ltd (G-JOEE)	
G-TCDB	Airbus A.321-211	Thomas Cook Airlines Ltd	
G-TCDC	Airbus A.321-211	Thomas Cook Airlines Ltd	
G-TCEE	Hughes 369HS	Aviation Styling Ltd (G-AZVM)	
G-TCHI	VS.509 Spitfire Tr.9	M. B. Phillips	
G-TCHO	VS Spitfire Mk.IX	B. Phillips	
G-TCHZ	VS.329 Spitfire IIA	M. B. Phillips	
G-TCNM	Tecnam P92-EA Echo	F. G. Walker	
G-TCNY	Mainair Pegasus Quik	L. A. Maynard	
G-TCTC	PA-28RT-200 Arrow IV	P. Salemis	
G-TCUB	Piper J-3C-65 Cub (modified)	C. Kirk	
G-TCXA	Airbus A.330-243	Thomas Cook Airlines Ltd	
G-TDJN	North American AT-6D Harvard III	D. J. Nock	

Notes	Reg.	Type	Owner or Operator
	G-TDJP	Van's RV-8	D. J. Pearson
	G-TDKI	CZAW Sportcruiser	D. R. Kendall
	G-TDOG	SA Bulldog Srs 120/121 (XX538:O)	G. S. Taylor
	G-TDRA	Cessna 172S Skyhawk	TDR Aviation Ltd
	G-TDSA	Cessna F.406 Caravan II	Nor Leasing
	G-TDVB	Dyn' Aero MCR-01ULC	D. V. Brunt
	G-TDYN	Aerospool Dynamic WT9 UK	A. A. & L. J. Rice
	G-TEBZ	PA-28R-201 Arrow III	Smart People Don't Buy Ltd
	G-TECA	Tecnam P2002-JF	Aeros Holdings Ltd
	G-TECB	Tecnam P2006T	Aeros Holdings Ltd
	G-TECC	Aeronca 7AC Champion	N. J. Orchard-Armitage
	G-TECH	Rockwell Commander 114	A. S. Turner (G-BEDH)
	G-TECI	Tecnam P2002-JF	Polarb Air Ltd
	G-TECK	Cameron V-77 balloon	M. W. A. Shemilt
	G-TECM	Tecnam P92-EM Echo	N. G. H. Staunton
	G-TECO	Tecnam P92-EM Echo	A. N. Buchan
	G-TECS	Tecnam P2002-EA Sierra	D. A. Lawrence
	G-TECT	Tecnam P2006T	Polarb Air Ltd
	G-TEDB	Cessna F.150L	R. Nightingale (G-AZLZ)
	G-TEDI	Best Off Skyranger J2.2(1)	P. W. Reid
	G-TEDW	Kiss 450-582 (2)	S. S. Pratt
	G-TEDY	Evans VP-1	N. K. Marston (G-BHGN)
	G-TEFC	PA-28 Cherokee 140	Foxtrot Charlie Flyers
	G-TEGS	Bell 206B JetRanger III	HC Services Ltd
	G-TEHL	CFM Streak Shadow	L. T. Flower (G-MYJE)
	G-TEKK	Tecnam P2006T	Aeros Holdings Ltd
	G-TELC	Rotorsport UK MT-03	C. M. Jones
	G-TELY	Agusta A109A-II	Castle Air Ltd
	G-TEMB	Tecnam P2000-EA Sierra	M. B. Hill
	G-TEMP	PA-28 Cherokee 180	F. R. Busch & M. Khoshkou (G-AYBK)
	G-TEMT	Hawker Tempest II (MW763)	Tempest Two Ltd
	G-TENG	Extra EA.300/L	D. McGinn
	G-TENT	Auster J/1N Alpha	R. Callaway-Lewis (G-AKJU)
	G-TERA	Vulcanair P68 Observer 2	APEM Aviation Ltd
	G-TERN	Shaw Europa	J. Smith
	G-TERR	Mainair Pegasus Quik	M. Faulkner
	G-TERY	PA-28-181 Archer II	J. R. Bratherton (G-BOXZ)
	G-TESI	Tecnam P2002 EA Sierra	C. C. Burgess
	G-TESR	Tecnam P2002-RG Sierra	C. D. Meek
	G-TEST	PA-34-200 Seneca	Stapleford Flying Club Ltd (G-BLCD)
	G-TEWS	PA-28-140 Cherokee	D. Barron (G-KEAN/G-AWTM)
	G-TEXN	North American T-6G Texan (3072:72)	Boultbee Vintage LLP (G-BHTH)
	G-TEZZ	CZAW Sportcruiser	T. D. Baker
	G-TFCC	Cub Crafters Carbon Cub SS CC11-160	Patina Ltd
	G-TFIX	Mainair Pegasus Quantum 15-912	T. G. Jones
	G-TFLX	P & M Quik GT450	L. A. Wood
	G-TFLY	Air Creation Kiss 450-582 (1)	A. J. Ladell
	G-TFOG	Best Off Skyranger 912(2)	T. J. Fogg
	G-TFRA	Cessna 525 Citationjet CJ1+	Blu Halkin Ltd
	G-TFRB	Air Command 532 Elite	F. R. Blennerhassett
	G-TFUN	Valentin Taifun 17E	North West Taifun Group
	G-TFYN	PA-32RT-300 Lance II	R. C. Poolman
	G-TGER	AA-5B Tiger	D. T. Pangbourne (G-BFZP)
	G-TGGR	Eurocopter EC 120B	Messiah Corporation Ltd
	G-TGJH	Pitts S-1S Special	R. S. Taylor
	G-TGRA	Agusta A109A	Tiger Helicopters Ltd
	G-TGRD	Robinson R22 Beta II	Tiger Helicopters Ltd (G-OPTS)
	G-TGRE	Robinson R22A	Tiger Helicopters Ltd (G-SOLD)
	G-TGRS	Robinson R22 Beta	Tiger Helicopters Ltd (G-DELL)
	G-TGRZ	Bell 206B JetRanger 3	Tiger Helicopters Ltd (G-BXZX)
	G-TGTT	Robinson R44 II	Air'Opale (G-STUS)
	G-TGUN	Aero AT-3 R100	Medcentres Property Portfolio Ltd
	G-THAT	Raj Hamsa X'Air Falcon 912 (1)	E. E. Colley
	G-THEA	Boeing E75 Stearman	S. Bennett
	G-THEO	TEAM mini-MAX 91	G. Evans
	G-THFC	Embraer RJ135BJ Legacy	Raz Air Ltd (G-RRAZ/G-RUBN)
	G-THFW	Bell 206B-3 JetRanger III	Fly Heli Wales Ltd

Reg.	Type	Owner or Operator	Notes
G-THIN	Cessna FR.172E	I. C. A. Ussher (G-BXYY)	
G-THLA	Robinson R22 Beta	Thurston Helicopters Ltd & J. W. F. Tuke	
G-THOM	Thunder Ax-6-56 balloon	T. H. Wilson	
G-THOC	Boeing 737-59D	TAG Aviation (Stansted) Ltd (G-BVKA)	
G-THOT	Avtech Jabiru SK	S. G. Holton	
G-THRE	Cessna 182S	J. P. Monjalet	
G-THRM	Schleicher ASW-27	C. G. Starkey (G-CJWC)	
G-THSL	PA-28R-201 Arrow III	D. M. Markscheffe	
G-TIAC	Tiger Cub RL5A LW Sherwood Ranger	The Light Aircraft Co.Ltd	
G-TICH	Taylor JT.2 Titch	R. Davitt	
G-TIDS	Jodel 150	M. R. Parker	
G-TIDY	Best Off Sky Ranger Nynja 912S(1)	P. Rigby	
G-TIFG	Ikarus C42 FB80	The Ikarus Flying Group	
G-TIGA	DH.82A Tiger Moth	D. E. Leatherland (G-AOEG)	
G-TIGC	AS.332L Super Puma	Bristow Helicopters Ltd (G-BJYH)	
G-TIGE	AS.332L Super Puma	Bristow Helicopters Ltd (G-BJYJ)	
G-TIGS	AS.332L Super Puma	Bristow Helicopters Ltd	
G-TIGV	AS.332L Super Puma	Bristow Helicopters Ltd	
G-TIII	Aerotek Pitts S-2A Special	Treble India Group	
G-TILE	Robinson R22 Beta	Heli Air Ltd	
G-TIMC	Robinson R44	T. Clark Aviation LLP (G-CDUR)	
G-TIMH	Robinson R22	Central Helicopters Ltd	
G-TIMK	PA-28-181 Archer II	Minimal Risk Consultancy Ltd	
G-TIMM	Folland Gnat T.1 (XM693)	Heritage Aircraft Ltd	
G-TIMP	Aeronca 7BCM Champion	R. B. Valler	
G-TIMS	Falconar F-12A	T. Sheridan	
G-TIMX	Head AX8-88B balloon	T. S. Crowdy	
G-TIMY	Gardan GY-80 Horizon 160	R. G. Whyte	
G-TINA	SOCATA TB10 Tobago	A. Lister	
G-TINK	Robinson R22 Beta	Airtask Group PLC	
G-TINS	Cameron N-90 balloon	J. R. Clifton	
G-TINT	Aerotechnik EV-97 Team Eurostar UK	I. A. Cunningham	
G-TINY	Z.526F Trener Master	D. Evans	
G-TIPJ	Cameron Z-77 balloon	J. R. Lawson	
G-TIPS	Nipper T.66 Srs.3	F. V. Neefs	
G-TIVS	Rans S.6-ES Coyote II	A. P. Michell & C. W. Bridge	
G-TIVV	Aerotechnik EV-97 Team Eurostar UK	I. Shulver	
G-TJAL	Jabiru SPL-430	D. W. Cross	
G-TJAV	Mainair Pegasus Quik	D. Allan & J. Hunter	
G-TJAY	PA-22 Tri-Pacer 135	D. Pegley	
G-TJDM	Van's RV-6A	J. D. Michie	
G-TKAY	Shaw Europa	A. M. Kay	
G-TKEV	P & M Quik R	S. J. Thompson	
G-TKIS	Tri-R Kis	T. J. Bone	
G-TKNO	UltraMagic S-50 balloon	P. Dickinson	
G-TLAC	Sherwood Ranger ST	The Light Aircraft Co.Ltd	
G-TLDL	Medway SLA 100 Executive	D. T. Lucas	
G-TLET	PA-28-161 Cadet	ADR Aviation (G-GFCF/G-RHBH)	
G-TLOY	Alpi Pioneer 400	A. R. Lloyd	
G-TLST	TL 2000UK Sting Carbon	I. Foster	
G-TLTL	Schempp-Hirth Discus CS	E. K. Armitage	
G-TMAN	Roadster/Adventure Funflyer Quattro	P. A. Mahony	
G-TMAX	Evektor EV-97 Sportstar Max	G-TMAX Group	
G-TMCB	Best Off Skyranger 912 (2)	J. R. Davis	
G-TMCC	Cameron N-90 balloon	M. S. Jennings	
G-TMHK	PA-38-112 Tomahawk	J. T. Mountain (G-GALL/G-BTEV)	
G-TMRB	Short SD3-60 Variant 100	HD Air Ltd (G-SSWB/G-BMLE)	
G-TNGO	Van's RV-6	R. Marsden	
G-TNJB	P & M Quik R	C. J. Shorter	
G-TNRG	Tanarg/Ixess 15 912S(2)	J. E. McGee	
G-TNTN	Thunder Ax6-56 balloon	H. M. Savage & J. F. Trehern	
G-TOBA	SOCATA TB10 Tobago	E. Downing	
G-TOBI	Cessna F.172K	TOBI Group (G-AYVB)	
G-TODD	ICA IS-28M2A	C. I. Roberts & C. D. King	

BRITISH CIVIL REGISTRATIONS

Notes	Reg.	Type	Owner or Operator
	G-TODG	Flight Design CTSW	S. J. Sykes
	G-TOFT	Colt 90A balloon	C. S. Perceval
	G-TOGO	Van's RV-6	I. R. Thomas
	G-TOLI	Robinson R44 II	Coleman Cantle Partnership
	G-TOLL	PA-28R-201 Arrow III	Arrow Aircraft Ltd
	G-TOLS	Robinson R44	K. N. Tolley (G-CBOT)
	G-TOLY	Robinson R22 Beta ★	Helicopter Services Ltd (G-NSHR)
	G-TOMC	NA AT-6D Harvard III	A. A. Marshall
	G-TOMJ	Flight Design CT2K	K. Brown
	G-TOMX	MCR-01 VLA Sportster	P. T. Knight
	G-TOMZ	Denney Kitfox Mk.2	S. J. Spavins
	G-TONE	Pazmany PL-4	P. I. Morgans
	G-TONN	Mainair Pegasus Quik	T. D. Evans
	G-TOOB	Schempp-Hirth Discus 2b	M. F. Evans
	G-TOOL	Thunder Ax8-105 balloon	D. V. Howard
	G-TOPB	Cameron Z-140 balloon	Anana Ltd
	G-TOPC	AS.355F1 Twin Squirrel	Kinetic Avionics Ltd
	G-TOPK	Shaw Europa XS	P. J. Kember
	G-TOPO	PA-23-250 Turbo Aztec	Blue Sky Investments Ltd (G-BGWW)
	G-TOPS	AS.355F1 Twin Squirrel	Sterling Helicopters (G-BPRH)
	G-TORC	PA-28R Cherokee Arrow 200	Pure Aviation Support Services Ltd
	G-TORE	P.84 Jet Provost T.3A ★	Instructional airframe/City University, Islington
	G-TORO	Best Off Skyranger Nynja 912S(1)	B. J. Nortje
	G-TORI	Zenair CH.701SP	M. J. Maddock (G-CCSK)
	G-TORK	Cameron Z-105 balloon	M. E. Dunstan-Sewell
	G-TORN	Flight Design CTSW	J. A. Moss
	G-TOSH	Robinson R22 Beta	Heli Air Ltd
	G-TOTN	Cessna 210M	Quay Financial Strategies Ltd (G-BVZM)
	G-TOTO	Cessna F.177RG	TOTO Flying Group (G-OADE/G-AZKH)
	G-TOUR	Robin R.2112	A. Carnegie
	G-TOWS	PA-25 Pawnee 260	Lasham Gliding Society Ltd
	G-TOYD	Boeing 737-33V	bmi Baby (G-EZYT) (stored)
	G-TOYG	Boeing 737-36N	bmi Baby (G-IGOJ) (stored)
	G-TOYI	Boeing 737-3Q8	bmi Baby (stored)
	G-TOYK	Boeing 737-33R	Aergo Trading Ltd
	G-TOYZ	Bell 206B JetRanger 3	Potter Aviation Ltd (G-RGER)
	G-TPAL	P & M Aviation Quik GT450	R. Robertson
	G-TPPW	Van's RV-7	P. Wright
	G-TPSL	Cessna 182S	A. N. Purslow
	G-TPSY	Champion 8KCAB Super Decathlon	G. R. Potts (G-CEOE)
	G-TPTP	Robinson R44	A. N. Purslow
	G-TPWL	P & M Quik GT450	The G-TPWL Group
	G-TPWX	Heliopolis Gomhouria Mk.6 (TP+WX)	W. H. Greenwood
	G-TRAC	Robinson R44	C. J. Sharples
	G-TRAM	Pegasus Quantum 15-912	G-TRAM Group
	G-TRAN	Beech 76 Duchess	Multiflight Ltd (G-NIFR)
	G-TRAT	Pilatus PC-12/45	Flew LLP
	G-TRAW	Augusta A.109E	Castle Air Ltd
	G-TRAX	Cessna F.172M	Skytrax Aviation Ltd
	G-TRBO	Schleicher ASW-28-18E	A. Cluskey
	G-TRCY	Robinson R44	Sugarfree Air Ltd
	G-TRDS	Guimbal Cabri G2	W. R. Harford
	G-TREC	Cessna 421C	Sovereign Business Integration PLC (G-TLOL)
	G-TREE	Bell 206B JetRanger 3	Bush Woodlands
	G-TREK	Jodel D.18	R. H. Mole
	G-TREX	Alpi Pioneer 300	S. R. Winter
	G-TRIG	Cameron Z-90 balloon	Hedge Hoppers Balloon Group
	G-TRIM	Monnett Moni	E. A. Brotherton-Ratcliffe
	G-TRIN	SOCATA TB20 Trinidad	M. Hardy & M. J. Porter
	G-TRJB	Beech A36 Bonanza	G. A. J. Bowles
	G-TRLL	Groppo Trail	P. M. Grant
	G-TRNG	Agusta A109E Power	Castle Air Ltd (G-NWOY/G-JMXA)
	G-TROY	NA T-28A Fennec (51-7692)	S. G. Howell & S. Tilling
	G-TRTM	DG Flugzeugbau DG-808C	D. T. S. Walsh
	G-TRUE	MDH Hughes 369E	N. E. Bailey
	G-TRUK	Stoddard-Hamilton Glasair RG	M. P. Jackson
	G-TRUX	Colt 77A balloon	Servowarm Baloon Syndicate
	G-TRVR	Van's RV-7	The Richard Ormonde Shuttleworth Remembrance Trust

Reg.	Type	Owner or Operator	Notes
G-TRYX	Enstrom 480B	Trans Holdings Ltd	
G-TSAC	Tecnam P2002-EA Sierra	A. G. Cozens	
G-TSDS	PA-32R-301 Saratoga SP	I. R. Jones (G-TRIP/G-HOSK)	
G-TSGA	PA-28R-201 Arrow III	TSG Aviation Ltd (G-ONSF/G-EMAK)	
G-TSGJ	PA-28-181 Archer II	Golf Juliet Flying Club	
G-TSHO	Ikarus C42 FB80	A. P. Shoobert	
G-TSIM	Titan T-51 Mustang	B. J. Chester-Master	
G-TSIX	AT-6C Harvard IIA (111836:JZ-6)	Century Aviation Ltd	
G-TSJF	Cessna 525B CitationJet CJ3	Lunar Jet Ltd	
G-TSKD	Raj Hamsa X'Air Jabiru J.2.2.	T. Sexton & K. B. Dupuy	
G-TSKS	EV-97 TeamEurostar UK	Purple Aviation Ltd	
G-TSKY	Beagle B.121 Pup 2	R. G. Hayes (G-AWDY)	
G-TSLC	Schweizer 269C-1	Bournemouth Helicopters Ltd	
G-TSOB	Rans S.6-ES Coyote II	S. Luck	
G-TSOL	EAA Acrosport 1	D. F. Cumberlidge & H. Stuart (G-BPKI)	
G-TSUE	Shaw Europa	H. J. C. Maclean	
G-TSWI	Lindstrand LBL-90A balloon	R. J. Gahan	
G-TSWZ	Cameron Z-77 balloon	Group 1st Ltd	
G-TTAT	ICP MXP-740 Savannah VG Jabiru(1)	A. N. Green	
G-TTDD	Zenair CH.701 STOL	D. B. Dainton & V. D. Asque	
G-TTFG	Colt 77B balloon	T. J. & M. J. Turner (G-BUZF)	
G-TTJF	Dassault Falcon 2000S	TAG Aviation (UK) Ltd	
G-TTOB	Airbus A.320-232	British Airways PLC	
G-TTOE	Airbus A.320-232	British Airways PLC	
G-TTOM	Zenair CH.601HD Zodiac	T. M. Bootyman	
G-TTOY	CFM Streak Shadow SA	J. Softley	
G-TTRL	Van's RV-9A	J. E. Gattrell	
G-TTUG	Aeropro Eurofox 912(S)	R. M. Cornwell (G-WTUG)	
G-TUBB	Avtech Jabiru UL	A. H. Bower	
G-TUCK	Van's RV-8	N. G. R. Moffat	
G-TUGG	PA-18 Super Cub 150	Ulster Gliding Club Ltd	
G-TUGI	CZAW Sportcruiser	T. J. Wilson	
G-TUGS	PA-25-235 Pawnee D	J. A. Stephen (G-BFEW)	
G-TUGY	Robin DR.400/180	TUGY Group	
G-TUGZ	Robin DR.400/180R	Buckminster Gliding Club Ltd	
G-TUIA	Boeing 787-8	Thomson Airways Ltd	
G-TUIB	Boeing 787-8	Thomson Airways Ltd	
G-TUIC	Boeing 787-8	Thomson Airways Ltd	
G-TUID	Boeing 787-8	Thomson Airways Ltd	
G-TUNE	Robinson R22 Beta	Heli Air Ltd (G-OJVI)	
G-TURF	Cessna F.406	Reconnaissance Ventures Ltd	
G-TUTU	Cameron O-105 balloon	A. C. K. Rawson & J. J. Rudoni	
G-TVAM	MBB Bo105DBS-4	South Georgis Heritage Trust (G-SPOL)	
G-TVBF	Lindstrand LBL-310A balloon	Virgin Balloons Flights	
G-TVCO	Gippsland GA-8 Airvan	Zyox Ltd	
G-TVHB	Eurocopter EC 135 P2+	Police & Crime Commissioner for West Yorkshire	
G-TVHD	AS.355F2 Ecureuil 2	Arena Aviation Ltd	
G-TVII	Hawker Hunter T.7 (XX467:86)	G-TVII Group/Exeter	
G-TVIJ	CCF Harvard IV (T-6J) (28521:TA-521)	R. W. Davies (G-BSBE)	
G-TVSI	Campbell Cricket Replica	C. Smith	
G-TWAZ	Rolladen-Schneider LS7-WL	S. Derwin	
G-TWEL	PA-28-181 Archer II	International Aerospace Engineering Ltd	
G-TWIN	PA-44-180 Seminole	Transport Command Ltd	
G-TWIS	Silence Twister	C. S. & K. D. Rhodes	
G-TWIZ	Rockwell Commander 114	B. C. & P. M. Cox	
G-TWLV	Van's RV-12	G-TWLV Group	
G-TWNN	Beech 76 Duchess	Folada Aero and Technical Services Ltd	
G-TWOA	Schempp-Hirth Discus 2a	P. Krumm	
G-TWOC	Schempp-Hirth Ventus 2cT	D. Heslop	
G-TWOO	Extra EA.300/200	Skyboard Aerobatics Ltd (G-MRKI)	
G-TWOP	Cessna 525A Citationjet CJ2	Centreline Air Charter Ltd (G-ODAG)	
G-TWRL	Pitts S-1S Special	C. Dennis	
G-TWSR	Silence Twister	J. A. Hallam	
G-TWSS	Silence Twister	A. P. Hatton	
G-TWTR	Robinson R44 II	Heli Aviation Ltd	

Notes	Reg.	Type	Owner or Operator
	G-TWTW	Denney Kitfox Mk.2	R. M. Bremner
	G-TXAN	AT-6D Harvard III (FX301)	P. J. Lawton (G-JUDI)
	G-TXAS	Cessna A.150L	R. S. Grace
	G-TYAK	IDA Bacau Yakovlev Yak-52	S. J. Ducker
	G-TYER	Robin DR.400/500	Robin Group
	G-TYGA	AA-5B Tiger	G-TYGA Group (G-BHNZ)
	G-TYGR	Best Off Skyranger Swift 912S(1)	M. J. Poole
	G-TYKE	Avtech Jabiru UL-450	D. R. Harper
	G-TYNA	PA-28-181 Archer II	Winged Bull Aviation
	G-TYNE	SOCATA TB20 Trinidad	N. V. Price
	G-TYPH	BAe.146-200	BAE Systems (Corporate Air Travel) Ltd (G-BTVT)
	G-TYRE	Cessna F.172M	J. S. C. English
	G-TZEE	SOCATA TB10 Tobago	Zytech Ltd
	G-TZII	Thorp T.211B	M. J. Newton
	G-UACA	Best Off Skyranger 912(2)	R. G. Hicks
	G-UAKE	NA P-51D-5-NA Mustang	P. S. Warner
	G-UANO	DHC.1 Chipmunk 22	Advanced Flight Training Ltd (G-BYYW)
	G-UANT	PA-28 Cherokee 140	Air Navigation & Trading Co Ltd
	G-UAPA	Robin DR.400/140B	Fluirdados Sociedade Aeronautica/Portugal
	G-UAPO	Ruschmeyer R.90-230RG	P. Randall
	G-UART	Moravan Zlin Z-242L	Oxford Aviation Academy (Oxford) Ltd (G-EKMN)
	G-UAVA	PA-30 Twin Comanche	Small World Aviation Ltd
	G-UCAM	PA-31-350 Navajo Chieftain	Blue Sky Investments Ltd (G-NERC/G-BBXX)
	G-UCCC	Cameron 90 Sign SS balloon	Unipart Group of Companies Ltd
	G-UCLU	Schleicher ASK-21	University College London Union
	G-UDET	Replica Fokker E.111	M. J. Clark
	G-UDGE	Thruster T.600N	G-UDGE Syndicate (G-BYPI)
	G-UDMS	PA-46R-350T Malibu Matrix	J. C. M. Critchley & S. Harding
	G-UDOG	SA Bulldog Srs 120/121 (XX518:S)	M. van den Broek
	G-UFAW	Raj Hamsa X'Air 582 (5)	P. Batchelor
	G-UFCB	Cessna 172S	The Cambridge Aero Club Ltd
	G-UFCF	Cessna 172S	PAF Pontoise Aero Formation/France
	G-UFCG	Cessna 172S	Ulster Flying Club (1961) Ltd
	G-UFCI	Cessna 172S	Ulster Flying Club (1961) Ltd
	G-UFCL	Tecnam P2002-JF Sierra	Ulster Flying Club (1961) Ltd
	G-UFCM	Tecnam P2002-JF Sierra	Ulster Flying Club (1961) Ltd
	G-UFLY	Cessna F.150H	Westair Flying Services Ltd (G-AVVY)
	G-UFOE	Grob G.115	Swiftair Maintenance Ltd
	G-UFOX	Aeropro Eurofox 912(1)	G-UFOX Group
	G-UHGB	Bell 205A-1	Heli-Lift Services
	G-UHIH	Bell UH-1H Iroquois (21509)	MSS Holdings Ltd
	G-UHOP	UltraMagic H-31 balloon	S. J. Roake
	G-UIKR	P & M Quik R	A. M. Sirant
	G-UILD	Grob G.109B	K. Butterfield
	G-UILE	Lancair 320	R. J. Martin
	G-UILT	Cessna T.303	D. L. Tucker (G-EDRY)
	G-UIMB	Guimbal Cabri G2	Helitrain Ltd
	G-UINN	Stolp SA.300 Starduster Too	J. D. H. Gordon
	G-UIRI	Aeropro Eurofox 912(S)	P. Crawley
	G-UJAB	Avtech Jabiru UL	C. A. Thomas
	G-UJGK	Avtech Jabiru UL	W. G. Upton & J. G. Kosak
	G-UKAL	Cessna F.406 Caravan II	Aero Lease UK
	G-UKAW	Agusta A.109E	Agusta Westland Ltd
	G-UKFT	Cameron Z-77 balloon	A. M. Holly
	G-UKOZ	Avtech Jabiru SK	D. J. Burnett
	G-UKPS	Cessna 208 Caravan 1	UK Parachute Services Ltd
	G-UKRB	Colt 105A balloon	Virgin Airship & Balloon Co Ltd

Reg.	Type	Owner or Operator	Notes
G-UKUK	Head Ax8-105 balloon	P. A. George	
G-ULAS	DHC.1 Chipmunk 22 (WK517)	ULAS Flying Club Ltd	
G-ULFS	Gulfstream VI	Profred Partners LLP	
G-ULHI	SA Bulldog Srs.100/101	Kryten Systems Ltd (G-OPOD/G-AZMS)	
G-ULIA	Cameron V-77 balloon	J. T. Wilkinson	
G-ULPS	Everett Srs 1 gyroplane	C. J. Watkinson (G-BMNY)	
G-ULSY	Ikarus C.42 FB 80	B. W. Rooke	
G-ULTA	Ultramagic M-65C	G. A. Board	
G-ULTR	Cameron A-105 balloon	P. Glydon	
G-ULUL	Rotorsport UK Calidus	P. J. Troy-Davies (G-HTBT)	
G-UMAS	Rotorsport UK MT-03	BAE Systems (Operations) Ltd	
G-UMBO	Thunder Ax7-77A balloon	Virgin Airship & Balloon Co Ltd	
G-UMBY	Hughes 369E	HQ Aviation Ltd	
G-UMKA	Dassault Falcon 7X	Hyperion Aviation Ltd	
G-UMMI	PA-31-310 Turbo Navajo	2 Excel Aviation Ltd (G-BGSO)	
G-UMMS	EV-97 TeamEurostar UK	A. C. Lees (G-ODRY)	
G-UMMY	Best Off Skyranger J2.2(2)	A. R. Williams	
G-UMPY	Shaw Europa	GDBMK Ltd	
G-UNDD	PA-23 Aztec 250E	G. J. & D. P. Deadman (G-BATX)	
G-UNER	Lindstrand LBL-90A balloon	St. Dunstans	
G-UNES	Van's RV-6	C. A. Greatrex	
G-UNGE	Lindstrand LBL-90A balloon	Silver Ghost Balloon Club (G-BVPJ)	
G-UNGO	Pietenpol Air Camper	A. R. Wyatt	
G-UNIN	Schempp-Hirth Ventus b	U9 Syndicate	
G-UNIX	VPM M16 Tandem Trainer	A. P. Wilkinson	
G-UNKY	Ultramagic S-50 balloon	A. M. Holly	
G-UNNA	Jabiru UL-450WW	N. D. A. Graham	
G-UNRL	Lindstrand LBL-RR21 balloon	Alton Aviation Ltd	
G-UORO	Shaw Europa	D. Dufton	
G-UPFS	Waco UPS-7	D. N. Peters & N. R. Finlayson	
G-UPHI	Best Off Skyranger Swift 912S(1)	Flylight Airsports Ltd	
G-UPID	Bowers Fly Baby 1A	R. D. Taylor	
G-UPOI	Cameron TR-84 S1 balloon	Beatwax Ltd	
G-UPTA	Skyranger 912S (1)	S. J. Joseph	
G-UPUP	Cameron V-77 balloon	S. F. Burden/Netherlands	
G-UPUZ	Lindstrand LBL-120A balloon	C.J. Sanger-Davies	
G-UROP	Beech 95-B55 Baron	S. C. Smith	
G-URRR	Air Command 582 Sport	L. Armes	
G-URSA	Sikorsky S-76C	Capital Air Services Ltd (G-URSS)	
G-URUH	Robinson R44	Heli Air Ltd	
G-USAA	Cessna F.150G	R. E. C. Hawkins (G-OIDW)	
G-USAR	Cessna 441 Conquest	I. Annenskiy	
G-USIL	Thunder Ax7-77 balloon	Window On The World Ltd	
G-USKY	Aviat A-1B Husky	L. W. H. Griffith	
G-USMC	Cameron Chestie 90 SS balloon	J. W. Soukup	
G-USRV	Van's RV-6	W. D. Garlick & R. J. Napp	
G-USSY	PA-28-181 Archer II	The Leicestershire Aero Club Ltd	
G-USTH	Agusta A109A-II	Stratton Motor Co.(Norfolk) Ltd	
G-USTS	Agusta A109A-II	MB Air Ltd (G-MKSF)	
G-USTY	FRED Srs 2	I. Pearson	
G-UTRA	Ultramagic M-77 balloon	Ultrait Ltd	
G-UTSI	Rand-Robinson KR-2	K. B. Gutridge	
G-UTSY	PA-28R-201 Arrow III	J. P. Quoniam	
G-UTZI	Robinson R44 II	S. K. Miles/Spain	
G-UURO	Aerotechnik EV-97 Eurostar	Romeo Oscar Syndicate	
G-UVBF	Lindstrand LBL-400A balloon	Virgin Balloon Flights	
G-UVIP	Cessna 421C	MM Air Ltd (G-BSKH)	
G-UVNR	BAC.167 Strikemaster Mk 87	P. Turek (G-BXFS)	
G-UZLE	Colt 77A balloon	G. B. Davies	

Notes	Reg.	Type	Owner or Operator
	G-UZUP	Aerotechnik EV-97A Eurostar	G-UZUP EV-97 Flying Group
	G-VAAC	PA-28-181 Archer III	J. N. D. de Jager (G-CCDN)
	G-VAAV	P & M Quik R	A. Voyce
	G-VAIR	Airbus A.340-313	Virgin Atlantic Airways Ltd *Maiden Tokyo*
	G-VALS	Pietenpol Air Camper	J. R. D. Bygraves
	G-VALY	SOCATA TB21 Trinidad GT Turbo	R. J. Thwaites and Westflight Aviation Ltd
	G-VALZ	Cameron N-120 balloon	J. D. & K. Griffiths
	G-VANA	Gippsland GA-8 Airvan	P. Marsden
	G-VANC	Gippsland GA-8 Airvan	Irish Skydiving Club Ltd
	G-VAND	Gippsland GA-8 Airvan	Irish Skydiving Club Ltd
	G-VANN	Van's RV-7A	D. N. & J. A. Carnegie
	G-VANS	Van's RV-4	R. J. Marshall
	G-VANX	Gippsland GA-8 Airvan	Airkix Aircraft Ltd
	G-VANZ	Van's RV-6A	S. J. Baxter
	G-VARG	Varga 2150A Kachina	J. Denton
	G-VAST	Boeing 747-41R	Virgin Atlantic Airways Ltd *Ladybird*
	G-VATL	Airbus A.340-642	Avaio 376 Leasing Ltd
	G-VBAA	Cameron A-400 balloon	Virgin Balloon Flights
	G-VBAB	Cameron A-400 balloon	Virgin Balloon Flights
	G-VBAD	Cameron A-300 balloon	Virgin Balloon Flights
	G-VBAE	Cameron A-400 balloon	Virgin Balloon Flights
	G-VBAF	Cameron A-300 balloon	Virgin Balloon Flights
	G-VBAG	Cameron A-400 balloon	Virgin Balloon Flights
	G-VBAH	Cameron A-400 balloon	Virgin Balloon Flights
	G-VBCA	Cirrus SR22	C. A. S. Atha
	G-VBCD	Beech C90 King Air	Aerolease APS
	G-VBFA	Ultramagic N-250 balloon	Virgin Balloon Flights
	G-VBFB	Ultramagic N-355 balloon	Virgin Balloon Flights
	G-VBFC	Ultramagic N-250 balloon	Virgin Balloon Flights
	G-VBFD	Ultramagic N-250 balloon	Virgin Balloon Flights
	G-VBFE	Ultramagic N-255 balloon	Virgin Balloon Flights
	G-VBFF	Lindstrand LBL-360A balloon	Virgin Balloon Flights
	G-VBFG	Cameron Z-350 balloon	Virgin Balloon Flights
	G-VBFH	Cameron Z-350 balloon	Virgin Balloon Flights
	G-VBFI	Cameron Z-350 balloon	Virgin Balloon Flights
	G-VBFJ	Cameron Z-350 balloon	Virgin Balloon Flights
	G-VBFK	Cameron Z-350 balloon	Virgin Balloon Flights
	G-VBFL	Cameron Z-400 balloon	Virgin Balloon Flights
	G-VBFM	Cameron Z-375 balloon	Virgin Balloon Flights
	G-VBFN	Cameron Z-375 balloon	Virgin Balloon Flights
	G-VBFO	Cameron Z-375 balloon	Virgin Balloon Flights
	G-VBFP	Ultramagic N-425 balloon	Virgin Balloon Flights
	G-VBFR	Cameron Z-375 balloon	Virgin Balloon Flights
	G-VBFS	Cameron Z-375 balloon	Virgin Balloon Flights
	G-VBFT	Cameron Z-375 balloon	Virgin Balloon Flights
	G-VBFU	Cameron A-400 balloon	Virgin Balloon Flights
	G-VBFV	Cameron Z-400 balloon	Virgin Balloon Flights
	G-VBFW	Cameron Z-77 balloon	Virgin Balloon Flights
	G-VBFX	Cameron Z-400 balloon	Virgin Balloon Flights
	G-VBFY	Cameron Z-400 balloon	Virgin Balloon Flights
	G-VBFZ	Cameron A-300 balloon	Virgin Balloon Flights
	G-VBIG	Boeing 747-4Q8	Virgin Atlantic Airways Ltd *Tinkerbelle*
	G-VBLU	Airbus A.340-642	Virgin Atlantic Airways Ltd *Soul Sister*
	G-VBPM	Cirrus SR22	S. Perkes
	G-VBUG	Airbus A.340-642	Virgin Atlantic Airways Ltd
	G-VCAN	Bombardier BD100-1A10 Challenger 300	London Executive Aviation Ltd
	G-VCIO	EAA Acro Sport II	C. M. Knight
	G-VCJH	Robinson R22 Beta	Heli Air Ltd
	G-VCML	Beech 58 Baron	St. Angelo Aviation Ltd
	G-VCXT	Schempp-Hirth Ventus 2cT	R. F. Aldous/Germany
	G-VDIR	Cessna T.310R	J. Driver
	G-VDOG	Cessna 305C Bird Dog (24582)	D. K. Shead
	G-VECD	Robin R.1180T	B. Lee
	G-VECG	Robin R.2160	I. A. Anderson
	G-VECT	Cessna 560XL Citation Excel	Fly Vectra Ltd
	G-VEGA	Slingsby T.65A Vega	R. A. Rice (G-BFZN)

Reg.	Type	Owner or Operator	Notes
G-VEIL	Airbus A.340-642	Virgin Atlantic Airways Ltd *Queen of the Skies*	
G-VEIT	Robinson R44 II	Field Marshall Helicopters Ltd	
G-VELA	SIAI-Marchetti S.205-22R	G-VELA Group	
G-VELD	Airbus A.340-313	Virgin Atlantic Airways Ltd *African Queen*	
G-VELO	Velocity 173RG	J. Bergin	
G-VENC	Schempp-Hirth Ventus 2cT	J. B. Giddins	
G-VENM	DH.112 Venom FB.50 (WK436)	Aviation Heritage Ltd (G-BLIE)	
G-VERA	Gardan GY-201 Minicab	D. K. Shipton	
G-VETS	Enstrom 280C-UK Shark	B. G. Rhodes (G-FSDC/G-BKTG)	
G-VEYE	Robinson R22	K. A. Jones (G-BPTP)	
G-VEZE	Rutan Vari-Eze	Go Eze Flying	
G-VFAB	Boeing 747-4Q8	Virgin Atlantic Airways Ltd *Lady Penelope*	
G-VFAR	Airbus A.340-313	Virgin Atlantic Airways Ltd *Diana*	
G-VFAS	PA-28R-200 Cherokee Arrow	P. Wood (G-MEAH/G-BSNM)	
G-VFDS	Van's RV-8	S. T. G. Lloyd	
G-VFIT	Airbus A.340-642	Virgin Atlantic Airways Ltd *Dancing Queen*	
G-VFIZ	Airbus A.340-642	Virgin Atlantic Airways Ltd *Bubbles*	
G-VFOX	Airbus A.340-642	Blue Aviation Ltd	
G-VGAG	Cirrus SR20 GTS	Alfred Graham Ltd	
G-VGAL	Boeing 747-443	Virgin Atlantic Airways Ltd *Jersey Girl*	
G-VGAS	Airbus A.340-542	Virgin Atlantic Airways Ltd *Varga Girl*	
G-VGBR	Airbus A.330-343	Virgin Atlantic Airways Ltd	
G-VGEM	Airbus A.330-343	Virgin Atlantic Airways Ltd	
G-VGMC	Eurocopter AS.355N Ecureuil II	Cheshire Helicopters Ltd (G-HEMH)	
G-VGMG	Eurocopter AS.350B Ecureuil II	Lomas Helicopters (G-KELY/G-WKRD/G-BUJG/ G-HEAR)	
G-VGOA	Airbus A.340-642	Avaio 371 Ltd	
G-VGVG	Savannah VG Jabiru(1)	M. A. Jones	
G-VHOT	Boeing 747-4Q8	Virgin Atlantic Airways Ltd *Tubular Belle*	
G-VICC	PA-28-161 Warrior II	Freedom Aviation Ltd (G-JFHL)	
G-VICM	Beech F33C Bonanza	Velocity Engineering Ltd	
G-VICT	PA-31-310 Turbo Navajo	Aviation Leasing ACS (G-BBZI)	
G-VIEW	Vinten-Wallis WA-116/100	K. H. Wallis	
G-VIIA	Boeing 777-236	British Airways	
G-VIIB	Boeing 777-236	British Airways	
G-VIIC	Boeing 777-236	British Airways	
G-VIID	Boeing 777-236	British Airways	
G-VIIE	Boeing 777-236	British Airways	
G-VIIF	Boeing 777-236	British Airways	
G-VIIG	Boeing 777-236	British Airways	
G-VIIH	Boeing 777-236	British Airways	
G-VIIJ	Boeing 777-236	British Airways	
G-VIIK	Boeing 777-236	British Airways	
G-VIIL	Boeing 777-236	British Airways	
G-VIIM	Boeing 777-236	British Airways	
G-VIIN	Boeing 777-236	British Airways	
G-VIIO	Boeing 777-236	British Airways	
G-VIIP	Boeing 777-236	British Airways	
G-VIIR	Boeing 777-236	British Airways	
G-VIIS	Boeing 777-236	British Airways	
G-VIIT	Boeing 777-236	British Airways	
G-VIIU	Boeing 777-236	British Airways	
G-VIIV	Boeing 777-236	British Airways	
G-VIIW	Boeing 777-236	British Airways	
G-VIIX	Boeing 777-236	British Airways	
G-VIIY	Boeing 777-236	British Airways	
G-VIIZ	CZAW Sportcruiser	Skyview Systems Ltd	
G-VIKE	Bellanca 1730A Viking	R. Waas	
G-VIKS	Maule MT-7-235 Super Rocket	V. Sharma	
G-VILL	Lazer Z.200 (modified)	The G-VILL Group (G-BOYZ)	
G-VINA	Aeroprakt A-22L Foxbat	J. M. Davidson	
G-VINB	Agusta AW.139	Bond Offshore Helicopters Ltd	
G-VINC	Agusta AW.139	Bond Offshore Helicopters Ltd	
G-VINE	Airbus A.330-343	Virgin Atlantic Airways Ltd	
G-VING	Sikorsky S-92A	Bond Offshore Helicopters Ltd	
G-VINJ	Agusta AW.139	Bond Offshore Helicopters Ltd	
G-VIPA	Cessna 182S	Stallingborough Aviation Ltd	

Notes	Reg.	Type	Owner or Operator
	G-VIPH	Agusta A109C	Cheqair Ltd(G-BVNH/G-LAXO)
	G-VIPI	BAe 125 Srs 800B	Yeates of Leicester Ltd
	G-VIPP	PA-31-350 Navajo Chieftain	Capital Air Charter Ltd
	G-VIPR	Eurocopter EC 120B Colibri	Amey Aviation LLP
	G-VIPU	PA-31-350 Navajo Chieftain	Capital Air Charter Ltd
	G-VIPV	PA-31-350 Navajo Chieftain	Capital Air Charter Ltd
	G-VIPW	PA-31-350 Navajo Chieftain	Capital Air Charter Ltd
	G-VIPX	PA-31-350 Navajo Chieftain	Capital Air Charter Ltd
	G-VIPY	PA-31-350 Navajo Chieftain	Capital Air Charter Ltd
	G-VIRR	Robin DR.400/500	R. A. Walters (G-IYCO)
	G-VITA	Dassault Falcon 7X	Casanova Air 7X Ltd
	G-VITE	Robin R.1180T	G-VITE Flying Group
	G-VITL	Lindstrand LBL-105A balloon	Vital Resources
	G-VIVA	Thunder Ax7-65 balloon	R. J. Mitchener
	G-VIVI	Taylor JT.2 Titch	D. G. Tucker
	G-VIVM	P.84 Jet Provost T.5	Victor Mike Group (G-BVWF)
	G-VIVO	Nicollier HN700 Menestrel II	D. G. Tucker
	G-VIVS	PA-28-151 Cherokee Warrior	S. J. Harrison & V. A. Donnelly
	G-VIXN	DH.110 Sea Vixen FAW.2 (XS587) ★	P. G. Vallance Ltd/Charlwood
	G-VIXX	Alpi Pioneer 300	B. F. Walker & S. R. Neale (G-CESE/G-CERJ)
	G-VIZA	LBL-260A balloon	A. Nimmo
	G-VIZZ	Sportavia RS.180 Sportsman	Exeter Fournier Group
	G-VJET	Avro 698 Vulcan B.2 (XL426) ★	Vulcan Restoration Trust
	G-VKIT	Shaw Europa	T. H. Crow
	G-VKSS	Airbus A.330-343	Virgin Atlantic Airways Ltd *Mademoiselle Rouge*
	G-VKUP	Cameron Z-90 balloon	A. & H. A. Evans
	G-VLCC	Schleicher ASW-27-18E	Viscount Cobham
	G-VLCN	Avro 698 Vulcan B.2 (XH558) ★	Vulcan to the Sky Trust/Bruntingthorpe
	G-VLIP	Boeing 747-443	Virgin Atlantic Airways Ltd *Hot Lips*
	G-VLTT	Diamond DA.42 Twin Star	The Leninton Company
	G-VLUU	Airbus A.330-343	Virgin Atlantic Airways Ltd
	G-VMCG	PA-38-112 Tomahawk	Pure Aviation Support Services Ltd (G-BSVX)
	G-VMEG	Airbus A.340-642	Blue Aviation Ltd
	G-VMIJ	VS 349 Spitfire Mk.VC	I. D. Ward
	G-VMJM	SOCATA TB10 Tobago	S. C. Brown (G-BTOK)
	G-VMVM	Cessna Z-77 balloon	Virgin Balloon Flights
	G-VNAP	Airbus A.340-642	Virgin Atlantic Airways Ltd *Sleeping Beauty*
	G-VNOM	DH.112 Venom FB.50 (J-1632) ★	de Havilland Heritage Museum/London Colney
	G-VNON	Escapade Jabiru (3)	P. A. Vernon
	G-VNTS	Schempp-Hirth Ventus bT	911 Syndicatem
	G-VNYC	Airbus A.330-343	Virgin Atlantic Airways Ltd
	G-VOAR	PA-28-181 Archer III	E. A. Dwarka
	G-VOCE	Robinson R22	J. J. Voce (G-BSCL)
	G-VODA	Cameron N-77 balloon	H. Cusden
	G-VOGE	Airbus A.340-642	Blue Aviation Ltd
	G-VOID	PA-28RT-201 Arrow IV	Doublecube Aviation LLP
	G-VOIP	Westland SA.341G Gazelle	Q. Milne (G-HOBZ/G-CBSJ)
	G-VOLO	Alpi Pioneer 300	J. Buglass
	G-VONE	Eurocopter AS355N Twin Squirrel	London Helicopter Centres Ltd (G-LCON)
	G-VONG	AS.355F1 Twin Squirrel	Airbourne Solutions Ltd (G-OILX/G-RMGN/G-BMCY)
	G-VONH	AS.355F1 Twin Squirrel	London Helicopter Centres Ltd (G-BKUL/G-FFHI/G-GWHH)
	G-VONK	AS.355F1 Squirrel	Airbourne Solutions Ltd (G-BLRI/G-NUTZ)
	G-VONS	PA-32R-301T Saratoga IITC	W. S. Stanley
	G-VOOM	Pitts S-1S Special	VOOM Syndicate
	G-VORN	Aerotechnik EV-97 Eurostar	J. Parker (G-ODAV)
	G-VPAT	Evans VP-1 Srs 2	A. P. Twort
	G-VPCM	Dassault Falcon 2000LX	Executive Jet Charter Ltd
	G-VPPL	SOCATA TB20 Trinidad	J. M. Thorpe (G-BPAS)
	G-VPSJ	Shaw Europa	J. D. Bean
	G-VRAY	Airbus A.330-343	Virgin Atlantic Airways Ltd

Reg.	Type	Owner or Operator	Notes
G-VRCW	Cessna P.210N	M. Mignini/Italy	
G-VRED	Airbus A.340-642	Virgin Atlantic Airways Ltd *Scarlet Lady*	
G-VROC	Boeing 747-41R	Virgin Atlantic Airways Ltd *Mustang Sally*	
G-VROE	Avro 652A Anson T.21 (WD413)	Air Atlantique Ltd (G-BFIR)	
G-VROM	Boeing 747-443	Virgin Atlantic Airways Ltd	
G-VROS	Boeing 747-443	Virgin Atlantic Airways Ltd *English Rose*	
G-VROY	Boeing 747-443	Virgin Atlantic Airways Ltd *Pretty Woman*	
G-VRVB	Van's RV-8	R. J. Verrall (G-CETI)	
G-VRVI	Cameron O-90 balloon	Gone Ballooning	
G-VSGE	Cameron O-105 balloon	G. Sbocchelli	
G-VSIX	Schempp-Hirth Ventus 2cT	V6 Group	
G-VSOZ	Yakovlev Yak-18T	N. R. Parsons	
G-VSSH	Airbus A.340-642	Virgin Atlantic Airways Ltd *Sweet Dreamer*	
G-VSTR	Stolp SA-900 V-Star	R. L. Hanreck	
G-VSUN	Airbus A.340-313	Virgin Atlantic Airways Ltd *Rainbow Lady*	
G-VSXY	Airbus A.330-343	Virgin Atlantic Airways Ltd *Beauty Queen*	
G-VTAL	Beech V35 Bonanza	M. Elsey	
G-VTCT	Schempp-Hirth Ventus-2cT	V26 Syndicate	
G-VTGE	Bell 206L LongRanger	Vantage Helicopters Ltd (G-ELIT)	
G-VTII	DH.115 Vampire T.11 (XX507:74)	Vampire Preservation Group, Bournemouth	
G-VTOL	Hawker Siddeley Harrier T.52 ★	Brooklands Museum of Aviation/Weybridge	
G-VTUS	Schempp-Hirth Ventus 2cT	Ventus 02 Syndicate	
G-VTWO	Schempp-Hirth Ventus 2c	The G-VTWO Flyiing Group	
G-VUEA	Cessna 550 Citation II	Marshall of Cambridge Aerospace Ltd (G-BWOM)	
G-VUEZ	Cessna 550 Citation II	AD Aviation Ltd	
G-VUFO	Airbus A.330-343	Virgin Atlantic Airways Ltd	
G-VULC	Avro 698 Vulcan B.2A (XM655) ★	Radarmoor Ltd/Wellesbourne	
G-VVBA	AS.355F2 Ecureuil II	Hinde Holdings Ltd (G-DBOK)	
G-VVBE	Robinson R22 Beta	Hinde Holdings Ltd (G-OTOY/G-BPEW)	
G-VVBF	Colt 315A balloon	Virgin Balloon Flights	
G-VVBK	PA-34-200T Seneca II	Ravenair Aircraft Ltd (G-BSBS/G-BDRI)	
G-VVBL	Robinson R44 II	Hinde Holdings Ltd	
G-VVBO	Bell 206L-3 LongRanger III	Hinde Holdings Ltd	
G-VVIP	Cessna 421C	Cranfield Aerospace Ltd (G-BMWB)	
G-VVPA	Bombardier CL600-2B16	TAG Aviation (UK) Ltd	
G-VVTV	Diamond DA42 Twin Star	A. D. R. Northeast	
G-VVVV	Skyranger 912 (2)	J. Thomas	
G-VVWW	Enstrom 280C Shark	P. J. Odendaal	
G-VWAG	Airbus A.330-343	Virgin Atlantic Airways Ltd	
G-VWEB	Airbus A.340-642	Virgin Atlantic Airways Ltd *Surfer Girl*	
G-VWIN	Airbus A.340-642	Virgin Atlantic Airways Ltd *Lady Luck*	
G-VWKD	Airbus A.340-642	Virgin Atlantic Airways Ltd *Miss Behavin'*	
G-VWOW	Boeing 747-41R	Virgin Atlantic Airways Ltd *Cosmic Girl*	
G-VXLG	Boeing 747-41R	Virgin Atlantic Airways Ltd *Ruby Tuesday*	
G-VYAK	Yakovlev Yak-18T	A. I. McRobbie	
G-VYGG	Airbus A.330-243	Air Tanker Ltd	
G-UYGH	Airbus A.330-243	Air Tanker Ltd	
G-VYOU	Airbus A.340-642	Virgin Atlantic Airways Ltd *Emmeline Heaney born August 2006*	
G-VZIM	Alpha R2160	I. M. Hollingsworth	
G-VZON	ATR-72-212A	Aurigny Air Services Ltd	
G-WAAS	MBB Bö.105DBS-4	South Georgia Heritage Trust (G-ESAM/G-BUIB/G-BDYZ)	
G-WABH	Cessna 172S Skyhawk	Blackhawk Aviation Ltd	
G-WACB	Cessna F.152 II	Booker Aircraft Leasing Ltd	
G-WACE	Cessna F.152 II	Booker Aircraft Leasing Ltd	
G-WACF	Cessna 152 II	Booker Aircraft Leasing Ltd	
G-WACG	Cessna 152 II	Booker Aircraft Leasing Ltd	
G-WACH	Cessna FA.152 II	Booker Aircraft Leasing Ltd	
G-WACI	Beech 76 Duchess	K. A. O'Connor	
G-WACJ	Beech 76 Duchess	K. A. O'Connor	

BRITISH CIVIL REGISTRATIONS

Notes	Reg.	Type	Owner or Operator
	G-WACL	Cessna F.172N	A. G. Arthur (G-BHGG)
	G-WACO	Waco UPF-7	R. F. L. Cuypers/Belgium
	G-WACT	Cessna F.152 II	N. Clark (G-BKFT)
	G-WACU	Cessna FA.152	Booker Aircraft Leasing Ltd (G-BJZU)
	G-WACW	Cessna 172P	Technical Power & Maintenance Ltd
	G-WACY	Cessna F.172P	The Vintage Wings Aviation Co.Ltd
	G-WADI	PA-46-350P Malibu Mirage	Air Malibu AG/Liechtenstein
	G-WADS	Robinson R22 Beta	Whizzard Helicopters (G-NICO)
	G-WADZ	Lindstrand LBL-90A balloon	A. K. C., J. E. H., M. H. & Y. K. Wadsworth (G-CGVN)
	G-WAGA	Wag-Aero Wagabond	A. I. Sutherland (G-BNJA)
	G-WAGG	Robinson R22 Beta II	N. J. Wagstaff Leasing
	G-WAGN	Stinson 108-3 Voyager	S. E. H. Ellcome
	G-WAHL	QAC Quickie	A. A. A. Wahlberg
	G-WAIR	PA-32-301 Saratoga	Finningley Aviation
	G-WAIT	Cameron V-77 balloon	C. P. Brown
	G-WAKE	Mainair Blade 912	J. E. Rourke
	G-WAKY	Cyclone AX2000	S. Perks & A. Munn
	G-WALI	Robinson R44 II	Casdron Enterprises Ltd
	G-WALY	Maule MX-7-180	J. R. Colthurst
	G-WALZ	Best Off Sky Ranger Nynja 912S(1)	R. J. Thomas
	G-WAMS	PA-28R-201 Arrow	Stapleford Flying Club Ltd
	G-WAPA	Robinson R44 II	Aerocorp Ltd
	G-WARA	PA-28-161 Warrior III	KN Singles & Twins Aviation Consultants BV/Netherlands
	G-WARB	PA-28-161 Warrior III	OSF Ltd
	G-WARD	Taylor JT.1 Monoplane	R. P. J. Hunter
	G-WARE	PA-28-161 Warrior II	I. D. Wakeling
	G-WARH	PA-28-161 Warrior III	KN Singles & Twins Aviation Consultants BV
	G-WARO	PA-28-161 Warrior III	T. G. D. Leasing Ltd
	G-WARP	Cessna 182F Sylane	R. D. Fowden (G-ASHB)
	G-WARR	PA-28-161 Warrior II	R. N. Brown
	G-WARS	PA-28-161 Warrior III	Blaneby Ltd
	G-WARU	PA-28-161 Warrior III	Smart People Don't Buy Ltd
	G-WARV	PA-28-161 Warrior III	Bickertons Aerodromes Ltd
	G-WARW	PA-28-161 Warrior III	Lomac Aviators Ltd
	G-WARX	PA-28-161 Warrior III	C. M. A. Clark
	G-WARY	PA-28-161 Warrior III	Target Aviation Ltd
	G-WARZ	PA-28-161 Warrior III	Target Aviation Ltd
	G-WASC	Eurocopter EC.135 T2+	Bond Air Services Ltd
	G-WASN	Eurocopter EC.135 T2+	Bond Air Services Ltd
	G-WASS	Eurocopter EC.135 T2+	Bond Air Services Ltd
	G-WATR	Christen A1 Husky	S. N. Gregory
	G-WATT	Cameron Cooling Tower SS balloon	C. G. Dobson
	G-WAVA	Robin HR.200/120B	Smart People Don't Buy Ltd
	G-WAVE	Grob G.109B	C. G. Wray
	G-WAVS	PA-28-161 Warrior III	TGD Leasing Ltd (G-WARC)
	G-WAVV	Robon HR200/120B	TGD Leasing Ltd (G-GORF)
	G-WAVY	Grob G.109B	G-WAVY Group
	G-WAWW	P & M Quik GT450	P. Knowles
	G-WAYS	Lindstrand LBL-105A balloon	Lindstrand Hot Air Balloons Ltd
	G-WAZP	Skyranger 912 (2)	L. V. McClune
	G-WAZZ	Pitts S-1S Special	J. P. Taylor (G-BRRP)
	G-WBEV	Cameron N-77 balloon	T. J. & M. Turner (G-PVCU)
	G-WBLY	Mainair Pegasus Quik	A. J. Lindsey
	G-WBTS	Falconar F-11	M. K. Field (G-BDPL)
	G-WBVS	Diamond DA.4D Star	G. W. Beavis
	G-WCAO	Eurocopter EC 135T2	Police & Crime Commissioner for West Yorkshire
	G-WCAT	Colt Flying Mitt SS balloon	I. Chadwick
	G-WCCP	Beech B200 Super King Air	William Cook Aviation Ltd
	G-WCEI	MS.894E Rallye 220GT	R. A. L. Lucas (G-BAOC)
	G-WCKD	Eurocopter EC130 B4	Batchelor Aviation Ltd (G-CFWX)
	G-WCKM	Best Off Sky Ranger 912(1)	J. Depree & B. Janson
	G-WCME	Grumman FM-2 Wildcat	Bygone Engineering Ltd
	G-WCMI	Grumman FM-2 Wildcat	Bygone Engineering Ltd
	G-WCMO	Grumman FM-2 Wildcat	Bygone Engineering Ltd
	G-WCRD	Aérospatiale SA.341G Gazelle	MW Helicopters Ltd
	G-WCUB	PA-18 Super Cub 150	P. A. Walley

Reg.	Type	Owner or Operator	Notes
G-WDEB	Thunder Ax-7-77 balloon	A. Heginbottom	
G-WDGC	Rolladen-Schneider LS8-18	W. D. G. Chappel (G-CEWJ)	
G-WDKR	AS.355F1 Ecureuil 2	Cheshire Helicopters Ltd (G-NEXT/G-OMAV)	
G-WEAT	Robinson R44 II	R. F. Brook	
G-WEBI	Hughes 369E	M. Webb	
G-WEBY	Ace Magic Cyclone	B. W. Webster	
G-WEBS	American Champion 7ECA Citabria	Flugsportclub Odenwald	
G-WEED	Ace Magic Laser	R. D. Leigh	
G-WEEE	Ace Magic Cyclone	K. G. Grayson & R. D. Leigh	
G-WEEK	Skyranger 912(2)	D. J. Prothero	
G-WEFR	Alpi Pioneer 200-M	Cardiff Backpacker Caerdydd Ltd	
G-WELY	Agusta A109E Power	Titan Airways Ltd	
G-WENA	AS.355F2 Ecureuil II	Multiflight Ltd (G-CORR/G-MUFF/G-MOBI)	
G-WEND	PA-28RT-201 Arrow IV	Tayside Aviation Ltd	
G-WERY	SOCATA TB20 Trinidad	R-Aviation SARL/France	
G-WESX	CFM Streak Shadow	M. Catania	
G-WETI	Cameron N-31 balloon	C. A. Butter & J. J. T. Cooke	
G-WEWI	Cessna 172	T. J. Wassell (G-BSEP)	
G-WEZZ	Taylor JT.1 Monoplane	W. A. Tierney (G-BDRF)	
G-WFFW	PA-28-161 Warrior II	S. Letheren & D. Jelly	
G-WFLY	Mainair Pegasus Quik	A. C. R. Drayton	
G-WFOX	Robinson R22 Beta II	Rotorfun Aviation	
G-WGCS	PA-18 Super Cub 95	S. C. Thompson	
G-WGSC	Pilatus PC-6/B2-H4 Turbo Porter	D. M. Penny	
G-WGSI	Tanarg/Ixess 13 912S(1)	J. A. Ganderton	
G-WGSZ	Tanarg/Bionix 13 912S(1)	J. A. Ganderton	
G-WHAL	QAC Quickie	A. A. M. Wahiberg	
G-WHAM	AS.350B3 Ecureuil	Horizon Helicopter Hire Ltd	
G-WHAT	Colt 77A balloon	M. A. Scholes	
G-WHEE	Pegasus Quantum 15-912	Airways Airsports Ltd	
G-WHEN	Tecnam P92-EM Echo	N. Harrison	
G-WHIL	Balony Kubicek BB-S Cup SS balloon	A. M. Holly	
G-WHIM	Colt 77A balloon	D. L. Morgan	
G-WHOG	CFM Streak Shadow	B. R. Cannell	
G-WHOO	Rotorway Executive 162F	J. White	
G-WHRL	Schweizer 269C	P. A. Adams & T. S. Davies	
G-WHST	AS.350B2 Ecureuil	Kelair (IoM) Ltd (G-BWYA)	
G-WHYS	ICP MXP-740 Savannah VG Jabiru(1)	D. J. Whysall	
G-WIBB	Jodel D.18	C. J. Bragg	
G-WIBS	CASA 1-131E Jungmann 2000	C. Willoughby	
G-WICH	Clutton FRED Srs II	L. A. Tomlinson	
G-WIFE	Cessna R.182 RG II	Wife 182 Group (G-BGVT)	
G-WIFI	Cameron Z-90 balloon	A. R. Rich	
G-WIGY	Pitts S-1S Special	R. E. Welch (G-ITTI)	
G-WIII	Schempp-Hirth Ventus bT	I. G. Carrick	
G-WIIZ	Augusta-Bell 206B JetRanger 2	M. Horne, V. Phillips & Kington Building Supplies Ltd (G-DBHH/G-AWVO)	
G-WIKI	Europa XS	J. Greenhaigh	
G-WILB	Ultramagic M-105 balloon	A. S. Davidson, B. N. Trowbridge & W. C. Bailey	
G-WILG	PZL-104 Wilga 35	M. H. Bletsoe-Brown (G-AZYJ)	
G-WILT	Ikarus C42 FB80	A. E. Lacy-Hulbert	
G-WIMP	Colt 56A balloon	D. M. Wade	
G-WINE	Thunder Ax7-77Z balloon ★	Balloon Preservation Group/Lancing	
G-WINH	EV-97 TeamEurostar UK	H. M. Wooldridge	
G-WINI	SA Bulldog Srs.120/121 (XX546:03)	A. Bole (G-CBCO)	
G-WINK	AA-5B Tiger	B. St. J. Cooke	
G-WINN	Stolp SA.300 Starduster Too	H. Feeney	
G-WINR	Robinson R22	Heli Air Ltd (G-BTHG)	
G-WINS	PA-32 Cherokee Six 300	Cheyenne Ltd	
G-WINV	Eurocopter EC155 B1	Starspeed Ltd (G-WJCJ)	
G-WIRG	Embraer EMB-135BJ Legacy 650	Air Charter Scotland Ltd	
G-WIRL	Robinson R22 Beta	Rivermead Aviation Ltd/Switzerland	
G-WISZ	Steen Skybolt	G. S. Reid	
G-WIXI	Avions Mudry CAP-10B	A. R. Harris	
G-WIZI	Enstrom 280FX	AAA Pest Control GmbH	
G-WIZR	Robinson R22 Beta II	Fly Executive Ltd	

Notes	Reg.	Type	Owner or Operator
	G-WIZS	Mainair Pegasus Quik	R. P. Offord
	G-WIZY	Robinson R22 Beta	Subacoustech Ltd (G-BMWX)
	G-WIZZ	Agusta-Bell 206B JetRanger 2	Rivermead Aviation Ltd
	G-WJAC	Cameron TR-70 balloon	S. J. & J. A. Bellaby
	G-WJAN	Boeing 757-21K	Thomas Cook Airlines Ltd
	G-WJCM	CASA 1.131E Jungmann 2000 (S5+B06)	G. W. Lynch (G-BSFB)
	G-WJET	HpH Glasflugel 304 S Shark	P. Thomson
	G-WKNS	Shaw Europa XS	A. L. Wickens
	G-WLAC	PA-18 Super Cub 150	White Waltham Airfield Ltd (G-HAHA/G-BSWE)
	G-WLDN	Robinson R44 Raven	R. D. Masters
	G-WLGC	PA-28-181 Archer III	E. F. Mangion (G-FLUX)
	G-WLKI	Lindstrand LBL-105A balloon	C. Wilkinson
	G-WLKS	Schleicher ASW-20L	S. E. Wilks (G-IUMB)
	G-WLLS	Rolladen-Schneider LS8-18	L & A Wells
	G-WLMS	Mainair Blade 912	G. Zerrun
	G-WLSN	Best Off Skyranger 912S (1)	A. Wilson & ptnrs
	G-WMAS	Eurocopter EC 135T1	Bond Air Services Ltd
	G-WMTM	AA-5B Tiger	G. R. Balls
	G-WNCH	Beech B200 Super King Air	Winch Air Ltd (G-OMGI)
	G-WNSE	Sikorsky S-92A	CHC Scotia Ltd
	G-WNSG	Sikorsky S-92A	CHC Scotia Ltd
	G-WNSI	Sikorsky S-92A	CHC Scotia Ltd
	G-WNSJ	Sikorsky S-92A	CHC Scotia Ltd
	G-WNSN	Eurocopter EC.225LP Super Puma	CHC Scotia Ltd
	G-WNSO	Eurocopter EC.225LP Super Puma	CHC Scotia Ltd (G-PNEO)
	G-WNSP	Eurocopter EC.225LP Super Puma	CHC Scotia Ltd
	G-WNTR	PA-28-161 Warrior II	Fleetlands Flying Group (G-BFNJ)
	G-WOCO	Waco YMF-5C	Classic Aviation Ltd
	G-WOFM	Agusta A109E Power	Quinnasette Ltd (G-NWRR)
	G-WOLF	PA-28 Cherokee 140	G-WOLF Ltd
	G-WONE	Schempp-Hirth Ventus 2cT	J. P. Wright
	G-WONN	Eurocopter EC135 T2	Bond Air Services Ltd
	G-WOOD	Beech 95-B55A Baron	M. S. Choskey (G-AYID)
	G-WOOF	Enstrom 480	Netcopter.co.uk Ltd & Curvature Ltd
	G-WOOL	Colt 77A balloon	Whacko Balloon Group
	G-WOOO	CZAW Sportcruiser	J. J. Nicholson
	G-WORM	Thruster T.600N	C. Childs
	G-WOSY	MBB Bö.105DBS/4	Redwood Aviation Ltd (G-PASD/G-BNRS)
	G-WOTW	Ultramagic M-77 balloon	Window on the World Ltd
	G-WOWI	Van's RV-7	P. J. Wood
	G-WPAS	MDH MD-900 Explorer	Police Aviation Services Ltd
	G-WPDA	Eurocopter EC135 P1	WPD Helicopter Unit
	G-WPDB	Eurocopter EC135 P1	WPD Helicopter Unit
	G-WPDC	Eurocopter EC135 P1	WPD Helicopter Unit
	G-WPDD	Eurocopter EC135 P1	WPD Helicopter Unit
	G-WPIE	Enstrom 280FX Shark	Wrights Pies (Shelton) Ltd (G-RCAR/G-BXRD)
	G-WREN	Pitts S-2A Special	Modi Aviation Ltd
	G-WRFM	Enstrom 280C-UK Shark	A. J. Clark (G-CTSI/G-BKIO)
	G-WRIT	Thunder Ax7-77A balloon	G. Pusey
	G-WRLY	Robinson R22 Beta	Burman Aviation Ltd (G-OFJS/G-BNXJ)
	G-WRWR	Robinson R22 Beta II	MFH Helicopters Ltd
	G-WSKY	Enstrom 280C-UK-2 Shark	B. J. Rutterford (G-BEEK)
	G-WSMW	Robinson R44	M. Wass (G-SGPL)
	G-WSSX	Ikarus C42 FB100	J. M. Crane
	G-WSTY	Lindstrand LBL-77A balloon	C. Westwood
	G-WTAV	Robinson R44 II	T. Levitan
	G-WTSN	Van's RV-8	S. R. Watson
	G-WTWO	Aquila AT01	J. P. Wright
	G-WUFF	Shaw Europa	W. H. Bliss

Reg.	Type	Owner or Operator	Notes
G-WVBF	Lindstrand LBL-210A balloon	Virgin Balloon Flights Ltd	
G-WVIP	Beech B.200 Super King Air	Capital Air Charter Ltd	
G-WWAL	PA-28R Cherokee Arrow 180	White Waltham Airfield Ltd (G-AZSH)	
G-WWAY	Piper PA-28-181 Archer II	R. A. Witchell	
G-WWFC	Dassault Falcon 2000LX	London Executive Aviation Ltd	
G-WWLF	Extra EA.300/L	P. Sapignoli	
G-WWZZ	CZAW Sportcruiser	L. Hogan	
G-WYAT	CFM Streak Shadow Srs SA	N. L. Phillips	
G-WYDE	Schleicher ASW-20BL	461 Syndicate	
G-WYKD	Tanarg/Ixess 15 912S(2)	D. L. Turner	
G-WYND	Wittman W.8 Tailwind	R. S. Marriott	
G-WYNE	BAe 125 Srs 800B	Global Flight Solutions Ltd (G-CJAA/G-HCFR/ G-SHEA/G-BUWC)	
G-WYNT	Cameron N-56 balloon	P. Richardson	
G-WYPA	MBB Bö.105DBS/4	Police Aviation Services Ltd	
G-WYSZ	Robin DR.400/100	Exavia Ltd (G-FTIM)	
G-WYVN	DG Flugzeugbau DG-1000S	Army Gliding Association	
G-WZOL	RL.5B LWS Sherwood Ranger	D. Lentell (G-MZOL)	
G-WZOY	Rans S.6-ES Coyote II	S. P. Read	
G-WZRD	Eurocopter EC 120B Colibri	Conductia Enterprises Ltd	
G-XAIM	Ultramagic H-31 balloon	G. Everett	
G-XALT	PA-38-112 Tomahawk	P. J. Crowther	
G-XALZ	Rans S6S-116 Super Six	M. R. McNeil	
G-XARA	Czech Sport Aircraft PS-28 Cruiser	Andrew English PS-28 Group	
G-XARV	ARV Super 2	C. M. Rose (G-OPIG/G-BMSJ)	
G-XASH	Schleicher ASH-31 MI	R. C. Wilson	
G-XAVB	Cessna 510 Citation Mustang	Aviation Beauport Ltd	
G-XAVI	PA-28-161 Warrior II	J. R. Santamaria (G-SACZ)	
G-XAVV	Schempp-Hirth Ventus 2c	A. J. McNamara & O. Walters	
G-XBAL	Skyringer Nynja 912S(1)	W. G. Gill & N. D. Ewer	
G-XBCI	Bell 206B JetRanger 3	BCI Helicopter Charters Ltd	
G-XBGA	Glaser-Dirks DG500/22 Elan	N. Kelly	
G-XBJT	Aerotechnik EV-97 Eurostar	C. J. & J. A. Aldous (G-WHOA/G-DATH)	
G-XBLD	MBB Bo.105DB	PLM Dollar Group Ltd	
G-XBLU	Cessna 680 Citation Sovereign	Datel Holdings Ltd	
G-XBOX	Bell 206B JetRanger 3	Castle Air Ltd (G-OOHO/G-OCHC/G-KLEE/ G-SIZL/G-BOSW)	
G-XCBI	Schweizer 269C-1	B. Durkan	
G-XCCC	Extra EA.300/L	P. T. Fellows	
G-XCII	Sikorsky S-92A	Bristow Helicopters Ltd	
G-XCIT	Alpi Pioneer 300	A. Thomas	
G-XCJM	Embraer EMB-135BJ Legacy 650	Corporate Jet Management Ltd	
G-XCRJ	Van's RV-9A	R. Jones	
G-XCUB	PA-18 Super Cub 150	M. C. Barraclough	
G-XDEA	Diamond DA.42 Twin Star	Diamond Executive Aviation Ltd	
G-XDUO	Schempp-Hirth Duo Discus xT	G-XDUO Group	
G-XDWE	P & M Quik GT450	R. J. Harper	
G-XELA	Robinson R44 II	A. Schedl/Germany	
G-XELL	Schleicher ASW-27-18E	S. R. Ell	
G-XENA	PA-28-161 Warrior II	P. Brewer	
G-XERO	CZAW Sportcruiser	M. R. Mosley	
G-XFLY	Lambert Mission M212-100	Lambert Aircraft Engineering BVBA	
G-XFOX	Aeropro Eurofox 912(S)	G. J. Baker & R. F. Lyon	
G-XHOT	Cameron Z-105 balloon	S. F. Burden	
G-XIII	Van's RV-7	Icarus Flying Group	
G-XIIX	Robinson R22 Beta ★	(Static exhibit)/Blackbushe	
G-XINE	PA-28-161 Warrior II	P. Tee (G-BPAC)	
G-XIOO	Raj Hamsa X'Air 133 (1)	M. Ridgway	
G-XIXI	Evektor EV-97 TeamEurostar UK	J. A. C. Cockfield	
G-XIXX	Glaser-Dirks DG-300 Elan	S. D. Black	

Notes	Reg.	Type	Owner or Operator
	G-XJET	Learjet 45	CEGA Air Ambulance UK Ltd (G-IZAP/G-OLDK)
	G-XJJM	P & M Pegasus Quik	Mainair Microlight Centre Ltd
	G-XJON	Schempp-Hirth Ventus 2b	J. C. Bastin
	G-XKKA	Diamond KH36 Super Dimona	G-XKKA Group
	G-XLAM	Best Off Skyranger 912S	X-LAM Skyranger Syndicate
	G-XLEA	Airbus A.380-841	British Airways PLC
	G-XLEB	Airbus A.380-841	British Airways PLC
	G-XLEC	Airbus A.380-841	British Airways PLC
	G-XLEDd	Airbus A.380-841	British Airways PLC
	G-XLII	Schleicher ASW-27-18E	P. M. Wells
	G-XLLL	AS.355F1 Twin Squirrel	MW Helicopters Ltd (G-PASF/G-SCHU)
	G-XLNT	Zenair CH.601XL	Zenair G-XLNT Group
	G-XLTG	Cessna 182S	T. I. M. Paul
	G-XLTV	Cessna 560XL Citation XLS	Arena Aircraft Ltd
	G-XLXL	Robin DR.400/160	L. R. Marchant (G-BAUD)
	G-XMGO	Aeromot AMT-200S Super Ximango	G. McLean & R. P. Beck
	G-XMHD	Hawker Hunter T.Mk.7 (XL577/V)	Canberra 134 Ltd (G-BXKF)
	G-XOAR	Schleicher ASW-27-18E	R. A. Browne
	G-XOIL	AS.355N Twin Squirrel	Firstearl Marine and Aviation Ltd (G-LOUN)
	G-XONE	Canadair CL600-2B16	Gama Aviation Ltd
	G-XPBI	Letov LK-2M Sluka	R. M. C. Hunter
	G-XPDA	Cameron Z-120 balloon	M. Cowling
	G-XPII	Cessna R.172K	The Hawk Flying Group (G-DIVA)
	G-XPWW	Cameron TR-77 balloon	Chalmers Ballong Corps/Sweden
	G-XPXP	Aero Designs Pulsar XP	B. J. Edwards
	G-XRAY	Rand-Robinson KR-2	R. S. Smith
	G-XRED	Pitts S-1C Special	J. E. Rands (G-SWUN/G-BSXH)
	G-XRLD	Cameron A-250 balloon	The Cotswold Balloon Co.Ltd
	G-XRVB	Van's RV-8	P. G. Winters
	G-XRVX	Van's RV-10	N. K. Lamping
	G-XRXR	Raj Hamsa X'Air 582 (1)	R. J. Philpotts
	G-XSAM	Van's RV-9A	Parachuting Aircraft Ltd
	G-XSDJ	Europa XS	D. N. Joyce
	G-XSEA	Van's RV-8	H. M. Darlington
	G-XSEL	Silence Twister	Skyview Systems Ltd
	G-XSRF	Europa XS	R. L. W. Frank
	G-XTEE	Edge XT912-B/Streak III	Airborne Australia UK
	G-XTHT	Edge XT912-B/Streak III-B	H. A. Taylor
	G-XTME	Xtremeair XA42	Xtreme Aerobatics Ltd
	G-XTNI	AirBorne XT912-B/Streak	A. J. Parry
	G-XTRA	Extra EA.230	C. Butler
	G-XTUN	Westland-Bell 47G-3B1 (XT223)	P. A. Rogers (G-BGZK)
	G-XVAX	Tecnam P2006T	J. Byrne
	G-XVII	Schleicher ASW-17	C. A. & S. C. Noujaim (G-DCTE)
	G-XVOM	Van's RV-6	A. Baker-Munton
	G-XWEB	Best Off Skyranger 912 (2)	K. B. Woods
	G-XWON	Rolladen-Schneider LS8-18	P. K Carpenter
	G-XXBH	Agusta-Bell 206B JetRanger 3	Coln Aviation Ltd (G-BYBA/G-BHXV/G-OWJM)
	G-XXEB	Sikorsky S-76C	The Queen's Helicopter Flight
	G-XXIV	Agusta-Bell 206B JetRanger 3	Heliart Ltd
	G-XXIX	Schleicher ASW-27-18E	P. R. & A. H. Pentecost
	G-XXRG	Avid Speed Wing Mk.4	R. J. Grainger (G-BWLW)
	G-XXRS	Bombardier BD-700 Global Express	TAG Aviation (UK) Ltd
	G-XXRV	Van's RV-9	D. R. Gilbert & D. Slabbert
	G-XXTB	SOCATA TB20 Trinidad	N. Schaefer (G-KPTT)
	G-XXTR	Extra EA.300/L	Shoreham Extra Group (G-ECCC)
	G-XXVB	Schempp-Hirth Ventus b	R. Johnson
	G-XYAK	IDA Bacau Yakovlev Yak-52 (69 blue)	R. Davies

Reg.	Type	Owner or Operator	Notes
G-XYJY	Best Off Skyranger 912(1)	A. V. Francis	
G-XYZT	Aeromot AMT-200S Super Ximango	S. Marriott	
G-XZXZ	Robinson R44 II	Ashley Martin Ltd	
G-YAAK	Yakovlev Yak-50	D. J. Hopkinson (G-BWJT)	
G-YADA	Ikarus C42 FB100	Ikarus Flying Syndicate (Carlisle)	
G-YAKA	Yakovlev Yak-50	M. Chapman	
G-YAKB	Aerostar Yakovlev Yak-52	M. J. Gadsby	
G-YAKC	Yakovlev Yak-52	C. L. Jones	
G-YAKE	Yakovlev Yak-52	D. J. Hopkinson (G-BVVA)	
G-YAKF	Aerostar Yakovlev Yak-52	P. C. Henry	
G-YAKG	Yakovlev Yak-18T	A. Dunk	
G-YAKH	IDA Bacau Yakovlev Yak-52	Plus 7 minus 5 Ltd	
G-YAKI	IDA Bacau Yakovlev Yak-52 (100 blue)	Yak One Ltd	
G-YAKJ	Yakovlev Yak-18T	Teshka Aviation Syndicate	
G-YAKM	IDA Bacau Yakovlev Yak-50 (61 red)	Airborne Services Ltd	
G-YAKN	IDA Bacau Yakovlev Yak-52 (66 red)	Airborne Services Ltd	
G-YAKP	Yakovlev Yak-9	M. V. Rijkse & N. M. R. Richards	
G-YAKR	IDA Bacau Yakovlev Yak-52 (03 white)	G-YAKR Group	
G-YAKT	IDA Bacau Yakovlev Yak-52	G-YAKT Group	
G-YAKU	IDA Bacau Yakovlev Yak-50 (49 red)	D. J. Hopkinson (G-BXND)	
G-YAKV	IDA Bacau Yakovlev Yak-52 (31 grey)	P. D. Scandrett	
G-YAKX	IDA Bacau Yakovlev Yak-52 (27 red)	The X-Flyers Ltd	
G-YAKY	Aerostar Yakovlev Yak-52	W. T. Marriott	
G-YAKZ	IDA Bacau Yakovlev Yak-50 (33 red)	Airborne Services Ltd	
G-YANK	PA-28-181 Archer II	G-YANK Flying Group	
G-YARR	Mainair Rapier	D. Yarr	
G-YARV	ARV Super 2	A. M. Oliver (G-BMDO)	
G-YAWW	PA-28RT-201T Turbo Arrow IV	Barton Aviation Ltd	
G-YBAA	Cessna FR.172J	G-YBAA Flying Group	
G-YCII	LET Yakovlev C-11 (11 yellow)	R. W. Davies	
G-YCKF	Dassault Falcon 900EX	Execujet (UK) Ltd	
G-YCUB	PA-18 Super Cub 150	F. W. Rogers	
G-YCUE	Agusta A109A	Oldham Broadway Developments Ltd	
G-YDEA	DA-42 Twin Star	Diamond Executive Aviation Ltd	
G-YEDC	Cessna 525B Citationjet CJ3	Air Charter Scotland Ltd	
G-YEHA	Schleicher ASW-27	B. L. Cooper	
G-YELL	Murphy Rebel	A. H. Godfrey	
G-YELP	RL5A Sherwood Ranger ST	James Blunt Ltd	
G-YEOM	PA-31-350 Navajo Chieftain	A. B. Yeoman	
G-YEWS	Rotorway Executive 152	R. Turrell & P. Mason	
G-YFUT	Yakovlev Yak-52	W. Fuchshofer	
G-YFZT	Cessna 172S	AB Integro	
G-YIII	Cessna F.150L	Merlin Flying Club Ltd	
G-YIPI	Cessan FR.172K	J. Francis & M. T. Hodgson	
G-YIRO	Campbell Cricket Mk.4	R. Boese (G-KGED)	
G-YJET	Montgomerie-Bensen B.8MR	A. Shuttleworth (G-BMUH)	
G-YKSO	Yakovlev Yak-50	A. M. Holman-West	
G-YKSS	Yakovlev Yak-55	T. Ollivier	
G-YKSZ	Aerostar Yakovlev Yak-52 (01 yellow)	Tzarina Group	
G-YKYK	Aerostar Yakovlev Yak-52	K. J. Pilling	
G-YMFC	Waco YMF	S. J. Brenchley	
G-YMMA	Boeing 777-236ER	British Airways	
G-YMMB	Boeing 777-236ER	British Airways	
G-YMMC	Boeing 777-236ER	British Airways	
G-YMMD	Boeing 777-236ER	British Airways	
G-YMME	Boeing 777-236ER	British Airways	
G-YMMF	Boeing 777-236ER	British Airways	
G-YMMG	Boeing 777-236ER	British Airways	
G-YMMH	Boeing 777-236ER	British Airways	

Notes	Reg.	Type	Owner or Operator
	G-YMMI	Boeing 777-236ER	British Airways
	G-YMMJ	Boeing 777-236ER	British Airways
	G-YMMK	Boeing 777-236ER	British Airways
	G-YMML	Boeing 777-236ER	British Airways
	G-YMMN	Boeing 777-236ER	British Airways
	G-YMMO	Boeing 777-236ER	British Airways
	G-YMMP	Boeing 777-236ER	British Airways
	G-YMMR	Boeing 777-236ER	British Airways
	G-YMMS	Boeing 777-236ER	British Airways
	G-YMMT	Boeing 777-236ER	British Airways
	G-YMMU	Boeing 777-236ER	British Airways
	G-YNOT	D.62B Condor	T. Littlefair (G-AYFH)
	G-YNYS	Cessna 172S Skyhawk	T. V. Hughes
	G-YOBI	Schleicher ASH-25	J. Kangurs
	G-YODA	Schempp-Hirth Ventus 2cT	A. Charlier
	G-YOGI	Robin DR.400/140B	M. M. Pepper (G-BDME)
	G-YOLK	P & M Aviation Quik GT450	M. Austin
	G-YOLO	Aeroprakt A22-L2 Foxbat	J. W. Mann
	G-YORC	Cirrus SR-22	A. P. Von Croy
	G-YORK	Cessna F.172M	EIMH-Flying Group
	G-YOTS	IDA Bacau Yakovlev Yak-52	G-YOTS Group
	G-YOYO	Pitts S-1E Special	P. M. Jarvis (G-OTSW/G-BLHE)
	G-YPDN	Rotorsport UK MT-03	T. M. Jones
	G-YPOL	MDH MD-900 Explorer	Police & Crime Commissioner for West Yorkshire
	G-YPRS	Cessna 550 Citation Bravo	Executive Aviation Services Ltd (G-IPAC/ G-IPAL)
	G-YPSY	Andreasson BA-4B	M. J. Sharp
	G-YRAF	RAF 2000 GTX-SE gyroplane	J. R. Cooper
	G-YRAX	Magni M-24C	C. M. Jones
	G-YRIL	Luscombe 8E Silvaire	C. Potter
	G-YRKS	Robinson R44	N. Robson
	G-YROA	Rotorsport UK MTO Sport	J. P. R. McLaren
	G-YROC	Rotorsport UK MT-03	C. V. Catherall
	G-YROH	Rotorsport UK MTO Sport	J. W. G. Andrews
	G-YROI	Air Command 532 Elite	W. B. Lumb
	G-YROK	Magni M-16C	K. J. Yeadon
	G-YROM	Rotorsport UK MT-03	A. Wallace
	G-YRON	Magni M-16C Tandem Trainer	A. J. Brent & A. D. Mann
	G-YROO	RAF 2000 GTX-SE gyroplane	L. Mullin
	G-YROP	Magni M-16C Tandem Trainer	Magni Guernsey Flying Group
	G-YROR	Magni M.24C	R. M. Stanley
	G-YROX	Rotorsport UK MT-03	Surplus Art
	G-YROY	Montgomerie-Bensen B.8MR	S. S. Wilson
	G-YROZ	Rotorsport UK Calidus	C. J. Rose
	G-YRRO	AutoGyro Calidus	M. Black
	G-YRUS	Jodel D.140E	W. E. Massam (G-YRNS)
	G-YSMO	Mainair Pegasus Quik	F. Poirot
	G-YTLY	Rans S-6-ES Coyote II	Royal Aeronautical Society
	G-YUGE	Schempp-Hirth Ventus cT	E. P. Lambert (G-CFNN)
	G-YUGO	HS.125 Srs 1B/R-522 ★	Fire Section/Dunsfold (G-ATWH)
	G-YULL	PA-28 Cherokee 180E	C. J. Varley (G-BEAJ)
	G-YUMM	Cameron N-90 balloon	H. Stringer
	G-YUMN	Dassault Falcon 2000	Gama Aviation Ltd
	G-YUPI	Cameron N-90 balloon	MCVH SA/Belgium
	G-YURO	Shaw Europa ★	Yorkshire Air Museum/Elvington
	G-YVES	Alpi Pioneer 300	G-YVES Group
	G-YXLX	ISF Mistral C	R. R. Penman
	G-YYAK	Aerostar SA Yak-52	A. Bonnet
	G-YYRO	Magni M-16C Tandem Trainer	J. A. McGill
	G-YYYY	MH.1521C-1 Broussard	Aerosuperbatics Ltd

Reg.	Type	Owner or Operator	Notes
G-YZYZ	Mainair Blade 912	A. M. Beale	
G-ZAAP	CZAW Sportcruiser	H. Page	
G-ZAAZ	Van's RV-8	P. A. Soper	
G-ZABC	Sky 90-24 balloon	P. Donnelly	
G-ZACE	Cessna 172S	Sywell Aerodrome Ltd	
G-ZACH	Robin DR.400/100	A. P. Wellings (G-FTIO)	
G-ZADA	Best Off Skyranger 912S(1)	C. P. Lincoln	
G-ZAIR	Zenair CH 601HD	G-ZAIR Flying Group	
G-ZANY	Diamond DA40D Star	Altair Aviation Ltd	
G-ZAPK	BAe 146-200QC	Pionair Australia Pty Ltd (G-BTIA/G-PRIN)	
G-ZAPO	BAe 146-200QC	Trident Aviation Leasing Services (Jersey) Ltd (G-BWLG/G-PRCS)	
G-ZAPW	Boeing 737-3L9	Titan Airways Ltd (G-BOZB/G-IGOX)	
G-ZAPX	Boeing 757-256	Titan Airways Ltd	
G-ZAPY	Robinson R22 Beta	HQ Aviation Ltd (G-INGB)	
G-ZAPZ	Boeing 737-33A	Titan Airways Ltd	
G-ZARV	ARV Super 2	P. R. Snowden	
G-ZASH	Ikarus C42 FB80	J. W. D. Blythe	
G-ZAVI	Ikarus C42 FB100	B. & J. M. Cooper	
G-ZAZA	PA-18 Super Cub 95	G. J. Harry, The Viscount Goschen	
G-ZAZU	Diamond DA.42 Twin Star	NAL Asset Management Ltd (G-GFDA/G-CEFX)	
G-ZAZZ	Lindstrand LBL-120A balloon	Idea Balloon SAS Di Stefano Travaglia and Co/Italy	
G-ZBAA	Airbus A.320-214	Monarch Airlines Ltd	
G-ZBAB	Airbus A.320-214	Monarch Airlines Ltd	
G-ZBAD	Airbus A.321-231	Monarch Airlines Ltd	
G-ZBAE	Airbus A.321-231	Monarch Airlines Ltd	
G-ZBAF	Airbus A.321-231	Monarch Airlines Ltd	
G-ZBAG	Airbus A.321-231	Monarch Airlines Ltd	
G-ZBAH	Airbus A.320-214	Monarch Airlines Ltd	
G-ZBAI	Airbus A.321-231	Monarch Airlines Ltd	
G-ZBAJ	Airbus A.321-231	Monarch Airlines Ltd	
G-ZBAK	Airbus A.321-231	Monarch Airlines Ltd	
G-ZBAL	Airbus A.321-231	Monarch Airlines Ltd	
G-ZBAP	Airbus A.320-214	Monarch Airlines Ltd	
G-ZBED	Robinson R22 Beta	P. D. Spinks	
G-ZBJA	Boeing 787-836	British Airways PLC	
G-ZBJB	Boeing 787-836	British Airways PLC	
G-ZBJC	Boeing 787-836	British Airways PLC	
G-ZBJD	Boeing 787-836	British Airways PLC	
G-ZBLT	Cessna 182S Skylane	Cessna 182S Group/Ireland	
G-ZBOP	PZL-Bielsko SZD-36A Cobra 15	S. Bruce	
G-ZDEA	Diamond DA.42 Twin Star	Diamond Executive Aviation Ltd	
G-ZEBS	Aerospatiale ATR-42-320	Blue Islands Ltd	
G-ZEBY	PA-28 Cherokee 140	G. Gee (G-BFBF)	
G-ZECH	CZAW Sportcruiser	R. Stalker	
G-ZEIN	Slingsby T.67M Firefly 260	R. C. P. Brookhouse	
G-ZELE	Westland Gazelle HT.Mk.2	London Helicopter Centres Ltd (G-CBSA)	
G-ZENA	Zenair CH.701UL	I. D. Worthington	
G-ZENI	Zenair CH.601HD Zodiac	P. P. Plumley	
G-ZENR	Zenair CH.601HD Zodiac	N. L. Daniels (G-BRJB)	
G-ZENY	Zenair CH.601HD Zodiac	T. R. & B. K. Pugh	
G-ZEPI	Colt GA-42 gas airship	P. A. Lindstrand (G-ISPY/G-BPRB)	
G-ZERO	AA-5B Tiger	S. King & T. Boughton	
G-ZETA	Lindstrand LBL-105A balloon	S. Travaglia/Italy	
G-ZEXL	Extra EA.300/L	2 Excel Aviation Ltd	
G-ZFOX	Denney Kitfox Mk.2	S. M. Hall	
G-ZGZG	Cessna 182T	J. Noble	
G-ZGTK	Schleicher ASH-26E	P. M. Wells (G-BWBY)	
G-ZHKF	Escapade 912(2)	C. D. & C. M. Wills	
G-ZHWH	Rotorway Executive 162F	B. Alexander	
G-ZIGI	Robin DR.400/180	Aeroclub du Bassin D'Arcachon/France	
G-ZIGY	Europa XS	K. D. Weston	

Notes	Reg.	Type	Owner or Operator
	G-ZIII	Pitts S-2B	W. A. Cruickshank (G-CDBH)
	G-ZINC	Cessna 182S	J. Brown (G-VALI)
	G-ZINT	Cameron Z-77 balloon	D. Ricci
	G-ZION	Cessna 177B	S. C. Meacock
	G-ZIPA	Rockwell Commander 114A	R. Robson (G-BHRA)
	G-ZIPE	Agusta A109E Power Elite	Noble Foods Group Ltd
	G-ZIPI	Robin DR.400/180	A. J. Cooper
	G-ZIPY	Wittman W.8 Tailwind	K. J. Nurcombe
	G-ZIRA	Z-1RA Stummelflitzer	D. H. Pattison
	G-ZITZ	AS.355F2 Twin Squirrel	Heli Aviation Ltd
	G-ZIZI	Cessna 525 CitationJet	Ortac Air Ltd
	G-ZIZY	TL2000UK Sting Carbon S4	C. E. & R. P. Reeves
	G-ZIZZ	Agusta A.109 II	Fortis Property Investment LLP
	G-ZLLE	Aérospatiale SA.341G Gazelle	MW Helicopters Ltd
	G-ZLOJ	Beech A36 Bonanza	C. J. Parker
	G-ZMAM	PA-28-181 Archer II	Z. Mahmood (G-BNPN)
	G-ZMED	Learjet 35A	Air Medical Fleet Ltd, Argyll Ltd (G-JETL)
	G-ZNSF	Gulfstream 550	TAG Aviation UK Ltd
	G-ZODY	Zenair CH.601UL Zodiac	Sarum AX2000 Group
	G-ZOGT	Cirrus SR20	M. Banbury
	G-ZOIZ	Ultramagic M-105 balloon	British Telecommunications PLC
	G-ZONX	Moulai Sonex	FFFF Flyers Group
	G-ZOOG	Tecnam P2006T	Polarb Air Ltd
	G-ZOOL	Cessna FA.152	W. J. D. Tollett (G-BGXZ)
	G-ZORO	Shaw Europa	N. T. Read
	G-ZOSA	Champion 7GCAA	R. McQueen
	G-ZSDB	PA-28-236 Dakota	Dakota Air Services LLP (G-BPCX)
	G-ZSIX	Schleicher ASW-27-18E	C. Cowley & F. J. Davis
	G-ZSKD	Cameron Z-90 balloon	M. J. Gunston
	G-ZSKY	Best Off Sky Ranger Swift 912S(1)	J. E. Lipinski
	G-ZTED	Shaw Europa	J. J. Kennedy
	G-ZTWO	Staaken Z-2 Flitzer	S. J. Randle
	G-ZUFL	Lindstrand LBL-90A balloon	Zuffle Dog Balloon Team (G-CHLL)
	G-ZUMI	Van's RV-8	D. R. CairnsT
	G-ZVIP	Beech 200 Super King Air	Capital Air Charter Ltd (G-SAXN/G-OMNH)
	G-ZVKO	Edge 360	R. J. Allan, N. Jones & A. J. Maxwell
	G-ZWIP	Silence Twister	Zulu Glasstek Ltd (G-TWST)
	G-ZXCL	Extra EA.300/L	2 Excel Aviation Ltd
	G-ZXEL	Extra EA.300/L	2 Excel Aviation Ltd
	G-ZXLL	Extra EA.300/L	2 Excel Aviation Ltd
	G-ZXZX	Learjet 45	Gama Aviation Ltd
	G-ZYAK	IDA Bacau Yakovlev YAK-52	J. A. H. Van Rossom
	G-ZZAC	Aerotechnik EV-97 Eurostar	Cosmik Aviation Ltd
	G-ZZAJ	Schleicher ASH-26E	A. T. Johnstone
	G-ZZDD	Schweizer 269C	C. D. Reeves (G-OCJK)
	G-ZZDG	Cirrus SR20 G2	S. James
	G-ZZEL	Westland Gazelle AH.1	Tregenna Castle Hotel Ltd
	G-ZZIJ	PA-28-180 Cherokee C	G-ZZIJ Group (G-AVGK)
	G-ZZLE	Westland Gazelle AH.2	Estates (UK) Management Ltd (G-CBSE)
	G-ZZMM	Enstrom 480B	Fly 7 Helicopters LLP (G-TOIL)
	G-ZZOE	Eurocopter EC 120B	J. F. H. James
	G-ZZOW	Medway Eclipse	M. Belemet
	G-ZZSA	Eurocopter EC.225LP Super Puma	Bristow Helicopters Ltd
	G-ZZSB	Eurocopter EC.225LP Super Puma	Bristow Helicopters Ltd
	G-ZZSC	Eurocopter EC.225LP Super Puma	Bristow Helicopters Ltd
	G-ZZSD	Eurocopter EC.225LP Super Puma	Bristow Helicopters Ltd
	G-ZZSE	Eurocopter EC.225LP Super Puma	Bristow Helicopters Ltd
	G-ZZSF	Eurocopter EC.225LP Super Puma	Bristow Helicopters Ltd

Reg.	Type	Owner or Operator	Notes
G-ZZSG	Eurocopter EC.225LP Super Puma	Bristow Helicopters Ltd	
G-ZZSI	Eurocopter EC.225LP Super Puma	Bristow Helicopters Ltd (G-CGES)	
G-ZZSK	Eurocopter EC.225LP Super Puma	Bristow Helicopters Ltd	
G-ZZSJ	Eurocopter EC.225LP Super Puma	Bristow Helicopters Ltd	
G-ZZTT	Schweizer 269C	Heli Andaluz SL/Spain	
G-ZZXX	P & M Quik GT450	R. G. Street	
G-ZZZA	Boeing 777-236	British Airways	
G-ZZZB	Boeing 777-236	British Airways	
G-ZZZC	Boeing 777-236	British Airways	
G-ZZZS	Eurocopter EC.120B Colibri	London Helicopter Centres Ltd	

ISLE OF MAN REGISTER

Reg.	Type	Owner or Operator	Notes
M-AAAD	Bombardier CL600-2B16 Challenger	Gulf Wings (IOM) Ltd	
M-AAAL	Bombardier BD700-1A10 Global Express	ALM Jet Ltd	
M-AAES	Bombardier CL600-2B16 Challenger	Eliston Enterprises Ltd	
M-ABCD	Dassault Falcon 2000	ASP Aviation Ltd	
M-ABCM	Bombardier BD100-1A10 Challenger 300	Cameron Industries Inc	
M-ABCU	Bombardier CL600-2B16 Challenger	MeHoria Ltd	
M-ABDL	Hawker 4000	SB Leasing Ireland Ltd	
M-ABDP	Hawker 800XP	Kitlan Ltd	
M-ABDQ	Eurocopter EC.135 P2+	Knightspeed Ltd	
M-ABEC	Embraer EMB-135BJ Legacy 600	Carys Investment Group Ltd	
M-ABEU	Learjet 45	Aviation Leasing (IOM) Ltd	
M-ABEV	Aerospatiale ATR-72-212A	Hubli Aircraft Leasing Ltd	
M-ABEW	Aerospatiale ATR-72-212A	Hubli Aircraft Leasing Ltd	
M-ABFC	Aerospatiale ATR-72-212A	KP Aero	
M-ABFD	Aerospatiale ATR-72-212A	KP Aero	
M-ABFE	Aerospatiale ATR-72-212A	KP Aero	
M-ABFI	Aerospatiale ATR-72-212A	Plateau Aviation Ltd	
M-ABFJ	Aerospatiale ATR-72-212A	Plateau Aviation Ltd	
M-ABFO	Hawker 400XP	Porto Mediterranean Investments Ltd	
M-ABFQ	Bombardier BD700-1A10 Global 6000	AGT International GmbH	
M-ABFR	Bombardier BD700-1A10 Global 6000	AGT International GmbH	
M-ABGA	Airbus A,319-111	Celestial Aviation Trading 30 Ltd	
M-ABGB	Airbus A.319-111	Celestial Aviation Trading 30 Ltd	
M-ABGG	Bombardier CL600-2B16 Challenger	Zarox Holdings Ltd	
M-ABGH	Bombardier CL600-2B19 Challenger 800	Asia Aviation Holdings Ltd	
M-ABGI	Learjet 60	GE Capital Equipment Finance Ltd	
M-ABGM	Hawker 400XP	Ceau Ltd	
M-ABGN	Boeing 737-49R	KG Aircraft Leasing Co.Ltd	
M-ABGO	Dassault Falcon 7X	Dassault Aviation SA	
M-ABGS	Bombardier CL600-2B16 Challenger 605	Viking Travel Services Ltd	
M-ACHO	Bombardier CL600-2B16 Challenger	Zeta Aviation Ltd	
M-ACPT	BAe. 125 Srs.1000	Remo Investments Ltd	
M-ACRO	Eurocopter AS.350B3 Ecureuil	F. Allani	
M-ADEL	Bombardier CL600-2B16 Challenger	Blue Nightingale Trading Ltd	
M-AFAJ	Dassault Falcon 900EX	Elan Finance Management SA	
M-AGGY	Cessna 550 Citation II	Maudib GmbH Deutschland	
M-AGIC	Cessna 680 Citation Sovereign	Trustair Ltd	
M-AHAA	Bombardier BD700-IA10 Global 6000	AH Aviation Ltd	
M-AIRS	Learjet 60	Maiton Air LLP	
M-AJOR	Hawker 900XP	INEOS Aviation LLP	
M-AJWA	Bombardier BD700-1A11 Global Express	Global Express Management Ltd	
M-AKAK	Embraer EMB-135BJ Legacy	AAK Company	
M-AKAR	Sikorsky S-76C	Starspeed Ltd	
M-AKOL	Dassault Falcon 7X	Elise Continental Ltd	
M-ALAY	Gulfstream VP	Stonefel Trade & Invest Ltd	
M-ALCB	Pilatus PC-12/47E	M. S. Bartlett	
M-ALEN	Embraer EMB-135BJ Legacy	ATT Aviation Ltd	
M-ALMA	Dassault Falcon 7X	Armad Ltd	
M-ALRV	Dassault Falcon 2000EX	Lodgings 2000 LP	
M-ALUN	BAe 125 Srs.700A	Briarwood Products Ltd	
M-AMAN	Pilatus PC-12	Pilatus PC-12 Centre UK Ltd	
M-AMND	Dassault Falcon 2000EX	Doha Capital Ltd	

Notes	Reg.	Type	Owner or Operator
	M-AMRT	Bombardier CL600-2B16 Challenger	Eastern Heights Corporation
	M-ANGA	Embraer EMB-135BJ Legacy 600	Max Air Ltd
	M-ANGO	Bombardier BD700-1A11 Global 5000	Waylawn Ltd
	M-ANIE	Gulfstream 550	Pobedy Corporation
	M-ANTA	Bombardier CL600-2B190 Challenger 85	Tathra International Holdings Inc
	M-APLE	Embraer EMB-505 Phenom 300	Poseidon Finance Ltd
	M-AQUA	Bombardier BD700-1A11 Global 5000	Theberton Ltd
	M-ARAE	Gulfstream 450	Global Pipeline Services Ltd
	M-ARCH	Cessna 750 Citation X	Archildsa International Inc.
	M-ARDI	Gulfstream V-SP	LGM Property Services Ltd
	M-ARIA	Cessna 680 Citation Sovereign	Swiss Aviation IM Ltd
	M-ARIE	Beech B200GT Super King Air	Guernsey PC-12 Ltd
	M-ARKZ	Bombardier CL600-2B16 Challenger	Markz Jet Ltd
	M-ARRH	Bombardier BD100-1A10 Challenger 300	Eagle Aviation Ltd
	M-ARRJ	Bombardier BD700-1A10 Global Express	Sentonan Investments Ltd
	M-ARTY	Pilatus PC-12/47E	Creston (UK) Ltd
	M-ARVY	Dassault Falcon 7X	Almondine Ltd
	M-ASHI	Bombardier CL600-2B16 Challenger	Beckett Holding Ltd
	M-ASRI	Bombardier BD700-1A10 Global Express	YYA Aviation Ltd
	M-ASRY	Bombardier BD100-1A10 Challenger 300	Celina Aviation Ltd
	M-ATAK	Bombardier BD700-1A10 Global 5000	Greenway Investment Assets Ltd
	M-ATAR	Bombardier BD700-1A10 Global	AV West Aircraft Pty.Ltd
	M-ATHS	Pilatus PC-12/47E	Altis Partners (Aviation) Ltd
	M-ATOS	Dassault Falcon 900EX	Banton Overseas Ltd
	M-ATPS	Gulfstream V-SP	Tarona Ltd
	M-AVOS	Gulfstream IV-X	Helter Management Ltd
	M-AXIM	CessnaT.206H Turbo Stationair	C. D. B. Cope
	M-AYBE	Gulfstream 280	Maybe Aviation Ltd
	M-AYRU	Bombardier CL600-2B16 Challenger	Setfair Aviation Ltd
	M-AZAG	BAe.125 Srs.800B	Mazag
	M-AZIA	Cessna 525C CitationJet CJ4	Hunting Star Ltd
	M-AZIZ	Boeing 737-505	Azizi Group Ltd
	M-AZKL	Agusta A109S Grand	Azikel Dredging Nigeria Ltd
	M-BAEP	Bombardier CL600-2B16 Challenger	Swift Cloud Aviation Services Ltd
	M-BEST	Cessna 750 Citation X	Lanara Ltd
	M-BETS	Rockwell Commander 695A	Aldersey Aviation Ltd
	M-BETY	Dornier Do.328-310	Funfte XR-GmbH
	M-BIGG	Bombardier CL600-2B16 Challenger	Signal Aviation Ltd
	M-BISA	Pilatus PC-12/47	Pilatus PC-12 Centre UK Ltd
	M-BJEP	Gulfstream 550	M-BJEP Ltd
	M-BLUE	Bombardier BD700-1A11 Global 5000	Tetran Assets Ltd
	M-BONO	Cessna 172N Skyhawk II	J. McCandless
	M-BRRB	Bombardier BD700-1A11	Damstone Ltd
	M-BTAR	Bombardier BD700-1A10 Global Express	AVWest Aircraft Pty.Ltd
	M-BTLT	Bombardier BD100-1A10 Challenger 300	Bombardier Transportation GmbH
	M-CCCP	Bombardier BD700-1A11 Global 5000	Heda Airlines Ltd
	M-CDFY	Beech B.200 Super King Air	BAE Systems Marine Ltd
	M-CDZT	Beech B.200 Super King Air	BAE Systems Marine Ltd
	M-CELT	Dassault Falcon 7X	Cravant Ltd
	M-CESB	Cessna 560 Citation XLS	Cessna Spanish Citation Service Centre SL
	M-CESC	Cessna 560 Citation XLS	Cessna Spanish Citation Service Centre SL
	M-CESD	Cessna 560 Citation XLS	Cessna Spanish Citation Service Centre SL
	M-CHEM	Dassault Falcon 200EX	Hampshire Aviation LLP
	M-CICO	Dassault Falcon 50	BZ Air Ltd
	M-CIMO	Dassault Falcon 2000EX	Dassault Aviation SA
	M-CLAB	Bombardier BD100-1A10 Challenger 300	Shamrock Trading Ltd
	M-COOL	Cessna 510 Citation Mustang	E. Keats
	M-CRAO	Beech B.300 Super King Air 350	Dr. A. Oetker
	M-CRCR	Bombardier CL600-2B16 Challenger	Prophiol Holdings Ltd
	M-CTLX	Cessna 525A CitationJet CJ2	Hanover Beteiligungsgesellshaft mbH
	M-DADA	Bombardier BD700-1A10 Global 6000	STC Aviation Services Ltd
	M-DADI	Dassault Falcon 900DX	Rubicon Capital Consulting Co.Ltd

Reg.	Type	Owner or Operator	Notes
M-DARA	Dassault Falcon 200LX	Trident Investment Ltd	
M-DBOY	Agusta A.109C	Herair Ltd	
M-DEJB	Dassault Falcon 200	Baron Aircraft Management SA	
M-DKVL	Gulfstream 450	Fiordani Holding Ltd	
M-DMMH	Cessna 680 Citation Sovereign	Heerenknecht Aviation GmbH	
M-DRIL	Pilatus PC-12/47E	Drilling Systems Ltd	
M-DSCL	Embraer 135BJ Legacy	Legacy Aviation Ltd	
M-DTBP	Dassault Falcon 7X	Shangwin Investment Ltd	
M-DWSF	Bell 430	Dave Whelan Sports Ltd	
M-DWWW	Bombardier CL600-2B19 Challenger	Dragon Asset Global Investment Group Ltd	
M-EAGL	Dassault Falcon 900EX	Faycroft Finance	
M-EANS	Bombardier BD100-1A10 Challenger 300	YH Aviation Ltd	
M-EASY	Leajet 35A	PM Lutfahrzeugvermietung GmbH & Co KG	
M-EBRB	Dassault Falcon 900	Skyscraper Ltd	
M-ECJI	Dassault Falcon 10	Fleet International Aviation and Finance Ltd	
M-EDIA	Dassault Falcon 7X	M-EDIA Aviation Ltd	
M-EGGA	Beech B200 Super King Air	Langley Aviation Ltd	
M-ELON	Cessna 525B Citationjet CJ3	Sleepwell Aviation Ltd	
M-EMCT	Cessna 560 Citation V	Control Techniques Ltd	
M-EMLI	Agusta A109E Power	Tycoon Aviation Ltd	
M-ENTA	Dassault Falcon 200	Riviera Invest und Services SA	
M-ERCI	Bombardier CL600-2B16 Challenger	J & S Holding Ltd	
M-ERIL	Pilatus PC-12/47E	Confidentia Aviation Ltd	
M-ERRY	Sikorsky S-76B	Trustair Ltd	
M-ESGR	Embraer ERJ135 Legacy	Hermes Executive Aviation Ltd	
M-EVAN	Bombardier BD100-1A10 Challenger 300	Marcus Evans (Aviation) Ltd	
M-EXPL	Eurocopter AS.355N Ecureuil 2	Select Plant Hire Co.Ltd	
M-FAHD	Boeing 727-76	Prime Air Corporation	
M-FASH	Dassault Falcon 900B	Al Hokair Aviation Ltd	
M-FBVZ	Bombardier CL600-2B16 Challenger	Qaltin Enterprises Ltd	
M-FINK	BAe. 125 Srs.1000B	B. T. Fink	
M-FIVE	Beech B300 Super King Air 350	Larvotto LP	
M-FLYI	Cessna 525 Citationjet CJ4	Avtrade Ltd	
M-FRED	Piaggio P.180 Avanti	Ecologue Investments Ltd	
M-FROG	Beech 390 Premier 1	White and Cope Aviation LLP	
M-FRZN	Bombardier CL600-2B16 Challenger	Iceland Foods Ltd	
M-FTHD	Dassault Falcon 2000EX	Eagle Reach Group Ltd	
M-FTOH	Boeing 727-269A	Strong Aviation (BVI) Ltd	
M-FUAD	Gulfstream 550	Future Pipe Aviation Ltd	
M-FWIN	Pilatus PC-12/47E	DW Consulting GmbH & Co KG	
M-FZMH	Bombardier CL600-2B19 Global Express	AK VI Ltd	
M-GACB	Dassault Falcon 10	Valiant Aviation Ltd	
M-GASG	Gulfstream 150	PIV Global Holding Ltd	
M-GCCC	Beech B.350i King Air	NG2 SA	
M-GDRS	Beech 390 Premier 1	G. de Rooy	
M-GINI	Bombardier CL600-2B16 Challenger	Pak-Arab Fertilizers Ltd	
M-GLEX	Bombardier BD700-1A10 Global Express	Pytonian Trade & Invest SA	
M-GLFV	Gulfstream 550	G550 Investments General Partner Ltd	
M-GLFZ	Learjet 60	M-GLFZ Ltd	
M-GLOB	Bombardier BD700-1A10 Global Express	Colvic Investment Holdings Ltd	
M-GOLD	Eurocopter EC.120B Colibri	Wilpot Ltd	
M-GOLF	Cessna FR.182RG	P. R. Piggin & C. J. Harding	
M-GRAN	Bombardier BD700-1A11 Global 5000	Starflight Investments Ltd	
M-GSIX	Gulfstream 650	AC Executive Aircraft (2013) Ltd	
M-GSKY	Bombardier BD700-1A10 Global Express	Jerand Holdings Ltd	
M-GULF	Gulfstream 200	BIBBIENA 66 s.r.o.	
M-GVSP	Gulfstream 550	Business Universe Ltd	
M-GYQM	Bombardier BD700-1A10 Global Express	Head Win Group Ltd	
M-HARP	Pilatus PC-12/47E	Harpin Ltd	
M-HASL	Hawker 800XP	King Airshare SA	
M-HAWK	Bombardier BD700-1A10 Global 6000	Genetechma Finance Ltd	
M-HDAM	BAe 125 Srs.800B	ABG Air Ltd	
M-HELI	Eurocopter EC.155-B1	Flambards Ltd	
M-HHHH	Airbus A.318-112CJ	Kutus Ltd	

Notes	Reg.	Type	Owner or Operator
	M-HLAN	Bombardier CL600-2B19 Challenger 850	Wonder Air International Ltd
	M-HOIL	Learjet 60	Begal Air Ltd
	M-HOTB	Gulfstream V SP	Darwin Air Ltd
	M-HSNT	Bombardier BD100-1A10 Challenger 300	Unisky Ltd
	M-HSXP	Hawker 800XP	HEWE Ltd
	M-IABU	Airbus A.340-313	Klaret Aviation Ltd
	M-IBAD	Aerospatiale ATR-72-212A	INV JET Leasing Ltd
	M-IBAE	Aerospatiale ATR-72-212A	KF Turbo Leasing Ltd
	M-IBAF	Aerospatiale ATR-72-212A	KF Turbo Leasing Ltd
	M-IBAG	Aerospatiale ATR-72-212A	KF Turbo Leasing Ltd
	M-IBAH	Aerospatiale ATR-72-212A	KF Turbo Leasing Ltd
	M-IBAI	Aerospatiale ATR-72-212A	KF Turbo Leasing Ltd
	M-IBAJ	Aerospatiale ATR-72-212A	KF Turbo Leasing Ltd
	M-ICKY	Pilatus PC12/45	Saxon Logistics Ltd
	M-ICRO	Cessna 525A	Pektron Ltd
	M-IDAS	Agusta A109E Power	Trustair Ltd
	M-IFLY	Pilatus PC-12/47E	N. J. Vetch
	M-IGHT	Learjet 60	High Wing Aviation Ltd
	M-IGOR	Learjet 60	Condamine Enterprises Ltd
	M-IIII	Bombardier BD700-1A10 Global Express	Webberburn Corporation
	M-IKAT	Dassault Falcon 2000EX	F2000 LX Ltd
	M-IKEL	Dassault Falcon 2000LX	Second Aircraft Co.Ltd
	M-ILTD	Gulfstream 200	Flash Sky Ltd
	M-IMAK	Embraer EMB-135BJ Legacy 600	Donard Trading Ltd
	M-IMOR	Cessna 680 Citation Sovereign	JATO Aviation Ltd
	M-INER	Dassault Falcon 7X	Osprey Aviation Ltd
	M-INOR	Hawker 900XP	INEOS Aviation LLP
	M-INTS	Embraer EMB-135BJ Legacy	Swissport Systems Inc
	M-IPHS	Gulfstream 550	Islands Aviation Ltd
	M-IRNE	Hawker 850XP	R. N. Edmiston
	M-IRON	Embraer EMB-135BJ Legacy 600	Delino Investments Ltd
	M-ISKY	Cessna 550 Citation Bravo	MYSKY LLP
	M-ISLE	Cessna 680 Citation Sovereign	Bakewell Industries Ltd
	M-ISRK	Dassault Falcon 900LX	ISR Jet Ltd
	M-IVSP	Gulfstream IV SP	Travcorp Air Transportation Ltd
	M-IWPS	Cessna 525A Citationjet CJ2	Schneider Warenvertriebsgesellschaft mbH
	M-JACK	Beech B200GT King Air	Jetstream Aviation Ltd
	M-JANP	Bombardier BD700-1A10 Global Express	Joannou and Paraskevaides (Aviation) Ltd
	M-JCBA	Sikorsky S-76C	J C Bamford Excavators Ltd
	M-JCPO	HS.125 Srs.700A	Saucar Ltd
	M-JETI	BAe 125 Srs 800B	Cassel Invest Ltd
	M-JETT	Dassault Falcon 200	Piraeus Leasing Chrimatodotikes Mishoseis SA
	M-JETZ	Dassault Falcon 2000EX	Avtorita Holdings Ltd
	M-JIGG	Gulfstream 550	Hermes Executive Aviation Ltd
	M-JJTL	Pilatus PC-12/47E	L. Uggia, J. P. Huth & K. Giannamore
	M-JMMM	Dassault Falcon 900B	Executive Aviation (SPV) Ltd
	M-JNJL	Bombardier BD700-1A11 Global Express	Global Thirteen Worldwide Resources Ltd
	M-JOLY	Hawker 900XP	Rooksmead Capital Ltd
	M-JPLC	Dassault Falcon 900EX	Yolenal Aeronautics Ltd
	M-JSMN	Bombardier BD700-1A11 Global 5000	Jasmin Aviation Ltd
	M-JSTA	Bombardier CL600-2B16 Challenger	Jetsteff Aviation Ltd
	M-KARI	Bombardier CL600-2B16 Challenger	Timege Ltd
	M-KATE	Airbus A.319-133	Sophar Property Holding
	M-KBBG	Gulfstream 450	Golden Global Aviation Ltd
	M-KELY	Embraer EMB-500 Phenom 100	Kelly Air Ltd
	M-KENF	Hawker 4000 Horizon	Avalanche Aviation Ltd
	M-KING	Beech C.90A King Air	Villocq Investments Ltd
	M-KPCO	Embraer EMB-135BJ Legacy	M-KPCO Holding Co.Ltd
	M-KRRR	Learjet 55	R. Rogner
	M-KSSN	Gulfstream 650	NS Aviation Ltd
	M-LEFB	Cessna 550	Patagonia Assets Ltd
	M-LEKT	Robin DR.400/180	T. D. Allan, P. & J. P. Bromley
	M-LENR	Beech B.200GT Super King Air	BAE Systems Marine Ltd
	M-LEYS	Beech C.90GT King Air	Heres Aviation Ltd
	M-LIFE	Bombardier BD100-1A10 Challenger 300	NY Jets Transporter Ltd

Reg.	Type	Owner or Operator	Notes
M-LILJ	Bombardier CL600-2B19 Challenger 850	Raise in Development Ltd	
M-LILY	Bombardier CL600-2B19 Challenger 850	Bright Loysal Ltd/Offshore Incorporations (Cayman) Ltd	
M-LION	Hawker 900XP	Lion Invest and Trade Ltd	
M-LJGI	Dassault Falcon 7X	Milestown	
M-LOOK	Bombardier CL600-2B16 Challenger	Kennington Ltd	
M-LRJT	Learjet 40	Chemiplastica Aviation Ltd	
M-LRLR	Bombardier CL600-2B16 Challenger	L & B Conveyjet Ltd	
M-LUNA	Eurocopter MBB BK-117C-2	Flambards Ltd	
M-LVIA	Eurocopter AS.365N3 Dauphin 2	Flambards Ltd	
M-LWSA	Bombardier BD700-1A10 Global Express	Lynx Aviation (Isle of Man) Ltd	
M-MACH	Embraer EMB-500 Phenom 100	Mach Air Ltd	
M-MANX	Cessna 425 Conquest	Suas Investments Ltd	
M-MARI	Learjet 60XR	Rumit Aviation Ltd	
M-MDBD	Bombardier BD700-1A10 Global Express	Cozuro Holdings Ltd	
M-MDDE	CL-600-2B16 Challenger	Fielding Overseas Ltd	
M-MDMH	Embraer EMB-505 Phenom 300	Herrenknecht Aviation GmbH	
M-MHAC	Learjet 60	Trans Aviation Ltd	
M-MHDH	Cessna 510 Citation Mustang	Herrenknecht Aviation GmbH	
M-MHFZ	Embraer EMB-135BJ Legacy	AK VI Ltd	
M-MIDO	Raytheon Hawker 800XP	Barbican Holdings Ltd	
M-MIKE	Cessna 525B Citationjet CJ3	M. F. Jacobson	
M-MMAA	Bombardier BD700-1A10 Global Express	JAPAT AG (Isle of Man)	
M-MNAA	Bombardier BD700-1A10 Global Express	JAPAT AG (Isle of Man)	
M-MNBB	Dassault Falcon 7X	JAPAT AG (Isle of Man)	
M-MNCC	Dassault Falcon 7X	JAPAT AG (Isle of Man)	
M-MNDD	Dassault Falcon 900EX	JAPAT AG (Isle of Man)	
M-MNDG	Gulfstream 450	Oviation Ltd	
M-MNVN	Gulfstream 450	High Altitude Holdings Ltd	
M-MOMO	Gulfstream V SP	Fayair (Jersey) Co Ltd	
M-MOON	Cessna 750	Bambara Holding SA	
M-MRBB	Learjet 45	Boultbee Aviation 3 LLP	
M-MSGG	Gulfstream G200	ARTOC Prague	
M-MTOO	Bombardier BD100-1A10 Challenger 300	Nadremal Air Holding Ltd	
M-MTPO	Bombardier CL600-2A12 Challenger	Marimax Jets Ltd	
M-MYNA	Bombardier BD700-1A10 Global 6000	Tibit Ltd	
M-NACO	Eurocopter EC.155B1	Mosaics Industry Corporation	
M-NALE	Bombardier BD700-1A10 Global Express	Jover Ltd	
M-NELS	Gulfstream 450	Citylink Partners Ltd	
M-NGSN	Pilatus PC-12/47E	N. Stolt-Nielson	
M-NHOI	Bombardier CL600-2B16 Challenger	Hatta Investments Ltd	
M-NICE	Gulfstream 200	M-NICE Ltd	
M-NJSS	Embraer EMB-135BJ Legacy	Saby Finance Ltd	
M-NLYY	PA-42-1000 Cheyenne 400LS	Factory Leasing Ltd	
M-NSJS	Cessna 525C Citationjet CJ4	Ferncroft Ltd	
M-OBIL	Cessna 525C Citationjet C14	Popken Fashion Services GmbH	
M-ODKZ	Dassault Falcon 900EX	Skylane LP	
M-OEPL	Dassault Falcon 900DX	Cloud Services Ltd	
M-OGUL	Agusta A109S Grand	Medway Leasing Ltd	
M-OIWA	Bombardier BD100-1A10 Challenger	Delta A/S	
M-OLAR	Liberty XL-2	C. Partington	
M-OLEG	Embraer 135BJ Legacy	Hermitage Air Ltd	
M-OLLE	Hawker 750	Dunard Engineering Ltd	
M-OLLY	Cessna 525 Citationjet CJ1	MBK Maschinenbau GmbH/Bohnet GmbH	
M-OLOT	Bombardier CL600-2B16 Challenger	Kellie Aviation Ltd	
M-OLTT	Pilatus PC-12/47E	One Luxury Travel LLP	
M-OMAN	Dassault Falcon 7X	RUWI Ltd	
M-ONAV	Hawker 900XP	Monavia Ltd	
M-ONDE	Eurocopter MBB BK.117C2	Peyton Ltd	
M-ONEM	Gulfstream 550	G550 Ltd	
M-ONTY	Sikorsky S-76C	Trustair Ltd	
M-OOSE	PA-46-500TP Malibu Meridian	Global Domain Names Ltd	
M-OPED	PA-32-301XTC Saratoga	Hock Lai Cham	
M-ORAD	Dassault Falcon 2000EX	Swift Aviation Ltd	

Notes	Reg.	Type	Owner or Operator
	M-OSPB	Gulfstream G200	G200 Ltd
	M-OTOR	Beech C90A King Air	Pektron Group Ltd
	M-OUSE	Cessna 510 Citation Mustang	Mouse (IOM) Ltd
	M-OUTH	Diamond DA.42 Twin Star	Sky Fly LP Inc
	M-OZZA	Bombardier BD100-1A10 Challenger 300	Casam International Ltd
	M-PACF	Eurocopter EC135 P2+	Starspeed Ltd
	M-PBKI	Gulfstream IV SP	GIV-SP Air Service Ltd
	M-PCPC	Pilatus PC-12/45	Treetops Aviation LLP
	M-PHML	American General AG-5B Tiger	I. J. Ross & J. R. Shannon
	M-POWR	Beech C.90A King Air	Northside Aviation Ltd
	M-PPBA	Embraer EMB-135BJ Legacy 600	Zamin Aviation Ltd
	M-PREI	Raytheon RB390 Premier 1	Craft Air SA
	M-PRVT	Cessna 750 Citation X	Unifox Holdings Ltd
	M-PZPZ	Gulfstream IV	A. I. Eze
	M-RAFF	Airbus A.320-214	Air Salvage International Ltd
	M-RBUS	Airbus A.319-115CJ	Belville Investment Ltd
	M-RCCG	Embraer EMB-135BJ Legacy 650	Russian Copper Co. Holdings Ltd
	M-RIDE	BD-700-1A11 Global 5000	Jesper Continental SA
	M-RISE	Boeing 757-23N	Talos Aviation Ltd
	M-RKAY	Raytheon 390 Premier 1A	Sunseeker Corporate Aviation Ltd
	M-RLDR	Pilatus PC-12/45	RDLR Air Ltd
	M-RLIV	Bombardier CL600-2B16 Challenger	Mobyhold Ltd
	M-ROLL	Dassault Falcon 7X	Pacelli Beteiligungs GmbH and Co KG
	M-ROMA	Learjet 45	ArtJet Ltd
	M-RONE	Dassault Falcon 2000EX	Ocean Sky Aircraft Management Ltd
	M-RRBK	Embraer EMB-135BJ Legacy 650	Delino Investments Ltd
	M-RSKL	Bombardier BD700-1A10 Global Express	Angel Aviation Ltd
	M-SAID	Bombardier BD700-IA11 Global 5000	S & K Aviation Ltd
	M-SAIL	Pilatus PC-12/47E	G. G. & L. G. Gordon
	M-SAIR	Falcon 900B	W. A. Developments International Ltd
	M-SAPL	Bombardier CL600-2B16 Challenger	Sapetro Aviation Ltd
	M-SAWO	Gulfstream V-SP	Cloud Air Services Ltd
	M-SBAH	Embraer ERJ190ECJ Lineage 1000	National Lineage M-SBAH Holding Co.Ltd
	M-SCMG	Dassault Falcon 7X	BlueSky International Management Ltd
	M-SEAS	Bombardier BD700-1A11 Global 5000	Jana Aviation Ltd
	M-SFAM	McDonnell Douglas MD-87	Montavachi Ltd
	M-SGCR	Cessna 550 Citation Bravo	Labraid Ltd
	M-SHEP	SOCATA TBM-850	L. W. & J. K. Shephard
	M-SITM	BAe 125-800SP	SITM Jet Ltd
	M-SKSM	Bombardier BD700-1A11 Global	Tesker Management Ltd
	M-SMKM	Cirrus SR20	K. Mallet
	M-SNAP	Dassault Falcon 2000EASy	Aviation Holding Services Ltd
	M-SNER	Dassault Falcon 2000EX	Wincor Aviation Establishment
	M-SNSS	Dassault Falcon 50EX	Brookline Holdings Ltd
	M-SPEC	Beech B350 Super King Air	Specsavers Aviation Ltd
	M-SPEX	Beech B350 Super King Air	Specsavers Aviation Ltd
	M-SPOR	Beech B200 King Air	Select Plant Hire Co.Ltd
	M-SQAR	Gulfstream V-SP	M Square Aviation Ltd
	M-SRNE	Eurocopter MBB-BK.117C-2	Serena Aviation Ltd
	M-SSSR	Bombardier BD700-1A10 Global Express	VipJet Ltd
	M-STAR	Boeing 727-2X8	Starling Aviation Ltd
	M-STCO	Dassault Falcon 2000LX	STC IOM Ltd
	M-STEP	Gulfstream G150	ArtJet Ltd
	M-SVGN	Cessna 680 Citation Sovereign	Vocalion Ltd
	M-SWAN	IAI Gulfstream 200	Falcon Crest Resources Inc.
	M-SYGB	Beech B.200GT Super King Air	Rialus Ltd
	M-TAKE	Bombardier CL600-2B19 Challenger 850	Caropan Company SA
	M-TEAM	Cessna 525B Citationjet CJ1+	Mistral Aviation Ltd
	M-TINK	Dassault Falcon 2000EX	Stark Limited
	M-TNTJ	Learjet 55	TNT Airways SA
	M-TOMS	Pilatus PC-12/47E	C J Airways Ltd
	M-TOPI	Bombardier CL600-2B16 Challenger	Gladiator Flight Ltd
	M-TRBS	Bombardier CL600-2B16 Challenger	Arrow Management Property Corp
	M-TSRI	Beech C.90GTI King Air	Timpson Ltd
	M-UGIC	Gulfstream 550	Cityville Capital Ltd
	M-UKHA	Hawker 800XP	Nebula III Ltd
	M-UNIS	Bombardier BD700-1A10 Global Express	Lapwing Ltd

Reg.	Type	Owner or Operator	Notes
M-URAL	Learjet 60	Uralkali Trading (Gibralter) Ltd	
M-URKA	Sikorsky S-76B	Starspeed Ltd	
M-URUS	Boeing 737-7GC	Ingram Services Ltd	
M-USBA	Gulfstream V	Shukra Ltd	
M-USCA	SOCATA TBM-850	Sterna Aviation Ltd	
M-USHY	Cessna 441 Conquest	Flying Dogs Ltd	
M-USIC	Gulfstream 550	Hampshire Aviation Ltd	
M-USIK	Gulfstream 650	OS Aviation Ltd	
M-USTG	Cessna 510 Citation Mustang	OSM Aviation Ltd	
M-UTIN	Pilatus PC-12/45	Myriel Aviation SA	
M-VANG	Bombardier BD700-1A10 Global Express	Elderberry Ltd	
M-VBPO	Beech 390 Premier 1A	Asia Universal Jet Ltd	
M-VGIN	Dassault Falcon 50EX	Charter Air Ltd	
M-VITO	Hawker 800XP	Beratex Group Ltd	
M-VQBI	Bombardier BD700-1A10 Global Express	Altitude X3 Ltd	
M-VRNY	Gulfstream 550	Mirtos Ltd	
M-WATJ	Beech B.200GT Super King Air	Saxonhenge Ltd	
M-WFAM	Bombardier CL600-2B16 Challenger	Multibird Overseas Ltd	
M-WHAT	Eurocopter EC.135T2+	Starspeed Ltd	
M-WING	Dassault Falcon 900LX	Certeco Aviation Ltd	
M-WINT	Pilatus PC-12/43E	Air Winton Ltd	
M-WMWM	Cessna 525A Citationjet CJ2	Standard Aviation Ltd	
M-WOOD	Cessna 550 Citation Bravo	Horizon Air LLP	
M-XHEC	Eurocopter EC155B	Flambards Ltd	
M-YBBJ	Boeing 737-7HE BBJ	Hamilton Jets Ltd	
M-YBLS	Pilatus PC-12/45	B. L. Schroder	
M-YBST	Bombardier CL600-2B16 Challenger	Kilmarnock Management Ltd	
M-YCEF	Hawker 800XP	Spirit Ltd	
M-YCUP	Embraer EMB-135BJ Legacy	Reatex Invest SA	
M-YEDT	Gulfstream 100	Opal Consulting LLC	
M-YFLY	Bombardier BD700-1A10 Global Express	Glenn Eagles Research LLP	
M-YGIV	Gulfstream IV	Al-Sahab Ltd	
M-YGLK	Gulfstream 450	Overseas Operation Ltd	
M-YGVI	Gulfstream 650	LTS Holding Ltd	
M-YJET	Dassault Falcon 2000Easy	My Jet Ltd	
M-YLEO	Pilatus PC-12/47E	Guernsey PC-12 Ltd	
M-YMCM	Bell 429	T. J. Morris Ltd	
M-YNNS	Dassault Falcon 7X	NS Falcon Ltd	
M-YORK	Falcon 7X	Lead Universal Ltd	
M-YRGN	Aerospatiale ATR-72-212A	Turbo 72-500 Leasing Ltd	
M-YRGP	Embraer ERJ-170-200LR	ECC Leasing Co.Ltd	
M-YSAI	Bombardier BD700-1A10 Global 5000	Capital Investment Worldwide	
M-YTAF	Beech B.36TC Bonanza	FBS Aviation Ltd	
M-YTOY	Embraer EMB-500 Phenom 100	TD Aviation IOM Ltd	
M-YULI	Bombardier BD700-1A11 Global Express	Primevalue Trading Ltd	
M-YUNI	Bombardier CL600-2B16 Challenger	Unitrans Management Ltd	
M-YWAA	Aerospatiale ATR-72-212A	Veling Narain Ltd	
M-YWAY	Gulfstream IV SP	Blue Sky Leasing Ltd	
M-YZZT	Cirrus SR22T	Stamp Aviation Ltd	
M-ZELL	Cessna 208 Caravan	Ridler Verwaltungs und Vermittlungs GmbH	
M-ZUMO	Pilatus PC-12/47	C. C. H. Way Ltd	

CHANNEL ISLANDS REGISTER

2-HIGH	Cirrus SR20		
2-KOOL	PA-28-181 ArcherII		
2-OFUS	Cirrus SR22		
2-PLAY	SOCATA TBM-700C-1		

G-AAZP DH.80A Puss Moth. *Peter R. March*

G-ACTF ComperCLA.7 Swift. *Peter R. March*

G-AHKX Avro 19 Srs.2. *Peter R. March*

G-ALWB DHC.1Chipmunk 22A. *Peter R. March*

G-BWDB Aerospatiale ATR-72-202 of Aurigny Air Services. *Allan S. Wright*

G-CBYH Aeroprakt A.22 Foxbat. *Allan S. Wright*

G-CEWM DHC.6 Twin Otter 300 of Isles of Scilly Skybus. *Peter R. March*

G-CFEZ CZAW Sportcruiser. *Allan S. Wright*

G-ECAN DH.84 Dragon. *Peter R. March*

G-FBJH Embraer ERJ170-200STD of Flybee. *Allan S. Wright*

G-HAAT MDH MD.900 Explorer. *Tom Cole*

G-ISSV Eurocopter EC.155B1. *Allan S. Wright*

G-JMCP Boeing 737-3TO of West Atlantic. *Allan S. Wright*

G-TATR Replica Travelair R Type. *Peter R. March*

G-TUIC Boeing 787-8 of Thompson Airways. *Allan S. Wright*

M-YULI Bombardier BD700-1A11 Global Express. *Tom Cole*

16693/G-BLPG AusterJ/1N Alpha. *Peter R. March*

JV579/G-RUMW Grumman FM-2. *Allan S. Wright*

Military to Civil Cross-Reference

Serial carried	Civil identity	Serial carried	Civil identity
001	G-BYPY	854 (USAAC)	G-BTBH
1	G-BPVE	897:E (USN)	G-BJEV
6	G-CAMM	99+26 (Luftwaffe)	G-BZGL
6G-ED (Luftwaffe)	G-BZOB	99+32 (Luftwaffe)	G-BZGK
9 (Soviet AF)	G-OYAK	1018 (Polish AF)	G-ISKA
03 (Soviet AF)	G-YAKR	1102:102 (USN)	G-AZLE
07 (Soviet AF)	G-BMJY	1104 (Royal Saudi AF)	G-SMAS
09 (DOSAAF)	G-BVMU	1125 (Kuwaiti AF)	G-CFBK
10 (DOSAAF)	G-BTZB	1130 (Royal Saudi AF)	G-VPER
10 (DOSAAF)	G-CBMD	1164:64 (USAAC)	G-BKGL
11 (Soviet AF)	G-YCII	1211(North Korean AF)	G-MIGG
21 (Soviet AF)	G-CDBJ	1342 (Soviet AF)	G-BTZD
23 (Soviet AF)	G-YKSO	1365 (Portuguese AF)	G-DHPM
26 (USAAC)	G-BAVO	1373 (Portuguese AF)	G-CBJG
26 (DOSAAF)	G-BVXK	1377 (Portuguese AF)	G-BARS
27 (Soviet AF)	G-YAKX	1747 (Portuguese AF)	G-BGPB
27 (USN)	G-BRVG	2345 (RFC)	G-ATVP
27 (USAAC)	G-AGYY	3066	G-AETA
27 (Soviet AF)	G-YAKX	3072:72 (USN)	G-TEXN
33 (grey) (Soviet AF)	G-YAKH	3303 (Portuguese AF)	G-CBGL
33 (red) (Soviet AF)	G-YAKZ	3349 (RCAF)	G-BYNF
42 (Soviet AF)	G-CBRU	3397:174 (USN)	G-OBEE
43:SC (USAF)	G-AZSC	4034 (Luftwaffe)	G-CDTI
44 (DOSAAF)	G-BXAK	4406:12 (USN)	G-ONAF
49 (USAAF)	G-KITT	4513:1 (French AF)	G-BFYO
49 (Soviet AF)	G-YAKU	5964 (RFC)	G-BFVH
50 (DOSAAF)	G-CBPM	6136:205 (USN)	G-BRUJ
50 (DOSAAF)	G-CBRW	7198/18 (Luftwaffe)	G-AANJ
50 (DOSAAF)	G-EYAK	7797 (USAAF)	G-BFAF
52 (Soviet AF)	G-BWVR	8178:FU-178 (USAF)	G-SABR
52 (Soviet AF)	G-CCJK	8449M (RAF)	G-ASWJ
52 (Soviet AF)	G-YAKY	9917	G-EBKY
55 (Soviet AF)	G-BVOK	01420 (Polish AF but in Korean colours)	G-BMZF
61 (Soviet AF)	G-YAKM	14863 (USAAC)	G-BGOR
66 (Soviet AF)	G-YAKN	16693:693 (RCAF)	G-BLPG
67 (DOSAAF)	G-CBSL	18393:393 (RCAF)	G-BCYK
68 (Chinese AF)	G-BVVG	18671:671 (RCAF)	G-BNZC
69 (Russian AF)	G-XYAK	20310:310 (RCAF)	G-BSBG
78 (French Army)	G-BIZK	21261:261 (RCAF)	G-TBRD
82:8 (French AF)	G-CCVH	21509 (US Army)	G-UHIH
93 (DOSAAF)	G-JYAK	24550 (US Army)	G-PDOG
100 (DOSAAF)	G-YAKI	24582 (US Army)	G-VDOG
104 (South Arabian AF)	G-PROV	28521:TA-521 (USAF)	G-TVIJ
112 (USAAC)	G-BSWC	30146 (Yugoslav Army)	G-BSXD
113 (Kuwait AF)	G-CFBK	30149 (Yugoslav Army)	G-SOKO
118 (USAAC)	G-BSDS	31145:G-26 (USAAF)	G-BBLH
124 (French Army)	G-BOSJ	3-1923 (USAAF)	G-BRHP
143 (French AF)	G-MSAL	31952 (USAAF)	G-BRPR
156 (French AF)	G-NIFE	39624:D-39 (USAAF)	G-BVMH
161 (Irish Air Corps)	G-CCCA	40467:19 (USN)	G-BTCC
168 (RFC)	G-BFDE	56321:U-AB (Royal Norwegian AF)	G-BKPY
174 (Royal Netherlands Navy)	G-BEPV	80105 (US Air Service)	G-CCBN
177 (Irish Air Corps)	G-BLIW	80425:WT-4 (USN)	G-RUMT
311 (Singapore AF)	G-MXPH	111836:JZ-6 (USN)	G-TSIX
347	G-AWYI	115042:TA-042 (USAF)	G-BGHU
354	G-BZNK	115227 (USN)	G-BKRA
379 (USAAC)	G-ILLE	115302:TP (USMC)	G-BJTP
422/15 (Luftwaffe)	G-AVJO	115373 (USAAF)	G-AYPM
423 / 427 (Royal Norwegian AF)	G-AMRK	115684 (USAAF)	G-BKVM
425 (Oman AF)	G-SOAF	121714:201-B (USN)	G-RUMM
441 (USN)	G-BTFG	124485:DF-A (USAAF)	G-BEDF
450/17 (Luftwaffe)	G-BVGZ	126922:503 (USN)	G-RADR
503 (Hungarian AF)	G-BRAM	150225:123 (USMC)	G-AWOX
540 (USAAF)	G-BCNX	18-2001 (USAAF)	G-BIZV
669 (USAAC)	G-CCXA	18-5395:CDG (French Army)	G-CUBJ
781-32 (Spanish AF)	G-BPDM	238410:A-44 (USAAF)	G-BHPK

Serial carried	Civil identity	Serial carried	Civil identity
314887 (USAAF)	G-AJPI	C5430	G-CCXG
315509:W7-S (USAAF)	G-BHUB	C9533:M	G-BUWE
329405:A-23 (USAAF)	G-BCOB	D-692	G-BVAW
329417 (USAAF)	G-BDHK	D5397/17 (Luftwaffe)	G-BFXL
329471:F-44 (USAAF)	G-BGXA	D7889	G-AANM
329601:D-44 (USAAF)	G-AXHR	D8084	G-ACAA
329854:R-44 (USAAF)	G-BMKC	D8096:D	G-AEPH
329934:B-72 (USAAF)	G-BCPH	E-15 (Royal Netherlands AF)	G-BIYU
330238:A-24 (USAAF)	G-LIVH	E3B-143 (Spanish AF)	G-JUNG
330485:C-44 (USAAF)	G-AJES	E3B-153:781-75 (Spanish AF)	G-BPTS
343251:27 (USAAC)	G-NZSS	E3B-350:05-97 (Spanish AF)	G-BHPL
379994:J-52 (USAAF)	G-BPUR	E449	G-EBJE
413521:5Q-B (USAAF)	G-MRLL	E3273	G-ADEV
413704: 87-H (USAAF)	G-BTCD	E8894	G-CDLI
413926: E2-S (USAAF)	G-CGOI	F141:G	G-SEVA
414419:LH-F (USAAF)	G-MSTG	F235:B	G-BMDB
433915 (USAAF)	G-PBYA	F904	G-EBIA
436021 (USAAF)	G-BWEZ	F938	G-EBIC
454467:J-44 (USAAF)	G-BILI	F943	G-BIHF
454537:J-04 (USAAF)	G-BFDL	F943	G-BKDT
461748:Y (USAF)	G-BHDK	F5447:N	G-BKER
472035 (USAAF)	G-SIJJ	F5459:Y	G-INNY
472216:HO-M (USAAF)	G-BIXL	F8010:Z	G-BDWJ
474008:VF-R (USAAF)	G-PSIR	F8614	G-AWAU
479744:M-49 (USAAF)	G-BGPD	G-48-1 (Class B)	G-ALSX
479766:D-63 (USAAF)	G-BKHG	J-1605 (Swiss AF)	G-BLID
479897:JD(USAAF)	G-BOXJ	J-1632 (Swiss AF)	G-VNOM
480015:M-44 (USAAF)	G-AKIB	J-1758 (Swiss AF)	G-BLSD
480133:B-44 (USAAF)	G-BDCD	J-4021 (Swiss AF)	G-HHAC
480173:57-H (USAAF)	G-RRSR	J-4083 (Swiss AF)	G-EGHH
480321:H-44 (USAAF)	G-FRAN	J7326	G-EBQP
480480:E-44 (USAAF)	G-BECN	J9941:57	G-ABMR
480636:A-58 (USAAF)	G-AXHP	K1786	G-AFTA
480723:E5-J (USAAF)	G-BFZB	K1930	G-BKBB
480752:E-39 (USAAF)	G-BCXJ	K2048	G-BZNW
493209 (US ANG)	G-DDMV	K2050	G-ASCM
542447 (USAF)	G-SCUB	K2059	G-PFAR
2632019 (Chinese AF)	G-BXZB	K2075	G-BEER
41-19841:X-17	G-CGZP	K2227	G-ABBB
41-33275:CE (USAAF)	G-BICE	K2567	G-MOTH
42-10855 (USAAF)	G-KITT	K2572	G-AOZH
42-35870:129 (USN)	G-BWLJ	K2585	G-ANKT
42-58678:IY (USAAF)	G-BRIY	K2587	G-BJAP
42-78044 (USAAF)	G-BRXL	K3241	G-AHSA
42-84555:EP-H (USAAF)	G-ELMH	K3661	G-BURZ
43-35943 (USN)	G-BKRN	K3731	G-RODI
44-79609:44-S (USAAF)	G-BHXY	K4259:71	G-ANMO
44-80594 (USAAF)	G-BEDJ	K5054	G-BRDV
44-83184 (USAAF)	G-RGUS	K5414:XV	G-AENP
51-7692 (French AF)	G-TROY	K5600	G-BVVI
51-11701A:AF258 (USAF)	G-BSZC	K5673	G-BZAS
51-15319 (USAAF)	G-FUZZ	K5674	G-CBZP
51-15527 (USN)	G-BKRA	K7985	G-AMRK
51-15555 (US Army)	G-OSPS	K8203	G-BTVE
54-2445 (USAF)	G-OTAN	K8303:D	G-BWWN
69-16011 (USAAF)	G-OHGA	L2301	G-AIZG
A-10 (Swiss AF)	G-BECW	L6906	G-AKKY
A11-301 (RAN)	G-ARKG	N-294 (RNeth AF)	G-KAXF
A16-199:SF-R (RAAF)	G-BEOX	N500	G-BWRA
A17-48 (RAAF)	G-BPHR	N1854	G-AIBE
A-57 (Swiss AF)	G-BECT	N1977:8 (French AF)	G-BWMJ
A-806 (Swiss AF)	G-BTLL	N3200	G-CFGJ
A8226	G-BIDW	N3788	G-AKPF
B595:W	G-BUOD	N4877:MK-V	G-AMDA
B1807	G-EAVX	N5182	G-APUP
B2458:R	G-BPOB	N5195	G-ABOX
B6401	G-AWYY	N5719	G-CBHO
C1904:Z	G-PFAP	N5903:H	G-GLAD
C3009	G-BFWD	N6290	G-BOCK
C3011:S	G-SWOT	N6452	G-BIAU
C4918	G-BWJM	N6466	G-ANKZ
C4994	G-BLWM	N6537	G-AOHY

Serial carried	Civil identity	Serial carried	Civil identity
N6720:VX	G-BYTN	AR213:PR-D	G-AIST
N6797	G-ANEH	AR501:NN-A	G-AWII
N6847	G-APAL	BB697	G-ADGT
N6965:FL-J	G-AJTW	BB807	G-ADWO
N9191	G-ALND	BE505:XP-L	G-HHII
N9192:RCO-N	G-DHZF	BI-005 (RNethAF)	G-BUVN
P2902:DX-X	G-ROBT	BM597:JH-C	G-MKVB
P3717:SW-P	G-HITT	CW-BG (Luftwaffe)	G-BXBD
P3886:UF-K	G-CHTK	DE208	G-AGYU
P6382:C	G-AJRS	DE470	G-ANMY
P9374	G-MKIA	DE623	G-ANFI
P9398	G-CEPL	DE673	G-ADNZ
R-55 (RNethAF)	G-BLMI	DE992	G-AXXV
R-151 (RNethAF)	G-BIYR	DF112	G-ANRM
R-156 (RNethAF)	G-ROVE	DF128:RCO-U	G-AOJJ
R-163 (RNethAF)	G-BIRH	DF198	G-BBRB
R-167 (RNethAF)	G-LION	DG590	G-ADMW
R1914	G-AHUJ	EM720	G-AXAN
R3821:UX-N	G-BPIV	EN224	G-FXII
R4118:UP-W	G-HUPW	EN961:SD-X	G-CGIK
R4922	G-APAO	EP120:AE-A	G-LFVB
R4959:59	G-ARAZ	ES.1-4 (Spanish AF)	G-BUTX
R5136	G-APAP	FB226:MT-A	G-BDWM
R5172:FIJ-E	G-AOIS	FE695:94	G-BTXI
R5250	G-AODT	FE788	G-CTKL
S1287	G-BEYB	FH153	G-BBHK
S1579:571	G-BBVO	FJ777 (RCAF)	G-BIXN
S1581:573	G-BWWK	FR886	G-BDMS
T5854	G-ANKK	FS628	G-AIZE
T5879:RUC-W	G-AXBW	FT391	G-AZBN
T6562	G-ANTE	FX301:FD-NQ	G-TXAN
T6953	G-ANNI	FZ626:YS-DH	G-AMPO
T7230	G-AFVE	HB275	G-BKGM
T7281	G-ARTL	HB751	G-BCBL
T7290	G-ANNK	HD-75 (R Belgian AF)	G-AFDX
T7793	G-ANKV	HG691	G-AIYR
T7794	G-ASPV	HM580	G-ACUU
T7798	G-ANZT	JV579:F	G-RUMW
T7842	G-AMTF	KB889:NA-I	G-LANC
T7909	G-ANON	KD345:130-A	G-FGID
T7997	G-AHUF	KF584:RAI-X	G-RAIX
T8191	G-BWMK	KF729	G-BJST
T9707	G-AKKR	KG651	G-AMHJ
T9738	G-AKAT	KK116	G-AMPY
T9768	G-AIUA	KN353	G-AMYJ
U-0247 (Class B identity)	G-AGOY	LB264	G-AIXA
U-80 (Swiss AF)	G-BUKK	LB312	G-AHXE
U-95 (Swiss AF)	G-BVGP	LB323	G-AHSD
U-99 (Swiss AF)	G-AXMT	LB367	G-AHGZ
U-108 (Swiss AF)	G-BJAX	LB375	G-AHGW
U-110 (Swiss AF)	G-PTWO	LF858	G-BLUZ
V-54 (Swiss AF)	G-BVSD	LZ766	G-ALCK
V3388	G-AHTW	LZ842:EF-F	G-CGZU
V7497	G-HRLI	MB293	G-CFGI
V9312	G-CCOM	MH434:ZD-B	G-ASJV
V9367:MA-B	G-AZWT	MJ627:9G-P	G-BMSB
V9673:MA-J	G-LIZY	ML407:OU-V	G-LFIX
W2718	G-RNLI	MP425	G-AITB
W3257:FY-E	G-CENI	MS824 (French AF)	G-AWBU
W5856:A2A	G-BMGC	MT197	G-ANHS
W9385:YG-L	G-ADND	MT438	G-AREI
X4276	G-CDGU	MT818	G-AIDN
X4650	G-CGUK	MV268:JE-J	G-SPIT
Z2033:N/275	G-ASTL	MW401	G-PEST
Z5140:HA-C	G-HURI	MW763:HF-A	G-TEMT
Z5207	G-BYDL	NJ633	G-AKXP
Z5252:GO-B	G-BWHA	NJ673	G-AOCR
Z7015:7-L	G-BKTH	NJ695	G-AJXV
Z7197	G-AKZN	NJ719	G-ANFU
AB196	G-CCGH	NJ889	G-AHLK
AP506	G-ACWM	NL750	G-AOBH
AP507:KX-P	G-ACWP	NL985	G-BWIK

Serial carried	Civil identity	Serial carried	Civil identity
NM138	G-ANEW	WA577	G-ALST
NM181	G-AZGZ	WA591:FMK-Q	G-BWMF
NX534	G-BUDL	WB565:X	G-PVET
NX611:LE-C/DX-C	G-ASXX	WB569:R	G-BYSJ
PL965:R	G-MKXI	WB585:M	G-AOSY
PL983	G-PRXI	WB588:D	G-AOTD
PS853:C	G-RRGN	WB615:E	G-BXIA
PT462:SW-A	G-CTIX	WB652:V	G-CHPY
PT879	G-BYDE	WB654:U	G-BXGO
PV303:ON-B	G-CCJL	WB671:910	G-BWTG
RB142:DW-B	G-CEFC	WB697:95	G-BXCT
RG333	G-AIEK	WB702	G-AOFE
RG333	G-AKEZ	WB703	G-ARMC
RH377	G-ALAH	WB711	G-APPM
RK855	G-PIXY	WB726:E	G-AOSK
RL962	G-AHED	WB763:14	G-BBMR
RM221	G-ANXR	WD286	G-BBND
RN218:N	G-BBJI	WD292	G-BCRX
RR232	G-BRSF	WD305	G-ARGG
RT486:PF-A	G-AJGJ	WD310:B	G-BWUN
RT520	G-ALYB	WD327	G-ATVF
RT610	G-AKWS	WD331:J	G-BXDH
RX168	G-BWEM	WD363:5	G-BCIH
SM520:KJ-1	G-ILDA	WD373:12	G-BXDI
SM969:D-A	G-BRAF	WD379:K	G-APLO
SX336:105-VL	G-KASX	WD390:68	G-BWNK
TA634:8K-K	G-AWJV	WD413	G-VROE
TA719:6T	G-ASKC	WE569	G-ASAJ
TA805:FX-M	G-PMNF	WE724:062	G-BUCM
TD248:CR-S	G-OXVI	WF118	G-DACA
TD314: FX-P	G-CEYJ	WF877	G-BPOA
TE184:D	G-MXVI	WG308:8	G-BYHL
TE517	G-JGCA	WG316	G-BCAH
TJ534	G-AKSY	WG321:G	G-DHCC
TJ569	G-AKOW	WG348	G-BBMV
TJ652	G-AMVD	WG350	G-BPAL
TJ672:TS-D	G-ANIJ	WG407:67	G-BWMX
TJ704:JA	G-ASCD	WG422:16	G-BFAX
TS798	G-AGNV	WG465	G-BCEY
TW439	G-ANRP	WG469:72	G-BWJY
TW467	G-ANIE	WG472	G-AOTY
TW501	G-ALBJ	WG655	G-CHFP
TW511	G-APAF	WG719	G-BRMA
TW536:TS-V	G-BNGE	WJ358	G-ARYD
TW591:N	G-ARIH	WJ368	G-ASZX
TW641	G-ATDN	WJ945:21	G-BEDV
TX213	G-AWRS	WK163	G-BVWC
TX310	G-AIDL	WK436	G-VENM
VF512:PF-M	G-ARRX	WK512:A	G-BXIM
VF516	G-ASMZ	WK514	G-BBMO
VF526:T	G-ARXU	WK517	G-ULAS
VF581	G-ARSL	WK522	G-BCOU
VL348	G-AVVO	WK549	G-BTWF
VL349	G-AWSA	WK577	G-BCYM
VM360	G-APHV	WK585	G-BZGA
VN799	G-CDSX	WK586:V	G-BXGX
VP955	G-DVON	WK590:69	G-BWVZ
VP981	G-DHDV	WK609:93	G-BXDN
VR192	G-APIT	WK611	G-ARWB
VR249:FA-EL	G-APIY	WK624	G-BWHI
VR259:M	G-APJB	WK628	G-BBMW
VS356	G-AOLU	WK630	G-BXDG
VS610:K-L	G-AOKL	WK633:A	G-BXEC
VS623	G-AOKZ	WK635	G-HFRH
VX113	G-ARNO	WK640:C	G-BWUV
VX118	G-ASNB	WK642:94	G BXDP
VX147	G-AVIL	WL626:P	G-BHDD
VX281	G-RNHF	WM167	G-LOSM
VX927	G-ASYG	WP308:572CU	G-GACA
VZ638:HF	G-JETM	WP321	G-BRFC
VZ728	G-AGOS	WP788	G-BCHL
WA576	G-ALSS	WP790:T	G-BBNC

Serial carried	Civil identity	Serial carried	Civil identity
WP795:901	G-BVZZ	XL587	G-HPUX
WP800:2	G-BCXN	XL602	G-BWFT
WP803	G-HAPY	XL621	G-BNCX
WP805:D	G-MAJR	XL714	G-AOGR
WP808	G-BDEU	XL809	G-BLIX
WP809:78 RN	G-BVTX	XL929	G-BNPU
WP857:24	G-BDRJ	XL954	G-BXES
WP859:E	G-BXCP	XM223:J	G-BWWC
WP860:6	G-BXDA	XM370:10	G-BVSP
WP870:12	G-BCOI	XM424	G-BWDS
WP896	G-BWVY	XM479:54	G-BVEZ
WP901:B	G-BWNT	XM553	G-AWSV
WP903	G-BCGC	XM575	G-BLMC
WP925:C	G-BXHA	XM655	G-VULC
WP928:D	G-BXGM	XM685:513/PO	G-AYZJ
WP929:F	G-BXCV	XM819	G-APXW
WP930:J	G-BXHF	XN351	G-BKSC
WP971	G-ATHD	XN437	G-AXWA
WP983:B	G-BXNN	XN441	G-BGKT
WP984:H	G-BWTO	XN498	G-BWSH
WR410:N	G-BLKA	XN637:03	G-BKOU
WR470	G-DHVM	XP242	G-BUCI
WR963	G-SKTN	XP254	G-ASCC
WT333	G-BVXC	XP279	G-BWKK
WT933	G-ALSW	XP282	G-BGTC
WV198:K	G-BJWY	XP355	G-BEBC
WV318:D	G-FFOX	XP907	G-SROE
WV322:Y	G-BZSE	XP924	G-CVIX
WV372:R	G-BXFI	XR240	G-BDFH
WV493:29	G-BDYG	XR241	G-AXRR
WV740	G-BNPH	XR246	G-AZBU
WV783	G-ALSP	XR267	G-BJXR
WZ507:74	G-VTII	XR486	G-RWWW
WZ662	G-BKVK	XR537:T	G-NATY
WZ711	G-AVHT	XR538:01	G-RORI
WZ847:F	G-CPMK	XR595:M	G-BWHU
WZ868:H	G-ARMF	XR673:L	G-BXLO
WZ872:E	G-BZGB	XR724	G-BTSY
WZ879	G-BWUT	XR944	G-ATTB
WZ882:K	G-BXGP	XR991	G-MOUR
XA880	G-BVXR	XS104	G-FRCE
XD693:Z-Q	G-AOBU	XS111	G-TIMM
XE489	G-JETH	XS165:37	G-ASAZ
XE685:861/VL	G-GAII	XS235	G-CPDA
XE856	G-DUSK	XS587	G-VIXN
XE956	G-OBLN	XS765	G-BSET
XF114	G-SWIF	XT223	G-XTUN
XF597:AH	G-BKFW	XT420:606	G-CBUI
XF603	G-KAPW	XT435:430	G-RIMM
XF690	G-MOOS	XT626	G-CIBW
XF785	G-ALBN	XT634	G-BYRX
XF836:J-G	G-AWRY	XT671	G-BYRC
XG160:U	G-BWAF	XT787	G-KAXT
XG194:A	G-PRII	XT788:316	G-BMIR
XG452	G-BRMB	XV134:P	G-BWLX
XH134	G-OMHD	XV137	G-CRUM
XH558	G-VLCN	XV138	G-SASM
XJ389	G-AJJP	XV268	G-BVER
XJ398	G-BDBZ	XW289:73	G-JPVA
XJ615	G-BWGL	XW293:Z	G-BWCS
XJ729	G-BVGE	XW310	G-BWGS
XJ771	G-HELV	XW324:K	G-BWSG
XK417	G-AVXY	XW325:E	G-BWGF
XK895:19/CU	G-SDEV	XW333:79	G-BVTC
XK896	G-RNAS	XW354	G-JPTV
XK940:911	G-AYXT	XW422:3	G-BWEB
XL426	G-VJET	XW423:14	G-BWUW
XL500	G-KAEW	XW433	G-JPRO
XL502	G-BMYP	XW612	G-KAXW
XL571:V	G-HNTR	XW613	G-BXRS
XL573	G-BVGH	XW635	G-AWSW
XL577:V	G-XMHD	XW784:VL	G-BBRN

Serial carried	Civil identity	Serial carried	Civil identity
XW853	G-IBNH	XX695:3	G-CBBT
XW854:46/CU	G-TIZZ	XX698:9	G-BZME
XW858:C	G-ONNE	XX699:F	G-CBCV
XW866:E	G-BXTH	XX700:17	G-CBEK
XX406:P	G-CBSH	XX702:P	G-CBCR
XX432	G-CDNO	XX704	G-BCUV
XX467:86	G-TVII	XX707:4	G-CBDS
XX513:10	G-CCMI	XX885	G-HHAA
XX514	G-BWIB	XZ239	G-BZYD
XX515:4	G-CBBC	XZ934:U	G-CBSI
XX518:S	G-UDOG	XZ937:Y	G-CBKA
XX521:H	G-CBEH	ZA250	G-VTOL
XX522:06	G-DAWG	ZA634:C	G-BUHA
XX524:04	G-DDOG	ZA652	G-BUDC
XX528:D	G-BZON	ZA730	G-FUKM
XX534:B	G-EDAV	ZB500	G-LYNX
XX537:C	G-CBCB	ZB627:A	G-CBSK
XX538:O	G-TDOG	ZB646:59/CU	G-CBGZ
XX543:F	G-CBAB	HKG-5 (Royal Hong Kong AAF)	G-BULL
XX546:03	G-WINI	HKG-6 (Royal Hong Kong AAF)	G-BPCL
XX549:6	G-CBID	HKG-11 (Royal Hong Kong AAF)	G-BYRY
XX550:Z	G-CBBL	HKG-13 (Royal Hong Kong AAF)	G-BXKW
XX551:E	G-BZDP	2+1:7334 Luftwaffe)	G-SYFW
XX554	G-BZMD	3+ (Luftwaffe)	G-BAYV
XX561:7	G-BZEP	4+ (Luftwaffe)	G-BSLX
XX611:7	G-CBDK	4-97/MM52801 (Italian)	G-BBII
XX612:A, 03	G-BZXC	07 (Russian AF)	G-BMJY
XX614:V	G-GGRR	F+IS (Luftwaffe)	G-BIRW
XX619:T	G-CBBW	BU+CC (Luftwaffe)	G-BUCC
XX621:H	G-CBEF	BU+CK (Luftwaffe)	G-BUCK
XX622:B	G-CBGZ	CF+HF (Luftwaffe)	EI-AUY
XX624:E	G-KDOG	DM+BK (Luftwaffe)	G-BPHZ
XX626:02, W	G-CDVV	GM+AI (Luftwaffe)	G-STCH
XX628:9	G-CBFU	LG+01 (Luftwaffe)	G-AYSJ
XX629:V	G-BZXZ	LG+03 (Luftwaffe)	G-AEZX
XX630:5	G-SIJW	KG+EM (Luftwaffe)	G-ETME
XX631:W	G-BZXS	NJ+C11 (Luftwaffe)	G-ATBG
XX636:Y	G-CBFP	S4+A07 (Luftwaffe)	G-BWHP
XX638	G-DOGG	S5+B06 (Luftwaffe)	G-WJCM
XX658:07	G-BZPS	TP+WX (Luftwaffe)	G-TPWX
XX667:16	G-BZFN	6J+PR (Luftwaffe)	G-AWHB
XX668:1	G-CBAN	57-H (USAAC)	G-AKAZ
XX692:A	G-BZMH	97+04 (Luftwaffe)	G-APVF
XX693:07	G-BZML	+14 (Luftwaffe)	G-BSMD
XX694:E	G-CBBS		
		146-11083 (5) G-BNAI	

Republic of Ireland Civil Registrations

Reg.	Type (†False registration)	Owner or Operator	Notes
EI-ABI	DH.84 Dragon	Aer Lingus Charitable Foundation (EI-AFK)	
EI-AED	Cessna 120	E. McNeill & P. O'Reilly	
EI-AEE	Auster 3/1 Autocrat	O. & N. A. O'Sullivan	
EI-AEF	Cessna 120	J. Halligan	
EI-AEI	Aeronca 65-TAC	S. Hudson & Partners	
EI-AEJ	PA-16	J. Dolan	
EI-AFE	Piper J3C-65 Cub	4 of Cubs Flying Group	
EI-AFF	B.A. Swallow 2	J. J. Sullivan & ptnrs	
EI-AGD	Taylorcraft Plus D	B. & K. O'Sullivan	
EI-AGJ	Auster J/1 Autocrat	T. G. Rafter	
EI-AHI	DH.82A Tiger Moth	High Fidelity Flyers	
EI-AII	Cessna 150F	L. Bagnell	
EI-AKM	Piper J-3C-65 Cub	J. A. Kent	
EI-ALP	Avro 643 Cadet	J.C. O'Loughlin (stored)	
EI-AMK	Auster J/1 Autocrat	Iona National Airways	
EI-ANT	Champion 7ECA Citabria	T. Croke & ptnrs	
EI-ANY	PA-18 Super Cub 95	Bogavia Group	
EI-AOB	PA-28 Cherokee 140	Knock Flying Group	
EI-APS	Schleicher ASK.14	E. Shiel & ptnrs	
EI-ARW	Jodel D.R.1050	J. Davy	
EI-ATJ	B.121 Pup Srs 2	L. O'Leary	
EI-AUM	Auster J/1 Autocrat	T. G. Rafter	
EI-AUO	Cessna FA.150K Aerobat	S. Burke & L. Bagnell	
EI-AVM	Cessna F.150L	Opax Ltd	
EI-AWH	Cessna 210J	Rathcoole Flying Club	
EI-AWP	DH.82A Tiger Moth	A. P. Bruton	
EI-AWR	Malmö MFI-9 Junior	C. O'Shea	
EI-AYB	GY-80 Horizon 180	J. B. Smith	
EI-AYI	MS.880B Rallye Club	J. McNamara	
EI-AYN	BN-2A-8 Islander	Aer Arann	
EI-AYR	Schleicher ASK-16	B. O'Broin & ptnrs	
EI-AYT	MS.894A Rallye Minerva	K. A. O'Connor	
EI-AYY	Evans VP-1	R. Dowd	
EI-BAJ	Stampe SV.4C	W. Rafter & Partners	
EI-BAT	Cessna F.150M	J. Reilly	
EI-BAV	PA-22 Colt 108	E. Finnamore	
EI-BBC	PA-28 Cherokee 180C	Vero Beach	
EI-BBE	Champion 7FC Tri-Traveler (tailwheel)	P. Ryan	
EI-BBI	MS.892 Rallye Commodore	Ossory Flying & Gliding Club	
EI-BBV	Piper J-3C-65 Cub	F. Cronin	
EI-BCE	BN-2A-26 Islander	Aer Arann	
EI-BCF	Bensen B.8M	P. Flanagan	
EI-BCJ	Aeromere F.8L Falco 1 Srs 3	M. P. McLoughlin	
EI-BCK	Cessna F.172N II	K. A. O'Connor	
EI-BCM	Piper J-3C-65 Cub	M. Bergin & Partners	
EI-BCN	Piper J-3C-65 Cub	H. Diver	
EI-BCP	D.62B Condor	T. Delaney	
EI-BDL	Evans VP-2	P. Buggle	
EI-BDR	PA-28 Cherokee 180	Cherokee Group	
EI-BEN	Piper J-3C-65 Cub	Capt. J. J. Sullivan	
EI-BHI	Bell 206B JetRanger 2	G. Tracey	
EI-BHV	Champion 7EC Traveler	P. O'Donnell & ptnrs	
EI-BIB	Cessna F.152	Sligo Aeronautical Club Ltd	
EI-BID	PA-18 Super Cub 95	A. Connaire & Partners	
EI-BIK	PA-18 Super Cub 180	Dublin Gliding Club	
EI-BIO	Piper J-3C-65 Cub	H. Duggan & Partners	
EI-BIR	Cessna F.172M	Figile Flying Group	
EI-BIV	Bellanca 8KCAB	Atlantic Flight Training Ltd	
EI-BJB	Aeronca 7AC Champion	A. W. Kennedy	
EI-BJC	Aeronca 7AC Champion	A. E. Griffin	
EI-BJK	MS.880B Rallye 110ST	M. Keenen	
EI-BJM	Cessna A.152	K. A. O'Connor	
EI-BJO	Cessna R.172K	The XP Group	
EI-BKC	Aeronca 15AC Sedan	G. Hendrick & M. Farrell	
EI-BKK	Taylor JT.1 Monoplane	R. Klimcke	

Notes	Reg.	Type	Owner or Operator
	EI-BMI	SOCATA TB9 Tampico	A. Breslin
	EI-BMN	Cessna F.152 II	K. A. O'Connor
	EI-BMU	Monnet Sonerai IIL	N. O'Donnell
	EI-BNL	Rand-Robinson KR-2	K. Hayes
	EI-BNU	MS.880B Rallye Club	J. Cooke
	EI-BOE	SOCATA TB10 Tobago	Tobago Group
	EI-BOV	Rand-Robinson KR-2	G. O'Hara & G. Callan
	EI-BPL	Cessna F.172K	Phoenix Flying
	EI-BPP	Quicksilver MX	J. A. Smith
	EI-BRS	Cessna P.172D	P. Mathews
	EI-BRU	Evans VP-1	C. O'Shea
	EI-BSB	Wassmer Jodel D.112	S. Byrne
	EI-BSC	Cessna F.172N	M. Foreman
	EI-BSG	Bensen B.80	J. Todd
	EI-BSK	SOCATA TB9 Tampico	T. Drury
	EI-BSL	PA-34-220T Seneca III	P. Sreenan
	EI-BSN	Cameron O-65 balloon	C. O'Neill & T. Hooper
	EI-BSO	PA-28 Cherokee 140B	S. Brazil
	EI-BSW	Solar Wings Pegasus XL-R	E. Fitzgerald
	EI-BUA	Cessna 172M	K. A. O'Connor
	EI-BUC	Jodel D.9 Bébé	B. Lyons & M. Blake
	EI-BUE	Boeing 737-348	Mistral Air
	EI-BUF	Cessna 210N	210 Group
	EI-BUG	SOCATA ST.10 Diplomate	J. Cooke
	EI-BUL	Whittaker MW5 Sorcerer	J. Culleton
	EI-BUN	Beech 76 Duchess	K. A. O'Connor
	EI-BUT	MS.893A Commodore 180	T. Keating
	EI-BVJ	AMF Chevron 232	A. Dunn
	EI-BVK	PA-38-112 Tomahawk	B. Lowe
	EI-BVT	Evans VP-2	P. Morrison
	EI-BVY	Zenith 200AA-RW	J. Matthews & M. Skelly
	EI-BYG	SOCATA TB9 Tampico	M. McGinn
	EI-BYL	Zenith CH.250	M. McLoughlin
	EI-BYO	Aérospatiale ATR-42-310	Aer Arann
	EI-BYX	Champion 7GCAA	P. J. Gallagher
	EI-BYY	Piper J-3C-85 Cub	The Cub Club
	EI-CAC	Grob G.115A	C. Phillips
	EI-CAD	Grob G.115A	C. Phillips
	EI-CAE	Grob G.115A	O. O'Reilly
	EI-CAN	Aerotech MW5 Sorcerer	V. A. Vaughan
	EI-CAP	Cessna R.182RG	K. K. Skorupski
	EI-CAU	AMF Chevron 232	J. Tarrant
	EI-CAX	Cessna P.210N	K. A. O'Connor
	EI-CBK	Aérospatiale ATR-42-310	Aer Arann
	EI-CCF	Aeronca 11AC Chief	G. McGuinness
	EI-CCM	Cessna 152 II	E. Hopkins
	EI-CDP	Cessna 182L	Irish Parachute Club
	EI-CDV	Cessna 150G	K. A. O'Connor
	EI-CEG	MS.893A Rallye 180GT	M. Jarrett
	EI-CES	Taylorcraft BC-65	G. Higgins & Partners
	EI-CFF	PA-12 Super Cruiser	J. & T. O'Dwyer
	EI-CFG	CP.301B Emeraude	F. Doyle
	EI-CFH	PA-12 Super Cruiser	G. Treacy
	EI-CFO	Piper J-3C-65 Cub	J. T. Wilson & ptnrs
	EI-CFP	Cessna 172P (floatplane)	S. Collins & Partners
	EI-CFY	Cessna 172N	K. A. O'Connor
	EI-CGD	Cessna 172M	J. Kelly
	EI-CGF	Luton LA-5 Major	P. White
	EI-CGH	Cessna 210N	J. Smith
	EI-CGP	PA-28 Cherokee 140C	L. A. Tattan
	EI-CHR	CFM Shadow Srs BD	B. Kelly
	EI-CIF	PA-28 Cherokee 180C	AA Flying Group
	EI-CIG	PA-18 Super Cub 150	K. A. O'Connor
	EI-CIM	Avid Flyer Mk IV	P. Swan
	EI-CIN	Cessna 150K	K. A. O'Connor
	EI-CJJ	Slingsby T-31M	J. J. Sullivan
	EI-CJR	SNCAN Stampe SV.4A	P. McKenna
	EI-CJS	Jodel D.120A	A. Flood
	EI-CJT	Slingsby Motor Cadet III	J. Tarrant
	EI-CKH	PA-18 Super Cub 95	G. Brady

Reg.	Type	Owner or Operator	Notes
EI-CKI	Thruster TST Mk 1	S. Woodgates	
EI-CKJ	Cameron N-77 balloon	A. F. Meldon	
EI-CKZ	Jodel D.18	J. O'Brien	
EI-CLA	HOAC Katana DV.20	J. Cooke	
EI-CLQ	Cessna F.172N	E. Finnamore	
EI-CMB	PA-28 Cherokee 140	K. Furnell & Partners	
EI-CML	Cessna 150M	P. Donohoe	
EI-CMN	PA-12 Super Cruiser	A. McNamee & ptnrs	
EI-CMR	Rutan LongEz	F. & C. O'Caoimh	
EI-CMT	PA-34-200T Seneca II	Atlantic Flight Training	
EI-CMU	Mainair Mercury	Bill O'Neill	
EI-CMV	Cessna 150L	K. A. O'Connor	
EI-CMW	Rotorway Executive	B. McNamee	
EI-CNC	TEAM mini-MAX	A. M. S. Allen	
EI-CNG	Air & Space 18A gyroplane	P. Joyce	
EI-CNU	Pegasus Quantum 15-912	M. Ffrench	
EI-COT	Cessna F.172N	Tojo Air Leasing	
EI-COY	Piper J-3C-65 Cub	W. Flood	
EI-CPE	Airbus A.321-211	Aer Lingus St Enda	
EI-CPG	Airbus A.321-211	Aer Lingus St Aidan	
EI-CPH	Airbus A.321-211	Aer Lingus St Dervilla	
EI-CPI	Rutan LongEz	D. J. Ryan	
EI-CPP	Piper J-3C-65 Cub	E. Fitzgerald	
EI-CPT	Aérospatiale ATR-42-320	Aer Arann	
EI-CPX	I.I.I. Sky Arrow 650T	M. McCarthy	
EI-CRB	Lindstrand LBL-90A balloon	J. & C. Concannon	
EI-CRG	Robin DR.400/180R	D. & B. Lodge	
EI-CRR	Aeronca 11AC Chief	L. Maddock & ptnrs	
EI-CRV	Hoffman H-36 Dimona	The Dimona Group	
EI-CRX	SOCATA TB-9 Tampico	Hotel Bravo Flying Club	
EI-CSG	Boeing 737-8AS	CIT Aerospace International	
EI-CTL	Aerotech MW-5B Sorcerer	M. Wade	
EI-CUA	Boeing 737-4K5	Aerco Ireland/Blue Panorama	
EI-CUJ	Cessna 172N	M. Nally	
EI-CUN	Boeing 737-4K5	Aerco Ireland/Blue Panorama	
EI-CUS	AB-206B JetRanger 3	R. Lyons	
EI-CUW	BN-2B-20 Islander	Aer Arann	
EI-CVA	Airbus A.320-214	Aer Lingus St Schira	
EI-CVB	Airbus A.320-214	Aer Lingus St Mobhi	
EI-CVC	Airbus A.320-214	Aer Lingus St Kealin	
EI-CVL	Ercoupe 415CD	V. O'Rourke	
EI-CVM	Schweizer S.269C	Helicopter Support Ireland Ltd	
EI-CVW	Bensen B.8M	F. Kavanagh	
EI-CXC	Raj Hamsa X'Air 502T	R. Dunleavy	
EI-CXK	Boeing 737-4S3	Transaero	
EI-CXN	Boeing 737-329	Transaero	
EI-CXR	Boeing 737-329	Transaero	
EI-CXS	Sikorsky S-61N	CHC Ireland Ltd	
EI-CXV	Boeing 737-8CX	MASL Ireland(14)Ltd/MIAT Mongolian Airlines	
EI-CXY	Evektor EV-97 Eurostar	G. Doody & ptnrs	
EI-CXZ	Boeing 767-216ER	Transaero	
EI-CZA	ATEC Zephyr 2000	M. Higgins & Partners	
EI-CZC	CFM Streak Shadow Srs II	M. Culhane & D. Burrows	
EI-CZD	Boeing 767-216ER	Transaero	
EI-CZK	Boeing 737-4Y0	Transaero	
EI-CZN	Sikorsky S-61N	CHC Ireland	
EI-CZP	Schweizer 269C-1	T. Ng Kam	
EI-DAA	Airbus A.330-202	Aer Lingus St Keeva	
EI-DAC	Boeing 737-8AS	Ryanair	
EI-DAD	Boeing 737-8AS	Ryanair	
EI-DAE	Boeing 737-8AS	Ryanair	
EI-DAF	Boeing 737-8AS	Ryanair	
EI-DAG	Boeing 737-8AS	Ryanair	
EI-DAH	Boeing 737-8AS	Ryanair	
EI-DAI	Boeing 737-8AS	Ryanair	
EI-DAJ	Boeing 737-8AS	Ryanair	
EI-DAK	Boeing 737-8AS	Ryanair	
EI-DAL	Boeing 737-8AS	Ryanair	
EI-DAM	Boeing 737-8AS	Ryanair	
EI-DAN	Boeing 737-8AS	Ryanair	
EI-DAO	Boeing 737-8AS	Ryanair	

Notes	Reg.	Type	Owner or Operator
	EI-DAP	Boeing 737-8AS	Ryanair
	EI-DAR	Boeing 737-8AS	Ryanair
	EI-DAS	Boeing 737-8AS	Ryanair
	EI-DBF	Boeing 767-3Q8ER	Transaero
	EI-DBG	Boeing 767-3Q8ER	Transaero
	EI-DBH	CFM Streak Shadow SA-11	M. O'Mahony
	EI-DBI	Raj Hamsa X'Air Mk.2 Falcon	E. Hamilton
	EI-DBJ	Huntwing Pegasus XL Classic	P. A. McMahon
	EI-DBK	Boeing 777-243ER	Alitalia
	EI-DBL	Boeing 777-243ER	Alitalia
	EI-DBM	Boeing 777-243ER	Alitalia
	EI-DBO	Air Creation Kiss 400	E. Spain
	EI-DBP	Boeing 767-35H	Alitalia
	EI-DBU	Boeing 767-37EER	Transaero
	EI-DBV	Rand Kar X' Air 602T	S. Scanlon
	EI-DBW	Boeing 767-201	Transaero
	EI-DCA	Raj Hamsa X'Air	S. Cahill
	EI-DCF	Boeing 737-8AS	Ryanair
	EI-DCG	Boeing 737-8AS	Ryanair
	EI-DCH	Boeing 737-8AS	Ryanair
	EI-DCI	Boeing 737-8AS	Ryanair
	EI-DCJ	Boeing 737-8AS	Ryanair
	EI-DCK	Boeing 737-8AS	Ryanair
	EI-DCL	Boeing 737-8AS	Ryanair
	EI-DCM	Boeing 737-8AS	Ryanair
	EI-DCN	Boeing 737-8AS	Ryanair
	EI-DCO	Boeing 737-8AS	Ryanair
	EI-DCP	Boeing 737-8AS	Ryanair
	EI-DCR	Boeing 737-8AS	Ryanair
	EI-DCW	Boeing 737-8AS	Ryanair
	EI-DCX	Boeing 737-8AS	Ryanair
	EI-DCY	Boeing 737-8AS	Ryanair
	EI-DCZ	Boeing 737-8AS	Ryanair
	EI-DDA	Robinson R44 II	Eirecopter Helicopters Ltd
	EI-DDC	Cessna F.172M	Trim Flying Club
	EI-DDD	Aeronca 7AC	J. Sullivan & M. Quinn
	EI-DDH	Boeing 777-243ER	Alitalia
	EI-DDI	Schweizer S.269C-1	B. Hade
	EI-DDJ	Raj Hamsa X'Air 582	J. P. McHugh
	EI-DDK	Boeing 737-4S3	Transaero
	EI-DDP	Southdown International microlight	M. Mannion
	EI-DDR	Bensen B8V	P. MacCabe & Partners
	EI-DDX	Cessna 172S	Atlantic Flight Training
	EI-DDY	Boeing 737-4Y0	Transaero
	EI-DEA	Airbus A.320-214	Aer Lingus St Fidelma
	EI-DEB	Airbus A.320-214	Aer Lingus St Nathy
	EI-DEC	Airbus A.320-214	Aer Lingus St Fergal
	EI-DEE	Airbus A.320-214	Aer Lingus St Fintan
	EI-DEF	Airbus A.320-214	Aer Lingus St Declan
	EI-DEG	Airbus A.320-214	Aer Lingus St Fachtna
	EI-DEH	Airbus A.320-214	Aer Lingus St Malachy
	EI-DEI	Airbus A.320-214	Aer Lingus St Kilian
	EI-DEJ	Airbus A.320-214	Aer Lingus St Oliver Plunkett
	EI-DEK	Airbus A.320-214	Aer Lingus St Eunan
	EI-DEL	Airbus A.320-214	Aer Lingus St Ibar
	EI-DEM	Airbus A.320-214	Aer Lingus St Canice
	EI-DEN	Airbus A.320-214	Aer Lingus St Kieran
	EI-DEO	Airbus A.320-214	Aer Lingus St Senan
	EI-DEP	Airbus A.320-214	Aer Lingus St Eugene
	EI-DER	Airbus A.320-214	Aer Lingus St Mel
	EI-DES	Airbus A.320-214	Aer Lingus St Pappin
	EI-DEZ	Airbus A.319-112	Meridiana
	EI-DFA	Airbus A.319-112	Meridiana
	EI-DFM	Evektor EV-97 Eurostar	G. Doody
	EI-DFO	Airbus A.320-211	Windjet
	EI-DFS	Boeing 767-33AER	Transaero
	EI-DFX	Air Creation Kiss 400	L. Daly
	EI-DFY	Raj Hamsa R100 (2)	P. McGirr & R Gillespie
	EI-DGA	Urban Air UFM-11UK Lambada	Dr. P. & D. Durkin
	EI-DGG	Raj Hamsa X'Air 582	P. A. Weldon
	EI-DGH	Raj Hamsa X'Air 582	M. Garvey & T. McGowan

Reg.	Type	Owner or Operator	Notes
EI-DGJ	Raj Hamsa X'Air 582	N. Brereton	
EI-DGK	Raj Hamsa X'Air 133	B. Chambers	
EI-DGP	Urban Air UFM-11 Lambada	R. Linehan	
EI-DGT	Urban Air UFM-11UK Lambada	P. Walsh & Partners	
EI-DGV	ATEC Zephyr 2000	K. Higgins	
EI-DGW	Cameron Z-90 balloon	J. Leahy	
EI-DGX	Cessna 152 II	K. A. O'Connor	
EI-DGY	Urban Air UFM-11 Lambada	D. McMorrow	
EI-DHA	Boeing 737-8AS	Ryanair	
EI-DHB	Boeing 737-8AS	Ryanair	
EI-DHC	Boeing 737-8AS	Ryanair	
EI-DHD	Boeing 737-8AS	Ryanair	
EI-DHE	Boeing 737-8AS	Ryanair	
EI-DHF	Boeing 737-8AS	Ryanair	
EI-DHG	Boeing 737-8AS	Ryanair	
EI-DHH	Boeing 737-8AS	Ryanair	
EI-DHN	Boeing 737-8AS	Ryanair	
EI-DHO	Boeing 737-8AS	Ryanair	
EI-DHP	Boeing 737-8AS	Ryanair	
EI-DHR	Boeing 737-8AS	Ryanair	
EI-DHS	Boeing 737-8AS	Ryanair	
EI-DHT	Boeing 737-8AS	Ryanair	
EI-DHV	Boeing 737-8AS	Ryanair	
EI-DHW	Boeing 737-8AS	Ryanair	
EI-DHX	Boeing 737-8AS	Ryanair	
EI-DHY	Boeing 737-8AS	Ryanair	
EI-DHZ	Boeing 737-8AS	Ryanair	
EI-DIA	Solar Wings Pegasus XL-Q	P. Byrne	
EI-DIF	PA-31-350 Navajo Chieftain	Flightwise Aviation Ltd & Partners	
EI-DIP	Airbus A.330-202	Alitalia	
EI-DIR	Airbus A.330-202	Alitalia	
EI-DIY	Van's RV-4	J. A. Kent	
EI-DJL	Boeing 767-330ER	Blue Panorama	
EI-DJM	PA-28-161 Warrior II	Waterford Aero Club	
EI-DJY	Grob G.115	Atlantic Flight Training	
EI-DKC	Solar Wings Quasar	K. Daly	
EI-DKE	Air Creation Kiss 450-582	J. Bennett	
EI-DKI	Robinson R22 Beta	P. Gilboy	
EI-DKJ	Thruster T.600N	C. Brogan	
EI-DKK	Raj Hamsa X'Air Jabiru	M. Tolan	
EI-DKN	ELA Aviacion ELA-07 gyrocopter	S. Brennan	
EI-DKT	Raj Hamsa X'Air 582 (11)	S. O'Reilly	
EI-DKU	Air Creation Kiss 450-582 (1)	P. Kirwan	
EI-DKW	Evektor EV-97 Eurostar	Ormand Flying Club	
EI-DKY	Raj Hamsa X'Air 582	M. Clarke	
EI-DKZ	Reality Aircraft Escapade 912 (1)	J. Deegan	
EI-DLB	Boeing 737-8AS	Ryanair	
EI-DLC	Boeing 737-8AS	Ryanair	
EI-DLD	Boeing 737-8AS	Ryanair	
EI-DLE	Boeing 737-8AS	Ryanair	
EI-DLF	Boeing 737-8AS	Ryanair	
EI-DLG	Boeing 737-8AS	Ryanair	
EI-DLH	Boeing 737-8AS	Ryanair	
EI-DLI	Boeing 737-8AS	Ryanair	
EI-DLJ	Boeing 737-8AS	Ryanair	
EI-DLK	Boeing 737-8AS	Ryanair	
EI-DLN	Boeing 737-8AS	Ryanair	
EI-DLO	Boeing 737-8AS	Ryanair	
EI-DLR	Boeing 737-8AS	Ryanair	
EI-DLV	Boeing 737-8AS	Ryanair	
EI-DLW	Boeing 737-8AS	Ryanair	
EI-DLX	Boeing 737-8AS	Ryanair	
EI-DLY	Boeing 737-8AS	Ryanair	
EI-DMA	MS.892E Rallye 150	J. Lynn & Partners	
EI-DMB	Best Off Skyranger 912S (1)	Fun 2 Fly Ltd	
EI-DMC	Schweizer 269C-1	B. Hade	
EI-DMG	Cessna 441	Dawn Meats Group	
EI-DMR	Boeing 737-436	Air One	
EI-DMU	Whittaker MW6S Merlin	M. Heaton	
EI-DNM	Boeing 737-4S3	Transaero	
EI-DNN	Bede BD-5G	H. John & E. M. Cox	

Notes	Reg.	Type	Owner or Operator
	EI-DNO	Bede BD-5G	R. A. Gardiner
	EI-DNR	Raj Hamsa X'Air 582 (5)	N. Furlong & J. Grattan
	EI-DNV	Urban Air UFM-11UK Lambada	F. Maughan
	EI-DOB	Zenair CH-701	D. O'Brien
	EI-DOH	Boeing 737-31S	Transaero
	EI-DOT	Bombardier CL-600-2D24	Air One
	EI-DOU	Bombardier CL-600-2D24	Air One
	EI-DOW	Mainair Blade 912	G. D. Fortune
	EI-DOX	Solar Wings XL-R	T. Noonan
	EI-DOY	PZL Koliber 150A	V. O'Brien & Partners
	EI-DPB	Boeing 737-8AS	Ryanair
	EI-DPC	Boeing 737-8AS	Ryanair
	EI-DPD	Boeing 737-8AS	Ryanair
	EI-DPF	Boeing 737-8AS	Ryanair
	EI-DPG	Boeing 737-8AS	Ryanair
	EI-DPH	Boeing 737-8AS	Ryanair
	EI-DPI	Boeing 737-8AS	Ryanair
	EI-DPJ	Boeing 737-8AS	Ryanair
	EI-DPK	Boeing 737-8AS	Ryanair
	EI-DPL	Boeing 737-8AS	Ryanair
	EI-DPM	Boeing 737-8AS	Ryanair
	EI-DPN	Boeing 737-8AS	Ryanair
	EI-DPO	Boeing 737-8AS	Ryanair
	EI-DPP	Boeing 737-8AS	Ryanair
	EI-DPR	Boeing 737-8AS	Ryanair
	EI-DPS	Boeing 737-8AS	Ryanair
	EI-DPT	Boeing 737-8AS	Ryanair
	EI-DPV	Boeing 737-8AS	Ryanair
	EI-DPW	Boeing 737-8AS	Ryanair
	EI-DPX	Boeing 737-8AS	Ryanair
	EI-DPY	Boeing 737-8AS	Ryanair
	EI-DPZ	Boeing 737-8AS	Ryanair
	EI-DRA	Boeing 737-852	Aeromexico
	EI-DRC	Boeing 737-852	Aeromexico
	EI-DRD	Boeing 737-852	Aeromexico
	EI-DRE	Boeing 737-752	Aeromexico
	EI-DRH	Mainair Blade	J. McErlain
	EI-DRI	Bombardier CL-600-2D24	Air One
	EI-DRJ	Bombardier CL-600-2D24	Air One
	EI-DRK	Bombardier CL-600-2D24	Air One
	EI-DRL	Raj Hamsa X'Air Jabiru	J. O'Connor
	EI-DRM	Urban Air UFM-10 Samba	S. Brennan
	EI-DRT	Air Creation Tanarg 912	P. McMahon
	EI-DRU	Tecnam P92/EM Echo	P. Gallogly
	EI-DRW	Evektor EV-97R Eurostar	Eurostar Flying Club
	EI-DRX	Raj Hamsa X'Air 582 (5)	M. Sheelan & D. McShane
	EI-DSA	Airbus A.320-216	Alitalia
	EI-DSB	Airbus A.320-216	Alitalia
	EI-DSC	Airbus A.320-216	Alitalia
	EI-DSD	Airbus A.320-216	Alitalia
	EI-DSE	Airbus A.320-216	Alitalia
	EI-DSF	Airbus A.320-216	Alitalia
	EI-DSG	Airbus A.320-216	Alitalia
	EI-DSH	Airbus A.320-216	Alitalia
	EI-DSI	Airbus A.320-216	Alitalia
	EI-DSJ	Airbus A.320-216	Alitalia
	EI-DSK	Airbus A.320-216	Alitalia
	EI-DSL	Airbus A.320-216	Alitalia
	EI-DSM	Airbus A.320-216	Alitalia
	EI-DSN	Airbus A.320-216	Alitalia
	EI-DSO	Airbus A.320-216	Alitalia
	EI-DSP	Airbus A.320-216	Alitalia
	EI-DSR	Airbus A.320-216	Alitalia
	EI-DSS	Airbus A.320-216	Alitalia
	EI-DST	Airbus A.320-216	Alitalia
	EI-DSU	Airbus A.320-216	Alitalia
	EI-DSV	Airbus A.320-216	Alitalia
	EI-DSW	Airbus A.320-216	Alitalia
	EI-DSX	Airbus A.320-216	Alitalia
	EI-DSY	Airbus A.320-216	Alitalia
	EI-DSZ	Airbus A.320-216	Alitalia

Reg.	Type	Owner or Operator	Notes
EI-DTA	Airbus A.320-216	Alitalia	
EI-DTB	Airbus A.320-216	Alitalia	
EI-DTC	Airbus A.320-216	Alitalia	
EI-DTD	Airbus A.320-216	Alitalia	
EI-DTE	Airbus A.320-216	Alitalia	
EI-DTF	Airbus A.320-216	Alitalia	
EI-DTG	Airbus A.320-216	Alitalia	
EI-DTH	Airbus A.320-216	Alitalia	
EI-DTI	Airbus A.320-216	Alitalia	
EI-DTJ	Airbus A.320-216	Alitalia	
EI-DTK	Airbus A.320-216	Alitalia	
EI-DTL	Airbus A.320-216	Alitalia	
EI-DTM	Airbus A.320-216	Alitalia	
EI-DTN	Airbus A.320-216	Alitalia	
EI-DTO	Airbus A.320-216	Alitalia	
EI-DTR	Robinson R44	R & M Quarries Ltd	
EI-DTS	PA-18 Super Cub	P. Dunne, K. Synnott & M. Murphy	
EI-DTT	ELA-07 R-100 Gyrocopter	N. Steele	
EI-DTV	Boeing 737-5Y0	Transaero	
EI-DTW	Boeing 737-5Y0	Transaero	
EI-DTX	Boeing 737-5Q8	Transaero	
EI-DUA	Boeing 757-256	Kras Air/AiRUnion	
EI-DUC	Boeing 757-256	Kras Air/AiRUnion	
EI-DUD	Boeing 757-256	Kras Air/AiRUnion	
EI-DUH	Scintex CP.1310C3 Emeraude	W. Kennedy	
EI-DUJ	Evektor EV-97 Eurostar	E. Fitzpatrick	
EI-DUK	Bombardier CL-600-2D24	myAir	
EI-DUL	Alpi Aviation Pioneer	J. Hackett	
EI-DUO	Airbus A.330-203	Aer Lingus	
EI-DUV	Beech 55	J. Given	
EI-DUZ	Airbus A.330-203	Aer Lingus	
EI-DVA	Boeing 737-33A	Mistral Air	
EI-DVC	Boeing 737-33A	Mistral Air	
EI-DVE	Airbus A.320-214	Aer Lingus	
EI-DVG	Airbus A.320-214	Aer Lingus	
EI-DVH	Airbus A.320-214	Aer Lingus	
EI-DVI	Airbus A.320-214	Aer Lingus	
EI-DVJ	Airbus A.320-214	Aer Lingus	
EI-DVK	Airbus A.320-214	Aer Lingus	
EI-DVL	Airbus A.320-214	Aer Lingus	
EI-DVM	Airbus A.320-214	Aer Lingus	
EI-DVN	Airbus A.320-214	Aer Lingus	
EI-DVO	Barnett J4B2	T. Brennan	
EI-DVP	CL-600-2D24	Air One	
EI-DVR	CL-600-2D24	Air One	
EI-DVS	CL-600-2D24	Air One	
EI-DVT	CL-600-2D24	Air One	
EI-DVZ	Robinson R44 II	D. McAuliffe	
EI-DWA	Boeing 737-8AS	Ryanair	
EI-DWB	Boeing 737-8AS	Ryanair	
EI-DWC	Boeing 737-8AS	Ryanair	
EI-DWD	Boeing 737-8AS	Ryanair	
EI-DWE	Boeing 737-8AS	Ryanair	
EI-DWF	Boeing 737-8AS	Ryanair	
EI-DWG	Boeing 737-8AS	Ryanair	
EI-DWH	Boeing 737-8AS	Ryanair	
EI-DWI	Boeing 737-8AS	Ryanair	
EI-DWJ	Boeing 737-8AS	Ryanair	
EI-DWK	Boeing 737-8AS	Ryanair	
EI-DWL	Boeing 737-8AS	Ryanair	
EI-DWM	Boeing 737-8AS	Ryanair	
EI-DWO	Boeing 737-8AS	Ryanair	
EI-DWP	Boeing 737-8AS	Ryanair	
EI-DWR	Boeing 737-8AS	Ryanair	
EI-DWS	Boeing 737-8AS	Ryanair	
EI-DWT	Boeing 737-8AS	Ryanair	
EI-DWV	Boeing 737-8AS	Ryanair	
EI-DWW	Boeing 737-8AS	Ryanair	
EI-DWX	Boeing 737-8AS	Ryanair	
EI-DWY	Boeing 737-8AS	Ryanair	
EI-DWZ	Boeing 737-8AS	Ryanair	

Notes	Reg.	Type	Owner or Operator
	EI-DXA	Ikarus C42	M. Kirrane
	EI-DXL	CFM Shadow	F. Lynch
	EI-DXM	Raj Hamsa X'Air 582	B. Nugent
	EI-DXN	Zenair CH.601HD	N. Gallagher
	EI-DXP	Cyclone AX3/503	J. McCann
	EI-DXS	CFM Shadow	R. W. Frost
	EI-DXT	UrbanAir UFM-10 Samba	N. Irwin
	EI-DXV	Thruster T.600N	P. Higgins
	EI-DXX	Raj Hamsa X'AIR 582(5)	D. Hanly & C. Wright
	EI-DXY	Airbus A.320-212	Rossiya
	EI-DXZ	UrbanAir UFM-10 Samba	D. O'Leary
	EI-DYA	Boeing 737-8AS	Ryanair
	EI-DYB	Boeing 737-8AS	Ryanair
	EI-DYC	Boeing 737-8AS	Ryanair
	EI-DYD	Boeing 737-8AS	Ryanair
	EI-DYE	Boeing 737-8AS	Ryanair
	EI-DYF	Boeing 737-8AS	Ryanair
	EI-DYH	Boeing 737-8AS	Ryanair
	EI-DYI	Boeing 737-8AS	Ryanair
	EI-DYJ	Boeing 737-8AS	Ryanair
	EI-DYK	Boeing 737-8AS	Ryanair
	EI-DYL	Boeing 737-8AS	Ryanair
	EI-DYM	Boeing 737-8AS	Ryanair
	EI-DYN	Boeing 737-8AS	Ryanair
	EI-DYO	Boeing 737-8AS	Ryanair
	EI-DYP	Boeing 737-8AS	Ryanair
	EI-DYR	Boeing 737-8AS	Ryanair
	EI-DYS	Boeing 737-8AS	Ryanair
	EI-DYT	Boeing 737-8AS	Ryanair
	EI-DYV	Boeing 737-8AS	Ryanair
	EI-DYW	Boeing 737-8AS	Ryanair
	EI-DYX	Boeing 737-8AS	Ryanair
	EI-DYY	Boeing 737-8AS	Ryanair
	EI-DYZ	Boeing 737-8AS	Ryanair
	EI-DZA	Colt 21A balloon	P. Baker
	EI-DZB	Colt 21A balloon	P. Baker
	EI-DZE	UrbanAir UFM-10 Samba	P. Keane
	EI-DZF	Pipistrel Sinus 912	Light Sport Aviation Ltd
	EI-DZH	Boeing 767-3Q8ER	Rossiya
	EI-DZK	Robinson R22B2 Beta	Skywest Aviation Ltd
	EI-DZL	Urban Air Samba XXL	M. Tormey
	EI-DZM	Robinson R44 II	A. & G. Thomond Builders Ltd
	EI-DZN	Bell 222	B. McCarty & A. Dalton
	EI-DZO	Dominator Gyroplane Ultrawhite	P. O'Reilly
	EI-DZR	Airbus A.320-212	Rossiya
	EI-DZS	BRM Land Africa	M. Whyte
	EI-EAG	Pipistrel Virus 912	R. Armstrong
	EI-EAJ	RAF-2000GTX-SE	J. P. Henry
	EI-EAK	Airborne Windsports Edge XT	M. O'Brien
	EI-EAM	Cessna 172R	Atlantic Flight Training Ltd
	EI-EAP	Mainair Blade	H. D. Lynch
	EI-EAR	Boeing 767-3Q8ER	Rossiya
	EI-EAV	Airbus A.330-302	Aer Lingus
	EI-EAX	Raj Hamsa X'Air 582 (2)	M. Murphy
	EI-EAY	Raj Hamsa X'Air 582 (5)	R. Smith
	EI-EAZ	Cessna 172R	Atlantic Flight Training Ltd
	EI-EBA	Boeing 737-8AS	Ryanair
	EI-EBB	Boeing 737-8AS	Ryanair
	EI-EBC	Boeing 737-8AS	Ryanair
	EI-EBD	Boeing 737-8AS	Ryanair
	EI-EBE	Boeing 737-8AS	Ryanair
	EI-EBF	Boeing 737-8AS	Ryanair
	EI-EBG	Boeing 737-8AS	Ryanair
	EI-EBH	Boeing 737-8AS	Ryanair
	EI-EBI	Boeing 737-8AS	Ryanair
	EI-EBK	Boeing 737-8AS	Ryanair
	EI-EBL	Boeing 737-8AS	Ryanair
	EI-EBM	Boeing 737-8AS	Ryanair
	EI-EBN	Boeing 737-8AS	Ryanair
	EI-EBO	Boeing 737-8AS	Ryanair
	EI-EBP	Boeing 737-8AS	Ryanair

Reg.	Type	Owner or Operator	Notes
EI-EBR	Boeing 737-8AS	Ryanair	
EI-EBS	Boeing 737-8AS	Ryanair	
EI-EBT	Boeing 737-8AS	Ryanair	
EI-EBV	Boeing 737-8AS	Ryanair	
EI-EBW	Boeing 737-8AS	Ryanair	
EI-EBX	Boeing 737-8AS	Ryanair	
EI-EBY	Boeing 737-8AS	Ryanair	
EI-EBZ	Boeing 737-8AS	Ryanair	
EI-ECB	Boeing 767-3Q8ER	ILFC Ireland	
EI-ECC	Cameron Z-90 balloon	J. J. Daly	
EI-ECG	BRM Land Africa	J. McGuinness	
EI-ECK	Raj Hamsa X'Air Hawk	N. Geh	
EI-ECP	Raj Hamsa X'Air Hawk	R. Gillespie & Partners	
EI-ECR	Cessna 525	Aircraft International Renting Ltd	
EI-ECV	Raj Hamsa X'Air Hawk	D. P. Myers	
EI-ECX	Airbus A.319-132	ILFC Ireland Ltd	
EI-ECY	Airbus A.319-132	ILFC Ireland Ltd	
EI-ECZ	Raj Hamsa X'Air Hawk	M. Tolan	
EI-EDA	Raj Hamsa X'Air Hawk	S. M. Eochgain	
EI-EDB	Cessna 152	K. O'Connor	
EI-EDC	Cessna FA.152	K. O'Connor	
EI-EDI	Ikarus C42	M. Owens	
EI-EDJ	CZAW Sportcruiser	Croftal Ltd	
EI-EDP	Airbus A.320-214	Aer Lingus	
EI-EDR	PA-28R Cherokee Arrow 200	Dublin Flyers	
EI-EDS	Airbus A.320-214	Aer Lingus	
EI-EDY	Airbus A.330-302	Aer Lingus	
EI-EDZ	Boeing 737-8K5	Transaero	
EI-EEA	Boeing 737-8K5	Transaero	
EI-EEB	Boeing 737-73S	AIRES Colombia	
EI-EEH	BRM Land Africa	R. Duffy	
EI-EEO	Van's RV-7	A. Butler	
EI-EES	ELA-07R	D. Doyle & Partners	
EI-EEU	Osprey II	P. Forde & S. Coughlan	
EI-EEV	Boeing 737-73S	AIRES Colombia	
EI-EEW	Boeing 737-375	Blue Panorama	
EI-EEZ	Bombardier CL-600-2B19	Airlink Airways Ltd	
EI-EFA	Boeing 737-8AS	Ryanair	
EI-EFB	Boeing 737-8AS	Ryanair	
EI-EFC	Boeing 737-8AS	Ryanair	
EI-EFD	Boeing 737-8AS	Ryanair	
EI-EFE	Boeing 737-8AS	Ryanair	
EI-EFF	Boeing 737-8AS	Ryanair	
EI-EFG	Boeing 737-8AS	Ryanair	
EI-EFH	Boeing 737-8AS	Ryanair	
EI-EFI	Boeing 737-8AS	Ryanair	
EI-EFJ	Boeing 737-8AS	Ryanair	
EI-EFK	Boeing 737-8AS	Ryanair	
EI-EFL	Boeing 737-8AS	Ryanair	
EI-EFM	Boeing 737-8AS	Ryanair	
EI-EFN	Boeing 737-8AS	Ryanair	
EI-EFO	Boeing 737-8AS	Ryanair	
EI-EFP	Boeing 737-8AS	Ryanair	
EI-EFR	Boeing 737-8AS	Ryanair	
EI-EFS	Boeing 737-8AS	Ryanair	
EI-EFT	Boeing 737-8AS	Ryanair	
EI-EFV	Boeing 737-8AS	Ryanair	
EI-EFW	Boeing 737-8AS	Ryanair	
EI-EFX	Boeing 737-8AS	Ryanair	
EI-EFY	Boeing 737-8AS	Ryanair	
EI-EFZ	Boeing 737-8AS	Ryanair	
EI-EGA	Boeing 737-8AS	Ryanair	
EI-EGB	Boeing 737-8AS	Ryanair	
EI-EGC	Boeing 737-8AS	Ryanair	
EI-EGD	Boeing 737-8AS	Ryanair	
EI-EHG	Robinson R22 Beta	G. Jordan	
EI-EHH	Aerospatiale ATR-42-300	Aer Arran	
EI-EHK	Magni Gyro M-22 Voyager	M. Concannon	
EI-EHL	Air Creation Tanarg/Ixess 15 912S	S. Woods	
EI-EHM	Rand KR-2T	A. Lagun	
EI-EHV	CZAW Sportcruiser	G. Doody & Partners	

Notes	Reg.	Type	Owner or Operator
	EI-EHY	Urban Air Samba XXL	J. K. Woodville
	EI-EIA	Airbus A.320-216	Alitalia
	EI-EIB	Airbus A.320-216	Alitalia
	EI-EIC	Airbus A.320-216	Alitalia
	EI-EID	Airbus A.320-216	Alitalia
	EI-EIE	Airbus A.320-216	Alitalia
	EI-EIG	Airbus A.320-216	Alitalia
	EI-EJG	Airbus A.330-202	Alitalia
	EI-EJH	Airbus A.330-202	Alitalia
	EI-EJI	Airbus A.330-202	Alitalia
	EI-EJJ	Airbus A.330-202	Alitalia
	EI-EJK	Airbus A.330-202	Alitalia
	EI-EJL	Airbus A.330-202	Alitalia
	EI-EJM	Airbus A.330-202	Alitalia
	EI-EJN	Airbus A.330-202	Alitalia
	EI-EJO	Airbus A.330-202	Alitalia
	EI-EJP	Airbus A.330-202	Alitalia
	EI-EKA	Boeing 737-8AS	Ryanair
	EI-EKB	Boeing 737-8AS	Ryanair
	EI-EKC	Boeing 737-8AS	Ryanair
	EI-EKD	Boeing 737-8AS	Ryanair
	EI-EKE	Boeing 737-8AS	Ryanair
	EI-EKF	Boeing 737-8AS	Ryanair
	EI-EKG	Boeing 737-8AS	Ryanair
	EI-EKH	Boeing 737-8AS	Ryanair
	EI-EKI	Boeing 737-8AS	Ryanair
	EI-EKJ	Boeing 737-8AS	Ryanair
	EI-EKK	Boeing 737-8AS	Ryanair
	EI-EKL	Boeing 737-8AS	Ryanair
	EI-EKM	Boeing 737-8AS	Ryanair
	EI-EKN	Boeing 737-8AS	Ryanair
	EI-EKO	Boeing 737-8AS	Ryanair
	EI-EKP	Boeing 737-8AS	Ryanair
	EI-EKR	Boeing 737-8AS	Ryanair
	EI-EKS	Boeing 737-8AS	Ryanair
	EI-EKT	Boeing 737-8AS	Ryanair
	EI-EKV	Boeing 737-8AS	Ryanair
	EI-EKW	Boeing 737-8AS	Ryanair
	EI-EKX	Boeing 737-8AS	Ryanair
	EI-EKY	Boeing 737-8AS	Ryanair
	EI-EKZ	Boeing 737-8AS	Ryanair
	EI-ELA	Airbus A.330-302	Aer Lingus
	EI-ELB	Raj Hamsa X'Air 582 (1)	G. McLaughlin
	EI-ELC	Ikarus C42B	R. Maclaughlin
	EI-ELL	Medway Eclipser	P. McMahon
	EI-ELM	PA-18-95 Super Cub	S. Coughlan
	EI-ELV	Pegasus XL-R	D. Minnock
	EI-ELZ	Boeing 737-4Q8	Mistral Air
	EI-EMA	Boeing 737-8AS	Ryanair
	EI-EMB	Boeing 737-8AS	Ryanair
	EI-EMC	Boeing 737-8AS	Ryanair
	EI-EMD	Boeing 737-8AS	Ryanair
	EI-EME	Boeing 737-8AS	Ryanair
	EI-EMF	Boeing 737-8AS	Ryanair
	EI-EMH	Boeing 737-8AS	Ryanair
	EI-EMI	Boeing 737-8AS	Ryanair
	EI-EMJ	Boeing 737-8AS	Ryanair
	EI-EMK	Boeing 737-8AS	Ryanair
	EI-EML	Boeing 737-8AS	Ryanair
	EI-EMM	Boeing 737-8AS	Ryanair
	EI-EMN	Boeing 737-8AS	Ryanair
	EI-EMO	Boeing 737-8AS	Ryanair
	EI-EMP	Boeing 737-8AS	Ryanair
	EI-EMR	Boeing 737-8AS	Ryanair
	EI-EMT	PA-16 Clipper	J. Dolan
	EI-EMU	Cessna F.152	K. O'Connor
	EI-EMV	CZAW Sportcruiser	L. Doherty & partners
	EI-ENA	Boeing 737-8AS	Ryanair
	EI-ENB	Boeing 737-8AS	Ryanair
	EI-ENC	Boeing 737-8AS	Ryanair
	EI-ENE	Boeing 737-8AS	Ryanair

Reg.	Type	Owner or Operator	Notes
EI-ENF	Boeing 737-8AS	Ryanair	
EI-ENG	Boeing 737-8AS	Ryanair	
EI-ENH	Boeing 737-8AS	Ryanair	
EI-ENI	Boeing 737-8AS	Ryanair	
EI-ENJ	Boeing 737-8AS	Ryanair	
EI-ENK	Boeing 737-8AS	Ryanair	
EI-ENL	Boeing 737-8AS	Ryanair	
EI-ENM	Boeing 737-8AS	Ryanair	
EI-ENN	Boeing 737-8AS	Ryanair	
EI-ENO	Boeing 737-8AS	Ryanair	
EI-ENP	Boeing 737-8AS	Ryanair	
EI-ENR	Boeing 737-8AS	Ryanair	
EI-ENS	Boeing 737-8AS	Ryanair	
EI-ENT	Boeing 737-8AS	Ryanair	
EI-ENV	Boeing 737-8AS	Ryanair	
EI-ENW	Boeing 737-8AS	Ryanair	
EI-ENX	Boeing 737-8AS	Ryanair	
EI-ENY	Boeing 737-8AS	Ryanair	
EI-ENZ	Boeing 737-8AS	Ryanair	
EI-EOA	Raj Hamsa X'Air Jabiru	B. Lynch Jnr	
EI-EOB	Cameron Z-69 balloon	J. Leahy	
EI-EOC	Van's RV-6	D. McCann	
EI-EOE	Boeing 737-505	Engaly Ltd	
EI-EOF	Jabiru SP430	J. Bermingham	
EI-EOH	BRM Land Africa	P. J. Piling	
EI-EOI	Take Off Merlin 1100	N. Fitzmaurice	
EI-EOJ	Boeing 737-8BK	Air Italy Polska	
EI-EOO	Ikarus C42 FB UK	B. Gurnett & Partners	
EI-EOU	Evektor EV-97 Eurostar SL	E. McEvoy	
EI-EOW	Flight Design CTSW	J. Moriarty	
EI-EOZ	Boeing 737-3Q8	Celestial Aviation Trading 21 Ltd	
EI-EPA	Boeing 737-8AS	Ryanair	
EI-EPB	Boeing 737-8AS	Ryanair	
EI-EPC	Boeing 737-8AS	Ryanair	
EI-EPD	Boeing 737-8AS	Ryanair	
EI-EPE	Boeing 737-8AS	Ryanair	
EI-EPF	Boeing 737-8AS	Ryanair	
EI-EPG	Boeing 737-8AS	Ryanair	
EI-EPH	Boeing 737-8AS	Ryanair	
EI-EPI	Medway Hybred 44XLR	H. J. Long	
EI-EPJ	Mainair/Gemini Flash IIA	L. Flannery	
EI-EPK	Pegasus Quantum 15-912	R. A. Atkinson	
EI-EPN	Jodel DR.1050	Conor Airpark Developments Ltd	
EI-EPP	PA-22-160	P. McCabe	
EI-EPR	Airbus A.319-111	Aer Lingus	
EI-EPS	Airbus A.319-111	Aer Lingus	
EI-EPT	Airbus A.319-111	Aer Lingus	
EI-EPU	Airbus A.319-111	Aer Lingus	
EI-EPW	MXP-740 Savannah Jabiru(5)	L. Reilly	
EI-EPY	UFM-11 Lambada	P. Kearney	
EI-EPZ	Jodel DR.1050M1	A. Dunne & Partners	
EI-ERD	Boeing 737-36N	Aircraft Finance Trust Ireland Ltd	
EI-ERE	Pegasus Quantum 15-912	M. Carter	
EI-ERF	Boeing 757-256	I-Fly	
EI-ERH	Airbus A.320-232	New Livingston	
EI-ERI	Air Creation Clipper/Kiss 400-582(1)	E. Redmond	
EI-ERJ	Southdown Raven X	M. Hanley	
EI-ERL	Best Off Sky Ranger 912	B. Chambers	
EI-ERM	Ikarus C42B	C42 Club	
EI-ERO	Pegasus XL-R	M. Doyle	
EI-ERP	Boeing 737-3S3	Transaero	
EI-ERZ	Flight Design CT-2K	M. Bowden	
EI-ESB	Urban Air Samba XXL	G. Creegan	
EI-ESC	BRM Land Africa	D. Killian	
EI-ESD	Mainair Blade	O. Farrell	
EI-ESE	Zenair CH.601XL Zodiac	O. Haslett & Partners	
EI-ESF	PA-22-160	J. Dolan	
EI-ESL	Boeing 737-8AS	Ryanair	
EI-ESM	Boeing 737-8AS	Ryanair	
EI-ESN	Boeing 737-8AS	Ryanair	
EI-ESO	Boeing 737-8AS	Ryanair	

Notes	Reg.	Type	Owner or Operator
	EI-ESP	Boeing 737-8AS	Ryanair
	EI-ESR	Boeing 737-8AS	Ryanair
	EI-ESS	Boeing 737-8AS	Ryanair
	EI-EST	Boeing 737-8AS	Ryanair
	EI-ESV	Boeing 737-8AS	Ryanair
	EI-ESW	Boeing 737-8AS	Ryanair
	EI-ESX	Boeing 737-8AS	Ryanair
	EI-ESY	Boeing 737-8AS	Ryanair
	EI-ESZ	Boeing 737-8AS	Ryanair
	EI-ETB	Ikarus C42B	S. Ryan & Partners
	EI-ETD	Raj Hamsa X'Air Hawk	T. McDevitt
	EI-ETE	MS.880B Rallye	Wicklow Wings Ltd
	EI-ETF	Samba XXL	V. Vaughan
	EI-ETH	Airbus A.321-211	Wilmington Trust SP Services (Dublin) Ltd
	EI-ETI	Airbus A.330-322	Constitution Aircraft Leasing (Ireland) 3 Ltd
	EI-ETJ	Airbus A.321-231	Kolavia
	EI-ETK	Airbus A.321-231	Kolavia
	EI-ETL	Airbus A.321-231	Kolavia
	EI-ETN	Airbus A.319-112	Rossiya
	EI-ETO	Airbus A.319-112	Rossiya
	EI-ETP	Airbus A.319-111	Rossiya
	EI-ETT	Boeing 737-4K5	Mistral Air
	EI-ETU	Ikarus C42 FB UK	A. Leadley
	EI-ETV	Raj Hamsa X'Air Hawk	P. Higgins & Partners
	EI-ETX	Boeing 737-7Q8	Wilmington Trust SP Services (Dublin) Ltd
	EI-EUA	Airbus A.320-232	New Livingston
	EI-EUB	Airbus A.320-232	Palma Aviation Ltd
	EI-EUW	Boeing 737-7Q8	Transaero
	EI-EUX	Boeing 737-7Q8	Transaero
	EI-EUY	Boeing 737-7Q8	Transaero
	EI-EUZ	Boeing 737-7Q8	Transaero
	EI-EVA	Boeing 737-8AS	Ryanair
	EI-EVB	Boeing 737-8AS	Ryanair
	EI-EVC	Boeing 737-8AS	Ryanair
	EI-EVD	Boeing 737-8AS	Ryanair
	EI-EVE	Boeing 737-8AS	Ryanair
	EI-EVF	Boeing 737-8AS	Ryanair
	EI-EVG	Boeing 737-8AS	Ryanair
	EI-EVH	Boeing 737-8AS	Ryanair
	EI-EVI	Boeing 737-8AS	Ryanair
	EI-EVJ	Boeing 737-8AS	Ryanair
	EI-EVK	Boeing 737-8AS	Ryanair
	EI-EVL	Boeing 737-8AS	Ryanair
	EI-EVM	Boeing 737-8AS	Ryanair
	EI-EVN	Boeing 737-8AS	Ryanair
	EI-EVO	Boeing 737-8AS	Ryanair
	EI-EVP	Boeing 737-8AS	Ryanair
	EI-EVR	Boeing 737-8AS	Ryanair
	EI-EVS	Boeing 737-8AS	Ryanair
	EI-EVT	Boeing 737-8AS	Ryanair
	EI-EVV	Boeing 737-8AS	Ryanair
	EI-EVW	Boeing 737-8AS	Ryanair
	EI-EVX	Boeing 737-8AS	Ryanair
	EI-EVY	Boeing 737-8AS	Ryanair
	EI-EVZ	Boeing 737-8AS	Ryanair
	EI-EWB	Ikarus C42B	E. Maguire
	EI-EWC	Beech 76	K. A. O'Connor
	EI-EWI	Boeing 717-2BL	Volotea Airlines
	EI-EWJ	Boeing 717-2BL	Volotea Airlines
	EI-EWO	Airbus A.320-232	Sunflower Aircraft Leasing Ltd
	EI-EWT	Boeing 757-28A	I-Fly
	EI-EWV	Ikarus C42 FB100 VLA	D. Parke
	EI-EWX	Aeropro Eurofox	J. L. Pearson
	EI-EWY	Van's RV-6A	D. Horan & Partners
	EI-EWZ	MB-2 Colibri	Colibri Group
	EI-EXA	Boeing 717-2BL	Volotea Airlines
	EI-EXB	Boeing 717-2BL	Volotea Airlines
	EI-EXD	Boeing 737-8AS	Ryanair
	EI-EXE	Boeing 737-8AS	Ryanair
	EI-EXF	Boeing 737-8AS	Ryanair
	EI-EXI	Boeing 717-2BL	Volotea Airlines

Reg.	Type	Owner or Operator	Notes
EI-EXJ	Boeing 717-2BL	Volotea Airlines	
EI-EXK	Airbus A.320-232	New Livingston	
EI-EXR	Airbus A.300-B4622RF	ILFC Ireland Ltd	
EI-EXY	Urban Air Samba XXL	M. Tormey	
EI-EYD	Airbus A.320-232	ILFC Ireland Ltd	
EI-EYE	Airbus A.320-232	ILFC Ireland Ltd	
EI-EYI	PA-28-181	C. Rooney	
EI-EYJ	Cessna F.172N	K. Fagan	
EI-EYK	Airbus A.300B4-622R	Wilmington Trust SP Services (Dublin) Ltd	
EI-EYL	Airbus A.319-111	Rossiya	
EI-EYM	Airbus A.319-111	Rossiya	
EI-EYN	Murphy Renegade Spirit	L. Blair	
EI-EYO	Airbus A.330-243	Continuity Air Finance (Ireland) 1 Ltd	
EI-EYR	Airbus A.320-214	Rossiya	
EI-EYS	Airbus A.320-214	Rossiya	
EI-EYT	Ikarus C42B	Croom C42 Club	
EI-EYW	Thruster T600N 450	M. O'Carroll	
EI-EYZ	Boeing 757-2Q8	ILFC Ireland Ltd	
EI-EZC	Airbus A.319-112	Celestial Aviation Trading 5 Ltd	
EI-EZD	Airbus A.319-112	Celestial Aviation Trading 5 Ltd	
EI-EZK	Aerospatiale ATR-72-212A	Aircraft International Renting (A.I.R.) Ltd	
EI-EZL	Airbus A.330-223	CIT Aerospace International Ltd	
EI-EZR	Airbus A.320-214	Meridiana	
EI-EZS	Airbus A.320-214	Meridiana	
EI-EZT	Airbus A.320-214	Meridiana	
EI-EZU	Cessna FR.172K	The Hawk Group	
EI-EZV	Airbus A.320-214	Virgin Atlantic Airways *Tartan Lassie*	
EI-EZW	Airbus A.320-214	Virgin Atlantic Airways *Rosie Lee*	
EI-EZX	PA-22-108 Colt	M. Breen & Partners	
EI-EZY	Dominator Ultrawhite	J. Dowling	
EI-EZZ	Raj Hamsa X'Air 582	K. Lannery	
EI-FAB	Eurocopter EC.120B	Billy Jet Ltd	
EI-FAD	Van's RV-7A	J. Lynch & Partners	
EI-FAJ	Airbus A.320-214	CIT Aerospace International	
EI-FAS	Aerospatiale ATR-72-212A	Aer Arran	
EI-FAT	Aerospatiale ATR-72-600	Aer Arran	
EI-FAU	Aerospatiale ATR-72-600	Aer Arran	
EI-FAV	Aerospatiale ATR-72-600	Aer Arran	
EI-FAW	Aerospatiale ATR-72-600	Aer Arran	
EI-FAX	Aerospatiale ATR-72-600	Aer Arran	
EI-FAZ	Aerospatiale ATR-72-600	Aer Arran	
EI-FBA	Airbus A.320-233	Jet-1 34898 Leasing Ltd	
EI-FBB	Airbus A.320-233	Jet-1 35211 Leasing Ltd	
EI-FBC	Cessna 172N	K. O'Connor	
EI-FBF	Airbus A.321-231	Kolavia	
EI-FBH	Airbus A.321-231	Kolavia	
EI-FBJ	Boeing 717-200	Volotea Airlines	
EI-FBK	Boeing 717-2BL	Volotea Airlines	
EI-FBL	Boeing 717-200	Volotea Airlines	
EI-FBM	Boeing 717-2BL	Volotea Airlines	
EI-FBN	Boeing 737-4Q8	Triton Aviation Ireland Ltd	
EI-FBU	Airbus A.330-322	I-Fly	
EI-FBV	Airbus A.321-211	Kolavia	
EI-FBX	BRM Citius	P. Higgins	
EI-FBY	BRM Citius	D. Bolger	
EI-FBZ	Thruster T.600N	V. Vaughan	
EI-FCA	Urban Air UFM-11 Lambada	S. Walshe	
EI-FCB	Boeing 717-200	Volotea Airlines	
EI-FCH	Boeing 737-83N	Alrosa Airlines	
EI-FCI	Zenair CH-601HD	J. Kenny	
EI-FCL	Embraer ERJ190-100LR	SMBC Aviation Capital Leasing Ireland Ltd	
EI-FCM	Embraer ERJ190-100LR	SMBC Aviation Capital Leasing Ireland Ltd	
EI-FCN	Embraer ERJ190-100LR	SMBC Aviation Capital Leasing Ireland Ltd	
EI-FCO	Embraer ERJ190-100LR	SMBC Aviation Caoital Leasing Ireland Ltd	
EI-FCS	Airbus A.320-232	BOC Aviation (Ireland) Ltd	
EI-FCU	Boeing 717-2BL	Volotea Airlines	
EI-FCV	Boeing 767-3X2ER	Blue Panorama	
EI-FCW	Boeing 737-3U3	KV MSN 28733 Aircraft Ltd	
EI-FCY	Aerospatiale ATR-72	Aer Arran	
EI-FDD	Cameron Z-105 balloon	The Travel Department	
EI-FDF	Urban Air Samba XXL	K. Dardis	

Notes	Reg.	Type	Owner or Operator
	EI-FDG	Airbus A.320-232	BOC Aviation (Ireland) Ltd
	EI-FDH	Airbus A.320-232	BOC Aviation (Ireland) Ltd
	EI-FDK	Airbus A.320-214	AWAS Aviation Trading Ltd
	EI-FDN	Airbus A.320-232	Q Aircraft Leasing 2475 Ltd
	EI-FII	Cessna 172RG	K. O'Connor
	EI-FLA	Rotor Flight Dominator	P. Flanagan
	EI-FXA	Aérospatiale ATR-42-300	Air Contractors (Ireland) Ltd
	EI-FXB	Aérospatiale ATR-42-300	Air Contractors (Ireland) Ltd
	EI-FXC	Aérospatiale ATR-42-300	Air Contractors (Ireland) Ltd
	EI-FXD	Aérospatiale ATR-42-300	Air Contractors (Ireland) Ltd
	EI-FXE	Aérospatiale ATR-42-300	Air Contractors (Ireland) Ltd
	EI-FXG	Aérospatiale ATR-72-202	Air Contractors (Ireland) Ltd
	EI-FXH	Aérospatiale ATR-72-202	Air Contractors (Ireland) Ltd
	EI-FXI	Aérospatiale ATR-72-202	Air Contractors (Ireland) Ltd
	EI-FXJ	Aérospatiale ATR-72-202	Air Contractors (Ireland) Ltd
	EI-FXK	Aérospatiale ATR-72-202	Air Contractors (Ireland) Ltd
	EI-GCE	Sikorsky S-61N	CHC Ireland Ltd
	EI-GDJ	Piper J-4E	Ballyboughal J4 Flying Group
	EI-GDL	Gulfstream GV-SP (G550)	Westair Aviation
	EI-GER	Maule MX7-180A	R. Lanigan & J.Patrick
	EI-GJL	AS.365N3	Anglo Beef Processors Ireland
	EI-GLA	Schleicher ASK-21	Dublin Gliding Club Ltd
	EI-GLB	Schleicher ASK-21	Dublin Gliding Club Ltd
	EI-GLC	Centrair 101A Pegase	Dublin Gliding Club Ltd
	EI-GLD	Schleicher ASK-13	Dublin Gliding Club Ltd
	EI-GLF	Schleicher K-8B	Dublin Gliding Club Ltd
	EI-GLG	Schleicher Ka 6CR	C. Sinclair
	EI-GLH	AB Sportine LAK-17A	S. Kinnear
	EI-GLL	Glaser-Dirks DG-200	P. Denman & C. Craig
	EI-GLM	Schleicher Ka-6CR	P. Denman, C. Craig & J. Finnan
	EI-GLO	Scheibe Zugvogel IIIB	J. Walsh, J. Murphy & N. Short
	EI-GLP	Olympia 2B	J. Cashin
	EI-GLS	Rolladen-Schneider LS-7	M. McHugo
	EI-GLT	Schempp-Hirth Discus b	D. Thomas
	EI-GLU	Schleicher Ka-6CR	K. Cullen & Partners
	EI-GLV	Schleicher ASW-19B	C. Sinclair & B. O'Neill
	EI-GMB	Schleicher ASW-17	ASW-17 Group
	EI-GMC	Schleicher ASK-18	The Eighteen Group
	EI-GMD	Phoebus C	F. McDonnell & Partners
	EI-GMF	Schleicher ASK-13	Dublin Gliding Club Ltd
	EI-GML	Grob G.103 Twin Astir	D. McCarthy
	EI-GMN	DG Flugzeugbau DG-808C	K. Houlihan
	EI-GPT	Robinson R22 Beta	Treaty Plant & Tool (Hire & Sales)
	EI-GSE	Cessna F.172M	K. A. O'Connor
	EI-GSM	Cessna 182S	Westpoint Flying Group
	EI-GVM	Robinson R22 Beta	G. V. Maloney
	EI-GWY	Cessna 172R	Atlantic Flight Training
	EI-HCS	Grob G.109B	H. Sydner
	EI-HUM	Van's RV-7	G. Humphreys
	EI-IAN	Pilatus PC-6/B2-H4	Irish Parachute Club
	EI-ICA	Sikorsky S-92A	CHC Ireland Ltd
	EI-ICD	Sikorsky S-92A	CHC Ireland Ltd
	EI-ICG	Sikorsky S-92A	CHC Ireland Ltd
	EI-ICR	Sikorsky S-92A	CHC Ireland Ltd
	EI-ICU	Sikorsky S-92A	CHC Ireland Ltd
	EI-IGN	Boeing 737-84P	Air Italy
	EI-IGP	Boeing 737-7GL	Air Italy
	EI-IGR	Boeing 737-36N	Air Italy
	EI-IGS	Boeing 737-36N	Air Italy
	EI-IGT	Boeing 737-73V	Air Italy
	EI-IGU	Boeing 737-73V	Air Italy
	EI-IKB	Airbus A.320-214	Alitalia
	EI-IKF	Airbus A.320-214	Alitalia
	EI-IKG	Airbus A.320-214	Alitalia
	EI-IKL	Airbus A.320-214	Alitalia
	EI-IKU	Airbus A.320-214	Alitalia
	EI-ILS	Eurocopter EC.135T2+	Irish Helicopters Ltd
	EI-IMB	Airbus A.319-112	Alitalia
	EI-IMC	Airbus A.319-112	Alitalia
	EI-IMD	Airbus A.319-112	Alitalia
	EI-IME	Airbus A.319-112	Alitalia

Reg.	Type	Owner or Operator	Notes
EI-IMF	Airbus A.319-112	Alitalia	
EI-IMG	Airbus A.319-112	Alitalia	
EI-IMH	Airbus A.319-112	Alitalia	
EI-IMI	Airbus A.319-112	Alitalia	
EI-IMJ	Airbus A.319-112	Alitalia	
EI-IML	Airbus A.319-112	Alitalia	
EI-IMM	Airbus A.319-112	Alitalia	
EI-IMN	Airbus A.319-111	Alitalia	
EI-IMO	Airbus A.319-111	Alitalia	
EI-IMP	Airbus A.319-111	Alitalia	
EI-IMR	Airbus A.319-111	Alitalia	
EI-IMS	Airbus A.319-111	Alitalia	
EI-IMT	Airbus A.319-111	Alitalia	
EI-IMU	Airbus A.319-111	Alitalia	
EI-IMV	Airbus A.319-111	Alitalia	
EI-IMW	Airbus A.319-111	Alitalia	
EI-IMX	Airbus A.319-111	Alitalia	
EI-ING	Cessna F.172P	21st Century Flyers	
EI-ISA	Boeing 777-243ER	Alitalia	
EI-ISB	Boeing 777-243ER	Alitalia	
EI-ISD	Boeing 777-243ER	Alitalia	
EI-ISE	Boeing 777-243ER	Alitalia	
EI-ISO	Boeing 777-243ER	Alitalia	
EI-IXB	Airbus A.321-112	Alitalia	
EI-IXC	Airbus A.321-112	Alitalia	
EI-IXD	Airbus A.321-112	Alitalia	
EI-IXF	Airbus A.321-112	Alitalia	
EI-IXG	Airbus A.321-112	Alitalia	
EI-IXH	Airbus A.321-112	Alitalia	
EI-IXI	Airbus A.321-112	Alitalia	
EI-IXJ	Airbus A.321-112	Alitalia	
EI-IXO	Airbus A.321-112	Alitalia	
EI-IXU	Airbus A.321-112	Alitalia	
EI-IXV	Airbus A.321-112	Alitalia	
EI-IXZ	Airbus A.321-112	Alitalia	
EI-JIM	Urban Air Samba XLA	J. Smith	
EI-JIV	L.382G-44K-30 Hercules	Air Contractors (Ireland)	
EI-JOR	Robinson R44 II	Skywest Aviation Ltd	
EI-JPK	Tecnam P2002-JF	Limerick Flying Club (Coonagh) Ltd	
EI-KDH	PA-28-181 Archer II	K. O'Driscoll & D. Harris	
EI-KEL	Eurocopter EC.135T2+	Bond Air Services (Ireland) Ltd	
EI-KEV	Raj Hamsa X'Air Jabiru(3)	P. Kearney	
EI-LAD	Robinson R44 II	J. Harney & Partners	
EI-LAX	Airbus A.330-202	Aer Lingus St Mella	
EI-LBR	Boeing 757-2Q8	Air Contractors (Ireland) Ltd	
EI-LCM	TBM-700N	G. Power	
EI-LEM	SOCATA TB9 Tampico	M. Fleing	
EI-LFC	Tecnam P.2002-JF	Limerick Flying Club (Coonagh) Ltd	
EI-LIR	Airbus A.319-132	Belle Air	
EI-LIS	Airbus A.320-214	Belle Air	
EI-LNA	Boeing 787-8	Norwegian Air Shuttle	
EI-LNB	Boeing 787-8	Norwegian Air Shuttle	
EI-LNC	Boeing 787-8	Norwegian Air Shuttle	
EI-LOW	AS.355N	Executive Helicopter Maintenance Ltd	
EI-LSA	Cub Crafters CC11-160	Directsky Aviation Ltd	
EI-MCF	Cessna 172R	K. O'Connor	
EI-MCG	Cessna 172R	Galway Flying Club	
EI-MIR	Roko Aero NG 4HD	H. Goulding	
EI-MPW	Robinson R44	Connacht Helicopters	
EI-MSG	Agusta A.109E	Beckdrive Ltd	
EI-MTZ	Urban Air Samba XXL	M. Motz	
EI-NFW	Cessna 172S	Galway Flying Club	
EI-NJA	Robinson R44 II	Nojo Aviation Ltd	
EI-NVL	Jora spol S. R. O. Jora	A. McAllister & partners	
EI-ODD	Bell 206B JetRanger	Dwyer Nolan Developments Ltd	
EI-OFM	Cessna F.172N	C. Phillips	
EI-OOR	Cessna 172S	M. Casey	
EI-OZD	Airbus A.300B4-203F	Air Contractors/DHL	
EI-OZE	Airbus A.300B4-203F	Air Contractors/DHL	
EI-OZF	Airbus A.300B4-203F	Air Contractors/DHL	
EI-OZJ	Airbus A.300B4-622R	Air Contractors/DHL	

Notes	Reg.	Type	Owner or Operator
	EI-OZK	Airbus A.300B4-622RF	Air Contractors/DHL
	EI-PCI	Bell 206B JetRanger	Malcove Ltd
	EI-PJD	AS.350B2 Twin Squirrel	New World Plant
	EI-PMI	Agusta-Bell 206B JetRanger III	Eirland Ltd
	EI-POP	Cameron Z-90 balloon	The Travel Department
	EI-RCA	Roko Aero NG4UL	Racecrest Ltd
	EI-RCG	Sikorsky S-61N	CHC Ireland
	EI-RDA	Embraer ERJ170-200LR	Alitalia Cityliner
	EI-RDB	Embraer ERJ170-200LR	Alitalia Cityliner
	EI-RDC	Embraer ERJ170-200LR	Alitalia Cityliner
	EI-RDD	Embraer ERJ170-200LR	Alitalia Cityliner
	EI-RDE	Embraer ERJ170-200LR	Alitalia Cityliner
	EI-RDF	Embraer ERJ170-200LR	Alitalia Cityliner
	EI-RDG	Embraer ERJ170-200LR	Alitalia Cityliner
	EI-RDH	Embraer ERJ170-200LR	Alitalia Cityliner
	EI-RDI	Embraer ERJ170-200LR	Alitalia Cityliner
	EI-RDJ	Embraer ERJ170-200LR	Alitalia Cityliner
	EI-RDK	Embraer ERJ170-200LR	Alitalia Cityliner
	EI-RDL	Embraer ERJ170-200LR	Alitalia Cityliner
	EI-RDM	Embraer ERJ170-200LR	Alitalia Cityliner
	EI-RDN	Embraer ERJ170-200LR	Alitalia Cityliner
	EI-RDO	Embraer ERJ170-200LR	Alitalia Cityliner
	EI-REH	Aérospatiale ATR-72-201	Aer Arann
	EI-REI	Aérospatiale ATR-72-201	Aer Arann
	EI-REJ	Aérospatiale ATR-72-201	Air Contractgors (Ireland) Ltd
	EI-REL	Aerospatiale ATR-72-212	Aer Arann
	EI-REM	Aerospatiale ATR-72-212	Aer Arann
	EI-REX	Learjet 60	Airlink Airways
	EI-RHM	Bell 407	A. Morrin
	EI-RJA	Avro RJ85	Cityjet
	EI-RJB	Avro RJ85	Cityjet Bere Island
	EI-RJC	Avro RJ85	Cityjet
	EI-RJD	Avro RJ85	Cityjet
	EI-RJE	Avro RJ85	Cityjet
	EI-RJF	Avro RJ85	Cityjet
	EI-RJG	Avro RJ85	Cityjet
	EI-RJH	Avro RJ85	Cityjet
	EI-RJI	Avro RJ85	Cityjet
	EI-RJJ	Avro RJ85	Cityjet
	EI-RJN	Avro RJ85	Cityjet
	EI-RJO	Avro RJ85	Cityjet
	EI-RJR	Avro RJ85	Cityjet
	EI-RJS	Avro RJ85	Cityjet Dursey Island
	EI-RJT	Avro RJ85	Cityjet
	EI-RJU	Avro RJ85	Cityjet
	EI-RJW	Avro RJ85	Cityjet Garinish Island
	EI-RJX	Avro RJ85	Cityjet
	EI-RJY	Avro RJ85	Cityjet
	EI-RJZ	Avro RJ85	Cityjet
	EI-RMC	Bell 206B JetRanger	Westair Aviation
	EI-RNA	Embraer ERJ190-100STD	Alitalia Cityliner
	EI-RNB	Embraer ERJ190-100STD	Alitalia Cityliner
	EI-RNC	Embraer ERJ190-100STD	Alitalia Cityliner
	EI-RND	Embraer ERJ190-100STD	Alitalia Cityliner
	EI-RNE	Embraer ERJ190-100STD	Alitalia Cityliner
	EI-ROB	Robin R.1180TD	Extras Ltd
	EI-ROK	Roko Aero NG 4UL	K. Harley
	EI-RUA	Boeing 737-86J	Transaero
	EI-RUB	Boeing 737-85P	Transaero
	EI-RUC	Boeing 737-86R	Transaero
	EI-RUD	Boeing 737-86R	Transaero
	EI-RUE	Boeing 737-85P	Transaero
	EI-RUF	Boeing 737-85P	Transaero
	EI-RUG	Boeing 737-86N	Transaero
	EI-RUH	Boeing 737-8K5	Transaero
	EI-RUI	Boeing 737-85P	Transaero
	EI-RUJ	Boeing 737-81Q	Transaero
	EI-RUK	Boeing 737-86N	Transaero
	EI-RUL	Boeing 737-7K9	Transaero
	EI-RUM	Boeing 737-7K9	Transaero

Reg.	Type	Owner or Operator	Notes
EI-RUY	Boeing 767-3Q8ER	Transaero	
EI-RUZ	Boeing 767-3Q8ER	Transaero	
EI-SAC	Cessna 172P	Sligo Aero Club	
EI-SAI	Eurocopter SA.330J	Heavylift Charters Ltd	
EI-SAR	Sikorsky S-61N	CHC Ireland	
EI-SEA	SeaRey	J. Brennan	
EI-SKB	PA-44-180 Seminole	Shemburn Ltd	
EI-SKC	PA-44-180 Seminole	Shemburn Ltd	
EI-SKE	Robin DR400/140B	Shemburn Ltd	
EI-SKR	PA-44-180 Seminole	Shemburn Ltd	
EI-SKS	Robin R.2160	Shemburn Ltd	
EI-SKT	PA-44-180 Seminole	Shemburn Ltd	
EI-SKV	Robin R.2160	Shemburn Ltd	
EI-SKW	PA-28-161 Warrior II	Shemburn Ltd	
EI-SLA	Aérospatiale ATR-42-310	Air Contractors (Ireland) Ltd	
EI-SLF	Aérospatiale ATR-72-201	Air Contractors (Ireland) Ltd	
EI-SLG	Aérospatiale ATR-72-202	Air Contractors (Ireland) Ltd	
EI-SLH	Aerospatiale ATR-72-202	Air Contractors (Ireland) Ltd	
EI-SLJ	Aerospatiale ATR-72-201	Air Contractors (Ireland) Ltd	
EI-SLK	Aerospatiale ATR-72-212	Air Contractors (Ireland) Ltd	
EI-SLN	Aerospatiale ATR-72-212	Air Contractors (Ireland) Ltd/Aer Arran	
EI-SMK	Zenair CH701	S. King	
EI-SPB	Cessna T206H	P. Morrissey	
EI-SSF	Bombardier BD700-1A10	Airlink Airways Ltd	
EI-STA	Boeing 737-31S	Air Contractors (Ireland) Ltd/Europe Airpost	
EI-STB	Boeing 737-476F	Air Contractors (Ireland) Ltd	
EI-STC	Boeing 737-476	Air Contractors (Ireland) Ltd	
EI-STD	Boeing 737-476F	Air Contractors (Ireland) Ltd	
EI-STE	Boeing 737-4YOF	Air Contractors (Ireland) Ltd	
EI-STT	Cessna 172M	Trim Flying Club	
EI-SYM	Van's RV-7	E. Symes	
EI-TAT	Bombardier CL600-2B16	Bandon Aircraft Leasing Ltd	
EI-TDV	Dassault Falcon 2000LX	Herodias Executive Aircraft	
EI-TIM	Piper J-5A	N. & P. Murphy	
EI-TKI	Robinson R22 Beta	J. McDaid	
EI-TLP	Airbus A.320-232	Flying Fortress Ireland Leasing Ltd	
EI-TON	M. B. Cooke 582 (5)	T. Merrigan	
EI-UFO	PA-22 Tri-Pacer 150 (tailwheel)	W. Treacy	
EI-UNA	Boeing 767-3P6ER	Transaero	
EI-UNB	Boeing 767-3P6ER	Transaero	
EI-UNC	Boeing 767-319ER	Transaero	
EI-UND	Boeing 767-2P6ER	Transaero	
EI-UNE	Boeing 767-3Q8ER	Transaero	
EI-UNF	Boeing 767-3P6ER	Transaero	
EI-UNG	Boeing 737-524	Transaero	
EI-UNH	Boeing 737-524	Transaero	
EI-UNI	Robinson R44 II	Unipipe (Irl) Ltd	
EI-UNJ	Boeing 737-86J	Transaero	
EI-UNK	Boeing 737-86J	Transaero	
EI-UNL	Boeing 777-312	Transaero	
EI-UNM	Boeing 777-312	Transaero	
EI-UNN	Boeing 777-312	Transaero	
EI-UNP	Boeing 777-312	Transaero	
EI-UNR	Boeing 777-212ER	Transaero	
EI-UNS	Boeing 777-212ER	Transaero	
EI-UNT	Boeing 777-212ER	Transaero	
EI-UNU	Boeing 777-222ER	Transaero	
EI-UNV	Boeing 777-222ER	Transaero	
EI-UNW	Boeing 777-222	Transaero	
EI-UNX	Boeing 777-222	Transaero	
EI-UNY	Boeing 777-222	Transaero	
EI-UNZ	Boeing 777-222	Transaero	
EI-VII	Vans RV-7	B. Sheane	
EI-VLN	PA-18A-150	D. O'Mahony	
EI-WAC	PA-23 Aztec 250E	Westair Aviation	
EI-WAT	Tecnam P.2002-JF	Waterford Aero Club Ltd	
EI-WAV	Bell 430	Westair Aviation	
EI-WFD	Tecnam P.2002-JF	Waterford Aero Club Ltd	
EI-WFI	Bombardier CL600-2B16 Challenger	Midwest Atlantic/Westair	
EI-WIG	Sky Ranger 912	M. Brereton	
EI-WMN	PA-23 Aztec 250F	Westair Aviation	

Notes	Reg.	Type	Owner or Operator
	EI-WOT	Currie Wot	D. Doyle & Partners
	EI-WWI	Robinson R44 II	J. Murtagh
	EI-WXA	Avro RJ85	Cityjet Ltd
	EI-WXP	Hawker 800XP	Westair Aviation Ltd
	EI-XLA	Urban Air Samba XLA	K. Dardis
	EI-XLB	Boeing 747-446	Transaero
	EI-XLC	Boeing 747-446	Transaero
	EI-XLD	Boeing 747-446	Transaero
	EI-XLE	Boeing 747-446	Transaero
	EI-XLF	Boeing 747-446	Transaero
	EI-XLG	Boeing 747-446	Transaero
	EI-XLH	Boeing 747-446	Transaero
	EI-XLI	Boeing 747-446	Transaero
	EI-XLJ	Boeing 747-446	Transaero
	EI-XLK	Boeing 747-412	Transaero
	EI-XLL	Boeing 747-412	Transaero
	EI-XLM	Boeing 747-412	Transaero
	EI-XLN	Boeing 747-412	Transaero
	EI-XLO	Boeing 747-412	Transaero
	EI-XLP	Boeing 777-312	Transaero
	EI-XLS	Cessna 560XL	Airlink Airways Ltd
	EI-XLZ	Boeing 747-444	Transaero
	EI-YLG	Robin HR.200/120B	Leinster Aero Club
	EI-ZMA	Falcon 900EX	Airlink Airways Ltd
	EI-ZZZ	Bel222	Executive Helicopter Maintenance Ltd

EI-EZV Airbus A.320-214 of Virgin Atlantic. *Allan S. Wright*

EI-EZX Piper PA-22-108 Colt. *Allan S. Wright*

EI-JIV Lockheed L.382G-44K-30 Hercules of Air Contractors. *Tom Cole*

Reg.	Type	Owner or Operator	Notes

(Aircraft included in this section are those most likely to be seen at UK and nearby European airports or overflying UK airspace.)

A6 (Arab Emirates)

Reg.	Type	Owner or Operator
A6-AFA	Airbus A.330-343X	Etihad Airways
A6-AFB	Airbus A.330-343X	Etihad Airways
A6-AFC	Airbus A.330-343X	Etihad Airways
A6-AFD	Airbus A.330-343X	Etihad Airways
A6-AFE	Airbus A.330-343X	Etihad Airways
A6-AFF	Airbus A.330-343X	Etihad Airways
A6-EAD	Airbus A.330-243	Emirates Airlines
A6-EAE	Airbus A.330-243	Emirates Airlines
A6-EAF	Airbus A.330-243	Emirates Airlines
A6-EAG	Airbus A.330-243	Emirates Airlines
A6-EAH	Airbus A.330-243	Emirates Airlines
A6-EAI	Airbus A.330-243	Emirates Airlines
A6-EAK	Airbus A.330-243	Emirates Airlines
A6-EAM	Airbus A.330-243	Emirates Airlines
A6-EAO	Airbus A.330-243	Emirates Airlines
A6-EAP	Airbus A.330-243	Emirates Airlines
A6-EAQ	Airbus A.330-243	Emirates Airlines
A6-EAR	Airbus A.330-243	Emirates Airlines
A6-EAS	Airbus A.330-243	Emirates Airlines
A6-EBA	Boeing 777-31HER	Emirates Airlines
A6-EBB	Boeing 777-36NER	Emirates Airlines
A6-EBC	Boeing 777-36NER	Emirates Airlines
A6-EBD	Boeing 777-31HER	Emirates Airlines
A6-EBE	Boeing 777-36NER	Emirates Airlines
A6-EBF	Boeing 777-31HER	Emirates Airlines
A6-EBG	Boeing 777-36NER	Emirates Airlines
A6-EBH	Boeing 777-31HER	Emirates Airlines
A6-EBI	Boeing 777-36NER	Emirates Airlines
A6-EBJ	Boeing 777-36NER	Emirates Airlines
A6-EBK	Boeing 777-31HER	Emirates Airlines
A6-EBL	Boeing 777-31HER	Emirates Airlines
A6-EBM	Boeing 777-31HER	Emirates Airlines
A6-EBN	Boeing 777-36NER	Emirates Airlines
A6-EBO	Boeing 777-36NER	Emirates Airlines
A6-EBP	Boeing 777-31HER	Emirates Airlines
A6-EBQ	Boeing 777-36NER	Emirates Airlines
A6-EBR	Boeing 777-31HER	Emirates Airlines
A6-EBS	Boeing 777-31HER	Emirates Airlines
A6-EBT	Boeing 777-31HER	Emirates Airlines
A6-EBU	Boeing 777-31HER	Emirates Airlines
A6-EBV	Boeing 777-31HER	Emirates Airlines
A6-EBW	Boeing 777-36NER	Emirates Airlines
A6-EBX	Boeing 777-31HER	Emirates Airlines
A6-EBY	Boeing 777-36NER	Emirates Airlines
A6-EBZ	Boeing 777-31HER	Emirates Airlines
A6-ECA	Boeing 777-36NER	Emirates Airlines
A6-ECB	Boeing 777-31HER	Emirates Airlines
A6-ECC	Boeing 777-36NER	Emirates Airlines
A6-ECD	Boeing 777-36NER	Emirates Airlines
A6-ECE	Boeing 777-31HER	Emirates Airlines
A6-ECF	Boeing 777-31HER	Emirates Airlines
A6-ECG	Boeing 777-31HER	Emirates Airlines
A6-ECH	Boeing 777-31HER	Emirates Airlines
A6-ECI	Boeing 777-31HER	Emirates Airlines
A6-ECJ	Boeing 777-31HER	Emirates Airlines
A6-ECK	Boeing 777-31HER	Emirates Airlines
A6-ECL	Boeing 777-31NER	Emirates Airlines
A6-ECM	Boeing 777-31NER	Emirates Airlines
A6-ECN	Boeing 777-31NER	Emirates Airlines
A6-ECO	Boeinb 777-31NER	Emirates Airlines
A6-ECP	Boeing 777-31HER	Emirates Airlines
A6-ECQ	Boeing 777-31HER	Emirates Airlines
A6-ECR	Boeing 777-31HER	Emirates Airlines
A6-ECS	Boeing 777-31HER	Emirates Airlines

Notes	Reg.	Type	Owner or Operator
	A6-ECT	Boeing 777-31HER	Emirates Airlines
	A6-ECU	Boeing 777-31HER	Emirates Airlines
	A6-ECV	Boeing 777-31HER	Emirates Airlines
	A6-ECW	Boeing 777-31HER	Emirates Airlines
	A6-ECX	Boeing 777-31HER	Emirates Airlines
	A6-ECY	Boeing 777-31HER	Emirates Airlines
	A6-ECZ	Boeing 777-31HER	Emirates Airlines
	A6-EDA	Airbus A.380-861	Emirates Airlines
	A6-EDB	Airbus A.380-861	Emirates Airlines
	A6-EDC	Airbus A.380-861	Emirates Airlines
	A6-EDD	Airbus A.380-861	Emirates Airlines
	A6-EDE	Airbus A.380-861	Emirates Airlines
	A6-EDF	Airbus A.380-861	Emirates Airlines
	A6-EDG	Airbus A.380-861	Emirates Airlines
	A6-EDH	Airbus A.380-861	Emirates Airlines
	A6-EDI	Airbus A.380-861	Emirates Airlines
	A6-EDJ	Airbus A.380-861	Emirates Airlines
	A6-EDK	Airbus A.380-861	Emirates Airlines
	A6-EDL	Airbus A.380-861	Emirates Airlines
	A6-EDM	Airbus A.380-861	Emirates Airlines
	A6-EDN	Airbus A.380-861	Emirates Airlines
	A6-EDO	Airbus A.380-861	Emirates Airlines
	A6-EDP	Airbus A.380-861	Emirates Airlines
	A6-EDQ	Airbus A.380-861	Emirates Airlines
	A6-EDR	Airbus A.380-861	Emirates Airlines
	A6-EDS	Airbus A.380-861	Emirates Airlines
	A6-EDT	Airbus A.380-861	Emirates Airlines
	A6-EDU	Airbus A.380-861	Emirates Airlines
	A6-EDV	Airbus A.380-861	Emirates Airlines
	A6-EDW	Airbus A.380-861	Emirates Airlines
	A6-EDX	Airbus A.380-861	Emirates Airlines
	A6-EDY	Airbus A.380-861	Emirates Airlines
	A6-EDZ	Airbus A.380-861	Emirates Airlines
	A6-EEA	Airbus A.380-861	Emirates Airlines
	A6-EEB	Airbus A.380-861	Emirates Airlines
	A6-EEC	Airbus A.380-861	Emirates Airlines
	A6-EED	Airbus A.380-861	Emirates Airlines
	A6-EEE	Airbus A.380-861	Emirates Airlines
	A6-EEF	Airbus A.380-861	Emirates Airlines
	A6-EEG	Airbus A.380-861	Emirates Airlines
	A6-EEH	Airbus A.380-861	Emirates Airlines
	A6-EEI	Airbus A.380-861	Emirates Airlines
	A6-EEJ	Airbus A.380-861	Emirates Airlines
	A6-EEK	Airbus A,380-861	Emirates Airlines
	A6-EEL	Airbus A.380-861	Emirates Airlines
	A6-EEM	Airbus A.380-861	Emirates Airlines
	A6-EEN	Airbus A.380-861	Emirates Airlines
	A6-EEO	Airbus A.380-861	Emirates Airlines
	A6-EEP	Airbus A.380-861	Emirates Airlines
	A6-EEQ	Airbus A.380-861	Emirates Airlines
	A6-EER	Airbus A.380-861	Emirates Airlines
	A6-EES	Airbus A.380-861	Emirates Airlines
	A6-EET	Airbus A.380-861	Emirates Airlines
	A6-EEU	Airbus A.380-861	Emirates Airlines
	A6-EEV	Airbus A.380-861	Emirates Airlines
	A6-EEW	Airbus A.380-861	Emirates Airlines
	A6-EFD	Boeing 777-21H	Emirates Airlines
	A6-EFE	Boeing 777-21H	Emirates Airlines
	A6-EFF	Boeing 777-21H	Emirates Airlines
	A6-EFG	Boeing 777-21H	Emirates Airlines
	A6-EFH	Boeing 777-21H	Emirates Airlines
	A6-EFI	Boeing 777-21H	Emirates Airlines
	A6-EFJ	Boeing 777-21H	Emirates Airlines
	A6-EGA	Boeing 777-31HER	Emirates Airlines
	A6-EGB	Boeing 777-31HER	Emirates Airlines
	A6-EGC	Boeing 777-31HER	Emirates Airlines
	A6-EGD	Boeing 777-31HER	Emirates Airlines
	A6-EGE	Boeing 777-31HER	Emirates Airlines
	A6-EGF	Boeing 777-31HER	Emirates Airlines
	A6-EGG	Boeing 777-31HER	Emirates Airlines
	A6-EGH	Boeing 777-31HER	Emirates Airlines
	A6-EGI	Boeing 777-31HER	Emirates Airlines

Reg.	Type	Owner or Operator	Notes
A6-EGJ	Boeing 777-31HER	Emirates Airlines	
A6-EGK	Boeing 777-31HER	Emirates Airlines	
A6-EGL	Boeing 777-31HER	Emirates Airlines	
A6-EGM	Boeing 777-31HER	Emirates Airlines	
A6-EGN	Boeing 777-31HER	Emirates Airlines	
A6-EGO	Boeing 777-31HER	Emirates Airlines	
A6-EGP	Boeing 777-31HER	Emirates Airlines	
A6-EGQ	Boeing 777-31HER	Emirates Airlines	
A6-EGR	Boeing 777-31HER	Emirates Airlines	
A6-EGS	Boeing 777-31HER	Emirates Airlines	
A6-EGT	Boeing 777-31HER	Emirates Airlines	
A6-EGU	Boeing 777-31HER	Emirates Airlines	
A6-EGV	Boeing 777-31HER	Emirates Airlines	
A6-EGW	Boeing 777-31HER	Emirates Airlines	
A6-EGX	Boeing 777-31HER	Emirates Airlines	
A6-EGY	Boeing 777-31HER	Emirates Airlines	
A6-EGZ	Boeing 777-31HER	Emirates Airlines	
A6-EHA	Airbus A.340-541	Etihad Airways	
A6-EHB	Airbus A.340-541	Etihad Airways	
A6-EHC	Airbus A.340-541	Etihad Airways	
A6-EHD	Airbus A.340-541	Etihad Airways	
A6-EHE	Airbus A.340-642	Etihad Airways	
A6-EHF	Airbus A.340-642	Etihad Airways	
A6-EHH	Airbus A.340-642	Etihad Airways	
A6-EHI	Airbus A.340-642	Etihad Airways	
A6-EHJ	Airbus A.340-642	Etihad Airways	
A6-EHK	Airbus A.340-642	Etihad Airways	
A6-EHL	Airbus A.340-642	Etihad Airways	
A6-EKQ	Airbus A.330-243	Emirates Airlines	
A6-EKR	Airbus A.330-243	Emirates Airlines	
A6-EKS	Airbus A.330-243	Emirates Airlines	
A6-EKT	Airbus A.330-243	Emirates Airlines	
A6-EKU	Airbus A.330-243	Emirates Airlines	
A6-EKV	Airbus A.330-243	Emirates Airlines	
A6-EKW	Airbus A.330-243	Emirates Airlines	
A6-EKX	Airbus A.330-243	Emirates Airlines	
A6-EKY	Airbus A.330-243	Emirates Airlines	
A6-EMD	Boeing 777-21H	Emirates Airlines	
A6-EME	Boeing 777-21H	Emirates Airlines	
A6-EMF	Boeing 777-21H	Emirates Airlines	
A6-EMG	Boeing 777-21HER	Emirates Airlines	
A6-EMH	Boeing 777-21HER	Emirates Airlines	
A6-EMI	Boeing 777-21HER	Emirates Airlines	
A6-EMJ	Boeing 777-21HER	Emirates Airlines	
A6-EMK	Boeing 777-21HER	Emirates Airlines	
A6-EML	Boeing 777-21HER	Emirates Airlines	
A6-EMM	Boeing 777-31H	Emirates Airlines	
A6-EMN	Boeing 777-31H	Emirates Airlines	
A6-EMO	Boeing 777-31H	Emirates Airlines	
A6-EMP	Boeing 777-31H	Emirates Airlines	
A6-EMQ	Boeing 777-31H	Emirates Airlines	
A6-EMR	Boeing 777-31H	Emirates Airlines	
A6-EMS	Boeing 777-31H	Emirates Airlines	
A6-EMT	Boeing 777-31H	Emirates Airlines	
A6-EMU	Boeing 777-31H	Emirates Airlines	
A6-EMV	Boeing 777-31H	Emirates Airlines	
A6-EMW	Boeing 777-31H	Emirates Airlines	
A6-EMX	Boeing 777-31H	Emirates Airlines	
A6-ENA	Boeing 777-31HER	Emirates Airlines	
A6-ENB	Boeing 777-31HER	Emirates Airlines	
A6-ENC	Boeing 777-31HER	Emirates Airlines	
A6-END	Boeing 777-31HER	Emirates Airlines	
A6-ENE	Boeing 777-31HER	Emirates Airlines	
A6-ENF	Boeing 777-31HER	Emirates Airlines	
A6-ENG	Boeing 777-31HER	Emirates Airlines	
A6-ENH	Boeing 777-31HER	Emirates Airlines	
A6-ENI	Boeing 777-31HER	Emirates Airlines	
A6-ENJ	Boeing 777-31HER	Emirates Airlines	
A6-ENK	Boeing 777-31HER	Emirates Airlines	
A6-ENL	Boeing 777-31HER	Emirates Airlines	
A6-ENM	Boeing 777-31HER	Emirates Airlines	
A6-ENN	Boeing 777-31HER	Emirates Airlines	

Notes	Reg.	Type	Owner or Operator
	A6-ERA	Airbus A.340-541	Emirates Airlines
	A6-ERB	Airbus A.340-541	Emirates Airlines
	A6-ERC	Airbus A.340-541	Emirates Airlines
	A6-ERD	Airbus A.340-541	Emirates Airlines
	A6-ERE	Airbus A.340-541	Emirates Airlines
	A6-ERF	Airbus A.340-541	Emirates Airlines
	A6-ERG	Airbus A.340-541	Emirates Airlines
	A6-ERH	Airbus A.340-541	Emirates Airlines
	A6-ERI	Airbus A.340-541	Emirates Airlines
	A6-ERJ	Airbus A.340-541	Emirates Airlines
	A6-ERM	Airbus A.340-313X	Emirates Airlines
	A6-ERN	Airbus A.340-313X	Emirates Airlines
	A6-ERO	Airbus A.340-313X	Emirates Airlines
	A6-ERP	Airbus A.340-313X	Emirates Airlines
	A6-ETA	Boeing 777-3FXER	Etihad Airways
	A6-ETB	Boeing 777-3FXER	Etihad Airways
	A6-ETC	Boeing 777-3FXER	Etihad Airways
	A6-ETD	Boeing 777-3FXER	Etihad Airways
	A6-ETE	Boeing 777-3FXER	Etihad Airways
	A6-ETF	Boeing 777-3FXER	Etihad Airways
	A6-ETG	Boeing 777-3FXER	Etihad Airways
	A6-ETH	Boeing 777-3FXER	Etihad Airways
	A6-ETI	Boeing 777-3FXER	Etihad Airways
	A6-ETJ	Boeing 777-3FXER	Etihad Airways
	A6-ETK	Boeing 777-3FXER	Etihad Airways
	A6-ETL	Boeing 777-3FXER	Etihad Airways
	A6-ETM	Boeing 777-3FXER	Etihad Airways
	A6-ETN	Boeing 777-3FXER	Etihad Airways
	A6-ETO	Boeing 777-3FXER	Etihad Airways
	A6-ETP	Boeing 777-3FXER	Etihad Airways
	A6-ETQ	Boeing 777-3FXER	Etihad Airways
	A6-ETR	Boeing 777-3FXER	Etihad Airways
	A6-EWA	Boeing 777-21HLR	Emirates Airlines
	A6-EWB	Boeing 777-21HLR	Emirates Airlines
	A6-EWC	Boeing 777-21HLR	Emirates Airlines
	A6-EWD	Boeing 777-21HLR	Emirates Airlines
	A6-EWE	Boeing 777-21HLR	Emirates Airlines
	A6-EWF	Boeing 777-21HLR	Emirates Airlines
	A6-EWG	Boeing 777-21HLR	Emirates Airlines
	A6-EWH	Boeing 777-21HER	Emirates Airlines
	A6-EWI	Boeing 777-21HER	Emirates Airlines
	A6-EWJ	Boeing 777-21HLR	Emirates Airlines
	A6-EYD	Airbus A.330-243	Etihad Airways
	A6-EYE	Airbus A.330-243	Etihad Airways *Blue Moon Rising*
	A6-EYF	Airbus A.330-243	Etihad Airways
	A6-EYG	Airbus A.330-243	Etihad Airways
	A6-EYH	Airbus A.330-243	Etihad Airways
	A6-EYI	Airbus A.330-243	Etihad Airways
	A6-EYJ	Airbus A.330-243	Ethiad Airways
	A6-EYK	Airbus A.330-243	Etihad Airways
	A6-EYL	Airbus A.330-243	Etihad Airways
	A6-EYM	Airbus A.330-243	Etihad Airways
	A6-EYN	Airbus A.330-243	Etihad Airways
	A6-EYO	Airbus A.330-243	Etihad Airways
	A6-EYP	Airbus A.330-243	Etihad Airways
	A6-EYQ	Airbus A.330-243	Etihad Airways
	A6-EYR	Airbus A.330-243	Ethiad Airways
	A6-EYS	Airbus A.330-243	Ethiad Airways
	A6-EYT	Airbus A.330-243	Ethiad Airways
	A6-HAZ	Airbus A.300B4-622RF	Maximus Air Cargo
	A6-NIN	Airbus A.300B4-622RF	Maximus Air Cargo
	A6-SUL	Airbus A.300B4-622RF	Maximus Air Cargo

A7 (Qatar)

	A7-ACA	Airbus A.330-202	Qatar Airways *Al Wajba*
	A7-ACB	Airbus A.330-202	Qatar Airways *Al Majida*
	A7-ACC	Airbus A.330-202	Qatar Airways *Al Shahaniya*
	A7-ACD	Airbus A.330-202	Qatar Airways *Al Wusell*
	A7-ACE	Airbus A.330-202	Qatar Airways *Al Dhakira*
	A7-ACF	Airbus A.330-202	Qatar Airways *Al Kara'anah*

Reg.	Type	Owner or Operator	Notes
A7-ACG	Airbus A.330-202	Qatar Airways Al Wabra	
A7-ACH	Airbus A.330-202	Qatar Airways Al Mafjar	
A7-ACI	Airbus A.330-202	Qatar Airways Muathier	
A7-ACJ	Airbus A.330-202	Qatar Airways Zikreet	
A7-ACK	Airbus A.330-202	Qatar Airways	
A7-ACL	Airbus A.330-202	Qatar Airways	
A7-ACM	Airbus A.330-202	Qatar Airways	
A7-AEA	Airbus A.330-302	Qatar Airways Al Muntazah	
A7-AEB	Airbus A.330-302	Qatar Airways Al Sayliyah	
A7-AEC	Airbus A.330-302	Qatar Airways Al Markhiya	
A7-AED	Airbus A.330-302	Qatar Airways Al Nu'uman	
A7-AEE	Airbus A.330-302	Qatar Airways Semaisma	
A7-AEF	Airbus A.330-302	Qatar Airways Al Rumellah	
A7-AEG	Airbus A.330-302	Qatar Airways Al Duhell	
A7-AEH	Airbus A.330-302	Qatar Airways	
A7-AEI	Airbus A.330-302	Qatar Airways	
A7-AEJ	Airbus A.330-302	Qatar Airways	
A7-AEM	Airbus A.330-302	Qatar Airways	
A7-AEN	Airbus A.330-302	Qatar Airways	
A7-AEO	Airbus A.330-302	Qatar Airways	
A7-AFL	Airbus A.330-202	Qatar Airways Al Messilah	
A7-AFM	Airbus A.330-202	Qatar Airways Al Udaid	
A7-AFP	Airbus A-330-202	Qatar Airways Al Shamal	
A7-AGA	Airbus A.340-642	Qatar Airways	
A7-AGB	Airbus A.340-642	Qatar Airways	
A7-AGC	Airbus A.340-642	Qatar Airways	
A7-AGD	Airbus A.340-642	Qatar Airways	
A7-BAA	Boeing 777-3DZ ER	Qatar Airways	
A7-BAB	Boeing 777-3DZ ER	Qatar Airways	
A7-BAC	Boeing 777-3DZ ER	Qatar Airways	
A7-BAE	Boeing 777-3DZ ER	Qatar Airways	
A7-BAF	Boeing 777-3DZ ER	Qatar Airways	
A7-BAG	Boeing 777-3DZ ER	Qatar Airways	
A7-BAH	Boeing 777-3DZ ER	Qatar Airways	
A7-BAI	Boeing 777-3DZ ER	Qatar Airways	
A7-BAJ	Boeing 777-3DZ ER	Qatar Airways	
A7-BAK	Boeing 777-3DZ ER	Qatar Airways	
A7-BAL	Boeing 777-3DZ ER	Qatar Airways	
A7-BAM	Boeing 777-3DZ ER	Qatar Airways	
A7-BAN	Boeing 777-3DZ ER	Qatar Airways	
A7-BAO	Boeing 777-3DZ ER	Qatar Airways	
A7-BAP	Boeing 777-3DZ ER	Qatar Airways Al Qattard	
A7-BAQ	Boeing 777-3DZ ER	Qatar Airways	
A7-BAS	Boeing 777-3DZ ER	Qatar Airways	
A7-BAT	Boeing 777-3DZ ER	Qatar Airways	
A7-BAU	Boeing 777-3DZ ER	Qatar Airways	
A7-BAW	Boeing 777-3DZ ER	Qatar Airways	
A7-BAX	Boeing 777-3DZ ER	Qatar Airways	
A7-BAY	Boeing 777-3DZ ER	Qatar Airways	
A7-BAZ	Boeing 777-3DZ ER	Qatar Airways	
A7-BBA	Boeing 777-2DZ LR	Qatar Airways	
A7-BBB	Boeing 777-2DZ LR	Qatar Airways	
A7-BBC	Boeing 777-2DZ LR	Qatar Airways	
A7-BBD	Boeing 777-2DZ LR	Qatar Airways	
A7-BBE	Boeing 777-2DZ LR	Qatar Airways	
A7-BBF	Boeing 777-2DZ LR	Qatar Airways	
A7-BBG	Boeing 777-2DZ LR	Qatar Airways	
A7-BBH	Boeing 777-2DZ LR	Qatar Airways A.Calail	
A7-BBI	Boeing 777-2DZ LR	Qatar Airways Jaow Alsalam	
A7-BBJ	Boeing 777-2DZ LR	Qatar Airways	
A7-BCA	Boeing 787-8	Qatar Airways	
A7-BCB	Boeing 787-8	Qatar Airways	
A7-BCC	Boeing 787-8	Qatar Airways	
A7-BCD	Boeing 787-8	Qatar Airways	
A7-BCE	Boeing 787-8	Qatar Airways	
A7-BCF	Boeing 787-8	Qatar Airways	
A7-BCG	Boeing 787-8	Qatar Airways	
A7-BCH	Boeing 787-8	Qatar Airways	
A7-BCI	Boeing 787-8	Qatar Airways	
A7-BCK	Boeing 787-8	Qatar Airways	
A7-BCL	Boeing 787-8	Qatar Airways	
A7-BEA	Boeing 777-3DZ ER	Qatar Airways	

Notes	Reg.	Type	Owner or Operator
	A7-BFA	Boeing 777-FDZ	Qatar Airways Cargo
	A7-BFB	Boeing 777-FDZ	Qatar Airways Cargo
	A7-BFC	Boeing 777-FDZ	Qatar Airways Cargo
	A7-BFD	Boeing 777-FDZ	Qatar Airways Cargo
	A7-BFE	Boeing 777-FDZ	Qatar Airways Cargo

A9C (Bahrain)

	A9C-KA	Airbus A.330-243 (501)	Gulf Air
	A9C-KB	Airbus A.330-243 (502)	Gulf Air
	A9C-KC	Airbus A.330-243 (503)	Gulf Air
	A9C-KD	Airbus A.330-243 (504)	Gulf Air
	A9C-KE	Airbus A.330-243 (505)	Gulf Air
	A9C-KF	Airbus A.330-243 (506)	Gulf Air *Aldafra*

A40 (Oman)

	A40-DA	Airbus A.330-243	Oman Air
	A40-DB	Airbus A.330-343	Oman Air
	A40-DC	Airbus A.330-243	Oman Air
	A40-DD	Airbus A.330-343	Oman Air
	A40-DE	Airbus A.330-343	Oman Air
	A40-DF	Airbus A.330-243	Oman Air
	A40-DG	Airbus A.330-243	Oman Air

AP (Pakistan)

	AP-BDZ	Airbus A.310-308	Pakistan International Airlines
	AP-BEC	Airbus A.310-308	Pakistan International Airlines
	AP-BEG	Airbus A.310-308	Pakistan International Airlines
	AP-BEQ	Airbus A.310-308	Pakistan International Airlines
	AP-BEU	Airbus A.310-308	Pakistan International Airlines
	AP-BGJ	Boeing 777-240ER	Pakistan International Airlines
	AP-BGK	Boeing 777-240ER	Pakistan International Airlines
	AP-BGL	Boeing 777-240ER	Pakistan International Airlines
	AP-BGY	Boeing 777-240LR	Pakistan International Airlines
	AP-BGZ	Boeing 777-240LR	Pakistan International Airlines
	AP-BHV	Boeing 777-340ER	Pakistan International Airlines
	AP-BHW	Boeing 777-340ER	Pakistan International Airlines
	AP-BHX	Boeing 777-240ER	Pakistan International Airlines
	AP-BID	Boeing 777-340ER	Pakistan International Airlines

B (China/Taiwan/Hong Kong)

	B-HKT	Boeing 747-412	Cathay Pacific Airways
	B-HKU	Boeing 747-412	Cathay Pacific Airways
	B-HKV	Boeing 747-412	Cathay Pacific Airways
	B-HKX	Boeing 747-412	Cathay Pacific Airways
	B-HOP	Boeing 747-467	Cathay Pacific Airways
	B-HOR	Boeing 747-467	Cathay Pacific Airways
	B-HUA	Boeing 747-467	Cathay Pacific Airways
	B-HUB	Boeing 747-467	Cathay Pacific Airways
	B-HUE	Boeing 747-467	Cathay Pacific Airways
	B-HUF	Boeing 747-467	Cathay Pacific Airways
	B-HUG	Boeing 747-467	Cathay Pacific Airways
	B-HUI	Boeing 747-467	Cathay Pacific Airways
	B-HUJ	Boeing 747-467	Cathay Pacific Airways
	B-HUL	Boeing 747-467F (SCD)	Cathay Pacific Airways
	B-HUO	Boeing 747-467F (SCD)	Cathay Pacific Airways
	B-HUP	Boeing 747-467F (SCD)	Cathay Pacific Airways
	B-HXA	Airbus A.340-313X	Cathay Pacific Airways
	B-HXB	Airbus A.340-313X	Cathay Pacific Airways
	B-HXC	Airbus A.340-313X	Cathay Pacific Airways
	B-HXD	Airbus A.340-313X	Cathay Pacific Airways
	B-HXE	Airbus A.340-313X	Cathay Pacific Airways
	B-HXF	Airbus A.340-313X	Cathay Pacific Airways
	B-HXG	Airbus A.340-313X	Cathay Pacific Airways
	B-HXH	Airbus A.340-313X	Cathay Pacific Airways

Reg.	Type	Owner or Operator	Notes
B-HXI	Airbus A.340-313X	Cathay Pacific Airways	
B-HXJ	Airbus A.340-313X	Cathay Pacific Airways	
B-HXK	Airbus A.340-313X	Cathay Pacific Airways	
B-KPA	Boeing 777-367ER	Cathay Pacific Airways	
B-KPB	Boeing 777-367ER	Cathay Pacific Airways	
B-KPC	Boeing 777-367ER	Cathay Pacific Airways	
B-KPD	Boeing 777-367ER	Cathay Pacific Airways	
B-KPE	Boeing 777-367ER	Cathay Pacific Airways	
B-KPF	Boeing 777-367ER	Cathay Pacific Airways	
B-KPG	Boeing 777-367ER	Cathay Pacific Airways	
B-KPH	Boeing 777-367ER	Cathay Pacific Airways	
B-KPI	Boeing 777-367ER	Cathay Pacific Airways	
B-KPJ	Boeing 777-367ER	Cathay Pacific Airways	
B-KPK	Boeing 777-367ER	Cathay Pacific Airways	
B-KPL	Boeing 777-367ER	Cathay Pacific Airways	
B-KPM	Boeing 777-367ER	Cathay Pacific Airways	
B-KPN	Boeing 777-367ER	Cathay Pacific Airways	
B-KPO	Boeing 777-367ER	Cathay Pacific Airways	
B-KPP	Boeing 777-367ER	Cathay Pacific Airways	
B-KPQ	Boeing 777-367ER	Cathay Pacific Airways	
B-KPR	Boeing 777-367ER	Cathay Pacific Airways	
B-KPS	Boeing 777-367ER	Cathay Pacific Airways	
B-KPT	Boeing 777-367ER	Cathay Pacific Airways	
B-KPU	Boeing 777-367ER	Cathay Pacific Airways	
B-KPV	Boeing 777-367ER	Cathay Pacific Airways	
B-KPW	Boeing 777-367ER	Cathay Pacific Airways	
B-KPX	Boeing 777-367ER	Cathay Pacific Airways	
B-KPY	Boeing 777-367ER	Cathay Pacific Airways	
B-KPZ	Boeing 777-367ER	Cathay Pacific Airways	
B-KQA	Boeing 777-367ER	Cathay Pacific Airways	
B-KQB	Boeing 777-367ER	Cathay Pacific Airways	
B-KQC	Boeing 777-367ER	Cathay Pacific Airways	
B-KQD	Boeing 777-367ER	Cathay Pacific Airways	
B-KQE	Boeing 777-367ER	Cathay Pacific Airways	
B-KQF	Boeing 777-367ER	Cathay Pacific Airways	
B-KQG	Boeing 777-367ER	Cathay Pacific Airways	
B-KQH	Boeing 777-367ER	Cathay Pacific Airways	
B-KQI	Boeing 777-367ER	Cathay Pacific Airways	
B-KQJ	Boeing 777-367ER	Cathay Pacific Airways	
B-KQK	Boeing 777-367ER	Cathay Pacific Airways	
B-KQL	Boeing 777-367ER	Cathay Pacific Airways	
B-LIA	Boeing 747-467ERF	Cathay Pacific Airways	
B-LIB	Boeing 747-467ERF	Cathay Pacific Airways	
B-LIC	Boeing 747-467ERF	Cathay Pacific Airways	
B-LID	Boeing 747-467ERF	Cathay Pacific Airways	
B-LIE	Boeing 747-467ERF	Cathay Pacific Airways	
B-LIF	Boeing 747-467ERF	Cathay Pacific Airways	
B-LJA	Boeing 747-867F	Cathay Pacific Airways	
B-LJB	Boeing 747-867F	Cathay Pacific Airways	
B-LJC	Boeing 747-867F	Cathay Pacific Airways	
B-LJD	Boeing 747-867F	Cathay Pacific Airways	
B-LJE	Boeing 747-867F	Cathay Pacific Airways	
B-LJF	Boeing 747-867F	Cathay Pacific Airways	
B-LJG	Boeing 747-867F	Cathay Pacific Airways	
B-LJH	Boeing 747-867F	Cathay Pacific Airways	
B-LJI	Boeing 747-867F	Cathay Pacific Airways	
B-LJJ	Boeing 747-867F	Cathay Pacific Airways	
B-LJK	Boeing 747-867F	Cathay Pacific Airways	
B-LJL	Boeing 747-867F	Cathay Pacific Airways	
B-LJM	Boeing 747-867F	Cathay Pacific Airways	
B-2031	Boeing 777-39LER	Air China	
B-2032	Boeing 777-39LER	Air China	
B-2033	Boeing 777-39LER	Air China	
B-2035	Boeing 777-39LER	Air China	
B-2036	Boeing 777-39LER	Air China	
B-2037	Boeing 777-39LER	Air China	
B-2038	Boeing 777-39LER	Air China	
B-2039	Boeing 777-39LER	Air China	
B-2040	Boeing 777-39LER	Air China	
B-2043	Boeing 777-39LER	Air China	
B-2046	Boeing 777-39LER	Air China	
B-2085	Boeing 777-39LER	Air China	

Reg.	Type	Owner or Operator
B-2086	Boeing 777-39LER	Air China
B-2087	Boeing 777-39LER	Air China
B-2088	Boeing 777-39LER	Air China
B-2089	Boeing 777-39LER	Air China
B-2090	Boeing 777-39LER	Air China
B-2387	Airbus A.340-313X	Air China
B-2388	Airbus A.340-313X	Air China
B-2389	Airbus A.340-313X	Air China
B-2390	Airbus A.340-313X	Air China
B-2409	Boeing 747-412F (SCD)	Air China Cargo
B-2453	Boeing 747-412BCF	Air China Cargo
B-2456	Boeing 747-4J6BCF	Air China Cargo
B-2458	Boeing 747-4J6BCF	Air China Cargo
B-2460	Boeing 747-4J6BCF	Air China Cargo
B-2475	Boeing 747-4FTF (SCD)	Air China Cargo
B-2476	Boeing 747-4FTF (SCD)	Air China Cargo
B-2725	Boeing 787-8	China Southern Airlines
B-2726	Boeing 787-8	China Southern Airlines
B-2727	Boeing 787-8	China Southern Airlines
B-2732	Boeing 787-8	China Southern Airlines
B-2733	Boeing 787-8	China Southern Airlines
B-2735	Boeing 787-8	China Southern Airlines
B-2736	Boeing 787-8	China Southern Airlines
B-2737	Boeing 787-8	China Southern Airlines
B-5902	Airbus A.330-243	China Eastern Airlines
B-5903	Airbus A.330-243	China Eastern Airlines
B-5908	Airbus A.330-243	China Eastern Airlines
B-5918	Airbus A.330-243	Air China
B-5920	Airbus A.330-243	China Eastern Airlines
B-5921	Airbus A.330-243	China Eastern Airlines
B-5925	Airbus A.330-243	Air China
B-5926	Airbus A.330-243	China Eastern Airlines
B-5927	Airbus A.330-243	Air China
B-5930	Airbus A.330-243	China Eastern Airlines
B-5931	Airbus A.330-243	China Eastern Airlines
B-5932	Airbus A.330-243	Air China
B-5933	Airbus A.330-243	Air China
B-5936	Airbus A.330-243	China Eastern Airlines
B-5937	Airbus A.330-243	China Eastern Airlines
B-5938	Airbus A.330-243	China Eastern Airlines
B-6070	Airbus A.330-243	Air China
B-6071	Airbus A.330-243	Air China
B-6072	Airbus A.330-243	Air China
B-6073	Airbus A.330-243	Air China
B-6075	Airbus A.330-243	Air China
B-6076	Airbus A.330-243	Air China
B-6079	Airbus A.330-243	Air China
B-6080	Airbus A.330-243	Air China
B-6081	Airbus A.330-243	Air China
B-6082	Airbus A.330-243	China Eastern Airlines
B-6090	Airbus A.330-243	Air China
B-6091	Airbus A.330-243	Air China
B-6092	Airbus A.330-243	Air China
B-6093	Airbus A.330-243	Air China
B-6099	Airbus A.330-243	China Eastern Airlines
B-6113	Airbus A.330-243	Air China
B-6115	Airbus A.330-243	Air China
B-6117	Airbus A.330-243	Air China
B-6121	Airbus A.330-243	China Eastern Airlines
B-6122	Airbus A.330-243	China Eastern Airlines
B-6123	Airbus A.330-243	China Eastern Airlines
B-6130	Airbus A.330-243	Air China
B-6131	Airbus A.330-243	Air China
B-6132	Airbus A.330-243	Air China
B-6505	Airbus A.330-243	Air China
B-6533	Airbus A.330-243	Air China
B-6536	Airbus A.330-243	Air China
B-6537	Airbus A.330-243	China Eastern Airlines
B-6538	Airbus A.330-243	China Eastern Airlines
B-6540	Airbus A.330-243	Air China
B-6541	Airbus A.330-243	Air China
B-6543	Airbus A.330-243	China Eastern Airlines

Reg.	Type	Owner or Operator	Notes
B-6549	Airbus A.330-243	Air China	
B-16401	Boeing 747-45E	EVA Air Cargo	
B-16402	Boeing 747-45E	EVA Air Cargo	
B-16406	Boeing 747-45E	EVA Air Cargo	
B-16407	Boeing 747-45E	EVA Air Cargo	
B-16462	Boeing 747-45E	EVA Air Cargo	
B-16463	Boeing 747-45E	EVA Air Cargo	
B-16481	Boeing 747-45E	EVA Air Cargo	
B-16482	Boeing 747-45E	EVA Air Cargo	
B-16483	Boeing 747-45E	EVA Air Cargo	
B-16701	Boeing 777-35EER	EVA Airways	
B-16702	Boeing 777-35EER	EVA Airways	
B-16703	Boeing 777-35EER	EVA Airways	
B-16705	Boeing 777-35EER	EVA Airways	
B-16706	Boeing 777-35EER	EVA Airways	
B-16707	Boeing 777-35EER	EVA Airways	
B-16708	Boeing 777-35EER	EVA Airways	
B-16709	Boeing 777-35EER	EVA Airways	
B-16710	Boeing 777-35EER	EVA Airways	
B-16711	Boeing 777-35EER	EVA Airways	
B-16712	Boeing 777-35EER	EVA Airways	
B-16713	Boeing 777-35EER	EVA Airways	
B-16715	Boeing 777-35EER	EVA Airways	
B-16716	Boeing 777-35EER	EVA Airways	
B-16717	Boeing 777-35EER	EVA Airways	

C (Canada)

Reg.	Type	Owner or Operator	Notes
C-FCAB	Boeing 767-375ER (681)	Air Canada	
C-FCAE	Boeing 767-375ER (682)	Air Canada	
C-FCAF	Boeing 767-375ER (683)	Air Canada	
C-FCAG	Boeing 767-375ER (684)	Air Canada	
C-FDAT	Airbus A.310-308 (305)	Air Transat	
C-FITL	Boeing 777-333ER (731)	Air Canada	
C-FITU	Boeing 777-333ER (732)	Air Canada	
C-FITW	Boeing 777-3Q8ER (733)	Air Canada	
C-FIUA	Boeing 777-233LR (701)	Air Canada	
C-FIUF	Boeing 777-233LR (702)	Air Canada	
C-FIUJ	Boeing 777-233LR (703)	Air Canada	
C-FIUL	Boeing 777-333ER (734)	Air Canada	
C-FIUR	Boeing 777-333ER (735)	Air Canada	
C-FIUV	Boeing 777-333ER (736)	Air Canada	
C-FIUW	Boeing 777-333ER (737)	Air Canada	
C-FIVK	Boeing 777-233LR (704)	Air Canada	
C-FIVM	Boeing 777-333ER (738)	Air Canada	
C-FIVQ	Boeing 777-333ER (740)	Air Canada	
C-FIVR	Boeing 777-333ER (741)	Air Canada	
C-FIVS	Boeing 777-333ER (742)	Air Canada	
C-FIVW	Boeing 777-333ER (743)	Air Canada	
C-FIVX	Boeing 777-333ER (744)	Air Canada	
C-FMWP	Boeing 767-333ER (631)	Air Canada	
C-FMWQ	Boeing 767-333ER (632)	Air Canada	
C-FMWU	Boeing 767-333ER (633)	Air Canada	
C-FMWV	Boeing 767-333ER (634)	Air Canada	
C-FMWY	Boeing 767-333ER (635)	Air Canada	
C-FMXC	Boeing 767-333ER (636)	Air Canada	
C-FNND	Boeing 767-233ER (705)	Air Canada	
C-FNNH	Boeing 777-233LR (706)	Air Canada	
C-FNNQ	Boeing 777-333ER (745)	Air Canada	
C-FNNU	Boeing 777-333ER (746)	Air Canada	
C-FNNW	Boeing 777-333ER	Air Canada	
C-FOCA	Boeing 767-375ER (640)	Air Canada	
C-FPCA	Boeing 767-375ER (637)	Air Canada	
C-FRAM	Boeing 777-333ER (739)	Air Canada	
C-FTCA	Boeing 767-375ER (638)	Air Canada	
C-FXCA	Boeing 767-375ER (639)	Air Canada	
C-GBZR	Boeing 767-38EER (645)	Air Canada	
C-GCTS	Airbus A.330-342	Air Transat	
C-GDUZ	Boeing 767-38EER (646)	Air Canada	
C-GEOQ	Boeing 767-375ER (647)	Air Canada	
C-GEOU	Boeing 767-375ER (648)	Air Canada	

Notes	Reg.	Type	Owner or Operator
	C-GFAF	Airbus A.330-343X (931)	Air Canada
	C-GFAH	Airbus A.330-343X (932)	Air Canada
	C-GFAJ	Airbus A.330-343X (933)	Air Canada
	C-GFAT	Airbus A.310-304 (301)	Air Transat
	C-GFUR	Airbus A.330-343X (934)	Air Canada
	C-GGTS	Airbus A.330-243 (101)	Air Transat
	C-GHKR	Airbus A.330-343X (935)	Air Canada
	C-GHKW	Airbus A.330-343X (936)	Air Canada
	C-GHKX	Airbus A.330-343X (937)	Air Canada
	C-GHLA	Boeing 767-35HER (656)	Air Canada
	C-GHLK	Boeing 767-35HER (657)	Air Canada
	C-GHLM	Airbus A.330-343X (938)	Air Canada
	C-GHLQ	Boeing 767-333ER (658)	Air Canada
	C-GHLT	Boeing 767-333ER (659)	Air Canada
	C-GHLU	Boeing 767-333ER (660)	Air Canada
	C-GHLV	Boeing 767-333ER (661)	Air Canada
	C-GHOZ	Boeing 767-375ER (685)	Air Canada
	C-GHPE	Boeing 767-33AER	Air Canada Rouge
	C-GHPN	Boeing 767-33AER	Air Canada Rouge
	C-GHPQ	Boeing 787-8 (801)	Air Canada
	C-GITS	Airbus A.330-243 (102)	Air Transat
	C-GKTS	Airbus A.330-342 (100)	Air Transat
	C-GLAT	Airbus A.310-308 (302)	Air Transat
	C-GLCA	Boeing 767-375ER (641)	Air Canada
	C-GPAT	Airbus A.310-308 (303)	Air Transat
	C-GPTS	Airbus A.330-243 (103)	Air Transat
	C-GSAT	Airbus A.310-308 (304)	Air Transat
	C-GSCA	Boeing 767-375ER (642)	Air Canada
	C-GTSD	Airbus A.330-343	Air Transat
	C-GTSF	Airbus A.310-304 (345)	Air Transat
	C-GTSH	Airbus A.310-304 (343)	Air Transat
	C-GTSI	Airbus A.330-243	Air Transat
	C-GTSJ	Airbus A.330-243	Air Transat
	C-GTSN	Airbus A.330-243	Air Transat
	C-GTSO	Airbus A.330-342	Air Transat
	C-GTSR	Airbus A.330-243	Air Transat
	C-GTSW	Airbus A.310-304	Air Transat
	C-GTSY	Airbus A.310-304 (344)	Air Transat
	C-GTSZ	Airbus A.330-243	Air Transat

Note: Airline fleet number when carried on aircraft is shown in parentheses.

CN (Morocco)

	CN-NMA	Airbus A.320-214	Air Arabia Maroc
	CN-NMB	Airbus A.320-214	Air Arabia Maroc
	CN-NMF	Airbus A.320-214	Air Arabia Maroc
	CN-RGA	Boeing 747-428	Royal Air Maroc
	CN-RGE	Boeing 737-86N	Royal Air Maroc
	CN-RGF	Boeing 737-86N	Royal Air Maroc
	CN-RGG	Boeing 737-86N	Royal Air Maroc
	CN-RGH	Boeing 737-86N	Royal Air Maroc
	CN-RGI	Boeing 737-86N	Royal Air Maroc
	CN-RGJ	Boeing 737-8B6	Royal Air Maroc
	CN-RGK	Boeing 737-8B6	Royal Air Maroc
	CN-RGM	Boeing 737-8B6	Royal Air Maroc
	CN-RGN	Boeing 737-8B6	Royal Air Maroc
	CN-RNJ	Boeing 737-8B6	Royal Air Maroc
	CN-RNK	Boeing 737-8B6	Royal Air Maroc
	CN-RNL	Boeing 737-7B6	Royal Air Maroc
	CN-RNM	Boeing 737-8B6	Royal Air Maroc
	CN-RNP	Boeing 737-8B6	Royal Air Maroc
	CN-RNQ	Boeing 737-7B6	Royal Air Maroc
	CN-RNR	Boeing 737-7B6	Royal Air Maroc
	CN-RNS	Boeing 767-3B6ER	Royal Air Maroc
	CN-RNT	Boeing 767-3B6ER	Royal Air Maroc
	CN-RNU	Boeing 737-8B6	Royal Air Maroc
	CN-RNV	Boeing 737-7B6	Royal Air Maroc
	CN-RNW	Boeing 737-8B6	Royal Air Maroc
	CN-RNZ	Boeing 737-8B6	Royal Air Maroc
	CN-ROA	Boeing 737-8B6	Royal Air Maroc
	CN-ROB	Boeing 737-8B6	Royal Air Maroc

Reg.	Type	Owner or Operator	Notes
CN-ROC	Boeing 737-8B6	Royal Air Maroc	
CN-ROD	Boeing 737-7B6	Royal Air Maroc	
CN-ROE	Boeing 737-8B6	Royal Air Maroc	
CN-ROH	Boeing 737-8B6	Royal Air Maroc	
CN-ROJ	Boeing 737-8B6	Royal Air Maroc	
CN-ROK	Boeing 737-8B6	Royal Air Maroc	
CN-ROL	Boeing 737-8B6	Royal Air Maroc	
CN-ROP	Boeing 737-8B6	Royal Air Maroc	
CN-ROR	Boeing 737-8B6	Royal Air Maroc	
CN-ROS	Boeing 737-8B6	Royal Air Maroc	
CN-ROT	Boeing 737-8B6	Royal Air Maroc	
CN-ROU	Boeing 737-8B6	Royal Air Maroc	
CN-ROV	Boeing 767-3Q8ER	Royal Air Maroc	
CN-ROW	Boeing 767-343ER	Royal Air Maroc	
CN-ROY	Boeing 737-8B6	Royal Air Maroc	
CN-ROZ	Boeing 737-8B6	Royal Air Maroc	

CS (Portugal)

Reg.	Type	Owner or Operator	Notes
CS-TEX	Airbus A.310-304	HiFly	
CS-TFS	Boeing 767-3YOER	Euro Atlantic Airways	
CS-TFT	Boeing 767-3YOER	Euro Atlantic Airways	
CS-TFU	Airbus A.319-115	White Airways	
CS-TFW	Airbus A.340-542	Arik Air	
CS-TFX	Airbus A.340-542	Arik Air *Captain Bob Hayes,OON*	
CS-TGU	Airbus A.310-304	SATA International *Terceira*	
CS-TGV	Airbus A.310-304	SATA International	
CS-TJE	Airbus A.321-211	TAP Portugal *Pero Vaz de Caminha*	
CS-TJF	Airbus A.321-211	TAP Portugal *Luis Vaz de Camoes*	
CS-TJG	Airbus A.321-211	TAP Portugal *Amelia Rodrigues*	
CS-TKJ	Airbus A.320-212	SATA International *Pico*	
CS-TKK	Airbus A.320-214	SATA International *Corvo*	
CS-TKM	Airbus A.310-304	SATA International *Autonomia*	
CS-TKN	Airbus A.310-325	SATA International *Macaronesia*	
CS-TKO	Airbus A.320-214	SATA International	
CS-TKP	Airbus A.320-214	SATA International	
CS-TLO	Boeing 767-383ER	Euro Atlantic Airways/TAP Portugal	
CS-TLU	Airbus A.319-133	White Airways	
CS-TMW	Airbus A.320-214	TAP Portugal *Luisa Todi*	
CS-TNG	Airbus A.320-214	TAP Portugal *Mouzinho da Silveira*	
CS-TNH	Airbus A.320-214	TAP Portugal *Almada Negreiros*	
CS-TNI	Airbus A.320-214	TAP Portugal *Aquilino Ribiera*	
CS-TNJ	Airbus A.320-214	TAP Portugal *Florbela Espanca*	
CS-TNK	Airbus A.320-214	TAP Portugal *Teofilo Braga*	
CS-TNL	Airbus A.320-214	TAP Portugal *Vitorino Nermesio*	
CS-TNM	Airbus A.320-214	TAP Portugal *Natalia Correia*	
CS-TNN	Airbus A.320-214	TAP Portugal *Gil Vicente*	
CS-TNP	Airbus A.320-214	TAP Portugal *Alexandre O'Neill*	
CS-TNQ	Airbus A.320-214	TAP Portugal *Jose Regio*	
CS-TNR	Airbus A.320-214	TAP Portugal	
CS-TNS	Airbus A.320-214	TAP Portugal *D.Alfonso Henriques*	
CS-TNT	Airbus A.320-214	TAP Portugal	
CS-TNU	Airbus A.320-214	TAP Portugal	
CS-TNV	Airbus A.320-214	TAP Portugal	
CS-TOA	Airbus A.340-312	TAP Portugal *Fernao Mendes Pinto*	
CS-TOB	Airbus A.340-312	TAP Portugal *D Joao de Castro*	
CS-TOC	Airbus A.340-312	TAP Portugal *Wenceslau de Moraes*	
CS-TOD	Airbus A.340-312	TAP Portugal *D Francisco de Almeida*	
CS-TOE	Airbus A.330-223	TAP Portugal *Pedro Alvares Cabal*	
CS-TOF	Airbus A.330-223	TAP Portugal *Infante D Henrique*	
CS-TOG	Airbus A.330-223	TAP Portugal *Bartolomeu de Gusmão*	
CS-TOH	Airbus A.330-223	TAP Portugal *Nuno Gongalves*	
CS-TOI	Airbus A.330-223	TAP Portugal *Damiao de Gois*	
CS-TOJ	Airbus A.330-223	TAP Portugal *D.Ja-o II 'O Principe Perfeito*	
CS-TOK	Airbus A.330-223	TAP Portugal *Padre Antonio Vieira*	
CS-TOL	Airbus A.330-202	TAP Portugal *Joao Goncalves Zarco*	
CS-TOM	Airbus A.330-202	TAP Portugal *Vasco da Gama*	
CS-TON	Airbus A.330-202	TAP Portugal *Ja-o XXI*	
CS-TOO	Airbus A.330-202	TAP Portugal *Fernao de Magalhaes*	
CS-TOP	Airbus A.330-202	TAP Portugal *Pedro Nunes*	
CS-TOQ	Airbus A.330-203	TAP Portugal	

Notes	Reg.	Type	Owner or Operator
	CS-TOR	Airbus A.330-203	TAP Portugal
	CS-TQD	Airbus A.320-214	TAP Portugal
	CS-TQJ	Airbus A.319-115	White Airways
	CS-TQM	Airbus A.340-313	HiFly/Livingston
	CS-TQP	Airbus A.330-202	HiFly/Livingston
	CS-TQU	Boeing 737-8K2	Euro Atlantic Airways
	CS-TQV	Airbus A.310-304	White Airways
	CS-TQZ	Airbus A.340-313	HiFly/Jetairfly
	CS-TPA	Fokker 100	PGA Portugalia Airlines
	CS-TPB	Fokker 100	PGA Portugalia Airlines
	CS-TPC	Fokker 100	PGA Portugalia Airlines
	CS-TPD	Fokker 100	PGA Portugalia Airlines
	CS-TPE	Fokker 100	PGA Portugalia Airlines
	CS-TPF	Fokker 100	PGA Portugalia Airlines
	CS-TRH	Airbus A.330-343	Orbest
	CS-TRI	Airbus A.330-322	HiFly
	CS-TRN	Boeing 767-333AER	Euro Atlantic Airways
	CS-TTA	Airbus A.319-111	TAP Portugal *Vieira da Silva*
	CS-TTB	Airbus A.319-111	TAP Portugal *Gago Coutinho*
	CS-TTC	Airbus A.319-111	TAP Portugal *Fernando Pessoa*
	CS-TTD	Airbus A.319-111	TAP Portugal *Amadeo de Souza-Cardoso*
	CS-TTE	Airbus A.319-111	TAP Portugal *Francisco d'Ollanda*
	CS-TTF	Airbus A.319-111	TAP Portugal *Calouste Gulbenkian*
	CS-TTG	Airbus A.319-111	TAP Portugal *Humberto Delgado*
	CS-TTH	Airbus A.319-111	TAP Portugal *Antonio Sergio*
	CS-TTI	Airbus A.319-111	TAP Portugal *Eca de Queiros*
	CS-TTJ	Airbus A.319-111	TAP Portugal *Eusebio*
	CS-TTK	Airbus A.319-111	TAP Portugal *Miguel Torga*
	CS-TTL	Airbus A.319-111	TAP Portugal *Almeida Garrett*
	CS-TTM	Airbus A.319-111	TAP Portugal *Alexandre Herculano*
	CS-TTN	Airbus A.319-111	TAP Portugal *Camilo Castelo Branco*
	CS-TTO	Airbus A.319-111	TAP Portugal *Antero de Quental*
	CS-TTP	Airbus A.319-111	TAP Portugal *Josefa d'Obidos*
	CS-TTQ	Airbus A.319-112	TAP Portugal *Agostinho da Silva*
	CS-TTR	Airbus A.319-112	TAP Portugal
	CS-TTS	Airbus A.319-112	TAP Portugal *Guilhermina Suggia*
	CS-TTU	Airbus A.319-112	TAP Portugal
	CS-TTV	Airbus A.319-112	TAP Portugal

D (Germany)

	D-AALA	Boeing 777-FZN	AeroLogic
	D-AALB	Boeing 777-FZN	AeroLogic
	D-AALC	Boeing 777-FZN	AeroLogic
	D-AALD	Boeing 777-FZN	AeroLogic
	D-AALE	Boeing 777-FZN	AeroLogic
	D-AALF	Boeing 777-FZN	AeroLogic
	D-AALG	Boeing 777-FZN	AeroLogic
	D-AALH	Boeing 777-FZN	AeroLogic
	D-ABAF	Boeing 737-86J	Air Berlin
	D-ABAG	Boeing 737-86J	Air Berlin
	D-ABBG	Boeing 737-86J	Air Berlin
	D-ABBJ	Boeing 737-86Q	Air Berlin
	D-ABBK	Boeing 737-8BK	Air Berlin
	D-ABBX	Boeing 737-808	Air Berlin
	D-ABBY	Boeing 737-808	Air Berlin
	D-ABCA	Airbus A.321-211	Air Berlin
	D-ABCB	Airbus A.321-211	Air Berlin
	D-ABCC	Airbus A.321-211	Air Berlin
	D-ABCF	Airbus A.321-211	Air Berlin
	D-ABCG	Airbus A.321-211	Air Berlin
	D-ABCH	Airbus A.321-211	Air Berlin
	D-ABCI	Airbus A.321-231	Air Berlin
	D-ABCJ	Airbus A.321-231	Air Berlin
	D-ABCK	Airbus A.321-231	Air Berlin
	D-ABDB	Airbus A.320-214	Air Berlin
	D-ABDO	Airbus A.320-214	Air Berlin
	D-ABDP	Airbus A.320-214	Air Berlin
	D-ABDQ	Airbus A.320-214	Air Berlin
	D-ABDU	Airbus A.320-214	Air Berlin
	D-ABDW	Airbus A.320-214	Air Berlin

Reg.	Type	Owner or Operator	Notes
D-ABDY	Airbus A.320-214	Air Berlin	
D-ABEB	Boeing 737-330	Lufthansa *Xanten*	
D-ABEC	Boeing 737-330	Lufthansa *Karlsrühe*	
D-ABED	Boeing 737-330	Lufthansa *Hagen*	
D-ABEH	Boeing 737-330	Lufthansa *Bad Kissingen*	
D-ABEK	Boeing 737-330	Lufthansa *Wuppertal*	
D-ABEN	Boeing 737-330	Lufthansa *Neubrandenburg*	
D-ABEW	Boeing 737-330	Lufthansa *Detmold*	
D-ABFA	Airbus A.320-214	Air Berlin	
D-ABFC	Airbus A.320-214	Air Berlin	
D-ABFE	Airbus A.320-214	Air Berlin	
D-ABFF	Airbus A.320-214	Air Berlin	
D-ABFG	Airbus A.320-214	Air Berlin	
D-ABFK	Airbus A.320-214	Air Berlin	
D-ABFN	Airbus A.320-214	Air Berlin	
D-ABFO	Airbus A.320-214	Air Berlin	
D-ABFP	Airbus A.320-214	Air Berlin	
D-ABFT	Airbus A.320-214	Air Berlin	
D-ABFU	Airbus A.320-214	Air Berlin	
D-ABFZ	Airbus A.320-214	Air Berlin	
D-ABGJ	Airbus A.319-112	Air Berlin	
D-ABGK	Airbus A.319-112	Air Berlin	
D-ABGN	Airbus A.319-112	Air Berlin	
D-ABGO	Airbus A.319-112	Air Berlin	
D-ABGP	Airbus A.319-112	Air Berlin	
D-ABGS	Airbus A.319-112	Air Berlin	
D-ABIF	Boeing 737-530	Lufthansa *Landau*	
D-ABIH	Boeing 737-530	Lufthansa *Bruchsal*	
D-ABIL	Boeing 737-530	Lufthansa *Memmingen*	
D-ABIN	Boeing 737-530	Lufthansa *Langenhagen*	
D-ABIR	Boeing 737-530	Lufthansa *Anklam*	
D-ABIS	Boeing 737-530	Lufthansa *Rendsburg*	
D-ABIT	Boeing 737-530	Lufthansa *Neumünster*	
D-ABIU	Boeing 737-530	Lufthansa *Limburg a.d. Lahn*	
D-ABIW	Boeing 737-530	Lufthansa *Bad Nauheim*	
D-ABIX	Boeing 737-530	Lufthansa *Iserlohn*	
D-ABIY	Boeing 737-530	Lufthansa *Lingen*	
D-ABJB	Boeing 737-530	Lufthansa *Rheine*	
D-ABKA	Boeing 737-82R	Air Berlin	
D-ABKD	Boeing 737-86J	Air Berlin	
D-ABKI	Boeing 737-86J	Air Berlin	
D-ABKJ	Boeing 737-86J	Air Berlin	
D-ABKK	Boeing 737-86J	Air Berlin	
D-ABKM	Boeing 737-86J	Air Berlin	
D-ABKN	Boeing 737-86J	Air Berlin	
D-ABKP	Boeing 737-86J	Air Berlin	
D-ABKQ	Boeing 737-86J	Air Berlin	
D-ABKS	Boeing 737-86J	Air Berlin	
D-ABKT	Boeing 737-86J	Air Berlin	
D-ABKW	Boeing 737-86J	Air Berlin	
D-ABLA	Boeing 737-76J	Air Berlin	
D-ABLC	Boeing 737-76J	Air Berlin	
D-ABLD	Boeing 737-76J	Air Berlin	
D-ABMB	Boeing 737-86J	Air Berlin	
D-ABMC	Boeing 737-86J	Air Berlin	
D-ABMD	Boeing 737-86J	Air Berlin	
D-ABME	Boeing 737-86J	Air Berlin	
D-ABMF	Boeing 737-86J	Air Berlin	
D-ABMI	Boeing 737-86J	Air Berlin	
D-ABMK	Boeing 737-86J	Air Berlin	
D-ABML	Boeing 737-86J	Air Berlin	
D-ABMO	Boeing 737-86J	Air Berlin	
D-ABMP	Boeing 737-86J	Air Berlin	
D-ABMQ	Boeing 737-86J	Air Berlin	
D-ABMR	Boeing 737-86J	Air Berlin	
D-ABMS	Boeing 737-86J	Air Berlin	
D-ABMU	Boeing 737-86J	Air Berlin	
D-ABMV	Boeing 737-86J	Air Berlin	
D-ABNA	Airbus A.320-214	Air Berlin	
D-ABNB	Airbus A.320-214	Air Berlin	
D-ABNE	Airbus A.320-214	Air Berlin	
D-ABNF	Airbus A.320-214	Air Berlin	

Notes	Reg.	Type	Owner or Operator
	D-ABOA	Boeing 757-330	Condor
	D-ABOB	Boeing 757-330	Condor
	D-ABOC	Boeing 757-330	Condor
	D-ABOE	Boeing 757-330	Condor
	D-ABOF	Boeing 757-330	Condor
	D-ABOG	Boeing 757-330	Condor
	D-ABOH	Boeing 757-330	Condor
	D-ABOI	Boeing 757-330	Condor
	D-ABOJ	Boeing 757-330	Condor
	D-ABOK	Boeing 757-330	Condor
	D-ABOL	Boeing 757-330	Condor
	D-ABOM	Boeing 757-330	Condor
	D-ABON	Boeing 757-330	Condor
	D-ABQA	DHC.8Q-402 Dash Eight	Air Berlin
	D-ABQB	DHC.8Q-402 Dash Eight	Air Berlin
	D-ABQC	DHC.8Q-402 Dash Eight	Air Berlin
	D-ABQD	DHC.8Q-402 Dash Eight	Air Berlin
	D-ABQE	DHC.8Q-402 Dash Eight	Air Berlin
	D-ABQF	DHC.8Q-402 Dash Eight	Air Berlin
	D-ABQG	DHC.8Q-402 Dash Eight	Air Berlin
	D-ABQH	DHC.8Q-402 Dash Eight	Air Berlin
	D-ABQI	DHC.8Q-402 Dash Eight	Air Berlin
	D-ABQJ	DHC.8Q-402 Dash Eight	Air Berlin
	D-ABTF	Boeing 747-430 (SCD)	Lufthansa *Thuringen*
	D-ABTK	Boeing 747-430 (SCD)	Lufthansa *Kiel*
	D-ABTL	Boeing 747-430 (SCD)	Lufthansa *Dresden*
	D-ABUA	Boeing 767-330ER	Condor
	D-ABUB	Boeing 767-330ER	Condor
	D-ABUC	Boeing 767-330ER	Condor
	D-ABUD	Boeing 767-330ER	Condor
	D-ABUE	Boeing 767-330ER	Condor
	D-ABUF	Boeing 767-330ER	Condor
	D-ABUH	Boeing 767-330ER	Condor
	D-ABUI	Boeing 767-330ER	Condor
	D-ABUK	Boeing 767-343ER	Condor
	D-ABUL	Boeing 767-31BER	Condor
	D-ABUM	Boeing 767-31BER	Condor
	D-ABUZ	Boeing 767-330ER	Condor
	D-ABVH	Boeing 747-430	Lufthansa *Düsseldorf*
	D-ABVK	Boeing 747-430	Lufthansa *Hannover*
	D-ABVL	Boeing 747-430	Lufthansa *Muenchen*
	D-ABVN	Boeing 747-430	Lufthansa *Dortmund*
	D-ABVO	Boeing 747-430	Lufthansa *Mulheim a.d.Ruhr*
	D-ABVP	Boeing 747-430	Lufthansa *Bremen*
	D-ABVR	Boeing 747-430	Lufthansa *Koln*
	D-ABVS	Boeing 747-430	Lufthansa *Saarland*
	D-ABVT	Boeing 747-430	Lufthansa *Rheinland Pfalz*
	D-ABVU	Boeing 747-430	Lufthansa *Bayern*
	D-ABVW	Boeing 747-430	Lufthansa *Wolfsburg*
	D-ABVX	Boeing 747-430	Lufthansa *Schleswig-Holstein*
	D-ABVY	Boeing 747-430	Lufthansa *Nordrhein Westfalen*
	D-ABVZ	Boeing 747-430	Lufthansa *Niedersachsen*
	D-ABXA	Airbus A.330-223	Air Berlin
	D-ABXB	Airbus A.330-223	Air Berlin
	D-ABXC	Airbus A.330-243	Air Berlin
	D-ABXD	Airbus A.330-223	Air Berlin
	D-ABXU	Boeing 737-330	Lufthansa *Seeheim-Jugenheim*
	D-ABXX	Boeing 737-330	Lufthansa *Bad Homburg v.d. Höhe*
	D-ABYA	Boeing 747-830	Lufthansa
	D-ABYC	Boeing 747-830	Lufthansa
	D-ABYD	Boeing 747-830	Lufthansa
	D-ABYF	Boeing 747-830	Lufthansa
	D-ABYG	Boeing 747-830	Lufthansa
	D-ABYH	Boeing 747-830	Lufthansa
	D-ABYI	Boeing 747-830	Lufthansa
	D-ABYJ	Boeing 747-830	Lufthansa
	D-ABYK	Boeing 747-830	Lufthansa
	D-ACKA	Canadair CRJ900ER	Lufthansa Regional *Pfaffenhofen a.d.ilm*
	D-ACKB	Canadair CRJ900ER	Lufthansa Regional *Schliersee*
	D-ACKC	Canadair CRJ900ER	Lufthansa Regional *Mettmann*
	D-ACKD	Canadair CRJ900ER	Lufthansa Regional *Wittlich*
	D-ACKE	Canadair CRJ900ER	Lufthansa Regional *Weningerode*

Reg.	Type	Owner or Operator	Notes
D-ACKF	Canadair CRJ900ER	Lufthansa Regional *Prenzlau*	
D-ACKG	Canadair CRJ900ER	Lufthansa Regional *Glucksburg*	
D-ACKH	Canadair CRJ900ER	Lufthansa Regional *Radebuel*	
D-ACKI	Canadair CRJ900ER	Lufthansa Regional *Tuttlingen*	
D-ACKJ	Canadair CRJ900ER	Lufthansa Regional *Ilmenau*	
D-ACKK	Canadair CRJ900ER	Lufthansa Regional *Furstenwalde*	
D-ACKL	Canadair CRJ900ER	Lufthansa Regional *Bad Bergzabern*	
D-ACNA	Canadair CRJ900ER	Eurowings/Germanwings	
D-ACNB	Canadair CRJ900ER	Eurowings/Germanwings	
D-ACNC	Canadair CRJ900ER	Eurowings/Germanwings	
D-ACND	Canadair CRJ900ER	Eurowings/Germanwings	
D-ACNE	Canadair CRJ900ER	Eurowings/Germanwings	
D-ACNF	Canadair CRJ900ER	Eurowings/Germanwings	
D-ACNG	Canadair CRJ900ER	Lufthansa Regional	
D-ACNH	Canadair CRJ900ER	Lufthansa Regional	
D-ACNI	Canadair CRJ900ER	Lufthansa Regional	
D-ACNJ	Canadair CRJ900ER	Lufthansa Regional	
D-ACNK	Canadair CRJ900ER	Lufthansa Regional	
D-ACNL	Canadair CRJ900ER	Lufthansa Regional	
D-ACNM	Canadair CRJ900ER	Lufthansa Regional	
D-ACNN	Canadair CRJ900ER	Lufthansa Regional	
D-ACNO	Canadair CRJ900ER	Lufthansa Regional	
D-ACNP	Canadair CRJ900ER	Lufthansa Regional	
D-ACNQ	Canadair CRJ900ER	Lufthansa Regional	
D-ACNR	Canadair CRJ900ER	Lufthansa Regional	
D-ACNT	Canadair CRJ900ER	Lufthansa Regional	
D-ACNU	Canadair CRJ900ER	Lufthansa Regional	
D-ACNV	Canadair CRJ900ER	Lufthansa Regional	
D-ACNW	Canadair CRJ900ER	Lufthansa Regional	
D-ACNX	Canadair CRJ900ER	Lufthansa Regional	
D-ACPB	Canadair CRJ700ER	Lufthansa Regional *Rudesheim a. Rhein*	
D-ACPC	Canadair CRJ700ER	Lufthansa Regional *Espelkamp*	
D-ACPD	Canadair CRJ700ER	Lufthansa Regional *Vilshofen*	
D-ACPE	Canadair CRJ700ER	Lufthansa Regional *Belzig*	
D-ACPF	Canadair CRJ700ER	Lufthansa Regional *Uhingen*	
D-ACPG	Canadair CRJ700ER	Lufthansa Regional *Leinfelden-Echterdingen*	
D-ACPH	Canadair CRJ700ER	Lufthansa Regional *Eschwege*	
D-ACPI	Canadair CRJ700ER	Lufthansa Regional *Viernheim*	
D-ACPJ	Canadair CRJ700ER	Lufthansa Regional *Neumarkt i. d. Oberpfalz*	
D-ACPK	Canadair CRJ700ER	Lufthansa Regional *Besigheim*	
D-ACPL	Canadair CRJ700ER	Lufthansa Regional *Halberstadt*	
D-ACPM	Canadair CRJ700ER	Lufthansa Regional *Heidenheim an der Brenz*	
D-ACPN	Canadair CRJ700ER	Lufthansa Regional *Quedlinburg*	
D-ACPO	Canadair CRJ700ER	Lufthansa Regional *Spaichingen*	
D-ACPP	Canadair CRJ700ER	Lufthansa Regional *Torgau*	
D-ACPQ	Canadair CRJ700ER	Lufthansa Regional *Lübbecke*	
D-ACPR	Canadair CRJ700ER	Lufthansa Regional *Weinheim an der Bergstrasse*	
D-ACPS	Canadair CRJ700ER	Lufthansa Regional *Berchtesgarten*	
D-ACPT	Canadair CRJ700ER	Lufthansa Regional *Altötting*	
D-AEAB	Airbus A.300B4-622R	EAT Leipzig/DHL	
D-AEAC	Airbus A.300B4-622R	EAT Leipzig/DHL	
D-AEAD	Airbus A.300B4-622R	EAT Leipzig/DHL	
D-AEAE	Airbus A.300B4-622R	EAT Leipzig/DHL	
D-AEAF	Airbus A.300B4-622R	EAT Leipzig/DHL	
D-AEAG	Airbus A.300B4-622R	EAT Leipzig/DHL	
D-AEAH	Airbus A.300B4-622R	EAT Leipzig/DHL	
D-AEAI	Airbus A.300B4-622R	EAT Leipzig/DHL	
D-AEAJ	Airbus A.300B4-622R	EAT Leipzig/DHL	
D-AEAK	Airbus A.300B4-622R	EAT Leipzig/DHL	
D-AEAL	Airbus A.300B4-622R	EAT Leipzig/DHL	
D-AEAM	Airbus A.300B4-622R	EAT Leipzig/DHL	
D-AEAN	Airbus A.300B4-622R	EAT Leipzig/DHL	
D-AEAO	Airbus A.300B4-622R	EAT Leipzig/DHL	
D-AEAP	Airbus A.300B4-622R	EAT Leipzig/DHL	
D-AEAQ	Airbus A.300B4-622R	EAT Leipzig/DHL	
D-AEAR	Airbus A.300B4-622R	EAT Leipzig/DHL	
D-AEAS	Airbus A.300B4-622R	EAT Leipzig/DHL	
D-AEAT	Airbus A.300B4-622R	EAT Leipzig/DHL	
D-AEBA	Embraer ERJ190-200LR	Lufthansa Regional	
D-AEBB	Embraer ERJ190-200LR	Lufthansa Regional	
D-AEBC	Embraer ERJ190-200LR	Lufthansa Regional	
D-AEBD	Embraer ERJ190-200LR	Lufthansa Regional	

Notes	Reg.	Type	Owner or Operator
	D-AEBE	Embraer ERJ190-200LR	Lufthansa Regional
	D-AEBF	Embraer ERJ190-200LR	Lufthansa Regional
	D-AEBG	Embraer ERJ190-200LR	Lufthansa Regional
	D-AEBH	Embraer ERJ190-200LR	Lufthansa Regional
	D-AEBI	Embraer ERJ190-200LR	Lufthansa Regional
	D-AEBJ	Embraer ERJ190-200LR	Lufthansa Regional
	D-AEBK	Embraer ERJ190-200LR	Lufthansa Regional
	D-AEBL	Embraer ERJ190-200LR	Lufthansa Regional
	D-AEBM	Embraer ERJ190-200LR	Lufthansa Regional
	D-AEBN	Embraer ERJ190-200LR	Lufthansa Regional
	D-AEBO	Embraer ERJ190-200LR	Lufthansa Regional
	D-AEBP	Embraer ERJ190-200LR	Lufthansa Regional
	D-AEBQ	Embraer ERJ190-200LR	Lufthansa Regional
	D-AEBR	Embraer ERJ190-200LR	Lufthansa Regional
	D-AEBS	Embraer ERJ190-200LR	Lufthansa Regional
	D-AECA	Embraer ERJ190-100LR	Lufthansa Regional *Deidesheim*
	D-AECB	Embraer ERJ190-100LR	Lufthansa Regional *Meiben*
	D-AECC	Embraer ERJ190-100LR	Lufthansa Regional *Eisleben*
	D-AECD	Embraer ERJ190-100LR	Lufthansa Regional *Schkeuditz*
	D-AECE	Embraer ERJ190-100LR	Lufthansa Regional *Kronach*
	D-AECF	Embraer ERJ190-100LR	Lufthansa Regional
	D-AECG	Embraer ERJ190-100LR	Lufthansa Regional
	D-AECH	Embraer ERJ190-100LR	Lufthansa Regional
	D-AECI	Embraer ERJ190-100LR	Lufthansa Regional
	D-AEMA	Embraer ERJ190-200LR	Lufthansa Regional
	D-AEMB	Embraer ERJ190-200LR	Lufthansa Regional
	D-AEMC	Embraer ERJ190-200LR	Lufthansa Regional
	D-AEMD	Embraer ERJ190-200LR	Lufthansa Regional
	D-AEME	Embraer ERJ190-200LR	Lufthansa Regional
	D-AEMF	Embraer ERJ190-100LR	Lufthansa Regional
	D-AEMG	Embraer ERJ190-100LR	Lufthansa Regional
	D-AGEB	Boeing 737-76J	Germania
	D-AGEC	Boeing 737-76J	Air Berlin
	D-AGEL	Boeing 737-75B	Germania
	D-AGEN	Boeing 737-75B	Air Berlin
	D-AGEP	Boeing 737-75B	Germania
	D-AGEQ	Boeing 737-75B	Germania
	D-AGER	Boeing 737-75B	Germania
	D-AGES	Boeing 737-75B	Germania
	D-AGET	Boeing 737-75B	Germania
	D-AGEU	Boeing 737-75B	Germania
	D-AGEY	Boeing 737-7L9	Germania
	D-AGWA	Airbus A.319-132	Germanwings
	D-AGWB	Airbus A.319-132	Germanwings
	D-AGWC	Airbus A.319-132	Germanwings
	D-AGWD	Airbus A.319-132	Germanwings
	D-AGWE	Airbus A.319-132	Germanwings
	D-AGWF	Airbus A.319-132	Germanwings
	D-AGWG	Airbus A.319-132	Germanwings
	D-AGWH	Airbus A.319-132	Germanwings
	D-AGWI	Airbus A.319-132	Germanwings
	D-AGWJ	Airbus A.319-132	Germanwings
	D-AGWK	Airbus A.319-132	Germanwings
	D-AGWL	Airbus A.319-132	Germanwings
	D-AGWM	Airbus A.319-132	Germanwings
	D-AGWN	Airbus A.319-132	Germanwings
	D-AGWO	Airbus A.319-132	Germanwings
	D-AGWP	Airbus A.319-132	Germanwings
	D-AGWQ	Airbus A.319-132	Germanwings
	D-AGWR	Airbus A.319-132	Germanwings
	D-AGWS	Airbus A.319-132	Germanwings
	D-AGWT	Airbus A.319-132	Germanwings
	D-AGWU	Airbus A.319-132	Germanwings
	D-AGWV	Airbus A.319-132	Germanwings
	D-AGWW	Airbus A.319-132	Germanwings
	D-AGWX	Airbus A.319-132	Germanwings
	D-AGWY	Airbus A.319-132	Germanwings
	D-AHFH	Boeing 737-8K5	TUIfly
	D-AHFI	Boeing 737-8K5	TUIfly
	D-AHFO	Boeing 737-8K5	Air Berlin
	D-AHFP	Boeing 737-8K5	TUIfly
	D-AHFR	Boeing 737-8K5	TUIfly

Reg.	Type	Owner or Operator	Notes
D-AHFS	Boeing 737-86N	Air Berlin	
D-AHFT	Boeing 737-8K5	TUIfly	
D-AHFV	Boeing 737-8K5	TUIfly	
D-AHFW	Boeing 737-8K5	TUIfly	
D-AHFX	Boeing 737-8K5	TUIfly	
D-AHFY	Boeing 737-8K5	TUIfly	
D-AHFZ	Boeing 737-8K5	TUIfly	
D-AHHA	Airbus A.319-111	Hamburg Airways	
D-AHHB	Airbus A.319-112	Hamburg Airways	
D-AHHC	Airbus A.320-214	Hamburg Airways	
D-AHHD	Airbus A.320-214	Hamburg Airways	
D-AHHF	Airbus A.320-214	Hamburg Airways	
D-AHIA	Boeing 737-73S	Air Berlin	
D-AHIL	Airbus A.319-112	Germania	
D-AHIM	Airbus A.319-112	Germania	
D-AHLK	Boeing 737-8K5	TUIfly	
D-AHXC	Boeing 737-7K5	Air Berlin	
D-AHXE	Boeing 737-7K5	Air Berlin	
D-AHXF	Boeing 737-7K5	Air Berlin	
D-AHXG	Boeing 737-7K5	Air Berlin	
D-AHXH	Boeing 737-7K5	Air Berlin	
D-AHXJ	Boeing 737-7K5	Air Berlin	
D-AIAA	Airbus A.321-211	Condor	
D-AIAC	Airbus A.321-211	Condor	
D-AIAD	Airbus A.321-211	Condor	
D-AIBA	Airbus A.319-114	Lufthansa	
D-AIBB	Airbus A.319-114	Lufthansa	
D-AIBC	Airbus A.319-114	Lufthansa	
D-AIBD	Airbus A.319-114	Lufthansa *Pirmasens*	
D-AIBE	Airbus A.319-114	Lufthansa *Schonfeld*	
D-AIBF	Airbus A.319-112	Lufthansa	
D-AIBG	Airbus A.319-112	Lufthansa	
D-AIBH	Airbus A.319-112	Lufthansa	
D-AIBI	Airbus A.319-112	Lufthansa	
D-AIBJ	Airbus A.319-112	Lufthansa	
D-AICA	Airbus A.320-212	Condor	
D-AICC	Airbus A.320-212	Condor	
D-AICD	Airbus A.320-212	Condor	
D-AICE	Airbus A.320-212	Condor	
D-AICF	Airbus A.320-212	Condor	
D-AICG	Airbus A.320-212	Condor	
D-AICH	Airbus A.320-212	Condor	
D-AICI	Airbus A.320-212	Condor	
D-AICJ	Airbus A.320-212	Condor	
D-AICK	Airbus A.320-212	Condor	
D-AICL	Airbus A.320-212	Condor	
D-AICN	Airbus A.320-214	Condor	
D-AIDA	Airbus A.321-231	Lufthansa	
D-AIDB	Airbus A.321-231	Lufthansa	
D-AIDC	Airbus A.321-231	Lufthansa	
D-AIDD	Airbus A.321-231	Lufthansa	
D-AIDE	Airbus A.321-231	Lufthansa	
D-AIDF	Airbus A.321-231	Lufthansa	
D-AIDG	Airbus A.321-231	Lufthansa	
D-AIDH	Airbus A.321-231	Lufthansa	
D-AIDI	Airbus A.321-231	Lufthansa	
D-AIDJ	Airbus A.321-231	Lufthansa	
D-AIDK	Airbus A.321-231	Lufthansa	
D-AIDL	Airbus A.321-231	Lufthansa	
D-AIDM	Airbus A.321-231	Lufthansa	
D-AIDN	Airbus A.321-231	Lufthansa	
D-AIDO	Airbus A.321-231	Lufthansa	
D-AIDP	Airbus A.321-231	Lufthansa	
D-AIDQ	Airbus A.321-231	Lufthansa	
D-AIDT	Airbus A.321-231	Lufthansa	
D-AIDU	Airbus A.321-231	Lufthansa	
D-AIDV	Airbus A.321-231	Lufthansa	
D-AIFA	Airbus A.340-313X	Lufthansa *Dorsten*	
D-AIFC	Airbus A.340-313X	Lufthansa *Gander/Halifax*	
D-AIFD	Airbus A.340-313X	Lufthansa *Giessen*	
D-AIFE	Airbus A.340-313X	Lufthansa *Passau*	
D-AIFF	Airbus A.340-313X	Lufthansa *Delmenhorst*	

Notes	Reg.	Type	Owner or Operator
	D-AIGF	Airbus A.340-311	Lufthansa *Gottingen*
	D-AIGH	Airbus A.340-311	Lufthansa *Koblenz*
	D-AIGI	Airbus A.340-311	Lufthansa *Worms*
	D-AIGL	Airbus A.340-313X	Lufthansa *Herne*
	D-AIGM	Airbus A.340-313X	Lufthansa *Görlitz*
	D-AIGN	Airbus A.340-313X	Lufthansa *Solingen*
	D-AIGO	Airbus A.340-313X	Lufthansa *Offenbach*
	D-AIGP	Airbus A.340-313X	Lufthansa *Paderborn*
	D-AIGS	Airbus A.340-313X	Lufthansa *Bergisch-Gladbach*
	D-AIGT	Airbus A.340-313X	Lufthansa *Viersen*
	D-AIGU	Airbus A.340-313X	Lufthansa *Castrop-Rauxei*
	D-AIGV	Airbus A.340-313X	Lufthansa *Dinslaken*
	D-AIGW	Airbus A.340-313X	Lufthansa *Gladbeck*
	D-AIGX	Airbus A.340-313X	Lufthansa *Duren*
	D-AIGY	Airbus A.340-313X	Lufthansa *Lünen*
	D-AIGZ	Airbus A.340-313X	Lufthansa *Villingen-Schwenningen*
	D-AIHA	Airbus A.340-642	Lufthansa *Nurnberg*
	D-AIHB	Airbus A.340-642	Lufthansa *Bremerhaven*
	D-AIHC	Airbus A.340-642	Lufthansa *Essen*
	D-AIHD	Airbus A.340-642	Lufthansa *Stuttgart*
	D-AIHE	Airbus A.340-642	Lufthansa *Leverkusen*
	D-AIHF	Airbus A.340-642	Lufthansa *Lübeck*
	D-AIHH	Airbus A.340-642	Lufthansa
	D-AIHI	Airbus A.340-642	Lufthansa
	D-AIHK	Airbus A.340-642	Lufthansa
	D-AIHL	Airbus A.340-642	Lufthansa
	D-AIHM	Airbus A.340-642	Lufthansa
	D-AIHN	Airbus A.340-642	Lufthansa
	D-AIHO	Airbus A.340-642	Lufthansa
	D-AIHP	Airbus A.340-642	Lufthansa
	D-AIHQ	Airbus A.340-642	Lufthansa
	D-AIHR	Airbus A.340-642	Lufthansa
	D-AIHS	Airbus A.340-642	Lufthansa
	D-AIHT	Airbus A.340-642	Lufthansa
	D-AIHU	Airbus A.340-642	Lufthansa
	D-AIHV	Airbus A.340-642	Lufthansa
	D-AIHW	Airbus A.340-642	Lufthansa
	D-AIHX	Airbus A.340-642	Lufthansa
	D-AIHY	Airbus A.340-642	Lufthansa
	D-AIHZ	Airbus A.340-642	Lufthansa
	D-AIKA	Airbus A.330-343X	Lufthansa *Minden*
	D-AIKB	Airbus A.330-343X	Lufthansa *Cuxhaven*
	D-AIKC	Airbus A.330-343X	Lufthansa *Hamm*
	D-AIKD	Airbus A.330-343X	Lufthansa *Siegen*
	D-AIKE	Airbus A.330-343X	Lufthansa *Landshut*
	D-AIKF	Airbus A.330-343X	Lufthansa *Witten*
	D-AIKG	Airbus A.330-343X	Lufthansa *Ludwigsburg*
	D-AIKH	Airbus A.330-343X	Lufthansa
	D-AIKI	Airbus A.330-343X	Lufthansa
	D-AIKJ	Airbus A.330-343X	Lufthansa
	D-AIKK	Airbus A.330-343X	Lufthansa
	D-AIKL	Airbus A.330-343X	Lufthansa
	D-AIKM	Airbus A.330-343X	Lufthansa
	D-AIKN	Airbus A.330-343X	Lufthansa
	D-AIKO	Airbus A.330-343X	Lufthansa
	D-AIKP	Airbus A.330-343X	Lufthansa
	D-AIKQ	Airbus A.330-343X	Lufthansa
	D-AIKR	Airbus A.330-343X	Lufthansa
	D-AIKS	Airbus A.330-343X	Lufthansa
	D-AILA	Airbus A.319-114	Lufthansa *Frankfurt (Oder)*
	D-AILB	Airbus A.319-114	Lufthansa *Lutherstadt Wittenburg*
	D-AILC	Airbus A.319-114	Lufthansa *Russelsheim*
	D-AILD	Airbus A.319-114	Lufthansa *Dinkelsbühl*
	D-AILE	Airbus A.319-114	Lufthansa *Kelsterbach*
	D-AILF	Airbus A.319-114	Lufthansa Italia
	D-AILH	Airbus A.319-114	Lufthansa Italia *Norderstedt*
	D-AILI	Airbus A.319-114	Lufthansa Italia *Roma*
	D-AILK	Airbus A.319-114	Lufthansa *Landshut*
	D-AILL	Airbus A.319-114	Lufthansa *Marburg*
	D-AILM	Airbus A.319-114	Lufthansa *Friedrichshafen*
	D-AILN	Airbus A.319-114	Lufthansa *Idar-Oberstein*
	D-AILP	Airbus A.319-114	Lufthansa *Tubingen*

Reg.	Type	Owner or Operator	Notes
D-AILR	Airbus A.319-114	Lufthansa *Tegernsee*	
D-AILS	Airbus A.319-114	Lufthansa *Heide*	
D-AILT	Airbus A.319-114	Lufthansa *Straubing*	
D-AILU	Airbus A.319-114	Lufthansa *Verden*	
D-AILW	Airbus A.319-114	Lufthansa *Donaueschingen*	
D-AILX	Airbus A.319-114	Lufthansa *Feilbach*	
D-AILY	Airbus A.319-114	Lufthansa *Schweinfurt*	
D-AIMA	Airbus A.380-841	Lufthansa *Frankfurt am Main*	
D-AIMB	Airbus A.380-841	Lufthansa	
D-AIMC	Airbus A.380-841	Lufthansa	
D-AIMD	Airbus A.380-841	Lufthansa	
D-AIME	Airbus A.380-841	Lufthansa *Johannesburg*	
D-AIMF	Airbus A.380-841	Lufthansa *Zurich*	
D-AIMG	Airbus A.380-841	Lufthansa	
D-AIMH	Airbus A.380-841	Lufthansa	
D-AIMI	Airbus A.380-841	Lufthansa	
D-AIMJ	Airbus A.380-841	Lufthansa *Brussel*	
D-AIMK	Airbus A.380-841	Lufthansa	
D-AIML	Airbus A.380-841	Lufthansa	
D-AIPA	Airbus A.320-211	Lufthansa *Buxtehude*	
D-AIPB	Airbus A.320-211	Lufthansa *Heidelberg*	
D-AIPC	Airbus A.320-211	Lufthansa *Braunschweig*	
D-AIPD	Airbus A.320-211	Lufthansa *Freiburg*	
D-AIPE	Airbus A.320-211	Lufthansa *Kassel*	
D-AIPF	Airbus A.320-211	Lufthansa *Deggendorf*	
D-AIPH	Airbus A.320-211	Lufthansa *Munster*	
D-AIPK	Airbus A.320-211	Lufthansa *Wiesbaden*	
D-AIPL	Airbus A.320-211	Lufthansa *Ludwigshafen am Rhein*	
D-AIPM	Airbus A.320-211	Lufthansa *Troisdorf*	
D-AIPP	Airbus A.320-211	Lufthansa *Starnberg*	
D-AIPR	Airbus A.320-211	Lufthansa *Kaufbeuren*	
D-AIPS	Airbus A.320-211	Lufthansa (for Germanwings)	
D-AIPT	Airbus A.320-211	Lufthansa *Cottbus*	
D-AIPU	Airbus A.320-211	Lufthansa (for Germanwings)	
D-AIPW	Airbus A.320-211	Lufthansa (for Germanwings)	
D-AIPX	Airbus A.320-211	Germanwings	
D-AIPY	Airbus A.320-211	Lufthansa (for Germanwings)	
D-AIPZ	Airbus A.320-211	Germanwings	
D-AIQA	Airbus A.320-211	Lufthansa (for Germanwings)	
D-AIQB	Airbus A.320-211	Lufthansa (for Germanwings)	
D-AIQC	Airbus A.320-211	Lufthansa (for Germanwings)	
D-AIQD	Airbus A.320-211	Lufthansa (for Germanwings)	
D-AIQE	Airbus A.320-211	Lufthansa (for Germanwings)	
D-AIQF	Airbus A.320-211	Lufthansa (for Germanwings)	
D-AIQH	Airbus A.320-211	Germanwings	
D-AIQK	Airbus A.320-211	Germanwings	
D-AIQL	Airbus A.320-211	Lufthansa (for Germanwings)	
D-AIQM	Airbus A.320-211	Lufthansa (for Germanwings)	
D-AIQN	Airbus A.320-211	Lufthansa (for Germanwings)	
D-AIQP	Airbus A.320-211	Lufthansa (for Germanwings)	
D-AIQR	Airbus A.320-211	Lufthansa *Lahr/Schwarzwald*	
D-AIQS	Airbus A.320-211	Germanwings	
D-AIQT	Airbus A.320-211	Lufthansa *Gotha*	
D-AIQU	Airbus A.320-211	Lufthansa *Backnang*	
D-AIQW	Airbus A.320-211	Lufthansa *Kleve*	
D-AIRA	Airbus A.321-131	Lufthansa *Finkenwerder*	
D-AIRB	Airbus A.321-131	Lufthansa *Baden-Baden*	
D-AIRC	Airbus A.321-131	Lufthansa *Erlangen*	
D-AIRD	Airbus A.321-131	Lufthansa *Coburg*	
D-AIRE	Airbus A.321-131	Lufthansa *Osnabrueck*	
D-AIRF	Airbus A.321-131	Lufthansa *Kempten*	
D-AIRH	Airbus A.321-131	Lufthansa *Garmisch-Partenkirchen*	
D-AIRK	Airbus A.321-131	Lufthansa *Freudenstadt/Schwarzwald*	
D-AIRL	Airbus A.321-131	Lufthansa *Kulmbach*	
D-AIRM	Airbus A.321-131	Lufthansa *Darmstadt*	
D-AIRN	Airbus A.321-131	Lufthansa *Kaiserslautern*	
D-AIRO	Airbus A.321-131	Lufthansa *Konstanz*	
D-AIRP	Airbus A.321-131	Lufthansa *Lüneburg*	
D-AIRR	Airbus A.321-131	Lufthansa *Wismar*	
D-AIRS	Airbus A.321-131	Lufthansa *Husum*	
D-AIRT	Airbus A.321-131	Lufthansa *Regensburg*	
D-AIRU	Airbus A.321-131	Lufthansa *Würzburg*	

Notes	Reg.	Type	Owner or Operator
	D-AIRW	Airbus A.321-131	Lufthansa *Heilbronn*
	D-AIRX	Airbus A.321-131	Lufthansa *Weimar*
	D-AIRY	Airbus A.321-131	Lufthansa *Flensburg*
	D-AISB	Airbus A.321-231	Lufthansa *Hamein*
	D-AISC	Airbus A.321-231	Lufthansa *Speyer*
	D-AISD	Airbus A.321-231	Lufthansa *Chemnitz*
	D-AISE	Airbus A.321-231	Lufthansa *Neustadt an der Weinstrasse*
	D-AISF	Airbus A.321-231	Lufthansa *Lippstadt*
	D-AISG	Airbus A.321-231	Lufthansa *Dormagen*
	D-AISH	Airbus A.321-231	Lufthansa
	D-AISI	Airbus A.321-231	Lufthansa
	D-AISJ	Airbus A.321-231	Lufthansa
	D-AISK	Airbus A.321-231	Lufthansa
	D-AISL	Airbus A.321-231	Lufthansa Arnsberg
	D-AISN	Airbus A.321-231	Lufthansa *Goppingen*
	D-AISO	Airbus A.321-231	Lufthansa
	D-AISP	Airbus A.321-231	Lufthansa
	D-AISQ	Airbus A.321-231	Lufthansa
	D-AISR	Airbus A.321-231	Lufthansa
	D-AIST	Airbus A.321-231	Lufthansa
	D-AISU	Airbus A.321-231	Lufthansa *Nordlingen*
	D-AISV	Airbus A.321-231	Lufthansa *Bingen*
	D-AISW	Airbus A.321-231	Lufthansa
	D-AISX	Airbus A.321-231	Lufthansa
	D-AISZ	Airbus A.321-231	Lufthansa
	D-AIUA	Airbus A.320-214	Lufthansa
	D-AIUB	Airbus A.320-214	Lufthansa
	D-AIUC	Airbus A.320-214	Lufthansa
	D-AIUD	Airbus A.320-214	Lufthansa
	D-AIZA	Airbus A.320-214	Lufthansa
	D-AIZB	Airbus A.320-214	Lufthansa
	D-AIZC	Airbus A.320-214	Lufthansa
	D-AIZD	Airbus A.320-214	Lufthansa
	D-AIZE	Airbus A.320-214	Lufthansa
	D-AIZF	Airbus A.320-214	Lufthansa
	D-AIZG	Airbus A.320-214	Lufthansa
	D-AIZH	Airbus A.320-214	Lufthansa
	D-AIZI	Airbus A.320-214	Lufthansa
	D-AIZJ	Airbus A.320-214	Lufthansa
	D-AIZK	Airbus A.320-214	Lufthansa
	D-AIZL	Airbus A.320-214	Lufthansa
	D-AIZM	Airbus A.320-214	Lufthansa
	D-AIZN	Airbus A.320-214	Lufthansa
	D-AIZO	Airbus A.320-214	Lufthansa
	D-AIZP	Airbus A.320-214	Lufthansa
	D-AIZQ	Airbus A.320-214	Lufthansa
	D-AIZR	Airbus A.320-214	Lufthansa
	D-AIZS	Airbus A.320-214	Lufthansa
	D-AIZT	Airbus A.320-214	Lufthansa
	D-AIZU	Airbus A.320-214	Lufthansa
	D-AIZV	Airbus A.320-214	Lufthansa
	D-AIZW	Airbus A.320-214	Lufthansa
	D-AIZX	Airbus A.320-214	Lufthansa
	D-AIZY	Airbus A.320-214	Lufthansa
	D-AIZZ	Airbus A.320-214	Lufthansa
	D-AKNF	Airbus A.319-112	Germanwings
	D-AKNG	Airbus A.319-112	Germanwings
	D-AKNH	Airbus A.319-112	Germanwings
	D-AKNI	Airbus A.319-112	Germanwings
	D-AKNJ	Airbus A.319-112	Germanwings
	D-AKNK	Airbus A.319-112	Germanwings
	D-AKNL	Airbus A.319-112	Germanwings
	D-AKNM	Airbus A.319-112	Germanwings
	D-AKNN	Airbus A.319-112	Germanwings
	D-AKNO	Airbus A.319-112	Germanwings
	D-AKNP	Airbus A.319-112	Germanwings
	D-AKNQ	Airbus A.319-112	Germanwings
	D-AKNR	Airbus A.319-112	Germanwings *Spirit of T-Com*
	D-AKNS	Airbus A.319-112	Germanwings *Spirit of T Mobile*
	D-AKNT	Airbus A.319-112	Germanwings *City of Hamburg*
	D-AKNU	Airbus A.319-112	Germanwings
	D-AKNV	Airbus A.319-112	Germanwings

Reg.	Type	Owner or Operator	Notes
D-ALCA	McD Douglas MD-11F	Lufthansa Cargo	
D-ALCB	McD Douglas MD-11F	Lufthansa Cargo	
D-ALCC	McD Douglas MD-11F	Lufthansa Cargo	
D-ALCD	McD Douglas MD-11F	Lufthansa Cargo	
D-ALCF	McD Douglas MD-11F	Lufthansa Cargo	
D-ALCG	McD Douglas MD-11F	Lufthansa Cargo	
D-ALCH	McD Douglas MD-11F	Lufthansa Cargo	
D-ALCI	McD Douglas MD-11F	Lufthansa Cargo	
D-ALCJ	McD Douglas MD-11F	Lufthansa Cargo	
D-ALCK	McD Douglas MD-11F	Lufthansa Cargo	
D-ALCL	McD Douglas MD-11F	Lufthansa Cargo	
D-ALCM	McD Douglas MD-11F	Lufthansa Cargo	
D-ALCN	McD Douglas MD-11F	Lufthansa Cargo	
D-ALCP	McD Douglas MD-11F	Lufthansa Cargo	
D-ALCR	McD Douglas MD-11F	Lufthansa Cargo	
D-ALCS	McD Douglas MD-11F	Lufthansa Cargo	
D-ALEA	Boeing 757-236SF	EAT Leipzig/DHL	
D-ALEB	Boeing 757-236SF	EAT Leipzig/DHL	
D-ALEC	Boeing 757-236SF	EAT Leipzig/DHL	
D-ALED	Boeing 757-236SF	EAT Leipzig/DHL	
D-ALEE	Boeing 757-236SF	EAT Leipzig/DHL	
D-ALEF	Boeing 757-236SF	EAT Leipzig/DHL	
D-ALEG	Boeing 757-236SF	EAT Leipzig/DHL	
D-ALEH	Boeing 757-236SF	EAT Leipzig/DHL	
D-ALEI	Boeing 757-236SF	EAT Leipzig/DHL	
D-ALEJ	Boeing 757-23APF	EAT Leipzig/DHL	
D-ALEK	Boeing 757-236SF	EAT Leipzig/DHL	
D-ALFA	Boeing 777FBT	Lufthansa Cargo	
D-ALFB	Boeing 777FBT	Lufthansa Cargo	
D-ALFC	Boeing 777FBT	Lufthansa Cargo	
D-ALPA	Airbus A.330-223	Air Berlin	
D-ALPB	Airbus A.330-223	Air Berlin	
D-ALPC	Airbus A.330-223	Air Berlin	
D-ALPD	Airbus A.330-223	Air Berlin	
D-ALPE	Airbus A.330-223	Air Berlin	
D-ALPF	Airbus A.330-223	Air Berlin	
D-ALPG	Airbus A.330-223	Air Berlin	
D-ALPH	Airbus A.330-223	Air Berlin	
D-ALPI	Airbus A.330-223	Air Berlin	
D-ALPJ	Airbus A.330-223	Air Berlin	
D-ALSB	Airbus A.321-211	Air Berlin	
D-ALSC	Airbus A.321-211	Air Berlin	
D-AMGL	BAe 146-200	WDL Aviation	
D-APBB	Boeing 737-8FH	PrivatAir/Lufthansa	
D-APBC	Boeing 737-8BK	PrivatAir/Lufthansa	
D-APBD	Boeing 737-8BK	PrivatAir/Lufthansa	
D-ARJF	Embraer ERJ190-100LR	Niki	
D-ASTA	Airbus A.319-112	Gambia Bird	
D-ASTB	Airbus A.319-112	Germania	
D-ASTC	Airbus A.319-112	Germania	
D-ASTD	Airbus A.321-211	Germania	
D-ASTE	Airbus A.321-211	Germania	
D-ASTX	Airbus A.319-112	Germania	
D-ASTY	Airbus A.319-112	Germania	
D-ASTZ	Airbus A.319-112	Germania	
D-ATUA	Boeing 737-8K5	TUIfly	
D-ATUB	Boeing 737-8K5	TUIfly	
D-ATUC	Boeing 737-8K5	TUIfly	
D-ATUD	Boeing 737-8K5	TUIfly	
D-ATUE	Boeing 737-8K5	TUIfly	
D-ATUF	Boeing 737-8K5	TUIfly	
D-ATUG	Boeing 737-8K5	TUIfly	
D-ATUH	Boeing 737-8K5	TUIfly	
D-ATUI	Boeing 737-8K5	TUIfly	
D-ATUJ	Boeing 737-8K5	TUIfly	
D-ATUK	Boeing 737-8K5	TUIfly	
D-ATUL	Boeing 737-8K5	TUIfly	
D-AWBA	Bae 146-300	WDL Aviation	
D-AWUE	BAe 146-200	WDL Aviation	
D-CCAS	Short SD3-60-300	Night Express	
D-CIRD	Dornier 328-110	Loganair/British Airways	
D-CIRI	Dornier 328-110	Sun-Air/British Airways	

Notes	Reg.	Type	Owner or Operator
	D-CIRP	Dornier 328-120	Sun-Air/British Airways
	D-CRAS	Short SD3-60-300	Night Express
	D-IEXB	Beech 99	Night Express

EC (Spain)

	Reg.	Type	Owner or Operator
	EC-ELT	BAe 146-200QT	Pan Air/TNT Airways
	EC-FGR	Airbus A.320-211	Iberia Express
	EC-FLP	Airbus A.320-211	Iberia Express
	EC-FVY	BAe 146-200QT	Pan Air/TNT Airways
	EC-FZE	BAe 146-200QT	Pan Air/TNT Airways
	EC-GJT	Airbus A.340-313	Iberia *Rosa Chacel*
	EC-GLE	Airbus A.340-313	Iberia *Concepcion Arenal*
	EC-GQO	BAe 146-200QT	Pan Air/TNT Airways
	EC-GRH	Airbus A.320-211	Vueling Airlines
	EC-GUP	Airbus A.340-313X	Iberia *Agustina De Aragon*
	EC-GUQ	Airbus A.340-313X	Iberia *Beatriz Galindo*
	EC-GYI	Canadair CRJ200ER	Air Nostrum/Iberia Regional
	EC-HDH	BAe 146-200QT	Pan Air/TNT Airways
	EC-HDS	Boeing 757-256	Iberia *Paraguay*
	EC-HGR	Airbus A.319-111	Iberia *Ribeira Sacra*
	EC-HGV	Airbus A.340-313X	Iberia *Maria Guerrero*
	EC-HGZ	Airbus A.320-214	Vueling Airlines
	EC-HHA	Airbus A.320-214	Vueling Airlines
	EC-HJH	BAe 146-200QT	Pan Air/TNT Airways
	EC-HKO	Airbus A.319-111	Iberia *Gorbia*
	EC-HQI	Airbus A.320-214	Vueling Airlines *Merce Sune*
	EC-HQJ	Airbus A.320-214	Vueling Airlines
	EC-HQL	Airbus A.320-214	Vueling Airlines *Click on Vueling*
	EC-HSH	Canadair CRJ200ER	Air Nostrum/Iberia Regional
	EC-HTB	Airbus A.320-214	Iberia Express
	EC-HTC	Airbus A.320-214	Vueling Airlines
	EC-HTD	Airbus A.320-214	Vueling Airlines *Unos Vuelan,otros Vueling*
	EC-HUH	Airbus A.321-211	Iberia *Benidorm*
	EC-HUI	Airbus A.321-211	Iberia *Comunidad Autonoma de la Rioja*
	EC-HZS	Boeing 737-86Q	Air Europa
	EC-IBM	Canadair CRJ200ER	Air Nostrum/SAS
	EC-IDA	Boeing 737-86Q	Air Europa
	EC-IDC	Canadair CRJ200ER	Air Nostrum/SAS
	EC-IDF	Airbus A.340-313X	Iberia *Mariana Pineda*
	EC-IDT	Boeing 737-86Q	Air Europa
	EC-IEF	Airbus A.320-214	Iberia *Castillo de Loarre*
	EC-IEG	Airbus A.320-214	Iberia *Costa Brava*
	EC-IEI	Airbus A.320-214	Vueling Airlines
	EC-IGK	Airbus A.321-211	Iberia *Costa Calida*
	EC-IGO	Canadair CRJ200ER	Air Nostrum/SAS
	EC-IIH	Airbus A.340-313X	Iberia *Maria Barbara de Braganza*
	EC-III	Boeing 737-86Q	Air Europa
	EC-IJN	Airbus A.321-211	Iberia *Merida*
	EC-ILO	Airbus A.321-211	Iberia *Cueva de Nerja*
	EC-ILP	Airbus A.321-211	Iberia *Peniscola*
	EC-ILQ	Airbus A.320-214	Vueling Airlines
	EC-ILR	Airbus A.320-214	Iberia *San Juan de la Pena*
	EC-ILS	Airbus A.320-214	Iberia *Sierra de Cameros*
	EC-INO	Airbus A.340-642	Iberia *Gaudi*
	EC-IOB	Airbus A.340-642	Iberia *Julio Romanes de Torres*
	EC-IQR	Airbus A.340-642	Iberia *Salvador Dali*
	EC-ISN	Boeing 737-86Q	Air Europa
	EC-ITN	Airbus A.321-211	Iberia *Empuries*
	EC-IXD	Airbus A.321-211	Iberia *Vall d'Aran*
	EC-IZD	Airbus A.320-214	Vueling Airlines
	EC-IZH	Airbus A.320-214	Iberia *San Pere de Roda*
	EC-IZR	Airbus A.320-214	Iberia *Urkiola*
	EC-IZX	Airbus A.340-642	Iberia *Mariano Benlliure*
	EC-IZY	Airbus A.340-642	Iberia *I. Zuloaga*
	EC-JAP	Boeing 737-85P	Air Europa
	EC-JAZ	Airbus A.319-111	Iberia *Las Medulas*
	EC-JBA	Airbus A.340-642	Iberia *Joaquin Rodrigo*
	EC-JBJ	Boeing 737-85P	Air Europa
	EC-JBK	Boeing 737-85P	Air Europa
	EC-JBL	Boeing 737-85P	Air Europa

Reg.	Type	Owner or Operator	Notes
EC-JCY	Airbus A.340-642	Iberia *Andrés Segovia*	
EC-JCZ	Airbus A.340-642	Iberia *Vicente Aleixandre*	
EC-JDL	Airbus A.319-111	Iberia *Los Llanos de Aridane*	
EC-JDM	Airbus A.321-211	Iberia *Cantabria*	
EC-JDR	Airbus A.321-211	Iberia	
EC-JEI	Airbus A.319-111	Iberia *Xátiva*	
EC-JEJ	Airbus A.321-211	Iberia *Río Frío*	
EC-JFF	Airbus A.320-214	Vueling Airlines *Vueling the world*	
EC-JFG	Airbus A.320-214	Iberia Express	
EC-JFH	Airbus A.320-214	Iberia Express	
EC-JFN	Airbus A.320-214	Iberia *Sirrea de las Nieves*	
EC-JFX	Airbus A.340-642	Iberia *Jacinto Benavente*	
EC-JGM	Airbus A.320-214	Vueling Airlines *The joy of vueling*	
EC-JGS	Airbus A.321-211	Iberia *Guadelupe*	
EC-JHK	Boeing 737-85P	Air Europa	
EC-JHL	Boeing 737-85P	Air Europa	
EC-JLE	Airbus A.340-642	Iberia *Santiago Ramon y Cajal*	
EC-JLI	Airbus A.321-211	Iberia *Delta del Llobregrat*	
EC-JMR	Airbus A.321-211	Iberia *Aranjuez*	
EC-JNB	Canadair CRJ900ER	Air Nostrum/Iberia Regional	
EC-JNF	Boeing 737-85P	Air Europa *Mutua Madrileqa*	
EC-JNI	Airbus A.321-211	Iberia *Palmeral de Eiche*	
EC-JNQ	Airbus A.340-642	Iberia *Antonio Machado*	
EC-JNX	Canadair CRJ200ER	Air Nostrum/Iberia Regional	
EC-JPF	Airbus A.330-202	Air Europa	
EC-JPU	Airbus A.340-642	Iberia *Pio Baroja*	
EC-JQG	Airbus A.330-202	Air Europa *Estepona – Costa del Sol*	
EC-JQQ	Airbus A.330-202	Air Europa	
EC-JQZ	Airbus A.321-211	Iberia *Generalife*	
EC-JRE	Airbus A.321-211	Iberia *Villa de Uncastillo*	
EC-JSK	Airbus A.320-214	Iberia Express	
EC-JSY	Airbus A.320-214	Vueling Airlines	
EC-JTQ	Airbus A.320-214	Vueling Airlines *Vueling, que es gerundio*	
EC-JTR	Airbus A.320-214	Vueling Airlines *No Vueling no party*	
EC-JTS	Canadair CRJ900ER	Air Nostrum/Iberia Regional	
EC-JTT	Canadair CRJ900ER	Air Nostrum/Iberia Regional	
EC-JTU	Canadair CRJ900ER	Air Nostrum/Iberia Regional	
EC-JVE	Airbus A.319-111	Vueling Airlines	
EC-JXJ	Airbus A.319-111	Iberia	
EC-JXV	Airbus A.319-111	Vueling Airlines	
EC-JXZ	Canadair CRJ900ER	Air Nostrum/Iberia Regional	
EC-JYA	Canadair CRJ900ER	Air Nostrum/Iberia Regional	
EC-JYV	Canadair CRJ900ER	Air Nostrum/Iberia Regional	
EC-JYX	Airbus A.320-214	Vueling Airlines *Elisenda Masana*	
EC-JZI	Airbus A.320-214	Vueling Airlines *Vueling in love*	
EC-JZL	Airbus A.330-202	Air Europa	
EC-JZM	Airbus A.321-211	Iberia *Águila Imperial Ibérica*	
EC-JZQ	Airbus A.320-214	Vueling Airlines *I want to Vueling*	
EC-JZS	Canadair CRJ900ER	Air Nostrum/Iberia Regional	
EC-JZT	Canadair CRJ900ER	Air Nostrum/Iberia Regional	
EC-JZU	Canadair CRJ900ER	Air Nostrum/Iberia Regional	
EC-JZV	Canadair CRJ900ER	Air Nostrum/Iberia Regional	
EC-KBX	Airbus A.319-111	Iberia *Oso Pardo*	
EC-KCG	Boeing 737-85P	Air Europa	
EC-KCU	Airbus A.320-216	Vueling Airlines	
EC-KDG	Airbus A.320-214	Vueling Airlines	
EC-KDH	Airbus A.320-214	Vueling Airlines *Ain't no Vueling high enough*	
EC-KDT	Airbus A.320-216	Vueling Airlines	
EC-KDX	Airbus A.320-216	Vueling Airlines *Francisco Jose Ruiz Cortizo*	
EC-KFI	Airbus A.320-216	Vueling Airlines	
EC-KHM	Airbus A.319-111	Iberia *Buho Real*	
EC-KHN	Airbus A.320-216	Vueling Airlines	
EC-KJD	Airbus A.320-216	Vueling Airlines	
EC-KKS	Airbus A.319-111	Iberia *Halcon Peregrino*	
EC-KKT	Airbus A.320-214	Vueling Airlines *Vueling Together*	
EC-KLB	Airbus A.320-214	Vueling Airlines *Vuela Punto*	
EC-KLR	Boeing 737-3Q8	Swiftair	
EC-KLT	Airbus A.320-214	Vueling Airlines	
EC-KMD	Airbus A.319-111	Iberia *Petirrojo*	
EC-KMI	Airbus A.320-216	Vueling Airlines *How are you? I'm Vueling!*	
EC-KOH	Airbus A.320-214	Iberia Express	
EC-KOM	Airbus A.330-202	Air Europa	

Notes	Reg.	Type	Owner or Operator
	EC-KOU	Airbus A.340-313	Iberia
	EC-KOY	Airbus A.319-111	Iberia *Vencejo*
	EC-KRH	Airbus A.320-214	Vueling Airlines *Vueling me softly*
	EC-KRJ	Embraer RJ190-200SR	Air Europa
	EC-KTG	Airbus A.330-203	Air Europa
	EC-KTZ	Boeing 737-375	Swiftair
	EC-KUB	Airbus A.319-111	Iberia
	EC-KVD	Boeing 737-306	Swiftair
	EC-KXD	Embraer RJ190-200SR	Air Europa
	EC-KYO	Embraer RJ190-200SR	Air Europa
	EC-KYP	Embraer RJ190-200SR	Air Europa
	EC-KZI	Airbus A.340-642	Iberia *Miguel Hernandez*
	EC-LAA	Airbus A.320-214	Vueling Airlines
	EC-LAB	Airbus A.320-214	Vueling Airlines
	EC-LAC	Boeing 737-3M8	Swiftair
	EC-LAV	Boeing 737-408	AlbaStar
	EC-LCQ	Embraer ERJ190-20LR	Air Europa
	EC-LCZ	Airbus A.340-642	Iberia
	EC-LEA	Airbus A.320-214	Iberia Express
	EC-LEI	Airbus A.319-111	Iberia *Vison Europeo*
	EC-LEK	Embraer ERJ190-200LR	Air Europa
	EC-LEU	Airbus A.340-642	Iberia
	EC-LEV	Airbus A.340-642	Iberia
	EC-LFS	Airbus A.340-642	Iberia
	EC-LFZ	Embraer ERJ190-200LR	Air Europa
	EC-LIN	Embraer ERJ190-200LR	Air Europa
	EC-LJI	Boeing 737-301F	Swiftair
	EC-LJR	Canadair CRJ1000ER	Air Nostrum/Iberia Regional
	EC-LJS	Canadair CRJ1000ER	Air Nostrum/Iberia Regional
	EC-LJT	Canadair CRJ1000ER	Air Nostrum/Iberia Regional
	EC-LJX	Canadair CRJ1000ER	Air Nostrum/Iberia Regional
	EC-LKF	Canadair CRJ1000ER	Air Nostrum/Iberia Regional
	EC-LKG	Airbus A.320-214	Iberia *Santiago de Compostela*
	EC-LKH	Airbus A.320-214	Iberia Express
	EC-LKM	Embraer ERJ190-200LR	Air Europa
	EC-LKS	Airbus A.340-313	Iberia *Placido Domingo*
	EC-LKX	Embraer ERJ190-200LR	Air Europa
	EC-LLE	Airbus A.320-214	Iberia Express
	EC-LLM	Airbus A.320-216	Vueling Airlines *Be happy, be Vueling*
	EC-LLR	Embraer ERJ190-200LR	Air Europa
	EC-LML	Airbus A.320-216	Vueling Airlines
	EC-LMN	Airbus A.330-243	Air Europa
	EC-LMR	BAe 146-300QT	Panair/TNT Airways
	EC-LNC	Boeing 737-4K5	AlbaStar
	EC-LNH	Airbus A.330-243	Air Europa
	EC-LOB	Airbus A.320-232	Vueling Airlines
	EC-LOC	Airbus A.320-232	Vueling Airlines *Vueling on heaven's door*
	EC-LOF	BAe 146-300QT	Panair/TNT Airways
	EC-LOJ	Canadair CRJ1000ER	Air Nostrum/Iberia Regional
	EC-LOP	Airbus A.320-214	Vueling Airlines
	EC-LOV	Canadair CRJ1000ER	Air Nostrum/Iberia Regional
	EC-LOX	Canadair CRJ1000ER	Air Nostrum/Iberia Regional
	EC-LPG	Canadair CRJ1000ER	Air Nostrum/Iberia Regional
	EC-LPM	Boeing 717-2BL	Volotea
	EC-LPN	Canadair CRJ1000ER	Air Nostrum/Iberia Regional
	EC-LPQ	Boeing 737-85P	Air Europa
	EC-LPR	Boeing 737-85P	Air Europa
	EC-LQI	Boeing 717-2BL	Volotea
	EC-LQJ	Airbus A.320-232	Vueling Airlines
	EC-LQK	Airbus A.320-232	Vueling Airlines
	EC-LQL	Airbus A.320-232	Vueling Airlines
	EC-LQM	Airbus A.320-232	Vueling Airlines
	EC-LQN	Airbus A.320-232	Vueling Airlines
	EC-LQO	Airbus A.330-243	Air Europa
	EC-LQP	Airbus A.330-243	Air Europa
	EC-LQS	Boeing 717-2BL	Volotea
	EC-LQX	Boeing 737-85P	Air Europa
	EC-LQZ	Airbus A.320-232	Vueling Airlines
	EC-LRA	Airbus A.320-232	Vueling Airlines
	EC-LRE	Airbus A.320-232	Vueling Airlines
	EC-LRG	Airbus A.320-214	Iberia Express
	EC-LRM	Airbus A.320-232	Vueling Airlines

Reg.	Type	Owner or Operator	Notes
EC-LRN	Airbus A.320-214	Vueling Airlines	
EC-LRS	Airbus A.319-112	Vueling Airlines	
EC-LRY	Airbus A.320-232	Vueling Airlines	
EC-LRZ	Airbus A.319-112	Vueling Airlines	
EC-LSA	Airbus A.320-214	Vueling Airlines	
EC-LTG	Boeing 737-4K5	AlbaStar	
EC-LTM	Boeing 737-85P	Air Europa	
EC-LTO	Boeing 737-301F	Swiftair	
EC-LUB	Airbus A.330-302	Iberia	
EC-LUC	Airbus A.320-214	Iberia Express	
EC-LUD	Airbus A.320-214	Iberia Express	
EC-LUK	Airbus A.330-302E	Iberia Costa Rica	
EC-LUL	Airbus A.320-216	Iberia	
EC-LUN	Airbus A.320-232	Vueling Airlines	
EC-LUO	Airbus A.320-232	Vueling Airlines	
EC-LUS	Airbus A.320-216	Iberia Express	
EC-LUT	Boeing 737-85P	Air Europa	
EC-LUX	Airbus A.330-302E	Iberia	
EC-LVA	Airbus A.320-214	Vueling Airlines	
EC-LVB	Airbus A.320-214	Vueling Airlines	
EC-LVC	Airbus A.320-214	Vueling Airlines	
EC-LVD	Airbus A.320-216	Iberia Valle de Mena	
EC-LVL	Airbus A.330-243	Air Europa	
EC-LVO	Airbus A.320-214	Vueling Airlines	
EC-LVP	Airbus A.320-214	Vueling Airlines	
EC-LVQ	Airbus A.320-216	Iberia Express	
EC-LVR	Boeing 737-85P	Air Europa	
EC-LVS	Airbus A.320-214	Vueling Airlines	
EC-LVT	Airbus A.320-214	Vueling Airlines	
EC-LVU	Airbus A.320-214	Vueling Airlines	
EC-LVV	Airbus A.320-214	Vueling Airlines	
EC-LVX	Airbus A.320-214	Vueling Airlines	
EC-LXA	Airbus A.330-343	Air Europa	
EC-LXK	Airbus A.330-302E	Iberia	
EC-LXQ	Airbus A.320-216	Iberia	
EC-LXR	Airbus A.330-343	Air Europa	
EC-LXV	Boeing 737-86N	Air Europa	
EC-LYE	Airbus A.320-216	Iberia Express	
EC-LYF	Airbus A.330-302E	Iberia	
EC-LYM	Airbus A.320-216	Iberia Express	
EC-LYR	Boeing 737-85P	Air Europa	
EC-LZD	Airbus A.320-214	Evelop Airlines	
EC-LZE	Airbus A.320-214	Vueling Airlines	
EC-LZF	Airbus A.320-214	Vueling Airlines	
EC-LZJ	Airbus A.330-343	Iberia	
EC-LZN	Airbus A.320-214	Vueling Airlines	

EP (Iran)

EP-IBA	Airbus A.300B4-605R	Iran Air	
EP-IBB	Airbus A.300B4-605R	Iran Air	
EP-IBC	Airbus A.300B4-605R	Iran Air	
EP-IBD	Airbus A.300B4-605R	Iran Air	
EP-IBK	Airbus A.310-304	Iran Air	
EP-IBL	Airbus A.310-304	Iran Air	

ER (Moldova)

ER-AXP	Airbus A.320-211	Air Moldova	
ER-AXV	Airbus A.320-211	Air Moldova	
ER-ECB	Embraer ERJ190-100AR	Air Moldova	
ER-ECC	Embraer ERJ190-100AR	Air Moldova	

ES (Estonia)

ES-ACB	Canadair CRJ900ER	Estonian Air	
ES-ACC	Canadair CRJ900ER	Estonian Air	
ES-ACD	Canadair CRJ900ER	Estonian Air	
ES-AEA	Embraer ERJ170-100LR	Estonian Air	

Notes	Reg.	Type	Owner or Operator
	ES-AEB	Embraer ERJ170-100LR	Estonian Air
	ES-AEC	Embraer ERJ170-100LR	Estonian Air
	ES-AED	Embraer ERJ170-100LR	Estonian Air

ET (Ethiopia)

ET-ANN	Boeing 777-260LR	Ethiopian Airlines
ET-ANO	Boeing 777-260LR	Ethiopian Airlines
ET-ANP	Boeing 777-260LR	Ethiopian Airlines
ET-ANQ	Boeing 777-260LR	Ethiopian Airlines
ET-ANR	Boeing 777-260LR	Ethiopian Airlines
ET-AOO	Boeing 787-8	Ethiopian Airlines
ET-AOP	Boeing 787-8	Ethiopian Airlines
ET-AOQ	Boeing 787-8	Ethiopian Airlines
ET-AOR	Boeing 787-8	Ethiopian Airlines
ET-AOS	Boeing 787-8	Ethiopian Airlines
ET-APX	Boeing 777-36NER	Ethiopian Airlines
ET-APY	Boeing 777-36NER	Ethiopian Airlines
ET-AQL	Boeing 777-260LR	Ethiopian Airlines

EW (Belarus)

EW-100PJ	Canadair CRJ200LR	Belavia
EW-250PA	Boeing 737-524	Belavia
EW-251PA	Boeing 737-5Q8	Belavia
EW-252PA	Boeing 737-524	Belavia
EW-253PA	Boeing 737-524	Belavia
EW-254PA	Boeing 737-3Q8	Belavia
EW-276PJ	Canadair CRJ200ER	Belavia
EW-277PJ	Canadair CRJ200ER	Belavia
EW-282PA	Boeing 737-3Q8	Belavia
EW-283PA	Boeing 737-3Q8	Belavia
EW-290PA	Boeing 737-5Q8	Belavia
EW-294PA	Boeing 737-505	Belavia
EW-303PJ	Canadair CRJ200LR	Belavia
EW-308PA	Boeing 737-3K2	Belavia
EW-336PA	Boeing 737-3Q8	Belavia
EW-340PO	Embraer ERJ170-200LR	Belavia
EW-341PO	Embraer ERJ170-200LR	Belavia
EW-366PA	Boeing 737-31S	Belavia
EW-386PA	Boeing 737-3K2	Belavia

EZ (Turkmenistan)

EZ-A010	Boeing 757-23A	Turkmenistan Airlines
EZ-A011	Boeing 757-22K	Turkmenistan Airlines
EZ-A012	Boeing 757-22K	Turkmenistan Airlines
EZ-A014	Boeing 757-22K	Turkmenistan Airlines

F (France)

F-GEXB	Boeing 747-4B3	Air France
F-GFKY	Airbus A.320-211	Air France *Ville de Toulouse*
F-GFUF	Boeing 737-3B3	Europe Airpost
F-GHQL	Airbus A.320-211	Air France
F-GITD	Boeing 747-428	Air France
F-GITE	Boeing 747-428	Air France
F-GITF	Boeing 747-428	Air France
F-GITH	Boeing 747-428	Air France
F-GITI	Boeing 747-428	Air France
F-GITJ	Boeing 747-428	Air France
F-GIUA	Boeing 747-428ERF (SCD)	Air France Cargo
F-GIUC	Boeing 747-428ERF (SCD)	Air France Cargo
F-GIUG	Boeing 747-428ERF (SCD)	Air France Cargo
F-GIXB	Boeing 737-33A	Europe Airpost
F-GIXC	Boeing 737-38B	Europe Airpost
F-GIXE	Boeing 737-3B3	Europe Airpost
F-GIXN	Boeing 737-4Y0F	Europe Airpost

Reg.	Type	Owner or Operator	Notes
F-GIXS	Boeing 737-3H6F	Europe Airpost	
F-GIXT	Boeing 737-39M	Europe Airpost	
F-GIXU	Boeing 737-4Y0F	Europe Airpost	
F-GJVW	Airbus A.320-211	Air France	
F-GKXA	Airbus A.320-211	Air France	
F-GKXE	Airbus A.320-214	Air France	
F-GKXG	Airbus A.320-214	Air France	
F-GKXH	Airbus A.320-214	Air France	
F-GKXI	Airbus A.320-214	Air France	
F-GKXJ	Airbus A.320-214	Air France	
F-GKXK	Airbus A.320-214	Air France	
F-GKXL	Airbus A.320-214	Air France	
F-GKXM	Airbus A.320-214	Air France	
F-GKXN	Airbus A.320-214	Air France	
F-GKXO	Airbus A.320-214	Air France	
F-GKXP	Airbus A.320-214	Air France	
F-GKXR	Airbus A.320-214	Air France	
F-GKXS	Airbus A.320-214	Air France	
F-GKXT	Airbus A.320-214	Air France	
F-GKXU	Airbus A.320-214	Air France	
F-GKXV	Airbus A.320-214	Air France	
F-GKXY	Airbus A.320-214	Air France	
F-GKXZ	Airbus A.320-214	Air France	
F-GLZC	Airbus A.340-312	Air France	
F-GLZH	Airbus A.340-312	Air France	
F-GLZI	Airbus A.340-312	Air France	
F-GLZJ	Airbus A.340-313X	Air France	
F-GLZK	Airbus A.340-313X	Air France	
F-GLZM	Airbus A.340-313X	Air France	
F-GLZN	Airbus A.340-313X	Air France	
F-GLZO	Airbus A.340-313X	Air France	
F-GLZP	Airbus A.340-313X	Air France	
F-GLZR	Airbus A.340-313X	Air France	
F-GLZS	Airbus A.340-313X	Air France	
F-GLZU	Airbus A.340-313X	Air France	
F-GMZA	Airbus A.321-111	Air France	
F-GMZB	Airbus A.321-111	Air France	
F-GMZC	Airbus A.321-111	Air France	
F-GMZD	Airbus A.321-111	Air France	
F-GMZE	Airbus A.321-111	Air France	
F-GNII	Airbus A.340-313X	Air France	
F-GPEK	Boeing 757-236	Open Skies	
F-GPMA	Airbus A.319-113	Air France	
F-GPMB	Airbus A.319-113	Air France	
F-GPMC	Airbus A.319-113	Air France	
F-GPMD	Airbus A.319-113	Air France	
F-GPME	Airbus A.319-113	Air France	
F-GPMF	Airbus A.319-113	Air France	
F-GRGC	Embraer RJ145EU	HOP!	
F-GRGD	Embraer RJ145EU	HOP!	
F-GRGE	Embraer RJ145EU	HOP!	
F-GRGF	Embraer RJ145EU	HOP!	
F-GRGG	Embraer RJ145EU	HOP!	
F-GRGH	Embraer RJ145EU	HOP!	
F-GRGI	Embraer RJ145EU	HOP!	
F-GRGJ	Embraer RJ145EU	HOP!	
F-GRGK	Embraer RJ145EU	HOP!	
F-GRGL	Embraer RJ145EU	HOP!	
F-GRGQ	Embraer RJ135ER	HOP!	
F-GRGR	Embraer RJ135ER	HOP!	
F-GRHA	Airbus A.319-111	Air France	
F-GRHB	Airbus A.319-111	Air France	
F-GRHC	Airbus A.319-111	Air France	
F-GRHD	Airbus A.319-111	Air France	
F-GRHE	Airbus A.319-111	Air France	
F-GRHF	Airbus A.319-111	Air France	
F-GRHG	Airbus A.319-111	Air France	
F-GRHH	Airbus A.319-111	Air France	
F-GRHI	Airbus A.319-111	Air France	
F-GRHJ	Airbus A.319-111	Air France	
F-GRHK	Airbus A.319-111	Air France	
F-GRHL	Airbus A.319-111	Air France	

Notes	Reg.	Type	Owner or Operator
	F-GRHM	Airbus A.319-111	Air France
	F-GRHN	Airbus A.319-111	Air France
	F-GRHO	Airbus A.319-111	Air France
	F-GRHP	Airbus A.319-111	Air France
	F-GRHQ	Airbus A.319-111	Air France
	F-GRHR	Airbus A.319-111	Air France
	F-GRHS	Airbus A.319-111	Air France
	F-GRHT	Airbus A.319-111	Air France
	F-GRHU	Airbus A.319-111	Air France
	F-GRHV	Airbus A.319-111	Air France
	F-GRHX	Airbus A.319-111	Air France
	F-GRHY	Airbus A.319-111	Air France
	F-GRHZ	Airbus A.319-111	Air France
	F-GRJG	Canadair CRJ100ER	HOP !
	F-GRJM	Canadair CRJ100ER	HOP !
	F-GRJN	Canadair CRJ100ER	HOP !
	F-GRJO	Canadair CRJ100ER	HOP !
	F-GRJP	Canadair CRJ100ER	HOP !
	F-GRJQ	Canadair CRJ100ER	HOP !
	F-GRJT	Canadair CRJ100ER	HOP !
	F-GRSQ	Airbus A.330-243	XL Airways France
	F-GRXA	Airbus A.319-111	Air France
	F-GRXB	Airbus A.319-111	Air France
	F-GRXC	Airbus A.319-111	Air France
	F-GRXD	Airbus A.319-111	Air France
	F-GRXE	Airbus A.319-111	Air France
	F-GRXF	Airbus A.319-111	Air France
	F-GRXJ	Airbus A.319-115LR	Air France
	F-GRXK	Airbus A.319-115LR	Air France
	F-GRXL	Airbus A.319-111	Air France
	F-GRXM	Airbus A.319-111	Air France
	F-GRZC	Canadair CRJ700	HOP !
	F-GRZD	Canadair CRJ700	HOP !
	F-GRZE	Canadair CRJ700	HOP !
	F-GRZF	Canadair CRJ700	HOP !
	F-GRZG	Canadair CRJ700	HOP !
	F-GRZH	Canadair CRJ700	HOP !
	F-GRZI	Canadair CRJ700	HOP !
	F-GRZJ	Canadair CRJ700	HOP !
	F-GRZK	Canadair CRJ700	HOP !
	F-GRZL	Canadair CRJ700	HOP !
	F-GRZM	Canadair CRJ700	HOP !
	F-GRZN	Canadair CRJ700	HOP !
	F-GRZO	Canadair CRJ700	HOP !
	F-GSEU	Airbus A.330-243	XL Airways France
	F-GSPA	Boeing 777-228ER	Air France
	F-GSPB	Boeing 777-228ER	Air France
	F-GSPC	Boeing 777-228ER	Air France
	F-GSPD	Boeing 777-228ER	Air France
	F-GSPE	Boeing 777-228ER	Air France
	F-GSPF	Boeing 777-228ER	Air France
	F-GSPG	Boeing 777-228ER	Air France
	F-GSPH	Boeing 777-228ER	Air France
	F-GSPI	Boeing 777-228ER	Air France
	F-GSPJ	Boeing 777-228ER	Air France
	F-GSPK	Boeing 777-228ER	Air France
	F-GSPL	Boeing 777-228ER	Air France
	F-GSPM	Boeing 777-228ER	Air France
	F-GSPN	Boeing 777-228ER	Air France
	F-GSPO	Boeing 777-228ER	Air France
	F-GSPP	Boeing 777-228ER	Air France
	F-GSPQ	Boeing 777-228ER	Air France
	F-GSPR	Boeing 777-228ER	Air France
	F-GSPS	Boeing 777-228ER	Air France
	F-GSPT	Boeing 777-228ER	Air France
	F-GSPU	Boeing 777-228ER	Air France
	F-GSPV	Boeing 777-228ER	Air France
	F-GSPX	Boeing 777-228ER	Air France
	F-GSPY	Boeing 777-228ER	Air France
	F-GSPZ	Boeing 777-228ER	Air France
	F-GSQA	Boeing 777-328ER	Air France
	F-GSQB	Boeing 777-328ER	Air France

Reg.	Type	Owner or Operator	Notes
F-GSQC	Boeing 777-328ER	Air France	
F-GSQD	Boeing 777-328ER	Air France	
F-GSQE	Boeing 777-328ER	Air France	
F-GSQF	Boeing 777-328ER	Air France	
F-GSQG	Boeing 777-328ER	Air France	
F-GSQH	Boeing 777-328ER	Air France	
F-GSQI	Boeing 777-328ER	Air France	
F-GSQJ	Boeing 777-328ER	Air France	
F-GSQK	Boeing 777-328ER	Air France	
F-GSQL	Boeing 777-328ER	Air France	
F-GSQM	Boeing 777-328ER	Air France	
F-GSQN	Boeing 777-328ER	Air France	
F-GSQO	Boeing 777-328ER	Air France	
F-GSQP	Boeing 777-328ER	Air France	
F-GSQR	Boeing 777-328ER	Air France	
F-GSQS	Boeing 777-328ER	Air France	
F-GSQT	Boeing 777-328ER	Air France	
F-GSQU	Boeing 777-328ER	Air France	
F-GSQV	Boeing 777-328ER	Air France	
F-GSQX	Boeing 777-328ER	Air France	
F-GSQY	Boeing 777-328ER	Air France	
F-GSTA	Airbus A.300-608ST Beluga (1)	Airbus Transport International	
F-GSTB	Airbus A.300-608ST Beluga (2)	Airbus Transport International	
F-GSTC	Airbus A.300-608ST Beluga (3)	Airbus Transport International	
F-GSTD	Airbus A.300-608ST Beluga (4)	Airbus Transport International	
F-GSTF	Airbus A.300-608ST Beluga (5)	Airbus Transport International	
F-GTAD	Airbus A.321-211	Air France	
F-GTAE	Airbus A.321-211	Air France	
F-GTAH	Airbus A.321-211	Air France	
F-GTAI	Airbus A.321-211	Air France	
F-GTAJ	Airbus A.321-211	Air France	
F-GTAK	Airbus A.321-211	Air France	
F-GTAL	Airbus A.321-211	Air France	
F-GTAM	Airbus A.321-211	Air France	
F-GTAN	Airbus A.321-211	Air France	
F-GTAO	Airbus A.321-211	Air France	
F-GTAP	Airbus A.321-212	Air France	
F-GTAQ	Airbus A.321-211	Air France	
F-GTAR	Airbus A.321-211	Air France	
F-GTAS	Airbus A.321-211	Air France	
F-GTAT	Airbus A.321-211	Air France	
F-GTAU	Airbus A.321-211	Air France	
F-GTAV	Airbus A.321-211	Air France	
F-GTAX	Airbus A.321-211	Air France	
F-GTAY	Airbus A.321-211	Air France	
F-GTAZ	Airbus A.321-211	Air France	
F-GTUI	Boeing 747-422	Corsair	
F-GUAA	Airbus A.321-211	Aigle Azur	
F-GUBC	Embraer RJ145MP	HOP !	
F-GUBD	Embraer RJ145MP	HOP !	
F-GUBE	Embraer RJ145MP	HOP !	
F-GUBF	Embraer RJ145MP	HOP !	
F-GUBG	Embraer RJ145MP	HOP !	
F-GUEA	Embraer RJ145MP	HOP !	
F-GUFD	Embraer RJ145MP	HOP !	
F-GUGA	Airbus A.318-111	Air France	
F-GUGB	Airbus A.318-111	Air France	
F-GUGC	Airbus A.318-111	Air France	
F-GUGD	Airbus A.318-111	Air France	
F-GUGE	Airbus A.318-111	Air France	
F-GUGF	Airbus A.318-111	Air France	
F-GUGG	Airbus A.318-111	Air France	
F-GUGH	Airbus A.318-111	Air France	
F-GUGI	Airbus A.318-111	Air France	
F-GUGJ	Airbus A.318-111	Air France	
F-GUGK	Airbus A.318-111	Air France	
F-GUGL	Airbus A.318-111	Air France	
F-GUGM	Airbus A.318-111	Air France	
F-GUGN	Airbus A.318-111	Air France	
F-GUGO	Airbus A.318-111	Air France	
F-GUGP	Airbus A.318-111	Air France	
F-GUGQ	Airbus A.318-111	Air France	

Notes	Reg.	Type	Owner or Operator
	F-GUGR	Airbus A.318-111	Air France
	F-GUOB	Boeing 777-F28	Air France Cargo
	F-GUOC	Boeing 777-F28	Air France Cargo
	F-GVHD	Embraer RJ145MP	HOP !
	F-GXAH	Airbus A.319-132	Aigle Azur
	F-GYAN	Airbus A.321-111	Air Mediterranée
	F-GYAP	Airbus A.321-111	Air Mediterranée
	F-GYAQ	Airbus A.321-211	Air Mediterranée
	F-GYAR	Airbus A.321-211	Air Mediterranée
	F-GYAZ	Airbus A.321-111	Air Mediterranée
	F-GZCA	Airbus A.330-203	Air France
	F-GZCB	Airbus A.330-203	Air France
	F-GZCC	Airbus A.330-203	Air France
	F-GZCD	Airbus A.330-203	Air France
	F-GZCE	Airbus A.330-203	Air France
	F-GZCF	Airbus A.330-203	Air France
	F-GZCG	Airbus A.330-203	Air France
	F-GZCH	Airbus A.330-203	Air France
	F-GZCI	Airbus A.330-203	Air France
	F-GZCJ	Airbus A.330-203	Air France
	F-GZCK	Airbus A.330-203	Air France
	F-GZCL	Airbus A.330-203	Air France
	F-GZCM	Airbus A.330-203	Air France
	F-GZCN	Airbus A.330-203	Air France
	F-GZCO	Airbus A.330-203	Air France
	F-GZHA	Boeing 737-8GJ	Transavia France
	F-GZHB	Boeing 737-8GJ	Transavia France
	F-GZHC	Boeing 737-8GJ	Transavia France
	F-GZHD	Boeing 737-8K2	Transavia France
	F-GZHE	Boeing 737-8K2	Transavia France
	F-GZHF	Boeing 737-8HX	Transavia France
	F-GZHG	Boeing 737-8K2	Transavia France
	F-GZHI	Boeing 737-8K2	Transavia France
	F-GZHJ	Boeing 737-8K2	Transavia France
	F-GZHN	Boeing 737-8K2	Transavia France
	F-GZHV	Boeing 737-85H	Transavia France
	F-GZNA	Boeing 777-328ER	Air France
	F-GZNB	Boeing 777-328ER	Air France
	F-GZNC	Boeing 777-328ER	Air France
	F-GZND	Boeing 777-328ER	Air France
	F-GZNE	Boeing 777-328ER	Air France
	F-GZNF	Boeing 777-328ER	Air France
	F-GZNG	Boeing 777-328ER	Air France
	F-GZNH	Boeing 777-328ER	Air France
	F-GZNI	Boeing 777-328ER	Air France
	F-GZNJ	Boeing 777-328ER	Air France
	F-GZNK	Boeing 777-328ER	Air France
	F-GZNL	Boeing 777-328ER	Air France
	F-GZNN	Boeing 777-328ER	Air France
	F-GZNO	Boeing 777-328ER	Air France
	F-GZTA	Boeing 737-33V	Europe Airpost
	F-GZTB	Boeing 737-33V	Europe Airpost
	F-GZTC	Boeing 737-73V	Europe Airpost
	F-GZTD	Boeing 737-73V	Europe Airpost
	F-GZTI	Boeing 737-408F	Europe Airpost
	F-GZTJ	Boeing 737-4S3F	Europe Airpost
	F-HAVI	Boeing 757-26D	Open Skies *Violette*
	F-HAVN	Boeing 757-230	Open Skies
	F-HAXL	Boeing 737-8Q8	XL Airways France
	F-HBAF	Airbus A.321-211	Aigle Azur
	F-HBAL	Airbus A.319-111	Aigle Azur
	F-HBAO	Airbus A.320-214	Aigle Azur
	F-HBAP	Airbus A.320-214	Aigle Azur
	F-HBIB	Airbus A.320-214	Aigle Azur
	F-HBII	Airbus A.320-214	Aigle Azur
	F-HBIL	Airbus A.330-243	Corsair
	F-HBIO	Airbus A.320-214	Aigle Azur
	F-HBIS	Airbus A.320-214	Aigle Azur
	F-HBLA	Embraer RJ190-100LR	HOP !
	F-HBLB	Embraer RJ190-100LR	HOP !
	F-HBLC	Embraer RJ190-100LR	HOP !
	F-HBLD	Embraer RJ190-100LR	HOP !

Reg.	Type	Owner or Operator	Notes
F-HBLE	Embraer RJ190-100LR	HOP !	
F-HBLF	Embraer RJ190-100LR	HOP !	
F-HBLG	Embraer RJ190-100LR	HOP !	
F-HBLH	Embraer RJ190-100LR	HOP !	
F-HBLI	Embraer RJ190-100LR	HOP !	
F-HBLJ	Embraer RJ190-100LR	HOP !	
F-HBMI	Airbus A.319-114	Aigle Azur	
F-HBNA	Airbus A.320-214	Air France	
F-HBNB	Airbus A.320-214	Air France	
F-HBNC	Airbus A.320-214	Air France	
F-HBND	Airbus A.320-214	Air France	
F-HBNE	Airbus A.320-214	Air France	
F-HBNF	Airbus A.320-214	Air France	
F-HBNG	Airbus A.320-214	Air France	
F-HBNH	Airbus A.320-214	Air France	
F-HBNI	Airbus A.320-214	Air France	
F-HBNJ	Airbus A.320-214	Air France	
F-HBNK	Airbus A.320-214	Air France	
F-HBNL	Airbus A.320-214	Air France	
F-HBNM	Airbus A.320-214	Air France	
F-HBNN	Airbus A.320-214	Air France	
F-HBXA	Embraer RJ170-100LR	HOP !	
F-HBXB	Embraer RJ170-100LR	HOP !	
F-HBXC	Embraer RJ170-100LR	HOP !	
F-HBXD	Embraer RJ170-100LR	HOP !	
F-HBXE	Embraer RJ170-100LR	HOP !	
F-HBXF	Embraer RJ170-100LR	HOP !	
F-HBXG	Embraer RJ170-100LR	HOP !	
F-HBXI	Embraer RJ170-100LR	HOP !	
F-HBXJ	Embraer RJ170-100LR	HOP !	
F-HBXK	Embraer RJ170-100LR	HOP !	
F-HBXL	Embraer RJ170-100LR	HOP !	
F-HBXM	Embraer RJ170-100LR	HOP !	
F-HBXN	Embraer RJ170-100LR	HOP !	
F-HBXO	Embraer RJ170-100LR	HOP !	
F-HBXP	Embraer RJ170-100LR	HOP !	
F-HCAT	Airbus A.330-243	Corsair	
F-HCOA	Boeing 737-5L9	Air Mediterranee	
F-HCOB	Boeing 737-59D	Air Mediterranee	
F-HCZI	Airbus A.319-112	Aigle Azur	
F-HEPA	Airbus A.320-214	Air France	
F-HEPB	Airbus A.320-214	Air France	
F-HEPC	Airbus A.320-214	Air France	
F-HEPD	Airbus A.320-214	Air France	
F-HEPE	Airbus A.320-214	Air France	
F-HEPF	Airbus A.320-214	Air France	
F-HEPG	Airbus A.320-214	Air France	
F-HEPH	Airbus A.320-214	Air France	
F-HJER	Boeing 737-86N	XL Airways France	
F-HJUL	Boeing 737-8Q8	XL Airways France	
F-HMLA	Canadair CRJ1000	HOP !	
F-HMLC	Canadair CRJ1000	HOP !	
F-HMLD	Canadair CRJ1000	HOP !	
F-HMLE	Canadair CRJ1000	HOP !	
F-HMLF	Canadair CRJ1000	HOP !	
F-HMLG	Canadair CRJ1000	HOP !	
F-HMLH	Canadair CRJ1000	HOP !	
F-HMLI	Canadair CRJ1000	HOP !	
F-HMLJ	Canadair CRJ1000	HOP !	
F-HMLK	Canadair CRJ1000	HOP !	
F-HMLL	Canadair CRJ1000	HOP !	
F-HMLM	Canadair CRJ1000	HOP !	
F-HMLN	Canadair CRJ1000	HOP !	
F-HPJA	Airbus A.380-861	Air France	
F-HPJB	Airbus A.380-861	Air France	
F-HPJC	Airbus A.380-861	Air France	
F-HPJD	Airbus A.380-861	Air France	
F-HPJE	Airbus A.380-861	Air France	
F-HPJF	Airbus A.380-861	Air France	
F-HPJG	Airbus A.380-861	Air France	
F-HPJH	Airbus A.380-861	Air France	
F-HPJI	Airbus A.380-861	Air France	

Notes	Reg.	Type	Owner or Operator
	F-HPJJ	Airbus A.380-861	Air France
	F-HPJK	Airbus A.380-861	Air France
	F-HSEA	Boeing 747-422	Corsair
	F-HSKY	Airbus A.330-343	Corsair
	F-HSUN	Boeing 747-422	Corsair
	F-HXLF	Airbus A.330-303	XL Airways France
	F-HZEN	Airbus A.330-343	Corsair
	F-OMRA	Airbus A.320-214	Middle East Airlines
	F-OMRB	Airbus A.320-214	Middle East Airlines
	F-OMRC	Airbus A.320-214	Middle East Airlines
	F-OMRD	Airbus A.320-214	Middle East Airlines
	F-OMRN	Airbus A.320-232	Middle East Airlines

HA (Hungary)

HA-LKG	Boeing 737-8CX	Travel Service Airlines
HA-LPD	Airbus A.320-233	Wizz Air
HA-LPE	Airbus A.320-233	Wizz Air
HA-LPF	Airbus A.320-233	Wizz Air
HA-LPI	Airbus A.320-233	Wizz Air
HA-LPJ	Airbus A.320-232	Wizz Air
HA-LPK	Airbus A.320-231	Wizz Air
HA-LPL	Airbus A.320-232	Wizz Air
HA-LPM	Airbus A.320-232	Wizz Air
HA-LPN	Airbus A.320-232	Wizz Air
HA-LPO	Airbus A.320-232	Wizz Air
HA-LPQ	Airbus A.320-232	Wizz Air
HA-LPR	Airbus A.320-232	Wizz Air
HA-LPS	Airbus A.320-232	Wizz Air
HA-LPT	Airbus A.320-232	Wizz Air
HA-LPU	Airbus A.320-232	Wizz Air
HA-LPV	Airbus A.320-232	Wizz Air
HA-LPW	Airbus A.320-232	Wizz Air
HA-LPX	Airbus A.320-232	Wizz Air
HA-LPY	Airbus A.320-232	Wizz Air
HA-LPZ	Airbus A.320-232	Wizz Air
HA-LWA	Airbus A.320-232	Wizz Air
HA-LWB	Airbus A.320-232	Wizz Air
HA-LWC	Airbus A.320-232	Wizz Air
HA-LWD	Airbus A.320-232	Wizz Air
HA-LWE	Airbus A.320-232	Wizz Air
HA-LWF	Airbus A.320-232	Wizz Air
HA-LWG	Airbus A.320-232	Wizz Air
HA-LWH	Airbus A.320-232	Wizz Air
HA-LWI	Airbus A.320-214	Wizz Air
HA-LWJ	Airbus A.320-214	Wizz Air
HA-LWK	Airbus A.320-232	Wizz Air
HA-LWL	Airbus A.320-232	Wizz Air
HA-LWM	Airbus A.320-232	Wizz Air
HA-LWN	Airbus A.320-232	Wizz Air
HA-LWO	Airbus A.320-232	Wizz Air
HA-LWP	Airbus A.320-232	Wizz Air
HA-LWQ	Airbus A.320-232	Wizz Air
HA-LWR	Airbus A.320-232	Wizz Air
HA-LWS	Airbus A.320-232	Wizz Air
HA-LWT	Airbus A.320-232	Wizz Air
HA-LWU	Airbus A.320-232	Wizz Air

HB (Switzerland)

HB-AEO	Dornier Do.328-110	Sky Work Airlines
HB-AER	Dornier Do.328-110	Sky Work Airlines
HB-AES	Dornier Do.328-110	Sky Work Airlines
HB-AEV	Dornier Do.328-110	Sky Work Airlines
HB-AEY	Dornier Do.328-130	Sky Work Airlines
HB-IHX	Airbus A.320-214	Edelweiss Air *Calvaro*
HB-IHY	Airbus A.320-214	Edelweiss Air *Upali*
HB-IHZ	Airbus A.320-214	Edelweiss Air *Viktoria*
HB-IJD	Airbus A.320-214	Swiss International
HB-IJE	Airbus A.320-214	Swiss International *Arosa*

Reg.	Type	Owner or Operator	Notes
HB-IJF	Airbus A.320-214	Swiss International	
HB-IJH	Airbus A.320-214	Swiss International	
HB-IJI	Airbus A.320-214	Swiss International *Basodino*	
HB-IJJ	Airbus A.320-214	Swiss International *Les Diablerets*	
HB-IJK	Airbus A.320-214	Swiss International *Wissigstock*	
HB-IJL	Airbus A.320-214	Swiss International *Pizol*	
HB-IJM	Airbus A.320-214	Swiss International *Schilthorn*	
HB-IJN	Airbus A.320-214	Swiss International *Vanil Noir*	
HB-IJO	Airbus A.320-214	Swiss International *Lissengrat*	
HB-IJP	Airbus A.320-214	Swiss International *Nollen*	
HB-IJQ	Airbus A.320-214	Swiss International *Agassizhorn*	
HB-IJR	Airbus A.320-214	Swiss International *Dammastock*	
HB-IJS	Airbus A.320-214	Swiss International *Creux du Van*	
HB-IJU	Airbus A.320-214	Swiss International *Bietschhorn*	
HB-IJV	Airbus A.320-214	Edelweiss Air	
HB-IJW	Airbus A.320-214	Swiss International *Bachtel*	
HB-IJX	Airbus A.320-214	Swiss International *Davos*	
HB-IOC	Airbus A.321-111	Swiss International *Eiger*	
HB-IOD	Airbus A.321-111	Swiss International	
HB-IOF	Airbus A.321-111	Swiss International	
HB-IOH	Airbus A.321-111	Swiss International *Piz Palu*	
HB-IOK	Airbus A.321-111	Swiss International *Biefertenstock*	
HB-IOL	Airbus A.321-111	Swiss International *Kaiseregg*	
HB-IOM	Airbus A.321-212	Swiss International	
HB-ION	Airbus A.321-212	Swiss International *Lugano*	
HB-IOP	Airbus A.320-214	Air Berlin/Belair	
HB-IOQ	Airbus A.320-214	Air Berlin/Belair	
HB-IOR	Airbus A.320-214	Air Berlin/Belair	
HB-IOS	Airbus A.320-214	Air Berlin/Belair	
HB-IOX	Airbus A.319-112	Air Berlin/Belair	
HB-IOZ	Airbus A.320-214	Air Berlin/Belair	
HB-IPT	Airbus A.319-112	Swiss International *Stadel*	
HB-IPU	Airbus A.319-112	Swiss International *Hochfelden*	
HB-IPV	Airbus A.319-112	Swiss International *Rumlang*	
HB-IPX	Airbus A.319-112	Swiss International *Steinmaur*	
HB-IPY	Airbus A.319-112	Swiss International *Hori*	
HB-IQI	Airbus A.330-223	Edelweiss Air *Kiburi*	
HB-IXN	Avro RJ100	Swiss European Airlines *Balmhorn 3699m*	
HB-IXO	Avro RJ100	Swiss European Airlines *Brisen 2404m*	
HB-IXP	Avro RJ100	Swiss European Airlines *Chestenberg 647m*	
HB-IXQ	Avro RJ100	Swiss European Airlines *Corno Gries 2969m*	
HB-IXR	Avro RJ100	Swiss European Airlines *Hoho Winde 1204m*	
HB-IXS	Avro RJ100	Swiss European Airlines *Mont Velan 3731m*	
HB-IXT	Avro RJ100	Swiss European Airlines *Ottenberg 681m*	
HB-IXU	Avro RJ100	Swiss European Airlines *Pfannenstiel 853m*	
HB-IXV	Avro RJ100	Swiss European Airlines *Saxer First 2151m*	
HB-IXW	Avro RJ100	Swiss European Airlines *Shafarnisch 2107m*	
HB-IXX	Avro RJ100	Swiss European Airlines *Silberen 2319m*	
HB-IYD	Saab 2000	Darwin Airline	
HB-IYI	Saab 2000	Darwin Airline	
HB-IYQ	Avro RJ100	Swiss European Airlines *Piz Buin 3312m*	
HB-IYR	Avro RJ100	Swiss European Airlines *Vrenelisgärtli 2904m*	
HB-IYS	Avro RJ100	Swiss European Airlines *Churfirsten 2306m*	
HB-IYT	Avro RJ100	Swiss European Airlines *Bluemlisalp 3663m*	
HB-IYU	Avro RJ100	Swiss European Airlines *Rot Turm 2002m*	
HB-IYV	Avro RJ100	Swiss European Airlines *Pizzo Barone 2864m*	
HB-IYW	Avro RJ100	Swiss European Airlines *Spitzmeilen 2501m*	
HB-IYY	Avro RJ100	Swiss European Airlines *Titlis 3238m*	
HB-IYZ	Avro RJ100	Swiss European Airlines *Tour d'Ai 2331m*	
HB-IZG	Saab 2000	Darwin Airline	
HB-IZH	Saab 2000	Darwin Airline	
HB-IZJ	Saab 2000	Darwin Airline	
HB-IZP	Saab 2000	Darwin Airline	
HB-IZU	Saab 2000	Darwin Airline	
HB-IZW	Saab 2000	Darwin Airline	
HB-IZX	Saab 2000	Darwin Airline	
HB-IZZ	Saab 2000	Darwin Airline	
HB-JHA	Airbus A.330-343	Swiss International	
HB-JHB	Airbus A.330-343	Swiss International *Sion*	
HB-JHC	Airbus A.330-343	Swiss International *Bellinzona*	
HB-JHD	Airbus A.330-343	Swiss International *St.Gallen*	
HB-JHE	Airbus A.330-343	Swiss International *Fribourg*	

Notes	Reg.	Type	Owner or Operator
	HB-JHF	Airbus A.330-343	Swiss International
	HB-JHG	Airbus A.330-343	Swiss International *Glarus*
	HB-JHH	Airbus A.330-343	Swiss International *Neuchatel*
	HB-JHI	Airbus A.330-343	Swiss International *Geneve*
	HB-JHJ	Airbus A.330-343	Swiss International *Appenzell*
	HB-JHK	Airbus A.330-343	Swiss International
	HB-JHL	Airbus A.330-343	Swiss International
	HB-JHM	Airbus A.330-343	Swiss International
	HB-JHN	Airbus A.330-343	Swiss International
	HB-JHQ	Airbus A.330-343	Edelweiss Air *Chamsin*
	HB-JIJ	DHC.8Q-402 Dash Eight	Sky Work Airlines
	HB-JIK	DHC.8Q-402 Dash Eight	Sky Work Airlines
	HB-JLP	Airbus A.320-214	Swiss International *Allschwil*
	HB-JLQ	Airbus A.320-214	Swiss International *Bllach*
	HB-JLR	Airbus A.320-214	Swiss International
	HB-JLS	Airbus A.320-214	Swiss International
	HB-JLT	Airbus A.320-214	Swiss International *Grenchen*
	HB-JMA	Airbus A.340-313X	Swiss International *Matterhorn*
	HB-JMB	Airbus A.340-313X	Swiss International *Zurich*
	HB-JMC	Airbus A.340-313X	Swiss International *Basel*
	HB-JMD	Airbus A.340-313X	Swiss International *Liestal*
	HB-JME	Airbus A.340-313X	Swiss International *Dom*
	HB-JMF	Airbus A.340-313X	Swiss International *Liskamm*
	HB-JMG	Airbus A.340-313X	Swiss International *Luzern*
	HB-JMH	Airbus A.340-313X	Swiss International *Chur*
	HB-JMI	Airbus A.340-313X	Swiss International *Schaffhausen*
	HB-JMJ	Airbus A.340-313X	Swiss International *City of Basel*
	HB-JMK	Airbus A.340-313X	Swiss International *Aarau*
	HB-JML	Airbus A.340-313X	Swiss International *Liestal*
	HB-JMM	Airbus A.340-313X	Swiss International
	HB-JMN	Airbus A.340-313X	Swiss International
	HB-JMO	Airbus A.340-313X	Swiss International
	HB-JOY	Airbus A.319-112	Air Berlin/Belair
	HB-JOZ	Airbus A.320-214	Air Berlin/Belair
	HB-JVC	Fokker 100	Helvetic Airways
	HB-JVE	Fokker 100	Helvetic Airways
	HB-JVF	Fokker 100	Helvetic Airways
	HB-JVG	Fokker 100	Helvetic Airways
	HB-JVH	Fokker 100	Helvetic Airways
	HB-JVI	Fokker 100	Helvetic Airways
	HB-JVK	Airbus A.319-112	Helvetic Airways
	HB-JXA	Airbus A.320-214	easyJet Switzerland
	HB-JYA	Airbus A.320-214	easyJet Switzerland
	HB-JYB	Airbus A.319-111	easyJet Switzerland
	HB-JYC	Airbus A.319-111	easyJet Switzerland
	HB-JYD	Airbus A.320-214	easyJet Switzerland
	HB-JYE	Airbus A.320-214	easyJet Switzerland
	HB-JZF	Airbus A.319-111	easyJet Switzerland
	HB-JZI	Airbus A.319-111	easyJet Switzerland
	HB-JZJ	Airbus A.319-111	easyJet Switzerland
	HB-JZL	Airbus A.319-111	easyJet Switzerland
	HB-JZM	Airbus A.319-111	easyJet Switzerland
	HB-JZO	Airbus A.319-111	easyJet Switzerland
	HB-JZP	Airbus A.319-111	easyJet Switzerland
	HB-JZQ	Airbus A.319-111	easyJet Switzerland
	HB-JZR	Airbus A.320-214	easyJet Switzerland
	HB-JZS	Airbus A.319-111	easyJet Switzerland
	HB-JZT	Airbus A.319-111	easyJet Switzerland
	HB-JZU	Airbus A.319-111	easyJet Switzerland
	HB-JZV	Airbus A.319-111	easyJet Switzerland
	HB-JZW	Airbus A.319-111	easyJet Switzerland
	HB-JZX	Airbus A.320-214	easyJet Switzerland
	HB-JZY	Airbus A.320-214	easyJet Switzerland
	HB-JZZ	Airbus A.320-214	easyJet Switzerland

HL (Korea)

HL7400	Boeing 747-4B5F		Korean Air Cargo
HL7402	Boeing 747-4B5		Korean Air
HL7403	Boeing 747-4B5F		Korean Air Cargo
HL7404	Boeing 747-4B5		Korean Air

Reg.	Type	Owner or Operator	Notes
HL7413	Boeing 747-48EBCF	Asiana Airlines Cargo	
HL7414	Boeing 747-48EBCF	Asiana Airlines Cargo	
HL7415	Boeing 747-48EBCF	Asiana Airlines Cargo	
HL7417	Boeing 747-48EBCF	Asiana Airlines Cargo	
HL7419	Boeing 747-48EF (SCD)	Asiana Airlines Cargo	
HL7420	Boeing 747-48EF (SCD)	Asiana Airlines Cargo	
HL7434	Boeing 747-4B5F	Korean Air Cargo	
HL7436	Boeing 747-48EF (SCD)	Asiana Airlines Cargo	
HL7437	Boeing 747-4B5F	Korean Air Cargo	
HL7438	Boeing 747-4B5ERF	Korean Air Cargo	
HL7439	Boeing 747-4B5ERF	Korean Air Cargo	
HL7448	Boeing 747-4B5F (SCD)	Korean Air Cargo	
HL7449	Boeing 747-4B5F (SCD)	Korean Air Cargo	
HL7460	Boeing 747-4B5	Korean Air	
HL7461	Boeing 747-4B5	Korean Air	
HL7466	Boeing 747-4B5F	Korean Air Cargo	
HL7467	Boeing 747-4B5F	Korean Air Cargo	
HL7472	Boeing 747-4B5	Korean Air	
HL7473	Boeing 747-4B5	Korean Air	
HL7485	Boeing 747-4B5BCF	Korean Air Cargo	
HL7486	Boeing 747-4B5BCF	Korean Air Cargo	
HL7489	Boeing 747-4B5	Korean Air	
HL7490	Boeing 747-4B5	Korean Air	
HL7491	Boeing 747-4B5	Korean Air	
HL7492	Boeing 747-4B5	Korean Air	
HL7493	Boeing 747-4B5	Korean Air	
HL7494	Boeing 747-4B5	Korean Air	
HL7495	Boeing 747-4B5	Korean Air	
HL7498	Boeing 747-4B5	Korean Air	
HL7499	Boeing 747-4B5ERF	Korean Air Cargo	
HL7500	Boeing 777-28EER	Asiana Airlines	
HL7526	Boeing 777-2B5ER	Korean Air	
HL7530	Boeing 777-2B5ER	Korean Air	
HL7531	Boeing 777-2B5ER	Korean Air	
HL7574	Boeing 777-2B5ER	Korean Air	
HL7575	Boeing 777-2B5ER	Korean Air	
HL7596	Boeing 777-28EER	Asiana Airlines	
HL7597	Boeing 777-28EER	Asiana Airlines	
HL7598	Boeing 777-2B5ER	Korean Air	
HL7600	Boeing 747-4B5ERF	Korean Air Cargo	
HL7601	Boeing 747-4B5ERF	Korean Air Cargo	
HL7602	Boeing 747-4B5ERF	Korean Air Cargo	
HL7603	Boeing 747-4B5ERF	Korean Air Cargo	
HL7605	Boeing 747-4B5ERF	Korean Air Cargo	
HL7616	Boeing 747-446F	Asiana Airlines Cargo	
HL7618	Boeing 747-446F	Asiana Airlines Cargo	
HL7620	Boeing 747-419F	Asiana Airlines Cargo	
HL7700	Boeing 777-28EER	Asiana Airlines	
HL7714	Boeing 777-2B5ER	Korean Air	
HL7715	Boeing 777-2B5ER	Korean Air	
HL7721	Boeing 777-2B5ER	Korean Air	
HL7732	Boeing 777-28EER	Asiana Airlines	
HL7733	Boeing 777-2B5ER	Korean Air	
HL7734	Boeing 777-2B5ER	Korean Air	
HL7739	Boeing 777-28EER	Asiana Airlines	
HL7743	Boeing 777-2B5ER	Korean Air	
HL7750	Boeing 777-2B5ER	Korean Air	
HL7751	Boeing 777-2B5ER	Korean Air	
HL7752	Boeing 777-2B5ER	Korean Air	
HL7755	Boeing 777-28EER	Asiana Airlines	
HL7756	Boeing 777-28EER	Asiana Airlines	
HL7764	Boeing 777-2B5ER	Korean Air	
HL7765	Boeing 777-2B5ER	Korean Air	
HL7766	Boeing 777-2B5ER	Korean Air	
HL7775	Boeing 777-28EER	Asiana Airlines	
HL7782	Boeing 777-3B5ER	Korean Air	
HL7783	Boeing 777-3B5ER	Korean Air	
HL7784	Boeing 777-3B5ER	Korean Air	
HL7791	Boeing 777-28EER	Asiana Airlines	
HL8208	Boeing 777-3B5ER	Korean Air	
HL8209	Boeing 777-3B5ER	Korean Air	
HL8210	Boeing 777-3B5ER	Korean Air	

Notes	Reg.	Type	Owner or Operator
	HL8216	Boeing 777-3B5ER	Korean Air
	HL8217	Boeing 777-3B5ER	Korean Air
	HL8218	Boeing 777-3B5ER	Korean Air
	HL8226	Boeing 777-FB5	Korean Air Cargo
	HL8250	Boeing 777-3B5ER	Korean Air
	HL8251	Boeing 777-FB5	Korean Air Cargo
	HL8252	Boeing 777-FB5	Korean Air Cargo
	HL8254	Boeing 777-28EER	Asiana Airlines
	HL8274	Boeing 777-3B5ER	Korean Air
	HL8275	Boeing 777-3B5ER	Korean Air
	HL8284	Boeing 777-28EER	Asiana Airlines
	HL8285	Boeing 777-FB5	Korean Air Cargo

HS (Thailand)

HS-TGA	Boeing 747-4D7		Thai Airways International *Srisuriyothai*
HS-TGB	Boeing 747-4D7		Thai Airways International *Si Satchanulai*
HS-TGF	Boeing 747-4D7		Thai Airways International *Sri Ubon*
HS-TGG	Boeing 747-4D7		Thai Airways International *Pathoomawadi*
HS-TGL	Boeing 747-4D7		Thai Airways International *Theparat*
HS-TGM	Boeing 747-4D7		Thai Airways International
HS-TGN	Boeing 747-4D7		Thai Airways International *Simongkhon*
HS-TGO	Boeing 747-4D7		Thai Airways International *Bowonrangsi*
HS-TGP	Boeing 747-4D7		Thai Airways International *Thepprasit*
HS-TGR	Boeing 747-4D7		Thai Airways International *Siriwatthana*
HS-TGT	Boeing 747-4D7		Thai Airways International *Watthanothai*
HS-TGW	Boeing 747-4D7		Thai Airways International *Visuthakasatriya*
HS-TGX	Boeing 747-4D7		Thai Airways International *Sirisobhakya*
HS-TGY	Boeing 747-4D7		Thai Airways International *Dararasmi*
HS-TGZ	Boeing 747-4D7		Thai Airways International *Phimara*
HS-TNA	Airbus A.340-642		Thai Airways International *Watthana Nakhon*
HS-TNB	Airbus A.340-642		Thai Airways International *Saraburi*
HS-TNC	Airbus A.340-642		Thai Airways International *Chon Buri*
HS-TND	Airbus A.340-642		Thai Airways International *Phetchaburi*
HS-TNE	Airbus A.340-642		Thai Airways International *Nonthaburi*
HS-TNF	Airbus A.340-642		Thai Airways International
HS-TUA	Airbus A.380-841		Thai Airways International
HS-TUB	Airbus A.380-841		Thai Airways International
HS-TUC	Airbus A.380-841		Thai Airways International
HS-TUD	Airbus A.380-861		Thai Airways International
HS-TUE	Airbus A.380-861		Thai Airways International
HS-TUF	Airbus A.380-861		Thai Airways International

HZ (Saudi Arabia)

HZ-AK11	Boeing 777-368ER		Saudi Arabian Airlines
HZ-AK12	Boeing 777-368ER		Saudi Arabian Airlines
HZ-AK13	Boeing 777-368ER		Saudi Arabian Airlines
HZ-AK14	Boeing 777-368ER		Saudi Arabian Airlines
HZ-AK15	Boeing 777-368ER		Saudi Arabian Airlines
HZ-AK16	Boeing 777-368ER		Saudi Arabian Airlines
HZ-AK17	Boeing 777-368ER		Saudi Arabian Airlines
HZ-AK18	Boeing 777-368ER		Saudi Arabian Airlines
HZ-AK19	Boeing 777-368ER		Saudi Arabian Airlines
HZ-AK20	Boeing 777-368ER		Saudi Arabian Airlines
HZ-AK21	Boeing 777-368ER		Saudi Arabian Airlines
HZ-AK22	Boeing 777-368ER		Saudi Arabian Airlines
HZ-AKA	Boeing 777-268ER		Saudi Arabian Airlines
HZ-AKB	Boeing 777-268ER		Saudi Arabian Airlines
HZ-AKC	Boeing 777-268ER		Saudi Arabian Airlines
HZ-AKD	Boeing 777-268ER		Saudi Arabian Airlines
HZ-AKE	Boeing 777-268ER		Saudi Arabian Airlines
HZ-AKF	Boeing 777-268ER		Saudi Arabian Airlines
HZ-AKG	Boeing 777-268ER		Saudi Arabian Airlines
HZ-AKH	Boeing 777-268ER		Saudi Arabian Airlines
HZ-AKI	Boeing 777-268ER		Saudi Arabian Airlines
HZ-AKJ	Boeing 777-268ER		Saudi Arabian Airlines
HZ-AKK	Boeing 777-268ER		Saudi Arabian Airlines
HZ-AKL	Boeing 777-268ER		Saudi Arabian Airlines
HZ-AKM	Boeing 777-268ER		Saudi Arabian Airlines

Reg.	Type	Owner or Operator	Notes
HZ-AKN	Boeing 777-268ER	Saudi Arabian Airlines	
HZ-AKO	Boeing 777-268ER	Saudi Arabian Airlines	
HZ-AKP	Boeing 777-268ER	Saudi Arabian Airlines	
HZ-AKQ	Boeing 777-268ER	Saudi Arabian Airlines	
HZ-AKR	Boeing 777-268ER	Saudi Arabian Airlines	
HZ-AKS	Boeing 777-268ER	Saudi Arabian Airlines	
HZ-AKT	Boeing 777-268ER	Saudi Arabian Airlines	
HZ-AKU	Boeing 777-268ER	Saudi Arabian Airlines	
HZ-AKV	Boeing 777-268ER	Saudi Arabian Airlines	
HZ-AKW	Boeing 777-268ER	Saudi Arabian Airlines	
HZ-ANA	McD Douglas MD-11F	Saudi Arabian Airlines Cargo	
HZ-ANB	McD Douglas MD-11F	Saudi Arabian Airlines Cargo	
HZ-ANC	McD Douglas MD-11F	Saudi Arabian Airlines Cargo	
HZ-AND	McD Douglas MD-11F	Saudi Arabian Airlines Cargo	

I (Italy)

Reg.	Type	Owner or Operator	Notes
I-ADJK	Embraer ERJ190-200LR	Air Dolomiti	
I-ADJL	Embraer ERJ190-200LR	Air Dolomiti	
I-ADJM	Embraer ERJ190-200LR	Air Dolomiti	
I-ADJN	Embraer ERJ190-200LR	Air Dolomiti	
I-ADJO	Embraer ERJ190-200LR	Air Dolomiti	
I-ADJP	Embraer ERJ190-200LR	Air Dolomiti	
I-ADJQ	Embraer ERJ190-200LR	Air Dolomiti	
I-ADJR	Embraer ERJ190-200LR	Air Dolomiti	
I-ADJS	Embraer ERJ190-200LR	Air Dolomiti	
I-ADJT	Embraer ERJ190-200LR	Air Dolomiti	
I-AIGH	Boeing 767-23BER	Air Italy	
I-BIKA	Airbus A.320-214	Alitalia *Johann Sebastian Bach*	
I-BIKC	Airbus A.320-214	Alitalia *Zefiro*	
I-BIKD	Airbus A.320-214	Alitalia *Maestrale*	
I-BIKI	Airbus A.320-214	Alitalia *Girolamo Frescobaldi*	
I-BIKO	Airbus A.320-214	Alitalia *George Bizet*	
I-BIMA	Airbus A.319-112	Alitalia *Isola d'Elba*	
I-BIXA	Airbus A.321-112	Alitalia *Piazza del Duomo Milano*	
I-BIXE	Airbus A.321-112	Alitalia *Piazza di Spagna Roma*	
I-BIXM	Airbus A.321-112	Alitalia *Piazza di San Franceso Assisi*	
I-BIXP	Airbus A.321-112	Alitalia *Carlo Morelli*	
I-BIXQ	Airbus A.321-112	Alitalia *Domenico Colapietro*	
I-BIXR	Airbus A.321-112	Alitalia *Piazza dell Campidoglio-Roma*	
I-BIXS	Airbus A.321-112	Alitalia *Piazza San Martino-Lucca*	
I-DISU	Boeing 777-243ER	Alitalia *Madonna di Campiglio*	
I-EEZH	Airbus A.320-214	Meridiana Fly	
I-EEZI	Airbus A.320-214	Meridiana Fly	
I-EEZK	Airbus A.320-214	Meridiana Fly	
I-EEZP	Airbus A.320-233	Meridiana Fly	
I-NEOS	Boeing 737-86N	Neos	
I-NEOT	Boeing 737-86N	Neos	
I-NEOU	Boeing 737-86N	Neos	
I-NEOW	Boeing 737-86N	Neos	
I-NEOX	Boeing 737-86N	Neos	
I-NEOZ	Boeing 737-86N	Neos *Monte Rosa*	
I-NDMJ	Boeing 767-306ER	Neos	
I-NDOF	Boeing 767-306ER	Neos	
I-SMEB	McD Douglas MD-82	Meridiana Fly	
I-SMEL	McD Douglas MD-82	Meridiana Fly	
I-SMEM	McD Douglas MD-82	Meridiana Fly	
I-SMEN	McD Douglas MD-83	Meridiana Fly	
I-SMEP	McD Douglas MD-82	Meridiana Fly	
I-SMER	McD Douglas MD-82	Meridiana Fly	
I-SMES	McD Douglas MD-82	Meridiana Fly	
I-SMET	McD Douglas MD-82	Meridiana Fly	
I-SMEV	McD Douglas MD-82	Meridiana Fly	
I-SMEZ	McD Douglas MD-82	Meridiana Fly	
I-WEBA	Airbus A.320-214	Air One	
I-WEBB	Airbus A.320-214	Air One	

JA (Japan)

Reg.	Type	Owner or Operator	Notes
JA01KZ	Boeing 747-481F	Nippon Cargo Airlines	

Notes	Reg.	Type	Owner or Operator
	JA03KZ	Boeing 747-4KZF	Nippon Cargo Airlines
	JA04KZ	Boeing 747-4KZF	Nippon Cargo Airlines
	JA05KZ	Boeing 747-4KZF	Nippon Cargo Airlines *NCA Apollo*
	JA06KZ	Boeing 747-4KZF	Nippon Cargo Airlines
	JA07KZ	Boeing 747-4KZF	Nippon Cargo Airlines *NCA Andromeda*
	JA08KZ	Boeing 747-4KZF	Nippon Cargo Airlines *NCA Aries*
	JA11KZ	Boeing 747-8KZF	Nippon Cargo Airlines
	JA12KZ	Boeing 747-8KZF	Nippon Cargo Airlines
	JA13KZ	Boeing 747-8KZF	Nippon Cargo Airlines
	JA14KZ	Boeing 747-8KZF	Nippon Cargo Airlines
	JA15KZ	Boeing 747-8KZF	Nippon Cargo Airlines
	JA731A	Boeing 777-381ER	All Nippon Airways
	JA731J	Boeing 777-346ER	Japan Airlines
	JA732A	Boeing 777-381ER	All Nippon Airways
	JA732J	Boeing 777-346ER	Japan Airlines
	JA733A	Boeing 777-381ER	All Nippon Airways
	JA733J	Boeing 777-346ER	Japan Airlines
	JA734A	Boeing 777-381ER	All Nippon Airways
	JA734J	Boeing 777-346ER	Japan Airlines
	JA735A	Boeing 777-381ER	All Nippon Airways
	JA735J	Boeing 777-346ER	Japan Airlines
	JA736A	Boeing 777-381ER	All Nippon Airways
	JA736J	Boeing 777-346ER	Japan Airlines
	JA737J	Boeing 777-346ER	Japan Airlines
	JA738J	Boeing 777-346ER	Japan Airlines
	JA739J	Boeing 777-346ER	Japan Airlines
	JA740J	Boeing 777-346ER	Japan Airlines
	JA741J	Boeing 777-346ER	Japan Airlines
	JA742J	Boeing 777-346ER	Japan Airlines
	JA743J	Boeing 777-346ER	Japan Airlines
	JA777A	Boeing 777-381ER	All Nippon Airways
	JA778A	Boeing 777-381ER	All Nippon Airways
	JA779A	Boeing 777-381ER	All Nippon Airways
	JA780A	Boeing 777-381ER	All Nippon Airways
	JA781A	Boeing 777-381ER	All Nippon Airways
	JA782A	Boeing 777-381ER	All Nippon Airways
	JA783A	Boeing 777-381ER	All Nippon Airways
	JA784A	Boeing 777-381ER	All Nippon Airways
	JA785A	Boeing 777-381ER	All Nippon Airways
	JA786A	Boeing 777-381ER	All Nippon Airways
	JA787A	Boeing 777-381ER	All Nippon Airways
	JA788A	Boeing 777-381ER	All Nippon Airways
	JA789A	Boeing 777-381ER	All Nippon Airways

JY (Jordan)

	JY-AGM	Airbus A.310-304	Royal Jordanian *Princess Alia bin Al-Hussein*
	JY-AGQ	Airbus A.310-304F	Royal Jordanian Cargo
	JY-AGR	Airbus A.310-304F	Royal Jordanian Cargo
	JY-AIE	Airbus A.330-223	Royal Jordanian *Jordan River*
	JY-AIF	Airbus A.330-223	Royal Jordanian *Prince Ali bin Al Hussein*
	JY-AIG	Airbus A.330-223	Royal Jordanian *Prince Feisal Ibn Al-Hussein*
	JY-AYJ	Airbus A.321-231	Royal Jordanian *Ramtha*
	JY-AYK	Airbus A.321-231	Royal Jordanian
	JY-AYL	Airbus A.319-132	Royal Jordanian
	JY-AYM	Airbus A.319-132	Royal Jordanian *Ma'an*
	JY-AYN	Airbus A.319-132	Royal Jordanian
	JY-AYP	Airbus A.319-132	Royal Jordabian *Ajloun*
	JY-AYQ	Airbus A.320-232	Royal Jordanian *Mount Nebo*
	JY-AYR	Airbus A.320-232	Royal Jordanian
	JY-AYS	Airbus A.320-232	Royal Jordanian
	JY-AYT	Aitbus A.321-231	Royal Jordanian
	JY-AYU	Airbus A.320-232	Royal Jordanian
	JY-AYV	Airbus A.321-231	Royal Jordanian *Madaba*
	JY-AYW	Airbus A.320-232	Royal Jordanian
	JY-AYX	Airbus A.320-232	Royal Jordanian

LN (Norway)

	LN-BKA	Boeing 787-8	Norwegian Air Shuttle

Reg.	Type	Owner or Operator	Notes
LN-BKB	Boeing 787-8	Norwegian Air Shuttle	
LN-BKC	Boeing 787-8	Norwegian Air Shuttle	
LN-BKD	Boeing 787-8	Norwegian Air Shuttle	
LN-BRE	Boeing 737-405	SAS *Haakon V Magnusson*	
LN-BRX	Boeing 737-505	SAS *Sigurd Munn*	
LN-DYA	Boeing 737-8JP	Norwegian Air Shuttle *Erik Bye*	
LN-DYB	Boeing 737-8JP	Norwegian Air Shuttle *Bjørnstjerne Bjornson*	
LN-DYC	Boeing 737-8JP	Norwegian Air Shuttle *Max Manus*	
LN-DYD	Boeing 737-8JP	Norwegian Air Shuttle *Hans Christian Andersen*	
LN-DYE	Boeing 737-8JP	Norwegian Air Shuttle *Arne Jacobsen*	
LN-DYF	Boeing 737-8JP	Norwegian Air Shuttle *Fridtjof Nansen*	
LN-DYG	Boeing 737-8JP	Norwegian Air Shuttle *Jenny Lind*	
LN-DYH	Boeing 737-8JP	Norwegian Air Shuttle *Soren Kierkegaard*	
LN-DYI	Boeing 737-8JP	Norwegian Air Shuttle *Aasmund Olavson Vinje*	
LN-DYJ	Boeing 737-8JP	Norwegian Air Shuttle *Georg Brandes*	
LN-DYK	Boeing 737-8JP	Norwegian Air Shuttle *Karl Larsson*	
LN-DYL	Boeing 737-8JP	Norwegian Air Shuttle *Amalie Skram*	
LN-DYM	Boeing 737-8JP	Norwegian Air Shuttle *Andre Bjerke*	
LN-DYN	Boeing 737-8JP	Norwegian Air Shuttle *Karen Blixen*	
LN-DYO	Boeing 737-8JP	Norwegian Air Shuttle *Otto Sverdrup*	
LN-DYP	Boeing 737-8JP	Norwegian Air Shuttle *Aksel Sandemose*	
LN-DYQ	Boeing 737-8JP	Norwegian Air Shuttle *Helge Ingstad*	
LN-DYR	Boeing 737-8JP	Norwegian Air Shuttle *Peter C Asbjornsen/Jorgen Moe*	
LN-DYS	Boeing 737-8JP	Norwegian Air Shuttle *Niels Henrik Abel*	
LN-DYT	Boeing 737-8JP	Norwegian Air Shuttle *Kirsten Flagstad*	
LN-DYU	Boeing 737-8JP	Norwegian Air Shuttle *Jorn Utzon*	
LN-DYV	Boeing 737-8JP	Norwegian Air Shuttle *Elsa Beskow*	
LN-DYW	Boeing 737-8JP	Norwegian Air Shuttle	
LN-DYX	Boeing 737-8JP	Norwegian Air Shuttle	
LN-DYY	Boeing 737-8JP	Norwegian Air Shuttle	
LN-DYZ	Boeing 737-8JP	Norwegian Air Shuttle	
LN-KHA	Boeing 737-31S	Norwegian Air Shuttle	
LN-KHB	Boeing 737-31S	Norwegian Air Shuttle	
LN-KHC	Boeing 737-31S	Norwegian Air Shuttle	
LN-KKD	Boeing 737-33V	Norwegian Air Shuttle	
LN-KKJ	Boeing 737-36N	Norwegian Air Shuttle *Sonja Henie*	
LN-KKL	Boeing 737-36N	Norwegian Air Shuttle *Roald Amundsen*	
LN-KKM	Boeing 737-3Y0	Norwegian Air Shuttle *Thor Heyerdahl*	
LN-KKN	Boeing 737-3Y0	Norwegian Air Shuttle *Sigrid Undset*	
LN-KKW	Boeing 737-3K9	Norwegian Air Shuttle	
LN-KKX	Boeing 737-33S	Norwegian Air Shuttle	
LN-NGA	Boeing 737-8JP	Norwegian Air Shuttle	
LN-NGB	Boeing 737-8JP	Norwegian Air Shuttle	
LN-NGC	Boeing 737-8JP	Norwegian Air Shuttle	
LN-NGD	Boeing 737-8JP	Norwegian Air Shuttle	
LN-NGE	Boeing 737-8JP	Norwegian Air Shuttle	
LN-NGF	Boeing 737-8JP	Norwegian Air Shuttle	
LN-NGG	Boeing 737-8JP	Norwegian Air Shuttle	
LN-NGH	Boeing 737-8JP	Norwegian Air Shuttle	
LN-NGI	Boeing 737-8JP	Norwegian Air Shuttle	
LN-NGJ	Boeing 737-8JP	Norwegian Air Shuttle	
LN-NGK	Boeing 737-8JP	Norwegian Air Shuttle	
LN-NGL	Boeing 737-8JP	Norwegian Air Shuttle	
LN-NGM	Boeing 737-8JP	Norwegian Air Shuttle	
LN-NGN	Boeing 737-8JP	Norwegian Air Shuttle	
LN-NGO	Boeing 737-8JP	Norwegian Air Shuttle	
LN-NGP	Boeing 737-8JP	Norwegian Air Shuttle	
LN-NGQ	Boeing 737-8JP	Norwegian Air Shuttle	
LN-NGR	Boeing 737-8JP	Norwegian Air Shuttle	
LN-NGS	Boeing 737-8JP	Norwegian Air Shuttle	
LN-NGT	Boeing 737-8JP	Norwegian Air Shuttle	
LN-NGU	Boeing 737-8JP	Norwegian Air Shuttle	
LN-NIA	Boeing 737-8JP	Norwegian Air Shuttle	
LN-NIB	Boeing 737-8JP	Norwegian Air Shuttle *Helmer Hanssen*	
LN-NIC	Boeing 737-8JP	Norwegian Air Shuttle	
LN-NID	Boeing 737-8JP	Norwegian Air Shuttle	
LN-NIE	Boeing 737-8JP	Norwegian Air Shuttle	
LN-NIF	Boeing 737-8JP	Norwegian Air Shuttle	
LN-NOB	Boeing 737-8FZ	Norwegian Air Shuttle *Edward Grieg*	
LN-NOC	Boeing 737-81Q	Norwegian Air Shuttle *Ole Bull*	
LN-NOD	Boeing 737-8Q8	Norwegian Air Shuttle *Sonje Henie*	
LN-NOE	Boeing 737-8Q8	Norwegian Air Shuttle *Henrik Wergeland*	

Notes	Reg.	Type	Owner or Operator
	LN-NOF	Boeing 737-86N	Norwegian Air Shuttle *Edvard Munch*
	LN-NOG	Boeing 737-86N	Norwegian Air Shuttle *Henrik Ibsen*
	LN-NOH	Boeing 737-86N	Norwegian Air Shuttle *Selma Lagerlof*
	LN-NOI	Boeing 737-86N	Norwegian Air Shuttle *Sam Eyde*
	LN-NOJ	Boeing 737-86N	Norwegian Air Shuttle *Tycho Brahe*
	LN-NOL	Boeing 737-8Q8	Norwegian Air Shuttle
	LN-NOM	Boeing 737-86N	Norwegian Air Shuttle *Greta Garbo*
	LN-NON	Boeing 737-86N	Norwegian Air Shuttle *Anders Celcius*
	LN-NOO	Boeing 737-86Q	Norwegian Air Shuttle *Gustav Vigeland*
	LN-NOP	Boeing 737-86N	Norwegian Air Shuttle *Camilla Collett*
	LN-NOQ	Boeing 737-86N	Norwegian Air Shuttle *Kristian Birkeland*
	LN-NOR	Boeing 737-86N	Norwegian Air Shuttle *Povel Ramel*
	LN-NOT	Boeing 737-8JP	Norwegian Air Shuttle *Piet Hein*
	LN-NOU	Boeing 737-8FZ	Norwegian Air Shuttle *Carl von Linne*
	LN-NOV	Boeing 737-8FZ	Norwegian Air Shuttle *Evart Taube*
	LN-NOW	Boeing 737-8JP	Norwegian Air Shuttle *Oda Krohg*
	LN-NOX	Boeing 737-8JP	Norwegian Air Shuttle *Christian Krohg*
	LN-NOY	Boeing 737-8JP	Norwegian Air Shuttle
	LN-NOZ	Boeing 737-8JP	Norwegian Air Shuttle
	LN-RCN	Boeing 737-883	SAS *Hedrun Viking*
	LN-RCT	Boeing 737-683	SAS *Fridlev Viking*
	LN-RCU	Boeing 737-683	SAS *Sigfrid Viking*
	LN-RCW	Boeing 737-683	SAS *Yngvar Viking*
	LN-RCX	Boeing 737-883	SAS *Hottur Viking*
	LN-RCY	Boeing 737-883	SAS *Eylime Viking*
	LN-RCZ	Boeing 737-883	SAS *Glitne Viking*
	LN-RDV	DHC.8-402 Dash Eight	Wideroe's Flyveselskap
	LN-RDY	DHC.8-402 Dash Eight	Wideroe's Flyveselskap
	LN-RDZ	DHC.8-402 Dash Eight	Wideroe's Flyveselskap
	LN-RGA	Boeing 737-883	SAS
	LN-RGB	Boeing 737-883	SAS
	LN-RGC	Boeing 737-883	SAS *Cecilia Viking*
	LN-RGD	Boeing 737-883	SAS
	LN-RGE	Boeing 737-883	SAS
	LN-RGF	Boeing 737-883	SAS
	LN-RGG	Boeing 737-883	SAS *Asgerd Viking*
	LN-RGH	Boeing 737-883	SAS
	LN-RGI	Boeing 737-883	SAS
	LN-RGK	Boeing 737-683	SAS
	LN-RKF	Airbus A.340-313X	SAS *Godfred Viking*
	LN-RKG	Airbus A.340-313X	SAS *Gudrod Viking*
	LN-RKH	Airbus A.330-343X	SAS *Emund Viking*
	LN-RKI	Airbus A.321-231	SAS *Gunnhild Viking*
	LN-RKK	Airbus A.321-231	SAS *Viger Viking*
	LN-RKM	Airbus A.330-343	SAS
	LN-RKN	Airbus A.330-343	SAS
	LN-RKO	Airbus A.330-343	SAS
	LN-RKP	Airbus A.340-313	SAS
	LN-RNL	Canadair CRJ900ER	SAS *Fafner Viking*
	LN-RNN	Boeing 737-783	SAS *Borgny Viking*
	LN-RNO	Boeing 737-783	SAS *Gjuke Viking*
	LN-RNU	Boeing 737-783	SAS *Hans Viking*
	LN-RNW	Boeing 737-783	SAS *Granmar Viking*
	LN-RPA	Boeing 737-683	SAS *Arnljot Viking*
	LN-RPB	Boeing 737-683	SAS *Bure Viking*
	LN-RPE	Boeing 737-683	SAS *Edla Viking*
	LN-RPF	Boeing 737-683	SAS *Frede Viking*
	LN-RPG	Boeing 737-683	SAS *Geirmund Viking*
	LN-RPH	Boeing 737-683	SAS *Hamder Viking*
	LN-RPJ	Boeing 737-783	SAS *Grimhild Viking*
	LN-RPK	Boeing 737-783	SAS *Heimer Viking*
	LN-RPL	Boeing 737-883	SAS *Svanevit Viking*
	LN-RPM	Boeing 737-883	SAS *Frigg Viking*
	LN-RPN	Boeing 737-883	SAS *Bergfora Viking*
	LN-RPO	Boeing 737-883	SAS *Thorleif Viking*
	LN-RPR	Boeing 737-883	SAS *Ore Viking*
	LN-RPS	Boeing 737-683	SAS *Gautrek Viking*
	LN-RPT	Boeing 737-683	SAS *Ellida Viking*
	LN-RPW	Boeing 737-683	SAS *Alvid Viking*
	LN-RPX	Boeing 737-683	SAS *Nanna Viking*
	LN-RPY	Boeing 737-683	SAS *Olof Viking*
	LN-RPZ	Boeing 737-683	SAS *Bera Viking*

Reg.	Type	Owner or Operator	Notes
LN-RRA	Boeing 737-783	SAS Steinar Viking	
LN-RRB	Boeing 737-783	SAS Cecilia Viking	
LN-RRC	Boeing 737-683	SAS Sindre Viking	
LN-RRD	Boeing 737-683	SAS Embla Viking	
LN-RRE	Boeing 737-883	SAS Knut Viking	
LN-RRF	Boeing 737-883	SAS Froydis Viking	
LN-RRG	Boeing 737-883	SAS Einar Viking	
LN-RRH	Boeing 737-883	SAS Freja Viking	
LN-RRJ	Boeing 737-883	SAS Frida Viking	
LN-RRK	Boeing 737-883	SAS Gerud Viking	
LN-RRL	Boeing 737-883	SAS Jarlabanke Viking	
LN-RRM	Boeing 737-783	SAS Erland Viking	
LN-RRN	Boeing 737-783	SAS Solveig Viking	
LN-RRO	Boeing 737-683	SAS Bernt Viking	
LN-RRP	Boeing 737-683	SAS Vilborg Viking	
LN-RRR	Boeing 737-683	SAS Torbjorn Viking	
LN-RRS	Boeing 737-883	SAS Ymir Viking	
LN-RRT	Boeing 737-883	SAS Lodyn Viking	
LN-RRU	Boeing 737-883	SAS Vingolf Viking	
LN-RRW	Boeing 737-883	SAS Saga Viking	
LN-RRX	Boeing 737-683	SAS Ragnfast Viking	
LN-RRY	Boeing 737-683	SAS Signe Viking	
LN-RRZ	Boeing 737-683	SAS Gisla Viking	
LN-TUA	Boeing 737-705	SAS Ingeborg Eriksdatter	
LN-TUD	Boeing 737-705	SAS Margrete Skulesdatter	
LN-TUF	Boeing 737-705	SAS Tyra Haraldsdatter	
LN-TUH	Boeing 737-705	SAS Margrete Ingesdatter	
LN-TUI	Boeing 737-705	SAS Kristin Knudsdatter	
LN-TUJ	Boeing 737-705	SAS Eirik Blodoks	
LN-TUK	Boeing 737-705	SAS Inge Bardsson	
LN-TUL	Boeing 737-705	SAS Haakon IV Haakonson	
LN-TUM	Boeing 737-705	SAS Oystein Magnusson	
LN-WDE	DHC.8-402 Dash Eight	Wideroe's Flyveselskap	
LN-WDF	DHC.8-402 Dash Eight	Wideroe's Flyveselskap	
LN-WDG	DHC.8-402 Dash Eight	Wideroe's Flyveselskap	
LN-WDH	DHC.8-402 Dash Eight	Wideroe's Flyveselskap	
LN-WDI	DHC.8-402 Dash Eight	Wideroe's Flyveselskap	
LN-WDJ	DHC.8-402 Dash Eight	Wideroe's Flyveselskap	
LN-WDK	DHC.8-402 Dash Eight	Wideroe's Flyveselskap	
LN-WDL	DHC.8-402 Dash Eight	Wideroe's Flyveselskap	
LN-WFC	DHC.8-311 Dash Eight	Wideroe's Flyveselskap	
LN-WFD	DHC.8-311 Dash Eight	Wideroe's Flyveselskap	
LN-WFH	DHC.8-311 Dash Eight	Wideroe's Flyveselskap	
LN-WFO	DHC.8Q-311 Dash Eight	Wideroe's Flyveselskap	
LN-WFP	DHC.8Q-311 Dash Eight	Wideroe's Flyveselskap	
LN-WFS	DHC.8Q-311 Dash Eight	Wideroe's Flyveselskap	
LN-WFT	DHC.8Q-311 Dash Eight	Wideroe's Flyveselskap	
LN-WFU	DHC.8Q-311 Dash Eight	Wideroe's Flyveselskap	

LX (Luxembourg)

LX-ACV	Boeing 747-4B5BCF	Cargolux	
LX-DCV	Boeing 747-4B5CF	Cargolux	
LX-ECV	Boeing 747-4HQERF	Cargolux	
LX-LGE	DHC.8Q-402 Dash Eight	Luxair	
LX-LGF	DHC.8Q-402 Dash Eight	Luxair	
LX-LGG	DHC.8Q-402 Dash Eight	Luxair	
LX-LGH	DHC.8Q-402 Dash Eight	Luxair	
LX-LGI	Embraer RJ145LU	Luxair	
LX-LGJ	Embraer RJ145LU	Luxair	
LX-LGM	DHC.8Q-402 Dash Eight	Luxair	
LX-LGN	DHC.8Q-402 Dash Eight	Luxair	
LX-LGQ	Boeing 737-7C9	Luxair Chateau de Burg	
LX-LGR	Boeing 737-7C9	Luxair Chateau de Fischbach	
LX-LGS	Boeing 737-7C9	Luxair Chateau de Senningen	
LX-LGU	Boeing 737-8C9	Luxair	
LX-LGV	Boeing 737-8C9	Luxair	
LX-LGW	Embraer RJ145LU	Luxair	
LX-LGX	Embraer RJ145LU	Luxair	
LX-LGY	Embraer RJ145LU	Luxair	
LX-LGZ	Embraer RJ145LU	Luxair	

Notes	Reg.	Type	Owner or Operator
	LX-OCV	Boeing 747-4R7F (SCD)	Cargolux City of Differdange
	LX-RCV	Boeing 747-4R7F (SCD)	Cargolux City of Schengen
	LX-SCV	Boeing 747-4R7F (SCD)	Cargolux City of Niederanven
	LX-TCV	Boeing 747-4R7F (SCD)	Cargolux City of Sandweiler
	LX-UCV	Boeing 747-4R7F (SCD)	Cargolux City of Bertragne
	LX-VCA	Boeing 747-8R7F	Cargolux City of Vianden
	LX-VCB	Boeing 747-8R7F	Cargolux City of Esch-sur-Aizette
	LX-VCC	Boeing 747-8R7F	Cargolux City of Troisvierges
	LX-VCD	Boeing 747-8R7F	Cargolux City of Luxembourg
	LX-VCE	Boeing 747-8R7F	Cargolux
	LX-VCF	Boeing 747-8R7F	Cargolux City of Grevenmacher
	LX-VCG	Boeing 747-8R7F	Cargolux City of Diekirch
	LX-VCH	Boeing 747-8R7F	Cargolux City of Dudelange
	LX-VCI	Boeing 747-8R7F	Cargolux
	LX-VCV	Boeing 747-4R7F (SCD)	Cargolux City of Walferdange
	LX-WAE	BAe ATP	West Air Europe
	LX-WCV	Boeing 747-4R7F (SCD)	Cargolux City of Petange
	LX-YCV	Boeing 747-4R7F	Cargolux City of Contem

LY (Lithuania)

	LY-AQX	Boeing 737-322	Small Planet Airlines
	LY-BGC	Boeing 737-35B	Grand Cru Airlines
	LY-COM	Airbus A.320-212	Avion Express
	LY-FLC	Boeing 737-31S	Small Planet Airlines
	LY-FLE	Boeing 737-3L9	Small Planet Airlines
	LY-FLH	Boeing 737-382	Small Planet Airlines
	LY-GGC	Boeing 737-3Q8	Grand Cru Airlines
	LY-SPA	Airbus A.320-232	Small Planet Airlines
	LY-SPC	Airbus A.320-231	Small Planet Airlines
	LY-VER	Airbus A.320-212	Avion Express
	LY-VES	Airbus A.320-212	Avion Express
	LY-VET	Airbus A.319-112	Avion Express
	LY-VEU	Airbus A.319-112	Avion Express
	LY-VEV	Airbus A.320-211	Avion Express
	LY-VEX	Airbus A.320-212	Avion Express
	LY-VEY	Airbus A.320-212	Avion Express
	LY-VEZ	Airbus A.320-212	Avion Express

LZ (Bulgaria)

	LZ-BHG	Airbus A.320-232	BH Air
	LZ-BHH	Airbus A.320-232	BH Air
	LZ-BUR	Embraer ERJ190-100IGW	Bulgaria Air
	LZ-FBA	Airbus A.319-112	Bulgaria Air
	LZ-FBB	Airbus A.319-112	Bulgaria Air
	LZ-FBC	Airbus A.320-214	Bulgaria Air
	LZ-FBD	Airbus A.320-214	Bulgaria Air
	LZ-FBE	Airbus A.320-214	Bulgaria Air
	LZ-LDG	McD Douglas MD-83	Bulgarian Air Charter
	LZ-LDK	McD Douglas MD-82	Bulgarian Air Charter
	LZ-LDM	McD Douglas MD-82	Bulgarian Air Charter
	LZ-LDN	McD Douglas MD-82	Bulgarian Air Charter
	LZ-LDP	McD Douglas MD-82	Bulgarian Air Charter
	LZ-LDS	McD Douglas MD-82	Bulgarian Air Charter
	LZ-LDT	McD Douglas MD-82	Bulgarian Air Charter
	LZ-LDU	McD Douglas MD-82	Bulgarian Air Charter
	LZ-LDW	McD Douglas MD-82	Bulgarian Air Charter
	LZ-LDY	McD Douglas MD-82	Bulgarian Air Charter
	LZ-MDA	Airbus A.320-232	Air VIA/Wizz Air
	LZ-MDB	Airbus A.320-232	Air VIA
	LZ-MDC	Airbus A.320-232	Air VIA/WOW Air
	LZ-MDD	Airbus A.320-232	Air VIA/WOW Air
	LZ-PLO	Embraer ERJ190-100STD	Bulgaria Air
	LZ-SOF	Embraer ERJ190-100IGW	Bulgaria Air
	LZ-VAR	Embraer ERJ190-100IGW	Bulgaria Air

Reg.	Type	Owner or Operator	Notes

N (USA)

N104UA	Boeing 747-422	United Airlines	
N105UA	Boeing 747-451	United Airlines	
N107UA	Boeing 747-422	United Airlines	
N116UA	Boeing 747-422	United Airlines	
N117UA	Boeing 747-422	United Airlines	
N118UA	Boeing 747-422	United Airlines	
N119UA	Boeing 747-422	United Airlines	
N120UA	Boeing 747-422	United Airlines	
N121UA	Boeing 747-422	United Airlines	
N122UA	Boeing 747-422	United Airlines	
N127UA	Boeing 747-422	United Airlines	
N128UA	Boeing 747-422	United Airlines	
N152DL	Boeing 767-3P6ER	Delta Air Lines	
N153DL	Boeing 767-3P6ER	Delta Air Lines	
N154DL	Boeing 767-3P6ER	Delta Air Lines	
N155DL	Boeing 767-3P6ER	Delta Air Lines	
N156DL	Boeing 767-3P6ER	Delta Air Lines	
N169DZ	Boeing 767-332ER	Delta Air Lines	
N171DN	Boeing 767-332ER	Delta Air Lines	
N171DZ	Boeing 767-332ER	Delta Air Lines	
N171UA	Boeing 747-422	United Airlines	
N172AJ	Boeing 757-223ET	American Airlines	
N172DN	Boeing 767-332ER	Delta Air Lines	
N172DZ	Boeing 767-332ER	Delta Air Lines	
N173AN	Boeing 757-223ET	American Airlines	
N173DZ	Boeing 767-332ER	Delta Air Lines	
N174AA	Boeing 757-223ET	American Airlines	
N174DN	Boeing 767-332ER	Delta Air Lines	
N174DZ	Boeing 767-332ER	Delta Air Lines	
N174UA	Boeing 747-422	United Airlines	
N175AN	Boeing 757-223ET	American Airlines	
N175DN	Boeing 767-332ER	Delta Air Lines	
N175DZ	Boeing 767-332ER	Delta Air Lines	
N175UA	Boeing 747-422	United Airlines	
N176AA	Boeing 757-223ET	American Airlines	
N176DN	Boeing 767-332ER	Delta Air Lines	
N176DZ	Boeing 767-332ER	Delta Air Lines	
N177AN	Boeing 757-223ET	American Airlines	
N177DN	Boeing 767-332ER	Delta Air Lines	
N177DZ	Boeing 767-332ER	Delta Air Lines	
N177UA	Boeing 747-422	United Airlines	
N178AA	Boeing 757-223ET	American Airlines	
N178DN	Boeing 767-332ER	Delta Air Lines	
N178DZ	Boeing 767-332ER	Delta Air Lines	
N178UA	Boeing 747-422	United Airlines	
N179AA	Boeing 757-223ET	American Airlines	
N179DN	Boeing 767-332ER	Delta Air Lines	
N179UA	Boeing 747-422	United Airlines	
N180DN	Boeing 767-332ER	Delta Air Lines	
N180UA	Boeing 747-422	United Airlines	
N181DN	Boeing 767-332ER	Delta Air Lines	
N181UA	Boeing 747-422	United Airlines	
N182DN	Boeing 767-332ER	Delta Air Lines	
N182UA	Boeing 747-422	United Airlines	
N183DN	Boeing 767-332ER	Delta Air Lines	
N184DN	Boeing 767-332ER	Delta Air Lines	
N185AN	Boeing 757-223ET	American Airlines	
N185DN	Boeing 767-332ER	Delta Air Lines	
N186AN	Boeing 757-223ET	American Airlines	
N186DN	Boeing 767-332ER	Delta Air Lines	
N187AN	Boeing 757-223ET	American Airlines	
N187DN	Boeing 767-332ER	Delta Air Lines	
N188AN	Boeing 757-223ET	American Airlines	
N188DN	Boeing 767-332ER	Delta Air Lines	
N189AN	Boeing 757-223ET	American Airlines	
N189DN	Boeing 767-332ER	Delta Air Lines	
N190AA	Boeing 757-223ET	American Airlines	
N190DN	Boeing 767-332ER	Delta Air Lines	
N191AN	Boeing 757-223ET	American Airlines	

Notes	Reg.	Type	Owner or Operator
	N191DN	Boeing 767-332ER	Delta Air Lines
	N192DN	Boeing 767-332ER	Delta Air Lines
	N193DN	Boeing 767-332ER	Delta Air Lines
	N194DN	Boeing 767-332ER	Delta Air Lines
	N195AN	Boeing 757-223ET	American Airlines
	N195DN	Boeing 767-332ER	Delta Air Lines
	N196DN	Boeing 767-332ER	Delta Air Lines
	N197AN	Boeing 757-223ET	American Airlines
	N197DN	Boeing 767-332ER	Delta Air Lines
	N197UA	Boeing 747-422	United Airlines
	N198AA	Boeing 757-223ET	American Airlines
	N198DN	Boeing 767-332ER	Delta Air Lines
	N199AN	Boeing 757-223ET	American Airlines
	N199DN	Boeing 767-332ER	Delta Air Lines
	N199UA	Boeing 747-422	United Airlines
	N200UU	Boeing 757-2B7	US Airways
	N201UU	Boeing 757-2B7	US Airways
	N202UW	Boeing 757-2B7	US Airways
	N203UW	Boeing 757-23N	US Airways
	N204UA	Boeing 777-222ER	United Airlines
	N204UW	Boeing 757-23N	US Airways
	N205UW	Boeing 757-23N	US Airways
	N206UA	Boeing 777-222ER	United Airlines
	N206UW	Boeing 757-2B7	US Airways
	N209UA	Boeing 777-222ER	United Airlines
	N216UA	Boeing 777-222ER	United Airlines
	N217UA	Boeing 777-222ER	United Airlines
	N218UA	Boeing 777-222ER	United Airlines
	N219CY	Boeing 767-383ER	ABX Air/DHL
	N220CY	Boeing 767-383ER	ABX Air/DHL
	N219UA	Boeing 777-222ER	United Airlines
	N220UA	Boeing 777-222ER	United Airlines
	N221UA	Boeing 777-222ER	United Airlines
	N222UA	Boeing 777-222ER	United Airlines
	N223UA	Boeing 777-222ER	United Airlines
	N224UA	Boeing 777-222ER	United Airlines
	N225UA	Boeing 777-222ER	United Airlines
	N226UA	Boeing 777-222ER	United Airlines
	N227UA	Boeing 777-222ER	United Airlines
	N228UA	Boeing 777-222ER	United Airlines
	N229UA	Boeing 777-222ER	United Airlines
	N245AY	Boeing 767-201ER	US Airways
	N246AY	Boeing 767-201ER	US Airways
	N248AY	Boeing 767-201ER	US Airways
	N249AU	Boeing 767-201ER	US Airways
	N250AY	Boeing 767-201ER	US Airways
	N251AY	Boeing 767-2B7ER	US Airways
	N252AU	Boeing 767-2B7ER	US Airways
	N253AY	Boeing 767-2B7ER	US Airways
	N255AY	Boeing 767-2B7ER	US Airways
	N256AY	Boeing 767-2B7ER	US Airways
	N270AY	Airbus A.330-323X	US Airways
	N271AY	Airbus A.330-323X	US Airways
	N271WA	McD Douglas MD-11 (271)	World Airways
	N272AY	Airbus A.330-323X	US Airways
	N272WA	McD Douglas MD-11 (272)	World Airways
	N273AY	Airbus A.330-323X	US Airways
	N274AY	Airbus A.330-323X	US Airways
	N275AY	Airbus A.330-323X	US Airways
	N276AY	Airbus A.330-323X	US Airways
	N277AY	Airbus A.330-323X	US Airways
	N278AY	Airbus A.330-323X	US Airways
	N279AY	Airbus A.330-243	US Airways
	N280AY	Airbus A.330-243	US Airways
	N281AY	Airbus A.330-243	US Airways
	N282AY	Airbus A.330-243	US Airways
	N283AY	Airbus A.330-243	US Airways
	N284AY	Airbus A.330-243	US Airways
	N285AY	Airbus A.330-243	US Airways
	N286AY	Airbus A.330-243	US Airways
	N287AY	Airbus A.330-243	US Airways
	N288AY	Airbus A.330-243	US Airways

Reg.	Type	Owner or Operator	Notes
N289AY	Airbus A.330-243	US Airways	
N290AY	Airbus A.330-243	US Airways	
N291AY	Airbus A.330-243	US Airways	
N301UP	Boeing 767-34AFER	United Parcel Service	
N302UP	Boeing 767-34AFER	United Parcel Service	
N303UP	Boeing 767-34AFER	United Parcel Service	
N304UP	Boeing 767-34AFER	United Parcel Service	
N305UP	Boeing 767-34AFER	United Parcel Service	
N306UP	Boeing 767-34AFER	United Parcel Service	
N307UP	Boeing 767-34AFER	United Parcel Service	
N308UP	Boeing 767-34AFER	United Parcel Service	
N309UP	Boeing 767-34AFER	United Parcel Service	
N310UP	Boeing 767-34AFER	United Parcel Service	
N311UP	Boeing 767-34AFER	United Parcel Service	
N312UP	Boeing 767-34AFER	United Parcel Service	
N313UP	Boeing 767-34AFER	United Parcel Service	
N314UP	Boeing 767-34AFER	United Parcel Service	
N315UP	Boeing 767-34AFER	United Parcel Service	
N316UP	Boeing 767-34AFER	United Parcel Service	
N317UP	Boeing 767-34AFER	United Parcel Service	
N318UP	Boeing 767-34AFER	United Parcel Service	
N319UP	Boeing 767-34AFER	United Parcel Service	
N320UP	Boeing 767-34AFER	United Parcel Service	
N322UP	Boeing 767-34AFER	United Parcel Service	
N323UP	Boeing 767-34AFER	United Parcel Service	
N324UP	Boeing 767-34AFER	United Parcel Service	
N325UP	Boeing 767-34AFER	United Parcel Service	
N326UP	Boeing 767-34AFER	United Parcel Service	
N327UP	Boeing 767-34AFER	United Parcel Service	
N328UP	Boeing 767-34AFER	United Parcel Service	
N329UP	Boeing 767-34AER	United Parcel Service	
N330UP	Boeing 767-34AER	United Parcel Service	
N331UP	Boeing 767-34AER	United Parcel Service	
N332UP	Boeing 767-34AER	United Parcel Service	
N334UP	Boeing 767-34AER	United Parcel Service	
N335UP	Boeing 767-34AF	United Parcel Service	
N336UP	Boeing 767-34AF	United Parcel Service	
N337UP	Boeing 767-34AF	United Parcel Service	
N338UP	Boeing 767-34AF	United Parcel Service	
N339UP	Boeing 767-34AF	United Parcel Service	
N340UP	Boeing 767-34AF	United Parcel Service	
N341UP	Boeing 767-34AF	United Parcel Service	
N342AN	Boeing 767-323ER	American Airlines	
N342UP	Boeing 767-34AF	United Parcel Service	
N343AN	Boeing 767-323ER	American Airlines	
N343UP	Boeing 767-34AF	United Parcel Service	
N344AN	Boeing 767-323ER	American Airlines	
N344UP	Boeing 767-34AF	United Parcel Service	
N345AN	Boeing 767-323ER	American Airlines	
N345UP	Boeing 767-34AF	United Parcel Service	
N346AN	Boeing 767-323ER	American Airlines	
N346UP	Boeing 767-34AF	United Parcel Service	
N347AN	Boeing 767-323ER	American Airlines	
N347UP	Boeing 767-34AF	United Parcel Service	
N348AN	Boeing 767-323ER	American Airlines	
N348UP	Boeing 767-34AF	United Parcel Service	
N349AN	Boeing 767-323ER	American Airlines	
N349UP	Boeing 767-34AF	United Parcel Service	
N350AN	Boeing 767-323ER	American Airlines	
N350UP	Boeing 767-34AF	United Parcel Service	
N351AA	Boeing 767-323ER	American Airlines	
N351UP	Boeing 767-34AF	United Parcel Service	
N352AA	Boeing 767-323ER	American Airlines	
N352UP	Boeing 767-34AF	United Parcel Service	
N353AA	Boeing 767-323ER	American Airlines	
N353UP	Boeing 767-34AF	United Parcel Service	
N354AA	Boeing 767-323ER	American Airlines	
N354UP	Boeing 767-34AF	United Parcel Service	
N355AA	Boeing 767-323ER	American Airlines	
N355UP	Boeing 767-34AF	United Parcel Service	
N356UP	Boeing 767-34AF	United Parcel Service	
N357AA	Boeing 767-323ER	American Airlines	

Notes	Reg.	Type	Owner or Operator
	N357UP	Boeing 767-34AF	United Parcel Service
	N358AA	Boeing 767-323ER	American Airlines
	N358UP	Boeing 767-34AF	United Parcel Service
	N359AA	Boeing 767-323ER	American Airlines
	N359UP	Boeing 767-34AF	United Parcel Service
	N360AA	Boeing 767-323ER	American Airlines
	N360UP	Boeing 767-34AF	United Parcel Service
	N361AA	Boeing 767-323ER	American Airlines
	N361UP	Boeing 767-34AF	United Parcel Service
	N362AA	Boeing 767-323ER	American Airlines
	N363AA	Boeing 767-323ER	American Airlines
	N366AA	Boeing 767-323ER	American Airlines
	N368AA	Boeing 767-323ER	American Airlines
	N369AA	Boeing 767-323ER	American Airlines
	N370AA	Boeing 767-323ER	American Airlines
	N371AA	Boeing 767-323ER	American Airlines
	N372AA	Boeing 767-323ER	American Airlines
	N373AA	Boeing 767-323ER	American Airlines
	N374AA	Boeing 767-323ER	American Airlines
	N376AN	Boeing 767-323ER	American Airlines
	N377AN	Boeing 767-323ER	American Airlines
	N378AN	Boeing 767-323ER	American Airlines
	N379AA	Boeing 767-323ER	American Airlines
	N380AN	Boeing 767-323ER	American Airlines
	N381AN	Boeing 767-323ER	American Airlines
	N382AN	Boeing 767-323ER	American Airlines
	N383AN	Boeing 767-323ER	American Airlines
	N384AA	Boeing 767-323ER	American Airlines
	N385AM	Boeing 767-323ER	American Airlines
	N386AA	Boeing 767-323ER	American Airlines
	N387AM	Boeing 767-323ER	American Airlines
	N388AA	Boeing 767-323ER	American Airlines
	N389AA	Boeing 767-323ER	American Airlines
	N390AA	Boeing 767-323ER	American Airlines
	N391AA	Boeing 767-323ER	American Airlines
	N392AN	Boeing 767-323ER	American Airlines
	N393AN	Boeing 767-323ER	American Airlines
	N394AN	Boeing 767-323ER	American Airlines
	N394DL	Boeing 767-324ER	Delta Air Lines
	N395AN	Boeing 767-323ER	American Airlines
	N396AN	Boeing 767-323ER	American Airlines
	N397AN	Boeing 767-323ER	American Airlines
	N398AN	Boeing 767-323ER	American Airlines
	N399AN	Boeing 767-323ER	American Airlines
	N412MC	Boeing 747-47UF	Atlas Air
	N415MC	Boeing 747-47UF	Atlas Air
	N418MC	Boeing 747-47UF	Atlas Air
	N429MC	Boeing 747-481	Atlas Air
	N475MC	Boeing 747-47U	Atlas Air
	N476MC	Boeing 747-47U	Atlas Air
	N477MC	Boeing 747-47U	Atlas Air
	N493MC	Boeing 747-47UF	Atlas Air
	N496MC	Boeing 747-47UF	Atlas Air
	N497MC	Boeing 747-47UF	Atlas Air
	N498MC	Boeing 747-47UF	Atlas Air/Polar Air Cargo
	N499MC	Boeing 747-47UF	Atlas Air/Polar Air Cargo
	N521FE	McD Douglas MD-11F	Federal Express
	N522FE	McD Douglas MD-11F	Federal Express
	N523FE	McD Douglas MD-11F	Federal Express
	N524FE	McD Douglas MD-11F	Federal Express
	N525FE	McD Douglas MD-11F	Federal Express
	N527FE	McD Douglas MD-11F	Federal Express
	N528FE	McD Douglas MD-11F	Federal Express
	N529FE	McD Douglas MD-11F	Federal Express
	N572FE	McD Douglas MD-11F	Federal Express
	N573FE	McD Douglas MD-11F	Federal Express
	N574FE	McD Douglas MD-11F	Federal Express
	N575FE	McD Douglas MD-11F	Federal Express
	N576FE	McD Douglas MD-11F	Federal Express
	N577FE	McD Douglas MD-11F	Federal Express
	N578FE	McD Douglas MD-11F	Federal Express *Stephen*
	N579FE	McD Douglas MD-11F	Federal Express *Nash*

Reg.	Type	Owner or Operator	Notes
N580FE	McD Douglas MD-11F	Federal Express *Ashton*	
N582FE	McD Douglas MD-11F	Federal Express *Jamie*	
N583FE	McD Douglas MD-11F	Federal Express *Nancy*	
N584FE	McD Douglas MD-11F	Federal Express *Jeffrey Wellington*	
N585FE	McD Douglas MD-11F	Federal Express *Katherine*	
N586FE	McD Douglas MD-11F	Federal Express *Dylan*	
N587FE	McD Douglas MD-11F	Federal Express *Jeanna*	
N588FE	McD Douglas MD-11F	Federal Express *Kendra*	
N589FE	McD Douglas MD-11F	Federal Express *Shaun*	
N590FE	McD Douglas MD-11F	Federal Express	
N591FE	McD Douglas MD-11F	Federal Express *Giovanni*	
N592FE	McD Douglas MD-11F	Federal Express *Joshua*	
N593FE	McD Douglas MD-11F	Federal Express *Harrison*	
N594FE	McD Douglas MD-11F	Federal Express	
N595FE	McD Douglas MD-11F	Federal Express *Avery*	
N596FE	McD Douglas MD-11F	Federal Express	
N597FE	McD Douglas MD-11F	Federal Express	
N598FE	McD Douglas MD-11F	Federal Express	
N599FE	McD Douglas MD-11F	Federal Express *Mariana*	
N601FE	McD Douglas MD-11F	Federal Express *Jim Riedmeyer*	
N602FE	McD Douglas MD-11F	Federal Express *Malcolm Baldridge 1990*	
N603FE	McD Douglas MD-11F	Federal Express *Elizabeth*	
N604FE	McD Douglas MD-11F	Federal Express *Hollis*	
N605FE	McD Douglas MD-11F	Federal Express *April Star*	
N606FE	McD Douglas MD-11F	Federal Express *Charles & Theresa*	
N607FE	McD Douglas MD-11F	Federal Express *Christina*	
N608FE	McD Douglas MD-11F	Federal Express *Karen*	
N609FE	McD Douglas MD-11F	Federal Express *Scott*	
N610FE	McD Douglas MD-11F	Federal Express *Marisa*	
N612FE	McD Douglas MD-11F	Federal Express *Alyssa*	
N613FE	McD Douglas MD-11F	Federal Express *Krista*	
N614FE	McD Douglas MD-11F	Federal Express *Christy Allison*	
N615FE	McD Douglas MD-11F	Federal Express *Max*	
N616FE	McD Douglas MD-11F	Federal Express *Shanita*	
N617FE	McD Douglas MD-11F	Federal Express *Travis*	
N618FE	McD Douglas MD-11F	Federal Express *Justin*	
N619FE	McD Douglas MD-11F	Federal Express *Lyndon*	
N620FE	McD Douglas MD-11F	Federal Express	
N621FE	McD Douglas MD-11F	Federal Express *Connor*	
N623FE	McD Douglas MD-11F	Federal Express *Meghan*	
N624FE	McD Douglas MD-11F	Federal Express	
N625FE	McD Douglas MD-11F	Federal Express	
N628FE	McD Douglas MD-11F	Federal Express	
N631FE	McD Douglas MD-11F	Federal Express	
N641UA	Boeing 767-322ER	United Airlines	
N642FE	McD Douglas MD-11F	Federal Express	
N642UA	Boeing 767-322ER	United Airlines	
N643FE	McD Douglas MD-11F	Federal Express	
N643UA	Boeing 767-322ER	United Airlines	
N644FE	McD Douglas MD-11F	Federal Express	
N644UA	Boeing 767-322ER	United Airlines	
N645FE	McD Douglas MD-11F	Federal Express	
N646UA	Boeing 767-322ER	United Airlines	
N647UA	Boeing 767-322ER	United Airlines	
N648UA	Boeing 767-322ER	United Airlines	
N649UA	Boeing 767-322ER	United Airlines	
N651UA	Boeing 767-322ER	United Airlines	
N652UA	Boeing 767-322ER	United Airlines	
N653UA	Boeing 767-322ER	United Airlines	
N654UA	Boeing 767-322ER	United Airlines	
N655UA	Boeing 767-322ER	United Airlines	
N656UA	Boeing 767-322ER	United Airlines	
N657UA	Boeing 767-322ER	United Airlines	
N658UA	Boeing 767-322ER	United Airlines	
N659UA	Boeing 767-322ER	United Airlines	
N660UA	Boeing 767-322ER	United Airlines	
N661UA	Boeing 767-322ER	United Airlines	
N662UA	Boeing 767-322ER	United Airlines	
N663UA	Boeing 767-322ER	United Airlines	
N664UA	Boeing 767-322ER	United Airlines	
N665UA	Boeing 767-322ER	United Airlines	
N666UA	Boeing 767-322ER	United Airlines	

Notes	Reg.	Type	Owner or Operator
	N667UA	Boeing 767-322ER	United Airlines
	N668UA	Boeing 767-322ER	United Airlines
	N669UA	Boeing 767-322ER	United Airlines
	N670UA	Boeing 767-322ER	United Airlines
	N671UA	Boeing 767-322ER	United Airlines
	N672UA	Boeing 767-322ER	United Airlines
	N673UA	Boeing 767-322ER	United Airlines
	N674UA	Boeing 767-322ER	United Airlines
	N675UA	Boeing 767-322ER	United Airlines
	N676UA	Boeing 767-322ER	United Airlines
	N677UA	Boeing 767-322ER	United Airlines
	N704CK	Boeing 747-246F	Kalitta Air
	N717AN	Boeing 777-323ER	American Airlines
	N718AN	Boeing 777-323ER	American Airlines
	N719AN	Boeing 777-323ER	American Airlines
	N720AN	Boeing 777-323ER	American Airlines
	N721AN	Boeing 777-323ER	American Airlines
	N722AN	Boeing 777-323ER	American Airlines
	N723AN	Boeing 777-323ER	American Airlines
	N724AN	Boeing 777-323ER	American Airlines
	N725AN	Boeing 777-323ER	American Airlines
	N726AN	Boeing 777-323ER	American Airlines
	N727AN	Boeing 777-323ER	American Airlines
	N728AN	Boeing 777-323ER	American Airlines
	N729AN	Boeing 777-323ER	American Airlines
	N730AN	Boeing 777-323ER	American Airlines
	N731AN	Boeing 777-323ER	American Airlines
	N732AN	Boeing 777-323ER	American Airlines
	N740CK	Boeing 747-4H6BCF	Kalitta Air
	N741CK	Boeing 747-4H6F	Kalitta Air
	N742CK	Boeing 747-446BCF	Kalitta Air
	N743CK	Boeing 747-446BCF	Kalitta Air
	N744CK	Boeing 747-446BCF	Kalitta Air
	N745CK	Boeing 747-446BCF	Kalitta Air
	N746CK	Boeing 747-246B	Kalitta Air
	N748CK	Boeing 747-221F	Kalitta Air
	N750AN	Boeing 777-223ER	American Airlines
	N751AN	Boeing 777-223ER	American Airlines
	N752AN	Boeing 777-223ER	American Airlines
	N753AN	Boeing 777-223ER	American Airlines
	N754AN	Boeing 777-223ER	American Airlines
	N755AN	Boeing 777-223ER	American Airlines
	N756AM	Boeing 777-223ER	American Airlines
	N757AN	Boeing 777-223ER	American Airlines
	N758AN	Boeing 777-223ER	American Airlines
	N759AN	Boeing 777-223ER	American Airlines
	N760AN	Boeing 777-223ER	American Airlines
	N761AJ	Boeing 777-223ER	American Airlines
	N762AN	Boeing 777-223ER	American Airlines
	N765AN	Boeing 777-223ER	American Airlines
	N766AN	Boeing 777-223ER	American Airlines
	N767AJ	Boeing 777-223ER	American Airlines
	N768AA	Boeing 777-223ER	American Airlines
	N768UA	Boeing 777-222	United Airlines
	N769CK	Boeing 747-430	Kalitta Air
	N769UA	Boeing 777-222	United Airlines
	N770AN	Boeing 777-223ER	American Airlines
	N771AN	Boeing 777-223ER	American Airlines
	N771UA	Boeing 777-222	United Airlines
	N772AN	Boeing 777-223ER	American Airlines
	N772UA	Boeing 777-222	United Airlines
	N773AN	Boeing 777-223ER	American Airlines
	N773UA	Boeing 777-222	United Airlines
	N774AN	Boeing 777-223ER	American Airlines
	N774UA	Boeing 777-222	United Airlines
	N775AN	Boeing 777-223ER	American Airlines
	N775UA	Boeing 777-222	United Airlines
	N776AN	Boeing 777-223ER	American Airlines
	N776UA	Boeing 777-222	United Airlines
	N777AN	Boeing 777-223ER	American Airlines
	N777UA	Boeing 777-222	United Airlines
	N778AN	Boeing 777-223ER	American Airlines

Reg.	Type	Owner or Operator	Notes
N778UA	Boeing 777-222	United Airlines	
N779AN	Boeing 777-223ER	American Airlines	
N779UA	Boeing 777-222	United Airlines	
N780AN	Boeing 777-223ER	American Airlines	
N780UA	Boeing 777-222	United Airlines	
N781AN	Boeing 777-223ER	American Airlines	
N781UA	Boeing 777-222	United Airlines	
N782AN	Boeing 777-223ER	American Airlines	
N782CK	Boeing 747-4HQF	Kalitta Air	
N782UA	Boeing 777-222ER	United Airlines	
N783AN	Boeing 777-223ER	American Airlines	
N783UA	Boeing 777-222ER	United Airlines	
N784AN	Boeing 777-223ER	American Airlines	
N784UA	Boeing 777-222ER	United Airlines	
N785AN	Boeing 777-223ER	American Airlines	
N785UA	Boeing 777-222ER	United Airlines	
N786AN	Boeing 777-223ER	American Airlines	
N786UA	Boeing 777-222ER	United Airlines	
N787AL	Boeing 777-223ER	American Airlines	
N787UA	Boeing 777-222ER	United Airlines	
N788AN	Boeing 777-223ER	American Airlines	
N788UA	Boeing 777-222ER	United Airlines	
N789AN	Boeing 777-223ER	American Airlines	
N790AN	Boeing 777-223ER	American Airlines	
N791AN	Boeing 777-223ER	American Airlines	
N791UA	Boeing 777-222ER	United Airlines	
N792AN	Boeing 777-223ER	American Airlines	
N792UA	Boeing 777-222ER	United Airlines	
N793AN	Boeing 777-223ER	American Airlines	
N793CK	Boeing 747-222BF	Kalitta Air	
N793UA	Boeing 777-222ER	United Airlines	
N794AN	Boeing 777-223ER	American Airlines	
N794UA	Boeing 777-222ER	United Airlines	
N795AN	Boeing 777-223ER	American Airlines	
N795CK	Boeing 747-251B	Kalitta Air	
N795UA	Boeing 777-222ER	United Airlines	
N796AN	Boeing 777-223ER	American Airlines	
N796UA	Boeing 777-222ER	United Airlines	
N797AN	Boeing 777-223ER	American Airlines	
N797UA	Boeing 777-222ER	United Airlines	
N798AN	Boeing 777-223ER	American Airlines	
N798UA	Boeing 777-222ER	United Airlines	
N799AN	Boeing 777-223ER	American Airlines	
N799UA	Boeing 777-222ER	United Airlines	
N801NW	Airbus A.330-323X	Delta Airlines	
N802NW	Airbus A.330-323X	Delta Airlines	
N803NW	Airbus A.330-323X	Delta Air Lines	
N804NW	Airbus A.330-323X	Delta Air Lines	
N805NW	Airbus A.330-323X	Delta Air Lines	
N806NW	Airbus A.330-323X	Delta Air Lines	
N807NW	Airbus A.330-323X	Delta Air Lines	
N808NW	Airbus A.330-323X	Delta Air Lines	
N809NW	Airbus A.330-323E	Delta Air Lines	
N810NW	Airbus A.330-323E	Delta Air Lines	
N811NW	Airbus A.330-323E	Delta Air Lines	
N812NW	Airbus A.330-323E	Delta Air Lines	
N813NW	Airbus A.330-323E	Delta Air Lines	
N814NW	Airbus A.330-323E	Delta Air Lines	
N815NW	Airbus A.330-323E	Delta Air Lines	
N816NW	Airbus A.330-323E	Delta Air Lines	
N817NW	Airbus A.330-323E	Delta Air Lines	
N818NW	Airbus A.330-323E	Delta Air Lines	
N819NW	Airbus A.330-323E	Delta Air Lines	
N820NW	Airbus A.330-323E	Delta Air Lines	
N821NW	Airbus A.330-323E	Delta Air Lines	
N825MH	Boeing 767-432ER (1801)	Delta Air Lines	
N826MH	Boeing 767-432ER (1802)	Delta Air Lines	
N827MH	Boeing 767-432ER (1803)	Delta Air Lines	
N828MH	Boeing 767-432ER (1804)	Delta Air Lines	
N829MH	Boeing 767-432ER (1805)	Delta Air Lines	
N830MH	Boeing 767-432ER (1806)	Delta Air Lines	
N831MH	Boeing 767-432ER (1807)	Delta Air Lines	

Notes	Reg.	Type	Owner or Operator
	N832MH	Boeing 767-432ER (1808)	Delta Air Lines
	N833MH	Boeing 767-432ER (1809)	Delta Air Lines
	N834MH	Boeing 767-432ER (1810)	Delta Air Lines
	N835MH	Boeing 767-432ER (1811)	Delta Air Lines
	N836MH	Boeing 767-432ER (1812)	Delta Air Lines
	N837MH	Boeing 767-432ER (1813)	Delta Air Lines
	N838MH	Boeing 767-432ER (1814)	Delta Air Lines
	N839MH	Boeing 767-432ER (1815)	Delta Air Lines
	N840MH	Boeing 767-432ER (1816)	Delta Air Lines
	N841MH	Boeing 767-432ER (1817)	Delta Air Lines
	N842MH	Boeing 767-432ER (1818)	Delta Air Lines
	N843MH	Boeing 767-432ER (1819)	Delta Air Lines
	N844MH	Boeing 767-432ER (1820)	Delta Air Lines
	N845MH	Boeing 767-432ER (1821)	Delta Air Lines
	N850FD	Boeing 777-2S2LRF	Federal Express
	N850GT	Boeing 747-87UF	Atlas Air/Panalpina World Transport
	N851FD	Boeing 777-2S2LRF	Federal Express
	N851GT	Boeing 747-87UF	Atlas Air/Panalpina World Transport
	N851NW	Airbus A.330-223	Delta Air Lines
	N852FD	Boeing 777-2S2LRF	Federal Express
	N852GT	Boeing 747-87UF	Atlas Air/Polar Air Cargo
	N852NW	Airbus A.330-223	Delta Air Lines
	N853FD	Boeing 777-2S2LRF	Federal Express
	N853GT	Boeing 747-87UF	Atlas Air/Polar Air Cargo
	N853NW	Airbus A.330-223	Delta Air Lines
	N854FD	Boeing 777-2S2LRF	Federal Express
	N854GT	Boeing 747-87UF	Atlas Air
	N854NW	Airbus A.330-223	Delta Air Lines
	N855FD	Boeing 777-2S2LRF	Federal Express
	N855NW	Airbus A.330-223	Delta Air Lines
	N856FD	Boeing 777-2S2LRF	Federal Express
	N856NW	Airbus A.330-223	Delta Air Lines
	N857FD	Boeing 777-2S2LRF	Federal Express
	N857NW	Airbus A.330-223	Delta Air Lines
	N858FD	Boeing 777-2S2LRF	Federal Express
	N858NW	Airbus A.330-223	Delta Air Lines
	N859FD	Boeing 777-2S2LRF	Federal Express
	N859NW	Airbus A.330-223	Delta Air Lines
	N860NW	Airbus A.330-223	Delta Air Lines
	N861FD	Boeing 777-2S2LRF	Federal Express
	N861NW	Airbus A.330-223	Delta Air Lines
	N862FD	Boeing 777-2S2LRF	Federal Express
	N863FD	Boeing 777-2S2LRF	Federal Express
	N864FD	Boeing 777-2S2LRF	Federal Express
	N880FD	Boeing 777-2S2LRF	Federal Express
	N882FD	Boeing 777-2S2LRF	Federal Express
	N883FD	Boeing 777-2S2LRF	Federal Express
	N884FD	Boeing 777-2S2LRF	Federal Express
	N885FD	Boeing 777-2S2LRF	Federal Express
	N886FD	Boeing 777-2S2LRF	Federal Express
	N887FD	Boeing 777-2S2LRF	Federal Express
	N889FD	Boeing 777-2S2LRF	Federal Express
	N890FD	Boeing 777-2S2LRF	Federal Express
	N892FD	Boeing 777-2S2LRF	Federal Express
	N895FD	Boeing 777-2S2LRF	Federal Express
	N901FD	Boeing 757-2B7	Federal Express
	N903FD	Boeing 757-2B7	Federal Express
	N913FD	Boeing 757-28A	Federal Express
	N915FD	Boeing 757-236	Federal Express
	N916FD	Boeing 757-27B	Federal Express
	N917FD	Boeing 757-23A	Federal Express
	N919CA	Boeing 747-428BCF	National Airlines
	N919FD	Boeing 757-23A	Federal Express
	N920FD	Boeing 757-23A	Federal Express
	N922FD	Boeing 757-23A	Federal Express
	N923FD	Boeing 757-204	Federal Express
	N934FD	Boeing 757-21B	Federal Express
	N937UW	Boeing 757-2B7	US Airways
	N938UW	Boeing 757-2B7	US Airways
	N939UW	Boeing 757-2B7	US Airways
	N940UW	Boeing 757-2B7	US Airways
	N941UW	Boeing 757-2B7	US Airways

Reg.	Type	Owner or Operator	Notes
N942UW	Boeing 757-2B7	US Airways	
N952CA	Boeing 747-428BCF	National Airlines	
N961AM	Boeing 787-8	Aeromexico	
N964AM	Boeing 787-8	Aeromexico	
N965AM	Boeing 787-8	Aeromexico	
N1200K	Boeing 767-332ER (200)	Delta Air Lines	
N1201P	Boeing 767-332ER (201)	Delta Air Lines	
N1501P	Boeing 767-3P6ER (1501)	Delta Air Lines	
N1602	Boeing 767-332ER (1602)	Delta Air Lines	
N1603	Boeing 767-332ER (1603)	Delta Air Lines	
N1604R	Boeing 767-332ER (1604)	Delta Air Lines	
N1605	Boeing 767-332ER (1605)	Delta Air Lines	
N1607B	Boeing 767-332ER (1607)	Delta Air Lines	
N1608	Boeing 767-332ER (1608)	Delta Air Lines	
N1609	Boeing 767-332ER (1609)	Delta Air Lines	
N1610D	Boeing 767-332ER (1610)	Delta Air Lines	
N1611B	Boeing 767-332ER (1611)	Delta Air Lines	
N1612T	Boeing 767-332ER (1612)	Delta Air Lines	
N1613B	Boeing 767-332ER (1613)	Delta Air Lines	
N7375A	Boeing 767-323ER	American Airlines	
N12109	Boeing 757-224	United Airlines	
N12114	Boeing 757-224	United Airlines	
N12116	Boeing 757-224	United Airlines	
N12125	Boeing 757-224	United Airlines	
N13110	Boeing 757-224	United Airlines	
N13113	Boeing 757-224	United Airlines	
N13138	Boeing 757-224	United Airlines	
N14102	Boeing 757-224	United Airlines	
N14106	Boeing 757-224	United Airlines	
N14107	Boeing 757-224	United Airlines	
N14115	Boeing 757-224	United Airlines	
N14118	Boeing 757-224	United Airlines	
N14120	Boeing 757-224	United Airlines	
N14121	Boeing 757-224	United Airlines	
N16065	Boeing 767-332ER (1606)	Delta Air Lines	
N17104	Boeing 757-224	United Airlines	
N17105	Boeing 757-224	United Airlines	
N17122	Boeing 757-224	United Airlines	
N17126	Boeing 757-224	United Airlines	
N17128	Boeing 757-224	United Airlines	
N17133	Boeing 757-224	United Airlines	
N17139	Boeing 757-224	United Airlines	
N18112	Boeing 757-224	United Airlines	
N18119	Boeing 757-224	United Airlines	
N19117	Boeing 757-224	United Airlines	
N19130	Boeing 757-224	United Airlines	
N19136	Boeing 757-224	United Airlines	
N19141	Boeing 757-224	United Airlines	
N20904	Boeing 787-8	United Airlines	
N21108	Boeing 757-224	United Airlines	
N26123	Boeing 757-224	United Airlines	
N26902	Boeing 787-8	United Airlines	
N26906	Boeing 787-8	United Airlines	
N26909	Boeing 787-8	United Airlines	
N26910	Boeing 787-8	United Airlines	
N27015	Boeing 777-224ER	United Airlines	
N27901	Boeing 787-8	United Airlines	
N27903	Boeing 787-8	United Airlines	
N27908	Boeing 787-8	United Airlines	
N27910	Boeing 787-8	United Airlines	
N29124	Boeing 757-224	United Airlines	
N29129	Boeing 757-224	United Airlines	
N29907	Boeing 787-8	United Airlines	
N33103	Boeing 757-224	United Airlines	
N33132	Boeing 757-224	United Airlines	
N34131	Boeing 757-224	United Airlines	
N34137	Boeing 757-224	United Airlines	
N37018	Boeing 777-224ER	United Airlines	
N39356	Boeing 767-323ER	American Airlines	
N39364	Boeing 767-323ER	American Airlines	
N39365	Boeing 767-323ER	American Airlines	
N39367	Boeing 767-323ER	American Airlines	

Notes	Reg.	Type	Owner or Operator
	N41135	Boeing 757-224	United Airlines
	N41140	Boeing 757-224	United Airlines
	N45905	Boeing 787-8	United Airlines
	N47905	Boeing 787-8	United Airlines
	N48127	Boeing 757-224	United Airlines
	N57016	Boeing 777-224ER	United Airlines
	N57111	Boeing 757-224	United Airlines
	N58101	Boeing 757-224	United Airlines
	N59053	Boeing 767-424ER	United Airlines
	N66051	Boeing 767-424ER	United Airlines
	N66056	Boeing 767-424ER	United Airlines
	N66057	Boeing 767-424ER	United Airlines
	N67052	Boeing 767-424ER	United Airlines
	N67058	Boeing 767-424ER	United Airlines
	N67134	Boeing 757-224	United Airlines
	N67157	Boeing 767-224ER	United Airlines
	N68061	Boeing 767-424ER	United Airlines
	N68155	Boeing 767-224ER	United Airlines
	N68159	Boeing 767-224ER	United Airlines
	N68160	Boeing 767-224ER	United Airlines
	N69020	Boeing 777-224ER	United Airlines
	N69059	Boeing 767-424ER	United Airlines
	N69063	Boeing 767-424ER	United Airlines
	N69154	Boeing 767-224ER	United Airlines
	N74007	Boeing 777-224ER	United Airlines
	N76010	Boeing 777-224ER	United Airlines
	N76021	Boeing 777-224ER	United Airlines
	N76054	Boeing 767-424ER	United Airlines
	N76055	Boeing 767-424ER	United Airlines
	N76062	Boeing 767-424ER	United Airlines
	N76064	Boeing 767-424ER	United Airlines
	N76065	Boeing 767-424ER	United Airlines
	N76153	Boeing 767-224ER	United Airlines
	N77006	Boeing 777-224ER	United Airlines
	N77012	Boeing 777-224ER	United Airlines
	N77014	Boeing 777-224ER	United Airlines
	N77019	Boeing 777-224ER	United Airlines
	N77022	Boeing 777-224ER	United Airlines
	N77066	Boeing 767-424ER	United Airlines
	N78001	Boeing 777-224ER	United Airlines
	N78002	Boeing 777-224ER	United Airlines
	N78003	Boeing 777-224ER	United Airlines
	N78004	Boeing 777-224ER	United Airlines
	N78005	Boeing 777-224ER	United Airlines
	N78008	Boeing 777-224ER	United Airlines
	N78009	Boeing 777-224ER	United Airlines
	N78013	Boeing 777-224ER	United Airlines
	N78017	Boeing 777-224ER	United Airlines
	N78060	Boeing 767-424ER	United Airlines
	N79011	Boeing 777-224ER	United Airlines

OD (Lebanon)

	OD-MEA	Airbus A.330-243	Middle East Airlines
	OD-MEB	Airbus A.330-243	Middle East Airlines
	OD-MEC	Airbus A.330-243	Middle East Airlines
	OD-MED	Airbus A.330-243	Middle East Airlines
	OD-MRL	Airbus A.320-232	Middle East Airlines
	OD-MRM	Airbus A.320-232	Middle East Airlines
	OD-MRO	Airbus A.320-232	Middle East Airlines
	OD-MRR	Airbus A.320-232	Middle East Airlines
	OD-MRS	Airbus A.320-232	Middle East Airlines
	OD-MRT	Airbus A.320-232	Middle East Airlines
	OD-RMI	Airbus A.321-231	Middle East Airlines
	OD-RMJ	Airbus A.321-231	Middle East Airlines
	OD-TMA	Airbus A.300F4-605R	TMA – Trans Mediterranean Airways

OE (Austria)

	OE-IAP	Boeing 737-4MO	TNT Airways

Reg.	Type	Owner or Operator	Notes
OE-IAQ	Boeing 737-4MO	TNT Airways	
OE-IAR	Boeing 737-4MO	TNT Airways	
OE-IAS	Boeing 737-4MO	TNT Airways	
OE-IAT	Boeing 737-4MO	TNT Airways	
OE-IBZ	Boeing 737-34SF	TNT Airways	
OE-IHA	Embraer ERJ190-100LR	Niki *Samba*	
OE-IHB	Embraer ERJ190-100LR	Niki *Lambada*	
OE-IHD	Embraer ERJ190-100LR	Niki *Calypso*	
OE-IHE	Embraer ERJ190-100LR	Niki *Rumba*	
OE-IXC	Embraer ERJ190-100LR	Niki	
OE-IXF	Embraer ERJ190-100LR	Niki	
OE-IXG	Embraer ERJ190-100LR	Niki	
OE-LAE	Boeing 767-3Z9ER	Austrian Airlines *Malaysia*	
OE-LAT	Boeing 767-31AER	Austrian Airlines *Enzo Ferrari*	
OE-LAW	Boeing 767-3Z9ER	Austrian Airlines *China*	
OE-LAX	Boeing 767-3Z9ER	Austrian Airlines *Thailand*	
OE-LAY	Boeing 767-3Z9ER	Austrian Airlines *Japan*	
OE-LAZ	Boeing 767-3Z9ER	Austrian Airlines *India*	
OE-LBA	Airbus A.321-111	Austrian Airlines *Salzkammergut*	
OE-LBB	Airbus A.321-111	Austrian Airlines *Pinzgau*	
OE-LBC	Airbus A.321-111	Austrian Airlines *Sudtirol*	
OE-LBD	Airbus A.321-111	Austrian Airlines *Steirisches Weinland*	
OE-LBE	Airbus A.321-111	Austrian Airlines *Wachau*	
OE-LBF	Airbus A.321-111	Austrian Airlines *Wien*	
OE-LBI	Airbus A.320-214	Austrian Airlines *Marchfeld*	
OE-LBJ	Airbus A.320-212	Austrian Airlines *Hohe Tauern*	
OE-LBK	Airbus A.320-214	Austrian Airlines	
OE-LBL	Airbus A.320-214	Austrian Airlines	
OE-LBM	Airbus A.320-214	Austrian Airlines	
OE-LBN	Airbus A.320-214	Austrian Airlines *Osttirol*	
OE-LBO	Airbus A.320-214	Austrian Airlines *Pyhrn-Eisenwurzen*	
OE-LBP	Airbus A.320-214	Austrian Airlines *Neusiedler See*	
OE-LBQ	Airbus A.320-214	Austrian Airlines *Wienerwald*	
OE-LBR	Airbus A.320-214	Austrian Airlines *Frida Kahle*	
OE-LBS	Airbus A.320-214	Austrian Airlines *Waldviertel*	
OE-LBT	Airbus A.320-214	Austrian Airlines *Worthersee*	
OE-LBU	Airbus A.320-214	Austrian Airlines *Muhlviertel*	
OE-LBV	Airbus A.320-214	Austrian Airlines *Weinviertel*	
OE-LBW	Airbus A.320-214	Austrian Airlines *Innviertel*	
OE-LBX	Airbus A.320-214	Austrian Airlines *Mostviertel*	
OE-LDA	Airbus A.319-112	Austrian Airlines *Sofia*	
OE-LDB	Airbus A.319-112	Austrian Airlines *Bucharest*	
OE-LDC	Airbus A.319-112	Austrian Airlines *Kiev*	
OE-LDD	Airbus A.319-112	Austrian Airlines *Moscow*	
OE-LDE	Airbus A.319-112	Austrian Airlines *Baku*	
OE-LDF	Airbus A.319-112	Austrian Airlines *Sarajevo*	
OE-LDG	Airbus A.319-112	Austrian Airlines *Tbilisi*	
OE-LEA	Airbus A.320-214	Niki *Rock 'n Roll*	
OE-LEB	Airbus A.320-214	Niki *Polka*	
OE-LEC	Airbus A.320-214	Niki *Flamenco*	
OE-LEE	Airbus A.320-214	Niki *Reggae*	
OE-LEF	Airbus A.320-214	Niki *Sirtaki*	
OE-LEG	Airbus A.320-214	Niki *Bolero*	
OE-LEH	Airbus A.320-214	Niki *Gospel*	
OE-LEL	Airbus A.320-214	Niki	
OE-LEP	Airbus A.320-214	Niki	
OE-LER	Airbus A.320-214	Niki	
OE-LES	Airbus A.321-211	Niki *Boogie Woogie*	
OE-LET	Airbus A.321-211	Niki *Heavy Metal*	
OE-LEU	Airbus A.320-214	Niki *Cancan*	
OE-LEW	Airbus A.321-211	Niki *Cancan*	
OE-LEX	Airbus A.320-214	Niki *Jazz*	
OE-LEY	Airbus A.320-214	Niki	
OE-LEZ	Airbus A.321-211	Niki *Blues*	
OE-LFH	Fokker 70	Austrian Airlines *Salzburg*	
OE-LFI	Fokker 70	Austrian Airlines *Klagenfurt*	
OE-LFJ	Fokker 70	Austrian Airlines *Graz*	
OE-LFP	Fokker 70	Austrian Airlines *Wels*	
OE-LFQ	Fokker 70	Austrian Airlines *Dornbirn*	
OE-LFR	Fokker 70	Austrian Airlines *Steyr*	
OE-LGA	DHC.8Q-402 Dash Eight	Austrian Airlines *Karnten*	
OE-LGB	DHC.8Q-402 Dash Eight	Austrian Airlines *Tirol*	

Notes	Reg.	Type	Owner or Operator
	OE-LGC	DHC.8Q-402 Dash Eight	Brussels Airlines
	OE-LGD	DHC.8Q-402 Dash Eight	Austrian Airlines *Steiermark*
	OE-LGE	DHC.8Q-402 Dash Eight	Austrian Airlines *Oberosterreich*
	OE-LGF	DHC.8Q-402 Dash Eight	Austrian Airlines *Niederosterreich*
	OE-LGG	DHC.8Q-402 Dash Eight	Austrian Airlines *Budapest*
	OE-LGH	DHC.8Q-402 Dash Eight	Austrian Airlines *Vorarlberg*
	OE-LGI	DHC.8Q-402 Dash Eight	Austrian Airlines *Eisenstadt*
	OE-LGJ	DHC.8Q-402 Dash Eight	Austrian Airlines *St Pölten*
	OE-LGK	DHC.8Q-402 Dash Eight	Austrian Airlines *Burgenland*
	OE-LGL	DHC.8Q-402 Dash Eight	Austrian Airlines *Altenrhein*
	OE-LGM	DHC.8Q-402 Dash Eight	Austrian Airlines *Villach*
	OE-LGN	DHC.8Q-402 Dash Eight	Austrian Airlines *Gmunden*
	OE-LIB	Aerospatiale ATR-72-600	Inter Sky
	OE-LID	Aerospatiale ATR-72-600	Inter Sky
	OE-LPA	Boeing 777-2Z9	Austrian Airlines *Melbourne*
	OE-LPB	Boeing 777-2Z9	Austrian Airlines *Sydney*
	OE-LPC	Boeing 777-2Z9ER	Austrian Airlines *Donald Bradman*
	OE-LPD	Boeing 777-2Z9ER	Austrian Airlines *America*
	OE-LVA	Fokker 100	Austrian Airlines *Riga*
	OE-LVB	Fokker 100	Austrian Airlines *Vilnius*
	OE-LVC	Fokker 100	Austrian Airlines *Tirana*
	OE-LVD	Fokker 100	Austrian Airlines *Belgrade*
	OE-LVE	Fokker 100	Austrian Airlines *Zagreb*
	OE-LVF	Fokker 100	Austrian Airlines *Yerevan*
	OE-LVG	Fokker 100	Austrian Airlines *Krakow*
	OE-LVH	Fokker 100	Austrian Airlines *Minsk*
	OE-LVI	Fokker 100	Austrian Airlines *Prague*
	OE-LVJ	Fokker 100	Austrian Airlines *Bratislava*
	OE-LVK	Fokker 100	Austrian Airlines *Timisoara*
	OE-LVL	Fokker 100	Austrian Airlines *Odessa*
	OE-LVM	Fokker 100	Austrian Airlines *Krasnodar*
	OE-LVN	Fokker 100	Austrian Airlines *Dnepropetrovsk*
	OE-LVO	Fokker 100	Austrian Airlines *Chisinau*

OH (Finland)

	OH-BLG	Boeing 717-2CM	Blue 1
	OH-BLH	Boeing 717-2CM	Blue 1
	OH-BLI	Boeing 717-2CM	Blue 1
	OH-BLJ	Boeing 717-23S	Blue 1
	OH-BLM	Boeing 717-23S	Blue 1
	OH-BLN	Boeing 717-2K9	Blue 1
	OH-BLO	Boeing 717-2K9	Blue 1
	OH-BLP	Boeing 717-23S	Blue 1
	OH-BLQ	Boeing 717-2K9	Blue 1
	OH-LEI	Embraer RJ170-100STD	Finnair
	OH-LEK	Embraer RJ170-100STD	Finnair
	OH-LGC	McD Douglas MD-11F	Nordic Global Airlines
	OH-LGD	McD Douglas MD-11F	Nordic Global Airlines
	OH-LKE	Embraer RJ190-100LR	Finnair
	OH-LKF	Embraer RJ190-100LR	Finnair
	OH-LKG	Embraer RJ190-100LR	Finnair
	OH-LKH	Embraer RJ190-100LR	Finnair
	OH-LKI	Embraer RJ190-100LR	Finnair
	OH-LKK	Embraer RJ190-100LR	Finnair
	OH-LKL	Embraer RJ190-100LR	Finnair
	OH-LKM	Embraer RJ190-100LR	Finnair
	OH-LKN	Embraer RJ190-100LR	Finnair
	OH-LKO	Embraer RJ190-100LR	Finnair
	OH-LKP	Embraer RJ190-100LR	Finnair
	OH-LKR	Embraer RJ190-100LR	Finnair
	OH-LQA	Airbus A.340-311	Finnair
	OH-LQB	Airbus A.340-313X	Finnair
	OH-LQC	Airbus A.340-313E	Finnair
	OH-LQD	Airbus A.340-313E	Finnair
	OH-LQE	Airbus A.340-313E	Finnair
	OH-LQF	Airbus A.340-313X	Finnair
	OH-LQG	Airbus A.340-313X	Finnair
	OH-LTM	Airbus A.330-302	Finnair
	OH-LTN	Airbus A.330-302	Finnair
	OH-LTO	Airbus A.330-302	Finnair

Reg.	Type	Owner or Operator	Notes
OH-LTP	Airbus A.330-302	Finnair	
OH-LTR	Airbus A.330-302	Finnair	
OH-LTS	Airbus A.330-302	Finnair	
OH-LTT	Airbus A.330-302	Finnair	
OH-LTU	Airbus A.330-302	Finnair	
OH-LVA	Airbus A.319-112	Finnair	
OH-LVB	Airbus A.319-112	Finnair	
OH-LVC	Airbus A.319-112	Finnair	
OH-LVD	Airbus A.319-112	Finnair	
OH-LVG	Airbus A.319-112	Finnair	
OH-LVH	Airbus A.319-112	Finnair	
OH-LVI	Airbus A.319-112	Finnair	
OH-LVK	Airbus A.319-112	Finnair	
OH-LVL	Airbus A.319-112	Finnair	
OH-LXA	Airbus A.320-214	Finnair	
OH-LXB	Airbus A.320-214	Finnair	
OH-LXC	Airbus A.320-214	Finnair	
OH-LXD	Airbus A.320-214	Finnair	
OH-LXF	Airbus A.320-214	Finnair	
OH-LXH	Airbus A.320-214	Finnair	
OH-LXI	Airbus A.320-214	Finnair	
OH-LXK	Airbus A.320-214	Finnair	
OH-LXL	Airbus A.320-214	Finnair	
OH-LXM	Airbus A.320-214	Finnair	
OH-LZA	Airbus A.321-211	Finnair	
OH-LZB	Airbus A.321-211	Finnair	
OH-LZC	Airbus A.321-211	Finnair	
OH-LZD	Airbus A.321-211	Finnair	
OH-LZE	Airbus A.321-211	Finnair	
OH-LZF	Airbus A.321-211	Finnair	
OH-LZG	Airbus A.321-231	Finnair	
OH-LZH	Airbus A.321-231	Finnair	
OH-LZI	Airbus A.321-231	Finnair	
OH-NGA	McD Douglas MD-11F	Nordic Global Airlines	
OH-NGB	McD Douglas MD-11F	Nordic Global Airlines	

OK (Czech Republic)

Reg.	Type	Owner or Operator	Notes
OK-ASA	Let L410UVP-E	Brighton City Airways	
OK-HCB	Airbus A.320-214	Travel Service Airlines Slovakia	
OK-LEE	Airbus A.320-214	Holidays Czech Airlines	
OK-LEF	Airbus A.320-214	Holidays Czech Airlines	
OK-LEG	Airbus A.320-214	CSA Czech Airlines	
OK-MEH	Airbus A.320-214	CSA Czech Airlines	
OK-MEI	Airbus A.320-214	CSA Czech Airlines	
OK-MEJ	Airbus A.320-214	CSA Czech Airlines	
OK-MEK	Airbus A.319-112	CSA Czech Airlines	
OK-MEL	Airbus A.319-112	CSA Czech Airlines	
OK-NEM	Airbus A.319-112	CSA Czech Airlines	
OK-NEN	Airbus A.319-112	CSA Czech Airlines	
OK-NEO	Airbus A.319-112	CSA Czech Airlines	
OK-NEP	Airbus A.319-112	CSA Czech Airlines	
OK-OER	Airbus A.319-112	CSA Czech Airlines	
OK-PET	Airbus A.319-112	CSA Czech Airlines	
OK-RDA	Let L410UVP-E9	Citywing	
OK-REQ	Airbus A.319-112	CSA Czech Airlines	
OK-SWT	Boeing 737-7Q8	Smart Wings	
OK-SWW	Boeing 737-7Q8	Smart Wings	
OK-TCA	Let L410UVP-E	Citywing	
OK-TSA	Boeing 737-8S3	Travel Service Airlines	
OK-TSC	Boeing 737-8FH	Smart Wings	
OK-TSE	Boeing 737-81D	Travel Service Airlines	
OK-TVD	Boeing 737-86N	Travel Service Airlines	
OK-TVE	Boeing 737-86Q	Travel Service Airlines	
OK-TVG	Boeing 737-8Q8	Travel Service Airlines	
OK-TVK	Boeing 737-86N	Travel Service Airlines	
OK-TVL	Boeing 737-8FN	Travel Service Airlines	
OK-TVM	Boeing 737-8FN	Travel Service Airlines	
OK-TVO	Boeing 737-8CX	Travel Service Airlines	
OK-TVP	Boeing 737-8K5	Smart Wings	

Notes	Reg.	Type	Owner or Operator
	OK-TVR	Boeing 737-86N	Travel Service Airlines
	OK-TVS	Boeing 737-86N	Travel Service Airlines
	OK-TVT	Boeing 737-86N	Travel Service Airlines
	OK-TVU	Boeing 737-86N	Travel Service Airlines
	OK-TVV	Boeing 737-86N	Travel Service Airlines
	OK-TVW	Boeing 737-86Q	Smart Wings
	OK-TVX	Boeing 737-8Z9	Travel Service Airlines
	OK-TVY	Boeing 737-8Q8	Smart Wings

OM (Slovakia)

	OM-AEX	Boeing 737-4YO	AirExplore
	OM-CEX	Boeing 737-436	AirExplore
	OM-DEX	Boeing 737-46J	AirExplore
	OM-HCA	Airbus A.320-214	Travel Service Airlines
	OM-SAA	Boeing 737-476	Samair

OO (Belgium)

	OO-DWA	Avro RJ100	Brussels Airlines
	OO-DWB	Avro RJ100	Brussels Airlines
	OO-DWC	Avro RJ100	Brussels Airlines
	OO-DWD	Avro RJ100	Brussels Airlines
	OO-DWE	Avro RJ100	Brussels Airlines
	OO-DWF	Avro RJ100	Brussels Airlines
	OO-DWG	Avro RJ100	Brussels Airlines
	OO-DWH	Avro RJ100	Brussels Airlines
	OO-DWI	Avro RJ100	Brussels Airlines
	OO-DWJ	Avro RJ100	Brussels Airlines
	OO-DWK	Avro RJ100	Brussels Airlines
	OO-DWL	Avro RJ100	Brussels Airlines
	OO-JAA	Boeing 737-8BK	Jetairfly
	OO-JAD	Boeing 737-8K5	Jetairfly *Magnificent*
	OO-JAF	Boeing 737-8K5	Jetairfly *Smile*
	OO-JAH	Boeing 737-8K5	Jetairfly *Perspective*
	OO-JAN	Boeing 737-76N	Jetairfly *Revelation*
	OO-JAO	Boeing 737-7K5	Jetairfly *Playing to Win*
	OO-JAP	Boeing 767-38EER	Jetairfly
	OO-JAQ	Boeing 737-8K5	Jetairfly *Vision*
	OO-JAR	Boeing 737-7K5	Jetairfly *Enjoy*
	OO-JAS	Boeing 737-7K5	Jetairfly *Emotion*
	OO-JAU	Boeing 737-8K5	Jetairfly
	OO-JAV	Boeing 737-8K5	Jetairfly *Happiness*
	OO-JAX	Boeing 737-8K5	Jetairfly *Brightness*
	OO-JAY	Boeing 737-8K5	Jetairfly *Elegance*
	OO-JBG	Boeing 737-8K5	Jetairfly *Gerard Brack*
	OO-JBV	Boeing 737-8K5	Jetairfly *Evasion*
	OO-JDL	Boeing 787-8K5	Jetairfly
	OO-JEB	Embraer ERJ190-100STD	Jetairfly
	OO-JEM	Embraer ERJ190-100STD	Jetairfly
	OO-JLO	Boeing 737-8K5	Jetairfly *Grace*
	OO-JPT	Boeing 737-8K5	Jetairfly *Sky*
	OO-SFM	Airbus A.330-301	Brussels Airlines
	OO-SFN	Airbus A.330-301	Brussels Airlines
	OO-SFO	Airbus A.330-301	Brussels Airlines
	OO-SFU	Airbus A.330-223	Brussels Airlines
	OO-SFV	Airbus A.330-322	Brussels Airlines
	OO-SFW	Airbus A.330-322	Brussels Airlines
	OO-SFY	Airbus A.330-223	Brussels Airlines
	OO-SFZ	Airbus A.330-223	Brussels Airlines
	OO-SNA	Airbus A.320-214	Brussels Airlines
	OO-SNB	Airbus A.320-214	Brussels Airlines
	OO-SNC	Airbus A.320-214	Brussels Airlines
	OO-SND	Airbus A.320-214	Brussels Airlines
	OO-SNF	Airbus A.320-214	Brussels Airlines
	OO-SNG	Airbus A.320-214	Brussels Airlines
	OO-SSA	Airbus A.319-111	Brussels Airlines
	OO-SSB	Airbus A.319-111	Brussels Airlines
	OO-SSC	Airbus A.319-112	Brussels Airlines
	OO-SSD	Airbus A.319-112	Brussels Airlines

Reg.	Type	Owner or Operator	Notes
OO-SSG	Airbus A.319-112	Brussels Airlines	
OO-SSK	Airbus A.319-112	Brussels Airlines	
OO-SSM	Airbus A.319-112	Brussels Airlines	
OO-SSN	Airbus A.319-112	Brussels Airlines	
OO-SSP	Airbus A.319-112	Brussels Airlines	
OO-SSQ	Airbus A.319-112	Brussels Airlines	
OO-SSR	Airbus A.319-112	Brussels Airlines	
OO-SSU	Airbus A.319-111	Brussels Airlines	
OO-SSV	Airbus A.319-111	Brussels Airlines	
OO-SSW	Airbus A.319-111	Brussels Airlines	
OO-TAD	BAe 146-300QT	TNT Airways	
OO-TAF	BAe 146-300QT	TNT Airways	
OO-TAH	BAe 146-300QT	TNT Airways	
OO-TAJ	BAe 146-300QT	TNT Airways	
OO-TAS	BAe 146-300QT	TNT Airways	
OO-TAU	BAe 146-200QT	TNT Airways	
OO-TAW	BAe 146-200QT	TNT Airways	
OO-TCH	Airbus A.320-214	Thomas Cook Airlines Belgium *experience*	
OO-TCI	Airbus A.320-214	Thomas Cook Airlines Belgium *relax*	
OO-TCJ	Airbus A.320-214	Thomas Cook Airlines Belgium *inspire*	
OO-TCP	Airbus A.320-214	Thomas Cook Airlines Belgium *desire*	
OO-TCS	Airbus A.319-132	Thomas Cook Airlines Belgium	
OO-TFA	Boeing 757-28A	TNT Airways	
OO-THA	Boeing 747-4HAERF	TNT Airways	
OO-THB	Boeing 747-4HAERF	TNT Airways	
OO-THC	Boeing 747-4HAERF	TNT Airways	
OO-THD	Boeing 747-4HAERF	TNT Airways	
OO-TNC	Boeing 737-3T0F	TNT Airways	
OO-TNL	Boeing 737-34SF	TNT Airways	
OO-TNN	Boeing 737-45D	TNT Airways	
OO-TNO	Boeing 737-49RF	TNT Airways	
OO-TNP	Boeing 737-45D	TNT Airways	
OO-TNQ	Boeing 737-4MOF	TNT Airways	
OO-TSA	Boeing 777-FHT	TNT Airways	
OO-TSB	Boeing 777-FHT	TNT Airways	
OO-TSC	Boeing 777-FHT	TNT Airways	
OO-VLF	Fokker 50	Cityjet	
OO-VLI	Fokker 50	Cityjet	
OO-VLJ	Fokker 50	Cityjet	
OO-VLL	Fokker 50	Cityjet	
OO-VLM	Fokker 50	Cityjet	
OO-VLN	Fokker 50	Cityjet	
OO-VLO	Fokker 50	Cityjet	
OO-VLP	Fokker 50	Cityjet	
OO-VLR	Fokker 50	Cityjet	
OO-VLQ	Fokker 50	Cityjet	
OO-VLS	Fokker 50	Cityjet	
OO-VLZ	Fokker 50	Cityjet	

OY (Denmark)

Reg.	Type	Owner or Operator	Notes
OY-BJP	Swearingen SA.227AC Metro III	Benair	
OY-JJB	Dornier 328-300 JET	Sun-Air	
OY-JTA	Boeing 737-33A	Jet Time	
OY-JTB	Boeing 737-3Y0	Jet Time	
OY-JTC	Boeing 737-3L9	Jet Time	
OY-JTD	Boeing 737-3Y0	Jet Time	
OY-JTE	Boeing 737-3L9	Jet Time	
OY-JTF	Boeing 737-382	Jet Time	
OY-JTH	Boeing 737-3YO	Jet Time	
OY-JTI	Boeing 737-448F	Jet Time/TNT Airways	
OY-JTS	Boeing 737-7K2	Jet Time	
OY-JTT	Boeing 737-73S	Jet Time	
OY-JTU	Boeing 737-7L9	Jet Time	
OY-JTV	Boeing 737-7L9	Jet Time	
OY-JTW	Boeing 737-7L9	Jet Time	
OY-JTY	Boeing 737-7Q8	Jet Time	
OY-JTZ	Boeing 737-73S	Jet Time	
OY-KAL	Airbus A.320-232	SAS	
OY-KAM	Airbus A.320-232	SAS	
OY-KAN	Airbus A.320-232	SAS	

Notes	Reg.	Type	Owner or Operator
	OY-KAO	Airbus A.320-232	SAS
	OY-KAP	Airbus A.320-232	SAS *Viglek Viking*
	OY-KAR	Airbus A.320-232	SAS
	OY-KAS	Airbus A.320-232	SAS
	OY-KAT	Airbus A.320-232	SAS
	OY-KAU	Airbus A.320-232	SAS
	OY-KAW	Airbus A.320-232	SAS
	OY-KAY	Airbus A.320-232	SAS
	OY-KBA	Airbus A.340-313X	SAS *Adalstein Viking*
	OY-KBB	Airbus A.321-231	SAS *Hjorulf Viking*
	OY-KBC	Airbus A.340-313X	SAS *Fredis Viking*
	OY-KBD	Airbus A.340-313X	SAS *Toste Viking*
	OY-KBE	Airbus A.321-231	SAS *Emma Viking*
	OY-KBF	Airbus A.321-231	SAS *Skapti Viking*
	OY-KBH	Airbus A.321-231	SAS *Sulke Viking*
	OY-KBI	Airbus A.340-313X	SAS *Rurik Viking*
	OY-KBK	Airbus A.321-231	SAS *Arne Viking*
	OY-KBL	Airbus A.321-231	SAS *Gynnbjorn Viking*
	OY-KBM	Airbus A.340-313X	HiFly
	OY-KBO	Airbus A.319-131	SAS *Christian Valdemar Viking*
	OY-KBP	Airbus A.319-131	SAS *Viger Viking*
	OY-KBR	Airbus A.319-132	SAS *Finnboge Viking*
	OY-KBT	Airbus A.319-131	SAS *Ragnvald Viking*
	OY-KFA	Canadair CRJ900ER	SAS *Johan Viking*
	OY-KFB	Canadair CRJ900ER	SAS *Alfhild Viking*
	OY-KFC	Canadair CRJ900ER	SAS *Bertil Viking*
	OY-KFD	Canadair CRJ900ER	SAS *Estrid Viking*
	OY-KFE	Canadair CRJ900ER	SAS *Ingemar Viking*
	OY-KFF	Canadair CRJ900ER	SAS *Karl Viking*
	OY-KFG	Canadair CRJ900ER	SAS *Maria Viking*
	OY-KFH	Canadair CRJ900ER	SAS *Ella Viking*
	OY-KFI	Canadair CRJ900ER	SAS *Rolf Viking*
	OY-KFK	Canadair CRJ900ER	SAS *Hardeknud Viking*
	OY-KFL	Canadair CRJ900ER	SAS *Regin Viking*
	OY-KKS	Boeing 737-683	SAS *Ramveig Viking*
	OY-NCL	Dornier 328-300 JET	Sun-Air/British Airways
	OY-NCM	Dornier 328-300 JET	Sun-Air/British Airways
	OY-NCN	Dornier 328-300 JET	Sun-Air/British Airways
	OY-NCO	Dornier 328-300 JET	Sun-Air/British Airways
	OY-NCP	Dornier 328-300 JET	Sun-Air/British Airways
	OY-NCT	Dornier 328-300 JET	Sun-Air/British Airways
	OY-NCV	Dornier 328-300 JET	Sun-Air/British Airways
	OY-NCW	Dornier 328-300 JET	Sun-Air/British Airways
	OY-PBH	Let L410UVP-E20	Benair
	OY-PBI	Let L410UVP-E20	Benair
	OY-PSA	Boeing 737-8Q8	Primera Air Scandinavia
	OY-PSB	Boeing 737-8Q8	Primera Air Scandinavia
	OY-PSC	Boeing 737-86N	Primera Air Scandinavia
	OY-PSD	Boeing 737-86N	Primera Air Scandinavia
	OY-PSE	Boeing 737-809	Primera Air Scandinavia
	OY-PSF	Boeing 737-7Q8	Primera Air Scandinavia
	OY-PSG	Boeing 737-7BX	Primera Air Scandinavia
	OY-PSH	Boeing 737-86N	Primera Air Scandinavia
	OY-RCC	Avro RJ100	Atlantic Airways
	OY-RCG	Airbus A.319-112	Atlantic Airways
	OY-RCH	Airbus A.319-112	Atlantic Airways
	OY-RCI	Airbus A.319-112	Atlantic Airways
	OY-RUE	McD Douglas MD-83	Danish Air Transport
	OY-SRF	Boeing 767-219 (SF)	Star Air
	OY-SRG	Boeing 767-219 (SF)	Star Air
	OY-SRH	Boeing 767-204 (SF)	Star Air
	OY-SRI	Boeing 767-25E (SF)	Star Air
	OY-SRJ	Boeing 767-25E (SF)	Star Air
	OY-SRK	Boeing 767-204 (SF)	Star Air
	OY-SRL	Boeing 767-232 (SF)	Star Air
	OY-SRM	Boeing 767-25E (SF)	Star Air
	OY-SRN	Boeing 767-219 (SF)	Star Air
	OY-SRO	Boeing 767-25E (SF)	Star Air
	OY-SRP	Boeing 767-232 (SF)	Star Air
	OY-VKA	Airbus A.321-211	Thomas Cook Airlines
	OY-VKB	Airbus A.321-211	Thomas Cook Airlines
	OY-VKC	Airbus A.321-211	Thomas Cook Airlines

Reg.	Type	Owner or Operator	Notes
OY-VKD	Airbus A.321-211	Thomas Cook Airlines	
OY-VKE	Airbus A.321-211	Thomas Cook Airlines	
OY-VKF	Airbus A.330-243	Thomas Cook Airlines	
OY-VKG	Airbus A.330-343X	Thomas Cook Airlines	
OY-VKH	Airbus A.330-343X	Thomas Cook Airlines	
OY-VKI	Airbus A.330-343X	Thomas Cook Airlines	
OY-VKM	Airbus A.320-214	Thomas Cook Airlines	
OY-VKS	Airbus A.320-214	Thomas Cook Airlines	
OY-VKT	Airbus A.321-211	Thomas Cook Airlines	

P4 (Aruba)

Reg.	Type	Owner or Operator	Notes
P4-EAS	Boeing 757-2G5	Air Astana	
P4-FAS	Boeing 757-2G5	Air Astana	
P4-GAS	Boeing 757-2G5	Air Astana	
P4-KCA	Boeing 767-306ER	Air Astana	
P4-KCB	Boeing 767-306ER	Air Astana	
P4-KCU	Boeing 757-23N	Air Astana	
P4-MAS	Boeing 757-28A	Air Astana	

PH (Netherlands)

Reg.	Type	Owner or Operator	Notes
PH-AHQ	Boeing 767-383ER	TUI Airlines Nederland/Arkefly	
PH-AHX	Boeing 767-383ER	TUI Airlines Nederland/Arkefly	
PH-AKA	Airbus A.330-303	KLM *Times Square – New York*	
PH-AKB	Airbus A.330-303	KLM *Piazza Navona-Roma*	
PH-AKD	Airbus A.330-303	KLM *Plaza de la Catedral-La Habana*	
PH-AKE	Airbus A.330-303	KLM	
PH-AOA	Airbus A.330-203	KLM *Dam – Amsterdam*	
PH-AOB	Airbus A.330-203	KLM *Potsdamer Platz – Berlin*	
PH-AOC	Airbus A.330-203	KLM *Place de la Concorde – Paris*	
PH-AOD	Airbus A.330-203	KLM *Plazza del Duomo – Milano*	
PH-AOE	Airbus A.330-203	KLM *Parliament Square – Edinburgh*	
PH-AOF	Airbus A.330-203	KLM *Federation Square – Melbourne*	
PH-AOH	Airbus A.330-203	KLM *Senaatintori/Senate Square-Helsinki*	
PH-AOI	Airbus A.330-203	KLM *Plaza de la Independencia-Madrid*	
PH-AOK	Airbus A.330-203	KLM *Radhuspladsen-Kobenhavn*	
PH-AOL	Airbus A.330-203	KLM *Picadilly Circus – London*	
PH-AOM	Airbus A.330-203	KLM	
PH-AON	Airbus A.330-203	KLM *Museumplein-Amsterdam*	
PH-BCA	Boeing 737-8K2	KLM *Flamingo*	
PH-BCB	Boeing 737-8BK	KLM *Grote Pijlstormvogel/Great Shearwater*	
PH-BCD	Boeing 737-8BK	KLM	
PH-BFA	Boeing 747-406	KLM *City of Atlanta*	
PH-BFB	Boeing 747-406	KLM *City of Bangkok*	
PH-BFC	Boeing 747-406 (SCD)	KLM *City of Calgary*	
PH-BFD	Boeing 747-406 (SCD)	KLM *City of Dubai*	
PH-BFE	Boeing 747-406 (SCD)	KLM *City of Melbourne*	
PH-BFF	Boeing 747-406 (SCD)	KLM *City of Freetown*	
PH-BFG	Boeing 747-406	KLM *City of Guayaquil*	
PH-BFH	Boeing 747-406 (SCD)	KLM *City of Hong Kong*	
PH-BFI	Boeing 747-406 (SCD)	KLM *City of Jakarta*	
PH-BFK	Boeing 747-406 (SCD)	KLM *City of Karachi*	
PH-BFL	Boeing 747-406	KLM *City of Lima*	
PH-BFM	Boeing 747-406 (SCD)	KLM *City of Mexico*	
PH-BFN	Boeing 747-406	KLM *City of Nairobi*	
PH-BFO	Boeing 747-406 (SCD)	KLM *City of Orlando*	
PH-BFP	Boeing 747-406 (SCD)	KLM *City of Paramaribo*	
PH-BFR	Boeing 747-406 (SCD)	KLM *City of Rio de Janeiro*	
PH-BFS	Boeing 747-406 (SCD)	KLM *City of Seoul*	
PH-BFT	Boeing 747-406 (SCD)	KLM *City of Tokyo*	
PH-BFU	Boeing 747-406 (SCD)	KLM *City of Beijing*	
PH-BFV	Boeing 747-406	KLM *City of Vancouver*	
PH-BFW	Boeing 747-406	KLM *City of Shanghai*	
PH-BFY	Boeing 747-406	KLM *City of Johannesburg*	
PH-BGA	Boeing 737-8K2	KLM *Tureluur/Redshank*	
PH-BGB	Boeing 737-8K2	KLM *Whimbrel/Regenwulg*	
PH-BGC	Boeing 737-8K2	KLM *Pijlstaart/Pintail*	
PH-BGD	Boeing 737-706	KLM *Goldcrest/Goadhaantje*	
PH-BGE	Boeing 737-706	KLM *Ortolan Bunting/Ortolaan*	

Notes	Reg.	Type	Owner or Operator
	PH-BGF	Boeing 737-7K2	KLM Great White Heron/Grote Ziverreiger
	PH-BGG	Boeing 737-706	KLM King Eider/Koening Seider
	PH-BGH	Boeing 737-7K2	KLM Grutto/Godwit
	PH-BGI	Boeing 737-7K2	KLM Vink/Finch
	PH-BGK	Boeing 737-7K2	KLM Noordse Stormvogel/Fulmar
	PH-BGL	Boeing 737-7K2	KLM Rietzangler/Warbler
	PH-BGM	Boeing 737-7K2	KLM Aabscholver/Cormorant
	PH-BGN	Boeing 737-7K2	KLM Jan van Gent/Gannet
	PH-BGO	Boeing 737-7K2	KLM Paradijsvogel/Bird of Paradise
	PH-BGP	Boeing 737-7K2	KLM Pelikaan/Pelican
	PH-BGQ	Boeing 737-7K2	KLM Wielewaal/Golden Oriole
	PH-BGR	Boeing 737-7K2	KLM Zwarte Wouw/Black Kite
	PH-BGT	Boeing 737-7K2	KLM Zanglijster/Song Thrush
	PH-BGU	Boeing 737-7K2	KLM Koekoek/Cuckoo
	PH-BGW	Boeing 737-7K2	KLM
	PH-BGX	Boeing 737-7K2	KLM Scholekster/Oystercatcher
	PH-BQA	Boeing 777-206ER	KLM Albert Plesman
	PH-BQB	Boeing 777-206ER	KLM Borobudur
	PH-BQC	Boeing 777-206ER	KLM Chichen-Itza
	PH-BQD	Boeing 777-206ER	KLM Darjeeling Highway
	PH-BQE	Boeing 777-206ER	KLM Epidaurus
	PH-BQF	Boeing 777-206ER	KLM Ferrara City
	PH-BQG	Boeing 777-206ER	KLM Galapagos Islands
	PH-BQH	Boeing 777-206ER	KLM Hadrian's Wall
	PH-BQI	Boeing 777-206ER	KLM Iguazu Falls
	PH-BQK	Boeing 777-206ER	KLM Mount Kilimanjaro
	PH-BQL	Boeing 777-206ER	KLM Litomysl Castle
	PH-BQM	Boeing 777-206ER	KLM Macchu Picchu
	PH-BQN	Boeing 777-206ER	KLM Nahanni National Park
	PH-BQO	Boeing 777-206ER	KLM Old Rauma
	PH-BQP	Boeing 777-206ER	KLM Pont du Gard
	PH-BVA	Boeing 777-206ER	KLM National Park De Hoge Veluwe
	PH-BVB	Boeing 777-306ER	KLM Fulufjallet National Park
	PH-BVC	Boeing 777-306ER	KLM National ParkSian Ka'an
	PH-BVD	Boeing 777-306ER	KLM Amboseli National Park
	PH-BVF	Boeing 777-306ER	KLM Yakushima
	PH-BVG	Boeing 777-306ER	KLM
	PH-BVI	Boeing 777-306ER	KLM Nationaal Park Vuurland
	PH-BVK	Boeing 777-306ER	KLM Yellowstone National Park
	PH-BXA	Boeing 737-8K2	KLM Zwaan/Swan
	PH-BXB	Boeing 737-8K2	KLM Valk/Falcon
	PH-BXC	Boeing 737-8K2	KLM Korhoen/Grouse
	PH-BXD	Boeing 737-8K2	KLM Arend/Eagle
	PH-BXE	Boeing 737-8K2	KLM Harvik/Hawk
	PH-BXF	Boeing 737-8K2	KLM Zwallou/Swallow
	PH-BXG	Boeing 737-8K2	KLM Kraanvogel/Crane
	PH-BXH	Boeing 737-8K2	KLM Gans/Goose
	PH-BXI	Boeing 737-8K2	KLM Zilvermeeuw
	PH-BXK	Boeing 737-8K2	KLM Gierzwallou/Swift
	PH-BXL	Boeing 737-8K2	KLM Sperwer/Sparrow
	PH-BXM	Boeing 737-8K2	KLM Kluut/Avocet
	PH-BXN	Boeing 737-8K2	KLM Merel/Blackbird
	PH-BXO	Boeing 737-8K2	KLM Plevier/Plover
	PH-BXP	Boeing 737-9K2	KLM Meerkoet/Crested Coot
	PH-BXR	Boeing 737-9K2	KLM Nachtegaal/Nightingale
	PH-BXS	Boeing 737-9K2	KLM Buizerd/Buzzard
	PH-BXT	Boeing 737-9K2	KLM Zeestern/Sea Tern
	PH-BXU	Boeing 737-8BK	KLM Albatros/Albatross
	PH-BXV	Boeing 737-8K2	KLM Roodborstje
	PH-BXW	Boeing 737-8K2	KLM Patrijs/Partridge
	PH-BXY	Boeing 737-8K2	KLM Fuut/Grebe
	PH-BXZ	Boeing 737-8K2	KLM Uil/Owl
	PH-CKA	Boeing 747-406ERF	KLM Cargo/Martinair Eendracht
	PH-CKB	Boeing 747-406ERF	KLM Cargo/Martinair Leeuwin
	PH-CKC	Boeing 747-406ERF	KLM Cargo/Martinair Oranje
	PH-CKD	Boeing 747-406ERF	KLM Cargo/Martinair Wapen van Amsterdam
	PH-EXA	Embraer ERJ190-STD	KLM CityHopper
	PH-EZA	Embraer ERJ190-100STD	KLM CityHopper
	PH-EZB	Embraer ERJ190-100STD	KLM CityHopper
	PH-EZC	Embraer ERJ190-100STD	KLM CityHopper
	PH-EZD	Embraer ERJ190-100STD	KLM CityHopper
	PH-EZE	Embraer ERJ190-100STD	KLM CityHopper

Reg.	Type	Owner or Operator	Notes
PH-EZF	Embraer ERJ190-100STD	KLM CityHopper	
PH-EZG	Embraer ERJ190-100STD	KLM Cityhopper	
PH-EZH	Embraer ERJ190-100STD	KLM CityHopper	
PH-EZI	Embraer ERJ190-100STD	KLM CityHopper	
PH-EZK	Embraer ERJ190-100STD	KLM CityHopper	
PH-EZL	Embraer ERJ190-100STD	KLM CityHopper	
PH-EZM	Embraer ERJ190-100STD	KLM CityHopper	
PH-EZN	Embraer ERJ190-100STD	KLM CityHopper	
PH-EZO	Embraer ERJ190-100STD	KLM CityHopper	
PH-EZP	Embraer ERJ190-100STD	KLM CityHopper	
PH-EZR	Embraer ERJ190-100STD	KLM CityHopper	
PH-EZS	Embraer ERJ190-100STD	KLM CityHopper	
PH-EZT	Embraer ERJ190-100STD	KLM CityHopper	
PH-EZU	Embraer ERJ190-100STD	KLM CityHopper	
PH-EZV	Embraer ERJ190-100STD	KLM CityHopper	
PH-EZW	Embraer ERJ190-100STD	KLM CityHopper	
PH-EZX	Embraer ERJ190-100STD	KLM CityHopper	
PH-EZY	Embraer ERJ190-100STD	KLM CityHopper	
PH-EZZ	Embraer ERJ190-100STD	KLM CityHopper	
PH-GUA	Boeing 737-8EH	Transavia	
PH-HSA	Boeing 737-8K2	Transavia	
PH-HSB	Boeing 737-8K2	Transavia	
PH-HSC	Boeing 737-8K2	Transavia	
PH-HSD	Boeing 737-8K2	Transavia	
PH-HSE	Boeing 737-8K2	Transavia	
PH-HSF	Boeing 737-8K2	Transavia	
PH-HSG	Boeing 737-8K2	Transavia	
PH-HSI	Boeing 737-8K2	Transavia	
PH-HSW	Boeing 737-8K2	Transavia	
PH-HZD	Boeing 737-8K2	Transavia	
PH-HZE	Boeing 737-8K2	Transavia	
PH-HZF	Boeing 737-8K2	Transavia	
PH-HZG	Boeing 737-8K2	Transavia	
PH-HZI	Boeing 737-8K2	Transavia	
PH-HZJ	Boeing 737-8K2	Transavia	
PH-HZK	Boeing 737-8K2	Transavia	
PH-HZL	Boeing 737-8K2	Transavia	
PH-HZN	Boeing 737-8K2	Transavia	
PH-HZO	Boeing 737-8K2	Transavia	
PH-HZW	Boeing 737-8K2	Transavia	
PH-HZX	Boeing 737-8K2	Transavia	
PH-JCH	Fokker 70	KLM CityHopper	
PH-JCT	Fokker 70	KLM CityHopper	
PH-KCA	McD Douglas MD-11	KLM *Amy Johnson*	
PH-KCB	McD Douglas MD-11	KLM *Maria Montessori*	
PH-KCD	McD Douglas MD-11	KLM *Florence Nightingale*	
PH-KCE	McD Douglas MD-11	KLM *Audrey Hepburn*	
PH-KZA	Fokker 70	KLM CityHopper	
PH-KZB	Fokker 70	KLM CityHopper	
PH-KZC	Fokker 70	KLM CityHopper	
PH-KZD	Fokker 70	KLM CityHopper	
PH-KZE	Fokker 70	KLM CityHopper	
PH-KZF	Fokker 70	KLM CityHopper	
PH-KZH	Fokker 70	KLM CityHopper	
PH-KZI	Fokker 70	KLM CityHopper	
PH-KZK	Fokker 70	KLM CityHopper	
PH-KZL	Fokker 70	KLM CityHopper	
PH-KZM	Fokker 70	KLM CityHopper	
PH-KZN	Fokker 70	KLM CityHopper	
PH-KZO	Fokker 70	KLM CityHopper	
PH-KZP	Fokker 70	KLM CityHopper	
PH-KZR	Fokker 70	KLM CityHopper	
PH-KZS	Fokker 70	KLM CityHopper	
PH-KZT	Fokker 70	KLM CityHopper	
PH-KZU	Fokker 70	KLM CityHopper	
PH-KZW	Fokker 70	KLM CityHopper	
PH-MCP	McD Douglas MD-11CF	Martinair Cargo	
PH-MCR	McD Douglas MD-11CF	Martinair Cargo	
PH-MCS	McD Douglas MD-11CF	Martinair Cargo	
PH-MCU	McD Douglas MD-11F	Martinair Cargo	
PH-MCW	McD Douglas MD-11F	Martinair Cargo	
PH-MCY	McD Douglas MD-11F	Martinair Cargo	

Notes	Reg.	Type	Owner or Operator
	PH-MPS	Boeing 747-412BCF	Martinair Cargo
	PH-OYE	Boeing 767-304ER	TUI Airlines Nederland/Arkefly
	PH-OYI	Boeing 767-304ER	TUI Airlines Nederland/Arkefly
	PH-OYJ	Boeing 767-304ER	TUI Airlines Nederland/Arkefly
	PH-TFA	Boeing 737-8FH	TUI Airlines Nederland/Arkefly
	PH-TFB	Boeing 737-8K5	TUI Airlines Nederland/Arkefly
	PH-TFC	Boeing 737-8K5	TUI Airlines Nederland/Arkefly
	PH-TFD	Boeing 737-86N	TUI Airlines Nederland/Arkefly
	PH-TFF	Boeing 737-86N	TUI Airlines Nederland/Arkefly
	PH-WXA	Fokker 70	KLM CityHopper
	PH-WXC	Fokker 70	KLM CityHopper
	PH-WXD	Fokker 70	KLM CityHopper
	PH-XRA	Boeing 737-7K2	Transavia *Leontien van Moorsel*
	PH-XRB	Boeing 737-7K2	Transavia
	PH-XRC	Boeing 737-7K2	Transavia
	PH-XRD	Boeing 737-7K2	Transavia
	PH-XRE	Boeing 737-7K2	Transavia
	PH-XRV	Boeing 737-7K2	Transavia
	PH-XRX	Boeing 737-7K2	Transavia
	PH-XRY	Boeing 737-7K2	Transavia
	PH-XRZ	Boeing 737-7K2	Transavia

PK (Indonesia)

	PK-GIA	Boeing 777-3U3ER	Garuda Indonesia
	PK-GIC	Boeing 777-3U3ER	Garuda Indonesia
	PK-GID	Boeing 777-3U3ER	Garuda Indonesia
	PK-GIE	Boeing 777-3U3ER	Garuda Indonesia

PP/PR/PT (Brazil)

	PT-MSV	Boeing 767-316ER	TAM Linhas Aereas
	PT-MSW	Boeing 767-316ER	TAM Linhas Aereas
	PT-MSX	Boeing 767-316ER	TAM Linhas Aereas
	PT-MSY	Boeing 767-316ER	TAM Linhas Aereas
	PT-MUA	Boeing 777-32WER	TAM Linhas Aereas
	PT-MUB	Boeing 777-32WER	TAM Linhas Aereas
	PT-MUC	Boeing 777-32WER	TAM Linhas Aereas
	PT-MUD	Boeing 777-32WER	TAM Linhas Aereas
	PT-MUE	Boeing 777-32WER	TAM Linhas Aereas
	PT-MUF	Boeing 777-32WER	TAM Linhas Aereas
	PT-MUG	Boeing 777-32WER	TAM Linhas Aereas
	PT-MUH	Boeing 777-32WER	TAM Linhas Aereas
	PT-MUI	Boeing 777-32WER	TAM Linhas Aereas
	PT-MUJ	Boeing 777-32WER	TAM Linhas Aereas
	PT-MVE	Airbus A.330-223	TAM Linhas Aereas
	PT-MVF	Airbus A.330-203	TAM Linhas Aereas
	PT-MVG	Airbus A.330-203	TAM Linhas Aereas
	PT-MVL	Airbus A.330-203	TAM Linhas Aereas
	PT-MVM	Airbus A.330-223	TAM Linhas Aereas
	PT-MVN	Airbus A.330-223	TAM Linhas Aereas
	PT-MVO	Airbus A.330-223	TAM Linhas Aereas
	PT-MVP	Airbus A.330-223	TAM Linhas Aereas
	PT-MVQ	Airbus A.330-223	TAM Linhas Aereas
	PT-MVR	Airbus A.330-223	TAM Linhas Aereas
	PT-MVS	Airbus A.330-223	TAM Linhas Aereas
	PT-MVT	Airbus A.330-223	TAM Linhas Aereas
	PT-MVU	Airbus A.330-223	TAM Linhas Aereas
	PT-MVV	Airbus A.330-223	TAM Linhas Aereas

RA (Russia)

	RA-61701	Antonov An-148-100B	Rossiya
	RA-61702	Antonov An-148-100B	Rossiya
	RA-61703	Antonov An-148-100B	Rossiya
	RA-61704	Antonov An-148-100B	Rossiya
	RA-61705	Antonov An-148-100B	Rossiya
	RA-61706	Antonov An-148-100B	Rossiya
	RA-82042	An-124	Volga-Dnepr

Reg.	Type	Owner or Operator	Notes
RA-82043	An-124	Volga-Dnepr	
RA-82044	An-124	Volga-Dnepr	
RA-82045	An-124	Volga-Dnepr	
RA-82046	An-124	Volga-Dnepr	
RA-82047	An-124	Volga-Dnepr	
RA-82068	An-124	Polet	
RA-82074	An-124	Volga-Dnepr	
RA-82075	An-124	Polet	
RA-82077	An-124	Polet	
RA-82078	An-124	Volga-Dnepr	
RA-82079	An-124	Volga-Dnepr	
RA-82080	An-124	Polet	
RA-82081	An-124	Volga-Dnepr	

RP (Philippines)

Reg.	Type	Owner or Operator	Notes
RP-C7772	Boeing 777-3F6ER	Philippine Airlines	
RP-C7773	Boeing 777-3F6ER	Philippine Airlines	
RP-C7774	Boeing 777-3F6ER	Philippine Airlines	
RP-C7775	Boeing 777-3F6ER	Philippine Airlines	
RP-C7776	Boeing 777-36NER	Philippine Airlines	
RP-C7777	Boeing 777-36NER	Philippine Airlines	

S2 (Bangladesh)

Reg.	Type	Owner or Operator	Notes
S2-ADF	Airbus A.310-325	Bangladesh Biman *City of Chittagong*	
S2-ADK	Airbus A.310-324	Bangladesh Biman	
S2-AFO	Boeing 777-3E9ER	Bangladesh Biman	
S2-AFP	Boeing 777-3E9FR	Bangladesh Biman	
S2-AHM	Boeing 777-3E9FR	Bangladesh Biman	

S5 (Slovenia)

Reg.	Type	Owner or Operator	Notes
S5-AAD	Canadair CRJ200LR	Adria Airways	
S5-AAE	Canadair CRJ200LR	Adria Airways	
S5-AAF	Canadair CRJ200LR	Adria Airways	
S5-AAG	Canadair CRJ200LR	Adria Airways	
S5-AAJ	Canadair CRJ200LR	Adria Airways	
S5-AAK	Canadair CRJ900LR	Adria Airways	
S5-AAL	Canadair CRJ900LR	Adria Airways	
S5-AAN	Canadair CRJ900LR	Adria Airways	
S5-AAO	Canadair CRJ900LR	Adria Airways	
S5-AAP	Airbus A.319-132	Adria Airways	
S5-AAR	Airbus A.319-132	Adria Airways	
S5-AAS	Airbus A.320-231	Adria Airways	

SE (Sweden)

Reg.	Type	Owner or Operator	Notes
SE-DNX	Boeing 737-683	SAS *Torvald Viking*	
SE-DOR	Boeing 737-683	SAS *Elisabeth Viking*	
SE-DZN	Boeing 737-804	TUIfly Nordic	
SE-DZV	Boeing 737-804	TUIfly Nordic	
SE-KXP	BAe ATP	West Air Sweden	
SE-LFX	BAe ATP	West Air Sweden	
SE-LGX	BAe ATP	West Air Sweden	
SE-LGY	BAe ATP	West Air Sweden	
SE-LGZ	BAe ATP	West Air Sweden	
SE-LHX	BAe ATP	West Air Sweden	
SE-LHZ	BAe ATP	West Air Sweden	
SE-LNX	BAe ATP	West Air Sweden	
SE-LNY	BAe ATP	West Air Sweden	
SE-LPR	BAe ATP	West Air Sweden	
SE-LPS	BAe ATP	West Air Sweden	
SE-LPT	BAe ATP	West Air Sweden	
SE-LPU	BAe ATP	West Air Sweden	
SE-LPV	BAe ATP	West Air Sweden	
SE-LPX	BAe ATP	West Air Sweden	
SE-MAF	BAe ATP	West Air Sweden	

Notes	Reg.	Type	Owner or Operator
	SE-MAH	BAe ATP	West Air Sweden
	SE-MAJ	BAe ATP	West Air Sweden
	SE-MAO	BAe ATP	West Air Sweden
	SE-MAR	BAe ATP	West Air Sweden
	SE-MAY	BAe ATP	West Air Sweden
	SE-RDN	Airbus A.321-231	Novair Airlines
	SE-RDO	Airbus A.321-231	Novair Airlines
	SE-RDP	Airbus A.321-231	Novair Airlines
	SE-RER	Boeing 737-7BX	SAS
	SE-RES	Boeing 737-7BX	SAS
	SE-RET	Boeing 737-76N	SAS
	SE-REU	Boeing 737-76N	SAS
	SE-REX	Boeing 737-76N	SAS
	SE-REY	Boeing 737-76N	SAS
	SE-REZ	Boeing 737-76N	SAS
	SE-RFR	Boeing 767-38AER	TUIfly Nordic
	SE-RFS	Boeing 767-304ER	TUIfly Nordic
	SE-RFT	Boeing 737-8K5	TUIfly Nordic
	SE-RFU	Boeing 737-8K5	TUIfly Nordic
	SE-RFV	Boeing 737-86N	TUIfly Nordic
	SE-RFX	Boeing 737-8K5	TUIfly Nordic
	SE-RJE	Airbus A.320-232	SAS
	SE-RJF	Airbus A.320-232	SAS
	SE-RJU	Boeing 737-76N	SAS

SP (Poland)

Notes	Reg.	Type	Owner or Operator
	SP-ENA	Boeing 737-4Q8	Enter Air
	SP-ENB	Boeing 737-4Q8	Enter Air
	SP-ENC	Boeing 737-4Q8	Enter Air
	SP-ENE	Boeing 737-4Q8	Enter Air
	SP-ENF	Boeing 737-4C9	Enter Air
	SP-ENH	Boeing 737-405	Enter Air
	SP-ENI	Boeing 737-43Q	Enter Air
	SP-ENK	Boeing 737-46J	Enter Air
	SP-ENV	Boeing 737-8BK	Enter Air
	SP-ENW	Boeing 737-86J	Enter Air
	SP-ENX	Boeing 737-8Q8	Enter Air
	SP-ENY	Boeing 737-86N	Enter Air
	SP-ENZ	Boeing 737-85F	Enter Air
	SP-LDA	Embraer RJ170 100ST	LOT
	SP-LDB	Embraer RJ170 100ST	LOT
	SP-LDC	Embraer RJ170 100ST	LOT
	SP-LDD	Embraer RJ170 100ST	LOT
	SP-LDE	Embraer RJ170 100LR	LOT
	SP-LDF	Embraer RJ170 100LR	LOT
	SP-LDG	Embraer RJ170 100LR	LOT
	SP-LDH	Embraer RJ170 100LR	LOT
	SP-LDI	Embraer RJ170 100LR	LOT
	SP-LDK	Embraer RJ170 100LR	LOT
	SP-LIA	Embraer RJ170-200STD	LOT
	SP-LIB	Embraer RJ170-200STD	LOT
	SP-LIC	Embraer RJ170-200STD	LOT
	SP-LID	Embraer RJ170-200STD	LOT
	SP-LIE	Embraer RJ170-200STD	LOT
	SP-LIF	Embraer RJ170-200STD	LOT
	SP-LII	Embraer RJ170-200STD	LOT
	SP-LIK	Embraer RJ170-200STD	LOT
	SP-LIL	Embraer RJ170-200STD	LOT
	SP-LIM	Embraer RJ170-200STD	LOT
	SP-LIN	Embraer RJ170-200STD	LOT
	SP-LIO	Embraer RJ170-200STD	LOT
	SP-LLE	Boeing 737-45D	LOT
	SP-LLF	Boeing 737-45D	LOT
	SP-LLG	Boeing 737-45D	LOT
	SP-LNA	Embraer RJ190-200LR	LOT
	SP-LNB	Embraer RJ190-200LR	LOT
	SP-LNC	Embraer RJ190-200LR	LOT
	SP-LND	Embraer RJ190-200LR	LOT
	SP-LNE	Embraer RJ190-200LR	LOT
	SP-LNF	Embraer RJ190-200LR	LOT

Reg.	Type	Owner or Operator	Notes
SP-LRA	Boeing 787-8	LOT	
SP-LRB	Boeing 787-8	LOT	
SP-LRC	Boeing 787-8	LOT	
SP-LRD	Boeing 787-8	LOT	
SP-LRE	Boeing 787-8	LOT	

SU (Egypt)

SU-GAC	Airbus A.300B4-203F	EgyptAir Cargo *New Valley*	
SU-GAS	Airbus A.300F4-622RF	EgyptAir Cargo *Cheops*	
SU-GAY	Airbus A.300B4-622RF	EgyptAir Cargo *Seti I*	
SU-GBR	Boeing 777-266ER	EgyptAir *Nefertari*	
SU-GBS	Boeing 777-266ER	EgyptAir *Tyie*	
SU-GBT	Airbus A.321-231	EgyptAir *Red Sea*	
SU-GBU	Airbus A.321-231	EgyptAir	
SU-GBV	Airbus A.321-231	EgyptAir	
SU-GBW	Airbus A.321-231	EgyptAir *The Nile*	
SU-GBX	Boeing 777-266ER	EgyptAir *Neit*	
SU-GBY	Boeing 777-266ER	EgyptAir *Titi*	
SU-GCE	Airbus A.330-243	EgyptAir	
SU-GCF	Airbus A.330-243	EgyptAir	
SU-GCG	Airbus A.330-243	EgyptAir	
SU-GCH	Airbus A.330-243	EgyptAir	
SU-GCI	Airbus A.330-243	EgyptAir	
SU-GCJ	Airbus A.330-243	EgyptAir	
SU-GCK	Airbus A.330-243	EgyptAir	
SU-GCM	Boeing 737-866WIN	EgyptAir	
SU-GCN	Boeing 737-866WIN	EgyptAir	
SU-GCO	Boeing 737-866WIN	EgyptAir	
SU-GCP	Boeing 737-866WIN	EgyptAir	
SU-GCR	Boeing 737-866WIN	EgyptAir	
SU-GCS	Boeing 737-866WIN	EgyptAir	
SU-GCZ	Boeing 737-866WIN	EgyptAir	
SU-GDA	Boeing 737-866WIN	EgyptAir	
SU-GDB	Boeing 737-866WIN	EgyptAir	
SU-GDC	Boeing 737-866WIN	EgyptAir	
SU-GDD	Boeing 737-866WIN	EgyptAir	
SU-GDE	Boeing 737-866WIN	EgyptAir	
SU-GDL	Boeing 777-36NER	EgyptAir	
SU-GDM	Boeing 777-36NER	EgyptAir	
SU-GDN	Boeing 777-36NER	EgyptAir	
SU-GDO	Boeing 777-36NER	EgyptAir	
SU-GDP	Boeing 777-36NER	EgyptAir	
SU-GDR	Boeing 777-36NER	EgyptAir	
SU-GDS	Airbus A.330-343X	EgyptAir	
SU-GDT	Airbus A.330-343X	EgyptAir	
SU-GDU	Airbus A.330-343X	EgyptAir	
SU-GDV	Airbus A.330-343X	EgyptAir	
SU-GDX	Boeing 737-866WIN	EgyptAir	
SU-GDY	Boeing 737-866WIN	EgyptAir	
SU-GDZ	Boeing 737-866WIN	EgyptAir	
SU-GEA	Boeing 737-866WIN	EgyptAir	
SU-GEB	Boeing 737-866WIN	EgyptAir	
SU-GEC	Boeing 737-866WIN	EgyptAir	
SU-GED	Boeing 737-866WIN	EgyptAir	
SU-GEE	Boeing 737-866WIN	EgyptAir	

SX (Greece)

SX-BHS	Airbus A.321-111	Air Mediterranee	
SX-BHT	Airbus A.321-211	Hermes Airlines	
SX-BHV	Airbus A.320-211	Air Mediterranee	
SX-DGA	Airbus A.321-231	Aegean Airlines	
SX-DGB	Airbus A.320-232	Aegean Airlines	
SX-DGC	Airbus A.320-232	Aegean Airlines	
SX-DGD	Airbus A.320-232	Aegean Airlines	
SX-DGE	Airbus A.320-232	Aegean Airlines	
SX-DGF	Airbus A.319-132	Aegean Airlines	
SX-DGI	Airbus A.320-232	Aegean Airlines	
SX-DGJ	Airbus A.320-232	Aegean Airlines	

Notes	Reg.	Type	Owner or Operator
	SX-DGK	Airbus A.320-232	Aegean Airlines
	SX-DGL	Airbus A.320-232	Aegean Airlines
	SX-DGN	Airbus A.320-232	Aegean Airlines
	SX-DVG	Airbus A.320-232	Aegean Airlines *Ethos*
	SX-DVH	Airbus A.320-232	Aegean Airlines *Nostos*
	SX-DVI	Airbus A.320-232	Aegean Airlines *Kinesis*
	SX-DVJ	Airbus A.320-232	Aegean Airlines *Kinesis*
	SX-DVK	Airbus A.320-232	Aegean Airlines
	SX-DVL	Airbus A.320-232	Aegean Airlines
	SX-DVM	Airbus A.320-232	Aegean Airlines
	SX-DVN	Airbus A.320-232	Aegean Airlines
	SX-DVO	Airbus A.321-232	Aegean Airlines *Philoxenia*
	SX-DVP	Airbus A.321-232	Aegean Airlines
	SX-DVQ	Airbus A.320-232	Aegean Airlines
	SX-DVR	Airbus A.320-232	Aegean Airlines
	SX-DVS	Airbus A.320-232	Aegean Airlines
	SX-DVT	Airbus A.320-232	Aegean Airlines
	SX-DVU	Airbus A.320-232	Aegean Airlines *Pheidias*
	SX-DVV	Airbus A.320-232	Aegean Airlines *Cleisthenes*
	SX-DVW	Airbus A.320-232	Aegean Airlines
	SX-DVX	Airbus A.320-232	Aegean Airlines
	SX-DVY	Airbus A.320-232	Aegean Airlines
	SX-DVZ	Airbus A.321-232	Aegean Airlines

TC (Turkey)

Notes	Reg.	Type	Owner or Operator
	TC-AAE	Boeing 737-82R	Pegasus Airlines *Hayirli*
	TC-AAH	Boeing 737-82R	Pegasus Airlines
	TC-AAI	Boeing 737-82R	Pegasus Airlines
	TC-AAJ	Boeing 737-82R	Pegasus Airlines
	TC-AAL	Boeing 737-82R	Pegasus Airlines
	TC-AAN	Boeing 737-82R	Pegasus Airlines *Merve*
	TC-AAO	Boeing 737-86N	Pegasus Airlines
	TC-AAR	Boeing 737-86N	Pegasus Airlines
	TC-AAS	Boeing 737-82R	Pegasus Airlines
	TC-AAT	Boeing 737-82R	Pegasus Airlines
	TC-AAU	Boeing 737-82R	Pegasus Airlines *Duru*
	TC-AAV	Boeing 737-82R	Pegasus Airlines
	TC-AAY	Boeing 737-82R	Pegasus Airlines
	TC-AAZ	Boeing 737-82R	Pegasus Airlines *Mina*
	TC-ABK	Airbus A.300B4-203F	ULS Cargo *Adiyaman*
	TC-ABP	Boeing 737-82R	Pegasus Airlines *Nisa*
	TC-ACF	Boeing 747-481F	myCargo Airlines
	TC-ACG	Boeing 747-481F	myCargo Airlines
	TC-ACH	Boeing 747-433F	myCargo Airlines
	TC-ACP	Boeing 737-82R	Pegasus Airlines
	TC-ADP	Boeing 737-82R	Pegasus Airlines *Nisa Nur*
	TC-AEP	Boeing 737-82R	Pegasus Airlines
	TC-AGP	Boeing 737-82R	Pegasus Airlines *Sebnem*
	TC-AHP	Boeing 737-82R	Pegasus Airlines *Iram Naz*
	TC-AIP	Boeing 737-82R	Pegasus Airlines *Hante*
	TC-AIS	Boeing 737-82R	Pegasus Airlines *Sevde Nil D*
	TC-AJP	Boeing 737-82R	Pegasus Airlines *Masal*
	TC-AMP	Boeing 737-82R	Pegasus Airlines *Nil*
	TC-ANP	Boeing 737-82R	Pegasus Airlines *Sena*
	TC-ARP	Boeing 737-82R	Pegasus Airlines *Nehir*
	TC-ASP	Boeing 737-82R	Pegasus Airlines
	TC-ATB	Airbus A.321-211	Atlasjet Airlines
	TC-ATD	Airbus A.319-112	Atlasjet Airlines
	TC-ATE	Airbus A.321-211	Atlasjet Airlines
	TC-ATF	Airbus A.321-211	Atlasjet Airlines
	TC-ATH	Airbus A.321-231	Atlasjet Airlines
	TC-ATJ	Airbus A.320-233	Atlasjet Airlines
	TC-ATK	Airbus A.320-232	Atlasjet Airlines
	TC-ATM	Airbus A.320-232	Atlasjet Airlines
	TC-ATR	Airbus A.321-211	Atlasjet Airlines
	TC-ATT	Airbus A.320-233	Atlasjet Airlines
	TC-ATZ	Airbus A.321-211	Atlasjet Airlines
	TC-AVP	Boeing 737-82R	Pegasus Airlines
	TC-AZP	Boeing 737-82R	Pegasus Airlines *Maya*
	TC-CCP	Boeing 737-86J	Pegasus Airlines

Reg.	Type	Owner or Operator	Notes
TC-CPA	Boeing 737-82R	Pegasus Airlines *Sena*	
TC-CPB	Boeing 737-82R	Pegasus Airlines *Doge*	
TC-CPC	Boeing 737-82R	Pegasus Airlines *Oyku*	
TC-CPD	Boeing 737-82R	Pegasus Airlines *Berra*	
TC-CPE	Boeing 737-82R	Pegasus Airlines *Bade*	
TC-CPF	Boeing 737-82R	Pegasus Airlines *Zeynep*	
TC-CPG	Boeing 737-82R	Pegasus Airlines	
TC-CPI	Boeing 737-82R	Pegasus Airlines	
TC-CPJ	Boeing 737-82R	Pegasus Airlines *Beren K*	
TC-CPK	Boeing 737-82R	Pegasus Airlines	
TC-DCA	Airbus A.320-214	Pegasus Airlines	
TC-DCB	Airbus A.320-214	Pegasus Airlines	
TC-ETF	Airbus A.321-211	Atlasjet Airlines	
TC-ETH	Airbus A.321-211	Atlasjet Airlines	
TC-ETJ	Airbus A.321-211	Atlasjet Airlines	
TC-ETM	Airbus A.321-131	Atlasjet Airlines	
TC-ETN	Airbus A.321-131	Atlasjet Airlines	
TC-ETV	Airbus A.321-211	Atlasjet Airlines	
TC-FBG	Airbus A.321-131	Freebird Airlines	
TC-FBH	Airbus A.320-214	Freebird Airlines	
TC-FBJ	Airbus A.320-232	Freebird Airlines	
TC-FBO	Airbus A.320-214	Freebird Airlines	
TC-FBR	Airbus A.320-232	Freebird Airlines	
TC-FBT	Airbus A.321-131	Freebird Airlines	
TC-FBV	Airbus A.320-214	Freebird Airlines	
TC-FHE	Airbus A.320-232	Freebird Airlines	
TC-IZD	Boeing 737-83N	Pegasus Airlines	
TC-IZE	Boeing 737-86J	Pegasus Airlines	
TC-JAI	Airbus A.320-232	Turkish Airlines	
TC-JBI	Airbus A.320-232	Turkish Airlines	
TC-JDJ	Airbus A.340-311	Turkish Airlines *Istanbul*	
TC-JDK	Airbus A.340-311	Turkish Airlines *Diyarbakir*	
TC-JDL	Airbus A.340-311	Turkish Airlines *Ankara*	
TC-JDM	Airbus A.340-311	Turkish Airlines *Izmir*	
TC-JDN	Airbus A.340-313X	Turkish Airlines *Adana*	
TC-JFC	Boeing 737-8F2	Turkish Airlines *Diyarbakir*	
TC-JFD	Boeing 737-8F2	Turkish Airlines *Rize*	
TC-JFE	Boeing 737-8F2	Turkish Airlines *Hatay*	
TC-JFF	Boeing 737-8F2	Turkish Airlines *Afyon*	
TC-JFG	Boeing 737-8F2	Turkish Airlines *Mardi*	
TC-JFH	Boeing 737-8F2	Turkish Airlines *Igdir*	
TC-JFI	Boeing 737-8F2	Turkish Airlines *Sivas*	
TC-JFJ	Boeing 737-8F2	Turkish Airlines *Agri*	
TC-JFK	Boeing 737-8F2	Turkish Airlines *Zonguldak*	
TC-JFL	Boeing 737-8F2	Turkish Airlines *Ordu*	
TC-JFM	Boeing 737-8F2	Turkish Airlines *Nigde*	
TC-JFN	Boeing 737-8F2	Turkish Airlines *Bitlis*	
TC-JFO	Boeing 737-8F2	Turkish Airlines *Batman*	
TC-JFP	Boeing 737-8F2	Turkish Airlines	
TC-JFR	Boeing 737-8F2	Turkish Airlines	
TC-JFT	Boeing 737-8F2	Turkish Airlines *Kastamonu*	
TC-JFU	Boeing 737-8F2	Turkish Airlines *Elazig*	
TC-JFV	Boeing 737-8F2	Turkish Airlines *Tunceli*	
TC-JFY	Boeing 737-8F2	Turkish Airlines *Manisa*	
TC-JFZ	Boeing 737-8F2	Turkish Airlines *Bolu*	
TC-JGA	Boeing 737-8F2	Turkish Airlines	
TC-JGB	Boeing 737-8F2	Turkish Airlines *Eskisehir*	
TC-JGC	Boeing 737-8F2	Turkish Airlines *Kocaeli*	
TC-JGD	Boeing 737-8F2	Turkish Airlines *Nevsehir*	
TC-JGF	Boeing 737-8F2	Turkish Airlines *Ardahan*	
TC-JGG	Boeing 737-8F2	Turkish Airlines *Erzincan*	
TC-JGH	Boeing 737-8F2	Turkish Airlines *Tokat*	
TC-JGI	Boeing 737-8F2	Turkish Airlines *Siirt*	
TC-JGJ	Boeing 737-8F2	Turkish Airlines	
TC-JGK	Boeing 737-8F2	Turkish Airlines	
TC-JGL	Boeing 737-8F2	Turkish Airlines	
TC-JGM	Boeing 737-8F2	Turkish Airlines	
TC-JGN	Boeing 737-8F2	Turkish Airlines	
TC-JGO	Boeing 737-8F2	Turkish Airlines	
TC-JGP	Boeing 737-8F2	Turkish Airlines *Bartin*	
TC-JGR	Boeing 737-8F2	Turkish Airlines *Usak*	
TC-JGS	Boeing 737-8F2	Turkish Airlines *Kahramanmaras*	

Notes	Reg.	Type	Owner or Operator
	TC-JGT	Boeing 737-8F2	Turkish Airlines *Avanos*
	TC-JGU	Boeing 737-8F2	Turkish Airlines *Bodrum*
	TC-JGV	Boeing 737-8F2	Turkish Airlines *Cesme*
	TC-JGY	Boeing 737-8F2	Turkish Airlines *Managvat*
	TC-JGZ	Boeing 737-8F2	Turkish Airlines *Midyat*
	TC-JHA	Boeing 737-8F2	Turkish Airlines *Mudanya*
	TC-JHB	Boeing 737-8F2	Turkish Airlines *Safranbolu*
	TC-JHC	Boeing 737-8F2	Turkish Airlines *Iskenderun*
	TC-JHD	Boeing 737-8F2	Turkish Airlines *Serik*
	TC-JHE	Boeing 737-8F2	Turkish Airlines *Burhaniye*
	TC-JHF	Boeing 737-8F2	Turkish Airlines *Ayvalik*
	TC-JHK	Boeing 737-8F2	Turkish Airlines *Yesilkoy*
	TC-JHL	Boeing 737-8F2	Turkish Airlines *Unye*
	TC-JHM	Boeing 737-8F2	Turkish Airlines *Burgaz*
	TC-JHN	Boeing 737-8F2	Turkish Airlines
	TC-JHO	Boeing 737-8F2	Turkish Airlines
	TC-JHP	Boeing 737-8F2	Turkish Airlines
	TC-JHR	Boeing 737-8F2	Turkish Airlines
	TC-JHS	Boeing 737-8F2	Turkish Airlines
	TC-JHT	Boeing 737-8F2	Turkish Airlines
	TC-JHU	Boeing 737-8F2	Turkish Airlines
	TC-JIH	Airbus A.340-313X	Turkish Airlines *Kocaeli*
	TC-JII	Airbus A.340-313X	Turkish Airlines *Mersin*
	TC-JJE	Boeing 777-3F2ER	Turkish Airlines *Dolmabahce*
	TC-JJF	Boeing 777-3F2ER	Turkish Airlines *Beylerbeyi*
	TC-JJG	Boeing 777-3F2ER	Turkish Airlines *Yildiz*
	TC-JJH	Boeing 777-3F2ER	Turkish Airlines *Rumeli*
	TC-JJI	Boeing 777-3F2ER	Turkish Airlines *Ede*
	TC-JJJ	Boeing 777-3F2ER	Turkish Airlines *Erzurum*
	TC-JJK	Boeing 777-3F2ER	Turkish Airlines *Akdeniz*
	TC-JJL	Boeing 777-3F2ER	Turkish Airlines *Karadeniz*
	TC-JJM	Boeing 777-3F2ER	Turkish Airlines *Mamara*
	TC-JJN	Boeing 777-3F2ER	Turkish Airlines *Anadolu*
	TC-JJO	Boeing 777-3F2ER	Turkish Airlines *Istanbul*
	TC-JJP	Boeing 777-3F2ER	Turkish Airlines *Ankara*
	TC-JKJ	Boeing 737-752	Turkish Airlines *Eyup*
	TC-JKK	Boeing 737-752	Turkish Airlines *Fatih*
	TC-JKN	Boeing 737-752	Turkish Airlines *Besiktas*
	TC-JKO	Boeing 737-752	Turkish Airlines *Kadikoy*
	TC-JLJ	Airbus A.320-232	Turkish Airlines *Sirnak*
	TC-JLK	Airbus A.320-232	Turkish Airlines *Kirklareli*
	TC-JLL	Airbus A.320-232	Turkish Airlines *Duzce*
	TC-JLM	Airbus A.319-132	Turkish Airlines *Sinop*
	TC-JLN	Airbus A.319-132	Turkish Airlines *Karabuk*
	TC-JLO	Airbus A.319-132	Turkish Airlines *Ahlat*
	TC-JLP	Airbus A.319-132	Turkish Airlines *Koycegiz*
	TC-JLR	Airbus A.319-132	Turkish Airlines
	TC-JLS	Airbus A.319-132	Turkish Airlines *Salihli*
	TC-JLT	Airbus A.319-132	Turkish Airlines *Adilcevaz*
	TC-JLU	Airbus A.319-132	Turkish Airlines
	TC-JLV	Airbus A.319-132	Turkish Airlines
	TC-JLY	Airbus A.319-132	Turkish Airlines *Bergama*
	TC-JLZ	Airbus A.319-132	Turkish Airlines
	TC-JMH	Airbus A.321-232	Turkish Airlines *Didim*
	TC-JMI	Airbus A.321-232	Turkish Airlines *Milas*
	TC-JMJ	Airbus A.321-232	Turkish Airlines *Tekirdag*
	TC-JMK	Airbus A.321-232	Turkish Airlines *Uskudar*
	TC-JML	Airbus A.321-231	Turkish Airlines *Eminonu*
	TC-JNA	Airbus A.330-203	Turkish Airlines *Gaziantep*
	TC-JNB	Airbus A.330-203	Turkish Airlines *Konya*
	TC-JNC	Airbus A.330-203	Turkish Airlines *Bursa*
	TC-JND	Airbus A.330-203	Turkish Airlines *Antalya*
	TC-JNE	Airbus A.330-203	Turkish Airlines *Kayseri*
	TC-JNF	Airbus A.330-203	Turkish Airlines *Canakkale*
	TC-JNG	Airbus A.330-203	Turkish Airlines *Eskisehir*
	TC-JNH	Airbus A.330-343X	Turkish Airlines *Topkapi*
	TC-JNI	Airbus A.330-343X	Turkish Airlines *Konak*
	TC-JNJ	Airbus A.330-343X	Turkish Airlines *Kapadokya*
	TC-JNK	Airbus A.330-343X	Turkish Airlines *Sanliurfa*
	TC-JNL	Airbus A.330-343E	Turkish Airlines *Trabzon*
	TC-JNM	Airbus A.330-343X	Turkish Airlines *Samsun*
	TC-JNN	Airbus A.330-343	Turkish Airlines *Manisa*

Reg.	Type	Owner or Operator	Notes
TC-JNO	Airbus A.330-343	Turkish Airlines	
TC-JNP	Airbus A.330-343	Turkish Airlines *Gokceada*	
TC-JNR	Airbus A.330-343	Turkish Airlines *Halic Golden Horn*	
TC-JNS	Airbus A.330-303	Turkish Airlines	
TC-JNT	Airbus A.330-303	Turkish Airlines	
TC-JNU	Airbus A.330-243	Turkish Airlines	
TC-JNV	Airbus A.330-243	Turkish Airlines	
TC-JPA	Airbus A.320-232	Turkish Airlines *Mus*	
TC-JPB	Airbus A.320-232	Turkish Airlines *Rize*	
TC-JPC	Airbus A.320-232	Turkish Airlines *Erzurum*	
TC-JPD	Airbus A.320-232	Turkish Airlines *Isparta*	
TC-JPE	Airbus A.320-232	Turkish Airlines *Gumushane*	
TC-JPF	Airbus A.320-232	Turkish Airlines *Yozgat*	
TC-JPG	Airbus A.320-232	Turkish Airlines *Osmaniye*	
TC-JPH	Airbus A.320-232	Turkish Airlines *Kars*	
TC-JPI	Airbus A.320-232	Turkish Airlines *Dogubeyazit*	
TC-JPJ	Airbus A.320-232	Turkish Airlines *Edremit*	
TC-JPK	Airbus A.320-232	Turkish Airlines *Erdek*	
TC-JPL	Airbus A.320-232	Turkish Airlines *Goreme*	
TC-JPM	Airbus A.320-232	Turkish Airlines *Harput*	
TC-JPN	Airbus A.320-232	Turkish Airlines *Sarikamis*	
TC-JPO	Airbus A.320-232	Turkish Airlines *Kemer*	
TC-JPP	Airbus A.320-232	Turkish Airlines *Harran*	
TC-JPR	Airbus A.320-232	Turkish Airlines *Kusadasi*	
TC-JPS	Airbus A.320-232	Turkish Airlines *Adilcevaz*	
TC-JPT	Airbus A.320-232	Turkish Airlines *Urgup*	
TC-JPU	Airbus A.320-214	Turkish Airlines *Salihli*	
TC-JPV	Airbus A.320-214	Turkish Airlines *Sisli*	
TC-JPY	Airbus A.320-214	Turkish Airlines *Beykoz*	
TC-JRA	Airbus A.321-231	Turkish Airlines *Kutayha*	
TC-JRB	Airbus A.321-231	Turkish Airlines *Sanliurfa*	
TC-JRC	Airbus A.321-231	Turkish Airlines *Sakarya*	
TC-JRD	Airbus A.321-231	Turkish Airlines *Balikesir*	
TC-JRE	Airbus A.321-231	Turkish Airlines *Trabzon*	
TC-JRF	Airbus A.321-231	Turkish Airlines *Fethiye*	
TC-JRG	Airbus A.321-231	Turkish Airlines *Finike*	
TC-JRH	Airbus A.321-231	Turkish Airlines *Yalova*	
TC-JRI	Airbus A.321-232	Turkish Airlines *Adiyaman*	
TC-JRJ	Airbus A.321-232	Turkish Airlines *Corum*	
TC-JRK	Airbus A.321-231	Turkish Airlines *Batman*	
TC-JRL	Airbus A.321-231	Turkish Airlines *Tarsus*	
TC-JRM	Airbus A.321-232	Turkish Airlines *Afyonkarahisar*	
TC-JRN	Airbus A.321-232	Turkish Airlines *Sariyer*	
TC-JRO	Airbus A.321-231	Turkish Airlines *Uludag*	
TC-JRP	Airbus A.321-231	Turkish Airlines *Urgup*	
TC-JRR	Airbus A.321-231	Turkish Airlines *Emirgan*	
TC-JRS	Airbus A.321-231	Turkish Airlines *Datca*	
TC-JRT	Airbus A.321-231	Turkish Airlines *Alacati*	
TC-JRU	Airbus A.321-231	Turkish Airlines	
TC-JRV	Airbus A.321-232	Turkish Airlines	
TC-JRY	Airbus A.321-232	Turkish Airlines	
TC-JRZ	Airbus A.321-232	Turkish Airlines	
TC-JSA	Airbus A.321-232	Turkish Airlines	
TC-JSB	Airbus A.321-231	Turkish Airlines	
TC-JSC	Airbus A.321-231	Turkish Airlines	
TC-JSD	Airbus A.321-231	Turkish Airlines	
TC-JSE	Airbus A.321-231	Turkish Airlines	
TC-JSF	Airbus A.321-231	Turkish Airlines	
TC-JSG	Airbus A.321-231	Turkish Airlines	
TC-JSH	Airbus A.321-231	Turkish Airlines	
TC-JSI	Airbus A.321-231	Turkish Airlines	
TC-JSJ	Airbus A.321-232	Turkish Airlines	
TC-JSK	Airbus A.321-232	Turkish Airlines	
TC-JSL	Airbus A.321-232	Turkish Airlines	
TC-JSM	Airbus A.321-231	Turkish Airlines	
TC-JUA	Airbus A.319-132	Turkish Airlines	
TC-JUB	Airbus A.319-132	Turkish Airlines	
TC-JUD	Airbus A.319-132	Turkish Airlines	
TC-JUE	Airbus A.320-232	AnadoluJet	
TC-JUF	Airbus A.320-232	AnadoluJet	
TC-JUG	Airbus A.320-232	AnadoluJet	
TC-JUI	Airbus A.320-232	AnadoluJet	

Notes	Reg.	Type	Owner or Operator
	TC-JUJ	Airbus A.320-232	AnadoluJet
	TC-JUK	Airbus A.320-232	AnadoluJet
	TC-JYA	Boeing 737-9F2ER	Turkish Airlines *Amasya*
	TC-JYB	Boeing 737-9F2ER	Turkish Airlines *Debizli*
	TC-JYC	Boeing 737-9F2ER	Turkish Airlines *Eregu*
	TC-JYD	Boeing 737-9F2ER	Turkish Airlines
	TC-JYE	Boeing 737-9F2ER	Turkish Airlines
	TC-JYF	Boeing 737-9F2ER	Turkish Airlines
	TC-JYG	Boeing 737-9F2ER	Turkish Airlines
	TC-JYH	Boeing 737-9F2ER	Turkish Airlines
	TC-JYI	Boeing 737-9F2ER	Turkish Airlines *Mugla*
	TC-JYJ	Boeing 737-9F2ER	Turkish Airlines
	TC-LER	Airbus A.310-308F	ULS Cargo *Aras*
	TC-MCA	Airbus A.300B4-605R	MNG Cargo
	TC-MCC	Airbus A.300B4-622RF	MNG Cargo
	TC-MCD	Airbus A.300B4-605RF	MNG Cargo
	TC-MCE	Airbus A.300B4-605R	MNG Cargo
	TC-MCF	Boeing 737-4K5F	MNG Cargo
	TC-MCZ	Airbus A.330-243F	MNG Cargo
	TC-MNV	Airbus A.300B4-605R	MNG Cargo
	TC-OBF	Airbus A.321-231	Onur Air
	TC-OBG	Airbus A.320-233	Onur Air
	TC-OBH	Airbus A.320-233	Onur Air
	TC-OBI	Airbus A.320-233	Onur Air
	TC-OBJ	Airbus A.321-231	Onur Air
	TC-OBK	Airbus A.321-231	Onur Air
	TC-OBL	Airbus A.320-232	Onur Air
	TC-OBM	Airbus A.320-232	Onur Air
	TC-OBN	Airbus A.320-232	Onur Air
	TC-OBO	Airbus A.320-232	Onur Air
	TC-OBP	Airbus A.320-232	Onur Air
	TC-OBR	Airbus A.321-231	Onur Air
	TC-OBS	Airbus A.320-232	Onur Air
	TC-OBU	Airbus A.320-231	Onur Air
	TC-OBV	Airbus A.321-231	Onur Air
	TC-OBY	Airbus A.321-231	Onur Air
	TC-OBZ	Airbus A.321-231	Onur Air
	TC-ONJ	Airbus A.321-131	Onur Air
	TC-ONS	Airbus A.321-131	Onur Air
	TC-SAC	Boeing 737-76N	AnadoluJet
	TC-SAD	Boeing 737-76N	AnadoluJet
	TC-SAE	Boeing 737-76N	AnadoluJet
	TC-SAF	Boeing 737-73V	AnadoluJet
	TC-SAG	Boeing 737-73V	AnadoluJet
	TC-SAH	Boeing 737-8FH	AnadoluJet
	TC-SAI	Boeing 737-8AS	AnadoluJet
	TC-SAJ	Boeing 737-8AS	AnadoluJet
	TC-SAK	Boeing 737-8AS	AnadoluJet
	TC-SAL	Boeing 737-76N	AnadoluJet
	TC-SAO	Boeing 737-76N	AnadoluJet
	TC-SAP	Boeing 737-76N	AnadoluJet
	TC-SAU	Boeing 737-8GJ	AnadoluJet
	TC-SAV	Boeing 737-8GJ	AnadoluJet
	TC-SAZ	Boeing 737-7GL	AnadoluJet
	TC-SBB	Boeing 737-7GL	AnadoluJet
	TC-SBE	Boeing 737-8BK	AnadoluJet
	TC-SBF	Boeing 737-86Q	AnadoluJet
	TC-SBG	Boeing 737-86J	AnadoluJet
	TC-SBI	Boeing 737-8AS	AnadoluJet
	TC-SNE	Boeing 737-8HX	SunExpress
	TC-SNF	Boeing 737-8HC	SunExpress
	TC-SNG	Boeing 737-8HC	SunExpress
	TC-SNH	Boeing 737-8FH	SunExpress
	TC-SNI	Boeing 737-8FH	SunExpress
	TC-SNJ	Boeing 737-86J	SunExpress
	TC-SNL	Boeing 737-86N	SunExpress
	TC-SNM	Boeing 737-8BK	SunExpress
	TC-SNN	Boeing 737-8HC	SunExpress
	TC-SNO	Boeing 737-8HC	SunExpress
	TC-SNP	Boeing 737-8HC	SunExpress
	TC-SNR	Boeing 737-8HC	SunExpress
	TC-SNT	Boeing 737-8HC	SunExpress

Reg.	Type	Owner or Operator	Notes
TC-SNU	Boeing 737-8HC	SunExpress	
TC-SNV	Boeing 737-86J	AnadoluJet	
TC-SNY	Boeing 737-8K5	SunExpress	
TC-SUI	Boeing 737-8CX	SunExpress	
TC-SUL	Boeing 737-85F	SunExpress	
TC-SUM	Boeing 737-85F	SunExpress	
TC-SUO	Boeing 737-86Q	AnadoluJet	
TC-SUU	Boeing 737-86Q	SunExpress	
TC-SUV	Boeing 737-86N	SunExpress	
TC-SUY	Boeing 737-86N	SunExpress	
TC-SUZ	Boeing 737-8HX	SunExpress	
TC-TJB	Boeing 737-3Q8	Corendon Air	
TC-TJG	Boeing 737-86J	Corendon Air	
TC-TJH	Boeing 737-86J	Corendon Air	
TC-TJI	Boeing 737-8S3	Corendon Air	
TC-TJJ	Boeing 737-8S3	Corendon Air	
TC-TJL	Boeing 737-86J	Corendon Air	
TC-TJM	Boeing 737-8Q8	Corendon Air	
TC-TJN	Boeing 737-8Q8	Corendon Air	
TC-TLA	Boeing 737-4Q8	Tailwind Airlines	
TC-TLB	Boeing 737-4Q8	Tailwind Airlines	
TC-TLC	Boeing 737-4Q8	Tailwind Airlines	
TC-TLD	Boeing 737-4Q8	Tailwind Airlines	
TC-TLE	Boeing 737-4Q8	Tailwind Airlines	
TC-VEL	Airbus A.310-308F	ULS Cargo	

TF (Iceland)

Reg.	Type	Owner or Operator	Notes
TF-AAA	Boeing 747-236F	Air Atlanta Icelandic/Saudi Arabian Airlines	
TF-AAC	Boeing 747-481	Air Atlanta Icelandic/Saudi Arabian Airlines	
TF-AAD	Boeing 747-4H6	Air Atlanta Icelandic/Saudi Arabian Airlines	
TF-AAE	Boeing 747-4H6	Air Atlanta Icelandic/Saudi Arabian Airlines	
TF-AAG	Boeing 747-4H6	Air Atlanta Icelandic/Saudi Arabian Airlines	
TF-AMF	Boeing 747-412BCF	Air Atlanta Icelandic/Saudi Arabian Airlines	
TF-AMI	Boeing 747-412BCF	Air Atlanta Icelandic/Saudi Arabian Airlines	
TF-AML	Boeing 747-4H6SF	Air Atlanta Icelandic/Saudi Arabian Airlines	
TF-AMP	Boeing 747-481BCF	Air Atlanta Icelandic/Saudi Arabian Airlines	
TF-AMS	Boeing 747-481	Air Atlanta Icelandic/Saudi Arabian Airlines	
TF-AMT	Boeing 747-481	Air Atlanta Icelandic/Saudi Arabian Airlines	
TF-AMU	Boeing 747-48E	Air Atlanta Icelandic/Saudi Arabian Airlines	
TF-AMV	Boeing 747-412	Air Atlanta Icelandic/Saudi Arabian Airlines	
TF-AMX	Boeing 747-441BCF	Air Atlanta Icelandic/Saudi Arabian Airlines	
TF-AMY	Boeing 747-446	Air Atlanta Icelandic/Saudi Arabian Airlines	
TF-BBD	Boeing 737-3Y0F	Bluebird Cargo/TNT Airways	
TF-BBE	Boeing 737-36EF	Bluebird Cargo	
TF-BBF	Boeing 737-36EF	Bluebird Cargo	
TF-BBG	Boeing 737-36EF	Bluebird Cargo/TNT Airways	
TF-BBH	Boeing 737-4YO	Bluebird Cargo/TNT Airways	
TF-FIA	Boeing 757-256	Icelandair	
TF-FIC	Boeing 757-23N	Icelandair	
TF-FID	Boeing 757-23APF	Icelandair Cargo/TNT Airways	
TF-FIG	Boeing 757-23APF	Icelandair Cargo	
TF-FIH	Boeing 757-208PCF	Icelandair Cargo	
TF-FII	Boeing 757-208	Icelandair	
TF-FIJ	Boeing 757-208	Icelandair *Surtsey*	
TF-FIN	Boeing 757-208	Icelandair *Bryndis*	
TF-FIO	Boeing 757-208	Icelandair *Valdis*	
TF-FIP	Boeing 757-208	Icelandair *Leifur Eiriksson*	
TF-FIR	Boeing 757-256	Icelandair	
TF-FIU	Boeing 757-256	Icelandair	
TF-FIV	Boeing 757-208	Icelandair *Gudridur Porbjarnardottir*	
TF-FIW	Boeing 757-27B	Icelandair	
TF-FIX	Boeing 757-308	Icelandair *Snorri Porfinnsson*	
TF-FIY	Boeing 757-256	Icelandair	
TF-FIZ	Boeing 757-256	Icelandair	
TF-ISF	Boeing 757-223	Icelandair	
TF-ISK	Boeing 757-223	Icelandair	
TF-ISL	Boeing 757-223	Icelandair *Oraefajokull*	
TF-LLX	Boeing 757-256	Icelandair	
TF-WOW	Airbus A.320-232	WOW Air	

TS (Tunisia)

Reg.	Type	Owner or Operator
TS-IEF	Airbus A.319-112	Syphax Airlines
TS-IEG	Airbus A.319-112	Syphax Airlines
TS-IMC	Airbus A.320-211	Tunis Air 7 Novembre
TS-IMD	Airbus A.320-211	Tunis Air Khereddine
TS-IME	Airbus A.320-211	Tunis Air Tabarka
TS-IMF	Airbus A.320-211	Tunis Air Djerba
TS-IMG	Airbus A.320-211	Tunis Air Abou el Kacem Chebbi
TS-IMH	Airbus A.320-211	Tunis Air Ali Belhaouane
TS-IMI	Airbus A.320-211	Tunis Air Jughurta
TS-IMJ	Airbus A.319-114	Tunis Air El Kantaoui
TS-IMK	Airbus A.319-114	Tunis Air Kerkenah
TS-IML	Airbus A.320-211	Tunis Air Gafsa el Ksar
TS-IMM	Airbus A.320-211	Tunis Air Le Bardo
TS-IMN	Airbus A.320-211	Tunis Air Ibn Khaldoun
TS-IMO	Airbus A.319-114	Tunis Air Hannibal
TS-IMP	Airbus A.320-211	Tunis Air La Galite
TS-IMQ	Airbus A.319-114	Tunis Air/Afriqiyah Airways
TS-IMR	Airbus A.320-211	Tunis Air Habib Bourguiba
TS-IMS	Airbus A.320-214	Tunis Air Dougga
TS-IMT	Airbus A.320-214	Tunis Air
TS-IMU	Airbus A.320-214	Tunis Air Sousse
TS-IMV	Airbus A.320-214	Tunis Air Ibn Eljazzar
TS-INA	Airbus A.320-214	Nouvelair
TS-INB	Airbus A.320-214	Nouvelair
TS-INC	Airbus A.320-214	Nouvelair
TS-INF	Airbus A.320-212	Nouvelair
TS-INH	Airbus A.320-214	Nouvelair
TS-INL	Airbus A.320-212	Nouvelair
TS-INN	Airbus A.320-212	Libyan Airlines
TS-INO	Airbus A.320-214	Nouvelair
TS-INP	Airbus A.320-214	Libyan Airlines
TS-IOK	Boeing 737-6H3	Tunis Air Kairouan
TS-IOL	Boeing 737-6H3	Tunis Air Tozeur-Nefta
TS-IOM	Boeing 737-6H3	Tunis Air Carthage
TS-ION	Boeing 737-6H3	Tunis Air Utique
TS-IOP	Boeing 737-6H3	Tunis Air El Jem
TS-IOQ	Boeing 737-6H3	Tunis Air Bizerte
TS-IOR	Boeing 737-6H3	Tunis Air Tahar Haddad
TS-IQA	Airbus A.321-211	Nouvelair
TS-IQB	Airbus A.321-211	Nouvelair
TS-IRA	Airbus A.330-243	Syphax Airlines

UK (Uzbekistan)

Reg.	Type	Owner or Operator
UK-67001	Boeing 767-33PER	Uzbekistan Airways
UK-67002	Boeing 767-33PER	Uzbekistan Airways
UK-67003	Boeing 767-33PER	Uzbekistan Airways
UK-67004	Boeing 767-33PER	Uzbekistan Airways
UK-67005	Boeing 767-33PER	Uzbekistan Airways
UK-67006	Boeing 767-33PER	Uzbekistan Airways
UK-75701	Boeing 757-23P	Uzbekistan Airways
UK-75702	Boeing 757-23P	Uzbekistan Airways

UN (Kazakhstan)

Note: Air Astana operates P4- registered Boeing 757s and 767s.

UR (Ukraine)

Reg.	Type	Owner or Operator
UR-GAH	Boeing 737-32Q	Ukraine International Mayrni
UR-GAK	Boeing 737-5Y0	Ukraine International
UR-GAN	Boeing 737-36N	Ukraine International
UR-GAO	Boeing 737-4Z9	Ukraine International
UR-GAP	Boeing 737-4Z9	Ukraine International
UR-GAQ	Boeing 737-33R	Ukraine International

Reg.	Type	Owner or Operator	Notes
UR-GAS	Boeing 737-528	Ukraine International	
UR-GAT	Boeing 737-528	Ukraine International	
UR-GAU	Boeing 737-5Y0	Ukraine International	
UR-GAV	Boeing 737-4C9	Ukraine International	
UR-GAW	Boeing 737-5Y0	Ukraine International	
UR-GAX	Boeing 737-4Y0	Ukraine International	
UR-GAZ	Boeing 737-55D	Ukraine International	
UR-GBA	Boeing 737-36N	Ukraine International	
UR-GBB	Boeing 737-529	Ukraine International	
UR-GBC	Boeing 737-5L9	Ukraine International	
UR-GBD	Boeing 737-36Q	Ukraine International	
UR-GBE	Boeing 737-548	Ukraine International	
UR-GBF	Boeing 737-548	Ukraine International	
UR-PSA	Boeing 737-8HX	Ukraine International	
UR-PSB	Boeing 737-8HX	Ukraine International	
UR-PSC	Boeing 737-8HX	Ukraine International	
UR-PSD	Boeing 737-89P	Ukraine International	
UR-PSE	Boeing 737-84R	Ukraine International	
UR-PSF	Boeing 737-84R	Ukraine International	
UR-PSG	Boeing 737-85R	Ukraine International	
UR-PSH	Boeing 737-85R	Ukraine International	
UR-PSI	Boeing 737-9KVER	Ukraine International	
UR-PSJ	Boeing 737-9KV	Ukraine International	
UR-PSK	Boeing 737-94XER	Ukraine International	
UR-PSL	Boeing 737-94XER	Ukraine International	
UR-WUA	Airbus A.320-232	Wizz Air Ukraine	
UR-WUB	Airbus A.320-232	Wizz Air Ukraine	
UR-WUC	Airbus A.320-232	Wizz Air Ukraine	
UR-WUD	Airbus A.320-232	Wizz Air Ukraine	
UR-82007	Antonov An-124	Antonov Airlines	
UR-82008	Antonov An-124	Antonov Airlines	
UR-82009	Antonov An-124	Antonov Airlines	
UR-82027	Antonov An-124	Antonov Airlines	
UR-82029	Antonov An-124	Antonov Airlines	
UR-82060	Antonov An-225	Antonov Airlines	
UR-82072	Antonov An-124	Antonov Airlines	
UR-82073	Antonov An-124	Antonov Airlines	

V8 (Brunei)

V8-BLC	Boeing 777-212ER	Royal Brunei Airlines	
V8-BLF	Boeing 777-212ER	Royal Brunei Airlines	
V8-DLA	Boeing 787-8	Royal Brunei Airlines	
V8-DLB	Boeing 787-8	Royal Brunei Airlines	

VH (Australia)

VH-OQA	Airbus A.380-841	QANTAS	
VH-OQB	Airbus A.380-841	QANTAS	
VH-OQC	Airbus A.380-841	QANTAS	
VH-OQD	Airbus A.380-841	QANTAS	
VH-OQE	Airbus A.380-841	QANTAS	
VH-OQF	Airbus A.380-841	QANTAS	
VH-OQG	Airbus A.380-841	QANTAS	
VH-OQH	Airbus A.380-841	QANTAS	
VH-OQI	Airbus A.380-841	QANTAS	
VH-OQJ	Airbus A.380-841	QANTAS	
VH-OQK	Airbus A.380-841	QANTAS	
VH-OQL	Airbus A.380-841	QANTAS	
VH-OQM	Airbus A.380-841	QANTAS	
VH-OQN	Airbus A.380-841	QANTAS	

VN (Vietnam)

VN-A141	Boeing 777-2Q8ER	Vietnam Airlines	
VN-A142	Boeing 777-2Q8ER	Vietnam Airlines	
VN-A143	Boeing 777-26KER	Vietnam Airlines	
VN-A144	Boeing 777-26KER	Vietnam Airlines	
VN-A145	Boeing 777-26KER	Vietnam Airlines	

Notes	Reg.	Type	Owner or Operator
	VN-A146	Boeing 777-26KER	Vietnam Airlines
	VN-A147	Boeing 777-2Q8ER	Vietnam Airlines
	VN-A149	Boeing 777-2Q8ER	Vietnam Airlines
	VN-A150	Boeing 777-2Q8ER	Vietnam Airlines
	VN-A151	Boeing 777-2Q8ER	Vietnam Airlines

VP-B/VQ-B (Bermuda)

Notes	Reg.	Type	Owner or Operator
	VP-BDC	Airbus A.321-211	Aeroflot Russian International V. Alekseev
	VP-BDD	Airbus A.330-343	Aeroflot Russian International A. Mozhaysky
	VP-BDE	Airbus A.330-343	Aeroflot Russian International L. Kantorovich
	VP-BDK	Airbus A.320-214	Aeroflot Russian International G. Sviridov
	VP-BDM	Airbus A.319-111	Aeroflot Russian International A. Borodin
	VP-BDN	Airbus A.319-111	Aeroflot Russian International A. Dargomyzhsky
	VP-BDO	Airbus A.319-111	Aeroflot Russian International I. Stravinsky
	VP-BID	Airbus A.320-214	Aeroflot Russian International I. Tamm
	VP-BIQ	Airbus A.319-111	Rossiya
	VP-BIT	Airbus A.319-111	Rossiya
	VP-BIU	Airbus A.319-114	Rossiya
	VP-BJA	Airbus A.320-214	Aeroflot Russian International I. Mechnikov
	VP-BKC	Airbus A.320-214	Aeroflot Russian International I. Kruzenshtern
	VP-BKX	Airbus A.320-214	Aeroflot Russian International G. Sedov
	VP-BKY	Airbus A.320-214	Aeroflot Russian International M. Rostropovich
	VP-BLH	Airbus A.320-214	Aeroflot Russian International P. Cherenkov
	VP-BLL	Airbus A.320-214	Aeroflot Russian International N. Basov
	VP-BLP	Airbus A.320-214	Aeroflot Russian International A. Popov
	VP-BLR	Airbus A.320-214	Aeroflot Russian International P. Yablochkov
	VP-BLX	Airbus A.330-243	Aeroflot Russian International E. Svetlanov
	VP-BLY	Airbus A.330-243	Aeroflot Russian International V. Vysotskly
	VP-BME	Airbus A.320-214	Aeroflot Russian International N. Mikluho-Maklay
	VP-BMF	Airbus A.320-214	Aeroflot Russian International G. Shelihov
	VP-BNL	Airbus A.320-214	Aeroflot Russian International A. Suvorov
	VP-BNT	Airbus A.320-214	Aeroflot Russian International Dobrolet
	VP-BOC	Airbus A.321-231	Aeroflot Russian International S. Mikhalkov
	VP-BOE	Airbus A.321-211	Aeroflot Russian International G. Vishnevskaya
	VP-BPA	Boeing 737-5K5	Transaero
	VP-BPD	Boeing 737-5K5	Transaero
	VP-BQP	Airbus A.320-214	Aeroflot Russian International A. Rublev
	VP-BQR	Airbus A.321-211	Aeroflot Russian International I. Repin
	VP-BQS	Airbus A.321-211	Aeroflot Russian International I. Kramskoi
	VP-BQT	Airbus A.321-211	Aeroflot Russian International I. Shishkin
	VP-BQU	Airbus A.320-214	Aeroflot Russian International A. Nikitin
	VP-BQV	Airbus A.320-214	Aeroflot Russian International V. Vasnetsov
	VP-BQW	Airbus A.320-214	Aeroflot Russian International V. Vereshchagin
	VP-BQX	Airbus A.321-211	Aeroflot Russian International I. Ayvazovsky
	VP-BRW	Airbus A.321-211	Aeroflot Russian International N. Rerih
	VP-BRX	Airbus A.320-214	Aeroflot Russian International V. Surikov
	VP-BRY	Airbus A.320-214	Aeroflot Russian International K. Brulloff
	VP-BRZ	Airbus A.320-214	Aeroflot Russian International V. Serov
	VP-BTG	Airbus A.321-211	Aeroflot Russian International K. Stanivlaskey
	VP-BTI	Airbus A.320-214	Aeroflot Russian International V. Meyerhold
	VP-BTL	Airbus A.321-211	Aeroflot Russian International E. Vakhtangov
	VP-BTR	Airbus A.321-211	Aeroflot Russian International S. Diaghilev
	VP-BUE	Boeing 767-3CBER	Uzbekistan Airways
	VP-BUF	Boeing 767-33PER	Uzbekistan Airways
	VP-BUH	Boeing 757-231	Uzbekistan Airways
	VP-BUI	Boeing 757-231	Uzbekistan Airways
	VP-BUJ	Boeing 757-231	Uzbekistan Airways
	VP-BUK	Airbus A.319-111	Aeroflot Russian International Yuri Senkevich
	VP-BUM	Airbus A.321-211	Aeroflot Russian International A.Deineka
	VP-BUN	Airbus A.319-112	Aeroflot Russian International
	VP-BUO	Airbus A.319-111	Aeroflot Russian International K. Malevich
	VP-BUP	Airbus A.321-211	Aeroflot Russian International M. Shagal
	VP-BWA	Airbus A.319-111	Aeroflot Russian International S. Prokofiev
	VP-BWD	Airbus A.320-214	Aeroflot Russian International A. Aliabiev
	VP-BWE	Airbus A.320-214	Aeroflot Russian International H. Rimsky-Korsakov
	VP-BWF	Airbus A.320-214	Aeroflot Russian International D. Shostakovich
	VP-BWH	Airbus A.320-214	Aeroflot Russian International M. Balakirev
	VP-BWI	Airbus A.320-214	Aeroflot Russian International A. Glazunov
	VP-BWJ	Airbus A.319-111	Aeroflot Russian International A. Shnitke
	VP-BWK	Airbus A.319-111	Aeroflot Russian International S. Taneyev

Reg.	Type	Owner or Operator	Notes
VP-BWL	Airbus A.319-111	Aeroflot Russian International A. Grechaninov	
VP-BWM	Airbus A.320-214	Aeroflot Russian International S. Rakhmaninov	
VP-BWN	Airbus A.321-211	Aeroflot Russian International A. Skriabin	
VP-BWO	Airbus A.321-211	Aeroflot Russian International P. Chaikovsky	
VP-BWP	Airbus A.321-211	Aeroflot Russian International M. Musorgsky	
VP-BWW	Boeing 767-306ER	Aeroflot Russian International S. Esenin	
VP-BWX	Boeing 767-306ER	Aeroflot Russian International A. Blok	
VP-BYI	Boeing 737-524	Transaero	
VP-BYJ	Boeing 737-524	Transaero	
VP-BYN	Boeing 737-524	Transaero	
VP-BYO	Boeing 737-524	Transaero	
VP-BYP	Boeing 737-524	Transaero	
VP-BYQ	Boeing 737-524	Transaero	
VP-BYT	Boeing 737-524	Transaero	
VP-BZO	Airbus A.320-214	Aeroflot Russian International V. Bering	
VP-BZP	Airbus A.320-214	Aeroflot Russian International E. Habarov	
VP-BZQ	Airbus A.320-214	Aeroflot Russian International Yu. Lisiansky	
VP-BZR	Airbus A.320-214	Aeroflot Russian International F. Bellinsgauzen	
VP-BZS	Airbus A.320-214	Aeroflot Russian International M. Lazarev	
VQ-BAQ	Airbus A.319-112	Rossiya	
VQ-BAR	Airbus A.319-112	Rossiya	
VQ-BAS	Airbus A.319-112	Rossiya	
VQ-BAT	Airbus A.319-112	Rossiya	
VQ-BAU	Airbus A.319-112	Rossiya	
VQ-BAV	Airbus A.319-112	Rossiya	
VQ-BAX	Airbus A.320-214	Aeroflot Russian International G. Nevelskoy	
VQ-BAY	Airbus A.320-214	Aeroflot Russian International S. Krasheninnikov	
VQ-BAZ	Airbus A.320-214	Aeroflot Russian International V. Obruchev	
VQ-BBA	Airbus A.319-112	Aeroflot Russian International S. Cheliuskin	
VQ-BBB	Airbus A.320-114	Aeroflot Russian International Yu. Gagarin	
VQ-BBC	Airbus A.320-214	Aeroflot Russian International N. Przhevalsky	
VQ-BBD	Airbus A.319-112	Aeroflot Russian International V. Golovnin	
VQ-BBE	Airbus A.330-243	Aeroflot Russian International I. Brodsky	
VQ-BBF	Airbus A.330-243	Aeroflot Russian International A. Griboedov	
VQ-BBG	Airbus A.330-243	Aeroflot Russian International N. Gogol	
VQ-BBM	Airbus A.320-214	Rossiya	
VQ-BCM	Airbus A.320-214	Aeroflot Russian International G. Titov	
VQ-BCN	Airbus A.320-214	Aeroflot Russian International V. Chelomey	
VQ-BCO	Airbus A.319-111	Aeroflot Russian International A. Hachaturian	
VQ-BCP	Airbus A.319-112	Aeroflot Russian International D. Mendeleev	
VQ-BCQ	Airbus A.330-343	Aeroflot Russian International	
VQ-BCU	Airbus A.330-343	Aeroflot Russian International W. Majakowski	
VQ-BCV	Airbus A.330-343	Aeroflot Russian International B. Pasternak	
VQ-BDQ	Airbus A.320-214	Rossiya	
VQ-BDR	Airbus A.320-214	Rossiya	
VQ-BDY	Airbus A.320-214	Rossiya	
VQ-BEA	Airbus A.321-211	Aeroflot Russian International I. Michurin	
VQ-BED	Airbus A.321-211	Aeroflot Russian International N. Pirogov	
VQ-BEE	Airbus A.321-211	Aeroflot Russian International I. Sechenov	
VQ-BEF	Airbus A.321-211	Aeroflot Russian International N. Zhukovsky	
VQ-BEG	Airbus A.321-211	Aeroflot Russian International K. Tsiolkovsky	
VQ-BEH	Airbus A.320-214	Aeroflot Russian International I. Pavlov	
VQ-BEI	Airbus A.321-211	Aeroflot Russian International S. Korolev	
VQ-BEJ	Airbus A.320-214	Aeroflot Russian International I. Kurchatov	
VQ-BEK	Airbus A.330-343	Aeroflot Russian International A. Tvardovsky	
VQ-BEL	Airbus A.330-343	Aeroflot Russian International F. Tyutchev	
VQ-BHK	Airbus A.321-211	Aeroflot Russian International M. Keldysh	
VQ-BHL	Airbus A.320-214	Aeroflot Russian International S. Vavilov	
VQ-BHM	Airbus A.321-211	Aeroflot Russian International N. Vavilov	
VQ-BHN	Airbus A.320-214	Aeroflot Russian International N. Lobachevsky	
VQ-BIR	Airbus A.320-214	Aeroflot Russian International S. Kovalevskaya	
VQ-BIT	Airbus A.320-214	Aeroflot Russian International L. Landau	
VQ-BIU	Airbus A.320-214	Aeroflot Russian International K. Timiryazev	
VQ-BIV	Airbus A.320-214	Aeroflot Russian International A. Kolmogorov	
VQ-BIW	Airbus A.320-214	Aeroflot Russian International V. Glushko	
VQ-BKS	Airbus A.320-214	Aeroflot Russian International A. Chizhevsky	
VQ-BKT	Airbus A.320-214	Aeroflot Russian International V. Vernadsky	
VQ-BKU	Airbus A.320-214	Aeroflot Russian International A. Nikolaev	
VQ-BMV	Airbus A.330-343	Aeroflot Russian International P. Kapitsa	
VQ-BMX	Airbus A.330-343	Aeroflot Russian International A. Sakharov	
VQ-BMY	Airbus A.330-343	Aeroflot Russian International Ilya Frank	
VQ-BNS	Airbus A.330-343	Aeroflot Russian International A. Bakulev	

Notes	Reg.	Type	Owner or Operator
	VQ-BOH	Airbus A.321-211	Aeroflot Russian International *A. Prokhorov*
	VQ-BOI	Airbus A.321-211	Aeroflot Russian International *N. Semenov*
	VQ-BPI	Airbus A.330-343	Aeroflot Russian International *L. Yashin*
	VQ-BPJ	Airbus A.330-343	Aeroflot Russian International *V.Brumel*
	VQ-BPK	Airbus A.330-343	Aeroflot Russian International *I.Kulibin*
	VQ-BPV	Airbus A.320-214	Aeroflot Russian International
	VQ-BPW	Airbus A.320-214	Aeroflot Russian International
	VQ-BQX	Airbus A.330-343	Aeroflot Russian International *O. Mandelshtam*
	VQ-BQY	Airbus A.330-343X	Aeroflot Russian International *M. Sholohov*
	VQ-BQZ	Airbus A.330-343	Aeroflot Russian International *N. Burdenko*
	VQ-BRV	Airbus A.320-214	Aeroflot Russian International

VT (India)

Notes	Reg.	Type	Owner or Operator
	VT-ALA	Boeing 777-237LR	Air-India *State of Andhra Pradesh*
	VT-ALB	Boeing 777-237LR	Air-India *Arunachal Pradesh*
	VT-ALC	Boeing 777-237LR	Air-India *State of Assam*
	VT-ALD	Boeing 777-237LR	Air-India *Gujarat*
	VT-ALE	Boeing 777-237LR	Air India *Haryana*
	VT-ALF	Boeing 777-237LR	Air India *Jharkhand*
	VT-ALG	Boeing 777-237LR	Air India *Kerala*
	VT-ALJ	Boeing 777-337ER	Air India *Bihar*
	VT-ALK	Boeing 777-337ER	Air India *Chattisgarh*
	VT-ALL	Boeing 777-337ER	Air-India *State of Assam*
	VT-ALM	Boeing 777-337ER	Air India *Himachel Pradesh*
	VT-ALN	Boeing 777-337ER	Air India *Jammu & Kashmir*
	VT-ALO	Boeing 777-337ER	Air India *Karnataka*
	VT-ALP	Boeing 777-337ER	Air India *Madhya Pradesh*
	VT-ALQ	Boeing 777-337ER	Air India *Manpur*
	VT-ALR	Boeing 777-337ER	Air India *Meghalaya*
	VT-ALS	Boeing 777-337ER	Air India *Mizoram*
	VT-ALT	Boeing 777-337ER	Air India *Nagaland*
	VT-ALU	Boeing 777-337ER	Air India *Orissa*
	VT-ALV	Boeing 777-337ER	Air India
	VT-ALW	Boeing 777-337ER	Air India
	VT-ALX	Boeing 777-337ER	Air India
	VT-ANA	Boeing 787-8	Air India
	VT-ANB	Boeing 787-8	Air India
	VT-AND	Boeing 787-8	Air India
	VT-ANE	Boeing 787-8	Air India
	VT-ANG	Boeing 787-8	Air India
	VT-ANH	Boeing 787-8	Air India
	VT-ANI	Boeing 787-8	Air India
	VT-ANJ	Boeing 787-8	Air India
	VT-ANK	Boeing 787-8	Air India
	VT-ANL	Boeing 787-8	Air India
	VT-ANM	Boeing 787-8	Air India
	VT-ANN	Boeing 787-8	Air India
	VT-ANO	Boeing 787-8	Air India
	VT-JEG	Boeing 777-35RER	Jet Airways
	VT-JEH	Boeing 777-35RER	Jet Airways
	VT-JEK	Boeing 777-35RER	Jet Airways
	VT-JEL	Boeing 777-35RER	Jet Airways
	VT-JEM	Boeing 777-35RER	Turkish Airlines
	VT-JEN	Boeing 777-35RER	Turkish Airlines
	VT-JEP	Boeing 777-35RER	Turkish Airlines
	VT-JEQ	Boeing 777-35RER	Jet Airways
	VT-JER	Boeing 777-35RER	Jet Airways
	VT-JWH	Airbus A.330-203	Jet Airways
	VT-JWL	Airbus A.330-203	Jet Airways
	VT-JWN	Airbus A.330-203	Jet Airways
	VT-JWP	Airbus A.330-203	Jet Airways
	VT-JWR	Airbus A.330-302	Jet Airways
	VT-JWS	Airbus A.330-302	Jet Airways
	VT-JWT	Airbus A.330-302	Jet Airways
	VT-JWU	Airbus A.330-302	Jet Airways

XA (Mexico)

Notes	Reg.	Type	Owner or Operator
	XA-FRJ	Boeing 767-283	Aeromexico

Reg.	Type	Owner or Operator	Notes
XA-JBC	Boeing 767-284	Aeromexico	
XA-OAM	Boeing 767-2B1	Aeromexico	

YI (Iraq)

YI-AGR	Airbus A.321-231	Iraqi Airways	
YI-AGS	Airbus A.321-231	Iraqi Airways	
YI-AQY	Airbus A.330-202	Iraqi Airways	

YL (Latvia)

YL-BBD	Boeing 737-53S	Air Baltic	
YL-BBE	Boeing 737-53S	Air Baltic	
YL-BBI	Boeing 737-33A	Air Baltic	
YL-BBJ	Boeing 737-36Q	Air Baltic	
YL-BBL	Boeing 737-33V	Air Baltic	
YL-BBM	Boeing 737-522	Air Baltic	
YL-BBN	Boeing 737-522	Air Baltic	
YL-BBO	Boeing 737-33V	Air Baltic	
YL-BBQ	Boeing 737-522	Air Baltic	
YL-BBR	Boeing 737-31S	Air Baltic	
YL-BBS	Boeing 737-31S	Air Baltic	
YL-BBX	Boeing 737-36Q	Air Baltic	
YL-BBY	Boeing 737-36Q	Air Baltic	

YR (Romania

YR-ASA	Airbus A.318-111	Tarom	
YR-ASB	Airbus A.318-111	Tarom	
YR-ASC	Airbus A.318-111	Tarom	
YR-ASD	Airbus A.318-111	Tarom	
YR-BAE	Boeing 737-46N	Blue Air	
YR-BAF	Boeing 737-322	Blue Air	
YR-BAG	Boeing 737-5L9	Blue Air	
YR-BAJ	Boeing 737-430	Blue Air	
YR-BAK	Boeing 737-430	Blue Air	
YR-BAO	Boeing 737-42C	Blue Air	
YR-BAR	Boeing 737-4Q8	Blue Air	
YR-BAZ	Boeing 737-405	Blue Air	
YR-BBA	Boeing 737-36M	Carpatair	
YR-BGA	Boeing 737-38J	Tarom *Alba Iulia*	
YR-BGB	Boeing 737-38J	Tarom *Bucuresti*	
YR-BGD	Boeing 737-38J	Tarom *Deva*	
YR-BGE	Boeing 737-38J	Tarom *Timisoara*	
YR-BGF	Boeing 737-78J	Tarom *Braila*	
YR-BGG	Boeing 737-78J	Tarom *Craiova*	
YR-BGH	Boeing 737-78J	Tarom *Hunedoara*	
YR-BGI	Boeing 737-78J	Tarom *Iasi*	
YR-BGS	Boeing 737-8GJ	Tarom	
YR-LCA	Airbus A.310-325	Tarom	
YR-TIB	Boeing 737-3L9	Air Bucharest	

YU (Serbia and Montenegro)

YU-ANI	Boeing 737-3H9	Air Serbia	
YU-ANJ	Boeing 737-3H9	Air Serbia	
YU-ANK	Boeing 737-3H9	Air Serbia	
YU-ANL	Boeing 737-3H9	Air Serbia	
YU-ANV	Boeing 737-3H9	Air Serbia	
YU-AON	Boeing 737-3Q4	Air Serbia	
YU-AOU	Boeing 737-322	Air Serbia	
YU-AOV	Boeing 737-341	Air Serbia	
YU-APB	Airbus A.319-132	Air Serbia	
YU-APC	Airbus A.319-131	Air Serbia	
YU-APE	Airbus A.319-132	Air Serbia	

Notes	Reg.	Type	Owner or Operator

ZK (New Zealand)

ZK-OKA	Boeing 777-219ER	Air New Zealand
ZK-OKB	Boeing 777-219ER	Air New Zealand
ZK-OKC	Boeing 777-219ER	Air New Zealand
ZK-OKD	Boeing 777-219ER	Air New Zealand
ZK-OKE	Boeing 777-219ER	Air New Zealand
ZK-OKF	Boeing 777-219ER	Air New Zealand
ZK-OKG	Boeing 777-219ER	Air New Zealand
ZK-OKH	Boeing 777-219ER	Air New Zealand
ZK-OKM	Boeing 777-319ER	Air New Zealand
ZK-OKN	Boeing 777-319ER	Air New Zealand
ZK-OKO	Boeing 777-319ER	Air New Zealand
ZK-OKP	Boeing 777-319ER	Air New Zealand
ZK-OKQ	Boeing 777-319ER	Air New Zealand

ZS (South Africa)

ZS-SLF	Airbus A.340-211	South African Airways
ZS-SNA	Airbus A.340-642	South African Airways
ZS-SNB	Airbus A.340-642	South African Airways
ZS-SNC	Airbus A.340-642	South African Airways
ZS-SND	Airbus A.340-642	South African Airways
ZS-SNE	Airbus A.340-642	South African Airways
ZS-SNF	Airbus A.340-642	South African Airways
ZS-SNG	Airbus A.340-642	South African Airways
ZS-SNH	Airbus A.340-642	South African Airways
ZS-SNI	Airbus A.340-642	South African Airways
ZS-SXA	Airbus A.340-313E	South African Airways
ZS-SXB	Airbus A.340-313E	South African Airways
ZS-SXC	Airbus A.340-313E	South African Airways
ZS-SXD	Airbus A.340-313E	South African Airways
ZS-SXE	Airbus A.340-313E	South African Airways
ZS-SXF	Airbus A.340-313E	South African Airways
ZS-SXG	Airbus A.340-313X	South African Airways
ZS-SXH	Airbus A.340-313X	South African Airways
ZS-SXU	Airbus A.330-243	South African Airways
ZS-SXV	Airbus A.330-243	South African Airways
ZS-SXW	Airbus A.330-243	South African Airways
ZS-SXX	Airbus A.330-243	South African Airways
ZS-SXY	Airbus A.330-243	South African Airways
ZS-SXZ	Airbus A.330-243	South African Airways

3B (Mauritius)

3B-NAU	Airbus A.340-312	Air Mauritius *Pink Pigeon*
3B-NAY	Airbus A.340-313X	Air Mauritius *Cardinal*
3B-NBD	Airbus A.340-313X	Air Mauritius *Parakeet*
3B-NBE	Airbus A.340-313X	Air Mauritius *Paille en Queue*
3B-NBI	Airbus A.340-313E	Air Mauritius *Le Flamboyant*
3B-NBJ	Airbus A.340-313E	Air Mauritius *Le Chamarel*

4K (Azerbaijan)

4K-AZ03	Airbus A.319-111	Azerbaijan Airlines
4K-AZ04	Airbus A.319-111	Azerbaijan Airlines
4K-AZ05	Airbus A.319-111	Azerbaijan Airlines
4K-AZ11	Boeing 757-22L	Azerbaijan Airlines
4K-AZ12	Boeing 757-22L	Azerbaijan Airlines
4K-AZ38	Boeing 757-256	Azerbaijan Airlines
4K-AZ43	Boeing 757-2M6	Azerbaijan Airlines
4K-AZ54	Airbus A.320-214	Azerbaijan Airlines
4K-AZ77	Airbus A.320-214	Azerbaijan Airlines
4K-AZ78	Airbus A.320-214	Azerbaijan Airlines
4K-AZ79	Airbus A.320-214	Azerbaijan Airlines
4K-AZ80	Airbus A.320-214	Azerbaijan Airlines
4K-AZ81	Boeing 767-32LER	Azerbaijan Airlines
4K-AZ82	Boeing 767-32LER	Azerbaijan Airlines

Reg.	Type	Owner or Operator	Notes
4K-AZ83	Airbus A.320-214	Azerbaijan Airlines	
4K-AZ84	Airbus A.320-214	Azerbaijan Airlines	
4K-AZ85	Airbus A.340-542	Azerbaijan Airlines	
4K-AZ86	Airbus A.340-542	Azerbaijan Airlines	

4O (Montenegro)

4O-AOA	Embraer ERJ190-200LR	Montenegro Airlines	
4O-AOB	Embraer ERJ190-200LR	Montenegro Airlines	
4O-AOC	Embraer ERJ190-200LR	Montenegro Airlines	
4O-AOK	Fokker 100	Montenegro Airlines	
4O-AOM	Fokker 100	Montenegro Airlines	
4O-AOP	Fokker 100	Montenegro Airlines	
4O-AOT	Fokker 100	Montenegro Airlines	

4R (Sri Lanka)

4R-ADA	Airbus A.340-311	SriLankan Airlines	
4R-ADB	Airbus A.340-311	SriLankan Airlines	
4R-ADC	Airbus A.340-311	SriLankan Airlines	
4R-ADE	Airbus A.340-313X	SriLankan Airlines	
4R-ADF	Airbus A.340-313X	SriLankan Airlines	
4R-ADG	Airbus A.340-313X	SriLankan Airlines	
4R-ALA	Airbus A.330-243	SriLankan Airlines	
4R-ALB	Airbus A.330-243	SriLankan Airlines	
4R-ALC	Airbus A.330-243	SriLankan Airlines	
4R-ALD	Airbus A.330-243	SriLankan Airlines	
4R-ALG	Airbus A.330-243	SriLankan Airlines	
4R-ALH	Airbus A.330-243	SriLankan Airlines	
4R-ALJ	Airbus A.330-243	SriLankan Airlines	

4X (Israel)

4X-ABF	Airbus A.320-232	Israir	
4X-ABG	Airbus A.320-232	Israir	
4X-EAJ	Boeing 767-330ER	El Al	
4X-EAK	Boeing 767-3Q8ER	El Al	
4X-EAL	Boeing 767-33AER	El Al	
4X-EAM	Boeing 767-3Q8ER	El Al	
4X-EAP	Boeing 767-3Y0ER	El Al	
4X-EAR	Boeing 767-352ER	El Al	
4X-ECA	Boeing 777-258ER	El Al Galilee	
4X-ECB	Boeing 777-258ER	El Al Negev	
4X-ECC	Boeing 777-258ER	El Al Hasharon	
4X-ECD	Boeing 777-258ER	El Al Carmel	
4X-ECE	Boeing 777-258ER	El Al Sderot	
4X-ECF	Boeing 777-258ER	El Al Kiryat Shmona	
4X-EHA	Boeing 737-958ER	El Al	
4X-EHB	Boeing 737-958ER	El Al	
4X-EKA	Boeing 737-858	El Al Tiberias	
4X-EKB	Boeing 737-858	El Al Eilat	
4X-EKC	Boeing 737-858	El Al Beit Shean	
4X-EKD	Boeing 737-758	El Al Ashkelon	
4X-EKE	Boeing 737-758	El Al Nazareth	
4X-EKF	Boeing 737-858	El Al Kinneret	
4X-EKH	Boeing 737-85P	El Al Yarden	
4X-EKI	Boeing 737-86N	El Al	
4X-EKJ	Boeing 737-85P	El Al Degania	
4X-EKL	Boeing 737-85P	El Al Nahalal	
4X-EKM	Boeing 737-804	El Al	
4X-EKO	Boeing 737-86Q	El Al	
4X-EKP	Boeing 737-8Q8	El Al	
4X-EKR	Boeing 737-804	El Al	
4X-EKS	Boeing 737-8Q8	El Al Caesarea	
4X-EKT	Boeing 737-8BK	El Al	
4X-EKU	Boeing 737-8Z9	El Al	
4X-ELA	Boeing 747-458	El Al Tel Aviv-Jaffa	
4X-ELB	Boeing 747-458	El Al Haifa	
4X-ELC	Boeing 747-458	El Al Beer Sheva	

Notes	Reg.	Type	Owner or Operator
	4X-ELD	Boeing 747-458	El Al *Jerusalem*
	4X-ELE	Boeing 747-458	El Al *Rishon Letsion*
	4X-ELF	Boeing 747-412F	El Al Cargo
	4X-ELH	Boeing 747-412	El Al

5B (Cyprus)

	5B-DBB	Airbus A.320-231	Cyprus Airways *Akamas*
	5B-DCH	Airbus A.320-232	Cyprus Airways *Lefkosia*
	5B-DCJ	Airbus A.320-232	Cyprus Airways *Amathus*
	5B-DCK	Airbus A.320-232	Cyprus Airways *Pafos*
	5B-DCL	Airbus A.320-232	Cyprus Airways *Pentadaktylos*
	5B-DCM	Airbus A.320-232	Cyprus Airways *Troodos*

5N (Nigeria)

	5N-JIC	Airbus A.330-223	Arik Air
	5N-JID	Airbus A.330-223	Arik Air
	5N-MJN	Boeing 737-86N	Arik Air
	5N-MJO	Boeing 737-86N	Arik Air
	5N-MJP	Boeing 737-8JE	Arik Air
	5N-MJQ	Boeing 737-8JE	Arik Air

5Y (Kenya)

	5Y-KQS	Boeing 777-2U8ER	Kenya Airways
	5Y-KQT	Boeing 777-2U8ER	Kenya Airways
	5Y-KQU	Boeing 777-2U8ER	Kenya Airways
	5Y-KQX	Boeing 767-36NER	Kenya Airways
	5Y-KQZ	Boeing 767-36NER	Kenya Airways
	5Y-KYV	Boeing 767-3Q8ER	Kenya Airways
	5Y-KYW	Boeing 767-319ER	Kenya Airways
	5Y-KYX	Boeing 767-3P6ER	Kenya Airways
	5Y-KYZ	Boeing 777-2U8ER	Kenya Airways
	5Y-KZZ	Boeing 777-36NER	Kenya Airways

7T (Algeria)

	7T-VJG	Boeing 767-3D6ER	Air Algerie
	7T-VJH	Boeing 767-3D6ER	Air Algerie
	7T-VJI	Boeing 767-3D6ER	Air Algerie
	7T-VJJ	Boeing 737-8D6	Air Algerie *Jugurtha*
	7T-VJK	Boeing 737-8D6	Air Algerie *Mansourah*
	7T-VJL	Boeing 737-8D6	Air Algerie *Illizi*
	7T-VJM	Boeing 737-8D6	Air Algerie
	7T-VJN	Boeing 737-8D6	Air Algerie
	7T-VJO	Boeing 737-8D6	Air Algerie
	7T-VJP	Boeing 737-8D6	Air Algerie
	7T-VJQ	Boeing 737-6D6	Air Algerie *Kasbah d'Alger*
	7T-VJR	Boeing 737-6D6	Air Algerie
	7T-VJS	Boeing 737-6D6	Air Algerie
	7T-VJT	Boeing 737-6D6	Air Algerie
	7T-VJU	Boeing 737-6D6	Air Algerie
	7T-VJV	Airbus A.330-202	Air Algerie *Tinhinan*
	7T-VJW	Airbus A.330-202	Air Algerie *Lalla Setti*
	7T-VJX	Airbus A.330-202	Air Algerie *Mers el Kebir*
	7T-VJY	Airbus A.330-202	Air Algerie *Monts des Beni Chougrane*
	7T-VJZ	Airbus A.330-202	Air Algerie *Teddis*
	7T-VKA	Boeing 737-8D6	Air Algerie
	7T-VKB	Boeing 737-8D6	Air Algerie
	7T-VKC	Boeing 737-8D6	Air Algerie
	7T-VKD	Boeing 737-8D6	Air Algerie
	7T-VKE	Boeing 737-8D6	Air Algerie
	7T-VKF	Boeing 737-8D6	Air Algerie
	7T-VKG	Boeing 737-8D6	Air Algerie
	7T-VKH	Boeing 737-8D6	Air Algerie
	7T-VKI	Boeing 737-8D6	Air Algerie

Reg.	Type	Owner or Operator	Notes
7T-VKJ	Boeing 737-8D6	Air Algerie	

9A (Croatia)

9A-CTF	Airbus A.320-211	Croatia Airlines/Syphax Airlines	
9A-CTG	Airbus A.319-112	Croatia Airlines *Zadar*	
9A-CTH	Airbus A.319-112	Croatia Airlines *Zagreb*	
9A-CTI	Airbus A.319-112	Croatia Airlines *Vukovar*	
9A-CTJ	Airbus A.320-214	Croatia Airlines *Dubrovnik*	
9A-CTK	Airbus A.320-214	Croatia Airlines *Split*	
9A-CTL	Airbus A.319-112	Croatia Airlines *Pula*	

9H (Malta)

9H-AEF	Airbus A.320-214	Air Malta	
9H-AEG	Airbus A.319-112	Air Malta	
9H-AEH	Airbus A.319-111	Air Malta *Floriana*	
9H-AEK	Airbus A.320-214	Air Malta *San Giljan*	
9H-AEL	Airbus A.319-111	Air Malta *Marsaxlokk*	
9H-AEM	Airbus A.319-111	Air Malta *Birgu*	
9H-AEN	Airbus A.320-214	Air Malta	
9H-AEO	Airbus A.320-214	Air Malta	
9H-AEP	Airbus A.320-214	Air Malta	
9H-AEQ	Airbus A.320-214	Air Malta	

9K (Kuwait)

9K-ADE	Boeing 747-469 (SCD)	Kuwait Airways *Al-Jabariya*	
9K-AMA	Airbus A.300B4-605R	Kuwait Airways *Failaka*	
9K-AMB	Airbus A.300B4-605R	Kuwait Airways *Burghan*	
9K-AMC	Airbus A.300B4-605R	Kuwait Airways *Wafra*	
9K-AMD	Airbus A.300B4-605R	Kuwait Airways *Wara*	
9K-AME	Airbus A.300B4-605R	Kuwait Airways *Al-Rawdhatain*	
9K-ANA	Airbus A.340-313	Kuwait Airways *Warba*	
9K-ANB	Airbus A.340-313	Kuwait Airways *Bayan*	
9K-ANC	Airbus A.340-313	Kuwait Airways *Meskan*	
9K-AND	Airbus A.340-313	Kuwait Airways *Al-Riggah*	
9K-AOA	Boeing 777-269ER	Kuwait Airways *Al-Grain*	
9K-AOB	Boeing 777-269ER	Kuwait Airways *Garouh*	

9M (Malaysia)

9M-MNA	Airbus A.380-841	Malaysian Airlines	
9M-MNB	Airbus A.380-841	Malaysian Airlines	
9M-MNC	Airbus A.380-841	Malaysian Airlines	
9M-MND	Airbus A.380-841	Malaysian Airlines	
9M-MNE	Airbus A.380-841	Malaysian Airlines	
9M-MNF	Airbus A.380-841	Malaysian Airlines	
9M-MPR	Boeing 747-4H6F	Malaysian Airlines Cargo	
9M-MPS	Boeing 747-4H6F	Malaysian Airlines Cargo	
9M-MRA	Boeing 777-2H6ER	Malaysian Airlines	
9M-MRB	Boeing 777-2H6ER	Malaysian Airlines	
9M-MRC	Boeing 777-2H6ER	Malaysian Airlines	
9M-MRD	Boeing 777-2H6ER	Malaysian Airlines	
9M-MRE	Boeing 777-2H6ER	Malaysian Airlines	
9M-MRF	Boeing 777-2H6ER	Malaysian Airlines	
9M-MRG	Boeing 777-2H6ER	Malaysian Airlines	
9M-MRH	Boeing 777-2H6ER	Malaysian Airlines	
9M-MRJ	Boeing 777-2H6ER	Malaysian Airlines	
9M-MRL	Boeing 777-2H6ER	Malaysian Airlines	
9M-MRM	Boeing 777-2H6ER	Malaysian Airlines	
9M-MRN	Boeing 777-2H6ER	Malaysian Airlines	
9M-MRO	Boeing 777-2H6ER	Malaysian Airlines	
9M-MRP	Boeing 777-2H6ER	Malaysian Airlines	
9M-MRQ	Boeing 777-2H6ER	Malaysian Airlines	

Notes	Reg.	Type	Owner or Operator

9V (Singapore)

9V-SFD	Boeing 747-412F	Singapore Airlines Cargo
9V-SFF	Boeing 747-412F	Singapore Airlines Cargo
9V-SFG	Boeing 747-412F	Singapore Airlines Cargo
9V-SFK	Boeing 747-412F	Singapore Airlines Cargo
9V-SFM	Boeing 747-412F	Singapore Airlines Cargo
9V-SFN	Boeing 747-412F	Singapore Airlines Cargo
9V-SFO	Boeing 747-412F	Singapore Airlines Cargo
9V-SFP	Boeing 747-412F	Singapore Airlines Cargo
9V-SFQ	Boeing 747-412F	Singapore Airlines Cargo
9V-SKA	Airbus A.380-841	Singapore Airlines
9V-SKB	Airbus A.380-841	Singapore Airlines
9V-SKC	Airbus A.380-841	Singapore Airlines
9V-SKD	Airbus A.380-841	Singapore Airlines
9V-SKE	Airbus A.380-841	Singapore Airlines
9V-SKF	Airbus A.380-841	Singapore Airlines
9V-SKG	Airbus A.380-841	Singapore Airlines
9V-SKH	Airbus A.380-841	Singapore Airlines
9V-SKI	Airbus A.380-841	Singapore Airlines
9V-SKJ	Airbus A.380-841	Singapore Airlines
9V-SKK	Airbus A.380-841	Singapore Airlines
9V-SKL	Airbus A.380-841	Singapore Airlines
9V-SKM	Airbus A.380-841	Singapore Airlines
9V-SKN	Airbus A.380-841	Singapore Airlines
9V-SKP	Airbus A.380-841	Singapore Airlines
9V-SKQ	Airbus A.380-841	Singapore Airlines
9V-SKR	Airbus A.380-841	Singapore Airlines
9V-SKS	Airbus A.380-841	Singapore Airlines
9V-SKT	Airbus A.380-841	Singapore Airlines
9V-SWA	Boeing 777-312ER	Singapore Airlines
9V-SWB	Boeing 777-312ER	Singapore Airlines
9V-SWD	Boeing 777-312ER	Singapore Airlines
9V-SWE	Boeing 777-312ER	Singapore Airlines
9V-SWF	Boeing 777-312ER	Singapore Airlines
9V-SWG	Boeing 777-312ER	Singapore Airlines
9V-SWH	Boeing 777-312ER	Singapore Airlines
9V-SWI	Boeing 777-312ER	Singapore Airlines
9V-SWJ	Boeing 777-312ER	Singapore Airlines
9V-SWK	Boeing 777-312ER	Singapore Airlines
9V-SWL	Boeing 777-312ER	Singapore Airlines
9V-SWM	Boeing 777-312ER	Singapore Airlines
9V-SWN	Boeing 777-312ER	Singapore Airlines
9V-SWO	Boeing 777-312ER	Singapore Airlines
9V-SWP	Boeing 777-312ER	Singapore Airlines
9V-SWQ	Boeing 777-312ER	Singapore Airlines
9V-SWR	Boeing 777-312ER	Singapore Airlines
9V-SWS	Boeing 777-312ER	Singapore Airlines
9V-SWT	Boeing 777-312ER	Singapore Airlines
9V-SWU	Boeing 777-312ER	Singapore Airlines
9V-SWV	Boeing 777-312ER	Singapore Airlines

9Y (Trinidad and Tobago)

9Y-LGW	Boeing 767-316ER	Caribbean Airlines
9Y-LHR	Boeing 767-316ER	Caribbean Airlines

A6-EYR A330-243 of Etihad Airways. *Allan S. Wright*

D-AHHC Airbus A.320-214 of Hamburg Airways. *Tom Cole*

D-ALCC McD Douglas MD-11F of Lufthansa Cargo. *Allan S. Wright*

EC-LYE Airbus A.320-216 of Iberia Express. *Allan S. Wright*

LY-FLH Boeing 737-382 of Small Planet Airlines. *Allan S. Wright*

N850GT Boeing 747-87UF of Panalpina World Transport. *Allan S. Wright*

OE-LFP Fokker 70 of Austrian Airlines. *Allan S. Wright*

OY-KFC Canadair CRJ900ER of SAS. *Allan S. Wright*

SP-LID Embraer ERJ 170-200STD of LOT. *Peter R. March*

TC-OBU Airbus A.320-231 of Onur Air. *Allan S. Wright*

Radio Frequencies

The frequencies used by the larger airfields/airports are listed below. Abbreviations used: TWR – Tower, APP – Approach, A/G – Air-Ground advisory. It is possible that changes will be made from time to time with the frequencies allocated, all of which are quoted in Megahertz (MHz).

Airfield	TWR	APP	A/G
Aberdeen	118.1	119.05	
Alderney	125.35	128.65	
Andrewsfield			130.55
Barton			120.25
Barrow			123.2
Beccles			120.375
Belfast International	118.3	128.5	
Belfast City	130.75	130.85	
Bembridge			123.25
Biggin Hill	134.8	129.4	
Birmingham	118.3	118.05	
Blackbushe			122.3
Blackpool	118.4	119.95	
Bodmin			122.7
Bourn			124.35
Bournemouth	125.6	119.475	
Breighton			129.80
Bristol/Filton	132.35	122.725	
Bristol/Lulsgate	133.85	127.25	
Bruntingthorpe			122.825
Caernarfon			122.25
Cambridge	122.2	123.6	
Cardiff	125.0	126.625	
Carlisle	123.6		
Clacton			118.15
Compton Abbas			122.7
Conington			129.725
Cosford	128.65	135.875	
Coventry	124.8	119.25	
Cranfield	134.925	122.85	
Cumbernauld	120.6		
Denham			130.725
Doncaster RHA	128.775	126.225	
Dundee	122.9		
Dunkeswell			123.475
Durham Tees Valley	119.8	118.85	
Duxford			122.075
Earls Colne			122.425
Edinburgh	118.7	121.2	
Elstree			122.4
Exeter	119.8	128.975	
Fairoaks			123.425
Farnborough	122.5	134.35	
Fenland			122.925
Fowlmere			135.7
Gamston			130.475
Gatwick	124.225	126.825	
Glasgow	118.8	119.1	
Gloucester/Staverton	122.9	128.55	
Goodwood			122.45
Guernsey	119.95	128.65	
Haverfordwest			122.2
Hawarden	124.95	123.35	
Henstridge			130.25
Headcorn			122.0
Heathrow	118.5	119.725	
Hethel			122.35
Hucknall			130.8
Humberside	124.9	119.125	
Inverness			122.6
Jersey	119.45	120.3	
Kemble			118.9
Land's End	120.25		
Lasham			125.25
Leeds Bradford	120.3	123.75	
Leicester			122.125
Liverpool	126.35	119.85	
London City	118.075	132.7	
Luton	132.55	129.55	
Lydd			120.7
Manchester	118.625	119.575	
Manston	119.925	126.35	
Netherthorpe			123.275
Newcastle	119.7	124.375	
Newquay	123.4	128.725	
North Denes			123.4
North Weald			123.525
Norwich	124.25	119.35	
Nottingham EMA	124.0	134.175	
Old Warden			130.7
Oxford	133.425	125.325	
Penzance			118.1
Perth	119.8		
Popham			129.8
Prestwick	118.15	120.55	
Redhill	119.6		
Rochester			122.25
Ronaldsway IOM	118.9	120.85	
Sandown			119.275
Sandtoft			130.425
Scilly Isles	123.825		
Seething			122.6
Sheffield City			128.525
Sherburn			122.6
Shipdham			132.25
Shobdon			123.5
Shoreham	125.4	123.15	
Sibson			122.3
Sleap			122.45
Southampton	118.2	128.85	
Southend	127.725	130.775	
Stansted	123.8	120.625	
Stapleford			122.8
Sumburgh	118.25	131.3	
Swansea			119.7
Sywell			122.7
Tatenhill			124.075
Thruxton			130.45
Tollerton			134.875
Wellesbourne			124.025
Welshpool			128.0
White Waltham			122.6
Wick			119.7
Wickenby			122.45
Wolverhampton			123.3
Woodford	120.7	130.75	
Woodvale	119.75	121.0	
Wycombe Air Park			126.55
Yeovil	125.4	130.8	

Airline Flight Codes

Those listed below identify many of the UK and overseas carriers appearing in the book

Code	Airline	Reg	Code	Airline	Reg	Code	Airline	Reg
AAF	Aigle Azur	F	CES	China Eastern	B	KAC	Kuwait Airways	9K
AAG	Atlantic Air Transport	G	CFG	Condor	D	KAL	Korean Air	HL
AAL	American Airlines	N	CKS	Kalitta Air	N	KBR	Koral Blue	AP
AAR	Asiana Airlines	HL	CLH	Lufthansa CityLine	D	KLC	KLM CityHopper	PH
ABD	Air Atlanta Icelandic	TF	CLX	Cargolux	LX	KLM	KLM	PH
ABQ	AirBlue	AP	CPA	Cathay Pacific	B	KQA	Kenya Airways	5Y
ABR	Air Contractors	EI	CRB	Air Astana	UN	KZR	Air Astana	UN
ACA	Air Canada	C	CRL	Corsair	F	KZU	Kuzu Airlines Cargo	TC
ADB	Antonov Airlines	UR	CSA	CSA Czech Airlines	OK	LBT	Nouvelair	TS
ADH	Air One	I	CTN	Croatia Airlines	9A	LDA	Lauda Air	OE
ADR	Adria Airways	S5	CUB	Cubana	CU	LGL	Luxair	LX
AEA	Air Europa	EC	CYP	Cyprus Airways	5B	LLC	Small Planet Airlines	LY
AEE	Aegean Airlines	SX	DAH	Air Algerie	7T	LOG	Loganair	G
AEY	Air Italy	I	DAL	Delta Air Lines	N	LOT	Polish Airlines (LOT)	SP
AFL	Aeroflot	RA	DHL	DHL Express	D/G/N	LSK	Aurela	LY
AFR	Air France	F	DLH	Lufthansa	D	LZB	Bulgaria Air	LZ
AHY	Azerbaijan Airlines	4K	DTR	Danish Air Transport	OY	MAH	Malev	HA
AIC	Air-India	VT	EDW	Edelweiss Air	HB	MAS	Malaysian Airlines	9M
AJA	Anadolujet	TC	EIN	Aer Lingus	EI	MAU	Air Mauritius	3B
AKL	Air Kilroe	G	ELL	Estonian Air	ES	MEA	Middle East Airlines	OD
ALK	SriLankan Airlines	4R	ELY	El Al	4X	MGX	Montenegro Airlines	4O
AMC	Air Malta	9H	ETD	Etihad Airways	A6	MLD	Air Moldova	ER
ANA	All Nippon Airways	JA	ETH	Ethiopian Airlines	ET	MMZ	Euro Atlantic Airways	CS
ANE	Air Nostrum	EC	EUK	Air Atlanta Europe	TF	MNB	MNG Airlines	TC
ANZ	Air New Zealand	ZK	EVA	EVA Airways	B	MON	Monarch Airlines	G
ARA	Arik Air	5N	EWG	Eurowings	D	MPH	Martinair	PH
AUA	Austrian Airlines	OE	EXS	Jet2	G	MSR	EgyptAir	SU
AUI	Ukraine International	UR	EZE	Eastern Airways	G	NAX	Norwegian Air Shuttle	LN
AUR	Aurigny A/S	G	EZS	easyJet Switzerland	HB	NCA	Nippon Cargo Airlines	JA
AWC	Titan Airways	G	EZY	easyJet	G	NEX	Northern Executive	G
AZA	Alitalia	I	FDX	Federal Express	N	NLY	Niki	OE
AZW	Air Zimbabwe	Z	FHE	Hello	HB	NMB	Air Namibia	V5
BAW	British Airways	G	FHY	Freebird Airlines	TC	NOA	Olympic Air	SX
BBC	Biman Bangladesh	S2	FIF	Air Finland	OH	NOS	Neos	I
BBD	Bluebird Cargo	TF	FIN	Finnair	OH	NPT	Atlantic Airlines	G
BCS	European A/T	OO	FLI	Atlantic Airways	OY	NVR	Novair Airlines	SE
BCY	CityJet	EI	GEC	Lufthansa Cargo	D	OAE	Omni Air International	N
BDI	BenAir A/S	OY	GFA	Gulf Air	A9C	OAS	Oman Air	A40
BEE	Flybe	G	GHA	Ghana Airways	9G	OAW	Helvetic Airways	HB
BEL	Brussels Airlines	OO	GMI	Germania	D	OBS	Orbest	CS
BER	Air Berlin	D	GTI	Atlas Air	N	OGE	Atlasjet	TC
BGA	Airbus Tpt International	F	GWI	Germanwings	D	OHY	Onur Air	TC
BGH	Balkan Holidays	LZ	GWL	Great Wall Airlines	B	PAC	Polar Air Cargo	N
BHP	Belair	HB	GXL	XL Airways Germany	D	PGT	Pegasus Airlines	TC
BID	Binair	D	HAY	Hamburg Airways	D	PIA	Pakistan International A/L	AP
BIE	Air Mediterranee	F	HCC	Holidays Czech Airlines	OK	PLK	Rossiya	RA
BIH	CHC Scotia	G	HFY	HiFly	CS	POT	Polet	RA
BLC	TAM Linhas Aereas	PT	HVN	Vietnam Airlines	VN	PRI	Primera Airlines	OY
BLF	Blue 1	OH	IBE	Iberia	EC	PTG	PrivatAir	D
BMR	bmi regional	G	ICB	Islandsflug	TF	PTI	PrivatAir	HB
BOS	Open Skies	F	ICE	Icelandair	TF	QFA	QANTAS	VH
BOX	AeroLogic	D	IOS	Isles of Scilly Skybus	G	QTR	Qatar Airways	A7
BPA	Blue Panorama	I	IRA	Iran Air	EP	RAE	Regional Airlines	F
BRT	BA Citiexpress	G	ISS	Meridianafly	I	RAM	Royal Air Maroc	CN
BRU	Belavia	EW	IWD	Orbest	EC	RBA	Royal Brunei Airlines	V8
BTI	Air Baltic	YL	IYE	Yemenia	7O	RCF	Aeroflot Cargo	RA
BUC	Bulgarian Air Charter	LZ	JAI	Jet Airways	VT	REA	Aer Arann	EI
BWA	Caribbean Airlines	9Y	JAL	Japan Airlines	JA	RJA	Royal Jordanian	JY
CAI	Corendon Airlines	TC	JAT	JAT Airways	YU	RNV	Armavia	EK
CAL	China Airlines	B	JOR	Blue Air	YR	ROT	Tarom	YR
CCA	Air China	B	JTG	Jet Time	OY	RYR	Ryanair	EI

RZO	SATA International	CS	TAP	TAP Portugal	CS	UAE	Emirates Airlines	A6
SAA	South African Airways	ZS	TAR	Tunis Air	TS	UBD	United Airways	S2
SAS	SAS	SE/ OY/ LN	TAY	TNT Airways	OO	UPS	United Parcel Service	N
SCW	Malmo Aviation	SE	TCW	Thomas Cook Belgium	OO	USA	US Airways	N
SDM	Rossiya	RA	TCX	Thomas Cook Airlines	G	UZB	Uzbekistan Airways	UK
SEY	Air Seychelles	S7	TFL	Arkefly	PH	VDA	Volga-Dnepr	RA
SVA	Singapore Airlines	9V	THA	Thai Airways International	HS	VIR	Virgin Atlantic	G
SLM	Surinam Airways	PZ	THY	Turkish Airlines	TC	VLG	Vueling	EC
SQC	Singapore Airlines Cargo	9V	TOM	Thomson Airways	G	VLM	VLM	OO
SRK	SkyWork Airlines	HB	TRA	Transavia	PH	WDL	WDL Aviation	D
SRR	Starair	OY	TSC	Air Transat	C	WIF	Wideroe's	LN
SUD	Sudan Airways	ST	TSO	Transaero	RA	WHT	White Airways	CS
SUS	Sun-Air	OY	TUA	Turkmenistan Airlines	EZ	WLX	West Air Europe	LX
SVA	Saudi Arabian Airlines	HZ	TUB	TUI Airlines Belgium	OO	WOA	World Airways	N
SVK	Air Slovakia	OM	TUI	TUIfly	D	WZZ	Wizz Air	HA/LZ
SWN	West Air Sweden	SE	TVF	Transavia France	F			
SWR	Swiss	HB	TVS	Travel Service/Smart Wings	OK	XL	XL Airways France	F
SXS	SunExpress	TC	TWI	Tailwind Airlines	TC			
SYR	Syrianair	YK	TYR	Austrian Arrows	OE			

4X-EKT Boeing 737-8BK of El Al. *Tom Cole*

British Aircraft Preservation Council Register

The British Aircraft Preservation Council was formed in 1967 to co-ordinate the works of all bodies involved in the preservation, restoration and display of historical aircraft. Membership covers the whole spectrum of national, Service, commercial and voluntary groups, and meetings are held regularly at the bases of member organisations. The Council is able to provide a means of communication, helping to resolve any misunderstandings or duplication of effort. Every effort is taken to encourage the raising of standards of both organisation and technical capacity amongst the member groups to the benefit of everyone interested in aviation. To assist historians, the B.A.P.C. register has been set up and provides an identity for those aircraft which do not qualify for a Service serial or inclusion in the UK Civil Register.

Aircraft on the current B.A.P.C. Register are as follows:

Reg.	Type	Owner or Operator	Notes
1	Roe Triplane Type 4 (replica)	Shuttleworth Collection as G-ARSG (not carried)	
2	Bristol Boxkite (replica)	Shuttleworth Collection as G-ASPP (not carried)	
3	Bleriot Type XI	Shuttleworth Collection as G-AANG (not carried)	
4	Deperdussin Monoplane	Shuttleworth Collection as G-AANH (not carried)	
5	Blackburn Monoplasne	Shuttleworth Collection as G-AANI (not carried)	
6	Roe Triplane Type IV (replica)	Manchester Museum of Science & Industry	
7	Southamton University MPA	Solent Sky, Southampton	
8	Dixon ornithopter	The Shuttleworth Collection	
9	Humber Monoplane (replica)	Midland Air Museum/Coventry	
10	Hafner R.II Revoplane	International Helicopter Museum/ Weston-Super-Mare	
11	English Electric Wren Composite	Shuttleworth Collection	
12	Mignet HM.14	Manchester Museum of Science and Industry	
13	Mignet HM.14	Brimpex Metal Treatments	
14	Addyman Standard Training Glider	A. Lindsay & N. H. Ponsford	
15	Addyman Standard Training Glider	The Aeroplane Collection	
16	Addyman ultra-light aircraft	N. H. Ponsford	
17	Woodhams Sprite	BB Aviation/Canterbury	
18	Killick MP Gyroplane	A. Lindsay & N. H. Ponsford	
19	Bristol F.2b Fighter	Musee Royal de l'Armee Brussels	
20	Lee-Richards annular biplane (replica)	Visitor Centre Shoreham Airport	
21	D.H.82A Tiger Moth	Newark Air Museum	
22	Mignet HM.14 (G-AEOF)	Aviodome/Netherlands	
23	SE-5A Scale Model	Newark Air Museum	
24	Currie Wot (replica)	Newark Air Museum	
25	Nyborg TGN-III glider	Warwick	
28	Wright Flyer (replica)	Yorkshire Air Museum Elvington	
29	Mignet HM.14 (replica) (G-ADRY)	Brooklands Museum of Aviation/Weybridge	
32	Crossley Tom Thumb	Midland Air Museum	
33	DFS.108-49 Grunau Baby IIb	Denmark	
34	DFS.108-49 Grunau Baby IIb	D. Elsdon	
35	EoN primary glider	–	
36	Fieseler Fi 103 (V-1) (replica)	Kent Battle of Britain Museum/Hawkinge	
37	Blake Bluetit (G-BXIY)	The Shuttleworth Collection/Old Warden	
38	Bristol Scout replica (A1742)	Shuttleworth Trust	
39	Addyman Zephyr sailplane	A. Lindsay & N. H. Ponsford	
40	Bristol Boxkite (replica)	Bristol City Museum	
41	B.E.2C (replica) (6232)	Yorkshire Air Museum/Elvington	
42	Avro 504 (replica) (H1968)	Yorkshire Air Museum/Elvington	
43	Mignet HM.14	Newark Air Museum/Winthorpe	
44	Miles Magister (L6906)	Museum of Berkshire Aviation (G-AKKY)/ Woodley	
45	Pilcher Hawk (replica)	Percy Pilcher Museum Rugby	
47	Watkins Monoplane	National Waterfront Museum Swansea	
48	Pilcher Hawk (replica)	Glasgow Museum of Transport	
49	Pilcher Hawk	Royal Scottish Museum/East Fortune	
50	Roe Triplane Type 1	Science Museum/South Kensington	
51	Vickers Vimy IV	Science Museum/South Kensington	
52	Lilienthal glider	National Museum of Science and Industry/Wroughton	
53	Wright Flyer (replica)	Science Museum/South Kensington	
54	JAP-Harding monoplane	Science Museum/South Kensington	

Notes	Reg.	Type	Owner or Operator
	55	Levavasseur Antoinette VII	Science Museum/South Kensington
	56	Fokker E.III (210/16)	Science Museum/South Kensington
	57	Pilcher Hawk (replica)	Duxford
	58	Yokosuka MXY7 Ohka II (15-1585)	F.A.A. Museum/Yeovilton
	59	Sopwith Camel (replica) (D3419)	East Fortune
	60	Murray M.1 helicopter	International Helicopter Museum/ Weston-super-Mare
	61	Stewart man-powered ornithopter	Boston Lincolnshire
	62	Cody Biplane (304)	Science Museum/South Kensington
	63	Hurricane (replica) (P3208)	Kent Battle of Britain Museum/Hawkinge
	64	Hurricane (replica) (P3059)	Kent Battle of Britain Museum/Hawkinge
	65	Spitfire (replica) (N3289)	Kent Battle of Britain Museum/Hawkinge
	66	Bf 109 (replica) (1480)	Kent Battle of Britain Museum/Hawkinge
	67	Bf 109 (replica) (14)	Kent Battle of Britain Museum/Hawkinge
	68	Hurricane (replica) (H3426)	-
	69	Spitfire (replica) (N3313)	Kent Battle of Britain Museum/Hawkinge
	70	Auster AOP.5 (TJ398)	North East Aircraft Museum/Usworth
	71	Spitfire (replica) (P8140)	Norfolk & Suffolk Aviation Museum
	72	Hurricane (model) (V6779)	Gloucestershire Aviation Collection
	73	Hurricane (replica)	New Zealand
	74	Bf 109 (replica) (6357)	Kent Battle of Britain Museum/Hawkinge
	75	Mignet HM.14 (G-AEFG)	N. H. Ponsford
	76	Mignet HM.14 (G-AFFI)	Yorkshire Air Museum/Elvington
	77	Mignet HM.14 (replica) (G-ADRG)	Lower Stondon Transport Museum
	78	Hawker Hind (K5414) (G-AENP)	The Shuttleworth Collection/Old Warden
	79	Fiat G.46-4B (MM53211)	Norfolk
	80	Airspeed Horsa (KJ351)	Museum of Army Flying/Middle Wallop
	81	Hawkridge Dagling	stored Bedford
	82	Hawker Hind (Afghan)	RAF Museum/Cosford
	83	Kawasaki Ki-100-1b (24)	RAF Museum/Hendon
	84	Nakajima Ki-46 (Dinah III)(5439)	RAF Museum/Hendon
	85	Weir W-2 autogyro	Museum of Flight/East Fortune
	86	de Havilland Tiger Moth (replica)	Yorkshire Aircraft Preservation Society
	87	Bristol Babe (replica) (G-EASQ)	Bristol Aero Collection/Kemble
	88	Fokker Dr 1 (replica) (102/17)	F.A.A. Museum/Yeovilton
	89	Cayley glider (replica)	Yorkshire Air Museum/Elvington
	90	Colditz Cock (replica)	Imperial War Museum/South Lambeth
	91	Fieseler Fi 103 (V-1)	Germany
	92	Fieseler Fi 103 (V-1)	RAF Museum/Hendon
	93	Fieseler Fi 103 (V-1)	Imperial War Museum/Duxford
	94	Fieseler Fi 103 (V-1)	RAF Museum/Cosford
	95	Gizmer autogyro	F. Fewsdale
	96	Brown helicopter	North East Aircraft Museum
	97	Luton L.A.4A Minor	North East Aircraft Museum
	98	Yokosuka MXY7 Ohka II (997)	Manchester Museum of Science & Industry
	99	Yokosuka MXY7 Ohka II (8486M)	RAF Museum/Cosford
	100	Clarke Chanute biplane gliderr	RAF Museum/Hendon
	101	Mignet HM.14	Newark Air Museum/Winthorpe
	102	Mignet HM.14	Not completed
	103	Hulton hang glider (replica)	Personal Plane Services Ltd
	105	Blériot XI (replica)	San Diego Aerospace Museum
	106	Blériot XI (164)	RAF Museum/Hendon
	107	Blériot XXVII	RAF Museum/Hendon
	108	Fairey Swordfish IV (HS503)	Stafford
	109	Slingsby Kirby Cadet TX.1	-
	110	Fokker D.VII replica (static) (5125)	USA
	111	Sopwith Triplane replica (static) (N5492)	F.A.A. Museum/Yeovilton
	112	DH.2 replica (static) (5964)	Museum of Army Flying/Middle Wallop
	113	S.E.5A replica (static) (B4863)	Orlando Florida
	114	Vickers Type 60 Viking (static) (G-EBED)	Brooklands Museum of Aviation/Weybridge
	115	Mignet HM.14	Norfolk & Suffolk Aviation Museum/Flixton
	116	Santos-Dumont Demoiselle (replica)	-
	117	B.E.2C (replica)(1701)	Stored Hawkinge
	119	Bensen B.7	North East Aircraft Museum

Reg.	Type	Owner or Operator	Notes
120	Mignet HM.14 (G-AEJZ)	South Yorkshire Aviation Museum/Doncaster	
121	Mignet HM.14 (G-AEKR)	South Yorkshire Aviation Society	
122	Avro 504 (replica) (1881)	Stored	
123	Vickers FB.5 Gunbus (replica)	A. Topen (stored)/Cranfield	
124	Lilienthal Glider Type XI (replica)	Science Museum/South Kensington	
126	D.31 Turbulent (static)	Midland Air Museum/Coventry	
127	Halton Jupiter MPA	Wannock Eastbourne	
128	Watkinson Cyclogyroplane Mk IV	IHM/Weston-super-Mare	
129	Blackburn 1911 Monoplane (replica)	-	
130	Blackburn 1912 Monoplane (replica)	Yorkshire Air Museum/Elvington	
131	Pilcher Hawk (replica)	C. Paton	
132	Blériot XI (G-BLXI)	Montelimar France	
133	Fokker Dr 1 (replica) (425/17)	Kent Battle of Britain Museum/Hawkinge	
134	Pitts S-2A static (G-AXNZ)	Istanbul Turkey	
135	Bristol M.1C (replica) (C4912)	Stored	
136	Deperdussin Seaplane (replica)	Planes of Fame Musem Chino/USA	
137	Sopwith Baby Floatplane (replica) (8151)	Stored	
138	Hansa Brandenburg W.29 Floatplane (replica) (2292)	Stored	
139	Fokker Dr 1 (replica) 150/17	Orlando Florida	
140	Curtiss 42A (replica)	Planes of Fame Museum Chino USA	
141	Macchi M39 (replica)	Planes of Fame Museum Chino USA	
142	SE-5A (replica) (F5459)	Switzerland	
143	Paxton MPA	-	
144	Weybridge Mercury MPA	-	
145	Oliver MPA	Stored	
146	Pedal Aeronauts Toucan MPA	Stored	
147	Bensen B.7	Norfolk & Suffolk Aviation Museum/Flixton	
148	Hawker Fury II (replica) (K7271)	High Ercall Aviation Museum	
149	Short S.27 (replica)	F.A.A. Museum (stored)/Yeovilton	
150	SEPECAT Jaguar GR.1 (replica) (XX728)	Oman	
151	SEPECAT Jaguar GR.1 (replica) (XZ363)	RAF M & R Unit/St. Athan	
152	BAe Hawk T.1 (replica) (XX227)	RAF M & R Unit/Bottesford	
153	Westland WG.33	IHM/Weston-super-Mare	
154	D.31 Turbulent	Lincolnshire Aviation Museum/E. Kirkby	
155	Panavia Tornado GR.1 (model) (ZA556)	RAF M & R Unit/St. Athan	
156	Supermarine S-6B (replica)	Planes of Fame Museum Chino/USA	
157	Waco CG-4A(237123)	Yorkshire Air Museum/Elvington	
158	Fieseler Fi 103 (V-1)	Defence Ordnance Disposal School/Chattenden	
159	Yokosuka MXY7 Ohka II	Imperial War Museum/Duxford	
160	Chargus 18/50 hang glider	Museum of Flight/East Fortune	
161	Stewart Ornithopter Coppelia	stored Louth	
162	Goodhart MPA	Science Museum/Wroughton	
163	AFEE 10/42 Rotabuggy (replica)	Museum of Army Flying/Middle Wallop	
164	Wight Quadruplane Type 1 (replica)	Solent Sky, Southampton	
165	Bristol F.2b (E2466)	RAF Museum/Hendon	
166	Bristol F.2b (D7889)	Canada	
167	Bristol SE-5A	USA	
168	DH.60G Moth (static replica)	Stored Hawkinge (G-AAAH)	
169	BAC/Sepecat Jaguar GR.1 (XX110)	RAF Training School/Cosford	
170	Pilcher Hawk (replica)	-	
171	BAe Hawk T.1 (model) (XX308)	RAF Marketing & Recruitment Unit/Bottesford	
172	Chargus Midas Super 8 hang glider	Science Museum/Wroughton	
173	Birdman Promotions Grasshopper	Science Museum/Wroughton	
174	Bensen B.7	Science Museum/Wroughton	
175	Volmer VJ-23 Swingwing	Manchester Museum of Science & Industry	
176	SE-5A (replica) (A4850)	Bygone Times Antiques Warehouse/Eccleston	
177	Avro 504K (replica) (G-AACA)	Brooklands Museum of Aviation/Weybridge	
178	Avro 504K (replica) (E373)	-	
179	Sopwith Pup (replica) (A7317)	Sywell	
180	McCurdy Silver Dart (replica)	Reynolds Pioneer Museum/Canada	
181	RAF B.E.2b (replica) (687)	RAF Museum/Hendon	

Notes	Reg.	Type	Owner or Operator
	182	Wood Ornithopter	Manchester Museum of Science & Industry
	183	Zurowski ZP.1 helicopter	Newark Air Museum/Winthorpe
	184	Spitfire IX (replica) (EN398)	Sleap
	185	Waco CG-4A (243809)	Museum of Army Flying/Middle Wallop
	186	DH.82B Queen Bee (LF789)	de Havilland Aircraft Heritage Museum/ London Colney
	187	Roe Type 1 biplane (replica)	Brooklands Museum of Aviation/Weybridge
	188	McBroom Cobra 88	Science Museum/Wroughton
	189	Bleriot XI (replica)	Stored
	190	Spitfire (replica) (K5054)	P. Smith/Hawkinge
	191	BAe Harrier GR.7 (model) (ZH139)	RAF M & R Unit/St. Athan
	192	Weedhopper JC-24	The Aeroplane Collection
	193	Hovey WD-11 Whing Ding	The Aeroplane Collection
	194	Santos Dumont Demoiselle (replica)	Deutches Technikmuseum/Berlin
	195	Moonraker 77 hang glider	Museum of Flight/East Fortune
	196	Sigma 2M hang glider	Museum of Flight/East Fortune
	197	Scotkites Cirrus III hang glider	Museum of Flight/East Fortune
	198	Fieseler Fi 103 (V-1)	Imperial War Museum/Duxford
	199	Fieseler Fi 103 (V-1)	Science Museum/South Kensington
	200	Bensen B.7	stored Leeds
	201	Mignet HM.14	stored Hooton Park
	202	Spitfire V (model) (MAV467)	-
	203	Chrislea LC.1 Airguard (G-AFIN)	stored Dunkeswell
	204	McBroom hang glider	stored Hooton Park
	205	Hurricane (replica) (Z3427)	RAF Museum/Hendon
	206	Spitfire (replica) (MH486)	RAF Museum/Hendon
	207	Austin Whippet (replica) (K.158)	South Yorkshire Aviation Museum/Doncaster
	208	SE-5A (replica) (D276)	Prince's Mead Shopping Precinct/Farnborough
	209	Spitfire IX (replica) (MJ751)	Niagara Falls Canada
	210	Avro 504J (replica) (C4451)	Solent Sky, Southampton
	211	Mignet HM.14 (replica) (G-ADVU)	North East Aircraft Museum
	212	Bensen B.8	IHM/Weston-super-Mare
	213	Vertigo MPA	IHM/Weston-super-Mare
	214	Spitfire prototype (replica) (K5054)	Tangmere Military Aviation Museum
	215	Airwave hang-glider prototype	Solent Sky, Southampton
	216	DH.88 Comet (replica) (G-ACSS)	de Havilland Heritage Museum/London Colney
	217	Spitfire (replica) (K9926)	RAF Museum/Bentley Priory
	218	Hurricane (replica) (P3386)	RAF Museum/Bentley Priory
	219	Hurricane (replica) (L1710)	Northolt
	220	Spitfire 1 (replica) (N3194)	Shirleywich
	221	Spitfire LF.IX (replica) (MH777)	RAF Museum/Northolt
	222	Spitfire IX (replica) (BR600)	RAF Museum/Uxbridge
	223	Hurricane 1 (replica) (V7467)	RAF High Wycombe
	224	Spitfire V (replica) (BR600)	National Air Force Museum Trenton Canada
	225	Spitfire IX (replica) (P8448)	RAF Museum/Cranwell
	226	Spitfire XI (replica) (EN343)	RAF Museum/Benson
	227	Spitfire 1A (replica) (L1070)	RAF Museum/Turnhouse
	228	Olympus hang-glider	North East Aircraft Museum/Usworth
	229	Spitfire IX (replica) (MJ832)	RAF Museum/Digby
	230	Spitfire (replica) (AA550)	Eden Camp/Malton
	231	Mignet HM.14 (G-ADRX)	South Copeland Aviation Group
	232	AS.58 Horsa I/II	de Havilland Heritage Museum/London Colney
	233	Broburn Wanderlust sailplane	Museum of Berkshire Aviation/Woodley
	234	Vickers FB.5 Gunbus (replica)	Sywell
	235	Fieseler Fi 103 (V-1) (replica)	Eden Camp Wartime Museum
	236	Hurricane (replica) (P2793)	Eden Camp Wartime Museum
	237	Fieseler Fi 103 (V-1)	Netherlands
	238	Waxflatter ornithopter	Wycombe Air Park
	239	Fokker D.VIII 5/8 scale replica	Norfolk & Suffolk Aviation Museum/Flixton
	240	Messerschmitt Bf.109G (replica)	Yorkshire Air Museum/Elvington
	241	Hurricane 1 (replica) (L1679)	Tangmere Military Aviation Museum
	242	Spitfire Vb (replica) (BL924)	Tangmere Military Aviation Museum
	243	Mignet HM.14 (replica) (G-ADYV)	stored Malvern Wells
	244	Solar Wings Typhoon	Museum of Flight/East Fortune
	245	Electraflyer Floater hang glider	Museum of Flight/East Fortune
	246	Hiway Cloudbase hang glider	Museum of Flight/East Fortune

Reg.	Type	Owner or Operator	Notes
247	Albatross ASG.21 hang glider	Museum of Flight/East Fortune	
248	McBroom hang glider	Museum of Berkshire Aviation/Woodley	
249	Hawker Fury 1 (replica) (K5673)	Brooklands Museum of Aviation/Weybridge	
250	RAF SE-5A (replica) (F5475)	Brooklands Museum of Aviation/Weybridge	
251	Hiway Spectrum hang glider (replica)	Manchester Museum of Science & Industry	
252	Flexiform Wing hang glider	Manchester Museum of Science & Industry	
253	Mignet HM.14 (G-ADZW)	Solent Sky/Southampton	
254	Hawker Hurricane (P3873)	Yorkshire Air Museum/Elvington	
255	NA P-51D Mustang (replica) (463209)	American Air Museum/Duxford	
256	Santos Dumont Type 20 (replica)	Brooklands Museum of Aviation/Weybridge	
257	DH.88 Comet (G-ACSS)	Sywell	
258	Adams balloon	British Balloon Museum	
259	Gloster Gamecock (replica)	Jet Age Museum Gloucestershire	
260	Mignet HM280	–	
261	GAL Hotspur (replica)	Museum of Army Flying/ Middle Wallop	
262	Catto CP-16	Museum of Flight/East Fortune	
263	Chargus Cyclone	Ulster Aviation Heritage/Langford Lodge	
264	Bensen B.8M	IHM/Weston-super-Mare	
265	Spitfire 1 (P3873)	Yorkshire Air Museum/Elvington	
266	Rogallo hang glider	Ulster Aviation Heritage	
267	Hurricane (model)	Imperial War Museum/Duxford	
268	Spifire (model)	stored St.Mawgan	
269	Spitfire (model) USAF	RAF Lakenheath	
270	DH.60 Moth (model)	Yorkshire Air Museum/Elvington	
271	Messerschmitt Me 163B	Shuttleworth Collection/Old Warden	
272	Hurricane (model)	Kent Battle of Britain Museum/Hawkinge	
273	Hurricane (model)	Kent Battle of Britain Museum/Hawkinge	
274	Boulton & Paul P.6 (model)	Pendeford Wolverhampton	
275	Bensen B.7 gyroglider	Doncaster Museum	
276	Hartman Ornithopter	Science Museum/Wroughton	
277	Mignet HM.14	Visitor Centre Shoreham Airport	
278	Hurricane (model)	Kent Battle of Britain Museum/Hawkinge	
279	Airspeed Horsa	RAF Shawbury	
280	DH.89A Dragon Rapide (model)	Crowne Plaza Hotel Speke	
281	Boulton & Paul Defiant (model)	Pendeford	
282	Manx Elder Duck	Isle of Man Airport Terminal	
283	Spitfire (model	Jurby, Isle of Man	
284	Gloster E.28/39 (model)	Lutterworth Leics	
285	Gloster E.28/39 (model)	Farnborough	
286	Mignet HM.14	Caernarfon Air Museum	
287	Blackburn F.2 Lincock (model)	Street Life Museum/Hull	
288	Hurricane (model)	Wonderland Pleasure Park, Mansfield	
289	Gyro Boat	IHM Weston-super-Mare	
290	Fieseler Fi 103 (V1) (model)	Dover Museum	
291	Hurricane (model)	National Battle of Britain Memorial, Capel-le-Ferne, Kent	
292	Eurofighter Typhoon (model)	RAF Museum/Hendon	
293	Spitfire (model)	RAF Museum/Hendon	
294	Fairchild Argus (model)	Visitor Centre, Thorpe Camp, Woodhall Spa	
295	Da Vinci hang glider (replica)	Skysport Engineering	
296	Army Balloon Factory NuIII (replica)	RAF Museum, Hendon	
297	Spitfire (replica)	Kent Battle of Britain Museum/Hawkinge	
298	Spitfire IX (Model)	RAF Cosford Parade Ground	
299	Spitfire 1 (model).	National Battle of Britain Memorial, Capel-le-Ferne, Kent	
300	Hummingbird (replica)	Shoreham Airport Historical Association	
301	Spitfire V FSM (replica)	Thornaby Aerodrome Memorial, Thornaby-on-Tees	
302	Mignet HM.14 reproduction	Shoreham Airport Historical Association	
303	Goldfinch 161 Amphibian	Norfolk and Suffolk Aviation Museum, Flixton	
305	Mersnier pedal powered airship Reproduction	British Balloon Museum and Library	
306	Lovegrove Autogyro trainer	Norfolk and Suffolk Aviation Museum, Flixton	

Note: Registrations/Serials carried are mostly false identities.
MPA = Man Powered Aircraft, IHM = International Helicopter Museum. The aircraft, listed as 'models' are generally intended for exhibition purposes and are not airworthy although they are full scale replicas. However, in a few cases the machines have the ability to taxi when used for film work

Future Allocations Log

The grid provides the facility to record future registrations as they are issued or seen. To trace a particular code, refer to the left hand column which contains the three letters following the G prefix. The final letter can be found by reading across the columns headed A to Z. For example, the box for G-CIFT is located 6 rows down (CIF) and then 19 across to the T column.

G-	A	B	C	D	E	F	G	H	I	J	K	L	M	N	O	P	R	S	T	U	V	W	X	Y	Z
CIE																									
CIF																									
CIG																									
CIH																									
CII																									
CIJ																									
CIK																									
CIL																									
CIM																									
CIN																									
CIO																									
CIP																									
CIR																									
CIS																									
CIT																									
CIU																									
CIV																									
CIW																									
CIX																									
CIY																									
CIZ																									
CJA																									
CJB																									
CJC																									
CJD																									
CJE																									
CJF																									
CJG																									
CJH																									
CJI																									
CJJ																									
CJK																									
CJL																									
	A	B	C	D	E	F	G	H	I	J	K	L	M	N	O	P	R	S	T	U	V	W	X	Y	Z

Credit: *Wal Gandy*